KINGDOM OF JUDAH
REUBEN
SIMEON
PHILISTINES
MOAB
SEA OF SALT
PLAINS OF MOAB
BNE BRAK
TIMNAT SERAH
LOD
lower BETH HORON
upper BETH HORON
BETH EL
BEEROTH
MITSPAH
RAMAH
MICHMAS
GEBAH
Gilgol
Jericho
YABNEH
NAAMA
GEZER
GEDERA
AYALON
YITLAH
GIVATH SHAUL
Kiriath Jearim
MOTZAH
ANATOTH
ASHDOD
EKRON
ESHTAOL
KESALON
JERUSALEM
TIMNAH
BETH SHEMESH
BETAR
SHAPHIR
ASEKAH
ZANOAH
Beth Lehem
ETAM
KIDRON
ASHKELON
LIBNAH
ADULAM
GEDOR
TEKOA
BETH GUBRIN
GILO
BETH TSUR
GATH
KEILAH
MARESHAH
CHALCHUL
BETHANOTH
LACHISH
HEBRON
EGLON
BETH TAPUAH
SIPH
GAZA
MAKEDAH
JUTAH
ESHTEMOA
CARMEL
EnGedi
ANAB
ZIKLAG
SOCHO
MAON
JANOAH
ANIM
JETER
AROD
BEER SHEBA
REHOBOTH
Mt. Halak
Tamar
KADESH BARNEA
TSOAR (Bela)
RABAT BNE AMON
BET NIMRAH
Elaleh
EBEL HASHITIM
HESHBON
BETH HARAM
MEDBA
BETH HAJESHIMOTH
YAHATS
ATAROTH
Zereth Hashahar
KIRJATHAIM
KEDEMOTH
DIBON
AROER
Arnon R.
RABAT MOAB
KIR MOAB
AMM
M

מקראות גדולות

מלכים ב׳

KINGS II

מקראות גדולות

מלכים ב׳

תורגם מחדש לאנגלית

מתורגם ומבואר עם כל דבורי
רש״י ולקט המפרשים על ידי

הרב אברהם י. ראזענבערג

הוצאת יודאיקא פרעסס

Mikraoth Gedoloth

KINGS II

A NEW ENGLISH TRANSLATION

TRANSLATION OF TEXT, RASHI
AND OTHER COMMENTARIES BY
RABBI A. J. ROSENBERG

THE JUDAICA PRESS, INC.

ISBN 0-910818-31-2

First Printing, 1980
Second Printing, 1985
Third Printing, 1989
Fourth Printing, 1993
Fifth Printing, 1998
Sixth Printing, 2005

The Judaica Press, Inc.
123 Ditmas Avenue
Brooklyn, NY 11218
718-972-6200 • 800-972-6201
Fax 718-972-6204
info@judaicapress.com
www.judaicapress.com

Manufactured in the United States of America

״ויעש . . . הישר בעיני ה׳ כל ימיו.״
מלכים ב׳ יב:ג

הוצאת ספר מלכים ב׳ זה מוקדש לזכר נשמת

הרב משה חיים ב״ר יעקב מרדכי לוסטיג ע״ה

איש חביב ונחמד
שכל ימיו עבד את בוראו בשמחה ולב טוב
ידיד נאמן לכל מכריו
בעל ואב נאמן ומסור לזוגתו שתחי׳, ולילדיו שיחיו.

"He . . . did what was proper in the eyes of the Lord all his days."
Kings II 12:3

This edition of Kings II is dedicated
to the eternal memory
of

Rabbi Murray H. Lustig ע״ה

Faithful and good humored friend
devoted husband and father
whose life was dedicated to serving his creator
joyfully and wholeheartedly.

CONTENTS

משה פיינשטיין
ר"מ תפארת ירושלים
בנוא יארק

RABBI MOSES FEINSTEIN
455 F. D. R. DRIVE
New York 2, N. Y.
OREGON 7-1222

בע"ה

הנה ידוע ומפורסם טובא בשער בת רבים ספרי הוצאת יודאיקא פרעסס על תנ"ך שכבר יצא לאור על ספרי יהושע ושמואל ועכשיו בחסדי השי"ת סדרו לדפוס ג"כ על ספר שופטים והוא כולל הפירושים המקובלים בתנ"ך הנקוב בשם מקראות גדולות ועל זה הוסיפו תרגום אנגלית שהוא השפה המדוברת במדינה זו על פסוקי תנ"ך וגם תרגום לפרש"י מלה במלה עם הוספות פירושים באנגלית הנצרכים להבנת פשוטו של קרא והכל נערך ע"י תלמידי היקר הרב הגאון ר' אברהם יוסף ראזענבערג שליט"א שהוא אומן גדול במלאכת התרגום, והרבה עמל השקיע בכל פרט ופרט בדקדוק גדול, וסידר את הכל בקצור כדי להקל על הלומדים שיוכלו לעיין בנקל ואפריון נמטיה למנהל יודאיקא פרעסס מהור"ר יעקב דוד גאלדמאן שליט"א שזכה ומזכה את הרבים בלימוד התנ"ך שמעורר לומדיה לאהבה וליראה את שמו הגדול ולהאמין בו ובעבדיו הנביאים שהוא יסוד ושורש בעבודתו יתברך ואמינא לפעלא טבא יישר ויתברכו כל העוסקים בכל ברכות התורה וחכמינו ז"ל בברוך אשר יקים את דברי התורה הזאת.

וע"ז באתי עה"ח

FOREWORD

In this volume, the sixth and last of our series of the Early Prophets, we present the second book of Kings. Halachically and historically, this is actually one book together with I Kings. Neither in the Talmud (*Baba Bathra* 14–15), nor in any of the mediaeval commentaries is it treated as a separate book. *Abarbanel* mentions that Jerome divided Samuel and Kings into two books respectively. This was adopted by the Christians from his Latin translation known as the Vulgate, translated between 388 and 405. Jerome was also the originator of the chapter divisions throughout the entire Bible. For want of a better division, this system was utilized by Isaac Nathan in his *Concordance,* printed in the year 5198, whence it was adopted by Jacob ben Haim in the first edition of *Mikraoth Gedoloth,* printed in Venice 5286. He apologized for using this non-Jewish division of *Tenach,* but excused himself by stating that he had found no Jewish, Masoretic division until after the printing, when he obtained a copy of the original *sedarim.* To avoid confusion and for the sake of convenience, we are using this widespread system despite its non-Jewish origin. See *Moda Labinah* by Wolf Heidenheim, end of Genesis.

As in the first five volumes, we have translated the text into modern, comprehensible English, but as literal as necessary to preserve the sense of the original Hebrew. Where there are variant renditions given by various exegetes and translators, we usually translate the text according to *Rashi,* the most popular of all Biblical exegetes. Other views are presented in the Commentary Digest.

Since *Rashi's* commentary is the most popular and widely accepted, it is translated verbatim, to enable the student to master it in the original. Where the wording is difficult, we have resorted to the version of *Rashi* ms., printed in *Mikraoth Gedoloth,* published by *Etz Haim,* Jerusalem, 1974. We also used the commentaries of R. Joseph Kara, a contemporary of *Rashi,* whose commentary of Joshua, Judges, and Kings, follows *Rashi* almost word for word, with the exception of certain significant differences. One version of this commentary appears in *Nach* Lublin, the Hebrew volume we are using for this work. A second version was published by Mossad Harav Kook, Jerusalem 1972. We refer to both of these editions in our Commentary Digest, as variations of *Rashi.* To assist us in this work, we have also utilized *Shem Ephraim,* emendations to *Rashi,* by R. Ephraim Zalman Margolioth, printed in Israel in 5732.

As in our other volumes, we have drawn mostly from the commentaries appearing in *Nach* Lublin, viz. *Redak, Ralbag,* and *Mezudoth.* In addition to these, we have often quoted from *Malbim* and *Abarbanel.* We have also obtained a rare volume of *K'li Y'kar* by R. Samuel Laniado. In this volume we find an evaluation of all early commentaries, in addition to original exegeses by the author. For this privilege we are indebted to our dear friend, Rabbi Sidney Krinsky, who was kind enough to lend us this valuable tome from his library.

Other sources used can be found in the bibliography.

We wish to thank Dr. Paul Forchheimer for enlightening us concerning the Old French expressions in *Rashi.* His extensive knowledge of Romance languages was invaluable to us.

We take this opportunity to thank the Almighty for granting us the ability to complete this series, the first milestone in our *Nach* series. We hope that we have inspired many to study the Early Prophets, and have given them the proper perspective regarding these Books.

INTRODUCTION

Kings and Chronicles:

The period covered by the Books of Kings extends from King David's last days until the destruction of the first Temple and the Babylonian exile. This same period is covered by the two Books of Chronicles. Yet, by comparing the two accounts, we find many differences. Many events concerning the kings of Israel are not even mentioned in Chronicles, and many important events of the kings of Judah are omitted from the Books of Kings. Moreover, Scripture often mentions the books of chronicles of the kings of Judah and of the kings of Israel. Obviously, many facts included in these books were omitted in the Biblical accounts. The reasons for the differences between these books are not found in the early commentaries, let alone in the Midrashic and Talmudic literature.

The first commentator to attempt to solve this difficulty was Don Isaac Abarbanel. He discounts the chronicles of the kings of Judah and the kings of Israel as secular books, which delineated the material accomplishments of each king, the cities he built, his military prowess, and other political events. (See II Kings 15:23.) Therefore, God did not instruct Jeremiah the prophet, the author of Kings, to include them in his prophetic Book. Likewise, Ezra the scribe, the author of Chronicles, was not divinely inspired to record these facts in his book of Chronicles.

Moreover, the two aforementioned books were probably written subjectively, according to the relationship of the author to the kings whose history he was recording. Therefore, they were excluded from the Biblical canon.

As regards Kings and Chronicles, Abarbanel establishes the premise that Jeremiah's intention in authoring Kings was to record the chronology of the kings, both of Judah and of Israel, their righteousness or their wickedness, and the prophecies issued concerning them. Ezra, on the other hand, was interested in the returnees from Babylonian exile, their lineage, and the kings of the house of David, the forebears of Zerubabel son of Shealtiel, leader of the Jews at the beginning of the Second Commonwealth. Since he was the grandson of Jehoiachin, the lineage of the kings is recorded, in addition to their good deeds. Many of these good deeds and exemplary accomplishments are omitted from the account in Kings.

Aaron Marcus, in his book *"Kadmonioth," Antiquities,* theorizes that the Book of Kings was meant primarily to record the events of the kings of

Israel, whereas Chronicles dwells mainly on the kings of Judah. This would account for the detailed narratives of the prophets of Samaria and the kings in whose reign they flourished. Abarabanel's reason does not account for this. The differences between the two books concerning the wickedness and righteousness of the kings will be discussed below.

Idolatry in the Days of the First Commonwealth:

Reading through the books of Kings and Chronicles, we are constantly confronted with mention of idolatry and paganism. We find this in King Solomon's reign when his wives worshipped their native deities, through the days of Jeroboam son of Nebat, who erected the golden calves in Bethel and in Dan, through Ahab's reign, when the Baal cult was introduced into Israel, and on and on. This question has been discussed in the introduction to Judges and I Kings. There is, however, no harm in refreshing our memories, and in introducing new facets, not discussed prior to this volume. Although many of these facts are mentioned in the volume in their proper places, we will discuss them briefly here.

First, one must bear in mind that it is absurd to suspect King Solomon, the wisest of all men, of having any tendencies toward idolatry. Scripture rebukes him for not preventing his foreign wives from continuing their previous practice. For King Solomon, this was considered tantamount to idolatry. This is discussed at length in the introduction to I Kings and in Chapter 11.

Even Jeroboam the son of Nebat did not intend to worship strange deities. As explained by *Redak,* I Kings 12:29, he intended merely to create tangible objects upon which the Shechinah would rest. Since the house of David had fallen into disfavor, he conjectured that the Temple, too, was to be displaced by sanctuaries located in the northern kingdom. He, therefore, erected two santuaries, one in Bethel and one in Dan, where he set up two golden calves, the same vehicle used by the Israelites in the desert to bring down the Shechinah upon them during Moses' absence. *Abarbanel* points out that the calf was the symbol of Jeroboam's tribe, the tribe of Ephraim. It was the national symbol of the northern kingdom. Eventually, however, the populace considered these calves as gods, and became attracted to the worship of other pagan deities. Jeroboam, however, never believed in the calves as gods. We find him entreating the prophet Iddo to pray for him that his arm be healed. He also sent his wife to Ahijah the Shilonite to inquire of God concerning their son's welfare. Yet, for a person of his stature, this was considered tantamount to idolatry, and Jeroboam is branded as the prototype of the one who sins and causes others to sin.

The worship of the calves continued in Israel until the reign of Ahab, when the Baal worship was introduced through his wife Jezebel. According to *Abarbanel,* this was a type of sun-worship. Even the Baal was worshipped as an intermediary between the people and God. Although this was, nevertheless, considered a grave sin, it was not the acceptance of other deities as substitutes for the Almighty. We find that Ahab, despite all his shortcomings, respected Torah scholars and assisted them with material gifts. This atoned for half his sins (*San.* 103a). Evidence of Ahab's belief in God is demonstrated by his humility before Elijah when he rebuked him for the murder of Naboth the Jezreelite.

Ahaziah the son of Ahab followed his father's footsteps, whereas his brother Jehoram retained only the sins of Jeroboam the son of Nebat. We find Jehoram addressing Elisha as *avi—My father,* or *My master.* He asks him for instuctions concerning the Aramean prisoners of war. He wears sackcloth as a symbol of mourning and remorse for his sins. Yet, he still wishes to execute Elisha. Later, he asks Gehazi to relate to him Elisha's wonders. Hence there is no doubt of his belief in God.

This trend continued all through the kings of Israel until the eventual exile to Assyria.

Jehu, who destroyed the house of Ahab and the Baal cult, nevertheless, continued to worship the calves erected by Jeroboam the son of Nebat.

Joash, son of Jehoahaz, who also continued the sins of Jeroboam, nevertheless, visited Elisha during the latter's terminal illness, and wept in his presence out of sorrow concerning his imminent demise. He uttered the identical words uttered by Elisha upon Elijah's ascent to heaven. "My master! My master! Israel's chariots and riders!" Can we imagine an idolatrous king weeping over the impending death of a prophet of the Lord? An idolatrous king leaving his palace to visit a dying prophet of the Lord? What attracted all these kings to idol worship, while they were so conscious of the existence of God and His messages through His prophets? The Talmud (*San.* 102b) tells us that during this period the temptation to worship idols was extremely potent. Menasseh, king of Judah, appeared to Rav Ashi in a dream and told him that he, too, had he been living at that time, would have picked up the skirt of his coat and run after him. Additionally, the kings of Israel feared the restoration of the Davidic dynasty in the northern kingdom. They, therefore, maintained the shrines in Bethel and Dan.

This trend continued until the exile to Assyria. Despite the motives for this type of idolatry and the excuses for it, they were, nonetheless, inadequate for acceptance by God, and the kingdom of Israel met its ultimate downfall.

Among the kings of Judah, however, there was much less idolatry. We find that Asa and Jehoshaphat were indeed righteous kings, following King David's footsteps. Joash, too, was a righteous king during his early years. Later, however, the princes of Judah worshipped him and accepted him as a deity. He was held guilty for the murder of Zechariah the propeht, but not for idol worship. Uzziah-Azariah was a God-fearing man until he made his fatal mistake of entering the Temple to burn the incense. He did this in good faith, thinking that the king was not subject to the regulation limiting the service to the priests. Nevertheless, he was severely punished for this sin, and he remained a *mezora* for the rest of his life. Jotham, Hezekiah, and Josiah were again outstanding holy men. Thus we have seven righteous kings among the kings of Judah. *Abarbanel* claims that all the other kings were idolatrous. This is, however, not in accordance with the Rabbinic teachings that Zedekiah was a perfect, righteous man. Also, Jehoiachin repented his sins and was forgiven, as will be discussed at the very end of this volume.

Daath Soferim attributes the sins of the kingdom of Judah after Solomon's death, to the letdown they experienced after the division of the kingdom. When the Temple was built, they could actually perceive the presence of the Shechinah. They were conscious of the superiority of Israel over the other nations of the world. They could virtually feel Divine Providence guiding them. Following Solomon's demise, when the preponderant majority of Israel broke away from the house of David, they felt an overwhelming letdown. They felt that they had lost their superiority over the other nations, and they sank to a much lower spiritual level than they had occupied during the reign of Solomon.

It must be kept in mind, however, that all during this period, even at its lowest ebb, there were always many people faithful to the Torah and to the observance of its tenets. Even in the northern kingdom, Obadiah was able to conceal one hundred prophets of God in two caves, without being informed upon by the people, surely there were many faithful in the southern kingdom.

Asa was known as a very righteous king, who abolished idolatry in his time. His son Jehoshaphat conducted a revival campaign throughout the land, and encouraged many Judeans to return to the ways of God. He made one mistake, however, by associating with the house of Ahab, for which he was reprimanded by Jehu the son of Hanani, the seer. Because of this mistake, his son Jehoram followed in the footsteps of the kings of Israel. Ahaziah his son went so far as to hide in Samaria, to cut the Names of God out of the Torah scrolls. He was afraid to do so in Judah, where the people were faithful to God.

During this entire period, no king dared tamper with the Temple service, which was conducted by the priests and the people as prescribed by the

Torah. The first to tamper with the Temple was Athaliah. She and her sons broke into the walls of the Temple. For this reason, it required repairs during the reign of Joash.

Ahaz was considered a very wicked king, who spread idolatry throughout the land. He placed an image in the attic of the Temple. He was afraid to place it in the Temple proper, lest the populace oppose him. He did, however, manage to seal the Torah. I.e. he closed the synagogues and the study-halls. He knew that if the children would not learn Torah, there would be no scholars to lead the people. Thus, there would be no synagogues where the Shechinah would rest upon the Jewish people. For this reason, he was called Ahaz, an expression of holding, since he held the synagogues closed. See *San.* 103b, Ruth *Rabbah,* Introduction 3.

Incidentally, according to Assyrian inscriptions, his name was Jehoahaz. Because of his evil deeds, however, Scripture omitted the letters of his name that represented God's Name. *Kadmonioth* by Aaron Marcus

Additionally, Ahaz abolished the Temple service and permitted incest. Yet, in spite of all his evil deeds, he was not listed among the kings who have no share in the world to come. This was either because of the merits of his father Jotham and his son Hezekiah, or because he was ashamed to look at Isaiah in the face. This indicated that he still believed in God and His prophets. He even called his son Hezekiah, "May God strengthen him." With all his evil, he still had God in mind. It was the overwhelming temptation to worship idols that he could not overpower.

Rabbi Avigdor Miller, in his book, "Behold a People," attributes Ahaz' tendency to evil to his father's failure to enter the Temple, as is mentioned in II Chron. 27:2. Since his father did not enter the Temple, although he was a very righteous man, Ahaz did not experience the sanctity emanating from this holy edifice. I see no basis for this theory, since the obvious meaning of the passage is that Jotham did not enter the Temple proper to burn incense as his father Uzziah had done. See *Mezudath David* ad loc. We have no indication that he did not enter the temple court.

Aaron Marcus claims that there was a great opposition to the priesthood. Uzziah-Azariah was a beloved king. Until his mistake, his record was impeccable. When he attempted to enter the Temple to burn incense, the *kohanim* called him by name and warned him to beware of entering the *heichal,* which was reserved for the seed of Aaron. Not heeding their admonition, Uzziah entered the *heichal* with his incense and was immediately stricken with *zaraath.* (II Chron. 26:16–20) The populace was very much incensed against the priests for their audacity in opposing their beloved king. Jotham, being a passive person, did not rise up against the priests, but kept his distance from the *heichal* and the sacrifical service. His son, Ahaz, however, was more aggressive, and opposed the priests. This led him to rebel against Torah in general. This, too, is hard to believe. Since the populace witnessed with their own eyes how Uzziah became a *mezora* upon entering the *heichal,* and experienced an earthquake at that very moment, how could they blame the priests for their opposition to their king. Was it not obvious that God had punished him for this act? I, am therefore, inclined to believe that Ahaz, as many others, was under the influence of the temptation to commit idolatry, which was extremely potent during that period.

His grandson Menasseh surpassed him in wickedness. Whereas Ahaz had sealed the Torah, Menasseh cut out the Names of God. Whereas Ahaz had abolished the Temple worship, Menasseh dismantled the altar. Whereas Ahaz had permitted incest, Menasseh was actually intimate with his own sister. Whereas Ahaz placed an image in the Temple attic, Menasseh placed it in the Temple proper. This was an indication that the people were more acquiescent to his idolatrous practices than they had been to those of Ahaz his grandfather. He could, therefore, dare to place his image in the Temple proper. Menasseh was guilty also of bloodshed. According to some, he murdered Isaiah the prophet, whose murder was tantamount to filling the streets of Jerusalem with blood. According to others, he made an idol, which required one thousand people to carry it. By doing so, they were crushed under its weight. He repeated this daily, thus murdering countless people.

This very wicked king had one redeeming factor, however. He was captured by the king of Assyria and carried off in irons. According to the *Targum* and *Pirkei d'R. Eliezer,* he was about to be burnt to death in a pan. When his gods would not respond to his prayers, he finally turned to the God of his fathers. Immediately, God accepted his prayers, and he was returned to Jerusalem to his kingdom. Whether he received a share in the world to come is disputed in the Talmud, *San.* 103. Because of his many sins, God had to hunt for a "tunnel," so to speak, to be able to accept his repentance. Some say that God accepted his penitence in order to set him up as an example for others to follow. Yet, according to others, his repentance was not accepted because it was a result of coercion, or because he repented only of his sins of idolatry, not of his other sins. For these reasons, Jeremiah does not mention it in Kings. Only the Chronicler mentions that Menasseh repented.

Whether or not Menasseh's repentance was genuine, his previous sins, however, left an indelible impression on his successors, such as Amon and Jehoiakim, and eventually brought about the destruction of the Temple and the Babylonian exile.

The last kings are discussed adequately in the Commentary Digest, and it is unnecessary to add anything here.

The Names of the Kings, the events that transpired during their reigns, the years of their reigns, their capitals, and the tribes of their origins.

Saul—the first king after the era of the judges—from Benjamin—reigned two years (2882–2884 See Seder Hadoroth, p. 88) — in Gibeath Saul in territory of Benjamin—died in war with Philistines on Mt. Gilboa.

IshBosheth son of Saul—reigned two years (See II Sam. 2:11 Com. Dig.) over all Israel (except tribe of Judah) in Mahanaim in the land of Gilead — assassinated by two officers of troops, Benjamites. The entire kingdom was then under David's rule.

David—from Judah — reigned forty years, (2884–2924) seven in Hebron. After Jerusalem was taken from the Jebusites, he transferred his capital there, where it remained.

Solomon son of David—reigned forty years (2924–2964) — built first Temple which existed 410 years, and was destroyed by king of Babylonia.

After Solomon's death, the kingdom was divided in two, two tribes assuming the name of the kingdom of Judah and ten tribes assuming the name of the kingdom of Israel or Ephraim. The kings of Judah were all scions of the House of David.

Kings of Judah

Rehoboam son of Solomon—ruled over Judah and Benjamin seventeen years. (2964–2981).

Abijah or *Abijam* his son — ruled three years. (2981–2983)

Asa — his son — reigned forty-one years. (2983–3024)

Jehoshaphat his son — reigned twenty-five years. (3024–3047)

Jehoram his son — reigned eight years. (3047–3055)

Ahaziah his son — reigned one year (3055) went to meet Jehoram king of Israel and was assassinated by Jehu.

Athaliah daughter of Ahab king of Israel — mother of Ahaziah — after her son's death reigned six years (3056–3061) was slain by order of Jehoiada the priest in order to obtain the throne for Joash the son of Ahaziah.

Joash son of Ahaziah — reigned forty years — (3061–3101) insurrection in Jerusalem — fled to Lachish — slain there.

Uzziah or *Azariah* his son — reigned fifty-two years. (3115–3167)

Jotham his son —reigned sixteen years. (3167–3183)

Ahaz his son — reigned sixteen years. (3183–3199)

Hezekiah his son —twenty-nine years. (3199–3228)

Menasseh his son —fifty-five years. (3283–3285)

Amon his son —two years (3283–3285) — slain by servants who rebelled.

Josiah his son —ruled thirty-one years (3285–3316) — killed by king of Egypt in war.
Jehoahaz his son —reigned three months (3316) —deposed by king of Egypt, who replaced him with his brother Eliakim, whose name he changed to Jehoiakim.
Jehoiakim son of Josiah - reigned eleven years (3317–3327) —bound by king of Babylonia to take to Babylonia —died on the way.
Jehoiachin his son — reigned three months (3327) — exiled to Babylonia with princes of Judah — succeeded by his uncle Mataniah, whose name was changed to Zedekiah.
Zedekiah son of Josiah — ruled eleven years (3327–3338) —chained and blinded by Babylonian king —taken to Babylonia — Nebuzaradan officer of king of Babylonia burned Temple, palace, and all houses in Jerusalem, demolished walls of Jerusalem, exiled the entire populace with all the Temple vessels, left Jerusalem desolate until the first year of Cyrus king of Persia.

Kings of Israel

Jeroboam son of Nebat — from tribe of Ephraim — ruled over ten tribes of Israel — twenty-two years — in Tirzah. (2964–2985)
Nadab his son — ruled two years — slain by Baasa son of Ahijah of Issachar, who rebelled against him and ruled in his stead. (2985–2986)
Baasa son of Ahijah — from tribe of Issachar — reigned twenty-four years. (2986–3009)
Elah his son — ruled two years (3009–3010) — slain by Zimri the captain of half his chariots, who rebelled and ruled in his stead.
Zimri — ruled seven days (3010) — attacked by Omri, general of the army — when he saw that the city was captured, he went into the king's palace, whereupon he (See I Kings 16:18), Comm. Dig.) burned the palace about him and he died, and Omri ruled in his stead.
Omri — from Ephraim — ruled twelve years (3010–3021) — six years in Tirzah, then he built up Samaria and moved his capital to that location, where it remained until the exile.
Ahab — his son — ruled twenty-two years (3021–3041) — perished in battle with Aram in Ramoth-Gilead.
Ahaziah his son — ruled two years (3041–3043) — fell through the lattice of his upper chamber, took sick and died — succeeded by his brother Jehoram.
Jehoram son of Ahab —reigned twelve years (3043–3055) — slain by Jehu son of Nimshi, who rebelled and reigned in his stead.
Jehu son of Jehoshaphat son of Nimshi — from tribe of Menasseh — reigned twenty-eight years. (3055–3083)
Jehoahaz his son — seventeen years. (3083–3097)

Jehoash his son — sixteen years. (3098–3115)
Jeoboam his son — forty-one years. (3115–3153)
Zechariah his son — reigned six months (3153) — slain by Shallum son of Jabesh, who rebelled against him and replaced him.
Shallum son of Jabesh — reigned one month (3154) — attacked by Menahem son of Gadi, who slew him and ruled in his stead.
Menahem son of Gadi — ruled ten years. (3154–3164)
Pekahiah his son —ruled two years (3164–3165) — succeeded by Pekah son of Remaliah, his aide, who rebelled against him and slew him.
Pekah son of Remaliah — reigned twenty years (3166–3186) — king of Assyria attacked and took land of Zebulun and Naphtali, exiled populace to Assyria — succeeded by Hoshea son of Elah who rebelled against him and slew him.
Hoshea son of Elah — from tribe of Reuben — ruled nineteen years (3187–3206) — in eighth year attacked by king of Assyria, who exiled the Reubenties, the Gadites, and half the tribe of Menasseh — in nineteenth year king of Assyria conquered Samaria, exiled Israel to Assyria, settled them in Halah, Habor, etc.

The Prophets Who Prophesied during the Reign of each King

Kings who reigned over all Israel
Saul son of Kish — Samuel the seer
David son of Jesse — Samuel the seer, Gad the seer, and Nathan the prophet
Solomon son of David — Nathan the prophet, Ahijah the Shilonite, and Iddo the seer
Kings of Judah
Rehoboam son of Solomon —Shemaiah the prophet and Iddo the seer
Abijah son of Rehoboam — Iddo
Asa son of Abijah — Azariah son of Oded, Hanani the seer, and Jehu the son of Hanani
Jehoshaphat son of Asa — Obadiah, Jehiel son of Zechariah, of the sons of Asaph, Micaiah son of Imla, and Jehu son of Hanani
Jehoram son of Jehoshaphat — Elijah the prophet
Ahaziah son of Jehoram — Elisha the prophet
Athaliah mother of Ahaziah — Elisha the prophet
Joash son of Ahaziah — Zechariah son of Jehoiada
Amaziah — Amoz father of Isaiah, brother of Amaziah
Uzziah-Azariah son of Amaziah — Hosea, Amos, and Isaiah
Jotham — Hosea, Amos, Isaiah, Micah the Morashtite
Ahaz — Hosea, Amos, Isaiah, Oded, and Micah

Hezekiah — Hosea, Amos, Isaiah, and Micah
Menasseh son of Hezekiah — Joel, Nahum, Habakkuk, and Hozai
Amon son of Menasseh — Nahum, Habakkuk, and Hozai
Josiah son of Amon — Jeremiah, Zephaniah, and Huldah the prophetess
Joahaz son of Josiah — Jeremiah
Jehoiakim son of Josiah — Jeremiah and Uriah
Jehoiachin son of Jehoiakim — Jeremiah
Zedekiah son of Josiah — Jeremiah and Ezekiel

KINGS OF ISRAEL

Jeroboam son of Nebat — Ahijah the Shilonite and Iddo the seer
Nadab son of Jeroboam — Jehu son of Hanani the seer
Baasha son of Ahijah — Jehu son of Hanani the seer
Elah son of Baasha — Jehu son of Hanani the seer
Zimri — Jehu son of Hanani the seer
Omri — Jehu son of Hanani
Ahab son of Omri — Elijah the Tishbite, Micaiah son of Imla, and Obadiah
Ahaziah son of Ahab — Elijah
Jehoram son of Ahab — Elijah and Elisha son of Shaphat
Jehu son of Nimshi — Elisha son of Shaphat and Jonah son of Amittai
Jehoahaz son of Jehu — Elisha son of Shaphat and Jonah son of Amittai
Jehoash son of Jehoahaz — Elisha son of Shaphat and Jonah son of Amittai
Jeroboam son of Joash — Jonah son of Amittai, Hosea, and Amos
Zechariah son of Jeroboam — Jonah son of Amittai, Hosea, and Amos
Shallum son of Jabesh — Hosea, Amos, and Micah
Menahem son of Gadi — Hosea, Amos, Isaiah, and Micah
Pekahiah son of Menahem — Hosea, Amos, Isaiah, and Micah
Pekah son of Remaliah — Hosea, Amos, Isaiah, and Micah
Hoshea son of Elah — Hosea, Amos, Isaiah, and Micah

Reminder: It is imperative that the reader consult all Biblical references cited for a fuller understanding.

An asterisk (*) in the Commentary Digest indicates additional corresponding notations cited in the Appendix in back of the volume.

OUTLINE OF KINGS II

I. End of Ahaziah's reign (I).
   A. Ahaziah's injury and subsequent illness (I:1–2).
   B. Elijah's message (I:3–8).
   C. Ahaziah's disastrous attempts to capture Elijah (I:9–12).
   D. Third delegation to Elijah, who follows them to the king (I:13–15).
   E. Prophecy of doom to Ahaziah (I:16).
   F. Ahaziah's death and succession of Jehoram (I:17–18).

II. Elijah's ascent to heaven (II:1–12).
   A. Trip to Bethel (III:1–3).
   B. Trip to Jericho (II:3–5).
   C. Splits the Jordan (II:6–8).
   D. Promise to Elisha (II:9–10).
   E. Actual ascent (II:11–12).

III. Elisha succeeds Elijah (II:13–18).
   A. Splits the Jordan (II:13–14).
   B. Accepted by disciples (II:15).
   C. Conducts fruitless search for Elijah (II:16–18).

IV. Elisha cures the waters of Jericho (II:19–22).

V. Elisha curses youths who jeer him (II:23–25).

VI. War against Moab (III).
   A. Jehoram's ascent to the throne of Israel (III:1).
   B. Jehoram's sins (III:2–3).
   C. Moab's tribute (III:4).
   D. Moab's revolt (III:5).
   E. War with Moab (III:6–27).
      1. Jehoram's alliance with Jehohaphat (III:6–7).
      2. Thirst in the Desert of Edom (III:8–10).
      3. Summoning Elisha (III:11–14).
      4. Elisha's prophecies (III:15–19).
      5. Fulfillment of prophecies (III:20–25).
         a. Water appearing red as blood (III:20–22).
         b. Defeat of Moab (III:23–25).
      6. Moab's final attempt to defeat Edom (III:26).
      7. Moabite king's sacrifice (III:27).

VII. Miracle of the oil (IV:1–7).
- A. Destitute widow whose sons were to be enslaved as payment of debt (IV:1).
- B. Vessels fill with oil (IV:2–7).

VIII. The son of the Shunemitess (IV:8–37).
- A. Elisha's lodging in Shunem (IV:8).
- B. Elisha's chamber (IV:9–11).
- C. Elisha's blessing (IV:12–17).
- D. Child's illness and death (IV:18–21).
- E. Mother's journey to Elisha (IV:22–28).
- F. Gehazi's mission (IV:29–31).
- G. Resurrection (IV:32–36).

IX. Miracle of the pot (IV:37–41).

X. Miracle of the loaves (IV:41–44).

XI. Naaman's cure (V:1–19).
- A. Naaman's affliction (V:1).
- B. Advice of Israelite girl (V:2–4).
- C. Naaman's journey to Samaria (V:5–9).
- D. Elisha's instruction (V:10).
- E. Naaman's refusal (V:11–12).
- F. Naaman's compliance and cure (V:13, 14).
- G. Naaman's acceptance of God (V:15–19).

XII. Gehazi's downfall (V:20–27).
- A. Gehazi requests gifts from Naaman (V:20–24).
- B. Elisha's curse (V:25–27).

XIII. Miracle of the ax-blade (VI:1–7).

XIV. War with Aram (VI:8–23).
- A. Elisha's warnings to Jehoram (VI:9–12).
- B. Aram's attempt to capture Elisha (VI:13–15).
- C. Elisha's miraculous capture of the Arameans and their release (VI:16–23).

XV. Aram's siege of Samaria (VI:24–33).
- A. Severe famine (VI:24–30).
- B. Jehoram's attempt to capture Elisha (VI:31–33).

XVI. Elisha's prophecy of plenty (VII:1–2).

XVII. Story of the four *mezoraim* (VII).

A. Discovery of vacated camp of Aram (VII:1–5).
B. Noises which led Arameans to vacate (VII:6–8).
C. Report to king (VII:9–15).
D. Populace loot camp (VII:16).
E. Prophecy fulfilled (VII:17–20).

XVIII. Shunemitess' fields confiscated during famine (VIII:1–6).
A. Leaves on Elisha's orders (VIII:1, 2).
B. Returns after famine (VIII:3).
C. Appeals to king (4–6).

XIX. Ben-hadad's illness and death (VIII:4–6).
XX. Jehoram son of Jehoshaphat reigns over Judah (VIII:16–23).
A. Edom's revolt (VIII:20–22).

XXI. Ahaziah's reign over Judah (VIII:23–29).
A. Alliance with Joram son of Ahab (VIII:28).
B. Joram wounded in battle with Aram (VIII:28).
C. Ahaziah visits Joram in Jezreel (VIII:29).

XXII. Jehu's coup (IX, X).
A. Jehu's anointment and charge to destroy Ahab's dynasty (IX:1–10).
B. Jehu's conspiracy (IX:11–14).
C. Massacre of Joram, Ahaziah, Jezebel in Jezreel (IX:15–37).
D. Massacre of Ahab's children in Samaria (X:1–12).
E. Massacre of Ahaziah's nephews (X:13–14).
F. Massacre of the remnant of Ahab's dynasty in Samaria (X:15–17).
G. Massacre of Baal cult (X:18–28).
H. Jehu's shortcomings and death (X:29–36).

XXIII. Athaliah (XI).
A. Massacre of Judean royal family (XI:1).
B. Concealment of Joash (XI:2, 3).

XXIV. Restoration of throne to Joash (XI:4–20).
XXV. Joash's reign (XII).
A. Repair of Temple (XII:1–17).
B. Tribute to Hazael (XII:18–19).
C. Death (XII:20–22).

XXVI. Jehoahaz, king of Israel (XIII:1–9).
A. Battles with Aram (XIII:3–7).

XXVII. Joash, king of Israel (XIII:10–13).
XXVIII. Elisha's terminal illness and prophecy to Joash (XIII:14–21).
XXIX. Restoration of cities seized by Aram (XIII:22–25).
XXX. Amaziah, king of Judah (XIV:1–20).
- A. Avenges father's death (XIV:5–6).
- B. Defeats Edom (XIV:7).
- C. War with Jehoash (XIV:8–14).
- D. Death (XIV:15–20).

XXXI. Uzziah-Azariah, king of Judah (XIV:21–22).
XXXII. Jeroboam son of Joash, king of Israel (XIV:23–29).
XXXIII. Uzziah-Azariah (XV:1–7).
- A. Afflicted with *zaraath* (XV:5).
- B. Jotham regent (XV:5).

XXXIV. Zechariah king of Israel (XV:8–12).
XXXV. Shallum son of Jabesh king of Israel (XV:13).
XXXVI. Menahem son of Gadi king of Israel (XV:14–22).
- A. Tribute to Pul king of Assyria (XV:19–20).

XXXVII. Pekahiah king of Israel (XV:21–26).
- A. First exile to Assyria (XV:29).

XXXIX. Jotham king of Judah (XV:32–38).
XL. Ahaz king of Judah (XVI).
- A. Idolatry (XVI:1–4).
- B. War with Aram, tribute to Assyria (XVI:5–9).
- C. New altar modeled after Damascan, other alterations in Temple (XVI:10–20).

XLI. Hoshea king of Israel (XVII:1–4).
XLII. Assyrian siege and exile (XVII:5–6).
XLIII. Causes of exile (XVII:7–23).
XLIV. New occupants of Samaria (XVII:24–41).
- A. Worshipped idols and were attacked by lions (XVII:24–25).
- B. Receive instruction from Israelite priests (XVII:26–28).
- C. Retain idolatry (XVII:29–41).

XLV. Hezekiah king of Judah (XVIII:XX).
- A. Abolished idolatry (XVIII:1–6).
- B. Made Judah independent of Assyria (XVIII:7).
- C. Defeated Philistines (XVIII:8).

D. Assyrian exile repeated (XVIII:9–12).
E. Assyria seizes Judean cities (XVIII:13).
F. Hezekiah pays tribute (XVIII:14–16).
G. Assyrian delegation blasphemes and warns people to surrender (XVIII-17–37).
H. Encouraged by Isaiah who predicts the withdrawal of Assyria (XIX:1–7).
I. Delegation warns Judah of Sennacherib's return (XIX:8–14).
J. Hezekiah prays (XIX:15–19).
K. Isaiah prophesies downfall of Sennacherib (XIX:20–37).
L. Hezekiah's illness and recovery (XX:1–11).
M. Babylonian delegation to Hezekiah (XX:12–13).
N. Rebuke by Isaiah (XX:14–21).

XLVI. Menasseh king of Judah (XXI:1–18).
A. Idolatry (XXI:1–9).
B. Doom predicted by prophets (XXI:10–15).
C. Much bloodshed (XXI:16–18).

XLVII. Amon idolatrous king (XXI:19–26).
XLVIII. Josiah (XXII–XXIII:30).
A. Repair of Temple and discovery of scroll (XXII:1–11).
B. Huldah prophesies destruction and exile after Josiah's demise (XXII:12–20).
C. Covenant with God and purification of Temple and land (XXIII:1–20).
D. Momentous Passover celebration (XXIII:21–29).
E. Killed by Egyptians in Megiddo (XXIII:29–30).

XLIX. Jehoahaz succeeds Josiah (XXIII:30–33).
A. Imprisoned by Pharaoh-neco (XXIII:33).
B. Tribute imposed on land (XXIII:33).

L. Jehoiakim (XXIII:34–XXIV:6).
A. Appointed by Pharaoh-neco (XXIII:34).
B. Pays tribute to Egypt (XXIII:35).
C. Commits evil deeds (XXIII:37).
D. Vanquished by Nebuchadnezzar and rebels (XXIV:1).
E. Attacked by armed bands (XXIV:2).
F. Punished for continuing sins of Menasseh (XXIV:3–4).
G. Dies at the hands of the Chaldees (XXIV:6).

LI. Jehoiachin succeeds Jehoiakim (XXIV:6–16).
- A. No aid from Egypt (XXIV:7).
- B. Nebuchadnezzar besieges Jerusalem (XXIV:10–11).
- C. Captured by Babylonians (XXIV:12).
- D. Temple looted (XXIV:13).
- E. Exile king and all important people (XXIV:14–16).

LII. Zedekiah appointed by Nebuchadnezzar (XXIV:17–20).
- A. Sinned (XXIV:19).
- B. Rebelled against Nebuchadnezzar (XXIV:20).

LIII. Destruction of Jerusalem (XXV:1–10).
- A. Siege (XXV:1–3).
- B. Breach of walls (XXV:4).
- C. Capture of Zedekiah (XXV:4–7).
- D. Destruction of city and Temple (XXV:8–10).

LIV. Exile remnant except poor (XXV:18–21).
LV. Loot Temple (XXV:13–17).
LVI. Important people executed (XXV:18–21).
LVII. Gedaliah son of Ahikam (XXV:22–26).
- A. Appointed by Nebuchadnezzar over remnant (XXV:22).
- B. Swears to protect people from Chaldees (XXV:23–24).
- C. Assassinated by Ishmael son of Nethaniah (XXV:25).
- D. Jews flee to Egypt to escape Nebuchadnezzar's vengeance (XXV:26).

LVIII. Jehoiachin released from prison with honors and sustenance (XXV:27–30).

ספר מלכים ב

•

מקראות גדולות

II KINGS

א א וַיִּפְשַׁע מוֹאָב בְּיִשְׂרָאֵל אַחֲרֵי מוֹת אַחְאָב: ב וַיִּפֹּל אֲחַזְיָה בְּעַד הַשְּׂבָכָה בַּעֲלִיָּתוֹ אֲשֶׁר בְּשֹׁמְרוֹן וַיָּחַל וַיִּשְׁלַח מַלְאָכִים וַיֹּאמֶר אֲלֵהֶם לְכוּ דִרְשׁוּ בְּבַעַל זְבוּב אֱלֹהֵי עֶקְרוֹן אִם־אֶחְיֶה מֵחֳלִי זֶה: ג וּמַלְאַךְ יְהוָה דִּבֶּר אֶל־אֵלִיָּה הַתִּשְׁבִּי קוּם עֲלֵה לִקְרַאת מַלְאֲכֵי מֶלֶךְ־שֹׁמְרוֹן וְדַבֵּר אֲלֵהֶם הֲמִבְּלִי אֵין־אֱלֹהִים בְּיִשְׂרָאֵל אַתֶּם הֹלְכִים לִדְרֹשׁ בְּבַעַל זְבוּב אֱלֹהֵי עֶקְרוֹן: ד וְלָכֵן כֹּה־אָמַר יְהוָה הַמִּטָּה אֲשֶׁר־עָלִיתָ שָּׁם לֹא־תֵרֵד מִמֶּנָּה כִּי מוֹת תָּמוּת וַיֵּלֶךְ אֵלִיָּה: ה וַיָּשׁוּבוּ

תרגום

א וּמְרָדוּ מוֹאֲבָאֵי בְּיִשְׂרָאֵל בָּתַר דְּמִית אַחְאָב: ב וּנְפַל אֲחַזְיָה מִן סְרִגְתָּא בְּעִילִּיתֵיהּ דִּי בְשָׁמְרוֹן וְאִתְמְרַע וּשְׁלַח אִזְגַּדִּין וַאֲמַר לְהוֹן אֱזִילוּ תְּבְעוּ בְּבַעַל זְבוּב טַעֲוַת עֶקְרוֹן אִם אֱחֵי מִמַּרְעִי דֵּין: ג וּמַלְאֲכָא דַּיְיָ מַלֵּיל עִם אֵלִיָּהוּ דְּמִן תּוֹשָׁב קוּם סַק לְקַדָּמוּת אִזְגַּדֵּי מַלְכָּא דְשָׁמְרוֹן וּמַלֵּיל עִמְּהוֹן הֲלָא אֱלָהָא קַיָּם דִּשְׁכִנְתֵּיהּ שַׁרְיָא בְּיִשְׂרָאֵל אַתּוּן אָזְלִין לְמִתְבַּע בְּבַעַל זְבוּב טַעֲוַת עֶקְרוֹן: ד וּבְכֵן כִּדְנַן אֲמַר יְיָ עַרְסָא דִסְלֵיקְתָּא תַּמָּן לָא תֵיחוּת מִנַּהּ אֲרֵי מְמָת תְּמוּת וַאֲזַל אֵלִיָּה: ה וְתָבוּ אִזְגַּדַּיָּא לְוָתֵיהּ

ת"א המבלי. פקידה שער ק:

רש"י

א (ב) בעד השבכה. גרא"ד"ה בלע"ז. אומר אני שרגילים לאורגו שתי וערב בנסרים ארוכים וקלרים שקורין (לטש) קנטיגל"י בלע"ז ועושין נקבים נקבים כעין שבכה וקרוי פרדוג"י בלע"ז. ואני שמעתי שבכה ווי"ן בלע"ז ובלשון אשכנז שווינדל שטיג כמו שפירשתי ובלולים יעלו (מלכים א' ו' ח'): ויחל. לשון חולי:

רד"ק

(א) ויפשע מואב. לפי שהיה עובד אחאב כמו שאמר למטה והשיב למלך ישראל מאה אלף כרים וכיון שמת אחאב פשע בבנו: (ב) בעד השבכה. השבכה היתה בעלית והיא ארובה ואורגים אותם בעצים שתי וערב ומניחים נקבים להאיר בבית התחתון ומפני זה נקראת שבכה שהיא עשויה

רלב"ג

(א) ויפשע מואב בישראל אחרי מות אחאב. ספר זה להעיר שיותר רעות היו פעלות אחזיה מפעלות אחאב כי אחאב עם קלת מרוע מעשיו אבל זה היה מחזיק בכל אותן הפעלות הרעות שעשו אביו ואמו וכאילו היה זה סבה שפשע מואב בישראל ולא נתנו למלך ישראל המס שהיו נותנים לו מקודם: (ב) בעד השבכה. הוא מעשה רשת עשוי על הארובה שיכנס האור דרך הנקבים אשר בשבכה בבית אשר תחת העלייה: (ד) וילך אליה. ר"ל שככר הלך לקראת מלאכי מלך שומרון ואמר להם מה שלוהו הש"י:

מנחת שי

א (ג) המבלי. הס"א בחטף פתח ובמאריך וכן חבריו שבפנין. ורבים כמותם כמ"ש בסוף מאמר המאריך ובפרשת בשלח על המבלי אין קברים:

מצודת דוד

א (א) ויפשע מואב. כי מאז היו עבדים לישראל ואחרי מות אחאב מרדו: (ב) בעד השבכה. ארובה היתה ברלפת העליה והיתה סתומה מעלים דקים עשויה כעין שבכה ובעברו דרך עליה נשברה ונפל דרך בה: ויחל. נעשה חולה: (ג) המבלי אין. המלה כפול לתוספת ביאור ור"ל וכי בעבור שאין אלהים בישראל כו' בתמיה הלא יש אלהים בישראל ומדוע לא דרשתם בנביאיו: (ד) וילך. הלך לדרכו:

מצודת ציון

א (ב) השבכה. מעשה רשת וכן שבכים מעשה שבכה (מ"א ז): בבעל זבוב. כן שם הע"ג: (ג) מלאכי. שלוחי:

upper chamber, Ahaziah should have taken heed of God's retribution. Instead, he sent to inquire of Baal-zebub, the god of Ekron. He did this because he received no response from Baal, the local deity [*Malbim*].

Baal-zebub was made in the shape of a fly and was as small as a fly. It was made small enough to be

1

1. Moab rebelled against Israel after Ahab's death. 2. Now Ahaziah fell through the lattice in his upper chamber that was in Samaria, and he became ill; and he sent messengers and said to them, "Go inquire of Baal-zebub, the god of Ekron, whether I will recover from this illness." 3. But an angel of the Lord spoke to Elijah the Tishbite [saying], "Arise, go up toward the king of Samaria's messengers, and speak to them, [saying], 'Is it because there is no God in Israel, that you go to inquire of Baal-zebub the god of Ekron? 4. Therefore, so has the Lord said, "From the bed upon which you have ascended you will not descend, for you shall die."'" And Elijah went.

1. **Moab rebelled** — See below 3:4 for a detailed account of Mesha's tribute to Israel. As long as Ahab lived, Mesha paid tribute. After Ahab's death, however, he rebelled [*Redak*].

after Ahab's death — Just as Ahaziah rebelled against God, so did Moab rebel against him [*Abarbanel*].

Although Ahab too had sinned, since he repented of his sins, God did not lead Moab to rebel against him. Ahaziah, however, persisted in his evil ways. [*Ralbag*]

2. **Now Ahaziah fell** — This too was part of his punishment for rebelling against God [*Abarbanel*].

through the lattice — *"grata" in Medieval Latin, lattice. I say that they were accustomed to weave it as a warp and a woof with long boards and short ones, which is called "lattes, lathe* in *Fr., cancelli* in Latin: *cancel in O.F., space behind the grating, and they would make it all of holes like a sort of net, and it is called* "prodnè" in O.F. *And I heard that* שְׂבָכָה *is vis in Fr. a screw, and in German "schwindel stieg," a spiral staircase, as I explained in* (I Kings 6:8) *"and with winding stairs they would go up . . ."* [*Rashi*].

According to the first and generally accepted interpretation, Ahaziah fell through the latticework in the floor of his upper chamber. According to the second he fell down the stairs which led up to the upper chamber.

and he became ill — Heb. וַיָּחַל *an expression of sickness.* — *Rashi,* see also *Redak.*

Although the final "he" is omitted, it is, nevertheless, derived from the root חלה, meaning *to become ill.*

"Go inquire of Baal-zebub the god of Ekron — After falling from his

הַמַּלְאָכִים אֵלָיו וַיֹּאמֶר אֲלֵיהֶם מַה־
זֶּה שַׁבְתֶּם: ו וַיֹּאמְרוּ אֵלָיו אִישׁ׀ עָלָה
לִקְרָאתֵנוּ וַיֹּאמֶר אֵלֵינוּ לְכוּ שׁוּבוּ אֶל־
הַמֶּלֶךְ אֲשֶׁר־שָׁלַח אֶתְכֶם וְדִבַּרְתֶּם
אֵלָיו כֹּה אָמַר יְהוָה הֲמִבְּלִי אֵין־אֱלֹהִים
בְּיִשְׂרָאֵל אַתָּה שֹׁלֵחַ לִדְרֹשׁ בְּבַעַל
זְבוּב אֱלֹהֵי עֶקְרוֹן לָכֵן הַמִּטָּה אֲשֶׁר־
עָלִיתָ שָּׁם לֹא־תֵרֵד מִמֶּנָּה כִּי־מוֹת
תָּמוּת: ז וַיְדַבֵּר אֲלֵהֶם מֶה מִשְׁפַּט
הָאִישׁ אֲשֶׁר עָלָה לִקְרַאתְכֶם וַיְדַבֵּר
אֲלֵיכֶם אֶת־הַדְּבָרִים הָאֵלֶּה: ח וַיֹּאמְרוּ
אֵלָיו אִישׁ בַּעַל שֵׂעָר וְאֵזוֹר עוֹר אָזוּר

נְאָמַר לְהוֹן מָא בֵין
תְּבִתּוּן: ו וַאֲמָרוּ לֵיהּ
גַּבְרָא סְלֵיק לְקַדָּמוּתָנָא
וַאֲמַר לָנָא אֱזִילוּ תוּבוּ
לְוָת מַלְכָּא דִשְׁלַח יָתְכוֹן
וּתְמַלְּלוּן עִמֵּיהּ כִּדְנַן
אֲמַר יְיָ הֲלָא אֱלָהָא קַיָּם
דִּשְׁכִנְתֵּיהּ שַׁרְיָא
בְּיִשְׂרָאֵל אַתְּ שָׁלַח
לְמִתְבַּע בְּבַעַל זְבוּב
טָעֲוַת עֶקְרוֹן בְּכֵן עַרְסָא
דִּסְלֵיקְתָּא תַמָּן לָא
תֵיחוּת מִנַהּ אֲרֵי מְמָת
תְּמוּת: ז וּמַלֵּיל עִמְּהוֹן
מָא נִמוּסָא דְגַבְרָא
דִּסְלֵיק לְקַדָּמוּתְכוֹן
וּמַלֵּיל עִמְּכוֹן יָת
פִּתְגָמַיָּא הָאִלֵּין:
ח וַאֲמָרוּ לֵיהּ גְּבַר בְּעֵיל
סְעַר וְזַרְזָא דְמַשְׁכָא
אסיר

ת״א ואזור עור. פקידה שער פד:

רד״ק

שעשה שבכה שהוא חרשת: ויחל. מן חלה על משקל ויעל מן ׳תארו ותרגומו מה נמיסא דגברא ונראה כי אלישע לא היה או
גלה ונקמצ׳ היו״ד מפני ההפסק: (ז) מה משפט האיש. מה עמו כי פעמים היה מניחו באחת המקומות והיה הולך יחידי

רלב״ג

(ז) מה משפט האיש. ר״ל מה מנהג האיש וכן וכה משפטו כל הימים:

מצודת דוד

(ז) מה משפט האיש. מה תארו ומלבושיו: (ח) בעל שער.

מצודת ציון

(ז) משפט. ר״ל מנהג:

for sending them, whereas in reality, the prophet had reprimanded them for obeying him [*Malbim*].

Therefore — Since you have profaned the name of God by sending to inquire of pagan deities, you shall not recover from your illness [*Daath Soferim*].

7. **"What was the manner of the man** — What was his description? *Jonathan* renders: "What was his behavior?" [*Redak*].

who came up toward you — and did not come directly to speak to me. Not only did he show disrespect toward me by not appearing, but he also did not execute his mission [*Malbim*].

8. **"He was a hairy man** — He had not groomed his hair. He was, therefore, ashamed to appear before a king in his unkempt condition [*Malbim*].

with a leather belt — not appropriate attire for audience with a king [*Malbim*].

5. And the messengers returned to him, and he said, "Why have you returned?" 6. And they said to him, "A man came up toward us and said to us, 'Go return to the king who sent you, and you shall speak to him, [saying,] "So has the Lord said, 'Is it because there is no God in Israel that you send to inquire of Baal-zebub, the god of Ekron? Therefore, from the bed upon which you have ascended, you will not descend, for you will die.'" 7. And he spoke to them, saying, "What was the manner of the man who came up toward you, and spoke these words to you?" 8. And they said, "He was a hairy man, with a leather belt girded . . .

carried in the pocket of its worshippers. [*Shabbath* 83b].

The renowned Kabalist, Rabbi Moshe Kordiviro, related the origin of this deity. When Pharaoh's daughter asked Solomon to give something to her gods, he replied derisively, "Take the fly that has alighted on my robe." She deliberately took the fly and established a religion of fly worshippers. This fly worship was adopted by the Philistines in Ekron [*K'li Y'kar*].

Although the Talmud (*Shabbath* 83b) identifies Baal-berith (Jud. 8:33) with Baal-zebub (it is possible that this worship had been abandoned until Pharaoh's daughter reestablished it.

6. **"A man came up toward us** — Perhaps they did not recognize Elijah, who had not appeared for many years, especially not in Samaria, where Jezebel would have captured him [*Redak*]. Alternatively, it is possible that they did recognize him. Yet, they feared that Ahaziah would deal harshly with them for allowing him to go free [*Daath Soferim*].

'Go return — The fact the king sent you is no justification of your act. God's words must be obeyed rather than the king's [*Daath Soferim*].

"So has the Lord said — Although, according to the original prophecy, Elijah was to scold the messengers on his own, without mentioning that this was the word of God, they were afraid to reveal to the king that they were scolded for obeying his orders. Rather, they quoted the prophet as saying this in the name of the Lord. They, therefore, were not afraid to say that he had reprimanded the king himself

במתניו ויאמר אליה התשבי הוא:
ט וישלח אליו שר חמשים וחמשיו
ויעל אליו והנה ישב על־ראש ההר
וידבר אליו איש האלהים המלך
דבר רדה: י ויענה אליהו וידבר אל־
שר החמשים ואם־איש אלהים אני
תרד אש מן־השמים ותאכל אתך
ואת־חמשיך ותרד אש מן־השמים
ותאכל אתו ואת־חמשיו: יא וישב
וישלח אליו שר־חמשים אחר וחמשיו
ויען וידבר אליו איש האלהים כה־
אמר המלך מהרה רדה: יב ויען אליה
וידבר אליהם אם־איש האלהים אני

תרגום

אסיר בחרציה ואמר
אליה דמן תושב הוא:
ט ושלח לותיה רב
חמשין וחמשין דעמיה
וסליק לותיה והוא יתיב
על ריש טורא ומליל
עמיה נביא דיי מלכא
מליל חות: י ואתיב
אליה ומליל עם רב
חמשין אם נביא דיי
אנא תיחות אשתא מן
שמיא ותיכול יתך וית
חמשין דעמך ונחתת
אשתא מן שמיא ואכלת
יתיה וית חמשין דעמיה:
יא ותב ושלח לותיה רב
חמשין אוחרנין וחמשין
דעמיה ואתיב ומליל
עמיה נביא דיי כדנן
אמר מלכא אוחי חות:
יב ואתיב אליה ומליל
עמהון אם נביא דיי
אנא

רד"ק

על ההרים להתבודד בנבואה: (ח) אליהו התשבי. כי יודע היה כי מנהגו לאזור אזור עור והיה ידוע כי בעל שער היה ותימ' הוא היאך לא היו מכירים אותו מלאכי מלך ישראל והלא הוא היה רגיל עם אחאב ובשמרון ואפשר כי אלו האנשים ששלח מלך ישראל לא היו אז בשמרון כשהיה אליהו רגיל שם וזמן רב הי' לאליהו שלא היה בשמרון מפני איזבל שאמר' להרגו שהרי במלחמת בן הדד ראינו שלא הי' שם ולא במלחמות רמות גלעד כי מיכיהו בן ימלא הי' להם אז הנביא לה' אשר בשמרון: (יב)ויען אליה וידבר אליהם. ויען כמו ויען איוב הראשון ועניתה ואמרת לשון צעקה בדבור:

רלב"ג

(ט) וישלח אליו שר חמשים וחמשיו. ר"ל שבלח לאליהו לכבודו לקרוא לו שר גדול שהיו חמשים איש הולכים לפניו והלכו עמו החמשים איש ההם: איש האלהים המלך דבר רדה. ידמה מדבריהם שהם היו רוצים להביאו עמהם בהכרח מצד מצות המלך ולזה אמרו לו שיבא כמצות המלך והרגיש אליהו מעניהם שאם לא יסכים ללכת מעצמו יקחוהו בכח למלאת מצות המלך ולזאת אמר להם כי מאחר שהם קוראי' אותו איש אלהים הנה מזה הצד אינו תחת המלך ולא יועילו לחזקם עמו ולזה אמר ואם איש אלהים אני תרד אש מן השמים ותאכל אותך ואת חמשיך. ולפי שהשר השני דבר אליו ג"כ כאופן שדבר אליו הראשון עשה אליהו שירדה אש ג"כ ואכלה אותו ואת חמשיו אמנם השר הג'

מצודת דוד

מגודל בשער הרבה ומגור הוא כחגורה של עור: (ט) וחמשיו. עם חמשים האנשים אשר הוא שר עליהם: המלך דבר רדה. כאומר רד

let a fire come down from heaven — Elijah understood that were he not to comply with the king's order, the captain and his fifty men would force him to accompany them. He therefore punished them as he had punished the prophets of Baal on Mt. Carmel. [*Abarbanel, Mezudath David*].

11. **he raised his voice** — This one did not dare to climb the mountain. Instead, he stood at the foot of the mountain and shouted. Also, he did not command Elijah to come down. He merely quoted the king as saying, "Come down quickly!" [*Malbim.* See also *Redak*].

12. **and spoke to them** — Since they all stood at the foot of the mountain, Elijah raised his voice

around his waist." And he said, "He is Elijah the Tishbite."
9. And he sent to him a captain of fifty men and his fifty men; and he went up to him, and behold, he was sitting on a mountain top, and he spoke to him, saying, "O man of God, the King has spoken; come down!"
10. And Elijah replied, and spoke to the captain of fifty, "Now, if I am a man of God, let a fire come down from the heaven and consume you and your fifty men!" And a fire came down from heaven and consumed him and his fifty men.
11. And again he sent to him another captain of fifty and his fifty men, and he raised and spoke to him, saying, "O man of God, so said the King, 'Come down quickly!'"
12. And Elijah raised his voice and spoke to them, [saying,] "If I am a man of God,

"He is Elijah the Tishbite" — who is surely not ashamed to appear before me. It is but because of his hatred toward the house of Ahab that he refuses to appear before me [*Malbim*].

Elijah originated from a city named Toshav. Hence the appelation *Tishbite.* See I Kings 17:1, Comm. Dig.

Elijah was noted for the leather belt which he always wore around his waist. This was taken from the ram sacrificed instead of Isaac on Mt. Moriah (*Pirke d'R. Eliezer* ch. 31). It was Elijah's spirit that sacrificed the ram. It was therefore given to him as his priestly due. [*Asarah Maamaroth, Maamar Hikur Din,* part 4, ch. 19. See Lev. 7:8].

Although Elisha was Elijah's disciple, he was not with him at this time since Elijah sometimes left him in seclusion on the mountains to meditate and prepare himself for prophecy [*Redak*].

and he went up to him — The first captain had the audacity to climb the mountain and order Elijah to come down. Moreover, he spoke disrespectfully to him. "The king has spoken; therefore I say, 'Come down!'" [*Malbim*].

Abarbanel points out that the prophet to whom God speaks is equal to the sanctuary of the Lord. Hence the captain had committed a grave sin by approaching him.

10. **and spoke to the captain** — He spoke to the captain only, since he alone had climbed to the mountain top. His men remained at the foot of the mountain [*Malbim*].

"Now if I am a man of God — I am not under the king's jurisdiction. Therefore . . . [*Abarbanel*].

תֵּרֶד אֵשׁ מִן־הַשָּׁמַיִם וְתֹאכַל אֹתְךָ וְאֶת־חֲמִשֶּׁיךָ וַתֵּרֶד אֵשׁ־אֱלֹהִים מִן־הַשָּׁמַיִם וַתֹּאכַל אֹתוֹ וְאֶת־חֲמִשָּׁיו׃
יג וַיָּשָׁב וַיִּשְׁלַח שַׂר־חֲמִשִּׁים שְׁלִשִׁים וַחֲמִשָּׁיו וַיַּעַל וַיָּבֹא שַׂר־הַחֲמִשִּׁים הַשְּׁלִישִׁי וַיִּכְרַע עַל־בִּרְכָּיו לְנֶגֶד אֵלִיָּהוּ וַיִּתְחַנֵּן אֵלָיו וַיְדַבֵּר אֵלָיו אִישׁ הָאֱלֹהִים תִּיקַר־נָא נַפְשִׁי וְנֶפֶשׁ עֲבָדֶיךָ אֵלֶּה חֲמִשִּׁים בְּעֵינֶיךָ׃
יד הִנֵּה יָרְדָה אֵשׁ מִן־הַשָּׁמַיִם וַתֹּאכַל אֶת־שְׁנֵי שָׂרֵי הַחֲמִשִּׁים הָרִאשֹׁנִים וְאֶת־חֲמִשֵּׁיהֶם וְעַתָּה תִּיקַר נַפְשִׁי בְּעֵינֶיךָ׃
טו וַיְדַבֵּר מַלְאַךְ יְהוָה אֶל־אֵלִיָּהוּ רֵד אוֹתוֹ אַל־תִּירָא מִפָּנָיו וַיָּקָם וַיֵּרֶד אוֹתוֹ אֶל־הַמֶּלֶךְ׃
טז וַיְדַבֵּר אֵלָיו כֹּה־אָמַר יְהוָה

אֲנָא מֵיחוּת אֶשָּׁתָא מִן שְׁמַיָא וְתֵיכוּל יָתָךְ וְיַת חַמְשִׁין דְעִמָךְ וּנְחָתַת אֶשָּׁתָא מִן שְׁמַיָא וַאֲכָלַת יָתֵיהּ וְיַת חַמְשִׁין דְעִמֵיהּ׃ יג וְתָב וּשְׁלַח רַב חַמְשִׁין תְּלִיתָאֵי, וְחַמְשִׁין דְעִמֵיהּ וּסְלִיק וַאֲתָא רַב חַמְשִׁין תְּלִיתָאִין וּכְרַע עַל בִּרְכּוֹהִי לָקֳבֵיל אֵלִיָהוּ וּבְעָא מִן קֳדָמוֹהִי וּמַלֵיל עִמֵיהּ נְבִיָא דַיְיָ תֵּיקַר כְּעַן נַפְשִׁי וְנַפְשָׁא דְעַבְדָךְ אִלֵין חַמְשִׁין בְּעֵינָךְ׃ יד הָא נְחָתַת אֶשָּׁתָא מִן שְׁמַיָא וַאֲכָלַת יַת תְּרֵין רַבְּנֵי חַמְשִׁין קַדְמָאִין וְיַת חַמְשִׁין דְעִמְהוֹן וּכְעַן תֵּיקַר נַפְשִׁי בְּעֵינָךְ׃ טו וּמַלֵיל מַלְאֲכָא דַיְיָ עִם אֵלִיָהוּ חוּת עִמֵיהּ לָא תִדְחַל מִן קֳדָמוֹהִי וְקָם וּנְחַת עִמֵיהּ לְוַת מַלְכָּא׃ טז וּמַלֵיל עִמֵיהּ כִּדְנַן אָמַר

ת״א שרי החמשים. פקידה שער קנ:

רד״ק

(טו) רד אותו. פי׳ עמו וכן וירד אתו אל המלך ירד עמו והלך אל המלך כי השר עלה אל קצה ההר ואליהו היה בראש ההר: אל תירא מפניו.

מנחת שי

(יג) תיקר נא נפשי. תיקר ב׳ חד מלעיל וחד מלרע וכענין. ועיין מ״ש במאריך במאריך בתירוץ תקירה ראשונה: (יד) הנה ירדה אש מן השמים. ברוב ספרי הדפוס וכ״י שופר הפוך ביו״ד ובלא טעם אחר בדל״ת:

רלב״ג

לא הראה שיבא אליו בכח אבל בא אליו בתחנונים ולזה לא עשה אליהו דבר כנגדו וגם לא היה מסכים לבא עם השר הסוא אל המלך

מצודת ציון

(יג) שר חמשים שלשים וחמשיו. הוא הפוך כמו שר חמשים וחמשיו שלישים:

מצודת דוד

במלות המלך כי אקחך עם אנשי: (יג) תיקר נא נפשי. תהא נפשי יקרה וחשובה בעיניך לבל תמית אותי: (יד) ותאכל וגו׳. על שדברו בזדון: ועתה. הואיל ואני באתי בהכנעה: (טו) רד אותו. רד עמו: וירד אותו. וילך עמו:

— If the purpose of the fire was to demonstrate your power and to cast your fear upon us, you have already accomplished it through the first two incidents. If it was a punishment for the audacity demonstrated by my predecessors, unlike them, I have come with humility. Therefore, I implore you to have pity on your servants and not to bring down another fire from heaven [*Malbim*].

now may my soul be precious in your eyes — Please accompany me to the king lest he put me to death for failing to bring you to him [*Malbim*].

let a fire come down from heaven and consume you and your fifty men!" And an enormous fire came down from heaven and consumed him and his fifty men. 13. And again he sent a third captain of fifty and his fifty men; and the third captain of fifty climbed up and came and kneeled on his knees opposite Elijah and implored him and spoke to him, saying, "O man of God, may my soul and the soul of these fifty servants of yours be precious in your eyes. 14. Behold, a fire has come down from heaven and consumed the first two captains of fifty and their fifties; now may my soul be precious in your eyes." 15. And the angel of the Lord spoke to Elijah, saying, "Go down with him; fear him not." And he arose and went down with him to the king. 16. And he spoke to him, saying, "So has the Lord said,

and addressed all of them, both the captain and his fifty men. Although the second captain was not as audacious as the first, since he thought that he was standing at a safe distance where the fire could not reach him, Elijah let him know that he was still vulnerable to God's fire [*Malbim.* See also *Redak*].

And an enormous fire — lit. a fire of God, a fire which burnt over a great distance [*Malbim*].

This expression is often used to denote enormity. See *Redak,* Jonah 3:3.

Alternatively, the word *E-lohim* denotes the divine attribute of justice. The fire meted out the full measure of justice against those who had already seen or heard the punishment visited upon their predecessors [*Daath Soferim, K'li Y'kar*].

Alternatively, since the second captain added the word מְהֵרָה, *quickly* he was consumed by a greater conflagration than was the first captain [*Abarbanel*].

13. **And again he sent** — Ahaziah did not despair of subordinating Elijah despite the fate of the first two companies he had sent [*Daath Soferim*].

climbed up and came — This one came up to the mountain top with humility, unlike his two predecessors [*Malbim*].

these fifty servants of yours — We are your servants. We have not come to coerce you to come down to Ahaziah. Possibly, even Ahaziah himself had not sent these soldiers to bring Elijah to him by force. The conspicuous omission of the phrase, *to him,* mentioned in the first two cases, *he sent to him,* lends support to this conjecture [*K'li Y'kar*].

14. **"Behold, a fire has come down**

יַעַן אֲשֶׁר־שָׁלַחְתָּ מַלְאָכִים לִדְרֹשׁ
בְּבַעַל זְבוּב אֱלֹהֵי עֶקְרוֹן הֲמִבְּלִי אֵין־
אֱלֹהִים בְּיִשְׂרָאֵל לִדְרֹשׁ בִּדְבָרוֹ לָכֵן
הַמִּטָּה אֲשֶׁר־עָלִיתָ שָּׁם לֹא־תֵרֵד
מִמֶּנָּה כִּי־מוֹת תָּמוּת׃ וַיָּמָת כִּדְבַר
יְהוָה אֲשֶׁר־דִּבֶּר אֵלִיָּהוּ וַיִּמְלֹךְ יְהוֹרָם
תַּחְתָּיו בִּשְׁנַת שְׁתַּיִם לִיהוֹרָם בֶּן־
יְהוֹשָׁפָט מֶלֶךְ יְהוּדָה כִּי לֹא־הָיָה לוֹ׃

אֲמַר יְיָ חֲלַף דִּשְׁלַחְתָּא
אִזְגַּדִּין לְמִשְׁאַל בְּבַעַל
זְבוּב טַעֲוַת עֶקְרוֹן הֲלָא
אֱלָהָא קַיָּם דִּשְׁכִנְתֵּיהּ
שַׁרְיָא בְּיִשְׂרָאֵל לְמִשְׁאַל
בְּפִתְגָמֵיהּ בְּכֵן עַרְסָא
דִּסְלֵיקְתָּא תַמָּן לָא
תֵיחוֹת מִנֵּהּ אֲרֵי מֵימַת
תְּמוּת׃ יז וּמִית כְּפִתְגָמָא
דַּיְיָ דְּמַלֵּיל אֵלִיָּהוּ וּמְלַךְ
יְהוֹרָם תְּחוֹתוֹהִי בִּשְׁנַת
תַּרְתֵּין לִיהוֹרָם בַּר
יְהוֹשָׁפָט מַלְכָּא דְבֵית
יְהוּדָה אֲרֵי לָא הֲוָה לֵיהּ
בר

רש"י

(יז) וימלוך יהורם תחתיו. אחיו היה: בשנת שתים ליהורם בן יהושפט. אפשר לומר כן והלא מלך בשנת י"ט ליהושפט שהרי אחזיהו מלך בי"ז ומלך שנתים ובסמוך כתיב בשנת י"ח ליהושפט מלך יהורם ויהושפט מלך עשרים וחמש שנים קודם שמלך יהורם בנו אלא ראוי היה יהושפט ליהרג ברמות גלעד ובשכר שזעק תלה לו שבע שנים ומאותה שעה הוא מונה לבנו:

רד"ק

כי מתיירא הי' שיוליכנו למלך והי' ירא מן המלך מפני שהתנבא עליו רע שימות או היה ירא מפני איזבל אמו: (יז) בשנת ב' ליהורם בן יהושפט. היאך הי' זה והלא אמר למטה כי מלך בשנת י"ה ליהושפט ויהושפט הלך עמו למלחמת מואב והנה הי' מלך בימי יהושפט שבע שנים כי יהושפט מלך כ"ה שנים אלא שיהושפט המליך את יהורם בנו בחייו מפני מחלוקת אחיו כמו שאומר בדברי הימים ואת הממלכה נתן ליהורם כי הוא הבכור ומה הי' צריך לומר זה ידוע הוא כי המלוכה היא לבכור אלא שנראה כי היה מחלוקת בין בניו לפיכך נתן לו המלוכה בחייו ומלך בחיי אביו שבע שנים ובשנת שתים למלכות יהורם זו שמלך בחיי אביו מלך יהורם בן אחאב על ישראל: כי לא היה לו בן. לא היה לאחזיהו בן לפיכך מלך יהורם אחיו תחתיו. ובסדר עולם בשנת שתים ליהורם בן יהושפט אפשר לומר כן והלא הוא מלך משנת שמונה עשרה ליהושפט אלא לענין שנאמר ויעזור יהושפט וה' עזרו ויסירם אלהים ממנו ראוי היה יהושפט ליהרג באותו שעה לפי שהי' עוזר לרשע ובשכר שזעק

רלב"ג

לירֿאתו מהמלך ההוא ומאיזבל אמו: (יז) בשנת שתים ליהורם בן יהושפט מלך יהודה. יש בכאן ספק חזק והוא שלא יתכן שיהיה אחזיהו עד שנת שתים ליהורם בן יהושפט וזה שכבר מלך בשנת שבע עשרה ליהושפט ולא מלך כי אם שתים שנים כמו שקדם וכבר מלך יהושפט עשרים וחמש שנה ולזה לא יתכן שנאמר שהתחיל למלוך יהורם בן אחאב בשנת שתים ליהורם בן יהושפט ואם אמרנו שכבר התחיל למלוך יהורם בן יהושפט בחיי אביו מעת מות אחאב הנה לא יתכן מה שאמר ואת הממלכה נתן ליהורם כי הוא הבכור שהרי החזיק בה בחייו והנה זכר במה שיבא כי בשנת חמש ליורם בן אחאב מלך ישראל ויהושפט מלך יהודה מלך יהורם בן יהושפט מלך יהודה וזה ממה שיוסיף עוד ספק על זה ועוד שאחר זה כתב כי בשנת אחת עשרה ליורם בן אחאב מלך אחזיה על יהודה ובמקום אחר כתב כי בשנת שתים עשרה ליורם בן אחאב מלך אחזיה על יהודה וזה לאות כי כשיאמר בשנת כך למלך כך הנה פעם ירצה בו שעברו אותן שנים למלך פעם ירצה שהמליך בשנה ההוא ויהיה הרצון באמרו בשנת אחת עשרה ליורם בן אחאב שכבר עברו לו אחת עשרה שנה והיא בשנת שתים עשרה והרצון באמרו בשנת שתים עשרה הוא שכבר היה בשנה ההיא. והנראה בעיני כי מפני החתון שהיה ליהושפט עם אחאב היה יהושפט מולך אחרי מות אחאב עם מלך ישראל כל ימיו כי היו חולקים לו כבוד בני אחאב מפני היותו זקן והתחתן באחאב ולזה תמצא שאמר בשנת חמש ליורם בן אחאב מלך ישראל ויהושפט מלך יהודה והרצון בו שיהושפט היה מנהיג מלכות ישראל עמו וכאילו היה יהושפט מלך ישראל גם כן והוא מבואר שהוא מחוייב שיהיה פירושו כן כי אי אפשר שיהיה הרצון בו שתהיה שנת חמש ליהושפט כי שנת החמש ליהורם בן אחאב הוא שנת עשרים וחמש ליהושפט אחר שכבר מלך אז יהורם בן יהושפט ובזה הדרך נאמר שעד שהתחילה השנה השנית למלכות יהורם מלך יהודה היה מלך יהודה משתתף עם יהורם בן אחאב בהנהגת המלכות כי כבר תמצא במלחמותיו שהי' יהושפט תמיד עמהם. והנה ליישב כל אלו הפסוקים ידמה בעיני שהשנה שמלך בה אחזיה היתה י"ח ליהושפט ר"ל שכבר עברו לו שבע עשרה ובמלוך יהורם עברו ליהושפט י"ח שנה והיה בשנת התשע עשרה ובשנ' שעברו חמש שנים ליהורם בן אחאב מלך ישראל מלך יהורם בן יהושפט מלך יהודה ובזה לא יפול שום ספק כי כשעברו לאחאב ארבע שנים מלך יהושפט ונשארו לאחאב י"ח שנים מקוטעים ולזה לא עברו ליהושפט במותו כי אם י"ז שנים שלמים והיה בשנת י"ח ומלך אחזיה שתי שנים מקוטעים ומת כשהיה יהושפט בשנת התשע עשרה ואחר כן יהושפט פחות מחמש שנים כדרך שלקח מהשנה העשרים וחמש מעט ואז עברו חמש שנים ליהורם בן אחאב והיא בשנה הששי' וכשעברו לו אחת עשרה שנה והיה בשנת השתים עשרה כדרך שלקח מהשתים עשרה יותר ממה

מצודת דוד

(יז) וימליך יהורם. אחי אחזיה בן אחאב: בשנת שתים ליהורם בן יהושפט. הרז"ל מעת שהלך יהושפט אל רמות גלעד לעזור לאחאב מונין המלכות גם לבנו על כי היה ראוי ליהרג אז על שעזר לרשע ושעת ההיא הם שתי שנים כי אז נהרג אחאב ומיד מלך בנו אחזיה וימי מלכו שנתים ומת ומיד מלך יהורם אחיו: כי לא וגו'. שימלוך תחתיו ולזה מלך אחיו:

'Since you sent messengers to inquire of Baal-zebub the god of Ekron (Is it because there is no God in Israel to inquire of His word?), therefore, from the bed upon which you have risen, you will not get down, for you shall die.'" 17. And he died according to the word of the Lord that Elijah had spoken; and Jehoram reigned in his stead in the second year of Jehoram the son of Jehoshaphat, the king of Judah, for he had no son.

15. **"Go down with him** — from the mountain top [*Redak*].

fear him not — Elijah feared that he would bring him before Ahaziah who would put him to death for prophesying his doom, or before Jezebel his mother, who would put him to death to avenge the death of her prophets, whom Elijah had massacred on Mt. Carmel [*Redak*].

16. **'Since you sent messengers** — Now he did not precede his prophecy with words of rebuke, "Is it because there is no God in Israel . . ." Ahaziah could have answered that since no prophets appeared to him, he was forced to send to Ekron to inquire of Baal-zebub. This rebuke was applicable only in the case of the messengers to whom Elijah had appeared. Now that he came to Ahaziah, however, he began his prophecy immediately with God's message of his approaching demise. [He did, however, insert the rebuke as a sort of parenthetical phrase, to impress upon him the implication of his sending to inquire of pagan deities] [*Malbim*].

17. **and Jehoram reigned in his stead** — *He was his brother* [*Rashi*].

in the second year of Jehoram the son of Jehoshaphat — *Is it possible to say this? Did he not reign in the nineteenth year of Jehoshaphat, for Ahaziah reigned in the seventeenth* year of Jehoshaphat (I Kings 22:52), *and reigned for two years* (ibid.), *and in a nearby chapter also it is written* (3:1) *In the eighteenth year of Jehoshaphat, Jehoram reigned. Now Jehoshaphat reigned twenty-five years before Jehoram his son reigned. But, Jehoshaphat was deservant of being killed in Ramoth-Gilead, but as a reward for his crying out* to God, God *suspended his death for him seven years, and from that time Scripture counts* the years *to his son* [*Rashi* from *Seder Olam* ch. 17, Tosefta Sotah 12:2].

Redak maintains that Jehoshaphat gave over the throne to Jehoram during his lifetime to prevent conflict among the brothers. Because of this, the Chronicler states, " . . . and the kingdom he gave to Jehoram because he was the firstborn (II Chron. 21:3).

18. **And the remaining deeds** —

בן: יח וְיֶתֶר דִּבְרֵי אֲחַזְיָהוּ אֲשֶׁר עָשָׂה הֲלוֹא־הֵמָּה כְתוּבִים עַל־סֵפֶר דִּבְרֵי הַיָּמִים לְמַלְכֵי יִשְׂרָאֵל: ב א וַיְהִי בְּהַעֲלוֹת יְהֹוָה אֶת־אֵלִיָּהוּ בַּסְעָרָה הַשָּׁמָיִם וַיֵּלֶךְ אֵלִיָּהוּ וֶאֱלִישָׁע מִן־הַגִּלְגָּל: ב וַיֹּאמֶר אֵלִיָּהוּ אֶל־אֱלִישָׁע שֵׁב־נָא פֹה כִּי יְהֹוָה שְׁלָחַנִי עַד־בֵּית־אֵל וַיֹּאמֶר אֱלִישָׁע חַי־יְהֹוָה וְחֵי־נַפְשְׁךָ אִם־אֶעֶזְבֶךָּ וַיֵּרְדוּ בֵּית־אֵל: ג וַיֵּצְאוּ

תרגום

בר: יח וּשְׁאָר פִּתְגָמֵי אֲחַזְיָה דַעֲבַד הֲלָא אִינוּן כְּתִיבִין עַל סְפַר פִּתְגָמֵי יוֹמַיָּא לְמַלְכָּא דְיִשְׂרָאֵל: א וַהֲוָה בְּאַסָּקוּת יְיָ יָת אֵלִיָּהוּ בְּעַלְעוֹלָא לְצֵית שְׁמַיָּא וַאֲזַל אֵלִיָּהוּ וֶאֱלִישָׁע מִן גִּלְגְּלָא: ב וַאֲמַר אֵלִיָּהוּ לֶאֱלִישָׁע תּוּב כְּעַן הָכָא אֲרֵי יְיָ שַׁלְחַנִי עַד בֵּית אֵל וַאֲמַר אֱלִישָׁע קַיָּם הוּא יְיָ וְחַי נַפְשָׁךְ אִם אֶשְׁבְּקִינָךְ וּנְחַתוּ לְבֵית אֵל: ג וּנְפַקוּ תַּלְמִידֵי נְבִיָּא

רש"י

ב (א) בסערה. ברוח סערה: (ב) שב נא פה. חפץ היה לדחותו מחמת ענוה שלא יראה בהלקחו:

רד"ק

הס' בחטף קמץ

תלה לו' האל ז' שנים ועלו לבנו ועוד נכתבנו: (א) בסערה. בקמץ חטף הסמ"ך אמר בסערה ולא אמר כן למטה אלא רכב אש וסוסי אש רוח סערה היה עמהם כמו שאמר ויעל אליהו בסערה אלא הנראה לאלישע אמר רכב אש וסוסי אש אבל הרוח אינה נראית ורוח הסערה העלתה אותו מן הארץ אל האויר כמי שמעלה הדברים הקלים כן העלתה אותו ברצון האל על גלגל האש ושם נשרפו בגדיו זולתי האדרת וכלה בשרו ועצמו והרוח שבה אל האלהים אשר נתנה ומה שנראה רכב אש וסוסי אש לאלישע להודיע בו כי בהעלותו עלה מישראל רכבו ופרשיו כמו שאמר אלישע אבי אבי רכב ישראל ופרשיו ודעת המונינו גם חכמינו כי הכניסו האל בגן עדן עם גופו כמו שהיה אדם הראשון קודם שחטא וכן הכניס חנוך שם. ובדרש כי עשרה הם שנכנסו חיים לגן עדן: וילך אליהו. ואליהו נאמר לו ברוח הנבואה כי באותו היום ילקח ולא גלה הדבר לאלישע אבל אלישע נאמר לו גם כן ברוח נבואה שהרי אמר גם אני ידעתי החשו ושאר הנביאים נאמרה להם כל שכן הוא ומה שהיו הולכים מעבר הירדן נראה כי כן נאמרה לו לאליהו בנבואה כי מעבר לירדן ילקח אולי היה הלקחו במקום אשר נאסף משה רבינו לכבודו כי מעלתו היתה קרובה למעלת משה רבינו יכן הראה לו הכבוד בהר חורב כמו שהראה לו למשה רבינו וצם מ' יום ומ' לילה כמו שצם משה רבינו: (ב) חי ה' וחי נפשך מת שאמר וחי נפשך אחר שאמר חי ה' לא אמר כן אלא להגדיל כי השבועה הראשונה גדולה אלא נשבע בנפשו

מנחת שי

ב (א) את אליהו בסערה. רבו החילופים שנפלו בספרים על מלה זו והחברתה שבעינן כי במקלתם הבי"ת במאריך והסמ"ך רפה והשוא לבד. ובמקלתם בלא מאריך בבי"ת והסמ"ך דגושה ובשוא לבדו ורד"ק בפי' ובמכלול דף ר"ו ושרשים כתב שהסמ"ך בחטף קמץ והבי"ת מעמדת בגעיה ולא דבר מאומה מדגשות או רפיות הסמ"ך. אמנם ממה שכתב במכלול דף נ"א משמע בהדיא שהסמ"ך רפה יען נמנה זה עם מלין אחרין שנפל מהן הדגש ואות השמוש בגעיה:

רלב"ג

שלקח מהשנה הששית הנה ככר עברו ליהורם בן יהושפט יותר משש שנים שלמים והיותר היה קלתו מהשנה הראשונה ליהורם בן יהושפט וקלתו היה מהשנה השמינית ונחשב לו זה שמנה שנים ולא היה כי אם שש שנים ויותר מעט ולפי שהשנה הראשונה ליהורם בן יהושפט לא היתה אלא זמן מועט מאד כמו שבארנו הנה לא נראה בזמן ההוא היות מלך יהודה בלתי משתתף עם מלך ישראל בהנהגת ישראל ולא הראה לו זה עד בא השנה השנית ליהורם מלך יהודה והנה בזה הדרך נתישב כל זה בלי שום ספק: (א) בהעלות ה' את אליהו בסערה השמים. אי אפשר שיובן שהעלהו השמים כי לא יעלו שם אלו הגופות אבל הכוונה בו כנוגה המליץ כאמרו ערים גדולות ובצורות בשמים ומגדל וראשו בשמים והנה נשאהו רוח ה' אל מקום לא נודע עדיין והוא חי שם כמו שבארנו: (ב) שב נא פה כי ה' שלחני עד בית אל. ראוי שתדע שלא עשה זה אליהו לתכלית שלא יאציל עליו מן הרוח אשר עליו על אלישע שהרי לזה הש"י משחו אלישע כן שפט לנביא תחתיו ואמנם אמר לו זה כדי שלא יחרד אלישע בהפרד אליהו ממנו אם יראהו שינשא בסערה השמים:

מצודת דוד

ב (א) בהעלות. בעת בא הזמן שהעלה ה' את אליהו ע"י רוח סערה אל השמים הלך אז אליהו עם אלישע מן הגלגל: (ב) שב נא פה.

into heaven, he would become the recipient of the prophetic spirit, and all other prophets would receive their prophecy through him [*Malbim*].

as far as Bethel — one of the places where Elijah's disciples were located. He went there to convey the spirit of prophecy upon them. For this reason, he asked Elisha not to accompany him, as mentioned above. Elijah was careful to say, "as far as Bethel," rather than "to Bethel." He would not enter the city where Jeroboam's golden calf was standing. In v. 4, however, he states, "The Lord has sent me to Jericho." We find another contrast between

18. And the remaining deeds of Ahaziah that he did are written in the book of the chronicles of the kings of Israel.

2

1. And it was when the Lord was about to take Elijah up to heaven in a whirlwind, that Elijah and Elisha went from Gilgal.
2. And Elijah said to Elisha, "Stay here now for the Lord has sent me as far as Bethel," but Elisha said, "As the Lord lives and by the life of your soul, I will not leave you." And they went down to Bethel.

i.e. his military feats and his political accomplishments, matters unrelated to observance of the Torah's precepts, were recorded in the chronicles of the kings of Israel, a secular, noncanonical book used to record the day by day happenings of the kings of Israel. There was a corresponding volume used by the kings of Judah. See preface to I Kings.

1. **to take Elijah up to heaven** — *Redak* theorizes that when Elijah was taken up into heaven in a fiery chariot, his clothing, his flesh, and his bones were consumed by the fire, and his soul was returned to its Maker. He admits, however, that the popular belief, following Talmudic and Midrashic sources, is that Elijah was admitted into Paradise while living.

in a whirlwind — lit. in a storm, i.e. *in a storm wind.* [*Rashi*].

that Elijah and Elisha went — Elijah did not reveal to Elisha that God was going to take him up to heaven on that day. Elisha, however, received the same prophetic message and was aware of Elijah's impending departure. We find that even the disciples of the prophets were aware of this, certainly Elisha, Elijah's successor. He was informed that he would be taken up on the eastern bank of the Jordan, much as Moses had departed this world on the eastern bank of the Jordan. This indicated that Elijah had reached a level of spirituality near that of Moses. Just as Moses perceived God's glory on Mt. Sinai, so did Elijah. Just as Moses fasted for forty days, so did Elijah [*Redak*].

2. **"Stay here now** — *He wished to drive him away because of his (Elijah's) humility, so that he would not see him being taken away* [*Rashi*].

Alternatively, Elijah wished to spare Elisha the pain of seeing his master being taken away from him [*Ralbag*]

Alternatively, Elijah wished to convey his prophetic spirit to all his disciples equally, not necessarily through Elisha. If Elisha were alone with him at the time of his ascent

בְנֵי־הַנְּבִיאִים אֲשֶׁר־בֵּית־אֵל אֶל־
אֱלִישָׁע וַיֹּאמְרוּ אֵלָיו הֲיָדַעְתָּ כִּי הַיּוֹם
יְהוָה לֹקֵחַ אֶת־אֲדֹנֶיךָ מֵעַל רֹאשֶׁךָ
וַיֹּאמֶר גַּם־אֲנִי יָדַעְתִּי הֶחֱשׁוּ׃ ד וַיֹּאמֶר
לוֹ אֵלִיָּהוּ אֱלִישָׁע | שֵׁב־נָא פֹה כִּי יְהוָה
שְׁלָחַנִי יְרִיחוֹ וַיֹּאמֶר חַי־יְהוָה וְחֵי־
נַפְשְׁךָ אִם־אֶעֶזְבֶךָּ וַיָּבֹאוּ יְרִיחוֹ׃
ה וַיִּגְּשׁוּ בְנֵי־הַנְּבִיאִים | אֲשֶׁר בִּירִיחוֹ
אֶל־אֱלִישָׁע וַיֹּאמְרוּ אֵלָיו הֲיָדַעְתָּ כִּי
הַיּוֹם יְהוָה לֹקֵחַ אֶת־אֲדֹנֶיךָ מֵעַל
רֹאשֶׁךָ וַיֹּאמֶר גַּם־אֲנִי יָדַעְתִּי הֶחֱשׁוּ׃
ו וַיֹּאמֶר לוֹ אֵלִיָּהוּ שֵׁב־נָא פֹה כִּי יְהוָה

תרגום

נְבִיַיָא דִי בְּבֵית אֵל לְוַת אֱלִישָׁע וַאֲמַרוּ לֵיהּ הֲיָדַעְתָּא אֲרֵי יוֹמָא דֵין יְיָ דְבַר יַת רִבּוֹנָךְ מֵעַל רֵישָׁךְ וַאֲמַר אַף אֲנָא יָדַעְנָא שְׁתוּקוּ׃ ד וַאֲמַר לֵיהּ אֵלִיָהוּ אֱלִישָׁע תּוּב כְּעַן הָכָא אֲרֵי יְיָ שַׁלְחַנִי לִירִיחוֹ וַאֲמַר קַיָם הוּא יְיָ וְחֵי נַפְשָׁךְ אִם אֶשְׁבְּקִינָךְ וַאֲתוֹ לִירִיחוֹ׃ ה וּקְרִיבוּ תַּלְמִידֵי נְבִיַיָא דִי בִירִיחוֹ לְוַת אֱלִישָׁע וַאֲמַרוּ לֵיהּ הֲיָדַעְתָּא אֲרֵי יוֹמָא דֵין יְיָ דְבַר יַת רִבּוֹנָךְ מִנָךְ וַאֲמַר אַף אֲנָא יָדַעְנָא שְׁתוּקוּ׃ ו וַאֲמַר לֵיהּ אֵלִיָהוּ תּוּב כְּעַן הָכָא אֲרֵי יְיָ שַׁלְחַנִי עד

ת"א שלחני. ע׳ זידה סעד לח׃

רש"י

(ג) את אדוניך. ולא אדונינו מלמד שהיו שקולים כאליהו׃

רד"ק

להראות כי גדלה נפשו בעיניו והקדים חי ה׳ לכבוד׃ (ג) בני הנביאים. כתרגומו תלמידי נבייא׃ אשר בית אל. כמו בבית אל ומה שהיו בני הנביאים בבית אל וביריחו כן היו בערים אחרות אלא זכר אלה לפי שהיה דרכם עליהם ומה שהיו ברוב ערי ישראל כדי להוכיח את ישראל בכל עיר ועיר ונבואתם היתה לשעה לפיכך לא נכתבה נבואתם׃ החשו. פירשו בו צווי כמו בפתח הה"א וכן ת"י שתיקו ואדוני אבי ז"ל פירש כמשמעו בשאכר הוא להם גם אני ידעתי החשו הם ולא דברו

רלב"ג

(ג) היום ה׳ לוקח את אדוניך מעל ראשך. הנה באמרו בזה שלא בלקח אלא מעל ראשו וכן אמר אליהו לאלישע בטרם אלקח מאתך וזה עדה שלא לקחו אנשים כמוהלם אבל לקחו מעם אלישע׃ סנגשו.

מנחת שי

(ג) אשר בית אל. ד׳ בלישנא סבירין בבית מסורת כאן ובפרשת וארא׃

מצודת דוד

מגודל הענין חסן להיותו לכל יראה בהלקחו השמים׃ (ג) אשר בית אל. אשר בבית אל׃ הידעת. בלשון שאלה אמרו האם ידעת וגו׳׃ מעל ראשך. כאלו אמרו הנה היום לך לעטרה ויוסר העטרה מעל ראשך׃ החשו. שתקו ולא תדברו מזה על כי רצה באליהו שאין

מצודת ציון

ב (ג) החשו. שתקו כמו ואנחנו מחשים (לעיל כג)׃

to appear to others, so we find in the case of Elijah [*Abarbanel*]. See I Sam. 3:21, Comm. Digest.

from you — lit. from upon your head. The Lord will take away your master who is like a crown upon your head [*Mezudath David*].

Alternatively, He will take him away from you, but he will not die [*Ralbag*].

Be quiet — This is the imperative. Others render this as a past tense, they were silent [*Redak*].

Just as when a person dies, the extremities lose their sensations before the organs close to the heart, so it was when the greatest prophet was going to be taken away, the disciples who were the farthest from him would feel his impending absence before the greater prophets who were nearer to the master.

Therefore, the disciples told Elisha that they already felt the diminishing of their prophecy, a sure indication of Elijah's leaving them. They

3. And the disciples of the prophets who were in Bethel came out to Elisha and said to him, "Do you know that today the Lord will take your master from you?" And he said, "I know it too. Be quiet." 4. And Elijah said to him, "Stay here now, for the Lord has sent me to Jericho." And he said, "As the Lord lives and by your life, I will not leave you." And they came to Jericho. 5. And the disciples of the prophets who were in Jericho approached Elisha and said to him, "Do you know that today the Lord will take your master from you?" And he said, "I know it too. Be quiet." 6. And Elijah said to him, "Stay here now, for the Lord has sent me to

the expressions used in regard to his visit to Bethel and his visit to Jericho. In v. 3, "... the disciples ... in Bethel came out to Elisha," while in v. 5, "... the disciples ... in Jericho approached Elisha." This indicates that Elijah and Elisha stood outside Bethel, yet entered Jericho. It is very probable that these two groups were the one hundred prophets hidden by Obadiah in two caves, mentioned in I Kings, 18:4. In v. 16, we learn that the disciples of the prophets in Jericho were indeed fifty men, the identical number of prophets hidden in each cave [*Malbim*].

3. **the disciples of the prophets** — lit. the sons of the prophets. This teaches us that disciples are considered like one's own children. Similarly, the teacher is considered a father, as we find Elisha crying, "My father, my father." (v. 12) [*Yalkut Shimoni* from *Sifrei* Deut. 6:7].

who were in Bethel — These were not the only disciples of the prophets. Just as there were disciples of the prophets in Bethel and in Jericho, there were also in many cities. They would guide the people and admonish them to keep the precepts of the Torah. Since their prophecy was needed only for their time, it was not recorded with the prophecies of the forty-eight prophets. It so happened that Elijah passed through these two cities on his way to the Jordan [*Redak*]. Compare with *Malbim* v. 2.

your master — *but not our master. This teaches us that they were equal to Elijah* [*Rashi, Yalkut Shimoni* from *Tosefta Sotah* 12:5].

This verse is stated to prove that during this period prophecy was very prevalent and to illustrate the caliber of the prophets, who were equal in wisdom to Elijah. In prophecy, however, they were his subordinates and they prophesied only through him. Just as we find in the case of Samuel, that as soon as he became a prophet, God continued

שלחני הירדנה ויאמר חי־יהוה וחי־
נפשך אם־אעזבך וילכו שניהם:
ז וחמשים איש מבני הנביאים הלכו
ויעמדו מנגד מרחוק ושניהם עמדו על־
הירדן: ח ויקח אליהו את־אדרתו
ויגלם ויכה את־המים ויחצו הנה
והנה ויעברו שניהם בחרבה: ט ויהי
כעברם ואליהו אמר אל־אלישע
שאל מה אעשה־לך בטרם אלקח
מעמך ויאמר אלישע ויהי־נא פי־

תרגום

עד ירדנא ואמר קים
הוא יי וחי נפשך אם
אשבקינך ואזלו
תרויהון : ז וחמשין
גברא מתלמידי נביא
אזלו וקמו מקביל
מרחיק ותרויהון קמו על
ירדנא : ח ונסיב אליהו
ית שושיפיה ואחזר
ומחא ית מיא ואתפליגו
לכא ולכא ועברו
תרויהון ביבשתא :
ט והוה כמעברהון
ואליהו אמר לאלישע
שאל מה אעביד לך
עד דלא אידבר מלותך
ואמר אלישע ויהי כען
על חד תרין ברוח

ת"א ואליהו אמר. עקרים פ׳ יט : פי שנים. סנהדרין מז קכ חולין ז עקידה שער קד :

רש"י

(ח) ויגלום. כרכה כדי שתהא נוחה להכות בה : ויגלום. ולא כריכה ממש אלא קולט שקורין פיינד"ו בלע"ז :

רד"ק

יד עוד : (ח) ויגלום. כרכה והכה בה את המים וכן בגלומי תכלת פי׳ כרכי בגדים : (ט) פי שנים ברוחך אלי. פירשו רז"ל כפלים ממה שהיה באליהו והוא שהחיה שני מתים אחד בחייו ואחד במותו ולמי שאמר על רגליו עמד ולביתו לא הלך שרפא צרעת נעמן שהמצורע חשוב כמת שנאמר אל נא תהי כמת. ואדוני אבי ז"ל פירש פי שנים שני חלקים שאל שיהיה לו מרוח אליהו וכן הוא אומר פי שנים בכל אשר ימצא לו שני

רלב"ג

שתקו : (ח) ויגלם. ר"ל שכבר כרך אדרתו והכה בה במים : (ט) ויהי נא פי שנים ברוחך אלי. ר"ל כמה שהאצלת מרוחך על כל בני הנביאים יהיה הנאצל לי מרוחך פי שנים על כל אחד מהם

מנחת שי

(ט) ויהי כעברם ואליהו. יש מי שנסתפק אם כתוב כעברם בכ"ף או בבי"ת ולדידן פשיטא לן דכתוב בכ"ף ע"פ המדוייקים והמסורת דהוא חד מן מלין דנסבין כ"ף בריש׳ ולית דכוותא וסימנהון במסרת רבתא אות כ"ף :

מצודת דוד

הספו לגלות הדבר נגודל הענוה : (ז) מנגד מרחוק. כפל המלה לתוספת ביאור : (ח) ויגלום. כרך אדרתו שתהא נוחה להכות בה את המים : ויחצו הנה והנה. נבקעו המים ונחה הלכו להם ומזה נשארו במקומם ולא ירדו למטה : (ט) שאל וגו׳. ר"ל שאל בטרם

מצודת ציון

(ח) אדרתו. מלבוש יקר המיוחד לנביאים וכן וישלך אדרתו (שם י"ט) : ויגלום. כרכו כאחת וכן בגלומי תכלת (יחזקאל כז) ופי׳ בכריכת בגדי תכלת : בחרבה. ביבשה : (ט) פי. ענין חלק וכן פי שנים בכל אשר ימצא לו (דברים כ"א) :

strike with it and he rolled it — not exactly rolling but gathering together, which is called koulir in O.F. [*Rashi*].

Others render: folded — *Sefer haShorashim, Ibn Janah.* According to Shem Ephraim's emendation *Rashi* too should read: *not exactly rolling but creasing . . .*

9. **a double portion of your spirit**—According to the Talmud, Elisha actually was endowed with double the spirit of Elijah. Whereas Elijah resurrected one dead person, Elisha resurrected two, the son of the Shunemitess (ch. 4) and the dead man who was thrown into his grave (13:21), or Naaman, whose *zaraath* he cured, which is tantamount to resurrecting the dead (Chulin 7b). *R. Joseph Kimchi,* however, explains this to mean that Elisha would attain two thirds of Elijah's spirit and all others together would attain one third [*Redak*].

Others explain that Elisha requested double of any other prophet [*Ralbag*].

Still others explain that he requested that Elijah's spirit of

the Jordan." And he said, "As the Lord lives and by your life, I will not leave you." And they both went. 7. And fifty men of the disciples of the prophets went and stood opposite them from a distance, as they both stood at the Jordan. 8. And Elijah took his mantle and rolled it up, and struck the water, and it divided to this side and to that side; and they both crossed on dry land. 9. And it was when they crossed, that Elijah said to Elisha, "Ask what I shall do for you, while I am not yet taken away from you." And Elisha said, "Please let there be a double portion of your spirit on me."

wished to hear whether he had experienced the same phenomenon. If he had experienced it, it would indicate that Elijah's departure was imminent. Otherwise, it might be some time off. When Elisha informed them that he had shared in their experience, they knew that on that very day, Elijah would depart.

Moreover, if God were taking Elijah away because He was angry with his generation, and He wanted to deprive them of God's word, it would be appropriate to pray and supplicate Him to allow Elijah to remain with them. If, however, Elijah was to be taken away because he had attained perfection, there would be no reason to pray. Therefore, Elisha informed them that he knew of Elijah's imminent departure through prophecy. This indicated that the generation was not to be deprived of prophecy. Instead, Elijah was being taken away because he had attained perfection. Hence, he commanded them, "Be quiet and do not pray to God to permit Elijah to stay with us" [*Malbim*].

to the Jordan — Elijah again sought to send Elisha away from close proximity with him, so that the disciples would achieve prophecy directly through him, not through Elisha. Elisha, however, refused to leave his master [*Malbim*].

Abarbanel expounds that Elijah traveled through all these holy places before his departure, since he did not know the site from which he would ascend to heaven. He first went to Gilgal, where the Jews camped upon entering the Holy Land. There was the first sanctuary; there Joshua circumcized the people; there they sacrificed the first Passover sacrifice. Then he went to Bethel, where God had appeared to Jacob twice and where he had set up a monument as a sanctuary. He then went to Jericho, which had been taken by Israel miraculously, so would he be taken into heaven miraculously. Then he went to the Jordan, which had been split by a miracle [*Abarbanel*].

8. **and rolled it up** — *He rolled it up in order that it would be easy to*

שְׁנַיִם בְּרוּחֲךָ אֵלָי: י וַיֹּאמֶר הִקְשִׁיתָ לִשְׁאוֹל אִם־תִּרְאֶה אֹתִי לֻקָּח מֵאִתָּךְ יְהִי־לְךָ כֵן וְאִם־אַיִן לֹא יִהְיֶה: יא וַיְהִי הֵמָּה הֹלְכִים הָלוֹךְ וְדַבֵּר וְהִנֵּה רֶכֶב־אֵשׁ וְסוּסֵי אֵשׁ וַיַּפְרִדוּ בֵּין שְׁנֵיהֶם וַיַּעַל אֵלִיָּהוּ בַּסְּעָרָה הַשָּׁמָיִם: יב וֶאֱלִישָׁע רֹאֶה וְהוּא מְצַעֵק אָבִי | אָבִי רֶכֶב

נְבוּאָתָךְ עִמִּי: י וַאֲמַר אַקְשֵׁיתָא לְמִשְׁאַל אִם תֶּחֱזֵי יָתִי דְאִנָּא מִידַּבַּר מִלְּוָתָךְ יְהֵי לָךְ כֵּן וְאִם לָא לָא יְהֵי: יא וַהֲוָה עַד דְּאִינוּן אָזְלִין מֵיזַל וּמְמַלְּלִין וְהָא רְתִיכִין דְּאֶשָּׁתָא וְסוּסָוָן דְּאֶשָּׁתָא וְאַפְרִישׁוּ בֵּין תַּרְוֵיהוֹן וּסְלֵיק אֵלִיָּהוּ בְּעַלְעוֹלָא לְצֵית שְׁמַיָּא: יב וֶאֱלִישָׁע חָזֵי וְהוּא מְצַוַּח רִבִּי רִבִּי דְּטַב לְהוֹן לְיִשְׂרָאֵל

ת"א אם תראה. עקידה שם זוהר ויצב: והנה רכב אש. תענית י. סוטה מט (ברכות ח): ויעל אליהו. סוכה ה: ואלישע ראה. מועד קטן כו סנהדרין ס סא עקידה שער קד (מועד קטן יג): הס' בח"ק

רש"י

(י) הקשית לשאול. א"א לתת לך יותר ממה שיש לי בידי: אם תראה אותי לוקח מאתך. אז אוכל לעשות לך יותר ויותר: יהי לך כן ואם אין לא יהיה. שאין היכולת בידי: (יב) אבי אבי רכב ישראל. רבי רבי דטב להון

רד"ק

חלקי נכסיו כי הבכור נוטל שני חלקים מן הנכסים והפשוט נוטל חלק השלישי: (י) הקשית לשאול. די היה לך בחלק אחד מרוחי או בחצי רוחי אבל פי שנים דבר קשה שאלת ואעפ"כ אם יהיה בך כח רוח אלהים שתוכל לראותי כשאלקח מאתך ידעתי כי מאת האל יהיה שיהיה לך כמו ששאלת: לוקח. פעל עומד מבנין שלא נזכר פעלו לפיכך הוא קמוץ: (יא) ויעל אליהו בסערה. כמו שפירשנו ופי' השמים לענין הגוף האוירי כמו אשר תעוף בשמים ולענין הרוח השמים העליונים עם המלאכים שיכנו לחם השמים כמו הללו את ה' מן השמים ואליהו נעשה רוחני והגוף כלה באש העליוני ושב כל יסוד אל יסודו ואלישע ראה העלותו מן הארץ ובהיותו לאויר ראה דמיון רכב אש וסוסי אש שהפריד בין שניהם כלומר בראותו כי נפרד ממנו מעת אשר הועלה וכן בגדיו כלו באש זולתי האדרת שנפלה מעליו כדי שיקחנו אלישע להכות בה המים ואם כדברי רז"ל שהית לו כפלים ברוח ממה שהית לאליהו תימה הוא מה צורך היה לו אדרת לחצות בה המים והנה אפי' עם האדרת לא נחצת המי' עד שאמר איה ה' אלהי אליהו ואם תאמר לא נפלה האדרת לצורך אלישע אלא כיון שנעשה רוחני נפלה האדרת מעליו אם כן שאר בגדיו למה לא נפלו גם כן: (יב) ואלישע ראה. ראה העלותו מן הארץ ולא ראהו עוד כי רכב אש וסוסי אש הפרידו בין שניהם: אבי אבי.

רלב"ג

והוא מענין מה שאמר כי את הבכור בן השנואה יכיר לתת לו פי שנים בכל אשר ימצא לו: (י) אם תראה אותי לוקח מאתך. אמר לו זה על דרך המופתים המתחדשים כאילו יאמר שאם יראה אותו בעת הלקחו מעמו בהעלותו בסערה השמים אז יתחדש לו על זה המופת שיאצל מן הרוח אשר על אליהו מה שישלם בו מה שבקש אלישע ואז עזב אליהו אדרתו כדי שיחזיק בה אלישע ותהיה כלי מה להשלמת זה המופת הלא תראה כי אלישע היה מלוה גחזי שיקח משענת אלישע בידו להחיות בו בן השונמית וכן תמצא שעל זה המופת נתחדש באדר' אליהו מה שעזר אלישע בעשיית המופתים וכבר באר[ו] זולתנו באמרו אם תראה אותי לוקח מאתך יהי לך כן באורים אחרים ואשר נחשב אנחנו הוא מה שזכרנו והוא נאות ללשון ולענין וזה כי קלתם אמרו אם תראה אותי לוקח מאתך שתשכיל מציאות השכל הנפרד והוא שכל אליהו אחרי הפרדו מהחומר ואלו השכימו בהכרח שיהיה זה הענין מות לאליהו וכבר באר[נ]ו שזה בלתי אפשר וקלתם אמרו אם תראה אותי לוקח מאתך ר"ל שתחקור עמי בכל הסודות אשר אתם נבוך בהם מפני ראותך שאני לוקח מאתך ולא ימצא זה לך ממני זולתי בזה העת והנה יקשה לזה שאנחנו לא מצאנו שעמדו יחד אחר כל זה מה שיתכן בו זה הענין גם לא היה מספיק זמן קצר כמו זה לזה הענין לפי מה שאחשב: (יא) והנה רכב אש וסוסי אש ויפרדו בין שניהם. הנה נתחדש זה על דרך המופת לשאת אליהו אל אשר יהיה שמה רצון הש"י: (יב) אבי אבי רכב ישראל ופרשיו. הנה כמו שהתלמידים נקראים בנים כמו בני הנביאים כן הרב יקרא אב כי הוא המוליד שכל התלמיד וקראו רכב ישראל ופרשיו כאילו יאמר שהוא התוקף והחוזק של ישראל במלחמה ולזה הוא רכב והפרשים

מצודת דוד

אלקח מה טובה אעשה לך: פי שנים. שתשרה עלי רוח הנבואה במעלה כפולה על מה ששרתה עליך: (י) הקשית לשאול. כי איך אוכל להשפיע עליך דבר שאין בי: אם תראה. אך אם תראה אותי בעת אשר אהיה נלקח מאך יהיה לך כן כי אז נתכפלה מעלת אלישע מזה שהיתה מקודם ויוכל להשפיע לזולתו כל הדבר שיש בו אז: (יא) והנה רכב אש. והנה בא רכב אש וגו': (יב) ואלישע רואה. בעת שנלקח: אבי אבי. רבי רבי שהיה לישראל לעזור מול האויב כמו רכב ופרשים כת"י: לשנים קרעים. ר"ל לשני חתיכות:

מצודת ציון

(י) הקשית. מל' קשה: ואם אין. ואם לא:

spiritual. Only his mantle was cast down to earth in order to enable Elisha to split the Jordan, as is delineated below, v. 14 [*Redak*].

According to the *Zohar, Vayakhel* 197a, he was transformed into a spiritual body, known as *s'arah,* the whirlwind. Thus he was able to remain in the heavens.

12. **"My father! My father! The chariots of Israel** — *Jonathan* renders *My master! My master! who benefited Israel with his prayer more than chariots and riders* [*Rashi*].

As mentioned above, a teacher is considered like a father. Similarly, the disciples of the prophets were known as the sons of the prophets [*Redak*].

and rent them in two pieces — Just

10. And he said, "You have made a difficult request. If you see me taken from you, it will be so to you, and if not, it will not be." 11. And it was that they were going, walking and talking, and behold a fiery chariot and fiery horses, and they separated them both. And Elijah ascended to heaven in a whirlwind.
12. And Elisha saw, and he was crying, "My father! My father! The chariots

prophecy rest upon him while he still retained his own spirit of prophecy that he possessed previously [*Malbim*].

"You have made a difficult request — *It is impossible to give you more than I have in my possession — Rashi.*

If you see me taken away from you — *then I will be able to do for you more and more* [*Rashi*].

According to *Rashi ms., you will be able to do more and more.*

At the time of Elijah's ascent, he attained superior spiritual heights. If Elisha would see him then, he too would attain that level of prophecy [*Abarbanel, Mezudath David*].

This is probably *Rashi's* intention in stating, *Then I will be able to do . . . more and more.* According to Kara, the words *for you* are deleted. Thus Elijah is saying that he himself would be able to do more and more at that time. Therefore, if Elisha would be able to see him in his exalted state, he too would be granted his master's powers. This seems to be the most accurate version of *Rashi.* Compare *Kara, Nach Lublin.*

it will be so to you, and if not, it will not be — *for I have not the ability* [*Rashi*].

I.e. in my present state, I have not the ability to bestow upon you what I myself do not possess. If you do not see me when I am being taken from you, you will have no contact with me then, and will not be able to receive any powers from me at that time.

Redak interprets this passage somewhat differently. As mentioned above, Elisha requested two thirds of Elijah's spirit of prophecy. Elijah replied that this was a difficult request for anyone to achieve. If Elisha would see his master being taken away from him, however, this would indicate that he had great spiritual powers, and God would certainly grant him his wish.

11. **walking and talking** — discussing the Torah. Had they not been discussing matters of Torah, they would have deserved to be consumed by the fiery chariot and horses [*Taanith* 10b].

a fiery chariot — to transport Elijah to wherever it was God's will to transport him [*Ralbag*].

According to *Redak,* Elijah's body was lifted into the atmosphere by the whirlwind. Thereupon, the fiery chariot and horses appeared. He was taken up into the chariot where his body and clothing were consumed. He then became purely

ישראל ופרשיו ולא ראהו עוד ויחזק
בבגדיו ויקרעם לשנים קרעים: יג וירם
את־אדרת אליהו אשר נפלה מעליו
וישב ויעמד על־שפת הירדן: יד ויקח
את־אדרת אליהו אשר־נפלה מעליו
ויכה את־המים ויאמר איה יהוה אלהי
אליהו אף־הוא ויכה את־המים ויחצו
הנה והנה ויעבר אלישע: טו ויראהו
בני־הנביאים אשר־ביריחו מנגד
ויאמרו נחה רוח אליהו על־אלישע
ויבאו לקראתו וישתחוו־לו ארצה:

תרגום

בצלותיה סרתיכין ופרשין ולא חזהי עוד ואתקף בלבושיה וסדקינון לתרין סדקין: יג נארים ית שושיפא דאליהו די נפלת מניה ותב וקם על כיף ירדנא: יד ונסיב ית שושיפא דאליהו דנפלת מניה ומחא ית מיא ואמר קביל בעותי יי אלהיה דאליהו אף הוא ומחא ית מיא ואתפליגו לכא ולכא ועבר אלישע: טו וחזוהי תלמידי נביא דביריחו מקביל ואמרו נחת רוחיה דאליהו על אלישע ואתו לקדמותיה וסגידו

ת"א ולא ראהו עוד. מועד קטן שם: ויחזק בבגדיו. שם כב כו: אף הוא. עקרים פ' יט:

רש"י

לישראל בתפלותיו מרהיכין ופרשין: (יד) איה ה' אלהי אליהו. שהובטחתי שתשרה בי פי שנים ברוחו אלי: אף הוא ויכה את המים. אף הוא. בפרקי ר' אליעזר בנו

רד"ק

כתרגומו רבי וכן תלמידי הנביאים נקראו בני הנביאים: רכב ישראל ופרשיו. כתרגומו דטב להון לישראל בצלותיה מרתיכין ופרשין: ויקרעם לשנים קרעים. מכאן סמכו רז"ל שחייב אדם לקרוע על רבו שלמדו חכמה ואותו הקרע אינו מתאחה לעולם לפי שנאמר לשנים ממשמע שנא' ויקרעם איני יודע שהוא לשנים א"כ מה ת"ל לשנים שיראה בהן הקרע לעולם: (יד) איה ה' אלהי אליהו. ת"י כן ואמר קבל בעותיה' אלהיה דאליהו ולפי פשוטו איה הוא שאינו מראה כח האות לי כמו שעשה לאליהו בחצות המים: אף הוא ויכה את המים. אף הוא נעשה לו נס והכה המים פעם שנית אחר שאמר איה ה' אלהי ונחצו הנה והנה וי"מ אף הוא על אליהו שבא כמו שהיה רוחני והכה את המים ויחצו ויעבר אלישע. ובדרש אף הוא מלמד שנעשו נסים לאלישע בקריעת הירדן יותר מאליהו שבפעם ראשונה היתה זכות שניהם עומדת ופעם שנייה של אלישע היתה זכות צדיק אחד עומדת וכן הוא אומר ויהי נא פי שנים ברוחך אלי מכאן אתה דורש שבנה מופתים באליהו שש עשרה לאלישע: (טו) נחה רוח אליהו. כיון שראוהו שחצה

רלב"ג

אשר בהם יגברו במלחמה: (יד) אף הוא ויכה את המים ויחלו הנה והנה. ר"ל אף הוא כאשר הכה את המים הנה נחלו תכף הנה והנה. ואחשב כי לא הכה אותם אלא פעם אחת ובפעם ההיא אמר איה אלהי אליהו וספר הכתוב שגם אלישע הגיע לזאת המעלה שהגיע אליהו והוא שכאשר הכה את המים נחלו הנה והנה: (טו) נחה רוח אליהו על אלישע. ר"ל שכבר האצילו מרוחו מה שימשך ממנו שיעשה

מצודת ציון

(יג) וירם. מל' הרמה והגבהה: (טו) נחה. ענין חניה:

מצודת דוד

(יד) איה ה'. כאומר עם שנלקח אליהו הנה איה ה' הלא השגחתו ויכלתו לא כלה: אף הוא. ר"ל אף הוא בהוייתו בכל עת ולא בהנה ודוגמתו עתה יזנו תזנותיה והיא (יחזקאל כ"ג) ור"ל עדיין הוא בהוייתה כשהיתה מאז. או מוסב הוא על ויכה וכו' ור"ל אף אלישע עשה כמעשה אליהו וכשהכה המים נבקעו הנה והנה וכו'. (ומעתה הולך ומונה יחד כל הנפלאות שעשה אלישע): (טו) ויראהו.

praying to God and striking the water a second time.

Alternatively, Elijah too, in his spiritual state, struck the water, and it divided [*Redak*].

Mezudath David explains thus: Where is the Lord, the God of Elijah? *He* is still here. Although Elijah is no longer with us, where is his God? He is always with us and His power is unchanging.

15. **"Elijah's spirit has rested on Elisha"** — When they saw him split the Jordan and cross, just as Elijah had done, they realized that Elijah's spirit had rested upon him, and they came to pay homage to him [*Redak*].

of Israel and their riders!" And he saw him no longer. Now he
took hold of his garments and rent them in two pieces. 13. And
he picked up Elijah's mantle that had fallen off him, and he
returned and stood on the bank of the Jordan. 14. And he took
Elijah's mantle that had fallen off him, and he struck the water
and said, "Where is the Lord, the God of Elijah?" He too
struck the water and it divided on this side and on that side, and
Elisha crossed. 15. And the disciples of the prophets who were
in Jericho saw him from a distance, and they said, "Elijah's
spirit has rested on Elisha." And they came toward him and
prostrated themselves before him to the ground.

as one is required to rend his garments upon the demise of one of his parents, so is he required to do so upon the demise of his teacher who taught him Torah. Since Scripture specifies that he rent them in two pieces, we deduce that the rend must never be completely sewn up [*Redak* from *Moed Katan* 22b].

14. **"Where is the Lord, the God of Elijah?** — *that I was promised (who promised me — Kara) that a double portion of his spirit would rest upon me* [*Rashi*].

Alternatively, Where is God Who does not show me His miracles as He showed Elijah? [*Redak*].

Jonathan paraphrases: Accept my prayer, O God of Elijah!

He too struck the water — *He too. In the Chapters of Rabbi Eliezer the son of Rabbi Jose the Galilean,* (should read: *In the "Thirty-two Methods of Rabbi Eliezer the son of Rabbi Jose the Galilean. — Shem Ephraim), Elisha's splitting* the Jordan *was doubly as great as Elijah's, for in the beginning there was the merit of them both, while here was his merit alone* [*Rashi* from *Thirty-two Methods of R. Eliezer the son of R. Jose the Galilean,* Method 1].

This *Baraitha* enumerates the various ways the Aggadah is expounded. The first method is that of inclusive words, such as אֶת גַּם, and אַף. These words are stated to include something not mentioned specifically in the Scripture. Here the word אַף, *also,* means to include the greater power of Elisha through which he split the Jordan singlehandedly, not like Elijah, who split it in conjunction with Elisha. See *Rashi* below 3:1, *Yalkut Shimoni* vol. 1:92. The *Baraitha* in its entirety appears after the Tractate *Berachoth* in the Babylonian Talmud and before *Midrash Rabbah* in the Vilna edition.

According to *peshat,* the simple interpretation, Scripture tells us that Elisha too, performed the same miracle Elijah had performed, after

טז וַיֹּאמְרוּ אֵלָיו הִנֵּה־נָא יֵשׁ־אֶת־עֲבָדֶיךָ חֲמִשִּׁים אֲנָשִׁים בְּנֵי־חַיִל יֵלְכוּ נָא וִיבַקְשׁוּ אֶת־אֲדֹנֶיךָ פֶּן־נְשָׂאוֹ רוּחַ יְהוָה וַיַּשְׁלִכֵהוּ בְּאַחַד הֶהָרִים אוֹ בְּאַחַת הַגֵּיאָוֹת וַיֹּאמֶר לֹא תִשְׁלָחוּ׃ יז וַיִּפְצְרוּ־בוֹ עַד־בֹּשׁ וַיֹּאמֶר שְׁלָחוּ וַיִּשְׁלְחוּ חֲמִשִּׁים אִישׁ וַיְבַקְשׁוּ שְׁלֹשָׁה־יָמִים וְלֹא מְצָאֻהוּ׃ יח וַיָּשֻׁבוּ אֵלָיו וְהוּא יֹשֵׁב בִּירִיחוֹ וַיֹּאמֶר אֲלֵהֶם הֲלוֹא־אָמַרְתִּי אֲלֵיכֶם אַל־תֵּלֵכוּ׃ יט וַיֹּאמְרוּ

נסגידו ליה על ארעא: טז ואמרו ליה הא כען אית עם עבדך חמשין גברין בני חילא יזלון כען ויבעון ית רבונך דלמא נטליה רוח מן קדם יי ורמהי בחד מן טוריא או בחד מן חיליא ואמר לא תשלחון: יז ואתקיפו ביה עד בהיא ואמר שלחו ושלחו חמשין גברא ובעו תלתא יומין ולא אשכחוהי: יח ותבו לותיה והוא יתיב ביריחו ואמר להון הלא אמרית לכון לא תיזלון: יט ואמרו אנשי קרתא לאלישע

הגאיות קרי

רש"י

של רבי יוסי הגלילי גדולה אליית אלישע כפלים של אליהו שבתחלה זכות שניהם ועכשיו זכותו יחידי: (טז) פן נשאו רוח ה'. אפשר אמש אמרו לו הידעת כי היום ה' לוקח את אדוניך ועכשיו נעלם מהם היכן הוא מלמד מיום שנגנז אליהו הלכה ונסתלקה רוח הקודש מן הנביאים ושוב לא היתה רוח הקודש מרובה בישראל: (יז) עד בוש. נתבייש מהם שלא יאמרו אינו רוצה להקביל פני רבו לפי שנטל גדולתו אינו רוצה שישוב. כל זה ראיתי בתוספתא דסוטה:

רד"ק

המים ועבר הירדן ידעו כי נחה עליו רוח אליהו: (טז) נ' אנשים בני חיל. למה היו צריכים בני חיל וכי היה להם לעשות מלחמה אלא פירוש בני חיל בני כח שיהיה להם כח ללכת הנה והנה במעט זמן ואיך אמרו לו שיבקשוהו והלא הם אמרו לו כי היום ה' לוקח אדוניך מעל ראשך אלא חשבו שמא לא עלה השמים אלא נשאו רוח ה' והפרידו מבני אדם כמו שראו שנפרד מבני אדם מ' יום ומ' לילה ואולי פעמים רבות היה לו זה שהית נפרד מבני אדם ולא היו מוצאים אותו שהרי עובדיה אמר לו ורוח ה' ישאך על אשר לא אדע: (יז) ויפצרו בו. הרבו לו דברים עד ששמע אליהם: עד בוש. עד אשר בושש הרבת

רלב"ג

אלישע בדמיון המוספתים שעשה אליהו ולזה חלקו לו כבוד רב והשתחוו לו ארצה: (טז) וישלכהו באחד ההרים או באחת הגאיות. ר"ל נהתהלא שם כי היה רגיל אליהו בכך כמו שאמר עובדיה ורוח ה' ישאך אל אשר לא אדע: (יז) ויפצרו בו עד בוש. ר"ל הרבו כל כך דברים עד שהיה לו בשת מלחלוק תמיד על דבריהם ולזה אמר להם שלחו מלד המוסר להניחם לעשות רצונם אך דבריו היו באופן שכשאמר שלחו היה ראוי שיובן ממנו שלא ישלחו מלד דבורו כי פעמים יש הן שהוא כלאו ולזה אמר הלא אמרתי אליכם אל תלכו כי ידע אלישע שלא יראה לאדם אליהו בזה העת כי הסתירו ה':

מנחת ש"י

(טז) הגיאות. הגאיות ק' והספרים מתחלפים במילוי או חיסור יו"ד בתר גימ"ל: (יז) עד בש. ברוב הספרים חסר וא"ו: (יח) הלוא אמרתי אליכם. באיזה ספרים חסר וא"ו אבל ברובן מלא וכן הוא במסורת במנין י"ז מלאים

מצודת דוד

כאשר בוקע מי הירדן: (טז) בני חיל. אנשי חיל ובני כח ללכת הנה והנה במעט זמן: וישליכהו. חשבו שהרוח שבה אל האלהים וגופו הושלך מת ורצו לבקשו ולקברו: לא תשלחו. כי ראה בעלה עם הגוף ומגודל הענוה לא אמר להם מה שראה: (יז) עד בוש. עד אשר נתאחר זמן רב שהפצירו בו לתת להם רשות לשלוח:

מצודת ציון

(טז) הגאיות. מל' גיא ועמק: (יז) ויפצרו. ענין רבוי הדברים להעביר האדם מרצונו כמו ויפצר בו ויקח (בראשית ל"ג): בוש. ענין איחור כמו

16. And they said to him, "Behold now, there are with your servants fifty able men. Let them go now and seek your master, perhaps a wind from the Lord has carried him off and thrown him on one of the mountains or in one of the valleys." And he said, "You shall not send." 17. And they urged him until he was ashamed. And he said, "Send." And they sent fifty men, and they searched for three days but did not find him. 18. And they returned to him when he was staying in Jericho; and he said to them, "Did I not say to you, 'You shall not go'"?

16. **Able men** — strong men capable of journeying throughout the country at a rapid pace and returning quickly [*Redak*].

Perhaps a wind from the Lord has carried him off — *Is it possible that on the day before, they said to him, "Do you know that today the Lord will take your master from you?"* (v. 5) *and now they did not know where he was? This teaches us that since the day when Elijah was hidden, the holy spirit departed from the prophets, and the holy spirit was no longer widespread throughout Israel* [*Rashi* from *Tosefta Sotah* 12:5].

Redak theorizes that they were completely unaware of Elijah's being taken up into heaven. They thought that the Lord would take Elijah away perhaps to some distant mountain or valley where he would remain in seclusion for a period of time. We find that Obadiah mentions to Elijah (I Kings 18:11) "And a wind from the Lord will carry you off to a place I know not where." It must, therefore, have been usual for such things to transpire.

Abarbanel explains that the earlier statement was not actually prophetic. Since their prophecy came to them through Elijah, and now they felt it diminishing, they realized that he would soon be taken away from them. They did not know, however, whether he would be removed from the world or whether he would be transported to a distant location.

17. **until he was ashamed** — *He was ashamed because of them, lest they say that he does not want to go to meet his teacher. Since he took over his high position, he does not want him to return. All this I saw in Tosefta Sotah* (12:5) [*Rashi*]. This includes *Rashi's* commentaries on v. 3, 16, 17.

Others render: until he delayed them considerably, i.e., from sending out searching parties to seek Elijah [*Redak, Mezudoth*].

יט ויאמרו אנשי העיר אל־אלישע הנה־נא מושב העיר טוב כאשר אדני ראה והמים רעים והארץ משכלת: כ ויאמר קחו־לי צלחית חדשה ושימו שם מלח ויקחו אליו: כא ויצא אל־מוצא המים וישלך־שם מלח ויאמר כה־אמר יהוה רפאתי למים האלה לא־יהיה משם עוד מות ומשכלת: כב וירפו המים עד היום הזה כדבר אלישע אשר דבר: כג ויעל משם בית־אל והוא עלה בדרך

לאלישע הא כען מושב קרתא שפיר כמא דרבוני חזי ומיא בישין וארעא מתכלא: כ ואמר איתו לי צלוחיתא חדתא ושוו תמן מלחא ואיתיאו לותיה: כא ונפק למפקנא דמיא ורמא תמן מלחא ואמר כדנן אמר יי אסיתי למיא האלין ולא יהי מתמן עוד מותא ומתכלא: כב ואתסיאו מיא עד יומא הדין כפתגמא דאלישע דמליל: כג וסליק מתמן לבית אל והוא סליק באורחא וינקין

ת"א מושב העיר טוב. סוטה מז

רש"י

(יט) והמים רעים. ומחמת המים הארץ משכלת את יושביה לקברם אם כן מהו ומושב העיר טוב מכאן אמרו חן מקום על יושביו: (כא) אל מוצא המים. שהיו נובעים משם: וישלך שם מלח. והלא מלח דבר המקלקל את

רד"ק

מלומר להם שישלחו ותרגומו עד סגיא: (יט) הנה נא מושב העיר טוב. עד עתה לא ראינו כי יריחו היו בה מים רעים ולא שהיתה העיר משכלת שא"כ לא היו חומדים אותה ולא היו עוברים על החרם לבנית אותה ואליהו ג"כ היאך לא רפה אותה ואם היתה משכלת מכמה שנים שישבו בה היו מניחים אותה ולא היו יושבין בה אלא נראה שמקרוב היה זה חרע למים מרעת יושבי בה ומפני רוע המים היתה גם כן הארץ משכלת שהיו האנשים שותים המים והיו מתים ברוב. ובדרש אמר יריחו היתה משכלת ומקוללת ע"ש שארדה יהושע ובא אליהו והוסיף לקללה ע"י מעשה של חיאל כשמתו בניו והלכו שניהם הוא ואחאב ובקרוהו וכל הענין נזכר למעלה. ובדברי רז"ל מושב העיר טוב והמים רעים והארץ משכלת מאי טיבותיה אמר ר' יוחנן חן מקום על יושביו: (כ) מלח. נס בתוך נס היה כי המלח עושה המים רעים וכן ויורהו ה' עץ אמרו עץ מר היה ונס בתיך נס היה: (כא) אל מוצא המים. אל מקור המים המקום שהיו המים יוצאים ממנו: רפאתי. בחיר"ק הפ"א כבעלי הה"א: ומשכלת. ולא תהיה הארץ משכלת כי מן המים היה בה השכול: (כב) וירפו המים. נעלמה האל"ף והיה כבעלי

מנחת שי

בסיפרא וסי' נמסר לעיל סימן כ"ב במ"ג: (כא) רפאתי. בחירק הפ"א:

רלב"ג

(יט) והמים רעים והארץ משכלת. מפני באמר אחר זה רפאתי למים האלה ולא יהיה משם עוד מות ומשכלת ידענו כי הארץ משכלה מלד המים שהיו רעים. והנה אף על פי שקלל יהושע מי שיבנה הנה לא מנע האנשים משבת בה אחר שתבנה באם היה כן לא היו הנביאים יושבים שם והנה הכלון ג"ה הנה מושב העיר טוב כאשר אדוני רואה ולזה אין אויר העיר סבה אל שתהיה הארץ משכלת רק בהמת מים הרעים ומזה הלך קרה לארץ שתהיה משכלת: (כב) והנה רפא אלישע המים ההם. על דרך המופת בהשליכו אל מולא המים מלח מהמלח ששמו בצלוחית חדשה והחשוב שככר בחר אלישע שתהיה הצלוחית חדשה כדי שלא יחשבו שיהיה מבושל בה דבר ימתק המלח כחו ויהיה לו רושם על דרך הרפואה בתקון המים אך בחר לתקנם במה שאין בו רושם לתקונם כי אנחנו רואים שהמים המלוחים הם

מצודת ציון

ויחילו עד בוש (שופטים ג'):(יט) מושב. מלשון ישיבה: משכלת. הורגת אנשים כמו ומשכלת גויך (יחזקאל ל"ו): (כ) צלוחית. תרגום של צלחת (שמות ט"ז) היא צלוחית: (כא) מוצא. מקום הנביעה: מות ומשכלת, היא היא וכפל הדבר במ"ש: (כב) וירפו.

מצודת דוד

(יט) טוב. בשדות וכרמים וכו': והארץ משכלת. בסיבת המים משכלת יושביה: (כא) אל מוצא המים. אל המקום שהמים נובעים משם: רפאתי למים. אמרו רז"ל שהיה הנס כפול כי דרך המלח לקלקל המים: לא יהיה משם. לא יבוא עוד משכלת מסיבת המים:

observance of *commandments.* [*Rashi, Redak* from source mentioned below.]

little — people of little faith [*Redak* from same source].

"Go away, baldy — *"Go away from here, for you have made the place bald for us, for until now we would hire ourselves out to bring sweet water from a distance, and we would earn our livelihood thereby." And when the water became sweet, they lost their livelihood. Thus it is explained in Sotah* (46b) [*Rashi*].

According to *peshat,* they jeered at him because he looked so much

19. And the people of the city said to Elisha, "Behold the city is a good place to live in, as my lord sees, but the water is bad and the land causes people to die. 20. And he said, "Take me to a new jug and put salt therein," and they took to him. 21. And he went out to the source of the water and threw salt there; and he said, "So has the Lord said, 'I have cured these waters; there will no longer be death and bereavement from there.'" 22. And the water became cured to this day, according to the word of Elisha that he spoke. 23. And he went up from there to Bethel, and he was going up on the road

19. **but the water is bad** — *and because of the water, the land causes people to die, to send them to their graves. If so, what is the meaning of: "the city is a good place to live in?" From here we deduce that a place has charm for its inhabitants* [*Rashi* from *Sotah* 47a]. Since Adam decreed that every inhabitable place be inhabited, God bestows charm upon all inhabitable places for some people who wish to live there [*Maharsha ibid.*].

Redak cites unknown Midrashic source that since Joshua cursed anyone who would rebuild Jericho, and Elijah renewed this curse when Hiel rebuilt the city (I Kings 16:34), the water became poisonous and many of the inhabitants died. *Abarbanel* suggests the identical theory, but does not mention that it originates from a Midrash. In any case, the origin is unknown to us.

20. **a new jug** — Lest the people think that Elisha cooked a beneficial substance in the jug, he made sure to take a new one, in which nothing had ever been cooked [*Ralbag*].

21. **to the source of the water** — *from where the water flowed* [*Rashi, Redak, Mezudoth*].

and threw salt there — *Now is not salt a thing that spoils water? This was then a miracle within a miracle* [*Rashi, Ex. Rabbah* 50:3, *Deut. Rabbah* 10:3, *Yalkut Shimoni* vol. 1:255, vol. 2:226 from *Mechilta* Ex. 15:25].

I.e. in addition to the fact that salt cannot cure water that is unsuitable for drinking, it is indeed detrimental to drinking water. Hence, this was a double miracle.

We find a similar instance of such a miracle in Exodus 15, when the Israelites could not drink the water in Marah because it was bitter. God instructed Moses to throw a tree into the water. The Rabbis tell us that this was a tree whose wood was bitter. Yet, the water became sweet and drinkable [*Redak* from sources mentioned above].

23. **and some little boys** — Heb. וּנְעָרִים, people *emptied out of* any

ונערים קטנים יצאו מן־העיר ויתקלסו־
בו ויאמרו לו עלה קרח עלה קרח:
כד ויפן אחריו ויראם ויקללם בשם יהוה
ותצאנה שתים דבים מן־היער
ותבקענה מהם ארבעים ושני ילדים:
כה וילך משם אל־הר הכרמל ומשם
שב שמרון: ג א ויהורם בן־אחאב מלך
על־ישראל בשמרון בשנת שמנה
עשרה ליהושפט מלך יהודה וימלך

ונוקין זעירין נפקו מן קרתא ואתלעבו ביה ואמרו ליה סק קרחא סק קרחא: כד ואתפני לאחורוהי וחזינון ולטינון בשמא דיי ונפקו תרתין דובין מן חורשא ובזעא מנהון ארבעין ותרין ינקין: כה ואזל מתמן לטור כרמלא ומתמן תב לשמרון: א ויהורם בר אחאב מלך על ישראל בשמרון בשנת תמני עסרי ליהושפט מלך שבטא דבית יהודה

ת"א עלה קרח. סוטה מו זוהר פקודי: ויקללם. סוטה שם: שתים דובים. שם:

רש"י

המים הוא אלא נס בתוך נס: (כג) ונערים קטנים. המנוערין מן המצות: עלה קרח. עלה מכאן שהקרחת עלינו את המקום שעד עכשיו היינו משתכרין להביא מים מתוקים מרחוק ומתפרנסין בכך ומשהמתיקו אבדו פרנסתן כך מפורש בסוטה: (כד) ויראם. ראה שאין בהם ולא בזרעם לחלוחית של טובה:

ג (א) ויהורם בן אחאב. אף פרשה זו בשביל להגיד נס של מישע מלך מואב שנעשה ע"י אלישע נכתבה כאן שמנה באליהו שמונה נסים ובאלישע ט"ז לקיים פי שנים ברוחך אלי וכתבן כולם זו בצד זו. כך ראיתי בל"ב מדו' דר"א בנו דר' יוסי הגלילי והליית ירדן של אלישע

רד"ק

הה"א: (כג) ונערים קטנים. כי יש גדולים ויקראו נערים אמר כי אלה הנערים היו קטנים וכן ונער קטן עמו ורז"ל דרשו נערים שהיו מנוערין מן המצות קטנים שהיו מקטני אמנה: ויתקלסו בו. לעגו בו ובזוהו בדבריהם שהיו אומרים לו בעלותו בדרך עלה קרח עלה קרח וקרח היה אלישע. ובדרש קרח אתה שהקרחת עלינו את המקום: (כד) ויראם ויקללם. ונחלקו רז"ל בזה כי קשה אליהם היאך גרם מיתה עליהם על דבר זה מהם אמרו ע"ש שבזוהו נתן עיניו בהן ונענשו כמו שאמרו כל מקום שנתנו עיניהם חכמים או מיתה או עוני ומהם אמרו ראה שכלם נתעברו אמותיהם ביום הכפורים כלומר ראה כי מעבירה באו וראוין היו למיתה ולכך הפקירו עצמם לבזותו ולכך קללם ולא כפני שבזיהו ומהם אמרו בלורית ראה להם כע"ג ומהם אמרו שלא ראה בהם לחלוחית מצוה ולא עתידה להיות לא בהם ולא בזרעם לפיכך ארכם לסלקם מן העולם ואמר כי נענש על דבר זה שגרם מיתה לאלה הנערים ואמרו שלשה חלאים חלה אלישע אחד על שגרה דובים בתינוקות ואחת על שדהפו לגחזי בשתי ידיו ואחת אשר מת בו וסמכו זה לפסוק שאמר ואלישע חלה את חליו אשר ימות בו. חלה. הנה אחד. חליו. שנים. אשר ימות בו. ג': שתים דובים. נקבות היו ואומר הריבוי במ"ם כמו גמלים מניקות ובדברי רז"ל מהם אמרו כי מעשה נס היה כי באותו יער לא היו רגילים חיות רעות ומהם אמרו נס בתוך נס היה כי לא היה שם לא יער ולא דובים ואמרו בשביל ארבעים ושתים קרבנות שהקריב בלק מלך מואב הובקעו

רלב"ג

רעים לבתיה עם בלי אפשר במעט מלח שיתן רושם במולא מים אשר לא יכזבו מימיו אם לא היה זה על דרך המופת: (כג) ויתקלסו בו. ר"ל לעגו בו ובזוהו: (כד) ויפן אחריו ויראם. הנה לא קללם עד שראה אותם וידע וראה על דרך נבואה שהם ראויים לקללה מצד רוע מעשיהם: (א) ויהורם בן אחאב מלך על ישראל בשומרון בשנת שמונה עשרה ליהושפט. זה יורה שאחזיה לא מלך שתי שנים שלמות

מנחת שי

(כד) ויקללם. אין דגש בלמ"ד:

מצודת דוד

(כג) עלה קרח. לפי שאליהו רבו היה בעל שער ואלישע היה קרח אמרו בלעג והתול עלה קרה השמימה כאליהו רבך וכאלו אמרו אינך במעלה כמוהו כי הוא היה בעל שער ואתה קרח: (כד) ויראם. אמרו רבותינו ז"ל שראה ברוח הקודש שאין בהם לחלוחית טובה ולכן קללם: ג (א) בשנת שמונה עשרה. ר"ל כבר עבר שמונה ליהושפט כי אחזיה בן אחאב מלך אחר שעבר י"ז ליהושפט בתחלת י"ח ושנתים מלך והם מקצת הי"ח מיהושפט ומקצת הי"ט ומלך אחר כך אחיו יהורם בתחלת הי"ט מיד אחר שעבר שנת י"ח: שתים עשרה

מצודת ציון

ויתקלסו. ויתלוצצו כמו לחרפה ולקלס מלשון לעג: (כג) ויתקלסו. ויגלעו כמו לחרפה ולקלם (יחזקאל כ"ב): קרח. כן יקרא מי שאין בו שער הראש כמו קרח הוא (ויקרא י"ג): (כד) ותבקענה. מלשון בקיעה:

bears emerged from it. According to others, there was a forest which was not usually frequented by wild beasts [*Redak* from *Sotah* ibid.].

1. **And Jehoram the son of Ahab**—*This section too was written here to tell the miracle of Mesha the king of Moab, which was performed through Elisha, for Scripture enumerated for Elijah eight miracles and for Elisha sixteen, to fulfill "a double*

and some little boys came out of the city and jeered him, and said to him, "Go away, baldy; go away, baldy!" 24. And he turned around and saw them, and he cursed them in the name of God. And two she-bears came out of the forest and tore apart forty-two boys of them. 25. And he went from there to Mt. Carmel, and from there he returned to Samaria.

3

1. And Jehoram the son of Ahab reigned over Israel in Samaria in the eighteenth year of Jehoshaphat king of Judah, and he reigned twelve years.

different from his master Elijah, who was described as a hairy man. This was as though to say that he was not on a level comparable to his master Elijah [*Mezudath David*].

According to this, we may render literally: Go up, baldy; go up, baldy! Just as your hairy master ascended to heaven, you, the baldheaded disciple, may do so too. In Bethel, the site of Jeroboam's calf, people had little respect for God's prophets [*Abarbanel, Malbim*].

24. **and saw them** — *He saw that neither in them nor in their descendants would there be any "sap" of good deeds* [*Rashi* from *Sotah* ibid.].

They were considered as having little faith because they thought that since they were no longer needed to bring water, there was no other means by which to earn a livelihood — *Rashi Sotah* ibid. They did not realize that the Almighty, Who gave them life until now, would continue to make it possible for them to earn a livelihood in a different manner.

Others explain that they were grownup youths who behaved contemptibly like children. The Talmud avoided the obvious meaning of this verse, that small children ridiculed Elisha, and he cursed them and caused them to be killed by bears. Elisha would never have done such a cruel thing. Yet, despite Elisha's justification for cursing them, he became ill as a punishment for this act [*Sotah* 47a, quoted by *Redak*].

As stated above, Elisha perceived through the holy spirit with which he was endowed, that these youths would never have any *sap* of good deeds, neither would any of their descendants. Had there been even one *tzaddik* destined to be born many generations later, he would not have invoked God's wrath upon them.

And two she-bears came out of the forest — This too was a double miracle. At this site, there was no forest, nor were there bears. Suddenly, a forest sprung up, and two

שתים־עשרה שנה: ב ויעשה הרע בעיני יהוה רק לא כאביו וכאמו ויסר את־מצבת הבעל אשר עשה אביו: ג רק בחטאות ירבעם בן־נבט אשר־החטיא את־ישראל דבק לא־סר ממנה: ד ומישע מלך־מואב היה נקד והשיב למלך־ישראל מאה־אלף כרים ומאה אלף אילים צמר: ה ויהי כמות אחאב ויפשע מלך־מואב במלך ישראל: ו ויצא המלך יהורם ביום ההוא משמרון ויפקד את־כל־ישראל: ז וילך וישלח אל־יהושפט מלך־יהודה

מלא ואו

ומלך תרתא עסרי שנין: ב ועבד דביש קדם יי לחוד לא כאבוהי וכאמיה ואעדי ית קמת בעלא דעבד אבוהי: ג לחוד בחובי ירבעם בר נבט דחיב ית ישראל אתרעי לא סטא מנה: ד ומישע מלכא דמואב הוה מרי גיתין ומתיב תוקרבא למלכא דישראל שנא בשנא מאה אלפין תורין דפטמא ומאה אלפין דכרין דרעיא: ה והוה כד מית אחאב ומריד מלכא דמואב במלכא דישראל: ו ונפק מלכא יהורם ביומא ההוא משמרון ומנא ית כל ישראל: ז ואזל ושלח לות יהושפט מלכא דבית

ת״א ומישע (בלאים לא):

רד״ק

מישראל ארבעית ושנים ילדים: (ב) ויסר את מצבת הבעל. אבל האשרה לא הסיר. מפני אמו שהיתה עובדת ע״א שהרי נביאי האשרה היו אוכלי שלחנו אבל הוא לא עבד הבעל והאשרה אלא העגלים שעשה ירבעם: (ד) היה נוקד. כתרגומו מרי גיתין ונקרא בעל המקנה נוקד שהצאן נקודים ברוב והיה מנהגו שהיה משיב מנחה למלך ישראל מאה אלף כרים ומאה אלף אילים צמר כלומר עם צמרם שלא היה גוזזם ולא אמר הכתוב אם היה משיב לו מנחה זו בכל שנה או לזמן אחד ידוע ביניהם: (ה) ויהי כמות אחאב. בכ״ף וכאשר מת אחאב פשע

רש״י

כשתי׳ דשל אליהו: (ב) רק לא כאביו וכאמו. שהוסיפו את הבעל להכעיס: (ג) רק בחטאות ירבעם וגו׳ דבק. וכן כל מלכי ישראל מדאגה שלא תשוב הממלכה לבית דוד אם יעלו לרגל לכך עבדו את העגלים: (ד) נוקד. מרי גיתין: אילים צמר. דיכרין דרעיא. עם למרס:

מנחת שי

ג (ד) אלף אלים למר. לית וכתיב רי״ב: (ה) ויהי כמות. בכ״ף רד״ק והם ג׳ בכ״ף ע״פ המסורת:

רלב״ג

אך היו מקוטעות והנה באמרנו במה שקדם היך יתישב כל זה סהספון בלי שום ספק: (ב) רק לא כאביו וכאמו. ר״ל שהוא דבק לבד בחטאת ירבעם ועזב חטאת אחאב ואיזבל. והנה הסיר מצבת הבעל שעשה אביו אך לא הסיר האשרה שעשתה אמו כי לא יכול לפי שהיא היתה עדיין: (ד) היה נוקד. ר״ל בעל מקנה והיה עושה מס למלך ישראל מאה אלף כרים ומאה אלף אילים למר ר״ל בעלי למר ולא

מצודת ציון

ג (ב) מצבת. מלשון מלבה:

מצודת דוד

שנה. ומקוטעות היו: (ג) בחטאות ירבעם. בעגלי הזהב: (ד) היה נוקד. ר״ל בעל לאן הרבה ועל שרובם נקודים יקראו המתעסק בהם בשם נוקד כמו דברי עמוס אשר היה בנוקדים (עמוס א׳): והשיב. לפי שבכל שנה העלה לו המס הזה לכן אמר והשיב ר״ל נתן והזר ונתן: צמר. עם למרם לא גוזזים: (ו) ביום ההוא. בעת שבא אלישע לשומרון: (ז) כמוני כמוך. כמו שתעלה אתה

the Baal, but not with the intention of provoking the Almighty. He, therefore, emends *Rashi* to read: *They, therefore, worshipped the Baalim. Malbim,* too, draws this distinction between Jehoram and Ahab.

4. **a sheepman**—Since the sheep are usually spotted, נְקֻדִּים in Heb., the owner of sheep is called נֹקֵד—*Redak. Jonathan,* however, renders נֹקֵד as *an owner of livestock* [*Rashi, Redak*].

This includes both sheep and cattle. Indeed, *Jonathan* renders כָּרִים as *fattened bulls.*

rams with their wool—*Jonathan* renders: *pasture-fed rams,* i.e. *with their wool* [*Rashi*].

2. And he did what was bad in the eyes of the Lord, however, not like his father and mother; and he removed the monument of the Baal that his father had made. 3. Only to the sins of Jeroboam the son of Nebat, who caused Israel to sin did he cling; he did not turn away from it. 4. Now Mesha the king of Moab was a sheepman; and he would repeatedly pay tribute to the king of Israel one hundred thousand lambs and one hundred thousand rams with their wool. 5. And it was, that when Ahab died, the king of Moab rebelled against the king of Israel. 6. Now King Jehoram went out of Samaria on that day, and counted all Israel. 7. And he went and called Jehoshaphat, king of Judah, . . .

portion of your spirit to me (above 2:9)," *and he wrote them all one juxtaposed to the other. I saw this in the "Thirty-two Methods of R. Eliezer the son of R. Jose the Galilean." Now the dividing of the Jordan by Elisha is counted like two miracles of Elijah* [*Rashi*]. See above 2:14.

in the eighteenth year—i.e. after the eighteenth year had passed, for Ahaziah reigned after the seventeenth year of Jehoshaphat had passed, and he reigned two years, part of the eighteenth year of Jehoshaphat and part of the nineteenth. Immediately after his death, Jehoram reigned in the nineteenth year of Jehoshaphat [*Mezudath David*]. See above 1:17.

2. **however, not like his father and mother**—*who added the worship of the Baal in order to provoke* God [*Rashi* according to *Shem Ephraim*]. See I Kings 16:30–33.

and he removed the monument of the Baal—As mentioned in the above source, Ahab, under the influence of his Phoenician wife, Jezebel, introduced Baal worship in Israel. His son, Jehoram, abolished this foreign deity. It is also mentioned that Ahab erected an *asherah*. This Jehoram did not abolish, since the prophets of the *asherah* ate at Jezebel's table (I Kings 18:19). He, himself, however, worshiped only Jeroboam's calves as is mentioned below v. 3 [*Redak*].

He could not abolish the *asherah* cult because his mother Jezebel was still living [*Ralbag*].

3. **Only to the sins of Jeroboam . . . did he cling**—i.e. he worshipped the calves that Jeroboam had erected [*Mezudath David*].

And so did *all kings of Israel, for fear lest the kingdom return to the house of David if they would perform the pilgrimage on festivals. They, therefore, worshipped the calves* [*Rashi*]. *Shem Ephraim* maintains that the kings of Israel worshipped

לֵאמֹר מֶלֶךְ מוֹאָב פָּשַׁע בִּי הֲתֵלֵךְ
אִתִּי אֶל־מוֹאָב לַמִּלְחָמָה וַיֹּאמֶר אֶעֱלֶה
כָּמוֹנִי כָמוֹךָ כְּעַמִּי כְעַמֶּךָ כְּסוּסַי
כְּסוּסֶיךָ׃ ח וַיֹּאמֶר אֵי־זֶה הַדֶּרֶךְ נַעֲלֶה
וַיֹּאמֶר דֶּרֶךְ מִדְבַּר אֱדוֹם׃ ט וַיֵּלֶךְ
מֶלֶךְ יִשְׂרָאֵל וּמֶלֶךְ יְהוּדָה וּמֶלֶךְ אֱדוֹם
וַיָּסֹבּוּ דֶּרֶךְ שִׁבְעַת יָמִים וְלֹא־הָיָה מַיִם
לַמַּחֲנֶה וְלַבְּהֵמָה אֲשֶׁר בְּרַגְלֵיהֶם׃
י וַיֹּאמֶר מֶלֶךְ יִשְׂרָאֵל אֲהָהּ כִּי־קָרָא
יְהוָה לִשְׁלֹשֶׁת הַמְּלָכִים הָאֵלֶּה לָתֵת
אוֹתָם בְּיַד־מוֹאָב׃ יא וַיֹּאמֶר יְהוֹשָׁפָט
הַאֵין פֹּה נָבִיא לַיהוָה וְנִדְרְשָׁה אֶת־
יְהוָה מֵאוֹתוֹ וַיַּעַן אֶחָד מֵעַבְדֵי מֶלֶךְ־
יִשְׂרָאֵל וַיֹּאמֶר פֹּה אֱלִישָׁע בֶּן־שָׁפָט

דבית יהודה למימר מלכא דמואב מריד בי התיזיל עמי לנת מואב בקרבא ואמר אסק אנא כותך עמי כעמך סוסני כסוסנך: ח ואמר באידא אורחא ניסק ואמר אורח מדברא דאדום: ט ואזל מלכא דישראל ומלך שבטא דבית יהודה ומלכא דאדום ואסחרו מהלך שבעא יומין ולא הוה מיא למשריתא ולבעירא דעמהון: י ואמר מלכא דישראל ני ארי זמין יי להלתא מלכיא האלין למסר יתהון בידא דמואב: יא ואמר יהושפט הלית פא נביא דיי ונשאל ית פתגמא דיי מניה ואתיב חד מעבדי מלכא דישראל ואמר הכא אלישע

ת"א מלך מואב פשע בי. יומא ל שבועות יב: פה אלישע. ברכות ה פסחים סח (ערובין כב):

רש"י

(ח) דרך מדבר אדום. כי גם מלך אדום ילך עמנו: (י) להת אותם וגו'. שימותו בצמא: (יא) אשר יצק מים על ידי אליהו. בהר הכרמל וביליקתו נעשו אצבעותיו

רד"ק

מלך מואב באחזיהו בנו כמו שכתוב למעלה וכן ביורם אחיו ולא השיב לו: (ח) דרך מדבר אדום. לפי שמלך אדום היה לו ללכת עמהם: (י) לתת אותם ביד מואב. שאם לא נמצא מים יפוצו חיילותינו אילך ואילך למצוא מים ויבואו מואב ולא נוכל להמלט מידם: (יא) פה אלישע. אלישע הלך עמהם על פי הנבואה להראותם זה הנס הגדול אולי ישוב מלך ישראל מדרכו הרעה והם לא ידעו כי הוא הולך עמהם אבל בא לו בתוך העם:

רלב"ג

אזים: (ח) ויאמר דרך מדבר אדום. יתכן שבחר הדרך ההוא כדי שלא יבגישו והביא שם מלך יהודה עם מלך אדום כי היה תחתיו וסוא הנליב שסם בו מלך יהודה: (יא) פה אלישע בן שפט אשר ילק מים ע"י אליהו. אף על פי שהיה לאליהו תלמידים רבים הנה זכר אלישע שהיה תלמיד והיה ראוי שיקנס יותר מהשלמת מפני שסרת את אליסו כי המשרת הוא תמיד לפני רבו ולזה יתכן שילמד

מצודת דוד

פלה כן גם אני: (ט) ומלך אדום. הוא היה נלב נלך מתחת יד מלך יהודה: ויסבו דרך וגו'. ר"ל הלכו שבעת ימים ולא מלאו מים. (י) כי קרא ה'. ר"ל גזר ה' להפילם ביד מואב כי בעבור הלמאון לא יתגברו להלחם: (יא) האין פה. האם אין פה: אשר יצק מים. ר"ל שהיה משרתו והתבודד עמו בכל עת:

מצודת ציון

(ט) ברגליהם. ההולכים עמהם ואחריהם כמו לעם אשר ברגלי (שופטים ח'): (י) אהה. ענין לשון לעקת יללה: (יא) יצק. שפך:

performed for us through him concerning water [*Rashi* from *Elijah Rabba* ch. 17]. See I Kings 18:34. Although there is no indication whether Elijah's fingers became like springs or whether Elisha's became like springs, the commentaries on *Elijah Rabba* interpret this to mean that Elijah's fingers were the ones that became like springs of water. See *Zikukin d'nura, Yeshuoth Jaakov* ad loc.

saying, "The king of Moab has rebelled against me. Will you go
with me to war against Moab?" And he said, "I will go up. I
will be like you, my people like your people, my horses like
your horses." 8. And he said, "By which road shall we go up?"
And he said, "By way of the Desert of Edom." 9. And the king
of Israel and the king of Judah and the king of Edom went, and
they went around, a journey of seven days; and there was no
water for the camp or for the animals that were with them.
10. And the king of Israel said, "Alas! For the Lord has called
these three kings to deliver them into the hands of Moab!"
11. And Jehoshaphat said, "Is there no prophet of the Lord
here that we may inquire of the Lord through him?" And one of
the king of Israel's servants answered, "Here is Elisha the son
of Shaphat . . .

No doubt *Jonathan* objected to the generally accepted translation of: . . . lambs and . . . rams with their wool. If the tribute consisted of 100,000 unshorn rams, why were the lambs not given in the same condition? He, therefore, concludes that the tribute consisted of 100,000 fattened bulls and 100,000 pasture-fed rams, who, although not fattened, were valuable because of their wool, for which they were raised.

would repeatedly pay tribute—lit. would return. The intervals in which he would pay this tribute are not made clear. Perhaps this was a yearly payment. It is, however, uncertain [*Redak*].

8. **by way of the Desert of Edom**—*for the king of Edom, too, will go with us* [Rashi, Redak].

9. **the king of Edom**—He was actually a governor, appointed by the king of Judah [*Mezudath David*]. See Kings 22:48, *Rashi* ad loc.

10. **to deliver them** . . . *for they will die of thirst* [*Rashi*].

I.e. if we remain together, we surely die of thirst. If we scatter to search for water, we will be unprepared to fight against the Moabites [*Redak*].

11. **Here is Elisha the son of Shaphat**—He had located them through prophecy, and had come to show the great miracle, perhaps Jehoram would repent. He mingled unnoticed among the soldiers [*Redak*].

who poured water on Elijah's hands—*on Mt. Carmel, and with his pouring, his fingers became like springs of water, until the ditch filled up, and it is fitting for a miracle to be*

אֲשֶׁר־יָצַק מַיִם עַל־יְדֵי אֵלִיָּהוּ: יב וַיֹּאמֶר
יְהוֹשָׁפָט יֵשׁ אוֹתוֹ דְּבַר־יְהוָה וַיֵּרְדוּ
אֵלָיו מֶלֶךְ יִשְׂרָאֵל וִיהוֹשָׁפָט וּמֶלֶךְ
אֱדוֹם: יג וַיֹּאמֶר אֱלִישָׁע אֶל־מֶלֶךְ
יִשְׂרָאֵל מַה־לִּי וָלָךְ לֵךְ אֶל־נְבִיאֵי אָבִיךָ
וְאֶל־נְבִיאֵי אִמֶּךָ וַיֹּאמֶר לוֹ מֶלֶךְ יִשְׂרָאֵל
אַל כִּי־קָרָא יְהוָה לִשְׁלֹשֶׁת הַמְּלָכִים
הָאֵלֶּה לָתֵת אוֹתָם בְּיַד מוֹאָב: יד וַיֹּאמֶר
אֱלִישָׁע חַי־יְהוָה צְבָאוֹת אֲשֶׁר עָמַדְתִּי
לְפָנָיו כִּי לוּלֵי פְּנֵי יְהוֹשָׁפָט מֶלֶךְ־יְהוּדָה
אֲנִי נֹשֵׂא אִם־אַבִּיט אֵלֶיךָ וְאִם־אֶרְאֶךָּ:

ת"א לולא. פסחים סו מגלה כח:

אֱלִישָׁע בַּר שָׁפָט דְשַׁמֵשׁ
יָת אֵלִיָהוּ: יב וַאֲמַר
יְהוֹשָׁפָט אִית עִמֵיהּ
פִּתְגָמָא דַיְיָ וּנְחָתוּ
לְוָתֵיהּ מַלְכָּא דְיִשְׂרָאֵל
וִיהוֹשָׁפָט וּמַלְכָּא
דֶאֱדוֹם: יג וַאֲמַר אֱלִישָׁע
לְמַלְכָּא דְיִשְׂרָאֵל מַה לִי
וְלָךְ אֱזֵיל לְוַת נְבִיֵי אֲבוּךְ
וּלְוַת נְבִיֵי אִמָךְ וַאֲמַר
לֵיהּ מַלְכָּא דְיִשְׂרָאֵל
בְּבָעוּ לָא תִדְכַּר חוֹבִין
רִשְׁעֲתָא הַהִיא בְּעֵי
עֲלָנָא רַחֲמִין אֲרֵי זַמִין יְיָ
לִתְלָתָא מַלְכַיָא הָאִלֵין
לְמִמְסַר יַתְהוֹן בִּידָא
מוֹאֲבָאֵי: יד וַאֲמַר אֱלִישָׁע
קַיָם הוּא יְיָ צְבָאוֹת
דִמְשַׁמֵשְׁנָא קֳדָמוֹהִי אֲרֵי
אִלוּלָא פוּן אַפֵּי יְהוֹשָׁפָט
מַלְכָּא שִׁבְטָא דְבֵית
יְהוּדָה אֲנָא נְסֵיב אִם
אֶסְתַּכַּל בָּךְ וְאִם

ועתה

רד"ק

אשר יצק מים. ר"ל ששרת אותו ובדברי רז"ל למד לא נאמר אלא יצק מלמד ששמוש' גדול מלמוד'.ובדרש אמר עוד אשר יצק מים ע"י אליהו בהר הכרמל כשמלא המזבח והתעלה מים אלישע היה יוצק מים ע"י אליהו ונעשה נס ונעשו י' אצבעותיו כמעינו' מים עד שנתמלאה התעלה מים שנאמר ויצקו וכמו ששם נעשה נס על ידו במים לפיכך אמר אשר יצק מים ולא אמר אשר שמש או אשר למד ועוד בדרש אשר יצק מים ע"י אליהו אמרו אפילו הי' מבקש מים לפניו היה נותן לו: (יב) יש אותו דבר ה'. שהרי הוא לא בא לעשות מלחמה למה בא לא בא אלא ע"י נבואה באמת יש אותו דבר ה': וירדו. ירדו מרכבתם לכבודו לדבר עמו ולא קראו לו שיבא אצלו לפי שהיו בצרה גדולה חשו לכבוד הבורא ולכבוד נביאו: מלך ישראל ויהושפט ומלך אדום. לפי שדבר יהושפט בשמו לא נאמר בו מלך ומלך אדום הוא הנציב שהיו משימי' עלהם מלכי יהודה והיא היה להם מלך; ויש בו דרש למה לא נאמר ביהושפט מלך להודיע ענוותנותו של אותו צדיק שלא רצה לירד לפני הנביא בבגדי מלכות אלא כחבר הדיוט וי"א שנגזרה גזרה שיהרג עם אחאב והיה הכתוב מונה לבני מן אותה שעה לפיכך לא נקרא מלך ובשכר שירדו לפני הנביא זכו לראות כל אלו הנסים: (יג) אל כי קרא ה'. אל תאמר עתה לנו דברים אלו אמת הוא כי קרא ה' לשלשת המלכים הבאים הנה לתתם ביד מואב וי"ת אל לשון בקשה בבעו לא תידכר עלנא חובין רשעתא ההיא בעי עלנא רחמין ארי זמין ה' לתלתא מלכיא

רש"י

כמעיינות מים עד שנתמלאה התעלה וראוי הוא ליעשות לנו נס אל ידו במים: (יג) אל כי קרא ה' וגו'. בבעו לא

רלב"ג

יותר ולזה שפט יהושפט שיש את אלישע דבר ה' מלורף לזה כי לאה שנסע ממקומו עם אנשי המלחמה ואף על פי שלא היה איש מלחמ'

מצודת ציון

(יב) אותו. עמו: (יד) לולי. אם לא:

מצודת דוד

(יב) יש אותו דבר ה'. כי בוודאי לא בא אל המחנה להלחם כי אם בא מדבר ה': (יג) מה לי ולך. ר"ל מה הוא האהבה והקורבה אשר בינינו מהו הטובה דעשית לי ומה עשיתי לך ומדוע א"כ תשאל בי: לך אל נביאי אביך וגו'. הם נביאי הבעל: אל וגו'. ר"ל אל תאמר עתה כדברים האלה כי אנו בסכנה ואל תעורר הדין בהזכרת החטאים: (יד) אשר עמדתי לפניו. שאני רגיל לעמוד לפניו בתפלה: כי לולא וגו'. ר"ל אם לא היה הדבר הזה מה שאני נושא פני יהושפט: אם אביט וגו'. ר"ל אם הייתי מביט אליך

has summoned . . .—*Jonathan* paraphrases thus: *Please do not mention the sins of that wicked woman. Beg mercy for us, for the Lord has summoned . . .* [*Rashi*].

Redak explains that *Jonathan* renders: אַל, as *please,* rather than as *don't.* The rest of the *Targum* is paraphrased. *Redak* himself, however, interprets it as *don't,* paraphrasing thus: "Don't tell us those things now. The truth is that the Lord . . ." This is the basis for our translation.

14. **before Whom I have stood**—before Whom I have habitually stood in prayer [*Mezudath David*].

who poured water on Elijah's hands." 12. And Jehoshaphat said, "The word of the Lord is with him." And the king of Israel and Jehoshaphat and the king of Edom went down to him. 13. And Elisha said to the king of Israel, "What do I have [to do] with you? Go to your father's prophets and to your mother's prophets!" And the king of Israel said to him, "Don't [say that], for the Lord has summoned these three kings to deliver them into the hands of Moab." 14. And Elisha said, "As the Lord of Hosts, before Whom I have stood, lives, for were it not that I respect Jehoshaphat king of Judah, I would neither look at you nor would I see you."

Alternatively, this is an expression denoting Elisha's complete devotion, to his master, as *Jonathan renders:* who served Elijah. He was his personal servant, ministering to his needs to the extent that he would pour water on his hands. Since Scripture describes Elisha in this capacity rather than as the disciple of Elijah, it indicates that the ministering to Torah is greater than learning it [*Redak* from *Berachoth* 7b]. See Joshua 1:1, Commentary Digest.

12. **"The word of the Lord is with him."**—He has surely come with a prophetic message for us. Otherwise, he would not have come here. He is surely not here to participate in the war [*Redak, Mezudath David*].

and Jehoshaphat—Since he is identified by name, his title is omitted. According to our sages, the omission of Jehoshaphat's title indicates that out of humility, Jehoshaphat removed his royal robes and his crown, and appeared before Elisha as a commoner.

Alternatively, since he was condemned to die in the battle of Ramoth-Gilead, even though God spared him, the remaining years of his reign were counted to his son's reign. He was, therefore relieved of the title of king [*Redak* from *Tanhuma Pinchas* 3, *Tan. Buber* 5].

13. **"What have I [to do] with you**—What relationship is there between me and you? What favors did either one of us do for the other? Why, then, do you come to me now that you are in distress? [*Mezudath David*].

The prophet's prayer can only avail one who believes in God and His prophets, thereby creating a union between the prophet and the one for whom he is praying [*Malbim*].

Go to your father's prophets—the prophets of Baal [*Mezudath David*].

"Don't [say that], for the Lord

טו וְעַתָּה קְחוּ־לִי מְנַגֵּן וְהָיָה כְּנַגֵּן הַמְנַגֵּן
וַתְּהִי עָלָיו יַד יְהוָה׃ טז וַיֹּאמֶר כֹּה אָמַר
יְהוָה עָשֹׂה הַנַּחַל הַזֶּה גֵּבִים ׀ גֵּבִים׃ יז כִּי
כֹה ׀ אָמַר יְהוָה לֹא־תִרְאוּ רוּחַ וְלֹא־תִרְאוּ
גֶשֶׁם וְהַנַּחַל הַהוּא יִמָּלֵא מָיִם וּשְׁתִיתֶם
אַתֶּם וּמִקְנֵיכֶם וּבְהֶמְתְּכֶם׃ יח וְנָקַל
זֹאת בְּעֵינֵי יְהוָה וְנָתַן אֶת־מוֹאָב
בְּיֶדְכֶם׃ יט וְהִכִּיתֶם כָּל־עִיר מִבְצָר וְכָל־
עִיר מִבְחוֹר וְכָל־עֵץ טוֹב תַּפִּילוּ וְכָל־

אֲחָזֵינָךְ׃ טו וּכְעַן אַיְתוֹ
לִי גַּבְרָא דְּיָדַע לְנַגָּנָא
בְּכִנּוֹרָא וַהֲוָה כַּד נַגֵּן
דִּמְנַגֵּן וּשְׁרָא עֲלוֹהִי רוּחַ
נְבוּאָה מִן קֳדָם יְיָ׃
טז וַאֲמַר כִּדְנַן אֲמַר יְיָ
יִתְעֲבֵיד נַחְלָא הָדֵין
פְּצִידִין פְּצִידִין׃ יז אֲרֵי
כִּדְנַן אֲמַר יְיָ לָא תֶחֱזוּן
רוּחָא וְלָא תֶחֱזוּן מִטְרָא
וְנַחְלָא הַהוּא יִתְמְלֵי מַיָּא
וְתִשְׁתּוֹן אַתּוּן וְגֵיתֵיכוֹן
וּבְעִירְכוֹן׃ יח וּקְלִילָא
דָא קֳדָם יְיָ וְיִמְסַר יַת
מוֹאֲבָאֵי בִּידְכוֹן׃
יט וְתִמְחוֹן כָּל כְּרַךְ תַּקִּיף
וְכָל קִרְוִין כְּרִיכָן וְכָל
אִילָן דְּיָאֵי תְּעַקְרִין וְכָל

מבועי

ת"א קחו לי מנגן. שבת ל פסחים סו קיז עקרים מג פ' י: והיה כנגן. (ברכות ג) סוכה נה:

רש"י

תדכר חובין דעתהא ההיא בעי עלנא רחמין אחרי זמין ה' וכו': (טו) קחו לי מנגן. מפני הכעס נסתלק' שכינה ממנו: (טז) גבים גבים. בורות מלאים מים: (יח) ונקל זאת. ועוד נס זה נקל ומועט בעיני ה' והוסיף להפליא אתכם נס אחר ונתן את מואב בידכם: (יט) וכל עץ טוב תפילו. אע"פ שנאמר (דברים כ' י"ט) לא תשחית את עצה כאן התיר לכם שהיא אומה בזויה ונקלית לפניו וכן הוא אומר

רד"ק

וכן תרגם אונקלוס אל נא אדני בבעו כען רבוני: (טו) קחו לי מנגן. אמרו כי מיום שנסתלק אליהו רבו לא שרתה עליו רוח נבואה עדיין כי אבל היה ורוח הקדש אינה שורה אלא מתוך שמחה וי"א מפני הכעס שכעס על מלך ישראל היה עצב ואמרו כל הכועס אם נביא נבואתו מסתלקת ממנו מנא לן מאלישע ולשמחתו אמר קחו לי מנגן: (טז) עשה הנחל הזה גבים. מקום במקור צווי: גבים. חפירות כמו באו על גבים ותרגום בור גובא אמר להם שיעשו הנחל חפירות שימלאוהו מן המים שיבואו ותרגומו פצידין פצידין וכן תרגם אפיקיו פצידוהי: (יח) ונקל זאת בעיני ה'. נקל זאת בעיניו לעשות לכם זה הנס עד שיעשה לכם נס גדול יותר ונתן מואב בידכם: (יט) וכל עץ טוב תפילו. כי הכתוב לא אמר לא תשחית את עצה אלא כשיצורו על עיר כמ"ש הטעם כי ממנו תאכל ואע"פ שרז"ל קבלו כי בכל מקום ובכל זמן אסור להשחית עץ מאכל פשט

מנחת שי

(טו) כנגן המנגן. בספרים כ"י הה"א במאריך והמ"ס רפה וכן במקצת דפוסים: (יז) ובהמתכם. בספרים מדוייקים הוא"ו במאריך:

רלב"ג

ולזה ידמה העשה זה שאם ילטרכו ישראל לדבר ה' ימלאהו שם והנה לכבודו ירדו אליו שלשה המלכים ולכבוד השם יתברך: (טו) ועתה קחו לי מנגן. ידוע כי הכעס מונע ההתבודדות לשכל בעת הגעת הנבואה מפני טרדת המחשבות אשר יהיה בהם הכעס ולפי שכעס מאוד אלישע על יהורם מפני שדבק בחטאת ירבעם הולך לדבר יסיר כעסו וירחיב לבו ואז שרתה עליו רוח הקדש: (טז) עשה הנחל הזה גבים גבים. ר"ל שיעשו המישור הזה חפירות חפירות ובזולת רוח וגשם יעשה הש"י על דרך המופת שימלאו החפירות אשר במישור ההוא מים יספיקו להם לשתות הם ומקניהם שהביאו לאכול ממנו ובהמתם אשר ירכבו עליהם: (יח) ונקל זאת בעיני ה'. ר"ל שלא יספיק לש"י עשיית זה החסד לכם כי הוא קל בעיניו ביחס אל החסד שהוא רוצה לעשות והוא שכבר יתן את מואב בידכם: (יט) והכיתם כל עיר מבצר וגו'. ר"ל שאמר להם במלות הש"י שיכו כל עיר בצור' וכל עיר נבחרת ויפילו כל אילן טוב אף על פי

מצודת דוד

מצודת ציון

בזולת יהושפט יהיה עלי עונש השבועה: (טו) קחו לי מנגן. לשמחני בנגונו כי בעבור שכעס על יהורם לא חלה עליו הנבואה כי אין הנבואה שורה אלא מתוך שמחה והכעס באה היא עם העצבון: והיה כנגן. כאשר המנגן התחיל לנגן שרתה עליו רוח הנבואה: (טז) גבים גבים. להתאסף בהם המים הבאים: (יז) לא תראו רוח. ר"ל לא יבואו המים בדרך טבעי על ידי הרוח והגשם כי אם יבואו על פי נס: ומקניכם. מה שהביאו למאכלם: ובהמתכם. מה שהיו רוכבים עליהם: (יח) ונקל זאת. החסד הזה הוא נקל בעיני ה' כי עוד יעשה חסד גדול מזה בתת את מואב בידכם: (יט) מבחור. טובה ונבחרה: תכאיבו. תשחיתו אותה במה

(טו) מנגן. יודע לנגן: (טז) הנחל. העמק: גבים. בורות כמו

crimes against Israel are delineated.

you shall clutter—lit. you shall pain. *Jon.* renders: you shall stop up; i.e. you shall stifle the vegetation by piling stones upon it. See *Redak.*

good field—*sown field* (*Koumici in O.F.*) [*Rashi*].

20. **And it was in the morning**

15. "And now fetch me a musician." And it was that when the musician played, the hand of the Lord came upon him." 16. And he said, "So has the Lord said, 'This valley will be made full of pools.' 17. For so has the Lord said, 'You shall not see wind neither shall you see rain, yet that valley will be filled with water; and you and your cattle and your beasts shall drink. 18. And this will be slight in the eyes of the Lord, and He will deliver Moab into your hands. 19. And you shall strike every fortified city and every choice city, and you shall fell every good tree,

15. **fetch me a musician**—*Because of his anger, the Shechinah left him* [*Rashi* from *Pesachim* 66b].

The strong emotions involved in anger prevent the mind from concentrating on attaining prophecy. It is, therefore, impossible to prophesy while angry [*Ralbag*].

Alternatively, Elisha could not prophesy because he was mourning the departure of his beloved master, Elijah. The Shechinah rests on the prophets only out of joy involved in the fulfillment of a precept [*Redak*]. See *Pesachim* 117a, *Mid. Psalms* 24.

Jonathan renders: Fetch me a man who knows how to play the harp.

when the musician played—When he commenced to play, Elisha rejoiced and was able to receive the spirit of prophecy [*Mezudath David*].

that the hand of the Lord was upon him—i.e. a spirit of prophecy from the Lord rested upon him [*Targum Jonathan*].

16. **full of pools**—*pits full of water* [*Rashi*].

Others render: Make this valley many pits. I.e. dig many pits in this valley so that the water will gather in them [*Redak, Mezudath David*].

17. **'You shall not see wind . . .**—I.e. the water will not come through rain but in a miraculous manner [*Mezudath David*]. Compare commentaries below v. 20.

18. **And this will be slight**—*And furthermore, this miracle is slight and insignificant in the eyes of the Lord, and He will proceed to act wondrously with you* and perform *another miracle, and He will deliver Moab into your hands* [*Rashi*].

19. **and you shall fell every good tree**—*Even though it is stated:* (Deut. 20:19). *"You shall not destroy its trees," here He permitted it for you, for this is a contemptible and insignificant nation before Him. And so* Scripture *states:* (Deut. 23:7) *"You shall not seek their welfare and their good. These are the good trees that are among them"* [*Rashi* from *Midrash Tanhuma, Pinchas* 3, Buber's version *Pinchas* 5].

See Deut. 23:4–7, where Moab's

מַעְיְנֵי־מַיִם תִּסְתֹּמוּ וְכֹל הַחֶלְקָה הַטּוֹבָה תַּכְאִבוּ בָּאֲבָנִים: כ וַיְהִי בַבֹּקֶר כַּעֲלוֹת הַמִּנְחָה וְהִנֵּה־מַיִם בָּאִים מִדֶּרֶךְ אֱדוֹם וַתִּמָּלֵא הָאָרֶץ אֶת־הַמָּיִם: כא וְכָל־מוֹאָב שָׁמְעוּ כִּי־עָלוּ הַמְּלָכִים לְהִלָּחֶם בָּם וַיִּצָּעֲקוּ מִכֹּל חֹגֵר חֲגֹרָה וָמָעְלָה וַיַּעַמְדוּ עַל־הַגְּבוּל: כב וַיַּשְׁכִּימוּ בַבֹּקֶר וְהַשֶּׁמֶשׁ זָרְחָה עַל־הַמָּיִם וַיִּרְאוּ מוֹאָב מִנֶּגֶד אֶת־הַמַּיִם אֲדֻמִּים כַּדָּם:

מַבּוּעֵי מַיָּא תִּסְתְּמוּן וְכָל אַחְסַנְתָּא שַׁפִּרְתָּא תְּטוּמוּן בְּאַבְנַיָּא: כ וַהֲוָה בְּצַפְרָא כְּמִיסַּק מִנְחָתָא וְהָא מַיָּא אָתַן בְּאוֹרַח אֱדוֹם וְאִתְמְלִיאַת אַרְעָא יַת מַיָּא: כא וְכָל מוֹאֲבָאֵי שְׁמָעוּ אֲרֵי סְלִיקוּ מַלְכַיָּא לְאַגָּחָא קְרָבָא בְּהוֹן וְאִתְכְּנִישׁוּ מִכֹּל אֲסִירֵי סַיְפָא וּלְעֵילָא וְקָמוּ עַל תְּחוּמָא: כב וְאַקְדִּימוּ בְּצַפְרָא וְשִׁמְשָׁא נְחַת עַל מַיָּא וַחֲזוֹ מוֹאֲבָאֵי מִקֳּבֵל יַת מַיָּא סוּמְקִין כִּדְמָא

ת״א המים אדומים. שבת קח נדה יט:

רש״י
(דברים כ״ג ז׳) לא תדרוש שלומם וטובתם אלו האילנות הטובים שבהם: החלקה הטובה. שדה זרועה (קומל״י בלע״ז): (כ) ויהי בבקר כעלות המנחה. המים התחילו לירד מן השמים בבקר בארץ אדום וכעלות המנחה באין שוטפין ובאין לאותו הנחל לפי שאמר לא תראו רוח ולא תראו גשם. במדרש ר׳ תנחומא: (כא) על הגבול. על הספר שקורין מרק״א: (כב) אדומים כדם. כן דרך המים כשהשמש זורחת עליהם בבקר מאדימות: מנגד.

רד״ק
הכתוב הוא שלא אמר אלא בעת המצור ואפשר שהיתה מצוה לשעה כאליהו בהר הכרמל שהקריב עולה בחוץ בשעת איסור הבמות. ובדרש כשאמר להם הנביא וכל עץ טוב תפילו אמרו לו הרי הוא אומר לא תשחית את עצה ואתה אומר כן אמר להם על שאר האומות נאמרה זה אבל אומה זו נקלה ונבזה לפני ה׳ שנאמר ונקל זאת בעיני ה׳ ונאמר לא תדרוש שלומם וטובתם אלו אילנות טובות שלהם: תכאבו באבנים. על דרך השאלה וכן היחיו את האבנים וירפא את מזבח ה׳ ההרוס. ותרגומו תטומון: (כ) ויהי בבקר כעלות המנחה. כעלות בכ״ף ופירוש בבקר בעת עלות מנחת הבקר והמים האלה אפשר שהיו מגשמים שהיו רחוקים מהם בארץ אדום אבל המחנה הזה לא ראה לא רוח ולא גשם או נפרץ אחד מנהרות בארץ אדום ברצון הבורא ונברו המים עד הנחל הזה. ובדרש או בבקר או בעלות המנחה מהו בבקר כעלות המנחה אמר רבי תנחומא שטף של גשמים ירד באדום בבקר ובאו להם כעלות המנחה: (כא) מכל חוגר חגורה. כתרגומו מכל אסירי סיפא: על הגבול. על גבול ארצם להלחם אם יבואו עליהם המלכים:

מנחת שי
(כ) ויהי בבקר כעלות המנחה. כעלות בכ״ף. ובס״א כ״י מצאתי כתוב ויהי

רלב״ג
שהתורה אמרה לא תשחית את עצה הנה היה זה למצות השי״ת לפי שעה להשחית את מואב לפי היכולת ולזה לוה גם כן לסתם להם כל מעין מים ולהכות באבנים על חלקה טובה כדי שישחיתו תבואתה: (כ) ויהי בבקר כעלות המנחה. לפי שלא יתכן שיהיה דברי המלכים לאלישע בלילה ולא נכון ג״כ שנאמר שהמתינו לשתות עד למחרת היום ההוא שבאו שם מים מדרך אדום הנה הנבואה כפתי בזה שהרלון באמרו ויהי בבקר שזה הרגע שאמר לעשות למואב היה בבקר שאחר היום ההוא כמו שיבאר אחר זה אך יעוד בא המים שם נתקיים הכף בעת אשר יעלו בו מנחת ערב והוא תמיד של בין הערבים והוא שכבר הביא הש״י מדרך אדום מים ומלאה הארץ אתם: (כא) מכל חוגר חגורה ומעלה. ר״ל כל מי שראוי לחגור חגורה להלחם ומי שלמעלה מהם כלם נלעקו ויעמדו אצל גבול ארצם

מצודת ציון
ולחסוף מים מגבא (ישעיה ל׳): (יט) החלקה. השדה כמו ראו חלקת יואב (שמואל ב׳ י״ד): (כא) ויצעקו. נאספו על ידי צעקת המאסף:

מצודת דוד
שתשליכו בה אבנים והוא לשון מושאל מן ובעלי חיים הנבאבים בהשחתה: (כ) כעלות המנחה. כאשר בא זמן העלאת מנחת תמיד הבוקר: (כא) שמעו. כאשר שמעו שעלו למלחמה נאספו גם המה: מכל חוגר. מכל היודע לחגור החרב: ומעלה. והמעולים מהם הם הגבורים אנשי מלחמה ור״ל איש לא נעדר: (כב) על המים. הבאים אל הנחל כדבר ה׳: אדומים כדם. על ידי זריחת השמש

late afternoon, it appeared red as blood on the *following* morning. According to the exegetes who explain that the water came in the morning, it appeared like blood at that very time [*Malbim*].

and you shall stop up all springs of water, and you shall clutter
every good field with stones." 20. And it was in the morning
when the meal-offering was offered up, that, behold, water was
coming from the road of Edom; and the land became filled with
the water. 21. And all the Moabites heard that the kings had
come up to wage war with them; and they assembled, everyone
old enough to gird a sword and older, and they stood at the
border. 22. And they arose early in the morning, when the sun
shone on the water; and the Moabites saw the water from a distance, red as blood.

when the meal-offering was offered up—i.e. when the meal-offering of the daily morning sacrifice was offered up. This water may have been rain that fell in the land of Edom, far from the camp, hence they did not see it fall. It is also possible that one of the rivers of Edom overflowed its banks, and the valley near the campsite was filled with water [*Redak*].

The Rabbis, however, interpret the phrase, *when the meal-offering was offered up,* as referring to the meal-offering of the afternoon sacrifice. Therefore, they ask, "Either it took place in the morning or when the meal-offering was offered up. What is the meaning of *in the morning, when the meal-offering was offered up?*" Said R. Tanhuma, *"The water began falling from heaven in the morning in the land of Edom, and at the time of offering up the meal-offering, it came surging into that valley, since the prophet had said, "You shall not see wind neither shall you see rain* (v. 17)"—*In R. Tanhuma's Midrash*—[*Rashi* and *Redak,* source unknown].

21. **everyone old enough to gird a sword**—*Targum Jonathan,* lit. from who girded a girdle.

at the border—*at the border that is called "marche."*

They were standing at the border of their land, ready to fight if the three kings would attack them [*Redak*].

22. **red as blood** —*Such is the nature of water; when the sun shines on it in the morning, it appears red at a distance. Now, since they had never seen water in that valley, they, therefore, thought that it was blood* [*Rashi* according to *Kara*]. This appears to be more accurate than the usual version, which presents the words of the verse in inverted order.

According to the Rabbis, that the water flowed into the valley in the

כג ויאמרו דם זה החרב נחרבו המלכים ויכו איש את־רעהו ועתה לשלל מואב: כד ויבאו אל־מחנה ישראל ויקמו ישראל ויכו את־מואב וינסו מפניהם ויבו־בה והכות את־מואב: כה והערים יהרסו וכל־חלקה טובה ישליכו איש־אבנו ומלאוה וכל־מעין־מים יסתמו וכל־עץ־טוב יפילו עד־השאיר אבניה

ויכו קרי

פדמא: כג ואמרו דם דין אתגראה אתגריאו מלכיא וקטלו גבר ית חבריה וכען פוקו לביזתא מואבאי: כד ואתו למשריתא דישראל וקמו ישראל ומחו ית מואבאי ואפכו מן קדמיהון ומחו בהון וקטלו ית מואבאי: כה וקרוא פגרו וכל אחסנתא שפירא רמו גבר אבניה ומלאוהא וכל מבועי מיא סתמו וכל אילן דיאי עקרו עד דלא אשתארת אבנא

רש"י

מרחוק והם לא ראו באותו הנהל מים מעולם לפיכך היו סבורין שהוא דם: (כה) והערים יהרוסו. היו הורסין: ישליכו איש אבנו. שהיו נוטלין האבנים מן החומות עד השאיר כל אבני הקירות כקיר לעמוד על הרסית שלהן הוא הטיט כלומר שלא היתה עוד אבן בחומה ואחרי זאת ויסובו הקלעים ויכו את הנשאר בחלקה שלא נשברה החומה

רד"ק

(כג) דם זה. לפי שראו האדמימות ומים לא היו נובעים כי עתה באו המים שם שהרי לא היו שם מתמול שלשום התחזק בלבם כי דם הוא וחשבו כי נפלה קטטה בין המלכים והרגו אלו לאלו: החרב נחרבו. מענין חרב כלומר נהרגו ביניהם. החרב מבנין הפעל: (כד) ויבאו. באו כאנשים בוטחים ולא כנלחמים וישראל ואשר עמהם קמו עליהם והכום: ויבו בה. כן כתיב בבי"ת וקרי בכ"ף והכתוב לא מצאתי לו טעם אלא אם נאמר שהוי"ו תמורת אל"ף ויהיה כמו ויבא בה כלומר ישראל בא בה ופי' בה בעיר כלומר בכל עיר ועיר שהיו נסים אלה להמלט שם מפני ישראל והוא במסרה והוא אחד מתרין שקורין בה וסבירין בם והאחר הוא ותירוש יכחש בה: (כה) עד השאיר אבניה בקיר חרשת. קיר חרשת שם עיר גדולה בערי מואב זוכר אותה בכל מפלת מואב ולפי שהיתה בעלת שם זכר אותה ולא זכר הערים האחרות שהרסו ופירוש עד השאיר הכל הרסו והפילו עד השאיר קיר חרשת לבדה שהיתה עיר בצורה ובה לא השאירו אלא אבני החומה זהו אבניה אבני העיר הזאת כי כל מה שהיה מחוץ לעיר הרסו והפילו העצים וכל האבנים היו משליכים בחלקות הטובות ונשארה חומת העיר הזאת: ויסבו הקלעים ויכוה. הכו בחומה עד שהרסוה ידמה כי לשאר הערים לא היו צריכים להם קלעים אלא היו כובשים הערים ואחר כך היו הורסים אותם ולזאת שהיתה עיר בצורה הוצרכו הקלעים והקלעים האלה לא היו קלעים ביד אלא קלעים שמשליכים אבנים גדולות בדיק וכיוצא בו שבאבן אחת משא כבד ומשליכין באותן הכלים האבן לחומה עד שישברו

מנחת שי

(כד) ויבו. ויכו ק' והוא חד מן מלין דכתיבין בי"ת וקריין כ"ף: ויבו בה. ג' סבירין בם ואידך ותירוש יכחש בה (הושע ט'):

בבקר כזר ח ה ש מ ש וטעות הוא:

רלב"ג

(כג) ויאמרו דם זה וגו'. לפי שלא היה ממנהג המישור ההוא להיות בו מים חשבו שיהיו דם ולא נתנו לבם הכאת השמש במים: החרב נחרבו. ר"ל הכו זה את זה בחרב והרגו זה את זה: (כד) ויבאו אל מחנה ישראל. הנה סבב הש"י שבאו כלם שם לא כדרך האנשי' היוצאים למלחמה אך כדרך האנשים היוצאים לשלל ולזה הכום ישראל בקלות: (כד) ויכו בה והכות את מואב. הנה הכתיב ויבו בבי"ת וקרי ויכו בכ"ף והכוונה בהם שכבר הכום במחנה ההוא שבאו שם והוא מחנה ישראל ובא בלשון נקבה על דרך אם תחנה עלי מחנה ואחר זה השלימו להכות את מואב במקומותיהם: (כה) והערים יהרסו וגו'. עד השאיר אבניה בקיר הרשת. ר"ל שבעיר ההיא לבדה השאיר אבניה כי היה היתם חזקה מאד וכבר היו סובבים הקלעים ומכים אות' והנה היה שם מלך מואב וכראותו כי חזק ממנו דבר המלחמה לקח אתו שבע מאות איש שלף חרב להבקיע אל מלך אדום ולא יכולו אז לקח במחנה מלך אדום בנו הבכור של מלך אדום אשר ימלוך תחתיו והעלהו עולה על החומה ר"ל ששרף אותו כאמרו על שרפו את

מצודת ציון

(כג) החרב נחרבו. מלשון חרב: (כה) הקלעים. משליכי אבני

מצודת דוד

(כג) דם זה. היות כי מעולם לא היה שם מים לחשוב שנראים אדומים מזריחת השמש כי לא ידעו שבא על המים נראים הם אדומים: שמה מים בדרך נס: החרב נחרבו. ר"ל המלכים נהרגו בחרב כי הכו איש את רעהו בהלחמם זה בזה: ועתה. הואיל וכן הרי הם מוכנים לשלל מואב ולא יצטרכו מעתה להלח' בהם: (כד) ויבואו. כההולכים בבטחון מבלי הכין למלחמה: ויכו בה והכות וגו'. ר"ל הכו וחזרו והכו: (כה) איש אבנו. כל אחד השליך האבן אשר היה עליו להשליך: עד השאיר אבניה וגו'. ר"ל לא השאירו בעיר קיר הרשת

that there were no more stones in the wall. And afterwards the catapultists surrounded that which remained in the field where the wall was not broken, and broke it down [*Rashi*].

Thus, *Rashi* renders: בְּקִיר חֲרָשֶׂת as in the wall the clay, i.e. only the clay was left after all the stones had been removed by the Israelite soldiers.

Jonathan renders: *until a stone did not remain in a city, that they did not demolish*, explaining חֲרָשֶׂת, as being derived from the root הרס, to demolish.

23. And they said, "This is blood! The kings have fought with each other and have killed each other. And now, to the spoils, Moab!" 24. And they came to the Israelite camp, and the Israelites arose and struck the Moabites, and they fled from before them; and they attacked them, and slew the Moabites. 25. And they demolished the cities, and each one threw his stone on every fertile field and filled it up, and they stopped up every water spring and they felled every good tree until they left over its stones

23. **"This is blood!**—As explained above, they had never witnessed water in that valley. Therefore, they thought that the reddish looking water was actually blood [*Redak, Ralbag, Mezudath David*].

The kings have fought with each other—lit. they have been struck by the sword [*Redak, Ralbag, Mezudath David*].

24. **And they came to the Israelite camp**—not in military formation, prepared for battle, but with confidence, seeking spoils. They were, therefore, vulnerable to the Israelite attack [*Ralbag, Redak, Mezudath David*].

and they attacked them and slew the Moabites—This translation follows *Targum Jonathan.* Others render: and they repeatedly struck the Moabites [*Mezudath David*].

According to the *Kethib,* we render; and they entered them (i.e. the cities where the Moabites fled), and struck the Moabites [*Redak*].

25. **And they demolished the cities**—I.e. *they were demolishing the cities* [*Rashi*]. This accounts for the future form used in this verse, rather than the past.

until they left over its stones in Kir-Haresheth—i.e. they demolished all the cities by removing all the stones from their walls. The only remaining city was Kir-Haresheth, where only the stones in the wall remained [*Redak*].

and the catapultists surrounded and struck it—they hurled heavy stones with catapults from atop the bulwark. Since this city was strongly fortified, there was no way to demolish the walls except by means of the catapults—*Redak.*

Since this was the metropolis of Moab and the home of the king, they were particularly eager to destroy it [*Ralbag, Mezudath David*].

Rashi, however, renders בְּקִיר חֲרֶשֶׂת as a common noun, interpreting the verse thus: *and each one threw his stone—for they would take stones from the walls until they left all the stones of the walls in the wall* (*Kara*—Our edition reads: *like the wall,* which is unclear) *with only their clay, i.e. their mortar; that is to say*

בְּקִיר חֲרָשֶׂת וַיָּסֹבּוּ הַקַּלָּעִים וַיַּכּוּהָ׃
כו וַיַּרְא מֶלֶךְ מוֹאָב כִּי־חָזַק מִמֶּנּוּ
הַמִּלְחָמָה וַיִּקַּח אוֹתוֹ שְׁבַע־מֵאוֹת
אִישׁ שֹׁלֵף חֶרֶב לְהַבְקִיעַ אֶל־מֶלֶךְ
אֱדוֹם וְלֹא יָכֹלוּ׃ כז וַיִּקַּח אֶת־בְּנוֹ הַבְּכוֹר
אֲשֶׁר־יִמְלֹךְ תַּחְתָּיו וַיַּעֲלֵהוּ עֹלָה עַל־
הַחֹמָה וַיְהִי קֶצֶף־גָּדוֹל עַל־יִשְׂרָאֵל

תרגום: בְּקִרְתָּא דְלָא פַּגְרוּהָא וְאִסְתַּחֲרוּ קַלָּעַיָא וּמְחוֹהָא׃ כו וַחֲזָא מַלְכָּא דְמוֹאָב אֲרֵי תְקִיפוּ מִנֵּיהּ עָבְדֵי קְרָבָא וּדְבַר עִמֵּיהּ שְׁבַע מְאָה גַּבְרָא שָׁלְפֵי סֵיפָא לְאַפְגָּאָה לְוָת מַלְכָּא דֶאֱדוֹם וְלָא יְכִילוּ׃ כז וּנְסֵיב יָת בְּרֵיהּ בּוּכְרָא דַעֲתִיד דְּיִמְלוֹךְ תְּחוֹתוֹהִי וְאַסְקֵיהּ עֲלָתָא עַל שׁוּרָא וַהֲוָה רְגַז רַב עַל יִשְׂרָאֵל וְאִסְתַּלַּקוּ מִנֵּיהּ ותבו

ת״א ויקח את בנו. תענית ד סנהדרין לט: ויהי קלף. שם עב: כצ״ל

רד״ק

חחומה וכן עשו לקיר חרשת והכוה וי״ת עד דלא אשתארת אבנא בקרתא דלא פגרוה ואסתחרו קלעיא ומחוהא: (כו) וירא מלך מואב. מלך מואב היה בתוך העיר הזאת כמו שאמר למעלה כי נסו מפניהם וחשבו להשגב בעיר הזאת ובראותו כי חזק ממנו דבר המלחמה הזאת לקח עמו שבע מאות איש להבקיע אל מלך אדום לצאת מן העיר כי אפשר כי מלך אדום היה קרוב לעיר יותר משני המלכים: חזק ממנו המלחמה. פירוש דבר המלחמה וחזק פועל עבר כי חציו קמץ וחציו פתח: (כז) ויקח את בנו הבכור. פי׳ אדוני אבי ז״ל כי בן מלך אדום הראוי למלוך תחתיו היה ברשות מלך מואב ומפני זה בא עם שני המלכים כי חשב להוציא בעזרתם בנו מתחת יד מלך מואב וכשחשב מלך מואב להבקיע אל מלך אדום ולא יכול לקח בקצפו את בן מלך אדום והעלהו על החומה ושרפו לעיני אביו זהו ויעלהו עולה ששרפו כמו ששורפין העולה: ויהי קצף גדול על ישראל. ממלך אדום כי חשב כי בעזרתם יוציא בנו מתחת יד מלך מואב וזהו שאמר הכתוב על שרפו את עצמות מלך אדום לשיד. ורבי אחי ר׳ משה ז״ל פי׳ כי כאשר חשב להבקיע מלך מואב אל מלך אדום אז לקח בנו באותה המלחמה חטפו מהם והעלהו על החומה ושרפו לעיני אביו ויהי קצף

רש״י

והפילוה: (כז) ויקח את בנו הבכור. בפסיקתא דפרשת שקלים נדרש ששאל את עבדיו מה טיבה של אומה זו שנעשה להם נסים כאלה אמרו לו אביהם אברהם בן יחיד היה לו א״ל הקב״ה הקריבהו לפני ורצה להקריבו להקב״ה אמר להם אף אני בן בכור יש לי אלך ואקריבו לע״ג: על החמה. חסר וא״ו שהיה עובד לחמה: ויהי קצף גדול. שנזכרו עונותיהם שאף הם עובדין לעבודת כוכבים ואינן ראויין לנס:

מנחת שי

(כז) על החמה. חסר וא״ו וכן דרשו בפסיקתא וכילמדנו פרשת כי תשא החמה כתיב שהיה משתחוה לחמה ובסנהדרין סוף פ׳ אחד דיני ממונות פליגי רב ושמואל חד אמר לש״ש וח״א לשם ע״ז וכו׳ נוי דב״ר פ׳ ג״ה בהירה ליה כמאן דאמר לשם שמים: וישובו לארץ. בשוחר פירקה דר״א אמר ר׳ חנינא בר פפא הותה שעה ידעו שונאיהם של ישראל למדרגה התחתונה ופי׳ רש״י מדלא כתיב לארצה הכי קאמר לשפלות ולתחתית שבו שנגזר עליהם פורענות, ורד״ק מפיק לה לההי דרשה מדכתיב וישבו חסר וא״ו כלומר ישבו לארץ. כמו וישבו אתו לארץ. ישבו לארץ ידמו זקני בת ציון:

רלב״ג

עלמות מלך אדום לשיד: (כז) והנה הכיא זה הענין קלף גדול על ישראל ר״ל שכעסו מאד על שקרה זה המקרה הרע למלך אדום שבא לעזור להם או יהיה הרלון שהיה למלך אדום קלף גדול בעבור ישר׳

מצודת ציון

קלע: (כו) אותו. עמו: להבקיע. מלשון בקיעה ור״ל להפריד המחנה ולעבור דרך בה:

מצודת דוד

כי אם אבני החומה עם שהיתה מטרפולין של מואב: ויסובו. אחר זה הפילו גם החומה עם אבני הקלע: (כו) המלחמה. עם המלחמ׳ הבא עליו: להבקיע. ר״ל לעבור בתוך המחנ׳ אל מלך אדום להלח׳ עמו ולא יכלו לבוא עד מקומו: (כז) ויקח את בנו. כי בא למקום בנו ולקחו עמו ושרפו כליל כעולה על החומה מול אביו מלך אדום: ויהי קצף. מלך אדום קצף על ישראל כי בעבורם באה לו הרעה ההיא ולא באו להצילו. ורבותינו ז״ל אמרו שמלך מואב העלה בנו לעולה מהם אמרו לשמים והם אמרו לעבודת כוכבים ובעבור זה קצף ה׳ על ישראל וכו׳:

about great wrath on them.

Others explain that the king of Moab burnt the first-born son of the king of Edom. Some say that he was a prisoner of the king of Moab. The king of Edom had consented to accompany the two kings to war only because he hoped thereby to rescue his son. When his son was slain because of his aid to Israel, he vented his wrath on the Israelites [*R. Joseph Kimchi*].

Others say that when the king of Moab was unable to reach the king of Edom, he did manage to reach his son, the crown prince, the heir apparent to the throne [*R. Moshe Kimchi*]. To avenge himself against the king of Edom, he burnt his son atop the wall, in full view of the father. He burnt him completely, just as a burnt-offering is burnt. He blamed the Jews for the death of his son, since they did not save him, and

only in Kir-Haresheth; and the catapultists surrounded and struck it. 26. And the king of Moab saw that the men of war were stronger than he and he took with him seven hundred men who drew their swords, to break a way to the king of Edom, yet they were unable. 27. And he took his first-born who would reign after him, and brought him up for a burnt-offering on the wall. And there was great wrath upon Israel, and they withdrew from him and returned to the land.

26. **the men of war were stronger than he**—This follows *Jonathan. Mezudath David* explains: *the army was stronger than he,* thus causing the verb, which is masculine singular, to agree with the subject. *Redak* rectifies this by rendering: *the matter of the war was too strong for him.*

to the king of Edom—He was probably the closest of the three kings. The king of Moab hoped to penetrate the lines and reach the king of Edom. The other two kings were too far away [*Redak*].

27. **And he took his first-born son**—*In the Pesikta of the section of Shekalim it is expounded that he asked his servants* (in *Pesikta* and *Yalkut: his astrologers), "What is the character of this nation, that miracles such as these were performed for them?" They replied, "Their forefather, Abraham, had an only son. The Holy One, Blessed be He, said to him, 'Sacrifice him before me,' and he wanted to sacrifice him to the Holy One, Blessed be He." He said to them, "I too have a first-born son. I will go and sacrifice him to the gods"* [*Rashi* from *Pesikta d'Rav Kahana,* p. 13].

on the wall—Heb. *chomah—The vav is missing, for he worshipped the sun, chammah* in Heb. I.e. he sacrificed his son to the sun [*Rashi*].

and there was great wrath—*for their iniquities were remembered, that they too worship pagan deities and are not worthy of miracles* [*Rashi* from above source]. The *Pesikta,* however, expresses this concept in slightly different language, as follows: The Holy One, Blessed be He, said to Israel, "My children, the nations of the world do not recognize My power and they, therefore, rebel against Me, but you do recognize My power, and nevertheless, you rebel against Me."

In the Babylonian Talmud, it appears thus: Like the superior of the nations you did not do, but like the corrupt ones you did [*Sanhedrin* 39b]. I.e. the Jews were also guilty of sacrificing children to pagan deities [*Rashi ad loc.*].

In the latter source, there is also an opinion that the king of Moab sacrificed his son to God, intending to perform a deed acceptable to Him. Although his deed was definitely unacceptable to God, the contrast between his intention and that of the Israelites of that time, brought

וַיִּסְעוּ מֵעָלָיו וַיָּשֻׁבוּ לָאָרֶץ׃ ד א וְאִשָּׁה
אַחַת מִנְּשֵׁי בְנֵי־הַנְּבִיאִים צָעֲקָה אֶל־
אֱלִישָׁע לֵאמֹר עַבְדְּךָ אִישִׁי מֵת וְאַתָּה
יָדַעְתָּ כִּי עַבְדְּךָ הָיָה יָרֵא אֶת־יְהוָה
וְהַנֹּשֶׁה בָּא לָקַחַת אֶת־שְׁנֵי יְלָדַי לוֹ
לַעֲבָדִים׃ ב וַיֹּאמֶר אֵלֶיהָ אֱלִישָׁע מָה
אעשה

וְתָבוּ לְאַרְעָא׃ א וְאִתְּתָא חֲדָא מִנְּשֵׁי תַלְמִידֵי נְבִיַּיָא מְצַוְּחָא קֳדָם אֱלִישָׁע לְמֵימַר עַבְדָּךְ עוֹבַדְיָה בַּעֲלִי מִית וְאַתְּ יְדַעַתְּ אֲרֵי עַבְדָּךְ הֲוָה דָחִיל מִן קֳדָם יְיָ כַּד קַטְלַת אִיזֶבֶל יַת נְבִיַּיָא דַיְיָ דְּבַר מִנְּהוֹן מְאָה גֻבְרִין וְצַמְרִינוּן חַמְשִׁין חַמְשִׁין גֻבְרִין בִּמְעַרְתָּא וַהֲוָה יָזִיף וּמוֹכֵל לְהוֹן בְּדִיל דְּלָא לְאוֹכָלָא יַתְהוֹן מִנִּכְסוֹהִי דְּאַחְאָב מִן קֳדָם דְּאִינוּן אוּנְסָא וּכְעַן רַשְׁיָא אֲתָא לְמִדְבַּר יַת תְּרֵין בְּנַי לֵיהּ לְעַבְדִּין׃ ב וַאֲמַר לַהּ אֱלִישָׁע מָה אַעְבֵּיד לִיךְ חֲוִי לִי מָא אִית לִיךְ בְּבֵיתָא וַאֲמַרַת לֵית

רש״י

ד (א) מנשי בני הנביאים. אשת עובדיה היתה כל בני הנביאים שבמקרא תרגומו תלמידי נבייא: והנושה. הוא יהורם בן אחאב שהיה מלווהו ברבית מה שזן את הנביאים בימי אביו. במדרש רבי תנחומא לכך נאמר (לקמן ט׳ כ״ד)

רד״ק

לאמתך

גדול על ישראל ממלך אדום שלא עזרהו להצילו מידם. ובדרש ויעלהו עולה שאל מלך מואב מפני מה אומה זו ראויה לנסים האלה אמר לו אברהם אביהם העלה את בנו עולה אמר להם אף אני אעשה כן והעלה את בנו עולה. וחלקו בדבר זה מהם אמרו לשם שמים העלה אותו וזה שאמר ויהי קצף גדול על ישראל שנתקצף הקדוש ברוך הוא עליהם כי מלך מואב לא חמל על בנו כשחשב לעשות בו רצון האל וישראל היו מקציפים אותו בכל יום והוא חשב לעשות רצון האל ואינו כמו שאמרו אשר לא צויתי זה יפתח שהעלה את בתו ולא עלתה על לבי זה מישע מלך מואב שהעלה את בנו מהם אמרו כי לע״ג העלה ומפני זה חסר וי״ו החמה כי היה עובד לחמה והעלה את בנו לחמה ומה שאמר ויהי קצף גדול שנזכרו עונותיהן של ישראל באותה שעה שגם הם היו שורפים את בניהם לע״ג ולאשרה ואמר הכתוב וכמשפטי הגוים לא עשיתם ואמרו רז״ל כמתוקנים שבהם לא עשיתם כמקולקלים שבהם עשיתם: וישבו לארץ. כל אחד מהמלכים שב לארצו. ובדרש באותה שעה ירדו ישראל למדרגה התחתונה: וישבו. כתיב חסר כלומר ישבו לארץ כמו וישבו אתו לארץ: (א) ואשה אחת. אמרו שהיתה אשת עובדיה: עבדך אישי מת. י״ת עבדך עובדיה בעלי מית ואת ידעת ארי עבדך הוה דחיל מן קדם ה׳ כד קטילת איזבל רשיעתא וגו׳ כבעמוד. ובתרגום של תוספתא עוד מאתן ושתין וחמשא זמנין צוחת אתת עובדיה כהאי גונא ולא הוה משגח ולא ידעה מה למעבד עד דאזלא לבי קיבריה וצוחא דחלא דה׳ דחלא דה׳ ואשתמע לה קלא מביני מיתיא מאן הדין דחלא דה׳ דקא בעית ארבעה איקרי דחלא דה׳ אברהם ויוסף ואיוב ועובדיה אותיבה ואמרה לא בעינא אלא האי דכתיב ביה דחלא דה׳ להדא וכד אודעוה קבריה תות קא מתפלשא בקבריה וקא צוחא ואמרה מרי מרי היכא רוחצניך לי בשעתא די דמכתא ודמותא כד אמרית לך למאן את שביק לי וית תרין בני ואתיבתני דרבון דעלמא רחצן לי ואמרת לי שבוק יתמך ואנא אקיימינון וארמלתך עלי תתרחץ וכדו לא נהשכח משזיב ויתמי נמי צוחי ואמרי קבלן אבא קבלן אבא אתיב עובדיה ואמר לה זילי לגבי אלישע בפורתא דמשחא דאשתאיר גביך ולברכיך ביה דאנא כי אטמרתינהו למאה נביאיא וזנתיהו במערתא בלחמא ובמיא לא איספיין בוציניה דמשחא מינייהו לא ביממא ולא בליליא לידכר ליה נבייא מילי דידי לקודשא בריך הוא וישלים לכו מאן דאוזפיניה דהכי אמר קרא דמוזיף למרי עלמא ח׳ כל מאן דרחים על עניא ועל מסכינא ובכן אזלת ואודעתיה לאלישע כולי האי: והנשה בא לקחת. בדרש מי היה זה זה יהורם בן

רלב״ג

כי בהכתם קרה לו זה: (א) ואשה אחת מנשי בני הנביאים. ידוע כי בני הנביאים היו כלם יראים ה׳ ולזה אמר׳ כי עבדך היה ירא

מצודת דוד

ד (א) ואשה וגו׳. אמרו רבותינו שהיתה אשת עובדיה והנושה היה יהורם בן אחאב ובחיי אחאב הלוה לו ממון ברבית לכלכל

מצודת ציון

ד (א) והנשה. המלוה כמו והאיש אשר אתה נושה בו (דברים כ״ד):

man you seek? Four were called God-fearing, Abraham, Joseph, Job, and Obadiah." She replied, "I seek only the ones about whom it is written, "feared the Lord greatly (I Kings 18:3)." When they directed her to his grave, she rolled in the dust of his grave, and cried, "My husband, my husband! Where is your promise to me at the time of your death, when I asked you, 'With whom are you leaving me and my two sons?' And you replied, 'The Lord promised me and said to me, "Leave your orphans and I will sustain them, and your widow may trust in Me."' And now, we have no one to save us, and the orphans are crying, 'Father, take us! Father, take us!'" Obadiah replied and said to her, "Go to Elisha with the little oil that is left, and he will bless you with it, for when I concealed the one hundred prophets in the caves, and I

4

1. Now a woman, of the wives of the disciples of the prophets, cried out to Elisha, saying, "Your servant, my husband, has died, and you know that your servant did fear the Lord; and the creditor has come to take my two children for himself as slaves." 2. And Elisha said to her, "What

vented his wrath against them [*Redak*].

Many commentators identify Amos' castigation of Moab "for burning bones of the king of Edom to lime" as referring to this incident when the king of Moab burnt the bones of the crown prince of Edom [*Redak, Abarbanel*]. See also *Mezudath David,* Amos 2:1.

According to *Pesikta d'Rav Kahana* and *Tanhuma, Ki Thissa* 5, who explain that the king of Moab sacrificed his own son to the sun-god, and this brought about God's wrath against the Jews (see above), the Jews were in danger of being completely annihilated, were it not for the merit of the wife of Obadiah mentioned below in ch. 4. For this reason these chapters are juxtaposed [*Pesikta Shekalim* and *Tan. Ki Thissa*].

1. **of the wives of the disciples of the prophets**—*She was the wife of Obadiah* [*Rashi, Redak* from aforementioned sources].

Rashi concludes: *Every expression of b'nei han'viim, the sons of the prophets, in Scripture, is translated in Targum as the disciples of the prophets* (See above 2:2, 2:12) [*Rashi*].

and the creditor—*He was Jehoram the son of Ahab, who would lend him with interest what he used to sustain the prophets in his father's time. In R. Tanhuma's Midrash* (*Mishpatim* 9): *Therefore it is stated* (below 9:24): *And he struck Jehoram between his arms—which stretched out to take interest* [*Rashi*].

Targum Jonathan paraphrases thus: "Your servant, Obadiah, has died, and you know that your servant did fear the Lord. When Jezebel killed the prophets of the Lord, he took one hundred of them and hid them, fifty in a cave, and he would borrow and feed them in order not to feed them from Ahab's property which had been acquired through coercion. And now, the creditor . . .

Redak quotes an additional *Targum* which elaborates on this incident and adds the following: The wife of Obadiah cried thus 265 times, (according to *Midrash V'ishah achath* etc. found in *Otzar Midrashim* p. 144–5, 271 times, as the numerical value of לֵאמֹר) yet he did not pay attention to her. She did not know what to do, until she went to the cemetery and cried, "God-fearing man, God-fearing man!" A voice was heard from among the dead, "Who is this God-fearing

אֶעֱשֶׂה־לָּךְ הַגִּידִי לִי מַה־יֶּשׁ־לָכִי בַּבָּיִת
וַתֹּאמֶר אֵין לְשִׁפְחָתְךָ כֹל בַּבַּיִת כִּי
אִם־אָסוּךְ שָׁמֶן׃ ג וַיֹּאמֶר לְכִי שַׁאֲלִי־
לָךְ כֵּלִים מִן־הַחוּץ מֵאֵת כָּל־שְׁכֵנָיִכִי
כֵּלִים רֵקִים אַל־תַּמְעִיטִי׃ ד וּבָאת
וְסָגַרְתְּ הַדֶּלֶת בַּעֲדֵךְ וּבְעַד־בָּנַיִךְ
וְיָצַקְתְּ עַל כָּל־הַכֵּלִים הָאֵלֶּה וְהַמָּלֵא
תַּסִּיעִי׃ ה וַתֵּלֶךְ מֵאִתּוֹ וַתִּסְגֹּר הַדֶּלֶת
בַּעֲדָהּ וּבְעַד בָּנֶיהָ הֵם מַגִּישִׁים אֵלֶיהָ

לך קרי שכניך קרי

תרגום

לְאַמְתָךְ כָּל מִדַעַם בְּבֵיתָא אֱלָהֵין מָנָא דִמְשְׁחָא׃ ג וַאֲמַר אֱזִילִי שְׁאִילִי לִיךְ מָנִין מִן בָּרָא מִן כָּל שְׁבָבַיְכִי מָנִין רֵיקָנִין לָא תַזְעִירִין׃ ד וְתֵהָכִין וְתַגִיפִין דַשָׁא בְּאַפִּיךְ וּבְאַפֵּי בְּנַיִךְ וּתְרִיקִין עַל כָּל מָנַיָא הָאִלֵין וּמָנָא דְאִתְמְלֵי תְּסַלְקִין׃ ה וַאֲזַלַת מִלְוָתֵיהּ וַאֲגִפַת דַשָׁא בְּאַפָּהָא וּבְאַפֵּי בְנָהָא אִינוּן מְקָרְבִין לַהּ מָנַיָא והיא

תולדות אהרן

אין לשפחתך. זוהר יתרו ולך לך ולו׃

רד"ק

אחאב עובדיה קיים כספו לא נתן בנשך ויהורם שנתן ברבית אמר לו הקדוש ברוך הוא עד עכשיו הוא חי יבוא יהוא ויהרגהו שנאמר בנשך נתן ותרבית לקח לא יחיה וכתיב ויהוא מלא ידו בקשת ויך את יהורם בין זרעותיו ויצא החצי מלבו על שהקשה לבו ויפשט זרועותיו ליטול רבית׃ (ב) מה יש לכי. כתיב לכי וקרי לך וכן שכיניכי נשיכי ובניכי כתובין ביו"ד באחרונה כמו הסולח לכל עוניכי תחלואיכי חייכי והקרי אחר הרוב׃ אסוך שמן. לגין שיש בו שמן והאל"ף נוספת והוא מן סוך לא סכתי לפי שסכין ממנו נקרא כן׃ (ד) והמלא תסיעי. כתרגומו תסלקי כלומר שתסלקי אותו ממקומו ושימי כלי הריק תחתיו וכן לכל כלי וכלי ובאמר לה והמלא תסיעי הודיעה שלא תזוז היא ממקומה והאסוך בידה כי מעשה נס לא יהיה אלא במקום שהתחיל בו׃ (ה) מיצקת. כתוב ביו"ד על דרך הכתובין ביו"ד מבנין הפעיל מאין תמורת כמו מטיבים את לבם וקרי בוי"ו על דרך הרוב בבנין הפעיל מנחי הפ"א שמימרת בהם

רש"י

ויך את יהורם בין זרועיו שפשטו ליטול רבית׃ (ב) אסוך שמן. כדי סיכת שמן והאל"ף בתיבה מן היסוד כמו אל"ף של ואחותי באזניכם (איוב י"ג ז') והאל"ף של אבח' חרב (יחזקאל כ"א כ')׃ (ד) וסגרת הדלת. כבוד הנס הוא לבא בהצנע׃ והמלא תסיעי. מלפניך ותתני כלי אחר במקומו למלאותו ולצוחית השמן לא תזוזי ממקומו לפי שהקב"ה עושהו כמעין ואין דרך מעין לזוז ממקומו. מדרש אגדה שמעתי׃ (ה) הם מגישים אליה. הכלים׃

מנחת שי

ד (ב) מה יש לכי. לך קרי׃ (ג) שכניכי. שכיניך קרי ובספרים מדוייקים אין בהם יו"ד אחר כ"ף ראשונה׃ (ה) מגישים. מלא גם יו"ד קדמאה בספרים מדוייקים וכן ראוי על פי המסורת שנזכר כאן ואף במלכים א' ה'׃ מילקת. מוצקת קרי והוא בחולם כי הוא בינוני מההפעיל כמו שכתוב במכלול דף קכ"ט

רלב"ג

את ה' ולא היה עובד ע"ג ואמר' זה כי רוב ישראל עובדים ע"ג אז׃ (ב) כי אם אסוך שמן. הנה אסוך הוא כלי קטן יסימו בו שמן לסוך והנה היה זה המופת שהשריק הכלי הזה היה כל האויר הנכנס שם מתהפך לשמן בדקך ההפך המטה לנחש היה זה המופת בפעם אחת לבד ולזה לוה אותה שתשאל תחלה כלים רקים מאת כל שכניה כל מה שאפשר לה כדי שיהיה לה מהשמן שיעור רב והיא היתה מוצקת על הכלי ובהיותו מלא בניה מסיעים הכלי המלא ושמים הכלי הריק באופן שכיליקה אחת נמלאו כל הכלים זה אחר זה׃

מצודת ציון

(ב) אסוך. שם כלי השמן ויקרא כן על שם שסכין ומושהין ממנו׃ (ד) בעדך. כנגדך׃ תסיעי. תעקור ממקומו׃

מצודת דוד

(ב) מה יש לך. את הנביאים׃ לעבדים. בעבור חוב הממון׃ לשיהא הברכה שורה בו׃ כל בבית. כלל לא׃ (ג) מן החוץ. מן האנשים שחוץ לביתך ולתוספות ביאור אמר מאת כל שכניך׃ אל תמעיטי. אל תשאלי מעט כי אם הרבה כלים׃ (ד) והמלא תסיעי. הכלי אשר תמלא תסיע ממקומה להעמיד האחר תחתיה ולא תזוז האסוך ממקומה על כי האסוך נעשה כמעין ואין מדרך המעין לזוז׃ (ה) הם מגישים. את הכלים הריקים כי היא לא זזה ממקומה עם

not move from its place, for the Holy One, Blessed be He, is making it as a spring, and it is not customary for a spring to move from its place. I heard this Midrash Aggadah [*Rashi*].

Apparently, this was a rare Midrash which *Rashi* had heard but had never seen in writing. To us it is unknown.

Redak explains that a miracle continues only in the place where it started.

5. **they were bringing to her**—*the vessels* [*Rashi*].

shall I do for you? Tell me what you have in the house." And she said, "Your maidservant has nothing at all in the house except a jug of oil." 3. And he said, "Borrow vessels for yourself from outside, from all your neighbors; do not borrow only a few empty vessels. 4. And you shall come and close the door about yourself and about your sons, and you shall pour upon all these vessels; and the full one you shall carry away." 5. And she went away from him and closed the door about herself and about her sons; they were bringing [vessels] to her and she was pouring.

sustained them with bread and water, the oil lamps were never extinguished, neither by day nor by night. Let the prophet mention my deeds to the Holy One, Blessed be He, and the One to whom I lent will repay you, as Scripture says: (Prov. 19:17). He lends to the Lord, who is liberal to the poor." She then went and related all this to Elisha [*Redak* from *Targum*]. For variant versions of this narrative, see *Otzar Midrashim* pp. 144–5, *Midrash R. David haNagid* vol. 1, p. 39.

2. **"What shall I do for you?**—Now that she came as a messenger from Obadiah, he responded to her appeal [*K'li Y'kar*].

a jug of oil—Heb. אָסוּךְ. The root is סוּךְ, *to anoint.* The jug was called by this name because it was used for anointing oil [*Redak*].

Rashi relates it to the same root, yet interprets it to mean—*enough oil for anointment, yet the "aleph" is part of the root like the "aleph" of* (Job 13:17) *and my speech in your ears,* Heb. וְאַחְוָתִי, from חוה, *and the "aleph" of* (Ezek. 21:20) *the crying of* those struck down by *the sword,* Heb. אִבְחַת, from נבח, *to bark* [*Rashi*].

Redak considers the *aleph* an additional letter prefixed to the root. *Rashi* considers it part of the root even though it is usually absent. *Ralbag* explains that the miracle was brought about by God's converting all the air that entered the vessel into oil. Hence, as the oil left the vessel, more oil formed in its place.

The *Zohar* teaches us that God's blessing rests only on something already existing, not on an empty table, so to speak. Therefore, Elisha asked Obadiah's wife what she had in the house for the blessing to rest upon. According to the *Zohar,* she had just enough oil to anoint one little finger. This was sufficient foundation for the blessing [*Zohar Lech* p. 88a].

4. **And you shall close the door**—*It affords respect to the miracle if it comes about in secret.—[Rashi].*

and the full one you shall carry away—*from before you, and you shall place another vessel in its place to fill it, but the jug of oil you shall*

וְהִיא מוֹצָקֶת׃ ו וַיְהִי ׀ כִּמְלֹאת הַכֵּלִים וַתֹּאמֶר אֶל־בְּנָהּ הַגִּישָׁה אֵלַי עוֹד כֶּלִי וַיֹּאמֶר אֵלֶיהָ אֵין עוֹד כֶּלִי וַיַּעֲמֹד הַשָּׁמֶן׃ ז וַתָּבֹא וַתַּגֵּד לְאִישׁ הָאֱלֹהִים וַיֹּאמֶר לְכִי מִכְרִי אֶת־הַשֶּׁמֶן וְשַׁלְּמִי אֶת־נִשְׁיֵכִי וְאַתְּ בָּנַיִכִי תִּחְיִי בַּנּוֹתָר׃ ח וַיְהִי הַיּוֹם וַיַּעֲבֹר אֱלִישָׁע אֶל־שׁוּנֵם וְשָׁם אִשָּׁה גְדוֹלָה וַתַּחֲזֶק־בּוֹ לֶאֱכָל־

וְהִיא מְרִיקָא מִשְׁחָא׃ ו וַהֲוָה כְּמִשְׁלַם מָנַיָא וַאֲמָרַת לִבְרַהּ קָרִיב לִי עוֹד מָנָא וַאֲמַר לַהּ לֵית עוֹד מָנָא וּפְסַק מִשְׁחָא׃ ז וַאֲתַת וְחַוִּיאַת לִנְבִיָא דַיְיָ וַאֲמַר אֱזִילִי זַבִּינִי יָת מִשְׁחָא וְשַׁלְּמִי לְמָרֵי חוֹבָתִיךְ וְאַתְּ וּבְנַיִךְ הִתְפַּרְנְסִין מִדְּאִשְׁתְּאַר׃ ח וַהֲוָה יוֹמָא וַעֲבַר אֱלִישָׁע לְשׁוּנֵם וְתַמָּן אִתְּתָא דַחֲלַת חֶטְאִין וְאַתְקִיפַת בֵּיהּ לְמֵיכַל לחמא

ה"א אל שונם. זוהר בכלת:

מוצקת קרי נשיך קרי ובניך קרי

רש"י

(ו) ויעמוד השמן. מלהא עוד. ומדרש אגדה בב"ר הוקיר בער השמן: (ז) ותבא ותגד וגו'. באת ליטול עלה אם למכור אם להמתין עד שיוקר עוד אמר לה לכי מכרי כי יש די לכל נשייך ולהיות את ובניך בנותר עד שיחיו המתים: (ח) ושם אשה גדולה. השובה. וראיתי בפ' דר' אליעזר

רד"ק

היו"ד בוי"ו: (ו) ויהי כמלאת הכלים. באגדת ובתרגום של תוספתא והות כמשלם מניא ואמרת לבנה קריב לי עוד מאני תבירי דחספא דמאן דיגזר על מאנין ריקנין דימלון יגזר על מאני תבירי ויתקנון והוא לקיש מאני שבירי ומשוי חד על חד ומתחברי במימרא דה' קוב"ה ועמודא דמשחא טייף על כלהון עד דשלימו כל פסקי מאנייא אמר בוא לית עיד מנא ושמע עמודא דמישחא ופסק: (ז) ושלמי את נשיכי. ושלמי למרי חובותיך. ובתוספתא וכד אתרחיש לה ההוא ניסא אמרת ליה לנביא דה' אית עלי עשור מהאי מישחא או לא אמר לה בעליך זן נביאיא דה' במילתא דליכא עליה עשורא ואף את לית על משחך עשור דמן ניסא הוא הדרה ואמרה ליה מה נעביד מבני דאחאב אי שמעי אלי ואנסי לי מיתב ואמרה לה דסגר פומא דכלבי דמצרים ועתיד למיסגר פום אריותא דדניאל יטמטם עיניהי דבני אחאב ויסגר אדניהון דלא לבאשו לך יהבית אודיתא ותושבחתא ואזלת: (ח) אשה גדולה. חשובה בעלת נכסים

רלב"ג

(ז) ותבא ותגד לאיש האלהים. הנה לא רלתה לעשות מזה השמן דבר אם לא בעלת הנביא כי לא היתה יודעת מה רלון הנביא בזה: ושלמי את נשייך. ר"ל פרעי את הוביך כטעם לוה רשע ולא ישלם: (ח) ושם אשה גדולה. ר"ל אשה השובה ונכבדת: ותחזק בו לאכל לחם. אחשב שהשתדלה בכל עוז שיאכל לחם אז בבית' ושיבא שם בכל עת שיהיה בעיר שונם ואחשוב שלא נתפרס' לה עדיין מעלת אלישע אך היה דרכם להביא לביתה מה שתוכל מהאורחים הבאים בעיר וזה כי זה היה בתחלת ענין אלישע לפי מה שיראה מהזמן בהיה זה קודם מה שאמר אלישע מחר סאה סלת בשקל וסאתים שעורים בשקל בשער שומרון וזה שכבר בנתה העליה אחר זה ולקץ שנה מעת בא שם אלישע ילדה בן וגדל הבן ההוא עד שכבר יצא אל הקוצרים ואמר לאביו ראשי ראשי ואחר זה אמר לה שתצא לגור

מנחת שי

וכן לריך להגיה בשרשים: (ז) נשיכי. נשיך קרי: *בניכי. ובניך קרי:

מצודת דוד

האסוך: (ו) הכלים. אשר שאלה: הגישה וגו'. כי לא ידעה אשר כבר נתמלאו כולם: ויעמוד השמן. לא היה נשפך עוד: (ז) בנותר. בדמי השמן על דמי החוב: (ח) ויהי היום. ר"ל בא היום אשר עבר אלישע אל שונם: אשה גדולה. אשה חשובה:

מצודת ציון

(ז) נשיך. הלואתך: (ח) מדי. מתי ר"ל בכל זמן:

a miracle." I.e. not from olives.

She then proceeded to ask him, "What shall I do about Ahab's children? They will hear about me and rob me."

He replied, "The One who shut the mouths of the dogs in Egypt and is destined to shut the mouths of the lions so that they do not harm Daniel, will stop up the eyes of the sons of Ahab and close their ears, so that they do not harm you. Thereupon, she offered up thanksgiving and praise, and left.

8. **a prominent woman**—lit. a great woman, i.e. an *important* woman. *And I saw in Pirkei d'R. Eliezer* (ch. 33): *She was the sister of Abishag the Shunemitess* who warmed King David in his old age—*Rashi* and *Redak*.

Redak and *Yalkut Shimoni* quote *Pirkei d'R. Eliezer* as concluding: and the mother of Iddo the prophet. Our editions of *Pirkei d'R. Eliezer* read: the wife of Iddo the prophet. R. David Luria in his commentary on that work, questions both ver-

6. And it was when the vessels were full, that she said to her son, "Bring me another vessel," and he said to her, "There is no other vessel." And the oil stopped. 7. And she came and told the man of God; and he said, "Go sell the oil and pay your debt; and you and your sons will live with the remainder."
8. And it was that day that Elisha went as far as Shumen, and there was a prominent woman who prevailed upon him to eat a meal;

6. **when the vessels were full**—*Redak* quotes *Aggadah* from an additional *Targum* which states: When the vessels were full, she said to her son "Bring me more vessels, broken earthenware jugs, for He Who decreed that empty vessels fill up, will decree that broken vessels become whole." He gathered broken vessels and placed one upon the other, and they became whole through the command of the Holy One, Blessed be He. Now the stream of oil was dripping on all of them, until all the potsherds were full. Her son said, "There is no more vessel"; the stream of oil heard and stopped.

and the oil stopped—*coming anymore.* This is the *peshat. Mid-Aggadah in Gen. Rabbah* 35 explains it literally: and the oil stood up, meaning that *the price of oil went up* [*Rashi*]

7. **And she came and told . . .**—*She came to receive advice whether to sell or to wait until it would become more expensive. He said to her, "Go sell, for there is enough for all your debt, and for you and your sons to live with the remainder until the dead come to life* [*Rashi* from *Gen. Rabbah* 35].

I.e. he blessed them with eternal life until the resurrection of the dead. The *Midrash* comments that the latter blessing was greater than the former, and this was granted only because she returned to ask advice of the *tzaddik.* Had she sold the oil without asking, she would not have received this blessing [*Maharzav*].

Midrash R. David Hanagid draws two morals from this story: one, that if one receives a favor from another, he should keep him informed and obey him concerning this matter. The second moral is that if one comes upon a sum of money, he should first pay his debts and then use the remainder for his living expenses.

and pay your debt—*Jonathan* renders: and pay your creditors.

The additional *Targum* relates the entire dialogue between the woman and Elisha. When the miracle took place, she asked the prophet, "Must I tithe this oil or not?" He replied, "Your husband sustained the prophets of the Lord with something that does not require tithes. You too, on your oil there is no obligation to tithe, because it comes from

לחם ויהי מדי עברו יסר שמה לאכל־
לחם: ט ותאמר אל־אישה הנה־נא
ידעתי כי איש אלהים קדוש הוא
עבר עלינו תמיד: י נעשה־נא עלית־
קיר קטנה ונשים לו שם מטה ושלחן
וכסא ומנורה והיה בבאו אלינו יסור
שמה: יא ויהי היום ויבא שמה ויסר
אל־העליה וישכב־שמה: יב ויאמר
אל־גיחזי נערו קרא לשונמית הזאת
ויקרא־לה ותעמד לפניו: יג ויאמר
לו אמר־נא אליה הנה חרדת ׀ אלינו

לחמא והוה בזמן מעדוהי מתפני לתמן למיכל לחמא: ט ואמרת לבעלה הא כען ידענא ארי נביא דיי קדישא הוא מתפני לותנא תדירא: י נעביד כען עלית כתלא זעירא ונתקן ליה תמן אתר ערסא ופתורא וכורסיא ומנרתא ויהי במיתוהי לותנא יתפני לתמן: יא והוה יומא ועל לתמן וזר לעיליתא ושכיב תמן: יב ואמר לגיחזי עולימיה קרי לשונמיתא הדא וקרא לה וקמת קדמוהי: יג ואמר ליה אמר כען לה הא

ת"א קדוש הוא. עקידה שער מה זוהר תרומה (סנהדרין כט יבמות ג): עלית קיר. ברכות יח (ברכות ח) סנהדרין כט: הנה חרדת. עקידה שער מה:

רש"י

אחותה של אבישג השונמית היתה: ויהי מדי עברו. בלותה העיר יסור אל ביתה לאכל לחם: יסור. לשון הווה היה סר שם: (ט) הנה נא ידעתי. שלא ראתה זבוב על שלחנו וקרי על סדינו: (יא) ויהי היום. ויהי יום א': (יג) חרדת אלינו. בשבילנו: את כל החרדה הזאת.

רד"ק

ובעלת השם. ובדרש כי אחותה של אבישג השונמית היתה אמו של עדוא הנביא וי"ת דחלת חטאין: (ט) הנה נא ידעתי. כי היה ידוע אלישע בישראל כי איש אלהים הוא וקדוש ואע"פ שאמרה נא אינו אומר כי עתה ידעה ולא קודם זה אלא מלת נא ר"ל עתה צריך לנו לעשות לו דבר כיון שהוא רגיל אצלינו ידעתי כי איש אלהים קדוש הוא וצריך שנעשה לו כבוד ונייחד לו מקום בביתינו וכמוהו הנה נא העיר הזאת קרובה אינו אומר כי עתה תהיה קרובה ולא קודם זה אלא עתה צריך אני להמלט בה כיון שהיא קרובה ורז"ל דקדקו מלת נא ר"ל שעתה ידעת כי קדוש היא ולא קודם זה ואמרו מנא ידעה ואמרה שלא ראתה לו קרי במטתו: (י) עלית קיר. עלית בנויה בקירות אבנים או לבנים לא במסיפוס: (יג) חרדת אלינו. לשון תנועה והשתדלות על הדבר וכן ויחרדו זקני העיר לקראתו יחרדו

רלב"ג

אחר תגור כי קרא ה' לרעב וגם בא אל הארץ שבע שנים ואחר שבע שנים סר הרעב וכשתחקור בזה תמצא שזה היה אלל תחלת למיתת נבואת אלישע ולזה אינו מן הפלא אם לא היה מפורסם לה שיהיה נביא ויתכן שחקרה מעניניו כשראתה עברו אצלה תמיד מפני ראותה כל מנהגיו בתכלית מהשלמות ואז נתבאר לה שהוא איש אלהים קדוש: (י) נעשה נא עלית קיר קטנה. אחשוב שמסקיר בנוים היתה נמשכת העלייה כמו הענין בבנין הכפה (מאלט"ו בלע"ז): ונשים לו שם מטה ושלחן ומנור'. ר"ל כי למעלתו אין ראוי שישתתפו בני הבית עמו ולא להשתמש בכלים שהוא ישתמש בהם ולזה רצתה שיהיה לו שם כלי תשמישו מיוחדים לה: (יג) ויאמר לו אמר נא אליה. הנה לא רצה אלישע לדבר עם האשה אם לא כשהביאו לזה הכרח ואלו הדברים הספיק שיאמר לה גחזי ולזה לא קרא לה גחזי

מצודת ציון

(ט) אישה. בעלה: (י) קיר. כותל: ונשים. מלשון שימה:

מצודת דוד

ויהי מדי עברו. מיום ההוא והלאה מדי עברו וכו': (ט) הנה נא ידעתי. מכירה אני בו שהוא איש קדוש ואין מהראוי לשבת אתנו יחד ואמרו רז"ל האשה מכרת באורחים יותר מן האיש: עובר. אף הוא עובר עלינו תמיד בכל עת בואו פה ואיך ישב עמנו יחד פעמים רבות: (י) עלית קיר. עליה קטנה בנויה בקיר אבנים בנין מעולה: יסור שמה. להתבודד בחדרו לבד: (יא) ויהי היום. בא היום אשר בא שמה אחרי עשותה את העליה: (יג) אמר וגו'. לא רצה לדבר עם האשה פה אל פה: הנה חרדת וגו'. ר"ל בעבור

Garden of Eden, rather than malodorous as used linen usually is [*Zohar, Beshallach* p. 44a].

Redak maintains that everyone knew that Elisha was a holy man. The Shunemitess meant that since this holy man of God visits us often, it is now time to honor him by building a small walled upper chamber to be used exclusively by him.

10. **a small walled upper chamber**—a structure with permanent, sturdy walls, not temporary partitions [*Redak, Mezudath David*].

and it was, whenever he would pass, he would stop there to eat a meal. 9. And she said to her husband, "Behold now I know that he is a holy man of God, who passes by us regularly. 10. Now let us make a small walled upper chamber, and place there for him a bed, a table, a chair, and a lamp; and it will be that when he comes to us, he will turn into there. 11. And it was one day that he went there, that he turned into the upper chamber and lay down there. 12. And he said to Gehazi his servant, "Call this Shunemitess;" and he called her, and she stood before him. 13. And he said to him, "Please say to her, 'Behold you have busied yourself on our account

sions. Iddo the prophet was the man of God mentioned in I Kings 13. He prophesied against Jeroboam son of Nebat. He was later killed by a lion for returning to Bethel. If the Shunemitess was Iddo's wife, she obviously remarried after his death. Gehazi remarked that her husband was old. *She* would necessarily be very old according to this version. If she were the mother of Iddo, she would be still older. He theorizes that for Iddo, we substitute Oded, who prophesied during the reigns of Asa (II Chron. 15:8) and Ahaz (ibid. 28:9). He remarks further that according to *Zohar,* the Shunemitess was the mother of Habakkuk. *Pirkei d'R. Eliezer* obviously does not share that view, since it mentions only Iddo as her son, not Habakkuk. According to the version, the wife of Iddo, or Oded, there is no conflict. (In any case, if she was the mother of Oded, who prophesied during Asa's reign and still lived until Ahaz's reign, he was born before this incident. Yet, Gehazi remarks that she has no son.)

Redak goes on to quote *Jonathan's* translation: a God-fearing woman. I.e. great in good deeds, surpassing other women in hospitality—[*Zohar, Beshallach* p. 44a].

to eat a meal—lit. to eat bread.

and it was, whenever he would pass—*in that city, he would stop at her house to eat a meal—Rashi.*

he would stop—Heb. יסר, lit. he will stop. This is *the present tense,* i.e. *he would stop there* [*Rashi*]. We find *Rashi* referring to the imperfect as the present because it is continuous.

9. **"Behold now I know**—*for she never saw a fly on his table or semen on his sheet* [*Rashi* from *Berachoth* 10b].

His table was as holy as the altar upon which no fly ever appeared [*Maharshaad* loc.].

Alternatively, when she made his bed in the morning, she found the bedclothes sweet-smelling like the

אֶת־כָּל־הַחֲרָדָה הַזֹּאת מֶה לַעֲשׂוֹת
לָךְ הֲיֵשׁ לְדַבֶּר־לָךְ אֶל־הַמֶּלֶךְ אוֹ אֶל־
שַׂר הַצָּבָא וַתֹּאמֶר בְּתוֹךְ עַמִּי אָנֹכִי
יֹשָׁבֶת׃ יד וַיֹּאמֶר וּמֶה לַעֲשׂוֹת לָהּ
וַיֹּאמֶר גֵּיחֲזִי אֲבָל בֵּן אֵין־לָהּ וְאִישָׁהּ
זָקֵן׃ טו וַיֹּאמֶר קְרָא־לָהּ וַיִּקְרָא־לָהּ
וַתַּעֲמֹד בַּפָּתַח׃ טז וַיֹּאמֶר לַמּוֹעֵד הַזֶּה
כָּעֵת חַיָּה אַתִּי חֹבֶקֶת בֵּן וַתֹּאמֶר אַל־

עסקתא לנא ית כל עסקא הדא מה למעבד ליך הפתגם אית ליך למללא עם מלכא או עם רב חילא ואמרת בגו עסקי עמי אנא מסוברא: יד ואמר ומה למעבד לה ואמר גיחזי בקושטא בר לית לה ובעלה סיב: טו ואמר קרי לה וקרא לה וקמת בתרעא: טז ואמר לזמנא הדין בעדן דאתון קימין תהא מחבקא ברא ואמרת בבעו

את קרי

רש"י

לשום אל לבך את העסק הזה כמו וחרד על דברי (ישעיה ס"ו ב') זהיר על הדבר שיהא עשוי וכותנו אל לבו: מה לעשות לך. מה את צריכה שנעשה לך שבשבילנו עסקת כל זה: בתוך עמי. בתוך קרובי אין אדם מזיקני איני צריכה למלך ולא לשר הצבא: (יד) ויאמר. אלישע לגחזי: ומה לעשות לה. נגד הטובה הזאת: (טז) למועד הזה כעת חיה. כמו שאת קיימת היום ולשלום כך תהי קיימת למועד הזה וחובקת בן: אל אדוני. אל תאמר חובקת בן מה לי חבוקו אם סופי לקוברו וזה שאמרה לו כשמת הנא

רד"ק

כצפור ממצרים ובענין זה ת"י הא עסקת לנא ית כל עסקא הדא: היש לדבר לך. ר"ל שידבר בעבורה אם תצטרך והיא השיבה בתוך עמי אנכי יושבת כלומר בתוך עמי ומשפחתי והם ידברו בעבורי אם אצטרך ואמר אלישע לגחזי כי היא הלכה מלפניו אחר שענתה לו לפיכך שאל אלישע לגיחזי: (יד) ומה לעשות. כלומר במה נוכל לגמלה טובה לטובה שעשתה עמנו אמר גיחזי אבל בן אין לה כלומר לזה ששאלת אינה צריכה ולא לשום דבר אבל לזה הדבר צריכה כי בן אין לה ואישה זקן כלומר אם תאמר אין לה עתה יהיה לה בן לזמן שיבא אישה זקן ולא ידע יום מותו כי קרוב לפרקו הוא ואם תוכל שיהיה לה בן ממנו זו תהיה לה טובה גדולה וי"ת בתוך עמי אנכי יושבת בגו עסקי עמי אנא מסוברא: (טו) קרא לה. כי כבר הלכה מלפניו: (טז) ויאמר למועד הזה. אפשר שנאמר לו באותה העת בנבואה או אמר מלבו ובטח באל יתברך שיקיים דברו כמו שכתוב באדם הצדיק ותגזר אומר ויקם לך וכן כתיב בשמואל הנביא ולא הפיל מכל דבריו ארצה וכן אמר בדרש רצון יראיו יעשה עשה הקב"ה רצונו של נביא והרתה וילדה: כעת חיה. למועד הזה כעת שתהיה ראויה שתהיה יולדת לשבעה הדשים או לתשעה והיולדת תקרא חיה בדברי רז"ל וחחיה תנעול את הסנדל: חובקת בן. שתטלי אותו בחיקך: אל אדוני. אמרה

רלב"ג

ותעמד בפתח כי לא היה רצון אלישע לדבר עמה אבל עמדה בחוץ לפני גחזי הי' בחוץ קרו' לאלישע או היה סמוך לפתח העלייה:

מנחת שי

(טז) אתי חבקת בן. את קרי:

מצודת דוד

הנה חרדת אלינו את כל החרדה הזאת. ר"ל הנה פחד' שלא תוכלו לנו לעשות הראוי מהכבוד כל הפחד הזה עד שהביאך זה לעשות כל מה שעשית לי מהכבוד: מה לעשות לך. להשיב גמול על הטובה הזאת היש לדבר בעבורך אל המלך או אל שר הצבא ולדבר אליהם בעבורך ותאמר בתוך עמי ומשפחתי אנכי יושבת ולזה אין לי עסק עם אדם ילטרך לי בעבורו לדבר אל המלך או אל שר הצבא: (יד) ויאמר. אלישע לגחזי: ומה לעשות לה. מהטובות לתת גמול ע"ז. ויאמר גחזי באמת בן אין לה ואישה זקן ולזה אינו מוכן מאד אל ההולד' עם שמלדה אפשר ג"כ שימנע פרי בטן להיותה עקרה: (טו) ויקרא לה ותעמד בפתח. הנה זה המאמר מפני שהוא נבואה רצה אלישע בעצמו לאמרו לה: (טז) כעת חיה. ר"ל כעת הזה העומד וקרא העת הסיא חיה להיות זה החלק מהזמן לבדו נמצא כי את מטרחת עלמך הטרחה הזאת בעבורנו מהו הגמול לעשות לך האם יש לך דבר מה לדבר בעבורך אל המלך וגו': בתוך עמי. ר"ל אני יושבת בתוך בני משפחתי ואין מי מהם עושה רעה עמדי לשאצטרך לקבול ולהתרעם על מי: (יד) ומה לעשות לה. אחר שהלכה מפניו שאל לגיחזי ומהו א"כ הגמול שנעשה לה: אבל. באמת יש מקום לעשות לה גמול כי אין לה בן ואישה זקן ובדרך הטבע לא תלד עוד ואם תלד ע"י בן יחשב לגמול רב: (טו) בפתח. בראותה שאיננו מדבר פה אל פה הוסיפה להתרחק ועמדה בפתח: (טז) למועד הזה כעת חיה: ר"ל לזמן הבא כעת הראויה להיות חיה ר"ל יולדת והיא ככלות תשעה חדשים שהם ימי הריון: את חובקת בן. ר"ל תשעשע עלמך עם בנך לחבקו ואף כי בתחלה לא

מצודת ציון

(יג) חרדת. ענין תנועה חזקה ואם הוא מבלי פחד כמו ויחרדו זקני העיר לקראתו (שמואל א' ט"ז): (טז) חיה. כן נקראת היולדת

15. **and she stood at the doorway**—so as not to look at Elisha's face. See above v. 13.

16. **"At this time next year when you will be alive like now**—lit. like the time, alive, i.e. *just as you are alive today, and well, so will you be alive* next year *at this time and embracing a son* [*Rashi*].

"No—*Jonathan* renders: *Please.*

with all this trouble. What is there to do for you? Can we speak on your behalf to the king or to the general of the army?' " And she said, "I dwell in the midst of my people." 14. And he said, "Now what can we do for her?" And Gehazi said, "Indeed, she has no son, and her husband is old." 15. And he said, "Summon her," and he summoned her, and she stood at the doorway. 16. And he said, "At this time next year, when you will be alive like now, you will be embracing a son."

In the Talmud we find two other interpretations of this verse. According to one, קִיר is related to תִּקְרָה, *a ceiling*. They built a ceiling on an upper chamber which had heretofore been open at the top.

The other interpretation is that they partitioned an open porch, explaining עֲלִיַּת as the superior of the houses, i.e. a walled chamber in a house of superior quality [*Berachoth* 10b].

13. **You have busied yourself on our account**—lit. *to us* [*Rashi*].

with all this trouble—lit. all this shudder, i.e. *to put your heart into this task, like*" (Is. 66:2) *"and shudders concerning My word,"* i.e. *is diligent concerning the task that it be accomplished and puts his heart into it* [*Rashi*].

According to *Pirkei d'R. Eliezer* mentioned above, any woman who looked at Elisha's countenance, would die immediately. She actually shuddered when Elisha visited. She, therefore, wished to erect a room for him, where he could seclude himself. Consequently, no one would be in danger of dying by looking at him.

What is there to do for you?—*What do you need that we do for you, for you busied yourself with all this for us* [*Rashi*].

According to *R. Joseph Kara,* we read: *What do you need that we do for you, for which you busied yourself with all this.*

"I dwell in the midst of my people."—*amidst my relatives. No one harms me. I have need neither for the King nor for the general of the army* [*Rashi*].

Alternatively, if I require any request presented before the King, my relatives will do it on my behalf [*Redak*].

Alternatively, I occupy a prominent place among my people. I, therefore, need no representation. I can speak for myself [*Heidenheim* Gen. 23:10].

14. **And he said**—*Elisha to Gehazi* [*Rashi*].

"Now what can we do for her?"—*to reciprocate for this favor* [*Rashi*].

אֲדֹנִי אִישׁ הָאֱלֹהִים אַל־תְּכַזֵּב
בְּשִׁפְחָתֶךָ: יז וַתַּהַר הָאִשָּׁה וַתֵּלֶד בֵּן
לַמּוֹעֵד הַזֶּה כָּעֵת חַיָּה אֲשֶׁר־דִּבֶּר אֵלֶיהָ
אֱלִישָׁע: יח וַיִּגְדַּל הַיָּלֶד וַיְהִי הַיּוֹם
וַיֵּצֵא אֶל־אָבִיו אֶל־הַקֹּצְרִים: יט וַיֹּאמֶר
אֶל־אָבִיו רֹאשִׁי ׀ רֹאשִׁי וַיֹּאמֶר אֶל־
הַנַּעַר שָׂאֵהוּ אֶל־אִמּוֹ: כ וַיִּשָּׂאֵהוּ וַיְבִיאֵהוּ
אֶל־אִמּוֹ וַיֵּשֶׁב עַל־בִּרְכֶּיהָ עַד־הַצָּהֳרַיִם
וַיָּמֹת: כא וַתַּעַל וַתַּשְׁכִּבֵהוּ עַל־מִטַּת
אִישׁ הָאֱלֹהִים וַתִּסְגֹּר בַּעֲדוֹ וַתֵּצֵא:
כב וַתִּקְרָא אֶל־אִישָׁהּ וַתֹּאמֶר שִׁלְחָה

בְּבָעוּ רִבּוֹנִי נְבִיָא דַיָי לָא יִתְכַּדֵּיב פִּתְגָמָךְ בְּאַמְתָךְ: יז וְעַדִּיאַת אִתְּתָא וִילֵידַת בַּר לִזְמְנָא הָדֵין כְּעִדָּן דְהִיא קַיָמָא דִי מַלֵיל עִמַהּ אֱלִישָׁע: יח וּרְבָא רַבְיָא וַהֲוָה יוֹמָא וּנְפַק לְוָת אֲבוּהִי לְוָת חַצְדַיָא: יט וַאֲמַר לַאֲבוּהִי רֵישִׁי רֵישִׁי וַאֲמַר לְעוּלֵימָא סְבָהִי אוֹבִילֵיהּ לְאִמֵיהּ: כ וּנְסָבֵיהּ וְאוֹבִלֵיהּ לְאִמֵיהּ וִיתֵיב עַל בִּרְכָּהָא עַד עִדָּן טֵיהֲרָא וּמִית: כא וּסְלִיקַת וְאַשְׁכְּבְתֵיהּ עַל עַרְסָא דִנְבִיָא דַיָי וְאַנְפָּקַת בְּאַפּוֹהִי וּנְפָקַת: כב וּקְרָת לְבַעְלָהּ וַאֲמַרַת שַׁדַר כְּעַן לִי חַד מִן

ת"א איש האלהים. עקידה שער ג: אל הקוצרים. (יבמות יד):

רד"ק

שני פעמים אל לחזק הדבר. לבקש ממנו שלא יכזב בה שיהיה הדבר על כל פנים אחר שיחל אותה עליו ושיהיה בן של קיימא כי מה יועיל לה אם לא יהיה בן של קיימא ופי' אל תכזב בשפחתך כמו אשר לא יכזבו מימיו וי"ת אל אדוני בבעו רבוני ותרגם אל תכזב לא יתכדיב פתגמך באמתך: (יז) כעת חיה. כעדן דהיא קימא: (יט) ראשי ראשי. היה לו כאב הראש ודרך

רש"י

אמרתי לא תשלה אותי: אל תכזב. אל יתראני דבר שיפסוק יש בידך לבקש רחמים וינתן לי בן אך בבקשה ממך אל תתן לי אלא בן של קיימא: אל תכזב. כמו לא יכזבו מימיו (ישעיה נ"ח): (יז) כעת חיה. כעת הזאת שהיתה בחיים ובשלום ולכך נקוד כעת: (יט) ראשי ראשי. הנני חולה בראשי: ויאמר. אביו אל אחד מן הנערים שאהו אל אמו:

רלב"ג

בזמן החולף כבר נעדר והעתיד עדיין לא נכנס במציאות וכבר באמרנו זה בפרשת וירא אליו באלוני ממרא: אל אדני איש האלהים אל תכזב בשפחתך. ר"ל שהיא אומרת זה דרך בקשה לא יהיה זה אדני לא תכזב בשפחתך בעבור שפחתך להביא לי טובה שאינה טובה אם לא יתקיים הילד כי אלישע לא הבטיחה שיחיה כמו שהיה נראה מבקשת גחזי שאמר אבל בן אין לה וזהו ג"כ מה שזכרה אחר זה שאמרה לו לא תשלה אותי ר"ל בל תתן לי טובה שלא תהיה אלא לתת לי שלוה להניח לי מעולם תשוקתי אל שיהיה לי בן כי אינני הפלה בזה מזה הלד אם לא יתקיים הילד: (יט) ראשי ראשי. התחיל הילד לאביו שכבר היה כואב לו ראשו ואז אמר למשרתו שהיה שם שישא הנער אל אמו: (כא) ותשכיבהו על מטת איש האלהים. חשבה שבזכות הנביא יהיה הולד יותר נשמר שם:

מצודת ציון

ובדרז"ל והחיה תגעול את הסנדל (יומא עג): תכזב. ענינו דבר הנפסק כמו אשר לא יכזבו מימיו (ישעיה נ"ח):

מצודת דוד

דבר עמה פה אל פה אבל אחר שראה לגיעותה שעמדה בפתח חזר לדבר עמה: אל אדוני. אל תדבר כדברים האלה: אל תכזב. אל תאמר דבר הנפסק בעבור לשמח לב שפחתך ועל כי אמר חובקת בן המורה לשעשוע מה ולא הבטיחה שיתקיים לזה אמרה אל תשמחני בדבר שאינו מתקיים: (יז) אשר דבר. כפי אשר דבר אלישע: (יח) ויהי היום. בא היום אשר יצא אל אביו כשהיה עומד על הקוצרים: (יט) ראשי ראשי. יש לי כאב בראש וכפל המלה

this time that she was alive and well. Therefore, the word is voweled כָּעֵת; i.e. like *the* time [*Rashi*].

which Elisha had spoken to her—Here he is not referred to as the man of God. This was his own blessing, not a divine prophecy. He depended on God's fulfilling the decree of righteous man [*Daath Soferim*].

19. **"My head! My head!"**—*I am sick in my head!* [*Rashi*].

It is usual for those who experience pain to repeat their cries [*Redak, Mezudath David*].

And he said—*His father* said *to one of the servants, "Carry him to his mother"* [*Rashi*].

21. **and laid him on the bed of the**

And she said, "No, my lord, O man of God, do not fail your maidservant." 17. And the woman conceived and bore a son, at this time a year later, which Elisha had spoken to her. 18. And the child grew up; and it was one day that he went out to his father, to the reapers. 19. And he said to his father, "My head! My head!" And he said to the servant, "Carry him to his mother." 20. And he carried him and brought him to his mother, and he sat on her knees until noon, and he died. 21. And she went up and laid him on the bed of the man of God, and she closed about him and left. 22. And she called her husband and said,

It may, however, alternatively be rendered, *No.* It is used to strengthen her request to Elisha not to deceive her [*Redak*].

"No, my lord—*Do not say, "embracing a son." Why do I need to embrace him if I will end up burying him?" This is what she said to him when he died, "Did I not say, 'Do not mislead me'?"* [*Rashi*].

do not fail—*do not show me something that will fail. You have power to beg mercy, and a son will be given to me. I beseech you, do not give me any but a child who will live.*

do not fail—*like* (Is. 58:11) *"whose water will not fail"* [*Rashi*].

Since he used the expression "embracing a son," she suspected that she would have the son for a short time only, to embrace him and thereby to experience short-lived happiness. She, therefore, begged the prophet not to fail her [*Mezudath David*]. Otherwise, he would have said, "You will have a son" [*Malbim*].

Jonathan, too, renders: Let your word not fail.

Daath Soferim conjectures that she had had children previously, but none remained alive. This does not follow the exegetes who maintain that she was barren.

The *Midrash* maintains that the Shunemitess did not believe Elisha's prediction that she would bear a son. She questioned him thus: Those angels who brought the tidings to Sarah, said, "*I* will return to you next year at this time." She suspected that Elisha would forget the promise and never return to see it fulfilled. Thereupon, Elisha replied, "Those angels who live forever could promise to return. I, however, am but flesh and blood. Today I am alive. Tomorrow I may be dead. In any case, whether I am alive or dead, at this time next year, you will embrace a son [*Gen. Rabbah* 53:1, quoted in some editions of *Rashi* Gen. 18:10].

17. **at this time a year later**—*like*

עוּלֵימַיָא וַחֲדָא מִן אֲתָנַיָא וְאֶתְמְטֵי לְוַת נְבִיָא דַיְיָ וְאֶתוּב׃ כג וַאֲמַר מָא דֵין אַתְּ אָזְלָא לְוָתֵיהּ יוֹמָא דֵין לָא יְרַח וְלָא שַׁבְּתָא וַאֲמַרַת שְׁלָם׃ כד וְזָרֵיזַת אֲתָנָא וַאֲמַרַת לְעוּלֵימָהָא דַבַּר וְאֵזֵיל לָא תִדְחוֹק עֲלַי לְמִרְכַּב אֱלָהֵין כַּד אֵימַר לָךְ׃ כה וַאֲזַלַת וַאֲתַת לְוַת נְבִיָא דַיְיָ לְטוּר כַּרְמְלָא וַהֲוָה כַּד חֲזָא נְבִיָא דַיְיָ יָתַהּ מְקַבֵּיל וַאֲמַר לְגֵיחֲזִי עוּלֵימֵיהּ הָא שׁוּנַמִּית דֵיכִי׃ כו כְּעַן רְהוֹט כְּעַן לְקַדְמוּתַהּ וַאֲמַר לַהּ הַשְּׁלָם

נא לי אחד מן הנערים ואחת האתנות וארוצה עד איש האלהים ואשובה׃ כג ויאמר מדוע את הלכתי אליו היום לא חדש ולא שבת ותאמר שלום׃ כד ותחבש האתון ותאמר אל נערה נהג ולך אל תעצר לי לרכב כי אם אמרתי לך׃ כה ותלך ותבא אל איש האלהים אל הר הכרמל ויהי כראות איש האלהים אתה מנגד ויאמר אל גיחזי נערו הנה השונמית הלז׃ כו עתה רוץ נא לקראתה ואמר לה השלום לך

תולדות אהרן

מדוע את לא חודש ולא שבת. סוכה כ"ו וכ"ז ר"ה ט"ז וי"ז

רש"י　　　　את קרי הולכת קרי　　　　רד"ק

(כד) נהג ולך. מהר: אל תעצר לי. אל תעכב על ידי　הכואבים או הנוהים לכפול דבריהם וכן מעי מעי אוחילה׃
(כג) אתי. כתיב ביו"ד וכן הולכתי כתיב ביו"ד כמו שנמצאו יודי"ן נוספות כמו אהבתי לדוש מלאתי משפט והקרי הולך אחר הרוב: לא חדש ולא שבת. למדו רז"ל מזה כי חייב אדם להקביל פני רבו בשבת וברגל שנאמר לא חדש ולא שבת מכלל דבחדש ושבת היה לה ללכת אליו. ואדוני אבי ז"ל פירש לא עבר לא חדש ולא שבת שראית אותו מה לך ללכת אליו עתה: ותאמר שלום. לא רצתה לגלות לאדם עד שתראה הנביא׃
(כד) נהג ולך. י"מ כי היא היתה רוכבת ואמרה לנער שינהג הבהמה כלומר שיכה האתון במתג למהר ללכת. ופי' אל תעצור לי לרכוב אל תעצור האתון ללכת בנחת בעבור רכיבתי אלא אם אומר לך נהג לך בנחת וי"מ כי היתה הולכת ברגל במר נפשה ואמרת לנער שינהג האתון וילך לו אחרי האתון ולא יעצור האתון, כדי שתרכב היא אם לא תאמר לו ועל הדרך הזה ת"י אלא שתרגם אל תעצור על האשה שתרגם לא תדחוק עלי למירכב אלהין כד אומר לך׃

רלב"ג　　　　　　　　　　　　　　מנחת שי

(כג) היום לא חדש ולא שבת. ידמה שבימים האלו היו באים לפני הגדולים לשמוע דבריהם והם יורו אותם את הדרך ילכו בה ואת המעשה אשר יעשון: (כד) ותחבוש האתון. ר"ל שכאשר חבשה האתון על יד משרתה אמרה לו שינהג האתון וילך לפניה ולא יעצור בעבורה האתון מללכת כדי שתרכב על האתון אם לא תאמר לו שתרצה לרכוב בעבור העיפות: (כה) הנה השונמית הלז. ר"ל הנה זאת שאנו רואים היא　(כג) אתי הלכתי, את קרי. הלכת קרי׃

מצודת דוד　　　　　　　　　　　　　　מצודת ציון

הדרך הנוסע מכאב כמו מעי מעי אוחילה (ירמיה ד'): (כג) לא חדש ולא שבת. כי בראש חודש ושבת היתה רגילה לקבל פניו: ותאמר שלום. ר"ל אין דבר רע שאלך בעבורו אל הנביא ולא רצתה לגלות הדבר לבעלה כי חשבה מוטב שיעשה הנס בלעדו: (כד) ותחבוש. קשרה האוכף: נהג ולך. נהג האתון ולך אתה ואל תתעכב בעבורי שארכב אני בה כי אם כאשר אומר לך עמוד אז תעמוד: (כה) מנגד. מרחוק: הנה השונמית הלז. ר"ל　(כב) וארוצה. ענין מהירות ההליכה: (כד) תעצר. תעכב כמו נעצרה נא אותך (שופטים י"ג): (כה) הלז. הזאת׃

donkey's speed on her account, but to ride as quickly as possible. Alternatively, she was walking along bitterly while he was riding. She admonished him to continue riding and not to keep back the donkey so that she would not fall behind [*Redak*].

Jonathan renders: *Do not urge me to ride.* Apparently, he too understood that she was proceeding on foot [*Redak*].

"Please send me one of the servants and one of the she-asses;
and I will run up to the man of God and return." 23. And he
said, "Why are you going to him today; it is neither the New
Moon nor the Sabbath." And she said, "It's all right." 24. And
she saddled the she-ass, and she said to her servant, "Drive and
go forward. Don't keep back from riding because of me unless
I tell you." 25. And she went and came to the man of God, to
Mt. Carmel; and it was when the man of God saw her from
afar, that he said to Gehazi his servant, "Here is that Shunemmitess. 26. "Now please run toward her, and say to her, 'Are
you well?

man of God—She thought that in Elisha's merit he would be preserved. She, therefore, laid the child on his bed [*Ralbag*].

She wished to keep her son's death a secret. She, therefore, laid him on the prophet's bed in his room. She was confident that he would revive him [*Daath Soferim*].

and she closed about him—i.e. she closed the door to the room where he was lying. As mentioned earlier, she wanted to keep his death secret. Perhaps she feared that he would be buried before she could enlist Elisha's aid—[*Daath Soferim.*]

23. **it is neither the New Moon nor the Sabbath**—It was customary to greet one's master on the New Moon and the Sabbath [*Rosh Hashanah* 16a].

Although the Talmud states that one should greet his master on festivals, that was not mentioned here, since it was not deemed proper for a woman to visit the rabbi on the same day that the students were visiting him. On Sabbaths and New Moons, however, the students were dismissed from the studyhall, and were not found in the rabbi's quarters [*Hanukath Hatorah,* p. 79].

Alternatively, *it is not a month since you saw him last, neither is it a week* [*Redak* quoting his father].

"It's all right."—She did not wish to reveal to her husband the reason for her going to the prophet. She preferred that the miracle be performed secretively *[Mezudath David*]

"Drive and go forward—*quickly* [*Rashi*].

Don't keep back from riding because of me—*Do not keep back the riding because of me* [*Rashi*].

Perhaps the woman rode on the donkey with the servant. She admonished him not to hinder the

הַשָּׁלוֹם לְאִישֵׁךְ הֲשָׁלוֹם לַיָּלֶד וַתֹּאמֶר
שָׁלוֹם: כז וַתָּבֹא אֶל־אִישׁ הָאֱלֹהִים אֶל־
הָהָר וַתַּחֲזֵק בְּרַגְלָיו וַיִּגַּשׁ גֵּיחֲזִי לְהָדְפָהּ
וַיֹּאמֶר אִישׁ הָאֱלֹהִים הַרְפֵּה־לָהּ כִּי־
נַפְשָׁהּ מָרָה־לָהּ וַיהוָה הֶעְלִים מִמֶּנִּי
וְלֹא הִגִּיד לִי: כח וַתֹּאמֶר הֲשָׁאַלְתִּי בֵן
מֵאֵת אֲדֹנִי הֲלֹא אָמַרְתִּי לֹא תַשְׁלֶה
אֹתִי: כט וַיֹּאמֶר לְגֵיחֲזִי חֲגֹר מָתְנֶיךָ וְקַח
מִשְׁעַנְתִּי בְיָדְךָ וָלֵךְ כִּי תִמְצָא־אִישׁ
לֹא תְבָרְכֶנּוּ וְכִי־יְבָרֶכְךָ אִישׁ לֹא תַעֲנֶנּוּ

תרגום

הַשְׁלָם לִיךְ הַשְׁלָם לְבַעְלִיךְ הַשְׁלָם לְרַבְיָא וַאֲמַרַת שְׁלָם: כז וַאֲתַת לְוַת נְבִיָא דַיְיָ לְטוּרָא וְאִתְקֵיפַת בְּרִגְלוֹהִי וּקְרֵיב גֵיחֲזִי לְמִידְחָהּ וַאֲמַר נְבִיָא דַיְיָ שְׁבוֹק מִינָהּ אֲרֵי נַפְשָׁא מְרִירָא לָהּ וּמִן קֳדָם יְיָ אִתְכְּסָא מִנִי וְלָא אִתְחֲוָה לִי: כח וַאֲמַרַת הַשְׁאֵילִית בְּרָא מִן רִבּוֹנִי הֲלָא אֲמָרִית לָךְ אִם מִתְיְהֵב לִי בַּר קַיָם אִם לָא לָא תְנַסִים יָתִי: כט וַאֲמַר לְגֵיחֲזִי זְרִיז חַרְצָךְ וְסַב חוּטְרִי בִידָךְ וְאִיזִיל אֲרֵי תִשְׁכַּח גְבַר לָא תִשְׁאַל בִּשְׁלָמֵיהּ וַאֲרֵי יִשְׁאַל בִּשְׁלָמָךְ גַבְרָא לָא תְתִבִינֵיהּ

ת"א ויגש גחזי. ברכות יא (סנהדרין כט): תשלה אתי. עקידה שער ג:

רד"ק

(כז) להדפה. בעבור כבודה שלא תשק רגלי הנביא או לכבוד הנביא שלא תחזק ברגליו: העלים ממני. עד עתה כי באותה שעה שנפלה לרגליו נאמר לו בנבואה: (כח) לא תשלה אותי. כמו שאמרה אל תכזב בשפחתך ותשלה כמו תשגה תרגום שגגה שלו כלומר שלא תטעה אותי ומה לי לבן אם לא יחיה ות"י הלא אמרית לך אם מתיהיב לי בר קיים אם לא לא תנסים יתי: (כט) חגור מתניך. אמר לו זה לפי שילך במהרה בזריזות: כי תמצא איש לא תברכנו. זה אמר לו כדי שלא יתעכב בדרך ותהיה כוונתו בשליחותו ולא יפנה לבו לדבר אחר לא במעשה ולא בדבור. ובדרש שהיה כשחוק בעיניו וכל האדם שהיה פוגע בו היה אומר לו התאמן שהמטה הזה מחיה את המת לפיכך לא

רש"י

את הרכיב': (כו) ותאמר שלום. הרי זה מקרא קצר שהרי היה לו לכתוב וישאל לה ותאמר שלום: (כח) הלא אמרתי. לך אל תכזב בשפחתך: לא תשלה. לא תשגה אותי על דבר טעות: (כט) לא תברכנו. לא תשאל לשלום וכל זה שלא ירבה דברים וישאלוהו להיכן אתה הולך והוא אומר להחיות את המת ואין זה כבוד הנס להתהלל

מנחת שי

(כז) העלים ממני. העי"ן בגו"א לבדו מכלול דף פ"ב וכן הוא בספרים כתובי יד מדוייקים ובלא מאריך בה"א ועיין מה שכתוב באיכה על פסוק אל ת-ע ל ס אונך: (כח) הלוא אמרתי. בספרים מדוייקים בלא וא"ו שאינו מן י"ז מלאים בסיפרא: (כט) חגר מתניך. בספרים מדוייקים חסר וא"ו:

רלב"ג

השונמית: (כו) ותאמר שלום. לא רצתה לפתוח פיה לרע: (כז) ותחזק ברגליו. להשתחוות לו ולהתחנן לפניו בעד בנה והנה נגש גחזי לדחותה ולהסיר שלא תכנע לפני הנביא כל זה ההכנע או אולי עשה זה לכבוד אלישע כי יודע שאין רצונו שתתקרב אליו אשה כל כך: (כט) חגור מתניך וקח משענתי בידך. לוהו לחגור מתניו כדי שיוכל לרוץ יותר כי החגורה תמנע תנועת האברים הפנימיים ולזאת הסבה ג"כ מנעו שלא יברך איש מהאנשים שימצאו בדרכו גם לא יענה למברכים אותו כדי שלא יעכב בדרך וידמה שלא נשמר גחזי מכל מ"ש לו אלישע ולזה לא הועיל כשם מטה אלישע על פני הנער וידמה ג"כ שלא היה גחזי ראוי שיעשה זה הענין על ידו וזה יתבאר ממה שחטא בו בדבר

מצודת ציון

(כז) להדפה. לדחפה כמו אשר הדפנו רוח (תהלים א): (כח) תשלה. ענין שגגה ושכחה כמו על השל (שמואל ב' ו') ור"ל הטעאה: (כט) משענתי. המטה אשר נשען בו: תעננו.

מצודת דוד

הזאת הבאה היא השונמית: (כו) ותאמר שלום. אחר ששאלה אמרה לו הכל שלום ולא רצתה לגלות גם אליו: (כז) להדפה. בעבור כבוד הנביא שלא תחזיק ברגליו: הרפה לה. תן לה רפיון ואל תדפנה כי עושה קזאת בעבור מרירות נפשה ולא ידעתי מה היא כי ה' העלים ממני בעת נהית' וגם עתה לא הגיד לי: (כח) השאלתי. וכי באלהי אני על הבן עד שבע"כ הבטחתני אף בדב' שאינו מתקיים: הלא אמרתי. בעת ההבטחה אמרתי אל תטעה אותי להבטיח לי דבר הנפסק: (כט) חגור מתניך. ללכת מהרה ובזריזות: לא

sel than one that was filled and then spilled out." This is in keeping with Jewish practice to avoid reporting deaths explicitly. See *Shulchan Aruch Yoreh Deah* 402:12.

"Do not mislead me'"?—*Do not mislead me concerning a mistaken thing* [*Rashi*].

Rashi explains the root of the word תַּשְׁלֶה, which is the Aramaic for *mistake*. See also *Redak*.

Jonathan renders: If a living son will be given me. If not, do not grieve me.

29. **"Gird your loins**—to prevent the motion of the internal organs.

Is your husband well? Is the child well?'" And she said, "We are well." 27. And she came to the man of God to the mountain, and she took hold of his feet; and Gehazi approached to push her away. Now the man of God said, "Let her be, for her soul is bitter to her, and the Lord hid it from me and did not tell me." 28. And she said, "Did I ask for a son from my lord? Did I not say, 'Do not mislead me?'" 29. And he said to Gehazi, "Gird your loins and take my staff in your hand and go. If you meet anyone, do not greet him, and if anyone greets you, do not answer him;

26. **And she said, "We are well."**—*This is an abbreviated verse, for he should have written, "And he asked her, and she said, "We are well."—Rashi.* She hesitated to report the bad news [*Ralbag*].

27. **to push her away**—out of respect for the prophet, so that she should not grasp his feet [*Redak, Mezudath David, Ralbag*].

[We find (v. 13) that Elisha never spoke directly to the Shunemitess. He always communicated with her through Gehazi. He surely would not allow her to come in such proximity with him.]

Alternatively, out of respect for her, so that she should not humble herself to the extent of kissing Elisha's feet [*Redak*], or prostrating herself on the ground before him [*Abarbanel, Ralbag*].

According to the Rabbis, while Gehazi attempted to push the woman away from Elisha, he placed his hand on her bosom [*Berachoth* 10b, *Lev. Rabbah* 24, *Pirkei d'R. Eliezer* 33].

Obviously, Elisha did not detect Gehazi's indecent behavior, otherwise, he would have certainly castigated him [*K'li Y'kar*].

[Alternatively, although it is humiliating to her to kiss my feet or to prostrate herself on the ground, do not prevent her from doing so, for her soul is bitter . . .]

and the Lord hid it from me—until now. At this time, however, Elisha was informed by God of the demise of the son of the Shunemitess [*Redak*].

The news of the child's death had been hidden from Elisha as a punishment for promising his birth without divine sanction. He had, virtually, coerced God into fulfilling his promise [*Radal* on *Pirkei d'R. Eliezer* 33].

28. **Did I not say**—*to you, 'Do not fail your maidservant'?* [*Rashi*].

She reminds Elisha that she had expressed her desire for a child who would live, and that she would rather have remained childless than be granted one who would not live. *Pirkei d'R. Eliezer* expresses it thus, "I would rather have an empty ves-

וְשַׂמְתָּ מִשְׁעַנְתִּי עַל־פְּנֵי הַנָּעַר׃ ל וַתֹּאמֶר
אֵם הַנַּעַר חַי־יְהוָה וְחֵי־נַפְשְׁךָ אִם־
אֶעֶזְבֶךָּ וַיָּקָם וַיֵּלֶךְ אַחֲרֶיהָ׃ לא וְגֵחֲזִי
עָבַר לִפְנֵיהֶם וַיָּשֶׂם אֶת־הַמִּשְׁעֶנֶת
עַל־פְּנֵי הַנַּעַר וְאֵין קוֹל וְאֵין קָשֶׁב וַיָּשָׁב
לִקְרָאתוֹ וַיַּגֶּד־לוֹ לֵאמֹר לֹא הֵקִיץ
הַנָּעַר׃ לב וַיָּבֹא אֱלִישָׁע הַבָּיְתָה וְהִנֵּה
הַנַּעַר מֵת מֻשְׁכָּב עַל־מִטָּתוֹ׃ לג וַיָּבֹא
וַיִּסְגֹּר הַדֶּלֶת בְּעַד שְׁנֵיהֶם וַיִּתְפַּלֵּל אֶל־
יְהוָה׃ לד וַיַּעַל וַיִּשְׁכַּב עַל־הַיֶּלֶד וַיָּשֶׂם
פִּיו עַל־פִּיו וְעֵינָיו עַל־עֵינָיו וְכַפָּיו עַל־
כַּפָּו וַיִּגְהַר עָלָיו וַיָּחָם בְּשַׂר הַיָּלֶד׃

כפיו קרי

תרגום

תְּתֵבִינֵיהּ וּתְשַׁוֵּי חוּטְרֵי עַל אַפֵּי רַבְיָא׃ ל וַאֲמַרַת אִמֵּיהּ דְּרַבְיָא קַיָּם הוּא יְיָ וְחַי נַפְשָׁךְ אִם אֶשְׁבְּקִינָךְ וְקָם וַאֲזַל בַּתְרָאַהּ׃ לא וְגֵיחֲזִי עֲבַר קֳדָמֵיהוֹן וְשַׁוֵּי יַת חוּטְרָא עַל אַפֵּי רַבְיָא וְלֵית קָל וְלֵית דְּמָצִית וְתָב לְקַדָּמוּתֵיהּ וְחַוֵּי לֵיהּ לְמֵימַר לָא אִתְּעַר רַבְיָא׃ לב וַאֲתָא אֱלִישָׁע לְבֵיתָא וְהָא רַבְיָא מִית רְמֵי עַל עַרְסֵיהּ׃ לג וְעַל וַאֲגַף דָּשָׁא בְּאַפֵּי תַּרְוֵיהוֹן וְצַלִּי קֳדָם יְיָ׃ לד וּסְלִיק וּשְׁכִיב עַל רַבְיָא וְשַׁוִּי פּוּמֵיהּ עַל פּוּמֵיהּ וְעֵינוֹהִי עַל עֵינוֹהִי וִידוֹהִי עַל יְדוֹהִי וְאַלְהֵי עֲלוֹהִי וְחַם בִּיסְרֵיהּ

ת״א ושמת. פסחים סח: וילך אחריה. ברכות סא: משענתי. ערובין יח:

רש״י

בו מי שבא על ידו והוא לא עשה כן אלא לכל השואלו הוא אומר רבי שלחני להחיות את המת: (לד) ויגהר עליו. ת״י ואלהי עלוהי. הוא לשון עייפו׳. יש דוגמתו בברייתא דהאזינו ובספרי. ומנחם פתר ויגהר פתרון המלה כפי מהו שיטמא והיתה התשובה מת מטמא ואינו מטמא חי: (לד) וישם פיו על פיו. כמו שפירשנו באליהו שאמר ויתמודד על הנער והכל לכוין לשון התפלה על מי שמתפלל עליו כמו שאמר ביצחק לנכח אשתו ואפשר ג״כ להנשים על הנער לחממו

רד״ק

עלתה בידו: (לא) ואין קול. לענות: ואין קשב. לשמוע כי אילו היה שומע ולא היה יכול לענות היה מתנועע או רומז בעיניו או בידיו אבל זה לא היה בו לא זה ולא זה: לא הקיץ הנער. מצאנו הקיצה למת כמו הקיצו ורננו שוכני עפר והסברא אשר אמרנו בילד שהחיה אליהו היא הסברא עצמה בזה הנער שהחיה אלישע ומצאנו לו סמך בדברי רז״ל ששאלו בן השונמית

רלב״ג

כעמן: (לא) ואין קול ואין קשב. ר״ל שלא היה מדבר ולא שומע כשידברו אליו: (לג) ויסגור הדלת בעד שניהם. ר״ל שלא היו בבית כי אם שניהם כי לא רצה שיהיה שם שום אדם כדי שתהיה שם תפלתו יותר שלימה וכדי שלא יראה אדם מה שיעשה: (לד) וישם פיו על פיו. כאילו רצה שישפע חיות לנער מאברי אלישע והנה עשה זה אחר התפלה: ויגהר עליו. ר״ל שחזר להתפלל אחר זה והיה הולך בבית לכו וכוונתו בתפלה היה נמשך לו תנועת רגליו ללכת מתנועת קול

מנחת שי

(לא) ואין קשב. במקצת נוסחאות ספרדיות כ״י מלרע והמ״ן בלירי וכתב בלוח שכן הוא בספר מוגה ואם כן הוא תואר וכן פירשו רבי יונה כי מלאו מלרע בספר ירושלמי שנסמך עליו ורד״ק כתב עליו בשרשים שלא מלאו מלרע בשום ספר מדוייק כי אם באותו הירושלמי אשר סמך עליו רבי יונה והוא שב דבר כמו ואין קול ואין ענה ואין קשב (מלכים א׳ י״ח) וכן הוא בספרים שלנו מלעיל ובסגול: (לד) כפו

מצודת דוד

תברכנו. בכדי שלא תשהה בדרך: (ל) אם אעזבך. לבל תלך בעלמך עמדי: (לא) עבר לפניהם. הקדים להם: ואין קול. אמרו רבותינו ז״ל כי גיחזי לא שמע לדברי הנביא והיה עוד מגלגל בדרך כומר שהולך להחיות את המת: ואין קשב. היא היא כי כשאין קול אין מה להקשיב וכפל הדבר במ״ש: (לד) ויעל. על המטה: פיו על פיו. כאלו ישפיע מן החיות שבאיבריו אל איברי הנער:

מצודת ציון

מלשון עניה ותשובה: (לא) קשב. ענין האזנה: הקיץ. ענין הערה: (לד) ויגהר. ענין השתטחות הגוף כמו ויגהר ארצה (מלכים א׳ י״ח): ויחם. מלשון חמימה:

along, accompanied only by Gehazi and her servant [*Redal* ibid.].

after her—i.e. after her advice. It is not proper for a man to walk after a woman [*K'li Y'kar* acc. to *TB Berachoth* 41a].

31. **no sound nor any attention**—I.e. if the child had been able to hear, even though he could not speak, he would have indicated his awareness by blinking, or moving his limbs [*Redak*].

"The lad has not awakened"—The term "awakened" is sometimes

and you shall place my staff on the lad's face." 30. And the lad's mother said, "As the Lord lives and by your life, I will not leave you." And he rose and went after her. 31. And Gehazi went ahead of them, and he placed the staff on the lad's face, and there was no sound nor any attention; and he returned toward him and told him saying, "The lad has not awakened." 32. And Elisha came into the house, and behold the lad was dead, laid out on his bed. 33. And he came and closed the door about both of them; and he prayed to the Lord. 34. And he went up and lay on the child, and placed his mouth on his mouth and his eyes on his eyes and his palms on his palms, and he prostrated himself upon him; and the child's flesh became warm.

This will enable you to travel faster [*Ralbag*].

do not greet him—lit. do not bless him. *Do not ask him about his welfare. All this was done so that he would not be engaged in conversation, and he would ask him, "Where are you going?" And he would say, "To revive the dead."* (And since he gave him the staff, it is improper that he interrupt [*Kara*]) *Now, it is not respectful for the one through whom it is coming about, to praise himself. He, however, did not do so. Instead, to every inquirer he would say, "My master sent me to revive the dead"* [*Rashi*].

He was indeed forbidden to engage in any conversation, even to the extent of refraining from replying to a greeting. Instead, Gehazi took his mission very lightly. He considered it a joke. He would stop anyone he met and say, "Do you believe that this will resurrect the dead?" Therefore, he was unsuccessful in his attempt to effect the resurrection [*Redak* from *Pirkei d'Rabbi Eliezer*, ch. 33].

and take my staff—Elisha believed that the child had fallen into a coma. In that case, it would have sufficed for *his* agent to place *his* staff on the lad's face, to effect the revival. He admonished him to refrain from talking to anyone, in order to retain the power he had projected through him [*Malbim*].

30. **"I will not leave you."**—and allow you to refrain from going personally to effect the resurrection [*Mezudath David*].

Knowing Gehazi's character (See above v. 27), she was certain that he was not the one through whom a miracle would be performed. She, therefore, insisted that Elisha himself go along to perform the revival [*Zohar B'shallach* 44b].

Alternatively, she refused to go

לה וַיָּשָׁב וַיֵּלֶךְ בַּבַּיִת אַחַת הֵנָּה וְאַחַת
הֵנָּה וַיַּעַל וַיִּגְהַר עָלָיו וַיְזוֹרֵר הַנַּעַר עַד־
שֶׁבַע פְּעָמִים וַיִּפְקַח הַנַּעַר אֶת־עֵינָיו:
לו וַיִּקְרָא אֶל־גֵּיחֲזִי וַיֹּאמֶר קְרָא אֶל־
הַשּׁוּנַמִּית הַזֹּאת וַיִּקְרָאֶהָ וַתָּבוֹא אֵלָיו
וַיֹּאמֶר שְׂאִי בְנֵךְ: לז וַתָּבֹא וַתִּפֹּל עַל־
רַגְלָיו וַתִּשְׁתַּחוּ אָרְצָה וַתִּשָּׂא אֶת־
בְּנָהּ וַתֵּצֵא: לח וֶאֱלִישָׁע שָׁב הַגִּלְגָּלָה
וְהָרָעָב בָּאָרֶץ וּבְנֵי הַנְּבִיאִים יֹשְׁבִים
לְפָנָיו וַיֹּאמֶר לְנַעֲרוֹ שְׁפֹת הַסִּיר
הַגְּדוֹלָה וּבַשֵּׁל נָזִיד לִבְנֵי הַנְּבִיאִים:

בִּיסְרֵיהּ דְּרַבְיָא: לה וְתָב וְהַלֵּיךְ בְּבֵיתָא זִמְנָא חֲדָא לְכָא וְזִמְנָא חֲדָא לְכָא וּסְלֵיק וְאִלְהֵי עֲלוֹהִי וְאִתְמוֹרַךְ רַבְיָא עַד שְׁבַע זִמְנִין וּפְקַח רַבְיָא יָת עֵינוֹהִי: לו וּקְרָא לְגֵיחֲזִי וַאֲמַר קְרֵי לְשׁוּנַמִיתָא הָדָא וּקְרָא לַהּ וַאֲתַת לִקְדָמוֹהִי וַאֲמַר סְבִי בְרִיךְ: לז וַאֲתַת וּנְפָלַת קֳדָם רַגְלוֹהִי וּסְגִידַת עַל אַרְעָא וּנְסֵיבַת יָת בְּרַהּ וּנְפָקַת: לח וֶאֱלִישָׁע תָּב לְגִלְגְּלָא וְכַפְנָא בְּאַרְעָא וְתַלְמִידֵי נְבִיַּיָּא יָתְבִין קֳדָמוֹהִי וַאֲמַר לְעוּלֵימֵיהּ תְּפִי דוּדָא רַבָּא וּבַשֵּׁיל תַּבְשִׁילָא לתלמידי

רד"ק
בחום הטבעי היוצא מפיו ומעיניו כי רוב הנסים נעשים עם מעט תחבולה מדרך העולם: ויגהר עליו. התנפל והשתטח עליו כמו ויגהר ארצה אבל זה ת"י ואלהי עלוהי: (לה) וישב וילך בבית אחת הנה ואחת הנה. וישב לארץ להתפלל כי כבר עלה על המטה אשר הנער שם ושכב עליו והתנפל עליו עד שחם בשרו ואחר כך שב לארץ והתפלל והתנפל עוד ומה שהלך אחת הנה ואחת הנה לכוין לבו יותר וכן אמר דוד אתהלך בתום לבבי בקרב ביתי: ויזורר הנער. נתעטש ותרגום עטישותיו תהל אור זרירוהי: (לז) ותצא. מעלית אלישע: (לח) שפות הסיר. ערוך כלומר שים אותה על השפתים: נזיד. תבשיל כמו ויזד יעקב נזיד:

רש"י
עניכה נשתטח עליו: (לה) ויזורר. נתעטש: (לח) שפות הסיר. הושיבה על הכירה: נזיד. תבשיל: לבני

מנחת שי
כפיו קרי׳ (לו) קרא אל השונמית הזאת. בספר אחד מטוליטולא נכתב בלדו נסחא אחרינא קרא ל ש נ מ י ת וגם בספר אחד מספרד בכתב יד היה כתוב בראשונה אל השונמית ואחר כך עבר על הגרר ורוית עלמא טובא ללמ"ד בהגיהו ל ש נ מ י ת ופלא הוא בעיני:

רלב"ג
הסיר התנועה במחולות וזה מבואר מן החוש במי שיחשב מחשבות תתנועע נפשו בהם פעם כה ופעם כה שהוא תנועע ללכת במהירות בעת חשבו המחשבות יזכר שאחר התפילה היה עולה וכורע על הילד: (לה) והנה זכר הנער אחר זה. ר"ל שנתעטש וכן עשה אלישע כסדר הזה להתפלל ולכרוע על הילד להתמודד עליו עד שעשה זה שבע פעמים ואז פקח הילד את עיניו ונשלמה לו התחיה: (לח) שפות הסיר הגדולה. ר"ל הכן הסיר הגדולה לבשל בה תבשיל ובשל בה תבשיל לבני הנביאים והם תלמידי הנביאים:

מצודת ציון
(לה) ויזורר. ענין עטוש כמו עטישותיו תהל אור (איוב מ"א) תרגומו זרירוהי: ויפקח. פתח כמו עיניו פקח (שם כ"ו): (לח) שפות. ענין העמדת הסיר במקום מושבה כמו שפות הסיר שפות (יחזקאל כ"ד): הסיר. הקדרה: נזיד. תבשיל כמו ויזד יעקב

מצודת דוד
(לה) וישב. חזר לרדת מעל המטה: אחת הנה. פעם להעבר מזה ופעם להעבר מזה עד שבע פעמים נתעטש ז׳ פעמים ופתח אח"כ את עיניו: (לח) שפות הסיר. ערוך הסיר על מקום מושבה ובשל בה תבשיל:

ing. He was given this name because his birth was predicted by Elisha with the expression, "you will embrace a son." The double *kuf* signifies two embraces, his mother's and Elisha's. Elisha embraced him when he prostrated himself upon him.

38. **And Elisha**—Here he is not referred to as the man of God since this journey was not a prophetic mission. He went to Gilgal on his own volition to teach Torah, as is mentioned in this verse [*Daath Soferim*].

returned to Gilgal—after leaving with Elijah. See above 2:1. This may have been an academy for prophets or perhaps from time to time the disciples of the prophets would assemble to learn from one of the

35. And he returned and walked in the house once here and
once there, and he went up and prostrated himself upon him;
and the lad sneezed up to seven times, and the lad opened his
eyes. 36. And he summoned Gehazi and said, "Call this Shunemmitess." And he called her, and she came to him, and he
said, "Pick up your son." 37. And she came and fell at his feet
and bowed to the ground; and she picked up her son and
departed. 38. And Elisha returned to Gilgal; and the famine
was in the land, and the disciples of the prophets were sitting
before him. And he said to his servant, "Set the large pot on the
fire and cook a stew for the disciples of the prophets."

used in reference to the resurrection of the dead. See Isaiah 26:19. *Redak* expresses the view that the child had not died, but had lapsed into a deep coma. Although he refers to his commentary on I Kings 17:17, concerning the son of the widow whom Elijah revived, his conclusion there is that the child actually died. Indeed, it is the generally accepted view that both prophets revived the dead [*K'li Y'kar*].

32. **was dead, laid out on his bed**—Contrary to Elisha's original impression, the child was dead from the time he was laid on the bed [*Malbim*].

34. **his mouth on his mouth**—to direct his prayer toward the child, much as Isaac had done when praying on behalf of Rebecca (Gen. 25:21). Moreover, he may have intended to exhale on the body to warm it up and contribute in a natural way to the performance of the miracle [*Redak*].

and he prostrated himself upon him—Heb. וַיִּגְהַר. This is an unusual word, with little similarity in Scripture. *Jonathan renders:* וְאַלְהֵי עֲלוֹהִי. *This is an expression of weariness.* I.e. he lay exhausted upon him. *There is a similar word in the Baraitha of Haazinu and in Sifrei* (references obscure). *And Menahem interpreted* as follows: *The interpretation of the word according to its context, is: he prostrated himself upon him* [*Rashi* from *Machbereth Menahem* p. 53]. Compare with I Kings 18:42.

35. **And he returned**—to the floor to pray for the resurrection of the lad [*Redak*].

and he walked in the house—to intensify his concentration on his prayer [*Redak*].

and the lad sneezed—Heb. וַיְזוֹרֵר [*Rashi, Redak, Mezudath Zion*].

37. **and departed**—from Elisha's chamber [*Redak*].

It is noteworthy that the *Zohar* (Gen. 7b, Ex. 44a, 45a) identifies the son of the Shunemitess as the prophet Habakkuk. The name Habakkuk signifies *hibbuk*, embrac-

לט ויצא אחד אל־השדה ללקט ארת
ויִמצא גפן שדה וילקט ממנו פקעת
שדה מלא בגדו ויבא ויפלח אל־סיר
הנזיד כי־לא ידעו: מ ויצקו לאנשים
לאכול ויהי כאכלם מהנזיד והמה
צעקו ויאמרו מות בסיר איש האלהים
ולא יכלו לאכל: מא ויאמר וקחו־קמח
וישלך אל־הסיר ויאמר צק לעם ויאכלו
ולא היה דבר רע בסיר: מב ואיש בא

ו קמץ ברביע

לְתַלְמִידֵי נְבִיַּיָא: לט וּנְפַק חַד לְחַקְלָא לְלַקָּטָא ירוקין ואשכח גופנא בחקלא ולקיט מיניה פקעי חקלא מלי לבושיה ואתא ופרס ורמא לדודא דתבשילא ארי לא ידעו: מ ואריקו לגבריא למיכל והוה כמיכלהון מתבשילא ואינון צוחו ואמרו מותא בדודא נביא דיי ולא יכילו למיכל: מא ואמר איתו קמחא ורמו לדודא ואמר אריק לעמא וייכלון ולא הוה מדעם ביש בדודא: מב וגברא אתא מארע דרומא

ת"א ללקט ארת. יומא יח: (עס יח. נדרים פ') ואיש בא מבעל. כתובות כ קט סנהדרין יב מנחות סו:

רש"י

הנביאים. לתלמידי נבייא: (לט) ללקט אורות. גרגיר שקורין אורגא שמאיר את העינים. ויש שפותרין אורות ירקות כמו כחם לח עלי אור (ישעיה יח ד): וימצא גפן שדה. גופנא בחקלא: וילקט ממנו פקועות שדה. למהו ממנו פקועות שדה. הוא (בוליי"ן בלע"ז) סם המות.

רד"ק

(לט) ללקוט ארת. ללקט ירקות לאכול וכת"י ללקטא ירוקנין וכן כי טל אורת טלך טל הראוי לירקות ובדברי רז"ל מאי אורות תנא משמיה דרבי מאיר זה גרגיר אמר ר' יוחנן למה נקרא שמו אורות שמאירות את העינים והוא הנקרא אירוג"א בלע"ז והעלי' יצא ללקט לא הזרע: וימצא גפן שדה. ת"י ואשכח גופנא בחקלא ולקיט מניה פקעי חקלא וי"מ גפן כמשמעו ומפרשים פקיעות פטריות הידוע בדברי רבותינו ז"ל וגדלו הפטריות ההם אצל הגפן ומצאנו בפי' הגאונים ז"ל פקועות שדה כעין אבטיחים קטנים והם מרים ועושין מזרע שלהם שמן הוא שאמרו רז"ל בשמן פקועות והוא הנקרא בלשון ישמעאל חנד"ל אם כן לזה הפירוש ירצה לומר גפן שדה שהקנה ההוא שגדלין בו אלה הפקועות הוא כעין גפן ונקרא גפן שדה: וילקט ממני. נמצא גפן זכר ונקבה ברוב וזכר כמו זה שאמר ממנו וכן גפן בוקק ובעל המסרת חשבו עם הששה שקורין ממנו וסבירין ממנה: ויפלח. כמו ויבקע מן כפלח הרמון כמו פולח ובוקע בארץ: כי לא ידעו. שהם מרים: (מ) ויצקו לאנשים. היו"ד מעמדת בגעיא לחסרון היו"ד פ"א הפעל מהמכתב וענינו שיצקו התבשיל בקערות לאנשים לאכול: כאכלם. בכ"ף: מות בסיר. לפי שהיו מרים: (מא) וקחו קמח. הוי"ו כאותן הוי"ן שכתבנו שהם בראש ענין ואינם לתוספת ענין כמו וישא אברהם את עיניו והדומים לו או תור' מלה נסתרת עמו ופי' לכו וקחו: וישלך אל הסיר. והלא כבר יצקו התבשיל בקערית אלא נראה שצוה להחזיר התבשיל בסיר ואחר כך השליך הקמח בסיר שלא תצטרך לתת הקמח

רלב"ג

(לט) ללקט אורות. ר"ל ללקט ירקות: וימצא גפן שדה וילקט ממנו פקיעות שדה. פירשו קצת המפרשי' שהם קפואין(מריקגומ"רו בלע"ז) והם בתכלית הרוע והסכנה לאוכל מהם וקצתם פירשו שהם הנקראים קולקוינטידא"ש והם ג"כ כמו סם המות: ויפלח אל סיר הנזיד. ר"ל שכרת העשבים ההם ושמם בסיר הנזיד כי לא ידעו שיהיה בלתי נאות למזון: (מ) וילקו לאנשים לאכול. ר"ל שילקו מהסיר אל הקערה וכאשר אכלו ממנו לעקו שיש סם המות בסיר ועל צד המופת

מנחת שי

(לט) ללקט ארת. אין באלף מאריך: ממנו. ו' סבירין ממנה וקריין ממנו מסורת ריש פ' לו ועיין מ"ש ריש פ' תרומה: (מ) וילקו לאנשים. היו"ד מעמדת בגעיא לחסרון היו"ד פ"א הפועל מהמכתב רד"ק וכן הוא בספרים מדוייקים:

מצודת דוד

(לט) גפן שדה. מין גפנים הגדלים בשדה והפירות הם דבר ארסי וממית: ויפלח. בקע לחתיכות ונתנה אל הסיר כי לא הכיר בו שהוא דבר ארסי: (מ) ויצקו. שפכו הנזיד אל הקערו' לאכלה: מות בסיר וגו'. אתה איש האלהים הנה בסיר יש דבר הממית כי הרגישו במרירתו: (מא) ויאמר. אלישע אמר החזירו הנזיד אל הסיר וקחו קמח לתת בסיר ואז יוסר הארס: צק לעם. עתה שפוך אל הקערות ויאכלו: ולא היה. ר"ל וכן היה כי לא

מצודת ציון

נזיד (בראשית כ"ה): (לט) אורות. ענינו למחי שדה כמו טל אורות טלך (ישעיה כ"ו): פקועות שדה. הם הגדלים על גפן שדה והמה מרים ועושים מהם שמן ובדרז"ל נקרא שמן פקועות (שבת כ"ד): ויפלח. ענין בקיעה כמו כפלח הרמון (שיר השירים ד):

bitter fruit, whose seeds are used for oil.

and diced them—*split them* [*Rashi*]. Since the gourds were diced, they were not recognizable in the stew, and could therefore not be removed [*K'li Y'kar*].

40. **"Death is in the pot,—** Because it was bitter, they considered it like poison [*Redak*].

According to *Rashi,* it was indeed poison.

and they could not eat—Their mouths became immediately affected by the toxicity of the gourds or the mushrooms, and they could not

39. And one went out to the field to gather herbs; and he found a vine in the field and gathered from it wild mushrooms his garment full; and he came and diced them into the pot of stew, for they did not know. 40. And they poured for the people to eat; and it was when they were eating of the stew, that they cried out and said, "Death is in the pot, O man of God!" and they could not eat. 41. And he said, "Fetch flour," and he threw [it] into the pot, and he said, "Pour it for the people and let them eat." And there was no harmful substance in the pot. 42. And a man came

great prophets, previously from Elijah and now from Elisha [*Daath Soferim*].

the famine was in the land—the famine mentioned below in ch. 8. The cause of the famine is not mentioned. Perhaps there was a draught, or perhaps, the loss of Moabite wool created a depression, since it was an important source of income, which enabled Israel to barter with other nations for necessary commodities—*Daath Soferim.*

set the . . . pot—*Place it on the stove* [*Rashi*].

a stew—Heb. נָזִיד, *a cooked dish* [*Rashi* from *Jonathan*].

for the disciples of the prophets—*Rashi* from *Targum Jonathan.* Lit. for the sons of the prophets. It has been mentioned in a number of instances that a teacher who brings his students to everlasting life by teaching them Torah, is considered like a father. See above 2:12.

39. **to gather herbs**—Heb. *oroth, garden rocket, which they call eruca* in Latin, *which brightens the eyes, meir* in Heb. (*Yoma* 18b). *Others interpret 'oroth' as herbs, as* (Is. 18:4) *Like a clear heat on herbs (or)* [*Rashi*].

Redak, too, quotes these two opinions. He notes that according to the former, the edible part of the plant is the leaves, not the seeds. The latter opinion originates from *Targum Jonathan* and is shared by *Ralbag* and *Mezudath Zion.*

a vine in the field [*Rashi* after *Jonathan*].

and gathered from it wild mushrooms—*Wild mushrooms grew from it. That is boljic in O.F. It is poisonous.* It is common that mushrooms grow from old tree stumps and the like. In this case, they grew from a vine. *And in the name of Rabbi Menahem* (*ben Helbo,* according to *Kara*) *I heard, and he gathered in addition to the fruit that grew from it, wild mushrooms* [*Rashi*].

I.e. in addition to gathering fruit from the vine, he gathered wild mushrooms, which happened to be poisonous.

Redak quotes the *Geonim* as interpreting this as wild gourds, a very

מבעל שלשה ויבא לאיש האלהים
לחם בכורים עשרים לחם שערים
וכרמל בצקלנו ויאמר תן לעם ויאכלו:
מג ויאמר משרתו מה אתן זה לפני
מאה איש ויאמר תן לעם ויאכלו כי
כה אמר יהוה אכול והותר: מד ויתן
לפניהם ויאכלו ויותרו כדבר יהוה:
ה א ונעמן שר צבא מלך ארם היה
איש גדול לפני אדניו ונשא פנים
כי בו נתן יהוה תשועה לארם והאיש

תרגום

דרומא ואיתי לנביא דיי לחם בכורין עסרין טולמין דלחם סעורין ופירוכן בלבושיה ואמר הב לעמא וייכלון: מג ואמר משומשניה מא אתן דין קדם מאה גברא ואמר הב לעמא וייכלון ארי כדנן אמר יי ייכלון ויותרון: מד ויהב קדמיהון ואכלו ואותירו כפתגמא דיי: א ונעמן רב חילא דמלכא דארם הוה גבר רב קדם רבוניה ונסיב אפין ארי על ידיה עבד יי נצחנא לאנש ארם וגברא הוה גבר חילא והוא לקי

ת"א תן לעם. סנהדרין יב: ויאמר משרתו. כתובות קו: לפני מאה איש כתובות קו:

רד"ק

בכל קערת וקערה: (מב) מבעל שלשה. שם מקום הנזכר בספר שמואל ויעבר בארץ שלישה וי"ת זה וזה ארע דרומא: לחם בכורים. מן השעורים הראשונים שקצרו כי זמן קציר שעורים היה: וכרמל בצקלונו. בקליפתו כתרגומו ופירוכן בלבושיה: (א) כי בו. כתרגומו ארי על ידיה עבד ה' נצחנא לאנש ארם. ובדרש היה מושך את הקשת להתומו והרג את אחאב ועוד בדרש בשעה שגמלו חסד עם יעקב כמו שכתוב ויאסוף לבן את כל אנשי המקום ויעש משתה אמר להם הקדוש ברוך הוא גמלתם חסד עם יעקב אני אתן שכרכם לבניכם בשביל שלא יהיה שכר לרשעים בעולם הבא שנאמר כי בו נתן ה' תשועה

רש"י

ובשם ר' מנחם שמעתי וילקט לבד ממנו בלעדיו פקועו' שדה: ויפלח. ויבקע: (מב) מבעל שלשה. שם מדינה. ויונתן תרגם מארעא דרומא בעל לשון מישור והרבה במקרא: לחם בכורי'. בפסח שהתבואה מבכרת: בצקלונו. בלבושיה: לעם. לתלמידים שהיה זן: (מג) מה אתן זה. כל לחם ולחם:

ה (א) ונעמן שר צבא. נסים שנעשו על ידי אלישע מסדר והולך: תשועה לארם. הוא משך

מנחת שי

באלגים. בכ"ף רד"ק: (מב) לחם בכורים עשרים לחם שערים. חד מאלפ"א ביתא מן ב' ב' לא נסבין וא"ו בריש תיבותא ומטעין בהון וסימן במסרא רבתא: ה (א) היה איש גדול. בכל ספרים שלפני מלרע ומכלל יופי כתב בא מלרע שלא כמנהג ובמקצת ספרים מלעיל וכן מדברי המכלול בדף ו':

רלב"ג

לזה הנביא שיקחו קמח וישליכו אל הסיר וכאשר עשו זה נרפא הנזיד ולא היה דבר רע בסיר: (מב) לחם בכורים. הוא מקציר השעורים כי הם נקצרים ראשונה: וכרמל בצקלונו. אחשב שבכבר היו קולין השעורים ואח"כ טוחנין אותם והיו קושרים אותם לחבקים גדולים והוא הנקרא כרמל ואמר שהוא בצקלונו ר"ל בכלי שהיה לו לשאת בו אלו הדברים: (א) כי בו נתן ה' תשועה לארם. ידמה שהתשועה הזאת היא הריגת אחאב שנלחם שני פעמים והנה התשועה היא כי בלי מתכוין משך בקשת לתמו והמית אחאב:

מצודת ציון

(מב) מבעל שלשה. שם מקום: בכורים. מלשון בכור ור"ל דבר הנקלר ראשון: וכרמל. כן יקרא שבלים רכים: בצקלונו. תרגם יונתן בקליפותיהן:

מצודת דוד

היה מעתה דבר ארסי וממית: (מב) לחם בכורים. לחם העשוי מהקציר הנקצר שם ראשונה והיו במספר עשרים וממין השעורים: וכרמל בצקלונו. שבלים רכים ומלאים כשהם עדיין בקליפותיהן: (מג) מה אתן זה. ר"ל הלא מעט המה: אכול והותר. בהם יהיה די לאכול ועוד יהיה מותר: ה (א) איש גדול. ר"ל חשוב לפניו וגו': ונשא פנים. הכל היו נושאים לו פנים לכבדו כי ע"י בא תשועה לארם ואחז"ל שהוא משך הקשת לתומו והרג את אחאב: גבור חיל מצורע. כאומר הנה בהיותו גבור חיל חשק לרדת בכל עת אל

interpretation that each bread had to suffice for one hundred men, since he had 2,200 pupils. Twenty loaves would have to feed two thousand, and *bikkurim* another hundred, and *karmel* still another hundred [*Kethuboth* 106a, quoted by *Yalkut Shimoni*].

1. **Now, Naaman the general**—*He goes on to recount the miracles that were performed through Elisha* [*Rashi*].

and respected—i.e. everyone respected him [*Mezudath David*].

the victory to Aram—*He drew back his bow innocently and killed*

from Baal-Shalishah, and he brought to the man of God bread of the first-fruits, twenty loaves of barley bread and sheaves of fresh grain in their shells; and he said, "Give to the people and let them eat. 43. And his servant said, "How will I give this before one hundred men? And he said, "Give the people and let them eat, for so has the Lord said, 'They shall eat and leave over.'" 44. And he placed it before them, and they ate and left over, according to the word of the Lord.

5

1. Now Naaman, the general of the king of Aram, was a prominent man before his lord and respected, for through him had the Lord given victory to Aram; and the man

eat anything [*K'li Y'kar*].

41. **"Fetch flour,"**—lit. "And fetch flour," or, "Now fetch flour," [*Redak*].

and he threw [it] into the pot—After they had all poured their portions back into the pot, Elisha took the flour and threw it in, so that they would not have to put flour into each portion [*Redak*].

Since flour is used to make bread, the staff of life, it is the direct opposite of poison, and was therefore chosen as the antidote for the poisonous gourds or mushrooms [*Abarbanel*].

42. **from Ball-Shalishah** — *the name of a province. And Jonathan rendered: from the southland. "Baal" is an expression meaning a plain. There are many such expressions **in the Bible*** [*Rashi*].

The land of Shalishah is also mentioned in I Sam. 9:4. There too, *Jonathan* renders it as "the southland" [*Redak*].

bread of the first fruits—*It was during Passover, when the grain becomes ripe* [*Rashi*].

He brought from the first barley crops, which are reaped at that time [*Redak*].*

fresh grain—tender ears of grain [*Mezudath Zion*].

in their shells—*Jonathan* renders: *in their garments.* The shell is compared to a garment of the grain [*Rashi*].

Ralbag theorizes that the grain is toasted and then broken up into large pieces, which are placed in a vessel known as *ziklon.*

to the people—*to the students whom he sustained* [*Rashi*].

43. **"How will I give this**—i.e. *each bread* [*Rashi*]. This accounts for the singular expression.

Rashi alludes to the Talmudic

היה גבור חיל מצרע: ב וארם יצאו
גדודים וישבו מארץ ישראל נערה
קטנה ותהי לפני אשת נעמן: ג ותאמר
אל־גברתה אחלי אדני לפני הנביא
אשר בשמרון אז יאסף אתו מצרעתו:
ד ויבא ויגד לאדניו לאמר כזאת וכזאת
דברה הנערה אשר מארץ ישראל:
ה ויאמר מלך־ארם לך בא ואשלחה
ספר אל־מלך ישראל וילך ויקח בידו

בסניריתא: ב ואנש ארם
נפקו במשרין ושבו
מארעא דישראל
עולמתא זעירתא והות
משמשא קדם אתת
נעמן: ג ואמרת
למרתה טובי רבוני אם
יצלי קדם נביא די
בשמרון בכן יסי יתיה
מסגירותיה: ד ואתא
וחוי לרבוניה למימר
כדין וכדין מללת
עולמתא די מארעא
דישראל: ה ואמר מלכא
דארם איתא אזיל
ואשדר אגרתא לות
מלכא דישראל ואזל
ונסיב בידיה עשר ככרין
דכסף

ת"א וארם יצאו. סוטה מו חולין פ:

רש"י

בקשת לתומו והרג את אחאב: (ב) יצאו גדודים. כשהולכין מאה או מאתים מעצמן לשלול כאשר ימצאון הוא קרוי גדוד: נערה קטנה. ריבה קטנה מעיר נערון: ותהי לפני. והות משמשא קדם אתת נעמן: (ג) אחלי אדוני לפני הנביא. לשון ויחל משה (שמות לב יא) בקשות כל המתפללים עליו יהיו שיבא הנס לפני הנביא: אחלי. (סוהיידמנ"ס בלע"ז) כלומר זו היא בקשה שהוא צריך לה: (ד) ויבא. נעמן: ויגד לאדוניו. מלך ארם: (ה) ויקח

רד"ק

לארם: גבור חיל מצורע. כי היה גבור חיל והיה מצורע: (ב) נערה קטנה. מן השבי ששבו היתה זאת הנערה ואמר קטנה כי יש נערה גדולה. ובדברי רבותינו ז"ל קרי לה נערה וקרי לה קטנה אלא קטנה היתה יהיתה ממקום ששמו נערון: ותהי לפני. היתה משמשת לפניה: (ג) אחלי אדני. תחנות אדוני ובקשותיו יהיו לפני הנביא אשר בשמרון: אז יאסף אותו מצרעתו. כי הבורא יתברך עושה נסים על ידו. ואחלי שם בפלס אשרי ות"י טובי רבוני: יאסף אותו מצרעתו. כתרגומו יסי יתיה מסגירותיה ונקראת רפואת הצרעת אסיפה מפני שהמצורע ישב בדד ובהרפאו יאסף בין בני אדם: (ד) ויבא

רלב"ג

(ב) וארם יצאו גדודים. ר"ל שמבני ארם יצאו גדודים: נערה קטנה. הנה יקרא נער הקטן אמר בשמואל והנער נער ולא היו לו כי אם שתי שנים ולזה אמר ונער קטון נוהג בם ולזאת הסבה ג"כ בזה המקום נערה קטנה: ותהי לפני אשת נעמן. רוצה לומר לשרתה: (ג) אחלי אדני לפני הנביא וגו'. ר"ל אם תהיינה תחנות אדוני ובקשותיו לפני הנביא אשר בשמרון אז יאסוף אותו מצרעתו: (ד) ויבא ויגד לאדניו. ר"ל שנעמן בא והגיד זה לאדניו למלך ארם:

מצודת דוד

המלחמה ומפני צרעתו מנע והיה מיצר בעבור זה: (ב) יצאו גדודים. כשהולכין מעצמן מתי מספר לשלול כאשר ימצאו קרוי גדוד: נערה קטנה. גם קטנה תקרא נערה וכן ונער קטן נוהג בם (ישעיה י"א): ותהי וגו'. היתה משמשת לפני אשת נעמן: (ג) אחלי אדוני. אם בקשת אדוני תהיה לפני הנביא אז מבלי ספק ירפאו מצרעתו ונקרא רפואת המצורע בלשון אסיפה לפי שבעודו בצרעתו מחוץ למחנה מושבו וכאשר יתרפא יאסף ויכנס אל המחנה וכן נאמר עד האסף מרים (במדבר י"ב): (ד) ויבא וגו'. נעמן ספר הדבר לפני המלך: (ה) לך בא. אל הנביא: אל מלך ישראל. שהוא יצוה את הנביא על זאת:

מצודת ציון

ה(ב) וישבו. מל' שביה: (ג) גברתה. אשת אדונה: אחלי. ענין בקשה כמו ויחל משה (שמות לב): (ה) ספר. אגרת: חליפות. כן

Naaman's wife [*Rashi*].

3. **"My master's supplications**—*before the prophet*—Heb. אַחֲלֵי, *an expression similar to* וַיְחַל מֹשֶׁה, *and Moses prayed* (Ex. 32:11). *The supplications of all those who pray for him, shall be that the miracle shall come before the prophet* [*Rashi*]. This wording is difficult. *Shem Ephraim* suggests: *The supplications of all those who pray for him that the miracle shall come, shall be that he come before the prophet.*

According to *Rashi* ms.: *The supplications of all those who pray for him, shall be that they go before the prophet.*

the supplications—אַחֲלֵי *I.e. to say that this is the supplication that he requires* [*Rashi*].

Redak interprets: My master's supplications should be offered be-was a great warrior, and he was a *mezora.* 2. Now the Arameans went out in bands and captured from the land of Israel a young girl, who ministered to Naaman's wife. 3. And she said to her mistress, "The supplications for my master should be that he go before the prophet who is in Samaria; then he would cure him of his *zaraath.* 4. And he came and told his master, saying, "In the following manner has the girl from the land of Israel spoken." 5. And the king of Aram said, "Come, go and I will send a letter to the king of Israel." He went and took in his possession

Ahab [*Rashi* from *Midrash Psalms* 78:11]. See I Kings 22:34, Comm. Dig.

mezora—He was stricken with a skin disease known as *zaraath.* The symptoms are delineated in Lev. 13. Although it is usually identified with leprosy, we prefer to leave it untranslated. Since the symptoms delineated in the Torah, e.g. the white hairs and the white area, are not found in leprosy, neither is the spontaneous healing, we cannot identify it thus. Moreover, the decay and loss of limbs found in leprosy is never mentioned in the case of *zaraath.*

Naaman's disease was visited upon him as a penalty for having captured a young girl from the land of Israel [*Tanhuma* end of *Tazria*].

Alternatively, it was divinely visited upon him as a punishment for haughtiness [*Tan. Mezora* 4].

2. **went out in bands**—*When they go in groups of one hundred or two hundred by themselves, to plunder whatever they find, that is called a band* [*Rashi*].

a young girl—Heb. *naarah ketannah.* According to halachah, the term *naarah* applies to a girl who has reached puberty, but is not completely mature. This period usually commences at the age of twelve and terminates six months later, at the time of *bagruth,* maturity. The term *ketannah* applies to a minor, a girl under the age of twelve. Hence, these two terms are contradictory. The Talmud therefore explains that they captured *a young girl from the town of Naaran* [*Rashi* from *TB Hulin* 5a].

This town is referred to variantly as Naaran in I Chron. 7:28, and as Naarah, Naarath, or Naarathah in Jos. 16:7. It is situated in Ephraim's territory.

According to *peshat,* we can explain that she was a *naarah* at the beginning of *naaruth,* hence a small *naarah,* as opposed to one at the end of that age, who would be referred to as a big *naarah* [*Redak*].

who ministered to—lit. and she was before Naaman's wife. *Jonathan* renders: *and she was serving before*

עֶשֶׂר כִּכְּרֵי־כֶסֶף וְשֵׁשֶׁת אֲלָפִים זָהָב וְעֶשֶׂר חֲלִיפוֹת בְּגָדִים: ו וַיָּבֵא הַסֵּפֶר אֶל־מֶלֶךְ יִשְׂרָאֵל לֵאמֹר וְעַתָּה כְּבוֹא הַסֵּפֶר הַזֶּה אֵלֶיךָ הִנֵּה שָׁלַחְתִּי אֵלֶיךָ אֶת־נַעֲמָן עַבְדִּי וַאֲסַפְתּוֹ מִצָּרַעְתּוֹ:
ז וַיְהִי כִּקְרֹא מֶלֶךְ־יִשְׂרָאֵל אֶת־הַסֵּפֶר וַיִּקְרַע בְּגָדָיו וַיֹּאמֶר הַאֱלֹהִים אָנִי לְהָמִית וּלְהַחֲיוֹת כִּי־זֶה שֹׁלֵחַ אֵלַי לֶאֱסֹף אִישׁ מִצָּרַעְתּוֹ כִּי אַךְ־דְּעוּ־נָא וּרְאוּ כִּי־מִתְאַנֶּה הוּא לִי: ח וַיְהִי כִּשְׁמֹעַ

דִּכְסַף וְשִׁתָּא אַלְפִין דִּינְרִין דִּדְהַב וְעַסְרָא אִצְטְלָוָן דִּלְבוּשָׁא: ו וְאַיְתִי אִגַּרְתָּא לְמַלְכָּא דְיִשְׂרָאֵל לְמֵימַר וּכְעַן כְּתִיב בַּהּ וּכְעַן כְּמֵיתֵי אִגַּרְתָּא הָדָא לְוָתָךְ הָא שַׁדְּרִית לָךְ יַת נַעֲמָן עַבְדִּי וְתַסֵּינֵיהּ מִסְגִירוּתֵיהּ: ז וַהֲוָה כַּד קְרָא מַלְכָּא דְיִשְׂרָאֵל יַת אִגַּרְתָּא וּבְזַע יַת לְבוּשׁוֹהִי וַאֲמַר הֲצָרוֹךְ אִית בִּי מִן קֳדָם יְיָ לְמִקְטַל וּלְאַחָאָה אֲרֵי דֵין שְׁלַח לִי לְאַסָּאָה גַּבְרָא מִסְגִירוּתֵיהּ אֲרֵי בְּרַם דְּעוּ כְעַן וַחֲזוֹ אֲרֵי תוּסְקְפָא דֵין בָּעֵי לְאִתְגְּרָאָה בִּי: ח וַהֲוָה

ת"א הנה שלחתי . כל ענין נעמן עקידה שער סא :

רד"ק

ויגד. נעמן הגיד למלך ארם אדוניו דברי הנערה אחר שספרה לו אשתו: (ה) וששת אלפים זהב. כתרגומו ושתא אלפין דינרין דדהב: (ו) ויבא הספר אל מלך ישראל לאמר. הביא הספר אל מלך ישראל ודברי הספר היו ועתה כבוא הספר הזה אליך היו בתחלת הספר דברים אחרים אלא שהדברים הצריכין ספר הכתוב: (ז) האלהים אני. ולא נתן אל לבו דבר הנביא אעפ"י שהיה יודע שהקדוש ברוך הוא עושה נסים על ידו כי בוש לבא לפניו ולאמר לו להתחנן לאל בעבורו לפי שהוא לא היה שומע אליו להניח עבודת העגלים: מתאנה הוא לי. מתעולל עלי עלילות ומבקש ממני דבר שלא אוכל לעשותו כדי

רש"י

בידו. מנחה לנביא: וששת אלפים זהב. זהובים: (ו) לאמר ועתה כבוא הספר הזה וגו'. הספר אמר לו ועתה כבוא הספר הזה וגו': ואספתו מצרעתו. אסיפה במצורע היא לשון רפואתו כי בהתרפאתו הוא נאסף אל תוך בני אדם ובחליו הכל בדילין הימנו: (ז) האלהים אני. ה"א נקוד פת"ח ללמד שהוא בלשון תמיהה: מתאנה. מתעולל עלי עלילות ומבקש ממני דבר שלא אוכל לעשותו כדי

רלב"ג

(ו) ואספתו מצרעתו. ר"ל שתרפאהו מצרעתו ונקרא הרפואה מהצרעת אסיפה כי הצרעת תעשה מהאחד רבים כי מפני תגבורת החום העפושי יתלש מאד החום הטבעי הקושר איברי הב"ח ומשים אותם אחד ולזה תמצא במצורע שהבשר יפלו איבריו ולזה אמר בזה המקום ברפואת המצורע וישוב בשרך לך וטהר כי המצורע אין בשרו לו כמו שזכרנו כי אין בו הדבר שקושר בשרו בו: (ז) כי מתאנה

מצודת ציון

יקראו הבגדים כי בהסיר האחת יחלוף אחר תחתיה: (ז) מתאנה. מבקש עלילה כמו תואנה הוא מבקש (שופטים יד):

מצודת דוד

ויקח בידו. מנחה להנביא: (ו) ועתה. לא פירש הכתוב מה כתב בראשית אמריו כי היה כמנהג לפקדו בשלום וסוף דבריו היה באמר ועתה וגו': ואספתו. לא שהיה דעת מלך ארם שמלך ישראל יאספו מצרעתו רק דבריו היו שהוא יצוה את הנביא לאספו מצרעתו: (ז) ויקרע בגדיו. מחמת חרדה: האלהים אני. וכי אני אלהים להיות בידי להמית ולהחיות כי זה וכו' כי אין מי יוכל לרפאות המצורע אלא מי שבידו להמית ולהחיות ומגודל רשעו לא האמין בהנביא וחשב אשר שלח שהוא בעצמו ירפאו: כי אך דעו נא. כאומר הלא לא נעלם ממנו שלא אוכל לו אבל הכוונה למצוא עלילה

Naaman, since he had not heeded his admonition to abandon idolatry [*Redak*].

he is looking for a pretext—*He is looking for a pretext to engage in strife with me* [*Rashi*]. Heb. מִתְאַנֶּה—*an expression of pretext*—*Rashi*. See Jud. 14:4.

ten talents of silver and six thousand gold pieces, and ten suits of clothes. 6. And the letter came to the king of Israel, saying, "And now, when this letter comes to you, behold I have sent Naaman my servant to you, and you shall cure him of his *zaraath.* 7. And it was when the king of Israel read the letter, that he rent his garments, and said, "Do I have power from God to put to death and to bring to life, that this one sends to me to cure a man of his *zaraath?* Just know now and see that he is looking for a pretext against me."

fore the prophet who is in Samaria. *Jonathan* renders: My master would be fortunate were he to go before the prophet who is in Samaria.

And he came—i.e. *Naaman* came [*Rashi*].

and told his master—*the king of Aram* [*Rashi*].

5. **and he took in his possession**—*as a gift to the prophet.—Rashi*

and six thousand gold pieces—lit. *and six thousand gold* [*Rashi*]. *Jonathan* renders: six thousand dinars of gold. The meaning is probably the same.

6. **saying,** "And now, when this letter comes . . .—*The letter said to him, "And now, when this letter . . ."* [*Rashi*].

This was obviously the content of the letter, as is indicated in the following verse.

After the customary salutation, the letter continued, "And now . . ." [*Mezudath David*].

and you shall cure him of his zaraath—lit. and you shall gather him in from his zaraath. *Gathering, as applied to the mezora, is the expression of his cure, for when he is cured, he is gathered in among people, whereas during his illness, everyone stays away from him* [*Rashi*].

Not that the king of Aram expected the king of Israel to cure the *mezora,* but he expected him to send Naaman to Elisha who would cure him [*Mezudath David*].

7. **that he rent his garments**—out of fear [*Mezudath David*].

"Do I have power from God—after *Jonathan.* Lit. Am I God? *The 'he' at the beginning of the word* הַאֱלֹהִים*, is voweled with a 'pathah' to indicate that it is a question* [*Rashi*].

By tearing his clothes and lamenting [*Abarbanel* and *Mezudath David*] the king of Israel displayed his total disbelief in the prophet.

Alternatively, even though he knew that Elisha had performed miracles, he was ashamed to appear before him to beg him to cure

אֱלִישָׁע אִישׁ־הָאֱלֹהִים כִּי־קָרַע מֶלֶךְ־
יִשְׂרָאֵל אֶת־בְּגָדָיו וַיִּשְׁלַח אֶל־הַמֶּלֶךְ
לֵאמֹר לָמָּה קָרַעְתָּ בְּגָדֶיךָ יָבֹא־נָא
אֵלַי וְיֵדַע כִּי יֵשׁ נָבִיא בְּיִשְׂרָאֵל: ט וַיָּבֹא
נַעֲמָן בְּסוּסָו וּבְרִכְבּוֹ וַיַּעֲמֹד פֶּתַח־
הַבַּיִת לֶאֱלִישָׁע: י וַיִּשְׁלַח אֵלָיו אֱלִישָׁע
מַלְאָךְ לֵאמֹר הָלוֹךְ וְרָחַצְתָּ שֶׁבַע־
פְּעָמִים בַּיַּרְדֵּן וְיָשֹׁב בְּשָׂרְךָ לְךָ וּטְהָר:
יא וַיִּקְצֹף נַעֲמָן וַיֵּלַךְ וַיֹּאמֶר הִנֵּה אָמַרְתִּי
אֵלַי יֵצֵא יָצוֹא וְעָמַד וְקָרָא בְּשֵׁם־יְהוָה
אֱלֹהָיו וְהֵנִיף יָדוֹ אֶל־הַמָּקוֹם וְאָסַף

כַּד שְׁמַע אֱלִישָׁע נְבִיָּא
דַיְיָ אֲרֵי בְזַע מַלְכָּא
דְיִשְׂרָאֵל יַת לְבוּשׁוֹהִי
וּשְׁלַח לְוַת מַלְכָּא
לְמֵימַר לְמָא בְזַעְתָּא
לְבוּשָׁךְ יֵיתֵי כְעַן לְוָתִי
וְיִדַע דְאִית נְבִיָּא
בְּיִשְׂרָאֵל: ט וַאֲתָא נַעֲמָן
בְּסוּסוֹהִי וּבִרְתִיכוֹהִי
וְקָם בִּתְרַע בֵּיתָא
דֶאֱלִישָׁע: י וּשְׁלַח לְוָתֵיהּ
אֱלִישָׁע אִזְגַדָא לְמֵימַר
אֱזֵיל וּטְבוֹל שְׁבַע זִמְנִין
בְּיַרְדְּנָא וִיתוּב בִּסְרָךְ
לָךְ וְאִתַּדְּכֵי: יא וּרְגִיז
נַעֲמָן וַאֲזַל וַאֲמַר הָא
הֲוֵיתִי אֲמַר דִלְוָתִי יִפּוֹק
מִפַּק וִיקוּם וִיצַלֵּי בִּשְׁמָא
דַיְיָ אֱלָהֵיהּ וִירִים יְדֵיהּ
עַל אֲתַר בֵּית מַחֲתָא
ותתסי

בסוסיו קרי

רש"י

מבקש תואנה להתגרות בי: מתאנה. לשון עלילות (דברים כב יז): (יא) הנה אמרתי. סבור הייתי אלי יצא הנביא וידבר עמי ויראה את החולי: והניף ידו אל המקום.

רד"ק

שילחם עמי כי בשלום היה אז עמו: (ט) בסוסו. כן כתיב וקרי בסוסיו לשון רבים הכתוב אומר על עצמו שהיה הוא רוכב בסוסו והקרי הוא על הבאים עמו: (יא) והניף ידו אל המקום. ת"י וירים ידיה על אתר בית מחתא ותיתסי סגירותיה ופי׳

רלב"ג

הוא לי. ר"ל מבקש תואנה כדי שילחם עמי: (יא) והניף ידו אל

מנחת שי

(ט) בסוס״ו. בסוסיו קרי והכי איתא בירושלמי פרק חלק כענין גחזי:

מצודת דוד

להלחם בי: (ח) וידע. לא למענך ארפאו כ"א למען קדושת השם: (י) וישוב בשרך לך. כי ע"י הצרעת כזה משמן הבשר ומעתה ישוב לך הבשר ואף תהיה טהור מן הצרעת: (יא) אלי יצא וגו׳. חשבתי כי לכבודי יצא אלי ויעמוד לפני על רגליו כדרך הכבוד שעושים בני אדם לשרים הגדולים ובדבר הרפואה חשבתי שיקרא בשם ה׳ ויניף ידו אל מקום הצרעת להשפיע שם הרפואה ע"פ נס ובאופן זה יאסף

מצודת ציון

(י) מלאך. שליח: (יא) והניף. מל׳ הנפה והרמה:

"Go and immerse yourself—Since cold water usually aggravates such lesions, Elisha would show him God's greatness, that He would cure him in a completely unnatural manner [*Malbim, Abarbanel*].

seven times—Symbolic of the seven Noachic commandments. The prophet hinted that if he repent of his violation of these seven commandments, he would be cured [*Yalkut HaGershuni*].

and your flesh will be restored to you—The nature of the *mezora* was to become emaciated, for the body would not replace the flesh that had been worn away [*Abarbanel, Mezudath David*].

Ralbag explains that the limbs that had fallen off would replace themselves. Apparently, he identifies *zaraath* with leprosy.

11. **Now Naaman became incensed**—for the reasons given below [*Malbim*].

"Here I thought—I thought that *the prophet would come out and speak with me, and see the ailment* [*Rashi*].

I thought that the prophet wished

8. And it was when Elisha the man of God heard that the king
of Israel had rent his garments, that he sent to the king, saying,
"Why have you rent your garments? Let him come to me now,
and let him know that there is a prophet in Israel." 9. And
Naaman came with his horses and with his chariots, and he
stood at the doorway of Elisha's house. 10. And Elisha dispatched a messenger to him, saying, "Go and immerse yourself
seven times in the Jordan, and your flesh will be restored to
you, and you will become clean." 11. Now Naaman became
incensed, and he went away, and he said, "Here I thought that
he would come out to see me, and he would stand and call in
the name of YHVH his God, and he would raise his hand
toward the spot and cure the *mezora*."

8. **"Let him come to me now**—Elisha could have cured Naaman from afar. Yet, he ordered him to appear before him so that he would recognize that his cure was effected through the divine powers with which the prophet was endowed [*Malbim*].

and let him know that there is a prophet in Israel."—I am not curing him for your sake, but for the sake of sanctifying the Name of God [*Mezudath David*].

The presence of a prophet proves that God is with Israel [*Malbim*].

9. **And Elisha came with his horses**—This follows the *K'ri, b'susav.* The *K'thib,* however, is *b'suso,* with his horse. Elisha left his entourage at a distance and proceeded clandestinely to the prophet's dwelling. To avoid blatantly discrediting his idols by appealing to a prophet of the Jewish God, he came alone on his horse. Alternatively, his haughtiness and arrogance prevented him from publicizing to his soldiers and to all those around, his humility before the prophet [*K'li Y'kar*].

Alternatively, out of respect for the prophet, he came before him alone with but one horse, as a sign of humility [*Mid. Haseroth veetheroth, Wertheimer,* p. 300].

and he stood at the doorway—expecting Elisha to come out to him, as in v. 11 [*K'li Y'kar*].

10. **And Elisha dispatched a messenger**—Lest Naaman believe that Elisha had cured him through natural means or through sorcery, Elisha remained in his house and sent out a messenger. Thus, Naaman would learn that by merely obeying the prophet's orders, without any physical contact, his ailment would be cured [*Malbim*].

הַמְּצוֹרָע׃ יב הֲלֹא טוֹב אֲבָנָה וּפַרְפַּר נַהֲרוֹת דַּמֶּשֶׂק מִכֹּל מֵימֵי יִשְׂרָאֵל הֲלֹא־אֶרְחַץ בָּהֶם וְטָהָרְתִּי וַיִּפֶן וַיֵּלֶךְ בְּחֵמָה׃ יג וַיִּגְּשׁוּ עֲבָדָיו וַיְדַבְּרוּ אֵלָיו וַיֹּאמְרוּ אָבִי דָּבָר גָּדוֹל הַנָּבִיא דִּבֶּר אֵלֶיךָ הֲלוֹא תַעֲשֶׂה וְאַף כִּי־אָמַר אֵלֶיךָ רְחַץ וּטְהָר׃ יד וַיֵּרֶד וַיִּטְבֹּל בַּיַּרְדֵּן שֶׁבַע פְּעָמִים כִּדְבַר אִישׁ הָאֱלֹהִים וַיָּשָׁב בְּשָׂרוֹ כִּבְשַׂר נַעַר קָטֹן וַיִּטְהָר׃ טו וַיָּשָׁב אֶל־אִישׁ הָאֱלֹהִים הוּא וְכָל־מַחֲנֵהוּ וַיָּבֹא וַיַּעֲמֹד לְפָנָיו וַיֹּאמֶר הִנֵּה־נָא יָדַעְתִּי כִּי אֵין אֱלֹהִים בְּכָל־הָאָרֶץ

ת״א כי אין אלהים. עקידה שער פג:

וְתִתַּסִּי סְגִירוּתָא׃ יב הֲלָא טָבִין אֲמָנָא וּפַרְפַּר נַהְרֵי דְמַשֶּׂק מִכֹּל מֵי אַרְעָא דְיִשְׂרָאֵל הֲלָא אֶטְבּוֹל בְּהוֹן וְאֶתַּסֵּי וְאִתְפְּנִי וַאֲזַל בִּרְגַז׃ יג וּקְרִיבוּ עַבְדוֹהִי וּמַלִּילוּ עִמֵּיהּ וַאֲמָרוּ מָרִי אִלּוּ פִתְגָּמָא רַבָּא נְבִיָּא מַלֵּיל עִמָּךְ הֲלָא תַעֲבֵיד וְאַף אֲלָהֵין דַּאֲמַר לָךְ טְבוֹל וְאִתַּסֵּי׃ יד וּנְחַת וּטְבַל בְּיַרְדְּנָא שְׁבַע זִמְנִין כְּפִתְגָּמָא נְבִיָּא דַיָי וְתָב בִּסְרֵיהּ כִּבְסַר יְנִיק זְעֵיר וְאִתַּסֵּי׃ טו וְתָב לְוָת נְבִיָּא דַיָי הוּא וְכָל מַשְׁרִיתֵיהּ וַאֲתָא וְקָם קֳדָמוֹהִי וַאֲמַר הָא כְעַן יְדַעִית אֲרֵי לֵית אֱלָהָא קַיָּם בְּכָל

אמנה קרי

רד״ק

דאסף המצורע בשר המצורע כלומר מקום הצרעת: (יב) אבנה ופרפר. כתוב בבי״ת וקרי במ״ם והיה הנהר נקרא אבנה ואמנה עם בי״ת ועם מ״ם: הלא ארחץ בהם וטהרתי. אם בשבילה אטהר ארחץ בהם ואטהר. ואדוני אבי ז״ל פירש הלא בכל יום אני רוחץ: וטהרתי. בתמיה וכי אני טהור בעבור זה וכן פי׳ ר׳ יונה המדקדק: (יג) אבי. כמו אדוני וכת״י מרי וכן אבי ראה גם ראה: דבר גדול אליך. אם דבר גדול דבר אליך הנביא לעשות כדי שתרפא הלא תעשה כל שכן שדבר קטן דבר אליך שיש לך לעשותו שאמר אליך רחץ וטהר וכת״י אילו פתגמא רבא נביא מליל עמך: וטהר. ת״י ואתסי ר״ל כי רפואתו היא טהרתו: (טו) ברכה. מנחה וכן קח נא את ברכתי:

רש״י

הצרעת: (יג) אבי. כמו אדוני: הלא תעשה. וכי לא תעשהו אפילו אמר לך דבר טורח: ואף כי. קל וחומר

מנחת שי

(יב) אבנה. אמנה קרי:

רלב״ג

המקום. ר״ל אל המקום אשר הוא עובד הש״י: (יב) הלא ארחץ בהם וטהרתי. ר״ל הלא אני רוחץ בהם תמיד האם טהרתי מצרעתי מפני רחיצתי בהם: (יג) אבי דבר גדול הנביא דבר אליך. ר״ל אילו דבר אליך הנביא לעשות דבר גדול הלא תעשה כדי שתרפא אף כי אמר אליך שתרפא בדבר קל כזה והיא הרחיצה בירדן שבע פעמים שיש לך לעשות דבריו: (טו) קח נא ברכה מאת עבדך. ר״ל מנחה:

מצודת ציון

(יג) אבי. ר״ל שר וקורין כהאב על הבן: ואף כי. הוא כענין כל שכן:

מצודת דוד

המצורע: (יב) הלא טוב. ר״ל אבל באמרו רחץ וטהר נראה א״כ שאמר מדרך רפואה טבעית והלא בוודאי אין ממש בדבריו כי נהרות דמשק טובים המה מכל מימי ישראל והלא בתמידות אני רוחץ עצמי בהם וכי טהור אני בתמיה א״כ כמו שלא הועילה לי נהרות דמשק כן לא יועיל מי הירדן: (יג) דבר גדול. אם הנביא היה אומר לך דבר טורח גדול בכדי שתטהר הלא מהראוי היה שתעשה ומכ״ש שאמר לך דבר קל רחץ וכזה תטהר ומדוע א״כ תמנע לעשות: (יד) כבשר נער קטן. ר״ל לח ומזהיר: ויטהר. נעשה טהור מן הצרעת: (טו) ויעמוד לפניו. כעבד לפני האדון: ועתה. בעבור הרפואה וההודאה הזאת קח ממני מנחה:

sion, since he said to you to do an easy thing, viz. *immerse yourself and become clean* [*Rashi, Jonathan, Redak, Mezudath David*].

14. **like the flesh of a young lad**—clear and glistening [*Mezudath David*].

15. **and stood before him**—like a

12. Are not Amanah and Parpar, the rivers of Damascus, better than all the waters of Israel? Will I not immerse myself in them and become clean?" And he turned and went away in anger. 13. And his servants approached and spoke to him and said, "Master, if the prophet spoke to you to do a difficult thing, would you not do it? And surely since he said to you, 'Immerse yourself and become clean.'" 14. And he went down and immersed himself in the Jordan seven times according to the word of the man of God; and his flesh was restored like the flesh of a young lad, and he became clean. 15. And he returned to the man of God, he and his entire camp; and he came and stood before him; and he said, "Behold, now I know that there is no God in all the earth

to see me in order to direct his prayers to me, much as Isaac prayed opposite Rebecca. If he did not want to see me, he could have given the same instructions while I was at the king's palace [*Malbim*].

Alternatively, I thought that he would come out to me and stand before me out of respect for my position [*Abarbanel*].

and he would raise his hand toward the spot—of the *zaraath* [*Rashi*].

I thought that, in order to effect a cure, he would raise his hand toward the lesion and thereby cure me of the disease. Otherwise, why did he summon me to his dwelling? [*Malbim*].

Alternatively, he would raise his hand toward the place where he worships his God and cure me [*Ralbag*].

12. **Amanah**—also called Abanah, hence the *K'ri* and *K'thib* [*Redak*].

Will I not immerse myself in them and become clean?—If immersion will purify me, will not the immersion in Amanah and Parpar be just as effective? [*Redak*].

Alternatively, *Do I not immerse myself in them? And do I become clean?*—Do I not immerse myself daily in these rivers? How can immersion in the Jordan be more effective? [*Redak* quoting his father, *Ralbag, Mezudath David*].

13. **"Master**—lit. father [*Rashi* after *Jonathan, Redak, Mezudath Zion*].

would you not do it?—*Would you not do it even if he ordered you to do something requiring exertion?* [*Rashi*].

and surely—*by a fortiori conclu-*

כִּי אִם־בְּיִשְׂרָאֵל וְעַתָּה קַח־נָא בְרָכָה
מֵאֵת עַבְדֶּךָ: טז וַיֹּאמֶר חַי־יְהוָה אֲשֶׁר־
עָמַדְתִּי לְפָנָיו אִם־אֶקָּח וַיִּפְצַר־בּוֹ
לָקַחַת וַיְמָאֵן: יז וַיֹּאמֶר נַעֲמָן וָלֹא יֻתַּן
נָא לְעַבְדְּךָ מַשָּׂא צֶמֶד־פְּרָדִים אֲדָמָה
כִּי לוֹא־יַעֲשֶׂה עוֹד עַבְדְּךָ עֹלָה וָזֶבַח
לֵאלֹהִים אֲחֵרִים כִּי אִם־לַיהוָה:
יח לַדָּבָר הַזֶּה יִסְלַח יְהוָה לְעַבְדֶּךָ בְּבוֹא
אֲדֹנִי בֵית־רִמּוֹן לְהִשְׁתַּחֲוֺת שָׁמָּה
וְהוּא ׀ נִשְׁעָן עַל־יָדִי וְהִשְׁתַּחֲוֵיתִי בֵּית
רִמֹּן בְּהִשְׁתַּחֲוָיָתִי בֵּית רִמֹּן יִסְלַח־נָא*

בְּכָל אַרְעָא אֱלָהֵין
בְּיִשְׂרָאֵל וּכְעַן קַבֵּל כְּעַן
תִּקְרוּבְתָּא מִן עַבְדָּךְ:
טז וַאֲמַר קַיָּם הוּא יְיָ דִי
מְשַׁמֵּשְׁנָא קֳדָמוֹהִי אִם
אֲקַבֵּל וְאַתְקֵיף בֵּיהּ
לְקַבָּלָא וְלָא אֲבָא:
יז וַאֲמַר נַעֲמָן וְלָא
יִתְיְהֵיב כְּעַן לְעַבְדָּךְ
טְעוּן זוּג כּוּדְנָוָן מֵעֲפַר
אַדְמְתָא אֲרֵי לָא יַעְבֵּד
עוֹד עַבְדָּךְ עֲלָתָא וּדְבַח
לְטָעֲוַת עַמְמַיָּא אֱלָהֵין
לִשְׁמָא דַיְיָ: יח לְפִתְגָמָא
הָדֵין יִשְׁבּוֹק יְיָ לְעַבְדָּךְ
בְּמֵיעַל רִבּוֹנִי לְבֵית
רִמּוֹן לְמִסְגַּד תַּמָּן וְהוּא
סָמִיךְ עַל יְדִי וְאֶסְגּוֹד
בֵּית רִמּוֹן בְּמִסְגְּדִי בֵּית
רִמּוֹן

ת"א לדבר הזה. (שבועות לה): בית רמון. נדרים לז סנהדרין עד:

*כתיב ולא קרי

רש"י

שאמר לך דבר קל רחץ וטהר: (טו) ברכה. מנחת שלום של הקבלת פנים ששואל תלמיד או עבד בשלום הרב (שולד"ו בלע"ז): (טז) אם אקח. שדמי עבודת גלולים מעורבין בו: (יז) ולא. לשון בקשה לשון הלואי: יותן נא. מאדמה זו מארץ ישראל שהיא קדושה משא שני פרדים ואשאנה לעירי ואעשה אותה מזבח: (יח) בית רמון. שם עבודת גלולים: והשתחויתי. על כרחי כשנוה' אדוני והוא נשען על ידי:

רלב"ג

(יז) ולא יתן נא לעבדך משא צמד פרדים אדמה. רוצה לומר ניחא זה אחר שאין רצונך לקחת גמול על זה שעשית לי מן הטוב אך אשאל ממך שתתן לי דרך אוכל לעבוד בו השם יתברך שעשה לי זאת הטובה ולזה שאל מאלישע שיותן לו מביתו מה שיוכל לשאת שני פרדים מאדמה לבנות בה מזבח לה' כי לא יעבוד עוד אלהים אחרים כי אם הש"י לבדו ובקש לאלישע שיתפלל לש"י שיסלח לו לדבר הזה והוא השתחויתו בית רמון אשר הוא מוכרח בה מפני היות אדוניו נשען עליו בבאו

מצודת דוד

(טז) עמדתי לפניו. שאני רגיל לעמוד לפניו בתפלה: אם אקח. ר"ל עונש שבועה יהיה עלי אם אקח: (יז) ולא יותן. בבקשה אמר לתת לו אדמה מעפר א"י בשיעור משא שני פרדים לשאתם לארצו למלאות מהם מזבח לזבוח עליו לה' ולא רצה לקחת מבלי רשות הנביא: כי לא וגו'. כי מעתה לא אעשה עוד עולה: (יח) לדבר הזה. שאל מהנביא שיעתיר בעבורו לה' לסלוח לו על הדבר האמור בענין: והוא נשען על ידי. בעת בואי להשתחות ובע"כ אשתחוה גם

רד"ק

(טז) אשר עמדתי לפניו. שאני רגיל לעמוד ולהתפלל לפניו ולעבדו בלבי ושבועה זו למד מרבו אליהו ויש מפרשים אשר עמדתי לפניו על אליהו חי ה' וחי אליהו אשר עמדתי לפניו: (יז) ולא יתן נא לעבדך. שאלה וכן ולא ילך אתנו אמנון אחי: אדמה. לעשות מזבח בארצו וכי לא היה יכול הוא לקחתה בלא רשות אלא אמר שלא יעשה המזבח לה' בגזלה אם לא מרצון הנביא והמלך: (יח) בהשתחויתי. מלעיל בשני פשטין והוא שם יאמר ממנו השתחויה ובמשנה שלש עשרה השתחויות היו במקדש: יסלח ה' לעבדך. נא כתיב ולא קרי

מנחת שי

(יח) בהשתחויתי. כפי הנראה בחילופים שלנו לבן נפתלי מלרע בפשט א' לבד ולב"א שאנו סומכים עליו מלעיל בשני פשטין והפשט הראשון ראוי להיות על היו"ד וכ"כ רד"ק בפי' הפסוק מלעיל בשני פשטין והוא שם. ובעל מכלל יופי סעה שכתב שם כי הוא מלעיל בשני פשטין נראה מדבריו שהמלעיל מורה שהוא שם והדרבא איפכא מיבעי ליה כמ"ש במכלול דף קס"ו זה לשונו כי מלרע הוא שם בהשתחויתי בית רמון אך דבריו אלו סותרים למה שכתב בפירוש הפסוק כדלעיל ובכמה ספרי הדפוס וכתיבי יד מלאתיהו מלרע בפשט האחרון לבד וכגון דא לריכא רבא: בהשתחויתי בית רמון יסלח נא. נא כתיב ולא קרי ע"פ הגמרא פרק אין

מצודת ציון

(טו) ברכה. מנחה כמו קח נא את ברכתי (בראשית לג): (טז) ויפצר. ענין רבוי הדברים ופתוי: וימאן. לא רצה: (יז) ולא יתן. הוא מל' שאלה וכן ולא ילך אתנו אמנון (שמואל ב' יג): צמד. זוג: פרדים. הם הנולדים מן הסוס והחמור: (יח) בית רמון. בית עבודת

to your servant . . .? [*Targum Jonathan, Redak, Mezudath David*].

Redak points out that Naaman could have easily taken the wagon load of soil without asking permission. However, he wished to construct an altar that would be untainted by any theft or dishonesty [*Redak*].

18. **Beth-Rimmon**—*the name of a pagan deity* [*Rashi*].

I.e. Rimmon is the name of a

except in Israel. And now, accept a gift from your servant."
16. And he said, "As the Lord before Whom I have stood,
lives, I will not accept." And he urged him to accept, but he
refused. 17. And Naaman said, "Now, if only your servant be
given a load of earth as carried by a team of mules, for your servant will no longer offer up a burnt-offering or a sacrifice to
other deities, but to the Lord. 18. For this thing may the Lord
forgive your servant; when my master comes to Beth-Rimmon
to prostrate himself there, and he leans on my hand, and I will
prostrate myself in Beth-Rimmon; when I bow in Beth-
Rimmon, may the Lord

slave before his master [*Mezudath David*].

And now—as a token of thanksgiving for the miraculous cure you have effected [*Mezudath David*].

a gift—lit. a blessing, *a gift of peace, of greeting, when a disciple or a slave greets his master (sallud in O.F., a greeting)* [*Rashi*].

before Whom I have stood—i.e. before Whom I habitually stand in prayer. He learned this oath from Elijah. See I Kings 17:1, 18:15. Alternatively, As the Lord lives, and as my master Elijah, before whom I stood to minister . . . [*Redak*].

I will not accept—*for the price of idols was included in it—Rashi.*

I.e. money that had been used to purchase idols had been included in the silver and gold that Naaman offered to Elisha.

Alternatively, Elisha had cured Naaman in order to sanctify God's Name, not for worldly gain. Moreover, he had done nothing to accomplish the feat. It was performed by the Almighty Himself. Therefore, Elisha felt that he was not entitled to accept any gift for it [*Redak*].

and he urged him to accept—After Elisha had sworn not to accept a gift, why did Naaman urge him to accept? Did he expect him to violate his oath? Possibly, Naaman understood the oath to mean that Elisha would not take a gift if it was placed before him. If, however, it was pressed upon him, he did not swear to refuse it.

Alternatively, Elisha swore not to accept a gift for himself. Naaman urged him to accept it for his disciples. Elisha, however, refused it in all cases [*K'li Y'kar*].

17. **"Now, if only**—וְלֹא *an expression of a request, an expression of* הַלְוַאי [*Rashi*]. **"Now . . . be given**—*from this soil of the land of Israel, which is holy, a load of earth as carried by a team of mules, and I will carry it off to my city, and I will make it into an altar* [*Rashi*].

Others render: Will it not be given

יהוה לעבדך בדבר הזה: יט ויאמר לו לך לשלום וילך מאתו כברת ארץ:
כ ויאמר גיחזי נער אלישע איש־האלהים הנה חשך אדני את נעמן הארמי הזה מקחת מידו את אשר־הביא חי־יהוה כי־אם־רצתי אחריו ולקחתי מאתו מאומה: כא וירדף גיחזי אחרי נעמן ויראה נעמן רץ אחריו ויפל מעל המרכבה לקראתו ויאמר השלום: כב ויאמר שלום אדני שלחני לאמר הנה עתה זה באו אלי

תרגום

רמון ישבוק יי לעבדך בפתגמא הדין: יט ואמר ליה איזיל לשלם ואזל מלותיה כרוב ארעא: כ ואמר גיחזי תלמידא דאלישע נביא דיי הא מנע רבוני ית נעמן ארמאה הדין מלקבלא מניה ית דאיתי קים הוא יי אלהין ארהוט בתרוהי ואסב מניה מדעם: כא ורדף גיחזי בתר נעמן וחזא נעמן גברא רהיט בתרוהי ואתרכין מן רתיכא לקדמותיה ואמר השלם: כב ואמר שלם רבוני שלחני למימר הא כען דין אתו לותי תרין עולימין

ת"א כי אם רצתי. (סנהדרין כט):

רד"ק

נ"א מומה

כמו כן יסלח ה' לעבדך והכתוב רוצה לומר מעתה יסלח ה' לעבדך כלומר שאל מאל שיסלח לי: (יט) כברת ארץ. הוא שיעור מיל: (כ) ויאמר גיחזי. ויאמר בלבו:

רש"י

(יט) כברת ארץ. שם מדה של קרקע כמו למדי כרם (ארפינ"ט בלע"ז): (כ) מומה. חסר אל"ף לפי שהיתה לקיחה זו למום: (כא) ויפול. ואתרכין:

מנחת שי

בין המודר ועל פי המסורת וסימן נמכר ברוה: (כ) ולקחתי מאתו מאומה. במקרא גדולה כתוב מומה חסר אל"ף והוא כפירוש רש"י ז"ל שכתב מומה חסר אל"ף לפי שהיתה לקיחה זו למום עכ"ל. ובכל הספרים שבאו לידי כתיב מאומה באל"ף גם הגיה המדקדק בהגהת שרשים שרש מאם הבא לשון רש"י ואח"י אמר והני לא מצאתי כן בכל הספרים וגם אינו במנין מלות דלא מפקין אל"ף כמו שלתך ודומיהם עד כאן דבריו. ואע"פ שאין ראיה מוכחת לדברי רש"י ז"ל סמך לדבריו מצאתי ממדרש תנחומא וזה תוארו חי ה' כי אם רצתי אחריו ולקחתי מידו מאומה אמר הקדוש ברוך הוא אני אמרתי שלא יהא לך משלו מאומה ואתה הזרת ולקחת ממנו מאומה חייך מומו אתה נוטל שנאמר וצרעת נעמן תדבק בך. עוד מצאתי בויקרא רבה סדר מצורע פרק י"ז על י' דברים נגעים באים וכו' עד ועל חילול ה' מגיחזי ויאמר גיחזי נער אלישע וגו' מהו מאומה מן מומה דהות ביה פירש בנעמן ומנין שלקה בצרעת שנאמר וצרעת נעמן תדבק בך. ומאמר זה היתה נמי במדרש רבה פרשת נשא פ"ז בלישנא יתירה והכי איתמר התם ועל המחלל שם שמים זה גיחזי שכן אחר נעמן ליטול ממנו ממון שנאמר וירדף גיחזי אחרי נעמן וגו' אלישע קידש שמו של הקדוש ברוך הוא שלא רצה ליטול מנעמן כלום וגיחזי רדף אחריו ונשבע לו לשקר שלא הללו שישלח לו ממון נמצא זה מחלל שם שמים מה שקידש אלישע אמר לו הקדוש ברוך הוא לגיחזי רשע אתה אמרת חי ה' כי אם רצתי אחריו ולקחתי מאתו מאומה נשבעת בשמי כדי לחלל חייך מאומה אמרת ומומו אתה נוטל וצרעת נעמן תדבק בך ע"כ. ומתוך כל מאמרים אלו גמרתי אומר שבספר של רש"י היה כתוב מומה וקרי מאומה וסברתו היא שגם חכמינו ז"ל דרשוהו כן וכן ראיתי לבעל כלי יקר שכתב נראה כי פשוט הוא שהם ז"ל דרשו קרי וכתיב דקרינן מאומה וכתיב מומה לשון מום ע"כ. אך לפי דעתי אין זה מוכח בדברי רבותינו ז"ל אדרבא נוכל לקיים גירסתם כספרים שלנו אבל דרשו מאומה לשון מום כמו שדרשו גם כן בב"ר פ' כ"ו על פסוק אל תעש לו מאומה אל תעש לו מומה ובויקרא רבה פ' ל"ד בענין הצדקה א"ל הקב"ה לא דייך שלא נתת לו משלך מאומה אלא במה שנתתי לו אתה מכניס לו עין רעה לפיכך והוליד בן ואין בידו מאומה מן כל מה דהוא ליה לא ישבוק לבריה ונסיב מומה לנפשיה ויש להם ז"ל על מה שיסמוכו מאחרי קראי דכתיבין מאום למערבאי וקרי ומיתפרשן מום והלא הן ואחר עיני הלך לבי ובכפי דבק מאום (איוב ל"א) וחברו ילדים אשר אין בהם כל מאום בריש

רלב"ג

בית רמון להשתחוות: (יט) ויאמר לו לך לשלום. קבל הכתוב אך המובן מזה שנתן לו בקשתו במה שבקש לו לעבוד את השם יתברך: וילך מאתו כברת ארץ. היא הארץ הנעבדת אשר סביב העיר והרצון בו שלא הרחיק מן העיר כי לא היה בינו ובין העיר כי אם שדות

מצודת ציון

גלולים שבמה רמון: (יט) כברת. הוא מיל וכן כברת ארץ (בראשית מח): (כ) חשך. מנע כמו ולא חשכת (שם כב): (כא) ויפול. ענין הטיה כמו ותפול מעל הגמל (שם כד): השלום. בה"א השאלה:

מצודת דוד

אני עמו: בהשתחויתי. ובדבר ההשתחואה ההוא יסלח לי ה': (כ) ויאמר. חשב בלבו: הנה חשך. ר"ל מנע את נעמן מליתן הואיל ומנע עצמו מקחת מידו: חי ה'. כאומר הריני נשבע שלא

Rabbah 17, *Num. Rabbah* 7, *Tan. Tazria* 2. There is, however, no evidence that the word is written without an "aleph" [*Minhath Shai*].

21. **and he leaned over**—*Jonathan.* Lit. and he fell [*Rashi*].

forgive your servant for this thing." 19. And he said to him, "Go in peace"; and he went some distance away from him. 20. And Gehazi, the servant of Elisha the man of God, thought, "Here my master has stopped Naaman, this Aramean, from giving, by not taking from his hand what he brought. As the Lord lives, I will run after him and take something from him." 21. And Gehazi chased after Naaman; and Naaman saw him running after him, and he leaned over off the chariot toward him, and said, "Is all well?" 22. And he said, "All is well. My master sent me, saying, "Here, just now

pagan deity. Its temple was known as Beth-Rimmon, the house of Rimmon.

and I will prostrate myself—*against my will when my master bows, since he leans on my hand* [*Rashi*].

19. **And he said to him,**—*"Go in peace"*—Elisha assured him that he would be absolved of sin. Since Naaman did not convert to Judaism, he was not required to sacrifice his life rather than worship idols. Noachites are not enjoined to sanctify God's Name by sacrificing their lives for His commandments. [*San.* 74b, 75a; *Rambam,* Kings 10:2].

some distance—Heb. *kivrath eretz the name of a land measure, like* "(Is. 5:10) *ten acres of vineyard." (arpent in French),* an old French measure of land, equivalent to about an acre [*Rashi*].

Redak defines this as a *mil,* a measure equal to two thousand cubits, between three thousand and four thousand feet. *Rashi* Gen. 48:7, quotes *R. Moshe Hadarshan* as having expressed this opinion. *Rashi,* Gen. 35:16, defines it as a parasang, four *mils.* He also quotes *Onkelos* who defines it as the amount of ground that is plowed in one day. *Rashi* himself defines it as a "plowshare" of land, an arbitrary measure used in ancient times. *Ramban* ad loc. claims that it is even less than a *mil,* judging from the distance from Rachel's tomb to the town of Bethlehem, which the Torah describes as *kivrath eretz.*

20. **something**—Heb. מאומה, *The "aleph" is missing, since this taking was responsible for his being stricken with a blemish.* מום in Heb—*Rashi.* See below v. 27. Apparently, in *Rashi's* edition of Kings, there was no "aleph" in the word. It was written מוּמָה. In all prevalent editions, however, the "aleph" is found.

The comparison of the word *m'umah* to *mum* is found in *Lev.*

שני־נערים מהר אפרים מבני הנביאים תנה־נא להם ככר־כסף ושתי חלפות בגדים׃ כג ויאמר נעמן הואל קח ככרים ויפרץ־בו ויצר ככרים כסף בשני חרטים ושתי חלפות בגדים ויתן אל־שני נעריו וישאו לפניו׃ כד ויבא אל־העפל ויקח מידם ויפקד בבית וישלח את־האנשים וילכו׃ כה והוא־בא ויעמד אל־אדניו ויאמר אליו אלישע מא׳ן

עולימין מטורא דבית אפרים מתלמידי נבייא הב כען להון ככרא דכספא ותרין אצטלון דלבושא: כג ואמר נעמן שרי סב תרתין ככרין ואתקיף ביה וצר תרתין ככרין דכסף בתרין פלדסין ותרין אצטלון דלבושין ויהב לתרין עולימוהי ונסיבו קדמוהי: כד ועל לאתר כסי ונסיב מידהון ופקיד בביתא ושלח ית גבריא ואזלו: כה והוא אתא וקם קדם רבוניה ואמר ליה אלישע מנן

את

ת״א הואל קח ככרים. סוטה מז סנהדרין קז ערכין ט:

מאין קרי

רש״י

(כג) הואל. השבע שלהך: בשני חרטים. מיני בגדים וסודרין כמו המטפחות והחריטים (ישעיה ג כב) כך חברו מנחם אבל יונתן תרגם זה פלדסין ואת שבספר ישעיה תרגם מחכיא. והפותרין אומרין בשני הריטי׳ בשני כיסין ארוכים (פירדיי״ש בלע״ז): אל שני נעריו. של נעמן: וישאו לפניו. לפני גחזי: (כד) ויבא אל העופל. תרגם יונתן לאתר כסי: ויקח מידם. מיד שני נערי נעמן: וישלח את האנשי׳.

רד״ק

(כג) ככרים כסף. השוא אשר בכ״ף הוא סי׳ חסמיכות: בשני חריטים. קשר בשני כיסים ויונתן תרגם פלדסין וכן תרגם סדינים פלדסין: (כד) אל העופל. מקום גבוה שבו היה בית כמו עופל ובחן שהוא מקום גבוה וי״ת לאתר כסי תרגם אותו מן עפולים שפירשו תחתוניות שהוא מקום נסתר: ויפקד בבית. הפקיד הכסף והבגדים שם שרצה להעלים מאלישע וזה לבדו בענין פקדון מן הקל: (כה) מאן גחזי. מאן כתיב בלא יו״ד והקרי מאין ושניהם ענין אחד כי מאן כמו אן הלכתם אנה ואנה אילך ואילך:

רלב״ג

העיר וכרמיה וגניס: (כג) ויצר ככרים כסף בשני הריטים. רוצה לומר שצרר שני ככרים של כסף בשני חריטים או בשתי אמתחות: (כד) ויבא אל העופל ויקח מידם. הנה העופל הוא מקום גבוהה והיה שם בית חזק ולזה שם כספו שם כדי שיהיה יותר נשמר: ויפקוד בבית. אחשוב שהרצון בזה שכבר מנה בהיותו בבית סך המטבע שיש באלו ההריטים כאלו תאמר סך הדינרין או הסלעים או המעות או יהיה מענין פקדון ואם הוא מהקל והרצון בו שהפקידו בביתו או יהיה מענין פקידות והרצון בו שמנה שם איש או אנשים יקנו לו בכסף ההוא בגדים וזיתים וכרמים וצאן ובקר ועבדים ושפחות ולזה אמר לו אלישע העת לקחת את הכסף ולקחת הבגדים וזיתים וכרמים וצאן ובקר ועבדים ושפחות: (כה) מאן גחזי. כתוב וקרי מאין והרצון בו מאין בא והפסר כי אם לא היה משקר לו היה לוקח בחטא שחטא דכך אחרת כאלו תאמר שישיב לו מה שלקח באופן

מנחת שי

דיאלו ואינון מן נ״ת מלין דנסבין אלף באמצעות תיבותא ולא קריין וסימנהון במסרה רבתא ובחילופי המקרא שבין מערבאי למדנחאי כתוב בלוחו של איוב דלמדנחאי מאומה כתיב מום קרי. אחר כל אלה הדברים מצאתי סיוע לרש״י מהירושלמי דערק חלק דאמרינן התם אתא גיחזי ואמר חי ה׳ כי אם רצתי אחריו ולקחתי מאתו מאומה מומה כתיב ע״כ. אך בעל יפה מראה כתב מומה כתיב לא מצאתי כן בשום ספר ונראה שהוא כמו קרי ביה מומה דמשום דק״ל שלא מצינו לשון מאומה על מציאות דבר אלא על העדרו לא תתן לו מאומה. ולא ידע אתו מאומה. כי לא מצאתם בידי מאומה. להכי קאמר דה״ל כאילו כתיב מומה שרמ ביקח מומו דהיינו הלרעת: (כג) קח ככרים. חד מאל״פא ביתא מן ב׳ ב׳ לא נסבין וא״ו בריש תיבותא ומטעין בהון וסימן במסרה רבתא: ככרים כסף. הכ״ף בשוא מפני הסמיכות: (כה) מא״ן. מאין קרי: אנה ואנה. במקצת ספרי הדפוס הנו״ן בקמ״ץ בשתי המלות וטעות הוא כי בכל ספרים המדוייקים

מצודת דוד

יהיה כן כי אם ארוץ אחריו ואקח ממנו דבר מה: (כג) הואל. כי חפץ היה להרבות במנחה להנביא: ויפרץ בו. נעמן הפציר בגחזי לקחת ככרים ובתחילה מיאן גחזי לבל ירגיש נעמן שבא מדעת עצמו: ויצר. נעמן קשר ככרים וכו׳ ונתנם לעבדיו לשהם ישאו אותם: (כד) אל העופל. אל המגדל וכן עופל ובחן (ישעיה ל״ב). או כמו כאופל בחל״ם וכ״ל למקום חושך לבל יראה מי: ויפקד. הכניס בבית שמור: את האנשים. נערי נעמן: (כה) מאין. מאיכן תבוא:

מצודת ציון

(כג) הואל. רצה כמו הואל נא ולך (לקמן ו): ויפרץ. הוא הפוך מן ויפצר והיא היא: ויצר. וקשר כמו צור תעודה (ישעיה ח): חריטים. מין כיסים וכן והמטפחות והחריטים (שם ג): (כה) אנה ואנה. לפה ולפה:

Elisha indeed accused Gehazi of taking. See v. 26. The root פקד can have any of these meanings.

and he dismissed the men—*lest Elisha see them* [*Rashi*].

Malbim maintains that Naaman suspected Gehazi of taking the gifts for himself. He, therefore, sent two men to accompany him to Elisha, to see whether he gave them over to him. Gehazi, fearing that Elisha would see Naaman's servants,

two youths have come to me from Mt. Ephraim, of the disciples of the prophets. Please give them a talent of silver and two suits of clothing. 23. And Naaman said, "Please take two talents. And he urged him and he tied two talents of silver in two pockets, and two suits of clothing. And he gave his two servants, and they carried them before him. 24. And he came to a secret place, and he took [them] from their hands, and he deposited them in the house. And he dismissed the men, and they went away. 25. And he came and stood before his master, and Elisha said to him,

22. **Please give them**—Since Elisha had been adamant in his refusal to accept gifts from Naaman, even to the extent of swearing to that effect, Gehazi could not expect Naaman to believe that Elisha had altered his position. He had to invent two youths who had recently joined Elisha's academy, and to reinterpret Elisha's refusal as referring only to gifts for his own personal use, not to gifts for his disciples [*Malbim*]. See Comm. Dig. v. 16.

23. **"Please**—Consent to take two talents. Naaman sought to give Elisha as large a gift as possible [*Mezudath David* after *Jonathan*].

Rashi, however, explains הוֹאֵל as *swear that he sent you* [*Rashi* from *Midrash Samuel* 15]. See also *Num. Rabbah* 7:5. Apparently, Naaman did not believe Gehazi and insisted that he swear before granting his request.

in two pockets—Heb. חֲרִטִים *types of garments and kerchiefs,* like (Is. 3:22) *and the kerchiefs and the "haritim." Menahem classified it thus (p. 94). Jonathan, however, translated this as "paldesin," sheets* (See *Targum* Jud. 14:12), *and the one in the book of Isaiah as "mahachaia," a plate covering the genitals. The exegetes say that* בִּשְׁנֵי חֲרִטִים, means *"in two long pockets" brids in O.F.* [*Rashi*].

his two servants—i.e. *Naaman's*—*Rashi.*

and they carried them before him—*before Gehazi* [*Rashi*].

23. **And he came to a secret place**—*Jonathan renders: to a hidden place* [*Rashi*].

Redak derives this from *afolim,* hemorrhoids, an affliction of the hidden regions of the body. He suggests also that it may mean a tower, as in Is. 32:14.

and he took them from their hands—*from the hands of Naaman's two servants* [*Rashi*].

and he deposited them in the house—to conceal them from Elisha [*Redak*].

Ralbag suggests that he *counted* them in the house, or he *appointed* people in the house to take the money and buy various items, as

גֵּחֲזִי וַיֹּאמֶר לֹא־הָלַךְ עַבְדְּךָ אָנֶה וָאָנָה:
כו וַיֹּאמֶר אֵלָיו לֹא־לִבִּי הָלַךְ כַּאֲשֶׁר
הָפַךְ־אִישׁ מֵעַל מֶרְכַּבְתּוֹ לִקְרָאתֶךָ
הַעֵת לָקַחַת אֶת־הַכֶּסֶף וְלָקַחַת בְּגָדִים
וְזֵיתִים וּכְרָמִים וְצֹאן וּבָקָר וַעֲבָדִים
וּשְׁפָחוֹת: כז וְצָרַעַת נַעֲמָן תִּדְבַּק־בְּךָ
וּבְזַרְעֲךָ לְעוֹלָם וַיֵּצֵא מִלְּפָנָיו מְצֹרָע
כַּשָּׁלֶג: ו א וַיֹּאמְרוּ בְנֵי־הַנְּבִיאִים אֶל־
אֱלִישָׁע הִנֵּה־נָא הַמָּקוֹם אֲשֶׁר אֲנַחְנוּ
יֹשְׁבִים שָׁם לְפָנֶיךָ צַר מִמֶּנּוּ: ב נֵלְכָה־
נָּא עַד־הַיַּרְדֵּן וְנִקְחָה מִשָּׁם אִישׁ קוֹרָה

תרגום

אַתְּ אָתֵי גֵיחֲזִי וַאֲמַר לָא אֲזַל עַבְדָּךְ לְכָא וּלְכָא: כו וַאֲמַר לֵיהּ בְּרוּחַ נְבוּאָה אִתְחֲזָא לִי כַּד אִתְהַפִּיךְ גַּבְרָא מֵעַל רְתִיכֵיהּ לְקַדָּמוּתָךְ הַשְׁעָה הִיא לָךְ דְּנַסֵיבְתָּא כַּסְפָּא וּנְסֵיבְתָּא לְבוּשַׁיָא נַחֲשַׁבְתָּא בְּלִבָּךְ לְמִקְנֵי זֵיתִין וּכְרָמִין וְעָאן וְתוֹרִין וְעַבְדִין וְאַמְהָן: כז וּסְגִירוּת נַעֲמָן תִּדְבַּק בָּךְ וּבִבְנָךְ לְעָלַם וּנְפַק מִן קֳדָמוֹהִי חִוָּר כְּתַלְגָא: א וַאֲמַרוּ תַלְמִידֵי נְבִיַיָא לֶאֱלִישָׁע הָא כְעַן אַתְרָא דִי אֲנַחְנָא יָתְבִין תַּמָּן קֳדָמָךְ עַק לָנָא: ב נֵיזֵל כְּעַן עַד יַרְדְּנָא וְנִסַּב מִתַּמָּן גְּבַר כְּשׁוּרָא חֲדָא ונעביד

ת"א לא לבי הלך. שם. סוטה מז: ולרעת נעמן. שם שם ערכין טז זוהר תזריע (סנהדרין כט): ויאמרו בני הנביאים. כתובה שם (סנהדרין שם):

רד"ק

(כו) לא לבי הלך. בתמיה כלומר כי לבי ומחשבתי היה עמך בלכתך וידעתי מה שהלכת ועשית: העת. פתח הה"א והיא לתמיה כלומר אם עת שהלכת לקחת לא ידעתי: וזיתים וכרמים. כתרגומו וחשבתא בלבך למקני זיתין וכרמין ועאן ותורין וגו' כלומר חשבת מן הכסף לקנות לך כל זה: (כז) וצרעת נעמן. הוי"ו כמו הווי"ן הנוספים שפירשנו או יהיה דבר נסתר עמו ופירושו הכסף נתון לך והצרעת: ובזרעך לעולם. לא אמר בכל הבנים שיצאו ממנו עד עולם אלא באותן בנים שהיו לו שתדבק הצרעת בו ובהם לעולם שלא ירפאו ממנה ואם גחזי חטא בניו מה חטאו אלא מלמד שבניו ידעו בדבר וכבר הרחבנו בזה הענין בספר שמואל בקללה שקלל דוד ליואב: (א) צר ממנו. שהיו יושבים שם בדוחק כ"כ היו רבים התלמידים ואמרו רז"ל כי כאשר גורש גחזי מלפני אלישע אז רבו התלמידים כי גחזי היה רע להם והיו רבי' יראי' לבא לפני אלישע מפני רעת גחזי שהיה דוחה אותם וכשנפרד גחזי ממנו

רש"י

שלא יראה אותם אלישע: (כו) העת לקחת את הכסף. להתעשר ולקחת ממנו בגדים וזיתים וגו':

ו (א) ויאמרו בני הנביאים. נסים שנעשו לו מסדר והילך. רבותינו אמרו מכאן שהיה גיחזי דוחה התלמידים מלפניו. כשנטרד באו תלמידים רבים ונדחק

מנחת שי

אָנֶה וְאָנָה הראשון הנו"ן בסגול וכן לא תלא מאם ולא נה והלכת אָנֶה ולא נה (מלכים א' ב') והם שלשה במסורת: (כז) תדבק בך. התי"ו במאריך: ובזרעך. הוא"ו במאריך במדוייקים: ו (ב) נלכה נא. מאריך בנו"ן בנסחאות כתובי יד ודפוסים ישנים:

רלב"ג

שהתבאר לנעמן שלא היה מאלישע הדבר הזה אך גחזי עשאו מעצמו אך מפני שכחש לו והוסיף בעונו לקח ממנו זאת הנקמה: (כו) לא לבי הלך כאשר הפך איש מעל מרכבתו וגו'. ר"ל לא הלך ממני לבי שיעל' ממני מה שעשי' כאשר הפך איש מעל מרכבתו לקראתך והוא נעמן כי בודאי אני יודע כל זה ולזה נתן ענשו ע"ז שתדבק בו לרעת נעמן ובזרעו לעולם ר"ל כל ימיהם או עד היובל על דרך ועבדו לעולם: (א) צר ממנו. ר"ל דחוק ממנו וידמה כי מפני זה סמך זה לדבר גחזי להעי' כי לרוע תכונ' גחזי לא היו התלמידים רבים מאד

מצודת ציון

ו (ב) קורה. ענין עץ כמו קורות בתינו ארזים (שה"ש א):

מצודת דוד

(כו) לא לבי הלך. ר"ל עם שאני ישבתי פה וכי לא הלך לבי עמך כאשר הפך איש וגו': העת. וכי בעת הזאת ראוי לקבל ממנו את הכסף הלא באה היא בדבר הנס וכי ראוי להנות מן הנס במקום שאין דחק: ולקחת בגדים. ואפי' אם היה נותן לך בגדים וזיתים וגו' לא היה לך לקחת עם שהוא עובר כך: (כז) וצרעת. יחסר לאמית הדברים וכאומר הכסף נתון לך וגם הצרעת: כשלג. כי הצרעת לבנה היא וכמ"ש ואם בהרת לבנה (ויקרא י"ג): ו (א) המקום. בית מדרשם: צר ממנו. דחוק הוא להחזיק את כולנו: (ב) משם.

them [*Rashi* from *San.* 107b].

Ralbag and *Abarbanel* maintain that Gehazi did not actually reject the pupils. Because of his undesirable traits, however, many pupils were reluctant to enter the academy. Now, that Gehazi had been banished, many more pupils came to study under Elisha's tutelage.

2. **to the Jordan**—the place of Elijah's ascent to heaven. The disciples decided to relocate their study hall at that holy site and asked Elisha for his consent [*Abarbanel*].

"Where are you coming from, Gehazi?" And he said, "Your servant has gone neither here nor there." 26. And he said to him, "Did my heart not go when a man turned around off his chariot toward you? Is it time to take the silver, and to buy clothing and olive trees and vineyards and sheep and cattle and slaves and maidservants? 27. Now Naaman's *zaraath* shall cling to you and to your children forever." And he went away from before him, stricken with *zaraath,* [white] as snow.

6

1. And the disciples of the prophets said to Elisha, "Behold now the place where we are sitting before you is too narrow for us. 2. Let us go now to the Jordan and take from there each man one beam,

stopped at a tower and went through the motions of giving orders to servants of the house. Naaman's servants assumed that this was Elisha's academy, over which Gehazi was the manager. They, therefore, left him and returned to their master.

25. **"Where are you coming from, Gehazi?"**—Elisha wished to give him the opportunity to confess his sin. Had Gehazi done so, Elisha would probably have ordered him to return the gifts to Naaman, and to explain that he had requested and accepted them without his master's knowledge. Since he lied, however, Elisha punished him with *zaraath* [*Ralbag*].

26. **"Did my heart not go**—Do you think that I did not follow you with my thoughts when a man turned around off his chariot to you? [*Redak, Mezudath David*].

Jonathan renders: With the spirit of prophecy it was told to me . . .

Is it time to take the silver—*to become wealthy and to buy with it clothing and olive trees . . .* [*Rashi, Redak*].*

27. **to your children**—those who were with him and were aware of his activities [*Redak*].

forever—I.e. they will never be cured. This does not mean that later generations were to suffer with this affliction [*Redak*].

1. **And the disciples of the prophets said**—*He continues to enumerate the miracles that were performed for him* (sic). *Our Sages deduced from here that Gehazi would reject the pupils from before him, and when he was banished, many pupils came, and the place became too cramped for*

אחת ונעשה־לנו שם מקום לשבת
שם ויאמר לכו: ג ויאמר האחד הואל
נא ולך את־עבדיך ויאמר אני אלך:
ד וילך אתם ויבאו הירדנה ויגזרו
העצים: ה ויהי האחד מפיל הקורה
ואת־הברזל נפל אל־המים ויצעק
ויאמר אהה אדני והוא שאול: ו ויאמר
איש־האלהים אנה נפל ויראהו את־
המקום ויקצב־עץ וישלך שמה ויצף
הברזל: ז ויאמר הרם לך וישלח ידו

ונעביד לנא תמן אתרא
למתב תמן ואמר
אזילו: ג נאמר חד שרי
כען ואזיל עם עבדך
ואמר אנא איזיל: ד ואזל
עמהון ואתו לירדנא
וקצו אעיא: ה והוה חד
מחי בשיריתא ואשתליף
ברזלא ונפל למיא וצוח
ואמר בבעו רבוני והוא
משאל שאילתיה:
ו ואמר נביא דיי אן נפל
ואחזיה ית אתרא וקץ
אעא ורמא לתמן וקפא
ברזלא: ז ואמר טול לך
ואושיט ידיה ונסביה
ומלכא

ת"א מפיל הקורה. סוטה יג:

רש"י

המקום מהם: (ג) הואל. התרצה: (ה) ואת הברזל. הנסורת: והוא שאול. שאלתיו ואין לי ממה לשלם: (ו) ויצף. צף על המים:

רד"ק

רבו התלמידים עד שצר המקום להם שהיו יושבין בו מתחלה: (ה) ואת הברזל נפל אל המים. אין מלת את נופלת על הפועל כאשר חשבו רבי' ופירושו ואת הברזל ועם הברזל הקורה עם הברזל נפל במים: והוא שאול. אם היה שלי לא הייתי חושש כ"כ אלא שאלתיו ואלי לשלמו: (ו) ויקצב עץ. למה לא השליך שם עץ שהיה יד הברזל מתחלה למה הוצרך לקצוב עץ ונראה כי הנסים בדבר חדש יעשו וכן צלוחית חדשה. ויקצוב עץ להיותו יד הברזל שנפל ונכנס העץ בנקב הברזל שנכנס בו היד וצף הברזל עם ידו לפיכך אמר ויקצב שפירושו כריתת העץ במדה שצריך כמו מדה אחת וקצב אחת: ויצף. פועל עומד אשר הציף את מי ים סוף פועל יוצא ויש לפרש ויצף פוע' יוצא

רלב"ג

אך כאשר נפרד גחזי מאלישע אז רבו התלמידים: (ב) ונעשה לנו שם מקום לשבת שם. ר"ל שיבנו מהקורות האלו בית או אהל כשיעשו מקלתם עמודים או יבנו הכותלים מאבן ויקרו הבית באלו הקורות: (ג) הואל נא ולך את עבדיך. אמר זה כדי שיהיה להם לעזר במתחדש להם שם: (ה) ויהי האחד מפיל את הקורה והברזל נפל אל המים. ר"ל שבעת הכותו בגרזן להפיל הקורה נשל הברזל מיד הגרזן ונפל במי הירדן וצעק ואמר אהה אדני זה הגרזן לא היה שלי אך שאלתיהו מאחר: (ו) ויקצב עץ וישלך שמה ויצף הברזל. ר"ל שכבר חתך ותקנו במדה שיוכל להכנס בנקב הברזל ויהיה לו כמו יד והנה היה המופת הזה שכאשר השליכו שמה נכנס בנקב הברזל ונתקיים בו הברזל ולפי שכבר הושרש בדבר המופתים מצד העיון ומצד דברי רז"ל כמו שבארנו בששי מספר מלחמות ה' שלא יתחדש בהם דבר חדש כאילו תאמר עליית הברזל למעלה במים והוא ברזל או כדת העץ למטה במים והוא עץ בלתי ראוי שיצלול במים והנה הרלון באמרו וישלך שמה שכבר השליך שם העץ בכח כדי שירד מפני זאת התנועה ההכרחית והנה היה העץ בשיעור שהיה יכול לגלות כבדו' הברזל וליפהו עמו על המים ולזה הולרך שיהיה העץ גדול ולא הספי' לו גודל יד הברזל להשליכו שם ואחך מפני זה עץ גדול אך המופת היה כמו שזכרנו היותו נכנס בנקב הברזל בהשליכו אותו במים:

מנחת שי

(ז) הרם לך. הרי"ש בסגול והמלה מלעיל כמו שבא במסורת פרשת בשלח על פסוק ואתה הרם את מטך והוא ג"כ בשטה חדא דכל חד וחד מלעיל ולית דכותיה וסימן

מצודת דוד

מן היער הסמוך אל הירדן: (ה) מפיל הקורה. אל הירדן להשיטה אל מקום הבנין: ואת הברזל. הקורה נפל אל המים ועם הברזל הוא הגרזן: אהה. הוא ענין ל' לעקת יללה: והוא שאול. הגרזן שאולה בידי ואין לי לשלם מחירו: (ו) אנה נפל. איה המקום שנפל בה: ויקצב. חתך חתיכת עץ: (ז) הרם לך. הגבה לך את הברזל:

מצודת ציון

(ג) הואל. רצה: (ד) ויגזרו. ענין חתוך כמו גזרו את הילד (מלכים א ג): (ו) ויקצב. ענין כריתה וחתוך וכן כעדר הקצובות (שה"ש ד): ויצף. שט למעלה כמו אשר הציף (דברים יא):

floated—*floated on the water* [*Rashi*].

Others suggest: and he (the prophet) *caused* the axe blade to float [*Redak*].

Alternatively, it (the wood) *caused*

and let us make a place for ourselves to sit there." And he said,
"Go." 3. And one said, "Please be willing to go with your servants." And he said, "I will go." 4. And he went with them,
and they came to the Jordan, and cut down the trees. 5. One
was casting down the beam, and with the axe blade it fell into
the water. He cried out and said, "Alas, master, it is borrowed!" 6. And the man of God said to him, "Where did it
fall?" And he showed him the spot, and he cut off a piece of
wood and threw it there, and the axe blade floated. 7. And he
said, "Pick it up for yourself." And he stretched out his hand
and took it.

3. **be willing**—Heb. הואל [*Rashi*].

This word appears above 5:23, where *Rashi* interprets it as "swear." Here, however, this interpretation is inappropriate.

5. **casting down**—into the Jordan to float it to its destination [*Mezudath David*].

and with the axe blade—lit. the iron. We have followed the vast majority of commentaries in our translation. *Rashi,* however, renders: *the saw,* according to *Shem Ephraim*'s emendation.

it is borrowed—*I borrowed it, and I have not the wherewithal to pay* [*Rashi*].

Were it mine, I would not care so much, but I borrowed it and will have to pay for it [*Redak*].

6. **and he cut off a piece of wood**—the size of an axe handle, to fit into the hole of the axe head. He did not use the original handle because miracles are usually performed with new things, as above 2:20 [*Redak*].

Ralbag explains that he threw a large piece of wood into the water, so that it would sink momentarily and then bring up the sunken axe blade. The axe handle was too light and too small to accomplish either.

Abarbanel rejects the supposition that the wood had to fit into the axe blade to bring it up. It is mentioned nowhere in the text that the wood floated up. Rather, the prophet wished to demonstrate that nature is no power of its own. It is merely a tool of God. When he wills it, a light piece of wood can sink, and a heavy piece of iron can float. He, therefore, cast a small piece of wood into the Jordan. It sank to the bottom as though summoning the axe blade to the top.

וַיִּקָּחֵהוּ׃ ח וּמֶלֶךְ אֲרָם הָיָה נִלְחָם בְּיִשְׂרָאֵל וַיִּוָּעַץ אֶל־עֲבָדָיו לֵאמֹר אֶל־מְקוֹם פְּלֹנִי אַלְמֹנִי תַּחֲנֹתִי׃ ט וַיִּשְׁלַח אִישׁ הָאֱלֹהִים אֶל־מֶלֶךְ יִשְׂרָאֵל לֵאמֹר הִשָּׁמֶר מֵעֲבֹר הַמָּקוֹם הַזֶּה כִּי־שָׁם אֲרָם נְחִתִּים׃ י וַיִּשְׁלַח מֶלֶךְ יִשְׂרָאֵל אֶל־הַמָּקוֹם אֲשֶׁר אָמַר־לוֹ אִישׁ־הָאֱלֹהִים וְהִזְהִירֹה וְנִשְׁמַר שָׁם לֹא אַחַת וְלֹא שְׁתָּיִם׃ יא וַיִּסָּעֵר לֵב מֶלֶךְ־אֲרָם עַל־הַדָּבָר הַזֶּה וַיִּקְרָא אֶל־עֲבָדָיו

ח ומלכא דארם הות מגיח קרבא בישראל ואתמלך בעבדוהי למימר לאתר כסי טמיר יהי בית משרי: ט ושלח נביא דיי לות מלכא דישראל למימר אסתמר מלמעבר אתרא הדין ארי תמן אנש ארם כמן: י ושלח מלכא דישראל לאתרא די אמר ליה נביא דיי ואזהריה ואסתמר תמן לא חדא זימנא ולא תרתין זימנין: יא ואסתער לבא דמלכא דארם על פתגמא הדין וקרא לעבדוהי ואמר להון הלא

והזהירו קרי

רד"ק

כלומר הנביא הציפו: (ח) אל מקום פלני אלמני תחנותי. כתרגומו לאתר כסי וטמיר יהי בית מישרי: (ט) נחתים. מן הנחת ה' גבוריך ותרגום ויירד ונחת ופירוש יורדים וחונים שם ואמר נחתים כי במקום מורד חנו להסתר שם ודגש תי"ו נחתים מקום הנח בשרידים וי"ת נחתים כמן: (י) והזהירה. בה"א כמו אהלה: ונשמר שם. ונשמר משם כמו שהיה מזהירו הנביא: לא אחת ולא שתים. לא פעם אחת לבדה ולא שתים לבדו אלא פעמים רבות וכמוהו והוא איש אחד לא גוע בעונו שפירושו לא גוע לבדו: (יא) ויסער. היה מסתער על זה הדבר

רש"י

(ח) פלוני אלמוני. כסי וטמיר פלוני לשון כי יפלא (דברים י"ז י"ח) יתכסי: אלמוני. מבלי שם שלא היה רוצה להתגלות: תחנותי. שם אחנה ואארוב את מלך ישראל או את גדודיו העוברים לשלול בארצי דרך אותו המקום: (ט) מעבור המקום הזה. מלכת שם: נחתים. חונים: (י) וישלח מלך ישראל. היה שולח ורואה אם אמת הוא: והזהירו. שהזהיר איש האלהים מעבור שם: לא אחת ולא שתים.

רלב"ג

(ח) אל מקום פלני אלמני תחנתי. ר"ל שבכך יהיה חונה במקום נעלם כדי שלא ישמר מלך ישראל מעבר שם ויקחהו והנה פלוני מענין פלוני שהוא דבר מכוסה ונעלם ואלמוני הוא ג"כ מענין ההסתר וההעלם והוא נגזר מהאלמות כאלו יאמר שלא ידובר בזה כלל כדי שלא יודע לאיש או אפשר ע"ז הענין בעצמו כי אל"ף אלמוני בזה המקום ישמש במקום עי"ן כמו עלמוני והוא ענין נעלם וכזה מלאכו הוראת שמוש האותיות מזה הצד על זה הדרך: (ט) השמר מעבור המקום הזה כי שם ארם נחתים. ר"ל שתשמור מעבור במקום ההוא כי שם ארם נחתים שהיה בו מלך ארם ועבדיו כי שם ארם יורדים כמורד אשר שם להחבא שלא תשמר מהם והנה באומר נחתים יורדים וחונים תרגום ויירד ונחת או יהיה מענין נחת ונשארה התי"ו דקמון כמו שנשארה התי"ו במלת נחשתך והרצון בו שהם עומדים שם בנחת בדרך שיעלם היותם שם וכן היה שולח לו אלישע בכל מקום שהיו נסתרים שם מלך ארם ועבדיו לתפשו ולבחון אם היה דבר הנביא אמת שלח שם מלך ישראל אל המקום ההוא אשר הזהירו מעבור שם ומלא אמתות דברי הנביא תמיד לא פעם א' לבד ולא ב' פעמים לבד אך בחן זה פעמים רבות בדרך שנודע למלך ארם כי מלך ישראל היה יודע המקומות אשר יתחבא שם: (יא) ויסער לב מלך ארם. ר"ל אחזהו סער ומבוכה על זה הענין לחשבו כי

מנחת שי

בסוף מ"ג: (ט) השמר. יש ספרים מהדפוסים ראשונים שהמ"ם בצירי ומשובשים הם כי המלה מלעיל והמ"ם בסגול ואף בלבד נמצא בצירי כי הוא מלרע השמר והשקט (ישעיה ז'): (י) והזהירה. והזהירו קרי:

מצודת ציון

(ח) פלוני. מכוסה: אלמוני. מלשון אלם כי לא ידובר בו וכן ואת הנערים יודעתי אל מקום פלוני אלמוני (ש"א כא): (ט) נחתים. ענין ירידה כמו הנחת ה' גבוריך (יואל ד) כי במקום מורד ירדו

מצודת דוד

(ח) אל מקום פלוני אלמוני תחנותי. ר"ל נהיה חונים במקום מכוסה ונעלם ולא רצה לגלות בפני כולם וזהו בכדי לארוב על מלך ישראל: (י) וישלח. שלח אל המקום שאמר לו הנביא שבני ארם נסתרים בה והזהירו מלעבור בה ושלח שם לדעת אם האמת אתו: ונשמר שם. והיה המלך נשמר משם כאשר ראה שאמת הדבר: לא אחת. לא פעם אחת לבד וכו' כ"א פעמים רבות הזהירו הנביא ומלאם אמתיים ונשמר שמה: (יא) ויסער. אחזו רעדה כמרוח סערה בעבור זאת: מי משלנו

8. And the king of Aram was waging war with Israel; and he held council with his servants, saying, "In a hidden, secret place I will encamp." 9. And the man of God sent to the king of Israel, saying, "Beware of passing this place, for there the Arameans are encamped." 10. And the king of Israel sent to the place concerning which the man of God had told him and cautioned him, and he took precautions there, not once and not twice. 11. And the king of Aram was greatly disturbed about this matter, and he summoned his servants

the axe blade to float [*Ralbag*].

8. **hidden, secret**—*Jonathan* renders: *covered and hidden.* פְּלֹנִי *is an expression of* (Deut. 17:8) *"If it be concealed"* (יִפָּלֵא), which *Onkelos* renders: *it will be covered* [*Rashi*].

secret—*without a name, for he did not want it to be revealed* [*Rashi*].

I will encamp—*There I will encamp and ambush the king of Israel or his bands who pass to plunder in my land through that place* [*Rashi*].

This was top secret information, and was not disclosed to all of the king's servants, lest it be divulged to the enemy [*Mezudath David*].

9. **of passing this place**—i.e. *from going there* [*Rashi*].

are encamped—Heb. נְחִתִּים, [*Rashi*].

Others explain this as an expression of descent. They have descended into a low place, where they are concealed from view. *Jonathan* renders: are hidden [*Redak*].

10. **And the king of Israel sent**—*He would send and see whether it was true* [*Rashi*].

and cautioned him—*concerning which the man of God had cautioned him from passing* [*Rashi*].

not once and not twice—*did he do so for him, but many times* [*Rashi*].

Every time he sent agents to ascertain whether a certain place was indeed the Arameans' hiding place, as the prophet had said, he found it to be so [*Mezudath David*].

11. **was greatly disturbed**—lit. was stormed. I.e. he shuddered as though being blown by a storm wind [*Mezudath David*].

about this matter—*who was revealing his secret* [*Rashi*].

The king of Aram was greatly distressed because he suspected that one of his trusted servants was divulging his secrets to the king of Israel [*Abarbanel*].

וַיֹּאמֶר אֲלֵיהֶם הֲלוֹא תַּגִּידוּ לִי מִי מִשֶּׁלָּנוּ אֶל־מֶלֶךְ יִשְׂרָאֵל׃ יב וַיֹּאמֶר אַחַד מֵעֲבָדָיו לוֹא אֲדֹנִי הַמֶּלֶךְ כִּי־אֱלִישָׁע הַנָּבִיא אֲשֶׁר בְּיִשְׂרָאֵל יַגִּיד לְמֶלֶךְ יִשְׂרָאֵל אֶת־הַדְּבָרִים אֲשֶׁר תְּדַבֵּר בַּחֲדַר מִשְׁכָּבֶךָ׃ יג וַיֹּאמֶר לְכוּ וּרְאוּ אֵיכֹה הוּא וְאֶשְׁלַח וְאֶקָּחֵהוּ וַיֻּגַּד־לוֹ לֵאמֹר הִנֵּה בְדֹתָן׃ יד וַיִּשְׁלַח־שָׁמָּה סוּסִים וְרֶכֶב וְחַיִל כָּבֵד וַיָּבֹאוּ לַיְלָה וַיַּקִּפוּ עַל־הָעִיר׃ טו וַיַּשְׁכֵּם מְשָׁרֵת אִישׁ הָאֱלֹהִים לָקוּם וַיֵּצֵא וְהִנֵּה־חַיִל סוֹבֵב אֶת־הָעִיר וְסוּס וָרָכֶב וַיֹּאמֶר נַעֲרוֹ אֵלָיו אֲהָהּ אֲדֹנִי אֵיכָה נַעֲשֶׂה׃ טז וַיֹּאמֶר אַל־תִּירָא כִּי רַבִּים אֲשֶׁר אִתָּנוּ מֵאֲשֶׁר

הֲלָא תְחַווֹן לִי מָן מְדִילָנָא גָלֵי רָזֵי לְמַלְכָּא דְיִשְׂרָאֵל׃ יב וַאֲמַר חַד מֵעַבְדוֹהִי לָא רִבּוֹנִי מַלְכָּא אֲרֵי אֱלִישָׁע נְבִיָא דִי בְיִשְׂרָאֵל יְחַוֵי לְמַלְכָּא דְיִשְׂרָאֵל יָת פִּתְגָמַיָא דִי תְמַלֵיל בְּאִדְרוֹן בֵּית מִשְׁכְּבָךְ׃ יג וַאֲמַר אֱזִילוּ וְחֱזוֹ הֵיכָא הוּא וְאֶשְׁלַח וְאֶדְבְּרִינֵיהּ וְאִתְחֲוָא לֵיהּ לְמֵימַר הָא בְדוֹתָן׃ יד וּשְׁלַח תַּמָן סוּסְוָן וּרְתִיכִין וּמַשְׁרְיָן סַגִיאִין וַאֲתוֹ בְלֵילְיָא וְאַקִיפוּ עַל קַרְתָּא׃ טו וְאַקְדִים מְשׁוּמְשָׁנֵיהּ דִנְבִיָא דַיְיָ לְמֵיקָם וּנְפַק וְהָא מַשְׁרְיָן אַקִיפָא יָת קַרְתָּא סוּסְוָן וּרְתִיכִין וַאֲמַר עוּלֵימֵיהּ לֵיהּ בְּבָעוּ רִבּוֹנִי אֵיכְדֵין נַעְבֵיד׃ טז וַאֲמַר לָא תִדְחַל אֲרֵי סַגִיאִין דְעִמָּנָא מִדְעִמְּהוֹן׃ וצלי

תולדות אהרן

תי מבלנו . עקידה שער לו׃

איכו קרי

רש״י

עשה לו כך כ״א פעמים רבות׃ (יא) על הדבר הזה. מי הוא מגלה סודי׃ (יג) איכה. היכן הוא׃ (טז) אשר אתנו.

רד״ק

מי היה מגלה מסתריו׃ (יג) איכה הוא. כמו אנה הוא וכן ענין אנה איכה תרעה אלא שהוא קמץ וזה בחולם׃

רלב״ג

במשרתיו איש יגלה סתריו למלך ישראל׃ (יג) איכה הוא. איך הוא והכוון בו אם הוא בעיר בצורה וחיל רב עמו או איך הוא ענינו כי לפי שהוא בו אתחכם להביא עליו חיל לתפשו׃ (טו) והנה החיל שם בלילה כדי שלא ישמע דבר זה אלישע ויקבץ אנשים יותר עמו׃

מנחת שי

(יג) איכה. הכ״ף בחולם.(אמר המגיה מה מראות עיני בראותי החילופים שנמצאו בין הספרים במלה זו כי במקרא גדולה מוגהת נכתב בגליון איכו קרי ובאחרת איפה קרי. וכן בדפוסי אמשטרדם איפה קרי ובדפוסי ווינציאה קדמאה איכו ובקדמאה איפה ואין לי להכריע ממסורת אלא שבאיוב ריש סימן ל״ח נמסר בכמה אופנים אשר נכתב כ תיבת איפה ואילו בכ״ף לא נסדר שם. אבל הנראה לע״ד אין כאן קרי וכתיב כלל כיון שהרב המחבר דרכו להעיר על כל קרי וכתיב וכאן לא כתב אלא הכ״ף בחולם. וכן נראה דעת רד״ק בפירוש הפסוק וכן כתב בשרשים שרש איך ע״ש. וכן כתב המכלל יופי כמו איכה תרעה אלא שהוא קמ״ץ וזה בחולם ע״כ׃

and said to them, "Will you not tell me who of ours [reveals my secrets] to the king of Israel?" 12. And one of his servants said, "No, my master, the King, but Elisha the prophet who is in Israel tells the king of Israel the words that you speak in your bedroom." 13. And he said, "Go and see where he is, and I will send and take him." And it was told to him saying, "Behold he is in Dothan." 14. And he sent there horses and chariots and a great army; and they came at night and surrounded the city. 15. And the man of God arose early and went out, and behold an army with horses and chariots was surrounding the city. And his attendant said to him, "Alas, my master! What shall we do?" 16. And he said, "Have no fear, for those who are with us are more numerous than those who are with them."

to the king of Israel—*Jonathan* paraphrases: reveals my secrets to the king of Israel.

12. **"No**—There are no spies in our midst [*Mezudath David*].

tells the king of Israel—for he knows it through prophecy [*Mezudath David*].

13. **where he is** [*Rashi, Redak, Mezudath Zion*].

Ralbag explains: *How* he is, i.e. his situation, whether he is in a fortified city or any other information regarding his whereabouts.

and take him—I will capture him [*Ralbag, Abarbanel*].

Malbim questions the possibility of the king of Aram's attempt to capture Elisha. Since he believed that Elisha knew his thoughts, how could he possibly hope to capture him? He, therefore, renders: where he is and how he is? Is he rich or poor? If he is poor, I will be able to lavish wealth and honor upon him and win him over to my side. When he learned of his whereabouts, he sent a great army to protect Elisha lest the king of Israel prevent him from leaving.

15. **What shall we do?**—to escape [*Mezudath David*].

16. **who are with us**—i.e. *who are on our side* (helping us) [*Rashi*].

אותם: יז ויתפלל אלישע ויאמר יהוה פקח נא את עיניו ויראה ויפקח יהוה את עיני הנער וירא והנה ההר מלא סוסים ורכב אש סביבת אלישע: יח וירדו אליו ויתפלל אלישע אל יהוה ויאמר הך נא את הגוי הזה בסנורים ויכם בסנורים כדבר אלישע: יט ויאמר אלהם אלישע לא זה הדרך ולא זה העיר לכו אחרי ואוליכה אתכם אל האיש אשר תבקשון וילך אותם שמרונה: כ ויהי כבאם שמרון ויאמר אלישע יהוה פקח את עיני אלה

תרגום

יז וצלי אלישע ואמר יי גלי כען ית עינוהי ויחזי וגלא יי ית עיני רביא וחזא והא טורא מלי סוסון ורתיכין דאשתא סחרנות אלישע: יח ונחתו לותיה וצלי אלישע קדם יי ואמר מחי כען ית עמא הדין בשבריריא ומחנון בשבריריא כפתגמא דאלישע: יט ואמר להון אלישע לא דין אורחא ולא דא קרתא איתו בתרי ואוביל יתכון לות גברא די אתון בען ואוביל יתהון לשמרון: כ והוה כמיעלהון לשמרון ואמר אלישע יי גלי ית עיני אלין ויחזון

רש"י

בעזרתנו: (יח) ויאמר הך נא וגו'. על הקללה לא הזכיר את השם אבל על הפקיח' הזכיר את השם על שתיהן על של נער ועל של גדוד: בסנורים. חולי של שממון רואה ואינו יודע מה הוא רואה: (יט) ולא זה העיר. שהנביא בתוכה ואמת אמר להם שכבר יצא ממנה:

רד"ק

(יז) סביבות אלישע. והלא אלישע בעיר היה והסוסים ורכב אש חוץ לעיר בהר אלא הראה לו לנער כן שהיו סביבות אלישע יראה לו האל כן לחזק לבו שלא יפחד: (כ) כבאם. בכ"ף:

מנחת שי

(כ) כבואם. בכ"ף:

רלב"ג

(יז) סוסים ורכב אש סביבות אלישע. הנה אע"פ שלא נעזר אלישע בהם היה תועלת להראותם לנערו לשמרו מהפחד כדי שלא יצעק מפני הפחד ויהיה זה סבה שיתפחדו בני העיר כלם ויעזר פחדם אל מה שהיו רוצים לעשות כי אז יכירו כי אלישע שם: (יח) וירדו אליו ויתפלל אלישע. ר"ל כי בעת שהיו יורדים אל אלישע לתפשו התפלל אלישע אל ה' שיכה אות' בסנורים בדרך שלא ראו היטב ובזה האופן נדמה להם שהטעי' שהלכו שם לא היתה העיר שהיו מבקשים והיה אפשר זה לפי מחשבתם כי בלילה הלכו שם ויתכן שבבאם לאלישע שאלו לו האם העיר שהם בה היא דותן וענה לא כי טעית' בדרך ולא זו העיר אשר אלישע בה כי כבר הלך לעיר אחרת או הרצון בו

מצודת ציון

(יז) פקח. פתח: נא. עתה:

מצודת דוד

אשר הם בעזרתנו המה מרובים מאשר עמהם: (יז) פקח נא. לראות דבר רואהו: והנה ההר וגו'. ואע"פ שלא היה נעזר בזה כ"א במה שהוכו בסנורים מ"מ הועיל בזה להשתיק הנער מצעקתו כי הצעקה היה סיבה שירגישו הארמים אשר אלישע ישנו פה: (יח) וירדו. הארמים ירדו אל אלישע: בסנורים. הוא העדר הראיה וההכרה האמיתית וכן נאמר בסדום הכו בסנורים וכו' וילאו למצוא הפתח (בראשית י"ט): (יט) לא זה הדרך. ר"ל תעיתם בדרך בעת הלכתם אל דותן ולא זהו העיר דותן: אל האיש. הוא הנביא: (כ) פקח. ר"ל יוסר מהם מכת הסנורים:

believed him that they had strayed, since they came to Dothan at night [*Abarbanel*].

20. **open these people's eyes**—I.e. remove the affliction of blindness and confusion from them [*Mezudath David*].

and they saw—I.e. they recognized what they saw [*Malbim*].

and behold they were in

17. And Elisha prayed and said, "O Lord, please open his eyes
and let him see." And the Lord opened the lad's eyes and he
saw, and behold the mountain was full of fiery horses and
chariots around Elisha. 18. And they came down to him, and
Elisha prayed to the Lord and said, "Please strike this people
with blindness; and He struck them with blindness according to
the word of Elisha. 19. And Elisha said to them, "Neither is
this the way nor is this the city. Follow me and I will lead you to
the man you seek." And he led them to Samaria. 20. And it
was when they came to Samaria, that Elisha said, "O Lord,
open these people's eyes that they may see."

17. **"... please open his eyes**—Elisha did not pray for fiery horses and chariots. He knew that God would help him. He prayed merely that his attendant *see* fiery horses and chariots, in order to allay his fears, so that he would not jeopardize the inhabitants of the city by crying out and revealing Elisha's whereabouts [*Abarbanel, Ralbag, Mezudath David*].

Malbim points out that it is a great miracle for one not prepared for prophecy, to perceive spiritual beings. Indeed, the righteous are always surrounded by God's angels. In this case, however, they assumed the form of fiery horses and chariots to indicate that they would defeat the horses and chariots of Aram.

around Elisha—Although Elisha was in the city and the horses and chariots were surrounding the city upon the mountain, God showed them to Elisha's attendant as though they were surrounding Elisha, in order to allay his fears [*Redak*].

18. **And they came down to him**—The Arameans came down to Elisha [*Mezudath David*].

and said, "Please strike . . .—*On the curse he did not mention the Name* of God, *but on opening the eyes he mentioned the Name* of God *on both of them, concerning* opening *the attendant's* eyes, *and concerning* opening the eyes *of the troop* [*Rashi, Yalkut* from *Tan. Tazria* 9].

We mention God's Name for good, not for harm. See Gen. *Rabbah* 3:8, which states that God does not join His name with evil, only with good.

with blindness—*a sickness of confusion; one sees, yet does not know what he sees* [*Rashi*].

19. **"Neither is this the way**—You went astray when you went to Dothan [*Mezudath David*].

nor is this the city—*wherein the prophet is* found. *Now he told them the truth since he had already left it* [*Rashi*].

and he led them—They actually

ויראו ויפקח יהוה את־עיניהם ויראו
והנה בתוך שמרון: כא ויאמר מלך־
ישראל אל־אלישע כראתו אותם
האכה אכה אבי: כב ויאמר לא תכה
האשר שבית בחרבך ובקשתך
אתה מכה שים לחם ומים לפניהם
ויאכלו וישתו וילכו אל־אדניהם:
כג ויכרה להם כרה גדולה ויאכלו
וישתו וישלחם וילכו אל־אדניהם ולא־
יספו עוד גדודי ארם לבוא בארץ
ישראל: כד ויהי אחרי־כן ויקבץ בן־

נחזון וגלא יי ית עיניהון
נחזו והא בגו שמרון:
כא נאמר מלכא דישראל
לאלישע כד חזא יתהון
המקטול אקטול רבי:
כב נאמר לא תקטול הא
דשביתא בחרבך
ובקשתך את קטיל שוי
לחמא ומיא קדמיהון
וייכלון וישתון ויזלון
לרבוניהון: כג ואתקין
להון שירו רבא ואכלו
ושתיאו ושלחינון ואזלו
לות רבוניהון ולא
אוסיפו עוד משרית
ארם למיעל בתחום
ארעא דישראל:
כד והוה בתר כן וכנש
בר

תולדות אהרן

ויכרה להם. בבא בתרא עה נדה לא:

רש"י

(כב) האשר שבית וגו'. וכי דרכך להרוג אותה שאתה מביא בשביה (ומשבית אותם): (כג) ויכרה. לשון תקון

רד"ק

(כא) כראתו. בכ"ף: (כב) האשר שבית. מה דין יש לך בהם שתכה אותם וכי אתה שבית אותם בחרבך ובקשתך: (כג) ויכרה להם. תקן להם מאכל גדול וכן יכרו עליו חברים אלא כי ויכרה יוצא לשלישי ויכרו יוצא לשני: ולא יספו עוד. אינו אומר עוד לעולם שהרי אומר ויהי אחרי כן ויקבוץ בן הדד אלא פי' עוד באותו הזמן וכן ולא הוסיף עוד מלך מצרים לצאת מארצו ונאמר בירמיה וחיל פרעה יוצא ממצרים וישמעו הכשדים

רלב"ג

ולא זו העיר היא דותן והביאור הראשון הוא יותר נכון: (כב) האשר שבית בחרבך ובקשתך אתה מכה. ר"ל הנה אלו שביתי והנהגתי בכח גבורת הש"י ולמה תכה אותם האם תכה האנשים אשר תנהג בשבי בחרבך ובקשתך אין זה ראוי וכ"ש שאין ראוי זה באשר שבה אותם הש"י: (כג) ויכרה להם כרה גדולה. ר"ל שעשה להם סעודה גדולה: ולא יספו עוד גדודי ארם. ר"ל שלא יספו עוד לבא שם בזה האופן שהיו באים בתחלה בהעלם כי יראו ממה שראו מהנבואה אך בשרצו להלחם בישראל אסף מלך ארם כל מחנהו ולא באו שם

מנחת שי

(כא) כראותו. בכ"ף: (כב) ובקשתך. הוא"ו במאריך במדוייקים ב"י:

מצודת דוד

(כא) האכה. בשאלה אמר האם אכה אותם: (כב) האשר שבית. האם הם אשר שבית אתה לשתכה בהם הלא בנס הובאו ומה לך להם: (כג) ויכרה. עשה להם סעודה גדולה: ולא יספו וגו'. לא באו עוד באופן זה לארוב עליהם בראותם כי הנביא מגלה מסתורם: (כד) ויקבוץ. לבוא בגלוי ובפומבי ולזה קבץ כל עמו:

מצודת ציון

(כא) אבי. ר"ל רבי: (כב) האשר. הה"א התימה: (כג) ויכרה. עשה סעודה כמו יכרו עליו חברים (איוב מ):

sistent with the following episode [*Malbim*].

24. **that Ben-Hadad . . . mustered all his camp**—to engage Israel in open battle, instead of guerrilla warfare as previously [*Ralbag*].

and besieged Samaria—He built bulwarks against the city to prevent anyone from leaving. Apparently, he had already besieged many cities of Israel and had destroyed the produce in the fields. Therefore, the

And the Lord opened their eyes, and they saw, and behold they
were in Samaria. 21. Now the king of Israel said to Elisha when
he saw them, "Shall I slay them, my lord?" 22. And he said,
"You shall not slay. Do you slay those you have captured with
your sword and with your bow? Set food and water for them
and let them eat and drink and go to their masters. 23. And he
prepared for them a lavish feast, and they ate and drank, and he
sent them away and they went to their masters; and Aramean
troops no longer continued to invade the land of Israel.
24. And it was after this, that Ben-Hadad

Samaria—They were captives in the capital of Israel.

22. **Do you slay those you have captured with your sword and with your bow**—*Is it your custom to slay one whom you bring into captivity (and destroy them)?* [*Rashi*].

You have the right to slay only in battle, not after you have taken prisoners [*Malbim*].

Redak and *Abarbanel* explain thus: What right do you have to kill them? Did you capture them with your sword and bow, that you should have the right to kill them?

Others combine both interpretations. Even if you would have captured them yourself, you would have no right to kill them. Surely now, that you had no part in their capture [*Ralbag*].

23. **And he prepared**—Heb. וַיִּכְרֶה, *an expression of preparation of a meal* [*Rashi*].

The Rabbis explain כֵּרָה as an expression of peace. As an example of (Ecc. 9:18) "Wisdom is better than implements of war," the Rabbis laud Elisha's wisdom as opposed to Jehoram's request to slay the prisoners of war. Whereas Jehoram thought to discourage the Arameans from attacking Israel through bloodshed, Elisha accomplished it through friendliness [*Elijah Rabba*, ch. 7, quoted by *Yalkut Shimoni*, explained by *K'li Y'kar*].

and Aramean troops no longer continued—for some time to invade the land of Israel [*Redak*].

Others explain that the king of Aram no longer sent troops into the land of Israel to hide and engage in guerrilla warfare, because Elisha would reveal their whereabouts [*Abarbanel, Ralbag, Mezudath David*].

Others explain that no longer would the Arameans attack in small bands to pillage and murder. They, however, did not refrain from engaging in warfare. Hence this is con-

הדד מלך־ארם את־כל־מחנהו ויעל
ויצר על־שמרון: כה ויהי רעב גדול
בשמרון והנה צרים עליה עד היות
ראש־חמור בשמנים כסף ורבע הקב
חריונים בחמשה כסף: כו ויהי מלך
ישראל עבר על־החמה ואשה צעקה
אליו לאמר הושיעה אדני המלך:
כז ויאמר אל־יושעך יהוה מאין אושיעך

דביונים קרי

בר הדד מלכא דארם
ית כל משריתיה
וסליק וצר על שמרון:
כה והוה כפנא רבא
בשמרון והא צירין עלה
עד דהוה רישא דחמרא
מזדבן בתמנן כסף
ורבעת קבא דזבל
מפקת יוניא בחמשא
סלעין דכסף: כו והוה
מלכא דישראל עבר
על שורא ואתתא קבלא
קדמוהי למימר פריק
רבוני מלכא: כז ואמר
לא יפרקינך יי מנן

ת"א חריונים. מגלה כה:

רש"י

סעודה: (כה) דביונים. זבל הזב מן היונים: (כו) הושיעה אדני המלך. כסבור ששואלת מזונות:

רד"ק

זכן לא תוסיפו עוד לעלות וכן ועמלו לא יזכר עוד רוצה לומר כל זמן שהיה בו: (כה) ראש חמור. כמשמעו כי הבהמות הטמאו' והשקצים היו אוכלים מפני הרעב וכן ת"י רישא דחמרא וי"מ כמו מעשר החמר והוא רחוק: חריונים. כן כתיב וקרי דביונים ופי' צואת יונים והכתוב אומר מה שיוצא מחור היונים והקרי לשון נקי' יותר מה שזב מן היונים ותרגם זוב דיב וכת"י דזבל מפקת יוניא והיו מבערים אש בצואת היונים כי לא היו להם עצים כי מפני המצור לא היו יכולים לצאת מן העיר לחטוב עצים ביער. וא"א אבי ז"ל פי' דביונים מה שבזפק היונים שהיונים היו יוצאים ואוכלים התבואה ונכנסים לעיר והיו אנשי העיר לוקחים מה שבזפק היונים

מנחת שי

(כה) חרי יונים. דיב יונים קרי כן הוא בס"ס מדויקים כ"י וגם בדפוס ישן אבל גירסת הרי"ף וריא"ז בפרק הקורא את המגילה עומד. חירי יונים וכן כתב בעל הלשון כי הכתיב חורי יונים והקרי ד ב י ו' נ י ם על משקל גליונים. ובמקצת ספרים חדא מלה כתיב ובשני יודי"ן וי"ס ביו"ד אחד לבד וכן הוא ברד"ק בפי' ובשרשים שרש דב וזו היא גם כן גירסת רבינו ישעיה הראשון ז"ל מטראני:

רלב"ג

כמו שהיה שולה בתחלה: (כד) ויעל ויצר על שמרון. ר"ל שבנה עליה מצור בדרך שלא יוכל איש לצאת מן העיר וידמה שבכר שם במצור ג"כ עיירות רבות מישראל והיו משקיתים יבול כל הארץ בדרך שהיה הרעב כבד בארץ וזהו מה שאמר אלישע לשונמית כי קרא ה' לרעב וגם בא אל הארץ ז' שנים ואפשר שנתקבלו ברעב סבות אחרות כאלו תאמר חסרון התבואות וידמה שזמן המצור ארך מאד ולזה הגיע הענין בשמרון מחוזק הרעב שהיה שם ראש חמור שוה שמנים כסף והיו אוכלים אותו מפני הרעב כי התורה אסרה וחי בהם ולא שימות בהם: (כה) ורובע הקב חריונים. פי' בו צואת יונים כי היא יוצאת מהוריהם וכמוהו לאכול את חוריהם ולא אשער מה היה השתמשותם ברעב בצואת יונים ואפשר כי לרוב השחתת האויבים יבול הארץ היו גרגירי הזרעים נמצאים מאד בהון והיו היונים אוכלים מהם לשובע ומרוב אכלם מהם היו נמצאים מהזרעים ההם קלת בצואתם כי לא יוכלו לעכל כל הכמות ההוא: (כז) אל יושיעך ה'. ר"ל הנה ה' הוא אשר איננו מושיעך כי הוא הביא לנו הרעב החזק הזה אבל אני אין לי אשם במה שלא יושיעך: המן הגורן או מן היקב. והנה אמר זה לפי שלא היו יכולים לאסוף להם התבואות

מצודת ציון

(כה) דביונים. צואה הזב מן היונים כי אשר יזוב (ויקרא טו) תרגומו אדי ידוב ובהם היו מדליקין האש לחסרון העצים בעבור המצור: (כז) היקב. הוא גת היין:

מצודת דוד

(כה) והנה צרים. כאומר מלבד הרעב מסיבת חסרון התבואה נתוסף עוד הרעב בעבור שהיו צרים עליה ולא הניחו להביא מאכל אל העיר: עד היות. כ"כ נתחזק הרעב עד שהיה נמכר ראש חמור בשמונים שקלי כסף: (כז) אל יושיעך ה'. חשב אשר שאלתה על המזון ואמר לה ה' הוא אין מושיעך ועם שבידו להושיעך וכי בתבואה מן הגורן או ביין מן היקב הלא אין עמדי וכאומר לא יקרא אין מושיע כי אם מי שבידו להושיע ולא זולת:

Ralbag conjectures that the people would eat the undigested kernels found in the dung.

26. **"Save me, my lord the king!"**—He thought she was asking for food [*Rashi*].

27. **"If the Lord will not save you**—although He is able, whence will I save you? You know that we have no food [*Mezudath David*].

"From the threshing floor or from the winepress?"—Do I have grain from the threshing floor or wine from the winepress to give you? He mentioned these because they had not harvested grain nor gathered grapes during the famine [*Ralbag, Abarbanel*].

the king of Aram, mustered all his camp; and he went up and besieged Samaria. 25. Now there was a severe famine in Samaria, and behold they were besieging it, until a donkey's head sold for eighty silver pieces and a quarter of a *kab* of doves' dung sold for five silver pieces. 26. And the king of Israel was passing on the wall, when a woman cried out to him, saying, "Save [me] my lord the king!" 27. And he said, "If the Lord will not save you, whence shall I save you?

prophet warned the Shunemitess that there would be a severe famine for seven years (8:1). There may have been other causes in addition to the siege, to bring about such a severe famine as is depicted in the following section [*Ralbag*].

25. **they were besieging it**—I.e. in addition to the shortage of grain, which caused a severe famine, the Arameans were besieging Samaria, and did not permit food to be brought into the city [*Mezudath David*].

a donkey's head—The famine became so severe that a donkey's head was sold for eighty shekels of silver [*Mezudath David*].

Because of the acute famine, the people were forced to eat unclean animals, rodents, and reptiles, as is depicted in Com. Dig. 8:1 [*Redak*].

In order to save one's life, he may eat forbidden foods. The Torah states: (Lev. 18:5) "And you shall observe My statutes and My laws, which man shall perform and live with them . . ." This implies that man should live by observing the commandments, but not die through their observance [*Ralbag* from *TB Yoma* 85b].

a quarter of a kab—a small measure.

dove's dung—Heb. *divyonim. Rashi* interprets this as two words, *div,* meaning "a flow" and *yonim,* meaning "doves." Thus, he renders: *dung that flows from the doves* [*Rashi*].

The *K'thib* is *horyonim,* meaning, "what is excreted from the holes of the doves." As a euphemism, *divyonim* was set down as the *K'ri* [*Redak* from *Megillah* 25b].

This was used as kindling instead of wood. Since the city was under siege, it was impossible to obtain wood from the forests outside the city.

Others interpret this as the kernels of grain found in the doves' crop. Since the doves could fly outside the city, they would eat of the little grain found in the fields. Because of the acute famine, the people would buy these kernels for five silver pieces a quarter of a *kab* [*Redak*].

המן-הגרן או מן-היקב: כח ויאמר-לה
המלך מה-לך ותאמר האשה הזאת
אמרה אלי תני את-בנך ונאכלנו היום
ואת-בני נאכל מחר: כט ונבשל את-
בני ונאכלהו ואמר אליה ביום האחר
תני את-בנך ונאכלנו ותחבא את-
בנה: ל ויהי כשמע המלך את-דברי
האשה ויקרע את-בגדיו והוא עבר
על-החמה וירא העם והנה השק על-
בשרו מבית: לא ויאמר כה-יעשה-לי
אלהים וכה יסף אם-יעמד ראש

אפרקינך המן אדרא או
מן מעצרתא: כח ואמר
לה מלכא מה ליך
ואמרת איתתא הדא
אמרת לי הבי ית בריך
וניכלניה יומא דין וית
ברי ניכול מחר:
כט ובשילנא ית ברי
ואכלנוהי ואמרית לה
ביומא אוחרנא הבי
ית בריך וניכליניה
ואטמרת ית ברה:
ל והוה כד שמע מלכא
ית פתגמי איתתא
ובזע ית לבושוהי
והוא עבר על שורא
וחזא עמא והא סקא
אסיר על בסריה מלגיו:
לא ואמר כדין יעביד
לי יי וכדין יוסיף אם
יתקים

ת"א ויקרע את בגדיו. תענית יד:

רש"י

(כט) ותחבא את בנה. מת ורוצה לאוכלו לבדה: (ל) וירא העם. דרך הקרע את השק תחת בגדיו: (לא) אם יעמוד ראש אלישע. שהיכולת בידו לבקש

רד"ק

ואוכלים כי מפני המצור היה הרעב: (כט) ותחבא את בנה. שתאכלנו לבדה או רחמה עליו להחיותו: (ל) מבית. מבפנים: (לא) אם יעמוד ראש אלישע. שהיה עליו לבקש רחמים ואיננו מבקש:

רלב"ג

גרן ותבואת יקב: (כט) ותחבא את בנה. ר"ל למלטו שלא יאכלוהו כי אולי תהיה לה הצלה ממקום אחר: (לא) אם יעמוד ראש אלישע בן שפט עליו היום. ידמה כי אלישע בהוכיחו אותו אמר לו שיהיה רעב ולא הגיד לו שיהיה שבע שנים לבד כמו שאמר אליהו אם יהיה השנים האלה טל ומטר כי אם לפי דברי ולא הגיד לו גם כן שיסור בשנה השלישית ולזה כעס המלך עליו ואמר להמיתו מפני ראותו כי

מנחת שי

(ל) ויהי כשמע. פליגי ספרי אם הוא דגש או רפה ועיין מ"ש בשופטים י"ו:

מצודת דוד

(כח) ויאמר. חזר המלך לשאלה מהו המבוקש לך כי שוב חשב שמא שאלתה בדבר אחר: (ל) מבית. מבפנים לבגדיו וראוהו דרך הקריעה: (לא) כה יעשה וגו'. הוא ענין שבועה וגזם ולא אמר: אם יעמוד וגו'. כי אמרו על כי בידו לעתור לה' להסיר הרעב

מצודת ציון

(כט) ותחבא. הסתירה:

garb over the sackcloth [Abarbanel].

He displayed to the people that he had completely despaired of divine mercy, and was ready to kill the prophet Elisha, who had not prayed for the end of the famine [*Malbim*].

31. **"So shall God do to me**—This is an expression of an oath [*Mezudath David*].

if Elisha the son of Shaphat's head remain—*for he is able to beg for mercy* [*Rashi, Redak, Mezudath David*].

Abarbanel explains that Jehoram wished to slay Elisha for allowing the famine to last for seven years, as he predicted in 8:1. Since Elijah his master had also decreed a famine and brought it to an end after three years, he felt that Elisha was responsible for the long famine from which they were suffering.

Ralbag conjectures that Elisha had not revealed to Jehoram that the famine would end after seven years. He, therefore thought that it would last longer. When it became

From the threshing floor or from the winepress?" 28. And the king said to her, "What troubles you?" And she said, "This woman said to me, 'Give your son and let us eat him today, and we will eat my son tomorrow.' 29. And we cooked my son and ate him. And I said to her the next day 'Give up your son and let us eat him.' But she hid her son." 30. And it was when the king heard the woman's words that he rent his garments while he was passing on the wall, and the people saw, and behold there was sackcloth on his flesh underneath. 31. And he said, "So shall God do to me and so shall He continue, if Elisha the son of Shaphat's head remain on him today."

28. **"What troubles you?"**—Although I cannot help you, tell me what troubles you? [*Pesikta Rabbathi* 30:2].

Perhaps she had a different problem, which he would be able to solve [*Mezudath David*].

'Give your son'—In order to conserve wood or dove's dung, they agreed to cook the two children on the first day, and to eat one then and one on the morrow. Or, perhaps they cooked them together to avoid unnecessary publicity [*K'li Y'kar* as explanation of *Pesikta Rabbathi*].

29. **And we cooked my son**—According to *Pesikta,* they cooked both children, but ate only one.

But she hid her son—*dead, and wants to eat him alone* [*Rashi*].

Pesikta adds, slaughtered and cooked. *Redak* and *Ralbag* suggest that perhaps she had pity on him and attempted to save him alive; perhaps she would find food and be able to feed him.

K'li Y'kar, however, rejects this theory, for what did she expect the king to answer? Would he order the other woman to slaughter her son and to share him with her neighbor? It is, therefore, only plausible that he had already been slaughtered and cooked. The dispute was only concerning the sharing of the flesh.

30. **that he rent his garments while he was passing on the wall**—The king was so greatly grieved by the woman's story, that he rent his garments, even though he was passing on the wall in full view of the populace. Although he would probably harm the morale of the people when they would witness his act of despair, he did not hesitate to give vent to his grief [*Abarbanel, Malbim*].

and the people saw—*the sackcloth under his garments through the tear* [*Rashi*].

This indicates that Jehoram repented of his sins and wore sackloth to mortify his flesh. Out of respect for the throne, he wore his royal

אֱלִישָׁע בֶּן־שָׁפָט עָלָיו הַיּוֹם׃ לב וֶאֱלִישָׁע יֹשֵׁב בְּבֵיתוֹ וְהַזְּקֵנִים יֹשְׁבִים אִתּוֹ וַיִּשְׁלַח אִישׁ מִלְּפָנָיו בְּטֶרֶם יָבֹא הַמַּלְאָךְ אֵלָיו וְהוּא ׀ אָמַר אֶל־הַזְּקֵנִים הַרְּאִיתֶם כִּי־שָׁלַח בֶּן־הַמְרַצֵּחַ הַזֶּה לְהָסִיר אֶת־רֹאשִׁי רְאוּ ׀ כְּבֹא הַמַּלְאָךְ סִגְרוּ הַדֶּלֶת וּלְחַצְתֶּם אֹתוֹ בַּדֶּלֶת הֲלוֹא קוֹל רַגְלֵי אֲדֹנָיו אַחֲרָיו׃ לג עוֹדֶנּוּ מְדַבֵּר עִמָּם וְהִנֵּה הַמַּלְאָךְ יֹרֵד אֵלָיו וַיֹּאמֶר הִנֵּה־זֹאת הָרָעָה מֵאֵת יְהוָה

תרגום

יתקים רישא דאלישע בר שפט עלוהי יומא דין: לב ואלישע יתיב בביתיה וסביא יתבין עמיה ושלח גברא קדמוהי עד לא יתי אזגדא לותיה והוא אמר לסביא החזיתון ארי שלח בר קטולא הדין לאעדאה ית רישי חזו כמיתי אזגדא אחודו דשא ותדחקון יתיה בדשא הלא קל רגלי רבוניה בתרוהי: לג עד דהוא ממליל עמהון והא אזגדא נחית לותיה ואמר הא דא בישתא מן קדם יי מא אצלי קדם

רד"ק ריש דגושה

(לב) וישלח איש. המלך שלח איש מלפניו להסיר את ראש אלישע: בטרם. חסר וי"ו והוא יתירה במלת והוא אמר וכן ענין הפסוק המלך שלח איש מלפניו אל אלישע ובטרם יבא המלאך אליו והוא אמר אל הזקנים כי המלך שולח איש להסיר את ראשו כי נאמר לו ברוח הנבואה: הראיתם. בדגש הרי"ש וכן הראיתם אשר בחר בו ה': בן המרצח. בן אהאב שרצח נבות כן הוא רוצה לרצחני: הלא קול. תשמעו קול רגלי אדוניו שיבא אחריו: (לג) ויאמר. המלך הבא אחרי המלאך אמר הנה זאת הרעה מאת ה' עד שאוכלת הנשים בשר בניהם:

רש"י

רחמים: (לב) וישלח איש מלפניו. המלך שלח להרגו ובטרם יבא אותו המלאך אל אלישע והוא נגלה לו ברוח הקודש ואמר אל הזקנים. והנה המלאך יורד אליו והמלך אחריו: (לג) ויאמר. המלך: הנה זאת הרעה מאת ה'. זאת אחת מן הקללות שקלל ע"י משה ואכלת פרי בטנך במצור ובמצוק וגו' (דברים כ"ח נ"ג): מה אוחיל לה' עוד. להושיע הלא לא יועיל:

מנחת שי

(לב) הראיתם. הרי"ש בדגש על פי המסורת ומכלול דף ע"ב ודף ס"א: המרצח בה"ם רפויה והה"א סמוכה בגעיא מכלול דף כ':

רלב"ג

כבר הגיע מחוזק הרעב אל שהיו אוכלים בשר בניהם: (לב) בן המרצח הזה. קרא בן אחאב בן המרצח כי הוא הסכים בהריגת נבות ובהריגת נביאי ה' ע"י איזבל: (לג) והנה המלאך יורד אליו ויאמר הנה זאת הרעה מאת ה' מה אוחיל לה' עוד. ידמה שהמלאך שירד אליו אמר לאלישע כי הוא בא להרגו על דבר הרעב במלות המלך ואמר לו אלישע כי לא זו הדרך להמלט מהרעב אלא עד שיתפללו לש"י וענה המלאך כי אחר שזאת הרעה מאת ה' לשוא יתפלל אליו עוד וחשב כי התפלה לבד תועיל להציל מהרע שיעשהו אחר לא מהרעה שיעשה הש"י בעצמה ולזה ענה אלישע כי השם יצילם מהרע ההוא עד שבעת מחר ישוב בשער שומרון סאה סולת בשקל וסאתים שעורים בשקל ואפשר שיהיה הרצון בזה שכבר אמר המלאך שבא להמית אלישע כמו מתחרט על שבא להרגו הנה זאת הרעה באה לנו מאת ה' על חטאינו מה אחטא עוד ואקנה לעצמי חיל ורעה על הרעה הזאת בעבור שיכעס עלי השם והוא מענין מעי מעי אוחילה:

מצודת ציון

(לב) הראיתם. הה"א השאלה: ולחצתם. ענין דחק: (לג) אוחיל. אקוה כמו על כן אוחיל לו (איכה ג):

מצודת דוד

ואינו חושש: (לב) וישלח. המלך שלח אל אלישע לפני בואו שמה לשמרו לבל יברח עד יבא הוא ולהרגו בפניו: בטרם. עד לא בא השליח אמר אלישע אל הזקנים הראיתם ר"ל האם אתם נותנין לב לדבר הזה אשר שלח בן המרצח להסיר ראשי כי בנבואה נאמר לו: בן המרצח. את אחאב קורא מרצח לפי שמה שהרגה איזבל את כל הנביאים היה בהסכמת דעת אחאב: ראו וגו'. הסתכלו עת ביאת המלאך לפה וסגרו אז את הדלת ודחקוהו עם הדלת אל החוץ: הלא קול. עודו מדבר עמהם אמר הלא עתה נשמע בנבואה קול רגלי אדוניו המלך אשר הולך אחרי המלאך אשר שלח: (לג) יורד אליו. אל אלישע הביתה כי נשמעם שגם המלך יבוא הדלו מלסגור הדלת מפני כבוד המלכות ויאמר כאשר בא גם המלך אמר המלאך אל המלך הנה רעת הרעב באה היא מה' לתשלום גמול הפשעים ואם אוסיף לפשוע לשלוח יד בנביאו א"כ מה היא התקוה אשר אוחיל עוד לה' הלא לא יוסיף לרחם עוד בעבור העון הזה ומפני כבוד המלכות תלה הדבר בעצמו:

would arrive, so that the word of God would gain publicity [*Abarbanel*].

33. **was coming down to him**—Since they knew that the king was following closely behind, they did not hold the door, out of respect for the throne [*Mezudath David*].

And he said—*The king* said [*Rashi*].

"Behold, this calamity is from the Lord—*This is one of the curses that He cursed through Moses.* "(Deut. 28:53) *And you will eat the fruit of*

32. And Elisha was sitting in his house, and the elders were sitting with him; and he sent a man from before him. When the
messenger had not yet arrived, he said to the elders, "Have you
seen that this son of a murderer has sent to remove my head?
See that when the messenger comes that you close the door and
you shall hold the door fast against him. Surely, the sound of
his master's footsteps will follow him." 33. While he was still
speaking with them, behold the messenger was coming down to
him. And he said, "Behold, this calamity is from the Lord.

so acute that people were eating their own children, he became very angry at Elisha and was determined to kill him.

32. **in his house**—i.e. not in the study hall with his disciples [*Malbim*].

and the elders—the members of the Sanhedrin were sitting with him to judge the people [*Malbim*].

and he sent a man from before him—*The king sent* a man *to kill him, and when that messenger had not yet come to Elisha,* and he was *revealed to him through the divine spirit, and he said to the elders . . ., and behold the messenger was coming down to him and the king was after him* [*Rashi*].

Malbim explains that Elisha sent every man away from him. I.e. he sent away all those who had come before him for litigation, and left only the elders.

"Have you seen—I know that the king has sent him here to murder me. As judges, it is up to you to protest this attempted crime. We see from Naboth's trial that the king did not have the power to kill anyone arbitrarily. He would have to consult the Sanhedrin whether Elisha deserved to be put to death [*Malbim*].

this son of a murderer—Just as his father Ahab murdered Naboth, so does Jehoram wish to murder me [*Redak, Ralbag*].

I.e. he was considered a murderer for his involvement in Naboth's execution.

Surely, the sound of his master's footsteps will follow him—You will soon hear the sound of his master's footsteps following him [*Redak*].

Alternatively, I hear the sound of the king's footsteps in the prophetic message that is being conveyed to me [*Mezudath David*].

Elisha ordered the elders to hold the door and not to permit the king's messenger to enter the house. When the king would arrive shortly after him, they should both be granted admittance to the house. Elisha knew that the king would follow stealthily to hear the prophetic message. He had ordered the messenger to listen first to the message, and if favorable, not to harm the prophet. Elisha wished to keep the messenger outside until the king

קֳדָם יְיָ עוֹד: א וַאֲמַר אֱלִישָׁע קַבִּילוּ פִּתְגָמָא דַיְיָ כִּדְנַן אֲמַר יְיָ כְּעִדָּנָא הָדֵין מְחַר סְאָה סוּלְתָּא בְּסִלְעָא וְסָאתַן סְעוֹרִין בְּסִלְעָא בִּתְרַע דְשָׁמְרוֹן: ב וַאֲתֵיב גַּבְרָא דְמַלְכָּא דְסָמִיךְ עַל יְדוֹהִי יָת נְבִיָּא דַיְיָ וַאֲמַר אִילוּ יְיָ פָּתַח כַּוִּין וּמַחֵית טוּבָא מִן שְׁמַיָּא הֲיֶהֱוֵי פִּתְגָמָא הָדֵין וַאֲמַר הָא אַתְּ חָזֵי בְּעֵינָךְ וּמִתַּמָּן לָא תֵיכוֹל: ג וְאַרְבְּעָה גֻבְרִין הֲווֹ סְגִירִין יָתְבִין בְּמֵעֲלָנָא דְתַרְעָא וַאֲמַרוּ גְבַר לְחַבְרֵיהּ מָא אֲנַחְנָא יָתְבִין כָּא עַד דְנָמוּת

מַה־אוֹחִיל לַיהוָה עוֹד: ז א וַיֹּאמֶר אֱלִישָׁע שִׁמְעוּ דְּבַר־יְהוָה כֹּה | אָמַר יְהוָה כָּעֵת | מָחָר סְאָה־סֹלֶת בְּשֶׁקֶל וְסָאתַיִם שְׂעֹרִים בְּשֶׁקֶל בְּשַׁעַר שֹׁמְרוֹן:
ב וַיַּעַן הַשָּׁלִישׁ אֲשֶׁר־לַמֶּלֶךְ נִשְׁעָן עַל־יָדוֹ אֶת־אִישׁ הָאֱלֹהִים וַיֹּאמַר הִנֵּה יְהוָה עֹשֶׂה אֲרֻבּוֹת בַּשָּׁמַיִם הֲיִהְיֶה הַדָּבָר הַזֶּה וַיֹּאמֶר הִנְּכָה רֹאֶה בְּעֵינֶיךָ וּמִשָּׁם לֹא תֹאכֵל:
ג וְאַרְבָּעָה אֲנָשִׁים הָיוּ מְצֹרָעִים פֶּתַח הַשָּׁעַר וַיֹּאמְרוּ אִישׁ אֶל־רֵעֵהוּ מָה אֲנַחְנוּ יֹשְׁבִים פֹּה עַד־

ת"א שמעו. סנהדרין ל: ויען השליש. שם עקידה שער סא: וארבעה אנשים. סוטה מז סנהדרין קז (שם):

רש"י

ז (ג) **וארבעה אנשים**. גיחזי ובניו: **פתח השער**. כמו שנאמר בדד ישב מחוץ למחנה מושבו (ויקרא

רד"ק

מה אוחיל לה' עוד. כלומר מה אקוה לה' עוד ומה אקוה לו מה יועילני אחרי זאת הרעה וי"ת מה אצלי תרגם אוחיל כמו אחלה: (ב) **אשר למלך נשען על ידו**. דרך קצרה פי' השליש אשר למלך שהיה נשען על ידו: **ארובות בשמים**. להמטיר או בדרך הפלגה להוריד חטים ושעורים על דרך ירידת המן ותרגם יונתן אלו ה' פתח כוין ומחית טובא מן שמיא: **הנכה**. בה"א כמו הנצבת עמכה והדומי' להם: (ג) **וארבעה אנשים**. ארז"ל

רלב"ג

(ב) השליש אשר למלך נשען על ידו. ר"ל בעת שהיה המלך נשען על ידו בדרך ששמע המלך דבריו כאמרו מכחיש נבואת אלישע שזה לא יהיה כמו שלא יתכן שיעשה השם ארובות בשמים: (ג) וארבעה אנשים היו מצורעים פתח השער. לפי שהיו מוכרחים לעמוד מחוץ

מצודת דוד

ז (א) **ויאמר וגו'**. כשמוע דברי המלאך הממאן לשלוח בו יד מפחד ה' והמלך הסכים על ידו אמר הנה כעת הזאת ביום מחר יהיה סאה סולת בשקל וגו': **בשער**. מקום שמוכרין שם התבואה: (ב) **אשר למלך נשען**. מלת אשר עומדת במקום שתים כאלו אמר אשר למלך אשר היה נשען על ידו בבואו אל הנביא כמ"ש למעלה הלוא קול רגלי וגו': **הנה ה' עושה**. אף אם עושה ה' ארובות בשמים להשליך דרך שם על הארץ הסולת והשעורים וכי אפשר שיהיה הדבר הזה להיות כ"כ בזול: **רואה**. הזול ההוא: **ומשם לא תאכל**. כי תמות מיד ועל שלגלג על דבריו אמר לו כן: (ג) **פתח השער**. היו יושבים בפתח השער כדין המצורע כמ"ש

מצודת ציון

ז (ב) **השליש**. שר וחשוב כמו ומבחר שלישיו (שמות טו): **נשען**. נסמך: **ארובות**. חלונות כמו וכעשן מארבה (הושע יג): **הנכה**. הנה אתה והוא כמו הנך וכה"א נוספת ודוגמתו הנלכה

from it, as we find that the people trampled him and he never recovered from his injuries [*Abarbanel, Mezudath David*].

3. **Now there were four men**—*Gehazi and his sons* [*Rashi* from *San.* 107b].

The expression in Heb. means literally, four men became stricken with *zaraath*, implying that all four became stricken simultaneously. This statement could only apply to Gehazi and his sons upon whom Elisha had pronounced a curse, which took its toll immediately [*K'li Y'kar, Maharsha San.* ad loc.]

Alternatively, since Elisha was in Samaria, why did he not cure the four *mezoraim* as he had cured Naaman? The obvious answer is that these four were Gehazi and his three sons, upon whom the curse had been pronounced that they would forever remain stricken with

What more can I hope for from the Lord?"

7.

1. And Elisha said, "Hearken to the word of the Lord. So has the Lord said, "At this time tomorrow, a *seah* of fine flour will sell for a shekel and two *seahs* of barley will sell for a shekel in the gate of Samaria." 2. And the king's officer upon whose hand he would lean, answered the man of God, and said, "Behold, if the Lord makes windows in the sky, will this thing come about?" And he said, "Behold, you will see with your own eyes, but you shall not eat therefrom." 3. Now there were four men, stricken with *zaraath,* [at] the entrance of the gate. And they said to each other, "Why are we sitting here until we die?

your womb . . . during the siege and in the straitness . . . [*Rashi*].

What more can I hope for from the Lord?—*to save? It will surely not avail* [*Rashi*].

Jonathan renders: What more shall I pray to the Lord?

Alternatively, the messenger said to Elisha, "Since the famine is a direct act of God, what will it avail us to pray? Will God go back on His word? [*Abarbanel*].

Still others explain that the messenger said to the king, "Since this calamity is the act of God, visited upon us as retribution for our sins, if I harm the prophet, what hope would there be for me anymore? [*Mezudath David*].

1. **And Elisha said,**—When Elisha heard that the messenger refused to harm him because of fear of the Lord, and that the king agreed with him, he announced, "Hearken to the word of the Lord . . ." [*Mezudath David*].

in the gate of Samaria—in the market.

2. **makes windows**—through which it will rain copiously, or through which wheat and barley will fall like manna . . . [*Redak, Mezudath David*].

will this thing come about?—Is it possible that grain will become so cheap? [*Abarbanel, Mezudath David*].

Behold, you will see . . .—Elisha detected that the officer denied God's ability to perform a miracle and grant enough grain to bring the price down to a shekel for a *seah* of fine flour and a shekel for two *seahs* of barley. He, therefore, cursed him that he would see it, yet not benefit

מָתְנוּ: ד אִם־אָמַרְנוּ נָבוֹא הָעִיר וְהָרָעָב
בָּעִיר וָמַתְנוּ שָׁם וְאִם־יָשַׁבְנוּ פֹה וָמָתְנוּ
וְעַתָּה לְכוּ וְנִפְּלָה אֶל־מַחֲנֵה אֲרָם אִם־
יְחַיֻּנוּ נִחְיֶה וְאִם־יְמִיתֻנוּ וָמָתְנוּ: ה וַיָּקֻמוּ
בַנֶּשֶׁף לָבוֹא אֶל־מַחֲנֵה אֲרָם וַיָּבֹאוּ עַד־
קְצֵה מַחֲנֵה אֲרָם וְהִנֵּה אֵין־שָׁם אִישׁ:
ו וַאדֹנָי הִשְׁמִיעַ | אֶת־מַחֲנֵה אֲרָם קוֹל
רֶכֶב וְקוֹל סוּס קוֹל חַיִל גָּדוֹל וַיֹּאמְרוּ
אִישׁ אֶל־אָחִיו הִנֵּה שָׂכַר־עָלֵינוּ מֶלֶךְ
יִשְׂרָאֵל אֶת־מַלְכֵי הַחִתִּים וְאֶת־מַלְכֵי
מִצְרַיִם לָבוֹא עָלֵינוּ: ז וַיָּקוּמוּ וַיָּנוּסוּ

דנמות: ד אם נימר
ניעול לקרתא וכפנא
בקרתא ונמות תמן
ואם נתיב הכא ונמות
וכען אתו ונשתמע
למשרית ארם אם
יחיוננא ונחי אם
יקטלוננא ונתקטיל:
ה וקמו בקבלא למיעל
למשרית ארם ואתו עד
סיפי משרית ארם
והא לית תמן אנש:
ו ומן קדם יי אשתמע
למשרית ארם קל
רתיכין קל סוסון קל
משרין סגיאין ונאמרו
גבר לחבריה הא אגר
עלנא מלכא דישראל
ית מלכי חתאי וית
מלכי מצראי למיתי
עלנא: ז וקמו וערקו

ת"א אם אמרנו. בבא קמא ס ע"ב
כז עקידה שער סא:

רד"ק

כי אלה הארבעה היו גחזי וג׳ בניו: פתח השער. כמו שדרך המצורעים להיות חוץ לעיר כמו שכתוב מחוץ למחנה מושבו: עד מתנו. עד אשר מתנו: (ד) ונפלה. כמו אל הכשדים אתה נופל: (ו) השמיע את מחנה ארם. לפני בא המצורעים באותו לילה כי אם נסו מאתמול ביום ההוא היו רואי׳ ישראל וכן אומר ויקומו בנשף תכף כששמעו הקול נכנס פחד גדול בלבם ונסו:

רש"י

י"ג מ"ו): (ו) השמיע את מחנה ארם. נדמה להם

מנחת שי

ז (ו) קול רכב וקול סוס. בתרגום של יונתן כתוב וקל סוסין ובכל ספרים כ"י ודפוסים ישנים קול סוס בלא וא"ו בראש המלה וכן הוא במאיר נתיב ואני יגעתי לעמוד על בירורו של דבר עד שמצאתי בחסד אל מסרה משנים עשר פסוקים דמיין מן ג׳ ג׳ מלין קדמאה ותליתאה לא נסיב וא"ו ומציעאה נסיב ו׳ וסימן נמסר במסרה גדולה ישעיה מ"ט ופסוק זה אינו נחשב עמהם ומזה נלמד

רלב"ג

למחנה והיה שם מקום להם תוך שער העיר סמוך לפתח השער: (ז) ויקומו וינוסו בנשף. רוצה לומר כי בלילה שמעו הקולות אשר

מצודת ציון

מסכה (ס"א א) ומשפטו עמך: (ד) ונפלה. ענין נטיה כמו אל כשדים אתה נופל (ירמיה לז): (ה) בנשף. בערב כמו מאחרי

מצודת דוד

מחוץ למחנה מושבו (ויקרא י"ג): עד מתנו. עד אשר נמות ברעב: (ד) נחיה. כי שם נמלא לחם: ומתנו. כלומר מה בכך אם נמות הלא ממ"כ אנו מעותדים למיתה: (ו) וה׳ השמיע. הסיבה היה שלא מלאו שם איש כי ה׳ השמיע וגו׳ ר"ל בהשגחת ה׳ היה נדמה להם כאילו שומעים: לבוא עלינו. וזהו הקול שאנו שומעים:

caused the soldiers to hear the sound of a great army. Had this transpired by day, the Israelites would have been aware of it [*Redak*].

to attack us—That is the sound that we hear. Hence the Lord had performed two miracles; first, to cause them to hear imaginary noises; and secondly, to cause them to imagine them to be the sound of attacking armies [*Malbim*].

and their horses . . .—They imagined that the attackers had come to plunder the camp. They, therefore, left over their horses and donkeys to occupy the attackers, so that they would neglect to pursue them [*Malbim*].

and they fled for their lives—They did not take a minute to gather any of their belongings, but fled immediately, lest the attackers overtake them [*Redak*].

came to the edge of the camp—Now they came to the edge of the camp proper [*Malbim*].

4. If we say that we will come into the city, with the famine in the city, we will die there, and if we stay here we will die. So now, let us go and let us defect to the Aramean camp. If they spare us we will live, and if they kill us we will die." 5. And they arose in the evening to come to the Aramean camp. And they came to the edge of the Aramean camp, and behold, no one was there. 6. Now the Lord had caused the Aramean camp to hear the sound of chariots and the sound of horses, the sound of a great army. And they said to one another, "Behold, the king of Israel has hired for us the kings of the Hittites and the kings of the Egyptians to attack us."

the *zaraath* of Naaman [*Yalkut Hagershuni*].

at the entrance of the gate—*as it is said* (Lev. 13:46) *He shall live alone; outside the camp shall be his habitation* [*Rashi, Redak, Mezudath David, Malbim*].

Walled cities are considered as the camp of Israel, corresponding to the camp of the Israelites in the desert, whence those afflicted with *zaraath* were expelled. See Rashi Num. 5:2, Kelim 1:7.

until we die—from hunger [*Mezudath David*].

If they spare us we will live—If they spare us and give us food, we will gain our lives by defecting to the Aramean camp [*Abarbanel, Mezudath David*].

we will die—We will die in any case, whether or not we defect. Therefore, we have nothing to lose by defecting to the Aramean camp [*Abarbanel, Mezudath David*].

Alternatively, if the Arameans will kill us, we will die immediately, without suffering the pangs of hunger. Therefore, in any case, we will gain by defecting to the Arameans [*Kochav MiYaakov*].

5. **And they arose in the evening**—In order for the prophecy to be fulfilled, that on the morrow food would be plentiful, they had to go to the camp in the evening. Otherwise, had they gone in the morning and then notified the king, it would not have been fulfilled at the same time it was pronounced on the day before [*Malbim*].

to the edge of the Aramean camp—some distance from the camp, where usually a sentry is posted to observe all that transpires in the vicinity of the camp [*Malbim*].

no one was there—I.e. the sentry was not in his usual place [*Malbim*].

6. **had caused the Aramean camp to hear**—*It seemed to them as though they were hearing* [*Rashi*].

The camp was deserted because on that very evening, before the arrival of the *mezoraim,* God had

בַּנֶּשֶׁף וַיַּעַזְבוּ אֶת־אׇהֳלֵיהֶם וְאֶת־
סוּסֵיהֶם וְאֶת־חֲמֹרֵיהֶם הַמַּחֲנֶה כַּאֲשֶׁר
הִיא וַיָּנֻסוּ אֶל־נַפְשָׁם׃ ח וַיָּבֹאוּ הַמְצֹרָעִים
הָאֵלֶּה עַד־קְצֵה הַמַּחֲנֶה וַיָּבֹאוּ אֶל־
אֹהֶל אֶחָד וַיֹּאכְלוּ וַיִּשְׁתּוּ וַיִּשְׂאוּ מִשָּׁם
כֶּסֶף וְזָהָב וּבְגָדִים וַיֵּלְכוּ וַיַּטְמִנוּ וַיָּשֻׁבוּ
וַיָּבֹאוּ אֶל־אֹהֶל אַחֵר וַיִּשְׂאוּ מִשָּׁם וַיֵּלְכוּ
וַיַּטְמִנוּ׃ ט וַיֹּאמְרוּ אִישׁ אֶל־רֵעֵהוּ לֹא־כֵן
אֲנַחְנוּ עֹשִׂים הַיּוֹם הַזֶּה יוֹם־בְּשֹׂרָה
הוּא וַאֲנַחְנוּ מַחְשִׁים וְחִכִּינוּ עַד־אוֹר
הַבֹּקֶר וּמְצָאָנוּ עָווֹן וְעַתָּה לְכוּ וְנָבֹאָה
וְנַגִּידָה בֵּית הַמֶּלֶךְ׃ י וַיָּבֹאוּ וַיִּקְרְאוּ אֶל־
שֹׁעֵר הָעִיר וַיַּגִּידוּ לָהֶם לֵאמֹר בָּאנוּ

בְּקַבְלָא וּשְׁבָקוּ יָת
מַשְׁכְּנֵיהוֹן וְיָת
סוּסָוָתְהוֹן וְיָת חֲמָרֵיהוֹן
בְּמַשְׁרִיתָא כְּמָא דְהִיא
וַעֲרַקוּ לְשֵׁיזָבָא
נַפְשֵׁיהוֹן׃ ח נַאֲתוֹ
סְגִירַיָא הָאִלֵּין עַד סְיָפֵי
מַשְׁרִיתָא וְעָלוּ לְמַשְׁכְּנָא
חַד וַאֲכַלוּ וּשְׁתִיאוּ
וּנְסִיבוּ מִתַּמָּן כַּסְפָּא
וְדַהֲבָא וּלְבוּשִׁין
נַאֲזַלוּ וְאַטְמַרוּ וְתָבוּ
וְעָלוּ לְמַשְׁכְּנָא אוֹחֲרָנָא
וּנְסִיבוּ מִתַּמָּן נַאֲזַלוּ
וְאַטְמַרוּ׃ ט נַאֲמַרוּ
גְּבַר לְחַבְרֵיהּ לָא כְשַׁר
מָה דַאֲנַחְנָא עָבְדִין
יוֹמָא הָדֵין יוֹם בְּסוֹרָא
הוּא וְאִלּוּ אֲנַחְנָא
שָׁתְקִין וּמוֹרְכִין עַד
נְהוֹר צַפְרָא
וְיַשְׁכְּחוּנָנָא חוֹבָא וּכְעַן
אִיתוֹ וְנֵיתֵי וּנְחַוֵּי בֵּית
מַלְכָּא׃ י נַאֲתוֹ וּקְרוֹ
לְנָטְרֵי תְּרַע קַרְתָּא

ת"א יום בשורה. עקידה שער סה:

רש"י

כאלו שומעין: (ט) ומצאנו עון. מתחייבין אנו למלכות:

רד"ק

(ז) וינוסו אל נפשם. להציל נפשם לא חסו על הממון ואפילו הסוסים לא אסרו לרכוב עליהם: (ט) לא כן. לא טוב כתרגומו לא כשר מה דאנחנא עבדין: מחשים. שותקים מלבשר: וחכינו עד אור הבוקר. אם נחכה עד אור הבוקר מלבשר מצאנו עון בזה: עון. מלא בשני ווי"ן: (י) אל שוער העיר ויגידו להם. שוער דרך כלל כמו ויליד ביתו הם יאכלו בלחמו

מנחת שי

שכתוב קול בלא וא"ו: שכר עלינו. כתוב במכלול משקל פעל שהוא מלעיל שלא כמנהג ובסוף מסרה גדולה נמנה ג"כ בשטה חדא דכל חד וחד מלעיל ולית דכותיה: (ז) המחנה כאשר היא. כתיב וקרי ביו"ד בדפוסים ישנים וספרים כתובי יד: (ח) ויבאו המצרעים. בספרים מדוייקים המ"ם רפה והצ"א במאריך: (ט) ומצאנו עוון. מלא בשני ווי"ן והוא חד מן ד' מלא ע"פ המסורות וסימן נמסר

רלב"ג

השמיעם הש"י על דרך המופ' ובלילה ההוא נסו תכף ומרוב פחדם עזבו סוסיהם והמוריהם וברחו ברגליהם: (ט) לא כן אנחנו עושים. ר"ל אין אנחנו עושים דבר ראוי היום הזה הוא יום ראוי לבשר ואם אנחנו שותקים וממתין עד אור הבוקר ידעו זה ישראל וימצאנו עונש

מצודת דוד

(ז) המחנה כאשר היא. הכל בשלימות כאשר היתה היא בעוד שהיו שם: אל נפשם. להציל את נפשם: (ט) לא כן. לא טוב ויושר כמו ולא יכין לדבר כן (שופטים י"ב): היום הזה וגו'. כי היום יש בו מה לבשר טוב ואנחנו שותקים מלבשר ואם נמתין עד הבוקר הלא יודע למלך ע"י אחרים ונאשם בעיניו ע"מ שלא מהרנו לבוא ולבשר: (י) שוער העיר. שומר שער העיר: אסור. קשור אל האבום כדרכו: כאשר המה. כשהיו מאז כאשר היו שם:

מצודת ציון

בנשף (ישעיה ה): (ט) מחשים. שותקים. כמו גם אני ידעתי החשו (לעיל ב): וחכינו. ענין איחור והמתנה כמו ונכסה ולא תחכה

Alternatively, the four *mezoraim* were guilty of the crime of which the king's officer was guilty. They doubted the prophecy of the termination of the famine. Now they regretted their sin and decided to make amends the best they could. They, therefore, announced, "This day is a day of good news." This is the day Elisha prophesied would be the end of the famine, when a *seah* of fine flour would be sold for a shekel and two *seahs* of barley would be sold for a shekel.

If we keep quiet and do not report our discovery to the king, we will compound our first offense of taking gifts from Naaman the Aramean.

7. And they picked themselves up and fled at dusk, leaving behind their tents, their horses, and their donkeys, the camp as it was, and they fled for their lives. 8. Now these *mezoraim* came up to the edge of the camp, entered one tent, ate and drank, and carried off from there silver, gold, and clothing, and they went and hid [them]. And they returned and entered another tent, and carried off from there, and they went and hid [them].9. Now one said to another, "We are not doing right. This day is a day of good news, yet we are keeping quiet. If we wait until daybreak, we will incur guilt. Now, let us go and come and relate this in the king's palace." 10. And they came and called to the gatekeepers of the city and told them, saying,

9. **"We are not doing right**—by not disclosing our discovery of plentiful food with which we can revive the starving populace [*Malbim*].

This day . . .—Let us not give in to our greed today as we did by taking gifts from Naaman. Let us not add to our sins, but rather go immediately to report Israel's good fortune [*Malbim*].

is a day of good news—a day when we have good news to report [*Mezudath David*].

and we are keeping quiet—I.e. we refrain from reporting it [*Redak, Mezudath David*].

Alternatively, and if we keep quiet . . . [*Ralbag*].

If we wait until daybreak—I.e. if we do not go now, we will not be able to go during the night. Since it is unusual to enter the enemy's camp during the night, they will realize that we entered during the early evening. They will ask us why we delayed our report until night, and suspect us of looting the camp. We will therefore be forced to wait until morning before reporting our discovery [*Malbim*].

We will incur guilt—*We will be held guilty by the throne* [*Rashi*].

I.e. if others report this before us, we will be held guilty by the king, for our delay in reporting the good news [*Mezudath David*].

Alternatively, we will be held guilty for looting the camp [*Abarbanel*].

Alternatively, we will be guilty of the deaths of many starving people [*Malbim*].

The plene spelling of עָוֹון, *guilt,* indicates a serious crime, since they would leave Israel vulnerable to attack by their enemies, a condition that could be remedied if they would take supplies from the Aramean camp [*Pseudo-Rashi* I Chron. 21:8].

אל-מחנה ארם והנה אין-שם איש
וקול אדם כי אם-הסוס אסור והחמור
אסור ואהלים כאשר המה: יא ויקרא
השערים ויגידו בית המלך פנימה:
יב ויקם המלך לילה ויאמר אל-עבדיו
אגידה-נא לכם את אשר-עשו לנו
ארם ידעו כי-רעבים אנחנו ויצאו מן
המחנה להחבה בהשדה לאמר כי-
יצאו מן-העיר ונתפשם חיים ואל-
העיר נבא: יג ויען אחד מעבדיו ויאמר
ויקחו-נא חמשה מן-הסוסים
הנשארים אשר נשארו-בה הנם
ככל-ההמון ישראל אשר נשארו-בה

תרגום

וחויאו להון למימר
אתינא למשרית ארם
והא לית תמן גבר וקל
אנש אלהין סוסון
אסירין וחמרין אסירין
ומשכנין כמא דאינון:
יא וקרא נטרי תרעא
וחויאו בית מלכא לגיו:
יב וקם מלכא בליליא
ואמר לעבדוהי אחוי
כען לכון ית דעבדו לנא
אנש ארם ידעין ארי
כפנין אנחנא ונפקו מן
משריתא לאטמרא
בחקלא למימר אם
יפקון מן קרתא
וניחודונון כד חיין
ולקרתא ניעול:
יג ואתיב חד מעבדוהי
ואמר וידברון כען
חמשא מן סוסותא מן
שארא דאשתארו בה
הא אינון ככל המונא
דישראל דאשתארו בה

אם

ת"א ויען אחד מעבדיו. בס שער ל:

בשדה קרי המון קרי

רד"ק

או פירושו קראו אל שוער אחד מן השוערים וקמו כלם והגידו לחם זה הדבר: הסוס אסור והחמור אסור. דרך כלל כמו ויחי לי שור וחמור ופירושו שהיו אסורים על אבוסיהם: (יא) ויקרא השוערים. שוער העיר קרא אל שוערי בית המלך והם הגידו בית המלך פנימה: (יב) להחבה. בה"א: בהשדה. נכתב בה"א הידיעה כמשפט כמו להגדוד אשר בא עליו והדומים לו וקרי בשדה בלא ה"א הידיעה כמנהג ברוב להקל: (יג) ככל המון ישראל אשר נשארו בה. נכתב ההמון על הידיעה בסמיכות כמו העם המלחמה הארון הברית והדומים

רש"י

(י) כאשר המה. כמו שהיו מלאים מתחלתם לא הוציאו מה שבתוכם: (יב) כי רעבים אנחנו. ותאבים לצאת אל השלל ואל המזון: (יג) אשר נשארו בה. בתוך העיר

מנחת שי

בדברי הימים א' כ"א. ועיין בס בפי' רש"י ז"ל: (יב) בהשדה. בשדה קרי ועיין מ"ש בקהלת סימן ו' על שהתקיף: (יג) הנם ככל ההמון. בכ"ף וכן

רלב"ג

על אשר לא בשרנו הבשורה הזאת והנה אז היה עדיין לילה: (יא) ויקרא השוערים. רוצה לומר ששוער העיר קרא השוערים אשר שומרים שער המלך: (יג) הנם ככל המון ישראל. הנה ההמון כתוב והמון קרי והכל ענין אחד והרצון בכתבו ההמון המון ישראל כמו והכוונה עודד הנביא והרצון בזה אם ימלטו הנם ככל המון ישראל אשר נשארו בה בעיר ואין בזה נזק ואם יפסדו הנם ככל המון ישראל

מצודת ציון

(לקמן ט): (יג) הנם. הנה הם: המון. ענין רבוי עם: תמו.

מצודת דוד

(יא) ויקרא השוערי'. שוער העיר קרא אל שומרי שערי בית המלך ואמר להם הדברים האלה והם הגידו הדבר לבית הפנימי מקום מושב המלך: (יב) את אשר וגו'. הערמה והתחבולה אשר עשו: כי יצאו. להמציא מה לאכול כי לגודל הרעבון לא ימתינו עד יחקרו על הדבר: (יג) אשר נשארו בה וגו'. כלומר אף אם האויב ימית את הרוכבים אין היזק בדבר כי יהיו ככל המון ישראל

horses left, I will tell you that the horses perished like the multitude of Israel that likewise perished from hunger [*Redak* quoting his father].

Others explain: It is advisable to risk the horses and their riders, because they will eventually die of starvation if they remain in the city [*Abarbanel* and *Mezudath David*].

Although they may die earlier by the hands of the Arameans, they will be no less fortunate than—*all the*

"We came to the Aramean camp, and behold there is no man there nor the sound of a human, but the horses are tethered and the donkeys are tethered, and the tents are as they were." 11. And he called the gatekeepers; and they related it to the king's palace inside. 12. And the king arose at night and said to his servants, "Now I will tell you what the Arameans have done to us. They know that we are hungry. So they left the camp to hide in the field, saying, 'When they come out of the city, we will seize them alive and enter the city.'" 13. Now one of his servants called out and said, "Let them take now five of the remaining horses that are left there. Behold, they are like all the multitude of Israel that are left there,

Now, because of our greed, we will take plunder for ourselves, and not look forward to God's salvation to His people Israel. The double *vav* indicates the compounded sin of which Gehazi and his sons would be guilty [*Akedah,* ch. 61, *K'li Y'kar*].

10. **the gatekeepers**—Heb. שֹׁעֵר, a singular noun, applying to the body of gatekeepers. Alternatively, the *mezoraim* called one gatekeeper, and when they all gathered around, they related their story to them [*Redak*].

as they were—*as they were full at the beginning; they did not take out what was in them* [*Rashi*].

11. **And he called the gatekeepers**—Heb. singular. See Commentary Digest v. 10. The gatekeepers of the city called the gatekeepers of the palace [*Redak, Ralbag, Mezudath David*].

and they related it—I.e. the palace gatekeepers related it to those in the king's palace [*Redak, Mezudath David*].

Alternatively, the *mezoraim* told their story to the head gatekeeper, who in turn called the other gatekeepers, who relayed the information to those within the king's palace [*Malbim*].

12. **that we are hungry**—*and long to go out to the loot and to the food* [*Rashi*].

13. **that are left there**—*within the city, that did not die of hunger* [*Rashi*].

Behold, they are like all the multitude of Israel that are left there—*If they will say that they are imperiled lest the Arameans kill them, behold they are in this city in peril of famine like the rest of all the multitude of Israel that are left there, and if they die, they are like all the multitude of Israel that have perished from hunger* [*Rashi* after *Jonathan*].

Others explain; Behold, they are as thin and emaciated as all the multitude of Israel that is left in the city. If you ask why there are so few

הנם ככל־המון ישראל אשר־תמו
ונשלחה ונראה: יד ויקחו שני רכב
סוסים וישלח המלך אחרי מחנה־
ארם לאמר לכו וראו: טו וילכו אחריהם
עד־הירדן והנה כל־הדרך מלאה
בגדים וכלים אשר־השליכו ארם
בהחפזם וישבו המלאכים ויגדו למלך:
טז ויצא העם ויבזו את מחנה ארם ויהי
סאה סלת בשקל וסאתים שערים
בשקל כדבר יהוה: יז והמלך הפקיד
את־השליש אשר נשען על־ידו על־

אם יבדון הא אינון כבל המונא דישראל דספו ונשלח ונחזי: יד ודברו תרין רכבי סוסין ושלח מלכא בתר משרית ארם למימר איזילו וחזו: טו ואזלו בתריהון עד ירדנא והא כל אורחא מליא לבושין ומנין דרמו אנש ארם באתבעותהון למערק ותבו אזגדיא וחויאו למלכא: טז ונפק עמא ובזו ית משרית ארם והוה סאה סולתא בסלעא וסאתן סעורין בסלעא כפתגמא דיי: יז ומלכא מני ית גברא דסמיך על ידוהי על תרעא ודשוהי עמא בתרעא ומית כמא דמליל

בחפזם קרי

רש"י

שלא מתו ברעב: הנם ככל המון אשר נשארו בה. אם יאמרו מסוכנין הן שלא יהרגם ארם הרי הנם בעיר הזאת בסכנת הרעב כשאר כל המון ישראל אשר נשארו בה ואם ימותו הנה ככל המון ישראל אשר תמו ברעב: (טו) בחפזם. במהרם לנוס: (יז) אשר נשען על ידו. אתמול כשבא לבית אלישע:

רד"ק

להם יקרי בלא ה"א הידיעה כמנהג ברוב ופי' הפסוק כן הוא הנם ככל המון ישראל פירוש הסוסים כחושים ורעים ככל המון ישראל שנשארו בשמרון שהם כחושים מהרעב וא"ת היאך לא נשארו כי אם חמשה סוסים בשמרון הנם ככל המון ישראל אשר תמו כמו שתמו האנשים כן תמו הסוסים כן פירש אדוני אבי ז"ל. ויונתן תרגם אם יבדון הא אינון ככל המונא דישראל דספו: ככל המון ישראל. בכ"ף: (יד) ויקחו שני רכב סוסים. והלא אמר חמשת סוסים והיאך אמר שלא לקחו אלא שנים כי פירוש שני רכב סוסים שנים סוסים ורוכבים עליהם וכת"י תרין רכבי סוסין אלא מן החמשה שאמרו בחרו השנים הטובים שבהם: (טו) בהחפזם. הכתוב הוא עם ה"א ויהיה מבנין נפעל אם הה"א נקודה בצר"י והקרי הוא בלא ה"א מן הקל:

רלב"ג

אשר תמו ולא יוכל ההפסד הזה ביחס אל כל מה שנפסד מפני הרעב והנה לא הסכימו לשלוח כי אם שני רכב סוסים כי די בהם לעמוד על אמתת זה: (טו) אשר השליכו ארם בחפזם. ר"ל מפני היותם נחפזים ללכת: (יז) והמלך הפקיד את השליש. ר"ל שכבר הפקידו

מנחת שי

חברו שבפסוק: ההמון ישראל אשר נשארו בה. המון קרי: (טו) בהחפזם. בחפזם קרי והוא חד מן מלין דכתובין ה"א במלעות תיבותא ולא קריין כמ"ש

מצודת דוד

הנשארים בעיר כי כולנו מעותדים למות ברעב והרוכבים לאחד ממנו אם ישארו פה ואם לאחוז במה שיוקדם להם המיתה הלא יהיו ככל המון ישראל שכבר תמו קודם להם ולזאת נשלחה ונראה: (יד) שני רכב. כי עכ"ז לא רצו להכניס בסכנה כ"א שנים: אחרי מחנה. ר"ל בדרך ארם: (טו) אשר השליכו. להקל משאם בעבור מהירת הניסה: (יז) הפקיד. מינה אותו אז להיות שומר השער:

מצודת ציון

נשלמו: (טו) בחפזם. ענין מהירות כמו ויהי בחפזם לנוס (ש"ב ד):

Samaria, since those bringing in grain were required to pay a duty [*Malbim*].

which he spoke when the king had come down to him—Scripture delineates the magnitude of the officer's sins. He retorted when the king had come to the prophet. The prophet had not spoken to him, yet he retorted by scoffing at his prophecy. By rejecting Elisha's assurance that the famine would soon terminate he

behold they are like all the multitude of Israel that have perished; and let us send and we will see." 14. So they took two riders of horses, and the king sent them after the Aramean camp, saying, "Go and see." 15. And they followed them up to the Jordan, and behold all the way was full of garments and vessels that the Arameans had cast off in their haste; and the messengers returned and related it to the king. 16. And the people went out and plundered the Aramean camp; and a *seah* of fine flour was sold for a shekel and two *seahs* of barley were sold for a shekel, according to the word of the Lord. 17. Now the king appointed the officer upon whose hand he leaned, over

multitude of Israel that has perished of hunger in the city [*Mezudath David*].

14. **two riders of horses**—i.e. two horses with their riders. Out of the five horses suggested by the king's servant, they selected the two best to send into the Aramean camp [*Redak*].

Although it had been suggested that they send *five* horses with riders into the Aramean camp to spy out the camp and to learn whether the Arameans were hiding in the nearby fields, they decided that the same information could be obtained by risking but two [*Ralbag, Mezudath David, Abarbanel, Malbim*].

15. **And they followed them**—I.e. the two horsemen followed the tracks of the Arameans.

in their haste—*in their hurry to flee* [*Rashi*].

I.e. in order to lighten their load, they discarded garments and utensils, and fled as quickly as possible [*Mezudath David*].

17. **upon whose hand he leaned**—*on the day before, when he came to Elisha's house* [*Rashi*].

The king appointed him to stand guard at the gate to prevent the populace from looting the camp. Since the rule was that spoils of war must be turned over to the royal treasury, he appointed the officer to enforce this. Had he indeed done so, and the distribution of grain would have been in the hands of the king, he could have kept the price higher than that predicted by the prophet. Hence, the officer was attempting to prevent the fulfillment of the prophecy. Because of his sins, he was trampled by the populace. Although outside the camp the price had already dropped, it had not yet dropped in the marketplace of

השער וירמסהו העם בשער וימת
כאשר דבר איש האלהים אשר דבר
ברדת המלך אליו: יח ויהי כדבר איש
האלהים אל־המלך לאמר סאתים
שערים בשקל וסאה־סלת בשקל
יהיה כעת מחר בשער שמרון: יט ויען
השליש את־איש האלהים ויאמר
והנה יהוה עשה ארבות בשמים
היהיה כדבר הזה ויאמר הנך ראה
בעיניך ומשם לא תאכל: כ ויהי־לו
כן וירמסו אתו העם בשער וימת:
ח א ואלישע דבר אל־האשה אשר־
החיה את־בנה לאמר קומי ולכי אתי

דמליל נביא דיי דמליל
כד נחת מלכא לותיה:
יח והוה כד מליל נביא
דיי עם מלכא למימר
סאתין סעורין בסלעא
וסאה סולתא בסלעא
יהי בעדנא הדין מחר
בתרעא דשמרון:
יט ואתיב גברא ית
נביא דיי ואמר ואלו
יי פתח כוין ומחית
טובא מן שמיא היהי
כפתגמא הדין ואמר
הא את חזי בעינך
ומתמן לא תיכול:
כ והוה ליה כן ודשו
יתיה עמא בתרעא
ומית: א ואלישע מליל
עם אתתא דאחיי ית
ברה למימר קומי
ואזילו את ואנש
ביתיך ודירי באתר
דכשר למידר אתי
זמין

ת״א ויהיו לו כן. סנהדרין ל:

את קרי

רד״ק

(יח) ויהי כדבר. לפי שאמר כאשר דבר איש האלהים ספר היאך היו הדברים אע״פ שכבר כתב למעלה השיב עוד הדברים הנה על המעשה: (א) אתי וביתך. היו״ד בכתב

רש״י

ח (א) ואלישע דבר אל האשה. זה שבע שנים: כי קרא ה׳ לרעב. הוא הרעב אשר היה בימי

מנחת שי

בקהלת סימן ו׳: (יח) ויהי כדבר וגו׳ וסאה סלת. במקצת ספרים כתיב וסאה הסמ״ך בשוא לבדו וכספרים כתובי יד מדוייקים וגם בדפוסים ישנים הסמ״ך בחטף קמץ והוא״ו במאריך וכ״כ רד״ק בשרשים ויהי סאה סלת בשוא הסמ״ך. וסאה סלת בשקל. בחטף קמץ הסמ״ך: (יט) היהיה כדבר הזה. הרבו הספרים לפשוע בדבר הזה וברוך היודע אי זה יכשר הזה או זה כי בשתי מקראות כ״י משנים קדמוניות מצאתי כתוב הדבר הזה בה״א כמו שכתוב בתחלת הפרשה וגם בדפוס ישן שכתב בפנים כדבר נרשם מבחוץ הדבר להורות שנמצא חילוף זה בספרים. ולא ראיתי לאחד מהמפרשים כלום זולתי בעל כלי יקר שכתב וזה יובן שנוי הלשון שלמעלה אמר הדבר הזה וכאן הוא אומר כדבר הזה להכביד חטא השליש לומר שלא האמין כלל לא זה ולא כיוצא בו ולזה אמר כאן כדבר הזה בכ״ף הדמיון לא כן למעלה שכתוב היהיה הדבר הזה עכ״ל. וכן בתרגום יונתן הראשון פתגמא והשני כפתגמא אבל במאיר נתיב שניהם בה״א:
ח (א) אשר החיה. ברוב ספרים החי״ת בחטף סגול כמנהג ברוב כספ״א גרונית ויש ספרים בשוא לבדו: ולכי אתי. את קרי:

רלב״ג

לאנשים שישמרוהו שם באופן שבעבור העם שם ירמסוהו בעבור מה

מצודת דוד

וירמסוהו. מרוב הדחק העם ההולכים לשלול שלל רמסוהו ברגליהם: (יח) ויהי כדבר. חוזר ומפרש למה דבר הנביא שימות השליש ואמר לפי שכאשר דבר איש האלהים וכו׳: (יט) ויען. ואז השיב השליש וכו׳: ויאמר. ואז אמר לו הנביא הנך רואה וכו׳: (כ) ויהי לו כן. וכאשר אמר הנביא כן היה: ח (א) באשר תגורי. במקום שתרצה לגור: וגם בא. ככל

one as a messenger of God, but administered solely by the Lord Himself. The Lord gave these keys to Elijah, but only one at a time, never two, lest people say that the disciple has more power than the Master (*San.* 113a). Elisha too was given these powers. Had he not resurrected the son of the Shunemitess, he would have been eligible for the "key" of rainfall, thus avoiding the famine. However, since he had resurrected him, he was unable to prevent it. He, therefore, advised the mother to leave the land for the duration of the famine [*Malbim*].

in a place suitable for you to sojourn—[*Jonathan*].

the gate, and the people trampled him and he died, as the man of God had spoken, which he spoke when the king had come down to him. 18. And it was when the man of God had spoken to the king, saying, "Two *seahs* of barley will be sold for a shekel and a *seah* of fine flour will be sold at this time tomorrow in the gate of Samaria," . . . 19. That the officer answered the man of God and said, "And behold, if God makes windows in the sky, will this thing come about?" And he said, "Behold you will see it with your own eyes, yet you shall not eat therefrom." 20. And so it happened to him, that the people trampled him in the gate, and he died.

8

1. Now Elisha had spoken to the woman whose son he had revived, saying, "Get up and go, you

was advising the king to slay him as he had originally planned [*Malbim*].

18. **"Two seahs of barley . . . in the gate of Samaria."**—This price was not unusual in all of the land of Israel. It was only so in Samaria because there was a famine due to the siege. It would not be unusual for the siege to end, and for the price to drop to the level of the rest of the land [*Malbim*].

19. **if God makes windows in the sky**—The retort was most untimely, since the prophet did not prophesy that the price would fall below that of the rest of the land. Had he so stated it would indeed necessitate a miracle to provide such a plenty. Since he did not, however, the officer's statement was entirely inappropriate [*Malbim*].

will this thing come about?—By this question, he denied God's ability, and he also denied the prophecy. He was therefore liable to death at the hands of Heaven [*Malbim*].

and so it happened to him—that he was paid in kind [*Malbim*].

1. **Now Elisha had spoken to the woman**—*already seven years before* [*Rashi*].

whose son he had revived—The relevance of the revival of the woman's son can be explained thus: The Talmud states that there are three "keys" that are not given over to a messenger: (1) the key of childbirth, (2) the key of rainfall, and (3) the key of resurrection of the dead. Until the time of Elijah, these powers were not delegated to any-

וביתך וגורי באשר תגורי כי־קרא
יהוה לרעב וגם־בא אל־הארץ שבע
שנים: ב ותקם האשה ותעש כדבר
איש האלהים ותלך היא וביתה ותגר
בארץ־פלשתים שבע שנים: ג ויהי
מקצה שבע שנים ותשב האשה
מארץ פלשתים ותצא לצעק אל־
המלך אל־ביתה ואל־שדה: ד והמלך
מדבר אל־גחזי נער איש־האלהים
לאמר ספרה־נא לי את כל־הגדלות
אשר־עשה אלישע: ה ויהי הוא מספר
למלך את־אשר־החיה את־המת והנה
האשה אשר־החיה את־בנה צעקת
אל־המלך על־ביתה ועל־שדה ויאמר

תרגום

זמין יי כפנא ואף
עתיד למיתי על ארעא
שבע שנין: ב וקמת
אתתא ועבדת כפתגמא
דנביא דיי ואזלת היא
ואנש ביתה ואתותבת
בארעא פלשתאי שבע
שנין: ג והוה מסוף
שבע שנין ותבת אתתא
מארעא פלשתאי
ונפקת למיקבל קדם
מלכא על ביתה ועל
חקלה: ד ומלכא מליל
עם גחזי תלמידא
דנביא דיי למימר
אשתעי כען לי ית כל
רברבתא דעבד אלישע:
ה והוה הוא משתעי
למלכא ית דאחיי ית
מיתא והא אתתא
דאחיי ית ברה קבלא
קדם מלכא על ביתה
ועל חקלה ואמר
גחזי

תולדות אהרן

כי קרא . ברכות ה תענית ה : כפרה נא . מגלה כז :

רש"י

יואל בן פתואל: (ג) אל ביתה ואל שדה. שהחזיקו להם דין חזקה: אל ביתה ואל שדה. כמו על וכמוהו רבים אל במקום על וכן הוא הבא אחר זה צעקה אל המלך על ביתה ועל

רד"ק

נוספת כמו יודי"ן רבות כמו שכתבתי למעלה: שבע שנים. בדברי רז"ל אותן שבע שנים אכלו שנה ראשונה מה שבבתים שניה מה שבשדות שלישית בשר בהמה טהורה רביעית בשר בהמה טמאה חמשית בשר שקצים ורמשים ששית בשר בניהם ובנותיהם שביעית בשר זרועותיהם לקיים מה שנאמר איש בשר זרועו יאכלו: (ג) לצעוק אל המלך. יש מרז"ל שלמדו מזה הפסוק כי יש חזקה לבורח כיון שהיתה צריכה למלך להחזיר השדה והתבואות שמע מינה כי אותם שהחזיקו היו

רלב"ג

מדבר כנגד הנביא: (ג) ותצא לצעק אל המלך אל ביתה ואל שדה. ר"ל שהחזיקו בהם אנשים והיתה מבקשת קרקעותיה ופירותיה מיום

מנחת שי

(ה) החיה את המת. החי"ת בחטף סגול וכן החיה את בנה. אשר החיה אלישע שבפסוק ומתחלפים בשוא לבד כמ"ש למעלה: וזה־בנה. יפה דגש:

מצודת דוד

כתחיל לבוא אל הארץ ויתמיד שבע שנים: (ג) אל ביתה. כי החזיקו בם אחרים בהיותה בפלשתים: (ד) כל הגדולות. כל הנפלאות הגדולות אשר עשה כי לא ידע המלך מכולם: (ה) ויהי הוא מספר. בעת שספר למלך מה שהחיה אלישע את בן השונמית

relates how the merit of Elisha benefited her, for she came just when the king asked Gehazi to tell him all the wondrous deeds that Elisha had performed [*Malbim*].

all the great things . . .—The king had not heard of all the miracles that Elisha had performed. He therefore asked Elisha to tell him *all* of them [*Mezudath David*].

5. **that the woman**—At exactly the time that Gehazi was telling of Elisha's reviving her son, she appeared before the king to com-

and your household, and sojourn in a place suitable for you to sojourn, for the Lord has decreed a famine, and it is destined to come upon the land for seven years." 2. And the woman got up and did according to the word of the man of God; and she and her household went, and she sojourned in the land of Philistines for seven years. 3. And it came about at the end of seven years that the woman returned from the land of Philistines; and she went out to complain to the king about her house and about her field. 4. Now the king was speaking to Gehazi, the servant of the man of God, saying, "Please tell me all the great things that Elisha performed." 5. And it was that he was telling the king that he revived the dead, that the woman whose son he had revived complained to the king about her house and about her field.

Alternatively, any place where you wish to sojourn [*Mezudath David*].

for the Lord has decreed a famine—*This is the famine that took place in the days of Joel the son of Pethuel* [*Rashi*]. See *Taanith* 5a, Joel 1:1, *Rashi* ad loc.

The Rabbis delineate the progressive severity of the famine, by teaching us what the people ate each year. During the first year they ate what they had in the houses; during the second year they ate what was in the fields; during the third year they ate the flesh of clean animals; during the fourth year the flesh of unclean animals; during the fifth year they ate reptiles and rodents; during the sixth year they ate their sons and daughters; during the seventh year they ate the flesh of their arms [*Redak* from *Taanith* 5a].

and it is destined to come—[*Targum Jonathan*]. *Mezudath David* renders: and has already come.

2. **according to the word of the man of God**—She left the land of Israel only because the prophet had instructed her to do so. Otherwise, she would not have left, especially since she was a prominent woman. She feared she would be punished like Elimelech for leaving Eretz Israel during a famine [*Malbim*].

3. **about her house and about her field**—*which robbers occupied* [*Rashi*].

While she was in the land of the Philistines, strangers occupied her house and field [*Mezudath David*].

4. **Now the king . . .**—Scripture

גֵּיחֲזִי אֲדֹנִי הַמֶּלֶךְ זֹאת הָאִשָּׁה וְזֶה־בְּנָהּ
אֲשֶׁר־הֶחֱיָה אֱלִישָׁע׃ ו וַיִּשְׁאַל הַמֶּלֶךְ
לָאִשָּׁה וַתְּסַפֶּר־לוֹ וַיִּתֶּן־לָהּ הַמֶּלֶךְ
סָרִיס אֶחָד לֵאמֹר הָשֵׁיב אֶת־כָּל־אֲשֶׁר־
לָהּ וְאֵת כָּל־תְּבוּאֹת הַשָּׂדֶה מִיּוֹם
עָזְבָה אֶת־הָאָרֶץ וְעַד־עָתָּה׃ ז וַיָּבֹא
אֱלִישָׁע דַּמֶּשֶׂק וּבֶן־הֲדַד מֶלֶךְ־אֲרָם
חֹלֶה וַיֻּגַּד־לוֹ לֵאמֹר בָּא אִישׁ הָאֱלֹהִים
עַד־הֵנָּה׃ ח וַיֹּאמֶר הַמֶּלֶךְ אֶל־חֲזָהאֵל
קַח בְּיָדְךָ מִנְחָה וְלֵךְ לִקְרַאת אִישׁ
הָאֱלֹהִים וְדָרַשְׁתָּ אֶת־יְהוָה מֵאוֹתוֹ
לֵאמֹר הַאֶחְיֶה מֵחֳלִי זֶה׃ ט וַיֵּלֶךְ חֲזָהאֵל
לִקְרָאתוֹ וַיִּקַּח מִנְחָה בְיָדוֹ וְכָל־טוּב

לא מפיק ה׳

תרגום

גחזי רבוני מלכא דא אתתא ודין ברה דאחיי אלישע : ו ושאיל מלכא לאתתא ואשתעיאת ליה ומני לה מלכא גוזא חד למימר אתיב ית כל דילה וית כל עללת חקלא מיומא דשבקת ית ארעא ועד כען :
ז ואתא אלישע דמשק ובר הדד מלכא דארם מרע ואתחוא ליה למימר אתא נביא דיי עד הלכא : ח ואמר מלכא לחזאל סב בידך תקרובתא ואזיל לקדמות נביא דיי ותתבע ית פתגמא דיי מניה למימר האיחי ממרעי דין : ט ואזל חזאל לקדמותיה ונסיב תקרובתא בידיה וכל טוב

תולדות אהרן

זאת האשה. סנהדרין ק : ויבא אלישע. סוטה מז סנהדרין קז :

רד"ק

שדה : (ו) סרים אחד. כתרגומו גוזא חד והוא סרים כמשמעו שנכרתו ביציו ואע"פ שהמעשה הזה אסור בישראל היו להם למלכי ישראל סריסים שהיו לוקחים אותם מן הגוים ההם או שהיו סריסים מחמת חולי והם בבתי המלכים כדי לעמוד בפני הנשים כמו שכתוב סרים המלך שומר הנשים : מיום עזבה. מקור העי"ן נקרא בקמץ חטף וההא רפה ומשפטה במפיק :
(ז) ויבא אלישע דמשק. למשוח את חזאל כדבר ה׳ אשר דבר אל אליהו כמו שפירשתי למעלה. ובדרש כי גחזי הלך לדמשק ואם הלך שם אומר אני כי הלך אל נעמן שייטיב לו בעבור שנדבק בו צרעתו בקללת אלישע והם אמרו כי יצא מן הדת והלך שם אלישע כדי להחזירו בתשובה ולא רצה אמר לו כך מקובל אני ממך כל החוטא ומחטיא את הרבים אין מספיקין בידו לעשות תשובה ומה עשה שהחטיא את הרבים מהם אמרו אבן שואבת תלה לחטאת ירבעם והעמידה בין שמים לארץ ומהם אמרו שם חקק לה בפיה והיתה מכרזת ואומרת אנכי ולא יהיה לך :(ט) וכל טוב דמשק. על דרך הפלגת הרבוי כמו

רש"י

כה גזלנים : (ז) ויבא אלישע דמשק. להחזיר את

מנחת שי

(ו) מיום עזבה את הארץ. בספרים מדוייקים הה"א רפה וכ"כ רד"ק במכלול דף ל"ב ובפירוש ושרשים שהוא מקור והעי"ן נקראת בקמץ חטוף והה"א

רלב"ג

נסתה : (ו) וישאל המלך לאשה ותספר לו. ר"ל שהגיד שאל לה זה הענין שספר גחזי שעשה אלישע מהגדולות ותספר לו שהענין הוא כן : ויתן לה המלך סרים אחד. ר"ל שר אחד ולוה שישיב לה את כל אשר לה מהקרקעות ואת כל תבואת השדה מיום עזבה את הארץ והולם

מצודת ציון

ח (ו) סרים. שר : עזבה. הניחה :

מצודת דוד

קרה מקרה שבאה אז השונמית עם בנה לצעוק אל המלך בעבור ביתה : (ו) השיב. אמר להשיב לה הכל ואף תבואות השדה אשר גדל בה מעת עזבה את השדה עד עתה : (ט) וכל טוב דמשק. כל מיני מאכל טוב הנמצא בדמשק :

And Gehazi said, "My lord the king, this is the woman and this
is her son whom Elisha revived." 6. And the king asked the
woman and she told him; and the king appointed for her one
eunuch, saying, "Return all her property, and all the produce of
the field from the day she left the land until now." 7. And
Elisha came to Damascus when Ben-Hadad was ill; and it was
told to him, saying, "The man of God is coming here." 8. And
the king said to Hazael, "Take a gift in your hand and go
toward the man of God, and inquire of the Lord from him, saying, "Will I recover from this illness?" 9. And Hazael went
toward him and took a gift in his hand and all the bounty

plain that her property had been occupied by strangers during her absence [*Malbim*].

The Rabbis tell us that this was far from being a coincidence. Even if the woman had been at the opposite end of the world, God would have transported her miraculously to the king to tell her own story, so that Gehazi would not be the one to tell of the miracles and praise the Almighty. He was not worthy of this honor [Lev. *Rabbah* 16:4.]

6. **And the king asked the woman**—Since the stories coincided, he awarded her the property. Had it not been for the merit of Elisha, she would have been required to bring evidence that she had not sold the field, since the present occupant had dwelt there for over three years without any protest on her part [*Malbim*].

7. **And Elisha came to Damascus**—*to influence Gehazi to repent* [*Rashi* from *San.* 107b].

Redak opines that Gehazi went to Damascus to request favors from Naaman whose *zaraath* had clung to him.

The Talmud continues to relate that Gehazi refused to repent on the grounds that he had learned that if one sins and causes others to sin, he is not enabled to repent. Some say that Gehazi had suspended Jeroboam's calves in the air by means of a magnet, and others say that he engraved the Divine Name in its mouth, by which it announced, "I am the Lord your God; you shall have no other gods before me." A third opinion, not quoted by *Redak,* is that he repelled students from attending Elisha's academy. See 6:1.

According to *peshat,* he went to Damascus to anoint Hazael as king of Aram. He was to represent his

טוּב דַמֶשֶׂק טְעוּן אַרְבְּעִין גַמְלִין וַאֲתָא וְקָם קֳדָמוֹהִי וַאֲמַר בְּרָךְ בַּר הֲדַד מַלְכָּא דַאֲרָם שַׁלְחַנִי לְוָתָךְ לְמֵימַר הַאֵיחֵי מִמַרְעִי דֵין: י וַאֲמַר לֵיהּ אֱלִישָׁע אֱזֵיל אֱמַר לֵיהּ מֵיחָא תֵיחֵי וְאַחֲזְיַנִי יְיָ אֲרֵי מֵמַת יְמוּת: יא וְאַסְחַר יַת אַפּוֹהִי וְאוֹרִיךְ עַד סַגִי וּבְכָא נְבִיָא דַיְיָ: יב וַאֲמַר חֲזָאֵל מָא דֵין רִבּוֹנִי בָּכֵי וַאֲמַר אֲרֵי יְדַעְנָא יַת דְתַעֲבֵיד לִבְנֵי יִשְׂרָאֵל בִּישָׁא כְּרַכֵּיהוֹן תּוֹקִיד בְּנוּרָא וְעוּלֵימֵיהוֹן בְּחַרְבָּא תִקְטֵיל וְעוּלֵימֵיהוֹן תטרף

דַּמֶּשֶׂק מַשָּׂא אַרְבָּעִים גָּמָל וַיָּבֹא וַיַּעֲמֹד לְפָנָיו וַיֹּאמֶר בִּנְךָ בֶן־הֲדַד מֶלֶךְ־אֲרָם שְׁלָחַנִי אֵלֶיךָ לֵאמֹר הַאֶחְיֶה מֵחֳלִי זֶה: י וַיֹּאמֶר אֵלָיו אֱלִישָׁע לֵךְ אֱמָר־לא חָיֹה תִחְיֶה וְהִרְאַנִי יְהוָה כִּי־מוֹת יָמוּת: יא וַיַּעֲמֵד אֶת־פָּנָיו וַיָּשֶׂם עַד־בֹּשׁ וַיֵּבְךְּ אִישׁ הָאֱלֹהִים: יב וַיֹּאמֶר חֲזָאֵל מַדּוּעַ אֲדֹנִי בֹכֶה וַיֹּאמֶר כִּי־יָדַעְתִּי אֵת אֲשֶׁר־תַּעֲשֶׂה לִבְנֵי יִשְׂרָאֵל רָעָה מִבְצְרֵיהֶם תְּשַׁלַּח בָּאֵשׁ וּבַחֻרֵיהֶם בַּחֶרֶב תַּהֲרֹג וְעֹלְלֵיהֶם

רש״י　　לו קרי

גיחזי בתשובה: (י) חיה תחיה. כלפי חזאל אמר שיחיה תחת בן הדד למלכות: (יא) ויעמד את פניו. פניו של צער שלו שהיה מבקש לבכות העמיד שלא יבכה בפני חזאל ויסם לבו לעמוד להתאפק: עד בוש. כמו בושש ולא

רד״ק

וכל טוב אדוניו בידו וכל הארץ באו מצרימה והדומים לחם. ובדרש וכי כל טוב דמשק היה נושא ארבעים גמל אלא ללמדך שהיתה בידו אבן טובה שהיתה ראויה ליתן בדמיה כל טוב דמשק: (י) אמר לא חיה תחיה. כתוב באל״ף לפי שדעתו שלא יחיה וקרי לו בוי״ו כי אמר לו שיחיה: והראני ה׳ כי מות ימות. כלומר מן החולי יחיה אם לא יומת אבל הראני ה׳ כי ימיתוהו ולפיכך כשאמר אלישע לחזאל כי יהיה מלך על ארם אמר לו והראני ה׳ כי מות ימות הבין חזאל כי רצה לומר לו שהוא ימיתהו אלא שלא אמר לו בפירוש: (יא) ויעמד את פניו וישם עד בוש. פי׳ העמיד פניו לצד אחר שלא יראה חזאל ושם ידיו על פניו עד זמן שהיה מתאפק מלבכות ולא יכול ויבך וי״ת ואסחר ית אפוהי ואוריך עד סגי ובכא נביאה דה׳. ובוש פעל עבר מנחי העי״ן בשקל הבקר אור ובושש משה פעל עבר מן המרובע בשקל כונן: (יב) ועולליהם תרטש.

רלב״ג

מהכית לא לוה לתת לה שכירות וזאת קלת ראיה שהדר בחלר תכרו שלא מדעתו אינו חייב להעלות לו שכר: (ט) וכל טוב דמשק משא ארבעים גמל. והנה אחשוב שזאת היא המנחה שלקח בידו ר״ל תחת רשותו ותהיה וי״ו וכל טוב כפ״א רפה בלשון ישמעאל ר״ל שהיא לנא ענין והרלון בו פל טוב דמשק: (י) לך אמור לו חיה תחיה. ר״ל שכבר הראהו השם ית׳ כי מות ימות אך כדי שלא יאמרו כי מפחד מת אמר לו חיה תחיה וזה דבר ראוי לנביאים כי בזה יתאמת יותר אמתות נבואתם: (יא) ויעמד את פניו. ר״ל שכבר התאפק להעמיד פניו שלא יבכה ושם ידיו על פניו שלא יראהו חזאל בוכה ולא יכול להמנע מלבכות: (יב) מבלריהם תשלח באש. ר״ל העריס הבלורות אשר להם: ועולליהם תרטש. אחשוב שהרלון בזה

מנחת שי

רפה ומשפטה במפיק והמסורת עליו ב׳ לא מפיק ה״א וחברו עוזב יתומיך (ירמיה מ״ט) שהוא ליווי ומזה למדנו שהעי״ן חטופה ואין כה מאריך: (י) לא חיה תחיה. לו קרי:

מצודת דוד

(י) אמר לו. ר״ל נכחנו אמר לו שיחיה אבל האמת הוא אשר הראני ה׳ בנבואה כי מות ימות: (יא) ויעמד. העמיד את פניו לצד אחר לבלי ראה דמעות עיניו מזלפין: וישם עד בוש. שם פניו לצד האחר עד התעכב זמן רב וכשלא יכול עוד להתאפק הרים קול בבכי והחזיר פניו מעתה הואיל ולא״א עוד להסתיר הבכי: (יב) כי ידעתי וגו׳. וזוכר אני עתה בדבר ולזה אבכה: מבצריהם. ערי מבלריהם תבעיר

מצודת ציון

(ט) בנך. ר״ל מכניע לך כבן לאביו: (יא) בוש. ענין איחור כמו ויחולו עד בוש (שופטים ג): (יב) תשלח. הבעב קרוי שלוח כי עשה יעשה שליחותו שהולך ממקום למקום ושורף הכל: ועולליהם.

You will rip open the wombs of the pregnant women to remove the unborn infants [*Mezudath David*].

This was a display of extreme cruelty [*Redak, Ralbag*].

Alternatively, the walls of their mountain fortresses you will split [*Ralbag*].

of Damascus, a load of forty camels; and he came and stood before him and said, "Your son, Ben-Hadad, the king of Aram, has sent me to you, saying, 'Will I recover from this illness?'"
10. And Elisha said to him, "Go say to him, 'You will live,' but the Lord has shown me that he will die." 11. He made his face expressionless and held it a long time; then the man of God wept. 12. And Hazael said, "Why does my lord weep?" And he said, "Because I know the evil that you will do to the children of Israel. You will set fire to their fortresses, and you will slay their youths with the sword, and you will dash their infants,

master Elijah who had been commanded by God to do so (I Kings 19:15) [*Redak*].

10. **'You will recover,'**—*Toward Hazael he said that he would live instead of Ben-Hadad and occupy the throne* [*Rashi*].

In order to avoid the prophet's making a completely false statement, *Rashi* explains that he really meant that *Hazael* would live. See v. 14. *Redak* explains that Elisha meant that Ben-Hadad would not die of his illness. He would, however, die by assassination. Hazael understood the implication and went about to assassinate him.

11. **He made his face expressionless**—lit. he made his face stand. I.e. *he held in his expression of grief, for he wanted to cry, so as not to cry before Hazael, and he made an effort to stand and control himself* [*Rashi*].

Others explain that he turned his face aside so as not to weep in Hazael's presence [*Jonathan, Redak, Mezudath David*].

a long time—Heb. *ad bosh,* lit. until he delayed, *like "boshesh"* (Ex. 32:1), *and he could not control himself and wept* [*Rashi*].

12. **you will dash**—Heb. תְּרַטֵּשׁ, an expression of dashing against the wall or the ground [*Redak*].

Rashi explains it as *an expression of splitting the intestines. The origin of all of them* (i.e. the verse which presents conclusive evidence to this definition) is (Is. 13:18) . . . *and bows will split* (תְּרַטֵּשְׁנָה) *the youths* [*Rashi*].

Redak explains there that the Median bows would dash the youths by using them in lieu of arrows.

Another interpretation is: and their infants you will cause to be abandoned. I.e. by killing their parents you will cause them to be abandoned [*Ralbag*].

and their pregnant women—[*Rashi, Redak, Mezudath David*].

תרטש והרתיהם תבקע: יג ויאמר
חזהאל כי מה עבדך הכלב כי יעשה
הדבר הגדול הזה ויאמר אלישע
הראני יהוה אתך מלך על־ארם:
יד וילך ׀ מאת אלישע ויבא אל־אדניו
ויאמר לו מה־אמר לך אלישע ויאמר
אמר לי חיה תחיה: טו ויהי ממחרת
ויקח המכבר ויטבל במים ויפרש על־
פניו וימת וימלך חזהאל תחתיו:
טז ובשנת חמש ליורם בן־אחאב מלך

תרגום

תטרף ומעדיתיהון
תבזע: יג ואמר חזאל
ארי מה עבדך כלבא
ארי יעביד פתגמא רבא
הדין ואמר אלישע
אחזיני יי יתך מלכא על
ארם: יד ואזל מלות
אלישע ואתא לות
רבוניה ואמר ליה מה
אמר לך אלישע ואמר
אמר לי מחא תיחי:
טו והוה ביומא דבתרוהי
ונסיב גונבא וטבל
במיא ופרס על אפוהי
ומית ומלך חזאל
תחותוהי: טז ובשנת
חמש ליורם בר אחאב
מלכא דישראל
ויהושפט

רד"ק

ענין הפלת העוללים על הקרקע או בקירות דרך אכזריות ות"י תטרף דומה למה שארז"ל או שטרפה בכותל: והרותיהם תבקע הנשים ההרות וכן ת"י ומעדתיהון תבזע וזה מדרך אכזריות: (טו) ויקח המכבר ויטבל במים. הוא הכר כמו כביר העזים וטבלהו במים ופרשהו על פניו והיה אומר לו כי לרפואה היה עושה לו הדבר ההוא והוא היה עושה לצננו ולהמיתו: (טז) ובשנת חמש ליורם בן אחאב מלך ישראל ויהושפט. חמש שזכר עומד במקום ב' ופי' חמש ליהושפט ומאימתי מונה לו ליהושפט אלו ה' שנים ממלחמת רמות גלעד כן פי' בעל סדר עולם כי במלחמת רמות גלעד הי' ראוי ליהושפט שיהרג שהלך לעזור לרשע וכשזעק תלו לו שבע שנים ולבסוף ה' שנים מאותה שעה שהיו ה' שנים ליורם בן אחאב וחזר יהושפט ממלחמת עמון ומואב והר שעיר עם מלך ישראל מאחר שהרגו אותם באו והמליכו את יורם בן יהושפט על

רש"י

יכול להתאפק ויבך: (יב) תרטש. לשון ביקוע המעי' וזה לכולן וקשתות נערים תרטשנה (ישעיה י"ג י"ח): והרותיהם. מעוברות שלהם: (טו) המכבר. תירגם יונתן גונבא וכן ותכסהו בשמיכה (שופטים ד' י"ח) תרגום בגונבא והוא בגד: ויפרוש על פניו. להצטנן: (טז) ובשנת חמש וגו'. יהושפט המליך את יורם בחייו

רלב"ג

שיהיה סבה שיהיו רעשי' ועזובים כשיהרג אבותיהם ואמותיהם: והרותיהם תבקע. רוצה לומר הנשים ההרות וזה דרך אכזריות או יהיה הרצון בהרותיהם המגדלים החזקים הבלורים ובנויים בהרים ועניין בקוע הוא בקוע חומותיהם וכמוהו על בקעם את הרות הגלעד והנה זה הפי' השני הוא היותר נכון לפי מה שאחשוב: (יג) הראני ה' אותך מלך על ארם. הנה זאת היא מפיחת חזאל למלך באמר הנה יתברך לאליהו: (טו) ויהי ממחרת ויקח המכבר ויטבל במים ויפרש על פניו וימת. אחשוב כי המכבר הוא הנקרא גוא"ה בלע"ז והנה טבל אותו במים קרים כי היה מתלעס בן הדד מתגבהות החום הנכרי ועשה זה להשקיע החום ההוא וזה עוד למהר המות ומלך חזאל תחתיו כמו שאמר לו אלישע: (טז) ובשנת חמש ליורם בן אחאב מלך ישראל. כבר באורנו זה במה שקדם והרצון בו שכאשר

מצודת ציון

בניהם הקטנים: תרטש. ענין בקיעה כמו עולליהם ירוטשו (הושע י"ד): (טו) המכבר. ת"י גונבא והוא מין בגד עב כי ותכסהו

מצודת דוד

כאש: והרותיהם. הנשים ההרות תבקע בטנם להוציא הולדות: (יג) כי מה עבדך. וכי כוחי רב כ"כ לעשות כדבר הזה: מלך. ואז יהיה בידך הכח הרב הזה: (טו) ויפרש על פניו. להקיר חמימות אש החלי: וימות. בעבור זה מת כי סרה החום מן החוץ אל הפנים: (טז) ובשנת חמש ליורם בן אחאב. בנויה בס"ע שיהושפט המליך את יהורם בנו שתי שנים שלימות בחייו דהיינו בשנת כ"ג למלכו כי כ"ה מלך והיה א"כ בשנת ה' ליורם בן אחאב כי הוא מלך בי"ט ליהושפט ולזה אמר ובשנת חמש ליורם בן אחאב וכו' ור"ל אז יהושפט מלך את יהורם בנו ויהיה מלך כמו המליך. או מלת חמש עומדת במקום שתים וכאילו אמר וחמש ליהושפט וחושב מזמן מלחמות רמות גלעד שהיה ראוי למות לולא חמלת ה' עליו וכאלו נעשה אז בריה חדשה ומלך אז אבל ליורם בן אחאב הם חמש שנים מקוטעות והם קלת שנת י"ט מיהושפט וכ' וכ"א וכ"ב וקלת

during his lifetime. When they returned from the war they had waged with the king of Moab. So it was taught in Seder Olam (ch. 17), *in the fifth year of Jehoram, and as regards the fifth year since Jehoshaphat, it was decreed on Jehoshaphat to be killed in Ramoth-Gilead, but he was reprieved for seven years because he cried out* to God [*Rashi* according to ms.].

Seder Olam elaborates that after Jehoshaphat returned from waging war with Ammon, Moab, and Mt.

and you will rip open their pregnant women." 13. And Hazael said, "Now what is your servant, the dog, that he shall perform this mighty deed?" And Elisha said, "The Lord has shown you to me as king over Aram." 14. And he went away from Elisha and came to his master, and he said to him, "What did Elisha say to you?" And he said, "He said to me, 'You will live.'" 15. And it came about on the next day that he took a blanket, dipped it in water, and spread it on his face, [after which] he died; and Hazael reigned in his stead. 16. And in the fifth year of Joram the son of Ahab, the king of Israel

13. **"Now what is your servant—** What power do I have to perpetrate such harm upon the Jewish people?" [*Abarbanel, Mezudath David*].

He referred to himself as a dog, alluding to the expression in Ex. 11:7, And to all the children of Israel, no dog whetted his tongue . . ., thus inferring that he had no power at all against the Jewish people [*K'li Y'kar*].

king—In the capacity of king you will have power to perpetrate these deeds [*Abarbanel, Mezudath David*].

Alternatively, although I do not understand it, since it is a prophetic vision, it will inevitably be realized [*K'li Y'kar*].

By informing Hazael that he would become king of Aram, Elisha fulfilled the errand entrusted to him by his master Elijah, to anoint Hazael as king of Aram [*Ralbag*].

14. **"What did Elisha say to you?"—**In the case of the terminally ill, the physician will sometimes tell the patient's true condition to his relatives and intimates, but to the public he will give a favorable report. Ben-Hadad, therefore, stressed, "What did Elisha say to *you?*" Inadvertently, he fell into a trap, since this meant also, "What did Elisha say to you, concerning yourself?" Upon this, Hazael replied, "He said to me, 'You will live.'" I.e. he said concerning me that I will live to reign in your stead. Ben-Hadad, however, understood only the simple meaning, and was consoled [*K'li Y'kar*].

15. **a blanket—***Jonathan renders: "gunva."* Likewise, (Jud. 4:18) *"And she covered him with a blanket," he renders, "b'gunva." It is a garment* [*Rashi*].

Mezudath Zion adds that it is a thick garment. Hence it absorbed much water.

Redak renders: a pillow.

and spread it on his face—*so that he cool off* [*Rashi*].

He claimed to be doing this to lower the fever, while actually he did it to chill Ben-Hadad and bring about his death [*Redak*].

16. **And in the fifth year—***Jehoshaphat crowned Joram two years*

יִשְׂרָאֵל וִיהוֹשָׁפָט מֶלֶךְ יְהוּדָה מָלַךְ
יְהוֹרָם בֶּן־יְהוֹשָׁפָט מֶלֶךְ יְהוּדָה׃ יז בֶּן־
שְׁלֹשִׁים וּשְׁתַּיִם שָׁנָה הָיָה בְמָלְכוֹ
וּשְׁמֹנֶה שָׁנָה מָלַךְ בִּירוּשָׁלִָם׃ יח וַיֵּלֶךְ
בְּדֶרֶךְ ׀ מַלְכֵי יִשְׂרָאֵל כַּאֲשֶׁר עָשׂוּ בֵּית
אַחְאָב כִּי בַּת־אַחְאָב הָיְתָה־לּוֹ לְאִשָּׁה
וַיַּעַשׂ הָרַע בְּעֵינֵי יְהוָה׃ יט וְלֹא־אָבָה
יְהוָה לְהַשְׁחִית אֶת־יְהוּדָה לְמַעַן דָּוִד
עַבְדּוֹ כַּאֲשֶׁר אָמַר־לוֹ לָתֵת לוֹ נִיר
לְבָנָיו כָּל־הַיָּמִים׃ כ בְּיָמָיו פָּשַׁע אֱדוֹם

שנים קרי

תרגום

וִיהוֹשָׁפָט מָלֵךְ שִׁבְטָא דְבֵית יְהוּדָה מְלַךְ יְהוֹרָם בַּר יְהוֹשָׁפָט מָלֵךְ יְהוּדָה׃ יז בַּר תְּלָתִין וְתַרְתֵּין שְׁנִין הֲוָה כַּד מְלַךְ וְתַמְנֵי שְׁנִין מְלַךְ בִּירוּשְׁלֵם׃ יח וַאֲזַל בְּאוֹרַח מַלְכֵי יִשְׂרָאֵל כְּמָא דַעֲבַדוּ בֵּית אַחְאָב אֲרֵי בַת אַחְאָב הֲוַת לֵיהּ לְאִתּוּ וַעֲבַד דְבִישׁ קֳדָם יְיָ׃ יט וְלָא הֲוָה רַעֲוָא קֳדָם יְיָ לְחַבָּלָא יָת דְבֵית יְהוּדָה בְּדִיל דָוִד עַבְדֵיהּ כְּמָא דַאֲמַר לֵיהּ לְמִתַּן לֵיהּ מַלְכוּ וְלִבְנוֹהִי כָּל יוֹמַיָא׃ כ בְּיוֹמוֹהִי מרדו

רש"י

שתי שנים כשחזרו מן המלחמה שנלחמו במלך מואב כך שנויה בסדר עולם בשנת חמש ליהורם ויהושפט בשנת חמשים שנגזרה גזירה על יהושפט ליהרג ברמות גלעד אלא שתלה לו בשביל שזעק שבע שנים: (יט) ניר. ממשלה:

רד"ק

יהודה ומלך שתי שנים בחיי אחיו ומה שאמר למעלה וימלוך יהורם בשנת שתי' ליהורם בן יהושפט שידמה כי יהורם בן יהושפט מלך קידם יהורם בן אחאב שתי שנים הנה כי מלך יהורם בחיי יהושפט אביו שבעה שנים לא המליכו אז אלא כיון שהיה ראוי יהושפט ליהרג מנה מאותה השעה המלכות לבני אבל לא המליכו אלא שתי שנים בחייו ואני תמה מדבריו שהוא אומר כי במלחמת רמות גלעד נגזר עליו הגזרה ומאותה שעה מנה המלכות לבנו שבע שנים והנה בשנת חמש ליורם בן אחאב שלמו אותם שבע שנים שהרי אחזיהו בן אחאב מלך שנתים ואיך היה שנה חמישית לגזרה ליורם זה לא יתכן ואיך המליכו שתי שנים בחייו והלא כשהיו ליורם חמש שנים ממלכותו מת יהושפט כי לא היה אחר אחאב שבע שנים ועוד איך אמר מאחר שהרגו עמון ומואב והר שעיר בחזרתן באו והמליכו את יהורם בן יהושפט ואותה מלחמה לא ראינו שהיה שם מלך ישראל ועוד כי אותה מלחמה היתה בימי אחזיה בן אחאב ועדיין לא מלך יהורם בן אחאב עד מות אחזיהו אחיו כי כן מצאנו בדברי הימים שאחרי המלחמה הזאת התחבר יהושפט עם אחזיהו בן אחאב לעשות אניות אלא פי' ויהושפט ומת יהושפט כי בשנת ה' ליורם מת יהושפט ומלך יהורם בנו שנית כי כבר מלך בחיי אביו שבע שנים כמו שפירשנו ועתה כשמת אביו מלך מלכות שלמה בלא מערער כי הרג את אחיו והתחזק במלוכה כמו שכתוב בדברי הימים ואם חסרה מלת ומת אין תמה בזה כי הענין מובן מהפסוק וכמוהו רבים במקרא חסירי מלה לפי שיובן ענינם מהפסוק וכדומה לזה נגיד חסר תבונות ורב מעשקות שונא בצע יאריך ימים שחסר ימות פי' נגיד שהוא חסר תבונות ורב מעשקות ימות אבל נגיד שהוא שונא בצע יאריך ימים כן בזה הפסוק אחרי שזכר כי בשנת חמש ליורם בן אחאב מלך יהורם בן יהושפט מובן מהפסוק כי מת יהושפט כי אותה שנה מת ולפיכך אמר ויהושפט כאילו אמר ומת יהושפט ושמנה שני' מלך יהורם בן יהושפט: (יז) שנה. כתיב ושנים קרי: (יט) לתת לו ניר. כמו נר בצרי על דרך ערכתי נר למשיחי וי"ת מלכו וכן תרגם אונקלוס ונירם ומלכו: (כ) בימיו פשע. כי תחת מלכי יהודה היו היום הזה

רלב"ג

מלכו חמש שנים ליורם בן אחאב עם יהושפט מלך יהודה שהיה משתתף עמו בהנהגת מלכות ישראל אז מלך יהורם בן יהושפט מלך יהודה: (יח) כי בת אחאב היתה לו לאשה. והנה במה שאמר זה קראה בת עמרי ואחשוב כי היתה בת אחאב אך פעם יחסה אל אביה ופעם אל אבי אביה: (יט) לתת לו ניר לבניו כל הימים. רוצה לומר שיתן מלכות לבניו כל הימים: (כ) בימיו פשע אדום מתחת יד

מנחת שי

(יז) שנה. שנים קרי: (יט) לתת לו ניר. הטעם. בתי"ו: ניר ולבניו. במקצת ספרים כתובי יד וכמה דפוסים כתוב לבניו בלא וא"ו בראשית המלה וכן מטמע

מצודת דוד

כ"ג כי אז המליך את יהורם בנו והם שתי שנים לפני מותו כי בכ"ה מת וליהושפט עלמו הם חמש שנים שלימות מזמן מלחמת רמות גלעד והם מקצת שנת י"ח מתחלת מלכותו וי"ט וכ' וכ"א וכ"ב ומקצת שנת כ"ג: (יז) שמנה שנים. ומקוטעות היו ובהם כלולים שתי השנים אשר מלך בחיי אביו: (יט) ולא אבה. עם שהיו ראויים להשחתה כי יהורם וביתו עשו הרע: את יהודה. ר"ל מלכי יהודה: כל הימים. ר"ל כל ימי המלכות: (כ) וימליכו. כי עד

מצודת ציון

בממיכה (שופטים ה) תרגומו כמו כן בגונבא: (יט) ניר. כמו כך ור"ל מלך המאיר ככר:

"(II Sam. 8:14) *And he placed governors in Edom.*" *Eight kings reigned in Edom before a king reigned in Israel, viz. those enumerated in the Book of Genesis* (36:31). *Corresponding to them, eight kings reigned in Israel: Ish-bosheth, David, Solomon, Rehoboam, Abiam, Asa, Jehoshaphat, and Jehoram. And Edom had no king.* I.e. during these kings' reigns, Edom had no king, until the middle of Jehoram's reign. It is not clear why

and Jehoshaphat, king of Judah, Jehoram, king of Judah,
became king. 17. He was thirty-two years old when he became
king, and he reigned eight years in Jerusalem. 18. He went in
the way of the kings of Israel, as the house of Ahab had done,
for a daughter of Ahab became his wife; and he did what was
bad in God's eyes. 19. Now the Lord was unwilling to destroy
Judah, for the sake of His servant David, as he said to him to
give him a kingdom for his children for all times. 20. In his
days, Edom rebelled

Seir, which took five years, they crowned Joram king two years prior to Jehoshaphat's death.

Redak questions this calculation on the grounds that above 1:17, it is stated that Jehoram the son of Jehoshaphat reigned two years before Jehoram the son of Ahab. According to *Seder Olam,* Scripture is counting from the decree upon Jehoshaphat, thus counting Jehoram the son of Jehoshaphat as king seven years before his father's death although he actually did not reign at that time. Here we credit him with reigning five years after Jehoram the son of Ahab, making a difference of seven years, the exact number of years his father was reprieved. Thus, it follows that at this time, Jehoshaphat actually died. He therefore concludes that the earlier verse *considers* him king, whereas in this verse he was indeed a monarch, uncontested. Hence, we explain: And in the fifth year . . . and Jehoshaphat the king of Judah [died] . . . [*Redak*].

Malbim explains that the five years are counted from the coronation of Joram the son of Ahab, for both him and Jehoshaphat, for in his reign, Jehoshaphat exerted great influence over the kingdom of Israel. The chronicler states: (II Chron. 19:4) And Jehoshaphat dwelt in Jerusalem, and he returned and went out among the people from Beersheba up to Mt. Ephraim, and he returned them to the Lord God of their forefathers. Hence he went to Mt. Ephraim, which belonged to the kingdom of Israel.

17. **and eight years**—not complete years. These included the two years he reigned during his father's lifetime [*Mezudath David*].

18. **a daughter of Ahab**—See v. 26, where Athaliah is referred to as the daughter of Omri. Here she is called the daughter of Ahab, who was her father. Below she is called the daughter of Omri, who was actually her grandfather [*Ralbag*].

19. **a kingdom**—Heb. נִיר [*Rashi* from *Jonathan*].

Some associate this with נֵר, a candle, i.e. a king who will shine like a candle [*Redak, Mezudath David*].

20. **and they appointed a king over themselves**—*Since the time of David they did not have a king, as it is said:*

מִתַּחַת יַד־יְהוּדָה וַיַּמְלִכוּ עֲלֵיהֶם מֶלֶךְ׃
כא וַיַּעֲבֹר יוֹרָם צָעִירָה וְכָל־הָרֶכֶב עִמּוֹ
וַיְהִי־הוּא קָם לַיְלָה וַיַּכֶּה אֶת־אֱדוֹם
הַסֹּבֵיב אֵלָיו וְאֵת שָׂרֵי הָרֶכֶב וַיָּנָס
הָעָם לְאֹהָלָיו׃ כב וַיִּפְשַׁע אֱדוֹם מִתַּחַת
יַד־יְהוּדָה עַד הַיּוֹם הַזֶּה אָז תִּפְשַׁע

מְרַדוּ אֱדוֹמָאֵי מִתְּחוֹת יַד אֱנָשׁ יְהוּדָה וְאַמְלִיכוּ עֲלֵיהוֹן מַלְכָּא׃ כא וַעֲבַר יוֹרָם לִצְעִיר וְכָל רְתִיכַיָּא עִמֵּיהּ וַהֲוָה הוּא קָם בְּלֵילְיָא וּמְחָא יַת אֱנָשׁ אֱדוֹם דְּמַקְּפִין לֵיהּ וְיַת רַבָּנֵי רְתִיכַיָּא וְאַפֵּךְ עַמָּא לְקִירְווֹהִי׃ כב וּמְרַדוּ אֱדוֹמָאֵי מִתְּחוֹת יַד אֱנָשׁ יְהוּדָה

ת"א אז תפשע. יומא לו שבועות יב:

רד"ק

יתיר י'

ולא היה בחם מלך אלא מלכי יהודה היו נותנים עליהם נציב והוא היה להם מלך ומפני עונות יהורם פשעו מתחת ידו: (כא) צעירה. עיר מאדום ועבר שם יהורם להלחם עם מלך אדום: ויהי הוא קם לילה. פי' כשהלך יורם צעירה יצא לו חיל אדום וחנו אלה נוכח אלה עד למחר שילחמו אלה עם אלה וכאשר היה בלילה קם יורם עם מחנהו והכה במחנה אדום כל אותם שהיו סובבים אליו והכה שרי הרכב וכשהרגישו היו מבוהלים מחנה אדום כי בפתאום נפלו עליהם ונס עם אדום הנשארים איש לאהליו ואמר אחר כך ויפשע כלומר עם כל זה שעשה יורם לאדום מרדו עוד כל הימים מתחת יד יהודה ואדוני אבי ז"ל פירש ויהי הוא קם לילה על מלך אדום שהכה את אדום הסובב למלך ישראל כלומר שהיו בעזרתו שלא מרדו עדיין כי היו באדום עדיין שלא מרדו וקם מלך אדום והכה אותם ואת שרי הרכב אשר ליורם: וינס העם. ישראל נסו לאהליהם ואמרו לישראל אשר בערים פשע אדום מתחת יד יהודה: הסביב. ביו"ד המשך שלא כמנהג עם הצרי וכמוהו הקיף את העיר ובעל כנפים יגיד דבר והוליד און: (כב) אז תפשע לבנה. אם לבנה זו היא לאדום למה אמר תפשע הלא כבר אמר ויפשע אדום ואפשר כי היתה לבנה זו סמוכה לארץ ישראל יותר משאר ארץ אדום וכשפשע אדום זאת לא מרדה עדיין ואחרי המלחמה זאת מרדה לפיכך אמר בעת ההיא ורש"י ז"ל כתב כי על לבנה ההיא לישראל אמר שמרדה כשמרד

רש"י

(כ) וימליכו עליהם מלך. ומימי דוד לא היה להם מלך כמו שנאמר ומלך אין באדום ויסם באדום נציבים (שמואל ב' ח' ו') שמנה מלכים מלכו באדום לפני מלך מלך לישראל המנויים בספר בראשית (ל"ו ל"א) כנגדו מלכו בישראל שמנה מלכים. איש בושת. ודוד. ושלמה. ורחבעם. ואביה. ואסא. ויהושפט. ויהורם. ולא היה מלך לאדום ומה שכתוב למעלה שהלך מלך אדום עם יהורם בן אחאב ועם יהושפט למלחמה על מלך מואב לא מלך גמור הוא אלא נציב שאף הוא היה קרוי מלך וכמו שנאמר ומלך אין באדום נצב מלך (מלכים א' כ"ב מ"ח) הנציב היה להם במקום מלך: (כא) הסוביב אליו. הסמוכים אל הספר: (כב) תפשע לבנה. מרדו יושבי לבנה ומרדו במלך ואיני יודע מאיזה אומה היו שהרי לבנה מארץ ישראל היא

מנחת שי

מפי' רלב"ג. ובמקצת ספרים כ"י מדוייקים וגם בדפוס ישן כתוב ולבני ובוא"ו וכן הוא בתרגום ובמאיר נתיב וגם חברו שבדברי הימים ב' סימן כ"א כתוב בוא"ו

רלב"ג

יהודה. ר"ל כי בימי יורם פשע אדום מתחת יד יהודה ומרדו בהם והמליכו עליהם מלך והעבירו הנציב ששם עליהם מלך יהודה: (כא) והנה עבר יורם לצעירה וכל הרכב עמו להלחם עם אדום המורד בו והנה לא מרדו כולם בו אך קצתם הלכו בעזרתו כדי להלחם עם המורדים בו מהאדומים ובהיות זה שהיה מבתדל יהורם להלחם עם אדום המורד בו הנה קם אדום המורד לילה והכה את אדום הסובב אליו להלחם עמו והם אשר באו לעזור את יהורם מלך יהודה והכה בלילה שרי הרכב אשר ליורם וינוסו עם ישראל לאהליו וגם אז מרדה עיר

מצודת דוד

כנה היה עליהם נציב מלך מתחת יד מלכי יהודה: (כא) צעירה. שם מקום מארץ אדום: קם לילה. כי לא יכל כח ללחום עמהם ביום בפומבי: הסובב אליו. הסמוך אליו ולא יכל כח ללכת בעומק המלחמה: וינס. אחר שהכה מה שהכה נס מיד לאהליו כי פחד מאדום: (כב) אז. בעת ההיא פשע גם לבנה ונזכרת היא ביהושע בערי נחלת יהודה והיתה סמוכה לאדום ופשעה גם היא במלך

army lost courage and fled to their dwellings [*Abarbanel, Mezudath David, Malbim*].

22. **And Edom rebelled**—Because of Judah's weakness, Edom remained in a state of rebellion against them [*Abarbanel, Malbim*].

Libnah rebelled—*The inhabitants*

from under the power of Judah, and they appointed a king over themselves. 21. And Joram went over to Zair, and all the chariots were with him; and he got up at night and struck the Edomites who came around to him and the officers of the chariots; and the people fled to their dwellings. 22. And Edom rebelled from under the power of Judah until this day; then

Rashi does not count Saul as one of the kings during whose reign Edom had no king. *Rashi Gen.*, following Gen. *Rabbah,* ibid. does include Saul among the eight kings and excludes Jehoram in whose reign Edom crowned a king. *What is written above* (3:9) *that the king of Edom went with Jehoram the son of Ahab and with Jehoshaphat to war against the king of Moab, presents no difficulty because he was not a real king, but a governor, who is also called a king, and as it is said:* (I Kings 22:48) *There was no king in Edom; a governor was king. They had a governor in lieu of a king* [*Rashi*].

21. **And Joram went over to Zair**—an Edomite city, to wage war with the king of Edom [*Redak*].

he got up at night—Although Joram attacked with all his officers and his chariots, as is stated in II Chron. 21:9, he was, nevertheless, afraid to attack by day. This illustrates his utter weakness at this point [*Malbim*].

who came around to him—*those near the border* [*Rashi*].

I.e. he had no strength to penetrate the enemy lines to attack those farther away [*Mezudath David*].

Redak pictures the two armies facing each other, awaiting a confrontation on the morrow. During the night, Joram sprang a surprise attack on the front lines of the Edomites. Having been taken by surprise, the survivors panicked and fled, each man to his home.

He quotes his father who renders:

who defected to him—I.e. the king of Edom killed his own people who had defected to the king of Judah and had not yet rebelled.

Alternatively, Joram captured the mighty warriors of the Edomites and kept them with him to prevent them from returning to their countrymen. During the night, he arose and slew them. Thus, we render: *who* had come around to him [*Pseudo-Rashi,* II Chron. 21:9].

and the people fled to their dwellings—According to *Redak,* this refers to the remaining Edomites, as mentioned above. Alternatively, since Joram was able to attack only the Edomites on the border and the officers of the chariots, the Judean

לבנה בעת ההיא: כג ויתר דברי יורם וכל־אשר עשה הלא־הם כתובים על־ספר דברי הימים למלכי יהודה: כד וישכב יורם עם־אבתיו ויקבר עם־אבתיו בעיר דוד וימלך אחזיהו בנו תחתיו: כה בשנת שתים־עשרה שנה ליורם בן־אחאב מלך ישראל מלך אחזיהו בן־יהורם מלך יהודה: כו בן־עשרים ושתים שנה אחזיהו במלכו ושנה אחת מלך בירושלם ושם אמו

עד יומא הדין בכן מרדו יתבי לבנה בעדנא ההיא: כג ושאר פתגמי יורם וכל דעבד הלא אינון כתיבין על ספרא פתגמי יומיא למלכי דבית יהודה: כד ושכיב יורם עם אבהתוהי ואתקבר עם אבהתוהי בקרתא דדויד ומלך אחזיהו בריה תחותוהי: כה בשנת תרתא עסרי שנין ליורם בר אחאב מלכא דישראל מלך אחזיהו בר יהורם מלך שבטא דבית יהודה: כו בר עשרין ותרתין שנין אחזיה כד מלך ושתא חדא מלך בירושלם ושום

רש"י

והומר הני שהיו משבט יהודה ומרדו במלך: (כד) ויקבר עם אבותיו בעיר דויד. (ובדברי הימים ב' כ"א כ') אומר בעיר דוד ולא בקברות המלכים:

רד"ק

אדום מרדה גם היא במלך וזה הפירוש רחוק בעיני: (כד) בעיר דוד. אבל לא עם המלכי' וכן כתב בדברי הימים ולא בקבורת המלכים: (כה) בשנת שתים עשרה. ויהורם אביו מלך בשנת חמש ליורם בן אחאב ומלך שמנה שני' הנה י"ג אך לא שלמה שנת י"ג לפיכך לא מנאה לו וכן תמצא בכל המספרים כמו שכתבנו: (כו) בן עשרים ושתים. בדברי הימים בן ארבעים ושתים שנה אחזיהו במלכו היאך היה זה ועוד כי כל ימי אביו לא היו אלא ארבעים שנה שכן כתוב בן ל"ב שנה במלכו ושמנה שנים מלך הרי ארבעי' איך היה הוא בן מ"ב במלכו זה לא יתכן ואמר בסדר עולם כיון שהשיא אסא בתו של עמרי ליהושפט בנו נגזרה גזרה זו על מלכות בית דוד שתכלה עם בית אחאב וכן היה שמת אחזיהו מלך יהודה עם מלך ישראל שהרגם יהוא ועתליהו אם אחזיהו מלך יהודה ראתה כי מת בנה ותאבד כל זרע המלוכה לפיכך מנה מ"ב מיום שנגזרה הגזרה ובשנת ל"א לאסא נשאה שנאמר בשנת שלשים ואחת לאסא מלך עמרי על ישראל והלא קודם לכן ארבעים ושתים שנה מלך אלא ר"ל מלך מלכות שלמה על

רלב"ג

לבנה בישראל: (כו) בן עשרים ושתים שנה אחזיהו במלכו. והנה בד"ה אמר בן ארבעים ושתים שנה והנה מה שמנה בד"ה אינו ללידת אחזיהו אך לעת לצמיחת מלכות עמרי אבר בעבור היותו מזרעו קרה לו שנהרג עם מלך ישראל וזה שאמר בלשים ואחד שנה לאסא מלך עמרי על כל ישראל ואחר זה מלך שש שנים ואחאב בנו עשרים ושתים ואחזיה בנתים ויורם היה בשנת שתי' עשרה הרי ארבעים

מנחת שי

ושניהם הובאו כן במסורת שם: (כה) בשנת שתים עשרה שנה. בנביאים עם פירוש הרד"ן ליכא מלת שנה וכן בס"א כתובי יד אמנם ברוב הספרים איכא:

מצודת דוד

יהודה: (כה) בשנת שתים עשרה. כי יהורם בן יהושפט מלך בשנת ה' ליורם בן אחאב וח' שנים מקוטעות מלך הרי כלו בי"ב ליורם בן אחאב ואז מלך אחזיה: (כו) בן עשרים ושתים שנה. ובד"ה נאמר בן ארבעים ושתים שנה ושניה בס"ע שמנין הזה אינה ללידת אחזיה כ"א לצמיחת מלכות עמרי על כל ישראל שהיתה ע"י שנשא יהושפט את בתו לאשה כמ"ש שם (ויתכן שנשאה שנה אחת לפני מלוך עמרי על כל ישראל והיה א"כ מ"ב שנה מקוטעות) ובעבור היות אחזיה מזרעו קרה לו שנהרג עם מלך ישראל ע"י יהוא

the age given here, viz. twenty-two and that given in Chronicles, viz. forty-two (II Chron. 22:1). Since *Rashi* discusses the same problem below 9:29, we will, God willing, discuss it there.

and his mother's name was Athaliah—She was already mentioned as a daughter of Ahab who was married to Joram (v. 18). We mentioned before that this verse refers to her as the daughter of Omri who was actually her grandfather [*Ralbag*].

This is not unusual since grandchildren are considered like children. Additionally, it is possible that

Libnah rebelled at that time. 23. And the remaining events of Joram and all that he did, are written in the book of Chronicles of the kings of Judah. 24. And Joram slept with his forefathers and was buried with his forefathers in the city of David. And Ahaziah his son reigned in his stead. 25. In the twelfth year of Joram the son of Ahab, king of Israel, Ahaziah the son of Jehoram reigned over Judah. 26. Ahaziah was twenty-two years old when he reigned, and one year he reigned in Jerusalem; and his mother's name

of Libnah rebelled and rebelled (sic) *against the king. I do not know from what nation they were, since Libnah is from Eretz Israel. But I say that they were of the tribe of Judah and rebelled against the king* [*Rashi*].

When Edom rebelled, they too rebelled against Judah, and defected to Edom. Since their city was located near the Edomite border, as the territory of Judah was in the south near Edom (Jos. 15:21, 42) [*Pseudo-Rashi* II Chron. 21:10].

Redak opines that Libnah was part of Edom, but located near Judah. They did not participate in the initial rebellion, but after the war, they too, despite their proximity to Judah, entered a state of rebellion.

23. **And the remaining events**—how he murdered his brothers and some of the officers of Israel, how he led Judah astray, and how he was punished by the Almighty for his sins. He was attacked by the Philistines and the Arabs, and he was stricken with incurable illnesses [*Malbim* from II Chron. 21].

24. **and was buried with his forefathers in the city of David**—*And in* II *Chron.* (21:20) *is stated: in the city of David, but not in the graves of the kings* [*Rashi, Redak*].

And Ahaziah his son reigned in his stead—Ahaziah was Joram's youngest son. The older ones had been killed by the attacking Arabs, leaving only Ahaziah [II Chron. 22:1].

25. **In the twelfth year of Joram the son of Ahab**—His father Joram reigned in the fifth year of Joram the son of Ahab (v. 16) for eight years (v. 17). This brings us to the *thirteenth* year of Joram the son of Ahab. However, since the last year of Joram the son of Jehoshaphat was not a full year, it is not counted, and Ahaziah is considered as becoming king in the twelfth year [*Mezudath David*].

26. **Ahaziah was twenty-two years old**—*Redak* and other commentators discuss the discrepancy between

עֲתַלְיָהוּ בַּת־עָמְרִי מֶלֶךְ יִשְׂרָאֵל׃ כז וַיֵּלֶךְ
בְּדֶרֶךְ בֵּית אַחְאָב וַיַּעַשׂ הָרַע בְּעֵינֵי
יְהוָה כְּבֵית אַחְאָב כִּי חֲתַן בֵּית־אַחְאָב
הוּא׃ כח וַיֵּלֶךְ אֶת־יוֹרָם בֶּן־אַחְאָב
לַמִּלְחָמָה עִם־חֲזָאֵל מֶלֶךְ־אֲרָם בְּרָמֹת
גִּלְעָד וַיַּכּוּ אֲרַמִּים אֶת־יוֹרָם׃ כט וַיָּשָׁב
יוֹרָם הַמֶּלֶךְ לְהִתְרַפֵּא בְיִזְרְעֶאל מִן־
הַמַּכִּים אֲשֶׁר יַכֻּהוּ אֲרַמִּים בָּרָמָה
בְּהִלָּחֲמוֹ אֶת־חֲזָהאֵל מֶלֶךְ אֲרָם
וַאֲחַזְיָהוּ בֶן־יְהוֹרָם מֶלֶךְ יְהוּדָה יָרַד
לִרְאוֹת אֶת־יוֹרָם בֶּן־אַחְאָב בְּיִזְרְעֶאל

וְשׁוּם אִמֵּיהּ עֲתַלְיָהוּ בַּת עָמְרִי מַלְכָּא דְיִשְׂרָאֵל׃ כז וַאֲזַל בְּאוֹרַח בֵּית אַחְאָב וַעֲבַד דְּבִישׁ קֳדָם יְיָ כְּבֵית אַחְאָב אֲרֵי חֲתָנָא דְבֵית אַחְאָב הוּא׃ כח וַאֲזַל עִם יוֹרָם בַּר אַחְאָב לְאַגָּחָא קְרָבָא עִם חֲזָאֵל מַלְכָּא דַאֲרָם בְּרָמוֹת גִּלְעָד וּמְחוֹ אֱנָשׁ אֲרָם יָת יוֹרָם׃ כט וְתָב יוֹרָם מַלְכָּא לְאִתַּסָּאָה בְּיִזְרְעֶאל מִן מַחֲתָא דִמְחוֹהִי אֱנָשׁ אֲרָם בְּרָמְתָא כַּד אַגִּיחַ קְרָבָא עִם חֲזָאֵל מַלְכָּא דַאֲרָם וַאֲחַזְיָהוּ בַּר יְהוֹרָם מַלְכָּא שִׁבְטָא דְבֵית יְהוּדָה נְחַת לְמִסְעַד יָת יוֹרָם בַּר אַחְאָב בְּיִזְרְעֶאל אֲרֵי

מרע

רד"ק

ישראל שנתחתן עם אסא ונתעלה והרגו לתבני ומלך על ישראל ובשנת ל"א לאסא עד שבת אחזיהו מלך יהודה מ"ב שנים כיצד תשע שנים לאסא וכ"ה ליהושפט הרי ל"ד ושמנה שנים ליהורם הרי מ"ב וזהו רחוק מאד מדרך הפשט והפי' הנכון כי יהורם חיה יותר ממ' שנה ולא מנה מימי מלכותו אלא שבנה שנים שמלך בחזקתו אבל מעת שנפל ביד הערבים ונפל גם כן בחליו לא מנו לו ימי מלכותו והשלימו והמליכו אחזיהו בחייו מעת שנפל אביו ומלך בלא חמדה והיו עשרים שנה וכשהמליכו אחזיהו בחיי אביו היה בן עשרים ושתים שנה כמ"ש הנה ומ"ש ושנה אחת מלך בירושלם אחר מות אביו אבל בחיי אביו מלך עשרים שנה וכשמת אביו היה בן מ"ב שנה והמליכוהו פעם אחרת ולא מלך אחר מיתת אביו אלא שנה אחת: ושם אמו עתליהו בת עמרי. ולמעלה אמר כי יהורם אביו בת אחאב היתה לו לאשה נאמר כי בת אחאב היתה ואמר בת עמרי כי בני בנים הרי הם כבנים וכן ותבאנה אל רעואל שהיה אבי אביהן וכן זרובבל בן שאלתיאל והוא היה בן פדיה שהיה בן שאלתיאל ורבים ככה ומה שאמר בו חתן בית אחאב והוא היה בן חתן בית אחאב הוא ג"כ חתן להם כלומר כי ע"י חיתון היתה קרובתו עמהם: (כט) מן המכי'. שם כמו מן המכות ויאמר האחד מכה בסגול על משקל ומטה וכן

רלב"ג

ושתים שנה שעמדה מלכות עמרי: ושם אמו עתליהו בת עמרי. הנה היא אמר זכר כי היא בת אחאב: (כח) ויכו ארמים את יורם. הנה מבב השם יתעלה שברמות גלעד נפלו אחאב ויורם בנו כי יורם הלך להלחם ברמות גלעד ושם הוכה וזה היה כלי אל שהיה יכול יהוא

מצודת דוד

ולזה תלה מלכותו בלמיחת מלכות עמרי: בת עמרי. ולמעלה נאמר שיהורם אביו נשא בת אחאב וידמה שעמרי גדלה ונקראת בתו אף כי בני בנים הם כבנים: (כז) כי חתן. ר"ל ע"י החתון באה לו קורבתו עמהם כי אביו היה חתן בית אחאב: (כט) וישב. מן המלחמה: ברמה. היא רמות גלעד: לראות. ר"ל לבקרו על כי היה חולה מן המכים:

was Athaliah the daughter of Omri king of Israel. 27. And he went in the way of the house of Ahab, and he did what was evil in the eyes of the Lord, like the house of Ahab, for he was a son-in-law of the house of Ahab. 28. And he went with Joram the son of Ahab to war with Hazael, king of Aram, in Ramoth-Gilead; and the Arameans struck Joram. 29. And King Joram returned to recuperate in Jezreel, from the wounds that the Arameans had inflicted upon him in Ramah when he fought with Hazael, king of Aram; and Ahaziah the son of Jehoram, king of Judah, went down to see Joram the son of Ahab in Jezreel, because he was ill.

she was raised by her grandfather [*Mezudath David, Redak*].

27. **a son-in-law of the house of Ahab**—I.e. through intermarriage he became related to the house of Ahab, because his father was a son-in-law of the house of Ahab [*Redak, Mezudath David*].

28. **And he went with Joram the son of Ahab**—who advised him to accompany him to war. He was predestined to go to war in Ramoth-Gilead, in order to fall prey to Jehu the son of Nimshi, who destroyed the entire house of Ahab. Since he went in their ways, he too was to perish with them [*Ralbag* from II Chron. 22:3–10].

and the Arameans struck Joram—Just as his father Ahab had been struck by the Arameans in Ramoth-Gilead, so was Joram. As already mentioned, this was the preparation for his death at the hands of Jehu [*Ralbag*].

29. **from the wounds that the Arameans had inflicted upon him**—[*Targum Jonathan* and *Redak*].

There are two difficulties in this interpretation: (1) the word for wounds is usually *makkoth,* while here it is *makkim;* (2) the future tense is used instead of the past.

K'li Y'kar, therefore, suggests: because of the slayers, for the Arameans would slay him. I.e. if he were to remain on the battlefield in his weakened condition, the Arameans would surely slay him.

כִּֽי־חֹלֶ֖ה הֽוּא׃ ט א וֶאֱלִישָׁע֙ הַנָּבִ֔יא קָרָ֕א לְאַחַ֖ד מִבְּנֵ֣י הַנְּבִיאִ֑ים וַיֹּ֣אמֶר ל֗וֹ חֲגֹ֨ר מָתְנֶ֜יךָ וְקַ֨ח פַּ֤ךְ הַשֶּׁ֙מֶן֙ הַזֶּ֣ה בְּיָדֶ֔ךָ וְלֵ֖ךְ רָמֹ֥ת גִּלְעָֽד׃ ב וּבָ֣אתָ שָׁ֗מָּה וּרְאֵה־שָׁ֞ם יֵה֤וּא בֶן־יְהֽוֹשָׁפָט֙ בֶּן־נִמְשִׁ֔י וּבָ֗אתָ וַהֲקֵֽמֹתוֹ֙ מִתּ֣וֹךְ אֶחָ֔יו וְהֵבֵיאתָ֥ אֹת֖וֹ חֶ֥דֶר בְּחָֽדֶר׃ ג וְלָקַחְתָּ֤ פַךְ־הַשֶּׁ֙מֶן֙ וְיָצַקְתָּ֣ עַל־רֹאשׁ֔וֹ וְאָמַרְתָּ֙ כֹּֽה־אָמַ֣ר יְהוָ֔ה מְשַׁחְתִּ֥יךָ לְמֶ֖לֶךְ אֶל־יִשְׂרָאֵ֑ל וּפָתַחְתָּ֥ הַדֶּ֛לֶת וְנַסְתָּ֖ה וְלֹ֥א תְחַכֶּֽה׃

מְרַע הוּא׃ א וֶאֱלִישָׁע נְבִיָא קְרָא לְחַד מִתַּלְמִידֵי נְבִיַיָא וַאֲמַר לֵיהּ זָרֵיז חַרְצָךְ וְנְסִיב מָנָא דִמְשַׁחָא הָדֵין בִּידָךְ וְאֵיזֵיל לְרָמוֹת גִּלְעָד׃ ב וְתֵיתֵי לְתַמָן וְתֶחֱזֵי תַמָן יָת יֵהוּא בַּר יְהוֹשָׁפָט בַּר נִמְשִׁי וְתֵיעוֹל וּתְקִימִינֵיהּ מִגוֹ אֲחוֹהִי וְתָעֵיל יָתֵיהּ תְּוָן בְּגוֹ תְּוָן׃ ג וְתִסַּב מָנָא דִמְשַׁחָא וּתְרִיק עַל רֵישֵׁיהּ וְתֵימַר כִּדְנַן אֲמַר יְיָ מְשַׁחְתָּךְ לְמֶהֱוֵי מַלְכָּא עַל יִשְׂרָאֵל וְתִפְתַּח דַּשָּׁא וְתֵעֱרוֹק וְלָא תִסְבֵּי׃ ואזל

רש"י

ט (א) ואלישע הנביא קרא וגו'. באותו הפרק שהיה יהורם חולה ביזרעאל: לאחד מבני הנביאים. יונה בן אמתי היה: חגור מתניך. כל חגורת מתנים לשון זירוז גבורה הוא לפי שהוא שלוח לדבר הסכנה (צריך

רד"ק

אמר התרגום מן מחתא: אשר יכוהו. כמו הכותו עתיד במקום עבר וכמוהו רבי': (א) לאחד מבני הנביאים. אמרו כי יונה בן אמתי היה: חגור מתניך. אמר לו זה כדי שילך במהרה וישוב במהרה בעוד שאין יהורם שהלך להתרפא ביזרעאל וכן אמר ונסתה ולא תחכה: וקח פך השמן. ולמה צוה למשחו והלא אין מושחין מלכי ישראל אמרו רז"ל מפני מחלוקתו של יורם בן אחאב וזה השמן לא היה שמן המשחה כי לא היו מושחין בו אלא מלכי בית דוד אלא שמן אפרסמון היה ואמרו שאול ויהוא נמשחו בפך לא נמשכה מלכותן דוד ושלמה שנמשחו בקרן נמשכה מלכותן: ולך רמות גלעד. והלא רמו' גלעד היתה ביד מלך ארם ואחאב שהלך לקחת אותה מידו מת במלחמה ההיא ולא ראינו אחר כן שלקחה מלך ישראל מידו וא"ת במחנה היו ישראל לפני רמות גלעד שהיו חושבין לקחתה ומלך ארם היה בעיר וישראל בחוץ ושם הוכה מלך ישראל והלך לו להתרפא ביזרעאל והניח מחניהו שם ואמר אלישע לזה הנביא שילך שם למחנה ישראל שהי' ברמות גלעד וימשח שם את יהוא זה לא יתכן כי ידמה כי בתוך העיר היו ישראל שהרי אמר והבאת אותו חדר בחדר ואומר ויבא הביתה ואומר אל גרם המעלו' ואומר אל יצא פליט מן העיר ללכת להגיד ביזרעאל מכל אלו הפסוקים נראה כי ישראל היו בעיר וארם מבחוץ א"כ נאמר מלך ישראל לקחה מיד מלך ארם או יהואחז או יהורם וחזאל בא אחר כן להלחם בה והלך שם מלך ישראל עם מחנהו: (ב) ובאת שמה. חלוקה המלה בטרחא: חדר בחדר. חדר לפני' מחדר: (ג) אל ישראל. כמו על

רלב"ג

להמיתו: (א) ויאמר לו חגור מתניך. לוהו לחגור מתניו כדי שיוכל לרוץ: ולך רמות גלעד. ידמה שלקחוה מיד מלך ארם אחרי מות אחאב או בעת מות אחאב כי אז הלליחו ישראל במלחמה אלא שבכר מת אחאב והנה היה בזה העת חיל ישראל שם: (ב) והבאת אותו חדר בחדר. לוהו זה כדי שלא ישמע אדם דבריו: (ג) ונסתה ולא תחכה. ר"ל שלא תמתין לנום אבל תנום תכף השלימך הדברים והנה קלר בכאן ולא זכר הדברים שאמר אלישע שיאמר ליהוא אך מדבריו ליהוא למדנו שבכר לוהו אלישע לומר אותן הדברים:

מנחת שי

ט (ב) וראה שם יהוא. יש ספרים וראה במאריך הוא"ו: והביאת. בא מלא בעי"ן הפועל מכלול דף ק"ן וכן ראיתי במסורת הביאת והביאת ב' כתיבי כן וחברו לא הביאת לי שה עלתך (ישעיה מ"ג). ותימא שבישעיה סימן מ"ג במקרא גדולה לא נחשב זה עם אותם שכם מלאים יו"ד בלישן הבאה. ועיין עוד מ"ש בישעיה ל"ז: (ג) משחתיך למלך אל ישראל. במקצת ספרים כתובי יד ישנים וגם במקצת דפוסים ראשונים כתוב על ישראל ואתבריר לן דשגגה היא וצריך למיכתב אל ישראל דהכי איתא במסורה כל משחתיך למלך כתוב אל ישראל בר מן א' על ישראל וסימן ויאמר נתן אל דוד אתה האיש (שמואל ב' י"ב) פוק חזי במ"ג סימן ויחי וכן כתב רד"ק אל ישראל כמו על ישראל וכן כתב לקמן אל עם ה' אל ישראל כמו על:

מצודת דוד

ט (א) לאחד וגו'. אמרז"ל שהיה יונה בן אמתי: חגור מתניך. לילך ולבוא בזריזות כי המגור במתניו הוא קל ללכת ומזורז: (ב) והקמותו. אמור לו שיקום מבין רעיו ותביא אותו בחדר לפנים מחדר: (ג) ונסתה. תנום משם ולא תאחר מללכת שלא

מצודת ציון

ט (א) פך. שם כלי מיוחד לשמן: (ג) תחכה. תמתין ותאחר כמו

going into the house and into an inner chamber. We, therefore, conclude that Israel had taken Ramoth-Gilead from Aram, either during the reign of Jehoahaz or the reign of Joram. Hazael had attacked and was striving at that time to restore it to Aram [*Redak*].

2. **and raise him up**—I.e. you shall order him to rise from among his fellows [*Mezudath David*].

into an inner chamber—lit. in a

9

1. And Elisha the prophet summoned one of the disciples of the prophets and said to him, "Gird your loins and take this cruse of oil in your hand, and go to Ramoth-Gilead. 2. And you shall come there, and see there Jehu the son of Jehoshaphat the son of Nimshi, and you shall come and raise him up from among his brothers and bring him into an inner chamber." 3. And you shall take the cruse of oil and pour it on his head, and you shall say, "So said the Lord, 'I have anointed you as king over Israel.' And you shall open the door and flee; do not tarry."

1. **And Elisha the prophet summoned . . .**—*at that same time that Jehoram was ill in Jezreel* [*Rashi*].

one of the disciples of the prophets—*It was Jonah the son of Amittai* [*Rashi, Redak, Abarbanel,* from *Seder Olam* ch. 18].

"Gird your loins—*Every girding of the loins is an expression of quickening of mightiness* (sic, omitted by *R. Joseph Kara*). *Since he was a messenger for a perilous mission, (he needed quickening)* [*Rashi*].

The last three words, although enclosed in parentheses as an indication that they do not appear in all editions of *Rashi,* do indeed appear in the commentary of *R. Joseph Kara.*

As mentioned above 4:29, girding the loins prevents the abdomen from moving, and facilitates running.

He ordered his disciple to hurry to Ramoth-Gilead before Joram would return from recuperating in Jezreel. To ascertain his return before Joram's arrival, he ordered him to flee and not to tarry [*Redak*].

and take this cruse of oil—Because of the dispute with Joram, it was necessary to anoint Jehu. Otherwise, kings of Israel are never anointed. Even in this case, the genuine anointing oil was not used. Instead, oil of balsimum was used. The anointing oil was reserved for kings of the Davidic dynasty [*Redak* from *Kerithuth* 5b].

A cruse of oil was used rather than a horn of oil as in the case of David and Solomon. The Talmud notes that those kings who were anointed with a horn of oil, enjoyed unbroken dynasties, whereas those who were anointed with a cruse of oil, did not [*Redak* from *Kerithuth* 6a].

and go to Ramoth-Gilead—From this entire episode it appears that the Israelites were in possession of Ramoth-Gilead. It does not seem that they were encamped there during a battle to wrest it from Aram, since there are many references to

ד וַיֵּלֶךְ הַנַּעַר הַנַּעַר הַנָּבִיא רָמֹת גִּלְעָד׃
ה וַיָּבֹא וְהִנֵּה שָׂרֵי הַחַיִל יֹשְׁבִים וַיֹּאמֶר
דָּבָר לִי אֵלֶיךָ הַשָּׂר וַיֹּאמֶר יֵהוּא אֶל־מִי
מִכֻּלָּנוּ וַיֹּאמֶר אֵלֶיךָ הַשָּׂר׃ ו וַיָּקָם וַיָּבֹא
הַבַּיְתָה וַיִּצֹק הַשֶּׁמֶן אֶל־רֹאשׁוֹ וַיֹּאמֶר
לוֹ כֹּה־אָמַר יְהוָה אֱלֹהֵי יִשְׂרָאֵל
מְשַׁחְתִּיךָ לְמֶלֶךְ אֶל־עַם יְהוָה אֶל־
יִשְׂרָאֵל׃ ז וְהִכִּיתָה אֶת־בֵּית אַחְאָב
אֲדֹנֶיךָ וְנִקַּמְתִּי דְּמֵי ׀ עֲבָדַי הַנְּבִיאִים
וּדְמֵי כָּל־עַבְדֵי יְהוָה מִיַּד אִיזָבֶל׃
ח וְאָבַד כָּל־בֵּית אַחְאָב וְהִכְרַתִּי
לְאַחְאָב מַשְׁתִּין בְּקִיר וְעָצוּר וְעָזוּב
בְּיִשְׂרָאֵל׃ ט וְנָתַתִּי אֶת־בֵּית אַחְאָב
כְּבֵית יָרָבְעָם בֶּן־נְבָט וּכְבֵית בַּעְשָׁא

ד ואזל עולימא תלמידא דנביא ברמות גלעד׃ ה ואתא והא רבני חילא יתבין ואמר פתגם אית לי למללא עמך רבא ואמר יהוא למן מכולנא ואמר עמך רבא׃ ו וקם ועל לביתא ואריק משחא על רישיה ואמר ליה כדנן אמר יי אלהא דישראל משחתך למהוי מלכא על עמא דיי על ישראל׃ ז ותמחי ית בית אחאב רבונך ואתפרע פורענות דם עבדי נביא ודמי כל עבדיא דיי מידא דאיזבל׃ ח וייבד כל בית אחאב ואשיצי לאחאב ידע מדע ואחיד ושביק בישראל׃ ט ואתן ית בית אחאב כבית ירבעם בר נבט וכבית בעשא

ת"א והכרתי לאחאב. כ"ב יט:

רד"ק / רש"י

ישראל: ולא תחכת. שיאמר לך דבר אלא מיד תצא: (ד) וילך זירוז): (ד) הנער הנביא. נערו של אלישע הנביא כך
הנער הנביא. אמר בתחל׳ הנער ואח"כ פירש איזה נער
ואמר הנער הנביא ולדעת יונתן הנער הוא סמוך אל הנביא כאילו אמר נער הנביא שתרגם תלמידא דנביא: (ו) אל ראשו.
אל עם ה׳ אל ישראל כמו על: (ז) ודמי כל עבדי ה׳. ונבות בכללם: (ח) משתין בקיר ועצור ועזוב. פירשנו אותם למעלה:

מצודת ציון / מצודת דוד

זמכיתו עד אור הבקר (לעיל ז׳): (י) בחלק. הנחלה יקרא חסתכן כאשר יודע למלך: (ד) וילך הנער. והוזר ומפרש הנער
של הנביא: (ה) דבר לי. יש לי מה לדבר עמך: (ז) בית אחאב.
זרעו ובני ביתו: ונקמתי. על ידיך: (ח) משתין בקיר. זה הזכר שעושה קלוח: עצור. העוצר הכנוס בבית: ועזוב. המקנה העזוב
ע"פ השדה: בישראל. ר"ל בפירסום למען יקחו מוסר:

of the second *ha-naar*. Since the meaning is "the disciple of," the definite article is out of place. To account for the repetition, *Jonathan* renders: the lad, the disciple of . . . I.e. which lad? The lad, or disciple of the prophet. The *he* is not accounted for. It is considered an irregularity [*Redak*].

Malbim, however, explains thus: And the lad, the lad who was a prophet, went. He is first referred to as the lad, i.e. Elisha's attendant. He went on his mission as Elisha's agent.

Secondly, he himself was a prophet, as is apparent from the elaborate charge he imposed upon Jehu, much more elaborate and detailed than that delegated to him by Elisha, who did not mention destroying the house of Ahab.

4. And the lad, the disciple of the prophet, went to Ramoth-Gilead. 5. And he came, and behold, the officers of the army were sitting; and he said, "I have a message for you, officer," and Jehu said, "For which one of all of us?" And he said, "For you, officer." 6. And he arose and came to the house and poured oil on his head. And he said to him, "So said the Lord God of Israel, 'I have anointed you as king over the Lord's people, over Israel. 7. And you shall strike the house of Ahab your master, and I will avenge the blood of My servants the prophets and the blood of all the Lord's servants from Jezebel. 8. And the entire house of Ahab will perish; and I will cut off from Ahab all males and every restrained and free in Israel. 9. And I shall render the house of Ahab like the house of Jeroboam the son of Nebat, and like the house of Baasha the son of Ahijah.

room within a room. You shall bring him into a hidden place lest others hear the message [*Ralbag*].

Alternatively, he ordered him to keep the matter secret lest the king become aware of it [*Abarbanel*].

3. **"So said the Lord**—This refers to the mission assigned by God to Elijah on Mt. Horeb (I Kings 19:16). Since Ahab was given a reprieve, Elijah himself could not execute his mission, but gave it over to Elisha his successor. Elisha, in turn, delegated the mission to Jonah his disciple. Had he personally appeared in Ramoth-Gilead, he would have created a sensation, and the anointment would have become known. He, therefore, sent Jonah, who was relatively obscure [*Abarbanel*].

Moreover, the youth was faster than Elisha and could return in great haste before his doings would be discovered [*Azulai*].

To emphasize the prophetic status of this mission, Elisha is referred to as Elisha the prophet. This was necessary since he himself had not received the prophecy directly from the Almighty [*K'li Y'kar*].

do not tarry—lest the king learn of your actions [*Mezudath David*].

Alternatively, *do not wait,* i.e. do not wait for Jehu's answer [*Redak*].

4. **the lad, the disciple of the prophet**—*the disciple of Elisha the prophet, so did Jonathan render: and the lad, the disciple of the prophet, went* [*Rashi*].

The Hebrew is very difficult for two reasons: (1) the repetition of the word *ha-naar,* the lad, and (2) the *he*

בַּעְשָׁא בַּר אֲחִיָּה: י וְיָת איזבל יכלון כלביא באחסנת יזרעאל ולית דקביר ופתח דשא וערק: יא ויהוא נפק לות עבדי רבוניה ואמר ליה השלם מה דין אתא שטיא הדין לותך ואמר להון אתון ידעתון ית גברא וית שועיתיה: יב ואמרו שקרא את אמר חוי כען לנא ואמר כדין וכדין אמר לי למימר כדנן אמר יי משחתך למהוי מלכא על ישראל: יג ואוחיאו ונסיבו גבר לבושיה ושויאו תחותוהי לדרג שעיא

בֶּן־אֲחִיָּה: י וְאֶת־אִיזֶבֶל יֹאכְלוּ הַכְּלָבִים בְּחֵלֶק יִזְרְעֶאל וְאֵין קֹבֵר וַיִּפְתַּח הַדֶּלֶת וַיָּנֹס: יא וְיֵהוּא יָצָא אֶל־עַבְדֵי אֲדֹנָיו וַיֹּאמֶר לוֹ הֲשָׁלוֹם מַדּוּעַ בָּא־הַמְשֻׁגָּע הַזֶּה אֵלֶיךָ וַיֹּאמֶר אֲלֵיהֶם אַתֶּם יְדַעְתֶּם אֶת־הָאִישׁ וְאֶת־שִׂיחוֹ: יב וַיֹּאמְרוּ שֶׁקֶר הַגֶּד־נָא לָנוּ וַיֹּאמֶר כָּזֹאת וְכָזֹאת אָמַר אֵלַי לֵאמֹר כֹּה אָמַר יְהוָה מְשַׁחְתִּיךָ לְמֶלֶךְ אֶל־יִשְׂרָאֵל: יג וַיְמַהֲרוּ וַיִּקְחוּ אִישׁ בִּגְדוֹ וַיָּשִׂימוּ תַחְתָּיו אֶל־גֶּרֶם

רש"י

תרגם יונתן ואזל עולימא תלמידא דנביא: (יא) אתם ידעתם את האיש. אתם מכירים את האיש שהוא משוגע: (יב) ויאמרו שקר. אתה אומר מעלים אתה מה שאמר לך: (יג) אל גרם המעלות. על דרג שעיא כמין מעלות עשויה למול שעות היום לדעת על כל שעה ושעה כשהצל יורד שעה אחת. גרם. (אורל"ו בלע"ז) לשון פגם. והגרמה שבהלכות שחיטה מן הלשון הזה הוא ששורט והולך לך: (יג) אל גרם המעלות. אל המעלה העליונה שבמעלות וי"ת לדרג שעיא והוא האבן שמסמנין אותה לדעת השעות:

רד"ק

(י) ואין קובר. כי כשהלכו לקברה לא מצאו בה אלא הגלגלת וכפות הידים ולא קברו העצמות: (יא) ויאמר לו השלום. הגדול שבשרים שאל ממנו השלום: המשוגע הזה. היו קוראים לנביא משוגע לפי שפעמים בעת הנבואה היה מנהגם כמו המשוגע ושיצא מדעתו כמו שאמר ויפשט גם הוא בגדיו לפי שיש להם בטול ההרגשות והכחות הנפשיות ובני ישראל הרעים שהיה דעתם ולבם אחר הבעל היו קוראים לנביא ה' משוגע דרך בזיון: אתם ידעתם. אתם ידעתם את האיש ואת דבריו כי אני לא ידעתי מה דבריו ולא אמר לי דבר עיקר: (יב) שקר. כי אתה מעלים ממנו מה שאמר לך ודבר סוד אמר

רלב"ג

(יא) ויאמר לו השלום. ר"ל שכבר אמר לו זה אחד מהשרים אשר שם וחקר עמו אם הדבר שדבר אליו הוא שלום או ספק כי רגילים היו הנביאים ליעד רע לישראל והנה קראו הנביא משוגע לפי שמרוב התבודדו' שכלם בש"י היו שוגים בשאר הענינים: אתם ידעתם את האיש ואת שיחו. ר"ל אתם מכירים את האיש ואת דבריו שאין בהם ממש ולזה אין לכם לחקור על דבריו כי לא אמר דבר שיהי' לו שורש: (יב) ויאמרו שקר הגד נא לנו. ר"ל הנה דבריך הם שקר הגד נא לנו מה אמר לך כי דבר סוד אמר אליך: (יג) וימהרו ויקחו איש בגדו. ר"ל שכל אחד מהשרים אשר שם לקח בגדו ושמהו תחת יהוא לעולם המעלות אשר העלוהו שם כדי שיהיה גבוה מאד על כלם כמשפט המלך:

מנחת שי

(יא) ויאמר לו השלום. י"ב דסבירין ויאמרו ועיין מ"ש בסוף מסות: המשגע הזה. הספרים חלוקים במקצתם הה"א במאריך והמ"ם רפויה ובמקצתם במאריך ודגש ויש ספרים בלא מאריך ובלא דגש ורד"ק בספר מכלול דף נ' מנאו עם אותם שהם בדגש ובלא מאריך כה"א:

מצודת דוד

(יא) יצא. מן החדר: ויאמר. אחד מהם שאלו השלום ר"ל אם הנביא ניבא טוב ושלום מדוע א"כ בא אליך לבד ולא אמר לכולנו: המשוגע. כן קראו את הנביא לפי שבעת שהיה מתבודד בנבואה היה נדמה להם כמשתגע על כי לא פנה אז בעניני העולם: אתם ידעתם. כאומר הלא אתם מכירים אותו ואת דבריו שהמה של מה בכך לא שלום ולא למלחמה והיה חפץ להעלים הדבר עד עת יראה כי יש לאל ידו: (יב) שקר. אתה מדבר שקר כי לא דברי רוח היו ולזאת הגד לנו: כזאת וכזאת. וחזר ומפרש כה אמר ה' וגו': (יג) תחתיו. תחת יהוא לשבת למעלה מכולם כדרך המלך:

מצודת ציון

כן כי נהלך לו: (יא) שיחו. דברו כמו כי שיח וכי שיג לו (מ"א י"ח): (יג) גרם. עלם וגרם אחד הוא כמו תשבר גרם (משלי כ"ה) וכמו שעלמות הדבר נקרא בלשון עלם כמ"ש בעלם היום (בראשית ז) כ"כ נקרא בל' גרם: המעלות. המדרגות:

gerem, ourle in Old French, an expression of a notch. Similarly, the word *"Hagramah," in the laws of "shechitah" is from this derivation, that one slaughters in a straight line, and then cuts downwards, making an appearance of a hillock above* [*Rashi*].

According to *Rashi ms.*, this reads: *When the shade descends one step, it is one hour. R. Joseph Kara*'s version is very similar. *When the*

10. And the dogs will eat Jezebel in the territory of Jezreel and no one will bury her.'" And he opened the door and fled.
11. And Jehu went out to his master's servants, and one said to him, "Is all well? Why did this madman come to you?" And he said, "You know the man and his speech."
12. And they said, "It is a lie; please tell us." And he said, "He said to me thus and thus, saying, 'So said the Lord, "I have anointed you as king over Israel."'"
13. And they hastened, and each one took his garment and they put them under him on the top step,

8. **all males**—See above I Kings 21:21, 14:10, 16:11.

10. **and no one will bury her**—for when they went to bury her, they found only her skull and her hands (v. 35) [*Redak*].

11. **And Jehu went out**—of the inner chamber [*Mezudath David*].

and one said to him—I.e. one of the officers said to him [*Ralbag, Mezudath David*].

Alternatively, the chief officer asked him [*Redak*].

Alternatively, although the word appears in the singular form, the intention is that they all asked him [*Minhath Shai*].

"Is all well?—Did the prophet bring good news? They were accustomed to hearing the prophets predict calamity [*Ralbag*].

Why did this madman come to you?"—If all is well, why did he come to you alone and not disclose his mission to all of us? [*Mezudath David*].

They referred to him as a madman, because the prophets would sometimes lose their worldly sensations and be unconscious of all that was transpiring around them when they would receive a prophetic message from God [*Redak, Ralbag, Abarbanel, Mezudath David*].

Additionally, the people of the kingdom of Israel, who were inclined to worship Baal, were ready to call God's prophets madmen as a pejorative [*Redak*].

"You know the man—*You recognize the man, that he is mad* [*Rashi*].

and his speech—You know that his speech is unintelligible. He never says anything tangible [*Redak, Ralbag*].

Alternatively, he did not tell me anything concerning war or peace. You know that he always says trivial things. Jehu tried to conceal the prophecy until an opportune time would arrive [*Mezudath David*].

12. **And they said, "It is a lie**—*that you are saying. You are hiding what he said to you* [*Rashi, Redak, Ralbag, Mezudath David*].

13. **on the top step**—[*Redak*].

Jonathan renders: *on the step of the hours, a type of steps made corresponding to the hours of the day, to know each hour when the shade descends one hour.* It was a type of sundial. The word used for step is

הַמַּעֲלוֹת וַיִּתְקְעוּ בַּשּׁוֹפָר וַיֹּאמְרוּ מָלַךְ
יֵהוּא: יד וַיִּתְקַשֵּׁר יֵהוּא בֶּן־יְהוֹשָׁפָט בֶּן
נִמְשִׁי אֶל־יוֹרָם וְיוֹרָם הָיָה שֹׁמֵר בְּרָמֹת
גִּלְעָד הוּא וְכָל־יִשְׂרָאֵל מִפְּנֵי חֲזָאֵל מֶלֶךְ
אֲרָם: טו וַיָּשָׁב יְהוֹרָם הַמֶּלֶךְ לְהִתְרַפֵּא
בְיִזְרְעֶאל מִן־הַמַּכִּים אֲשֶׁר יַכֻּהוּ אֲרַמִּים
בְּהִלָּחֲמוֹ אֶת־חֲזָאֵל מֶלֶךְ אֲרָם וַיֹּאמֶר
יֵהוּא אִם־יֵשׁ נַפְשְׁכֶם אַל־יֵצֵא פָלִיט
מִן־הָעִיר לָלֶכֶת *לְגִיד בְּיִזְרְעֶאל:
טז וַיִּרְכַּב יֵהוּא וַיֵּלֶךְ יִזְרְעֶאלָה כִּי יוֹרָם
שֹׁכֵב שָׁמָּה וַאֲחַזְיָה מֶלֶךְ יְהוּדָה יָרַד
לִרְאוֹת אֶת־יוֹרָם: יז וְהַצֹּפֶה עֹמֵד עַל־

להגיד קרי

תרגום

שַׁעֲיָא וּתְקַעוּ בְּשׁוֹפָר נַאֲמַרוּ מְלַךְ יֵהוּא: יד וּמְרִיד יֵהוּא בַּר יְהוֹשָׁפָט בַּר נִמְשִׁי עַל יוֹרָם וְיוֹרָם הֲוָה נָטִיר בְּרָמוֹת גִּלְעָד הוּא וְכָל יִשְׂרָאֵל מִן קֳדָם חֲזָאֵל מַלְכָּא דַאֲרָם: טו וְתָב יְהוֹרָם מַלְכָּא לְאִתַּסָאָה בְּיִזְרְעֶאל מִן מַחֲתָא דִמְחוֹהִי אֱנָשׁ אֲרָם כַּד אַגִּיחַ קְרָבָא עִם חֲזָאֵל מַלְכָּא דַאֲרָם וַאֲמַר יֵהוּא אִם רְעוּת נַפְשְׁכוֹן לָא יִפּוֹק מְשֵׁיזְבָא מִן קַרְתָּא לְמֵיזַל לְחַוָאָה בְּיִזְרְעֶאל: טז וּרְכַב יֵהוּא וַאֲזַל לְיִזְרְעֶאל אֲרֵי יוֹרָם שְׁכִיב תַּמָּן וַאֲחַזְיָה מַלְכָּא דְבֵית יְהוּדָה נְחַת לְמִסְעַד יַת יוֹרָם: יז וְסַכְוָאָה קָאֵים עַל

רד"ק

(יד) ויתקשר. המורד יקרא קשר לפי שהמורד הוא בהתקשר זה עם זה להיות בלב אחד ובהסכמה אחת: ויורם היה שומר. עתה ספר היאך היה הקשר חזק כי אם היה יורם שם לא היה הקשר אז כי היו שרי החיל אשר שם יראים מיורם ולא היו נסכמים עם יהוא למרוד בו אלא שיורם שהיה שם ברמות גלעד שומר העיר מפני חזאל היה מקרהו שהוכה שם והוצרך לו לשוב להתרפא ביזרעאל ובין כך בא הנביא אל יהוא ומשחו והתקשרו עמו שרי החיל אשר שם: (טו) מן המכים. שם כמו מן המכות יאמ' האחת מכה בסגול וכן אמר התרגום מן מחתא: אשר יכוהו. כמו הכוהו עתיד במקום עבר וכמוהו רבים: אם יש נפשכם. אם רצונכם אתי להמליכני כאשר אתם מראים עזרוני בזה הדבר שלא יצא פליט מן העיר ללכת להגיד ביזרעאל ליהורם כי טוב הוא שנבא עליו פתאום ולא ישמר ממנו: לגיד. כן כתיב וקרי להגיד ושניהם נכונים כי מצאנו המקור בחסרון הה"א רבים כמו לשמוע בקול תורת

רש"י

ויורד ונראה כמין גבשושית למעלה: (טו) אם יש נפשכם. שאמלוך: מן העיר. מן רמות גלעד:

מנחת שי

(טו) ל*גיד. להגיד קרי ונראה שכן צריך להיות בחילופים למערבאי:

רלב"ג

(יד) ויתקשר יהוא בן יהושפט. ר"ל שהתקשר עם הסריס אשר שם כנגד יורם וזכר כי סבת זה הקשר היה היות יורם מוכה ברמות גלעד כי לולי זה כבר היה שומר ברמות גלעד וכל ישראל מפני חזאל שהיה רוצה לכבוש רמות גלעד ומפני יראת הסריס ממנו לא היה אפשר אז כל זה אך קרה שהוכה שם והוכרח מפני זה ללכת ביזרעאל וזה ממה שהישיר הדרך אל זה הקשר: (טו) אם יש נפשכם. ר"ל אם רצונכם להחזק בקשר הזה לא יצא שום אדם מן העיר שיוכל להגיד זה ביזרעאל כי זה יהיה סבה אל שיחזק יורם לנגדי ולא נוכל לעשות

מצודת ציון

(יד) ויתקשר. כן נקרא המרד כי רבים יתקשרו באגודה אחת: (טו) נפשכם. רצונכם כמו ואכלת ענבים כנפשך (דברים כ"ג): פליט. שם שארית וכן שריד ופליט (ירמיה מ"ב): (יז) והצופה. הוא העומד במקום גבוה להביט למרחוק: שפעת.

מצודת דוד

אל גרם המעלות. על המעלות עצמן: (יד) ויתקשר. עשה קשר עם הסריס שהיו עמו: ויורם היה שומר. אז היתה ישיבת קביעתו ברמות גלעד לשמור העיר מחיל חזאל: (טו) וישב. לפי שעה שב מרמות גלעד להתרפא ביזרעאל: אם יש נפשכם. אם יש

[*Rashi*]. According to *Redak*, and in most editions of Kings, the *K'ri is* לְהַגִּיד, the usual form. Apparently, *Rashi* differs. Otherwise, he would not explain the *K'thib* unless the *K'ri* is identical.

17. **a troop**—[*Jonathan, Rashi*]. Others explain *shif'ath* as a multitude, also used in reference to camels (Is. 60:6), and similar to *shefa*, abundance, as in Deut. 33:19 [*Redak*].

and they sounded the *shofar* and said, "Jehu has become
king!" 14. And Jehu son of Jehoshaphat son of Nimshi
revolted against Joram, while Joram was guarding in Ramoth-
Gilead, he and all Israel, against Hazael king of Aram. 15. And
King Jehoram returned to recuperate in Jezreel from the
wounds that the Arameans inflicted upon him when he fought
with Hazael king of Aram. And Jehu said, "If you so desire, let
no survivor leave the city to go and tell in Jezreel." 16. And
Jehu rode and went to Jezreel for Joram was lying there, and
Ahaziah king of Judah went down to see Joram. 17. And the
lookout was standing on

shade descends one step, it is the hour.

They placed their garments under Jehu to elevate him and symbolize his kingship over them [*Mezudath David*].

It was Divine Providence that caused the officers to accept Jehu as their monarch, upon the prophet's word, when a moment before, they called the prophet a madman [*Malbim*].

14. **revolted**—Heb. *vayithkasher,* an expression of being tied together. I.e. forming a group that conspires against the government [*Redak*].

while Joram was guarding—Had Joram been there, the conspiracy would not have come about because the officers feared him. Since Joram was wounded and was forced to go to Jezreel to recuperate, it became possible for the prophet to anoint Jehu and for the rebellion to burgeon [*Redak*].

Moreover, since Israel was preoccupied with the war against Aram, the rebels found no opposition.

In addition, since Joram was separated from his army, he was vulnerable to attack [*Malbim*].

15. —**from the wounds that the Arameans inflicted upon him**—For alternate translation see above 8:29.

"If you so desire—*that I reign* [*Rashi*].

If your desire is with me to crown me as king, as it appears, help me in this manner. Let no man escape from Ramoth-Gilead to report the revolt in Jezreel. It will be easier to overpower Joram if we take him by surprise [*Redak*].

If Joram learns of the revolt, he will escape from Jezreel and, perhaps, receive aid from his army [*Malbim*].

from the city—*from Ramoth-Gilead* [*Rashi*].

tell—Heb. לַגִּיד, *same as* לְהַגִּיד

המגדל ביזרעאל וירא את־שפעת
יהוא בבאו ויאמר שפעת אני ראה
ויאמר יהורם קח רכב ושלח לקראתם
ויאמר השלום: יח וילך רכב הסוס
לקראתו ויאמר כה־אמר המלך
השלום ויאמר יהוא מה־לך ולשלום
סב אל־אחרי ויגד הצפה לאמר בא־
המלאך עד־הם ולא־שב: יט וישלח
רכב סוס שני ויבא אלהם ויאמר כה־
אמר המלך שלום ויאמר יהוא מה־
לך ולשלום סב אל־אחרי: כ ויגד
הצפה לאמר בא עד־אליהם ולא־שב
והמנהג כמנהג יהוא בן־נמשי כי

על מגדלא ביזרעאל
נחזא ית משרית יהוא
במיתוהי ואמר משרית
אנא חזי ואמר יהורם
דבר רכבא ושלח
לקדמותהון ויימר
השלם: יח ואזל רכיב
סוסיא לקדמותיה ואמר
כדנן אמר מלכא השלם
ואמר יהוא מה לך
ולשלם אסתחר לאחורי
וחוי סכותא למימר אתא
אזגדא עד לותהון ולא
תב: יט ושלח רכיב
סוסיא תנינא ואתא
לותהון ואמר כדנן אמר
מלכא השלם ואמר
יהוא מה לך ולשלם
אסתחר לאחורי: כ וחוי
סכותא למימר אתא עד
לותהון ולא תב ודברא
כדברא דיהוא בר נמשי
ארי

כצ"ל בלא ה'

רש"י

לגיד. כמו להגיד: (יז) שפעת. גדוד:

רד"ק

שהוא כמו להשמיע לראותכם כמו להראותכם והדומים להם: (יז) את שפעת יהוא. רבוי עם שהיה בא עם יהוא וכן שפעת גמלי' שפע ימים ינקו: שפעת אני רואה. התי"ו כמו הה"א כי אינני סמוך וכמוהו חכמת ודעת, אם אתן שנת לעיני כשמחת בקציר והדומה לו שכתבנו בספר מכלל: רכב. משרת רוכב הסוס יקרא רכב ועתה רכב על סוס אדוניו ללכת לקראת יהוא: (יח) עד הם. הראשון וכן השני עד אליהם שלא כמנהג כי המנהג עדיהם מלה אחת ועד אליהם היא תוספת ביאור כי היה מספיק אם יאמר אליהם או עדיהם לבדו: (כ) והמנהג כמנהג יהוא. מנהג הרכב כמנהג יהוא שהוא

רלב"ג

הגדוד ממנו: (יז) ויראה את שפעת יהוא. ר"ל שפע עם שהיה בא עם יהוא: קח רכב ושלח לקראתם. ר"ל רוכב סוס: (יח) מה לך ולשלום סוב אל אחרי. עשה זאת כדי שלא ידע המלך דבר בזה כדי שיתכן לו יותר להמיתו: (כ) והמנהג כמנהג יהוא. ר"ל מנהג המלך אשר היה רוכב בו והוא היה נוהג מנהג יהוא כי הוא רכבו בשגעון

מנחת שי

(יז) ושלח לקראתם. בספרים כתובי יד הוא"ו במאריך ויש מהם שהשי"ן בשוא ופתח: (יט) וישלח רכב סוס שני ויבא אליהם ויאמר כה אמר המלך שלום עין מ"ש בשמואל ב' י"ח:

מצודת דוד

הלוככם שאמלוך אני שמרו לבל יצא מי מן העיר כי פן ילך ויגיד ביזרעאל ויהיה המלך נשמר: (יז) בבואו. בעת בוא רבוי העם אשר עם יהוא ראה אותם הצופה אבל עדיין לא הכיר אם של יהוא המה: ויאמר השלום. הרכב אמר להם השלום ר"ל אם בואם בעבור השלום או למלחמה: (יח) מה לך ולשלום. מה לך שתשאל השלום האם נוגע לך הדבר: סוב אל אחרי. ללכת עם אנשי ולא תשוב אל המלך: (כ) והמנהג. הנני רואה הנהגת העם הבא הוא כמנהג יהוא אשר הנהגתו בשגעון מבלי סדר וישוב הדעת: בן

מצודת ציון

מל' סבוב: (יח) עד הם. עד אליהם:

20. **His driving**—i.e. the manner in which he drives his chariot is like that of Jehu, who drives wildly [*Redak*].

Alternatively, he *leads* his band

K'li Y'kar, however, notes the omission of the interrogative *he*. He, therefore, renders thus: The king said, 'Peace!' He was ready to make peace at all costs.

the tower in Jezreel, and he saw Jehu's troop when it came, and he said, "I see a troop." And Jehoram said, "Take a rider and send him toward them, and let him say, 'Is there peace?'"
18. The horse rider went toward him and said, "So said the king, 'Is there peace?'" and Jehu said, "What is it to you whether there is peace? Fall in behind me." And the lookout reported saying, "The messenger came up to them and did not return."
19. And he sent a second horse rider, who came to them and said, "So said the king, 'Is there peace?'" And Jehu said, "What is it to you whether there is peace? Fall in behind me."
20. And the lookout reported saying, "He came up to them and did not return. His driving is like the driving of Jehu the son of Nimshi,

I.e. a disorganized band, as below v. 20 [*K'li Y'kar*].

when they came—He saw the band as soon as they came. Yet, he was unable to recognize them as Jehu's band [*Mezudath David*].

"Take a rider—Heb. רַכָּב. According to *Ralbag,* this is synonymous with רוֹכֵב. According to *Redak* and *Abarbanel,* however, this refers to a squire, who would ride alongside a knight, attend him, and bear his armor. Joram ordered the lookout to send out a squire to investigate the band seen in the distance.

"Is there peace?"—Do you come in peace or do you wish to wage war? [*Mezudath David*].

18. **"What is it to you whether there is peace? Fall in behind me."**—What does it concern you whether I come in peace? Do not concern yourself with these matters; just fall in behind me and join my service. Jehu wanted to make sure that his intentions would not become known until he would reach Joram [*Abarbanel*].

Alternatively, Jehu replied, "What is it to you? If you want peace, fall in behind me." You have reached the point of no return. If you wish to remain alive, join my ranks. I will not permit you to return to Joram [*K'li Y'kar*].

19. **a second horse rider**—This time Joram himself sent out a knight, not a squire. They feared that the leader of the band had taken offense by being greeted by a squire rather than a knight. He, therefore, sent a knight to greet him [*K'li Y'kar*].

'Is there peace?'"—[*Jonathan*].

בְשִׁגָּעוֹן יִנְהָג׃ כא וַיֹּאמֶר יְהוֹרָם אֱסֹר
וַיֶּאְסֹר רִכְבּוֹ וַיֵּצֵא יְהוֹרָם מֶלֶךְ־יִשְׂרָאֵל
וַאֲחַזְיָהוּ מֶלֶךְ־יְהוּדָה אִישׁ בְּרִכְבּוֹ וַיֵּצְאוּ
לִקְרַאת יֵהוּא וַיִּמְצָאֻהוּ בְּחֶלְקַת נָבוֹת
הַיִּזְרְעֵאלִי׃ כב וַיְהִי כִּרְאוֹת יְהוֹרָם אֶת־
יֵהוּא וַיֹּאמֶר הֲשָׁלוֹם יֵהוּא וַיֹּאמֶר מָה
הַשָּׁלוֹם עַד־זְנוּנֵי אִיזֶבֶל אִמְּךָ וּכְשָׁפֶיהָ
הָרַבִּים׃ כג וַיַּהֲפֹךְ יְהוֹרָם יָדָיו וַיָּנָס
וַיֹּאמֶר אֶל־אֲחַזְיָהוּ מִרְמָה אֲחַזְיָה׃
כד וְיֵהוּא מִלֵּא יָדוֹ בַקֶּשֶׁת וַיַּךְ אֶת־
יְהוֹרָם בֵּין זְרֹעָיו וַיֵּצֵא הַחֵצִי מִלִּבּוֹ
וַיִּכְרַע בְּרִכְבּוֹ׃ כה וַיֹּאמֶר אֶל־בִּדְקַר
שָׁלִשֹׁה שָׂא הַשְׁלִכֵהוּ בְּחֶלְקַת שְׂדֵה

תרגום

ארי בניח מדבר׃ כא ואמר יהורם אזדרזו ושקים רתיכיה ונפק יהורם מלכא דישראל ואחזיהו מלך שבטא דבית יהודה גבר ברתיכיה ונפקו לקדמות יהוא ואשכחוהי באחסנת חקל נבות יזרעאלה׃ כב נהוה כד חזא יהורם ית יהוא ואמר השלם יהוא ואמר מה השלם עד טעות איזבל אמך וחרשהא סגיאין׃ כג ואתחזר יהורם לאחורוהי ואפך ואמר לאחזיהו ניכלא אחזיה׃ כד ויהוא מלא ידיה בקשתא ומחא ית יהורם בין דרעוהי ונפק גירא מלביה וכרע ברתיכיה׃ כה ואמר לבדקר גבריה סב רמיהי באחסנת חקל

שלשו קרי

רד"ק

נוהג רכבו בשגעון וי"ת בשגעון ינהג בניח מדבר׃ (כב) השלום עד זנוני. מה ענין השלום שיגיע עד זנוני אמך לא יאות לה ילך שלום׃ (כג) ויהפוך יהורם ידיו. האוחזות ברסן הפכם להסב פניו ולנום׃ (כד) מלא ידו בקשת. משך הקשת בכל כחו׃ (כה) שלשה. בה"א במקום וי"ו כמו אהלה׃ כי זכור אני ואתה. זכור היום שאני ואתה היינו רוכבים יחדיו מחוברים כלומר שהיו רוכבים שניהם ברכב אחד או שניהם זה אצל זה ביחד זהו צמדים כמו צמד בקר ומלת את ר"ל עם כלומר אני

מנחת שי

(כה) בדקר שלשה. סה"א במקום וא"ו׃

רלב"ג

כזולת ישוב׃ (כג) ויהפוך יהורם ידו וינס. ר"ל שהפך הי' גם לשוב ליזרעאל אך מהר יהוא וירה לו חץ והכהו מאחוריו בין זרועיו ויצא מלבו ומת לשעתו וכרע ברכבו ואמר יהוא לבדקר שהיה השליש שלו שישא נבלת יורם וישליכהו בחלקת שדה נבות היזרעאלי ר"ל במקום

מצודת ציון

(כא) בחלקת. בנחלת שדה׃ (כה) שלשו. ענין שר כמו ומבחר שלישיו (שמות טו)׃ שא. הגבה אותו׃ צמדים.

מצודת דוד

נמשי. בן בנו של נמשי׃ (כא) אסור. קשור הסוסים אל הרכב׃ (כב) מה השלום. מהו השלום הראוי עד שיהא השלום גמול זנוני איזבל וכו'. וכאומר וכי ראוים אתם לשלום׃ (כג) ויהפוך. הפך ידיו האוחזות ברסני הסוסים להפכם לאחור ולנוס׃ מרמה. ר"ל הנה קשר ומרד ובמרמה היו מראים עצמם כאוהבים׃ (כד) מלא ידו. שם כל ידו במלואה בקשת לירות בכח רב׃ ויכרע. כרע על ברכיו׃ (כה) כי זכר. תן דעתך לזכור כי אני ואתה את אשר היינו

befitting Jezebel who is still committing harlotries? [*Redak*].

Alternatively, what peace can there be until Jezebel has been punished for her harlotries [*Mezudath David*].

As in many instances in the Prophets, idolatry is referred to symbolically as harlotry. Just as an unfaithful wife leaves her husband for her paramours, so do the idolators leave God for pagan deities. See *Jonathan*.

and her numerous sorceries—Although no mention was made of Jezebel practicing sorcery, undoubtedly she did so in conjunction with her idolatry.

23. **turned his hands around**—I.e. he turned his hands around to pull

for he drives madly. 21. And Jehoram said, "Hitch up!" And he hitched up his chariot. And Jehoram king of Israel and Ahaziah king of Judah, went out each in his own chariot; they went out toward Jehu, and they found him in the territory of Naboth the Jezreelite. 22. And it was when Jehoram saw Jehu, that he said, "Is there peace, Jehu?" And he said, "What peace is there with the harlotries of Jezebel your mother and her numerous sorceries?" 23. And Jehoram turned his hands around and fled. And he said to Ahaziah, "Treachery, Ahaziah!" 24. And Jehu put all his strength into his bow, and he hit Jehoram between his arms, and the arrow protruded from his heart, and he fell to his knees in his chariot. 25. And he said to Bidkar, his officer, "Pick him up! Throw him into the territory of the field of

wildly, without order [*Mezudath David*].

Jonathan renders: he drives slowly. His intention here is not clear.

the son of Nimshi —i.e. the grandson of Nimshi [*Mezudath David*].

21. **"Hitch up!"**—Hitch up the horses to the chariots [*Mezudath David*].

Jehoram ordered Ahaziah to hitch up his own chariot. When the lookout reported that the two riders did not return, Jehoram already suspected treachery. There was no time to stand on ceremony and wait for their attendants to hitch up their chariots. Since Ahaziah had come to visit Jehoram, it was only proper to warn him of the impending peril. He, therefore, urged him to hitch up his own chariot [*K'li Y'kar*].

went out—They went out to make sure that they would not be trapped in the city [*Malbim*].

Although Naboth's vineyard was adjacent to the royal palace, he had other fields that covered a large area of the surrounding territory. Jehu stopped at one of these fields [*Daath Soferim*].

Abarbanel, however, identifies this territory with the site of Naboth's execution. Jehu stood, pondering the crime that had been committed there, and his mission to avenge Naboth's death by destroying the house of Ahab.

22. **"Is there peace, Jehu?"**—He reiterates the question a third time. By now, Joram doubts very much that Jehu has come with peaceful intentions [*Daath Soferim*].

"What peace is there with the harlotries of Jezebel—What peace is

חקל נבות יזרעאלה
ארי דכיר אנא ואת כד
הוינא רכיבין זוגא חד
אזלין בתר אחאב אבוהי
ומן קדם יי אתנטל
עלוהי ית מטל נבואתא
הדין: כו אם לא ית דמי
נבות וית דמי בנוהי
גלן קדמי בקריב אמר
יי ואשלם לך באחסנתא
הדא אמר יי וכען כב
רמיהי באחסנתא
כפתגמא דיי: כז ואחזיה
מלכא שבטא דבית
יהודה חזא ואפך באורח
בית גנא ורדף בתרוהי
יהוא

ת"א דמי נבות. סנהד' מח:

נְבוֹת הַיִּזְרְעֵאלִי כִּי־זְכֹר אֲנִי וָאַתָּה אֵת
רֹכְבִים צְמָדִים אַחֲרֵי אַחְאָב אָבִיו
וַיהוָה נָשָׂא עָלָיו אֶת־הַמַּשָּׂא הַזֶּה׃
כו אִם־לֹא אֶת־דְּמֵי נָבוֹת וְאֶת־דְּמֵי בָנָיו
רָאִיתִי אֶמֶשׁ נְאֻם־יְהוָה וְשִׁלַּמְתִּי לְךָ
בַּחֶלְקָה הַזֹּאת נְאֻם־יְהוָה וְעַתָּה שָׂא
הַשְׁלִכֵהוּ בַּחֶלְקָה כִּדְבַר יְהוָה׃
כז וַאֲחַזְיָה מֶלֶךְ־יְהוּדָה רָאָה וַיָּנָס דֶּרֶךְ
בֵּית הַגָּן וַיִּרְדֹּף אַחֲרָיו יֵהוּא וַיֹּאמֶר גַּם־

רש"י

(כה) את רוכבים צמדים. את אשר אני ואתה היינו רוכבי' צמדים (ס"א מלומדים) אחר אחאב ביום שהרג את נבות: וה' נשא עליו. ביד אליהו הנביא המשא הזה ואנחנו

רד"ק

עמך ואתה עמי היינו רוכבים צמדים וי"ת ארי דכיר אנא ואת כד הוינא רכיבין זוגא חד אזלין: וה' נשא עליו. ומן קדם ה' אתנטל עלוהי ית מטל נבואתא הדין: (כו) את דמי נבות ואת דמי בניו. נחלקו רז"ל בדבר זה יש שאומרים בניו נהרגו עמו ומהם אמרו בנים העתידים לצאת ממנו וא"א ז"ל פי' ואת דמי בניו שגזל מהם נחלתם: ראיתי אמש. ת"י גלן קדמי בקריב וי"ל אמש כמשמעו הלילה שעבר ונאמר לאליהו ממחרת שמת נבות הנבואה הזאת כי ביום שמת נבות שלחו אל איזבל ולא ירד לכרם לרשתו עד למחרתו והנבואה באה אל אחאב בו ביום שהיה אחאב בכרם ואמר לא ראיתי הלילה דמי נבות ודמי בניו על דרך קול דמי אחיך צועקים אלי מן האדמה: (כז) וינס דרך בית הגן. ובדברי הימים הוא אומר והוא מתחבא בשמרון ויביאוהו אל יהוא וימיתוהו נראה כי בדרך הכוהו כמו שאמר להם הכוהו אל המרכבה והם הורו לו חצים והכוהו והוא נס מוכה אל מגדו וימת שם ולא מת ממש אלא נשתתק מחמת

רלב"ג

אשר סוקל שם נבות: (כה) אני ואתה את רוכבים צמדים אחרי אחאב אביו. ר"ל שאני ואתה היינו יחד את רוכבים אחרים מחוברים והולכים אחרי אחאב אביו: (כו) אם לא את דמי נבות ואת דמי בניו ראיתי אמש. אמר דמי בניו העתידים לצאת ממנו כמו שבארנו במה שקדם ואמר אליהו לו כדבר ה' שכבר ראה בלילה שעבר קודם מלאו אותו דמי נבות שהומת בעבור שלא רצה למכור כרמו או להחליפו: (כז) ואחזיהו מלך יהודה ראה וינס. ספר בד"ה שכבר היה אחזיהו מתחבא בשומרון ויביאוהו אל יהוא ואולם קצר בזה המקום והנה כשהביאוהו אל יהוא אמר להם שיכוהו אל המרכבה בחלים והנה אמר להם זה בהיותו בעליית גור אשר את יבלעם ושם הכוהו בחלים

מצודת דוד

רוכבים צמדים ומהולכים אחרי אחאב ואז נשא ה' עליו את המשא הזה ע"י אליהו: (כו) אם לא וגו'. ור"ל האם לא את דמי וכו' ראיתי אמש כי למהרת הריגת נבות ירד אחאב לרשת כרמו ואז אמר לו אליהו כדבר ה' אם לא את דמי וכו' ראיתי אמש והם צועקים ומבקשים עליו דין: ואת דמי בניו. יש מרז"ל אמרו שהרג גם בניו ומהם אמרו בניו שהיה עתיד להוליד: ושלמתי לך. גם זה דברי אליהו שאמר בשם ה' שיקבל גמולו בחלקת נבות: ועתה. הואיל ודבר ה' הוא השליכהו אל החלקה ההיא: (כז) גם אתו הכהו. כי גם הוא מבית אחאב עובד ע"ג כמוהם: אל המרכבה. בעודו

מצודת ציון

חבורים יחד כמו לצמיד פתיל (במדבר יט): נשא עליו. הטעים עליו: המשא. הנבואה: (כו) אמש. יאמר על הלילה העברה כמו

Therefore, God says to Elijah, "Did I not see . . . last night?" [*Redak, Ralbag, Mezudath David*]. See I Kings 21:13–21.

Malbim interprets this as an oath: I swear that I saw . . . last night, and I shall requite you in this plot. Therefore, since God's oath is irrevocable, I command you—And now pick him up and throw him into this plot.

27. **"Strike him . . . in the chariot . . .**—*And in* II *Chron.* (22:9), *it is said: And he sought Ahaziah, and they captured him when he was hiding in Samaria, and they brought him to Jehu.* The discrepancy between *the verses can be reconciled* thus: *And . . . fled by way of the garden* (sic) *from Jezreel to Samaria. Rashi* does not explain why it is stated here that he fled to Megiddo while in Chron. it says that he was brought from Samaria. *There is, however, an uncer-*

Naboth the Jezreelite, for remember that you and I were riding together after Ahab his father, when the Lord pronounced this prophecy upon him: 26. 'Did I not see the blood of Naboth and the blood of his children last night?' says the Lord. 'I shall requite you in this plot,' says the Lord. And now, pick [him] up and throw him into this plot according to the word of the Lord." 27. And Ahaziah king of Judah saw, and he fled by way of the garden-house, and Jehu pursued him, and he said,

the reins and to drive the horses in the opposite direction, in order to flee back to Jezreel [*Redak*].

24. **and the arrow protruded from his heart**—Since Joram turned to flee, the arrow hit him in the back. It hit between his arms slanting downward, and came out through his heart [*Daath Soferim*].

and he fell to his knees in his chariot—This is reminiscent of his father's death in his chariot. Their deaths illustrate that "a horse is vain for victory (Psalms 33:17)" [*Daath Soferim*].

25. **"Pick him up! Throw him into the territory . . .**—Before he was killed, Jehoram had fled past Naboth's territory. Jehu, therefore, ordered Bidkar to bring him back to that area [*Malbim*].

According to *Ralbag*, this was the site of Naboth's execution.

that . . . were riding together—*how you and I were riding together after Ahab on the day that he killed Naboth* [*Rashi*].

riding together—lit. riding paired. They were both riding in the same chariot, or side by side [*Redak*].

when the Lord pronounced . . . upon him—*this prophecy through the prophet Elijah, and we heard* [*Rashi*].

26. **and the blood of his children**—Some say that Ahab killed Naboth's children with him in order to prevent them from inheriting his estate. For want of any closer relative, Ahab his cousin inherited the property. Others say that Ahab was considered accountable for all the children Naboth would have begotten had he been allowed to live [*Redak, Ralbag, Mezudath David,* from *Sanhedrin* 48b].

Alternatively, the blood of his children whom he impoverished by confiscating their property [*Redak* quoting his father, *Abarbanel*]. This is in accordance with the Talmudic maxim that a pauper is considered as dead.

The prophet was speaking figuratively, just as God said to Cain, "The voice of your brother's blood cries to me from the earth (Gen. 4:10)."

last night—*Jonathan* renders: *was revealed to me recently.* It may, however, be understood literally. This prophecy was conveyed to Elijah on the day following Naboth's execution. On the day of the execution, Jezebel was notified. She, in turn, notified Ahab, who took possession of the vineyard on the morrow.

אֹתוֹ הַכֻּהוּ אֶל־הַמֶּרְכָּבָה בְּמַעֲלֵה־גוּר
אֲשֶׁר אֶת־יִבְלְעָם וַיָּנָס מְגִדּוֹ וַיָּמָת שָׁם׃
כח וַיַּרְכִּבוּ אֹתוֹ עֲבָדָיו יְרוּשָׁלְָמָה וַיִּקְבְּרוּ
אֹתוֹ בִקְבֻרָתוֹ עִם־אֲבֹתָיו בְּעִיר דָּוִד׃
כט וּבִשְׁנַת אַחַת עֶשְׂרֵה שָׁנָה לְיוֹרָם בֶּן־
אַחְאָב מָלַךְ אֲחַזְיָה עַל־יְהוּדָה׃ ל וַיָּבוֹא
יֵהוּא יִזְרְעֶאלָה וְאִיזֶבֶל שָׁמְעָה וַתָּשֶׂם

יְהוּא וַאֲמַר אַף יָתֵיהּ מְחוֹהִי בִּרְתִיכָא בְּמַסְקָנָא דְגוּר דְעִם יִבְלְעָם וַאֲפַךְ לִמְגִדּוֹ וּמִית תַּמָן׃ כח וְאַחִיתוּ יָתֵיהּ עַבְדוֹהִי לִירוּשְׁלֵם וּקְבָרוּ יָתֵיהּ בִּקְבוּרְתֵּיהּ עִם אֲבָהָתוֹהִי בְּקַרְתָּא דְדָוִד׃ כט וּבִשְׁנַת חֲדָא עַסְרֵי שְׁנִין לְיוֹרָם בַּר אַחְאָב מְלַךְ אֲחַזְיָה עַל דְבֵית יְהוּדָה׃ ל וַאֲתָא יְהוּא לְיִזְרְעֶאל וְאִיזֶבֶל שְׁמָעַת וּכְחָלַת בִּצְרִידָא

ירושלימה קרי

רד"ק

המכות כמו שאומר בנבל וימת לבו בקרבו ולא מת ממש עד **עשרה** ימים וכך פירשו ויכת שם שנשתתק ואחר כן נשאוהו עבדיו להחבא בשמרון מפני יהוא ועבדי יהוא שרדפו אחריו ומצאוהו מתחבא בשמרון הביאוהו אל יהוא ביזרעאל והמיתוהו שם כי עדיין לא מת ומה שאמר שם ויקברוהו כי אמרו בן יהושפט הוא לא שקברוהו שם אלא שנתנוהו לקבורה והניחו אותו שיוליכוהו עבדיו לירושלם כמו שאמר הנה וירכיבו אותו עבדיו ירושלימה ויקברו אותו בקבורתו וגו׳: **במעלה גור.** לא אמר להם שיכוהו במעלה גור אלא אמר לעבדיו שהיו רודפים הכוהו אל המרכבה והם לא השיגוהו כי הוא היה נס על המרכבה ולא השיגוהו עד מעלה גור שהשיגוהו בחצים שמה והוא נס עם כל זה עד מגידו וזהו שאמר ויכוהו במעלה גור אשר את יבלעם והפסוק חסר במלת ויכוהו ולפי שאמר הכוהו סמך על המבין וכמוהו הרבה במקרא: (כט) **ובשנת אחת עשרה.** ולמעלה אמר בשנת י"ב ולפי החשבון הוא בשנת י"ג כמו שכתב אלא שב׳ שנים היו בהם מקוטעות מה שאומר זה הנה אף על פי שאמר למעלה תחלת מלכותו וסופה עתה בעת מותו ספר ג"כ מלכותו להודיע כי בעונו קצרו ימי מלכותו ומת ולא מלך אחר אביו אלא שנה אחת: (ל) **ותשם בפוך עיניה.** ותשם פוך בעיניה וכמוהו שלחו באש מקדשך שלחו אש במקדשך או פי׳ ותשם והתקן בפוך עיניה והפוך הוא

רש"י

שמעני: (כז) **הכהו אל המרכבה וגו׳.** ובדברי הימים (ב"ב כ"ב) הוא אומר ויבקש את אחזיה וילכדוהו והוא מתחבא בשומרון ויביאוהו אל יהוא יש ליישב המקראות וינס דרך הגן מיזרעאל לשומרון וירדוף אחריו יהוא אך יש גמגום בדבר שהרי לא היתה ממשלת יהוא בשומרון עד יום המחרת כמו שמפורש בענין ויכתוב יהוא ספרים וישלח שומרון וגו׳ רבותינו פירשו באגדת חלק והוא מתחבא בשומרון שהיה קודר אזכרות וכותב עכו"ם תחתיהם ולפי דבריהם יש לומר שאין ההבאה זו מפני יהוא אלא כך פירושו ויבקש את אחזיהו וילכדוהו כשהיה נס דרך הגן והוא היה מרשיע לעשות מתחלה שהיה בא לשומרון והתחבא מפני שרי יהודה לעשות התועבה הזאת לפי שיושבי שומרון עובדי עכו"ם היו ויביאוהו אל יהוא אנשי יהוא שרדפו אחריו ויאמר הכהו אל המרכבה: **במעלה גור.** ששם הביאוהו אליו: **וינס מגדו.** מוכה בגליות: (כט) **ובשנת אחת עשרה שנה ליורם בן אחאב מלך אחזיה.** למעלה הוא אומר בשנת י"ב ועל כרחך יהורם אביו לא מת אלא בשנת י"ב ליורם שהרי בשנת חמש ליורם מלך ושמונה שנים מלך ומהו שאמר כאן בשנת אחד עשר אומר אני שמלך בחיי אביו שנה לפי שהיה נגוף בתחלואים רעים כמו שנאמר (בדברי הימים ב׳ כ"א י"ח) ואחרי כל זאת נגפו ה׳ לחלי לאין מרפא ויהי לימים מימים יצאו מעיו עם חליו וגו׳

רלב"ג

וגם מוכה אל מגדו וימת שם והנה זכה לקבורה מפני היותו בן יהושפט אשר דרש את ה׳ בכל לבו כמו שנזכר בספר ד"ה: (ל) ותשם בפוך עיניה. ר"ל שחור קשטה את עלמה ושמה פוך בעיניה להיטיב ראותה אולי עשתה כדי שתשא חן בעיניו ויחמול עליה ולא יהרגנה

מצודת דוד

יושב במרכבה: במעלה גור. כאלו אמר והכהו במעלת גור וקצר הכתוב וסמך על מ"ש גם אותו הכהו: את יבלעם. סמוך ליבלעם: וינס מגדו. אחרי אשר הכהו נס אל מגידו: וימת שם. ר"ל הומת בדבר הקשר ההוא של יהוא כי בד"ה נאמר שמת בשומרון כי נשם בא ממגידו: (כח) בקבורתו. אשר כרה לו בחייו: (כט) ובשנת אחת עשרה. ר"ל אחר שעבר שנת י"א כי בי"ב מלך וכמ"ש למעלה בשנת שתים עשרה וכו׳ כי יהורם אביו מלך בה׳ ליורם בן אחאב וימי מלכותו ח׳ שנים מקוטעות וכלו א"כ בי"ב ליורם בן אחאב ואז מלך אחזיה: (ל) ותשם בפוך עיניה. כמו ותשם פוך בעיניה וכן שלחו באש מקדשך (תהלים ע"ד) ומשפטו שלחו אש במקדשך:

buried him,'' this does not mean that Jehu and his men buried him, but that they permitted his servants to bury him in Jerusalem [*Redak*].

29. **And in the eleventh year of Joram son of Ahab, Ahaziah became king**—*Above* (8:25) *it is stated, ''In the twelfth year.'' And you are forced to say that Jehoram his father did not die until the twelfth year of Joram, for in the fifth year of Joram he became king* (8:16) *and he reigned for eight years* (8:17). *Now why does it say here, ''In the eleventh year?'' I say that he reigned one year during his father's lifetime since he was afflicted with severe maladies, as it is said: ''And after all this, the Lord*

"Strike him too in the chariot." [And they struck him] at the ascent of Gur which is near Ibleam, and he fled to Megiddo and died there. 28. And his servants carried him in a chariot to Jerusalem, and they buried him in his grave with his forefathers in the city of David. 29. And in the eleventh year of Joram son of Ahab, Ahaziah became king over Judah. 30. And Jehu came to Jezreel, and Jezebel heard, and she painted

tainty in the matter, for Jehu had no rule in Samaria until the next day, as it is explained in this account (10:1): *And Jehu wrote letters and sent to Samaria . . . Our Rabbis explained in the Aggadah of* the chapter *entitled "Helek": And he was hiding in Samaria, that he would cut out the Divine Names* from the Scriptures *and write* the names of *pagan deities in their place* (*San.* 102b). *According to them, we can say that this hiding was not because of Jehu, but thus is its explanation: And he sought Ahaziah, and they captured him when he was fleeing by way of the garden* (sic), *and he had been behaving wickedly from the beginning, for he would come to Samaria and hide from the Judean officers to commit this abomination, since the inhabitants of Samaria were idolators. "And they brought him to Jehu,"* i.e. *Jehu's men, who had pursued him. "And he said, 'Strike him . . . in the chariot.'"* [*Rashi*].

at the ascent of Gur—*for there they brought him to him* [*Rashi*].

As is to be noted in the translation, the words: *and they struck him,* do not appear in the text. Since it is obvious, they were omitted [*Redak, Mezudath David*].

and he fled to Megiddo—*struck by craft* [*Rashi*]. Perhaps this should read מוכה בלונכיות, struck by spears.

Rashi's intention is not very clear, but the general idea is that Jehu's men shot Ahaziah at the ascent of Gur, whence he fled in his wounded condition, until he succumbed to his wounds in Megiddo.

Redak reconciles the inconsistency somewhat differently. He explains that the soldiers shot him at the ascent of Gur, whence he fled in his wounded condition as far as Megiddo, where he fell into a coma. Although Scripture says that he died, a condition of paralysis is sometimes referred to as dying. See I Sam. 25:37. Thereupon, his servants whisked him away to Samaria, where they hid him. Jehu and his men became aware of his whereabouts, and brought him to Jehu in Jezreel, where he slew him.

Malbim explains that Ahaziah fled to Samaria, as is stated in Chron. When Jehu came to Samaria, Ahaziah fled to Megiddo. He was overtaken at Megiddo and brought to Jehu, who dispatched him there. *Malbim* does not make clear what happened in the ascent of Gur.

28. —**in his grave**—which he had dug for himself [*Mezudath David*].

Although the chronicler states: "And they slew him, and they

בַּפּוּךְ עֵינֶיהָ וַתֵּיטֶב אֶת־רֹאשָׁהּ
וַתַּשְׁקֵף בְּעַד הַחַלּוֹן: לא וְיֵהוּא בָּא
בַשָּׁעַר וַתֹּאמֶר הֲשָׁלוֹם זִמְרִי הֹרֵג
אֲדֹנָיו: לב וַיִּשָּׂא פָנָיו אֶל־הַחַלּוֹן וַיֹּאמֶר
מִי אִתִּי מִי וַיַּשְׁקִיפוּ אֵלָיו שְׁנַיִם שְׁלֹשָׁה
סָרִיסִים: לג וַיֹּאמֶר שִׁמְטֻהוּ וַיִּשְׁמְטוּהָ

עֵינָהָא וְתַקִּינַת יַת רֵישַׁהּ
וְאִסְתְּכִיאַת מִן חֲרַכָּא:
לא וְיֵהוּא עָל בְּתַרְעָא
נַאֲמֶרֶת הֲשָׁלָם זִמְרִי
קְטִיל רִבּוֹנֵיהּ: לב וּזְקַף
אַפּוֹהִי לַחֲרַכָּא וַאֲמַר
מַן הָכָא מִן וְאִסְתְּכִיאוּ
לְוָתֵיהּ תְּרֵין תְּלָתָא
גַּוְזָאִין: לג וַאֲמַר מִגְרוּהָא

ומגרוה

שמטוה קרי

רש"י

וימליכו יושבי ירושלים את אחזיהו כאן הוא אומר בן כ"ב שנה אחזיהו במלכו (ובדברי הימים ב' כ"ב ב') בן מ"ב שנה היה במלכו וכל ימי יהורם אביו מ' שנה היו ולא יותר שנאמר בו ל"ב שנה במלכו וח' שנה מלך והיאך אפשר לבן להיות גדול מאביו שתי שנים אלא כ' שנה לפני שנולד שהם ב' שנים קודם שנולד אביו נגזרה גזירה זו מיום שנשא אסא את בת עמרי ליהושפט בנו נגזרה גזירה על בית דוד שתכלה עם בית אחאב וכן הוא אומר (בדברי הימים ב' כ"ב ז') ומאלהים היתה תבוסת אחזיה לבא אל יורם וגו' כך שנויה בסדר עולם ובתוספתא דסוטה אך בכל המקרא לא מצינו שנשא יהושפט את בת עמרי אך מלאתי (בדברי הימים ב' י"ח א') ויתחתן לאחאב ושמא זו היא אחותו שנשא ובשנת שלשים ואחד לאסא נשאה שנאמר בשנת שלשים ואחת לאסא מלך עמרי (מלכים א' ט"ז כ"ג) ושנים בסדר עולם שמלך מלכות שלימה שהרי שש שנים קודם לכן מלך על חצי העם וכשנשא אסא את בתו ליהושפט נתעלה עמרי והרגו את תבני לא וחשוב משנת שלשים ואחת לאסא עד מות אחזיהו ותמצאם מ"ב: (ל) ותיטב את ראשה. ותקנת ית רישה כדי שתהא לחן בעיני יהוא וישאנה: (לא) ותאמר השלום. תרצה להיות עמי בשלום: זמרי הורג אדניו. אם הרגת את אדוניך אין זה דבר חדש שהרי זמרי גם הוא הרג את אלה בן בעשא: (לב) מי אתי. מי בכם לעזרתי: (לג) שמטוה. מן החלון ארצה:

רד"ק

הכחול: ותיטב את ראשה. ותתקן כלומר קשטה את עצמה כדי שתמצא חן בעיניו ולא יהרגה: (לא) זמרי הרג אדוניו. לפי שהרג זמרי את אלה בן בעשא אדוניו ויהוא ג"כ הרג אדוניו לפיכך קראה אותו כן: (לב) מי אתי. מי שם בעזרתי: (לג) שמטות. הפילוה מן החלון לארץ וכתוב בוי"ו שהוא כנוי לזכר והקרי בקמץ הה"א לנקבה והוי"ו נוספת והכתיב יש בו דרש רמז לנבות שצותה לשמוט אותו ולסקלו כן צות הוא לשמטה כי דין סקילה היה לה כי מתה בנפלה ורמסות ויז מדמה. בחיר"ק היו"ד מבנין הקל וכתב זה לגלות משפט האל ברשעה הזאת כי היה דמה נראה ימים בקיר: וירמסנה.

רלב"ג

או עשתה זה להחזיק המלוכה עדיין והוא יותר נכון ולזה אמרה בגאוה ליהוא השלום זמרי הורג אדוניו: (לג) שמטוה. כתוב שמטוה קרי והכתוב שב אל גוף איזבל כאילו יאמר שמטו גופה כדי שיפילוהו לארץ וזהו סקילה כמו שסוקל נבות כי הסקילה הוא אם בשליכת אבנים על הנסקל או בירית הנסקל על האבן כאמרו כי סקול יסקל או ירה יירה והנה זה הי' מדה כנגד מדה: וירמסנה

מנחת שי

(לג) שמטוהו. שמטוה קרי:

מצודת דוד

ותיטב את ראשה. תקנה לעיף ראשה וקשטה עצמה למצוא חן בעיני יהוא לבל יהרגנה: (לא) השלום. האם תרצה להיות עמי בשלום: זמרי הורג אדניו. לפי שגם זמרי הרג את המלך אלה בן בעשא לזה קראה אותו בשם זמרי וכאילו באה להקל אשמתו לומר שכבר היה לעולמים וכדי להחניפו אמרה כן: (לב) מי אתי כי. מי בעזרתי: וישקיפו אליו. כאומרים הננו למצותיך: (לג) שמטות. הזיזו אותה מן החלון להפילה לארץ: וירמסנה. יהוא

מצודת ציון

ויכח אמש (כראשי' לא): (ל) בפוך. הוא כחול שחור וכן כי תקרעי בפוך עיניך (ירמיה ד): ותיטב. ענין תקון כמו אם תיטבי דרכך (שם ג): ותשקף. לאתה והביטה: (לב) סריסים. סריס: (לג) שמטות. ענין הזזה מן המקום כמו שמטו הבקר (ש"ב י):

king, and he reigned eight years. After the eight years, Judah was attacked by the Arabs and the Philistines, as delineated in II Chron. 21:16. Then he was stricken with an incurable malady, as the chronicler continues to relate (v. 18, 19). At that time, Ahaziah, who was twenty-two years old, was appointed king. Twenty years later, when his father died, he was again appointed king.

Thus, all the discrepancies are reconciled.

30. **she adorned her head**—*she adorned her head in order to have charm in Jehu's eyes so that he would marry her* [*Rashi*].

Others explain that she beautified herself so that Jehu would spare her life [*Redak, Mezudath David*].

31. **"Is there peace**—*Do you wish to be with me in peace?* [Rashi].

her eyes and she adorned her head, and looked out of the window. 31. And Jehu came into the gate; and she said, "Is there
peace, Zimri, assassin of his master?" 32. And he lifted his face
to the window and said, "Who is with me? Who?" And two or
three eunuchs looked out to him. 33. And he said, "Push her
out!" And they pushed her out,

afflicted him with incurable illness. And it was by the end of a year, that his intestines went out because of his illness . . . And the inhabitants of Jerusalem made Ahaziah . . . king (II Chron. 21:18–22:1) [*Rashi*].

Hence Ahaziah was appointed king twice, one year preceding his father's demise, and after his father's demise. During his father's lifetime he was not accepted wholeheartedly by the populace, only by his father who had made him king. Even after his father's death, only the Jerusalemites supported him as king, not the population at large. His army, therefore, did not rush to his aid when he was pursued by Jehu. Because of its relevance to Ahaziah's death, this verse is inserted here, out of chronological order [*Malbim*].

Rashi continues—

Here (8:26) it is stated: "Ahaziah was twenty-two years old when he reigned, and in II *Chron.* (22:2) *"He was* (sic) *forty-two years old when he reigned." Now all the days of Jehoram his father was forty years, no more, as it is said concerning him: "He was thirty-two years old when he became king, and he reigned eight years (8:17)." Now how is it possible for a son to be two years older than his father? Rather, twenty years before he was born, which was two years before his father was born, this decree was issued. From the day that Asa took a daughter of Omri in marriage for Jehoshaphat his son, a decree was issued upon the house of David that it be destroyed with the house of Ahab. And thus it is stated in* II *Chron.* (22:7) *"And from God was Ahaziah's confusion, to come to Joram . . ." Thus it is taught in Seder Olam* (ch. 17) *and in the Tosefta of Sotah* (ch. 12). *Nowhere in the Scriptures, however, do we find that Jehoshaphat married Omri's daughter. I did find, however, in* II *Chron.* (18:1) *"And he* (Jehoshaphat) *intermarried with Ahab." Perhaps this refers to his sister whom he married. And in the thirty-first year of Asa he married her, as it is said: "In the thirty-first year of Asa . . . Omri reigned* (I Kings 15:23)." *And we learned in Seder Olam* (ch. 17) *that he reigned over the entire kingdom, for six years prior to then, he reigned over half the people, and when Asa took his daughter in marriage to Jehoshaphat, he gained prestige, and they assassinated Tibni. Proceed and calculate from the thirty-first year of Asa until the death of Ahaziah and you will find them to be forty-two* [*Rashi*].

Redak on 8:26 maintains that Jehoram lived longer than forty years. As mentioned above (8:17), he was thirty-two when he became

וַיִּז מִדָּמָהּ אֶל־הַקִּיר וְאֶל־הַסּוּסִים
וַיִּרְמְסֶנָּה׃ לד וַיָּבֹא וַיֹּאכַל וַיֵּשְׁתְּ וַיֹּאמֶר
פִּקְדוּ־נָא אֶת־הָאֲרוּרָה הַזֹּאת וְקִבְרוּהָ
כִּי בַת־מֶלֶךְ הִיא׃ לה וַיֵּלְכוּ לְקָבְרָהּ וְלֹא־
מָצְאוּ בָהּ כִּי אִם־הַגֻּלְגֹּלֶת וְהָרַגְלַיִם
וְכַפּוֹת הַיָּדָיִם׃ לו וַיָּשֻׁבוּ וַיַּגִּידוּ לוֹ
וַיֹּאמֶר דְּבַר־יְהוָה הוּא אֲשֶׁר דִּבֶּר בְּיַד־
עַבְדּוֹ אֵלִיָּהוּ הַתִּשְׁבִּי לֵאמֹר בְּחֵלֶק
יִזְרְעֶאל יֹאכְלוּ הַכְּלָבִים אֶת־בְּשַׂר
אִיזָבֶל׃ לז וְהָיְתָ נִבְלַת אִיזֶבֶל כְּדֹמֶן עַל־
פְּנֵי הַשָּׂדֶה בְּחֵלֶק יִזְרְעֶאל אֲשֶׁר לֹא־

וּמְנַרְוּהָא וּנְדָא מִדְמַהּ עַל כּוֹתְלָא וְעַל סוּסְוָתָא וְדַשׁוּהָ׃ לד וְעַל וַאֲכַל וּשְׁתִי וַאֲמַר סְעָדוּ כְעַן יַת אֲרוּרְתָּא הָדָא וְקַבְרוּהָא אֲרֵי בַת מַלְכָּא הִיא׃ לה וַאֲזַלוּ לְמִקְבְּרַהּ וְלָא אַשְׁכָּחוּ בַהּ אֱלָהֵין גוּלְגַלְתָּא וְרִגְלַיָּא וּפַסַּת יְדַיָּא׃ לו וְתָבוּ וְחַוִּיאוּ לֵיהּ וַאֲמַר פִּתְגָמָא דַיְיָ הוּא דְּמַלֵּיל בְּיַד עַבְדֵּיהּ אֵלִיָּהוּ דְּמִן תּוֹשָׁב לְמֵימַר בְּאַחְסָנַת יִזְרְעֶאל יֵיכְלוּן כַּלְבַיָּא יַת בִּסְרָא דְּאִיזֶבֶל׃ לז וּתְהֵי נְבִילְתָּא דְּאִיזֶבֶל כְּזֶבֶל מִכְבַּר עַל אַפֵּי חַקְלָא בְּאַחְסָנַת יִזְרְעֶאל דְּלָא יימרון

רד״ק (והיתה קרי)

יהוא רמסה בסוסו: (לד) כי בת מלך היא. ואף על פי שהיתה ממלכי אומות העולם צריך לנהוג כבוד בכל נכבד באומתו מדרך המוסר ולא תלה בכבוד בעלה לפי שהיא גרמה מיתתו ואבדון מלכותו: (לה) כי אם הגלגלת. כי שאר כל הגוף אכלו הכלבים ולא מצאו בה כי אם הגלגלת והרגלים וכפות הידים רשבו ותגידו ליהוא ולא קברו ממנה דבר כיון שהיה רוב גופה נאכל כמו שאמר הנביא ואין קובר. ובדרש למה נשאר בה הגלגלת והרגלים וכפות הידים שלא אכלו הכלבים לזכות שהיתה מרקדת לפני הכלות נשארו בה הרגלים ולפי שהיתה משפחות לפניהם נשארו בה כפות הידים ולפי שהיתה מכשכשת בראשה לפניהן נשאר בה הגלגלת ולדעת הדרש הנשאר בה קברו ומה שאמר ואין קובר כי קודם שיבואו לקבר נאכל רוב גופה: (לו) בחלק יזרעאל. כי החלק הזה היה פתוח אל כרם נבות כמו שאמר הכתוב כי הכרם היה אצל היכל אחאב: (לז) והית. הכתוב הוא בלא ה״א כמו ועשת את התבואת

רש״י

(לה) הגולגולת והרגלים. אמרו רבותינו שהיתה מרקדת לפני חתנים בידיה וברגליה ומכשכשת בראשה: (לז) כדומן. תרגומו כזבל:

מנחת שי

(לז) והית*. והיתה קרי ובס״ס הוא״ו בגעיא ובספרים אחרים כתובי יד מלאתי בב׳ יודין והיית ומסור עליו לית כתיב ב׳ יודין וכן הוא בחילופי המקרא [illegible] דמדינחאי:

רלב״ג

רמס אותה יהוא אחרי נפלה להמיתה בשלמות ולקיים מה שנאמר והיתה נבלת איזבל כדומן על פני השדה: (לו) בחלק יזרעאל. ידמה שבכרם נבות נפלה ושם אכלו בשדה הכלבים כי אצל בית אחאב היה

מצודת ציון

ויז. מל׳ הזאה ונטיפה: (לה) הגלגלת. הראש: (לז) כדומן. כזבל כמו לדומן על פני האדמה (ירמיה ח):

מצודת דוד

רמסה ברגליו: (לד) פקדו נא. זכרו את הארורה הזאת וקברוה כי בת מלך הוא ואין מדרך המוסר לנהוג בה בזיון אחר המיתה: (לה) כי אם הגולגולת וגו׳. ושאר כל הגוף אכלו הכלבים כדבר ח׳ ואמרו״ל בזכות שהיתה מרקדת ברגליה ומטפחת בידיה ומרכנת בראשה לפני הכלה לשמחה לזה נשארו ולא אכלום הכלבים: (לו) דבר ה׳ הוא. ולא במקרה בא: (לז) כדומן. כזבל המפוזר בארץ כן היו אבריה מפוזרים: זאת איזבל. כי רוב הגוף אכלו הכלבים והנשאר לא היה שמה עליה:

dogs, it is considered that she was not buried [*Redak*].

Redak mentions that were it not for the Midrash, he would assume that in order to fulfill the prophecy, even these limbs were not given burial.

According to *Pirkei d'R. Eliezer,* ch. 17, she would walk along to escort bridegrooms who passed by her window, and she would clap her hands and praise them. She would join funeral processions and clap and lament for the dead. Therefore, these limbs that participated in the *mitzvah* of performing kind deeds

and some of her blood splattered on the wall and on the horses,
and they trampled her. 34. And he came and ate and drank;
and he said, "Attend to this cursed woman and bury her, for
she is a king's daughter." 35. And they went to bury her, but
they did not find of her save the skull, the feet, and the palms of
the hands. 36. And they returned and told him; and he said, "It
is God's word which he spoke through his prophet, Elijah the
Tishbite, saying, 'In the territory of Jezreel the dogs will
devour Jezebel's flesh. 37. And Jezebel's corpse shall be as
dung upon the field in the territory of Jezreel, so that no one

Zimri, assassin of his master—*If you assassinated your master, this is nothing new, for Zimri too assassinated Elah son of Baasha* [*Rashi*].

According to others, she called him Zimri, since he too assassinated his master Elah. She attempted to flatter him by telling him that he had not committed a grave crime by assassinating Joram, since Zimri too had assassinated his master [*Redak, Mezudath David*].

32. **"Who is with me?"**—*Who among you will come to my aid?* [*Rashi, Redak, Mezudath David*].

looked out to him—as though to say, "We are ready to abide by your wishes" [*Mezudath David*].

33. **"Push her out!"**—*of the window to the ground* [*Rashi*].

According to the *K'thib,* we should render, "Push him out!" *Ralbag* explains that this refers to the body, which, grammatically, is masculine. *Redak* quotes a Midrash, unknown to us, that this alludes to her plot to stone Naboth, who, according to halachah, was first pushed off a building before stones were laid up on him. Both concur that for this crime she was paid in kind.

34. **for she is a king's daughter**—Even the daughter of a pagan king deserves respect as any prominent official in any country. He did not respect her because of her husband, since she was the cause of his downfall [*Redak*].

35. **the skull, the feet**—*Our Rabbis said, that she would dance before bridegrooms with her hands and feet, and shake her head* [*Rashi* from unknown Midrashic source].

Redak quotes Midrash as saying that the dogs did not devour her feet because she danced before brides. They did not devour her hands because she clapped her hands before them. They did not devour her skull because she shook her head before them. According to the Midrash these limbs were buried. Although Scripture states (v. 10): "And no one will bury her," since the great majority of her body was devoured by the

יֹאמְרוּ זֹאת אִיזָבֶל׃ י א וּלְאַחְאָב
שִׁבְעִים בָּנִים בְּשֹׁמְרוֹן וַיִּכְתֹּב יֵהוּא
סְפָרִים וַיִּשְׁלַח שֹׁמְרוֹן אֶל־שָׂרֵי יִזְרְעֶאל
הַזְּקֵנִים וְאֶל־הָאֹמְנִים אַחְאָב לֵאמֹר׃
ב וְעַתָּה כְּבֹא הַסֵּפֶר הַזֶּה אֲלֵיכֶם וְאִתְּכֶם
בְּנֵי אֲדֹנֵיכֶם וְאִתְּכֶם הָרֶכֶב וְהַסּוּסִים
וְעִיר מִבְצָר וְהַנָּשֶׁק׃ ג וּרְאִיתֶם הַטּוֹב
וְהַיָּשָׁר מִבְּנֵי אֲדֹנֵיכֶם וְשַׂמְתֶּם עַל־
כִּסֵּא אָבִיו וְהִלָּחֲמוּ עַל־בֵּית אֲדֹנֵיכֶם׃
ד וַיִּרְאוּ מְאֹד מְאֹד וַיֹּאמְרוּ הִנֵּה שְׁנֵי
הַמְּלָכִים לֹא עָמְדוּ לְפָנָיו וְאֵיךְ נַעֲמֹד

תרגום:

יֵימְרוּן דָא אִיזֶבֶל:
א וּלְאַחְאָב שִׁבְעִין בְּנִין
בְּשָׁמְרוֹן וּכְתַב יֵהוּא
אִגְּרָן וְשַׁדַּר לְשָׁמְרוֹן
לְרַבְרְבֵי יִזְרְעֶאל סָבַיָא
וּלְתוּרְבְּנַיָא דְאַחְאָב
לְמֵימַר: ב וּכְעַן כְּמֵיתֵי
אִגַּרְתָּא הָדֵין לְוָתְכוֹן
וְעִמְּכוֹן בְּנֵי רִבּוֹנֵיכוֹן
וְעִמְּכוֹן רְתִיכִין וְסוּסָוָן
וְקִרְוִין כְּרִיכָן וּמָאנֵי
זֵינָא: ג וְתֶחֱזוּן דְתַקִּין
וְדִכְשַׁר מִבְּנֵי רִבּוֹנְכוֹן
וּתְשַׁוּוּן עַל כּוּרְסֵי
מַלְכוּתָא דַאֲבוּהִי
וְתַגִּיחוּן קְרָב עַל בֵּית
רִבּוֹנְכוֹן: ד וּדְחִילוּ
לַחֲדָא לַחֲדָא וַאֲמַרוּ
הָא תְּרֵין מַלְכַיָא לָא
יְכִילוּ לְמֵיקַם קֳדָמוֹהִי
וְאֵכְדֵין נְקוּם אֲנַחְנָא:
ושלח

רש"י

י (א) ואל האומנים אחאב. אומניס את בניו: (ב) ואתכם הרכב והסוסים. ויש בהס כח להלחס: (ד) שני המלכים. יורס ואחזיהו:

רד"ק

והקרי בה"א על הרוב: כדומן. כתרגומו כזבל דמבדר על אפי חקלא: (א) אל שרי יזרעאל. שרי יזרעאל היו אז בשמרון אולי הלכו שם כששמעו המרד להתיעץ שם לפי ששמרון היתה עיר המלוכה: ואל האומני' אחאב. האומנים בני אחאב כמו שאמר גדולי העיר מגדלים אותם: (ג) והלחמו. לנסותם כתב להם כן:

רלב"ג

כרס נכות: (ב) והנשק. ר"ל כלי המלחמה:

מנחת שי

י (ד) ויראו מאוד מאוד. בספרים מדוייקים כתובי יד וגם דפוסים ישנים סיו"ד

מצודת דוד

י (א) האמנים אחאב. האמניס של אחאב: (ב) ועתה. לא הזכיר הכתוב לאשית הדברים שהיו כמנהג לפוקדס בשלוס ואח"ז כתב ועתה וכו': בני אדוניכם. יורשי המלוכה: הרכב וגו'. ואח"כ הכח בידכס להלחס: (ג) על בית. בעבור בית אדוניכס ובכדי לנסותס לדעת מה בלבס שלח אליהס כדברים האלה:

מצודת ציון

י (א) האמנים. כן יקראו מגדלי הילדים כמו על לד תאמנה (ישעיה ס) (ב): והנשק. כלי המלחמה כמו נשק בית היער (שם כב):

will say, "This is Jezebel.'"

10

1. Now Ahab had seventy sons in Samaria, and Jehu wrote letters and sent [them] to Samaria, to the officials of Jezreel, the elders, and to those who brought up Ahab's children, saying, 2. "And now, when this letter reaches you, and your master's sons are with you, and the chariots and the horses and the fortified city and arms are with you, 3. And you shall select the best and the most suitable of your master's sons, and place him on his father's throne, and fight for your master's house." 4. And they were very very frightened, and they said, "Behold the two kings were unable to resist him, now how will we resist him?"

were spared the degradation of being devoured by the dogs.

37. **"This is Jezebel."**—since she could not be recognized from her remains [*Mezudath David*].

1. —**seventy sons**—This probably includes his grandsons [*Zayith Ra'anan*].

to the officials of Jezreel—Perhaps they had gone to Samaria, the capital, to confer on ways and means of combatting the rebellion [*Redak*].

and to those who brought up Ahab's children—lit. to those who brought up Ahab [*Rashi, Redak*].

2. **And now**—This followed the customary salutation, after which Jehu continued, ". . . And now, . . ." [*Mezudath David*].

and the chariots and the horses . . . are with you—*and they have strength to wage war* [*Rashi*]. According to *R. Joseph Kara: And you have strength to wage war.*

and fight—He sent this letter to test them, and to ascertain whether they were planning to resist him [*Redak, Mezudath David*].

Malbim explains that Jehu wrote the letter in a sarcastic vein. He wrote it as though it were coming from Ahab, although they knew that he was the true author. He proceeded to write, "And with you are the chariots and the horses . . . to hint that only the horses, fortifications, and arms belonged to them, while the public support was on his side.

the two kings—*Joram and Ahaziah* [*Rashi*].

אֲנָחְנוּ׃ ה וַיִּשְׁלַח אֲשֶׁר־עַל־הַבַּיִת וַאֲשֶׁר
עַל־הָעִיר וְהַזְּקֵנִים וְהָאֹמְנִים אֶל־יֵהוּא
לֵאמֹר עֲבָדֶיךָ אֲנַחְנוּ וְכֹל אֲשֶׁר־תֹּאמַר
אֵלֵינוּ נַעֲשֶׂה לֹא־נַמְלִיךְ אִישׁ הַטּוֹב
בְּעֵינֶיךָ עֲשֵׂה׃ ו וַיִּכְתֹּב אֲלֵיהֶם סֵפֶר
שֵׁנִית לֵאמֹר אִם־לִי אַתֶּם וּלְקֹלִי
אַתֶּם שֹׁמְעִים קְחוּ אֶת־רָאשֵׁי אַנְשֵׁי
בְנֵי־אֲדֹנֵיכֶם וּבֹאוּ אֵלַי כָּעֵת מָחָר
יִזְרְעֶאלָה וּבְנֵי הַמֶּלֶךְ שִׁבְעִים אִישׁ
אֶת־גְּדֹלֵי הָעִיר מְגַדְּלִים אוֹתָם׃ ז וַיְהִי
כְּבֹא הַסֵּפֶר אֲלֵיהֶם וַיִּקְחוּ אֶת־בְּנֵי
הַמֶּלֶךְ וַיִּשְׁחֲטוּ שִׁבְעִים אִישׁ וַיָּשִׂימוּ
אֶת־רָאשֵׁיהֶם בַּדּוּדִים וַיִּשְׁלְחוּ אֵלָיו

תרגום

ה וּשְׁלַח דִמְמַנָא עַל בֵּיתָא וְדִמְמַנָא עַל קַרְתָּא וְסָבַיָא וְתוּרְבְּנַיָא לְוָת יֵהוּא לְמֵימַר עַבְדָךְ אֲנַחְנָא וְכֹל דְתֵימַר לָנָא נַעְבֵּיד לָא נַמְלִיךְ גְּבַר דְּתָקִין בְּעֵינָךְ עֲבֵיד׃
ו וּכְתַב לְהוֹן אִגַּרְתָּא תִּנְיָנוּת לְמֵימַר אִם דִּילִי אַתּוּן וּמִנִּי אַתּוּן מְקַבְּלִין סְבוּ יָת רֵישֵׁי גֻבְרֵי בְּנֵי רִבּוֹנְכוֹן וְתֵיתוֹן לְוָתִי כְּעִדָּנָא הָדֵין מְחַר לְיִזְרְעֶאל וּבְנֵי מַלְכָּא שַׁבְעִין גַּבְרָא יָת רַבְרְבֵי קַרְתָּא מְרַבַּן יָתְהוֹן׃
ז וַהֲוָה כְּמֵיתֵי אִגַּרְתָּא לְוָתְהוֹן וּדְבָרוּ יָת בְּנֵי מַלְכָּא וּנְכִיסוּ שַׁבְעִין גַּבְרָא וְשַׁוִּיאוּ יָת רֵישֵׁיהוֹן בְּסַלַּיָא וְשַׁדְּרִינוּן לְוָתֵיהּ לְיִזְרְעֶאל

רד"ק

(ו) את ראשי אנשי בני אדניכם. בני הוא פי' אנשי כי אם היה אומר אנשי אדניכם היו סוברים כי על כל אנשי ביתו אמר ואעפ"י שאינם בניו לפיכך אמר בני אדניכם: ובני המלך. לא היה זה בספר אלא ספור הכתוב הוא שמספר כי בני המלך שצוה יהוא להביא את ראשיהם היו שבעים איש עם גדולי העיר שהיו מגדלים אותם: (ז) בדודים. בסלים וכן ת"י בסליא

רש"י

(ו) ובני המלך שבעים איש את גדולי העיר וגו'. כל זה כתוב בספר ואני יודע שבונם שבעים איש והם עם גדולי העיר המגדלים אותם: (ז) בדודים. סירות:

מנחת שי

במאריך והוא חד מן ד' חסרים יו"ד על פי המסורת מלבד שמואל וסימן במסרה רבתא אות יו"ד:

רלב"ג

(ה) וישלח אשר על הבית. ר"ל שכבר שלח הממונים על בית אחאב והממונה על עיר שמרון וזקני העיר והאומנים ומגדלים בני אחאב שהיו גדולי העיר כמו שנזכר אחר זה שהם עבדיו וכל אשר יאמר להם יעשו: (ז) וישימו את ראשיהם בדודי'. ר"ל בסלי' כדי שיראום האנשים:

מצודת דוד

(ה) אשר על הבית. הממונה על בית המלך: (ו) אם לי אתם. אם אתם משלי ונכנעים אלי: כעת מחר. כעת הזאת ביום מחר: ובני המלך וגו'. גם זה מדברי יהוא שכתב להם יודע אני שהמה שבעים ובבית גדולי העיר ולא תוכלו להעלים ממני אף מי מהם:

מצודת ציון

(ז) בדודים. ענין קדירות וכן והכה בכיור או בדוד (ש"א ב):

them to Jehu and his officers, lest they suspect that not all Ahab's sons were slain.

and they sent them—The elders felt that although Jehu had instructed them to come personally, since they were not sure of his intentions, whether to honor them or to

5. And the one appointed over the palace and the one appointed over the city, and the elders and those who brought up the children, sent to Jehu, saying, "We are your servants, and everything you say to us we will do; we will not appoint anyone as king; do what pleases you." 6. And he sent them a letter a second time, saying, "If you are with me and you obey my orders, fetch the heads of the men—of your master's sons—and come to me at this time tomorrow, to Jezreel. Now the king's sons are seventy men. They are with the elders of the city, who are raising them." 7. And it came to pass when the letter reached them, that they took the king's sons and slaughtered [them], seventy men; and they placed their heads in pots and sent them to him to Jezreel.

5. **we will not appoint anyone as king**—since we are your servants [*Malbim*].

do what pleases you—Since we promised to do anything you say [*Malbim*].

6. **fetch the heads of the men**—I.e. to say that only by slaying Ahab's sons will you show your obedience to me [*Abarbanel*].

Now the king's sons are seventy men. They are with the elders of the city . . .—*All this was written in the letter* (according to *Kara: All this he wrote in the letter*), *"And I know their count—seventy men—and they are with the elders of the city who are bringing them up* [*Rashi, Mezudath David*].

Therefore, you will not be able to spare any of them [*Mezudath David*].

Alternatively, this is not part of the quotation. The author of Kings comments that the sons of Ahab were seventy, and that they were with the elders who were raising them [*Redak*].

in pots—*Rashi, Mezudath Zion.*

Others render: in baskets [*Jonathan, Redak, Ralbag, R. Jonah ibn Janah, Abarbanel*].

Abarbanel adds that they brought the heads in baskets as one brings the *bikkurim*—the first fruits—to Jerusalem. *Ralbag* adds that they brought them in baskets to display them. Probably, he means that they brought them in baskets to display

יִזְרְעֶאלָה׃ ח וַיָּבֹא הַמַּלְאָךְ וַיַּגֶּד־לוֹ
לֵאמֹר הֵבִיאוּ רָאשֵׁי בְנֵי־הַמֶּלֶךְ וַיֹּאמֶר
שִׂימוּ אֹתָם שְׁנֵי צִבֻּרִים פֶּתַח הַשַּׁעַר
עַד־הַבֹּקֶר׃ ט וַיְהִי בַבֹּקֶר וַיֵּצֵא וַיַּעֲמֹד
וַיֹּאמֶר אֶל־כָּל־הָעָם צַדִּקִים אַתֶּם הִנֵּה
אֲנִי קָשַׁרְתִּי עַל־אֲדֹנִי וָאֶהַרְגֵהוּ וּמִי
הִכָּה אֶת־כָּל־אֵלֶּה׃ י דְּעוּ אֵפוֹא כִּי לֹא
יִפֹּל מִדְּבַר יְהוָה אַרְצָה אֲשֶׁר־דִּבֶּר
יְהוָה עַל־בֵּית אַחְאָב וַיהוָה עָשָׂה אֵת
אֲשֶׁר דִּבֶּר בְּיַד עַבְדּוֹ אֵלִיָּהוּ׃ יא וַיַּךְ
יֵהוּא אֵת כָּל־הַנִּשְׁאָרִים לְבֵית־אַחְאָב
בְּיִזְרְעֶאל וְכָל־גְּדֹלָיו וּמְיֻדָּעָיו וְכֹהֲנָיו

לְיִזְרְעֶאל׃ ח וַאֲתָא
אִזְגַּדָּא וְחַוִּי לֵיהּ לְמֵימַר
אַיְתִיאוּ רֵישֵׁי בְּנֵי מַלְכָּא
וַאֲמַר שַׁווּ יַתְהוֹן תְּרֵין
דְּגוֹרִין בְּמַעֲלָנָא דְתַרְעָא
עַד צַפְרָא׃ ט וַהֲוָה
בְצַפְרָא וּנְפַק וְקָם וַאֲמַר
לְכָל עַמָּא זַכָּאִין אַתּוּן
הָא אֲנָא מְרָדִית עַל
רִבּוֹנִי וְקַטְלְתֵּיהּ וּמַן
קְטַל יַת כָּל אִלֵּין׃ י דְּעוּ
כְּעַן אֲרֵי לָא יִבְטַל
מִפִּתְגָּמָא דַּיְיָ דְּמַלִּיל
יְיָ עַל בֵּית אַחְאָב וַיְיָ
קַיֵּים יַת דְּמַלִּיל בְּיַד
עַבְדֵּיהּ אֵלִיָּהוּ׃ יא וּמְחָא
יֵהוּא יַת כָּל דְּאִשְׁתְּאָרוּ
לְבֵית אַחְאָב בְּיִזְרְעֶאל
וְכָל רַבְרְבוֹהִי וְקָרִיבוֹהִי
וְחַבְרוֹהִי עַד דְּלָא
אשתאר

רש"י

(ח) צבורים. המריקדגורין (מונטי' בלע"ז): (ט) צדיקים אתם. כולכם בעיניכם לדיקים ומחזיקים אותי בחזקת רשע על שהרגתי את המלך ועתה ראו הנה אני קשרתי על אדוני והרגתיו את כל אלה מי הכה אני לא הרגתים אך מאל תדעו אפוא כי גזרת המלך היא עליהם וההורג' יצא הדבר ואני ואתם צדיקים בדם כל בית אחאב:

רד"ק

וכמוהו שני דודאי תאנים הדוד האחד: (ח) שני צבורים. כמו גלים לפי שהם נאספים יחד כמו גל אבנים לפיכך נקרא צבורי' מן ויצבור יוסף אם יצבר כעפר כסף וי"ת דגורין כמו שתרגם אונקלוס חמרים חמרים: (ט) צדיקים אתם. אינכם חייבים בדם אלה האנשים תאמרו כי אני עשיתי רע וקשרתי על אדוני ואהרגהו אלה לא הכיתי אני אלא גדולי העיר הכו אותם ולא רצו להלחם עליהם תוכלו להכיר ולדעת כי מה' (יא) ומיודעיו. קרוביו כמו ולנעמי מודע לאישה וכת"י

רלב"ג

(ח) שימו אותם שני לבורים. הם כמו חמרים ר"ל שיעשו שני גלים מאלו הראשים והנה באו בעוד לילה להעליס הענין מההמון: (יא) וכהניו. הם כהני הבמות:

מנחת שי

(ח) שימו אתם. ברוב ספרים כתובי יד מדוייקים וגם בדפוסים קדמונים אתם חסר וא"ו וכן נכון על פי המסורת כי במלכים ב' סימן ג' נמסר ט' אותם מלאים בסיפרא ולא נחשב זה עמהם: (ט) ויאמר אל כל העם לדקים אתם. כתב המכלול יופי בא עם המ"ם לנדה בחסרון יו"ד בכתיבה והם דברי רד"ק במכלול דף י"ב. והמהני כי בכל הספרים חסר יו"ד קדמאה ומלא יו"ד בתראה וכן הביאו בעל המסורת בחהגים ל"ז על פסוק ותשועת לדיקים. וכבר השיג עליו רב אליה המדקדק וכתב בהגהותיו לספר מכלול זהו טעות כי חסר בו יו"ד הדמאה והיה לו לומר ואנשים לדיקם המה ישפטו (יחזקאל כ"ג):

מצודת דוד

את גדולי העיר. והמה עם גדולי העיר שהיו מגדלים אותם ר"ל שהיו בבית גדולי העיר: (ח) עד הבקר. להיות מונחים עד הבקר בכדי שיראום העם: (ט) צדיקים אתם. רולה לומר הנה תחשבו שאתם לדיקים ממני על שהרגתי את המלך ומי הרג את כל אלה הלא אנשי שמרון הרגום: (י) דעו אפוא. בזאת דעו עתה שלא יפול דבר ה' ארלה להיות בטל מה מדברו כ"א יפול על ראש מי אשר נגזר עליו: וה' עשה. הריגת המלך ובניו באה בהשגחה מה':

מצודת ציון

(ח) צבורים. קבולים כמו ויצבור יוסף (בראשית מב): (י) אפוא. ת"י כען והוא תרגום של עתה: (יא) ומידעיו. קרוביו כמו מודע

Malbim explains thus: According to the halachah, if one approaches a community and demands that they deliver one of their number into his hands that he may slay him, even if he designates a particular individual, they may not deliver him even though the entire community will be killed out. They may, however, deliver an individual who is condemned to die, like Sheba the son of Bichri (See II Sam. 20:21, Commentary Digest).

Jehu approached them with the following consolation: You are righteous! An entire community of

8. And the messenger came and told him, saying, "They have brought the heads of the king's sons." And he said, "Place them in two piles at the entrance of the gate until morning." 9. And it was in the morning, that he went out and stood, and he said, to all the people, "You are righteous. Behold I revolted against my master and slew him, but who slew all these? 10. Know then that nothing of the Lord's word shall fall to the ground, which the Lord spoke concerning the house of Ahab, and the Lord has done what He spoke through His servant Elijah." 11. And Jehu slew all those remaining of the house of Ahab in Jezreel, and all the notables and his relatives and his priests

kill them, they preferred to send their gory cargo through messengers [*K'li Y'kar*].

8. **two piles**—Heb. צִבֻּרִים. Synonymous with חֲמָרִים in Heb. and דְּגוֹרִין in Aramaic (*monticules in French, mounds*) [*Rashi*].

See Ex. 8:10, *Onkelos,* which is identical with *Targum Jonathan* here [*Redak*].

According to *Midrash* Samuel 2, Ahab had seventy sons in Jezreel in addition to his seventy sons in Samaria. See *Yalkut Shimoni.* Accordingly, the two mounds may represent the seventy in Jezreel and the seventy in Samaria [*K'li Y'kar*].

until morning—to display them before the people [*Mezudath David*].

The messengers brought the heads at night in order to conceal the massacre from the people. Jehu, however, insisted on showing the people that he had destroyed the house of Ahab [*Ralbag*].

Abarbanel maintains that they brought the heads during the daytime, and left them overnight according to Jehu's orders. He bases this on Jehu's order to bring them "at this time tomorrow." This proves that they brought them during the day. *Ralbag* probably explains that they hastened to bring them the night before they were ordered to do so. Therefore, the messenger, out of surprise, reported to Jehu that they had already brought the heads of the king's sons [*K'li Y'kar*].

9. **"You are righteous**—*You consider yourselves all righteous, and me you consider wicked since I slew the king. Now look, behold I revolted against my master and slew him. Now who slew all these? But from these you shall know then that it is a decree of the King upon them, and he who slays is righteous and fulfills the commandment of the Omnipresent* [*Rashi*].

but, who slew all these?—Not I but the people of Samaria [*Mezudath David*].

עַד־בִּלְתִּי הִשְׁאִיר־לוֹ שָׂרִיד׃ יב וַיָּקָם
וַיָּבֹא וַיֵּלֶךְ שֹׁמְרוֹן הוּא בֵּית־עֵקֶד
הָרֹעִים בַּדָּרֶךְ׃ יג וְיֵהוּא מָצָא אֶת־אֲחֵי
אֲחַזְיָהוּ מֶלֶךְ־יְהוּדָה וַיֹּאמֶר מִי אַתֶּם
וַיֹּאמְרוּ אֲחֵי אֲחַזְיָהוּ אֲנַחְנוּ וַנֵּרֶד לִשְׁלוֹם
בְּנֵי־הַמֶּלֶךְ וּבְנֵי הַגְּבִירָה׃ יד וַיֹּאמֶר
תִּפְשׂוּם חַיִּים וַיִּתְפְּשׂוּם חַיִּים וַיִּשְׁחָטוּם
אֶל־בּוֹר בֵּית־עֵקֶד אַרְבָּעִים וּשְׁנַיִם
אִישׁ וְלֹא־הִשְׁאִיר אִישׁ מֵהֶם׃ טו וַיֵּלֶךְ
מִשָּׁם וַיִּמְצָא אֶת־יְהוֹנָדָב בֶּן־רֵכָב
לִקְרָאתוֹ וַיְבָרְכֵהוּ וַיֹּאמֶר אֵלָיו הֲיֵשׁ

תרגום

אִשְׁתְּאַר לֵיהּ מְשֵׁיזֵיב׃
יב וְקָם וַאֲתָא וַאֲזַל
לְשָׁמְרוֹן הוּא בֵּית
כְּנִישַׁת רַעֲיָא בְּאוֹרְחָא׃
יג וְיֵהוּא אַשְׁכַּח יָת אֲחֵי
אֲחַזְיָה מַלְכָּא דְשִׁבְטָא
דְבֵית יְהוּדָה וַאֲמַר מַן
אַתּוּן וַאֲמַרוּ אֲחֵי
אֲחַזְיָהוּ אֲנַחְנָא וּנְחַתְנָא
לְמִשְׁאַל שְׁלָם בְּנֵי מַלְכָּא
וּבְנֵי מַלְכְּתָא׃ יד וַאֲמַר
אֲחוּדִינוּן כַּד חַיִּין
וְאַחֲדוּנוּן כַּד חַיִּין
וְנַכְסוּנוּן לְגוֹ בֵּית
כְּנִשְׁתָּא אַרְבְּעִין וּתְרֵין
גַּבְרָא וְלָא אִשְׁתְּאַר
אֱנָשׁ מִנְּהוֹן׃ טו וַאֲזַל
מִתַּמָּן וְאַשְׁכַּח יָת
יְהוֹנָדָב בַּר רֵכָב
לְקַדָּמוּתֵיהּ וּבָרְכֵיהּ
וּשְׁאֵיל בִּשְׁלָמֵיהּ וַאֲמַר
לֵיהּ

רד"ק

וקריבוהו: וכהניו. כהני במות וי"ת וחברוהי: (יב) בית עקד הרועים. ת"י בית כנישת רעיא וכתב א"א ז"ל כי נקרא כן לפי שהיו הרועים גוזזים שם את צאנם ובעת הגזיזה קושרים אותם ברגליהם מקום העקדה: (יג) מצא את אחי אחזיהו. בני אחי אחזיהו כמו שאומר בד"ה וימצא את שרי יהודה ואת בני אחי אחזיהו ובן אחיו קורא אחיו כמו ואת לוט אחיו: לשלום בני המלך ובני הגבירה. בני אחאב ובני איזבל ומ"ש ובני הגבירה אחר שאמר לשלום בני המלך לפי שהכבוד היה תלוי בה שאף בחיי אחאב היתה היא גבירה ואחאב היה נשמע אליה ועושה על פיה ולא ידעו ענין זה המרד ושהומתה איזבל ושהומת אחזיהו לפיכך לא נסו מיהוא אבל שמעו כי מת יהורם ברמות גלעד לפיכך אמר לשלום בני המלך וכן אמרו שם בדברי הימים משרתים לאחזיהו שהיו באים לעבודת אחזיהו לעזור לבית אחאב כמו שהיה הוא עמהם: (יד) תפשום חיים. ומה שצוה כן ובלבבו להרגם כמו שאמר וישחטום להגדיל הנקמה שלא ימיתום דרך מלחמה: (טו) ויברכהו. נתן לו

רש"י

לדיק הוא ומקיים את מצות המקום: (יב) בית עקד הרועים. בית כנישת רעיא: עקד. לשון קשר מקום אסיפת רועים: (יג) ובני הגבירה. איזבל: (טו) ויאמר אליו. יהוא: היש את לבבך ישר. ושלם מה שאני

רלב"ג

(יב) ויקם ויבא וילך שומרון. ר"ל שבשר קם יהוא ובא לביתו לקחת השלל והלך לשומרון ובדרכו הנה בהיותו בית עקד הרועים הוא הבית שהיו הרועים גוזזים שם את הצאן ולזה היו עוקדים אותם שם הנה מצא יהוא את אחי אחזיהו מלך יהודה ר"ל בני אחי אחזיהו כי כבר מתו אחיו כמו שנזכר בספר ד"ה: (יד) וישחטו' אל בור בית עקד. הנה הי' בור בבית ההוא שהיה בית

מצודת ציון

לאישה (רות ב): וכהניו. כהני הבעל: שריד. שארית: (יב) בית עקד הרועים. בית שהרועים גוזזים בו הצאן ולפי שהדרך לעקדם ולקושרם בעת הגזיזה קרוי עקד מל' ויעקוד את יצחק (בראשית כב):

מצודת דוד

(יב) הוא בית עקד. כשבא לבית עקד הרועי' אשר עומד' בדרך: (יג) ויהוא מצא. שם מצא יהוא את אחי אחזיהו ר"ל בני אחזיהו וכן נאמר בד"ה כי לא היו לו אחים כי כולם נהרגו מאז כמ"ש: לשלום. לשאול בשלום בני אחאב ואיזבל ולא ידעו כי נהרגו: (יד) וישחטום. כי גם המה היו מבית אחאב: בית עקד. העומד בבית העקד: (טו) היש את לבבך ישר. האם יש עם לבבך ישר

sons of the queen mother—*Jezebel* [*Rashi*].

Unaware of the revolt, they came to greet Ahab's children and Jezebel's. Although all of Jezebel's children were Ahab's they, nevertheless, referred to them as the children of the queen mother, who had exerted great influence even during Ahab's lifetime. Ahaziah's nephews had heard that Joram was killed by Aram, and they were completely unaware that Jehu had killed him and massacred the entire royal family of Israel. Had they known, they would surely have fled [*Redak*].

14. **"Seize them alive**—He first ordered them to be taken alive, and

until he did not leave over a survivor. 12. And he arose and came and went to Samaria. He was at the meeting-place of the shepherds on the road. 13. And Jehu found the brothers of Ahaziah, king of Judah, and he said, "Who are you?" And they said, "We are Ahaziah's brothers, and we have come down to greet the sons of the king and the sons of the queen mother." 14. And he said, "Seize them alive!" And they seized them alive, and slaughtered into the pit of the meeting-place, forty-two men. He did not leave over even one of them. 15. And he went from there and found Jehonadab the son of Rechab coming toward him, and he greeted him and he said to him,

Israel would not commit a sin. I may be considered the bad one for revolting against my master and slaying him, but you, an entire community of Israel, are surely righteous. Who then, slew all these people? It can only mean that this was the will of God. He then goes on to say:

10. **Know then that nothing of the Lord's word shall fall to the ground**—The fact that righteous people slay seventy men is proof that these seventy men were condemned by heaven to die [*Malbim*].

11. **and his priests**—the priests of the high places [*Redak, Ralbag*].

Alternatively, the priests of the Baal [*Mezudath Zion*].

Jonathan translates: וְחַבְרוֹהִי. This is probably according to Persian usage, to call a priest חָבֵר. See *Aruch*.

12. **And he arose and came**—He came home to get his chariot and proceed to Samaria [*Ralbag*].

He was at the meeting place of the shepherds—I.e. on his way to Samaria, he stopped at the meeting place of the shepherds, where he found Ahaziah's brothers [*Ralbag*].

the meeting-place of the shepherds—*Jonathan* renders: *the house of the gathering of the shepherds* [*Rashi*].

meeting—Heb. עקד, *an expression of binding, the place where the shepherds assemble* [*Rashi*].

Rashi apparently explains that the gathering of the shepherds is referred to figuratively as tying, or binding, since they all converge at this one spot. Others interpret this as the place where the shepherds bind the sheep to shear them [*Redak, Ralbag*].

13. **the brothers of Ahaziah**—actually his brothers' sons, as we find in II Chron. 22:8, for Ahaziah's brothers had been captured by the Arabs during the reign of Jehoram, as in 1:17, and were killed as in 22:1. They are referred to as Ahaziah's brothers just as Lot was referred to as Abraham's brother although he was his nephew [*Redak, Ralbag, Mezudath David*].

to greet the sons of the king and the

אֶת־לְבָבְךָ יָשָׁר כַּאֲשֶׁר לְבָבִי עִם־לְבָבֶךָ וַיֹּאמֶר יְהוֹנָדָב יֵשׁ וָיֵשׁ תְּנָה אֶת־יָדֶךָ וַיִּתֵּן יָדוֹ וַיַּעֲלֵהוּ אֵלָיו אֶל־הַמֶּרְכָּבָה: טז וַיֹּאמֶר לְכָה אִתִּי וּרְאֵה בְּקִנְאָתִי לַיהוָה וַיַּרְכִּבוּ אֹתוֹ בְּרִכְבּוֹ: יז וַיָּבֹא שֹׁמְרוֹן וַיַּךְ אֶת־כָּל־הַנִּשְׁאָרִים לְאַחְאָב בְּשֹׁמְרוֹן עַד־הִשְׁמִדוֹ כִּדְבַר יְהוָה אֲשֶׁר דִּבֶּר אֶל־אֵלִיָּהוּ: יח וַיִּקְבֹּץ יֵהוּא אֶת־כָּל־הָעָם וַיֹּאמֶר אֲלֵהֶם אַחְאָב עָבַד אֶת־הַבַּעַל מְעָט יֵהוּא יַעַבְדֶנּוּ הַרְבֵּה: יט וְעַתָּה כָל־נְבִיאֵי הַבַּעַל כָּל־עֹבְדָיו וְכָל־כֹּהֲנָיו קִרְאוּ אֵלַי אִישׁ אַל־יִפָּקֵד כִּי זֶבַח גָּדוֹל לִי לַבַּעַל כֹּל אֲשֶׁר־יִפָּקֵד לֹא יִחְיֶה וְיֵהוּא עָשָׂה

לֵיהּ הָאִית לִבָּךְ כָּשֵׁר כְּמָא דְלִבִּי עִם לִבָּךְ וַאֲמַר יְהוֹנָדָב אִית וְאִית הַב יָת יְדָךְ וִיהַב יְדֵיהּ וְאַסְּקֵיהּ לְוָתֵיהּ לִרְתִיכָא: טז וַאֲמַר אִיתָא עִמִּי וַחֲזִי בְּקִנְאָתִי דַּאֲנָא מְקַנֵּא קֳדָם יְיָ וְאַרְכִּיבוּ יָתֵיהּ בִּרְתִיכֵיהּ: יז וַאֲתָא לְשֹׁמְרוֹן וּמְחָא יָת כָּל דְּאִשְׁתְּאָרוּ לְאַחְאָב בְּשֹׁמְרוֹן עַד דִּי שֵׁיצְיֵהּ כְּפִתְגָמָא דַיְיָ דְּמַלֵּיל עִם אֵלִיָּהוּ: יח וּכְנַשׁ יֵהוּא יָת כָּל עַמָּא וַאֲמַר לְהוֹן אַחְאָב פְּלַח יָת בְּעֶלָא זְעֵיר יֵהוּא יִפְלְחִינֵּיהּ סַגִּי: יט וּכְעַן כָּל נְבִיֵּי בְעֶלָא וְכָל פָּלְחוֹהִי וְכָל כּוּמְרוֹהִי זַמִּינוּ לִי אֱנָשׁ לָא יִשְׁגֵּי אֲרֵי דְבַח רַב לִי לִבְעֶלָא כָּל דְּיִשְׁגֵּי לָא יִתְקַיַּם

תולדות אהרן

יסוא יעבדנו הרבה. סנהדרין קב:

רש"י

עושה כאשר לבבי שלם עם לבבך: ויאמר יהונדב יש ויש תנה את ידך. ואחוז בה והעלני אליך אל המרכבה:

רד"ק

שלום: ויאמר יהונדב יש ויש תנה את ידך. יהונדב אמר יש ויש כפל לחזק כי יש לבבו ואחר כן אמר לו יהוא תנה את ידך להעלותו למרכבה עמו או פירושו ויש תשיבת יהוא דרך שאלה כלומר כן הוא כמו שאתה אומר כי יש לבבך עם לבבי א"כ תנה ידך ויתן ידו ויעלהו אליו אל המרכבה: (יז) עד

רלב"ג

פקד הכועים ושם שמים אחר שהרגום: (יט) איש אל יפקד. ר"ל

מנחת שי

(טו) תנה את ידך. במקצת דפוסים אחרונים כתוב ידיך ביו"ד וטעות הוא:

מצודת דוד

ותמים עמי לאהוב אותי כאשר לבבי ישר עם לבבך: יש ויש. הכפל לחזק: תנה את ידך. כדרך אהבה לקיום ברית או להעלהו על המרכבה: (טז) בקנאתי. במה שאקנא קנאת ה׳ להנקם מבית אחאב ועובדי הבעל: (יח) אחאב עבד את הבעל מעט. כאומר והנה בעבור זה באה הרעה על ביתו: (יט) לי לבעל. יהיה לי

מצודת ציון

(טז) בקנאתי. ענין נקימה כמו בקנאו את קנאתי (במדבר כה):
(יט) אל יפקד. אל יחסר כמו ולא נפקד ממנו איש (שם לא):

prophet Jonah to destroy the house of Ahab, as above 9:7–9. The prophet had announced to him, "I have anointed you over the people of the Lord, over Israel." He took this to mean that he was to destroy all those who were not of the people of the Lord, but of the Baal cult. Thus Israel would be purely the people of God [*Malbim* 9:6].

"Ahab worshipped the Baal a little—Ahab was punished for neglecting the Baal worship. He worshipped him but a little. Jehu, however, will worship him much. The Rabbis (San. 102a) criticize him for this statement. Even though he did not mean it seriously, but as a means of beguiling the Baal worshippers, there is a covenant made with the

"Is your heart right as my heart is with your heart?" And Jehonadab said, "Indeed it is. Give [me] your hand." And he gave him his hand and lifted him up into the chariot to him.
16. And he said, "Come with me and see my zeal for the Lord." And they caused him to ride in the chariot. 17. And he came to Samaria and struck down all those of Ahab that remained in Samaria, until he destroyed [them], according to the word of the Lord which He had spoken to Elijah. 18. Now Jehu assembled all the people, and said to them, "Ahab worshipped the Baal a little; Jehu will worship him much. 19. And now summon to me all the prophets of the Baal, all his worshippers and all his priests; let no one be missing, for I have a great sacrifice for the Baal; anyone who will be absent shall not live." But Jehu was acting

then slaughtered them. He did this to intensify his vengeance against the royal family of Judah which had intermarried with the idolatrous house of Ahab [*Redak*].

15. **Jehonadab the son of Rechab**—a well-known person of that time, descended from Jethro. He is mentioned in Jeremiah 34:2, as having commanded his sons to refrain from drinking wine, and from building houses and planting vineyards. They were to live as nomads. See also I Chron. 2:55.

and he greeted him—Jehonadab greeted Jehu [*Abarbanel*].

and he said to him—i.e. *Jehu* said to Jehonadab [*Rashi*].

"Is your heart right—*and fully committed in what I am doing, as my heart is fully with your heart?* [*Rashi*].

Alternatively, do you love me wholeheartedly as I love you? [*Mezudath David*].

"Indeed it is. Give me your hand."—*and hold it and pick me up to you to the chariot* [*Rashi*].

Alternatively, Jehu said to Jehonadab, "Give me your hand, and he pulled him up into the chariot [*Redak*].

Others explain that Jehu asked for Jehonadab's hand to shake it as a symbol of agreement and love [*Mezudath David*].

It is also possible that Jehonadab replied, "It is," and Jehu answered, "If it is, give me your hand" [*Redak*].

18. **Now Jehu assembled all the people**—After having destroyed the house of Ahab, Jehu went about to abolish the Baal worship and annihilate the entire cult [*Abarbanel*].

He had been commanded by the

בְּעָקְבָּה לְמַעַן הַאֲבִיד אֶת־עֹבְדֵי
הַבָּעַל׃ כ וַיֹּאמֶר יֵהוּא קַדְּשׁוּ עֲצָרָה
לַבַּעַל וַיִּקְרָאוּ׃ כא וַיִּשְׁלַח יֵהוּא בְּכָל־
יִשְׂרָאֵל וַיָּבֹאוּ כָּל־עֹבְדֵי הַבַּעַל וְלֹא־
נִשְׁאַר אִישׁ אֲשֶׁר לֹא־בָא וַיָּבֹאוּ בֵּית
הַבַּעַל וַיִּמָּלֵא בֵית־הַבַּעַל פֶּה לָפֶה׃
כב וַיֹּאמֶר לַאֲשֶׁר עַל־הַמֶּלְתָּחָה הוֹצֵא
לְבוּשׁ לְכֹל עֹבְדֵי הַבָּעַל וַיֹּצֵא לָהֶם
הַמַּלְבּוּשׁ׃ כג וַיָּבֹא יֵהוּא וִיהוֹנָדָב בֶּן־
רֵכָב בֵּית הַבָּעַל וַיֹּאמֶר לְעֹבְדֵי הַבַּעַל
חַפְּשׂוּ וּרְאוּ פֶּן־יֶשׁ־פֹּה עִמָּכֶם מֵעַבְדֵי
יְהוָה כִּי אִם־עֹבְדֵי הַבַּעַל לְבַדָּם׃
כד וַיָּבֹאוּ לַעֲשׂוֹת זְבָחִים וְעֹלוֹת וְיֵהוּא

תרגום

יְתַקֵים וְיֵהוּא עֲבַד
בְּחוּכְמָא בְּדִיל לְאוֹבָדָא
יַת פָּלְחֵי בְעָלָא׃
כ וַאֲמַר יֵהוּא זַמִּינוּ
כְּנִשְׁתָּא לְבַעֲלָא וְזַמִּינוּ׃
כא וּשְׁלַח יֵהוּא בְּכָל
יִשְׂרָאֵל וַאֲתוֹ כָּל פָּלְחֵי
בְעָלָא וְלָא אִשְׁתְּאַר אֱנָשׁ
דְלָא אֲתָא וְעָלוּ לְבֵית
בְּעָלָא וְאִתְמְלֵי בֵּית
בְּעָלָא סְפָא בִּסְפָא׃
כב וַאֲמַר לִדְמְמָנָא עַל
קוּמְטְרַיָא אַפֵּיק לְבוּשָׁא
לְכָל פָּלְחֵי בְעָלָא וְאַפֵּיק
לְהוֹן לְבוּשָׁא׃ כג וַאֲתָא
יֵהוּא וִיהוֹנָדָב בַּר רֵכָב
לְבֵית בְּעָלָא וַאֲמַר
לְפָלְחֵי בְעָלָא בְּלוּשׁוּ
וְחַזוּ דִלְמָא אִית כָּא
עִמְּכוֹן מִפַּלְחַיָא דַיְיָ
אֱלָהִין פָּלְחֵי בְעָלָא
בִּלְחוֹדֵיהוֹן׃ כד וַאֲתוֹ
לְמֶעְבַּד נִכְסַת קוּדְשִׁין
ועלון

ת"א הואה לכים. גיטין נפ:

רד"ק

השמידו. בחיר"ק הה"א כי כן יבוא המקור פעמים: (יט) בעקבה. כתרגומו בחכמה וכן ויעקבני: (כ) קדשו עצרה. זמנו עצרה שיהיו נעצרים כל העם לפני הבעל: (כב) לאשר על המלתחה. ת"י לדממנא על קומטריא פי' גנזי הבגדים וכן בדברי רז"ל קומטרי דספרי פי' גנזי הספרים:

רש"י

(יט) בעקבה. במרמה לשון ויעקבני (בראשית כ"ז ל"ו): (כ) קדשו עצרה. הכריזו אסיפה להיות נעצרים לבית הבעל: (כב) על המלתחה. תרגם יונתן לדממנא על קומטריא ארגזים וקופסאות שכורכין בתוכן וגונזין תכשיטי

מנחת שי

(יט) בעקבה. בספרים כתובי יד ודפוסים ישנים העי"ן בקמץ חטו"ף והבית דגושה וה"ה רפה:

רלב"ג

שלא יחסר איש שלא יהיו כלם שם: עשה בעקב'. ר"ל במרמה: (כ) קדשו עצרה לבעל. זמנו וקראו יום שתהיו נעצרים בו כלכם לבעל: (כב) ויאמר לאשר על המלתחה. הוא הממונה על אוצר בגדי הכמרים יעובדי הבעל:

מצודת ציון

בעקבה. ת"י בחוכמא וכן ויעקבני זה פעמים (בראשית כז): (כ) קדשו. הזמינו: עצרה. אסיפה וקבוץ כמו עצרת בוגדים (ירמיה ט): (כב) המלתחה. הוא מקום גניזת כריכי מלבושי כהני הבעל והיא הפוך מן וערפל חתולתו (איוב לח) וכן ת"י קומטריא ובמשנה כסיו קמטרא טהור (כלים פי"ו): (כג) חפשו. חקרו

מצודת דוד

אל הבעל: בעקבה. בכדי שיקבצו כולם: (כ) קדשו עצרה. הזמינו יום להיות כולם נעצרים ונאספים: ויקראו. הכריזו יום קבוע: (כא) פה לפה. מהפתח מהעבר מזה עד הפתח שממולו: (כב) הוצא לבוש. הכוונה היה שיהיו נכרים במלבושיהם לבלא ימלט מי מהם: (כג) מעבדי ה'. כי חשש פן יבוא מי מהם

with cunning, in order to exterminate the Baal worshippers.
20. And Jehu said, "Proclaim an assembly for the Baal," and
they called. 21. And Jehu sent throughout all Israel, and all the
Baal worshippers came; no one was left who did not come. And
they came to the temple of the Baal, and the temple of the Baal
was filled from entrance to entrance. 22. And he said to the one
[appointed] over the wardrobe, "Bring out the vestments for all
the Baal worshippers." And he brought out the vestments for
them. 23. And Jehu and Jehonadab the son of Rechab came to
the temple of the Baal, and he said to the Baal worshippers,
"Search and see whether any of the servants of the Lord is here
with you, except the Baal worshippers only." 24. And they
came to perform sacrifices and burnt-offerings,

lips, that whatever they say may come true [*Abarbanel*].

19. **with cunning**—Heb. בְּעָקְבָּה, *with* guile, an expression of "(Gen. 27:36) וַיַּעְקְבֵנִי, *he beguiled me.*" [*Rashi, Redak, Ralbag, Mezudath Zion*].

20. **"Proclaim an assembly**—*Announce an assembly, that they assemble in the temple of the Baal* [*Rashi, Redak, Ralbag, Mezudath Zion*].

Alternatively, proclaim a work stoppage. This was to be a festive day on which people would only engage in sacrificial service [*Malbim*]. Compare Joel 2:15, *Taanith* 12b, where the word עֲצָרָה is interpreted as a work stoppage.

22. **over the wardrobe**—*Jonathan rendered: to the one appointed over the wardrobe, chests and boxes in which they wrap and store the vestments of the Baal worshippers* [*Rashi*].

Jehu instructed the Baal worshippers to don the special vestments in order to distinguish them from others, and prevent them from escaping [*Abarbanel, Malbim*].

24. **his life shall be forfeit for his life**—i.e. *the life of the guard shall be forfeit for the life of the escapee* [*Rashi, Redak*].

The life of the guard who neglects his watch will be forfeit for the life of the one who escaped because of *his* negligence [*Mezudath David*].

שָׂם־לוֹ בַחוּץ שְׁמֹנִים אִישׁ וַיֹּאמֶר הָאִישׁ אֲשֶׁר־יִמָּלֵט מִן־הָאֲנָשִׁים אֲשֶׁר אֲנִי מֵבִיא עַל־יְדֵיכֶם נַפְשׁוֹ תַּחַת נַפְשׁוֹ׃ כה וַיְהִי כְּכַלֹּתוֹ לַעֲשׂוֹת הָעֹלָה וַיֹּאמֶר יֵהוּא לָרָצִים וְלַשָּׁלִשִׁים בֹּאוּ הַכּוּם אִישׁ אַל־יֵצֵא וַיַּכּוּם לְפִי־חָרֶב וַיַּשְׁלִכוּ הָרָצִים וְהַשָּׁלִשִׁים וַיֵּלְכוּ עַד־עִיר בֵּית־הַבָּעַל׃ כו וַיֹּצִאוּ אֶת־מַצְּבוֹת בֵּית־הַבַּעַל וַיִּשְׂרְפוּהָ׃ כז וַיִּתְּצוּ אֵת מַצְּבַת הַבָּעַל וַיִּתְּצוּ אֶת־בֵּית הַבַּעַל וַיְשִׂמֻהוּ לְמַחֲרָאוֹת עַד־הַיּוֹם׃ כח וַיַּשְׁמֵד יֵהוּא אֶת־הַבַּעַל מִיִּשְׂרָאֵל׃ כט רַק

וְעָלַּוְן וְיֵהוּא מַנִי לֵיהּ בְּבָרָא תְּמָנַן גַּבְרָא וַאֲמַר גַּבְרָא דְיִשְׁתֵּיזִיב מִן גַּבְרַיָא דַּאֲנָא מַעֵיל עַל יְדֵיכוֹן נַפְשֵׁיהּ חֲלַף נַפְשֵׁיהּ׃ כה וַהֲוָה כַּד שֵׁיצֵי לְמֶעְבַּד עֲלָתָא וַאֲמַר יֵהוּא לְרַהֲטַיָא וּלְגִבָּרַיָא עוּלוּ מְחוֹנוּן אֱנַשׁ לָא יִפּוֹק וּמְחוֹנוּן לְפִתְגָם דְּחָרֶב וּרְמוֹ רְהַטַיָא וְגִבָּרַיָא קְטִילִין וַאֲזַלוּ עַד קִרְיַת בֵּית בַּעֲלָא׃ כו וְאַפִּיקוּ יָת קָמַת בֵּית בַּעֲלָא וְאוֹקִידוּהָ׃ כז וּתְרָעוּ יָת קָמַת בַּעֲלָא וּתְרָעוּ יָת בֵּית בַּעֲלָא וְשַׁוְיוּהָא לְבֵית מַפְקַת אֱנָשָׁא עַד יוֹמָא דֵין׃ כח וְשֵׁיצֵי יֵהוּא יָת בַּעֲלָא מִיִּשְׂרָאֵל׃ כט לְחוּד בְּחוֹבֵי יָרָבְעָם בר

למוצאות קרי

רש"י

עובדי הבעל: (כד) נפשו תחת נפשו. נפש השומר תחת הנפש הנמלט: (כה) וישלכו. ורמו רהטיא וגבריא קטילין השליכו הרצים את עובדי הבעל: (כז) למחראות. לשון בית הכסא וכן לאכול את חוריהם (ישעיה ל"ו י"ב): (כט) רק חטאי ירבעם וגו'. מדאגה שלא תשוב הממלכ'

רד"ק

(כד) נפשו תחת נפשו. נפש השומר תחת נפש הנמלט: (כה) וישליכו. הוא על דרך הרחבת הלשון מריב חפזם ומהירותם אותם לשלחם לעיר בית הבעל לנתוץ את המצבות: (כו) ויוציאו. הו אשון מצבות לשון רבים והשני מצבת לשון יחיד: וישרפוה. כל אחת מן המצבות: (כז) למחראות. כתיב וקרי למוצאות ושניהם ענין אחד אלא שהקרי לשון נקיה יותר והענין שהיו

רלב"ג

(כה) וישלכו הרצים והשלשים. ר"ל שככר השליכו הרצים והשלישים נבלת ההרוגים מבית הבעל בעת הכותם אותם: (כז) למחראות. ר"ל לבתי כסאות להפנות שם לבזות הע"ג:

מנחת שי

(כו) ויתצו את מצבות בית הבעל. לית חסר דחסר ועיין מה שכתוב בדברי הימים ב' סימן א': (כז) וישימהו. ברוב המדוייקים כן כתיב מלא יו"ד: למחראות. למוצאות קרי והכי איתא בשילהי פירקא דהקורא את המגילה עומד ואמרינן התם דר' יהושע בן קרחה היה אומר למחראות כשמה מפני שהוא גנאי לבעל דאמר רב

מצודת דוד

לראות מה נעשה ויאבד עמהם: כי אם. ר"ל עבדי ה' ילאו מפה ולא ישארו כ"א עובדי הבעל: (כד) על ידיכם. המסורים בידכם לשמרם לבל יברחו: נפשו. נפש השומר הפושע בשמירתו תחת נפש הנמלט בפשיעתו: (כה) ככלותו. כאשר השלים יהוא לעשות העולה על ידיהם כי אחר שעשו העולה התפרסם אמתת הדבר שהמה עובדי הבעל ומעתה לא יאמרו שהרג נקיים: וישליכו. אמר כן על דרך ההרחבה אשר מרוב החפזון כאילו השליכו א"ע ללכת עד העיר המיוחדת לבית הבעל: (כז) מצבת הבעל. הכהנים שעמדו

מצודת ציון

כמו נתפשה דרכינו (איכה ג): (כה) לרצים. הרצים רגלי לפני מרכבתו: ולשלשים. ולשרים: (כו) וישרפוה. כל אחת ואחת: (כז) ויתצו. ענ' נתילה ושבירה: למוצאות. להפנות שם לגדולים:

ed the temple of the Baal and burnt each one of them [*Malbim, Redak*].

27. **And they tore down the monument of the Baal**—one single stone monument, called the monument of the Baal [*Malbim*].

The monuments symbolized that the worshipper was always standing before the deity.

It seems to me that the Canaanites who were carried away by idolatry would make an altar in all their temples, upon which to offer up their sacrifices, and a huge rock at the entrance upon which the priests would stand, and a tree planted outside to direct those coming there [*Ramban*, Deut. 16:22].

and Jehu had appointed for himself eighty men outside. And he said, "The one from whom one of the people I bring into your hands will escape, his life shall be forfeit for his life." 25. And it was when he finished performing the burnt-offering, that Jehu said to the couriers and to the officers, "Come, strike them down; let no man out." And they struck them down by the blade of the sword, and the couriers and the officers cast them out and went up to the city of the temple of the Baal. 26. And they took out the monument of the temple of the Baal and burnt it. 27. And they tore down the monument of the Baal, and they tore down the temple of the Baal and made it for a privy until this day. 28. And Jehu abolished the Baal from Israel.

25. **And it was when he finished performing the burnt-offering**—I.e. when he finished the sacrifice through the Baal worshippers. Now the truth was established that each one who had participated in the sacrificial service, was a Baal worshipper beyond a doubt. No one could accuse Jehu of slaying innocent people [*Mezudath David, Abarbanel*].

"Come, strike them down—The couriers and the officers were to kill the Baal worshippers within the temple. Should anyone escape, he would be dispatched by the eighty guards awaiting him [*Malbim*].

. . . cast them out—*Jonathan* renders: *and the couriers and the mighty warriors cast cadavers,* i.e. *they cast the Baal worshippers down dead* [*Rashi*].

Or, they cast the cadavers out of the temple as they slew them [*Abarbanel, Malbim*].

Alternatively, since they rushed through the slaughter, it was as though they cast *themselves* out of the temple of the Baal and went to the city of the temple of the Baal [*Redak, Mezudath David*].

and they went up to the city of the temple of the Baal—I.e. the couriers and the officers went to every corner of the city to destroy the monuments of the Baal as delineated in the following verses [*Redak*].

Alternatively, the bodies, which were cast out of the temple virtually reached all corners of the city. There was probably blood flowing through the streets of the entire city [*Daath Soferim*].

26. **. . . the monument of . . . and burnt it**—I.e. they took out the wooden monuments that surround-

חטאי ירבעם בן־נבט אשר החטיא
את־ישראל לא־סר יהוא מאחריהם
עגלי הזהב אשר בית־אל ואשר בדן:
ל ויאמר יהוה אל־יהוא יען אשר־
הטיבת לעשות הישר בעיני ככל
אשר בלבבי עשית לבית אחאב בני
רבעים ישבו לך על־כסא ישראל:
לא ויהוא לא שמר ללכת בתורת־יהוה
אלהי־ישראל בכל־לבבו לא סר מעל
חטאות ירבעם אשר החטיא את־
ישראל: לב בימים ההם החל יהוה
לקצות בישראל ויכם חזאל בכל־גבול

תרגום

בר נבט דחייב ית ישראל לא סטא יהוא מבתריהון אשתעביד לעגלי דדהבא די בבית אל ודי בדן: ל ואמר יי ליהוא חלף דאתקינתא למעבד דכשר קדמי ככל דברעותי עבדתא לבית אחאב בגין רביעין יתבון לך על כורסי מלכותא דישראל: לא ויהוא לא נטר למהך באוריתא דיי אלהא דישראל בכל לביה לא סטא מעל חובי ירבעם דחייב ית ישראל: לב ביומיא האינון שרי רוגזא דיי למתקף בישראל ומחנון חזאל בכל תחום ארעא דישראל

תולדות אהרן

אשר הטיבות . סנהדרין קב:

רש"י

לבית דוד כמו סנחריב ירבעם: (ל) ויאמר ה' אל יהוא. ביד יונה: בני רבעים. ארבע דורות תחת שהשמדת את בית אחאב שמלכו ארבע דורות. עמרי. ואחאב. ואחזיהו. ויהורם: (לב) לקצות. כמו קלתי בחיי (בראשית כ"ז מ"ו):

כלא ואו

רד"ק

נפנין שם: (כט) אשר בית אל. כמו בבית אל וכן הנמצא בית ה': (ל) ויאמר ה' אל יהוא. ע"י נביא ובסדר עולם מי אמר לו יונה בן אמתי: בני רבעים. כמו בנים רבעים יהואחז יהואש ירבעם זכריהו ואמרו בזכות שהשחית בית אחאב שמלכו ארבעה דורות עמרי אחאב אחזיהו יהורם מלכו מבניו ארבעה דורות ויהוא בער הבעל ולא בער העגלים כי אותם עשו לשם ה' ואע"פ כן היה חטא גדול כמו שכתוב לא תעשון אתי וגו': (לב) לקצות בישראל. לחכרית כמו מקצה רגלים חמס שותה:

מנחת שי

(כט) אשר בית אל. ד' דספרין כבי"ם: נחסן כל לילנותא חסירה כר וגו':

רלב"ג

(ל) ויאמר ה' אל יהוא. אמר לו זה ע"י נביא כי לא היה יסוד נביאה: (לב) בימים ההם החל ה' לקצות בישראל. הנה מזה המקום יתבאר לך שמה שהמית יהוא מבית אחאב היה נמלט מחרב חזאל כי בימי בית אחאב לא שלטה חרבו בישראל אך בימי יהוא התחיל הש"י לקצץ ולהכרית בישראל על יד חזאל וסנה קצה וקצן הם שני שרשים בענין אחד:

מצודת ציון

(לב) לקצות. להכרית כמו וקצותה את כפה (דברים כה):

מצודת דוד

מלוי נורת הבעל: (כט) עגלי הזהב. מוסב על תחילת המקרא לומר ומה הם חטאי ירבעם עגלי הזהב אשר בבית אל וכו':

(ל) ויאמר ה'. ע"י נביא: הטיבות לעשות וגו'. הישר בעיני עשית בלב היותר טוב וכפי מחשבות לבבי עשית וכו': בני רבעים. ד' דורות מזרעך ימלכו: (לב) החל ה'. התחיל ה' להכרית בישראל: בכל גבול ישראל. לא במקום אחד לבד:

This is an example of the principle of *middah k'neged middah,* paying in kind.

The four generations of Jehu's descendants who would occupy the throne of Israel were Jehoahaz, Jehoash, Jeroboam, and Zechariah. Jehu was not castigated for retaining the golden calves because they were made with honorable intentions. Even though it is forbidden to make images, yet, since they were not meant for deities, God did not castigate him for failing to abolish them [*Redak*]. See above v. 29.

According to *Elijah Zuta,* Jehu was a God fearing man. He did not follow the golden calves until after

29. However, Jehu did not turn away from the sins of Jeroboam the son of Nebat that he caused Israel to sin; the golden calves that were in Bethel and that were in Dan. 30. And the Lord said to Jehu, "Since you did well by executing what was proper in My eyes; according to all that was in My heart you have done to the house of Ahab, your descendants of the fourth generation shall occupy the throne of Israel." 31. But Jehu did not observe to follow the law of the Lord God of Israel wholeheartedly; he did not turn away from the sins of Jeroboam, that he caused Israel to sin. 32. In those days, the Lord commenced to be vexed with Israel; and Hazael struck them throughout the entire border of Israel.

27. **for a privy**—the *K'thib* is לְמַחְרָאוֹת, *an expression meaning a privy, and likewise,* "(Isaiah 36:12) *to eat their excrement,* חוריהם." [*Rashi*].

These words stem from the word חוֹר, a hole, alluding to the orifice from which the solid wastes are excreted. The *K'ri* in this case is לְמוֹצָאוֹת, for excretions. In Isaiah, it is צוֹאָתָם, their excrement. It was instituted to read this version since it is euphimistic, rather than the written version, which is more explicit [*Redak*].

29. **However, . . . from the sins of Jeroboam . . .**—*for fear that the kingdom return to the house of David, as Jeroboam had feared* [*Rashi*].

that he caused Israel to sin—Those deeds that had been accepted as proper were not abolished, whereas those that Jeroboam himself had practiced, but not followed by the people, *were* abolished [*Malbim*].

Abarbanel explains that the calves were not erected as deities. Jeroboam himself never worshipped them. He erected them as a symbol of his tribe, Ephraim, and its sister tribe, Manasseh. Just as Solomon erected two pillars in the Temple in honor of himself and his father David, so did Jeroboam erect two golden calves in honor of the two tribes of the sons of Joseph. Eventually, the people commenced to worship them as deities. See *Abarbanel* I Kings 12:28.

Likewise, Jehu did not intend them to be deities, but mere symbols [*Abarbanel*].

30. **And the Lord said to Jehu**—through Jonah [*Rashi, Redak* from *Seder Olam* ch. 19].

your descendants of the fourth generation—*four generations as reward for your having destroyed the house of Ahab, which reigned for four generations: Omri, Ahab, Ahaziah, and Jehoram* [*Rashi* from *Baraitha* of *Thirty-two Methods,* no. 27, quoted by *Yalkut Shimoni,* Num. 14:34].

יִשְׂרָאֵל׃ לג מִן־הַיַּרְדֵּן מִזְרַח הַשֶּׁמֶשׁ
אֵת כָּל־אֶרֶץ הַגִּלְעָד הַגָּדִי וְהָרֻאוּבֵנִי
וְהַמְנַשִּׁי מֵעֲרֹעֵר אֲשֶׁר עַל־נַחַל אַרְנֹן
וְהַגִּלְעָד וְהַבָּשָׁן׃ לד וְיֶתֶר דִּבְרֵי יֵהוּא
וְכָל־אֲשֶׁר עָשָׂה וְכָל־גְּבוּרָתוֹ הֲלוֹא־
הֵם כְּתוּבִים עַל־סֵפֶר דִּבְרֵי הַיָּמִים
לְמַלְכֵי יִשְׂרָאֵל׃ לה וַיִּשְׁכַּב יֵהוּא עִם־
אֲבֹתָיו וַיִּקְבְּרוּ אֹתוֹ בְּשֹׁמְרוֹן וַיִּמְלֹךְ
יְהוֹאָחָז בְּנוֹ תַּחְתָּיו׃ לו וְהַיָּמִים אֲשֶׁר
מָלַךְ יֵהוּא עַל־יִשְׂרָאֵל עֶשְׂרִים־וּשְׁמֹנֶה
שָׁנָה בְּשֹׁמְרוֹן׃ יא א וַעֲתַלְיָה אֵם
אֲחַזְיָהוּ וְרָאֲתָה כִּי מֵת בְּנָהּ וַתָּקָם
וַתְּאַבֵּד אֵת כָּל־זֶרַע הַמַּמְלָכָה׃ ב וַתִּקַּח
יְהוֹשֶׁבַע בַּת־הַמֶּלֶךְ־יוֹרָם אֲחוֹת
אֲחַזְיָהוּ אֶת־יוֹאָשׁ בֶּן־אֲחַזְיָה וַתִּגְנֹב

דִיִשְׂרָאֵל׃ לג מִן יַרְדְנָא
מַדְנַח שִׁמְשָׁא יַת כָּל
אַרְעָא גִלְעָד שִׁבְטָא גָד
וְשִׁבְטָא רְאוּבֵן וְשִׁבְטָא
דִמְנַשֶׁה מֵעֲרוֹעֵר דְעַל
כֵּיף נַחְלָא דְאַרְנוֹן
וְאַרְעָא גִלְעָד וּמַתְנָן׃
לד וּשְׁאָר פִּתְגָמֵי יֵהוּא
וְכָל דַעֲבַד וּגְבוּרְתֵיהּ
הֲלָא אִנוּן כְּתִיבִין עַל
סְפַר פִּתְגָמֵי יוֹמַיָא
לְמַלְכֵי יִשְׂרָאֵל׃ לה וּשְׁכַב
יֵהוּא עִם אֲבָהָתוֹהִי
וּקְבָרוּ יָתֵיהּ בְּשֹׁמְרוֹן
וּמְלַךְ יְהוֹאָחָז בְּרֵיהּ
תְּחוֹתוֹהִי׃ לו וְיוֹמַיָא
דִמְלַךְ יֵהוּא עַל יִשְׂרָאֵל
עַסְרִין וּתְמָנֵי שְׁנִין
בְּשֹׁמְרוֹן׃ א וַעֲתַלְיָה
אִמֵיהּ דַאֲחַזְיָה חֲזַת אֲרֵי
מִית בְּרַהּ וְקָמַת וְאוֹבֵדַת
יַת כָּל זַרְעָא דְמַלְכוּתָא׃
ב וּנְסֵיבַת יְהוֹשֶׁבַע בַּת
מַלְכָּא יוֹרָם אֲחָתֵיהּ
דַאֲחַזְיָה יַת יוֹאָשׁ בַּר
אֲחַזְיָה וּגְנָבַת יָתֵיהּ מִגוֹ
בְּנֵי

ת"א ראתה. סנהדרין לה:

ראתה קרי

רד"ק

(א) וראתה כי מת בנה. כתוב בוי"ו וקרי בלא וי"ו והענין אחד: ותאבד. ובמקומו בדברי הימים ותדבר ופי' תאבד דוברי כזב: הממלכה. פי' ממלכות יהודה וכן אומר בדברי הימים:

רלב"ג

(א) ועתליהו אם אחזיהו ראתה כי מת בנה. הנה זה פי' מאת הש"י לכלו' הזרע הרע מאת בית אחאב כי הנותר שלא המית יהוא המיתה עתליה עד שגם יואש בן בנה הולרכה יהושבע בת המלך יורם לגנבו ולהסתירו מפני עתליהו שלא תמיתהו ולזה גנזה אותו ואת מניקתו בחדר המטות שהיו שם והסתירו אותו הוא ומניקתו מפני עתליהו ולא הומת והנה הסתירה אותם יהושבע בבית ה' כי שם היתה יושבת כי בעלה

מנחת שי

(לד) וכל גבורתו. יונתן תרגם וגבורתיה דומה שהוא גורס וגברתו ולא מצאתי כן לאחד מהספרים: יא (א) וראתה. ראתה קרי:

מצודת דוד

(לג) מזרח השמש. לצד המזרח הכה את כל ארץ הגלעד וכו': מערוער וגו'. מן ערוער הכה עד סוף הגבול: והגלעד. עיר הגלעד היתה מטרפולין לכל ארץ הגלעד ואמר מלבד שהכה ארץ הגלעד כמ"ש למעלה הכה גם עיר המטרפולין שלה: יא (א) כל זרע. בכדי

33. From the east side of the Jordan, the entire land of Gilead, the Gadites, the Reubenites, and the Manassites; from Aroer, which is by the Arnon River and the Gilead and the Bashan.
34. And the rest of the acts of Jehu and all that he did and all his might, are written in the book of the chronicles of the kings of Israel.
35. And Jehu slept with his forefathers, and they buried him in Samaria; and Jehoahaz his son reigned in his stead.
36. And the days that Jehu reigned over Israel were twenty-eight years in Samaria.

11

1. And Athaliah, Ahaziah's mother, saw that her son was dead, and she rose and destroyed all those of royal descent.
2. And Jehosheba, King Joram's daughter, Ahaziah's sister, took Joash the son of Ahaziah,

he had been exalted as king. Then he deteriorated—Ch. 7.

32. **to be vexed with Israel**—Heb. לְקַצּוֹת, *like* "(Gen. 27:46) קַצְתִּי בְחַיַּי, *I am vexed with my life*" [*Rashi*] after *Jonathan.* Others render: commenced to cut into Israel [*Redak, Mezudath Zion*].

Or, to strike those living at the border [*Malbim*].

throughout the entire border of Israel—not only in one place [*Mezudath David*].

33. **From the east side of the Jordan**—he attacked the entire land of Gilead [*Mezudath David*].

And the Gilead—the capital city of the region.

1. After completing the account of Jehu's usurping the throne of Israel and destroying the house of Ahab, we return to the account of the kingdom of Judah. As we learned before, Jehu had slain Ahaziah and his nephews, who were descended from Ahab [***Abarbanel***].

destroyed—In II Chron. 23:10 we read: she brought a plague upon those of royal descent of the house of Judah. *Pseudo-Rashi* ad loc explains that she poisoned them.

She wished to destroy anyone who had a claim to the throne of Judah in order to reign uncontested [*Mezudath David*]. Alternatively, she wished to destroy the Davidic dynasty [*Abarbanel*].

2. **the slain children**—Heb. הַמּוּמָתִים, the slain. This is the *K'ri,* the traditional reading. The *K'thib,* the Masoretic spelling is, however,

אתו מתוך בני־המלך הממותים אתו ואת־מינקתו בחדר המטות ויסתרו אתו מפני עתליהו ולא הומת: ג ויהי אתה בית יהוה מתחבא שש שנים ועתליה מלכת על־הארץ: ד ובשנה השביעית שלח יהוידע ויקח | את־שרי המאיות לכרי ולרצים ויבא אתם אליו בית יהוה ויכרת להם ברית וישבע אתם בבית יהוה וירא אתם

בני מלכא דמתקטלין ואטמרת יתיה וית מנקתיה באידרון בית ערסתא ואטמרו יתיה מן קדם עתליה ולא אתקטיל: ג והוה עמה בבית מקדשא דיי מטמר שית שנין ועתליה מלכת על ארעא: ד ובשתא שביעתא שלח יהוידע ודבר ית רבני מאותא לגבריא ולרהטיא ואעיל יתהון לותיה לבית מקדשא דיי וגזר להון קים ואומי יתהון בבית מקדשא דיי ואחזי יתהון

המומתים קרי המאות קרי

רד"ק

(ב) הממותים. כתוב וקרי המומתים והענין אחד אלא שהכתוב הוא תואר כמו ממותי תחלאים והקרי הוא מהפעלים מבנין הפעיל: בחדר המטות. חסר וענינו ותסתירהו ואת מניקתו בחדר המטות ופת"י ואטמרת יתיה וית מניקתית כאידרון בית ערסתא וכן בדברי הימים ותתן אותו ואת מניקתו בחדר המטות ואמר אחר כך ויסתירו אותו ר"ל היא הסתירה אותו לשעה ומכאן ואילך הסתירו אותו ג"כ היודעים שלא גלו הדבר לעתליה כל שש השנים ופי' בחדר המטות חדר שהיה בעזרת הלוים או הכהנים ובדברי רז"ל בחדר המטות בתאים ר' ישמעאל אומר בעליות בימות החמה שהיו שוכבים שם הכהנים והלוים ויש בו דרש בית המקדש קורא חדר המטות על שם בין שדי ילין ועוד כתיב אף ערשינו רעננה: (ד) שרי המאיות. כתוב ביו"ד וקרי בלא יו"ד המאות וכן כלם אשר בפרשה זאת עד ויכרת יהוידע כן כתוב וכן קרי והכתוב הוא בהראות היו"ד למ"ד הפעל הנסתרת ממלת מאה כי הה"א במאה לנקבה ות"א השרש נעלמת ואלה שרי המאות כהנים ולוים היו כי רבים היו כי דוד מנה מן הלוים ארבעת אלפים שוערים וארבעת אלפים משוררים ומהללים: לכרי ולרצים. כמו לכרים וכמוהו הרודד עמי תחתי כמו עמים והדומים להם שכתבנו בספר מכלל ות"י לכרי לגבריא ופי' לקח שרי המאות אשר בלוים וקרא ג"כ לשרים ולרצים לשרים להתיעץ עמהם וכן אומר בדברי הימים וראשי האבות לישראל

רש"י

יא (ב) בחדר המטות. בעליית בית קדשי הקדשים כמה שהוא אומר ויהי אתה בית ה' מתחבא וגו' (לקמן פסוק ג') עליו אמר דוד (תהלים כ"ז ה') כי יצפנני בסכה יסתירני בסתר אהלו וקורא אותה חדר המטות על שם בין שדי ילין (שיר השירים א' י"ג) וזהו שיסד ר' אליעזר כפן חדר המטות חורבן ביתך יכפר עליהם: (ד) לכרי. שרי המאות לגבורים ושרי מאות לרצים ולשון כרי שלא אמר לכרים שם דבר של קבוצת הגבורים (ברני"ר בלע"ז): ויכרות להם ברית. שיהיו בעזרתו להמליך את בן המלך:

מנחת שי

(ב) הממותים. המומתים קרי ובמקצת ספרים הכתיב בשני תוי"ן. אמנם ברוב ספרים כתובי יד מדוייקים ודפוסים ישנים בתי"ו אחד בלבד וכן ברד"ק כאן וכפי' רש"י דברי הימים ב' כ"ב והוא חד מן מלין דכתיבין מוקדם מאוחר וסימן במסרה רבתי אות וא"ו. ברם צריך להתישב בדבר שמצאתי במלכים א' י"ט מסרה מן ז' מלין דכתיבין תי"ו ולא קרינן. ומילין אלין אינון מתלתא גווני תרי מינייהו כתיבין תי"ו וקריין דל"ת וסימן ובאתו אליו באחת המקמות (שמואל ב' י"ז) באחד קרי ותבריה ויבא וישב תחת רותם אחת (מלכים א' י"ט) אחד קרי ותרתי אחריני כתיבין תי"ו וקריין ה"א בשנת הרביעית (ירמיה כ"ח) בשנת העשירית (ירמיה ל"ב) תרווייהו בשנה קרי ותלתא כתיבין תי"ו ולא קריין כלל וסימן ארבעת כנפות (יחזקאל י"ז) ארבע קרי. עפר התפלשתי (מיכה א') התפלשי קרי. הממותתים. הממותתים קרי. והמסרה בחד שמא כלליהא זאת אומרת שתיבה זו כתובה בשני תוי"ן וצריך עיון. ובסוף קהלת איכא נמי מסרה אחריתי חילופא דדא מן י"א מלין דקריין תי"ו ולא כתבן דאית בהון מכמה אנפי. ובמסרה גדולה כתיב שם ואני המאסף קשיא לי טובא וכו' ולדידן לא קשיא לן כלל דאורחיה הוא כדחזינן הכא: (ד) המאיות. המאות קרי:

רלב"ג

היה כהן גדול והנה החביאתם שש שנים ואז היתה עתליה מולכת על הארץ: (ד) שלח יהוידע ויקח את שרי המאות לכרי ולרצים. הרצון באמרו לכרי לכרים והרצון בו לשרים והם ראשי האבות לישראל כמו שנזכר בספר דברי הימים והנה הרצון בזה שכבר לקח יהוידע שרי המאות לכהנים וללוים ושלח בידם לראשי אבות ישראל ולרצים שיבאו אליו והנה הביא אותם אליו בית ה' וכרת להם ברית עם ה' ועם המלך כמו שזכר אחר זה שלא יגלה אותם

מצודת ציון

יא (ד) לכרי. כמו לכרים ויקראו כן השרים ע"ד השאלה וכמ"ש

מצודת דוד

שתמלוך היא מבלי מערער: (ב) אותו ואת מנקתו. את יואש ומניקתו החביאם בחדר המטות שהיה בבה"מ: ויסתרו. אף היודעים הסתירו אותו לבל יודע לעתליה, ולזה לא הומת: (ג) ויהי אתה. כי היא היתה אשת כ"ג והתמידם לשבת בבה"מ: (ג) ועתליה מולכת. וימי מלכותה ו' שנים מקוטעות: (ד) ובשנת השביעית. למספר השנים שהיה מתחבא: יהוידע. יתכן שהוא יוחנן הנזכר בד"ה (א' ה') ועיין בסוף הספר בחשבון הדורות: שרי המאות. מן הכהנים והלוים: לכרי ולרצים. גם לקח הכרים והרצים: ויכרות.

According to the aforementioned Midrash, Joash was hidden in the attic during the summer and in the side chambers during the winter.

and they concealed him—At first, Jehosheba concealed him. Later, others who were aware of his identity concealed him from his grandmother [*Redak*].

4. **Jehoiada sent**—Jehoiada was

and stole him away from among the slain children of the king,
[and she concealed] him and his nurse in the bed-chamber; and
they concealed him from Athaliah, and he was not slain.
3. And he was hiding with her in the house of the Lord for six
years, while Athaliah was ruling over the land. 4. And in the
seventh year, Jehoiada sent and took the officers of the hundreds of the mighty warriors and of the couriers, and he brought them to him to the house of the Lord; and he enacted a covenant with them, and adjured them in the house of the Lord, and showed them the king's son.

הַמְּמוּתִים, which *Pseudo-Rashi* in II Chron. 22:11 takes to mean the dying ones, i.e. those who were dying from the agony of poison or sorcery.

and his nurse—Athaliah attempted to poison the nurse so that her milk would in turn poison Joash [*Pseudo-Rashi ibid.*].

him and his nurse in the bed-chamber—*Jonathan* paraphrases: and she concealed him and his nurse in the bed-chamber. The Chronicler words it thus: and she placed him and his nurse in the bed-chamber.

in the bed-chamber—*in the attic of the Holy of Holies, as it says* (v. 3): *And he was . . . with her in the house of the Lord.* It was *concerning him that David said,* "(Ps. 27:5) *For He will conceal me in His Tabernacle, He will hide me in the secrecy of His tent"* [*Seder Olam,* ch. 18]. *He calls it the bed-chamber in the manner of* "(Song of Songs 1:13) *Between my breasts He lodges."* This alludes to the Holy of Holies, where the Shechinah rested between the two staves of the Ark (*Rashi* ad loc), which protruded into the curtain like a woman's breasts (*Rashi* I Kings 8:8 from Yoma 54a). Because of the expression, "He will lodge," the Holy of Holies is referred to as "the bed-chamber," the symbol of God's love for the Jewish people. *This is what R. Eliezer* (should read: "Eleazar" as per *Kara*) *instituted, "The destruction of the bed-chamber,* may He remember for an atonement; "i.e. *may the destruction of Your Temple atone for them* [*Rashi* from *Mid. Rabbah,* Song of Songs 1:16].

Rashi is referring to the *piyut* of *Zichronoth* for the first day of Rosh Hashanah. This was composed by R. Eleazar the Kalir. For his identity, see *Responsum Concerning Piyutim,* by R. Eleazar Flekles, found as an introduction to many *mahzorim.*

Redak considers Rashi's interpretation as *derash.* Taking this expression literally, it refers to the chambers where the *kohanim* or the Levites slept in the unsanctified area surrounding the Temple court.

יתהון ית בר מלכא: ה ופקדינון למימר דין פתגמא דתעבדון תלתא מנכון עלי שבא ונטרי מטרת בית מלכא: ו ותלתא בתרע גבריא ותלתא בתרעא דבתרוהי תרע רהטיא ותטרון ית מטרת ביתא מדאשתלי:
והרין

את־בן־המלך: ה ויצום לאמר זה הדבר אשר תעשון השלשית מכם באי השבת ושמרי משמרת בית המלך: ו והשלשית בשער סור והשלשית בשער אחר הרצים ושמרתם את־משמרת הבית מסח:

רש"י

(ה) השלשית מכם באי השבת. המשמרות היו מתחדשות ובאות בשבת משמרות כהונה ולויה אחת נכנסת ואחת יוצאת וצוה את המשמר הנכנס להתחלק לשלשה חלקים השלישית בבית המלך לשמור שלא יעמוד איש על המלך להרגו. והשלישית בשער סור הוא שער המזרחי שבעזרה שער הסרה. השלישית בשער אחר הרצים. אף הוא משערי העזרה ויונתן תרג' בתרעא דבתרוהי תרעא רהטיא ושער הרצים דרך שם באין מבית המלך לבית המקדש כמה שנאמר בסוף הענין ואותו שער העזרה שנאמר אחריו שער הרצים קראו (בדברי הימים ב' כ"ג ד') שער הספים: (ו) ושמרתם את משמרת הבית מסח. שמירה זו לוס על החלק הראשון שאמר עליו ושמרו את משמרת בית המלך: מסח. שמרוהו מאד שלא תסיחו דעתכם לשון נואש (שמואל א' כ"ז ב') שלא יהא יאוש בדבר ומ"ס של

רד"ק

וקרא לרצים נ"כ להכינם למשמרת המלך: וירא אותם. מבנין הפעיל בתשלומו ויראה בפתח הוי"ו: (ה) באי השבת ושומרי משמרת. שיתעסקו בעבודתם וישמרו משמרת הבית ופי' באי השבת כי משמרות קבועות היו בכהנים ובלוים מימי דוד ושמואל שתקנו אותם והיה משמר אחד עובד השבוע ויוצא בשבת אחר הקרבת המוספין ונכנס המשמר האחר ואמר להם יהוידע שישמרו המלך ויהיה השלישית מן השומרים מן באי השבת ושתי הידות כל יוצאי השבת כי יוצאי השבת יותר פנויים מן באי השבת שעל באי השבת עבודת השבוע ויהיה השלישית בבית המלך השלישית בשער סור והשלישית בשער אחר הרצים ולא חלק איזו שלישית יהיה כאן ואיזו שלישית יהיה כאן אלא שיחלקו באי השבת עם יוצאי השבת לשלשה חלקים ויהיו על השלש מקומות הנזכרים ויהיו מוכנים לשמור הנכנסים והיוצאים שלא יבואו עוזרי עתליהו להמית המלך: (ו) בשער סור. ובדברי הימים בשער היסוד ות"י בתרע גבריא ויש נסחאות בתרע נטוריא ובדברי רז"ל שהוא שער המזרחי ושבע שמות נקראו לו שער סור ששם היו טמאים פורשים הה"ד סורו טמא קראו למו שער היסוד ששם היו מיסדים את ההלכה. שער חרסית שהיה מכוון כנגד זריחת החמה הה"ד האומר לחרס ולא יזרח. שער האיתון שהוא משמש כניסה ויציאה. שער התוך, שהוא ממוצע בין שני שערים שער חדש ששם חדשו סופרים את ההלכה. שער עליון שהוא למעלה מעזרת ישראל: בשער אחר הרצים. ת"י בתרעא דבתרוהי תרע רהטיא ובדברי הימים לשוערי הספים והוא שער שהיה לדרום העזרה ועליו נאמר בדברי הימים בית האספים ומה שכנהו בשער הרצים לשעתו שהיו רצי המלך שם: מסח. פי' משמרת מסח שתשמרו מכסח והיא הנתיצה וההריסה כמו

רלב"ג

והשביע אותם בשם ה' לעשות מלותו להקים את בית המלך על כסא אביו ואחר זה הראה אותם את בן המלך והוא יואש: (ה) ויצום לאמר זה הדבר אשר תעשון השלשית. השלישית מהאנשים אשר לוה יהוידע לשמירת המלך הם מבאי השבת והם המשמר הנכנס לכהנים וללוים והשאר ישתדלו בעבודת בית המקדש וככר זכר אחר זה כי שתי הידות ההם הם כל יוצאי השבת והם משמר היוצא ולזה יהיו השלישית מהם אלו באי השבת כי כל יוצאי השבת הם שתי הידות והנה באר כי השלישית ישמרו משמרת בית המלך שלא יכנס שם אדם יוכל להזיק למלך והשלישית יעמדו בשער סור והוא השער המזרחי שהיו טמאי' בלתי יכולים להכנס שם ולזה היה נקרא שער סור כטעם סורו טמא ובד"ה נקרא שער היסוד כי הוא יסוד הראשון מהקדושה והשלישית בשער שהוא אחר הרצים והנה תשמרו את משמרת הבית בית מסה והוא המקום שפרלו בבית בני עתליה המרשעת כמו שזכר בספר ד"ה ואולם שתי הידות באלו השלשה חלקים שזכר הם כל יוצאי השבת ושמרו את משמרת בית ה' בעבור

מנחת שי

(ה) השלישית מכם וכן (ו) והשלישית בשער סור והשלישית בשער אחר הרצים. בשלשת' ראיתי חילופי' רבים ומשבת אני אותם שכתובים חסרים יו"ד קדמאה ומלא יו"ד בתראה ומסורת דפרשת שלא לך מסייעא להו זיל קרי התם במסרה גדולה.

מצודת דוד

להיות האהבה ביניהם ולהיות ידם עמו להמליך את בן המלך והשביעם על זאת: (ה) השלישית. חלק שלישי: באי השבת. כי משמורות הכהנים והלוים היו מתחלפים בכל שבת אלו יוצאים ואלו באים כמה שכתוב בדברי הימים וקרוים המה באי השבת ואמר להם השלישית מכם ר"ל הלק שלישי משומרי המלך יהיו מהנכנסים באי השבת: ושומרי וגו'. המה יהיו שומרי משמרת בית המלך שלא יהרג בבית המלך מאוחזי עתליה והשמירה ההיא תהיה אחר שיבוא המלך אל הבית: (ו) והשלישית. הלק שלישי השני ישמרו בשער סור ואמרז"ל שהוא שער המזרחי ויקרא כן ע"ש שמשם היו הטמאים פורשים ע"ש הכתוב סורו טמא קראו למו (איכה ד') ובד"ה נאמר שער היסוד והיא היא לפי שהיתה מקום התחלת הקדושה כמו יסוד להבנין: והשלישית. הלק שלישי השלישי ישמרו בהשער אשר אחריו שער הרצים כן ת"י: את משמרת הבית. לבל יבוא מי בו להרוג את המלך: מסח. ת"י מדאשתלי ור"ל שישמרו מבלי היסח הדעת:

מצודת ציון

מדס כריס ועתודים (ישעיה לד): (ו) מסח. מלשון היסח

[*Redak* from *Yerushalmi*] *Erubin* 5:1. For diagram of the Temple, see Blackman's Mishnayoth *Kodoshim* 2. During the days of the Second Temple, the eastern gate was known as Nicanor's Gate, since it was donated by a Jew named Nicanor. See *Yoma* 38a.

6. **and you shall keep the watch of the palace without taking your mind off it**—*This watch he commanded them* (sic) *the first division, concern-*

5. And he commanded them, saying, "This is the thing that you shall do: a third of you, of those who come on the Sabbath and the keepers of the watch of the king's palace. 6. And a third in the Sur gate, and a third in the gate behind which was the gate of the couriers; and you shall keep the watch of the palace without taking your mind off it.

the ***kohen gadol*, the high priest, after Jehoahaz. He was Jehosheba's husband. See II Chron. 22:11.**

of the mighty warriors—Heb. לְכָּרִי, *the officers of the hundreds of the mighty warriors and the officers of the hundreds of the couriers. The expression* כָּרִי, *which he used, and did not say* לְכָּרִים, *is a noun meaning a company of mighty warriors (barnéd in O.F.), nobility* [*Rashi*].

These officers are named in II Chron. 23:1. The Chronicler tells us that first he summoned the heads of the *kohanim* and the Levites, and then the heads of the Israelites [*Redak, Ralbag, Mezudath David*].

and he enacted a covenant with them—*that they would aid him in crowning the king's son* [*Rashi*].

5. **a third of you, of those who come on the Sabbath**—*The watches would be renewed on the Sabbath* (See *Taanith* 2:6,7), *the watches of the priests and the Levites. One would enter and one would leave. He ordered the "mishmar" that was entering, to separate into three parts, one third in the king's palace, to guard that no one rise up against the king to assassinate him, one third in the Sur Gate, that is the eastern gate of the Temple court, the Hasarah Gate* (sic). *Kara* mentions the Haserarah Gate. Neither of these is found in the Bible or the Talmud. See below other names of this gate. *One third in the gate* called, *"After the Couriers." That too was one of the gates of the Temple court. Jonathan rendered: in the gate behind which was the gate of the couriers. Through the gate of the couriers one would go from the royal palace to the Temple, as it is stated at the end of this episode* (v. 19). *And that gate about which it is stated that the Gate of the couriers was behind it, was called in* II *Chron.* (23:4) *the gate of the Sippim* [*Rashi*].

This gate was on the south of the Temple court. It was also called *Beth Haasuppim* in I Chron. 26:15.

The eastern gate was called by seven different names: (1) the *Sur* Gate, because the unclean were required to turn (*sur*) away from it; (2) the *Yesod* Gate, i.e. the foundation gate, because there the Sanhedrin would convene to found the Halachah. (See II Chron. 23:5); (3) *Heres* Gate, directed toward the rising sun, known as *heres*; (4) *Ethun* Gate, which served for coming and going (אתה); (5) Middle Gate, because it was between the two gates, the gate of the Women's Court and the gate of the Temple; (6) the New Gate, in which a new halacha was introduced by the Sanhedrin in Jehoshaphat's time; (7) the Upper Gate, because it was above the Court of the Israelites

ז וּשְׁתֵּי הַיָּדוֹת בָּכֶם כֹּל יֹצְאֵי הַשַּׁבָּת וְשָׁמְרוּ אֶת־מִשְׁמֶרֶת בֵּית־יְהוָה אֶל־הַמֶּלֶךְ׃ ח וְהִקַּפְתֶּם עַל־הַמֶּלֶךְ סָבִיב אִישׁ וְכֵלָיו בְּיָדוֹ וְהַבָּא אֶל־הַשְּׂדֵרוֹת יוּמָת וִהְיוּ אֶת־הַמֶּלֶךְ בְּצֵאתוֹ וּבְבֹאוֹ׃ ט וַיַּעֲשׂוּ שָׂרֵי הַמֵּאיוֹת כְּכֹל אֲשֶׁר־צִוָּה יְהוֹיָדָע הַכֹּהֵן וַיִּקְחוּ אִישׁ אֶת־אֲנָשָׁיו בָּאֵי הַשַּׁבָּת עִם יֹצְאֵי הַשַּׁבָּת וַיָּבֹאוּ אֶל־יְהוֹיָדָע הַכֹּהֵן׃ י וַיִּתֵּן הַכֹּהֵן לְשָׂרֵי

המאות קרי

ז וּתְרֵין חוּלְקִין בְּכוֹן כֹּל נָפְקֵי שַׁבְּתָא וְיִטְּרוּן יַת מַטְּרַת בֵּית מַקְדְּשָׁא דַיָי עַל מַלְכָּא׃ ח וְתַקְפוּן עַל מַלְכָּא סְחוֹר סְחוֹר גְבַר וְזֵינֵיהּ בִּידֵיהּ וּדְיֵעוֹל לְגוֹ מִן סִדְרָא יִתְקְטִיל וַהֲווֹ עִם מַלְכָּא בְּמַפְקֵיהּ וּבְמֵיעֲלֵיהּ׃ ט וַעֲבָדוּ רַבָּנֵי מָאוָתָא כְּכֹל דְּפַקִּיד יְהוֹיָדָע כַּהֲנָא וּדְבַרוּ גְּבַר יַת גֻּבְרוֹהִי עָלֵי שַׁבְּתָא עִם נָפְקֵי שַׁבְּתָא וַאֲתוֹ לְוָת יְהוֹיָדָע כַּהֲנָא׃ י וִיהַב יְהוֹיָדָע כַּהֲנָא לְרַבָּנֵי מאותא

רש״י

מסח מן היסוד: (ז) ושתי הידות בכם. שאמרתי שיהו בשער סור ובשער הרלים ועמהם כל יולאי השבת כל אנשי משמר היולא: ושמרו את משמרת בית ה׳ אל המלך. שלא יבואהו נזק מתוך בית ה׳ ולא הולרך לכל זאת אלא שבת ראשונה עד שהומתה עתליה וברחו עוזריה מן העיר: (ח) והבא אל השדרות. איש נכרי שיבא לתוך המחוז הקרוי שדרות והוא מקום מבוא המלך מביתו לבית ה׳. ולא ידעתי מהו ל׳ שדרות ויונתן תרגם סודריא:

רד״ק

ונסחתם מעל האדמה ובמקום הזה הוא הויסת המשמרה על דרך פן יהרסו לעלות אל ה׳ והזהירם שיהיו במשמרה כאחד זה אצל זה שלא יפרד אחד מסדר המשמרה ללכת אל מקום אחר או יהיה מסח מן הסיח הדעת שישמרו שלא יסיחו דעתם לענין אחר אלא דעתם יהיה למשמרת לשמור את המלך: (ז) אל המלך. בעבור המלך: (ח) והבא אל השדרות. כתרגום ודיעול לגו מן סדרא כלומר אדם אחר שיכנס תוך סדר משמרותיכם יומת ובדברי הימים והבא אל הבית יומת ואחד הוא כי כל הבית היה משמרתם כמ״ש מכנף הבית הימנית עד כנף הבית השמאלית למזבח ולבית: (ט) ויקחו איש את אנשיו. כל אחד משרי המאות לקח אנשיו עמו: (י) את החנית. שם כלל כי לא נתן להם חנית אחד לבד אלא ר״ל החניתים וכן אומר בדברי הימים את החניתים ואת

מנחת שי

(ט) שרי המאיות. המאות קרי: (י) לשרי המאיות. המאות קרי:

רלב״ג

המלך שלא יזוק על לד עוזרי עתליהו והקפת׳ אלא המלך סביב איש כלי מלחמתו בידו והנכנס מהזרים אל הסדרים והמערכות שיהיו מסדרים שומרי המלך יומת כדי לשמור המלך תכלית השמירה ואלו השומרים יהיו את המלך בלאתו ובבאו כדי שלא יקרהו נזק: (ט) ויקחו איש את אנשיו באי השבת עם יולאי השבת. והנה לקחו מבאי השבת מחליתם לזאת השמירה וכל יולאי השבת כמו שקדם והנה לא שטליה יסודע המשמרו׳ האחרות לזאת השמירה: (י) ויתן הכהן לשרי המאות את החנית ואת השלטים אשר למלך דוד. ר״ל שפקדים

מצודת ציון

סדעת: (ז) הידות. החלקים כמו וארבע הידות (בראשית מ״ז י״ח): (ח) והקפתם. וסבבתם: השדרות. כמו הסדרות בסמ״ך והוא מלשון סדור ועריכה וכמו שהחיל המסודר יקראו מערכת כמו כן

מצודת דוד

(ז) ושתי הידות בכם. שנים שלישים בשומרי המלך יהיו כל אנשי יולאי השבת על כי המה פנוים הם מעבודת המקדש כי באו ממקומם באי השבת והמה יעבדו עבודת המקדש ולזה לא יוכלו הם כולם לשמור על המלך כ״א מחליתם: ושמרו. יולאי השבת ישמרו בבית ה׳ בעבור המלך: (ח) וכליו. כלי זיינו: והבא. איש זר הבא אל תוך סדר מערכות השומרים יומת כי אולי הוא מאנשי עתליה ומבקש להרוג את המלך: בצאתו ובבואו. בלאתו מן הבית ובבואו אליו: (ט) איש את אנשיו. כל שר מאה מבאי השבת ויולאי

when he goes out and when he comes in—when he goes out of the Temple and when he comes into the Temple [*Mezudath David*].

9. **and each one took his men**—i.e. each of the officers of two hundred took all his men with him [*Redak*].

the spears—lit. the spear, i.e. the collection of spears that had belonged to King David. In II Chron. 23:9, it appears in the plural form [*Redak*].

and the shields—as in Chron. ad loc. See II Sam. 8:7, where *Rashi* renders שְׁלָטִים as quivers.

that had belonged to King David—which he captured from Hadadezer, king of Syria, and from his other enemies whom he had defeated. All these weapons and shields he dedi-

7. And two thirds of you, all those who leave on the Sabbath,
shall keep the watch of the house of the Lord, to [guard] the
king. 8. And you shall surround the king, each one with his
weapons in his hand; and the one who comes within the ranks
shall be put to death; and you shall be with the king when he
goes out and when he comes in. 9. And the officers of the
hundreds did according to all that Jehoiada the priest had commanded, and each one took his men, those coming in on the
Sabbath and those leaving on the Sabbath, and they came to
Jehoiada the priest. 10. And the priest gave the officers of

ing whom he said, "And they shall keep the watch of the king's palace" (sic) [*Rashi*].

According to *R. Joseph Kara, Rashi* should read: This watch he commanded the first division. The last quotation is incorrect. It should read: and the keepers of the watch of the king's palace (v. 5).

from taking your mind off it—*Guard it very diligently, that you do not take your mind off it, an expression of despair* (I Sam. 27:2), *that there should be no despair in this matter. The 'mem' of* מַסָּח *is part of the root.* I.e. it is part of a noun. It is not a prefix meaning *from* [*Rashi*].

Alternatively, keep the watch . . . without breaking ranks [*Redak*].

7. **And two thirds of you**—*who I said should be in the Sur Gate and in the Gate of the Couriers, and with them all those who leave on the Sabbath, the men of the departing mishmar* [*Rashi*].

shall keep the watch of the house of the Lord, to guard the king—*lest harm befall him from within the house of the Lord. Now he did not require all this except on the first Sabbath, until Athaliah was killed and her allies fled from the city* [*Rashi*].

8. **and the one who comes within the ranks**—*a stranger who comes within the boundary called "sederoth," which is the place of the king's entry from his palace to the house of the Lord. I did not know the origin of the word "sederoth," and Jonathan rendered it as "rows"* like *"sedarim"* with a *"samech"* [*Rashi*].

I.e. the rows, or ranks of the guards in charge of the king's safety. The Chronicler words it as: He who comes into the Temple shall be put to death," since the entire Temple was guarded by the king's guards [*Redak*].

According to *Pseudo-Rashi,* 23:14, this was the passage connecting the palace to the Temple. Anyone coming from the palace was assumed to be sympathetic with Athaliah.

All strangers were suspected of being faithful to Athaliah, and potential assassins of the king [*Mezudath David*].

הַמֵּאוֹת אֶת־הַחֲנִית וְאֶת־הַשְּׁלָטִים
אֲשֶׁר לַמֶּלֶךְ דָּוִד אֲשֶׁר בְּבֵית יְהוָה׃
יא וַיַּעַמְדוּ הָרָצִים אִישׁ ׀ וְכֵלָיו בְּיָדוֹ
מִכֶּתֶף הַבַּיִת הַיְמָנִית עַד־כֶּתֶף הַבַּיִת
הַשְּׂמָאלִית לַמִּזְבֵּחַ וְלַבָּיִת עַל־הַמֶּלֶךְ
סָבִיב׃ יב וַיּוֹצִא אֶת־בֶּן־הַמֶּלֶךְ וַיִּתֵּן עָלָיו
אֶת־הַנֵּזֶר וְאֶת־הָעֵדוּת וַיַּמְלִכוּ אֹתוֹ
וַיִּמְשָׁחֻהוּ וַיַּכּוּ־כָף וַיֹּאמְרוּ יְחִי הַמֶּלֶךְ׃
יג וַתִּשְׁמַע עֲתַלְיָה אֶת־קוֹל הָרָצִין הָעָם
וַתָּבֹא אֶל־הָעָם בֵּית יְהוָה׃ יד וַתֵּרֶא
וְהִנֵּה הַמֶּלֶךְ עֹמֵד עַל־הָעַמּוּד כַּמִּשְׁפָּט

מאותא ית מורניתא וית
שלטיא די למלכא דויד
די בבית מקדשא דיי׃
יא וקמו רהטיא גבר
וזייניה בידיה מעיבר
ביתא מימינא עד עיבר
ביתא מסמלא למדבחא
ולבית כפורי על מלכא
סחור סחור׃ יב ואפיק
ית בר מלכא ויהב
עלוהי ית כלילא וית
סהדותא ואמליכו יתיה
ומשחוהי וטפחו יד
ואמרו יצלח מלכא׃
יג ושמעת עתליה ית
קל דרקדנין עמא ואתת
לות עמא לבית מקדשא
דיי׃ יד וחזת והא
מלכא קאים על
אסטונא כהלכתא
ורבביא

המאות קרי קמץ בז"ק

רש"י

(יב) את הנזר ואת העדות. ספר התורה כמו שכתוב והיתה עמו וקרא בו כל ימי חייו (דברים י"ז י"ט) ורבותינו אמרו הנזר הוא העדות שכל הראוי למלכות הולמתו ושאינו ראוי למלכות אינו הולמתו: (יד) העמוד. הוא מעמד

רד"ק

המגנות ואת השלטים ופי' השלטים בדמות מגינים וכן כל שלטי הגבורים: (יא) אשר למלך דוד. שהיה לוקח דוד במלחמות היה מקדיש כמו שלטי הזהב אשר לקח מהדרעזר וזולתו והיו נתוני' לאוצרות בית ה': (יב) את הנזר ואת העדות. בגדי מלכות כן ועדית עדי עדות בשקל גאות וי"ת ית כלילא וית סהדותא. ובדברי רז"ל כי זה הנזר היה עדות למלכי בית דוד מי שראוי למלכות הולמתו ומי שאינו ראוי למלכות אינה הולמתו ואדניהו בקש להלמו ולא הולמתו: וימשחוהו. יהוידע ובניו וכן כתוב בדברי הימים וימשחוהו יהוידע ובניו ומפני מה משחוהו והלא אין מושחין מלך בן מלך מפני מחלוקת של עתליהו כמו שמשחו שלמה מפני מחלוקת של אדניהו: יחי המלך. ת"י יצלח מלכא: (יג) את קול הרצין העם. חסר הנסמך ומשפטו הרצים רצי העם כמו סיגים כסף אמרים אמת או הוא כמו הפוך כמו שהוא אומר בדברי הימים את קול העם הרצים או יהיה קול עומד במקום שנים ופירוש את קול הרצים ואת קול העם ונו"ן הרצין במקום מ"ם וכן לקץ הימין כמו הימים ופי' קול הרצין קול השמחה שהיו שמחים והיו אומרים יחי המלך ובדברי הימים את קול העם הרצים מהללים את המלך ות"י את קול הרצים העם ית קל דרקדנין עמא פי' שהיו מרקדים ומטפחין כמו שאמר ויכו כף: (יד) עומד על העמוד. פי' סמוך לעמוד וכן וזבחת עליו סמוך לו ועליו מטה מנשה סמוך לו וי"ת קאים על אסטונא ופי' סטיו שהוא

רלב"ג

אותם המלך דוד: (יא) על המלך סביב. ר"ל אצל המלך סביב: (יב) את הנזר ואת העדות. ר"ל הכתר והאפוד שנתן אצלו התורה שנקראת עדות שיקרא בה כל ימי חייו והיתה עמו כמו שנזכר בתורה: וימשחוהו. מפני מחלוקת עתליה הוצרכו למשחו מלוכה ליה שלא היה מפורסם מאד שיהיה בן המלך: (יג) את קול הרצין העם. ר"ל קול הרצין וקול העם. (יד) עומד על העמוד. ר"ל אצל העמוד:

מנחת שי

(יב) ויוצא. הלד"ד בחירק וחסר יו"ד על פי המסורת ו ד' כתובים כן וסימן

מצודת דוד

שהנה לקח את אנשיו: (י) החנית. ר"ל קבוצת החניתות: אשר למלך דוד. אשר עשאם דוד והיו מונחים בבית ה': (יא) ויעמדו הרצים. מלבד באי השבת ויוצאי השבת עמדו הרצים ע"פ רוחב הבית ור"ל בעזרה: למזבח. לפני המזבח והיכל: על המלך. כמוך למלך וסביבו: (יב) ויוצא. ממקום מהבואו: הנזר. כתר מלכות: העדות. היא התורה הנקראת עדות ותנו אותה בזרועו וכמ"ש רז"ל בס"ת היתירה של מלך. או הוא מלשון עדי וקבוע ור"ל קשט אותו בבגדי מלוכה מאבני יקר: ויכו כף. היא דרך שמחה: (יג) קול הרצין העם. קול מרוצת העם וכאלו אמר קול העם הרצין: (יד) על העמוד. ר"ל על מקום מיוחד למלך לעמוד שם וזהו כמשפט ר"ל כמנהג המלך וכן נאמר ד"ה על עמדו והיא היא:

מצודת ציון

יקראו סדרות: (י) השלטים. כעין מגינים: (יא) מכתף. מלד: (יב) הנזר. הכתר: העדות. מל' עדי וקשוט או על הס"ת יאמר:

Temple. This is described in II Chron. 6:13, as being atop the laver. Even today it is customary for dignitaries to stand on a high platform when speaking, in order to make it possible for the public to hear

the hundreds, the spears and the shields that had belonged to King David, which were in the house of the Lord. 11. And the couriers stood, each one with his weapons in his hand, from the right end of the house to the left end of the house, before the altar and the house, surrounding the king. 12. And he brought out the king's son, and placed the crown and the testimony, and they made him king and anointed him; and they clapped their hands and said, "Long live the king!" 13. Now Athaliah heard the sound of the running people; and she came to the people, to the house of the Lord. 14. And she saw, and behold, the king was standing on his stand as the custom was,

cated to the treasures of the house of God See II Sam. 8:7–12 [*Redak*].

David had dedicated all these weapons and shields to commemorate the salvation God had wrought for him. He thanked God for vanquishing each foe individually. There is no doubt that just as he had dedicated Goliath's sword to the Tabernacle, he had dedicated his spear as well. In allusion to this one special spear, the singular form is used in our text. However, since other spears also were used, the Chronicler uses the plural form [*K'li Y'kar*].

12. **the crown and the testimony**—*the scroll of the Law, as it is written: "And it shall be with him, and he shall read in it all the days of his life* (Deut. 17:19)." This refers to the *sefer Torah* which the king is required to write. Hence it is a symbol, or testimony of royalty. Alternatively, the *sefer Torah* is referred to as "testimony" in other Scriptural passages, e.g. Ex. 25:16, where *Rashi* explains: The Torah which serves as testimony between Me and you that I commanded you the commandments written therein. See also Deut. 31:26.

And our Rabbis said that the crown itself was the testimony, for anyone who is fit for the throne it would fit, whereas anyone unfit for the throne it would not fit [*Rashi* from *Abodah Zarah* 44a, *Yalkut Shimoni*].

Others identify עֵדוּת with עֲדִי, *adornments.* They adorned the king with his royal robes [*Redak, Mezudoth*].

14. **on his stand**—*That is the place where the king stands in the house of the Lord* [*Rashi*].

According to *Jonathan,* it was a bench made specially for kings and dignitaries. Upon this bench was an exalted place upon which the king would stand [*Redak*].

Others identify this stand with the place upon which King Solomon stood and upon which he knelt in prayer during the dedication of the

וְהַשָּׂרִים וְהַחֲצֹצְרוֹת אֶל־הַמֶּלֶךְ וְכָל־
עַם־הָאָרֶץ שָׂמֵחַ וְתֹקֵעַ בַּחֲצֹצְרוֹת
וַתִּקְרַע עֲתַלְיָה אֶת־בְּגָדֶיהָ וַתִּקְרָא
קֶשֶׁר קָשֶׁר׃ טו וַיְצַו יְהוֹיָדָע הַכֹּהֵן אֶת־
שָׂרֵי הַמֵּאיוֹת ׀ פְּקֻדֵי הַחַיִל וַיֹּאמֶר
אֲלֵיהֶם הוֹצִיאוּ אֹתָהּ אֶל־מִבֵּית
לַשְּׂדֵרֹת וְהַבָּא אַחֲרֶיהָ הָמֵת בֶּחָרֶב כִּי
אָמַר הַכֹּהֵן אַל־תּוּמַת בֵּית יְהוָה׃
טז וַיָּשִׂמוּ לָהּ יָדַיִם וַתָּבוֹא דֶּרֶךְ־מְבוֹא
הַסּוּסִים בֵּית הַמֶּלֶךְ וַתּוּמַת שָׁם׃
יז וַיִּכְרֹת יְהוֹיָדָע אֶת־הַבְּרִית בֵּין יְהוָה

תרגום

וְרַבְרְבַיָא עֲמִיה וַחֲצוֹצְרָתָא קֳדָם מַלְכָּא וְכָל עַמָא דְאַרְעָא חָדָן וְתָקְעִין בַּחֲצוֹצְרָתָא וּבְזָעַת עֲתַלְיָה יַת לְבוּשָׁהָא וּקְרַת מֵירְדָא מֵירְדָא: טו וּפַקֵיד יְהוֹיָדָע כַּהֲנָא יַת רַבָּנֵי מָאוָתָא דִמְמַנַן עַל חֵילָא וַאֲמַר לְהוֹן אַפִּיקוּ יָתַהּ לְגָיו מִן סִדְרָא וּדְיֵיעוּל בָּתְרָהָא יִתְקְטֵיל בְּחַרְבָּא אֲרֵי אֲמַר כַּהֲנָא לָא תִתְקְטֵיל בְּבֵית מַקְדְשָׁא דַיְיָ: טז וְשַׁוִיאוּ לַהּ אַתְרָא וַעֲלַת בְּאוֹרַח מַעֲלָנָא דְסוּסְיָא לְבֵית מַלְכָּא וְאִתְקְטִילַת תַּמָן: יז וּגְזַר יְהוֹיָדָע יַת קְיָמָא בֵּין מֵימְרָא דַיְיָ וּבֵין מלכא

המאות קרי

רד"ק

ספסל שיושבים בו השרים הגדולים ולדעתו יהיה פי' עמוד שהיה באותו הספיו מקום נכבד לעמוד שם המלך לפיכך נקרא עמוד וכן אומר בדברי הימים על עמדו כלומר מקום הראוי לו לעמוד בו: (טו) הוציאו אותה אל מבית לשדרות. הוציאו אותה מבית ה' ותצא דרך מקום השדרות שהיא מערכת השומרים ואם יצא איש אחריה לעזרתה המיתוהו בחרב: המת. מקור: (טז) וישימו לה ידים. נתנו לה מקום שתצא באותו הדרך אשר מבית ה' לבית המלך והוא דרך מבוא הסוסים לבית ושם המיתוה: (יז) בין ה' ובין המלך. מתחלה

רש"י

המלך בבית ה': קשר קשר. מרד מרד יש כאן: (טו) הוציאו אותה. מבית המקדש לשדרות והביאו אותה דרך בית השדרות לבית המלך ואל תניחוה לצאת דרך מוצאת העזרה אל העיר פן תמצא עוזרים ומתחברים אליה: והבא אחריה. בעזרתה: המת בחרב. להמית בחרב: (טז) וישמו לה ידים. מקום (אשטנג"א בלע"ז): (יז) בין ה' ובין המלך ובין העם. שיהו המלך והעם

מנחת שי

בפ"שת ואתחנן במקרא גדולה: (טו) את שרי המאיות. המאות קרי: פקדי החיל. כל פקודי מלא וא"ו בר מן חד חסר וילו יהוידע את שרי. מסורת ריש

רלב"ג

(טו) הוציאו אותה אל מבית לשדרות. ר"ל הוציאו אותה בדרך שהיה תמיד מכסים לסדרים ולמערכות השומרים את המלך כדי שלא תמלט ותנוס: והבא אחריה המת בחרב. ר"ל המתחבר אחריה לבא עמה תמיתו בחרב כדי שלא יאספו אליה ותתחזק מעט והנה שמו לה מקום לנוס אשר בחרו ולזה באה דרך כניסת הסוסים בית המלך ושם לא היתה יכולה לנטות אנה ואנה והרגוה שם כי לא רצה הכהן שתומת בית ה': (יז) ויכרת יהוידע את הברית. הנה ראשונה כרת ברית בין ה' ובין המלך והעם שיהיו לעם ה' ואחר כן כרת ברית בין

מצודת דוד

קשר קשר. מרד יש כאן וכפלה דבריה כדרך המחד: (טו) פקודי החיל. הממונים על החיל: הוציאו אותה אל מבית לשדרות. ר"ל הוציאו אותה מהון לבה"מ אולם תלך אל מבית לשדרות ר"ל מכסים למערכת השומרים לבל תמלט: והבא אחריה. להיות בעזרתה דתו להמית בחרב: כי אמר וגו'. ולזה לא הרגוה מיד: (טז) וישמו לה ידים. עשו לה מקום פנוי ללכת מבית ה' ובאה

and the officers and the trumpets before the king, and all the people of the land were rejoicing and sounding the trumpets; and Athaliah rent her garments and called out, "Revolt! Revolt!" 15. And Jehoiada the priest commanded the officers of the hundreds, those appointed over the army, and he said to them, "Take her out to within the ranks, and anyone who comes after her, is to be slain by the sword," for the priest had said, "Let her not be slain in the house of the Lord." 16. And they made a place for her, and she came by way of the horses' entrance into the king's palace, and she was executed there.

17. And Jehoiada enacted the covenant between the Lord

[*Pseudo-Rashi* II Chron. 23:13].

"Revolt! Revolt!"—*Revolt! There is a revolt here* [*Rashi*].

15. **"Take her out**—*of the Temple to the ranks and bring her by way of the areas within the ranks to the king's palace. Do not allow her to leave through the exit of the Temple court through the city, lest she find allies who will join her* [*Rashi*].

Alternatively, take her out of the Temple, but do not allow her to leave the area where the guards are stationed, lest she escape [*Redak, Ralbag, Mezudath David*].

As mentioned above, the *sedoroth* was the passage to the royal palace. Thus he coincides with *Rashi* that Athaliah was to be returned through the passage to the palace, not through the city.

and anyone who comes after her—*to her assistance* [*Rashi, Mezudath David*].

is to be slain—lit. *to slay* [*Rashi, Redak*].

They feared that a group would gather to her and help her regain power. They, therefore, decreed that anyone who joins her would be slain immediately. She was given the opportunity to flee through the entrance of the horses into the palace. She had, however, no place to flee on either side [*Ralbag*].

for the priest had said . . .—Therefore, they did not slay her immediately [*Mezudath David*].

16. **And they made a place for her**—Heb. יָדַיִם, lit. hands, *a place (ajjsnçes in O.F.)* [*Rashi*].

They gave her a way to leave the Temple through the entrance the horses used, and there they slew her [*Redak, Mezudath David*].

17. **between the Lord and between the king and (between) the people**—*that the king and the people will follow the Lord, and afterwards he enacted a covenant between the king and between the people that they should be servants of the king* [*Rashi*].

וּבֵין הַמֶּלֶךְ וּבֵין הָעָם לִהְיוֹת לְעָם
לַיהוָה וּבֵין הַמֶּלֶךְ וּבֵין הָעָם: יח וַיָּבֹאוּ
כָל־עַם הָאָרֶץ בֵּית־הַבַּעַל וַיִּתְּצֻהוּ אֶת־
מִזְבְּחֹתָו וְאֶת־צְלָמָיו שִׁבְּרוּ הֵיטֵב וְאֵת
מַתָּן כֹּהֵן הַבַּעַל הָרְגוּ לִפְנֵי הַמִּזְבְּחוֹת
וַיָּשֶׂם הַכֹּהֵן פְּקֻדֹּת עַל־בֵּית יְהוָה:
יט וַיִּקַּח אֶת־שָׂרֵי הַמֵּאוֹת וְאֶת־הַכָּרִי
וְאֶת־הָרָצִים וְאֵת ׀ כָּל־עַם הָאָרֶץ
וַיֹּרִידוּ אֶת־הַמֶּלֶךְ מִבֵּית יְהוָה וַיָּבוֹאוּ
דֶּרֶךְ־שַׁעַר הָרָצִים בֵּית הַמֶּלֶךְ וַיֵּשֶׁב

מזבחותיו קרי

מַלְכָּא וּבֵין עַמָּא לְמֶהֱוֵי
לְעַם מְשַׁמֵּשׁ קֳדָם יְיָ בֵּין
מַלְכָּא וּבֵין עַמָּא:
יח וְעָלוּ כָּל עַמָּא דְאַרְעָא
לְבֵית בְּעֲלָא וְסַתְרוּהִי
וְיַת אֱגוֹרוֹהִי וְיַת צַלְמוֹהִי
תַּבִּירוּ יָאוּת וְיַת מַתָּן
כּוּמְרָא דִבְעֲלָא קְטָלוּ
קֳדָם אֱגוֹרַיָּא וּמַנִּי כַּהֲנָא
מַטְרָן עַל בֵּית מַקְדְּשָׁא
דַּייָ: יט וּדְבַר יַת רַבָּנֵי
מָאוָתָא וְיַת גִּבָּרַיָּא וְיַת
רָהֲטַיָּא וְיַת כָּל עַמָּא
דְאַרְעָא וְאַחִיתוּ יַת
מַלְכָּא מִבֵּית מַקְדְּשָׁא
דַּייָ וְעָלוּ בְּאוֹרַח תְּרַע
רָהֲטַיָּא דְבֵית מַלְכָּא
ויתיב

רש"י

אחרי ה׳ ואחר כך בין המלך ובין העם שיהו עבדים למלך: (יח) פקודות. ממונים לשמור במקום משמרתן כהלכתן כי עתליהו בטלה את סדר משמרות הבית: (יט) ויבואו דרך שער הרצים. אל בית המלך:

רד"ק

כרת ברית בין ה׳ והמלך והעם שיהיו כלם לעבודת ה׳ ולהסיר הבעלים ואחר כך כרת ברית בין המלך והעם: (יח) ואת מתן. כהן הבעל היה שמו מתן: וישם הכהן פקדות. ת"י ומני כהנא מטרות ר"ל המשמרות אשר היו מתוקנות מתחילה כן הושיבם עתה כי נראה כי מפני שהיו עובדים הבעל המלכים אשר היו

רלב"ג

המלך ובין העם שהוא יהיה להם למלך והם יהיו לו לעם: (יח) ואת מתן כהן הבעל. אחשוב שהכלון בזה שהכתוב׳ לכהן לבעל והם שאר הכהנים שהיו שם עובדים עמו הרגום כלם לפני המזבחות: וישם הכהן פקודו על בית ה׳. ר"ל שמנה שם מנויים ופקידות כדי[שיהיה] ענינו מסודר בתכלי׳ הסדור והנה מענין אלו המנוים העמדת המשמרות על ענינם הראשון: (יט) ויבאו דרך שער הרצים. ידמה שזה השער

מנחת שי

פרשת פקודי: (יח) ויתצהו את מזבחתו. בספרים אחרים כתיבת יד היה כתוב את ואחר כך הוסיפו וא"ו ועשו ו את וכן נראה מהתרגום וכן מצאתי בשני דפוסים ישנים ובמאיר נתיב. אמנם ברוב הספרים כתוב את בלא וא"ו: מזבחתו. מזבחותיו קרי: (יט) ויקח את שרי המאות. לית כתיב כן בענין:

מצודת דוד

אל בית המלך בדרך אשר הסוסים באים בה ושם נהרגה: (יז) להיות לעם לה׳. מוסב גם על ובין המלך שגם הוא יעבוד את ה׳: ובין המלך ובין העם. שהמלך ילחום מלחמות העם והם יעבדוהו כמשפט הראוי למלך: (יח) פקדות על בית ה׳. ממונים כפי שתקן דוד כי בהיותם עובדים לבעל בטלו הממונים:

מצודת ציון

(יח) ויתצהו. מל׳ נתיצה ושבירה: היטב. ר"ל בחוזק וכן טחון היטב (שם לב): מתן. כך שמו:

hundreds—Now they fulfilled the second covenant, to pay allegiance to the king [*Malbim*].

and they came by way of the gate of the couriers—*to the king's palace* [*Rashi*].

Rashi inserts the word "to" not found in the text. He wishes to avoid rendering "of the king's palace," since he holds that the Gate of the Couriers was one of the gates of the Temple court, not of the palace. See above v. 5. Here *Rashi* deviates from *Targum Jonathan*.

Ralbag conjectures that this gate was constructed during the reign of Rehoboam, who instituted the chamber of the couriers where he

and between the king and [between] the people, to be the
people of the Lord, and between the king and between the
people. 18. And all the people of the land came to the temple of
the Baal and tore it down, its altars and its images they
smashed, and Mattan the priest of the Baal they slew before
the altars; and the priest set up appointees over the house of the
Lord. 19. And he took the officers of the hundreds and the
mighty warriors and the couriers and all the people of the land,
and they brought the king down from the house of the Lord,
and they came by way of the gate of the couriers to the king's
palace; and he sat on the throne of the kings.

and between the king and between the people—that the king wage wars for the people and the people give the proper allegiance to the king [*Mezudath David*].

He enacted the covenant in such a way that the second part should be contingent on the first. Therefore, when Joash later forsook the Lord, the people revolted and killed him [*Malbim*].

I.e. this covenant between the Lord and the king and the people, to be the people of the Lord, shall be between the king and the people, that if the king ignores his obligations to the Lord, there will be no obligations on the part of the people to the king [*K'li Y'kar*].

18. **And all the people of the land came**—This was the first step in fulfilling the first covenant [*Malbim*].

and Mattan the priest of the Baal—That was his name [*Redak*].

Ralbag explains that *those who were given,* or placed *under the jurisdiction of the priests of the Baal, they slew.* He explains מַתָּן as an expression of giving.

appointees—*appointed to watch in the place of their watch according to their law, since Athaliah had abolished the order of the watches of the Temple* [*Rashi*].

It would appear from *Rashi* that Jehoiada reinstated the priests and the Levites who would stand guard in various locations in the Temple. *Redak,* however, cites the parallel verse in Chronicles, which states specifically that Jehoiada reinstated the *mishmaroth,* the order of priestly families to come to Jerusalem to perform the sacrificial service. King David had instituted the order of the *mishmaroth,* dividing the priests into twenty-four families, each of whom would serve twice a year at different times. See II Chron. 23:18. During the reigns of the idolatrous kings, the Temple had been neglected, and the schedules had to be reinstated [*Redak, Mezudath David*].

19. **And he took the officers of the**

עַל־כִּסֵּא הַמְּלָכִים: כ וַיִּשְׂמַח כָּל־עַם־הָאָרֶץ וְהָעִיר שָׁקָטָה וְאֶת־עֲתַלְיָהוּ הֵמִיתוּ בַחֶרֶב בֵּית *מֶלֶךְ: יב א בֶּן־שֶׁבַע שָׁנִים יְהוֹאָשׁ בְּמָלְכוֹ: ב בִּשְׁנַת־שֶׁבַע לְיֵהוּא מָלַךְ יְהוֹאָשׁ וְאַרְבָּעִים שָׁנָה מָלַךְ בִּירוּשָׁלָםִ וְשֵׁם אִמּוֹ צִבְיָה מִבְּאֵר שָׁבַע: ג וַיַּעַשׂ יְהוֹאָשׁ הַיָּשָׁר בְּעֵינֵי יְהוָה כָּל־יָמָיו אֲשֶׁר הוֹרָהוּ יְהוֹיָדָע הַכֹּהֵן: ד רַק הַבָּמוֹת לֹא־סָרוּ עוֹד הָעָם מְזַבְּחִים וּמְקַטְּרִים בַּבָּמוֹת: ה וַיֹּאמֶר יְהוֹאָשׁ אֶל־הַכֹּהֲנִים כֹּל כֶּסֶף הַקֳּדָשִׁים

וִיתִיב עַל כּוּרְסֵי מַלְכַיָא: כ וַחֲדִי כָּל עַמָּא דְאַרְעָא וְקַרְתָּא שְׁדוּכַת וְיָת עֲתַלְיָה קְטַלוּ בְחַרְבָּא בֵּית מַלְכָּא: א בַּר שְׁבַע שְׁנִין יְהוֹאָשׁ כַּד מְלַךְ: ב בִּשְׁנַת שְׁבַע לְיֵהוּא מְלַךְ יְהוֹאָשׁ וְאַרְבְּעִין שְׁנִין מְלַךְ בִּירוּשְׁלֶם וְשׁוּם אִימֵּהּ צִבְיָה מִבְּאֵר שָׁבַע: ג וַעֲבַד יְהוֹאָשׁ דְּכָשַׁר קֳדָם יְיָ כָּל יוֹמוֹהִי כְּמָא דְאַלְפֵיהּ יְהוֹיָדָע כַּהֲנָא: ד לְחוֹד בָּמָתָא לָא עֲטָרָא עַד כְּעַן עַמָּא מְדַבְּחִין וּמַסְקִין בּוּסְמִין עַל בָּמָתָא: ה וַאֲמַר יְהוֹאָשׁ לְכַהֲנַיָא כָּל כְּסַף קוּדְשַׁיָא דְמִתַּעַל לְבֵית מקדשא

המלך קרי

רד"ק

לפני זה לא נשאר דבר בבית ה׳ על מכונו ועל סדורו וכן כתוב בדברי הימים וישם יהוידע פקדות בית ה׳ ביד הכהנים הלוים אשר חלק דוד על בית ה׳ להעלות עולות וגו׳ : (כ) בית מלך . כן כתיב וקרי המלך ואחד הוא אלא שבכתוב חסרין הידיעה : (ג) כל ימיו אשר הורהו יהוידע הכהן . לא כל ימיו כי אחרי מות יהוידע עשה הרע בעיני ה׳ כמו שכתוב בדברי הימים אלא פי׳ כל הימים אשר הורהו יהוידע הכהן כלומר כ׳ז שיהוידע היה חי וכן כתוב בד"ה כל ימי יהוידע הכהן : (ה) כל כסף הקדשים .

רש"י

יב (ג) כל ימיו אשר הורהו יהוידע. אבל משמת יהוידע אז באו שרי יהודה להשתחוות למלך ועשאוהו אלוה אמרו לו הנכנס לבית קדש הקדשים שעה אחת מסוכן למות ואתה נחבאת בו שש שנים כדאי אתה להיות אלוה אז שמע המלך אליהם (בדברי הימים ב׳ כ״ד אומר בדברי הימים . ויהי אחר כן היה עם לב

מנחת שי

(כ) בית *מלך. המלך קרי: יב (ד) ומקטרים. בספרים כתובי יד בוא״ו במאריך: (ה) כל כסף הקדשים . במקלת מדוייקים הקו״ף בחטף קמץ וגם לספרים שהיא בקמץ לבד קריאתה בחטף קמץ כמו שכתוב בסוף פרשת תלוה :

רלב"ג

היה נקרא כך מימי לחבעס כי אז עשה לחבעס מגויס והפקידם אל את הכליס : (ג) כל ימיו אשר הורהו וגו׳ . מגיד שכל מה שהיה מימיו אשר הורהו יהוידע הכהן עשה הישר בעיני ה׳ אך אחרי מות יהוידע לא עשה הישר בעיני ה׳ כמו שנזכר בספר ד"ה : (ה) כל כסף הקדשים אשר יובא בית ה׳ . הוא מחלית השקל לכל אחד ואחד שהיה

מצודת ציון

(כ) שקטה . נחה : יב (ג) הורהו . למדהו כמו את מי יורה דעה

מצודת דוד

(כ) והעיר שקטה . לא נתעורר עוד מלחמה בעבור זה כי את עתליה המיתו ולא היה עוד מי נעורר מלחמה :

יב (ב) בשנת שבע . כי כשמלך יהוא הרג את אחזיה . ועתליה לא קבלה המלוכה עד שנה השניה ליהוא והומתה בשנה הששית והיא התחלת השביעית ליהוא ואז מלך יהואש : (ג) אשר הורהו . ר״ל כל הימים אשר למדו יהוידע אולם אחרי מות יהוידע ולא היה בעולם ללמדו השחית דרכו כמ״ש בדברי הימים : (ד) רק הבמות . במות יחיד לשמים ואסור הוא משנבנה הבית : (ה) כסף

Ex. Rabbah 8:2, *Tan.* Buber Ex. *Va'era* 16]. These are the only two Midrashim in which the entire dialogue appears. Since it is fairly well established that *Rashi,* as well as other early authorities, never saw Exodus *Rabbah,* we are safe in assuming the *Rashi*'s source was Buber's *Tanhuma.*

The words, "all his days," obviously present a difficulty. *Redak* explains this passage as, "all the days that Jehoiada the priest instructed him."

Abarbanel explains it as, "all Jehoiada's days," as the Chronicler states explicitly, "all the days of Jehoiada the priest." (24:2)

Malbim points out that Jehoiada *instructed* Jehoash; he did not teach

20. And all the people of the land rejoiced, and the city quieted down, and Athaliah they had dispatched by the sword in the royal palace.

12

1. Jehoash was seven years old when he became king.
2. Jehoash became king in the seventh year of Jehu, and he reigned in Jerusalem for forty years; and his mother's name was Zibiah from Beersheba. 3. And Jehoash did what was proper
in the eyes of the Lord all his days, what Jehoiada the priest instructed him. 4. However, the high places were not removed.
The people were still slaughtering sacrifices and burning incense on the high places. 5. And Jehoash said to the priests,
"All money of the hallowed things

kept his shields. See I Kings 14:28.

20. **And the people of the land rejoiced**—because the rightful heir to the throne had been restored [*K'li Y'kar*].

and the city quieted down—because they had dispatched Athaliah by the sword. I.e. since they had dispatched Athaliah by the sword, there was no one to instigate strife and quarrels in the city [*Abarbanel*].

in the royal palace—lit. the king's house. Since the king's house had dispatched her, there was no one to seek revenge. Had strangers done so, the royal family would have sought to avenge her death [*K'li Y'kar*].

1. **Jehoash**—Now that he became king, he was called Jehoash instead of Joash as he had been called previously [*Daath Soferim*].

seven years old—In spite of his youth, he was capable of ruling the land [*Daath Soferim*].

2. **in the seventh year of Jehu**—When Jehu commenced to reign, he killed Ahaziah. Athaliah became queen the next year. She reigned for six years. Hence, Jehoash became king in the seventh year of Jehu's reign [*Mezudath David*].

and his mother's name was Zibiah—a pious woman who influenced him by her piety [*Abarbanel*].

3. **all his days, that Jehoiada the priest instructed him**—*but after Jehoiada died, the princes of Judah came to prostrate themselves before the king, and they defiled him. They said to him, "One who enters the Holy of Holies is in peril of dying. Yet you hid there for six years. You are fit to be a god." Then the king listened to them.* (II Chron. 24:17) [*Rashi* from

אֲשֶׁר יוּבָא בֵית־יְהוָה כֶּסֶף עוֹבֵר אִישׁ
כֶּסֶף נַפְשׁוֹת עֶרְכּוֹ כָּל־כֶּסֶף אֲשֶׁר יַעֲלֶה
עַל לֶב־אִישׁ לְהָבִיא בֵּית יְהוָה: ו יִקְחוּ
לָהֶם הַכֹּהֲנִים אִישׁ מֵאֵת מַכָּרוֹ וְהֵם
יְחַזְּקוּ אֶת־בֶּדֶק הַבַּיִת לְכֹל אֲשֶׁר־
יִמָּצֵא שָׁם בָּדֶק: ז וַיְהִי בִּשְׁנַת עֶשְׂרִים
וְשָׁלֹשׁ שָׁנָה לַמֶּלֶךְ יְהוֹאָשׁ לֹא־חִזְּקוּ
הַכֹּהֲנִים אֶת־בֶּדֶק הַבָּיִת: ח וַיִּקְרָא
הַמֶּלֶךְ יְהוֹאָשׁ לִיהוֹיָדָע הַכֹּהֵן וְלַכֹּהֲנִים

מַקְדְּשָׁא דַיְיָ כְּסַף
תִּקְלַיָא דְּעָבַר עַל מִנְיָן
גַּבְרַיָא כְּסַף פּוּרְקַן
נַפְשָׁתָא דְמִתַּן גְּבַר
פּוּרְקַן נַפְשֵׁיהּ אַף כָּל
כְּסַף דְּמִתְנְדַב גְּבַר
בְּלִבֵּיהּ לְאַיְתָאָה לְבֵית
מַקְדְּשָׁא דַיְיָ: ו יִסְּבוּן
לְהוֹן כָּהֲנַיָא גְּבַר מִן
מַכָּרֵיהּ וְאִנּוּן יִתַּקְּפוּן
יָת בִּדְקָא דְבֵיתָא לְכָל
אֲתַר דִּי יִשְׁתְּכַח תַּמָּן
בִּדְקָא: ז וַהֲוָה בִּשְׁנַת
עַסְרִין וּתְלָת שְׁנִין
לְמַלְכָּא יְהוֹאָשׁ לָא
תַקִּיפוּ כָּהֲנַיָא יָת בִּדְקָא
דְּבֵיתָא: ח וּקְרָא מַלְכָּא

ת"א נפשות ערכו. מגלה כ"ט:

רש"י

י"ז): (ה) כסף עובר איש כסף נפשות ערכו. שני כספים יש כאן כסף עובר הוא כסף השקלים שבכל שנה הנאמר בו (שמות ל' י"ג וי"ד) כל העובר על הפקודים ואיש שיתנדב ערכת נפשו האומר ערכי עלי: כל כסף אשר יעלה וגו'. כגון האומר הרי עלי מנה לבדק הבית: (ו) יקחו להם הכהנים. יהיה שלהם והם יקבלו עליהם לחזק את בדק הבית משלהם: מאת מכרו. מאת מכירו

רד"ק

יואש לחדש את בית ה' כי היה צריך חזוק כי שם אומר הטעם כי עתליהו המרשעת ובניה פרצו את בית האלהים לפיכך היה צריך חזוק כי לולי זה היה עדיין קיים הבנין כי מיום שנבנה הבית עד שבדקו יואש לא היה אלא מאה וחמשים וחמש שנה ובנין חזק כאות: בנין היה עומד יותר ויותר לולא שפרצוהו עתליהו ובניה הם שהיו לה מאיש אחר ולפי שעשו בו פירצות שם יואש על לבו לתקנם והיה צריך לקבץ קדשי ישראל שיקדישו שקלים או קדשי נדבות וההקדשות שהיו בבית ה' אומר בדברי הימים כי עתליהו ובני' עשו אותם לבעלים הרוב ומה שנשאר לא רצה יהואש להוציאו בבנין כדי שלא ישאר אוצר ה' ריק וחשב שיעשהו מקדשי החוץ ואמר לכהנים שיקבצו כל כסף המובא בית ה' וגם הכריז על השקלים שיביאו אותם כמו שאומר בדברי הימים ויתנו קול ביהודה ובירושלם להביא בית ה' משאת משה עבד האלהים ומשאת משה הוא כסף שקלים קראו משאה על שם כי תשא את ראש בני ישראל ושלשה כספים זכר הנה כסף עובר הוא מחצית השקל כמו שנאמר כל העובר על הפקודים איש כסף נפשות ערכו הוא האומר ערכי עלי או ערך פלוני עלי כל כסף אשר יעלה על לב איש הוא המתנדב לבדק הבית וכת"י הפסוק כל כסף קודשיא דמיתעל לבית מקדשא דה' וגו' כבעמוד וא"ת כיון שנתנו השקלים לבדק הבית ממה היה להם התמידים באותה שנה שהיו לוקחין אותן בכל שנה מתרומת השקלים ונראה כי נתרשלו מלהביא אותה תרומה אותן השנים שמלכה עתליהו והיה לבם ועבודתם לבעלים ולא לבית ה' ולא היו מעלים עולות תמיד כמו שאומר בדברי הימים והיו מעלים עולות תמיד בבית ה' כל ימי יהוידע נראה כי קודם לכן לא היו מעלים תמיד ומפני זה הוצרך יהואש להחזירם ולהעביר קול ולהביא משאת ה' והטובים שבהם שבו אל ה' בכל לבם חביאו מה שהם חייבין מהשנים שעברו והספיק לזה ולזה: (ו) איש מאת מכרו. כל איש ואיש מאת הכהנים יקח הכסף מאת ישראל המכיר אותו והרגיל אצלו שנותן לו מתנותיו ויקחו הכהנים מעט מעט כמו שבא לידם ויהיה עליהם לחזק את בדק

רלב"ג

מלאת משה עבד האלהים על ישראל במדבר כמו שנזכר בספר ד"ה: כסף עובר. הוא הכסף שהיה מוגבל בכל שנה ושנה כמו ההקדשות והערכין שיהיה נודר איש כסף נפשות ערכו וכל כסף אשר יעלה על לב איש להביא בית ה' והם הנדרים אם זה נדרים שיהיו ומכללם ההקדשות שהם לבדק הבית: (ו) מאת מכרו. ר"ל מאת מיודעו: לכל אשר ימצא שם בדק. ר"ל לכל דבר שיצטרכו לחזק הבית ולבדקו

מצודת דוד

עובר. בתחילת המקרא אמר כל כסף וכו' והוזר ומפרש מה הן הכספים ואמר כסף עובר רלה לומר מחלית השקל שנאמר בו זה יתנו כל העובר על הפקודים (שמות ל') : איש וגו'. גם הכסף הבא מהאיש אשר יערוך נפש שדמיו קלובים בתורה ולפי רוב השנים אשר יעלה וכו' גם הכסף העולה על לב איש להביא בנדבה: (ו) יקחו להם. כל הכספים האלו יקחו הכהנים לעצמם כ"א מאת מכירו

מצודת ציון

(ישעיה כה): (ז) בדק. מקום השבר והרעוע יקרא בדק כי מהלורך

damages need examination to determine how they should be repaired, they are called *bedek,* lit. examination.

Redak poses the question, why the damages of the Temple should have created an issue. The Temple was standing but one hundred fifty-five years. Since Solomon had constructed it with the sturdiest materials, it should not have required any major repairs. Solomon reigned forty years. He commenced the construction of the Temple in the fourth

which is brought to the house of the Lord, the money of anyone who passes [the numbering], each one the money of the value of the people [whose value he vows to donate,] all money which comes upon a man's heart to bring to the house of the Lord.
6. The priests shall take for themselves each one from his acquaintance; and they shall strengthen the damage of the house, wherever damage is found." 7. And it was that in the
twenty-third year of King Jehoash, the priests did not strengthen the damages of the house. 8. And King Jehoash
summoned Jehoiada the priest and the priests

him. He gave him day by day instructions, but did not teach him Torah thoroughly, so that he himself would understand how to behave in each situation. Therefore, after Jehoiada's demise, he was easily misled.

5. **the money of anyone who passes the numbering, each one the money of the value of the people, [whose value he vows to donate]**—*Two types of money are mentioned here:* (1) *the money of anyone who passes the numbering. That is the money of the shekels, concerning which it is stated,* "(Ex. 30:13, 14) *Everyone who passes the numbering,*" *and* (2) *anyone who volunteers the value of his person; i.e. one who says, "My value shall be incumbent upon me to donate* [*Rashi*].

Rashi refers to the section of the Torah dealing with vows of valuation (Lev. 27). One who vows to donate the value of his person, or of any other person, is obliged to give to the treasury of the Temple, a fixed amount, according to the age and sex of the person whose value has been vowed.

Thus, we are dealing with two types of money: the half-shekel, which every Jew was required to give to the Temple annually to pay for the communal sacrifices, and the money donated by those who vowed their own value or the value of others to the Temple.

all money which comes upon . . .—I.e. all money which one desires to give, *such as one who says, "It is incumbent upon me to donate a maneh* (twenty-five *selaim* or one hundred dinarim) *for the repairs of the Temple* [*Rashi*].

Thus, we have a third type of money, that which was donated for the repairs of the Temple.

6. **The priests shall take for themselves**—*It shall be theirs, and they shall take upon themselves to strengthen the damage of the Temple from their own* money [*Rashi*].

from his acquaintance—Heb. מַכָּרוֹ, like מַכִּירוֹ, i.e. *from his acquaintance who frequently visits him.*

damage—*splits and cracks in the wall* [*Rashi*].

Redak explains that since the

ויאמר אלהם מדוע אינכם מחזקים את־בדק הבית ועתה אל־תקחו־כסף מאת מכריכם כי־לבדק הבית תתנהו: ט ויאתו הכהנים לבלתי קחת־כסף מאת העם ולבלתי חזק את־בדק הבית: י ויקח יהוידע הכהן ארון אחד ויקב חר בדלתו ויתן אתו אצל המזבח בימין בבוא־איש בית יהוה ונתנו־שמה הכהנים שמרי הסף את־כל־הכסף המובא בית־יהוה:

יהואש ליהוידע כהנא ולכהניא ואמר להון מא דין ליתיכון מתקפין ית בדקא דביתא וכען לא תסבון כספא מן מכריכון ארי לבדקא דביתא תתנוניה: ט ואיטפסו כהניא בדיל דלא למסב כספא מן עמא ובדיל דלא לתקפא ית בדקא דביתא: י ונסיב יהוידע כהנא ארונא חד ונקב חורא בדשיה ויהב יתיה בסטר מדבחא מימינא במיעל גברא לבית מקדשא דיי ויהבון תמן כהניא אמרכליא ית כל כספא דמתעל לבית מקדשא דיי

ת"א ויקב חר. סנהדרין כו לב מנחות לד: מימין קרי

רד"ק

הבית פירוש בדק הבית מקום השבר וההריסה ונקרא בדק לפי שצריך לבדקו ולעמוד עליו מה יצטרך: (ח) מדוע אינכם מחזקים נראה שהיו הכהנים שומרים עד שיהיה הכסף רב בידם ואחר יחזקו את בדק הבית והמלך חשד אותם שהיו לוקחים הכסף לעצמם לפיכך אמר להם שלא יקחו הכסף לעצמם אלא מיד שיבא לידם יתנוהו לבדק הבית: (ט) ויאתו הכהנים. בזה וישר בעיניהם שלא יקחוהו כלל כדי שלא יהיו נחשדים בזה הדבר וכיון שלא יקחו הם לא יהיה מוטל עליהם לחזק את הבית וזהו שאמר ולבלתי חזק את בדק הבית לפיכך לקח יהוידע הארון ונתנו במבוא הבית שישימו אותו הכהנים שם הכסף שיבא לידם: (י) ארון אחד. ארון איש אחד: בימין. כתיב מימין קרי והוא אחד בענין: שומרי הסף. שומרי כלי הבית וסף הוא שם כלל לכלי השרת וי"ת אמרכליא והם הגזברים הגדולים אשר ממונים אחרים תחתיהם כמו שתרגם

רש"י

הרגיל אצלו: בדק. בקיעה וסדק החומה: (ח) ועתה אל תקחו כסף. עוד ואל תחזקו הבית משלכם: כי לבדק הבית תתנוהו. אם יפחות יפחות ואם יותיר יותיר: (י) אצל המזבח. בעזרה: מימין בבוא איש. מימין ביאת הנכנסים: שומרי הסף. סיפי העזרה הממונים על מפתחות העזרה שהרי תרגומו יונתן אמרכלין והאמרכלים שבעה היו לשבעה שערי העזרה. בתוספתא

מנחת שי

(י) בימין. מימין קרי:

רלב"ג

אם יחסר דבר מהרגלו לו: (ח) כי לבדק הבית תתנוהו. ר"ל שתשימו הכסף ההוא במקום מוכן בו לבדק הבית: (ט) ויאתו הכהנים. ר"ל שהם לא רצו לקבל עליהם חזוק בדק הבית ויקבלו על זה הכסף מאת מכריהם אך היה נאות בעיניהם שלא יקחו הכסף ולא יהיה עליהם לחזק את בדק הבית: (י) ויקב חור בדלתו. הנה דרך החור היו מבליעין שם הכסף והיה בדלת שהיה מכסה הארון כדי שלא

מצודת ציון

לבדוק ולחפש אחריו כמו מבקיר בדקך (יחזקאל כז): (ט) ויאותו. נתרצו כמו בזאת נאות לכם (בראשית לד): (י) ארון. ארגז: ויקב. עשה נקב ולתוספת ביאור אמר חור כי חור הוא נקב: שומרי הסף. שומרי מזוזות השערים כי סף הוא מזוזה וכן ת"י אמרכליא והאמרכלים היו שבעה לשבעה שערי העזרה:

מצודת דוד

ומיודעו והמוכר זה יחזקו משלהם את בדק הבית בכל מקום שימצא שם בדק: (ח) אל תקחו כסף. אל תקחו לעצמיכם אלא מיד כבואו לידכם תנו אותו לבדק הבית ר"ל הכניסו באוצר בית ה' עד יהיה בהם די לחזק הבדק: (ט) ויאתו הכהנים. נתרצו והוטב הדבר בעיניהם לבלי קחת הכסף לעצמם ולבלי לחזק משלהם: (י) ויקב. עשה נקב בד בדלת הארון לזרוק דרך בו את הכסף אל הארון: בבוא איש וגו'. ר"ל בימין הבא אל הבית לא בימין היוצא: ונתנו שמה. מיד כבואו לידם נתנו בארון דרך החור אבל לא יוכלו להוציא מם

your money [*Rashi*].

but give it for the damage of the house—*If it will be little, let it be little, and if it will be left over, let it be left over* [*Rashi*].

Do not retain the money, but give it immediately for the repairs of the Temple [*Redak*].

10. **one chest**—after *Jonathan.* The vowel points of the word indicate that the word should be rendered literally "a chest of one." Therefore, *Redak* explains it as a chest of one man. In addition to the difficulty involved in this interpretation, since it is irrelevant that the

and said to them, "Why are you not repairing the damage of the house? Now, take no money from your acquaintances, but give it for the damage of the house." 9. And the priests agreed not to take money from the people and not to repair the damage of the house. 10. And Jehoiada the priest took one chest and bored a hole in its door; and he placed it near the altar on the right, where a person enters the house of the Lord; and the priests, the guards of the threshold, would put all the money that was brought into the house of the Lord, into there.

year of his reign. The construction took seven years, leaving thirty-one years. Rehoboam reigned seventeen years, making forty-eight. Abijah reigned three years, making fifty-one years. Asa reigned forty-one years, making ninety-two. Jehoshaphat reigned twenty-five years, making one hundred seventeen years. Jehoram reigned eight years and Ahaziah one. Athaliah reigned six years, making one hundred thirty-two years. Since it was in the twenty-third year of Jehoash's reign that he decided to strengthen the Temple, we have a total of one hundred fifty-five years. He quotes the Chronicler, who informs us that Athaliah's sons had made breaches in the walls of the Temple. She had sons from another man, not King Jehoram (II Chron. 24:7).

Redak further questions how the *shekalim* could be used for repairing the Temple. Since the daily sacrifices were resumed, the *shekalim* had to be used for this purpose. He explains tht during Athaliah's reign, no sacrifices were offered in the Temple. Likewise, no *shekalim* were brought. When Jehoash became king, Jehoiada announced that all should bring the *shekalim* they had neglected to bring during the past six years. Many repented of their sins and paid their arrears. Hence there was sufficient money to pay for the current sacrifices and to give the priests to repair the breaches in the walls.

During these past six years, all moneys that had been donated to the Temple, were diverted to the Baal (II Chron. ibid). Consequently, Jehoash did not wish to use the money he found in the treasury from before his reign. In order not to empty the treasury completely, he therefore found it necessary to proclaim a campaign for the repairs of the Temple [*Redak*].

8. **"Why are you not repairing—** The priests were waiting for the money to accumulate, so they should not have to take money out of their own pockets to repair the Temple. Joash, however, suspected them of taking the money for themselves and neglecting to fulfill their part of the agreement [*Redak*].

Now, take no money—*anymore, and do not repair the Temple from*

יא וַיְהִי כִּרְאוֹתָם כִּי־רַב הַכֶּסֶף בָּאָרוֹן וַיַּעַל סֹפֵר הַמֶּלֶךְ וְהַכֹּהֵן הַגָּדוֹל וַיָּצֻרוּ וַיִּמְנוּ אֶת־הַכֶּסֶף הַנִּמְצָא בֵית־יְהוָה׃
יב וְנָתְנוּ אֶת־הַכֶּסֶף הַמְתֻכָּן עַל־יְדֵי עֹשֵׂי הַמְּלָאכָה הַפְּקֻדִים בֵּית יְהוָה וַיּוֹצִיאֻהוּ לְחָרָשֵׁי הָעֵץ וְלַבֹּנִים הָעֹשִׂים בֵּית יְהוָה׃ יג וְלַגֹּדְרִים וּלְחֹצְבֵי הָאֶבֶן וְלִקְנוֹת עֵצִים וְאַבְנֵי מַחְצֵב לְחַזֵּק אֶת־בֶּדֶק בֵּית־יְהוָה וּלְכֹל אֲשֶׁר־יֵצֵא עַל־

תרגום: דַיְיָ: יא וַהֲוָה כַּד חֲזוֹ אֲרֵי סַגִי כַסְפָּא בַּאֲרוֹנָא וּסְלִיק סָפְרָא דְמַלְכָּא וְכַהֲנָא רַבָּא וְצָרוּ וּמְנוֹ יָת כַּסְפָּא דְאִשְׁתְּכַח בֵּית מַקְדְּשָׁא דַיְיָ: יב וְיַהֲבִין יָת כַּסְפָּא דִמְתַקַּם עַל יְדֵי עָבְדֵי עֲבִידְתָּא דִי מְמַנַן עַל בֵּית מַקְדְּשָׁא דַיְיָ וּמַפְּקִין לְנַגָּרֵי אָעַיָא וּלְאַרְדִּיכְלַיָא דְעָבְדִין בֵּית מַקְדְּשָׁא דַיְיָ: יג וְלַאֲרְגוּבְלַיָא וּלְפַסְלֵי אַבְנַיָא וּלְמִזְבַּן אָעִין וְאַבְנִין פְּסִילָן לְתַקָּפָא יָת בִּדְקָא בֵּית מַקְדְּשָׁא דַיְיָ וּלְכֹל דְיִפּוֹק עַל

ת״א ויצורו. בבא בתרא ס:

ידי קרי המפקדים קרי

רש״י

דשקלים: (יא) ויהי. מיום אל יום (תמיד): כראותם כי רב הכסף בארון ויעל סופר המלך וגו׳: (יב) ונתנו את הכסף המתכן. היו נותנין אותו הכסף המנוי לאחר שהוציאו מן הארון ושקלוהו ומנאוהו היו נותנין אותו על ידי הגזברין הממונים על עושי המלאכה: המתכן. לשון מנין כמו ותוכן לבנים תתנו (שמות ה׳ י״ח): המפקדים. הממונים: ויוציאהו. לשון הוצאה לשכור חרשי העץ: ולבונים. הם הארדיכלין חרשי האבן שחבריהם עושים על פיהם ראשי האומנות: (יג) ולגדרים. לבוני החומה תלמידי הארדיכלין:

רד״ק

אונקלוס ונשיא נשיאי הלוי אלעזר בן אהרן הכהן ואמרכליא דממנא על רברבי ליואי: (יא) ויהי כראותם. יום יום כשהיו רואי׳ שהארון מלא היו מערים אותו ומשיבים אותו למקומו וכן כתוב בדברי הימים ויערו את הארון וישאוהו ויביאוהו אל מקומו כה עשו ליום ביום: ויצורו וימנו. היו מונין תחילה ואחר כך היו משימין אותו בצרורות כסף שהיה מטבע צרור לבדו ואשר לא היה מטבע צרור לבדו והיו נותנין הכסף המתוכן והיא שהיה עשו מטבע היו נותנין אותו על ידי עושי המלאכה והיו מוציאין אותו לחרשים ואשר לא היה מטבע היה עושין אותו מטבע או צורפין אותו במטבע כי בהוצאה לא יוציא אדם אלא המטבע לשכר האומנין ולקנות עצים ואבנים ופי׳ המתוכן מתוקן בצורה שהיה נשלם בצורתו יתבניתו ויש לפרש ויצורו מענין צורה כי הכסף שלא היה מטבע עשו אותו מטבע: (יב) על יד. כן כתיב וקרי ידי ואחד הוא בענין: הפקדים. כן כתיב וקרי המופקדים והכתוב הוא תואר כמו חכם חכמים והקרי הוא מהפעלים ואחד הוא: לחרשי העץ. הם כורתי העצים בלבנון ועושין אותם במקצועות: ולבתים. שבונים העצים בבית: (יג) ולגודרים. הבונים קירות האבנים: ולחוצבי האבן. שחוצבין האבנים בהר: ולקנות עצים ואבני מחצב. היו להם פוסלים בלבנון ובהר והיו קונין גם כן מאחרים שהיו

רלב״ג

יוכל אחד לקחת ממנו בזולת פתיחת הארון: שומרי הסף. הם שומרי כלי בית המקדש: (יא) ויצורו וימנו את הכסף. כבר נתבאר בספר ד״ה שכאשר היה הארון מלא היו מערים אותו ואח״כ היו נושאים אותו ומשיבים אותו אל מקומו וזה המקום באר שאחר שערו את הארון היו משימים את הכסף בצרורות והיו מונים: (יב) ונתנו את הכסף המתוכן. ר״ל הכסף הנמנה. מענין מתכונת הלבנים. והיו נותנים אותו על ידי עושי המלאכה הממונים בית ה׳ והם יוציאו את הכסף לחרשי העץ והם האומנים הכורתים העצים בתמונה שירצו: ולבונים. והם העושים בית ה׳ כמו ההיכל והדביר: (יג) ולגודרים. והם העושים הקירות והגדר לחצר הגדולה והעזרה: ולחוצבי האבן. הם החוצבים אותם מן המחצב ואע״פ שהיו שוכרים חרשי עץ וחוצבי אבן הנה היו צריכים לקנות העצים כרותים ואבני מחצב נחצבים כי

מנחת שי

(יב) את הכסף המתכן. הה״א במאריך בספרים כתובי יד: ידי. ידי קרי:

מצודת דוד

זולת פתיחת הדלת: (יא) ויהי כראותם. בכל עת כשראו שיש בו הרבה כסף: והכהן הגדול. לא בעלמו כ״א פקידו בא במקומו וכן מפורש בד״ה: ויצורו. עשו בהם צורת מטבע להוציא בהוצאה ומנו המטבעות: (יב) עושי המלאכה. הם האומנים הגדולים הממונים בבית ה׳ ומתחת ידם בונים האומנים הפועלים כפי אשר יורו אותם ובדרז״ל נקראים ארדיכלין: ויוציאהו. הם הוציאו את הכסף בשכר האומנים הפועלים: לחרשי העץ. הם כורתי העלים בתמונה הנרצה: ולבונים. הבונים העלים בקירות הבית: (יג) ולגדרים. הם הבונים קירות אבנים: ולחוצבי האבן. החוצבים את האבנים מן ההר: ואבני מחצב. אף ששכרו חוצבי אבן הוצרכו עוד לקנות אבנים חצובים: ולכל אשר יצא. לכל שאר הדברים הנצרכים להוציא על הבית לחזק אותו:

מצודת ציון

(יא) ויצורו. מל׳ צורה: וימנו. מל׳ מנין ומספר: (יב) המתכן. המנוי כמו מתכונת הלבנים (שמות ה): על ידי. אל ידי: לחרשי. לאומני: (יג) ולחוצבי. לכורתי:

counted—I.e. first they counted the money and then packed it in bags, each containing a certain amount [*Redak*].

Alternatively, they minted and counted. The silver coins that had no stamp, were minted so that they could be spent [*Mezudath David*].

11. And it was when they saw that there was much money in the chest, that the king's scribe and the high priest went up and packed and counted the money which was brought into the house of the Lord. 12. And they would give the counted money into the hands of the foremen of the work who were appointed in the house of the Lord; and they spent it for the carpenters and for the builders who work in the house of the Lord.
13. And for the masons and for the stonecutters and to buy wood and quarried stones to repair the damage of the house of the Lord, and for everything which would be spent for the house to strengthen it.

chest belongs to one man, it is more difficult to render this way in II Chron. 24:8, where it says, "They made אֲרוֹן אֶחָד," which cannot be rendered as "a chest of one man." *Redak* rectifies it by explaining it as "They fixed a chest of one man," referring to the boring not the hole in its door. *Malbim* points out that the numerical value of the word *echad* is thirteen, *aleph* equaling one, *heth* eight, and *daleth* four. This alludes to the thirteen chests, called *shofaroth* because of their shape, wide at the bottom and narrow at the top, that were used in the Temple for various funds (*Shekalim* 6:1,5). Thus, we render, "took a chest of the thirteen." This was the chest upon which was inscribed, "New shekels," the *shekalim* of the current year.

bored a hole—to prevent anyone from taking money out of the chest without opening it [*Ralbag*].

near the altar—*in the Temple court* [*Rashi*].

on the right, where a person comes—*on the right of the people's entrance* [*Rashi*].

the guards of the threshold—*the thresholds of the Temple court, those in charge of the keys of the Temple court, for Jonathan rendered it as "Amarkalia," and the "Amarkalim" were seven, for the seven gates of the Temple court. Tosefta Shekalim* 2:15 [*Rashi*].

The *Tosefta* delineates the various offices in the Temple. The *Amarkalim* were the keepers of the keys of the seven gates of the court, who would open the gates to admit the treasurers.

Others render: the keepers of the vessels [*Redak, Ralbag*].

11. **And it was**—*from day to day* [*Rashi*].

I.e. whenever they saw that much money had accumulated in the chest [*Redak*].

when they saw that there was much money in the chest, that the king's scribe . . . and they packed and

הַבָּיִת לְחִזְקָה: יד אַךְ לֹא יֵעָשֶׂה בֵּית יְהוָה סִפּוֹת כֶּסֶף מְזַמְּרוֹת מִזְרָקוֹת חֲצֹצְרוֹת כָּל־כְּלִי זָהָב וּכְלִי־כָסֶף מִן הַכֶּסֶף הַמּוּבָא בֵית־יְהוָה: טו כִּי־לְעֹשֵׂי הַמְּלָאכָה יִתְּנֻהוּ וְחִזְּקוּ־בוֹ אֶת־בֵּית יְהוָה: טז וְלֹא יְחַשְּׁבוּ אֶת־הָאֲנָשִׁים אֲשֶׁר יִתְּנוּ אֶת־הַכֶּסֶף עַל־יָדָם לָתֵת לְעֹשֵׂי הַמְּלָאכָה כִּי בֶאֱמֻנָה הֵם עֹשִׂים: יז כֶּסֶף אָשָׁם וְכֶסֶף חַטָּאוֹת לֹא יוּבָא

תרגום

בֵּיתָא לְתַקָּפוּתֵיהּ: יד בְּרַם לָא מִתְעֲבֵיד בֵּית מַקְדְּשָׁא דַיָי קוּלִין דִּכְסַף מְזַמְּרַיָא וּמָנֵי מְזַרְקַיָא חֲצוֹצְרָתָא כָּל מָאנֵי דַּהֲבָא וּמָאנֵי כַסְפָּא מִן כַּסְפָּא דְּמִתְּעַל לְבֵית מַקְדְּשָׁא דַיָי: טו אֲרֵי לְעָבְדֵי עֲבִידְתָּא יָהֲבִין לֵיהּ וּמְתַקְּפִין בֵּיהּ יַת בֵּית מַקְדְּשָׁא דַיָי: טז וְלָא מְחַשְּׁבִין עִם גֻּבְרַיָא דִּי יָהֲבִין יַת כַּסְפָּא עַל יְדֵיהוֹן לְמִתַּן לְעָבְדֵי עֲבִידְתָּא אֲרֵי בְּהֵימְנוּתָא אִינוּן עָבְדִין: יז כְּסַף אַשְׁמָא וּכְסַף חֶטְוָתָא לָא מִתְּעַל לְבֵית מקדשא

ת"א אך לא יעשה. כתובות קו (שקלים ג): כי לעושי. שם: ולא יחשבו. בבא בתרא ט: כסף אשם. שקלים ט:

רד"ק

להם עצים כרותים ואבני מחצב כלומר אבנים חצובות מחצב שם בשקל משען וי"ת ולבינים ולארדיכליא והם אומני האבן הגדולים אשר תחתיהם אומנים אחרים ותרגם ולגודרים ולארגובליא הם אומני האבן הגדולים בוני הקירות: (יד) אך לא יעשה בית ה' ספות כסף. ובדברי הימים אומר ויעשו כלים לבית ה' כלי שרת ורז"ל הקשו אלה הפסוקי' ותרצו כאן שגבו והותירו כאן שגבו ולא הותירו והוא שאמר ובכלותם הביאו לפני המלך ויהוידע כי לפני כלות המלאכה לא היו עושים כלים כמו שאומר הנה אך לא יעשה בית ה' ספות כסף כי לעושי המלאכה יתנוהו שעדיין לא נעשתה המלאכה אך כאשר נעשתה המלאכה כמו שאומר שם ויעמידו בית האלהים על מתכונתו וגו' ובכלותם עשו הנותר כלי שרת: (טז) ולא יחשבו את האנשים. מכאן ארז"ל שאין מחשבין עם גבאי צדקה כי כשממנין אנשים על הצדקה אנשים נאותין כמנין ואין מחשבין עמהם שאין חושדין בכשרין: כי באמונה הם עושים. ידועים היו כי אנשים נאמנים היו: (יז) כסף אשם. פירוש רז"ל

רש"י

ולחצבי האבן. מן ההר: (יד) ספות כסף מזמרות. והם כלי שיר: (טז) ולא יחשבו את האנשים. לא היו האמרכלין צריך להחשבון עם האנשים הגזברין אשר יתנו האמרכלין את הכסף תמיד על ידם לתתו לעושי המלאכה לפי שלא היו חשודים בעיניהם כי באמונה הם עושים: (יז) כסף אשם וכסף חטאות. המפריש מעות לחטאתו

מנחת שי

ה״מפקדים. המפקדים קרי: (יד) כלי זהב וכלי כסף. שניהם בחירק ובמסורה גדולה נמנו עם ז' מטעין דסבירין בלירי:

רלב"ג

בלתי נחלבים: (יד) אך לא יעשה בית ה' ספות כסף. הם כלים לקבל הדם או יין הנסכים ומה שידמה להם: מזמרות. הם כלי זמר: מזרקות. (בליג"ש בלע"ז): חצוצרות. הם היו נעשות לתקוע על המזבחות כמו שזכרה התורה ואמר שלא יעשה מזה הכסף אלו הכלים וזולתם אבל יתנוהו לעושי המלאכה לחזק את בית ה' ואולם התבאר בספר ד"ה שאחר שהזקו את בית ה' אם הותיר היו עושין מהנשאר כלי שרת ולא היו מסכימין לעשות מהכסף כלי שרת אם לא נשאר אחר חזוק הבית: (טז) ולא יחשבו את האנשים. ר"ל שהאנשים הנותנים הכסף לעושי המלאכה לא יחשבו עמהם אם נתנוהו כולו לעושי מלאכה אם לא כי בודאי באמונה הם עושים כי הקדש מבדל בדילי אינשי מיניה: (יז) כסף אשם וכסף חטאות. ר"ל שהאנשים המפרישים מעות לאשם או לחטאת והותירו הנה המותר

מצודת ציון

(יד) ספות. שם כלים עשוים כצורת כדים כי ת"י קולין וכן וכדה על שכמה (בראשית כד) ת"א וקולתה: מזמרות. כלי זמר: מזרקות. ספלים לזרוק מהם דם הקרבנות:

מצודת דוד

(יד) אך לא יעשה וגו'. מהכסף הזה לא עשו לצורך בית ה' ספות כסף וגו' ובד"ה נאמר שגם הכלים נעשו מן הכסף המובא ואמרו רז"ל בתחילת הבנין לא עשו כלי שרת ואחר שהשלימו יהי' מותר עשו כלי שרת: (טז) ולא יחשבו. לא עשו חשבון עם האנשים אשר נתנו להם הכסף לשהם יתנו לעושי המלאכה הבונים והגודרים וכו': כי באמונה. ידוע היה שעושים באמונה ולכך נבחרו אלו מתחילה: (יז) כסף אשם וגו'. מי שהיה מפריש ממון לאשמו או לחטאתו וקנה הקרבן והותיר מן הממון הנה המותר הזה לא בא

goes primarily for the communal sacrifices. The remainder is used for repairs. The money mentioned in Chronicles, however, is the shekel collection of the past years. That goes primarily for repairs. The remainder thereof is used for purchasing vessels to minister to the sacrificial service.

silver pitchers—vessels used to receive the blood of sacrifices or the wine for libations [*Ralbag*].

14. However, there would not be made for the house of the Lord, silver pitchers, musical instruments, basins, trumpets, or any golden or silver utensils, from the money brought into the house of the Lord. 15. But they would give it to the foremen over the work, and they would repair therewith the house of the Lord. 16. And they would not reckon with the men into whose hand they would give the money to give the foremen over the work, for they did [the work] honestly. 17. The money for guilt-offerings and the money for sin-offerings would not be

brought

12. **And they would give the counted money**—*They would give that counted money. After they would take it out of the chest and weigh it, they would give it into the hands of the treasurers who were in charge of the performers of the work* [*Rashi*].

the counted—Heb. הַמְּתֻכָּן, *an expression of a number, like* "(Ex. 5:18) *and the number* (וְתֹכֶן) *of bricks you shall give.*" [*Rashi*].

who were appointed—Heb. הַמֻּפְקָדִים. [*Rashi*].

This root sometimes is used in the sense of counting. Therefore, *Rashi* clarifies that here it means "appointed."

and they spent it—lit. and they took it out. *An expression of expenditure to hire carpenters* [*Rashi*].

and for the builders—*They are the architects, the stonesmiths whose colleagues would work under their orders, the supervisors of the crafts* [*Rashi*].

Others explain *the woodcutters and the builders.* The woodcutters would chop down the trees, and the builders would build the hewn wood into the building [*Redak*].

13. **And for the masons**—*for the builders of the wall, the apprentices of the architects* [*Rashi, Redak*].

and for the stonecutters—*from the mountain* [*Rashi*].

and to buy—I.e. in addition to hiring stonecutters to quarry the stones from the mountain, and woodcutters to hew the trees in the Lebanon, they purchased hewn stone and lumber from others [*Redak*].

14. **However, they would not make . . . any golden or silver utensils**—In order to reconcile this verse with II Chron. 24:14, which states that they made vessels to minister, the Rabbis conclude that the money was primarily earmarked for repairs. If, after making all necessary repairs, however, there was money left over, it could be used for making utensils to be used in the Temple [*Redak* from Ketuboth 106b].

Malbim maintains that the money mentioned here was the shekel collection of the current year, which

בֵּית יְהוָה לַכֹּהֲנִים יִהְיוּ׃ יח אָז יַעֲלֶה חֲזָאֵל מֶלֶךְ אֲרָם וַיִּלָּחֶם עַל־גַּת וַיִּלְכְּדָהּ וַיָּשֶׂם חֲזָאֵל פָּנָיו לַעֲלוֹת עַל־יְרוּשָׁלִָם׃

מִקְדְּשָׁא דַיְיָ לְכַהֲנַיָא יָהֲבִין לֵיהּ׃ יח בְּכֵן סְלִיק חֲזָאֵל מַלְכָּא דַאֲרָם וַאֲגִיחַ קְרָבָא עַל גַּת וּכְבָשַׁהּ וְשַׁוִי חֲזָאֵל אַפּוֹהִי לְמִיסַק לִירוּשְׁלֵם׃

רש"י

ולאשמו ולקח את הבהמה ונותר מן המעות: לא יובא בית ה'. לבדק הבית: לכהנים יהיו. והם לוקחים מהם עולות קיץ למזבח הבשר לעולה והעורות שלהם כך שנינו בתמורה זה מדרש דרש יהוידע הכהן כל הבא ממותר חטאת וממותר אשם ילקח בהן עולות: (יח) אז יעלה חזאל.

רד"ק

המפריש מעות לחטאתו או לאשמו ולקח הבהמה לחטאת או לאשם והותיר מן המעות המותר לא יובא בית ה' לבדק הבית אלא לכהנים יהיו אותו הכסף והם לוקחין מהם עולות לקיץ המזבח אמרו זה מדרש דרש יהוידע הכהן אשם הוא לה' אשם הוא לכהן להביא כל דבר הבא ממותר חטאת ואשם ילקח בדמיו עולות הבשר לה' ועורות לכהנים: (יח) אז יעלה חזאל. בדברי הימים כתיב כי אחרי מות יהוידע עשה יהואש הרע בעיני ה' וגם הרגו זכריה בנו במצות המלך לפי שהיה מוכיחם ולתקופת השנה עלה עליו חיל ארם וגו' ושתי מלחמות היו וזו המלחמה שאמר הנה היתה ראשונה ובאמרו אז יעלה חזאל פירוש כשעשה הרע בעיני ה' אחרי מות יהוידע והביא עליהם האל מלך ארם ונלחם על גת ולכדה והיא היתה למלכי יהודה כי דוד לקחה מיד פלשתים: וישם חזאל פניו לעלות לירושלם. ולא עלה כי יהואש לקח קדשי בית ה' הכסף והזהב הנמצא באוצרות בית ה' ואע"פ שאמר כל הזהב לא ר"ל כלי אלא רובו שהרי בימי אמציה בנו לקח יהואש מלך ישראל הכסף והזהב הנמצאים בבית ה' ובאוצרות המלך אלא הרוב לקח ושלח

רלב"ג

לא יביאו בית ה' לחזק הבית אך יהיה לכהנים והנה היה הדין שיקנו מהם חטאות או אשמות וימסרו לצרכי חטאת ואשם אך תקנו חכמים שיהיה המותר לעולת הבשר לה' והעור לכהנים: (יח) אז יעלה חזאל מלך ארם. הנה זאת המלחמה היא זולת המלחמה הנזכרת בספר ד"ה כי בזאת המלחמה לא עלה לירושלם ובמלחמה הנזכרת שם בא אל יהודה וירושלם וידמה שבתחלת הענין כשעשה יואש הרע בעיני ה' אחרי מות יהוידע הכהן היתה זאת המלחמה והמלחמה הנזכרת בספר ד"ה היתה לתקופת השנה אחר שהרג זכריה בן יהוידע ואמר שם כי אז עזבוהו חיל ארם במחלוים גדולים ואז התקשרו עליו עבדיו והכוהו על מטתו ומת והנה זכר באה המקום שבכר היה אז יואש בעיר שמה בית מלוא ולפי שהיה שם בית מלוא אחר זולת זה זכר בזה היה יורד אל סלא והנה היה שם מושכב על מטתו מפני המכות שהכוהו חיל ארם וזכר שכבר קברו אותו עם אבותיו בעיר דוד וזה ממה שלמדנו ממנו שלא קברוהו עם אבותיו בקברות המלכים וכן באר זה בדברי הימים וזכר שכבר מלך אמציה בנו תחתיו הנה זה באור מה שראינו לבארו בזאת הפרשה שהגבלנו באורה בזה המקום: ואולם התועלות המגיעות ממנה: הא' והוא כולל הרבה מדברי אלו הספורים הוא להודיע כי ההליכה בדרכי ה' ימשכו הטובות וההפך למי שסר מאחרי השם יתברך ולזה ספר כי יהושפט עשה הישר בעיני ה' ובער יתר הקדש אשר נשאר בימי אסא אביו ונמשכו לו מההשגחות והטובות והוא שלא מרדו בו האדומיים ומרדו תכף אחרי מותו ומה שקרה לו מהפחד והרע היה בהתחברו לרשע מלך הרשע ולזה היו עליו אימות מות במלחמת רמות גלעד ונשברו אניות בהתחברו עם מלך ישראל והתחתנו בו ולזאת הפנה גם כן ספר שאחזיהו בן אחאב מפני הפליגו לעשות הרע בעיני ה' ככל חטא אחאב פשע מואב בו אחרי מות אחאב ונפל בעד השבכה בעלייתו אשר בשומרון וחלה מפני זה חליו אשר מת בו מפני שהיה דורש בבעל זבוב אלהי עקרון היחיה מחלי זה והלך בלא המדה כי לא נשאר לו בן שימלוך תחתיו ולזה גם כן סיפר מהנערים הקטני' שהיו מחרפים הנביא שכבר נענשו על זה כשיצאו שני דובים מן היער ובקעו מהם ארבעים ושנים ולזה גם כן תמצא כי יהורם בן אחאב לא הפליג ברע כמו שהפליגו בו אביו ואמו והסיר את מצבת הבעל ואף על פי שדבק בחטאת ירבעם הנה מפני מה שמיעט מן הרע נתן השם יתברך שכרו שהאריך לו זמן הפורעניות עד שתים עשרה שנה ולא תמצא כן בבית ירבעם ובבית בעשא גם הצליח במלחמת מואב ושמרו השם יתברך מיד ארם במקומות אשר נחבאו שם לתפשו והיה זה פעמים רבות על יד נביאי השם יתברך ולזה ספר גם כן בגחזי כי בעבור שחלל כבוד השם יתברך לקחת כסף על המופת אשר עשה לנעמן ובעבור שלא הודה הענין לאלישע הנה נענש בהדבקם בו צרעת נעמן ובזרעו לעולם ולקיים זאת הפנה שזכרנו ספר גם כן

מצודת דוד

לבדק הבית כ"א לכהנים יהיו לקחת מהם עולות והיה הבשר כליל והעורות לכהנים כן דרז"ל: (יח) אז. בימי יהואש עלה חזאל וגו':

to the house of the Lord; they would go to the priests. 18. Then Hazael the king of Aram went up and fought with Gath and captured it; and Hazael set his face to ascend upon Jerusalem.

It is not clear how *Ralbag* accounts for pitchers and basins, since both were used for receiving the blood for sprinkling.

silver pitchers, musical instruments—[*Rashi, Ralbag, Mezudath Zion*].

According to *Rashi* (I Kings 7:50) and R. Joseph Kara here, *sippoth,* too, represent a type of musical instruments.

basins—for collecting the blood of sacrifices and sprinkling it on the altar [*Mezudath Zion*].

trumpets—to sound during the sacrificial service, as delineated in Num. 10:10 [*Ralbag*].

16. **And they would not reckon with the men**—*The supervisors would not make a reckoning with the men, the treasurers into whose hand the supervisors would always give the money to give it to the foremen over the work, since they were not suspicious in their eyes, for they did the work honestly* [*Rashi*].

From here we deduce that no account must be given by officers appointed to collect and distribute charity, because when these officers are appointed, great care is taken to appoint honest men in this capacity [*Redak* from *Baba Bathra* 9a].

Although there is no conclusive proof from our text, since these officers were known for their superior piety and honesty, there is, nonetheless, Biblical support for this practice [*Tos.* ad loc].

for they did [the work] honestly—*They were known to be honest men* [*Rashi*].

Therefore, they were chosen to start with [*Mezudath David*].

17. **The money for guilt-offerings and the money for sin-offerings**—*If one set aside money for his sin-offering or for his guilt-offering, and purchased an animal, and there remained of the money* [*Rashi*].

would not be brought to the house of the Lord—*to repair the damage of the Temple* [*Rashi*].

they would go to the priests—*who would in turn purchase therefrom burnt-offerings, "fruit" for the altar; the flesh was for a burnt-offering and the hides were theirs. Thus we learned in Temurah* (23b). *This interpretation Jehoiada the priest expounded on. Everything that comes from the remainder of a guilt-offering shall be used to purchase burnt-offerings* [*Rashi, Redak, Mezudath David*].

Jehoiada the priest expounded on the verse in Lev. 5:19. "It is a guilt-offering; he was guilty to the Lord." First Scripture states that the entire sum devoted for the guilt-offering must be used for a guilt-offering. The conclusion of the verse implies that the sacrifice must go entirely to the Lord; i.e. it must be burnt completely on the altar, unlike a guilt-

חוזק הרעב שהיה בימי יהורם עד שאכלו בשר בניהם ועם כל זה לא שב מחטאת ירבעם אשר דבק בהם אבל היה מפליג יותר ברע שהיה מגזם להמית נביא ה' על דבר זה הרעב ולזה גם כן ספר המשח חזאל למלך על ארם אשר היה לקוץ מכאיב לישראל בעבור מהרס את ברית הש"י כמו שאמר הש"י לאליהו וספר עם זה שכבר הודיע לו אלישע הרע שיעשה לישראל כי זה ממה שיישירו יותר לעשות להם אלו הרעות ולזאת הסבה גם כן ספר שיהורם בן יהושפט הלך בדרך בית אחאב ולזה נמשך לו מהרע שמרדו אדום בו ומרדה עיר לבנה וזכר בדברי הימים שכבר נהרגו בניו על יד הערבים לא נשאר לו זולת אחזיהו בנו הקטן וזה היה גמולו הראוי לו על המתתו אחיו כמו שנזכר שם ובסוף הענין נגפו ה' במעיו עד יצאו מעיו עם חליו וספר גם כן שאחזיהו בנו הלך בדרך בית אחאב ולזה נהרג עם בית אחאב ולא מלך כי אם כמו שנה ולזאת הסבה זכר איך סבב הש"י אשר לו נתכנו עלילות שיבא לבית אחאב ולאיזבל כדבר ה' אשר דבר על דבר חטאתיהם אשר הפליגו בהם. והנה סבב הש"י שנלחם יורם עם חזאל ברמות גלעד והכוהו ארמים והלך מפני זה להתרפאות ביזרעאל ואנשי החיל נשארו ברמות גלעד לשמור העיר מפני חיל הארמים והיה זה סבה אל שיתכן יותר שימשח הנביא את יהוא על ישראל ושיתקשר יהוא כנגד המלך וסבב הש"י כשראה הצופה שפעת יהוא שלח שם המלך רכב אחד וכן שני וכן שלישי עד שיהיה זה סבה אל שיצאו יהורם ואחזיהו לקראת יהוא ומצאוהו אצל חלקת נבות ומת שם יהורם כדבר ה' גם הרג אחזיהו ובני אחיו שהיו ארבעים ושנים והיה זה סבה אל שיראו ממנו הזקנים והאומנים את בני המלך אשר בשמרון ושלחו לו ראשי בני אדוניהם בדודים גם נהרגה איזבל ואכלו הכלבים את בשרה בחלק יזרעאל עד שכבר השמיד יהוא כל בית אחאב וכל גדוליו ומיודעיו וכהניו עד בלי השאיר לו שריד ואחרי כן השמיד כל נביאי הבעל וכל עובדיו וכל כהניו ולזה גם כן ספר שעתליה הרגה כל זרע המלוכה כי מבית אחאב היו וגם היא נהרגה בסוף באמצעות הסבות הראויות על ידי יהוידע ולזאת הסבה גם כן ספר כי מפני שעשה יהוא רצון הש"י באחאב נתן הש"י שכרו שיהיו לו בנים רבעים על כסא ישראל ולזאת הסבה זכר כי מפני שלא שמר יהוא ללכת בתורת ה' אלהי ישראל והלך בדרך ירבעם הנה התחיל הש"י אז להכרית את ישראל על יד חזאל ולזה גם כן תמצא כי יואש בכל עת שהלך אחר הש"י כמו שהורהו יהוידע הכהן לא קרה לו רק טוב ואחר שעשה הרע בעיני ה' הגיע לו מן הרעות הרבה ולעמו עד שכבר השאירוהו ארמים בתחלואים רבים וקשרו עליו עבדיו והרגוהו: הב' והוא במדות והוא להודיע שראוי לכל אדם לברוח מחברת רשעים ולזה ספר שלא הסכים יהושפט שילכו עבדי אחזיהו עם עבדיו באניות כי כבר קרה לו מחברתו נזק כמו שאמר הנביא ליהושפט לפי מה שנזכר בד"ה: השלישי הוא להודיע איך היה חומל הש"י על ישראל מפני השגחתו על האבות ולזה תמצא שכאשר ראה הש"י עוצם סור ישראל מעליו עד שכבר היו דורשים מאלהי העמים אשר המה הבל ידיעת הדברים העתידים ועזבו את ה' ונביאיו לזה ראה הש"י שיצא אליהו להגיד למלאכי מלך שמרון כי בעבור שדרש בבעל זבוב אלהי עקרון היחיה מחליו ועזב נביאי ה' הנה לא ירד מהמטה אשר עלה שם כי מות ימות ולזאת הסבה גם כן סבב שיראו ישראל את ה' במה שאמר אליהו לשר החמשים וחמשיו כשחשב לתפשו בכח למיעוט האמנתו בש"י ובנביאים אם איש אלהים אני תרד אש מן השמים ותאכל אותך ואת חמשיך והיה לו כן ונשאר החמשי' השני עד שבא השלישי והכיר לנביא מעלתו והתחנן לו שתיקר נפשו ונפש עבדיו אלה בעיניו לפי שכבר הגיע מזה זה התועלת אשר היה ראוי שיהי' זה כלי אל שישובו ישראל לטוב הנה תמצא ביהורם בן אחאב שעשה זה הענין בו רושם עד שמיעט הרבה מהחטאים שהיה חוטא בהם אחאב: הד' הוא להודיע שראוי לכל אדם שיהיה מפחד ממה שראוי שיפחד ממנו ולא יסמוך על הנס הלא תראה כי גם הנביא אליהו עם עוצם מעלתו בחדוש המופתים היה ירא מלבוא למלך אחזיהו ליעד לו זה היעוד הרע עד שהבטיחו הש"י שלא יירא מפניו: הה' הוא להודיע עוצם מעלת אליהו והפלא שהיה בענינו והוא שכבר העלה אותו הש"י בסערה גבוה מאד שנעלם מכל אדם והסתירהו הש"י מבני אדם עד עת קץ כי לו נגזר ארך חיים נפלא על דרך המופת והראיה שלא מת בהעלותו הסערה השמים אחר זה בא מכתב אליהו ליורם בן יהושפט אשר הורה בלי ספק היותו אז חי כמו שבארנו כמה שקדם: הו' הוא להודיע כי לא יעשה ה' דבר כי אם גלה סודו אל עבדיו הנביאים ולזה תמצא שהדברים העתידים יודעו לנביאים קודם חדושם ואע"פ שיהיה חדושם על דרך המופת הלא תראה כי הלקח אליהו מעל ראש אלישע ביום ההוא היה ידוע לבני הנביאים אשר בבית אל וביריחו ואלישע אע"פ שהיה חדושו על דרך המופת וכן גם כן תמצא שהודיע הש"י לאברהם את דבר המופתים אשר יעשה בהוציאו זרעו מעבודתם ולזה אמר וגם את הגוי אשר יעבודו דן אנכי כי אלו המופתים היו כלי אל שיאמין אברהם בירושת הארץ כמו שבארנו שם: הז' הוא במדות והוא להודיע שאין ראוי להקדים לאדם הידיעה בדבר מצער טרם הגיעו כי די לו בצער שיקרה לו ממנו בהגיעו לא שיקדים להצטער קודם זה אלא אם יגיע מההודעה תועלת מה ולזה תמצא כי מפני שלא היה מצער אליהו שיגיע תועלת לאלישע מהודעתו אותו כי ה' לוקח אותו מעמו היה מעלים ממנו זה לצערו שכבר יצטער מאד אלישע מזה וכאשר ראה שהגיע העת שלא יוכל להעלים הענין ממנו מפני עוצם דבקות אלישע בחברתו עד שלא רצה להפרד ממנו כלל רצה לתת לו מה שישאל כדי שיסור צערו בהפרדו ממנו לפי מה שאפשר והנה נתן לו הנביא שאלתו על דרך המופת כשבקש מהש"י שיהיה לאלישע כן והוא שיהיה לו ברוחו פי שנים על כל בני הנביאים אשר למדו לפניו והנה מה שנתן לו האות בזה שאם יראה אותו לוקח מאתו יהי לו כן אינו שיהיה זה הענין סבה אל היות נאצל מן הרוח אשר עליו לאלישע זה השיעור הנפלא אבל היה זה אות לו בהגיעו שכבר נתנו לו המתנה ששאל מאליהו וזה ממה שראוי שישמח בו אחר הפרד אליהו ממנו ואחשוב כי אליהו היה יודע שלא יעזוב אלישע חברתו אבל עשה זה לנסות לבבו אם רב חשקו כל כך בהשגת השלמות שלא יתרצה בשום ענין להניח אליהו וכזה תמצא שעשה אליהו לאלישע בתחלה כשהשליך אדרתו עליו והיה אלישע רוצה לידבק בו תכף הנה אמר לו אליהו לבחון ענינו לך שוב כי מה עשיתי לך ומפני ראותו רב חשקו בחברת אליהו נודע לו שכבר השיג מחכמתו יותר הרבה ממה שהשיגו ממנה שאר תלמידיו: הח' הוא במדות והוא להודיע שראוי לאדם שיחשק מאד בחברת הטובים הלא תראה המעלה שזכה בה אלישע מפני חשקו בחברת אליהו זה' החשק הנפלא עד שלא רצה להפרד ממנו כלל עד שלקחו ה' מאתו: התשיעי הוא להודיע ענין הנפלאות העצומות שבאו בזה הספור כי באמונת הנפלאו' יתקיימו הפנות התוריות ולזה ספר שכבר הכה אליהו באדרתו מי הירדן ונחלו הנה והנה ושכבר עשה זה גם כן אלישע ולזה גם כן ספר שכבר רפא אלישע מי יריחו שהיו רעים וממיתים בשבם במקום המוצא מעט מלח אשר לא היה בטבע המלח שיתקן המים אבל הוא מקלקל אותם ולזה ג"כ ספר שתכף שקלל אלישע הנערים הקטנים שחרפו אותו יצאו שתי דובים מן היער ובקעו מהנערים ההם ארבעים ושנים וזה עשאו אלישע לתועלת שיכירו ישראל זה וישובו אל ה' כי רובם היו עובדים ע"ג בזמנו ולזאת הסבה גם כן ספר המופת שעשה אלישע כשלא היה מים לשלש' המלכים והיו יראי' שימותו בצמא ובאו להם המים על דרך המופת שעשה אלישע שבאו מים נמלא מהם הנחל ההוא מזולת שיראו רוח ידחם שם ולא גשם יתחדשו ממנו כמו שיעד להם והיה מעלם המופת בזה שהיה כלי להפיל מלך מואב ביד המלכים ההם בזה האופן הנפלא שזכר וזה שהם ראו מנגד את המים אדומים כדם וחשבו שהחרב נחרבו המלכים ויצאו כדמות אנשים הולכים לקחת שלל והיה זה סבה אל שנעשה למואב כל הרע הנפלא שיעד אלישע ולזה ג"כ זכר מופת השמן שלא היה שם אלישע אבל כל עוד שהיתה האשה מוצקת היה מתחדש על דרך מופת שמן באסוך ההוא עד שמלאת כל הכלים שיכלה לקבץ אליה ולזה ג"כ זכר המופת שעשה לשונמית שלא היה לה בן והיה אישה זקן והיה מפני זה יותר רחוק שתתעבר והנה אלישע כשידע יעד אותה בזה הטוב שבעת חיה היא חובקת בן על צד השכ' הגמול לה על הטוב שהטיבה לו והיה לה בן ולזה ספר שהוא החיה בנה אחר שמת ולזה גם כן ספר שהסיר שהיה בו מות מפני פקועות השדה ששמו בו הנה עשה אלישע על דרך המופת שהסיר הרע ממנו בהשליכו קמח אל הסיר אשר אין לו רושם בהסרת זה הרוע ולזה ספר שהלחם שהיה מעט מאד לתת לפני מאה איש אכלו ושבעו ממנו והותירו כמו שייעד אלישע להם ולזה ספר מה שרפא לצרעת נעמן כשאמר לו שירחץ במי הירדן שבע פעמים ותשוב בשרו אליו ויטהר והיה לו כן ולזאת הסבה גם כן ספר שדבקה צרעת נעמן בגחזי ובבניו תכף שקללהו הנביא בזאת הקללה ולזה גם כן ספר שהברזל שנפל מן העץ תוך הירדן הנה חתך אלישע עץ בצורת יד הגרזן במקום שנכנס שם ותכף שהשליך אלישע העץ אל המים נכנס על דרך המופת בנקב הברזל והציף הברזל על המים ולזה גם כן ספר מה שהראה אלישע לנערו סוסי אש ורכב אש ומה שהכה בסנורים על דרך המופת הגוי כלו הבא אליו עד שהוליכם תוך שומרון והם לא הרגישו ולזה ג"כ ספר מה שהשמיע הש"י את מחנה ארם על דרך המופת קול רכב קול סוס קול חיל כבד בדרך שנסו כלם ברגליהם ועזבו כל המחנה כאשר היא והיה זה סבה שיהיה סאה סולת בשקל וסאתים שעורים בשקל בשער שומרון בעת שייעד להם אלישע ונתקיים גם כן מה שאמר לשליש אשר המלך נשען על ידו שכבר יראה בעיניו ומשם לא יאכל: הי' הוא להודיע שאין תלמידי חכמים הולכים בלא דברי תורה וחכמה ולזה אמר ויהי הם הולכים הלוך ודבר כי בוודאי לא היו דבריהם דבר הבאי אבל מרוב תשוקת אלישע ללמוד מאליהו היו מדברים בסודות התורה והחכמה והנבואה: הי"א הוא להודיע כי חייב אדם לקרוע על רבו כשמת הלא תראה כי אלישע קרע בגדיו בהלקח אליהו מאתו ואע"פ שלא מת כי היה ענינו לו כאילו מת שלא יוכל להשיג ממנו אחר זה שום דבר חכמה: הי"ב הוא להודיע שהקורע בגדיו על אבל רבו אינו מאחה לעולם שנא' ויחזק בבגדיו ויקרעם לשנים קרעים ולא היה צריך לומר לשנים קרעים אחר שאמר ויקרעם כי לכל הפחות יהיו שנים קרעים אך הרצון בו שתמיד הם נראים שנים קרעים: הי"ג הוא להודיע שהוא ראוי שלא לומר את שאינו נשמע ולזה תמצא כי בני הנביאים כאשר שאלו את אלישע אם ישלחו חמשים איש בני חיל לבקש את אליהו איפה נשאו רוח ה' היה המענה ממנו שלא ישלחו וכאשר הפצירו בו מאד והכיר שאין דעתם להמנע מזה לא רצה לחלוק על כוונתם ואמר להם שישלחו בצור' שהיו יכולים להכיר ממנו שאין דעתו שישלחו והיה להם בה התגלות ג"כ שלא עשו כנגד מצות

offering, whose flesh is consumed by the priests. Jehoiada reconciled this discrepancy by promulgating the following rule: All that remains after purchasing a guilt-offering or a sin-offering, must be used to purchase burnt-offerings. Thus, the flesh will go entirely on the altar to be burnt as an offering to the Lord, and the hide will be given to the priests, creating a similarity to the guilt-offering of which the priests partake. Our verse testifies to Jehoiada's oral interpretation, by stating that the money for a guilt-offering or for a sin-offering should go to the priests. Now, if the money was devoted for a sacrifice, how can it go to the priests? Rather, the verse alludes to the remainder of the money, which was used to purchase burnt-offerings of which the priests would receive the hides.

These offerings were brought when the altar was unemployed, when no one was bringing sacrifices. They were known as the "fruit" of the altar. They were compared to sweet fruit served as a dessert after the meal has been finished. See *Korban Haedah, Shekalim* 6:4. For laws of guilt-offerings and sin-offerings, see Lev. 4, 5, 7:1–10.

18. **Then Hazael the king of Aram went up**—*after the death of Jehoiada, when Joash made himself for a god* [*Rashi*].

See above 12:1, Commentary Digest.

and fought with Gath—a Philistine city that had been captured by King David. Since then it had been under Judean rule [*Redak, Abarbanel*].

and Hazael set his face to ascend upon Jerusalem—I.e. he planned to march on Jerusalem, but was bribed by Joash and turned back, abandoning his plans of attack. The Chronicler tells a different version of the war. He tells us that Hazael did indeed attack Jerusalem, killed its officers, and plundered the city. The commentaries reconcile this discrepancy by establishing the fact that there were two wars. The first war took place soon after Jehoiada's demise. When Joash heeded the princes and made himself a god, the Almighty became angered with Judah, as the Chronicler informs us. At that time, Hazael attacked Gath, but was deterred from attacking Jerusalem. Then God sent prophets to admonish the people to repent. One of these prophets was Zechariah the son of Jehoiada, who proclaimed, "So has God said, 'Why do you transgress the commandments of the Lord? You will not succeed, for you have forsaken the Lord, and He has forsaken you!'" For his unfavorable prophecy, the king ordered him stoned. At the time of his death, he said, "The Lord shall see and demand it!" A year later, Hazael again marched on Judah. This time, the Lord delivered the great Judean army into the hands of Hazael's small forces. It was this time that Judah was sorely defeated. Joash was deserted by his soldiers, severely wounded and suffering from acute illnesses. Then he was assassinated by his two servants, as below. Hence the war mentioned in Kings was the first war, and the war

יט וַיִּקַּח יְהוֹאָשׁ מֶלֶךְ־יְהוּדָה אֵת כָּל־הַקֳּדָשִׁים אֲשֶׁר־הִקְדִּישׁוּ יְהוֹשָׁפָט וִיהוֹרָם וַאֲחַזְיָהוּ אֲבֹתָיו מַלְכֵי יְהוּדָה

יט ונסב יהואש מלך שבטא דבית יהודה ית כל קודשיא די אקדישו יהושפט ויהורם ואחזיהו אבהתוהי מלכיא דבית יהודה

רלב"ג

הנביא ולזה אמר להם בסוף הלא אמרתי לכם אל תלכו: הי"ד הוא במדות והוא להודיע שאין ראוי לבזות החכמים והשלמים הלא תראה מה שקרה להנערים שבזו את אלישע במתו מהם הדבעים ובנים: הט"ו הוא במדות והוא להודיע שראוי לכל אדם שיתדבק לחכמים וישרתם כי בשירות אותם ילמד הרבה מחכמת' מפני היותו תמיד אצלם ישמעו כל דבריהם ולזה ספר כי כאשר שאל יהושפט היש פה נביא לה' ענוהו פה אלישע בן שפט אשר יצק מים על ידי אליהו ללמד כי מפני שירות אותו ובמגבו היה ראוי שיקלה מהשלמות אשר לאליהו הרבה ולזה ענה יהושפט ג"כ יש אותו דבר ה': הט"ז הוא להודיע עולם תשוקת הנביאים להוכיח כראוי עד שכבר תמצא שאע"פ שהלך מן הכבוד הרבה מלך ישראל לאלישע עד שכבר ירדו אליו מלך ישראל ויהושפט ומלך אדום ולא הסכימו שבאו לקרוא לו הנה עם כל זה ענהו הנביא קשה ויאמר לו שילך אל נביאי הבעל והאשרה ולא ישאל ממנו דבר אשר שכבר סר מאחרי ה' ללכת בחטאת ירבעם וכל זה היה מהנביא להועיל ליהורם שהם ישוב אל ה' אולי ינחם ה' על הרעה אשר דבר לעשות לו וכאשר ראה שלא היה אז עת תוכחת כי הם בסכנה עצומה הראה לו שהוא מואס אותו מפני רוע מעשיו ואמר כי לולא פני יהושפט הוא נושא לא יביט אליו ולא יראנו אך לכבוד יהושפט שעשה הישר בעיני ה' ישבה שאלתו וזה כלו להועיל ליהורם כמו שזכרנו: הי"ז הוא במדות והוא להודיע שהוא ראוי לכל שלם שימאס הרעים ויסור מחברתם ומהבטת ראיית פניהם פן ימשכוהו לרוע דרכיהם ולזה אמר לולי פני יהושפט אני נושא אם אביט אליך ואם אראך: הי"ח הוא במדות והוא להודיע שראוי להרחיק מדת הכעס כי הכעס מכבה אור השכל הלא תראה כי מפני כעס אלישע על מלך ישראל לא שרתה עליו שכינה עד שהסיר הכעס בנגון המנגן לפניו: הי"ט הוא להודיע כי הנביאים אף על פי שהם שליטים בעשיית הש"י המופתים על ידם לא ישתדלו להטיב בזה האופן כי אם למודים ולזה תמצא שהאשה שלעקה לפניו כי הנושה בא לקחת את שני ילדיה לו לעבדים אמרה לו שכבר ידע כי אבי הילדים היה ירא את ה' כי אם היה מאשר כרו מאחרי ה' לא היה מתעורר אלישע להיטיב לה בזה האופן הנפלא: הכ' הוא במדות והוא להודיע במדות הנדיבות מבוכחת הלא תראה מה שקרה לשונמית מפני נדיבותיה שהחזיקה באלישע לאכל לחם ושאלה ממנו שיסור שמה תמיד מדי עברו ואחר שנתבאר לה שהוא איש האלהים קדוש הלקה לו מהכבוד יותר כראוי לו כי זה היה סבה אל שיהיה לה בן והחיהו אלישע ובלא ימיתו ברעב כי הודיע לה שכבר קרא הש"י אל הרעב וגם בא אל הארץ שבע שנים ולזה נתן לה עלה שתלך לגור באשר יאות לה לגור שם עד עבור הרעב: הכ"א הוא להודיע שראוי למקבל שישתדל לשלם גמול ראוי למטיב ולזה תמצא בספר שכבר חקר אלישע מה לעשות לשונמית מן הטוב' על מה שהטיבה לו ולגלותו להשיב לה גמול גדול שאל מה לעשות לה והשתדל על כל פנים לעשות לה דבר גדול יהיה לה גמול גדול וראוי על הטוב שהטיבה לו: הכ"ב הוא להודיע שאין ראוי לשלם לדבר עם האשה אם לא יביאוהו לזה הכרח אבל ראוי להתרחק ממנה לפי מה שאפשר ולזה ספר שכאשר רצה אלישע לדעת אי זה גמול יתכן לו להשיב לה לא דבר אליה הוא בעצמו אבל אמר לגחזי שיקרא לה והוא יאמר אליה אלה הדברים עד אשר ראה אלישע שלא היה לו דרך להשיב לה גמול אם לא בדרך המופת אז קרא לה ועמדה בפתח כדי שתשמע ייעוד הנביא מפי הנביא: הכ"ג הוא להודיע שאין התכלית בבני' שישמח אדם בהם בחייו אבל הוא לקיום המין שישאר לאדם בהם זכר ולזה ספר שכבר אמרה השונמית לאלישע כשייעד לה שבעל דרך המופת תהיה חובקת בן כעת חיה שלא יכזב בה לתת לה טוב שאינו טוב כי אם לא יהיה אין לה חפץ בזה הטוב להבלות אותה ר"ל לתת לה שלוה בראותה שיש לה בן ולזה אמרה לו הלא אמרתי לא תשלה אותי: הכ"ד הוא להודיע כי המועדים והימים טובים מכוונים לעבוד בהם הש"י ולהשתדל בהשגות קנין השלמות לפי היכולת ולזה ספר שכבר אמר אישה לשונמית מדוע את הולכת אליו היום לא חדש ולא שבת למדנו בזה שבכמו אלו הימים ראוי ללכת אל החכמים ללמוד מהם: הכ"ה הוא להודיע שהצריך לדבר הצלת הנפש ראוי שיתעסק בו במהירות נפלא לפי מה שאפשר ולזה ספר דבר מהירות השונמית ללכת לאלישע וגם התנפלה לפניו והחזיקה ברגליו כדי שידרש הנביא לבקשתה לא רצתה להגיד לו בברור על מה באה לכבוד הנביא כי ידעה שהוא ידע זה בראותו אות' וגם לא הסתפקה במה שאמר הנביא לגחזי כי ירצה שמא אינו ראוי שיעשה זה על ידו ולזה נשבעה שלא תעזבהו כי רצתה לשלם לבנה ההצלה בלי שום ספק: הכ"ו הוא להודיע שאין ראוי שיפתח אדם פיו לרע הלא תראה מה שספר מהשונמית שאמרה להיטה שלום כששאל לה על מה ועל מה היא הולכת ולזה אמרה לגחזי: הכ"ז הוא להודיע שראוי לנביאים לפרסם עולם גבורת הש"י לגויי הארצות לעשות להם מופת אף על פי שאינם ראויים לו ולזה תמצא שכבר התעורר אלישע לרפאות נעמן מצרעתו למען ידע כי יש נביא בישראל כי בזה תועלת להיישירם לעבודת הש"י וכן מצאנו זה התועלת בברור בתפלת שלמה כמו שבארנו שם. הכ"ח היא להודיע שאין ראוי לנביא לקחת שכר על מה שיעשהו מן המופתים כי בזה יבא להאמין כי הוא הפועל בזה המופת ויסור מפני זה התועלת אשר נתחדש בעבורו והוא שיכירו מעלת הש"י וגבורתו ויבושו לאמונתו ולזה תמצא שלא רצה אלישע לקחת מנחה מנעמן אחר שרפא אותו מצרעתו וגם קלל גחזי כשקבל ממנו כסף על זה והנה תמצא כי מפני שרצה נעמן שלא רצה אלישע לקבל דבר מנעמן על זה להורות שלא היה הוא הפועל בזה אך הש"י התנדב נעמן שלא יעבוד כי אם לה': הכ"ט הוא להודיע שאין ראוי לאדם שיכפור העון אך יהיה מודה ועוזב ולזה תמצא שלא קלל אלישע גחזי בראותו אותו אע"פ שהוא יודע שעשה זה החטא אך קללו אחר שכפר עונו ולולי כפירת העון היה אפשר שיקח אלישע לתקן את אשר עיות: הל' במדות והוא להודיע שהוא ראוי שכאשר נפלו קצת אויבי האומה בידם שייטיבו להם כדי שיהיו בשלום עמהם בראותם שבעת נפלם בידם המלו עליהם והטיבו להם וכ"ש שראוי לעשות זה בהיות אויבי האומה יותר חזקים מהם: הל"א הוא להודיע שאין ראוי לאדם שיהיה מכחיש ובלתי מאמין מה שייעדו הנביאים הלא תראה מה שקרה לשליש מפני היותו מרחיק שיהיה מה שאמר אלישע לסוב למחרת ה' וס' ההוא סאה סולת בשקל וסאתים שעורים בשקל בשער שומרון והוא שכבר ראה זה בעיניו ומבש לא אכל כמו שאמר הנביא לו וזה היה עונש הראוי לו שהוא ראה אמות דברי הנבואה ההיא ולא נהנה בטוב שהגיע ממנה: הל"ב הוא במשפטים התוריים והוא להודיע שסדר בהלל חבירו שלא מדעתו אינו חייב להעלות לו שכר ולזה תמצא במה שספר שלעקה השונמית אל המלך על ביתה ועל שדה שהיו מחזיקים בהם אנשים שכבר צוה המלך להשיב לה את כל אשר לה ואת כל תבואות השדה מיום עזבה את הארץ ולא אמר להשיב לה שכירות ביתה: הל"ג הוא להודיע שאין ראוי גם לנביא לסמוך על הנס ולזה צוה אלישע לנביא שיביא חדר בחדר יהוא בן יהושפט בן נמשי למשחו למלך על ישראל כדי שלא יודע סודו פן יהרגנו מלך ישראל וכן תמצא בעשה אחיה לירבעם ושמואל הנביא לדוד ר"ל שלקחו להם דרך כדי להעלים סודם ועניינם: הל"ד הוא להודיע שאין עושין שררה בממון באחד לבד ולזה תמצא שכאשר היה הכסף בארון לחזק את בדק הבית שמוהו שם הכהנים שומרי הסף לא אחד לבד גם בהיליאם הכסף מהארון היה שם סופר המלך והכהן הגדול לא אחד לבד גם בחשם הכסף אחד זה נתנוהו על ידי עושי המלאכה

Shomer—*In* II *Chron.* (24:26) *it is written, "Shimeath the Ammonitess and Jehozabad the son of Shimrith the Moabitess." Now why did Scripture specify? To teach* us *that the Holy One, Blessed be He, requited him through people of his type. Let the ungrateful Ammonites and*

19. And Jehoash, the king of Judah, took all the hallowed things that Jehoshaphat, Jehoram, and Ahaziah, his forefathers, the kings of Judah, had hallowed

mentioned in Chronicles was the second one [*Redak*]. See II Chron. 24:15–27.

19. **and all the gold**—i.e. the great majority of the gold, for we find (below 14:14) that Joash king of Israel took the remaining gold and silver from Amaziah son of Joash king of Judah. If so, there must have been something left after sending a gift to Hazael [*Redak*].

he turned back—i.e. he was deterred from marching on Jerusalem [*Redak*].

As mentioned above, the Jews murdered Zechariah, and were again attacked by Hazael a year later [*Redak*].

20. **And the rest of the acts of Jehoash**—This alludes to all that transpired after the death of Jehoiada the priest, i.e. all the incidents related in the Book of Chronicles, how the princes bowed to Jehoash and deified him, how the people turned to idolatry, how Zechariah the prophet rebuked them and was murdered by the king's orders, and about the second war with Aram.

As discussed in the introduction, the purpose of the Book of Kings was not to relate all the incidents of every king's reign, his successes, his failures, his victories and his defeats, his good deeds and his misdeeds, but to relate the geneology of the dynasties, the years of each king's reign, in order to account for all the years until the present time. Since all these incidents were recorded in the chronicles of the kings, our author, Jeremiah, sufficed with an allusion to these events here and there. E.g. in v.3, he alludes to the fact that Jehoash did what was proper in the eyes of the Lord as long as Jehoiada the priest instructed him, but after the demise of Jehoiada he turned away from God. In v. 18, too, he alludes to Jehoash's decadence and to the ensuing wars. In later years, when these books were lost, the Chronicler recorded these events in the Book of Chronicles, complementing the Book of Kings. [*Abarbanel*]

21. **at Beth-millo**—*in that place* [*Rashi*].

Millo—*the name of a place* [*Rashi*].

Silla—*the name of a place* [*Rashi*].

Since there was another Beth-millo, the Scripture specifies that he was killed at the Beth-millo that leads down to Silla, [*Redak, Ralbag, Abarbanel*]

Beth-millo is mentioned in Judges 9:6 as a city in the vicinity of Shechem. Scripture specifies here that this Beth-millo was in the vicinity of Jerusalem. [*Malbim*]

The Chronicler tells us that Joash was assassinated in bed. First he was severely wounded in battle, and was deserted by his army. Later, he was carried on a litter. On the way to the capital, his servants assassinated him [*Redak*].

22. **And Jozacar the son of Shimeath and Jehozabad the son of**

ואת־קדשיו ואת כל־הזהב הנמצא באצרות בית־יהוה ובית המלך וישלח לחזאל מלך ארם ויעל מעל ירושלם: כ ויתר דברי יואש וכל־אשר עשה הלוא־הם כתובים על־ספר דברי הימים למלכי יהודה: כא ויקמו עבדיו ויקשרו־קשר ויכו את־יואש בית מלא היורד סלא: כב ויוזכר בן־שמעת ויהוזבד בן־שמר ׀ עבדיו הכהו

תרגום: יהודה וית קודשוהי וית כל דהבא דאשתכח באוצרי בית מקדשא דיי ובית גנזי מלכא ושדר לחזאל מלכא דארם ואסתלק מעל ירושלם: כ ושאר פתגמי יואש וכל דעבד הלא אינון כתיבין על ספר פתגמי יומיא למלכי דבית יהודה: כא וקמו עבדוהי ומרדו מירדא ומחו ית יואש בית מלו דנחת לסלא: כב ויוזכר בר שמעת ויהוזבד בר שמר עבדוהי מחוהי וקטלוהי וקברו

רד"ק

לחזאל: (יט) ויעל מעל ירושלם. כלומר נמנע מלעלות ירושלם ואחר כך כשהרגו זכריה שהיה מוכיחם לתקופת השנה עלה חיל ארם ויבואו אל יהודה וירושלם והשחיתו כל השרים ורבים מהעם ואת יואש עשו שפטים ועזבו אותו בתחלואים רבים ואז קשרו עליו עבדיו והרגוהו בעון שהרג זכריה כמו שאומר שם בדמי בני יהוידע: (כא) בית מלוא היורד סלא. בית מלוא שם מקום וסלא שם מקום ובאמרו היורד סלא נראה כי בית מלא אחר היה ובד"ה אמר ויהרגוהו על מטתו וכן היה כי במלחמה הוכה כמו שאומר שם ואת יואש עשו שפטים ובלכתם ממנו כי עזבו אותו בתחלואים רבים וגו' ונשאוהו במטה להוליכו לישראל ובדרך הרגוהו עבדיו על מטתו: (כב) ויוזכר. בכ"ף וברי"ש ויהוזבד בבי"ת ובדל"ת והרבה נמצא בשנוי הזה בשמות בני אדם ובדברי הימים בן שמעת העמונית ויהוזבד בן שמרית המואבית ויש בו דרש למה פירש שם אמותם ללמדך שנפרע ממנו הקב"ה ע"י אנשים כיוצא בו אמר יבואו עמונית ומואבית כפויי טובה שכפו בטובתו של אברהם אבינו שעשה ללוט שנלחם עם המלכים להצילו והם שכרו את בלעם לקלל את בניו ויפרע מיואש שכפר בטובתו של יהוידע הכהן

רש"י

אחר מות יהוידע ועשה יואש את עצמו אלוה. (כא) בית מלא. באותו המקום: מלא. שם מקום: סלא. שם מקום: (כב) ויוזכר בן שמעת ויהוזבר בן שמר. כתוב בד"ה ב' (כ"ד כ"ו) שמעת העמונית ויהוזבד בן שמרית המואבות ולמה פירשו הכתוב ללמד שנפרע ממנו הקב"ה על ידי אנשים כיוצא בו יבאו עמונים ומואבים כפויי טובה שכפו בטובתו של אברהם אבינו שעשה ללוט שנלחם עם המלכים להצילו והם שכרו את בלעם לקלל את בניו ויפרע מיואש שכפה בטובתו של יהוידע והרג את זכריהו בנו כמו שמפרש (בדברי הימים ב' כ"ד כ"ו) ומדרש זה בספרי:

מנחת שי

(כב) ויוזכר. בכ"ף וברי"ש ואין כיו"ד מלרע: ויהוזבד. בבי"ת ובדל"ת כן כתב רד"ק ואני מצאתי שניהם בבי"ת ובדל"ת בארבעה ספרים מדוייקים כתובי יד ודפוס א' ישן וכן בדברי הימים כתוב זבד בן שמעת בבי"ת ובדל"ת:

רלב"ג

והם הוציאוהו יחד לא אחד לבד: הל"ח הוא ללמד שהדברים הטלמיים בבית המקדש ראוי שיקדמו לדברים המשרתים להם לפי שהם מכוונים בעצמם וכו' היסר' לעמוד על סודות המליאות ולזה ספר שבדק הבית היה קודם עשיית הכלים המשרתים שאינם מכוונים בעצמם כמו הספות והמזמרות והמזרקים והחצוצרות ומה שידמה להם מכלי הכסף והזהב: הל"ו הוא להודיע שאין מחשבין עם הממונים על ההקדשות והדומה להם כי באמונה הם עושים להיות דבר ההקדש חמור להם ולזה אמר ולא יחשבו את האנשים אשר יתנו את הכסף על ידם לתת לעושי המלאכה כי באמונה הם עושים וכן הענין בגבאי צדקה לפי מה שאחשוב: הל"ז הוא להודיע שמותר חטאת לחטאת ומותר אשם לאשם שאם היה מותרם לאיזה דבר שילכו הבעלים לא היה לכהנים וככר אמר כסף אשם וכסף חטאת לא יובא בית ה' לכהנים יהיו ולמדנו מאמרו לכהנים יהיו שדיני אלו הכספים מתחלף

מצודת דוד

(כא) היורד סלא. העומדת בדרך היורד אל סלא:

in his burial by not interring him in the graves of the kings [*Redak*].

Although they buried him in the city of David, which is Zion, the site of the tombs of the kings, they did not bury him in the sepulcher in

and his own hallowed things, and all the gold that was found in the treasuries of the house of the Lord and the royal palace, and sent it to Hazael the king of Aram, for which he turned back from marching on Jerusalem. 20. And the rest of the acts of Joash and all that he did, are written in the book of the chronicles of the kings of Judah. 21. And his servants rose up and revolted; and they struck Joash at Bethmillo that leads down to Silla. 22. And Jozacar the son of Shimeath and Jehozabad the son of Shomer, his servants, struck him

Moabites, who ignored our father Abraham's favor, which he did for Lot, (viz. that he fought with the kings to rescue him, yet they hired Balaam to curse his descendants,) and requite Joash who ignored the favor of Jehoiada and killed Zechariah his son, as is explained in II *Chron.* (24:22). *This interpretation is in Sifrei* [*Rashi*].

This passage is not found in any edition of *Sifrei* we have today. It is found in an abridged form, however, in *Mechilta,* Ex. 17:8. *Pseudo-Rashi* on Chron. quotes *Mechilta.*

Our Sages imply that Jehoash's assassination by his servant was an example of divine retribution by the principle of מדה כנגד מדה *payment in kind,* i.e. just as Jehoash had Zechariah murdered through ungratefulness, so was he murdered through ungratefulness. If we delve into the assassanation, we find it to be a multifaceted example of payment in kind. Just as Jehoash violated the sanctity of the House of God by ordering his henchmen to murder the prophet within its confines, so did his assassins violate the sanctity of the royal quarters and entered to kill the king. Jehoash cast off the yoke of Heaven, and his assassins cast off the yoke of the kingdom. Jehoash forgot the benefits he had received from Zechariah's father, and his assassins forgot the benefits they had received from him. Jehoash disregarded Zechariah's station as prophet and priest, and his assassisns disregarded his station as a king of royal descent.

Thus, Jehoash's assassination was due to his engineering the murder of Zechariah the prophet. [*Abarbanel*]

in the city of David—The Chronicler specifies, "but they did not bury him in the graves of the kings (24:25)." The princes who had supported him and persuaded him to worship idols, were killed in the war with Hazael, as is related in Chronicles. The people realized that the death of the princes as well as that of Joash, was the result of a decree from Heaven, a punishment for idolatry and the murder of Zechariah. They, therefore, disgraced him

וַיָּמֹת וַיִּקְבְּרוּ אֹתוֹ עִם־אֲבֹתָיו בְּעִיר
דָּוִד וַיִּמְלֹךְ אֲמַצְיָה בְנוֹ תַּחְתָּיו׃
יג א בִּשְׁנַת עֶשְׂרִים וְשָׁלֹשׁ שָׁנָה לְיוֹאָשׁ
בֶּן־אֲחַזְיָהוּ מֶלֶךְ יְהוּדָה מָלַךְ יְהוֹאָחָז
בֶּן־יֵהוּא עַל־יִשְׂרָאֵל בְּשֹׁמְרוֹן שְׁבַע
עֶשְׂרֵה שָׁנָה׃ ב וַיַּעַשׂ הָרַע בְּעֵינֵי יְהוָה
וַיֵּלֶךְ אַחַר חַטֹּאת יָרָבְעָם בֶּן־נְבָט אֲשֶׁר־
הֶחֱטִיא אֶת־יִשְׂרָאֵל לֹא־סָר מִמֶּנָּה׃
ג וַיִּחַר־אַף יְהוָה בְּיִשְׂרָאֵל וַיִּתְּנֵם בְּיַד ׀
חֲזָאֵל מֶלֶךְ־אֲרָם וּבְיַד בֶּן־הֲדַד בֶּן־
חֲזָאֵל כָּל־הַיָּמִים׃ ד וַיְחַל יְהוֹאָחָז אֶת־

וּקְבָרוּ יָתֵיהּ עִם
אֲבָהָתוֹהִי בְּקַרְתָּא דְדָוִד
וּמְלַךְ אֲמַצְיָה בְּרֵיהּ
תְּחוֹתוֹהִי׃ א בִּשְׁנַת
עַסְרִין וּתְלַת שְׁנִין
לְיוֹאָשׁ בַּר אֲחַזְיָה מַלְכָּא
שִׁבְטָא דְבֵית יְהוּדָה
מְלַךְ יְהוֹאָחָז בַּר יֵהוּא
עַל יִשְׂרָאֵל בְּשֹׁמְרוֹן
שְׁבַע עַסְרֵי שְׁנִין׃
ב וַעֲבַד דְבִישׁ קֳדָם יְיָ
וַאֲזַל בָּתַר חוֹבֵי יָרָבְעָם
בַּר נְבָט דְחַיֵיב יַת
יִשְׂרָאֵל לָא סְטָא מִנְהוֹן׃
ג וּתְקֵיף רוּגְזָא דַיְיָ
בְּיִשְׂרָאֵל וּמַסְרִינוּן בְּיַד
חֲזָאֵל מַלְכָּא דַאֲרָם
וּבְיַד בַּר הֲדַד בַּר חֲזָאֵל
כָּל יוֹמַיָא׃ ד וְצַלִּי
יהואחז

רד"ק

והרג את זכריהו בנו: בעיר דוד. ובדברי הימים ולא קברוהו בקברות המלכים כי שרי יהודה שחזקו את ידו ופתו אותו לעשית הרעות שעשה מתו במלחמה כמו שאמר שם והכירו העם כי מאת ה' היה כל זה שלקח נקמה מן השרים ומן יואש על הרעות שעשי לעבוד ע"ג ולהרוג זכריה ולפיכך עשו לו העם זה הבזיון ולא נתנוהו שיקברוהו בקברות המלכים: (א) בשנת עשרים ושלש. היה לו לומר בשנת עשרים ואחת שהרי בשנת שבע ליהוא מלך יהואש וכ"ז ואחת הרי כ"ח וכ"ח שנה מלך יהוא א"כ בנו מלך בשנת כ"א ליואש מלך יהודה נאמר כי מה שאמר בשנת שבע ליהוא מלך יהואש ר"ל בתחלת

רלב"ג

ולזה לא יתערבו זה עם זה אמנם יהיה כשיהיה מותר אחם לאחם ומותר השאת לחטאת כמו שיראה חיובו מלד עלם הענין: (א) בשנת עשרים ושלש שנה ליואש עד סוף הספר. בשנת עשרים ושלש. ידוע כי בם שנים נחשב יואש ואלו השש שנים מלך יהוא קודם מלוך יואש ולזה יתבאר כי ברא"ב שנת עשרים ושלש ליואש מלך אחזיהו: (ד) ויחל יהואחז את פני ה'. אף על פי שלא היה יהואחז ראוי שתשמע תפלתו הנה שמע הש"י אליו מפני ראותו את לחץ ישראל שלחץ אותם מלך ארם כי לולא שמעו תפלתו היו כלים עשרת השבטים ותוספ' ברי' הש"י עם השבטים בעבור האבות ואולם אמרנו בריתו עם השבטים כי כבר התבאר בתורה שלא יכלה אחד מהם כמו שבארנו שם ואחשוב כי שמע הש"י תפלתו לשמור ישראל שלא יצר להם חזאל בזה האופן הנפלא שהיה משחית בהם והיה זה בחייו אך עם כל זה לחץ אותם כל ימי חייו כמו שנזכר אחר זה והקי' להם מושיע מידו אחרי מות יהואחז והוא יואש בנו כמו שנזכר אחר זה ואחר סרו מתחת יד ארם וישבו ישראל באהליהם כתמול שלשום אך לא סרו ישראל מחטאת בית ירבעם וגם הלך יהואחז וגם האשרה עמדה עדיין בשמרון שלא בער

מצודת דוד

יג (א) בשנת עשרים ושלש. כי יהואש מלך בתחלת שבע ליהוא ויהוא מת בסוף כ"ח למלכו והוא כ"ב ליהואש ובתחלת השנה הבאה מלך יהואחז א"כ היא כ"ג ליהואש: שבע עשרה שנה. ומקוטעות היו: (ג) כל הימים. כל ימי יהואחז: (ד) כי

מצודת ציון

יג (ד) ויחל. ויתפלל׳ לחץ. דחק:

and he died; and they buried him with his forefathers in the city of David; and his son Amaziah reigned in his stead.

13

1. In the twenty-third year of Joash the son of Ahaziah the king of Judah, Jehoahaz the son of Jehu reigned over Israel in Samaria seventeen years. 2. And he did what was evil in the eyes of the Lord; and he followed the sins of Jeroboam the son of Nebat which he caused Israel to sin; he did not turn away from it. 3. And the Lord became angry with Israel, and He delivered them into the hand of Hazael the king of Aram and into the hand of Ben-Hadad the son of Hazael all the days. 4. And Jehoahaz prayed.

which David and Solomon repose. That sepulcher was known as the "graves of the kings." [*Abarbanel*]

1. **In the twenty-third year**—Since Joash became king in the seventh year of Jehu's reign (12:2), and Jehu reigned altogether twenty-eight years (10:36), it follows that his son became king in the twenty-first year of Joash's reign. We are forced to say that Joash became king in the beginning of Jehu's seventh year, and Jehoahaz became king in the beginning of Joash's twenty-third year [*Redak*]. I.e. since Jehoash became king in the beginning of Jehu's seventh year, and Jehu lived until the end of his own twenty-eighth year, that would be twenty-two years for Jehoash. Jehoahaz became king at the very beginning of the next year, which was the twenty-third year of Jehoash [*Mezudath David*].

seventeen years—incomplete years [*Mezudath David*]. See below v. 10.

2. **And he did what was evil**—Since he followed in his father's footsteps, God punished him for both *his* sins and his father's. Therefore,—

3. . . . **God became angry with Israel**—[*Malbim*].

all the days—of Jehoahaz [*Mezudath David*].

Undoubtedly, God notified Israel of this decree through a prophet [*Malbim*].

4. **for He saw Israel's oppres-**

פְּנֵי יְהוָה וַיִּשְׁמַע אֵלָיו יְהוָה כִּי רָאָה
אֶת־לַחַץ יִשְׂרָאֵל כִּי־לָחַץ אֹתָם מֶלֶךְ
אֲרָם: ה וַיִּתֵּן יְהוָה לְיִשְׂרָאֵל מוֹשִׁיעַ
וַיֵּצְאוּ מִתַּחַת יַד־אֲרָם וַיֵּשְׁבוּ בְנֵי־
יִשְׂרָאֵל בְּאָהֳלֵיהֶם כִּתְמוֹל שִׁלְשׁוֹם:
ו אַךְ לֹא־סָרוּ מֵחַטֹּאת בֵּית־יָרָבְעָם
אֲשֶׁר־הֶחֱטִי אֶת־יִשְׂרָאֵל בָּהּ הָלָךְ וְגַם
הָאֲשֵׁרָה עָמְדָה בְּשֹׁמְרוֹן: ז כִּי לֹא
הִשְׁאִיר לִיהוֹאָחָז עָם כִּי אִם־חֲמִשִּׁים
פָּרָשִׁים וַעֲשָׂרָה רֶכֶב וַעֲשֶׂרֶת אֲלָפִים
רַגְלִי כִּי אִבְּדָם מֶלֶךְ אֲרָם וַיְשִׂמֵם כֶּעָפָר
לָדֻשׁ: ח וְיֶתֶר דִּבְרֵי יְהוֹאָחָז וְכָל־אֲשֶׁר
עָשָׂה וּגְבוּרָתוֹ הֲלוֹא־הֵם כְּתוּבִים עַל־

יְהוֹאָחָז קֳדָם יְיָ וְקַבֵּיל
צְלוֹתֵיהּ יְיָ אֲרֵי גְלֵי
קֳדָמוֹהִי דוּחְקָא דְיִשְׂרָאֵל
אֲרֵי דְחַק יַתְהוֹן מַלְכָּא
דַאֲרָם: ה וִיהַב יְיָ
לְיִשְׂרָאֵל פָּרִיק וּנְפַקוּ
מִתְּחוֹת יַד אֱנָשׁ אֲרָם
וִיתִיבוּ בְּנֵי יִשְׂרָאֵל
בְּקִרְוֵיהוֹן כְּמֵאתְמָלֵי
וּמִדְּקַדְמוֹהִי: ו בְּרַם לָא
סְטוֹ מֵחוֹבֵי יָרָבְעָם
דְחַיֵּיב יַת יִשְׂרָאֵל בְּהוֹן
אֲזָלוּ וְאַף אֲשֵׁירְתָא קָמַת
בְּשָׁמְרוֹן: ז אֲרֵי לָא
אַשְׁאַר לִיהוֹאָחָז עַם
אֱלָהֵין חַמְשִׁין פָּרָשִׁין
וַעֲסַר רְתִיכִין וְעַסְרָא
אַלְפִּין גְּבַר רַגְלִין אֲרֵי
אַבְדִינוּן מַלְכָּא דַאֲרָם
וְשַׁוִּינוּן כְּעַפְרָא לְדָיִשׁ:
ח וּשְׁאָר פִּתְגָמֵי יְהוֹאָחָז
וְכָל דַעֲבַד וּגְבוּרְתֵּיהּ
הֲלָא אִינּוּן כְּתִיבִין עַל
ספר

החטיא קרי

רש"י

יג (ה) ויתן ה' לישראל מושיע. את יואש בן יהואחז

רד"ק

שבע ובשנת כ"ג ליואש ר"ל בתחילת כ"ג: (ה) ויתן ה' לישראל מושיע. הוא יהואש בן יהואחז כי כל ימי יהואחז לחץ אותם מלך ארם: (ו) אשר החטי את ישראל בה הלך. חסר אל"ף וכמוהו ות' חפץ דכאו החלי: וגם האשרה. כי לא כרת אותה יהוא אלא הבעלים הוא שהשמיד: (ז) כי לא השאיר ליהואחז. אינו טעם לדבק אליו אלא למה שאמר למעלה כי

מנחת שי

יג (ו) אך לא סרו וגו' החטי. חסר אל"ף וכן בירמיה ל"ב: (ז) ועשרה רכב. מלעיל:

רלב"ג

אותן יהואחז והנה עם כל זה שמע ה' תפלת יהואחז להקל מהלחץ אשר היה לוחץ אותם חזאל בימיו ונתן לישראל אחרי יהואחז מושיע מיד מלך ארם והוא יואש מפני שברוב הלחץ שהיה לוחץ אותם חזאל היו ישראל כלים בקלות כמו שזכרנו והולך הש"י בעבור בריתו עם האבות שירחם עליהם כמו שנזכר אחר זה וזה כי לא השאיר חזאל ליהואחז עם כי אם חמשים פרשים ועשרה רכב ועשרת אלפים איש

מצודת ציון

(ה) שלשום. יום השלישי שלפני היום: (ז) לדוש. מל' דישה וכתישה:

מצודת דוד

ראה וגו'. ולולי זאת לא היתה תפלתו כדאי להתקבל: (ה) מושיע. יהואש בנו היה המושיע כמו שזכר אח"ז בימי מלכות יהואחז התחילה התשועה: (ו) אך לא סרו. חוזר על המקרא שלפניו לומר אף שחילה יהואחז את פני ה' אך לא סרו הוא ועמו מחטאת בית ירבעם והיה התפילה עם אחיזת העון: (ז) כי לא השאיר. כי בעבור זה לא השאיר ארם ליהואחז עם וגו': כעפר לדוש. כעפר הנידש ברגלי אדם: (ח) וגבורתו. בהלחמו ביתר העמים זולת ארם:

away—Even though Jehoahaz prayed to God, he and his people did not turn away from the sins of the house of Jeroboam [*Mezudath David*].

Daath Soferim notes that the beginning of this verse is written in the plural form, placing the blame on the people, not only on the king. Perhaps the king would have been ready to abandon them were it not for the people's tenacity.

they persisted in them—lit. he persisted. *Jonathan* interprets the singular form as collective, thus rendering: they persisted.

before the Lord; and the Lord hearkened to his prayer, for He saw Israel's oppression, for the king of Aram oppressed them. 5. And the Lord gave Israel a savior and they went free from under Aram's hands, and the children of Israel dwelt in their dwelling places as yesterday and the day before. 6. However, they did not turn away from the sins of the house of Jeroboam which he made Israel sin; they persisted in them; and also the Asherah stood in Samaria. 7. For he had not left to Jehoahaz but fifty riders and ten chariots, for the king of Aram had destroyed them and made them like dust to trample. 8. And the rest of the events of Jehoahaz and all that he did and his might, are written in the

sion—Otherwise, Jehoahaz' prayer was not fit to be accepted [*Mezudath David*].

Abarbanel states that Jehoahaz repented. He does not, however, explain the extent of his repentance. In any case, it was mainly because of Israel's oppression that God hearkened to Jehoahaz' prayer.

5. **And the Lord gave Israel a savior**—*Joash the son of Jehoahaz, concerning whom it is stated,* (v. 19) *Three times shall you strike Aram."* [*Rashi, Redak, Ralbag, Mezudath David*].

The savior mentioned here came on the scene after Jehoahaz' death. During his lifetime, however, Israel was oppressed "all the days," as mentioned above [*Abarbanel*].

Others maintain that the salvation commenced during the reign of Jehoahaz [*Mezudath David*].

Still others hold that Joash became king during his father's lifetime, at which time the salvation commenced [*Malbim*].

A fourth view is that during Jehoahaz' entire lifetime the Israelites were oppressed by Aram. However, after his prayer, the Arameans stopped destroying them as they had done previously. The Israelites were not emancipated from Aramean rule, however, until after Jehoahaz' death [*Ralbag*].

Later scholars identify the *moshia* with Adad-Narari II, king of Assyria, who attacked Aram at that time. Although he did not vanquish them, he, nevertheless, succeeded in occupying them in battle, thus breaking their hold on Israel.

in their dwelling places—lit. in their tents. The Israelites did not, however, dwell in tents during this period. *Jonathan* renders: *in their cities.* [*Daath Soferim*] takes this expression as poetic.

6. **However, they did not turn**

ספר דברי הימים למלכי ישראל:
ט וישכב יהואחז עם־אבתיו ויקברהו
בשמרון וימלך יואש בנו תחתיו:
י בשנת שלשים ושבע שנה ליואש
מלך יהודה מלך יהואש בן־יהואחז
על־ישראל בשמרון שש עשרה שנה:
יא ויעשה הרע בעיני יהוה לא סר מכל־
חטאות ירבעם בן־נבט אשר־החטיא
את־ישראל בה הלך: יב ויתר דברי
יואש וכל־אשר עשה וגבורתו אשר

מלא ואו

ספר פתגמי יומיא למלכי ישראל: ט ושכיב יהואחז עם אבהתוהי וקברוהי בשמרון ומלך יואש בריה תחותוהי: י בשנת תלתין ושבע שנין ליואש מלך שבטא דבית יהודה מלך יהואש בר יהואחז על ישראל בשמרון שית עסרי שנין: יא ועבד דביש קדם יי לא סטא מכל חובי ירבעם בר נבט דחיב ית ישראל בהון אזל: יב ושאר פתגמי יואש וכל דעבד וגבורתיה

רש"י

שנאמר בו שלש פעמים תכה את ארם: (י) בשנת שלשים ושבע וגו'. מקרא זה מוכחש משני לדדין ולא מצאתי לו מתקן שהיה לו לומר שלשים ותשע שהרי עודו אביו בשנת עשרים ושלש ליואש ומלך שבע עשרה שנה נמצא שמת בשנת שלשים ותשע ליואש ועוד הא אמור למטה בענין ובשנת שתים ליואש בן יהואחז מלך ישראל מלך אמציה בן יואש מלך יהודה נמצא שעמד יואש בן יהואחז בשנת הארבעים של יואש שהיתה שנה אחרונה לו ובשנה שנייה ליואש בן יהואחז מלך אמציה ואף כי תאמר שמלך אמציה בשנת מות אביו וקרא הכתוב שנת שתים ליואש למדת שלא מלך יואש מלך ישראל עד שנת שלשים ותשע של יואש מלך יהודה:

רד"ק

לחוץ אותם מלך ארם: (י) בשנת שלשים ושבע. היה לו לומר בשנת שלשים ותשע שהרי בתחילת שנת עשרים ושלש ליהואש מלך יהודה מלך יהואחז בן יהוא ומלך שבע עשרה שנה הנה כלו לו י"ז בשנת תשעה ושלשים ליואש מלך יהודה ונראה כי מלך יהואש בחיי יהואחז אביו שני שנים וזה שאמר ויתן ה' לישראל מושיע והמושיע הוא יהואש ואחרי שחלה יהואחז את פני ה' ואמר וישמע אליו ה' היאך ידע ששמע אליו ה' אם לא החלה התשועה בימיו אלא מל״ד שהחלה התשועה בימיו אך לא על ידו אלא ע"י בנו ואולי על ידי נביא המליכו בחייו שאמר לו כי על ידי בנו תהיה התשועה ובעבור שיראה תחלה הישועה המליכו בחייו: (יב) ויתר דברי יואש. למה הזכיר הנה סוף מלכות יואש והלא עתיד לזכור עדיין את אשר עשה ואחר כן ויתר דברי יהואש אלא סמך תהלת מלכות בנו להתחלת מלכותו ואמר וירבעם ישב על כסאו להודיע כי בימיו המליכו כמו שמלך הוא בחיי אביו אולי הרגיש בבנים אחרים שהיו לו שיהלקו עליו לפיכך טרם מותו הושיבו על כסאו וזהו שאמר ירבעם ישב על כסאו ולא אמר וימלוך ירבעם בנו תחתיו כמו שאמר בשאר המלכים אלא כיון שאמר בלשון זה נראה כי בנו ישב על כסאו לפני מותו ובסדר עולם אומר ירבעם מלך בחיי

רלב"ג

רגלי כי אבדם מלך ארם וישימם כעפר לדוש: (י) בשנת שלשים ושבע שנה. כבר קדם כי בהיות יואש מלך יהודה בראש שנת עשרים ושלש למלכו אז מלך יהואחז והוא מלך שבע עשרה שנה מקוטעים מבתי קצותיהן והם יתכן שיהיו בפחות משש עשרה שנה ולזה יחוייב שנכון אמרו בשנת שלשים ושבע שנה אחר עבור ליואש שלשים ושבע שנה והיתה שנת שלשים ושמנה לו בלתי שלימה וזה יתכן שיהיה פחות משש עשרה שנה מעט וידמה שהתחלת שנת מלכי בית יהוא היא זולת התחלת שנת מלכי בית דוד ובזה האופן היתה השנה ראשונה ליהואחז

מנחת שי

(יב) אשר נלחם עם אמציה. בדפוס ישן נכתב בגליון אמליהו וכן הוא במקצת ספרים כתובי יד וטעות הוא בידם שזהו אחד מן ט' הכתובים בלא וא"ו על פי המסורת

מצודת דוד

(י) בשנת שלשים ושבע. כי יהואש מלך ישראל מלך בחיי אביו ב' שנים לפי שבאה על ידו תשועה כמו שכתוב למעלה לזה המליכו בחייו שתי שנים והלא יהואחז מלך בכ"ג ליואש מלך יהודה וימי מלכותו י"ז שנים מקוטעות וכלו א"כ בל"ט ליואש מלך יהודה והלא יהואש מלך ישראל מלך בחיי אביו ב' שנים הרי מלך בל"ז ליואש מלך יהודה: שש עשרה שנה. נמספר השנים ההם מלך אחרי מות אביו: (יב) ויתר וגו'. אף שאח"ז יספר עוד ממעשה יואש ואף שתי המקראות האלו אמורים שם ואולי לפי שבזמן ענין בקלרס שיהי' מושיע לישראל מיד ארם וסמכה לספורי אביו כי באה בתפלתו ואף התחילה בימי מלכותו ולזה ראה להזכיר כל מעשיו בקצרה עד

that the salvation commenced during Jehoahaz' lifetime not through him, however, but through his son, Joash. Perhaps they crowned Joash during his father's lifetime because of prophecies that the salvation

book of the chronicles of the kings of Israel. 9. And Jehoahaz slept with his forefathers, and they buried him in Samaria; and his son Joash reigned in his stead. 10. In the thirty-seventh year of Joash the king of Judah, Jehoash the son of Jehoahaz reigned over Israel in Samaria sixteen years. 11. And he did what was evil in the eyes of the Lord; he did not turn away from all the sins of Jeroboam the son of Nebat, which he had made Israel sin; he persisted in it. 12. And the rest of the events of Joash and all that he did and his mighty deeds,

Daath Soferim, however, interprets this clause as referring to the king. The people did not turn away from the sins of Jeroboam, and the king followed them.

and also the Asherah stood in Samaria—It is not mentioned when the Asherah was planted or who planted it. It may have been a vestige oq the Canaanite civilization existing prior to the conquest. In any case, it was not an official shrine. The king is blamed, however, for not abolishing it [*Daath Soferim*].

7. **For he had not left**—God hearkened to Jehoahaz' prayer since Aram had not left to Jehoahaz but fifty riders . . . [*Mezudath David*].

8. **and his might**—in waging war with nations other than Aram [*Mezudath David*].

10. **In the thirty-seventh year . . .**—*This verse is contradicted from two sides, and I have not found any reconciliation, for he should have said, "thirty-nine," since his father rose in the twenty-third year of Joash, and reigned seventeen years. It is found that he died in the thirty-ninth year of Joash. Furthermore, it is stated below in this section,* "(14:1) *In the second year of Joash the son of Joahaz the king of Israel, Amaziah the son of Joash the king of Judah, became king." It is found that Joash the son of Jehoahaz rose in the fortieth year of Joash, which was his last year, and in the second year of Joash the son of Jehoahaz, Amaziah became king. And even if you say that Amaziah became king in the year of his father's death, and Scripture calls this the second year of Joash, you,* nevertheless, *deduce that Joash the king of Israel did not become king until the thirty-ninth year of Joash the king of Judah* [*Rashi*].

It seems to me that Joash reigned for two years during his father's lifetime. This is what Scripture means by telling us that "the Lord gave Israel a savior." As mentioned above, that savior was Joash. Now after Jehoahaz prayed to God, He "hearkened to him." How did Jehoahaz know that God hearkened to him unless the savior arose during his own lifetime? Thus we must say

נִלְחַם עִם אֲמַצְיָה מֶלֶךְ־יְהוּדָה הֲלֹא־
הֵם כְּתוּבִים עַל־סֵפֶר דִּבְרֵי הַיָּמִים
לְמַלְכֵי יִשְׂרָאֵל׃ יג וַיִּשְׁכַּב יוֹאָשׁ עִם־
אֲבֹתָיו וְיָרָבְעָם יָשַׁב עַל־כִּסְאוֹ וַיִּקָּבֵר
יוֹאָשׁ בְּשֹׁמְרוֹן עִם מַלְכֵי יִשְׂרָאֵל׃
יד וֶאֱלִישָׁע חָלָה אֶת־חָלְיוֹ אֲשֶׁר יָמוּת
בּוֹ וַיֵּרֶד אֵלָיו יוֹאָשׁ מֶלֶךְ־יִשְׂרָאֵל וַיֵּבְךְּ
עַל־פָּנָיו וַיֹּאמַר אָבִי׀ אָבִי רֶכֶב יִשְׂרָאֵל
וּפָרָשָׁיו׃ טו וַיֹּאמֶר לוֹ אֱלִישָׁע קַח קֶשֶׁת
וְחִצִּים וַיִּקַּח אֵלָיו קֶשֶׁת וְחִצִּים׃
טז וַיֹּאמֶר׀ לְמֶלֶךְ יִשְׂרָאֵל הַרְכֵּב יָדְךָ
עַל־הַקֶּשֶׁת וַיַּרְכֵּב יָדוֹ וַיָּשֶׂם אֱלִישָׁע
יָדָיו עַל־יְדֵי הַמֶּלֶךְ׃ יז וַיֹּאמֶר פְּתַח

וּגְבוּרָתֵיהּ דַּאֲגִיחַ עִם אֲמַצְיָה מַלְכָּא שִׁבְטָא דְבֵית יְהוּדָה הֲלָא אִינוּן כְּתִיבִין עַל סְפַר פִּתְגָמֵי יוֹמַיָּא לְמַלְכֵי יִשְׂרָאֵל׃ יג וּשְׁכִיב יוֹאָשׁ עִם אֲבָהָתוֹהִי וְיָרָבְעָם יְתֵיב עַל כּוּרְסֵיהּ וְאִתְקְבַר יוֹאָשׁ בְּשֹׁמְרוֹן עִם מַלְכֵי יִשְׂרָאֵל׃ יד וֶאֱלִישָׁע מְרַע יַת מַרְעֵיהּ דִּימוּת בֵּיהּ וּנְחַת לְוָתֵיהּ יוֹאָשׁ מַלְכָּא דְיִשְׂרָאֵל וּבְכָא עַל אַפּוֹהִי וַאֲמַר רַבִּי רַבִּי דְּטָב לֵיהּ לְיִשְׂרָאֵל בִּצְלוֹתֵיהּ מֵרְתִיכִין וּמִפָּרָשִׁין׃ טו וַאֲמַר לֵיהּ אֱלִישָׁע סַב קַשְׁתָּא וְגִרְרַיָּא וּנְסֵיב לְוָתֵיהּ קַשְׁתָּא וְגִרְרַיָּא׃ טז וַאֲמַר לְמַלְכָּא דְיִשְׂרָאֵל אַחֵית יְדָךְ עַל קַשְׁתָּא וְאַחֵית יְדֵיהּ וְשַׁוִּי אֱלִישָׁע יְדוֹהִי עַל יְדֵי מַלְכָּא׃ יז וַאֲמַר פְּתַח כַּוָּן לְמַדִינְחָא

ה״א את חליו. סוטה מז בבא מציעא ז סנהד׳ קז:

רד״ק

אביו שנה שנאמר וירבעם ישב על כסאו: (יד) ואלישע חלה. כבר כתבנו למעלה מה שדרשו בפסוק זה כי שלשה חלאים חלה אלישע ומזה החולי השלישי מת: (טז) ידיו על ידי המלך. לחזק לבו להאמין בסימן החצים: (יז) ויאמר פתח החלון.

רש״י

(יג) וירבעם ישב על כסאו. בנו היה. ויש לתמוה למה נכתבו כאן שני מקראות הללו שהרי עוד לפנינו הוא מספר והולך בדברי יואש וחוזר וכותב ויתר דברי יואש וגו׳ וישכב יואש עם אבותיו וגו׳ ואומר אני שלא נכתבו אלא להפסיק שלא לסמוך מיתת אלישע למקרא של עבודת כוכבים לומר ויעש הרע וגו׳ ואלישע חלה וגו׳: (יז) פתח החלון

מנחת שי

(יג) וְיָרָבְעָם ישב. כן נקוד: וסימן נמסר לקמן סימן י״ד כמ״ג:

רלב״ג

קטועה וגם האחרונה ובזה יתישר זה המספר וכבר כארנו במה שקדם שלפעמים יקרא בזה שאלה השנים עברו שלמות למלכותו ולפעמים יקרא שהוא בזאת השנה: (יד) אבי אבי רכב ישראל ופרשיו. כי הוא גבורת ישראל וכחם בו ינצחו מלחמותיהם בתפלותיו שיתן להם כבר ה׳: (טז) וישם אלישע ידיו על ידי המלך. להעיר כי ידיו תהיינה במלחמותיו על דרך המופת וההשגחה הפרטית בעבור הנביא והנה היו אלו המופתים אחר מותו כמו שנמשך מופת המן גם אחרי מות משה וכמו שהחיה השם יתברך האיש שנגע בעצמות אלישע בעבור כבודו אחר מותו: (יז) ויאמר פתח החלון קדמה. הנה היה זה רמז להכאת ארם כי הם היו מזרחיים להם: ויאמר אלישע ירה

מצודת דוד

(יד) אשר ימות בו. אשר היה מעותד למות מחולי זה: אבי אבי וגו׳. רבי רבי שעוזר ישראל בתפלתו כרכב ופרשים: (טז) הרכב. הנח ידך על הקשת ותפוש בו: (יז) קדמה. אל מול ארם היושב אחר מותו וחוזר שוב לפרש מעשיו בארוכה ועד אחר מותו:

14. **And Elisha became ill**—Elisha suffered three illnesses during his life: one after inciting bears to attack the little boys who jeered him, (above 2:23, 24), one after expelling Gehazi wholeheartedly (5:26), and the final illness of which he died [*Redak* from *Sotah* 47a].

Joash the king of Israel . . . wept—This incident was unprecedented, a king weeping in the house of a prophet. He wept because the Israelites were at the mercy of the Arameans. The king knew that although the Israelites were highly superior to the Arameans, they fell

how he fought with Amaziah the king of Judah, are written in
the book of chronicles of the kings of Israel. 13. And Joash
slept with his forefathers, and Jeroboam sat on his throne, and
Joash was buried in Samaria with the kings of Israel. 14. Now
Elisha became ill with the illness he was to die of; and Joash the
king of Israel went down to him and wept on his face, and said,
"My master, my master, Israel's chariots and riders!" 15. And
Elisha said to him, "Fetch a bow and arrows." And he fetched
him a bow and arrows. 16. And he said to the king of Israel,
"Place your hand on the bow," and he placed his hand; and
Elisha placed his hands on the king's hands. 17. And he said,

"Open

would come about through Joash, and they wished to hasten it [*Redak*].

13. **and Jeroboam sat on his throne**—*He was his son. There is* reason *to wonder why these two verses were written here, for Scripture continues to relate the events of Joash, and then repeats, "And the rest of the deeds of Jehoash . . . And Joash slept with his forefathers* . . . (14:15, 16).

I say that these two verses *were written for the sole purpose of breaking continuity, so as not to juxtapose Elisha's demise with a verse dealing with idolatry, by saying, "And he did what was evil . . . And Elisha became ill* . . . [*Rashi*].

Alternatively, these verses are inserted here, to point out that Joash placed his son Jeroboam on his throne during his lifetime, much as his father had done to him. Perhaps Joash foresaw that there would arise a conflict among his sons concerning the inheritance of the throne, and, in order to avoid it, he made Jeroboam king during his lifetime. For this reason, Scripture states, "And Jeroboam sat on his throne," rather than the usual, "and he reigned in his stead." This indicates that while Joash was still living, his son Jeroboam occupied the throne. This is substantiated by *Seder Olam* (ch. 19), where it is stated that Jeroboam occupied the throne for one year during his father's lifetime [*Redak*].

See below *Rashi* 15:8.

Abarbanel feels that this explanation is inadequate. Perhaps because the following narrative took place prior to Jeroboam's assuming kingship. He therefore suggests that the author of this book wished to sum up all Joash's deeds immediately following the statement that the Lord sent a savior, to indicate that he was the savior, and immediately following these verses we find the account of Joash's war with Aram.

הַחַלּוֹן קֵדְמָה וַיִּפְתָּח וַיֹּאמֶר אֱלִישָׁע
יְרֵה וַיּוֹר וַיֹּאמֶר חֵץ־תְּשׁוּעָה לַיהוָה
וְחֵץ תְּשׁוּעָה בַאֲרָם וְהִכִּיתָ אֶת־אֲרָם
בַּאֲפֵק עַד־כַּלֵּה׃ יח וַיֹּאמֶר קַח הַחִצִּים
וַיִּקָּח וַיֹּאמֶר לְמֶלֶךְ יִשְׂרָאֵל הַךְ אַרְצָה
וַיַּךְ שָׁלֹשׁ־פְּעָמִים וַיַּעֲמֹד׃ יט וַיִּקְצֹף
עָלָיו אִישׁ הָאֱלֹהִים וַיֹּאמֶר לְהַכּוֹת
חָמֵשׁ אוֹ־שֵׁשׁ פְּעָמִים אָז הִכִּיתָ אֶת־
אֲרָם עַד־כַּלֵּה וְעַתָּה שָׁלֹשׁ פְּעָמִים
תַּכֶּה אֶת־אֲרָם׃ כ וַיָּמָת אֱלִישָׁע

לְמָדִינְחָא וּפְתַח וַאֲמַר אֱלִישָׁע שְׁדֵי וּשְׁדָא וַאֲמַר הָדֵין גֵירָא יִתְעֲבֵיד לָנָא פּוּרְקָנָא מִן קֳדָם יְיָ וְהָדֵין גֵירָא יִתְעֲבֵיד לָנָא נִצְחָנָא בֶּאֱנָשׁ אֲרָם וְתִמְחֵי יַת אֱנָשׁ אֲרָם בַּאֲפֵיק עַד דִישְׁתֵּיצוּן׃ יח וַאֲמַר סַב גִּרְרַיָא וּנְסִיב וַאֲמַר לְמַלְכָּא דְיִשְׂרָאֵל מְחֵי לְאַרְעָא וּמְחָא תְּלָת זִמְנִין וּפְסַק׃ יט וּרְגֵיז עֲלוֹהִי נְבִיָא דַיְיָ וַאֲמַר הֲוָה חָזֵי לָךְ לְמִמְחֵי חֲמֵשׁ אוֹ שִׁית זִמְנִין בְּכֵן פּוֹן מַחֵיתָא יַת אֱנָשׁ אֲרָם עַד שֵׁיצָיוּתָא וּכְעַן תְּלָת זִמְנִין תִּמְחֵי יַת אֱנָשׁ אֲרָם׃ כ וּמִית

רש"י

קדמה. מול ארץ ארם שהם במזרח כמה שנאמר ארם מקדם (ישעיה ט' י"ב): ירה ויור. שדו ושדא: ויאמר חץ תשועה וגו'. אלישע אמר החץ הזה יהיה סי' תשועה לישראל: באפק. שם העיר: (יט) ויאמר להכות חמש או שש פעמים. היה לך: אז. אם כך עשית הכית את

רד"ק

כבר אמר לו טרם שירכיב ידו על הקשת או אמר פתח לאחד מן העומדים שם: קדמה. לפי שארם היה למזרח ארץ ישראל כמו שכתוב ארם מקדם והחץ הראשון הוא שירה דרך החלון אבל האחרים הכה בהם בארץ ואמר אלישע בהורותו החץ זה החץ יהיה תשועה שיושיע ישראל ובאיזה עם יפול החץ שתהיה תשועה ממנו לישראל בארם יפול החץ וזהו שאמר חץ תשועה לה' וחץ תשועה בארם: באפק עד כלה. אפק הוא מערי יהודה ואע"פ שהיה גם כן אפק בנחלת בני אשר זה היה לבני יהודה כמו שפירש למעלה בדבר אחאב והוא המקום שנלחמו בו ישראל עם מלך ארם בימי אחאב והכו בני ישראל את ארם מאה אלף רגלי ביום אחד ונאמר לאלישע בנבואה כי באותו מקום שהיתה אז התשועה תהיה עוד התשועה לישראל במלחמת ארם ואמר לו אלישע עד כלה כי כן נאמר לו בנבואה אם יורה המלך החצים פעמים רבות והיה סבור אלישע כי לא יעמוד מלירות החצים עד שיאמר לו עמוד ומפני זה קצף עליו אלישע כאשר עמד: (יט) להכות חמש. אם עלה בלבך להכו' חמש או שש פעמים אז הכית ארם עד כלה: (כ) וימת אלישע. בסדר עולם היא שנה עשירית ליואש וכאן אתה מחשב כמה שנים פרנס אלישע לישראל משנת י"ט ליהושפט עד עכשיו יותר מששים שנה ולא ידעתי מאין היה לו כי בשנה העשירית ליואש מת אבל נראה כי בתחילת מלכותו מת כי אז התחילה

רלב"ג

ויור ויאמר חץ תשועה לה'. העיר אותו כי בכחו זה שקנה מיד אלישע יגלה במלחמת ארם וזה החץ שירה עתה הוא סימן לזה ואמר שיכה באפק עד כלה הנה בחר שתהיה המלחמה באפק כי משם יתכן לו יותר לנלחם וכבר זכרנו שהש"י כשיעשה המופתים יעשה באופן אשר בו יהיה בהם יותר מעט מן הזרות: (יח) הך ארצה. הנה היו שם חצים רבים וחשב הנביא שיכה בכלם לארץ כיון שאמר לו קח החצים ומפני זה אמר לו שיכה את ארם באפק עד כלה אך יואש הכה שלש פעמים ועמד מלהכות עוד וקצף עליו איש האלהים כי הוא מיעט

מצודת דוד

מקדם כמ"ש ארם מקדם (ישעיה ט'): ירה. השלך החצים מהקשת: ויור. שמע לו וירה: ויאמר. בעת שירה אמר הנביא חץ תשועה וכו' ר"ל ע"י החץ יהיה תשועה המיוחדת לה' לבא מאתו ובאיזה עם יפול החץ שיהיה ע"י תשועה לישראל בארם יפול שמן: באפק. במקום אפק תכה אותם עד תכלם: (יח) הך ארצה. השלך עם הקשת את החצים לארץ: ויעמוד. פסק מלהשליך עוד: (יט) להכות חמש וגו'. היה לך להכות חמש וכו' ואז היית מכלה את ארם:

מצודת ציון

(יז) ירה ויור. ענין השלכת חצים.

[*Rashi*]. Aphek was a Judean city. Although there also existed a city by that name in the territory of Asher, it too belonged to Judah. In this place, Israel had defeated the Arameans during Ahab's reign. Again the prophet foresaw a victory for the Israelites at this identical site. The prophetic message was that if Joash would shoot arrows to the ground many times, Israel would defeat Aram to the point of annihilation. Elisha thought that Joash would continue to shoot arrows to the ground until instructed to cease. Therefore, when he ceased after shooting three arrows, the prophet was incensed against him [*Redak*].

the window to the east," and he opened it; and Elisha said, 'Shoot!" And he shot. And he said, "[This is] an arrow of salvation from the Lord, and an arrow of victory over Aram, and you shall strike the Arameans in Aphek until they are completely annihilated." 18. And he said, "Take the arrows." And he took them. And he said to the king of Israel, "Strike at the ground," and he struck three times and stopped. 19. And the man of God was incensed against him, and he said, "You should have struck five or six times, then you would strike the Arameans until you would annihilate them completely, but now, you shall strike the Arameans but three times." 20. And Elisha died

short of what God expected of them [*Daath Soferim*].

"My master, my master, Israel's chariots and riders!"—My master, my master, who benefited Israel with his prayer more than chariots and riders [*Jonathan*].

Alternatively, you are the power of Israel, who vanquishes their foes through your divinely inspired counsel [*Ralbag*].

This is the very expression that Elisha used when his master Elijah was taken away from him. See above 2:12. Apparently, it had become well known among the people [*Daath Soferim*].

Since Elisha had prophesied that Hazael would harm Israel, it was impossible for that decree to be repealed until after Elisha's demise [*Malbim*]. See above 8:12.

16. **his hands on the king's hands**—to strengthen his belief in the symbol of the arrows [*Redak*].

17. **"Open the window to the east**—*Opposite the land of Aram, as it is said, "(Is. 9:11) Aram from the east."* [*Rashi*].

Either Elisha had given this order prior to his laying his hands on Joash's hands, or he commanded one of those present to open the window when Joash already had his hands on the bow and arrows [*Redak*].

"Shoot!" and he shot—[*Rashi* from *Jonathan, Mezudath Zion*].

And he said, "This is an arrow of salvation . . .—*Elisha said, "This arrow is a symbol of salvation for Israel* [*Rashi*].

and an arrow of victory over Aram—*Jonathan* paraphrases: and through this arrow, victory will be wrought for us against the people of Aram.

Redak explains thus: and this arrow of salvation will land in Aram. Therefore, you shall strike . . .

in Aphek—*the name of the city*

וַיִּקְבְּרֻהוּ וּגְדוּדֵי מוֹאָב יָבֹאוּ בָאָרֶץ בָּא שָׁנָה׃ כא וַיְהִי הֵם ׀ קֹבְרִים אִישׁ וְהִנֵּה רָאוּ אֶת־הַגְּדוּד וַיַּשְׁלִיכוּ אֶת־הָאִישׁ בְּקֶבֶר אֱלִישָׁע וַיֵּלֶךְ וַיִּגַּע הָאִישׁ בְּעַצְמוֹת אֱלִישָׁע וַיְחִי וַיָּקָם עַל־רַגְלָיו׃
כב וַחֲזָאֵל מֶלֶךְ אֲרָם לָחַץ אֶת־יִשְׂרָאֵל כֹּל יְמֵי יְהוֹאָחָז׃ כג וַיָּחָן יְהוָה אֹתָם וַיְרַחֲמֵם וַיִּפֶן אֲלֵיהֶם לְמַעַן בְּרִיתוֹ אֶת־

תרגום

אֱלִישָׁע וּקְבַרוּהִי וּמַשִׁרְיַת מוֹאָב עָלַת בְּאַרְעָא בְּמֵיעַל שַׁתָּא׃
כא וַהֲוָה עַד דְּאִינוּן קָבְרִין גַּבְרָא וְהָא חֲזוֹ יַת מַשִׁרִיתָא וּרְמוֹ יַת גַּבְרָא בְּקִבְרָא דֶּאֱלִישָׁע וַאֲזַל וּקְרֵיב גַּבְרָא בְּגַרְמֵי דֶּאֱלִישָׁע וַחֲיָא וְקָם עַל רַגְלוֹהִי׃
כב וַחֲזָאֵל מַלְכָּא דַאֲרָם דְּחַק יַת יִשְׂרָאֵל כָּל יוֹמֵי יְהוֹאָחָז׃ כג וְחַס יְיָ עֲלֵיהוֹן וְרַחֵם עֲלֵיהוֹן וְאִתְפְּנֵי בְּמֵימְרֵיהּ לְאוֹטָבָא לְהוֹן בְּדִיל קְיָמֵיהּ

ת״א הם קוברים. סנהד׳ מז חולין ז׳: ותחאל. שבת כה: ויחן. שם (סנהד׳ כז):

רד״ק

התשועה שהרי מעת שחילה יהואחז אביו את פני ה׳ שמע ה׳ את תפלתו: וגדודי מואב. כיון שמת אלישע התחיל הפורענות לבא התחילו גדודי מואב לבא שעל ידו נושעו ישראל מיד מואב ועשו ישראל בהם רעה גדולה כמו שכתוב למעלה ומשמת הוא התחילו לבוא בארץ: בא שנה. כתרגומו במיעל שתא ואפשר שתהיה האל״ף תמורת ה״א הנקבה והוא כמו בה שנה כלומר באותה שנה עצמה שמת אלישע באו גדודי מואב בארץ וכמוהו על כן גבהא קומתו באל״ף במקום ה״א הנקבה וכן בה ברוב גלוליו בה״א במקום אל״ף: (כא) וישליכו את האיש. מרוב חפזם מפחד הגדוד השליכוהו בקבר אלישע כלומר במערת אלישע שנקבר בה ולא היה להם אלא לפתוח פי המערה ולהשליכו בתוכה והיה נקל להם לעשות זה מלהפור קבר לאיש ופירוש ויהי הם קוברים איש רוצים לקבור מתעסקים בקבורתו וכיון שפתחו פי המערה השליכוהו שם ונתגלגל האיש עד שנגע בעצמות אלישע וזהו וילך ויגע האיש בעצמות אלישע: ויחי ויקם על רגליו. מרז״ל כי חיה והוליד בנים והטעם שהיה לקיים ברכת אליהו שנתן לו פי שנים ברוחו ואליהו החיה מת אחד והוא החיה שנים אחד בחייו בן השונמית ואחד במותו זה האיש ואמרו כי הוליד בן והאיש הזה היה שלום בן תקוה והוא מגדולי הדור והיה עושה צדקות

רש״י

ארם חמש או שש פעמים שהרי לסימן תשועה הרכבתי ידיך על הקשת: (כ) יבאו בארץ. היו רגילין לבא ולשלול בארץ: בא שנה. במיעל שתא בתשובת השנה בעוד הארץ מליאה דשאים ויש מאכל לבהמתם דרך היילות לצאת:

רלב״ג

הסוגה שהיה נותן לו על ארם: (כ) וגדודי מואב יבאו בארץ בא שנה. הנה בא באל״ף כמו בה בה״א בחלוף ה״א באל״ף כי הם מתחלפות או יהיה הרצון בזה שבא אלישע אל קבר זה שנה ועם כל זה נעשה זה המופת לכבוד אלישע שלא יקבר רשע אצל צדיק והנה זכר שתכף שקברו אלישע התחילו גדודי מואב לבא בארץ להצר לישראל כי בימי אלישע נכנעו כמו שקדם: (כא) ויחי ויקם על רגליו. תחיה שלימה עד שהגבר קם על רגליו לא כמו שהיה הענין בבן השונמית שהיתה תחייתו מעט מעט אך זה שב תכף לכחו לעמוד על רגליו. או אפשר שיהיה הרצון בזה שהגבר חיה לקום על רגליו לא ללכת לביתו לענינו הראשון אך היה זה להוציאו מהקבר ההוא לכבוד אלישע: (כב) לחץ את ישראל כל ימי יהואחז. ידמה שתכף שמת סר לחצו מישראל והנה הושיעם ה׳ על יד יואש שנלחם בארם במלחמה שלש פעמים והשיב לישראל את עריהם שלקחו ארם מהם במלחמה ולא ידענו מתי היה זה אם בראשית מלכות יואש או אחר שמלך זמן מה וידמה ממה שכתוב פה כי אחר שמת יהואחז סר לחץ ארם מישראל לגמרי כי לא אבה השם השחיתם כמו שזכר ולזה לא היה זמן הלחץ כ״א כל ימי יהואחז אך אחר מות חזאל ומלך בן הדד היתה התשועה שהשיב יואש ממלך ארם את כל ערי ישראל אשר

מצודת ציון

(כג) ויחן. מל׳ חנינה והמלה: ולא אבה. ולא רצה:

מצודת דוד

(כ) יבואו בארץ. היו רגילין לבוא בארץ לשלול שלל: בא שנה. תרגום יונתן במיעל שתא ר״ל בתחילת השנה בעוד הארץ מלאה דשאים למאכל בהמתם: (כא) ויהי הם. ר״ל פעם אירע כשהיו קוברין איש אחד ראו גדוד מואב בא: בקבר. סמוך להקבר: וילך ויגע. כאשר השליכוהו נתגלגל עד הקבר ונגע בעצמות אלישע: ויחי. המת ההוא וזהו על כי לא רצה אלישע שישכב אצלו:

bones—I.e. he rolled from the impact, and touched Elisha's remains [*Redak*].

Alternatively, they dropped him on the ground near Elisha's grave, and he rolled onto the grave [*Mezudath David*].

and he came to life and stood up on his feet—According to *Pirkei d'R. Eliezer*, Ch. 33, he actually was restored to life, and subsequently begot children. This miracle was performed to fulfill Elijah's promise to Elisha that he would be granted "a double portion" of Elijah's spirit (2:9, 10). Since Elijah had revived the son of the widow of Zarephath, Elisha would have to revive two dead persons. He had already revived only the son of the Shunem-

and they buried him, and Moabite bands would invade the land at the beginning of the year. 21. And it came to pass that they were burying a man, and behold, they saw the band, and they threw the man into Elisha's grave, and he went and touched Elisha's bones, and he came to life and stood up on his feet. 22. Now Hazael the king of Aram oppressed Israel all the days of Jehoahaz. 23. And the Lord was gracious and merciful to them, and he turned to them for the sake of His covenant

19. **And he said, "You should have struck five or six times**—lit. to strike five or six times [*Rashi*].

Redak paraphrases: If it had entered your mind to strike five or six times . . .

then—*Had you done so, you would have struck Aram five or six times, for as a symbol of victory, I placed your hands on the bow* [*Rashi*].

According to *Rashi* ms., this should read: *I placed my hands on your hands on the bow.*

20. **And Elisha died**—According to *Seder Olam,* ch. 19, Elisha died in the tenth year of Joash's reign. Figuring from the nineteenth year of Jehoshaphat, Elisha led Israel more than sixty years.

Redak questions this date, since it appears that Joash waged war immediately upon his ascent to the throne, as a fulfillment of the prophecy of God's giving a savior to His people in response to Jehoahaz' prayer.

would invade the land—*were wont to come and plunder the land* [*Rashi*].

Through Elisha, Israel realized a great victory over Moab (above 3). Now that he had passed away, Moab started to invade and plunder the land [*Redak*].

at the beginning of the year—*Jonathan* renders: *at the entrance of the year. At the return of the year, when the earth is still full of vegetation, and there is food for their animals, it is customary for bands to set out* [*Rashi, Mezudath David*].

This is an unusual expression, not found anywhere else in the Bible. Moreover, the word בא is difficult in this setting, since it is the masculine form of the verb, and שָׁנָה, *year,* is a feminine noun. To reconcile this difficulty, *Redak* and *Ralbag* suggest that the *aleph* is a substitute for a *he,* and is to be translated *in that year*; i.e. in the very year that Elisha died, bands of Moabites would often invade the land and plunder it. *Ralbag* suggests also that it may mean, *when he had come* to his resting place *for a year.*

21. **they threw the man**—In their haste, out of fear for the troop, they threw him into Elisha's grave, i.e. into the cave wherein Elisha was interred. It was much easier to open the cave and cast him in, than to dig a fresh grave. Thus, we explain, "they were burying a man," to mean that they were preparing to bury a man [*Redak*].

and he went and touched Elisha's

אברהם יצחק ויעקב ולא אבה השחיתם ולא השליכם מעל פניו עד עתה: כד וימת חזאל מלך ארם וימלך בן הדד בנו תחתיו: כה וישב יהואש בן יהואחז ויקח את הערים מיד בן הדד בן חזאל אשר לקח מיד יהואחז אביו במלחמה שלש פעמים הכהו יואש וישב את ערי ישראל:

יד א בשנת שתים ליואש בן יואחז מלך ישראל מלך אמציהו בן יואש מלך יהודה: ב בן עשרים וחמש שנה היה במלכו ועשרים ותשע שנה מלך בירושלם ושם אמו יהועדין מן

יהועדן קרי

קימיה דעם אברהם יצחק ויעקב ולא אבה להבלותהון ולא אגלינון מארע בית שכינתיה עד כען: כד ומית חזאל מלכא דארם ומלך בר הדד בריה תחותוהי: כה ותב יהואש בר יהואחז ונסיב ית קירויא מיד בר הדד בר חזאל דינסיב מן יהואחז אבוהי בקרבא תלת זמנין מחהי יואש ואתיב ית קירוי ישראל: א בשנת תרתין ליואש בר יהואחז מלכא דישראל מלך אמציה בר יואש מלך שבטא דבית יהודה: ב בר עסרין וחמש שנין הוה כד מלך ועסרין ותשע שנין מלך בירושלם ושום אמיה

מנחת שי

יד (ב) יהועדין. יהועדן קרי:

רד"ק

בכל יום ומה צדקות היה עושה היה ממלא את החמת מים והיה יושב על פתח העיר וכל אדם שהיה בא מן הדרך היה משקה אותו ומשיב את נפשו ובזכות הצדקות שעשה שרתה רוח הקדש על אשתו שנאמר אל חולדה הנביאה אשת שלום בן תקוה וכשמת גמלו כל ישראל עמו חסד ויצאו עמו לקברו וראו הגדוד והשליכו האיש בקבר אלישע ויגע בעצמות אלישע וחיה ואחר כן הוליד את חנמאל שנאמר הנה חנמאל בן דודך וכן אמר בתרגומו של תוספתא דין הוא שלום בן תקוה והוליד ית חנמאל בתריה ומהם אמרו שלא חיה אלא שלא יקבר עם אלישע הצדיק והאיש הזה היה רשע הה"ד אל תאסוף עם חטאים נפשי ודקדקו ויקם על רגליו עמד ואל ביתו לא הלך א"כ לא חיה אלא כדי שלא יהיה נקבר אצל אלישע וכאשר יצא מן המערה מת ונקבר במקום אחר וברכת פי שנים נתקיימה כשרפא צרעת נעמן כי המצורע חשוב כמת: (א) בשנת שתים ליואש בן יואחז. כיצד בשנת תשעה ושלשים ליואש מלך יהודה מת אחזיהו ומלך יואש בנו ואף על פי שמלך בחיי אביו כמו שפירשנו אחר מיתת אביו כונה לו עתה המלוכה הנה תשעה ושלשים ושנת הארבעים שבה

מצודת דוד

(כג) עד עתה. ר"ל עד עולם כי כל הקורא במקרא הזה כ"א בזמנו אומר עד עתה: (כד) וימת חזאל. בכדי לבוא תשועה לישראל מת חזאל ומלך בן הדד ובימיו נושעו:

יד (א) בשנת שתים. אף כי יואש מלך ב' שנים בחיי אביו מ"מ החשבון ימי מלכותו התחילו אחרי מות אביו והוא בל"ח ליואש מלך יהודה ויואש מלך מ' שנה וכלו בתחלת השנה השנית

tion" of this spirit was fulfilled when Elisha cured Naaman of his *zaraath,* since a *mezora* is considered like a dead person [*Redak* from *San.* 47a]. See *Hullin* 7b for slight variation.

23. **until now**—I.e. forever, since every reader at every time reads, "until now," this holds true forever [*Mezudath David*].

1. **In the second year of Joash the son of Joahaz**—In the thirty-ninth year of Joash the king of Judah, Joahaz died, and his son Joash became king. Since Joash, king of Judah, reigned for forty years, he died in the second year of Joash king of Israel. Even though we wrote before that Joash ascended the throne two years before Joahaz' demise, these two years were not counted in the number of years of

with Abraham, Isaac, and Jacob, and He did not want to destroy them, and He did not cast them off from His presence until now. 24. And Hazael died, and his son Ben-Hadad reigned in his stead. 25. And Jehoash the son of Jehoahaz returned and took the cities from the hand of Ben-Hadad the son of Hazael, which he had taken from the hand of His father Jehoahaz in battle; Joash beat him three times and recovered the cities of Israel.

14

1. In the second year of Joash the son of Joahaz the king of Israel, Amaziah the son of Joash the king of Judah, became king. 2. He was twenty-five years old when he became king, and he reigned in Jerusalem twenty-nine years. His mother's name was Jehoadan of Jerusalem.

itess. He was therefore due to revive another dead person.

This man was called Shallum the son of Tikvah. He was one of the greatest of his generation, noted for his daily charitable acts. He would fill a skin bag of water and sit by the entrance of the city. Whenever a traveler would come along, he would offer him water and refresh him. As a reward for these charitable acts, he merited that his wife become a prophetess. She was Huldah the prophetess, mentioned below 22:14.

When he died, all Israel came out to escort him to his grave. When they threw him into Elisha's grave, he came back to life and went home. He subsequently begot Hanamel the son of Shallum, Jeremiah's cousin, mentioned in Jer. 32:7. This account is also found in the addendum of the *Targum.*

According to the Babylonian Talmud, *Sanhedrin* 47a, he just stood up but did not go home. He died immediately, and was buried in a suitable place for one of his spiritual level. Since we may not bury a wicked man near a righteous man, he was not permitted to repose next to the prophet Elisha [*Redak*]. *Rashi* ad loc explains that he was the false prophet from Samaria, who misled Iddo the prophet, causing him to be devoured by a lion (I Kings 13:11–31). According to *Mid.* Psalms, 26, this was the son of the Shunemmitess, whom Elisha had once before resurrected. Since he turned out to be a wicked man, he was unfit to lie next to the prophet.

Elijah's promise of "a double por-

יְרוּשָׁלִָם׃ ג וַיַּעַשׂ הַיָּשָׁר בְּעֵינֵי יְהוָה רַק
לֹא כְּדָוִד אָבִיו כְּכֹל אֲשֶׁר־עָשָׂה יוֹאָשׁ
אָבִיו עָשָׂה׃ ד רַק הַבָּמוֹת לֹא־סָרוּ עוֹד
הָעָם מְזַבְּחִים וּמְקַטְּרִים בַּבָּמוֹת׃ ה וַיְהִי
כַּאֲשֶׁר חָזְקָה הַמַּמְלָכָה בְּיָדוֹ וַיַּךְ אֶת־
עֲבָדָיו הַמַּכִּים אֶת־הַמֶּלֶךְ אָבִיו׃ ו וְאֶת־
בְּנֵי הַמַּכִּים לֹא הֵמִית כַּכָּתוּב בְּסֵפֶר
תּוֹרַת־מֹשֶׁה אֲשֶׁר־צִוָּה יְהוָה לֵאמֹר
לֹא־יוּמְתוּ אָבוֹת עַל־בָּנִים וּבָנִים לֹא־
יוּמְתוּ עַל־אָבוֹת כִּי אִם־אִישׁ בְּחֶטְאוֹ
יָמוּת׃ ז הוּא־הִכָּה אֶת־אֱדוֹם בְּגֵיא־הַמֶּלַח
עֲשֶׂרֶת אֲלָפִים וְתָפַשׂ אֶת־הַסֶּלַע

יומת קרי מלח קרי

תרגום

אמיה יהועדן מן ירושלם: ג ועבד דכשר קדם יי לחוד לא כדוד אבוהי ככל דעבד יואש אבוהי עבד: ד לחוד במתא לא עטרא עד כען עמא מדבחין ומסקין בוסמין על במתא: ה והוה כד תקיפת מלכותא בידיה וקטל ית עבדוהי די קטלוית מלכא אבוהי: ו וית בני קטליא לא קטל כמא דכתיב בספר אוריתא דמשה דפקיד יי למימר לא יומתון אבהן על פום בנין ובנין לא יומתון על פום אבהן אלהין אנש בחוביה ימות: ז הוא מחא ית אנש אדום בגי מלח עסרא אלפין וכבש ית כרכא בקרבא

רד"ק

יואש מלך יהודה ומלך אמציה בנו באותה שנה הנה בשנת שתים ליואש מלך ישראל מלך אמציהו: (ו) לא יומתו אבות על בנים. כי משמעות הכתוב כן הוא כמו שאמר איש בחטאו יומת אלא שרבותינו ז"ל קבלו כי בכלל לאו זה עדות הקרובים כמו שתרגם אונקלוס על פום בנין ועל פום אבוהון אבל עיקר ההזהרה הוא שלא יומתו האבות בעון הבנים והבנים בעון אבות כמו שהביא ראיה הנה מן הפסוק: ימות. כתיב וקרי יומת והענין אחד: (ז) בגי המלח. כתיב וקרי גי מלח והענין אחד: עשרת אלפים. זכר המוכים בגי מלח ולא זכר השאר שאומר בדברי הימים עוד עשרת אלפים שבו חיים ויביאום לראש הסלע וישליכום מראש הסלע וכלם הבקעו: ותפש את הסלע במלחמה. ת"י וכבש ית כרכא בקרבא המצודה היתה בסלע: יקתאל. אחר שלקח המצודה שנה את שמה וקרא את

רש"י

יד (ז) ויקרא את שמה יקתאל. שהיתה לו לקיהוי סיניס כמו שכתוב (בד"ה ב' כ"ה יד) אחרי בוא אמציהו מהכות את אדו מים ויבא את אלהי בני שעיר וגו' לאלהי' ולפניהם ישתחוה וגו' והוכיחו הנביא ואמר לו (ד"ה ב' כ"ה ט"ו) ידעתי כי יעץ אלהים להשחיתך ומה היא העלה שהביאו

מנחת שי

(ד) ומקטרים. בספרים מדוייקים הוא"ו במאריך: (ו) בספר. בספרים מדוייקים בסמ"ך בגלגל: תורת משה. התי"ו במאריך: לא יומתו. במקצת ספרים יש מאריך במלת לא ולא במלת יומתו וכן חברו שבסמוך: ימות. יומת קרי: (ז) בגי המלח. מלח קרי ומלת בגי במקצת ספרים מלא יו"ד ואל"ף. אך במסורת. נמנה במספר החסרים אל"ף בקריאה וסימן נמסר במ"ג ביהושע סימן י"ח וזכריה סימן י"ד: יקתאל. עיין מה שכתבתי ביהושע ט"ו:

רלב"ג

לקחו ממנו במלחמה: (ו) ואת בני המכים לא המית ככתוב בספר תורת משה. זה לאות כי כונת הכתוב באמרו לא יומתו אבות על בנים ובנים לא יומתו על אבות שלא יומתו האבות בחטא הבנים ולא

מצודת ציון

יד (ו) על בנים. בעבור בנים:

מצודת דוד

ליואש מלך ישראל ואז מלך אמציה: (ז) את הסלע. מבלר בני

suaded him to incite the king of Israel [*Rashi*].

I.e. since he refused to obey the prophet and to forsake his idolatry, God inspired him to antagonize the king of Israel and to challenge him to war, as is related in the following verses.

Apparently, later, Amaziah realized that he had sinned, and called the fortress Joktheel as a token of his repentance [*Daath Soferim*].

Amaziah had committed an act of unprecedented cruelty for a Jewish king. He dashed his prisoners to death on the rocks. He should have repented by begging God for forgiveness. Instead, he worshipped the

3. And he did what was right in the eyes of the Lord, however, not like his father David; like all that Joash his father did, he did. 4. However, the high places were not removed; the people were still slaughtering sacrifices and burning incense on the high places. 5. And it was, when the kingdom became well established in his hand, that he slew his servants who had assassinated his father. 6. But the sons of the assassins he did not execute, as it is written in the book of the Torah of Moses, which the Lord commanded saying: "Fathers shall not be put to death for sons, nor shall sons be put to death for fathers, but each man shall be put to death for his own sin." 7. He struck down ten thousand of the Edomites in the valley of salt, and he seized the rock

his reign [*Redak, Mezudath David*].

3. **not like his father David**—who served God out of his love for Him. He served God merely out of habit as the Chronicler (II, 25:2) states: "but not wholeheartedly." His father Joash, too, served God only when instructed to do so by Jehoiada the priest. When he died, Joash strayed, as delineated above 12:3. Likewise, Amaziah strayed in his later years [*Malbim*].

5. **who assassinated his father**—as stated above 12:21.

6. **as it is written**—in Deut. 24:16. Although the Rabbis expound that verse to mean that fathers shall not be put to death by the testimony of their sons, (see *Rashi* ad loc.) the simple meaning, however, is as stated here [*Redak, Malbim*].

7. **He struck down ten thousand**—In addition to the ten thousand whom he killed in battle, he captured ten thousand whom he dashed to death from the top of the rock [*Redak* from II Chron. 25:12].

he seized the rock—i.e. the fortress which was on top of the rock [*Redak* from *Jonathan*].

and he called its name Joktheel—I.e. after he seized it, he changed its name to Joktheel for a reason known only to Amaziah and his contemporaries [*Redak*].

Rashi explains the reason for changing the name of the fortress, as follows: *for it set his teeth on edge,* קְהוּי שִׁנַּיִם in Heb.; i.e. the results of this conquest were unfavorable for Amaziah, *as it is written:* "(*II Chron.* 25:14) *After Amaziah came from striking down the Edomites, he brought the gods of the children of Seir . . . for deities. And before them he would prostrate himself.*" *And the prophet castigated him and said to him,* "(v. 16) *I know that God has advised in order to destroy you.*" *Now what was the advice? That He per-*

בַּמִּלְחָמָה וַיִּקְרָא אֶת־שְׁמָהּ יָקְתְאֵל
עַד הַיּוֹם הַזֶּה׃ ח אָז שָׁלַח אֲמַצְיָה
מַלְאָכִים אֶל־יְהוֹאָשׁ בֶּן־יְהוֹאָחָז בֶּן
יֵהוּא מֶלֶךְ יִשְׂרָאֵל לֵאמֹר לְכָה נִתְרָאֶה
פָנִים׃ ט וַיִּשְׁלַח יְהוֹאָשׁ מֶלֶךְ־יִשְׂרָאֵל
אֶל־אֲמַצְיָהוּ מֶלֶךְ־יְהוּדָה לֵאמֹר הַחוֹחַ
אֲשֶׁר בַּלְּבָנוֹן שָׁלַח אֶל־הָאֶרֶז אֲשֶׁר
בַּלְּבָנוֹן לֵאמֹר תְּנָה אֶת־בִּתְּךָ לִבְנִי
לְאִשָּׁה וַתַּעֲבֹר חַיַּת הַשָּׂדֶה אֲשֶׁר
בַּלְּבָנוֹן וַתִּרְמֹס אֶת־הַחוֹחַ׃ י הַכֵּה הִכִּיתָ
אֶת־אֱדוֹם וּנְשָׂאֲךָ לִבֶּךָ הִכָּבֵד וְשֵׁב

בִּקְרָבָא וּקְרָא יַת שְׁמַהּ
יָקְתְאֵל עַד יוֹמָא הָדֵין׃
ח בְּכֵן שְׁלַח אֲמַצְיָה
אִזְגַּדִּין לְוַת יְהוֹאָשׁ בַּר
יְהוֹאָחָז בַּר יֵהוּא מַלְכָּא
דְיִשְׂרָאֵל לְמֵימַר אִיתָא
נְקַבֵּיל אַפִּין בִּקְרָבָא׃
ט וּשְׁלַח יְהוֹאָשׁ מַלְכָּא
דְיִשְׂרָאֵל לְוַת אֲמַצְיָה
מֶלֶךְ שִׁבְטָא דְבֵית
יְהוּדָה לְמֵימַר חוּחָא דִי
בְלִבְנָן שְׁלַח לְאַרְזָא דִי
בְלִבְנָן לְמֵימַר הַב יַת
בְּרַתָּךְ לִבְרִי לְאִתּוּ
וַעֲבָרַת חֵיוַת בָּרָא דִי
בְלִבְנָן וְדָשַׁת יַת חוּחָא׃
י מִמְחָא מְחֵיתָא יַת
אֱנָשׁ אֱדוֹם וְרָאֵים עֲלָךְ
לִבָּךְ אִתְיַקַּר וְתִיב
בְּבֵיתָךְ

רש"י

להתגרות במלך ישראל: (ח) אז שלח אמציה מלאכים
וגו' נתראה פנים. במלחמ': (ט) החוח אשר בלבנון.
שכם בן חמור: שלח אל הארז. יעקב: ותעבור חית
השדה. בני יעקב באו על ההללים אף כאן אתה בא
להתמשל אלי ומשל בזיון הוא שדימהו לחוח ואת עצמו לארז:
והעבור חית השדה אשר בלבנון ותרמוס וגו'. לפי

רד"ק

שמה יקתאל על ענין ידוע אצלם: (ח) לכה נתראה פנים. פי'
למלחמה והענין שרצה להלחם עמו אומר בדברי הימים כי
בלכת אמציהו להלחם באדום שכר מישראל מאה אלף גבורים
שילכו עמו והניחם במצות הנביא ואמר להם שילכו למקומם
וחרה אפם ופשטו בערי יהודה והכו מהם ג' אלפים ובזו בזה
רבה ומפני זה רצה להלחם אמציה עם מלך ישראל: (ט) החוח
אשר בלבנון. משלו משל זה וקרא מלך יהודה החוח וקרא
עצמו ארז ומשל תנה את בתך לבני כלומר אפילו רצה להתחבר

מנחת שי

(י) ונשאך. בספרים מדוייקים הוא"ו במאריך

רלב"ג

יומתו הבנים בחטא אבותיהם: (ח) לכה נתראה פנים. ר"ל התראות הפנים במלחמה: (ט) החוח אשר בלבנון. קרא עצמו ארז וקרא מלך יהודה חוח על צד הבוז ואמר ממשל שאפי' שאל ממנו להתחבר עמו כדי שיהיה שלום ביניהם אעפ"כ יהיה דבר זה נבזה בעיניו כמאמ ומהפלג' הבוז תעבור חית השדה אשר בלבנון ותרמוס את החוח כ"ש כשירצה להלחם עמו והנה היה מבזה אותו כל כך מפני היותו מזרע אחזיהו אשר היה מבית אחאב ולזאת הסבה תמצא בזה המקום כשנלחו יואש שיחס אותו אל אחזיה וזה אמרו את אמציהו מלך יהודה בן יואש בן אחזיהו תפש יהואש מלך ישראל עם שזה היתה סבת נלחו אותו כי הוא הלך בדרך אחזיהו וגם יואש היו אחרי מות יהוידע וכבר ספר בד"ה כי אמציה הביא אלהי בני שעיר ולפניהם ישתחו' ובסבת זה החטא נפל ביד יואש הוא ויהודה עמו: (י) הכבד ושב בביתך. הוא מענין הכבוד וכאילו יאמר שכבודו יהיה שישב בביתו כי ישיגהו קלון מזאת

מצודת דוד

בכלע: (ח) נתראה פנים. כי בד"ה נאמר שאנשי יואש פשטו בערי יהודה והכו בהם ולזה בלאכיו לאמר אין זה גבורה לבא פתאום ולהכות אך נתראה פנים בפנים ונדעה הגבורה עם מי: (ט) החוח. המשיל את אמציה לחוח ואת עצמו לארז וכאלו אמר אף אם דברת בשלום לכלימה יחשב לי להתחבר עמך ומכ"ש לרדת עמך למלחמה: ותרמוס. על אשר נשאו נבו לדבר כזאת ורמז לו שאנשיו ירמסו אותו: (י) הכה. בעבור שהכית את אדום נתגאה לבך: הכבד ושב בביתך. ר"ל אם תשב בביתך ותחדל מלהלחם כי אז תשאר בכבודך שקנית בנצחון אדום: ולמה תתגרה ברעה. למה תתגרה עמדי בעבור סבה

מצודת ציון

(ט) החוח. מין קוץ: ותרמוס. מלשון רמיסה ודריכה: (י) ונשאך לבך. ענין התרוממות וגאוה: תתגרה. ענין התחלת הריב:

invited him to a conference. Upon receiving this invitation, Joash replied that just as Shechem the son of Hamor spoke in a friendly manner to Jacob, asking for his daughter's hand in marriage, but really harboring intentions of robbing his possessions, so do you intend to rob me, despite your friendly invitation. Therefore, just as Jacob's sons trampled the city of Shechem, so will my armies trample you.

Alternatively, Joash replied that even if Amaziah had made a friendly request of him, it would be degrad-

in battle, and he called its name Joktheel until this day. 8. Then
Amaziah sent messengers to Jehoash the son of Jehoahaz the
son of Jehu the king of Israel, saying, "Come, let us confront
each other." 9. And Jehoash the king of Israel sent to Amaziah
the king of Judah, saying, "The thistle that was in Lebanon sent
to the cedar that was in Lebanon saying, 'Give your daughter
to my son for a wife,' and the wild beast that was in Lebanon
came and trampled the thistle. 10. You have defeated the
Edomites and your heart has made you arrogant. Retain your
honor by staying

god of his captives, as though to beg forgiveness of him for slaughtering his people.

8. **Then Amaziah sent messengers . . . ". . . let us confront each other."**—*in war* [*Rashi*].

Amaziah, before going to war against Edom, had hired one hundred thousand Israelite soldiers to aid him in battle. When the prophet admonished him to dismiss the Israelite soldiers, "because the Lord is not with Israel, all the children of Ephraim," Amaziah obeyed and dismissed them, angering the Israelites considerably.

After Amaziah returned from the war, the Israelite troop that had been slighted, invaded Judah, slew three thousand men, and plundered the land.

After the prophet's warning to abandon the deities of Seir, and Amaziah's refusal to comply, God inspired him to challenge Joash to battle [*Redak* from II Chron. 25:5–17].

He berated him for the clandestine attacks perpetrated by his men, and challenged him to show his might in open battle [*Mezudath David*].

9. **"The thistle that was in Lebanon**—*Shechem the son of Hamor* [*Rashi*].

sent to the cedar—*Jacob* [*Rashi*].

and the wild beast that was in Lebanon came—*Jacob's sons came upon the slain. Here too, you come to compare yourself to me. This was a degrading comparison, for he likened him to a thistle, and himself to a cedar* [*Rashi* from Gen. *Rabbah* 80:3].

and the wild beast that was in Lebanon came and trampled—*Because you are arrogant, you too, the troops of my armies will trample you* [*Rashi*].

The comparison of the parable to the case in question is not clear, neither is the incident of Shechem comparable to Amaziah's challenging Jehoash to battle. To reconcile these difficulties, *Mussar Haneviim* quotes *Nezer Hakodesh,* who explains that Amaziah did not challenge Jehoash to war. Rather, he

בְּבֵיתֶךָ וְלָמָּה תִתְגָּרֶה בְּרָעָה וְנָפַלְתָּה
אַתָּה וִיהוּדָה עִמָּךְ: יא וְלֹא־שָׁמַע
אֲמַצְיָהוּ וַיַּעַל יְהוֹאָשׁ מֶלֶךְ־יִשְׂרָאֵל
וַיִּתְרָאוּ פָנִים הוּא וַאֲמַצְיָהוּ מֶלֶךְ־
יְהוּדָה בְּבֵית שֶׁמֶשׁ אֲשֶׁר לִיהוּדָה:
יב וַיִּנָּגֶף יְהוּדָה לִפְנֵי יִשְׂרָאֵל וַיָּנֻסוּ אִישׁ
לְאֹהָלָו: יג וְאֵת אֲמַצְיָהוּ מֶלֶךְ־יְהוּדָה
בֶּן־יְהוֹאָשׁ בֶּן־אֲחַזְיָהוּ תָּפַשׂ יְהוֹאָשׁ
מֶלֶךְ־יִשְׂרָאֵל בְּבֵית שָׁמֶשׁ וַיָּבֹאוּ
יְרוּשָׁלַםִ וַיִּפְרֹץ בְּחוֹמַת יְרוּשָׁלַםִ בְּשַׁעַר
אֶפְרַיִם עַד־שַׁעַר הַפִּנָּה אַרְבַּע מֵאוֹת

בְּבֵיתָךְ וּלְמָא אַתְּ מִתְגָּרֵי בְּבִישְׁתָא וְתִתְקְטֵיל אַתְּ וּדְבֵית יְהוּדָה עִמָּךְ: יא וְלָא קַבֵּל אֲמַצְיָהוּ וּסְלֵיק יְהוֹאָשׁ מַלְכָּא דְיִשְׂרָאֵל וְאִקְבִילוּ אַפֵּיהוֹן בִּקְרָבָא הוּא וַאֲמַצְיָהוּ מַלְכָּא שִׁבְטָא דְבֵית יְהוּדָה בְּבֵית שֶׁמֶשׁ דִּי לְשִׁבְטָא דִיהוּדָה:
יב וְאִתְּבָרוּ אֱנָשׁ יְהוּדָה קֳדָם יִשְׂרָאֵל וְאַפִּיכוּ גְּבַר לְקִירְווֹהִי: יג וְיָת אֲמַצְיָהוּ מֶלֶךְ שִׁבְטָא דְבֵית יְהוּדָה בַּר יְהוֹאָשׁ בַּר אֲחַזְיָה אֲחַד יְהוֹאָשׁ מַלְכָּא דְיִשְׂרָאֵל בְּבֵית שֶׁמֶשׁ וַאֲתוֹ לִירוּשְׁלֵם וּפְרַץ בְּשׁוּרָא דִירוּשְׁלֵם בִּתְרַע שִׁבְטָא דְאֶפְרַיִם עַד תְּרַע זָוִיתָא אַרְבַּע

לאוהליו קרי ויבא קרי

רד"ק

עמו דרך שלום היה נבזה בעיניו להתחבר עמו כ"ש דרך מלחמה: (יא) בבית שמש אשר ליהודה. ולמה אמר אשר ליהודה כי ידוע כי בית שמש ליהודה אלא להודיע כי בגבול בני יהודה בא מלך ישראל להלחם עמו: (יב) וינגף יהודה. בעון שהביא מלך יהודה אלהי בני שעיר ולפניהם ישתחוה כמו שאומר בדברי הימים לפיכך אמר להשחיתו: (יג) בשער אפרים. שער היה בירושלים שהיה נקרא שער אפרים שהיה פתוח נוכח גבול אפרים ודרך אותו השער היו נכנסים בני

מנחת שי

(יב) לאהלו. לאהליו קרי: (יג) ויבאו ירושלם. ויבא קרי:

רלב"ג

המלחמה: (יא) בבית שמש אשר ליהודה. הנה מרוב בטחון יואש לנצח מלך יהודה הלך אליו להלחם בארצו ולזה ספר כי בבית שמש אשר ליהודה היתה המלחמה: (יג) בשער אפרים עד שער הפנה. ידמה שהיה שם שער היה נכנס בו שבט אפרים בבואם לירושלם ושער

מצודת דוד

עליך הרעה ותפול אתה ועמך: (יג) בשער אפרים. כן היה שם השער ומשם התחיל לפרוץ ופרץ עד השער העומד בפנה העיר

raimites would enter Jerusalem [*Redak, Ralbag*].

the corner gate—the gate situated at the corner of the wall, known also as "*Shaar Hapinnim* (Zach. 14:10)" [*Redak*].

The Chronicler refers to it as "Shaar Haponeh," the gate that faces both directions, since it was in the corner.

Others interpret this as the gate near the Temple, which was known as the cornerstone of the world [*Ralbag*].

home. Now why should you provoke evil and fall, you and
Judah with you?" 11. Amaziah did not heed, however, and
Jehoash the king of Israel went up and they confronted one
another, he and Amaziah the king of Judah, in Beth-shemesh,
which belongs to Judah. 12. And Judah was beaten before
Israel, and they fled each man to his dwelling places. 13. And
Jehoash the king of Israel seized Amaziah the king of Judah,
the son of Jehoash the son of Ahaziah, in Beth-shemesh, and he
came to Jerusalem and breached the wall of Jerusalem at the
gate of Ephraim until the corner gate, four hundred cubits.

ing, surely a challenge to confront him in battle, was even more so [*Redak, Mezudath David*].

Joash's contempt for Amaziah was due to his descent from the house of Ahab, whom his forebear Jehu had destroyed [*Ralbag*].

Others maintain that, on the contrary, Amaziah desired to battle Joash to avenge his grandfather Ahaziah's death at the hands of Jehu, Joash's grandfather [*Azulai*].

10. **You have defeated the Edomites**—Because you have defeated the Edomites, you have become arrogant [*Mezudath David*].

Retain your honor by staying home—By staying home, you will retain the honor you have gained from your victory over Edom. If you engage in battle, however, you will surely be disgraced [*Mezudath David*].

11. **in Beth-shemesh, which belongs to Judah**—I.e. the Israelites invaded Judean territory as far as Beth-shemesh [*Redak*].

Joash's great confidence prompted him to penetrate deeply into the land of Judah to confront Amaziah [*Ralbag*].

12. **And Judah was beaten**—as punishment for adopting the deities of Seir, as cited above from II Chron. [*Redak*].

13. **breached the wall of Jerusalem**—Joash did not intend to destroy the wall, but to achieve honor from his victory over Amaziah. It was the custom of the Caesars to breach the walls of every city they conquered even though they could easily have entered through the gate [*Abarbanel, Malbim*].

the gate of Ephraim—There was a gate in the wall of Jerusalem known as the gate of Ephraim. This gate was open toward the territory of Ephraim, and through it the Eph-

אַמָּה׃ יד וְלָקַח אֶת־כָּל־הַזָּהָב וְהַכֶּסֶף וְאֵת כָּל־הַכֵּלִים הַנִּמְצְאִים בֵּית־יְהוָה וּבְאֹוצְרוֹת בֵּית הַמֶּלֶךְ וְאֵת בְּנֵי הַתַּעֲרֻבוֹת וַיָּשָׁב שֹׁמְרוֹנָה׃ טו וְיֶתֶר דִּבְרֵי יְהוֹאָשׁ אֲשֶׁר עָשָׂה וּגְבוּרָתוֹ וַאֲשֶׁר נִלְחַם עִם אֲמַצְיָהוּ מֶלֶךְ־יְהוּדָה הֲלֹא־הֵם כְּתוּבִים עַל־סֵפֶר דִּבְרֵי הַיָּמִים לְמַלְכֵי יִשְׂרָאֵל׃ טז וַיִּשְׁכַּב יְהוֹאָשׁ עִם־אֲבֹתָיו וַיִּקָּבֵר בְּשֹׁמְרוֹן עִם מַלְכֵי יִשְׂרָאֵל וַיִּמְלֹךְ יָרָבְעָם בְּנוֹ תַּחְתָּיו׃ יז וַיְחִי אֲמַצְיָהוּ בֶן־יוֹאָשׁ מֶלֶךְ יְהוּדָה אַחֲרֵי מוֹת יְהוֹאָשׁ בֶּן־יְהוֹאָחָז מֶלֶךְ יִשְׂרָאֵל חֲמֵשׁ עֶשְׂרֵה שָׁנָה׃

מְאָה אַמִּין׃ יד וּנְסֵיב יַת כָּל דַּהֲבָא וְכַסְפָּא וְיַת כָּל מָנַיָא דְּאִשְׁתְּכַחוּ בֵּית מַקְדְּשָׁא דַיְיָ וּבְגִנְזֵי בֵּית מַלְכָּא וְיַת בְּנֵי רַבְרְבַיָא וְתָב לְשֹׁמְרוֹן׃ טו וּשְׁאָר פִּתְגָמֵי יְהוֹאָשׁ דִּי עֲבַד וּגְבוּרְתֵּיהּ וּדְאַגִּיחַ עִם אֲמַצְיָה מַלְכָּא שִׁבְטָא דְבֵית יְהוּדָה הֲלָא אִינּוּן כְּתִיבִין עַל סְפַר פִּתְגָמֵי יוֹמַיָא לְמַלְכֵי יִשְׂרָאֵל׃ טז וּשְׁכִיב יְהוֹאָשׁ עִם אֲבָהָתוֹהִי וְאִתְקְבַר בְּשֹׁמְרוֹן עִם מַלְכֵי יִשְׂרָאֵל וּמְלַךְ יָרָבְעָם בְּרֵיהּ תְּחוֹתוֹהִי׃ יז וַחֲיָא אֲמַצְיָהוּ בַּר יוֹאָשׁ מֶלֶךְ שִׁבְטָא דְבֵית יְהוּדָה בָּתַר דְּמִית יְהוֹאָשׁ בַּר יְהוֹאָחָז מַלְכָּא דְיִשְׂרָאֵל חֲמֵשׁ עסרי

רש"י

שנתגאות אף אתה ירמסוך גדודי חילותי: (יד) ואת בני התערובות. בני השרים שהיו נתונים בבית המלך לערבון שלא ימרדו אבותם בו וכן ת"י בני רברביא: (יז) ויחי

רד"ק

אפרים בבואם לירושלם: עד שער הפנה. הוא שער הפנים ונקרא כן לפי שהיה שם פנת החומה: (יד) הנמצאים בית ה׳. כמו בבית ה׳ וכמוהו רבים: ואת בני התערובות. בני השרים שמשימין ערבים למלך שלא ימרדו בו ות"י בני רברביא: וישב שומרונה. אומר בסדר עולם בו בפרק מת יהואש מלך ישראל ובא לו אמציה לירושלם ואמת הוא כי מלך ישראל מת בשנת ארבעה עשר לאמציה לפי חשבון השנים אבל לא נתברר לנו בכמה שנים לאמציהו היתה מלחמת אדום ומלחמת ישראל: (יז) חמש עשרת שנה. זה החשבון ישר כי אמציהו מלך

רלב"ג

הפנה היה שער אשר הוא סמוך לבית ה׳ והוא נקרא שער הפנה כי הוא היה פנה והיסוד לקדושת ישראל: (יד) ואת בני התערובו׳. הם בני השרים שהם לערבות למלך שלא ימרדו בו אבותיהם והנה זכר כי חיה אמציה אחרי יואש ט"ו שנה כאילו זכר להעיר כי מפני שנתגאה כל כך יואש ואמר לאמציה ונפלת אתה ויהודה עמך הנה הוא מת קודם אמציה ט"ו שנה והנה היה כן כי כבר מלך יואש קודם אמציהו שתי שנים וי"ד שנה מלך בימיו ונשארו לאמציה ט"ו שנה:

מנחת שי

(יד) הנמצאים בית. בנביאים עם פירוש הרי"א בבית וגם בדפוס אחד נרשם כן בחוץ אבל בכל שאר ספרים כתוב בית ובדברי הימים כתוב בבית האלהים: התערבות. בספרים אחרים כתובי יד הבי"ת דגושה וכן חברו שבדברי הימים ובשאר ספרים שניהם רפין: (טו) ויתר דברי יהואש וגו׳ ואשר נלחם עם אמציהו. בכל הספרים כתוב בוא"ו ובאחד מן הספרים כתובי יד היה כתוב בוא"ו ואחר כך עבר עליה קולמוס. ולפי דעתי נשתבש במה שנמלא כתוב במסורת ויתר דברי יואש דאשר נלחם וסדרא ממסרה אטעיתיה סבר דדין הוא ולא הוא דהכא כתיב יהואש ומסרה קתני ליה אפסוקא דלעיל (י"ב י"ג) דכתיב יואש:

מצודת דוד

וסיס הפרלה באורך ת׳ אמה: (יד) בני התערובות. בני השרים שהם ביד המלך לערבון שלא ימרדו בו אבותיהם: (יז) חמש עשרה שנה. כי אמציה מלך בב׳ ליואש ויואש מלך ט"ז שנה מלבד שתי השנים שמלך בחיי אביו וכלו א"כ בט"ו לאמציה ואמציה הלא מלך

מצודת ציון

(יד) התערובות. מל׳ ערבון ומשכון:

14. And he took all the gold and silver and all the vessels that were found in the house of the Lord and in the treasuries of the king's palace, and the hostage children; and he returned to Samaria. 15. And the rest of the deeds of Jehoash which he performed, and his might, and how he fought with Amaziah the king of Judah, are written in the book of the chronicles of the kings of Israel. 16. And Jehoash slept with his forefathers, and he was buried in Samaria with the kings of Israel, and Jeroboam his son reigned in his stead. 17. And Amaziah the son of Joash the king of Judah lived fifteen years after the death of Jehoash the son of Jehoahaz the king of Israel.

14. **and the hostage children**—*the children of the princes, who were placed in the king's palace as security that their fathers would not rebel against him. And so did Jonathan render: the children of the princes* [*Rashi, Redak, Mezudath David*].

and he returned to Samaria—According to *Seder Olam,* ch. 19, Joash died at this time, and Amaziah returned to Jerusalem. This is obviously an oral tradition, since the Scripture does not indicate what year of Amaziah's reign the wars against Edom and Israel transpired [*Redak*].

17. **And Amaziah . . . lived . . .**—*The entire fifteen years, Uzziah his son reigned during his lifetime, for so it is written in* II *Chron.* (25:26): *"And since the time that Amaziah turned away from following the Lord,* they rebelled against him in Jerusalem, and he fled to Lachish. And they sent after him to Lachish and assassinated him there" [*Rashi*].

According to *Rashi* ms., the reading is: *All those fifteen years.*

Pseudo-Rashi in Chron. cites this explanation from the commentaries of R. Joseph (Kara). He objects, however, on the grounds that Uzziah was but sixteen years old when Amaziah died. That would make him one year old when he occupied the throne. Moreover, Scripture does not state that he was made king. He therefore concludes that Uzziah's mother Jecoliah reigned during Amaziah's stay in Lachish. See below v. 22, *Rashi.*

Since Joash behaved arrogantly toward Amaziah, he was punished by dying fifteen years before him [*Ralbag*].

Amaziah reigned in the second year of Joash. He reigned twenty-nine years (v. 1, 2). Hence he reigned

יח ויתר דברי אמציהו הלא הם כתבים
על־ספר דברי הימים למלכי יהודה:
יט ויקשרו עליו קשר בירושלם וינס
לכישה וישלחו אחריו לכישה וימתהו
שם: כ וישאו אתו על־הסוסים ויקבר
בירושלם עם־אבתיו בעיר דוד:
כא ויקחו כל־עם יהודה את־עזריה והוא
בן־שש עשרה שנה וימלכו אתו תחת
אביו אמציהו: כב הוא בנה את־אילת
וישבה ליהודה אחרי שכב־המלך

עסרי שנין: יח ושאר
פתגמי אמציה הלא
אינון כתיבין על ספר
פתגמי יומיא למלכיא
דבית יהודה: יט ומרדו
עלוהי מירדא בירושלם
ואפיך ללכיש ושלחו
בתרוהי ללכיש
וקטלוהי תמן: כ ונטלו
יתיה על סוסיא
ואתקבר בירושלם עם
אבהתוהי בקרתא
דדוד: כא ודברו כל
עמא דיהודה ית עזריה
והוא בר שית עסרי
שנין ואמליכו יתיה
תחות אבוהי אמציהו:
כב הוא בנא ית אילת
ואתיבה לבית יהודה
בתר דשכיב מלכא

רד"ק

בשנת שתים ליואש ויואש מלך חמשה עשר שנה נמצא כי ארבעה עשר שנה מלך יואש בפני אמציהו ואמציה מלך כ"ט הנה כי ט"ו שנה חיה אמציהו אחרי יואש: (כ) על הסוסים. על רכב משני סוסים: (כב) הוא בנה את אילת. ובדברי הימים את אילות ואחד הוא והיתה למלך אדום כמו שכתוב בתורה מאת אחינו בני שעיר מאילת ומעציון גבר וכן אמר בדברי הימים אז הלך שלמה לעציון גבר ואל אילות על שפת הים בארץ אדום ואפשר כי דוד לקחה ממלך אדום כי מושל היה בכל ארץ אדום כמו שאומר וישם דוד באדו' נציבים ובימי יהורם בן יהושפט פשע אדום מתחת יד יהודה ואילות שלקחה דוד השיבוה אליהם ועתה כשמלך עוזיהו לקח אילת ממלך אדום וישיבה ליהודה ועוזיה בנה אותה אחר שהשיבה ליהודה כי לא בנה אותה והיא ביד אדום אלא לאחר שלקחה מידי אדום ואפשר שנהרסו חומותיה בעת הככוש עד שהוצרך לבנותה וכמו וי"ו זה הן אתה קצפת ונחטא אחר שחטאנו קצפת ובאמרו אחרי שכב המלך עם אבותיו נראה כי קודם שמת אביו מלך שאם לא כן לא הוצרך לומר אחרי שכב המלך ומתי היה אלא אחרי מות אביו אלא שמלך קודם כיון שנס אביו מירושלם מפני הקושרים עליו ולא ידענו מתי היא זה שקשרו עליו ונס לכישה והנה נראה מהפסוקי' כי תכף שנס שם שלחו אחריו והמיתוהו שם ונשאוהו לירושלם וקברוהו והמליכו את בנו ואפשר כי וישלחו אחריו שאמר לא היה תכף שהיה בלכיש אלא לאחר זמן ולדברי בעל סדר עולם נראה כי בשובו ממלחמת אדום ונלחם עם ישראל קשרו עליו עבדיו ומקרא מסייע בדברי הימים ומעת אשר סר אמציה מאחרי ה' ויקשרו עליו קשר וגו' ובשובו ממלחמת אדום הוא שסר מאחרי ה' שהביא אלהי שעיר ובעל סדר עולם אמר כי בשנת שלש עשרה לאמציהו עשה מלחמת אדום וא"כ הוא בשובו מן המלחמה אחרי שנלחם עם ישראל קשרו עליו עבדיו והמיתוהו כל זה היה בשנת שלש עשרה לאמציהו או בשנת ארבעה עשר והנה נשארו משני מלכותו י"ו שנה או ט"ו שנה כי הכתוב אומר כי עשרים ותשעה שנה מלך בירושלים והיאך היה זה ובסדר עולם אומר ג"כ מה ת"ל אחרי שכב המלך עם אבותיו אלא שמלך בחיי אביו ולא פירש כמה ועוד אמר בו טעם אחר מה

רש"י

אמציהו וגו'. כל חמש עשרה שנה מלך עוזיהו בנו בחייו שכן כתוב (בד"ה ב' כ"ה כ"ח) ומעת אשר סר אמציהו מאחר ה': (יט) ויקשרו עליו וגו'. משמעו מה שאמר הנביא כי יעץ ה' להשחיתך: וינס לכישה. שם היה כל ט"ו שנה: (כב) אחרי שכב המלך עם אבותיו. אחרי מות אמציה אביו מכאן אתה למד שמלך עוזיה בימי אביו ומ"מ לא נהגה אילת בידו עד לאחר מות אביו שאם לא מלך בחיי אביו למה לו לומ' אחרי שכב המלך עם אבותיו וכשאת' מונה ימי הבית ע"פ שנות המלכים אם אינך מחסר ט"ו שני' הללו שנמנית לאמציה ולעוזיהו תמצא בעמד ארבע מאות

מצודת דוד

כ"ט שנה א"כ עם השנה שמת בו יואש חי אחריו אמציה ט"ו שנה: (יט) בירושלם. כי אף שתפסו יואש מ"מ החזירו למלכותו: (כב) הוא בנה את אילת וישיבה ליהודה. יתכן שסיבה פעם א' משל יהודה ובני אדום לקחו מהם וכאשר הכה אמציה את אדום לקחה מידם ועזיה בנה את חומתה להיות עיר מבצר וכזה השיבה ליהודה כי בעודה פרוצה אין להתחזק בה ולהחזיק בבעלה: אחרי

Thus, *Rashi* maintains that Uzziah/Azariah was sixteen when he replaced his father during the latter's lifetime, not as the commentary ascribed to *Rashi* on Chron. understood, that he was sixteen on his father's death.

Redak questions this calculation on the grounds that v. 21 implies that Uzziah was sixteen when his father died, not when he ascended the throne fifteen years prior to his father's death. Moreover, v. 2 states that Amaziah reigned twenty-nine

18. And the rest of the deeds of Amaziah are written in the book of chronicles of the kings of Judah. 19. And they revolted against him in Jerusalem, and he fled to Lachish. And they sent after him to Lachish and assassinated him there. 20. And they carried him on the horses, and he was buried in Jerusalem with his forefathers in the city of David. 21. And the entire nation of Judah took Azariah, who was sixteen years old, and made him king instead of his father Amaziah. 22. He built up Elath and restored it to Judah, after the king had slept with his forefathers.

fourteen years during Joash's lifetime and fifteen years thereafter [*Redak*].

19. **And they revolted against him in Jerusalem**—*since they heard what the prophet said, "That God has given counsel to destroy you."* [*Rashi* from II Chron. 25:16].

R. Elijah of Vilna explains that עֵצָה, *counsel,* refers to a plan one perpetrates through others. Hence God had informed the prophet that He would inspire others to destroy Amaziah [*Beur HaGra* on *Seder Olam* ch. 19].

and he fled to Lachish—*He was there for the entire fifteen years* [*Rashi*].

Lachish was a fortified city, against which Sennacherib fought at a later date and captured (below 18:13, 14) [*Pseudo-Rashi,* II Chron. 25:27].

20. **on the horses**—on a chariot drawn by two horses [*Redak*].

22. **Elath**—also known as Eloth in II Chron. 25:20. Elath belonged to Edom, as in Deut. 2:8. In II Chron. 8:17, it is mentioned that Solomon went there. It was probably conquered by David, who conquered Edom and set up governors. When Edom rebelled against Jehoram the son of Jehoshaphat, Elath was restored to Edomite rule. Now, when Uzziah restored it to Judah, he rebuilt the walls that had been breached during the war. Naturally, he would not rebuild it while it still belonged to Edom [*Redak, Malbim*].

after the king had slept with his forefathers—*after the death of his father Amaziah. From here you deduce that Uzziah reigned during his father's lifetime. Nevertheless, Elath was not given into his hand until after his father's death, for if he did not reign during his father's lifetime, why was it necessary to state, "after the king had slept with his forefathers?" And when you count the days of the Temple according to the years of the kings, if you do not subtract these fifteen years, which are counted for Amaziah and Uzziah, you will find that it existed four hundred twenty-five years,* instead of the traditional four hundred ten (*Yoma* 9a) [*Rashi*].

עִם־אֲבֹתָיו׃ כג בִּשְׁנַת חֲמֵשׁ־עֶשְׂרֵה
שָׁנָה לַאֲמַצְיָהוּ בֶן־יוֹאָשׁ מֶלֶךְ יְהוּדָה
מָלַךְ יָרָבְעָם בֶּן־יוֹאָשׁ מֶלֶךְ־יִשְׂרָאֵל
בְּשֹׁמְרוֹן אַרְבָּעִים וְאַחַת שָׁנָה׃ כד וַיַּעַשׂ
הָרַע בְּעֵינֵי יְהוָה לֹא סָר מִכָּל־חַטֹּאות
יָרָבְעָם בֶּן־נְבָט אֲשֶׁר הֶחֱטִיא אֶת־
יִשְׂרָאֵל׃ כה הוּא הֵשִׁיב אֶת־גְּבוּל
יִשְׂרָאֵל מִלְּבוֹא חֲמָת עַד־יָם הָעֲרָבָה
כִּדְבַר יְהוָה אֱלֹהֵי יִשְׂרָאֵל אֲשֶׁר דִּבֶּר

מלא ואו

תרגום

עִם אֲבָהָתוֹהִי׃ כג בִּשְׁנַת חֲמֵשׁ עַסְרֵי שְׁנִין לַאֲמַצְיָה בַּר יוֹאָשׁ מֶלֶךְ שִׁבְטָא דְבֵית יְהוּדָה מְלַךְ יָרָבְעָם בַּר יוֹאָשׁ מַלְכָּא דְיִשְׂרָאֵל בְּשֹׁמְרוֹן אַרְבְּעִין וְחַדָא שְׁנִין׃ כד וַעֲבַד דְבִישׁ קֳדָם יְיָ לָא סְטָא מִכָּל חוֹבֵי יָרָבְעָם בַּר נְבָט דְחַטִיב יַת יִשְׂרָאֵל׃ כה הוּא אֲתִיב יַת תְּחוּם יִשְׂרָאֵל מִמַעֲלָנָא דַחֲמָת עַד יַמָא דְמִישְׁרָא כְּמָא דְמַלֵיל יְיָ אֱלָהָא דְיִשְׂרָאֵל דִי מַלֵיל בְּיַד

ת"א הוא השיב. יבמות לח (חלה נח):

רש"י

ועשרים וחמש: (כה) **הוא השיב**. מיד מלכי ארם: **יונה בן אמתי**. הוא שמשח את יהוא שאמר לו בני רבעים ישבו לך אבל רבותינו דקדקו ויהי דבר ה' אל יונה שנית (יונה ג' א') ולא שלישית לפי שתבע כבוד הבן ולא תבע כבוד האב והוקשה להם זה המקרא ותרצוהו כדבר ה' אשר דבר ביד יונה לניגוה ונהפכה גזרת רעה לטובה כך נהפך לישראל בימי ירבעם בן יואש מרעה שהיו בה אשר אבדם מלך ארם וישימם כעפר לדוש ועכשיו נהפך להם לטובה:

רד"ק

יהורם ואחזיהו ויואש מתו מיתת תחלואים ע"י אחרים אף אמציהו מת מיתת תחלואים ע"י אחרים לפיכך אמר אחרי שכב המלך עם אבותיו מת כמות אבותיו ורש"י ז"ל כתב כי אותן חמשה עשר שנה לאמציהו משקשרו עליו קשר ומלך עוזיהו ואמציה ישב בלכיש כל אותן חמשה עשר שנה ועוזיהו בנו מלך ולא נראה כן לפי הפסוקים כי הכתוב אומר כי אחר שנקבר אמציהו לקחו כל עם יהודה את עוזיהו בנו וימליכו אותו תחת אביו והוא בן י"ו שנה היאך מלך חמשה עשר שנה בחיי אביו ואם יאמר כי ויקחו כל עם יהודה את עוזיהו כשקשרו על אמציהו וגם לכישה אז המליכו בנו ואז היה בנו בן י"ו שנה לא נראה כן לא במלכים ולא בד"ה כי אחר מיתת אביו אומר שהמליכוהו ועוד היאך אומר הכתוב על אמציהו כי תשעה ועשרים מלך והוא לא מלך אלא י"ד שנה יאם היה מתחבא בלכיש ט"ו שנה מהמלכות היה זה ועוד כי לבנו אינו מונה אלא שתים וחמשים שנה והם אחר מות אביו כי כן כתוב כי בן ששה עשר היה במלכו ונ"ב שנה מלך ואותן ט"ו שנה אם תמנה אותן לבנו הרי מלך ס"ז והראיה שהוא מביא מהימים שעמד הבית אינה ראיה כי ב' חשבונות תמצא בימי הבית כי אם תמנה מתחלת בנין הבית עד ג' ליהויקים שבא עליו נבוכדנצר תמצא ארבע מאות ועשר ושלשה חדשים ואם תמנה עד שחרב הבית מכל וכל בי"א שנה לצדקיהו תמצא ארבע מאות ותשע וששה חדשים ועוד לדבריו כי היה הקשר ט"ו שנה והוא עומד בלכיש היאך היה זה והכתוב אומר כי בנוסו ללכיש שלחו אחריו והמיתוהו שם ואם אחר ט"ו שנה היה לא היה אומר וישלחו אחריו כי אחריו נראה מיד אחר שנס שם שלחו אחריו. אלא הנראה בזה כי מלחמת אמציהו עם אדום ועם ישראל היתה עד י"ד לאמציהו כי מארבעה עשר ואילך לא יכול להיות כי בשנת ארבעה עשר לאמציהו מת מלך ישראל ואם תרצה לומר כי בשנת שלש עשרה לאמציה היתה המלחמה כמו שאומר בסדר עולם אבל הקשר שקשרו עליו לא היה אלא סמוך למיתתו ומה שאמר בד"ה ומעת אשר סר אמציהו מאחרי ה' ויקשרו עליו ר"ל מעת אשר ס' מאחרי ה' החלה הרעה לבוא עליו שהרי נגף במלחמת ישראל ועוד בכל יום ויום ענינו היה ברע עד סוף ימיו שקשרו עליו עבדיו וזאת קשה מכלם שנס מפניהם לכישה וישלחו אחריו והמיתוהו שם והכתוב קצר וסיפר הרעה האחרונה כי כן דרך הכתוב בהרבה מקומות ומ"ש אחרי שכב המלך עם אבותיו לומר כי תכף שמת אביו החלה ההצלחה לבא כמו שהיה הפכה בחיי אביו כמו שאומר בד"ה ובימי דרשו את ה' הצליחו האלהים ותחלת הצלחתו הוא שהשיב אילת ליהודה: (כה) הוא השיב את גבול ישראל. והנה יואש אביו השיב ערי ישראל אלא שיואש השיב אותם הערים שלקח מלך ארם וירבעם בנו השיב מלבא חמת עד ים הערבה מיד מלכי הגוים שלקחו אותם ולא ראינו ביד מי היו ויש מחלוקת בדברי רז"ל בזה יש מי שאומר מה שכבש יהושע כבש זה ויש מי שאומר יותר ממה שכבש יהושע כבש זה ואנחנו רואים כי גבול לבא חמת וים הערבה הוא בארץ

רלב"ג

(כג) בשנת חמש עשרה שנה לאמציהו. זה מבואר כי ככר מלך י"ד שנה כשמת יואש מלך ישראל:

מנחת שי

(כג) מלך ירבעם בן יואש מלך ישראל. בספרים אחרים כתובי יד וגם בדפוס ישן מוגיליאה ובנביאים עם פירוש מהרי"א כתוב בן יואש על ישראל ובספרים אחרים כתיב מלך וכן תרגם יונתן:

מצודת דוד

שכב המלך. על אמציה יאמר כי אף שהוא לבדה עדיין לא הוחזר לידם להחזיק בה עד כימת ובא עזריה ועשאה עיר מבלר: (כג) בשנת חמש עשרה. כי אמציה מלך כב' ליואש וימי מלכות יואש ט"ו שנים וכלו א"כ בט"ו לאמציה ואז מלך ירבעם ארבעים וגו' ומקוטעות היו: (כה) הוא השיב. כי בימי אבותיו המלכים לקחו מלכי ע"ג את הגבול ההוא מישראל וחזר הוא והשיב להם: מלבוא חמת. מן המקום שבאים בה לחמת: עד ים הערבה. ר"ל כלפי ים הערבה והוא ים המלח: ביד עבדו יונה וגו'. הנבואה ההיא לא הוזכרה

to speak with him. *This verse was therefore difficult to them,* since this would make a third prophecy. *And they reconciled it thus: Just like the*

23. In the fifteenth year of Amaziah the son of Joash the king
of Judah, Jeroboam the son of Joash the king of Israel, ruled in
Samaria forty-one years. 24. And he did what was evil in the
eyes of the Lord; he did not turn away from all the sins of Jeroboam the son of Nebat that he had caused Israel to sin. 25. He
restored the boundary of Israel from the approach to Hamath
until the sea of the Arabah, according to the word of the Lord
God of Israel which He spoke

years. If he was hiding in Lachish for fifteen years, he was obviously not reigning during this time. Additionally, it appears from v. 19 that the rebels sent after Amaziah immediately, while he was fleeing, not after fifteen years. Otherwise, it would not say, "they sent after him." He therefore concludes that the wars with Edom and Israel were over in Amaziah's fourteenth year. They could not have ended later, since Joash died then. The revolt, however, did not take place until shortly before Amaziah's death. Although the Chronicler states that "from the time that Amaziah turned away from following the Lord, they revolted against him . . .," the intention is that as soon as he turned away from following the Lord, his power commenced to wane, until finally, his servants revolted against him, and he was forced to flee to Lachish, where they sent after him and assassinated him [*Redak*].

25. **He restored**—*from the hand of the kings of Aram* [*Rashi*].

Redak, however, states that Joash had already restored the Israelitish cities that had been taken by the kings of Aram. Jeroboam, however, restored those areas taken by kings of other nations whose identities were not disclosed in the Scriptures. In the Jerusalem Talmud we find a dispute whether Jeroboam restored only those areas conquered by Joshua or whether he conquered also areas yet unconquered by the Jews [*Redak* from *Yerushalmi Hallah* 2:1].

Jonah the son of Amittai—*He was the one who anointed Jehu, who said to him,* "(10:30) *Your descendants of the fourth generation will occupy . . ." Our Rabbis, however, deduced* from Jonah 3:1, *"And the word of the Lord came to Jonah a second time,"* i.e. a second time *but not a third time, since he demanded the honor of the son,* Israel, *but he did not demand the honor of the Father,* God. Jonah fled from before the Lord, in order to avoid prophesying the downfall of Nineveh, since he knew that the inhabitants of Nineveh would repent and be forgiven, unlike the Jews who did not heed the admonitions of the prophets. Since the honor of the Jews was dearer to Jonah than the honor of the Lord, Who demanded the obedience of the inhabitants of Nineveh, God ceased

בְּיַד עַבְדּוֹ יוֹנָה בֶן־אֲמִתַּי הַנָּבִיא אֲשֶׁר
מִגַּת הַחֵפֶר: כו כִּי־רָאָה יְהוָה אֶת־עֳנִי
יִשְׂרָאֵל מֹרֶה מְאֹד וְאֶפֶס עָצוּר וְאֶפֶס
עָזוּב וְאֵין עֹזֵר לְיִשְׂרָאֵל: כז וְלֹא־דִבֶּר
יְהוָה לִמְחוֹת אֶת־שֵׁם יִשְׂרָאֵל מִתַּחַת
הַשָּׁמָיִם וַיּוֹשִׁיעֵם בְּיַד יָרָבְעָם בֶּן־
יוֹאָשׁ: כח וְיֶתֶר דִּבְרֵי יָרָבְעָם וְכָל־
אֲשֶׁר עָשָׂה וּגְבוּרָתוֹ אֲשֶׁר־נִלְחָם
וַאֲשֶׁר הֵשִׁיב אֶת־דַּמֶּשֶׂק וְאֶת־חֲמָת
לִיהוּדָה בְּיִשְׂרָאֵל הֲלֹא־הֵם כְּתוּבִים
עַל־סֵפֶר דִּבְרֵי הַיָּמִים לְמַלְכֵי יִשְׂרָאֵל:

תרגום

ביד עבדיה יונה בר אמתי נביא די מגת חפר: כו ארי גלי קדם יי שעבודא דישראל תקיף לחדא ואינון מטלטלין ושביקין ולית דסעיד לישראל: כז ולא הוה רעוא קדם יי למימחי ית שמא דישראל מתחות שמיא ופרקינון על ידי ירבעם בר יואש: כח ושאר פתגמי ירבעם וכל דעבד וגבורתיה דאגיח ודאתיב ית דמשק וית חמת לדבית יהודה בישראל הלא אינון כתיבין על ספר פתגמי יומיא למלכי ישראל:
ושכיב

ת"א מגת החפר. שם (סוכה נב):

רד"ק קמץ בז"ק

הנכבשת בין משה ויהושע ועוד הכתוב אומר השיב מלמד שכבר היתה נכבשת: אשר דבר ביד עבדו יונה בן אמתי. לא נכתבה נבואה זו ויש בדבר זה מחלוקת בדברי רז"ל שהם אמרו יונה תבע כבוד הבן ולא כבוד האב ר"ל חשש לכבוד ישראל לפיכך ברח חוצה לארץ שאינה מקום נבואה כדי שלא ישלחהו האל לנינוה שידע שיהיו קרובי התשובה ויהיה בזה עונש לישראל ולא חשש לכבוד האל מה נאמר בו ויהי דבר ה' אל יונה בן אמתי שנית שני' דבר עמו ולא שלישי' והקשו והא כתיב אשר דבר ביד עבדו יונה בן אמתי הנביא ותרצו על עסקי נינוה לא דבר אלא פעם שנית ולא שלישית ומהם אמרו לא דבר עמו לא בנינוה ולא בדבר אחר אלא פעם שנית ומה שאמר אשר דבר ביד עבדו יונה בן אמתי ר"ל כמו שנתהפך להם בנינוה מרעה לטובה כך בימי ירבעם נהפך להם מרעה לטובה: (כו) כי ראה ה'. לא בשביל תשובה שעשו אלא שריחם עליהם כי ראה ענים: מרה מאד. משתנה ומתחלף מרעה אל רעה וי"ת שעבודא דישראל תקיף לחדא: (כח) ואשר השיב. דמשק וחמת לארם היו א"כ איך אמר השיב נאמר כי דוד המלך נלחם בארם והכה בהם מכה גדולה עד שהיו לו עבדים ושם נציבים בדמשק וגם בחמת אע"פ שלא נראה זה בכתוב כי בחמת שם נציבים נראה כי בחמת היתה המלחמה ואם דמשק לקח כ"ש חמת ואומר ותהי ארם עבדים לדוד וזה שאמר ליהודה כי מלך ישראל לקחם והשיבם ליהודה כי להם היה המשפט כיון שדוד לקחם ומה שאמר בישראל לומר אע"פ שהוא היה מלך ישראל והשיבם למלך יהודה לא הקפיד בזה

רש"י

(כו) מורה מאד. מילר מאד (קונטריאי"ש בלע"ז) כמו אשר ימרה את פיך ממרים היתם. ותהיין מורת רוח (בראשית כ"ו ל"ה) ויש פותרין מורה מאד ירוד מאד לשון ירה בים:

רלב"ג

(כו) כי ראה ה' את עני ישראל מורה מאד. ר"ל אע"פ שהיה מורה מאד את פי הש"י במה שעזבו את בריתו: ואפס עצור ואפס עזוב.

מצודת ציון

(כו) מורה. מל' תמורה וחלוף: ואפס. הוא כענין לא: (כז) למחות. מל' מחיה ומחיקה:

מצודת דוד

במקרא ורז"ל אמרו כמו שע"י יונה נהפך לנינוה מרעה לטובה כך נהפך לישראל בימי ירבעם: (כו) כי ראה וגו'. לא בזכותם רק כי ראה ענים המשתנה ומתחלף מרעה אל רעה ונכמרו רחמיו:
ואפס עצור. לא נשאר בידם העושר הכנוס בבית ולא המקנה העזוב ע"פ השדה: (כז) ולא דבר. ר"ל וה' לא רצה למחות את שמם ולזה הושיעם ביד ירבעם: (כח) ואשר השיב. כי מלכי יהודה כבשו מאז חמת ודמשק וחזרו ארם ולקחום מידם ועתה השיבם הוא ליהודה: בישראל. ר"ל בכח גבורי ישראל אנשי בני עמו ולא בכח אנשי יהודה:

quered Damascus, he surely conquered Hamath, the site of the battles. Therefore, it is appropriate to say that Jeroboam restored those territories that had at one time belonged to Israel [*Redak*].

(We do not find that David fought with Hamath. On the contrary, when David vanquished Hadadezer, Toi the king of Hamath sent his son to David with blessings and gifts, since he had vanquished

through his servant Jonah the son of Amittai the prophet, who was from Gath-hepher. 26. For the Lord saw the affliction of Israel becoming increasingly severe, with neither stored property nor free property, and no one to help Israel. 27. And the Lord did not speak to eradicate the name of Israel from under the heavens, and He saved them through Jeroboam the son of Joash. 28. And the rest of the events of Jeroboam and all that he did and his mighty deeds, how he fought, and how he restored Damascus and Hamath to Judah through Israel, are written in the book of the chronicles of the kings of Israel.

word of the Lord, which He had spoken through Jonah concerning Nineveh, and the evil decree was changed for good, so was it changed for Israel in the days of Jeroboam the son of Joash, from the distress in which they were found, i.e. *that "the king of Aram had destroyed them and made them like dust to trample* (13:7)," *and now it was changed for the good* [*Rashi* from *Yebamoth* 98a].

Another view stated there is that the Lord spoke to Jonah but twice concerning Nineveh. Concerning other matters, he may have spoken to him many times [*Redak*].

This view is consistent with the first interpretation stated by *Rashi,* that Jonah was the prophet who informed Jehu that four generations of his descendants would occupy the throne of Israel. This stems from *Seder Olam,* ch. 19. The view quoted by *Rashi* is apparently inconsistent with *Seder Olam. Tos.* ibid. presents one opinion that these two sources do indeed disagree. Another opinion is that God spoke to Jonah only twice regarding urgent prophecies. Other, minor, prophecies do not count.

26. **increasingly severe**—*very vexing (kontrarios in O.F.). Similar to* "(Jos. 1:18) *who will rebel* (יַמְרֶה) *against your command.*" "(Deut. 9:24) *You have been contrary* (מַמְרִים) *with the Lord,*" "(Gen. 26:38) *And they were of contrary spirit.*" (מֹרַת רוּחַ) *Others interpret* מֹרֶה מְאֹד *as "very low," an expression of* "(Ex. 15:4) *He cast* (יָרָה) *into the sea.*" [*Rashi*].

with neither stored property nor free property—They had neither wealth stored in their houses, nor livestock grazing free in the pastures [*Mezudath David*].

28. **restored Damascus and Hamath**—Since Damascus and Hamath originally belonged to Aram, the term "restored" is inappropriate. The fact is, however, that David had conquered Aram and had set up governors in Damascus and in Hamath. Although Scripture mentions only that he set up governors in Damascus (II Sam. 8:6), the war was in Hamath, and if he con-

כט וישכב ירבעם עם־אבתיו עם מלכי
ישראל וימלך זכריה בנו תחתיו:
טו א בשנת עשרים ושבע שנה
לירבעם מלך ישראל מלך עזריה בן
אמציה מלך יהודה: ב בן־שש עשרה
שנה היה במלכו וחמשים ושתים
שנה מלך בירושלם ושם אמו יכליהו
מירושלם: ג ויעש הישר בעיני יהוה
ככל אשר־עשה אמציהו אביו: ד רק
הבמות לא־סרו עוד העם מזבחים

כט ושכיב ירבעם עם אבהתוהי עם מלכי ישראל ומלך זכריה בריה תחותוהי: א בשנת עשרין ושבע שנין לירבעם מלכא דישראל מלך עזריה בר אמציה מלך שבטא דבית יהודה: ב בר שית עסרי שנין הוה כד מלך וחמשין ותרתין שנין מלך בירושלם ושום אמיה יכליה מירושלם: ג ועבד דכשר קדם יי ככל דעבד אמציה אבוהי: ד לחוד במתא לא עטרא עד כען עמא מדבחין ומסקין בוסמא על

רש"י

טו (א) בשנת עשרים ושבע שנים לירבעם וגו'. אפשר לומר כן והלא עוזיה וירבעם מלכו כאחת כמו שפי' בסמוך אלא מה ת"ל בשנת עשרים וז' לירבעם מלך עזריה שמלך מלכות מנוגעת למדנו שנתנגע בשנת כ"ז

רד"ק

כיון שהשיבם בישראל: (א) בשנת עשרי' ושבע. והלא בשנת י"ד שנה לירבעם מלך עזריה שהרי מלך ירבעם בשנת ט"ו לאמציהו ומלכות אמציהו כ"ט נמצא כי בשנת י"ד לירבעם מת אמציהו ומלך עזריה אלא פי' עשרים ושבע לירבעם בסוף מלכותו שהוא י"ד שנה לתחלת מלכותו מלך עזריה כי מ"א מלך ירבעם וי"ד וכ"ז הרי מ"א. ובסדר עולם בשנת עשרים ושבע לירבעם מלך ישראל מלך עזריה וגו' וכי אפשר לומר כן והלא ירבעם ועזריה מלכו כאחת אלא שמלך מליכה מנוגעת פי' וכן היו כ"ז או כ"ו לעצמו אם מלכו כאחת כיומר שתחלת מלכותם היתה בזמן אחד ומכאן ואילך מלך מלכות מנוגעת א"כ חצי מלכותו מלכות מנוגעת ואם כן לדבריו למה אמר בשנת עשרים ושבע לירבעם היה לו לומר בשנת כ"ז למלכו מלך מלכות מנוגעת למה תלה הדבר במלכות ירבעם ובדברי רז"ל ג"כ יותם לא היה לעוזיהו אלא בימי חלוטו שהרי בן כ"ה שנה היה במלכו כשמת אביו הנה שנה אחת היה לו לעוזיהו כשנצטרע כשנולד יותם אם כן שמש מטתו בימי חלוטו ולמדו מזה כי מותר למצורע לשמש מטתו בימי חלוטו ומה שאמר הכתוב וישב מחוץ לאהלו שבעת ימים בימי ספרו היא הנה הסכימה דעתם כדעת בעל סדר עולם כי ירבעם ועזיהו מלכו כאחת ולא ידעתי מאין היה להם זה ולא יתכן זה לפי הפסוקים אם לא מלך עוזיהו בימי אמציהו אביו י"ד שנה וכבר כתבנו למעלה כי לא יראה זה לפי הפסוקים שאפילו שנה אחת מלך

רלב"ג

בישראל. ר"ל שסרו קניניהם הגלולים בבית ובעזובים בשדה: (א) בשנת עשרים ושבע שנה לירבעם מלך ישראל מלך עזריה. ידוע כי כשמת אמציה מלך ירבעם ט"ו שנה ולזה יתבאר שכבר מלך עזריה בשנת י"ו למלכות ירבעם והנראה בעיני שהוא מונה כ"ז שנה שהיו עתידים לבא ואחר יכלה מלכות בית יהוא וזה כי ירבעם מלך אחר זה כ"ו שנה ובנו מלך ששה חדשים והם כ"ז שנה מקוטעין:

מנחת שי

טו (ד) ומקטרים בבמות. בספרים כתובי יד מהריך בוא"ו וכן ומקטרים

מצודת דוד

טו (א) בשנת עשרים ושבע. שנויה כס"ע שבשנת כ"ז לירבעם נתנגע עזריה ומלך מלכות מנוגעת אבל התחלת מלכות עזריה היתה כאחת עם מלכות ירבעם (ר"ל מה שמלך אחר מות אביו יואש ולא התחלת חשבון ימי מלכותו כי ירבעם מלך בשלשה שנים בחיי אביו מאז היתה חשבון ימי מלכותו) כי עזריה מלך ס"ו שנים בחיי אביו והוא בעת מת יואש (ולכך לא תלה מלכותו המנוגעת במלכות עצמו כי לא היינו יודעין אם חושב מהזמן שמלך בחיי אביו או משמת אביו אבל עתה כאילו יאמר בשנת כ"ז למלכותו והוא כ"ז לירבעם א"כ חושב מזמן שמלך הוא בחיי אביו והוא הזמן אשר מלך ירבעם משמת אביו): (ב) וחמשים ושתים. ט"ו בחיי אביו ובל"ביס

מצודת ציון

טו (א) עזריה. הוא עוזיהו האמור בדברי הימים ולמטה:

years together with Jeroboam.

3. **like all that Amaziah his father did**—Although Amaziah worshipped the idols of Seir during his later years, that sin was atoned for and is, therefore, not counted [*Daath Soferim*]. (Ed. note. It seems more likely that the intention is that Azariah did what was proper up to a point, just as his father had done. His father, too, is described as doing what was proper in the eyes of the Lord, like *his* father Jehoash (14:3), who turned to idolatry during his later years.)

According to other commentar-

29. And Jeroboam slept with his forefathers, with the kings of Israel, and his son Zechariah reigned in his stead.

15

1. In the twenty-seventh year of Jeroboam the king of Israel, Azariah the son of Amaziah the king of Judah, became king. 2. He was sixteen years old when he became king, and he reigned fifty-two years in Jerusalem, and his mother's name was Jecoliah of Jerusalem. 3. And he did what was right in the eyes of the Lord, like all that Amaziah his father did. 4. However, the high places were not removed; the people were still slaughtering sacrifices and burning incense on the high places.

his foe. See II Sam. 8:9,10. Ed. note.)

to Judah through Israel—Since these territories had belonged to Judah, Jeroboam restored them to their previous owners. This restoration was accomplished through the power of the Israelite forces [*Redak, Mezudath David*].

K'li Y'kar suggests that we render: in partnership with Israel. Israel did not return the territory completely to Judah, but retained a share as payment for their trouble of battling Aram.

1. **In the twenty-seventh year of Jeroboam**—*Is it possible to say so? Did not Uzziah and Jeroboam reign simultaneously, as I explained shortly before this* (14:22)? *What, then, is the meaning of the verse, "In the twenty-seventh year of Jeroboam . . . Azariah . . . became king"? That from that year, he reigned a plagued kingship. We learn that he was stricken with "zaraath" in the twenty-seventh year of his reign* [*Rashi* from *Seder Olam* ch. 19].

This is based on the statement of *Seder Olam* mentioned above, that Azariah, or Uzziah, as he is called below, reigned fifteen years prior to his father Amaziah's demise. According to that, Jeroboam, who became king in the fifteenth year of Amaziah, became king at the same time as Azariah. We mentioned above that *Redak* questioned this statement. According to him, Azariah did not reign during Amaziah's lifetime. Thus we arrive at the conclusion that Azariah became king in the fourteenth year of Jeroboam. *Redak* reconciles our verse by rendering thus: During twenty-seven years of Jeroboam, king of Israel, Azariah . . . reigned. Since Jeroboam reigned forty-one years, and Azariah became king during the fourteenth year of his reign, he reigned the remaining twenty-seven

וּמְקַטְּרִים בַּבָּמוֹת: ה וַיְנַגַּע יְהוָה אֶת־
הַמֶּלֶךְ וַיְהִי מְצֹרָע עַד־יוֹם מֹתוֹ וַיֵּשֶׁב
בְּבֵית הַחָפְשִׁית וְיוֹתָם בֶּן־הַמֶּלֶךְ עַל־
הַבַּיִת שֹׁפֵט אֶת־עַם הָאָרֶץ: ו וְיֶתֶר
דִּבְרֵי עֲזַרְיָהוּ וְכָל־אֲשֶׁר עָשָׂה הֲלֹא־הֵם
כְּתוּבִים עַל־סֵפֶר דִּבְרֵי הַיָּמִים לְמַלְכֵי
יְהוּדָה: ז וַיִּשְׁכַּב עֲזַרְיָה עִם־אֲבֹתָיו
וַיִּקְבְּרוּ אֹתוֹ עִם־אֲבֹתָיו בְּעִיר דָּוִד
וַיִּמְלֹךְ יוֹתָם בְּנוֹ תַּחְתָּיו: ח בִּשְׁנַת

תרגום

עַל בָּמָתָא: ה וְאַיְתִי יְיָ
מַכְתַּשׁ עַל מַלְכָּא וַהֲוָה
סְגִיר עַד יוֹם מוֹתֵיהּ
וִיתֵיב בַּר מִן יְרוּשְׁלֵם
וְיוֹתָם בַּר מַלְכָּא מְמַנָא
עַל בֵּיתָא דָאֵין יַת עַמָא
דְאַרְעָא: ו וּשְׁאַר פִּתְגָמֵי
עֲזַרְיָהוּ וְכָל דִי עֲבַד
הֲלָא אִינוּן כְּתִיבִין עַל
סְפַר פִּתְגָמֵי יוֹמַיָא
לְמַלְכֵי דְבֵית יְהוּדָה:
ז וּשְׁכִיב עֲזַרְיָה עִם
אֲבָהָתוֹהִי וּקְבָרוּ יָתֵיהּ
עִם אֲבָהָתוֹהִי בְּקִרְתָּא
דָדָוִד וּמְלַךְ יוֹתָם בְּרֵיהּ
תְּחוֹתוֹהִי: ח בִּשְׁנַת
תלתין

ת"א בבית החפשית. סוריוס:

רש"י

למלכותו: (ה) וינגע ה' את המלך. מפורש בדברי הימים שנכנס להיכל להקטיר על המזבח הקטורת: בבית החפשית. עשה לו בית בבית הקברות כמה דאת אמר במתים חפשי. בירושלמי: (ח) בשנת שלשים ושמנה

רד"ק

בחייו: (ה) וינגע ה' את המלך. בדברי הימים אומר למה נגעהו לפי שנכנס להיכל להקטיר קטורת ודרשו כי למשה רמז בזה הדבר וזהו שאמר במחלוקת קרח כאשר דבר ה' ביד משה לו כשלקתה יד משה בצרעת רמז לו כי כל החולק על הכהונה ילקה בצרעת לפיכך לקה עוזיהו בצרעת: וישב בבית החפשית. אמרו רז"ל כי המלכות היא עבודה שהרי צריך לשאת כל משא העם עליו ולשמיע אליהם ולשפוט משפטיהם בין ברצונו בין שלא ברצונו אם כן המלכות היא עבדות וכשנצטרע עוזיהו וישב לו בבית אחד לבדו הנה הוא חפשי מן העבודה שהיה בה לפיכך נקראת הבית בית החפשית ועוד אמרו שעשה לו בית בבית הקברות כד"א במתים חפשי וי"ת ויתב מברא לירושלם: שופט את עם הארץ. לדברינו כל הימים שאביו היה מצורע הוא היה שופט את עם הארץ וכן הוא משמעות הכתוב ולדברי רז"ל כי בשנה שנצטרע נולד ולא שפט את עם הארץ אלא אחר שגדל והיה בן דעת וקודם לכן היו הזקנים והשרים שופטים את עם הארץ: (ח) בשנת ל'

רלב"ג

(ה) וינגע ה' את המלך ויהי מצורע. כבר באר בד"ה כי זה קרה לו מפני חשבו להקטיר במזבח הקטורת והנה היה אז יותם בן המלך שופט את עם הארץ בחיי אביו ומהעת שהיה מצורע ישב בבית החפשית לפי שהיה צריך לישב בדד מחוץ למחנה והיתה נקראת בית המצורע בית החפשית לפי שהמצורע אין לו עסק עם בני אדם והוא מפני זה חפשי מהעסקים והמלאכות: (ח) בשנת שלשים ושמנה שנה לעזריהו מלך יהודה. לפי שככר מלך ירבעם בחייו עשרים ושש שנה הנה יהיה זה בשנת כ"ז לעזריהו ולזה ידמה שמלך עזריה בחיי אביו י"א שנה כי קשרו

מנחת שי

בסוף הסימן הזה: (ה) וישב בבית החפשית. סימן מלכים בבית החפשית דברי הימים בית החפשית וא' פסוק וסימן עיניכם הרואות אשר עשה ה' בבעל

מצודת דוד

ושנעה אחר מות אביו: (ה) וינגע ה'. ובד"ה נאמר שבא לו כועסו עם הכהנים בעת בא להקטיר ומיחו בו: בבית החפשית. ר"ל עזב הנהגת המלכות והיה חפשי מזה העמל וכמ"ש רז"ל שהמלכות יחשב לעבדות לפי רוב העמל: על הבית. היה ממונה על בית המלך להיות שופט משפט העם תחת המלך: (ח) בשנת שלשים ושמנה. כי ירבעם מלך שלש שנים בחיי אביו ולא אחרי מות אביו וכן כולם מ"א וכלו א"כ בל"ח לעזריה כי התחלת מלכות עזריה משמלך בחיי אביו והתחלת מלכות ירבעם משמת אביו היו בזמן אחד אם כן

in which Uzziah spent his last years, when he was afflicted with *zaraath*.

and Jotham the king's son—According to the Talmud, Jotham was born during the first year of Uzziah's affliction. Apparently, the elders and the princes ruled the land until he was old enough to assume that position [*Redak*].

judged the people of the land—He did not assume the title of king during his father's lifetime. Moreover, every verdict he issued, he said in his father's name [*Rashi, Sukkah* 45b].

7. **in the city of David**—in the royal graveyard, but not in the cave of the kings because of his affliction [*Pseudo-Rashi,* II Chron. 26:27].

5. And the Lord brought a plague upon the king, and he was stricken with *zaraath* until the day of his death, and he lived in a house of retirement, and Jotham the king's son, who was appointed over the palace, judged the people of the land.
6. And the rest of the events of Azariah and all that he did, are written in the book of the chronicles of the kings of Judah.
7. And Azariah slept with his forefathers, and they buried him with his forefathers in the city of David, and Jotham his son reigned in his stead.

ies, the intention is that Uzziah did the good deeds his father had done, but not the wicked deeds he had done [*Pseudo-Rashi, Mezudath David* II Chron. 26:4].

5. **And the Lord brought a plague upon the king**—*It is explained in Chronicles* (II 26:16–21) *that he entered the heichal, the Temple proper, to burn incense on the altar of incense* [*Rashi*].

Uzziah overstepped his boundary by attempting to assume the role of high priest and burn incense on the altar. Although the priests admonished him to refrain from doing so, he paid them no heed, until the lesion of *zaraath* literally "shone on his forehead," and he was forced to leave the Temple in haste. He received the punishment alluded to by the Torah, for any "stranger" who usurps the priesthood. See *Rashi* Num. 17:5.

in a house of retirement—lit. in a house of freedom. *He made himself a house in the cemetery, as it is said,* "(Ps. 88:6) *Among the dead a free man."*—*Rashi* quoting *Yerushalmi* (Palestinian Talmud). This statement is found nowhere in our editions of *Yerushalmi,* nor in any Midrash available today.

Our Rabbis (*Horioth* 10a) explain that Uzziah became free of the duties of the kingdom. The kingship is virtually a state of slavery, since the king has many burdens which he must bear whether he so wishes or not.

Jonathan renders: outside of Jerusalem [*Redak*].

Azulai correlates these two interpretations. By establishing his dwelling outside Jerusalem, he indicated that he had retired from the duties of the kingdom [*Homath Anach*].

As discussed above (7:3) that a *mezora* was forbidden to dwell in Jerusalem or in any other walled city. Therefore, Uzziah was forced to establish his residence outside. In the Kidron Valley, next to the tomb of Zechariah the prophet, is a house believed to be the *"beth hahofshith"*

שלשים ושמנה שנה לעזריהו מלך
יהודה מלך זכריהו בן־ירבעם על־
ישראל בשמרון ששה חדשים:
ט ויעש הרע בעיני יהוה כאשר עשו
אבתיו לא סר מחטאות ירבעם בן
נבט אשר החטיא את־ישראל:
י ויקשר עליו שלם בן־יבש ויכהו קבל־
עם וימיתהו וימלך תחתיו: יא ויתר
דברי זכריה הנם כתובים על־ספר
דברי הימים למלכי ישראל: יב הוא
דבר־יהוה אשר דבר אל־יהוא לאמר
בני רביעים ישבו לך על־כסא ישראל

תלתין ותמני שנין לעזריה מלכא דשבטא דבית יהודה מלך זכריהו בר ירבעם על ישראל בשמרון שתא ירחין: ט ועבד דביש קדם יי כמא דעבדו אבהתוהי לא סטא מחובי ירבעם בר נבט דחייב ית ישראל: י ומרד עלוהי שלם בר יבש ומחהי קדם עמא וקטליה ומלך תחותוהי: יא ושאר פתגמי זכריה הא אינון כתיבין על ספר פתגמי יומיא למלכי ישראל: יב הוא פתגמא דיי די מליל עם יהוא למימר בנין רביעאין יתבון לך על כורסי מלכותא דישראל

ת"א בני רביעים (סוריות מז):

מלא ואו

רש"י

שנה לעזריהו מלך יהודה מלך זכריהו. אף מכאן יש ללמוד שמלך עזריה משמת יואש מלך ישראל ט"ו שנה בחיי המליה אביו שאם לא עמד עד שמת אביו כמלא שלא עמד עד בשנת ט"ו לירבעם בן יואש וירבעם מלך ארבעים ואחת כמלא שמת ירבעם בשנת כ"ז לעוזיה והיאך הוא אומר בשנת ל"ח אלא ע"כ עוזיהו וירבעם מלכו כאחת אלא שירבעם מלך בחיי אביו יהואש ג' שנים לכך הוא אומר וירבעם ישב על כסאו שישב כבר ועוזיה עמד משמת יואש ומלך ירבעם מלבות שלמה ובסדר עולם ראיתי שירבעם מלך בחיי אביו שנה ואיני יודע אם שבוש הסופרים הוא שאיני יכול ליישב בשנת שלשים ושמנה לעזריה מלך זכריה אלא בענין זה: (י) ויכהו קבל עם. ומחהי קדם עמא. לעיני העם: (יב) ויהי כן. לא שהיתה כדאי מלכותו לימשך כ"כ אלא

רד"ק

ושמנה שנה לעזריהו. אם בדברי רז"ל שעזיהו וירבעם מלכו כאחת היה לו לומר בשנת ארבעים ואחת לעזריהו מלך זכריהו בן ירבעם אלא שנאמרה לדעתם כי זכריהו מלך בחיי אביו ג' שנים וזה לא מצאנו בכתוב וגם בעל סדר עולם לא דבר בזה דבר ואותם ג' שנים מנה אותם לזכריהו וגם לדברינו יתרים י"א שנה ונאמר כי אותם י"א שנה מלך זכריהו בימי אביו ולא ידענו למה אלא כן נראה לפי החשבון: (י) קבל עם. שתי מלות והוא כמו נגד העם תרגום נגד קבל ות"י קדם עמא: (יב) הוא דבר ה' אשר דבר. מלת הוא טעמו למעלה וימיתהו וימלך תחתיו כאשר דבר ה' וכיון שמלך רב או מעט כבר נתקיים דבר ה' והוסבה המלוכה לאחרים כי הם היו רשעים

רלב"ג

עליו קשר בירושלם מעת סר מאחרי ה' וינס לכיש ואז המליכו כל עם יהודה את עזריה ומלך בחיי אביו י"א שנה והעד הנאמן על זה הוא אמרו הוא בנה את אילת וישיבה ליהודה אחר שכב המלך עם אבותיו וזה לעדות קלת כי מלך בחיי אביו והיה בן ט"ז שנה כשהמליכוהו בחיי אביו:

מנחת שי

פעור כי כל האיש אשר הלך אחרי בעל פעור: (י) קבל עם. במקצת ספרים הוא מלה אחת אבל רד"ק כתב בפירוש ובשרשים שהן שתי מלות וכן תרגם יונתן

מצודת דוד

קדמה מלכות ירבעם למלכות עזריה שלש שנים מה שמלך בחיי אביו ולכן היתה שנת מ"א שלו בל"ח לעזריה ואז מלך זכריה: (יב) הוא דבר ה'. מוסב על המקרא שלפני פניו שנאמר וימלוך תחתיו והוא דבר ה' וגו': ויהי כן. כי מלכו יהואחז ויואש וירבעם וזכריה ונפסק

מצודת ציון

(י) קבל עם. תרגום של נגד הוא קבל:

and it was so—that Jehoahaz, Joash, Jeroboam, and Zechariah reigned. Then the dynasty was terminated [*Mezudath Zion*].

Rashi comments, *Not that his kingdom deserved to last that long, but to fulfill the word of the King, as it is said,* "(Is. 55:11) *So shall be My*

8. In the thirty-eighth year of Azariah the king of Judah, Zechariah the son of Jeroboam reigned over Israel in Samaria six months. 9. And he did what was evil in the eyes of the Lord, as his forefathers had done; he did not turn away from the sins of Jeroboam the son of Nebat, which he caused Israel to sin. 10. And Shallum the son of Jabesh revolted against him and struck him before the people and slew him, and reigned in his stead. 11. And the rest of the deeds of Zechariah are written in the book of chronicles of the kings of Israel. 12. This was the word of the Lord which he had spoken to Jehu, saying, "Your descendants of the fourth generation will sit on the throne of Israel," and it was so.

8. **In the thirty-eighth year of Azariah the king of Judah, Zechariah . . . reigned**—*From here too it is possible to deduce that Azariah reigned from the time that Joash king of Israel died, fifteen years during the lifetime of Amaziah his father, for if he did not rise until his father died, it follows that he did not rise until the fifteenth year of Jeroboam the son of Joash. Now, since Jeroboam reigned forty-one years, it follows that Jeroboam died in the twenty-seventh year of Uzziah. Now, how does Scripture say, "In the thirty-eighth year"? Rather, we are forced* to admit that *Uzziah and Jeroboam reigned simultaneously, except that Jeroboam reigned three years during the lifetime of his father Jehoash. Therefore, Scripture states,* "(13:13) *and Jeroboam had sat on his throne," meaning that he had already sat. Now Uzziah rose when Joash died and Jeroboam reigned as a full-fledged monarch* (lit. a full kingship). *I saw in Seder Olam* (ch. 19) *that Jeroboam reigned one year during his father's lifetime, and I do not know whether it is the copyists' error, for I cannot reconcile* the verse reading, *"In the thirty-eighth year of Azariah . . . Zechariah . . . reigned," except in this manner* [*Rashi*].

10. **and struck him before the people**—*Jonathan.* I.e. *before the eyes of the people* [*Rashi*].

Lit. opposite the people [*Redak, Mezudath Zion*].

12. **This was the word of the Lord**—This refers to v. 10, "and slew him, and reigned in his stead." As long as he reigned any period of time, the prophecy was fulfilled. Had they been righteous kings, their dynasty would have continued. Since they were wicked, however, their dynasty terminated as soon as the Lord had fulfilled the prophecy that Jehu's descendants would occupy the throne for four generations as reward for eradicating the Baal cult from Israel [*Redak*].

וַֽיְהִי־כֵֽן׃ יג שַׁלּ֣וּם בֶּן־יָבֵ֗ישׁ מָלַ֕ךְ בִּשְׁנַ֕ת שְׁלֹשִׁ֥ים וָתֵ֙שַׁע֙ שָׁנָ֔ה לְעֻזִיָּ֖ה מֶ֣לֶךְ יְהוּדָ֑ה וַיִּמְלֹ֥ךְ יֶֽרַח־יָמִ֖ים בְּשֹׁמְרֽוֹן׃ יד וַיַּעַל֩ מְנַחֵ֨ם בֶּן־גָּדִ֜י מִתִּרְצָ֗ה וַיָּבֹא֙ שֹׁמְר֔וֹן וַיַּ֛ךְ אֶת־שַׁלּ֥וּם בֶּן־יָבֵ֖ישׁ בְּשֹׁמְר֑וֹן וַיְמִיתֵ֖הוּ וַיִּמְלֹ֥ךְ תַּחְתָּֽיו׃ טו וְיֶ֙תֶר֙ דִּבְרֵ֣י שַׁלּ֔וּם וְקִשְׁר֖וֹ אֲשֶׁ֣ר קָשָׁ֑ר הִנָּ֣ם כְּתֻבִ֔ים עַל־סֵ֥פֶר דִּבְרֵ֛י הַיָּמִ֖ים לְמַלְכֵ֥י יִשְׂרָאֵֽל׃ טז אָ֣ז יַכֶּה־מְ֠נַחֵם אֶת־תִּפְסַ֨ח וְאֶת־כָּל־אֲשֶׁר־בָּ֤הּ וְאֶת־גְּבוּלֶ֙יהָ֙ מִתִּרְצָ֔ה כִּ֥י לֹ֖א פָתַ֑ח וַיַּ֕ךְ אֵ֥ת כָּל־הֶהָרוֹתֶ֖יהָ בִּקֵּֽעַ׃

תרגום

וַהֲוָה כֵן: יג שַׁלּוּם בַּר יָבֵשׁ מְלַךְ בִּשְׁנַת תְּלָתִין וּתְשַׁע שְׁנִין לְעֻזִּיָּה מַלְכָּא שִׁבְטָא דְבֵית יְהוּדָה וּמְלַךְ יַרְחֵי יוֹמִין בְּשָׁמְרוֹן: יד וּסְלֵיק מְנַחֵם בַּר גָּדִי מִתִּרְצָה וַאֲתָא לְשָׁמְרוֹן וּמְחָא יַת שַׁלּוּם בַּר יָבֵשׁ בְּשָׁמְרוֹן וְקַטְלֵיהּ וּמְלַךְ תְּחוֹתוֹהִי: טו וּשְׁאָר פִּתְגָּמֵי שַׁלּוּם וּמִרְדֵיהּ דִּי מְרַד הָא אִינוּן כְּתִיבִין עַל סְפַר פִּתְגָּמֵי יוֹמַיָּא לְמַלְכֵי יִשְׂרָאֵל: טז בְּכֵן מְחָא מְנַחֵם יַת תִּפְסַח וְיַת כָּל דִּי בַהּ וְיַת תְּחוּמָהָא מִתִּרְצָה אֲרֵי לָא פְתַחַת תַּרְעָהָא לְאַשְׁלָמָא וּמְחָא וְיַת כָּל מעדיתהא

רד"ק

כלם ואילו היו טובים ארכה מלכותם עוד וכבר היתה מלכותם ראויה להפסק קודם זה מפני עונותם ולא מלך זכריה אותם ששה חדשים אלא לקיים דבר ה' בעבור שידעו העם כי אמת דבר הנביא ליהוא בשם ה' כשאמר לו בני רבעים ישבו לך על כסא ישראל: (טז) את תפסח ואת כל אשר בה. תפסח לא היתה מארץ ישראל אלא מעבר הנהר מארם וכן כתוב כי הוא רודה בכל עבר הנהר מתפסח ועד עזה ונראה כי היתה לגבול ארץ ישראל נכח תרצה ותרצה היתה מארץ ישראל מקומו של מנחם ומנחם בא להלחם על תפסח וקרא לשלום אליה להיותה לו למס ולא פתחו לו עם העיר וזהו שאמר כי לא פתח ויך והכה אותה ואת כל גבוליה מתרצה כלומר מגבול תרצה ואילך כל הנמצא בכל גבוליה הכה ועוד כי כל ההרות שבה בקע דרך נקמה ובזיון: ההרותיה. בשתי ידיעות כמו בתוך האהלי:

רש"י

לקיים דבר מלך שנאמר כן יהיה דברי אשר יצא מפי וגו' (ישעיה נ"ה י"א): (טז) כי לא פתח. שר העיר לא פתח לו את העיר לקבלו למלך עליהם: ההרותיה. את הנשים ההרות שבה בקע:

מנחת שי

קדש עמה. וגם בספר ישן מסור עליו לית ואינון תרין מלין ולכל הנסחאות בקמץ חטוף: (יג) שלום בן יבש וגו' לעזיה מלך יהודה. בספר אחד כ"י כתוב לעזריה וכן בספר אחר נכתב בצדו ס"א לעזריה וכן הוא בתרגום אבל בספרים אחרים כתוב לעזיה וכן דינו מכח המסורת שנמנה עם הכתובים עזיה במסרה רבתא אות עי"ן וכן כתב מהרי"א ז"ל לעזיהו הוא עזרי' פעמים קורא אותו עזריה ופעמים עזיה ועיין מה שכתוב בדברי הימים א' ו': (יד) ויך את שלום בן יביש. במקצת ספרים מלא יו"ד וכן דינו על פי המסורת דבסוף שופטים נמסר כל החסרים בלישנהון ולא נמנה זה עמהם:

רלב"ג

(טז) ואת גבוליה מתרצה כי לא פתח. ידמה שתפסח לא היתה מארץ ישראל וקרא לה מנחם לשלום ולא הסכימה להשלים עמו ולא פתח לו ולזה הכה אותה ואת כל אשר בה ואת גבוליה אשר מחוץ לעיר מתרצה ואילך וגם כל המגדלים החזקים הבנויים בהרים אשר בה בקע:

מצודת ציון

(יג) ירח. חדש על שהוא נמנה במהלך הירח:

מצודת דוד

מזרעו המלוכה: (יג) בשנת שלשים ותשע. כי זכריה מלך בל"ח לעוזיה ונמלך ששה חדשים ואחריו מלך שלום והוא ל"ט לעוזיה:

(טז) מתרצה. מעבר תרצה: כי לא פתח. על שלא פתח שר תפסח את שער העיר לבוא בה ולזה הכה את תפסח ואת גבוליה אשר מעבר תרצה: בקע. פתח בטני ההרות להוציא וולדותיהן:

13. Shallum the son of Jabesh became king in the thirty-ninth
year of Uzziah the king of Judah, and he reigned a full month in
Samaria. 14. And Menahem the son of Gadi went up from Tirzah and came to Samaria; and he struck down Shallum the son
of Jabesh and slew him, and reigned in his stead. 15. And the
rest of the deeds of Shallum and his revolt that he revolted, are
written in the book of the chronicles of the kings of Israel.
16. Then Menahem attacked Tiphsah and all those therein and
its boundaries from Tirzah; since he did not open, he attacked
it; he ripped open all its pregnant women.

word, which will go forth from My mouth, it will not return *to Me empty . . .*" [*Rashi*].

13. **in the thirty-ninth year**—Since Zechariah reigned in the thirty-eighth year of Uzziah, and he reigned for six months, after which Shallum reigned, it was already the thirty-ninth year [*Mezudath David*].

16. **Tiphsah**—Tiphsah was not part of Eretz Israel, but across the river from Aram, as it is written, "(I Kings 5:4) for he ruled over the entire side of the river from Tiphsah up to Gaza." It appears to be on the border of Israel, opposite Tirzah, the place of Menahem's residence [*Redak*].

According to the map in *Kaftor Vaferah,* it is identical with Thapsacus, a city on the west bank of the Euphrates.

and its borders from Tirzah—I.e. he attacked the entire surrounding area from the borders of Tirzah and further [*Redak*].

since he did not open—I.e. *the mayor of the city did not open the city for him, to accept him as king over them* [*Rashi, Redak, Ralbag*].

its pregnant women—*The pregnant women therein, he ripped open* [*Rashi*].

Malbim explains that Menahem did not comply with the laws of war. When attacking a city, one side must be left open, to allow fugitives to escape. Additionally, the women and children must be spared. Menahem did not leave the fourth side open. That is the meaning of "since he did not open." I.e. he killed all those in the city since he did not leave the fourth side open to allow some to escape. In addition to this breach in observance, he ripped

יז בִּשְׁנַת שְׁלֹשִׁים וָתֵשַׁע שָׁנָה לַעֲזַרְיָה
מֶלֶךְ יְהוּדָה מָלַךְ מְנַחֵם בֶּן־גָּדִי עַל־
יִשְׂרָאֵל עֶשֶׂר שָׁנִים בְּשֹׁמְרוֹן׃ יח וַיַּעַשׂ
הָרַע בְּעֵינֵי יְהוָה לֹא סָר מֵעַל חַטֹּאות
יָרָבְעָם בֶּן־נְבָט אֲשֶׁר־הֶחֱטִיא אֶת־
יִשְׂרָאֵל כָּל־יָמָיו׃ יט בָּא פוּל מֶלֶךְ־אַשּׁוּר
עַל־הָאָרֶץ וַיִּתֵּן מְנַחֵם לְפוּל אֶלֶף כִּכַּר־
כָּסֶף לִהְיוֹת יָדָיו אִתּוֹ לְהַחֲזִיק הַמַּמְלָכָה
בְּיָדוֹ׃ כ וַיֹּצֵא מְנַחֵם אֶת־הַכֶּסֶף עַל־
יִשְׂרָאֵל עַל כָּל־גִּבּוֹרֵי הַחַיִל לָתֵת
לְמֶלֶךְ אַשּׁוּר חֲמִשִּׁים שְׁקָלִים כֶּסֶף
לְאִישׁ אֶחָד וַיָּשָׁב מֶלֶךְ אַשּׁוּר וְלֹא־
עָמַד שָׁם בָּאָרֶץ׃ כא וְיֶתֶר דִּבְרֵי מְנַחֵם
וְכָל־אֲשֶׁר עָשָׂה הֲלוֹא־הֵם כְּתוּבִים
עַל־סֵפֶר דִּבְרֵי הַיָּמִים לְמַלְכֵי יִשְׂרָאֵל׃
כב וַיִּשְׁכַּב מְנַחֵם עִם־אֲבֹתָיו וַיִּמְלֹךְ

מלא ואו

מְעַדִיתָהָא בְזַע׃ יז בִּשְׁנַת תְּלָתִין וּתְשַׁע שְׁנִין לַעֲזַרְיָה מַלְכָּא שִׁבְטָא דְבֵית יְהוּדָה מְלַךְ מְנַחֵם בַּר גָּדִי עַל יִשְׂרָאֵל עֲסַר שְׁנִין בְּשֹׁמְרוֹן׃ יח וַעֲבַד דְבִישׁ קֳדָם יְיָ לָא סָטָא מֵעַל חוֹבֵי יָרָבְעָם בַּר נְבָט דְּחַיֵיב יָת יִשְׂרָאֵל כָּל יוֹמוֹהִי׃ יט אֲתָא פוּל מַלְכָּא דְאַתּוּר עַל אַרְעָא וִיהַב מְנַחֵם לְפוּל אֲלַף כִּכְּרִין דִּכְסַף לְאִשְׁתְּלָמָא יְדוֹהִי עִמֵּיהּ לְאַתְקָפָא מַלְכוּתָא בִידֵיהּ׃ כ וּרְמָא מְנַחֵם יָת כַּסְפָּא עַל יִשְׂרָאֵל וְעַל כָּל גִּבָּרֵי חֵילָא לְמִתַּן לְמַלְכָּא דְאַתּוּר חַמְשִׁין סִלְעִין דִּכְסַף לְגַבְרָא חַד וְתָב מַלְכָּא דְאַתּוּר וְלָא אַנְזִיק תַּמָּן בְּאַרְעָא׃ כא וּשְׁאָר פִּתְגָמֵי מְנַחֵם וְכָל דִּי עֲבַד הֲלָא אִינוּן כְּתִיבִין עַל סְפַר פִּתְגָמֵי יוֹמַיָּא לְמַלְכֵי יִשְׂרָאֵל׃ כב וּשְׁכִיב מְנַחֵם עִם אֲבָהָתוֹהִי וּמְלַךְ פְּקַחְיָה
בריה

רד"ק

(כ) ולא עמד שם בארץ. לא נתעכב שם אלא שב לו לארצו כיון שקבל הכסף ולא שמרה מאויב אחר וי"ת ולא אנזיק תמן

מצודת דוד

(יז) בשנת שלשים ותשע. ר"ל אחר שעבר ל"ט לעזריה כי שלום מלך בסוף ל"ט לעזריה ונהרג אחר ירח ימים ובשנה הבאה בכלות ל"ט לעזריה בתחלת מ' מלך מנחם: עשר וגו'. ומקוטעות היו: (יט) בא פול. כאשר בא פול והבטיח מנחם לתת לו אלף ככר כסף לעזור לו על המלוכה: (כ) ויוצא מנחם. הוציא את הכסף מזולתו והטילו על ישראל ומפרש שעל גבורי החיל הטיל על כל אחד חמשים שקל: ולא

מצודת ציון

(יט) ידיו. כח ידיו: להחזיק. מל' חזק:

17. In the thirty-ninth year of Azariah the king of Judah, Menahem the son of Gadi reigned over Israel ten years in Samaria. 18. And he did what was evil in the eyes of the Lord; he did not turn away from the sins of Jeroboam the son of Nebat that he caused Israel to sin, all his days. 19. Pul the king of Assyria invaded the land, and Menahem gave Pul one thousand talents of silver that his hands might be with him to strengthen the kingdom in his hand. 20. Menahem exacted the money from Israel, from all the mighty warriors, that each man give fifty shekels of silver. And the king of Assyria returned and did not remain there in the land. 21. And the rest of the events of Menahem and all that he did, are written in the book of the chronicles of the kings of Israel. 22. And Menahem slept with his forefathers, and Pekahiah his son reigned in his stead.

open the pregnant women, in violation of the law to spare the women and childen [*Malbim*].

17. **In the thirty-ninth year**—i.e. after the thirty-ninth year. Shallum reigned at the end of the thirty-ninth year of Azariah, and was assassinated after one month. Menahem commenced his reign at the beginning of the fortieth year [*Mezudath David*].

ten years—incomplete years [*Mezudath David*].

19. **and Menahem gave Pul**—I.e. he promised to give Pul one thousand talents of silver to support him on his throne and protect him from his enemies [*Mezudath David*].

20. **Menahem exacted**—In order to obtain the money, he levied a tax on each of his mighty warriors [*Mezudath David*].

and did not remain there in the land—Once he received the money, he left the land, without adhering to his agreement to protect Menahem

פְּקַחְיָה בְנוֹ תַּחְתָּיו׃ כג בִּשְׁנַת חֲמִשִּׁים
שָׁנָה לַעֲזַרְיָה מֶלֶךְ יְהוּדָה מָלַךְ פְּקַחְיָה
בֶן־מְנַחֵם עַל־יִשְׂרָאֵל בְּשֹׁמְרוֹן שְׁנָתָיִם׃
כד וַיַּעַשׂ הָרַע בְּעֵינֵי יְהוָה לֹא סָר
מֵחַטֹּאות יָרָבְעָם בֶּן־נְבָט אֲשֶׁר
הֶחֱטִיא אֶת־יִשְׂרָאֵל׃ כה וַיִּקְשֹׁר עָלָיו
פֶּקַח בֶּן־רְמַלְיָהוּ שָׁלִישׁוֹ וַיַּכֵּהוּ
בְשֹׁמְרוֹן בְּאַרְמוֹן בֵּית־*מֶלֶךְ אֶת־
אַרְגֹּב וְאֶת־הָאַרְיֵה וְעִמּוֹ חֲמִשִּׁים אִישׁ
מִבְּנֵי גִלְעָדִים וַיְמִתֵהוּ וַיִּמְלֹךְ תַּחְתָּיו׃
כו וְיֶתֶר דִּבְרֵי פְקַחְיָה וְכָל־אֲשֶׁר עָשָׂה
הִנָּם כְּתוּבִים עַל־סֵפֶר דִּבְרֵי הַיָּמִים
לְמַלְכֵי יִשְׂרָאֵל׃ כז בִּשְׁנַת חֲמִשִּׁים
וּשְׁתַּיִם שָׁנָה לַעֲזַרְיָה מֶלֶךְ יְהוּדָה מָלַךְ

תרגום

בריה תחותוהי: כג בשנת חמשין שנין לעזריה מלך שבטא דבית יהודה מלך פקחיה בר מנחם על ישראל בשמרון תרתין שנין: כד ועבד דביש קדם יי לא סטא מחובי ירבעם בר נבט דחייב ית ישראל: כה ומרד עלוהי פקח בר רמליהו גבריה ומחהי בשמרון באידרון בית מלכא ית ארגוב וית אריא ועמיה חמשין גברא מבני גלעדאי וקטליה ומלך תחותוהי: כו ושאר פתגמי פקחיה וכל די עבד הא אינון כתיבין על ספר פתגמי יומיא למלכי ישראל: כז בשנת חמשין ותרתין שנין לעזריה מלך שבטא דבית

*מלא ואו המלך קרי

רד"ק

בארעא: (כה) בארמון בית מלך. כן כתיב וקרי המלך והענין אחד: את ארגב ואת האריה. עם ארגב ועם האריה ושני

רש"י

(כה) שלישו. גבור שלו: את ארגוב ואת האריה. כל ארגוב לשון פלטין החשובין וכל טרכונין בלשון ארמי פלטין החשובין למלכות בארמון הגדול אשר אצל הארגוב: ואת האריה. יש לומר שהיה אריה של זהב עומד באותו

מנחת שי

(כה) בית *מלך. המלך קרי:

רלב"ג

(כה) בארמון בית המלך את ארגב ואת האריה. אחשוב שארגוב קרא הממונה על כל חבל ארגוב והאריה קרא גבור אחד יקראוהו אריה על צד ההשאלה לרוב גבורתו. והנה קשר עליו פקח עם שני אלו השרים והיו עמו גם כן חמשים איש מבני גלעדים כי

מצודת ציון

(כה) שלישו. שר שלו:

מצודת דוד

עמד. לא נתעכב: (כג) בשנת חמשים שנה. כי מנחם מלך בשנת מ' לעזריה ומלך י' שנים מקוטעות וכלו אם כן במ"ט לעזריה ובשנה הבאה מלך פקחיה והיא נ' לעזריה: שנתים. ומקוטעות היו: (כה) בארמון. בהיכל של בית המלך: את ארגוב ואת האריה. עם הארגוב ועם האריה והם שמות בני גבורים ואולי נקרא ארגוב על שהיה מושל בחבל הארגוב והאריה ע"ש גבורתו ופקח התחבר עמהם ועוד היו עמו חמשים איש והמיתו את פקחיה: (כז) בשנת חמשים ושתים. כי פקחיה מלך בנ' לעזריה ומלך

Gileadites to execute his plot.

Others explain that Argov and Aryeh were two mighty warriors who were with Pekahiah when he

23. In the fiftieth year of Azariah the king of Judah, Pekahiah the son of Menahem reigned over Israel in Samaria for two years. 24. And he did what was evil in the eyes of the Lord; he did not turn away from the sins of Jeroboam the son of Nebat, that he caused the Israelites to sin. 25. And Pekah the son of Remaliah his officer, revolted against him, and he struck him down in Samaria in the inner chamber of the king's palace, near the palace and near the lion, and with him were fifty men of the Gileadites; and he slew him and reigned in his stead. 26. And the rest of the events of Pekahiah and all that he did, are written in the book of the chronicles of the kings of Israel. 27. In the fifty-second year of Azariah the king of Judah,

from his enemies. *Jonathan* renders: and he did not harm in the land [*Redak*].

23. **In the fiftieth year**—Since Menahem reigned in the fortieth year of Azariah, and reigned ten incomplete years, ending in the forty-ninth year, after which Pekahiah became king in the fiftieth year [*Mezudath David*].

two years—incomplete ones [*Mezudath David*].

25. **his officer**—[*Mezudath Zion*]. *Rashi,* following *Jonathan,* renders: *his mighty warrior.*

in the inner chamber of the king's palace—[*Jonathan*]. Lit. in the palace of the king's house.

near the palace (אַרְגֹּב) and near the lion—*Every "argov" is an expression of important palaces, and every* mention of *"terachunin" in Aramaic* (See *Rashi,* Deut. 3:4) *means palaces important for the kingdom.* Hence, he assassinated him *in the great chamber that was next to the palace* [*Rashi*].

and near the lion—*It is possible to say that a golden lion was standing in that palace* (or chamber) [*Rashi*].

Daath Soferim explains this to mean that there were two sections of the king's palace, the inner chamber and a hall named *"argov,"* probably named thus because it was built by the children of Argov who dwelt in Gilead on the east side of the Jordan. From this location, they would guard Israel from attack by external enemies. Since their symbol was alion, they erected a golden lion in the*"argov"* hall, symbolic of their protection of Israel. Pekah wished to avenge the death of Shallum the son of Jabesh, probably of Jabesh-Gilead, who was assassinated by Pekahiah's father, Menahem. He therefore brought with him fifty

פֶּקַח בֶּן־רְמַלְיָהוּ עַל־יִשְׂרָאֵל בְּשֹׁמְרוֹן
עֶשְׂרִים שָׁנָה: כח וַיַּעַשׂ הָרַע בְּעֵינֵי יְהוָה
לֹא סָר מִן־חַטֹּאות יָרָבְעָם בֶּן־נְבָט
אֲשֶׁר הֶחֱטִיא אֶת־יִשְׂרָאֵל: כט בִּימֵי
פֶּקַח מֶלֶךְ־יִשְׂרָאֵל בָּא תִּגְלַת פִּלְאֶסֶר
מֶלֶךְ אַשּׁוּר וַיִּקַּח אֶת־עִיּוֹן וְאֶת־אָבֵל
בֵּית־מַעֲכָה וְאֶת־יָנוֹחַ וְאֶת־קֶדֶשׁ וְאֶת־
חָצוֹר וְאֶת־הַגִּלְעָד וְאֶת־הַגָּלִילָה כֹּל
אֶרֶץ נַפְתָּלִי וַיַּגְלֵם אַשּׁוּרָה: ל וַיִּקְשָׁר־
קֶשֶׁר הוֹשֵׁעַ בֶּן־אֵלָה עַל־פֶּקַח בֶּן־
רְמַלְיָהוּ וַיַּכֵּהוּ וַיְמִיתֵהוּ וַיִּמְלֹךְ תַּחְתָּיו
בִּשְׁנַת עֶשְׂרִים לְיוֹתָם בֶּן־עֻזִּיָּה: לא וְיֶתֶר
דִּבְרֵי פֶקַח וְכָל־אֲשֶׁר עָשָׂה הִנָּם
כְּתוּבִים עַל־סֵפֶר דִּבְרֵי הַיָּמִים לְמַלְכֵי

תרגום

דְבֵית יְהוּדָה מְלַךְ פֶּקַח בַּר רְמַלְיָהוּ עַל יִשְׂרָאֵל בְּשֹׁמְרוֹן עַסְרִין שְׁנִין:
כח וַעֲבַד דְבִישׁ קֳדָם יְיָ לָא סְטָא מִן חוֹבֵי יָרָבְעָם בַּר נְבָט דְחַיֵיב יַת יִשְׂרָאֵל:
כט בְּיוֹמֵי פֶּקַח מַלְכָּא דְיִשְׂרָאֵל אֲתָא תִּגְלַת פִּלְאֶסֶר מַלְכָּא דְאַתּוּר וּשְׁבָא יַת עִיּוֹן וְיַת אָבֵל בֵּית מַעְכָא וְיַת יָנוֹחַ וְיַת קֶדֶשׁ וְיַת חָצוֹר וְיַת גִּלְעָדָא וְיַת גְלִילָא כָּל אַרְעָא שֵׁבֶט נַפְתָּלִי וְאַגְלִינוּן לְאַתּוּר:
ל וּמְרַד מֵירְדָא הוֹשֵׁעַ בַּר אֵלָה עַל פֶּקַח בַּר רְמַלְיָהוּ וּמְחָהִי וְקַטְלֵיהּ וּמְלַךְ תְּחוֹתוֹהִי בִּשְׁנַת עַסְרִין לְיוֹתָם בַּר עֻזִּיָּה:
לא וּשְׁאָר פִּתְגָמֵי פֶּקַח וְכָל דִי עֲבַד הָא אִינוּן כְּתִיבִין עַל סְפַר פִּתְגָמֵי יוֹמַיָא לְמַלְכֵי יִשְׂרָאֵל:

בשנת

רש"י

ארמון: (ל) בשנת עשרים ליותם. היה לו לומר בשנת ארבע לאחז שהרי כל ימי מלכות יותם שש עשרה שנה אלא לפי שהיה אחז רשע רצה הכתוב למנותם ליותם בקבר ולא לאחז בחייו כך הוא בסדר עולם:

רלב"ג

לבני גלעד היה הכל ארגב לפי מה שאחשוב: (כט) ויקח את עיון ואת אבל בית מעכה ואת ינוח ואת קדש. הנה זה היה לפי מה שאחשוב מה שזכר בספר ד"ה כי תגלת פלנאסר מלך אשור הגלה לראובני ולגדי ולחצי שבט המנשי ויביאם לחלח וחבור והרי מדי וכהר גוזן ולפי שאלו המדינות היו מהלאן אשור אמר כזה המקום ויגלם

מצודת דוד

בנתים מקוטעות וכלו כ"א לעוזיה ובשנה הבאה מלך פקח והיא כ"ב לעוזיה: עשרים שנה. ומקוטעות היו: (ל) בשנת עשרים ליותם. כי פקח מלך בכ"ב לעוזיה ובסוף השנה ההיא מת עוזיה ובתחלת השנה הבאה מלך יותם כנו וימי מלכותו ט"ז שנה ופקח מלך כ' שנה והם שנה אחת ממלכות עוזיה וט"ז ממלכות יותם וג' שנים אחרי מות יותם וכלו א"כ בי"ט מהתחלת מלכות יותם ובתחלת השנה הבאה מלך הושע והיא כ' להתחלת מלכות יותם ורצה הכתוב למנות שנות הושע לימי יותם הצדיק בקבר ולא לימי

רד"ק (מלא ואו)

גבורים היו שמם כך ועמהם בא ועם חמשים מבני גלעדים וימיתוהו: (ל) בשנת עשרים ליותם. והיאך היה זה והלא יותם לא מלך אלא י"ו והיאך מונה לו עשרים ועשרי' של פקח שלמו בשנת ד' לאחז א"כ היה לו לומר בשנת ד' לאחז ואומר בסדר עולם וכי אפשר לומר כן אלא שהיתה גזירה גזורה בימי יותם.

מנחת שי

(כט) את תגלת. בספרים אחרים כתובי יד כתוב תגלת וכגליון שלו ספרים אחרים תגלת ובספר אחד כתיבת יד כתוב בפנים תגלת ובחוץ תלגת קרי וככל שאר ספרים כתיב וקרי תגלת כתבירין שבעינן. ובדברי הימים ב' כ"ח כתיב

מצודת ציון

(כט) אבל בית מעכה. כן שם העיר: הגלילה. מלשון הגליל:

Alternatively, since Pekah's death was decreed during Jotham's reign, it is recorded as in the twentieth year counting from Jotham's coronation. This, too, is found in *Seder Olam* ad loc. [*Redak*].

Pekah the son of Remaliah reigned over Israel in Samaria twenty years. 28. And he did what was evil in the eyes of the Lord; he did not turn away from the sins of Jeroboam the son of Nebat, which he had caused Israel to commit. 29. In the days of Pekah the king of Israel, Tiglath-pileser the king of Assyria came and took Ijon, Abel-beth-maacah, Janoah, Kedesh, Hazor, Gilead, and Galilee, the entire land of Naphtali; and he exiled them to Assyria. 30. And Hoshea the son of Elah revolted against Pekah the son of Remaliah, and he struck him and slew him, and reigned in his stead, in the twentieth year of Jotham the son of Uzziah. 31. And the rest of the events of Pekah and all that he did are written in the book of the chronicles of the kings of Israel.

was assassinated. They, too, were slain with him [*Abarbanel* and probably *Jonathan*].

29. **the entire land of Naphtali**— All these cities, with the exception of Gilead, belonged to the tribe of Naphtali.

and he exiled them to Assyria— This was the first Assyrian exile, which took place in the fourth year of Ahaz, king of Judah. In the twelfth year of Ahaz, "the Lord incited Pul, the king of Assyria . . . and he exiled the Reubenites, the Gadites, and the half-tribe of Manasseh (I Chron. 5:26)." As mentioned, this took place in the twelfth year of Ahaz, at the beginning of Hoshea's revolt, as is stated, "And the king of Assyria found conspiracy in Hoshea (below 17:4)," after he had subordinated himself to him for eight years. Although the calculation is not explicit in the Bible, it is, nevertheless, possible to deduce it from the *Baraitha* of *Seder Olam* (ch. 22). The third exile took place in the sixth year of Hezekiah, the ninth year of Hoshea's revolt, when Samaria, the capital, was captured, and everyone was exiled [*Rashi,* Isaiah 8:23].

Rashi continues to explain that the first exile included the tribe of Zebulun as is mentioned by the prophet Isaiah.

30. **in the twentieth year of Jotham**—*He should have said, "in the fourth year of Ahaz," since Jotham's entire reign lasted sixteen years, but since Ahaz was wicked, Scripture preferred to count them (I.e. the years) to Jotham who was in the grave, rather than to Ahaz,* who was *alive. Thus it is stated in Seder Olam* (Ch. 22) [*Rashi*].

ישראל: לב בשנת שתים לפקח בן־
רמליהו מלך ישראל מלך יותם בן־
עזיהו מלך יהודה: לג בן־עשרים וחמש
שנה היה במלכו ושש עשרה שנה
מלך בירושלם ושם אמו ירושא בת־
צדוק: לד ויעש הישר בעיני יהוה ככל
אשר־עשה עזיהו אביו עשה: לה רק
הבמות לא סרו עוד העם מזבחים
ומקטרים בבמות הוא בנה את־שער
בית־יהוה העליון: לו ויתר דברי יותם
וכל־אשר עשה הלא־הם כתובים
על־ספר דברי הימים למלכי יהודה:
לז בימים ההם החל יהוה להשליח

תרגום

לב בשנת תרתין לפקח בר רמליהו מלכא דישראל מלך יותם בר עזיהו מלך שבטא דבית יהודה: לג בר עשרין וחמש שנין הוה כד מלך ושית עשרי שנין מלך בירושלם ושום אמיה ירושא בת צדוק: לד ועבד דכשר קדם יי ככל דעבד עזיה אבוהי עבד: לה לחוד במתא לא עטרא עד כען עמא מדבחין ומסקין בוסמיא על במתא הוא בנא ית תרע בית מקדשא דיי עלאה: לו ושאר פתגמי יותם וכל די עבד הלא אינון כתיבין על ספר פתגמי יומיא למלכי דבית יהודה: לז ביומיא האינון שרי יי לגראה בדבית

רד"ק

דבר אחר שרצה הכתוב למנות ליותם בקבר ולא לאחז בחיים: (לב) בשנת שתים לפקח. בתחלית שתים ופקח מלך בשנת חמשים ושתים לעזריה ועזריה מת בסוף נ"ב לו ומלך יותם הנה בשנת שתים לפקח מלך יותם: (לה) הוא בנה את שער בית ה' העליון. השער הזה היה בין בית ה' ובין בית המלך כמו שראינו בדבר יואש ויורידו את המלך מבית ה' ויבואו דרך שער הרצים בית המלך ומה שאמר כי הוא בנה אותו הוסיף בו בניין או נפל ובנהו שהרי שלמה בנה שער בין ביתו ובית ה' כמו שאמר ועולתו אשר יעלה בית ה': (לז) בימים ההם החל ה'. אחר שמת יותם:

רש"י

(לז) בימי' ההם. בסוף ימיו של יותם: להשליח. לגרות:

מנחת שי

סלנת: (לה) ומקטרים. הוא"ו במאריך כמו שכתבתי למעלה:

רלב"ג

אשורה: (לב) בשנת שתים לפקח בן רמליהו מלך ישראל מלך יותם. ר"ל בראש השנה השנית כי בראש שנת חמשים ושנים לעזיה מלך פקח ומת עזיה בשנה ההיא: (לז) בימים ההם החל ה' להשליח ביהודה רצין. ר"ל לגרות ביהודה או לשלח וזה היה אחרי מות יותם כי בימי אחז נתחברו אלה המלכים על ירושלם מפני רוב הטאי אחז כמו שנתבאר בספר ד"ה והם הכה בה מכה גדולה ואחר זה היו צרים על ירושלם ולא יכלו להלחם כי חמל הש"י על יהודה ולא אמר להשחיתו:

מצודת ציון

(לז) החל. התחיל: להשליח. לגרות ולהסית כמו הנני משליח בך (שמות ח):

מצודת דוד

אחז כמו הרשע בחיים: (לב) בשנת שתים. כי פקח מלך שנה אחת בימי עוזיה ויותם מלך בשנה הבאה והיא בשנת ב' לפקח: (לג) ושש וגו'. ומקוטעות היו: (לה) הוא בנה. ר"ל עשה עליו בנין נכבד וגדול ממה שהית' או שנפל ועשהו מחדש ואולי זהו הנקרא שער ה' החדש (ירמיה כ"ו): (לז) בימים ההם. אחרי מות יותם:

Manasseh did what was evil in the eyes of the Lord; Josiah did not heed the words of prophecy from G-d; Zedekiah did what was evil in the eyes of the Lord and did not humble himself before Jeremiah. In Jotham, however, no trace of sin was found. (R. Eliezer the son of Moses told me this.) [*Pseudo-Rashi* II Chron. 27:2].

35. **the upper gate of the house of the Lord**—He enhanced the building of the gate between the Temple and the royal palace. The gate itself had been built by King Solomon. Alternatively, he rebuilt the gate after it had collapsed [*Redak*].

32. In the second year of Pekah the son of Remaliah the king of Israel, Jotham the son of Uzziah the king of Judah became king. 33. He was twenty-five years old when he became king, and he reigned sixteen years in Jerusalem; and his mother's name was Jerusha the daughter of Zadok. 34. And he did what was right in the eyes of the Lord; like all that his father Uzziah did, he did. 35. However, the high places were not removed; the people were still slaughtering sacrifices and burning incense on the high places. He built the upper gate of the house of the Lord. 36. And the rest of the events of Jotham and all that he did, are written in the book of chronicles of the kings of Judah.

37. In those days, the Lord began to incite

32. **In the second year of Pekah**—I.e. at the beginning of the second year, since Pekah became king in the fifty-second year of Azariah, and Azariah died that very year, Jotham must have become king at the beginning of the second year of Pekah [*Redak*].

33. **sixteen years**—incomplete years [*Mezudath David*].

34. **like all that his father Uzziah did, he did**—i.e. like all the good deeds his father had done. That is what R. Shimeon the son of Yohai said in Tractate *Sotah* (sic. Should be *Sukkah* 45b), "If Abraham would take upon himself all the sins of the generations until his time, I would take upon myself the sins of the generations from Abraham until my time. And if Jotham the son of Uzziah were with me, we would take upon ourselves the sins of all the generations from Abraham until the end of all generations, for in all the kings before him and after him we find sin, except in Jotham. Concerning David it is written, "(I Kings 15:5) Only concerning the matter of Uriah the Hittite;" concerning Solomon it is written, "(Ibid 11:4) His wives turned his heart away;" Rehoboam forsook the Lord's Torah; Abijah "(Ibid 15:3) went in all his father's sins;" Asa took silver and gold from the treasuries of the house of the Lord, and put the prophet in prison; Jehoshaphat associated with a wicked man (Ahab and his son Ahaziah); Ahaziah's mother advised him to sin; Joash killed Zechariah and was (later punished by being) sexually molested (*Yer. Kid.* 1:7); Amaziah prostrated himself before the graven images of Seir; Uzziah entered the Temple to burn incense; Ahaz went in the ways of the kings of Israel and also made monuments for the *baalim*; Hezekiah became haughty and there was anger upon him, and the sages did not concur with him on three things that he did;

בִּיהוּדָה רְצִין מֶלֶךְ אֲרָם וְאֵת פֶּקַח בֶּן
רְמַלְיָהוּ׃ לח וַיִּשְׁכַּב יוֹתָם עִם־אֲבֹתָיו
וַיִּקָּבֵר עִם־אֲבֹתָיו בְּעִיר דָּוִד אָבִיו
וַיִּמְלֹךְ אָחָז בְּנוֹ תַּחְתָּיו׃ טז א בִּשְׁנַת
שְׁבַע־עֶשְׂרֵה שָׁנָה לְפֶקַח בֶּן־רְמַלְיָהוּ
מָלַךְ אָחָז בֶּן־יוֹתָם מֶלֶךְ יְהוּדָה׃ ב בֶּן
עֶשְׂרִים שָׁנָה אָחָז בְּמָלְכוֹ וְשֵׁשׁ־עֶשְׂרֵה
שָׁנָה מָלַךְ בִּירוּשָׁלִָם וְלֹא־עָשָׂה הַיָּשָׁר
בְּעֵינֵי יְהוָה אֱלֹהָיו כְּדָוִד אָבִיו׃ ג וַיֵּלֶךְ
בְּדֶרֶךְ מַלְכֵי יִשְׂרָאֵל וְגַם אֶת־בְּנוֹ
הֶעֱבִיר בָּאֵשׁ כְּתֹעֲבוֹת הַגּוֹיִם אֲשֶׁר
הוֹרִישׁ יְהוָה אֹתָם מִפְּנֵי בְּנֵי יִשְׂרָאֵל׃
ד וַיְזַבֵּחַ וַיְקַטֵּר בַּבָּמוֹת וְעַל־הַגְּבָעוֹת

בְּדְבֵית יְהוּדָה רְצִין
מַלְכָּא דַאֲרָם וְיָת פֶּקַח
בַּר רְמַלְיָהוּ׃ לח וּשְׁכִיב
יוֹתָם עִם אֲבָהָתוֹהִי
וְאִתְקְבַר עִם אֲבָהָתוֹהִי
בְּקַרְתָּא דְדָוִד אֲבוּהִי
וּמְלַךְ אָחָז בְּרֵיהּ
תְּחוֹתוֹהִי׃ א בִּשְׁנַת
שְׁבַע עַסְרֵי שְׁנִין לְפֶקַח
בַּר רְמַלְיָהוּ מְלַךְ אָחָז
בַּר יוֹתָם מַלְכָּא דְשִׁבְטָא
דְבֵית יְהוּדָה׃ ב בַּר
עַשְׂרִין שְׁנִין אָחָז כַּד
מְלַךְ וְשִׁית עַסְרֵי שְׁנִין
מְלַךְ בִּירוּשְׁלֵם וְלָא עֲבַד
דְּכָשַׁר קֳדָם יְיָ אֱלָהֵיהּ
כְּדָוִד אֲבוּהִי׃ ג וַאֲזַל
בְּאוֹרַח מַלְכֵי יִשְׂרָאֵל
וְאַף יָת בְּרֵיהּ אַעֲבַר
בְּנוּרָא כְּתוֹעֲבַת עַמְמַיָּא
דְתָרֵיךְ יְיָ יָתְהוֹן מִן קֳדָם
בְּנֵי יִשְׂרָאֵל׃ ד וּדְבַח
וְאַסִּיק בּוּסְמִין עַל
בָּמָתָא וְעַל רָמָתָא
ותחות

מנחת שי

(לח) וישכב יותם עם אבותיו ויקבר עם אבותיו בעיר דוד אביו. בספרים אחרים כתב יד וגם בדפוס ישן המשיטו ויקבר עם אבתיו ולף בדפוס ישן מונילוהא ליכא בתרגום ואתקבר עם אבהתוהי ובספרים אחרים איתנהו בפסוק ובתרגום:

מצודת דוד

טז (א) בשנת שבע עשרה. כי יותם מלך כב׳ לפקח וימי מלכותו ט״ז שנה וכלו בי״ז לפקח ואז מלך אחז: (ב) ושש וגו׳. ומקוטעות היו: (ג) העביר באש. היא עבודת המולך שמעביר בנו בין שתי מדורות אש:

מצודת ציון

טז (ג) הוריש. גירש:

This is the manner of worshipping the Molech, by passing a child between two fires [*Mezudath David*].

There is a dispute between *Rashi, San.* 64b, and *Ramban,* Lev. 18:21. *Rashi*'s view is that the custom of the Molech cult was to give the child to the priest, who would pass him between two fires, but not to burn him. There were, however, other cults who used to burn children as a sacrifice to their gods. These were the nations mentioned below 17:31, the Sefarvaim who burnt their children to Adramelech and Anamelech, the gods of Sefarvaim. It was to such a cult that Ahaz belonged, for the Talmud relates (*San.* 63b) that Ahaz attempted to sacrifice his son Hezekiah to the flames, but his mother saved him by anointing him with the oil of the salamander.

Ramban maintains that, according to the Molech ritual, the father would hand the child to the priests, who would wave him before the god, and then return him to the father, who would then pass him through the fire, a practice usually

Rezin the king of Aram and Pekah the son of Remaliah against Judah. 38. And Jotham slept with his forefathers, and he was buried with his forefathers in the city of David his father, and Ahaz his son reigned in his stead.

16

1. In the seventeenth year of Pekah the son of Remaliah, Ahaz the son of Jotham the king of Judah became king. 2. Ahaz was twenty years old when he became king, and he reigned sixteen years in Jerusalem; and he did not do what was proper in the eyes of the Lord his God like David his father. 3. He went in the ways of the kings of Israel, and also he passed his son through fire in the abominable manner of the nations whom the Lord had driven out from before the children of Israel. 4. And he slaughtered sacrifices and burnt incense on the high places and on the hills,

37. **In those days**—*at the end of Jotham's days* [*Rashi*].

According to others, after Jotham's death [*Redak, Mezudath David*].

to incite—[*Rashi, Mezudath Zion* after *Jonathan*]. Lest one render, *to send, Rashi* makes clear that the conjugation indicates that this is not the correct translation. *Ralbag,* however, suggests that either translation may be correct.

He goes on to explain that this took place after Jotham's death, as a punishment for Ahaz' sins, as is delineated in II Chron. 28:1–8.

1. **In the seventeenth year**—Since Jotham became king in the second year of Pekah, and he reigned sixteen years, which ended in the seventeenth year of Pekah [*Mezudath David*].

2. **sixteen years**—incomplete ones [*Mezudath David*].

and he did not do what was proper in the eyes of the Lord his God like David his father—Judging from the following verses, this seems to be a gross understatement. It is likely that the Scripture wishes to distinguish between Ahaz and other kings, such as Joash, Amaziah, and Uzziah, who, originally did what was proper in God's eyes, but later were misled. Ahaz, however, *never* did what was proper in the eyes of God like his father David [*K'li Y'kar*].

3. **he passed his son through fire—**

ותחת כל־עץ רענן: ה אז יעלה רצין
מלך־ארם ופקח בן־רמליהו מלך־
ישראל ירושלם למלחמה ויצרו על־
אחז ולא יכלו להלחם: ו בעת ההיא
השיב רצין מלך־ארם את־אילת
לארם וינשל את־היהודים מאילות
וארומים באו אילת וישבו שם עד
היום הזה: ז וישלח אחז מלאכים אל־
תגלת פלסר מלך־אשור לאמר עבדך
ובנך אני עלה והושעני מכף מלך־
ארם ומכף מלך ישראל הקומים עלי:
ח ויקח אחז את־הכסף ואת־הזהב

ואדומים קרי

ותחות כל אילן עבוף:
ה בכן סליק רצין מלכא
דארם ופקח בר רמליהו
מלכא דישראל
לירושלם לאגחא
קרבא וצרו על אחז ולא
יכילו לאגחא: ו בעדנא
ההיא אתיב רצין מלכא
דארם ית אילת לארם
ותריך ית יהודאי
מאילת וארמאי אתו
לאילת ויתיבו תמן עד
יומא הדין: ז ושלח אחז
אזגדין לות תגלת פלסר
מלכא דאתור למימר
עבדך וברך אנא סק
ופרוקני מיד מלכא
דארם ומיד מלכא
דישראל דקמו עלי:
ח ונסיב אחז ית כספא
וית דהבא דאשתכח
בבית

רד"ק

(ו) את אילת לארם. שכבר לקחה עזריה מלך יהודה: וינשל את היהודים מאילות. זהו אילת כי כן היתה נקראת אילת ואילות וכן בדברי הימים אילות ופי׳ וינשל כמו ונשל גוים רבים מפניך ענין גירושין ושילוח: ארומים באו אילות. כתיב ארמים לפי שמלך ארם לקחה ועל ידו ישבו הארמים וקרי ואדומים בדל"ת כי לבני אדום היתה כמו שפירשנו למעלה: (ז) הקומים עלי.

מנחת שי

טז (ו) וארומים. ואדומים קרי והוא חד מן ד׳ מלין כתיבין ריש וקרינן דל"ת וסימן נכדר במס"ג בירמיה סימן ל"א:

רלב"ג

(ו) וינשל את היהודים מאילות. ר"ל שכבר השליכם וגרשם משם והוא אילת שבנה עזריה כמו שקדם: (ז) הקומים עלי.

מצודת ציון

(ה) ויצרו. מלשון מצור: (ו) וינשל. ענין השלכה כמו ונשל גוים

מצודת דוד

(ה) ולא יכלו להלחם. לא התגברו במלחמ׳ על ירושלים: (ו) השיב וגו׳ את אילת. זו היא האמור למעלה אשר בנה עזריה והשיבה ליהודה ועתה בא רצין והשיבה לארם: וינשל. גלה משם היהודים והאדומים ישבו בה כאשר ישבו בה מאז

variations from our editions].

6. **restored Elath to Aram** —As mentioned above (14:22), Azariah had rebuilt Elath and restored it to Judah. Now Rezin recaptured it and restored it to Aram [*Redak, Mezudath David*].

Elath . . . Eloth—variant spellings of the same name. It is not unusual in the Bible for people or places to have two names, especially similar ones. The second spelling is used in Chron. [*Redak*].

and Edomites came to Elath—The *K'thib* is *Arameans*. Since the Arameans took it, they settled there. Since it had originally belonged to Edom (I Kings 9:26), the Edomites, too, were given that privilege [*Redak*].

Moreover, the Chronicler mentions that the Edomites attacked

and under every green tree. 5. Then Rezin the king of Aram
and Pekah the son of Remaliah the king of Israel, went up to
Jerusalem to wage war, and they besieged Ahaz, but could not
wage war [with him]. 6. At that time, Rezin the king of Aram
restored Elath to Aram, and drove out the Judeans from Eloth,
and Edomites came to Elath and dwelt there until this day.
7. And Ahaz sent messengers to Tiglath-pileser the king of
Assyria, saying, "I am your servant and your son. Come up and
save me from the hand of the king of Aram and from the hand
of the king of Israel who have risen up against me." 8. And
Ahaz took the silver and the gold

resulting in death. Adramelech and Anamelech were variations of Molech. Thus it was the Molech cult to whom Ahaz, belonged, and Molech was the deity to which he attempted to sacrifice his son Hezekiah.

Malbim notes that in this verse the singular form is used, "he passed his son." In II Chron. 28:3, however, the plural form is used, "he burned his sons in the fire." This implies that he attempted to burn his two sons, but succeeded only in burning one, since Hezekiah was saved by his mother.

5. **could not wage war [with him]**—According to the account in II Chron. 28, both Rezin and Pekah waged successful wars against Ahaz, taking a heavy toll of lives and captives. Our text informs us, however, that they were repulsed when they attempted to take Jerusalem and destroy the Davidic dynasty. They first attacked independently of each other. When they saw that they were unsuccessful, they joined forces, as the prophet Isaiah reports (Is. 7:2). Yet, they still found it impossible to vanquish the Holy City [*Malbim*].

Although our text does not trace Ahaz' lineage, the text of Isaiah describes him as "(7:1) Ahaz the son of Jotham the son of Uzziah, the king of Judah." *Rashi* cites a Midrashic passage to illustrate the necessity of tracing his lineage. "The ministering angels said before the Holy One, Blessed be He, 'Woe! Who is this wicked man who has become king?' He replied to them, 'He is the son of Jotham; he is the grandson of Uzziah. His forebears were righteous. I, therefore, do not wish to harm him.' This is the meaning of the words, 'and he could not wage war against it,' because of the merit of his forefathers.'" [*Rashi,* Is. 7:1, from *Gen. Rabbah* 63:1, with slight

הַנִּמְצָא בֵּית יְהוָה וּבְאֹצְרוֹת בֵּית הַמֶּלֶךְ וַיִּשְׁלַח לְמֶלֶךְ־אַשּׁוּר שֹׁחַד׃
ט וַיִּשְׁמַע אֵלָיו מֶלֶךְ אַשּׁוּר וַיַּעַל מֶלֶךְ אַשּׁוּר אֶל־דַּמֶּשֶׂק וַיִּתְפְּשֶׂהָ וַיַּגְלֶהָ קִירָה וְאֶת־רְצִין הֵמִית׃
י וַיֵּלֶךְ הַמֶּלֶךְ אָחָז לִקְרַאת תִּגְלַת פִּלְאֶסֶר מֶלֶךְ־אַשּׁוּר דּוּמֶּשֶׂק וַיַּרְא אֶת־הַמִּזְבֵּחַ אֲשֶׁר בְּדַמָּשֶׂק וַיִּשְׁלַח הַמֶּלֶךְ אָחָז אֶל־אוּרִיָּה הַכֹּהֵן אֶת־דְּמוּת הַמִּזְבֵּחַ וְאֶת־תַּבְנִיתוֹ לְכָל־מַעֲשֵׂהוּ׃
יא וַיִּבֶן אוּרִיָּה הַכֹּהֵן אֶת־הַמִּזְבֵּחַ כְּכֹל אֲשֶׁר־שָׁלַח הַמֶּלֶךְ אָחָז מִדַּמֶּשֶׂק כֵּן עָשָׂה אוּרִיָּה הַכֹּהֵן עַד־בּוֹא הַמֶּלֶךְ־אָחָז מִדַּמָּשֶׂק׃
יב וַיָּבֹא הַמֶּלֶךְ מִדַּמֶּשֶׂק וַיַּרְא הַמֶּלֶךְ אֶת־

תרגום

בְּבֵית מַקְדְּשָׁא דַיְיָ וּבְאוֹצְרֵי בֵּית מַלְכָּא וְשַׁדַּר לְמַלְכָּא דְאַתּוּר שׁוּחֲדָא׃ ט וְקַבֵּיל מִנֵּיהּ מַלְכָּא דְאַתּוּר וּסְלֵיק מַלְכָּא דְאַתּוּר עַל דַּמֶּשֶׂק וְאַחְדַהּ וְאַגְלֵי עַמָּא דִּי בַהּ לְקִירִינָא וְיַת רְצִין קְטַל׃ י וַאֲזַל מַלְכָּא אָחָז לְקַדָּמוּת תִּגְלַת פִּלְאֶסֶר מַלְכָּא דְאַתּוּר לְדוּמֶּשֶׂק וַחֲזָא יַת מַדְבְּחָא דִּי בְדַמֶּשֶׂק וְשַׁדַּר מַלְכָּא אָחָז לְוָת אוּרִיָּה כַּהֲנָא יַת דְּמוּת מַדְבְּחָא וְיַת טִיקוּסֵיהּ לְכָל עוֹבָדוֹהִי׃ יא וּבְנָא אוּרִיָּה כַהֲנָא יַת מַדְבְּחָא כְּכֹל דִּשְׁלַח מַלְכָּא אָחָז מִדַּמֶּשֶׂק כֵּן עֲבַד אוּרִיָּה כַּהֲנָא עַד דַּאֲתָא מַלְכָּא אָחָז מִדַּמֶּשֶׂק׃ יב וַאֲתָא מַלְכָּא מִדַּמֶּשֶׂק וַחֲזָא מַלְכָּא יַת מדבחא

רש"י

טז (ט) ויגלה קירה. את העם אשר בה הגלה למדינה ששמה קיר: (יא) עד בוא. לפני בוא המלך

כצ"ל

רד"ק

תואר בפלס טובים: (ט) ויגלה קירה. העם אשר בה הגלה אל קיר וקיר היתה מאשור הוא שאומר עמוס הנביא וגלו עם ארם

רלב"ג

ר"ל הקמים עלי: (ט) ויגלה קירה. ר"ל שהגלה העם אשר בדמשק אל קיר: (יא) ויבן אוריה הכהן. ר"ל ויבנה אוריה הכהן את המזבח בעוד שהיה בא המלך אחז מדמשק עד שכאשר בא מלאו בנוי:

מנחת שי

(י) דומשק. נכתב בוא"ו עם דגש במ"ם ונמסר עליו לית מלא:

מצודת דוד

טרם לקחה אמליה ולפי שבא ארם להחזיר לאדום לזה אמר השיב לארם כאלו היתה שלהם מאז כי באו במקום אדום: (ט) ויגלה. הגלה אנשים אל קיר והיא מארץ אשור: (י) אוריה הכהן. יתכן שהוא אמריה הנזכר בד"ה א' ה' ועיין בסוף הספר בחשבון סדורות: את דמות המזבח. כי ישרה בעיניו תבניתו ושלח הדמות אל הכהן לעשות מזבח כדמותו: לכל מעשהו. ר"ל את תבנית הליורים הפרטים שבו: (יא) ככל וגו'. אף הליורים הפרטים: עד בוא. טרם בוא המלך וגו': (יב) ויקרב. קרב אל המזבח והעלה עליו

מצודת ציון

רכים (דברים ז'): (ח) בית ה'. בבית ה':

Chron. 28:23). For this purpose, he desired an altar constructed in the manner of the one he saw in Damascus, in order to worship God in conjunction with pagan deities [*Malbim*].

Uriah the priest—*Mezudath David* conjectures that Uriah is to be identified with Amariah, mentioned in I Chron. 5:37. He was the son of Azariah, who heroically opposed King Uzziah when he entered the Temple to burn incense. The commentators point out that Azariah still served as high priest during the reign of Hezekiah (II Chron. 31:13.)

that was found in the house of the Lord and in the treasuries of the king's palace, and sent them to the king of Assyria as a bribe. 9. And the king of Assyria heeded him, and the king of Assyria went up to Damascus and seized it, and exiled [its inhabitants] to Kir, and he slew Rezin. 10. And King Ahaz went toward Tiglath-Pileser the king of Assyria to Damascus, and he saw the altar that was in Damascus, and King Ahaz sent to Uriah the priest the likeness of the altar and its pattern, according to all its workmanship. 11. And Uriah the priest built the altar, according to all that King Ahaz sent from Damascus, so did Uriah the priest make it until King Ahaz came from Damascus. 12. And the king came from Damascus, and the king saw

Judah and took captives (28:17). They may have had an alliance with Aram, and were given the privilege of settling territory that Aram had seized [*Malbim*].

9. **and exiled it to Kir**—*The people therein he exiled to a province named Kir* [*Rashi*].

Kir belonged to Assyria. This exile was prophesied by Amos (1:5), "and the people of Aram will be exiled to Kir." [*Redak*].

10. **And King Ahaz went toward Tiglath-Pileser**—Scripture does not indicate the reason for Ahaz going to Damascus to meet Tiglath-Pileser. Perhaps he went to appeal to him to restore the cities the Philistines had taken, or to beg him not to besiege Judah. The Chronicler states that "he troubled him and did not strengthen him. Although Ahaz had divided the house of the Lord and the house of the king and the princes, and given them to the king of Assyria, he was of no assistance to him (II Chron. 28:20, 21)." According to *Pseudo-Rashi,* he was of no assistance in that he did not restore to him the cities taken by the Philistines, and according to *Redak,* he was of no assistance to him since, although he defeated Aram and Israel, he himself attacked Judah. According to *Malbim,* he did protect him from any of his other adversaries. Had Ahaz heeded the prophet Isaiah, and trusted God to save him from Israel and Aram, he would not have been confronted by any of these difficulties, nor would he have thought it necessary to bribe the king of Assyria. See Isaiah 7.

and he saw the altar—The Chronicler relates that Ahaz brought offerings to the gods of Aram, hoping that they would aid him as they had previously done for Aram (II

הַמִּזְבֵּחַ וַיִּקְרַב הַמֶּלֶךְ עַל־הַמִּזְבֵּחַ וַיַּעַל עָלָיו׃ יג וַיַּקְטֵר אֶת־עֹלָתוֹ וְאֶת־מִנְחָתוֹ וַיַּסֵּךְ אֶת־נִסְכּוֹ וַיִּזְרֹק אֶת־דַּם־הַשְּׁלָמִים אֲשֶׁר־לוֹ עַל־הַמִּזְבֵּחַ׃ יד וְאֵת הַמִּזְבַּח הַנְּחֹשֶׁת אֲשֶׁר לִפְנֵי יְהוָה וַיַּקְרֵב מֵאֵת פְּנֵי הַבַּיִת מִבֵּין הַמִּזְבֵּחַ וּמִבֵּין בֵּית יְהוָה וַיִּתֵּן אֹתוֹ עַל־יֶרֶךְ הַמִּזְבֵּחַ צָפוֹנָה׃ טו וַיְצַוֵּהוּ הַמֶּלֶךְ אָחָז אֶת־אוּרִיָּה הַכֹּהֵן לֵאמֹר עַל הַמִּזְבֵּחַ הַגָּדוֹל הַקְטֵר אֶת־עֹלַת־הַבֹּקֶר וְאֶת־מִנְחַת הָעֶרֶב וְאֶת־

תרגום

מדבחא וקריב מלכא על מדבחא ואסיק עלוהי: יג ואסיק ית עלתיה וית מנחתיה ונסיך ית נסכיה וזרק ית דם נכסת קודשיא די ליה על מדבחא: יד וית מדבחא דנחשא די קדם יי וקריב מן קדם ביתא מבין מדבחא ומבין בית מקדשא דיי ויהב יתיה על צידא דמדבחא צפונא: טו ופקיד מלכא אחז ית אוריה כהנא למימר על מדבחא רבא אסיק ית עלת צפרא וית מנחת רמשא וית עלת

ויצוה קרי

רד״ק

קירה אמר ה׳: (יב) ויקרב המלך על המזבח. פועל יוצא וזה לבדו כן הקל יוצא ר״ל הקריב על המזבח קרבנותיו והעלה עולותיו או יהיה ויקרב פועל עומד כמשפטו ויהיה על המזבח כמו אל המזבח קרב הוא בעצמו אל המזבח והעלה עליו: (יד) ואת המזבח הנחשת אשר לפני ה׳. סמוך עם ה״א הידיעה וכמוהו הממלכו׳ כנען והוא המזבח שעשה שלמה כמו שפירשתי בבנין הבית אמר שזה המזבח נתן אותו עם המזבח אשר לפני ה׳ ופירוש ויקרב מאת פני הבית הקריב זה המזבח ממזבח הנחשת שהיה בעזרה את פני הבית הקריב זה יותר לצד הבית ונתן אותו בין המזבח ובין בית ה׳ על ירך המזבח לצד צפון: (טו) ויצוהו המלך אחז. כתיב בוי״ו וק׳ בלא וי״ו והכתוב הוא כמו יתראהו את הילד וענין אחד הוא הכתיב והקרי: על המזבח הגדול. זהו המזבח שעשה ואמר שיהיה הוא עקר ומזבח ה׳ כטפל לו

רש״י

מדמשק: (יד) ואת מזבח הנחשת וגו׳ ויקרב וגו׳. א״א לומר מזבח הנחשת שעשה משה שהרי נגנז. ואי אפשר לומר מזבח אבנים שעשה שלמה וקראו (בד״ה ב׳ ז׳ ז׳) מזבח הנחשת שהרי אי אפשר לקרבו מזוית לזוית אלא א״כ הורסו והרי שנינו אם שירדה בימי שלמה לא נסתלקה מעל המזבח עד שבא מנשה וסילקה שהוא הרס את המזבח כמו שמצינו באגדת חלק. אין לי לפרש מזבח זה אלא בכיורות ומכונות של נחשת שהיו צרכי מזבח והיו אצל המזבח הקודש וכשעשה אחז את המזבח לע״ג סילק את הכיור והקריבו לצד אהר מאת פני הבית שלא להפסיק בין המזבח שעשה ובין בית ה׳ ויתן אותו אצל מזבח הקודש לפונה ומצינו שפירשו רבותינו דוגמתו (במסכת שבת דף נ״ה) ויבאו ויעמדו אצל מזבח הנחשת (יחזקאל ט׳ ב׳) מזבח הנחושת מי הוה אמר להם

מנחת שי

(טו) ויצוהו ויצוה קרי: ואת עלת המלך. בספרים מדוייקים הוא״ו בגעיא:

רלב״ג

(יד) ואת המזבח הנחשת אשר לפני ה׳. ר״ל שזה המזבח שבנה אוריה היה במצר הכהנים עם מזבח הנחשת אשר לפני ה׳ שבנה שלמה והי׳ זה המזבח השני יותר קרב אל פני ההיכל כאלו היה מבין המזבח ומבין בית השם אלא שלא היה מכוון לפני הבית אבל אצל ירך המזבח לפונה היה ואפשר שעשהו לפאת צפון להיותם עובדים לצבא השמים והכוכבים הצפוניים הם היותר חזקים בפעולותיהם כזה

מצודת דוד

עולותיו: (יד) ואת המזבח. מזבח החדש שם עם מזבח הנחושת וגו׳ שעשה שלמה ר״ל מזבח אבנים שעשה שלמה תחת מזבח הנחושת אשר עשה משה במדבר: ויקרב. מזבח החדש משך ממול פני ההיכל וחוצה ומסרם שמשכו מבין מזבח הנחושת ומבין בית ה׳ כי מקומו הראוי לו היה בין מזבח הנחושת ובין ההיכל כי בו לוה להקריב ולזה מהראוי שלא יפסיק דבר בינו ובין ההיכל הנה הוא לא העמידו במקום הראוי לו כי העמידו בצד מזבח הנחושת בצפונו וקראת מזבח הנחושת הפסיק בינו לבין ההיכל: (טו) המזבח הגדול. כי את מזבח החדש עשהו גדול מזה של שלמה: עולת הבקר. הוא התמיד של שחר: מנחת הערב. זה תמיד של בין הערבים: לבקר. לדרשו

"*And they came and stood next to the copper altar* (Ezekiel 9:2)." *Did the copper altar exist* at that time? *He said to them, "Commence from the place where they recite songs before Me." Thus we see here that copper musical instruments are called an altar*. Similarly, the copper laver, also an accessory to the altar, is called "the copper altar" [*Rashi*].

Redak renders: *And with the copper altar* . . . I.e. he placed the new altar near the copper altar, i.e. near Solomon's altar, which was referred

the altar, and the king approached the altar and offered up [sacrifices] thereon. 13. And he burnt his burnt-offering and his meal-offering, and he poured his libation, and he sprinkled the blood of his peace-offering on the altar. 14. And the copper altar that was before the Lord, he brought near from before the Temple, from between the altar and the house of the Lord, and he placed it on the side of the altar to the north. 15. And King Ahaz commanded Uriah the priest, saying, "On the great altar burn the the morning burnt-offering and the evening meal-offering

If so, how does his son Amariah become high priest during Ahaz' reign? It is probable that Ahaz deposed Azariah, who would surely not permit him to practice idolatry in the Temple, and appointed his son Uriah, upon whom he could depend to comply with his wishes. When Hezekiah became king, he, in turn, banished the idolatrous priests, deposed Uriah, and reinstated his righteous father Azariah as high priest.

according to all its workmanship—i.e. according to its minutest details [*Mezudath David*].

11. **until King Ahaz came**—i.e. *before the king came from Damascus* [*Rashi*].

12. **approached the altar and offered up sacrifices thereon**—Alternatively, offered his sacrifices on the altar and offered up his burnt-offerings [*Redak*].

14. **And the copper altar . . . he brought near . . .**—*It is impossible to say that this was the copper altar that Moses made, since it was hidden. It is also impossible to say that this was the stone altar that Solomon made, and he called it in* II *Chron.* (7:7) the *copper altar, for it was impossible to move it from one corner to another without demolishing it. Indeed, we learned* (*Zebahim* 61b): *The fire that descended in Solomon's time, did not leave the altar until Manasseh came and removed it, for he demolished the altar, as we find in the Aggadah of the chapter entitled Helek.* That is "All Israel have a share in the World to come." This is the tenth chapter of *Sanhedrin.* The aforementioned statement is found p. 103b. *I have no way to explain this except as referring to the lavers and the laver stands of copper, which were accessories of the altar and were near the holy altar. Now when Ahaz made the altar for the idols, he removed the laver and brought it near to another side, farther away from the Temple, so as not to intervene between the altar he made and the house of the Lord, and he placed it next to the holy altar on the north. We find that our Rabbis explained* a passage *in a similar manner in Tractate Shabbath* 55a:

עֲלַת מַלְכָּא וְיָת מִנְחָתֵיהּ
וְיָת עֲלַת כָּל עַמָּא
דְאַרְעָא וּמִנְחָתְהוֹן
וְנִסְכֵּיהוֹן וְכָל דַם עֲלָתָא
וְכָל דַם נִכְסַת קוּדְשַׁיָּא
עֲלוֹהִי תִּזְרוֹק וּמַדְבְּחָא
דִנְחָשָׁא יְהֵי לִי לְבַקָרָא:
טו וַעֲבַד אוּרִיָּה כַּהֲנָא
כְּכֹל דְפַקִיד מַלְכָּא אָחָז:
יז וְקַצִּיץ מַלְכָּא אָחָז יָת
גִדְנְפֵי בְסִיסַיָּא וְאַעְדִּי
מִנְהוֹן יָת כִּיוֹרָא וְיָת יַמָּא
אַחִית מֵעַל תּוֹרַיָּא
דִנְחָשָׁא דִתְחוֹתוֹהִי וִיהַב
יָתֵיהּ עַל רְצָפַת אַבְנַיָּא:
יח וְיָת טִיקוּס שַׁבְּתָא דִי
בְנוֹ

עֹלַת הַמֶּלֶךְ וְאֶת־מִנְחָתוֹ וְאֵת עֹלַת כָּל־
עַם הָאָרֶץ וּמִנְחָתָם וְנִסְכֵּיהֶם וְכָל־דַּם
עֹלָה וְכָל־דַּם־זֶבַח עָלָיו תִּזְרֹק וּמִזְבַּח
הַנְּחֹשֶׁת יִהְיֶה־לִּי לְבַקֵּר: טז וַיַּעַשׂ
אוּרִיָּה הַכֹּהֵן כְּכֹל אֲשֶׁר־צִוָּה הַמֶּלֶךְ
אָחָז: יז וַיְקַצֵּץ הַמֶּלֶךְ אָחָז אֶת־
הַמִּסְגְּרוֹת הַמְּכֹנוֹת וַיָּסַר מֵעֲלֵיהֶם
וְאֶת־הַכִּיֹּר וְאֶת־הַיָּם הוֹרִד מֵעַל הַבָּקָר
הַנְּחֹשֶׁת אֲשֶׁר תַּחְתֶּיהָ וַיִּתֵּן אֹתוֹ עַל
מַרְצֶפֶת אֲבָנִים: יח וְאֶת־מֵיסַךְ הַשַּׁבָּת

את קרי מוסך קרי

רש"י

התחילו ממקום שאומרין שירה לפני הרי כאן לכלי שיר של נחושת קראו מזבח: (טו) לבקר. לפרקים לכשיעלה בלבו לבקרו: (יז) את המסגרות המכונות. אילטבלאות שהמכונות עשויות עליהם כמו שנאמר וזה מעשה המכונות מסגרות להם: (יח) מוסך השבת. גג אהל עשוי לצל

רד"ק

וזהו שאמר יהיה לי לבקר כלומר לפעמים כשארצה לבקרו ולהעלות עליו: (יז) את המסגרות המכונות. סמוך עם הה"א הידיעה כמו המזבח הנחשת ופירוש קצץ המסגרות המכונות שהיו סוגרות הכיורו' בתוכן וקצץ אותן כסגרות והסיר הכיורו' וכן הים הוריד מעל הבקר הנחשת ונתן אותו על מרצפת אבני' וכן הכיור נתן על מרצפת אבנים ובאמרו את הכיור הוא שם כלל כי עשרה כיורות היו ואחר שאמר המסגרות המכונות ידענו כי על הכיורות אמר כן כי אם אמר על כיור אחד לבדו לא הוה אומר המכונות כי אם חמכתה וכל זה שעשה לא עשה אלא דרך בזיון והכעסה כמו שעשה מן המזבח ג"כ וכמו שכבה את הנרות וכמו שסגר דלתות בית ה' כדי שלא יכנס שם אדם להקריב ועשה מזבחות בכל פנה בירושלם כמו שאומר בד"ה ומתחלה שם המזבח שעשה לפני מזבח ה' ועשה אותו עקר ומזבח ה' טפל לו וכאשר הכעים עוד השחית כלי בית האלהים וסגר הדלתות שלא יכנס אדם שם: אשר תחתיה. זכר הים בלשון נקבה ובשאר מקומות לשון זכר: מרצפת אבנים. כמו רצפת בהט ושש וקרקע ההיכל לא היה מרצפת אבנים כי אם מצופה זהב היה מרוקע על נסרים של ארז אלא מרצפות אבנים ר"ל שהוא עשה להם מרצפות אבנים במקום המכונות: (יח) ואת מיסך השבת. כתיב ביו"ד וקרי בוי"ו ואחד הוא ושרשו יסך מענין סכך שנים שרשים וענין אחד וי"ת טיקוס

רלב"ג

העולם לפי מה שסדר הש"י מענינם ולזה תמלא פעל השמש יותר חזק במזלות הלפוניים: (טו) והנה קרא אחז המזבח ההוא אשר בנה מזבח הגדול כי אולי היה יותר גדול השיעור או מפני שהיה אלל מחשבתו יותר נכבד: ומזבח הנחשת יהיה לי לבקר. ר"ל כי לפעמים אדלה לראותו ולבקרו להעלות עליו: (יז) את המסגרות המכונות. ר"ל המסגרות מסגרות המכונות והנה הסיר מהם את הכיור ועמד הכיור בזולת כנו וכן עשה לכל הכיורות אשר שם והים הסיר מעל שנים העשר הבקר אשר תחתיו ונתן אותו על רצפת אבנים: (יח) ואת מיסך השבת אשר בנו בבית. היה כמו אהל לעמוד שם מבמר היולא עד הערב: ואת מבוא המלך החילונה הסב בית ה'. הנה מפני יראתו ממלך אשור סתם מבוא דיתו מחוץ והיו נכנסין בבית המלך

מנחת שי

(יז) ואת הכיור. את קרי: (יח) מיסך. מוסך קרי: החילונה. במקצת ספרים מלרע ובמדוייקים מלעיל ונמסר עליו לית בטעם מלעיל וכך כתב רד"ק ונמנה גם כן בסוף מ"ג בשטה חדא דכל חד וחד מלעיל ולית דכוותיה:

מצודת דוד

בעת מן העתים שיעלה על לבו להקטיר עליו: (יז) ויקצץ. כרת את המסגרות של המכונות והמה הנבזבזין ומחילות המכונות אשר מתחת לכיורות האמור במ"א בעשה שלמה: את הכיור. מכל מכונה הסיר את הכיור הנתון עליו: מעל הבקר הנחושת. כי שלמה העמיד את הים על י"ב בקר נחשת כמ"ש במ"א והוא הסיר מהבקרי' ההם ונתנו על רצפת אבנים: (יח) ואת מוסך השבת. גם הוריד את מוסך השבת וגו' והוא היה בנין מסוכך ממעל לשבת תחתיו אנשי

מצודת ציון

(טו) לבקר. לדרוש כמו לא יבקר הכהן (ויקרא י"ג): (יז) ויקצץ. ענין כריתה: המכונות. מלשון כן וכסים: הכיור. כעין דוד גדול עשוי לרחצה: הים. עשוי כגיגית גדולה: מרצפת. ענין רצפת אבנים בקרקע: (יח) מוסך. מלשון סכך:

stone. Scripture tells us that Ahaz paved the floor with stones in place of the original supports for the lavers and the tank [*Redak*].

18. **And the Sabbath canopy**—*the roof of a tent, made for shade, to sit under it in the Temple court on the Sabbath day* [*Rashi*].

This was made for the priests of the *mishmar,* the family that had served during the week, and were not occupied on the Sabbath follow-

and the king's burnt-offering and his meal-offering and the burnt-offering of the entire people of the land, and their meal-offering and their libations and the blood of every burnt-offering and the blood of every sacrifice you shall sprinkle on it, and the copper altar shall be for me to visit. 16. And Uriah the priest did according to all that King Ahaz had commanded. 17. And King Ahaz cut off the insets of the laver stands, and he removed the lavers from upon them, and he took the tank off the copper cattle that were under it, and put it on a stone floor.

18. And the Sabbath canopy

to as the copper altar. And he brought it near the front of the Temple . . . I.e. he placed it nearer the Temple than the copper altar. [Since he could not move the copper altar,] he placed his altar on its north side.

15. **"On the great altar**—This was the new altar that Uriah had just made. In order to give it more importance than Solomon's altar, Ahaz ordered it made larger than Solomon's [*Mezudath David, Redak*].

shall be for me to visit—*at intervals, when it would enter his mind to visit it* [*Rashi*].

This would accentuate the difference between the importance of the two altars, making the new altar the main one, and the old altar of secondary importance [*Redak*].

17. **And King Ahaz cut off**—He altered the Temple to suit his whims, illustrating that he did not believe that the plan of the Temple was divinely inspired [*Malbim*].

the insets of the laver stands—*the rows upon which the laver stands were made, as it is said,* "(I Kings 7:28) *And this is the work of the laver stand, they had insets*" [*Rashi*]. See Commentary Digest ad loc.

Mezudath David explains that these were partitions upon which the lavers rested.

and he removed the lavers—lit. the laver. Although the singular form is used, we are sure that the plural is meant, since the text mentions the insets of the laver stands in the plural form. There were ten lavers, set up on stands, as is delineated in I Kings 7. This act was part of Ahaz' provocation campaign, as were the erecting of a new altar, extinguishing the lights of the *menorah,* and building altars on every corner in Jerusalem. Later, he intensified his efforts by closing the Temple completely. See II Chron. 28:24,25 [*Redak*].

off the copper cattle—the twelve copper cattle which Solomon had made to support it [*Mezudath David*].

on a stone floor—The floor of the temple court was made of boards of cedar wood, covered with gold, not

אֲשֶׁר־בָּנוּ בַבַּיִת וְאֶת־מְבוֹא הַמֶּלֶךְ
הַחִיצוֹנָה הֵסֵב בֵּית יְהוָה מִפְּנֵי מֶלֶךְ
אַשּׁוּר׃ יט וְיֶתֶר דִּבְרֵי אָחָז אֲשֶׁר עָשָׂה
הֲלֹא־הֵם כְּתוּבִים עַל־סֵפֶר דִּבְרֵי
הַיָּמִים לְמַלְכֵי יְהוּדָה׃ כ וַיִּשְׁכַּב אָחָז
עִם־אֲבֹתָיו וַיִּקָּבֵר עִם־אֲבֹתָיו בְּעִיר דָּוִד
וַיִּמְלֹךְ חִזְקִיָּהוּ בְנוֹ תַּחְתָּיו׃ יז א בִּשְׁנַת
שְׁתֵּים עֶשְׂרֵה לְאָחָז מֶלֶךְ יְהוּדָה מָלַךְ

מלעיל

תרגום

בְנוֹ בְבֵיתָא וְיָת מַעֲלָנָא דְמַלְכָּא בְרָאָה אַסְחַר לְבֵית מַקְדְשָׁא דַיְיָ מִן קֳדָם מַלְכָּא דְאַתּוּר׃ יט וּשְׁאָר פִּתְגָמֵי אָחָז דַעֲבַד הֲלָא אִינוּן כְּתִיבִין עַל סְפַר פִּתְגָמֵי יוֹמַיָא לְמַלְכַיָא דְבֵית יְהוּדָה׃ כ וּשְׁכִיב אָחָז עִם אֲבָהָתוֹהִי וְאִתְקְבַר עִם אֲבָהָתוֹהִי בְּקַרְתָּא דְדָוִד וּמְלַךְ חִזְקִיָהוּ בְרֵיהּ תְּחוֹתוֹהִי׃ א בִּשְׁנַת תַּרְתֵּי עַסְרֵי לְאָחָז מְלַךְ שִׁבְטָא דְבֵית יְהוּדָה

רד"ק

שבתא ובמקצת נסחאות ית מקס מדבחא דשבתא ועניינו בנין שעשו לאנשי המשמר לחסות תחתיו ובסמכו אותו לשבת נראה כי למשמר היוצא עשו אותו שהיה יוצא בשבת והיו כנויים מן העבודה מאיתו היום והיו יושבין שם עד פנית היום שהיו הולכים להם ולא אמר מה עשה בו אבל נראה שסתר אותו: ואת מבוא המלך החיצונה. מלעיל וההה"א נוספת כה"א השערה החדרה והוא סמיך למה שאמר שהוריד הכיור והים כן הוריד זה המסך ויסתר אותו. והוא כמו החיצון והיסב מבוא ביתו שהיה מחוץ הסב אותו בית ה' ולא היו נכנסין בו אלא דרך בית ה' להשגב בו מפני מלך אשור: (א) בשנת שתים עשרה. והלא מלך בשנת ארבע לאחז לפי החשבון כמו שכתבנו

רש"י

לשבת תחתיו בעזרה ביום השבת: ואת מבוא המלך. שהיה בא בו מביתו לבית ה' דרך החוץ הסב אותו במקום הגנוז מפני מלך אשור שלא יחמיד אותן הכלים וגם את המבוא הסב שמא יצטרך להחבא ויברח בהגנוז:
יז (א) בשנת שתים עשרה לאחז וגו'. אי אפשר לומר שמלך הושע בשנת שתים עשרה לאחז שהרי בשנת ד' לאחז הרג את פקח ומלך תחתיו ישתבדיק בשנות פקח תמלא כן ינס ה"א לומר שלא מלך אלא ט' שנים שהרי מלך משנת ד' לאחז עד שנת ו' לחזקיהו שנלכדה שמרון הרי יותר מט"ז שנה ומה תלמוד לומר ט' שנים משמרד במלך אשור כך שנויה בסדר עולם. ואי אפשר לומר שבשנת י"ב לאחז התחיל למרוד שא"כ תמצא את שני מרדו חמש שנים בימי אחז ושש שנים בימי חזקיהו הרי י"א וכאן הוא אומר תשע לא הוזכר שנת י"ב לאחז אלא לענין מקרא של אחריו עליו עלה שלמנאסר וגו' שבשנת י"ב לאחז עלה סנחריב על הושע והגלה לאותו שבעבר הירדן. וכך שנינו בסדר עולם ומקרא כתיב (בד"ה א' ה' כ"ו) ויער אלהי ישראל את רוח פול מלך אשור ויגלם לראובני ולגדי ולא פירש באיזה זמן וכאן פירש שבשנת י"ב לאחז היה. בלם גליית גלו עשרת השבטים בשנת עשרים לפקח כמו שכתוב למעלה בא תגלת פלאסר מלך אשור ויקח את עיון ואת דן וגו' וכל ארץ נפתלי

רלב"ג

דרך בית ה': (כ) ויקבר עם אבותיו בעיר דוד. באר בספר ד"ה כי לא הביאוהו לקברי מלכי בית ישראל: (א) בשנת שתים עשרה לאחז. ידענו כי הושע מלך עד שנת שש לחזקיה והיא שנת ט' להושע כמו שנזכר במה שאחר זה ולפי שכבר ידענו כי אחז מלך בשנת י"ז לפקח הנה נתבאר כי אחז מלך י"ד שנה נגד קודם שימלוך הושע ולזה לריכים אנו לומר כי אחר עבור י"ב שנה לאחז והיא אחז בשנת הי"ג כי לא נשארו לו כי אם ג' שנים אז מלך הושע אך קודם זה היה עבד מלך אשור ולא נחשב למלך כי אם כמו שגליב בשמאו מלך אשור

מצודת דוד

המשמר ה' ולא בשבת על כי היו פונים אז מעבודה כי משמר הנכנס באו במקומם ולזה ישבו תחת לא המוסך עד פנות היום עת הלכם לביתם: ואת מבוא המלך. מקום הכניסה של בית המלך בהיתה אל החוץ סבבה אל בית ה' להיות מקום הכניסה מבית ה' ועשה כן מפני מלך אשור שלא יבוא עליו מבחוץ פתאום:
יז (א) בשנת שתים עשרה. כי מתחלה היה הושע תשעה שנים מקוטעות נציב מלך מתחת יד מלך אשור ואח"ז מרד בו וימלך מעלמו ט' שנים מקוטעות ומ"ש למעלה שמלך הושע בכ' ליותם ר"ל אז נעשה נציב מלך והיה כן עד תחלת שנת י"ג לאחז תשעה שנים מקוטעות כי כ' ליותם הוא ה' לאחז כי יותם מת בי"ו למלכו ומיד

23). *Now it is impossible to say that in the twelfth year of Ahaz he started to rebel, for if so, you will find the years of his revolt five years during the days of Hezekiah, making eleven years, yet here he states that he reigned nine years. The twelfth year of Ahaz was mentioned only in connection with the following verse, "Shalmaneser the king of Assyria went up against him," that in the twelfth year of Ahaz, Sennacherib went up against Hoshea and exiled those who were on the eastern bank of the Jordan. Thus we learned in Seder Olam* (ch. 22), *and a verse is written in Chron. (I 5:26): "The God of Israel aroused Pul the king of Assyria . . . and he exiled the Reubenites and the Gadites . . ." And he*

that they built in the house and the king's outside entrance he switched to the house of the Lord because of the king of Assyria. 19. And the rest of Ahaz's deeds that he did are written in the book of chronicles of the kings of Judah. 20. And Ahaz slept with his forefathers and was buried with his forefathers in the city of David, and Hezekiah his son reigned in his stead.

17

1. In the twelfth year of Ahaz the king of Judah,

ing their shift. They would stay in the Temple court until after the Sabbath, when they would return home. This too, was destroyed by Ahaz [*Redak*].

and the king's . . . entrance—*through which he would come from his house to the house of the Lord through the outside, he switched to a concealed place because of the king of Assyria, lest he covet those vessels, and also the entrance he switched, perhaps he would have to hide and escape surreptitiously* [*Rashi*].

Rashi explains the phrase, "because of the king of Assyria," as referring to the two previous verses. Ahaz removed the insets, the laver stands, and the copper cattle out of fear for the king of Assyria. He did not do so to provoke God as *Redak* explains above. Therefore, he was not to blame for removing these valuable accessories [*K'li Y'kar*].

Redak explains that just as Ahaz removed the vessels of the Temple and hid them, so did he remove the Sabbath canopy and the entrance to the royal palace and conceal them. Instead of entering the king's palace through the outside, they would enter through the Temple. Thus, they would be able to hide there in the event of attack by Assyria. I.e. the entrance to the king's palace would not be revealed.

20. **in the city of David**—He was, however, not interred in the graves of the kings, where David and Solomon were buried [*Ralbag* from II Chron. 28:27].

1. **In the twelfth year of Ahaz . . .**—*It is impossible to say that Hoshea became king in the twelfth year of Ahaz, for in the fourth year of Ahaz, he assassinated Pekah and reigned in his stead* (See above 15:30), *and when you calculate Pekah's years you will find it so. Likewise, it is impossible to say that he did not reign more than nine years, for he reigned from the fourth year of Ahaz until the sixth year of Hezekiah, when Samaria was captured. This amounts to more than sixteen years. What then is the meaning of "nine years"? Since he rebelled against the king of Assyria. This is what we learned in Seder Olam* (ch.

הוֹשֵׁעַ בֶּן־אֵלָה בְשֹׁמְרוֹן עַל־יִשְׂרָאֵל
תֵּשַׁע שָׁנִים: ב וַיַּעַשׂ הָרַע בְּעֵינֵי יְהֹוָה
רַק לֹא כְּמַלְכֵי יִשְׂרָאֵל אֲשֶׁר הָיוּ לְפָנָיו:
ג עָלָיו עָלָה שַׁלְמַנְאֶסֶר מֶלֶךְ אַשּׁוּר
וַיְהִי־לוֹ הוֹשֵׁעַ עֶבֶד וַיָּשֶׁב לוֹ מִנְחָה:
ד וַיִּמְצָא מֶלֶךְ־אַשּׁוּר בְּהוֹשֵׁעַ קֶשֶׁר
אֲשֶׁר שָׁלַח מַלְאָכִים אֶל־סוֹא מֶלֶךְ־
מִצְרַיִם וְלֹא־הֶעֱלָה מִנְחָה לְמֶלֶךְ אַשּׁוּר
כְּשָׁנָה בְשָׁנָה וַיַּעַצְרֵהוּ מֶלֶךְ אַשּׁוּר

תרגום

יְהוּדָה מְלַךְ הוֹשֵׁעַ בַּר אֵלָה בְּשׁוֹמְרוֹן עַל יִשְׂרָאֵל תְּשַׁע שְׁנִין: ב וַעֲבַד דְּבִישׁ קֳדָם יְיָ לְחוֹד לָא כְּמַלְכֵי יִשְׂרָאֵל דַּהֲווֹ קֳדָמוֹהִי: ג עֲלוֹהִי סְלִיק שַׁלְמַנְאֶסֶר מַלְכָּא דְאַתּוּר וַהֲוָה לֵיהּ הוֹשֵׁעַ עַבְדָּא נָאתֵיב לֵיהּ תִּקְרוּבְתָּא: ד וְאַשְׁכַּח מַלְכָּא דְאַתּוּר בְּהוֹשֵׁעַ מִירְדָא דִּי שְׁלַח אִזְגַּדִין לְוַת סוֹא מַלְכָּא דְמִצְרַיִם וְלָא אַסֵּיק תִּקְרוּבְתָּא לְמַלְכָּא דְאַתּוּר בִּשְׁנָא בִּשְׁנָא וְצַחְדֵיהּ מַלְכָּא דאתור

ת"א רק לא כמלכי ישראל. גיטין פח:

רש"י

יגלם אשורה וזה היה שנת הארבע לאחז שהה שמנה שנים ובא עליהם שנת י"ב לאחז והגלם לראובני ולגדי וכשראה הושע בן אלה מרד בו ושלח מלאכים אל סוא מלך מצרים שהה שמנה שנים ובא וצר על שומרון ונלכדה לקץ שלש שנים וגלו כולן וזהו שנאמר (ישעיה ט׳ א׳) כעת הראשון הקל ארצה זבולון וארצה נפתלי הקל אף בשניה שלא הגלה אלא שני השבטים. אבל האחרין הכביד טיאטא את הכל כזה שמכבד את הבית ומכל מקום לפי החשבון שכתב כאן את מנין שני מרדו תשע שנים לא מרד בו עד שנת י"ד לאחז שהרי אחז מלך שש עשרה שלש שנים של אחז היה המרד ושש שנים בימי חזקיהו: (ב) רק לא כמלכי ישראל. שביטל פרדיסאות שישבו מימי ירבעם על הדרכים לשמור שלא יעלו ישראל לרגל וזה בטלן לפי שגלו עגלי הזהב כבר בשתי גליות בגלות ראשונה ויקח את עיון ואת דן הגלה עגל שבדן. ובשניה כשגלו ראובן וגד נטל עגל שבבית אל לקיים מה שנאמר גם אותו לאשור יובל (הושע י׳ ו׳) ולפי שבטלו פרדיסאות והם נמנעו מלעלות לרגל לפיכך נחתם גזר דינם לגלות בימיו שעד עכשיו תלו הקלקלה במלכיהם ועתה לא היה במי לתלות. וזהו שאמר הושע בן בארי (שם ה׳ ג׳) כי עתה הזנית אפרים נטמא ישראל עתה נגלית רעתכם:

רד"ק

למעלה ואמ׳ בסדר עולם שני׳ למרדו אבל הוא מלך משנת ארבע לאחז עד שנת שש לחזקיהו ובשנת י"ב לאחז שהיא שנת שמנה להושע מרד במלך אשור ומשנה שמרד בה עד סוף מלכותו ט׳ שנים: (ב) רק לא כמלכי ישראל אשר היו לפניו. אמרו שהעביר כל אותן פרדיסאות שהושיב ירבעם בן נבט על התחומין שלא לעלות ירושלם ואמר כי בט"ו באב ביטל אותן פרדיסאות לפיכך היו ישראל עושין י"ט בט"ו באב:

רלב"ג

ומרד בו כמו שזכר ואחר זה נמשך במלכותו במרדו תשע שנים: (ד) ויעלהו מלך אשור ויאסרהו בית כלא. אחשוב שהיה זה אחר עבור תשע שנים להושע כי כבר עלה מלך אשור שמרון ויצר עלי׳ ובסוף הענין לכד שומרון ואז עצר הושע ועלהו בבית כלא:

מצודת דוד

מלך אחז ומ"ש כאן בשנת שתים עשרה ר"ל אחר שעבר י"ב לאחז ובתחלת י"ג מלך הושע בעלמי ומרד במלך אשור: (ב) רק לא וגו׳. ארז"ל שבטל השומרים שהושיב ירבעם לבל יעלו לירושלים ברגלים: (ג) וישב לו מנחה. לפי שהיה קבוע עליו לכל שנה אמר וישב כי נתן וחזר ונתן: (ד) וימצא. נודע למלך אשור כי הושע רוצה שוב למרוד בו ושלח למלך מצרים לעוזרו אף לא העלה לו המנחה כמו

מצודת ציון

יז (ד) ויעצרהו. עכבו ומנעו כמו אל תעצר לי (לעיל ד׳): כלא.

involved those tribes on the east bank of the Jordan. Bethel, however, was on the west bank. Indeed, *Seder Olam* ch. 22 mentions that the golden calf of Dan was taken in the first exile, and the one in Bethel was taken in the second exile, but it does not quote the verses as *Rashi* does here. It was apparently an oral tradition.) *Since the sentries were abolished, and they* (the Israelites) *refrained from performing the pilgrimage, therefore, their verdict was sealed to be exiled in his days, for until now, they had blamed the corruption on their kings, but now they had no one to blame. This is what Hosea the son of Beeri said,* "(Hosea 5:3) *For now you have gone astray, Ephraim; Israel has become defiled.*" *Now your evil has been revealed* [*Rashi* from *Gittin* 88a, *Seder Olam*

Hoshea the son of Elah reigned over Israel for nine years. 2. And he did what was evil in the eyes of the Lord, though not like the kings of Israel who had preceded him. 3. Shalmaneser the king of Assyria went up against him, and Hoshea became his vassal, and he paid him tribute. 4. And the king of Assyria found conspiracy in Hoshea, that he sent messengers to So the king of Egypt and did not pay tribute to the king of Assyria as year by year, and the king of Assyria arrested him

did not explain at what time. Here he explains that it was in the twelfth year of Ahaz.

The ten tribes were exiled at three different times (lit. three exiles were the ten tribes exiled): (1) *in the twentieth year of Pekah, as it is written above,* "(15:29) . . . *Tiglath-Pileser the king of Assyria came and took Ijon and Dan . . . and the entire land of Naphtali* (sic) *and exiled them to Assyria." Now this was the fourth year of Ahaz.* (2) *He waited eight years and came upon them in the twelfth year of Ahaz, and exiled the Reubenites and the Gadites. When Hoshea the son of Elah saw this, he revolted against him and sent messengers to So the king of Egypt.* (3) *He waited eight years and came and laid siege to Samaria. After three years it was captured, and everyone was exiled. This is the meaning of that which is written: (Is. 8:23) Like the first time, he dealt mildly, the land of Zebulun and the land of Naphtali."* I.e. just as the king of Assyria dealt mildly with Israel in the first exile by exiling only Zebulun and Naphtali, *so did he deal mildly also in the second exile, for he exiled but two tribes. But "in the last one, he swept* (Heb. *hichbid)". He swept everything out like one who sweeps a house. In any case, according to the figures he wrote here as the number of years of his revolt,* i.e. *nine years, he did not revolt against him until the fourteenth year of Ahaz, for Ahaz reigned sixteen years; the revolt was three years of Ahaz and six years in the days of Hezekiah* [*Rashi*].

2. **though not like the kings of Israel**—*for he abolished the sentries who were stationed since the days of Jeroboam, on the roads, to guard lest the Israelites perform the pilgrimage for the festivals, and this one abolished them, for the golden calves had already been exiled in the two exiles. In the first exile "he took Ijon and Dan." He exiled the calf that was in Dan. And in the second, when Reuben and Gad were exiled, he took the calf that was in Bethel, to fulfill what was stated,* "(Hosea 10:6) *That too, to Assyria will be transported."* (Ed. note: I am at a loss to explain *Rashi*'s commentary. The verse *Rashi* quotes, that he took Ijon and Dan, reads, "Ijon and Abel Beth-Maacah." See above 15:29. The only place where Ijon and Dan are mentioned together, is I Kings 15:20, in reference to Ben-Hadad's attack on Israel. Moreover, the second exile

ויאסרהו בית כלא: ה ויעל מלך־אשור
בכל־הארץ ויעל שמרון ויצר עליה
שלש שנים: ו בשנת התשיעית
להושע לכד מלך־אשור את־שמרון
ויגל את־ישראל אשורה וישב אותם
בחלח ובחבור נהר גוזן וערי מדי:
ז ויהי כי־חטאו בני־ישראל ליהוה
אלהיהם המעלה אתם מארץ מצרים
מתחת יד פרעה מלך־מצרים וייראו
אלהים אחרים: ח וילכו בחקות הגוים
אשר הוריש יהוה מפני בני ישראל

תרגום

דאתור ואסריה בבית
אסירי: ה וסליק מלכא
דאתור בכל ארעא
וסליק לשמרון וצר עלה
תלת שנין: ו בשתא
תשיעתא להושע כבש
מלכא דאתור ית שמרון
ואגלי ית ישראל לאתור
ואותיב יתהון בחלח
ובחבור נהר גוזן וקירוי
מדי: ז והוה כד חבו
בני ישראל קדם יי
אלההון דאסיק יתהון
מארעא דמצרים מתחות
יד פרעה מלכא דמצרים
ודחילו טעות עממיא:
ח ואזלו בגזירת עממיא
דתריך יי מן קדם בני
ישראל

רד"ק

(ה) ויעל מלך אשור בכל הארץ. פי' וילכדה ואחר כך עלה שמרון וצר עליה: (ח) ומלכי ישראל אשר עשו. פי' ובחקות

רש"י

(ו) בשנת התשיעית. למרדו של הושע: ויגל את ישראל. ויגלה את ישראל וזה שעור כל תיבה שפעל שלה בה"א כגון פנה בנה גלה זנה רבה כשבא לתת בראש התיבה וא"ו יו"ד אם המלה מוסבת על הפועל תחת היו"ד נקודה בחיר"ק כגון ויבן שם מזבח (בראשית י"ב ח') ויפן וירד משה (שמות ל"ב ט"ו) ויגל יהודה מעל אדמתו (לקמן כה כא) ותלך ותזן גם היא (ירמיה ג' ח') וירב העם ויעצמו מאד (שמות א' כ') ואם הוא מדבר בלשון מפעיל תחת היו"ד נקודה בסגו"ל כגון ויפן זנב אל זנב (שופטים ט"ו ד') ויגל את ישראל אשורה (דהכא) ויזן את יושבי ירושלים (ד"ה ב' כ"א י"א) וירב בבת יהודה תאניה ואניה (איכה ב' ה'):

מנחת שי

יז (ו) ויגל את ישראל אשורה. היו"ד בסגול וכך כתב רש"י כאן ובאיכה ב' כתב שהוא בליר"י ויש גם ט"ס בכתוב ויגל מלך בבל את ישראל אשורה

רלב"ג

(ח) ומלכי ישראל אשר עשו. ר"ל ובחקות מלכי ישראל אשר עשו כמו ירבעם בן נבט וחבריו כי כבר הלכו ישראל בחקותיהם ועזבו

מצודת ציון

ענין תפיסה כמו אשר כלאו צדקיה (ירמיה ל"ב): (ה) ויצר. מלשון מצור: (ו) ויגל. מלשון גלות: ויושב. מלשון ישיבה: (ח) הוריש. גירש:

מצודת דוד

בכל שנה ושנה: ויעצרהו. כי אז כאשר נודע לו היה הושע עמו ועצרו מללכת לארצו ואסרו בבית הכלא: (ה) בכל הארץ. בכל ארץ ישראל לכבוש את הכל: (ו) בשנת התשיעית. מעת שמלך מלאו ולא מלך א"כ כל תשעת השנים כי הלא אסרו בבית הכלא עד לא עלה על שמרון ולר עליה ג' שנים ומ"ש למעלה מלך הושע וגו' תשע שנים ר"ל מהתחלת מלכותו עד הגלות היה תשע שנים): נהר גוזן. ר"ל בחלח ובחבור העומדות על נהר גוזן: (ז) ויהי כי חטאו וגו'. ר"ל הגלות הזה היתה על שחטאו ב"י כי עד לא מלך הושע היו קלת אנוסים כי המלכים הטיאום ולא הניחום לעלות לירושלים אבל הושע בטל השומרים ונתן הברירה ועכ"ז לא עלו לירושלים ועבדו עגלי הזהב א"כ החטא להם יחשב: (ח) ומלכי ישראל. מלת בחוקות עומדת במקום שתים וכאלו אמר ובחוקות מלכי ישראל אשר עשו

he caused the dwellers of Jerusalem to commit whoredom (ויזן) (II Chron. 21:11)"; *"And He increased* (וירב) *among the people of Judah grief and lamentation* (Lam. 2:5)" [*Rashi*].

the Gozan River—i.e. in Halah and Habor, which were situated on the Gozan River [*Mezudath David*].

7. **And it was . . .**—The prophet recounts the sins that eventually brought about the exile to Assyria [*Abarbanel*].

8. **and [of] the kings of Israel**—I.e. they followed also the statutes of the kings of Israel [*Ralbag, Mezudath David*].

and confined him in prison. 5. And the king of Assyria went up through the entire land, and he went up to Samaria and besieged it three years. 6. In the ninth year of Hoshea, the king of Assyria took Samaria and exiled the Israelites to Assyria, and he repatriated them in Halah, and in Habor, the Gozan River, and the cities of Media. 7. And it was, when the children of Israel sinned to the Lord their God, who brought them up from the land of Egypt, from under the hand of Pharaoh the king of Egypt, and they feared other gods. 8. And they followed the statutes of the nations whom the Lord had driven out from before the children of Israel,

ch. 22, *Elijah Zuta*, ch. 9].

Redak notes that the sentries were abolished on the fifteenth day of *Av*. For this reason, that day was proclaimed a holiday. See *Taanith* 30b, 31a, where this as well as other reasons for the day's festivities, are discussed.

4. **found conspiracy in Hoshea**—He discovered that Hoshea was planning to revolt [*Mezudath David*].

and did not pay tribute—Since he depended on So, the king of Egypt, to defend him, he deemed it unnecessary to pay tribute to Assyria [*Abarbanel*].

arrested him—Perhaps Hoshea visited the king of Assyria, or he found him in one of his cities outside the capital. He detained him and did not allow him to return home [*Abarbanel*].

5. **went up**—while Hoshea was in captivity [*Abarbanel*].

6. **In the ninth year**—*of Hoshea's revolt* [*Rashi* from *Seder Olam* ch. 22].

and exiled the Israelites—Heb. וַיֶּגֶל, *like* וַיַּגְלֶה אֶת יִשְׂרָאֵל. *This is the rule of every word whose verb root* ends *with a mute "he"*, e.g. פנה, to face, בנה, *to build,* גלה, *to go in exile,* זנה *to commit whoredom,* רבה, *to multiply, when one comes to prefix the word with "vav" "yud,"* i.e. the "vav" that converts the verb from future to past, *if the word applies to the doer,* i.e. if the verb appears in the light conjugation, involving only one doer, *the "yud" will be voweled with a "hirik," e.g. "and he built* (וַיִּבֶן) *there an altar* (Gen. 12:8)"; *"And Moses turned* (וַיִּפֶן) *and descended* (Ex. 32:15)"; *"And Judah was exiled* (וַיִּגֶל) *off its land* (below 25:21)"; *"And she too went and committed whoredom* (וַתִּזֶן) (Jer. 3:8)"; *"And the people multiplied* (וַיִּרֶב) *and became very strong* (Ex. 1:20)." *If, however, one is talking in the causitive conjugation, the "yud" will be voweled with a "segol"*, e.g. *"and turned* (וַיֶּפֶן) *tail to tail* (Jud. 15:4)"; *"And exiled* (וַיֶּגֶל) the Israelites to Assyria (here)"; *"And*

ומלכי ישראל אשר עשו: ט ויחפאו
בני־ישראל דברים אשר לא־כן על־
יהוה אלהיהם ויבנו להם במות בכל־
עריהם ממגדל נוצרים עד־עיר מבצר:
י ויצבו להם מצבות ואשרים על כל־
גבעה גבהה ותחת כל־עץ רענן:
יא ויקטרו־שם בכל־במות כגוים אשר־
הגלה יהוה מפניהם ויעשו דברים
רעים להכעיס את־יהוה: יב ויעבדו
הגללים אשר אמר יהוה להם לא
תעשו את־הדבר הזה: יג ויעד יהוה

ישראל ומלכי ישראל
דעבדו: ט ואמרו בני
ישראל מלין דלא
כשרין קדם יי אלההון
ובנו להון במן בכל
קרויהון ממגדל תקיף
עד קירוין כריכן:
י ואקימו להון קמן
ואשירין על כל רמא
מנטלא ותחות כל אילן
עבוף: יא ואסיקו בוסמין
תמן על כל במתא
כעממיא דאגלי יי מן
קדמיהון ועבדו קדמוהי
פתגמין בישין לארגזא
קדם יי: יב ופלחו ית
בעליא די אמר יי להון
לא תעבדון ית פתגמא
הדין: יג ואסהיד יי
בישראל

ת"א ויחפאו. מ"ק יח.

רש"י

(ט) ויחפאו. כלאו. פתרונו לפי ענינו: ממגדל נוצרים. שאינו עשוי אלא להעמיד צופה לנצור. בכל בית גביה העמידו עבודת גילולים: עד עיר מבצר. כמו מקטן ועד גדול: (יג) ויעד ה'. התרה בהם: נביאי כל

רד"ק

מלכי ישראל אשר עשו: (ט) ויחפאו בני ישראל דברים אשר לא כן על ה' אלהיהם. בדברי רז"ל מה אמרו אמרו העמוד הזה אינו רואה ואינו שומע והוי לשון ויחפאו שהסתירו הידיעה מהבורא כמו שאמר יחזקאל הנביא שהיו אומרים אין ה' רואה אותנו עזב ה' את הארץ וכן אמר ישעיהו ויאמרו מי רואני ומי יודענו ובא אל"ף ויחפאו תמורת ה"א למ"ד הפעל כן חפה עצי ברושים כי ענין אחד ושרש אחד הם: אשר לא כן. אשר לא טוב: ממגדל נוצרים עד עיר מבצר. ממגדל שעומדים בו השומרים וי"ת ממגדל תקיף עד קרוין כריכן: (יג) ויעד ה'. מבנין הפעיל מנחי העי"ן ענינו ההתראה ע"י

רלב"ג

את ברית ה': (ט) ויחפאו בני ישראל דברים אשר לא כן על ה' אלהיהם. הנה ויחפאו הוא מענין חפוי וכסוי והרצון בו שהם שמו נעלם ומכוסה נגד ה' דברים אשר אינם כן ר"ל שאינם נעלמים ממנו והמשל שהם חשבו שאין הש"י מבין אל מעשיהם ושהוא עוזב את הארץ ולזה היו עובדים לצבא השמים והיו עושין הפעלות המגונות ההם כמו שקדם מעניינם עד שבכר בנו במות בכל עריהם מהקטן עד הגדול והנה הקטן הוא מגדל נוצרים ר"ל מגדל שומרים שכאשר יהיו לאדם שדות רבות וכרמים זה אחר זה יבנה מגדל בתוכם לשמור פירותיהם ולהצלם שם וגם במגדל ההוא בנו במה ולא הספיק להם זה אבל מהון לעיר הליבו להם מצבות ואשרים על כל גבעה גבוהה ותחת כל עץ רענן וזה כלו בהפך כוונת התורה שלותה לעבוד הש"י לבדו ובמקום אחד לבד אחר הבנות בית המקדש: (יא) כגוים אשר הגלה ה' מפניהם. לא שלא נתנו אל לבם שאלו הפעלות המגונות לא הועיל לגוים אשר הגלה ה' מפניהם אך היו סבה שהקיאה אותם הארץ: (יג) ויעד ה' בישראל וביהודה ביד כל נביאי כל חוזה. ר"ל ביד כל נביאים וכל חוזה וידמה שהחוזה הוא יותר שלם מהנביא

מנחת שי

וצריך למחוק אלף בכל: בחלת. בספרים מדוייקים החי"ת בשו"א לבדו: (יב) ויעבדו הגלולים. תרגומו ופלחו ית בעליא דומה שהיה כתוב את הגלילים

מצודת דוד

לע"ג: (ט) ויחפאו. אמרו בסתר על ה' דברים שאינם ראויים להאמין כי כחשו בידיעתו והשגחתו וכמ"ש כי אומרים אין ה' רואה אותנו עזב ה' את הארץ (יחזקאל ח') ונאמר הוי המעמיקים מה' לסתיר עצה וגו' (ישעיה כ"ט): ממגדל נוצרים. אף במגדל שעומדים בו הצופים וקוראים נולרים כי ע"י נשמרים בני העיר עד עיר מבצר. ר"ל בכל מקום כקטן כגדול: (י) ותחת כל עץ רענן. על מלבות חוזר: (יג) ויעד ה'. התרה בהם ועל כי הדרך

מצודת ציון

(ט) ויחפאו. מלשון חפוי וכסוי ור"ל הסתירו כדבר המכוסה: כן. ראוי והגון כמו ולא יכין לדבר כן (שופטי' יב): (יב) הגלולים. מלשון

every green tree. The *asherim* were themselves trees [*Mezudath David*].

13. **And the Lord warned**—*He warned them* [*Rashi*].

Lit. he testified against them. I.e. He warned them before witnesses [*Redak*].

all prophets of all visions—heb.

and [of] the kings of Israel that they practiced. 9. And the children of Israel fabricated things which were not so about the
Lord their God, and they built themselves high places in all
their cities, from watchtower to fortified city. 10. And they
erected for themselves monuments and *asherim* on every high
hill and under every green tree. 11. And they burned incense
there on all the high places, like the nations that the Lord had
exiled from before them, and they did evil things to anger the
Lord. 12. And they worshipped the idols, which the Lord had
said to them, "You shall not do this thing." 13. And the Lord

warned

9. **And they fabricated**—*This interpretation is according to context* [*Rashi*].

Rashi indicates that he could not determine the etymological origin of this word. He interpreted it according to its context. *Jonathan* renders: And they said. We are not aware of the source of this interpretation. Others explain this word to mean "they attributed concealment ... upon the Lord." They claimed that God did not see them, nor was He aware of their deeds. We find the prophets admonishing the people for this sin, e.g. Isaiah (29:15) "... and they said, 'Who sees us and who knows us?'" Also, Ezekiel (8:12) mentions that the elders of the house of Israel, say, "... the Lord does not see us; the Lord has left the earth." The Rabbis tell us that the people said, "This pillar neither sees nor hears" [*Redak* from unknown *Midrash*].

Since they did not believe in Divine Providence, God forsook them and caused them to be exiled to a forgotten place, thus paying them in kind [*Abarbanel*].

which were not so—[*Abarbanel*].

Alternatively, which were not proper [*Jonathan, Redak, Mezudath Zion*].

Ralbag explains that many of the Israelites believed that God had forsaken them and delegated their supervision to the heavenly bodies. Therefore, they built high places all over Israel, in honor of these heavenly bodies.

from watchtower—*which is made only to station a lookout to watch. In every high house they erected idols* [*Rashi*].

to fortified city—*like "from small to big* (Gen. 19:11 and many other places)" [*Rashi*].

I.e. they erected idols all over the land, from the smallest places to the largest, most spacious ones [*Abarbanel*].

10. **and under every green tree**—I.e. they erected monuments under

בְּיִשְׂרָאֵל וּבִיהוּדָה בְּיַד כָּל־נְבִיאוֹ כָל־חֹזֶה לֵאמֹר שֻׁבוּ מִדַּרְכֵיכֶם הָרָעִים וְשִׁמְרוּ מִצְוֹתַי חֻקּוֹתַי כְּכָל־הַתּוֹרָה אֲשֶׁר צִוִּיתִי אֶת־אֲבֹתֵיכֶם וַאֲשֶׁר שָׁלַחְתִּי אֲלֵיכֶם בְּיַד עֲבָדַי הַנְּבִיאִים׃ יד וְלֹא שָׁמֵעוּ וַיַּקְשׁוּ אֶת־עָרְפָּם כְּעֹרֶף אֲבוֹתָם אֲשֶׁר לֹא הֶאֱמִינוּ בַּיהוָה אֱלֹהֵיהֶם׃ טו וַיִּמְאֲסוּ אֶת־חֻקָּיו וְאֶת־בְּרִיתוֹ אֲשֶׁר כָּרַת אֶת־אֲבוֹתָם וְאֵת עֵדְוֹתָיו אֲשֶׁר הֵעִיד בָּם וַיֵּלְכוּ אַחֲרֵי

תרגום

בְּיִשְׂרָאֵל וּבִיהוּדָה בְּיַד כָּל סָפְרֵי כָּל מַלִּיף לְמֵימַר תּוּבוּ מֵאוֹרְחַתְכוֹן בִּישְׁתָא וְטַרוּ פִקּוּדַי וּקְיָמַי כְּכָל אוֹרָיְתָא דְפַקֵּדִית יָת אֲבָהָתְכוֹן וְדִשְׁלָחִית לְוָתְכוֹן בְּיַד עַבְדַי נְבִיַיָא׃ יד וְלָא קַבִּילוּ וְאַקְשִׁיאוּ יָת קְדָלְהוֹן כִּקְדָלָא דַאֲבָהַתְהוֹן דְלָא הֵימִינוּ בְּמֵימְרָא דַיְיָ אֱלָהֲהוֹן׃ טו וְקָצוּ בִקְיָמוֹהִי וּבִגְזֵירַתֵיהּ דִּי גְזַר עִם אֲבָהַתְהוֹן וּבְסָהֲדְוָתֵיהּ דְאַסְהִיד בְּהוֹן וּטְעוֹ בָּתַר טָעוּתָא

נביאי קרי ב' טעמים במלה אחת

רד"ק

עדים וכן העד העיד בנו האיש העידותי בכם היום: ביד כל נביאו כל חוזה. כתוב בוי"ו ר"ל ביד כל מי שהיה נביאו לא נביאי השקר וקרי נביאי והוא כמו נביאים וכן חלוני שקופים כמו חלונים אנשי מחוקה כמו אנשים וענינו שהעיד בהם ביד כל חוזה ונביא, ובדרש ביד כל נביאו כמת נביאים העידותי בהם אחד בשחרית ואחד בין הערבים נביאו כתיב:

רש"י

חוזה. נביאי כל חזון יש חוזה שהוא שם דבר כמו ועם שאול

מנחת שי

הגללים חסר וא"ו: (יג) כל נביאו. נביאי קרי ויש בו דרש בפסיקתא עיין ילקוט ורד"ק וכלי יקר: ושמרו מצותי חקותי. יש ספרים שכתוב וחקותי בוא"ו בתחלת המלה והגהה הוא כי נמסר עליו ג' וסימנהון עקב אשר שמע אברהם וגו'. אם שוב תשובון דמלכים א' ט': ויעד ה'. וכן הוא בלא וא"ו בתחלה בספרים כתובי יד מדוייקים ודפוסים קדמונים. עוד באיזה ספרים חסר וא"ו שבאמצע

רלב"ג

כי הנביא יקרא נביא אפילו בא אליו דבר ה' בחלום כאמרו אם יהיה נביאכם ה' במראה אליו אתודע בחלום אדבר בו ואולם החוזה יקרא אשר יבא אליו דבר ה' במראה והוא למעלה מהחלום: (יד) כערף אבותם אשר לא האמינו בה' אלהיהם. המשילם למי שהיה מאבותם שלא האמינו בה' אלהיהם ולא הסכימו להאמין בו מפני דברי הנביאים: (טו) וימאסו את חקיו ואת בריתו. זה כלו עדות כי הם עשו מה שזכר הש"י שאם יעשוהו יביא עליהם אלו הקללות שבאו עליהם ולסוף הענין ישליכם אל ארץ אחרת כיו' הזה ולזה זכר ג"כ שהם עזבו כל מצות ה' כמו שזכר שם באותם הקללות: ואת עדותיו אשר העיד בם. הנה קרא עדות מה שהיה בתורה על דרך העדות להעיד נפלאות הש"י לישראל כמו פסח וסוכות שהם עדות על יציאת מצרים וקדושת בכור בהמה טהורה ופדיון בכור אדם ופטר חמור שהם

מצודת ציון

גלל וציאה והם הע"ג: (יד) ערפם. הוא אחורי הראש: (טו) בהם.

מצודת דוד

להתרות בפני עדים אמר לשון ויעד: כל נביאי. כל נביאים ולתוספת ביאור אמר כל חוזה כי שם נביא משותף הוא גם לנביאי הבעל מפא"כ חוזה כי הוא הבלתי לה' נבדו: ואשר שלחתי. שמרו אשר שלחתי וגו': (יד) ויקשו את ערפם. הוא מלשון הרחקה כאילו נתקשה העורף מבלי יוכלו להחזיר לאחור לפנות מול הנביא: כעורף אבותם. הם עובדי העגל במדבר: (טו) אשר כרת. על קיום התורה: ואת עדותיו. מאסו בהתראות שהתרה בהם ולא היו חוששין להם: ויהבלו. נעשו בעלי הבל ואדוקים לע"ג: ואחרי.

—like one fleeing and not being able to turn around to return [*Mezudath David*].

like the nape of their forefathers—who worshipped the golden calf in the desert [*Mezudath David*].

who did not believe—He compares them to those of their ancestors who did not believe in God, and could not be influenced by the prophets to believe in Him [*Ralbag*].

Abarbanel adds: like Terah and Nahor who had no concept of the true faith, and like the calf worshippers and other rebellious ancestors of the Jewish people.

15. **and His warnings**—They despised His warnings and did not heed them [*Mezudath David*].

Alternatively, they despised His testimonies which He testified about them. They despised His commandments that are known as testimonies; e.g. Sabbath, which testifies to

Israel and Judah through all prophets of all visions, saying, "Repent of your evil ways, and keep My commandments, My statutes, according to the entire Law that I commanded your forefathers, and that I sent to you through My servants, the prophets." 14. But they did not heed, and they hardened their nape like the nape of their forefathers who did not believe in the Lord their God. 15. And they despised His statutes and His covenant that He had enacted with their forefathers and His warnings that He had warned them, and they followed

נְבִיאֵי כָל חֹזֶה, *prophets of all visions.* Although חוֹזֶה usually means "seer," *there is* a word חוֹזֶה *that is a noun, such as* "(Is.28:5) *and with the grave have we made a boundary* (חוֹזֶה)." [*Rashi*].

Redak renders נְבִיאֵי like נְבִיאִים, *prophets,* i.e. through all prophets, every seer. The *k'thib* is נביאו, *His prophet,* i.e. the true prophets, not the false ones. According to the Midrash (*Pesikta d'Rav Kahana,* p. 124), the singular form is used to denote that God sent one prophet every morning and one prophet every evening. See *Yalkut Shimoni,* ad loc.; *Lam. Rabbah* 2:17, Buber's edition 2:13; *Pesikta Rabbathi* 34:9, p. 268.

Others maintain that two prophets appeared every morning and every evening to admonish Judah and Israel to repent. According to *Pesikta Rabbathi,* a new prophet would appear on the scene daily, accompanied by Jeremiah, to admonish the people. Hosea warned the kingdom of Israel for ninety years before their exile, through the fifty-two years of Uzziah-Azariah, the sixteen years of Jotham, the sixteen years of Ahaz, and six years of Hezekiah's reign, when they were exiled. The numerical value of the word, וַיָּעַד, equals ninety. *Vav*=6; *yud*=10; *ayin*=70; *daleth*=4, making a total of ninety years that Hosea the prophet admonished the kingdom of Israel to repent.

Ralbag differentiates between *navi* and *hozeh,* explaining that *navi* includes prophets of low prophetic achievements, who perceive their prophecy through dreams, whereas *hozeh,* a seer, denotes one to whom God's word appears in a vision. This is a higher form of prophecy. This interpretation fits very well with the aforementioned *Pesikta,* that new prophets appeared every day. In order to have new prophets every day, it was necessary to call upon even those of lower prophetic stature, since the superior ones would not suffice.

Malbim claims that the earlier prophets from the time of Elijah and Elisha are included in this verse. They already had prophesied the impending retribution which God was going to visit upon Israel.

14. **and they hardened their nape**

הַהֶבֶל וַיֶּהְבָּלוּ וְאַחֲרֵי הַגּוֹיִם אֲשֶׁר
סְבִיבֹתָם אֲשֶׁר צִוָּה יְהוָה אֹתָם לְבִלְתִּי
עֲשׂוֹת כָּהֶם: טז וַיַּעַזְבוּ אֶת־כָּל־מִצְוֹת
יְהוָה אֱלֹהֵיהֶם וַיַּעֲשׂוּ לָהֶם מַסֵּכָה
שְׁנַיִם עֲגָלִים וַיַּעֲשׂוּ אֲשֵׁירָה וַיִּשְׁתַּחֲווּ
לְכָל־צְבָא הַשָּׁמַיִם וַיַּעַבְדוּ אֶת־הַבָּעַל:
יז וַיַּעֲבִירוּ אֶת־בְּנֵיהֶם וְאֶת־בְּנוֹתֵיהֶם
בָּאֵשׁ וַיִּקְסְמוּ קְסָמִים וַיְנַחֵשׁוּ וַיִּתְמַכְּרוּ
לַעֲשׂוֹת הָרַע בְּעֵינֵי יְהוָה לְהַכְעִיסוֹ:
יח וַיִּתְאַנַּף יְהוָה מְאֹד בְּיִשְׂרָאֵל וַיְסִרֵם
מֵעַל פָּנָיו לֹא נִשְׁאַר רַק שֵׁבֶט יְהוּדָה

טַעֲוָתָא וַהֲווֹ לְמַגָּנָא
וּבָתַר עַמְמַיָּא דִּי
בְסַחֲרָנֵיהוֹן דִּי פַקֵּיד יְיָ
יָתְהוֹן בְּדִיל דְּלָא
לְמֶעְבַּד כְּוָתְהוֹן:
טז וּשְׁבַקוּ יָת כָּל
פִּקּוּדַיָּא דַּיְיָ אֱלָהֲהוֹן
וַעֲבַדוּ לְהוֹן מַתְּכָא תְּרֵין
עֶגְלִין וַעֲבַדוּ אֲשֵׁירְתָא
וּסְגִידוּ לְכָל חֵילֵי שְׁמַיָּא
וּפְלַחוּ יָת בְּעֵלָא:
יז וְאַעֲבַרוּ יָת בְּנֵיהוֹן וְיָת
בְּנָתֵיהוֹן בְּנוּרָא וְקַסְמוּ
קִסְמִין וְנַחִישׁוּ וְחַשִׁיבוּ
לְמֶעְבַּד דְּבִישׁ קֳדָם יְיָ
לְאַרְגָּזָא קֳדָמוֹהִי:
יח וַהֲוָה רְגַז מִן קֳדָם יְיָ
לַחֲדָא בְּיִשְׂרָאֵל וְאַגְלִינוּן
מֵאַרְעָא בֵּית שְׁכִנְתֵּיהּ
לָא אִשְׁתְּאַר לְחוֹד
שִׁבְטָא דְּבֵית יְהוּדָה
בלחודוהי

קמץ בז"ק שני קרי

רש"י

עשינו חוזה: (טז) שני עגלים. בבית אל ובדן: את הבעל. ע"ג ששמה בעל: (יז) ויתמכרו. מכרו עצמן לכך: (יח) ויסרם

רד"ק

(יז) ויתמכרו. כבר פירשנו בפסוק יען התמכרך וגו': (יח) רק שבט יהודה לבדו. ושבט בנימין טפל לו ונבלל עמו:

מנחת שי

אבל במדוייקים מלא וכן ראוי על פי המסורת דפרשת תולדות ילחק: (טז) שנים.

רלב"ג

עדות למכת בכורות וקרא גם כן מה שהעיד בהם הש"י בתורה את השמים ואת הארץ שאם יעברו על בריתו יבואו להם אלו הקללות עד השמידו אותם וקרא עדות ג"כ מה שבא בתורה מהספורים אשר הם עדות על מי שיעבור על דבר הש"י כזה האופן יענש עונש נפלא והנה רבו הספורים בתורה המעידים על זה ומי שיקיימה ישלם לו גמול טוב והם עזבו כל זה אשר נודע להם שלמותו וטובו והלכו אחרי ההבל והיא הע"ג ועשו גם כן פעולותיהם הכלים: (יז) ויקסמו קסמים וינחשו. ר"ל שהם עשו פעולות להוריד להם רוחניות הכוכבים לפי מהשבתם והי' בזה האופן המגונה מגיעים להם כח קסם וכן היו מנחשים בגוים והיו מסתפקים באלו ההודעות העתידות הבאות

מצודת דוד

מוסב על וילכו לומר שהלכו אחרי דרך העמים וגו': (טז) ויעשו להם מסכה וגו'. ילקו לצלמם העגלים: (יז) ויעבירו וגו' באש. זהו עבודת המולך: ויתמכרו. כ"כ התמידו לעשות הרע כאלו מכרו עצמם לכך: (יח) ויתאנף ה'. ובעבור כל זאת התאנף ה': מעל פניו. ר"ל מארצו: לא נשאר. כארצם:

מצודת ציון

כמו הם: (טז) מסכה. ענין יליקת מתכת כמו הפסל נסך חרש (ישעיה מ'): (יז) ויקסמו וגו' וינחשו. ענין כשוף וניחוש: (יח) ויתאנף. מלשון

This was the worship of the sun, which they adopted in Ahab's time [*Malbim*].

17. **And they passed their sons and daughters through fire**—This was the Molech cult. See above 16:3 [*Mezudath David*].

They continued to adopt all the abominable practices of the surrounding nations, as enumerated in Deut. 18:10 [*Malbim*].

and they practiced enchantment and divination—These were all methods of bringing down spiritual influences from the heavenly bodies, and thus foretelling the future. The prophet castigates them for engaging in the practices of the Gentiles to gain knowledge of the future, yet ignoring God's prophets, who relayed messages acquired directly from the Almighty Himself [*Ralbag*].

and they committed themselves—lit. *they sold themselves to that* [*Rashi*].

worthless things and became worthless, and after the nations that were around them, concerning whom the Lord had commanded them not to do like them. 16. And they forsook all the commandments of the Lord their God, and made for themselves two molten calves, and they made an *asherah,* and they prostrated themselves before the entire host of the heavens, and they worshipped the Baal. 17. And they passed their sons and daughters through fire, and they practiced enchantment and divination, and they committed themselves to do what was evil in the eyes of the Lord, to anger Him. 18. And the Lord became every much incensed against Israel, and He sent them away from before Him; none was left but the tribe of Judah alone.

the creation of the world, Passover and *Succoth,* which testify to the Exodus, redemption of the firstborn, which testifies to the slaying of the firstborn in Egypt. This includes too God's testimony that one who disobeys His commandments will be punished, and the incidents recorded in the Torah that substantiate this testimony [*Ralbag*].

and they followed worthless things—Since they abandoned God's Torah, they substituted for it a worthless faith, a faith of nonsense and abominations [*Malbim*].

They followed the demons [*Abarbanel*].

and became worthless—They became attached to their faith of worthless things [*Mezudath David*].

and after the nations—I.e. they followed the nations, the manners of the nations around them [*Mezudath David*].

16. **And they forsook**—Until now, the prophet has been delineating the transgressions of individuals. From here on, he is delineating the communal sins of the people [*Malbim*].

two molten calves—lit. a molten image, two calves—*in Bethel and in Dan* [*Rashi*].

This took place in the reign of Jeroboam, son of Nebat. This was the beginning of Israel's communal sins [*Malbim*].

Although some exegetes maintain that the calves were erected as a symbol of the kingdom of Ephraim, not as deities, as in I Kings 12:28, it was, nevertheless, a sin, and a stumbling block for the people.

and they made an asherah—After they made the calves, they planted the *asherah,* a symbol of moon worship [*Malbim*].

the Baal—*a pagan deity named Baal* [*Rashi*].

לְבַדּוֹ: יט גַּם־יְהוּדָה לֹא שָׁמַר אֶת־מִצְוֺת יְהוָה אֱלֹהֵיהֶם וַיֵּלְכוּ בְּחֻקּוֹת יִשְׂרָאֵל אֲשֶׁר עָשׂוּ: כ וַיִּמְאַס יְהוָה בְּכָל־זֶרַע יִשְׂרָאֵל וַיְעַנֵּם וַיִּתְּנֵם בְּיַד שֹׁסִים עַד אֲשֶׁר הִשְׁלִיכָם מִפָּנָיו: כא כִּי־קָרַע יִשְׂרָאֵל מֵעַל בֵּית דָּוִד וַיַּמְלִיכוּ אֶת־יָרָבְעָם בֶּן־נְבָט וַיַּדָּא יָרָבְעָם אֶת־יִשְׂרָאֵל מֵאַחֲרֵי יְהוָה וְהֶחֱטִיאָם חֲטָאָה גְדוֹלָה: כב וַיֵּלְכוּ בְּנֵי יִשְׂרָאֵל בְּכָל־חַטֹּאות יָרָבְעָם אֲשֶׁר עָשָׂה לֹא־סָרוּ מִמֶּנָּה: כג עַד אֲשֶׁר־הֵסִיר יְהוָה אֶת־יִשְׂרָאֵל מֵעַל פָּנָיו כַּאֲשֶׁר דִּבֶּר בְּיַד כָּל־

בִּלְחוֹדוֹהִי: יט אַף דְּבֵית יְהוּדָה לָא נְטָרוּ יָת פִּקּוֹדַיָּא דַּיְיָ אֱלָהֲהוֹן וַאֲזַלוּ בִּגְזֵירַת יִשְׂרָאֵל דַּעֲבָדוּ: כ וְקַץ יְיָ בְּכָל זַרְעָא דְיִשְׂרָאֵל וְעַנִּינוּן וּמַסְרִינוּן בְּיַד בָּזוֹזִין עַד דְּאַגְלִינוּן מֵאֲתַר בֵּית שְׁכִנְתֵּיהּ: כא אֲרֵי אִתְפְּלִיגוּ בֵּית יִשְׂרָאֵל עַל דְּבֵית יְהוּדָה וְאַמְלִיכוּ יָת יָרָבְעָם בַּר נְבָט וְאַטְעֵי יָרָבְעָם יָת יִשְׂרָאֵל מִבָּתַר פּוּלְחָנָא דַּיְיָ וְחַיֵּיבִינוּן חוֹבָא רַבָּא: כב וַאֲזַלוּ בְּנֵי יִשְׂרָאֵל בְּכָל חוֹבֵי יָרָבְעָם דַּעֲבַד לָא סְטוֹ מִנַּהּ: כג עַד דְּאַגְלֵי יְיָ יָת יִשְׂרָאֵל מֵאַרְעָא בֵּית שְׁכִנְתֵּיהּ כְּמָא דְמַלֵּל בְּיַד

ת״א וידח ירבעם. סנהדרין קב:

רד״ק
וידח קרי מלא ואו

(כא) וידא. כן כתיב וקרי וידח והכתוב פי׳ מן המנדים ליום

רש״י
מעל פניו. שגלו עם הושע בן אלה: (כג) ויגל ישראל.

מנחת שי
שני קרי: (כא) וידח. וידא קרי: (כג) ויגל ישראל מעל אדמתו. היו״ד בחירק וכן כתב רש״י ז״ל ובמסורת שלנו בסוף מלכים נמסר ויגל ד׳ וסימן יהודה מעל אדמתו וחברו דסוף ירמיה. ויגל האחרית דדברי הימים. ויגל אונס למוסר (איוב ל״ו). ומאי דמנו בהו ויגל את האחרית דדברי הימים טעותא הוא דבכולהו ספרי בסגול וכ״ג ויגל ישראל דהכא. והכי אשכחנא בהדיא במס׳ כ״י:

רלב״ג
והמגוגית בתכלית והיו עוזבים ההודעות השלמות שהיו מגיעים להם על ידי נביא: (כ) ויענם ויתנם ה׳ ביד שוסים. זכר זה כי כבר עשה הש״י בהדרגה כמו שזכר בתורה והוא שכבר ענה ישראל ברעב וכמה שידמה לו ואחר זה נתנם ביד אויבים היו שוללים אותם ואחר זה השליכם מעל פניו והגלה אותם אל ארץ אחרת: (כא) וימליכו את ירבעם בן נבט. אמר זה כי ישראל המליכוהו מעצמם אף על פי שכבר ייעד הש״י על יד נביאו הנה נבחר זה אז מעצמם לא ע״י נביא ואולם בעת ההוא נהפך לבב ירבעם לרע ולו היו שואלים פי נביא לא היה בוחר בו כמו שמלאהו בשאול שאף על פי שנמשך למלך אמר הש״י לשמואל כי נחם כי המליכו כ״ש בזה שלא נמשח: וידא ירבעם את ישראל. וידא כתוב וידח קרי והכתי׳ הוא מענין ידו גורל והרצון

מצודת ציון
אף ומימה כמו ואנפת בם (מ״א ח׳): (כ) ויענם. מלשון עינוי: שוסים. בוזזים כמו והמה שוסים (ש״א כ״ג):

מצודת דוד
(יט) גם יהודה. ר״ל אף שגם יהודה לא שמר וגו׳: אשר עשו. החוקים אשר עשו ישראל: (כ) וימאס. ר״ל עכ״ז לא מאס עתה רק בישראל: מפניו. מאצלו: (כא) כי קרע ישראל. ר״ל וזהו בעבור אשר כל ישראל התחילו בעבירה כי הם מעצמם קרעו ונפרדו ממלכות בית דוד ופי ה׳ לא שאלו: וידח ירבעם. וזה היתה סיבה שהדיחם ירבעם בעגלי הזהב כי בראותו שמרדו במלכות בית דוד חשש פן גם בו ימרדו כאשר יבואו לירושלים ולזה עשה העגלים למנעם מללכת לירושלים כמ״ש במ״א אבל אם היו שואלים בדבר ה׳ ומלך על פיו לא היה בא לכלל זה: (כב) לא סרו ממנה. אף אחר שבטל הושע את השומרים עכ״ז לא סרו ממנה מדעת עצמם: (כג) עד אשר. כ״כ הרשיעו עד שגרם החטא והסירם ה׳ מעל פניו: עד היום הזה. ר״ל והנם שם עד היום הזה ולא חזרו בבית השני כמו יהודה. וכל זה חוזר למעלה ליתן טעם מדוע חרה אף ה׳ בישר׳ ועדיין האריך אפו ליהודה והלא דרך א׳ להם. ואמר לפי שע״י כל ישראל באה מתחילה התקלה ולבסוף אחזו מעצמם מבלי מכריח ולזה הרה בם והגלה אותם ומבלי חזרה בבית השני אבל אנשי יהודה לא באה התקלה על ידם כ״א ע״י המלכים המכריחים ובסור המכריח אחזו עדיין בדרך ה׳ ולזה

and delivered them into the hands of plunderers—as transpired during the reign of Jehoahaz, when Israel was under the power of Aram (ch. 13) [*Malbim*].

until He cast them away—until He finally cast them away completely [*Malbim*].

21. **For Israel had torn away**—Israel was punished first because they had commenced to sin by tearing away from the house of David

19. Neither did Judah observe the commandments of the Lord
their God, and they followed the practices of Israel that they
did. 20. And the Lord despised all the seed of Israel, and He
afflicted them, and delivered them into the hands of plunderers
until He cast them away from before Him. 21. For Israel had
torn away from the house of David and had appointed Jeroboam the son of Nebat as king, and Jeroboam led Israel astray
from following the Lord and caused them to commit a grave
sin. 22. And the children of Israel followed all the sins of Jeroboam that he committed; they did not turn away from it.
23. Until the Lord removed Israel from His Presence, as He
had spoken through all

18. **And the Lord became very much incensed against Israel**—Because of their sins, the Lord became very much incensed against them [*Mezudath David*].

First He became incensed against Israel, the northern kingdom, as is evidenced by the fact that He sent them away [*Malbim*].

and He sent them away from before Him—*for they were exiled with Hoshea the son of Elah* [*Rashi*].

from before Him—from His land [*Mezudath David*].

Alternatively, from His Providence. He seemed to be hiding His face from them and not looking into their needs [*Malbim*].

none was left—on his land [*Mezudath David*].

Alternatively, none was left under Divine Providence [*Malbim*].

but the tribe of Judah alone—and the tribe of Benjamin, which was included in Judah and was secondary to it [*Redak*].

19. **Neither did Judah**—Even though Judah too did not observe the commandments, God exiled only Israel [*Mezudath David*].

20. **And the Lord despised all the seed of Israel**—Even though Judah too did not observe the commandments, God despised the seed of Israel only [*Mezudath David*].

from before him—from His land [*Mezudath David*].

Others explain: Also Judah did not observe . . . Afterwards, Judah was influenced by Israel, and they, too, did not observe the commandments . . . Thus, it was obvious that if Israel were not exiled, Judah would become corrupted by them [*Malbim*].

And the Lord despised—He, therefore, saw to punish them so that Judah would see their fate, and learn to avoid following after their practices [*Malbim*].

He afflicted them—with poverty [*Malbim*].

עֲבָדָיו הַנְּבִיאִים וַיִּגֶל יִשְׂרָאֵל מֵעַל אַדְמָתוֹ אַשּׁוּרָה עַד הַיּוֹם הַזֶּה׃
כד וַיָּבֵא מֶלֶךְ־אַשּׁוּר מִבָּבֶל וּמִכּוּתָה וּמֵעַוָּא וּמֵחֲמָת וּ*סְפַרְוַיִם וַיֹּשֶׁב בְּעָרֵי שֹׁמְרוֹן תַּחַת בְּנֵי יִשְׂרָאֵל וַיִּרְשׁוּ אֶת־שֹׁמְרוֹן וַיֵּשְׁבוּ בְּעָרֶיהָ׃
כה וַיְהִי בִּתְחִלַּת שִׁבְתָּם שָׁם לֹא יָרְאוּ אֶת־יְהוָה וַיְשַׁלַּח יְהוָה בָּהֶם אֶת־הָאֲרָיוֹת וַיִּהְיוּ הֹרְגִים בָּהֶם׃
כו וַיֹּאמְרוּ לְמֶלֶךְ אַשּׁוּר לֵאמֹר הַגּוֹיִם אֲשֶׁר הִגְלִיתָ וַתּוֹשֶׁב בְּעָרֵי שֹׁמְרוֹן לֹא יָדְעוּ אֶת־מִשְׁפַּט אֱלֹהֵי הָאָרֶץ וַיְשַׁלַּח־בָּם אֶת־הָאֲרָיוֹת וְהִנָּם מְמִיתִים אוֹתָם כַּאֲשֶׁר אֵינָם יֹדְעִים אֶת־מִשְׁפַּט אֱלֹהֵי

בְּיַד כָּל עַבְדוֹהִי נְבִיַּיָא וּגְלוֹ יִשְׂרָאֵל מֵעַל אַרְעֲהוֹן לְאַתּוּר עַד יוֹמָא הָדֵין׃ כד וְאַיְתִי מַלְכָּא דְאַתּוּר מִבָּבֶל וּמִכּוּתָה וּמֵעַוָה וּמֵחֲמָת וּמִסְפַרְוַיִם וְאוֹתֵיב בְּקִירְוֵי שֹׁמְרוֹן חֲלַף בְּנֵי יִשְׂרָאֵל וִירִיתוּ יָת שֹׁמְרוֹן וִיתִיבוּ בְּקִירְוָהָא׃ כה וַהֲוָה בִּשְׁרָיוּת לְמִיתַּבְהוֹן תַּמָּן לָא הֲווֹ דַחֲלִין מִן קֳדָם יְיָ וְגָרֵי יְיָ בְּהוֹן יָת אַרְיָוָתָא וַהֲווֹ קָטְלִין בְּהוֹן׃ כו וַאֲמַרוּ לְמַלְכָּא דְאַתּוּר לְמֵימַר עַמְמַיָּא דְאַגְלֵיתָא וְאוֹתֵבְתָּא בְּקִירְוֵי שֹׁמְרוֹן לָא הֲווֹ יָדְעִין יָת דִּין אֱלָהָא דְאַרְעָא וְגָרֵי בְּהוֹן יָת אַרְיָוָתָא וְהָא אִינוּן מְקַטְּלִין יָתְהוֹן בִּדְלֵית אִינוּן יָדְעִין יָת דִּין אלהא

ומספרוים קרי

רש"י

זה נקוד בחירק שהוא לשון גלה ואינו לשון הגלה: (כה) לא יראו את ה׳. אע"פ שהעמים עובדי גלולים הם יראים

רד"ק

רע שונאיכם מנדיכם ופי׳ הרחיק מאחרי ה׳ את ישראל ותקרי ידוע: (כד) ויושב בערי שמרון. ולא אמר בשמרון ובעריה וכן אמר וירשו את שמרון וישבו בעריה כי שמרון החריבה מלך אשור עד היסוד כמו שניבא עליהם מיכה המורשתי ושמתי שמרון לעי השדה למטעי כרם: (כו) אשר הגליתי. הניעותי וטלטלתי כי פעמים יאמר לשון גלות זולת השבי וכן ויגלם מנחת:

רלב"ג

כו וישליך וכן כונת הקרי מסכמת לזה הענין כי ההדת׳ מתיחסת מאד אל ההשלכה: (כד) ויבא מלך אשור מבבל. ר"ל שהביא אנשים

מנחת שי

(כד) ומעוא ומחמת. בכל הספרים כתוב ומעוא באל"ף ומסור עליה לית כתיב אל"ף וקשה בעיני כי בחילופי המקרא כתוב למערבאי בה"א ולמדנחאי באל"ף: ו*ספרוים. ומספרוים קרי: וירשו את שמרון. ביו"ד האית"ן לבד ונעדרה היו"ד פ"א הפעל מהמכתב ובמסורת וירשו ד׳ חסרין וסימנהון ואלה מלכי הארץ יהושע ריש סימן י"ב ויאא גבול בני דן מהם שם סוף סימן י"ט. ויבא מלך אשור מבבל דמלכים ויבאו וירשו אותם (ירמיה ל"ב) ואית דמסרי ז׳ חסרים בליגנא. וכן נמסר ביהושע סימן י"ט וסימן כ"א במ"ג וליכא בינייהו פלוגתא ובספרים כתובי יד מדוייקים וגם בדפוס קדמון היו"ד במאיך והוא נכון כחבירו:

מצודת דוד

מדיין לא נתמלא סאתם (ואף אחר שגלו חזרו בבית השני כי לא ידמו בהטאם לחטא ישראל כי תחילת התקלה לא באה על ידם כדרך שבאה ע"י ישראל): (כד) בערי שומרון. בהערים הסמוכים לשומרון: (כו) ויאמרו. עבדי המלך: אשר הגלית. מבבל ומכותה וגו׳: את משפט. חוק האלהים השוכן בהארץ ההיא: וישלח. ולזה שלח בהם את האריות בעוד כאשר אינם יודעים משפט וגו׳ אבל כאשר ידעו לא שלח בהם עוד (ואף כי מאז היו בארלם לא ידעו משפט ה׳ מ"מ לא הקפיד על העו"ג כ"א בהיותם בארלו המקודש ולא בארץ

מצודת ציון

(כו) ויורם. ענין למוד כמו יורה דעה (ישעיה כח):

strengthen his rule in the land, he exiled its inhabitants and resettled it with peoples who were already under his control. Perhaps, when the Babylonians conquered the land, these people had become well established there, and were an important factor in the beginning of the era of the Second Temple.

Jeremiah enumerates these peoples to inform the leaders of later generations that many of the inhabitants of Eretz Israel were of these nations and were not of Jewish lin-

His servants, the prophets, and Israel went in exile from their land to Assyria until this day. 24. And the king of Assyria brought [people] from Babylonia and from Cuthah and from Avva and from Hamath and from Sepharvaim, and he settled them in the cities of Samaria instead of the children of Israel, and they took possession of Samaria and dwelt in its cities. 25. And it was in the beginning of their dwelling there, that they did not fear the Lord, and the Lord incited lions against them, and they were killing them. 26. And they said to the king of Assyria, saying, "The nations that you exiled and settled in the cities of Samaria, do not know the law of the God of the land, and He has incited lions against them, and behold they are killing them, as they do not know the law of the God of the land."

without consulting God's prophet [*Mezudath David*].

Jeroboam led Israel astray—This was the reason he brought sin upon the people. Since he saw that the people had rebelled against the house of David, he feared they would rebel against him too. He, therefore, erected the two calves to keep them in his kingdom to celebrate the pilgrimage festivals, rather than go to Jerusalem. Had he asked the Lord for guidance in governing his kingdom, he would never have come to this sin [*Mezudath David*].

22. **they did not turn away from it**—Even after Hoshea the son of Elah had abolished the sentries instituted by Jeroboam the son of Nebat, to prevent the Israelites from making the pilgrimage to Jerusalem, they still neglected to make the pilgrimage [*Mezudath David*].

23. **Until the Lord removed Israel**—I.e. they continued to sin until the Lord removed them from before Him [*Mezudath David*].

and Israel went in exile—Heb. וַיִּגֶל. *This is voweled with a "hirik," which is an expression of "went in exile." It is not an expression of "exiled" [Rashi*]. See above v. 6, for the difference between וַיִּגֶל and וַיֶּגֶל.

until this day—and they did not return as Judah returned to rebuild the Temple. As explained above, Judah did not meet the fate of Israel, since Israel preceded them with their sins, and continued to sin after they were no longer coerced by their kings, to do so. Judah, however, sinned only because of coercion by their kings [*Mezudath David*].

24. **from Babylonia**—over which he ruled at the time. In order to

הָאָרֶץ׃ כז וַיְצַו מֶלֶךְ־אַשּׁוּר לֵאמֹר
הֹלִיכוּ שָׁמָּה אֶחָד מֵהַכֹּהֲנִים אֲשֶׁר
הִגְלִיתֶם מִשָּׁם וְיֵלְכוּ וְיֵשְׁבוּ שָׁם וְיֹרֵם
אֶת־מִשְׁפַּט אֱלֹהֵי הָאָרֶץ׃ כח וַיָּבֹא אֶחָד
מֵהַכֹּהֲנִים אֲשֶׁר הִגְלוּ מִשֹּׁמְרוֹן וַיֵּשֶׁב
בְּבֵית־אֵל וַיְהִי מוֹרֶה אֹתָם אֵיךְ יִירְאוּ
אֶת־יְהוָה׃ כט וַיִּהְיוּ עֹשִׂים גּוֹי גּוֹי אֱלֹהָיו
וַיַּנִּיחוּ ׀ בְּבֵית הַבָּמוֹת אֲשֶׁר עָשׂוּ

אֱלָהָא דְאַרְעָא׃ כז וּפַקִּיד
מַלְכָּא דְאַתּוּר לְמֵימַר
אוֹבִילוּ לְתַמָּן חַד
מִכָּהֲנַיָּא דְאַגְלֵיתִינוּן
מִתַּמָּן וְיֵזְלוּן וְיִתְּבוּן תַּמָּן
וְיַלְּפוּן יָת דִּין אֱלָהָא
דְאַרְעָא׃ כח וַאֲתָא חַד
מִכָּהֲנַיָּא דְאִתְגְּלִיאוּ
מִשָּׁמְרוֹן וִיתֵיב בְּבֵית
אֵל וַהֲוָה מַלִּיף יָתְהוֹן
אֵכְדֵין יִדְחֲלוּן מִן קֳדָם
יְיָ׃ כט וַהֲווֹ עָבְדִין עַמָּא
עַמָּא טַעֲוָתֵיהוֹן וְצַחִיתוּ
בְּבֵית בָּמָתָא דַעֲבָדוּ
שמרונאי

רד"ק

(כז) אחד מהכהנים. שהם מורי התורה: (כח) איך יראו את ה'. הורה אותם שאע"פ שהם עובדים איש אלהיו יהיה לבם לאל כי ישראל אע"פ שהיו עובדים העגלים לא היו עושים אלא להיותם אמצעיים בינם ובין האל כי כן היתה דעת האומות בזמן ההוא שעל כל פנים היה צריך אמצעי להתקרב אליו ולעבדו. וישראל טעו אחרי דעות האומות אם כן מה בין ישראל ובין האומות י"א כי האומות כשהיו עובדי' איש את אלהיו החכמים שבהם היו יודעים כי הצלמים לא יועילו אלא להיותם אמצעיים ולעבדם והעבודה ההיא אמרו כי תישר בעיני האלהים אבל המון עם לא היה להם לב וסבר' כי אם על הנעבד והיו חושבים כי הוא המטיב והמריע וישראל לא כן אלא כלם היו יודעים מירושת אבות כי האל יתברך היא אלהי האלהים אלא שהיו טועי' אחרי דעות האומות לפי שהיו נבדלים מכל שאר האומות וכשהיו רואים ההצלחה לאומות העולם היו סוברים כי אלהיהם האמצעיים היו גורמים להם ההצלחה ההוא והיו אומרים איכה יעבדו הגוים האלה את אלהיהם ואעשה כן גם אני כמ"ש אחז כי אלהי מלכי ארם הם מעזרים אותם להם אזבח ויעזרוני ואפילו הרשעים שבהם היו דורשים את ה' כי ירבעם אמר חל נא את פני ה' אלהיך כי כוונתו כי הוא המטיב והמריע ולא אמר כי יבושת ידו היה מקרה וכשחלה בנו שלח אשתו לדרוש את ה' מאחיה השילוני ואחאב נסכם עם אליהו בדבר נביאי הבעל וחרד לדברי הנביא שאמר לו והיתה נפשך תחת נפשו ומנבואת אליהו חרד וקרע את בגדיו וצם וישכב בשק ויהורם אמר כי קרא ה' לשלשת המלכים האלה לתת אותם ביד מואב יראת השם זאת היתה בלבם כי מאת האל יתברך הטוב והרע אע"פ שהיו בהם קצת כופרים שהיו אומרים לא ייטיב ה' ולא ירע והיו אומרים מי רואנו ומי יודענו אותם היו מעטים ודעת אחרת היתה בלבם והיו אומרים בסתר כמו שאמר ויחפאו בני ישראל ואותם היו מאמינים שהטוב ורע אינו בכוונת מכוין לא באל ולא באחד מן הנעבדים אבל המאמינים בע"ג והעובדים אותה היו רבים ואותם היתה דעתם לאל יתב' אלא שהיו עובדים ע"י אמצעי ויראת אלהים זאת לא היתה אתם כי האל צוה אותם לא תעשון אתי אלהי כסף ואלהי זהב ר"ל שתחשבו שיהיו אמצעיים ביני וביניכם ובזה היו טועים והולכים בחקות הגוים בדברים אחרים רבים שמנעם האל יתברך לפיכך הקיאה אותם הארץ כמו שאמר להם ה' יתברך ולא תלכו בחקות הגוים ולא תקיא הארץ אתכם ומפני מה היו נענשים הגוים האלה אשר באו בשמרון ולא היו נענשים בארצם כי ארץ ישראל מקודשת מכל הארצות ולא תסבול הארץ התועבות ההם כמו שאמר הכתוב אלהי נכר הארץ לפיכך אמר ויורם את משפט אלהי הארץ ונאמר כאשר קאה את הגוי אשר לפניכם וזה הכהן הבא להורות אלת הגוים בשמרון אם יאמר להם שלא יהיו עובדים ע"ג כלל לא היו מאמינים כי הוא דבר שגדלו בו כל האומות מקדם והוא אצלם כמו מושכל ראשון אך אמר להם שיהיו עובדים את אלהיהם כמו שהיו עובדים ובלבד שתהא כוונת האל בלבם כי אלת האלהים לא ירעו ולא ייטיבו כ"א ברצון האל אלא שעובדים אותם להיות אמצעיים בינם ובין הבורא והורה אותם ג"כ שישמרו מהתועבת הגדולות בטמאת הגוף כמשכב זכור ומשכב בהמה ומשכב הקרובות כמו שאמר הכתוב כי את כל התיעבות האל עשו אנשי הארץ אשר לפניכם ותטמא הארץ וזהו את משפט אלהי הארץ וזה יראת ה' שיראו ממנו ויתנו לו הכח כי הוא אל על כל אלהים ויזהרו מהטומאות האלה בעבור יראתו והזהרתו שלא יעשו בארץ ההיא יותר משאר הארצות: (כט) אשר עשו השמרונים. זה ישראל שהיו בשומרון ובאותם בתי הבמות שעשו הם הניחו אלו הגוים אלהיהם גוי גוי בעריהם אשר

רש"י

מפניו וקרו ליה אלהא דאלהיא כענין שנאמר ושמי נורא בגויים (מלאכי א') ואלו לא יראוני כי אמרו אלו היתה בו יראה לא נתן עמו לגלות: (כט) אשר עשו השומרונים.

מנחת שי

(כח) איך ייראו את ה'. בספרים מדוייקים ודפוסים ישנים בשני יודי"ן ובמאריך:

רלב"ג

מכל אלו המקומות להושיב בערי שמרון אשר הגלה משם ישראל: (כז) אחד מהכהנים אשר הגליתם משם. ידמה כי קלת כהני ה' היו שם במנשיהם והוא היה מורה הגוים האלו איך יתנהגו לפי משפטי התורה והם עושים עם זה גוי גוי אלהיו בערי שמרון והניחו הע"ג שלהם בבית הבמות אשר עשו השומרוני' ויהיו יראים את ה' ועשו להם מקצתם כהני במות כמו שעשה ירבעם והזכיר הכהנים מן הכהונה ידמה כי באלו הבמות היו מקריבים לשם יתעלה כמו שהיה הענין קודם אסור הבמות

מצודת דוד

(כז) וילכו וישבו שם. חוזר על הע"ג מבבל ומכותה וגו' ור"ל כאשר הלכו לשם כן נשארו יושבים בה והכהן ילמדם משפט ה': (כט) גוי גוי אלהיו. כל אומה עשה לעצמו ע"ג שעבד בארצו ולא היה הכהן מעבירם מהע"ג מכל וכל כי הוא היה מכהני הבמות

made—i.e. *the Israelites while they were still there* [Rashi, Redak, Mezudath David].

each nation its god (sic)—*Every nation* (as per *R. Joseph Kara*), *the deity they had worshipped in their land, here, too, each nation did so in the city* (as per *R. Joseph Kara*)

27. And the king of Assyria commanded, saying, "Bring there
one of the priests whom I have exiled from there, and let them
go and dwell there, and teach them the law of the God of the
land." 28. And one of the priests whom they had exiled from
Samaria came and settled in Bethel, and he would direct them
how they should fear the Lord. 29. Now each nation made its
god, and they placed [it] in the temple of the high places that

eage [*Daath Soferim*].

from Cuthah—They were from the land of Cuth, as in v. 30. Cuthah was a region in that land, bordering on the Euphrates, in the environs of Babylonia. Apparently the Cuthites outnumbered the others. For this reason, all these peoples are referred to as Cuthites in later times [*Daath Soferim*].

from Avva—This, too, was a region of Babylonia [*Daath Soferim*].

and from Hamath—not to be confused with Hamath mentioned in I Kings 8:65, and above 14:25. That one was a city of Aram, whereas this is a Babylonian city or region [*Daath Soferim*].

and he settled them in the cities of Samaria—but not in Samaria itself. Also, at the end of the verse, we read, "and they dwelt in its cities." This implies that they did not dwell in Samaria itself. Samaria had been razed to its foundations by the king of Assyria, as had been prophesied by Micah (1:6), "And I shall make Samaria into a heap in the field" [*Redak*].

25. **they did not fear the Lord**—*Even though the pagan nations fear him and call him the God of the gods, in the manner it is written,* "(Malachi 1:14) *and My Name is feared among the nations," these did not fear Me, for they said, "If He were worthy of fear, He would not have delivered His people into exile."* [*Rashi* based on TB *Menahoth* 110a].

26. **And they said**—I.e. the king's courtiers said . . . [*Mezudath David*].

that you exiled—from Babylonia, from Cuthah . . . [*Mezudath David*]. In this case, *exile* does not imply captivity [*Redak*].

the law of the God of the land—the law of the God Who dwells in that land [*Mezudath David*].

and He has incited lions against them—Therefore, He has incited lions against them, since they have not yet learned the law of the God of the land. When they will learn His laws, He will no longer plague them with lions [*Mezudath David*].

one of the priests—who are the teachers of the Torah [*Redak*].

28. **how they should fear the Lord**—He taught that although each one would worship his own god, his thoughts should be directed to the One true God, for Israel, although they worshipped the calves, they considered them only as intermediaries between themselves and God.*

29. **the people of Samaria had**

השמרנים גוי גוי בעריהם אשר הם
ישבים שם: ל ואנשי בבל עשו את־
סכות בנות ואנשי־כות עשו את־נרגל
ואנשי חמת עשו את־אשימא:
לא והעוים עשו נבחז ואת־תרתק
והספרוים שרפים את־בניהם באש
לאדרמלך וענמלך אלה ספר*ים:
לב ויהיו יראים את־יהוה ויעשו להם
מקצותם כהני במות ויהיו עשים להם
בבית הבמות: לג את־יהוה היו יראים

שמרונאי עמא עמא בקירויהון דאינון יתבין תמן: ל ואנשי בבל עבדו ית סכות בנות ואנשי כות עבדו ית נרגל ואנשי חמת עבדו ית אשימא: לא ועואי עבדו נבחז וית תרתק ואנש ספרואי מוקדין ית בניהון בנורא לאדרמלך וענמלך טעות ספרוים: לב והוו דחלין מן קדם יי ועבדו להון מקצתהון כומרי במתא והוו עבדין להון בבית במתא: לג מן קדם יי הוו דחלין וית טעותהון

ת"א סכות בנות. סנהדרין סג (ע"ג מג): נבחז. (שם): מקלותם. קדושין עד:

זין רבתי אלהי קרי ספרוים קרי

רש"י

ישראל בעודם שם: גוי גוי אלהיו. לאומה ואומה ע"ג שהיו עובדים בארצם אף כאן עשו כן כל גויי העיר אשר הורישם סנחריב שם בערי ישראל: (ל) סכות בנות. דמות תרנגולת עם אפרוחיה: נרגל. דמות תרנגול: אשימא. דמות תיש וכן קרויין בלשון כל אומה ואומה וכן פירשו רבותינו בסנהדרין: (לא) נבחז. דמות כלב: תרתק. דמות המור: לאדרמלך. דמות פרד: וענמלך. דמות

רד"ק

היו יושבים שם היה עושה כל אחד בעירו בארץ ישראל כמנהגם בארצם:(ל) את סכות בנות. כן היה שם ע"ג שהיו עובדים בארצם וראינו כי שם ע"ג של בבל היה שמה בל כמו שאומר הכ' כרע בל קורס נבו וזה היה בימי נבוכדנצר כשה"כ בלטשאצר כשם אלהי אבל בימי מלך אשור היה ע"ג שלהם סכות בנות ובדברי רבותינו ז"ל סכות בנות זה תרנגולת כלומר דמות תרנגולת היו עובדים והיה שמה סכות בנות וכמו שקורין לתרנגול סכוי כן היו קורין לתרנגולת סכות ובנות פי' עם אפרוחיה: אשימא. נרגל זה תרנגולת הבר. ובירושלמי את נרגל רגלי' דיעקב ורגלי' דיוסף: אשימא. ברחא קרחא והוא התייש ונקרא אשימא לפי שאין לו צמר והוא כמו שומם. ובירושלמי אשימא. אימרא כמה דתימא באיל האשם: (לא) נבחז. בזי"ן ויש ספרים כתוב בנו"ן ואינו כ"א בזי"ן וטעות הוא בספרים. ופי' נבחז הוא כלב והוא מלה מורכבת נובח חז נו_ח מן לא יכלו לנבוח חז לשון מראה שמראה שיניו: תרתק. פירשו בו צירת חמור: לאדרמלך וענמלך. אדרמלך הוא הפרד ונקרא כן דאדר ל"ה למאריה בטועניה פי' שנושא לרבו כל משאותיו. אדר כמודרי טוענא. ענמלך זה הסוס דעני ליה למריה בקרבא ובירושלמי אדרמלך וענמלך זה טווס ופסיוני וטווס הוא הנקרא בלשון לע"ז פאון וידוע הוא ופסיוני הוא שלו והתרגום שאל ויבא שלו שאלו בשרא ואייתו פסיונין: (לב) ויהיו עושים להם. הכהני' היו עושים להם עבודתם וקרבנותיהם בבמות:

מנחת שי

(לא) עשו נבחז. בנביאים עם פירוש הרי"א כתוב עשו את נבחז והוא טעות: והעוים עשו נבחז. כתב רד"ק בזי"ן ויש ספרים כתוב בנון וטעות הוא בספרים עכ"ל. ובמקראות גדולות בגליון כתוב לית זי"ן רבתי ואולי זאת היתה סבת הטעות הר נא מלאתיה כן בשום נוסח מהלפ"א ביתא רבתית ובספרים אחרים כתובי יד נמסר עליו לית כתיב זיי"ן ומלת רבתי איננה. ובעל דרך אמונה במאמר ה' ש' ב' כ' הפך זה וז"ל ונכתב בנו"ן זעירא עד שרבים תבאוה נו"ן וכו' ע"ש. ובנוסחא כ"י מאותיות קטנות נמנה בתוכם סי"ן והעוים עשו נבחז ואין כן במסורת אחרות: אלה*. אלהי קרי: ספר*ים. ספרוים קרי: (לב) מקצותם. הקו"ף רפה:

מצודת דוד

ועבד ע"ג כמותם: השמרנים. היהודים אנשי שומרון עד לא גלו: גוי גוי. כל אומה העמידה ע"ג שלה בבית הבמות בהעיר אשר התיישבה בה: (ל) סכות בנות. בלשון בבל הוא תרנגולת עם אפרוחיה: נרגל. בלשון כותי הוא התרנגול הזכר וכן כ"א נקרא לפי לשון האומה ההיא: אשימא. הוא תיש: (לא) נבחז. הוא כלב: תרתק. הוא המור: לאדרמלך וענמלך. הם הפרד והסוס: (לב) מקצותם. עשו מקצתם כהני במות לעשות עבודתם בבית הבמות:

they worshipped their idols as intermediaries [*Abarbanel, R. Joseph Kara*].

and they would practice their [rites]—I.e. the priests would perform their rites for them in the temple of the high places [*Redak, Mezudath David*].

33. **as was the custom of the nations whom they had exiled from there**—*Those deities that the nations whom Sennacherib and his armies had exiled from there, worshipped, these they would worship here* [*Rashi*].

I.e. the peoples who were repatriated to Samaria, would worship the same deities as the nations from

the people of Samaria had made, each nation in their cities wherein they were dwelling. 30. And the people of Babylonia made Succoth-benoth, and the people of Cuth made Nergal, and the people of Hamath made Ashima. 31. And the Avvites made Nibhaz and Tartak, and the Sepharvites burnt their children in fire to Adramelech and Anamelech, the gods of Sepharvaim. 32. And they feared the Lord, and they made some of them priests of the high places, and they would practice their [rites] in the temple of the high places. 33. They feared the Lord,

which Sennacherib had given them as a possession (or *had settled them—Kara*) *there in the cities of Israel* [*Rashi, Redak, Mezudath David*].

30. **Succoth-benoth**—*a likeness of a hen with her chicks* [*Rashi* from *San.* 63b].

Redak theorizes that *Succoth* stems from *sechvi,* a rooster. *Benoth* means daughters. Hence the name *Succoth-benoth* for a hen and its chicks.

Nergal—*the likeness of a rooster* [*Rashi*].

According to *Redak,* a wild hen.

Ashima—*the likeness of a goat. So they are called in the language of every nation, and so did our Rabbis explain in Sanhedrin* (63b) [*Rashi*].

Ashima stems from the root שמם, *desolation.* Since a goat has no wool like a sheep, he is given the name of desolation. According to *Talmud Yerushalmi, Abodah Zarah* 3:2, Ashima was a sheep, like one used for a guilt-offering (*asham*) [*Redak*].

31. **Nibhaz**—*the likeness of a dog* [*Rashi* from same source]. *Rashi* in *Sanhedrin* explains it as a barking dog. This stems from the root נבח, *to bark. Redak* explains this as a contraction of two words, נוֹבֵחַ and חָז, *a show of barking.* When a dog barks, he shows his teeth.

Tartak—*the likeness of a donkey* [*Rashi, Redak*].

to Adramelech—*the likeness of a mule* [*Rashi*].

This is a contraction of Aramaic words, meaning, one who bears for his master his burdens [*Sanhedrin* ibid. according to *Redak*]. According to *Rashi ad loc.,* one who honors his master by bearing his burdens.

Anamelech—*the likeness of a horse* [*Rashi*].

This, too, is a contraction of Aramaic words meaning, one who responds to his master in battle. According to *Yerushalmi,* the last two were likenesses of a peacock and a quail [*Redak*].

See above 16:3, for *Ramban*'s interpretation, that these were variations of the Molech.

32. **And they feared the Lord**—They feared the retribution He would mete out to them if they did not accept Him. They, therefore, directed their thoughts to Him when

וְאֶת־אֱלֹהֵיהֶם הָיוּ עֹבְדִים כְּמִשְׁפַּט
הַגּוֹיִם אֲשֶׁר־הִגְלוּ אֹתָם מִשָּׁם׃ לד עַד
הַיּוֹם הַזֶּה הֵם עֹשִׂים כַּמִּשְׁפָּטִים
הָרִאשֹׁנִים אֵינָם יְרֵאִים אֶת־יְהוָה
וְאֵינָם עֹשִׂים כְּחֻקֹּתָם וּכְמִשְׁפָּטָם
וְכַתּוֹרָה וְכַמִּצְוָה אֲשֶׁר צִוָּה יְהוָה אֶת־
בְּנֵי יַעֲקֹב אֲשֶׁר־שָׂם שְׁמוֹ יִשְׂרָאֵל׃
לה וַיִּכְרֹת יְהוָה אִתָּם בְּרִית וַיְצַוֵּם לֵאמֹר
לֹא תִירְאוּ אֱלֹהִים אֲחֵרִים וְלֹא־

תרגום

טַעֲוַתְהוֹן הֲווֹ פָּלְחִין כְּנִימוֹסֵי עַמְמַיָא דְאַגְלִיאוּ יַתְהוֹן מִתַּמָן׃ לד עַד יוֹמָא הָדֵין אִינוּן עָבְדִין כְּנִימוֹסֵי קַדְמָאֵי לֵיתֵינוּן דָחֲלִין מִן קֳדָם יְיָ וְלֵיתֵינוּן עָבְדִין כִּגְזֵירַתְהוֹן וְכִדְחָזֵי לְהוֹן וּכְאוֹרַיְתָא וּכְתַפְקֵידְתָּא דְפַקֵיד יְיָ יַת בְּנֵי יַעֲקֹב דְשַׁוִי שְׁמֵיהּ יִשְׂרָאֵל׃ לה וּגְזַר יְיָ עִמְהוֹן קְיָם וּפַקְדִינוּן לְמֵימַר לָא תִדְחֲלוּן לְטַעֲוַת עַמְמַיָא וְלָא

תסגדון

רד"ק

(לג)כמשפט הגוים אשר הגלו אותם משם. כמשפט ישר' שגלו משומרון כן היו עושים אלה הגוים שהיו יראים את ה' ועובדים אלהים אחרים כמו שפירשנו או יהיה פירושו כמשפט הגוים גויי ארצותם אשר באו משם ויהיה טעמו אל אלהיה' היו עובדי' לא אל ה' היו יראים כלו' כן היו עושים ועובדים אלהיהם כמו שהיה משפטם בארצם:(לד) עד היום הזה.לפי' הא' יהיה פי' עד היום הזה הם עושים על ישראל פי' ישראל אשר גלו לא שבו בגלותם מדרכם הרעה ועד היום הזה עושים במקום אשר גלו שם כמשפטי' הראשוני' שהיו עושים בשמרון אינם יראים את ה' שלא לעבוד ע"ג כי גם שם עובדים ע"ג בגלותם ולא יראו את ה' כי היראה היא לעבוד את ה' לבדו כמו שאמר להם יהושע ועתה יראו את ה' ועבדו אותו בתמים ובאמ' והסירו את אלהים אשר עבדו אבותיכם בעבר הנהר ובמצרים וכן אמר להם שמואל אך יראו את ה' ועבדתם אותו באמת ואינם עושים כחקים וכמשפטי' רק כחקות הגוים וכמשפטיהם ואינם עושים כתורה וכמצות אשר צוה ה' את בני יעקב ומת שאומר אשר שם שמו ישראל כי אז כשאמר יעקב לבניו הסירו את אלהי הנכר אשר בתוככם והטהרו והחליפו שמלותיכם אז נראה אליו ה' ואמר לו ישראל יהיה שמך ולפי' אחרון יהיה פי' אינם יראים את ה' על הגוים אע"פ שאמר את ה' היו יראים לא היו יראים את ה' בלב שלם כי אם מפחד האריות לפיכך קראו אותם גרי אריו' ואמר כמשפטים הראשונים היו עושים פי' כמשפטי' הראשוני' שהיו עושי' בארצם כן היו עושי' ולא היו עושי' כחקות' וכמשפט' וכתור' אשר צוה ה' שהיה עליהם לקבל הכל כיון שנתגיירו ולא קבלו והיה להם לקבל התורה כתורה וכמצוה אשר צוה ה' את בני יעקב וכל הענין וכיון שראו הגוים האלה כי ישראל גלו משם לפי שלא עשו כתורה וכמצוה אשר צוה ה' אותם היה להם ללמוד ולעשות כתורה וכמצוה ולא עשו כן והפי' הראשון נכון בעיני:

רש"י

סוס: (לג) כמשפט הגוים אשר הגלו אותם משם. אותם עכומ"ז שעובדים הגוים אשר הגלן סנחרב ואוכלוסיו (את אלו) משם היו אלו עובדין כאן: (לד) אינם יראים את ה'. יראה שלימה כמשפט ישראל ואף על פי שנתגיירו מיראת האריות אין יראתם את ה' יראה שלימה (כמשפט ישראל) כמו שמפרש והולך שאינם עוסקים בתורה ובמצות אשר צוה את בני יעקב ואינם עושים כחקותם וכמשפטם שהי' עליהם לעשות משנתגיירו אלא כמו שהורם הכהן שהי' מן השמרונים שהיו עו"ג: (לה) ויכרת ה' אתם ברית. כשנתן להם תורה בהר סיני:

רלב"ג

(לג) כמשפט הגוים אשר הגלו אותם משם. ר"ל שהם היו ג"כ עובדים לשם יתעלה ועובדים ע"ג ולזה אמר להם אליהו עד מתי אתם פוסחים על שתי הסעיפים אם ה' הוא האלהים לכו אחריו ואם הבעל לכו אחריו: (לד) עד היום הזה הם עושים כמשפטים הראשונים. ר"ל הנשארים הם ישראל כי לא הגלו כולם כמו שיראה מהספור אשר בענין חזקיה שסלח למס שנשאר

מצודת דוד

(לג) ואת אלהיהם. ע"ג שלהם: כמשפט וגו'. כל אחד עבד את הע"ג שבארצו אשר הגלה ממנה: (לד) כמשפטים הראשונים. כפי מה שהורם הכהן בעת נתיישבו שמה: אינם יראים וגו'. יראה שלמה כ"א מפחד האריות: ואינם וגו'. אינם עושים לחק וכמשפט הראוי להם לעשות לאחר שנתגיירו: וכתורה וגו'. אינם עושים כתורה וגו' וראוי היה שכן יעשו הואיל ונתגיירו: אשר שם שמו ישראל. כאומר הלא השם הזה היה ע"ש כי שרית עם האלהים וגו' ותוכל ומזה נראה שאין לעבוד לשרי מעלה כי הלא בעזר אלוה גבר על השר של מעלה: (לה) ויכרת. בעת שלוח את בני יעקב התורה והמצות כרת עמהם ברית והזהירם על ע"ג וחוזר הוא למעלה לומר הנה הע"ג הבאים לערי שומרון לא עשו כדבר ה' אשר צוה וגו' וכרת עמהם הברית וגו' וכל הענין עד סופו וכאומר

the strange gods that are in your midst, and purify yourselves, and change your garments," God appeared to him and changed his name to Israel (v. 9) [*Redak*].

Alternatively, Israel denotes superiority over all heavenly powers, such as angels and stars. Hence there is no justification for the Israelites to worship any heavenly body as an intermediary [*Malbim*].

35. **And the Lord enacted a cove-**

yet they worshipped their own gods, as was the custom of the nations whom they had exiled from there. 34. Until this day, they practice just as their earlier practices; they do not fear the Lord, neither do they practice according to their statutes and laws, nor according to the Law and the commandment that the Lord commanded the sons of Jacob, whose name He called Israel. 35. And the Lord enacted a covenant with them, saying, "You shall not fear other gods,

whose country they were exiled [*Redak*].

Alternatively, they would worship God in conjunction with pagan idols, much as the Israelites had done in the days of Elijah, who admonished them for "hopping on two branches" [*Redak, Ralbag, Malbim*].

34. **just as their earlier practices**—as the priests of Samaria had instructed them [*Mezudath David*].

they do not fear the Lord—*a complete fear as the custom of the Israelites. Even though they were converted because of the fear of the lions, their fear of the Lord was not a complete fear, (like Jewish practice) as Scripture goes on to elaborate, that they were not engaged in the Torah and the commandments which He (or, which the Lord) commanded the sons of Jacob, neither do they practice according to their statutes and according to their law, which they are dutibound to practice since they converted, but as the priest who was of the people of Samaria, who were idolatrous, instructed them* [*Rashi*].

According to the explanation that Scripture is referring to the Israelites, we interpret thus, Until this day, the Israelites in exile, have not repented of their idolatrous practices, but continue to adhere to their earlier practices of combining the worship of God with that of pagan deities [*Redak*].

Alternatively, the Israelites who were left in Samaria continue to practice according to their previous custom . . .[*Ralbag*].

Since they have not abandoned their idolatry, even though they worship the pagan deities as mere intermediaries, this is not considered as fearing the Lord, Who commanded them to worship Him only, not in conjunction with other "powers." Joshua admonished them, "(24:14) And now, fear the Lord, and serve Him with perfection and with truth, and remove the deities that your ancestors worshipped on the other side of the river and in Egypt." Likewise, Samuel admonished them by saying, "(I Sam. 12:24) Only fear the Lord and you shall serve Him in truth." Yet the Israelites were not following their statutes and laws, but those of their pagan neighbors [*Redak*].

whose name He called Israel—or made Israel. This is mentioned here because, when Jacob admonished his children, "(Gen. 35:2) Remove

תשתחוו להם ולא תעבדום ולא
תזבחו להם: לו כי אם־את־יהוה אשר
העלה אתכם מארץ מצרים בכח
גדול ובזרוע נטויה אתו תיראו ולו
תשתחוו ולו תזבחו: לז ואת־החקים
ואת־המשפטים והתורה והמצוה
אשר כתב לכם תשמרון לעשות כל־
הימים ולא תיראו אלהים אחרים:
לח והברית אשר־כרתי אתכם לא
תשכחו ולא תיראו אלהים אחרים:
לט כי אם־את־יהוה אלהיכם תיראו
והוא יציל אתכם מיד כל־איביכם:
מ ולא שמעו כי אם־כמשפטם הראשון
הם עשים: מא ויהיו | הגוים האלה

תרגום

תסגדון להון ולא
תפלחנון ולא תדבחון
להון: לו אלהין קדם
יי דאסיק יתכון מארעא
דמצרים בחיל רב
ובדרע מרמם יתיה
תדחלון וקדמוהי
תסגדון ועל מדבחיה
תדבחון: לז וית קימיא
וית דיניא ואוריתא
ותפקידתא דכתב לכון
תטרון למעבד כל
יומיא ולא תדחלון
לטעות עממיא:
לח וקימא דגזרית עמכון
לא תתנשון ולא
תדחלון לטעות עממיא:
לט אלהין מן קדם יי
אלהכון תדחלון והוא
ישיזיב יתכון מיד כל
בעלי דבביכון: מ ולא
קבילו אלהין
כנימוסיהון קדמאי
אינון עבדין: מא והוו
עממיא האילין דחלין
מן

רד"ק

(מ) כי אם כמשפטם הראשון. לא שמעו נביאים המוכיחים אותם והם עושים אחר התוכחה כמו לפני התוכחה:

רלב"ג

בם: (לז) תשמרון לעשות כל הימים. זה לאות שהתורה נתנה לעשות מצות ה' כל הימים לא שתשתנה בההלכת כמו שחשבו אנשים הנלוה אליה: (מ) ולא שמעו כי אם כמשפטם הראשון הם עושים. ר"ל כי ישראל לא שמעו לסור מע"ג ולזה מלא שם יאשיה כהני הבמות: (מא) ויהיו הגוים האלה יראים את ה'. ידמה שאמר שלא שמעו אלו הגוים לקול הכהן אך הרכיבו בין שתי האמונות ולזה הוא מבואר שלא היו יראים את ה' שאם היו יראים את ה' לא היו עובדים ע"ג ולזה לא נחשבו לגרים אמתיים כי הגרים האמתיים הם כמו ישראלים כי הם לא קבלו עליהם לקיים התורה אך עבודת אלהיהם ולזה הם משוללים מיראת הש"י ומהיות במדרגת ישראל כי הישראל

מצודת דוד

שלא הע"ג ההם נתגיירו וידעו מהאזהרות ההם והיה מהראוי להיות זהירים בהם מעתה: (מ) ולא שמעו. אבל הע"ג ההם לא השגיחו על כל הדברים האלה אף כי נתגיירו כי אם היו עושים כמשפטם הראשון לעבוד עבודת כוכבים כאשר עבדו מאז: (מא) ויהיו הגוים.

מצודת ציון

(לו) נטויה. המשיל לגבור הנוטה זרועו במלחמה:

sins after the admonition as before it [*Redak*].

Ed. note: We have rendered אלהים אחרים, as *strange gods*, rather than other gods, in keeping with *Rashi*, Deut. 11:17, who are strange to their worshippers; he cries to him and he does not answer him. The result that he is like a stranger to him.

41. **And these nations**—i.e. the Cuthites and their neighbors, who were not forbidden to worship idols in conjunction with their worship of God [*Malbim*].

neither shall you prostrate yourselves to them nor worship
them, and you shall not slaughter [sacrifices] to them. 36. Only
the Lord Who brought you up from the land of Egypt with
great might and with an outstretched arm, Him shall you fear,
and to Him shall you prostrate yourselves and to Him shall you
slaughter sacrifices. 37. And the statutes and the judgments,
and the Law and the commandment that He wrote for you, you
shall heed to perform all times, and you shall not fear strange
gods. 38. And the covenant that I enacted with you, you shall
not forget, neither shall you fear strange gods. 39. But the Lord
your God you shall fear, and He will deliver you from the hand
of all your enemies." 40. But they did not obey, but according
to their earlier practice they were doing. 41. And these nations

nant with them—*when He gave them the Torah on Mt. Sinai* [*Rashi*].

37. **all times**—The Torah is eternal. It will never change or be replaced by another one, contrary to Christian belief [*Ralbag*].

Malbim explains that Scripture presents three reasons forbidding Israel to worship heavenly bodies as intermediaries between God and themselves. First, the prophet states in v. 35, And the Lord enacted a covenant with them, saying, "You shall not fear strange gods . . . for the following reasons—

(1) **Only the Lord Who brought you up from the land of Egypt with great might . . .**i.e. He brought you up from the land of Egypt with a supernatural redemption, demonstrating that you are above the forces of nature.

(2) **And the statutes and the judgments . . .**i.e. He gave you His Torah, the observance of which guarantees God's personal Providence.

(3) **And the covenant that I enacted with you . . .**i.e. He enacted His covenant with you, a covenant which includes the observance of the Sabbath and the rite of circumcision, which guarantee God's love for you, His partners in the covenant. Therefore, you shall not forget, neither shall you fear other gods.

39. **But the Lord your God you shall fear**—for you are under His providence, and therefore,—

He will deliver you from the hand of all your enemies [*Malbim*].

40. **but according to their earlier practice**—They did not heed their prophets who admonished them; they continued to commit the same

יְרֵאִים אֶת־יְהוָה וְאֶת־פְּסִילֵיהֶם הָיוּ
עֹבְדִים גַּם־בְּנֵיהֶם ׀ וּבְנֵי בְנֵיהֶם כַּאֲשֶׁר
עָשׂוּ אֲבֹתָם הֵם עֹשִׂים עַד הַיּוֹם הַזֶּה׃
יח א וַיְהִי בִּשְׁנַת שָׁלֹשׁ לְהוֹשֵׁעַ בֶּן־אֵלָה
מֶלֶךְ יִשְׂרָאֵל מָלַךְ חִזְקִיָּה בֶן־אָחָז מֶלֶךְ
יְהוּדָה׃ ב בֶּן־עֶשְׂרִים וְחָמֵשׁ שָׁנָה הָיָה
בְמָלְכוֹ וְעֶשְׂרִים וָתֵשַׁע שָׁנָה מָלַךְ
בִּירוּשָׁלִָם וְשֵׁם אִמּוֹ אֲבִי בַּת־זְכַרְיָה׃
ג וַיַּעַשׂ הַיָּשָׁר בְּעֵינֵי יְהוָה כְּכֹל אֲשֶׁר־
עָשָׂה דָּוִד אָבִיו׃ ד הוּא ׀ הֵסִיר אֶת־
הַבָּמוֹת וְשִׁבַּר אֶת־הַמַּצֵּבֹת וְכָרַת
אֶת־הָאֲשֵׁרָה וְכִתַּת נְחַשׁ הַנְּחֹשֶׁת

תרגום

מן קדם יי וית צלמניהון הוו פלחין אף בניהון ובני בניהון כמא דעבדו אבהתהון אינון עבדין עד יומא הדין׃ א והוה בשנת תלת להושע בר אלה מלכא דישראל מלך חזקיה בר אחז מלכא דשבטא דבית יהודה׃ ב בר עסרין וחמש שנין הוה כד מלך ועסרין ותשע שנין מלך בירושלם ושום אמיה אבי בת זכריה׃ ג ועבד דכשר קדם יי ככל דעבד דוד אבוהי׃ ד הוא אעדי ית במתא ותבר ית קמתא וקץ ית אשירתא ופסיק ית חויא

ת"א נחש הנחשת. ע"ג מד חולין ו (דמאי כב ע"ג מב)׃

רד"ק

(א) ויהי בשנת שלש להושע בן אלה. שנת שלש למרדו כמו שפי׳׃ (ד) וכתת נחש הנחשת. יש מרז"ל שאמרו שוחק חור׳ לרוח כי היה אסו׳ בהנא׳ ומהם אמרו כי לא היה אסור בהנאה כי משה רבינו ע"ה משלו עשה אותו שנא׳ עשה לך שרף משלך שהעובדים אותו לא היו יכולי׳ לאוסרו כי אין אדם אוסר דבר שאינו שלו ובדין הוא נמי דכתותי לא הוה צרי׳ אלא כיון דחזא חזקיה דקא טעו ישראל בתרי׳ עמד וכתתו׃ כי עד הימי׳ ההמה היו בני ישר׳ מקטירים לו. מעת שהרעו מלכי יהודה וטעו ישראל אחר ע"ג עד הימי׳ ההמ׳ שמלך חזקיהו היו בני ישראל מקטרים לו כיון שמצאו כתו׳

רש"י

יח (א) בשנת שלש. למרדו של הושע׃ (ד) ויקרא לו

מנחת שי

יח (ד) וכתת נחש הנחושת. בספרים אחרים כתובי יד וכתת את נחש והתרגום מסייעו שתרגם ופסיק ית חויא. ולא ראיתי כן באחר ספרים. אדרבא יש להוכיח מהמסורת דלא כתיב את ונשמעיניה מן הדא דבמסרה רבתי נמסר סימן י"ט פסוקים בספר מלכים דכתיב בהו את את את ודין חד מנהון שמעת מינה דלא את זה מהכא דאי לאו הכי הוו להו ד׳ את בפסוקא הדין והוה לן לאמנינהו בהדי ט"ז פסוקים דאית בהו את את את את וסימנהון במסרה רבתא׃

רלב"ג

אף על פי שהושע זכו לו אבותיו אל שיהיה מישראל אך הגר לא יהיה גר אם לא יקבל עליו כל מצות התורה כי התורה זאת בלתי קבלת תוספת וגרעון כמו שנזכר במקומות מהתורה׃ (ג) ויעש הישר בעיני ה׳ ככל אשר עשה דוד אביו. הנה בזה הוסיף על דוד כי הוא לא חטא אך עשה תמיד הישר בעיני ה׳ ודוד הטא על דבר אוריה׃ (ד) הוא הסיר את הבמות. הם שנעשו להקריב בהם לש"י אשר לא סרו בימי מלכי יהודה הראשונים׃ ושבר את המצבות. כי התורה אמר׳ לא תקים לך מצבה ואעפ"י שהיא לש"י כ"ש כשהיתה לשם ע"ג כמו שאחשוב שהיה הענין באלו המצבות׃ היו בני ישראל מקטרים לו. הנה הבנו שהיה לזאת הצורה מדרגה אלהית מפני שעשאה משה

מצודת ציון

יח (ד) וכתת. ענין כתישה כמו וכתתו חרבותם (שם ב)׃

מצודת דוד

ר"ל כאשר עשו בעת בואם כן עשו כל ימיהם והיו יראים את ה׳ ועובדים הפסילים וגם בניהם וגו׳ כאשר עשו אבותם כן עושים גם המה עד היום הזה׃ יח (א) בשנת שלש. ר"ל אחר שעבר שלש להושע בתחילת ד׳ למלכו מעלמו כי הושע מלך מעלמו כי"ג לאחז וימי מלכות אחז היו י"ו שנה וכלו א"כ בד׳ להושע ואז מלך חזקיה׃ (ב) ועשרים וגו׳. ומקוטעות היו׃ (ד) את הבמות. מה שהקריבו עליהם לגבוה ובאיסור נעשו כי מעת שנבנה הבית נאסרו הבמות׃ אשר עשה משה. בעת נשלח בישראל הנחשים השרפים לוהו ה׳ לעשות

salem, it was forbidden to sacrifice anywhere but on the altar of the Holy Temple. People, nevertheless, continued to sacrifice on high places as they had been accustomed to doing during the presence of the *Mishkan* in Nob and Gibeon. The early kings, although righteous, never abolished this practice [*Ralbag, Mezudath David*].

and smashed the monuments—even those erected for worship of God. The Torah proscribes the use of monuments for worship (Deut.

feared the Lord, yet they worshipped their graven images; also their children and their grandchildren, as their forefathers had done, they are doing until this day.

18

1. And it was in the third year of Hoshea the son of Elah, the king of Israel, that Hezekiah the son of Ahaz the king of Judah, became king. 2. He was twenty-five years old when he became king, and he reigned twenty-nine years in Jerusalem, and his mother's name was Abi the daughter of Zechariah. 3. And he did what was right in the eyes of the Lord, like all that his father David had done. 4. He abolished the high places, and smashed the monuments, and cut down the *asherah,* and crushed the copper serpent

feared the Lord—For them, it was considered that they feared the Lord, even though—

they worshipped their graven images; also their children . . . until this day—God did not become wroth with them neither did He punish them, since they believed in Him and worshipped their idols as intermediaries, not ascribing to them any independent power. Therefore, they were safe from the lions which had previously plagued them. The Israelites, however, since they had been redeemed from Egyptian bondage and been given a Torah and a covenant by God, were prohibited from worshipping any power in conjunction with His worship. Failure to observe this prohibition, resulted in exile [*Malbim*].

1. **in the third year**—*of Hoshea's rebellion* [*Rashi, Redak*]. See above 17:1.

I.e. after three years of Hoshea's independent rule, when he was not subordinate to the king of Assyria. For nine years he had ruled as governor under the king of Assyria. Then he rebelled and reigned for nine years independently. Hezekiah became king of Judah after the third year of Hoshea's independent rule [*Mezudath David*].

3. **like all that his father David had done**—He did what was right like his father David. He did not sin, however, like David, who was guilty of the sin concerning Uriah the Hittite [*Ralbag*]. See II Sam. 11:3, Commentary Digest.

4. **He abolished the high places**—These were altars upon which the Jews offered sacrifices to God. When the Temple was built in Jeru-

אֲשֶׁר־עָשָׂה מֹשֶׁה כִּי עַד־הַיָּמִים הָהֵמָּה הָיוּ בְנֵי־יִשְׂרָאֵל מְקַטְּרִים לוֹ וַיִּקְרָא־לוֹ נְחֻשְׁתָּן: ה בַּיהוָה אֱלֹהֵי־יִשְׂרָאֵל בָּטָח וְאַחֲרָיו לֹא־הָיָה כָמֹהוּ בְּכֹל מַלְכֵי יְהוּדָה וַאֲשֶׁר הָיוּ לְפָנָיו: ו וַיִּדְבַּק בַּיהוָה לֹא־סָר מֵאַחֲרָיו וַיִּשְׁמֹר מִצְוֹתָיו אֲשֶׁר־צִוָּה יְהוָה אֶת־מֹשֶׁה: ז וְהָיָה יְהוָה עִמּוֹ בְּכֹל אֲשֶׁר־יֵצֵא יַשְׂכִּיל וַיִּמְרֹד בְּמֶלֶךְ־אַשּׁוּר וְלֹא עֲבָדוֹ: ח הוּא הִכָּה אֶת־פְּלִשְׁתִּים עַד־עַזָּה וְאֶת־גְּבוּלֶיהָ

תרגום

חִוְיָא דִנְחָשָׁא דַעֲבַד מֹשֶׁה אֲרֵי עַד יוֹמַיָא הָאִינוּן הֲווֹ בְנֵי יִשְׂרָאֵל מַסְקִין בּוּסְמִין לֵיהּ וַהֲווֹ קָרַן לֵיהּ נְחוּשְׁתָּן: ה בְּמֵימְרָא דַיְיָ אֱלָהָא דְיִשְׂרָאֵל אִתְרְחֵיץ וּבָתְרוֹהִי לָא הֲוָה כְוָתֵיהּ בְּכֹל מַלְכַיָא דְבֵית יְהוּדָה וְדַהֲווֹ קֳדָמוֹהִי: ו וְאִדְבַּק בְּדַחַלְתָּא דַיְיָ לָא סְטָא מִבָּתַר פּוּלְחָנֵיהּ וּנְטַר פִּקּוֹדוֹהִי דְפַקִּיד יְיָ יָת מֹשֶׁה: ז וַהֲוָה מֵימְרָא דַיְיָ בְּסַעֲדֵיהּ בְּכֹל אֲתַר דִנְפַק מַצְלַח וּמְרִיד בְּמַלְכָּא דְאַתּוּר וְלָא פַלְחֵיהּ: ח הוּא קְטַל יָת פְּלִשְׁתָּאֵי

רש"י

נחשתן. לשון בזיון כלומר מה צורך בזה אינו אלא נחש נחושת: (ז) ישכיל. יצליח:

רד"ק

ורא' אותו וחי היו חושבי' כי טוב להיו' אמצעי ולעבוד אותו והיה מונח מימות משה זה הנחש לזכרון הנס כמו צנצנת המן ואסא ויהושפט שלא בערוהו כאשר בערו שאר הע"ג מפני שלא מצאו כשמלכו שהיו עובדין ומקטרין לזה הנחש והיו מניחים אותו לזכרון הנס וחזקיהו ראה לבער אותו כשביער הע"ג כי בימי אביו היו עובדי' לו כמו לע"ג אע"פ שהטובים היו זוכרים בו הנס אמר טוב לבער אותו וישכח הנס מלהניחו ויטעו בני ישראל היום או מחר אחריו ורבותינו ז"ל אמרו אפשר בא אסא ולא בערו בא יהושפט ולא בערו והלא כל עבודת גלולים שבארץ יהודה אסא ויהושפט ביערום אלא מקום הניחו לו אבותיו להתגדר בו: ויקרא לו נחשתן. דרך בזיון כלומר אינו אלא נחשת מה כח יש בו להרע ולהטיב בעת שכתתו קרא לו כן אמר להם לישראל איך יעלה בלב אדם כי זה יועיל כי אינו אלא נחשת ותוספת הנו"ן להקטינו: כיו"ד האמינון וי"ו נו"ן אישון שבתון וי"ת והוו קרן ליה נהושתן כלומר ישראל שהיו עובדים אותו היו קורין אותו נחשתן: (ה) ואשר היו לפניו. ר"ל חוץ מדוד ושלמה אבל בשאר מלכי יהודה אשר היו לפניו אע"פ שהיו בהם מלכי' טובים והם אסא ויהושפט ויהואש כל ימי יהוידע ועזיהו ויותם לא היה בהם שעש' הישר בעיני ה' כמוהו שהרי אמר עליו ככל אשר עשה דוד אביו: (ז) ישכיל. יצליח: וימרוד במלך אשור. לפי שאחז אביו הי' עובדו אמר כי מרד בו ולא עבדו שבטח באל לבדו: (ח) ממגדל נוצרים עד עיר מבצר. ממגדל

רלב"ג

והיה כל הכבוד ורצה אותו וחי והנה קרא לו חזקיה נחשת שלהן כאלו יאמר שאין זאת הצורה כח כי אם מה שיש מהכח לנחשת: (ה) בכל מלכי יהודה ואשר היו לפניו. הנה הוי"ו אשר במלת ואשר מושכת הבי"ת אשר במלת בכל והרצון בו בכל מלכי יהודה ובאש' היו לפניו והוא אמר זה כי אפילו דוד לא היה כמוהו כי הוא חטא וזה לא הטא אך עשה הישר בעיני ה': (ו) וידבק בה' לא סר מאחריו. הנה הדבקות בה' הוא ההשגה וההליכה בדרכיו ואמרו לא סר מאחריו מעיד שלא חטא בדבר: (ז) והיה ה' עמו. זה היה מהש"י גמול לו על ישרא': בכל אשר יצא ישכיל. ר"ל בכל אשר יצא יצליח: וימרד במלך אשור ולא עבדו. לפי שאביו אחז עשה עצמו עבד לו כאמרו עבדך ובנך אני זכר כי הוא מרד במלך אשור וענין המרד הוא שלא עבדו: (ח) ממגדל נוצרים עד עיר מבצר. ר"ל שלא נשאר בהם מקום שלא הוכה מקטון ועד גדול והיותר קטן הוא מגדל הנוצרים ר"ל השומרים שעושים מחוץ לעיר לשמור פירות השדה

מצודת דוד

נחש נחושת להביט בו הנשוך וחי כמ"ש בתורה: מקטרים לו. כחשבם שיש בו אלהות על כי נתרפא הנשוך כאשר הביט בו: נחשתן. כאומר מה זה הלא הוא רק נחושת ולהקטין מעלתו הוסיף הנו"ן כי כן דרך המקרא וכן האמינון אחיך (שמואל ב' י"ג): (ז) ישכיל. יצליח כי המצליח נראה הוא להבריות כאלו עושה מעשיו בהשכל: (ח) ממגדל נוצרים. מן המגדל שהצופים עומדים

them equaled Hezekiah, whom the prophet compares to David [*Redak*].

Alternatively, Hezekiah excelled in the trait of *bitachon*, trust in God. Similarly, Josiah excelled in repentance, as below 23:25 [*Malbim*].

6. **He cleaved to the Lord**—in his understanding of God's ways and in following them [*Ralbag*].

Ramban (Deut. 11:22) explains *devekuth* as attaching one's thoughts to the Almighty, never forgetting Him and His love.

he did not turn away from following Him—Scripture testifies that Hezekiah did not sin [*Ralbag*].

7. **he succeeded**—Heb. יַשְׂכִּיל, usu-

that Moses had made, for until those days the children of Israel were burning incense to it; and he called it *Nehushtan.* 5. He trusted in the God of Israel there was none like him among all the kings of Judah who were after him, nor were there before him. 6. He cleaved to the Lord; he did not turn away from following Him; he kept His commandments, which He had commanded Moses. 7. Now the Lord was with him; in everything he ventured he succeeded; and he rebelled against the king of Assyria and did not serve him. 8. He slew the Philistines up to Gaza and its boundaries,

16:22), [since they were used by the heathens. See above 10:26, for elaboration on the function of monuments.] [*Ralbag*].

and crushed the copper serpent—There is a dispute in the Talmud as to the reason for Hezekiah's crushing the copper serpent. One view is that the serpent had become an object of idol worship, and it was, therefore, forbidden to derive any benefit from it. Consequently, it had to be crushed and scattered to the winds or cast into the sea. Another view is that since the serpent was fashioned from Moses' own property, no one could make it into an object of idolatry. Hezekiah, however, realized that it posed a serious obstacle for the public, and decided to do away with it (*Abodah Zarah,* 44a) [*Redak*].

which Moses had made—When serpents were biting the Israelites in the desert (Num. 21:6–9), God commanded Moses to make this copper serpent and place it on a pole. When any of the stricken gazed at it [and repented his sins of slandering God and His servant Moses], he would be miraculously cured. It had, therefore, been preserved as a memorial of the miracle [*Redak*].

for until those days—i.e. from the time the kings started to turn away from pure monotheism, and the people began to go astray [*Redak*].

the children of Israel were burning incense to it—Since a miracle had been performed through this copper serpent, the people believed it to be endowed with godly powers. Hence it would be an appropriate intermediary between them and the Almighty. They, therefore, commenced burning incense to it [*Redak, Ralbag, Mezudath David*].*

and he called it Nehushtan—*a pejorative, as though to say, "Why is this necessary? It is nothing but a copper serpent* [*Rashi*]".*

5. **nor were there before him**—with the exclusion of David and Solomon, who reigned over the entire kingdom of Israel. Over the kingdom of Judah, however, there was no king as righteous as he. Even the righteous kings, e.g. Asa, Jehoshaphat, Jehoash before the death of Jehoiada, Uzziah, Jotham, none of

מִמִּגְדַּל נוֹצְרִים עַד־עִיר מִבְצָר׃ ט וַיְהִי
בַּשָּׁנָה הָרְבִיעִית לַמֶּלֶךְ חִזְקִיָּהוּ הִיא
הַשָּׁנָה הַשְּׁבִיעִית לְהוֹשֵׁעַ בֶּן־אֵלָה
מֶלֶךְ יִשְׂרָאֵל עָלָה שַׁלְמַנְאֶסֶר מֶלֶךְ־
אַשּׁוּר עַל־שֹׁמְרוֹן וַיָּצַר עָלֶיהָ׃ י וַיִּלְכְּדֻהָ
מִקְצֵה שָׁלֹשׁ שָׁנִים בִּשְׁנַת־שֵׁשׁ
לְחִזְקִיָּה הִיא שְׁנַת־תֵּשַׁע לְהוֹשֵׁעַ מֶלֶךְ
יִשְׂרָאֵל נִלְכְּדָה שֹׁמְרוֹן׃ יא וַיֶּגֶל מֶלֶךְ־
אַשּׁוּר אֶת־יִשְׂרָאֵל אַשּׁוּרָה וַיַּנְחֵם
בַּחְלַח וּבְחָבוֹר נְהַר גּוֹזָן וְעָרֵי מָדָי׃
יב עַל׀ אֲשֶׁר לֹא־שָׁמְעוּ בְּקוֹל יְהוָה
אֱלֹהֵיהֶם וַיַּעַבְרוּ אֶת־בְּרִיתוֹ אֵת כָּל־
אֲשֶׁר צִוָּה מֹשֶׁה עֶבֶד יְהוָה וְלֹא שָׁמְעוּ

תרגום

עַד עַזָה וְיַת תְּחוּמַהָא
מִמִּגְדַּל תְּקוֹף עַד
קִירְוִין כְּרִיכָן׃ ט וַהֲוָה
בְּשַׁתָּא רְבִיעֵיתָא
לְמַלְכָּא חִזְקִיָּה הִיא
שַׁתָּא שְׁבִיעֵיתָא לְהוֹשֵׁעַ
בַּר אֵלָה מַלְכָּא
דְיִשְׂרָאֵל סְלֵיק
שַׁלְמַנְאֶסֶר מַלְכָּא
דְאַתּוּר עַל שֹׁמְרוֹן וְצָר
עֲלָהּ׃ י וְכַבְשׁוּהָ מִסוֹף
תְּלַת שְׁנִין בִּשְׁנַת שִׁית
לְחִזְקִיָּהוּ הִיא שְׁנַת
תְּשַׁע לְהוֹשֵׁעַ מַלְכָּא
דְיִשְׂרָאֵל אִתְכְּבִישַׁת
שֹׁמְרוֹן׃ יא וְאַגְלֵי מַלְכָּא
דְאַתּוּר יַת יִשְׂרָאֵל
לְאַתּוּר וְאַשְׁרִינוּן בַּחֲלַח
וּבְחָבוֹר נְהַר גּוֹזָן
וְקִירְוֵי מָדָי׃ יב עַל
דְלָא קַבִּילוּ לְמֵימַר דַיָי
אֱלָהֲהוֹן וַעֲבַרוּ יַת
קְיָמֵיהּ יַת כָּל דְפַקֵּיד
מֹשֶׁה עַבְדָא דַיָי וְלָא
קבילו

ת"א עלה שלמנאסר. (תענית כט): בחלח ובחבור. יבמות יז קדושין עב:

רד"ק

שעומדים בו השומרי׳ וי"ת ממגדל תקיף עד קרוין כריכן: (י) מקצה שלש שנים. מתחלת שנה שלישית וכמוהו מקץ שבע שנים תשלחו איש את עבדו יכן מקץ שבע שנים תעשה שמטה להשמטת קרקע ילשלוח עבדי׳ כי הוא עלה בשנ׳ הרביעית לחזקיהו היא שנת שביעית להושע ולכדה בשנת שש לחזקיהו היא שנת תשע להושע אין כאן כי אם שתי שנים והו"א מקצה שלש א"כ פירושו מתחלת שלש וי"ת מסוף תלת שנין וא"כ לדעתו בשנה הרביעית ובשנה השביעית ר"ל בתחלת השנה הרביעי׳ והשביעית: (יא) ויגל מלך אשור. מבנין הפעיל כי הוא כלו בסגול ובתשלומו ויגלהו:

מנחת שי

(יא) וינחם בחלח. בספרים מדוייקים החי"ת בגעיא לבדו:

מצודת ציון

(ט) ויצר. מלשון מצור: (יא) וינחם. הכניסם:

מצודת דוד

עליו ור"ל מקטן ועד גדול: (ט) היא השנה השביעית להושע. כי חזקיהו מלך בג׳ להושע: עלה שלמנאסר. עם שכבר נאמר למעלה חזר לספר שוב כאומר מה שעלה שלמנאסר וגו׳ וגבר אשור על ישראל ויגל את ישראל וגו׳ עד סוף הענין הנה זה לא היה בכח ידיו כ"א על אשר לא שמעו בקול ה׳ וגו׳ שהרי בימי חזקיה עלה אשור על ירושלים וספו תמו בבלות ה׳: (י) מקצה שלש שנים. כי צר עליה בתחלת ד׳ ולכדה בסוף ו׳: (יב) על אשר לא שמעו וגו׳. ולא בכח ידם: את בריתו. התורה אשר נתן בבריות:

Samaria, he merely alludes to an unknown conqueror, not mentioned previously. This is one example of the wonders of the *Masorah* [*Antiquities* by Aaron Marcus, p. 149–150].

at the end of three years—Actually at the beginning of the third year, since he commenced the siege in the fourth year of Hezekiah, which was the seventh year of Hoshea, and he captured it in the sixth year of Hezekiah, which was the ninth year of Hoshea. Thus we find that the siege lasted but two years. We find a similar usage in Deut. 15:1: "At the end of seven years you shall make a release." This, too, is actually at the beginning of the seventh year. *Jonathan,* however, apparently holds

from watchtower to fortified city. 9. And it was in the fourth year of King Hezekiah—that is the seventh year of Hoshea the son of Elah, king of Israel—that Shalmaneser the king of Assyria went up to Samaria and laid siege to it. 10. And they captured it at the end of three years; in the sixth year of Hezekiah, which is the ninth year of Hoshea, king of Israel, Samaria was captured. 11. And the king of Assyria exiled Israel to Assyria, and he settled them in Halah and in Habor, the Gozan River, and the cities of Media. 12. Because they did not obey the Lord their God and transgressed His covenant, all that He had commanded Moses the servant of the Lord, and they did not obey nor did they do [His will].

ally an expression of intelligence, but used in several places in this sense. See Jos. 1:8, I Sam. 18:14.

and he rebelled against the king of Assyria—Unlike his father Ahaz, who paid tribute to Assyria, Hezekiah put his full trust in God [*Redak, Ralbag*].

from watchtower to fortified city—from the small watchtower in which several lookouts are stationed, to the large fortified city, Hezekiah overpowered the Philistines [*Redak*].

that is the seventh year of Hoshea—for Hezekiah reigned in the fourth year of Hoshea [*Mezudath David*].

that Shalmaneser the king of Assyria went up . . .—Although Shalmaneser's siege on Samaria was already recorded above 17:5,6, it is repeated here to inform us that Shalmaneser did not vanquish Israel with his own strength, but only because Israel had sinned, for in Hezekiah's time, Assyria marched on Jerusalem and was completely wiped out by the will of God [*Mezudath David*].

10. **And they captured it**—The antecedent is not clear. If we were to read the word וַיִּלְכְּדָה, *and he captured it,* it would seem to make more sense. Indeed, many non-Jewish translators have adopted that reading and have rendered the word accordingly. Thanks to archeological discoveries, however, we learn tht Shalmaneser died during the siege. His general, Sargon, a scion of a deposed royal family, was appointed in his stead by the Chaldees. It is unknown whether Sargon assassinated Shalmaneser or whether he died of natural causes. In any case, the antecedent is the Chaldees. They are not mentioned explicitly, lest we think that Shalmaneser's death was punishment for attacking Samaria. Since it is not the intention of the prophet to defend the people of

וְלֹא עָשׂוּ׃ יג וּבְאַרְבַּע עֶשְׂרֵה שָׁנָה
לַמֶּלֶךְ חִזְקִיָּהוּ עָלָה סַנְחֵרִיב מֶלֶךְ־
אַשּׁוּר עַל כָּל־עָרֵי יְהוּדָה הַבְּצֻרוֹת
וַיִּתְפְּשֵׂם׃ יד וַיִּשְׁלַח חִזְקִיָּה מֶלֶךְ־יְהוּדָה
אֶל־מֶלֶךְ־אַשּׁוּר ׀ לָכִישָׁה ׀ לֵאמֹר ׀
חָטָאתִי שׁוּב מֵעָלַי אֵת אֲשֶׁר־תִּתֵּן
עָלַי אֶשָּׂא וַיָּשֶׂם מֶלֶךְ־אַשּׁוּר עַל־חִזְקִיָּה
מֶלֶךְ־יְהוּדָה שְׁלֹשׁ מֵאוֹת כִּכַּר־כֶּסֶף
וּשְׁלֹשִׁים כִּכַּר זָהָב׃ טו וַיִּתֵּן חִזְקִיָּה אֶת־
כָּל־הַכֶּסֶף הַנִּמְצָא בֵית־יְהוָה
וּבְאֹצְרוֹת בֵּית הַמֶּלֶךְ׃ טז בָּעֵת הַהִיא
קִצַּץ חִזְקִיָּה אֶת־דַּלְתוֹת הֵיכַל יְהוָה

קַבִּילוּ לְמֵימְרֵיהּ וְלָא
עֲבָדוּ רְעוּתֵיהּ׃
יג וּבְאַרְבַּע עַשְׂרֵי שְׁנִין
לְמַלְכָּא חִזְקִיָּה סְלִיק
סַנְחֵרִיב מַלְכָּא דְאַתּוּר
עַל כָּל קִירְוַיָא דְבֵית
יְהוּדָה כְּרִיכָתָא
וְאַחְדִינוּן׃ יד וּשְׁלַח
חִזְקִיָּה מֶלֶךְ שִׁבְטָא
דְבֵית יְהוּדָה לְוָת
מַלְכָּא דְאַתּוּר לְלָכִישׁ
לְמֵימַר חָבֵית אִסְתַּלַּק
מִנִּי יָת דְּתִרְמֵי עֲלַי
אֲקַבֵּל וּרְמָא מַלְכָּא
דְאַתּוּר עַל חִזְקִיָּה
מֶלֶךְ שִׁבְטָא דְבֵית
יְהוּדָה תְּלָת מְאָה
כִּכְּרִין דִּכְסַף וּתְלָתִין
כִּכְּרִין דְּדַהֲבָא׃
טו וִיהַב חִזְקִיָּה יָת כָּל
כַּסְפָּא דְאִשְׁתְּכַח בֵּית
מַקְדְּשָׁא דַיְיָ וּבְגִנְזֵי
בֵית מַלְכָּא׃ טז בְּעִדָּנָא
הַהִיא קַלִּיף חִזְקִיָּה יָת

רש"י

(טז) קציץ. את הדלתות שהיו של זהב: ואת האומנות. תרגום יונתן וית סקיפיה אסקופות:

רד"ק

(יג) ויתפשם. מה שאמר בדברי הימים ויאמר לבקע' אליו פירוש אמר לבקעם ובקעם וכן להרגו בערמה והרגו לשכב את בת יעקב ושכב כי תחל לזנות. וזנתה והדימ' להם: (יד) וישלח חזקי'. אחר שתפש ערי יהודה הבצורות ושם פניו ירושלם כמו שאומר בדברי הימים ופנה למלחמם על ירושלם. שלח לו חזקיה אל לכיש שהי' שם מלך אשור והיא מערי יהוד' ושלח לו חטאתי שוב מעלי כלו' חטאתי שמרדתי בך ולא עבדתיך שוב מעלי ואת אשר תגזר עלי אתן ושב לו בפע' ההי' אחר שנתן לו מה שהטיל עליו שלש מאות ככר כסף ושלשי' ככר זהב לאח' זמן שב לו לארץ יהוד' לאחר שפסק מלתת לו שנה בשנ' מה שהטיל עליו כמו שאמר לו רבשקה על מי בטח' כי מרד' בי ובא עד לכיש ומשם שלח מלאכיו עם קצת חיילותיו לירושל' ודבר מה שדבר ולא קבלו אותן הדברים ושב לו רבשקה עם חיילותיו ואמר כי אזהשלימו עמו שבנ' וסיעתו ועליה' נאמר לא תאמרון קשר לכל אשר יאמר העם הזה קשר ומצאו רבשקה כי נסע מלכיש ובא ונלחם על לבנה ושב באה לו שמוע' כי תרהקה מלך כוש יצא להלחם עמו ונסע משם ומשם שלח מלאכים אל חזקיהו פעם שניה והפחידו כי בשובו מכלחמת כוש יבא עם חיילתיו על ירושלם והלך לו ונלחם על כוש ומלך מצרים ועם כל השבי ההוא בא לו ירושלם וחנה על העיר ובלילה ההיא יצא מלאך ה' והכה במחנה אשור ויצאו ישראל ובזזו כל הבזה ההיא ועל זה אמר נתתי כפרך מצרים כוש וסבא תחתיך וכן נאמר יגיע מצרים וסחר כוש וסבאים אנשי מדה עליך יעברו ולך יהיו וגו' ואותם שנצלו מן המלחמה שבו לדת ישראל כמו שאמר אך בך אל ואין עוד אפס אלהים ועליהם נאמר והיו חמש ערים בארץ מצרים מדברות שפת כנען ונשבעות לה' צבאות וכל אותה הפר' בארתי כל הענין הזה כאחד לפי שאינו מבואר כלו במקום אחד לא בזה הספר ולא בישעיה ולא בד"ה: את אשר תתן עלי אשא. העינש אשר תתן עלי אשא אסבול אותו ואשאנו: (טז) קצץ חזקיהו את

רלב"ג

(טז) קצץ חזקיה את דלתות היכל ה'. ר"ל והכרמים אשר סביבו:

מנחת שי

(יג) ובארבע עשרה שנה וגו'. חילופים רבים יש בין פרשה זו לאותה שבישעיהו

מצודת דוד

(יד) חטאתי. במה שמרדתי בך: את אשר תתן וגו'. ר"ל העונש אשר תשים עלי אשא ואסבול: וישם. שם עליו עונש שלש מאות וגו': (טז) קצץ. קלף ציפוי הזהב מן הדלתות ומן מפתני הבית: אשר צפה

מצודת ציון

(יג) הבצורות. מל' מבצר: ויתפשם. לכדם: (טו) בית ה'. בבית ה': (טז) קצץ. כרת וקלף: האומנות. מפתני הבית וכת"י סקופיא:

which Hezekiah, king of Judah, had overlaid—Perhaps the gold that King Solomon had placed there had already worn off, and was, there-

13. And in the fourteenth year of King Hezekiah, Sennacherib the king of Assyria came up against all the fortified cities of Judah and seized them. 14. And Hezekiah the king of Judah sent to the king of Assyria to Lachish, saying, "I have sinned, withdraw from me; whatever you impose upon me, I will bear." And the king of Assyria imposed upon Hezekiah, king of Judah, three hundred talents of silver and thirty talents of gold.
15. And Hezekiah gave all the silver that was found in the house of the Lord and in the treasuries of the king's palace.
16. At that time, Hezekiah stripped the doors of the temple of the Lord,

that it was actually at the end of the third year. According to him, the siege took place at the beginning of the fourth year of Hezekiah, which was the beginning of the seventh year of Hoshea [*Redak*].

12. **Because they did not obey**—The only reason Assyria vanquished them was Israel's failure to comply with God's will, not Assyria's strength [*Mezudath David*].

His covenant—the Torah which He gave them with a covenant [*Mezudath David*]. **His will**—[paraphrased by *Jonathan*].

14. **And Hezekiah . . . sent to the king of Assyria to Lachish**—After Sennacherib had seized the fortified cities of Judah and began his march on Jerusalem, as the chronicler states it, "(II Chron. 32:2) and he directed his face to wage war against Jerusalem," Hezekiah sent messengers to him while he was in Lachish, a captured Judean city [*Redak*].

"I have sinned—by rebelling against you and failing to pay tribute [*Redak, Mezudath David*].*

whatever you impose upon me, I will bear—I.e. whatever penalty you impose upon me because of my rebelliousness, I will bear, and pay it to you [*Redak, Mezudath David*].

16. **stripped**—*the doors, which were of gold* [*Rashi*].

According to *R. Joseph Kara,* the reading is as follows: **Hezekiah stripped the doors of the Temple**—*which were of gold.*

The doors and the thresholds of the Temple were plated with gold. This gold plate he sent to Sennacherib [*Redak, Ralbag, Mezudath Zion, Mezudath David*].

and the thresholds—[*Rashi, Redak, Mezudath Zion,* based on *Jonathan*]. *Ralbag* includes both the threshold and the lintel. He also suggests that they were pillars overlaid with gold.

ואת־האמנות אשר צפה חזקיה מלך יהודה ויתנם למלך אשור:
יז וישלח מלך־אשור את־תרתן ואת־רב־סריס ואת־רבשקה מן־לכיש אל־המלך חזקיהו בחיל כבד ירושלם ויעלו ויבאו ירושלם ויעלו ויבאו ויעמדו בתעלת הברכה העליונה אשר במסלת שדה כובס:
יח ויקראו אל־המלך ויצא אלהם אליקים בן־חלקיהו אשר על־הבית

תרגום

דשי היכלא דיי וית סקופיא דחפי חזקיה מלכא דשבטא דבית יהודה ויהבינון למלכא דאתור:
יז ושלח מלכא דאתור ית תרתן וית רב סריס וית רבשקה מן לכיש לות מלכא חזקיה במשרין סגיאן לירושלם וסליקו ואתו לירושלם וסליקו ואתו וקמו במנקת בריכתא עליתא די בכיבש חקל משטח קצריא:
יח וקרו למלכא ונפק לותהון אליקים בר חלקיה דממנא על

רד"ק

דלתות ההיכל. קלף הזהב מעליהם כי הדלתות היו מצופות זהב והזהב הוא שלקח וכת"י קליף: ואת האומנות. ת"י וית סקופיא ותרגם את מפתן הבית סקוף בית מקדשא והאסקופות האלה אשר צפה חזקיהו זהב אפשר כי הזהב אשר עליהם מבנין שלמה הוסר או נפסד וחזקיהו צפה אותו זהב ועתה כשנצטרך לזהב לתת למלך אשר קלף אותו הזהב: (יז) את תרתן ואת רב סרים ואת רבשקה. ובישעיה אמר רבשקה לבדו נראה כי הוא היה עיקר השליחות והשנים טפלים לו וכן נראה הוא ג"כ רבשקה הוא היה המדבר ובסדר עולם הוא אומר כי רבשקה לבדו בא בשליחו' ראשונה כמו שאומר בישעיה ותרתן ורב סרים באו בשליחות שנייה ומה שזכר הנה תרתן ורב סרים לפי שגם הם היו שלוחים אבל לא בפעם הזאת אלא בשליחות שנית כשמצאו רבשקה נלחם על לבנה ולבנה היא מארץ ישראל כמו שנאמר במלכי כנען מלך לבנה אחד ואמרו רז"ל כי רבשקה ישראל מומר היה ואם אמרו מפני שהיה מדבר יהודית הרבה בני אדם ימצאו מדברים בלשון עם אחר והנה אליקים ושבנה ויואח היו מכירין בלשון ארמי אולי קבלה היתה בידם: בחיל כבד. בחיל עם כבד: בתעלת הברכה העליונה. הבריכה היא חריץ בנוי באבנים ובסיד ומתכנסין שם מים מן המעין או מושכין שם מי גשמים ובבריכה הזאת היו מכונסין המים ויש בבריכה הזאת נקב ויסתמו אותו עד זמן שירצו להוציא מים מן הבריכה והתעלה היא חפירה סמוכה לבריכה ומוציאי' כי"א מן הבריכ' לתעלה בזמן שירצו להשקות או לכבס בגדים: אשר במסלת שדה כובס. המסלה היא הדרך שמתקנים אותה באבנים כדי שיוכלו ללכת בה בימות הגשמים ועיקר הלשון הוא לשון הרמה מענין סלו לרוכב בערבות שענינו רוממות והמקום הזה היה בזה השדה והוא מורם ומתוקן באבנים ועל המקום הזה היו עומדים מכבסי הבגדים במי התעלה ובשדה היו שוטחים הבגדים לשמש וכת"י שדה כובס חקל משטח קצריא: (יח) ויקראו אל המלך. קראו לאשר על החומה או לאשר מצאו בשדה כובס שיאמרו למלך שיצא לדבר עמם ויצאו אליהם במצות המלך אליקים ושבנא ויואח: אליקים בן חלקיהו אשר

רש"י

(יז) את תרתן ואת רב סרים. למדנו בסדר עולם שלא באו שלשתם יחד אלא רבשקה לבדו כמו שכתב בס' (ישעיה ל"ז ב') ותרתן ורב סרים באו בשליחות שנייה כשבאה לו שמועה על תרהקה מלך כוש וישמע וישלח מלאכים אל חזקיהו וגו' (ישעיה ל"ז ט'): בתעלת. פוסקיר"ה בלע"ז בריכה שעושין לגיברי דגים: שדה כובס. שדה

מנחת שי

וממנו במסורת שם: (יז) שדה כבס. כתב בעל המסורת ג' ב' מלא וחד חסר ולא פירש איזהו החסר ובס"א כ"י מלאתי חסר אותו של ישעיה סימן ל"ז ובשני ספרים כ"י זהו החסר ובמ"ג שלנו בדפוס קטן ג' מלאים וסותרת למה שנמסר כאן במקרא גדולה ג' חד חסר:

רלב"ג

לקחת מהם הזהב אשר הם מלופות ממנו: ואת האומנות. הם עמודים מלופים זהב או אסקופו' השער התחתונות והעליונות: (יז) בתעלת הברכה העליונה. הברכה הוא חריץ בנוי שעוצרים בו מים והיה אלא המים תעלה ר"ל חפירה רחבה יתפשטו בו: במסלת שדה כובס. היא הדרך הבא לשדה הכובסים אשר שם ישטחו בגדיהם אחר שכבסו אותם: (יח) ויקראו אל המלך. ר"ל קראו שילא אליהם

מצודת ציון

(יז) כבד. ענין רבוי: בתעלת הברכה. הברכה היא מקום בנוי באבנים ובסיד ושם מתכנסים המים והתעלה היא החפירה הסמוך לה ובעת הצורך ממשיכים לה את המים מן הבריכה וכן אל קלס לנגדם: (יח) אל המלך. קראו אל המלך לצאת אליהם: על הבית. הממונה על בית המלך: המזכיר. הממונה על ספר הזכרונות:

מצודת דוד

חזקית. כי בכר היה נפסד הצפוי שעשה שלמה: (יז) וישלח מלך אשור. ובמרמה שם עליו העונש כי עכ"ז עלה עליו: בתעלת. בתעלה הנמשכת מהבריכה העליונה אשר היא במסילה ההולך אל השדה שמכבסים שם את הבגדים ושוטחים שמה מול השמש

in the washer's field, to summon the king to talk with them. Thereupon, the king delegated Eliakim, Shebnah, and Joah [*Redak*].

Eliakim the son of Hilkiah who was appointed over the palace—This agrees with the account in Isaiah 37:2. In Isaiah 22:15, the prophet refers to him as "Shebna who is appointed over the palace (or over the Temple, *Rashi* ad loc.)." He proceeds to rebuke him and prophesies that his position will be given over to Eliakim, son of Hilkiah. We can-

and the thresholds which Hezekiah the king of Judah had overlaid, and he gave them to the king of Assyria. 17. And the king of Assyria sent Tartan and Rabsaris, and Rabshakeh from Lachish to King Hezekiah with an army of a great [multitude] to Jerusalem, and they went up and came and stood near the conduit of the upper pool, which is on the road of the washer's field. 18. And they summoned the king, and Eliakim the son of Hilkiah who was appointed over the palace,

fore, replaced by Hezekiah [*Redak*].

17. The following account of Hezekiah's encounter with Sennacherib's ambassadors and the results thereof, are found also in Is. 35–39, with variations. It is also found in II Chron. 32. We will strive to reconcile the variations between the three accounts.

And the king of Assyria sent—Although Hezekiah had paid the tribute levied upon him, the king of Assyria, nevertheless, sent his officers to attack [*Mezudath David*].

According to *Redak,* as mentioned above, this took place after Hezekiah had ceased to send the tribute. *Malbim,* Is. 36:1, based on the account in Chron., theorizes that Hezekiah agreed to pay tribute in order to gain respite from Assyria, to give him time to mobilize his army and prepare for war. He closed all the springs that flowed outside of Jerusalem so that the Assyrians would not find any water. This indicated that he was preparing for battle. When Sennacherib learned of his tactics, he sent his emissaries to intimidate him and convince him and his people to humble themselves before Sennacherib.

Tartan and Rabsaris—*We learned in Seder Olam* (?) *that the three of them did not come together, but Rabshakeh came alone, as the prophet wrote in the Book of Isaiah* (36:2), *and Tartan and Rabsaris came on a second mission, when he received word concerning Tarhakah, king of Cush, "and he heard and sent emissaries to Hezekiah . . .* (Is. 37:9)" [*Rashi*].*

near the conduit—*fosed* (fossé) *in French. A ditch, a trench, a moat* [*Rashi*].*

Redak explains that the pool was a ditch dug out in the ground and built up with stones and plaster. There was an outlet which was usually closed with a stone until the water became necessary for drinking or washing. When the stone would be removed, the water would run into the conduit, where it could be utilized.

the road—this is a paved road, which could be used during the rainy season [*Redak*].

the washer's field—*a field where the washers stretch out garments. So did Jonathan render, "a field where the washers stretch out"* [*Rashi*].

18. **And they summoned the king**—They called the sentry on the wall, or perhaps, someone they met

ביתא ושבנא ספרא ויואח בר אסף דממנא על דכרניא: יט ואמר להון רבשקה אמרו כען לחזקיה כדנן אמר מלכא רבא מלכא דאתור מא רוחצנא הדין דאתרחיצתא: כ אמרת ברם במלל ספון במילך וגבורה אעביד קרבא כען על מן אתרחיצתא ארי מרידתא בי: כא כען הא אתרחיצתא לך על סמך קניא רעיעא

וְשֶׁבְנָה הַסֹּפֵר וְיוֹאָח בֶּן־אָסָף הַמַּזְכִּיר:
יט וַיֹּאמֶר אֲלֵהֶם רַבְשָׁקֵה אִמְרוּ־נָא אֶל־חִזְקִיָּהוּ כֹּה־אָמַר הַמֶּלֶךְ הַגָּדוֹל מֶלֶךְ אַשּׁוּר מָה הַבִּטָּחוֹן הַזֶּה אֲשֶׁר בָּטָחְתָּ:
כ אָמַרְתָּ אַךְ־דְּבַר־שְׂפָתַיִם עֵצָה וּגְבוּרָה לַמִּלְחָמָה עַתָּה עַל־מִי בָטַחְתָּ כִּי מָרַדְתָּ בִּי:
כא עַתָּה הִנֵּה בָטַחְתָּ לְּךָ עַל־מִשְׁעֶנֶת הַקָּנֶה הָרָצוּץ

רש"י

שהכיבסין בוטחין בו בגדים וכן תרגם יונתן חקל משטח קצריא: (יח) המזכיר. איזה משפט בא לפני המלך ראשון שיפסקנו ראשון: (כ) אמרת אך דבר שפתים וגו'. אמרת עד הנה (לא) אעבוד למלך אשור אך דבר שפתים היה כל זמן שלא יצא ממקומו לבוא עליך לא הוצרכת לעצה וגבורה אבל עכשיו שיצא ובא עצה וגבורה אתה צריך למלחמה הזאת עתה אמור על מי בטחת: (כא) ובא בכפו. כשאדם נסמך על משענת קנה רצוץ שנשבר בידו כאין ראשי הקרומיות

רד"ק

על הבית. וכן אמר בישעיה בזאת הפרשה אבל בפרשה שנאמרה על שבנא נאמר לך בא אל הסוכן הזה על שבנא אשר על הבית ונבא עליו שיהדפנו מהשררה שהיה בה שהיה על הבית ויתננה לאליקים בן חלקיהו ולא נוכל לומר כי קודם המעשה הזה מרד שבנא ונתנו שררתו לאליקים ומפני זה אמר אליקים אשר על הבית כי אלו היו המלאכים הראשונים אשר באו ממלך אשור לירושלם ושבנא יצא אליהם עם אליקים ואמרו לרבשקה דבר נא אל עבדיך ארמית כי שומעים אנחנו ונאמר ויבא אליקים ושבנא הסופר ויואח קרועי בגדים נראה כי עדיין לא מרד אלא בשוב רבשקה אומר שמרד ובסדר עולם אומר כשהלך לכוש שטף שבנא וסיעתו והלך לכוש ובדברי רז"ל כשבא סנחריב וצר על ירושלם כתב שבנא כת' והשליכו עם החץ שירד למחנ' אשור והיה כתוב בו שבנא וסיעתו השלימו חזקיהו וסיעתו לא השלימו וכאשר יצא עם סיעתו בא גבריאל וסגר דלתות העיר בפני סיעתו כשבא אצל סנחריב אמר לו היכן סיעתך אמר להם חזרו בהם נקבוהו בעקביו ותלאוהו בזנבי הסוסים והיו מגררים אותו על הקוצים ועל הברקנים וזה אינו כדברי בעל סדר עולם שאמר ששטף שבנא וסיעתו ואפשר כי קודם לכן מרד מעט שבא מלך אשור על ערי יהודה אבל נסתר ולא היה מראה עצמו וכן במעשה הזה שבא קרוע בגדים היה מראה הוא עצמו עצב ולבו לא נכון והנביא גלה דעתו לחזקיהו והורידו מפקידותו ונשאר סופר והפקיד אליקים על הבית: (כ) אמרת אך דבר שפתים. חשבת להנצל בדבר שפתים כלומר בתפלה אין זה כי אם עצה וגבורה צריך אדם למלחמה כך פירש אדוני אבי ז"ל והחכם רבי אברהם ב"ע פי' אמרת לאנשיך כי יש לך עצה וגבורה וזהו דבר שפתים והטעם כי גבורתך הו' בדבור לבד וי"ת ברם במלל סיפוו במילך וגבורה אעביד קרבא: כי מרדת בי. שלא נתן מה שהטיל עליו שנה בשנה: (כא) הרצוץ. שהוא רצוץ בראשו

רלב"ג

המלך: (יט) ויאמר אליהם רבשקה. אע"פ שבאו אהרים עמו והם תרתן ורב סרים לא דבר אלו הדברים כי אם רבשקה ולזה לא זכר זולתו בזה הכליהות וכספר ישעיה וידמה כי אחר שנתן חזקיה את כל הכסף הנמצא באוצרות ה' ובאוצרות המלך למלך אשור שב למרוד בו ולא נתן לו מדי שנה בשנה זה המס הנכבד שבם עליו: מה הבטחון הזה אשר בטחת. כי מרדת בי ולא קיימת מה שאמרת לי בהיותי נלחם עמך את אשר תתן עלי אשא: (כ) אמרת אך דבר שפתים הוא עצה וגבורה. שיתגבר האדם בו במלחמה ר"ל שבדברי שפתיו יסיר מעליו הנלחם עמו כמו שעשית אתה ממני ואחר זה יתחזק ויתגבר בעוזריו לעמוד כנגד מי שהיה נלחם עמו עתה על מי בטחת שיעזרך כי מרדת בי ולפי שהשב מלך אשור כי חשב חזקיה שמרדו בו על מלך מצרים שיעזרהו במלחמה אמר אליו הנה בטחת על משענת הקנה כמו

מצודת דוד

(יט) מה הבטחון וגו'. אמור מה בטחונך אשר בעבורה מרדת בי לבל השמע לי ללכת מחלך אל ארץ אחרת וכאשר אמר בסוף דבריו: (כ) אמרת. אתה חושב שאך בדבר שפתים בעלת יועלים נעשה המלחמה לא כן הוא כי לדבר אין עצה עם גבורה: עתה. הואיל והלוכך הוא גם אל הגבורה ואינה בך א"כ על מי בטחת ביתן בך גבורה: (כא) עתה הנה בטחת. הואיל ואין בך גבורה מעצמך הנה מהו בטחונך על מצרים הנה הוא כמו משענת קנה רצוץ כדאבו אחר אם יסמוך איש עליו באיש עוד

מצודת ציון

תעלת הבריכה (שם ז'): במסלת. בדרך הכבושה: (כא) משענת. ענין סמיכה: הקנה. המטה: הרצוץ. השבור ומרוסס

you have trusted?—to rebel against me, not to heed me to vacate your land and follow me to another land, as below v. 32 [*Mezudath David*].

According to *Redak*, he asked him in whom he had confidence to rebel by becoming delinquent in his payments of tribute. According to *Malbim,* he asked him in whom he had confidence in mobilizing for war.

20. **You have said but words of the lips . . .**—*Until now you have said, "I will not pay tribute to the king of*

and Shebna the scribe and Joah the son of Asaph the recorder, came out to them. 19. And Rabshakeh said to them, "Say now to Hezekiah, 'So has the great king, the king of Assyria, said, "What is this confidence that you have trusted? 20. You have said but words of the lips; counsel and might are needed for war. Now, on whom do you depend that you have rebelled against me? 21. Now, behold you have depended upon the support of this splintered reed,

not say that this took place after Shebna's betrayal, when the position had already been given to Eliakim, since this was the first encounter with Rabshakeh, when all three begged him to speak Aramaic so as not to destroy the people's morale. Moreover, Shebna and his colleagues all returned to Hezekiah with rent garments, as below 37. It appears then that he was still faithful. Also, the *Seder Olam* ch. 23 states that first when Sennacherib went to Cush, he took along Shebna and his company. Our Rabbis (San. 26a) relate that when Sennacherib laid siege to Jerusalem, Shebna took a note, attached it to an arrow, and shot it into the Assyrian camp. On it was written, "Shebna and his company wish to make peace; Hezekiah and his company do not wish to make peace." When he went out with his company, the angel Gabriel closed the doors in front of his company. When he came to Sennacherib, he asked him, "Where is your company?" He replied, "They have recanted." He retorted, "If so, you are mocking us." They punctured his heels and hung him on their horses' tails, and dragged him over the thorns and thistles. Incidentally, this does not agree with the account of *Seder Olam,* that Sennacherib took along Shebna and his company.

To return to the first difficulty, we may say that Shebna secretly revolted from the time Sennacherib seized the cities of Judah. No one knew of his betrayal except the prophet Isaiah, to whom God revealed it. He, in turn, revealed it to Hezekiah, who demoted Shebna to the position of scribe and promoted Eliakim to Shebna's former position. When Rabshakeh shouted his blasphemies, Shebna, who had not yet revealed his betrayal, feigned grief, and rent his garments with Eliakim and Joah his colleagues [*Redak*].

over the palace—[*Mezudath David, Ibn Ezra* Isaiah 22:15]. *Rashi,* however, explains that he was in charge of the Temple, either as High Priest or as treasurer [*Rashi* ad loc.].

the recorder—*which judgment came first before the king, that he should first adjudicate* [*Rashi*].

Rashi on Isaiah 36:3, explains it as the writer of the records, the annals.

19. **"What is this confidence that**

הַזֶּה עַל־מִצְרַיִם אֲשֶׁר יִסָּמֵךְ אִישׁ עָלָיו
וּבָא בְכַפּוֹ וּנְקָבָהּ כֵּן פַּרְעֹה מֶלֶךְ־
מִצְרַיִם לְכָל־הַבֹּטְחִים עָלָיו׃ כב וְכִי־
תֹאמְרוּן אֵלַי אֶל־יְהֹוָה אֱלֹהֵינוּ בָּטָחְנוּ
הֲלוֹא־הוּא אֲשֶׁר הֵסִיר חִזְקִיָּהוּ אֶת־
בָּמֹתָיו וְאֶת־מִזְבְּחֹתָיו וַיֹּאמֶר לִיהוּדָה
וְלִירוּשָׁלִַם לִפְנֵי הַמִּזְבֵּחַ הַזֶּה תִּשְׁתַּחֲווּ
בִּירוּשָׁלִָם׃ כג וְעַתָּה הִתְעָרֶב נָא אֶת־
אֲדֹנִי אֶת־מֶלֶךְ אַשּׁוּר וְאֶתְּנָה לְךָ
אַלְפַּיִם סוּסִים אִם־תּוּכַל לָתֶת לְךָ
רֹכְבִים עֲלֵיהֶם׃ כד וְאֵיךְ תָּשִׁיב אֵת פְּנֵי

תרגום

הָדֵין עַל מִצְרַיִם דְאִם יִסְתְּמֵיךְ גַּבְרָא עֲלוֹהִי וְיֵעוּל בִּידֵיהּ וִיבַזְעִינֵיהּ כֵּן פַּרְעֹה מַלְכָּא דְמִצְרַיִם לְכָל דְמִתְרַחֲצִין עֲלוֹהִי׃ כב וַאֲרֵי תֵימְרוּן לִי עַל מֵימְרָא דַייָ אֱלָהָנָא אִתְרְחֵיצְנָא הֲלָא הוּא דְאַעְדֵי חִזְקִיָּה יַת בָּמָתוֹהִי וְיַת מַדְבְּחוֹהִי וַאֲמַר לֶאֱנָשׁ יְהוּדָה וּלְיָתְבֵי יְרוּשְׁלֵם קֳדָם מַדְבְּחָא הָדֵין תִּסְגְּדוּן בִּירוּשְׁלֵם׃ כג וּכְעַן אִתְעָרַב כְּעַן עִם רִבּוֹנִי עִם מַלְכָּא דְאַתּוּר וְאֶתֵּן לָךְ תְּרֵין אַלְפִין סוּסְוָן אִם תִּכּוּל לְמִנְאֵה לָךְ רְכִיבִין עֲלֵיהוֹן׃ כד וְאֵיכְדֵין אַתְּ מְדַמֵּי לאתבא

רד"ק

ואותם קסמין נכנסין בכף האדם בהשען עליו: (כב) הלא הוא אשר הסיר. כלו' כשהסיר חזקיהו ונתץ המזבחות לא עשה כי אם לכבודו ולהנאתו כדי שיבואו כלם לירושלם כי המזבחו' בכל מקום לשם ה' היו וחזקיהו הסירם ונתצן איך תחשבו כי ה' יעזור אותו ואיך תבטחו עליו: ליהודה ולירושלם. כתרגומו לאנש יהודה וליתבי ירושלם: (כג) התערב נא. הכנס עמי בערבון בזה הדבר אם תוכל לעשותו: רוכבים עליהם. רוכבים

רש"י

ונוקבין את כפו: (כב) הלא הוא אשר הסיר חזקיהו וגו'. יש ללמוד מכאן דרבשקה ישראל מומר היה שהיה מודה שהקב"ה אלוה אלא שרצונו לע"ג: (כג) התערב נא. התפאר עליו בוא בערבון על מנת אם תוכל ליתן לך רוכבים על אלפים סוסים: התערב. (גוי"ר בלע"ז): (כד) ואיך תשיב את פני פחת אחד עבדי אדוני. שהרי כל הקטן שבהם שר על אלפים איש ואתה אינך משיג לאלפים איש למדנו מכאן על ראשי גייסות מאה ושמונים

מנחת שי

(כב) את במתיו. במקצת ספרים במותיו מלא וא"ו:

רלב"ג

משענת הקנה הרצוץ כי לא די שלא אפשר לאדם להשען בו אבל (לא) יזיק לעצמו בהשענו בו כי הקנה הרצוץ יכנס בכפו ונקבה כי כן פרעה מלך מצרים לכל הבוטחים עליו וכי תאמרון אלי אל ה' אלהינו בטחנו שיצילנו הלא הוא אשר הסיר חזקיהו את במותיו ואת מזבחותיו אשר היו מקריבים בהם לה' ויאמר ליהודה ולירושלם לפני המזבח הזה לבד תשתחוו ואיך יעזרהו והוא עשה כנגדו להשחית במותיו ומזבחותיו: (כג) ועתה התערב נא את אדני את מלך אשור. ר"ל תן לו ערבון שלא תמרוד בו ותהיה לו למס ואתנה לך אלפים סוסים אם תוכל לתת לך אנשים רוכבים עליהם והנה אמר זה על דרך הבוז והלעג כאילו אמר שלא ימצאו לחזקיה אלפים אנשים ראויים לרכוב על סוסים: (כד) ואיך תשיב את פני פחת אחד עבדי אדני הקטנים. כל זה אמר לירא אותם ולבהלם כאילו יאמר שמלך אשור הוא באופן

מצודת ציון

כמו הרוללות אביונים (עמוס ד'): ונקבה. מלשון נקב וחור: (כג) התערב. מלשון ערבון ומשכון כי כששנים חלוקים בדבר

מצודת דוד

הקסמין והקרומיות בכפו ונוקבין אותה כן עזרת פרעה נהפך עוד לרעה: (כב) הלוא הוא. הלא זה הוא אשר הסיר חזקיה את במותיו אשר היו בכל הארץ ואמר לישראל שרק למזבח העומד בבהמ"ק אשר בירושלי' תשתחוו ומיעט א"כ בעבודתו ונכאש בעיניו: (כג) התערב נא. התחייב עצמך עם אדוני אם תוכל למצוא הדבר אשר ישאל: לתת לך. לתת מאנשיך: (כד) ואיך תשיב. את פניך להלח' עם פני פחת וגו' הלא אף הקטן שבהם ממונה הוא על אלפי':

ening to go down to Egypt to obtain horses to use for fighting Assyria. Rabshakeh taunts them by offering them two thousand horses. He promises them horses without the trouble of going down to Egypt if they can only supply riders for them [*R. Joseph Kara*].

24. **And how can you repulse one captain of . . . my master's servants**—*for the smallest of them is captain over two thousand men, and you cannot obtain two thousand men. We deduce from here concerning the heads of the armies, who totaled 185,000, who fell with Sennacherib,*

upon Egypt, upon whom a man will lean and it will go into his palm and puncture it; so is Pharaoh the king of Egypt to all those who trust in him. 22. And if you say to me, 'We trust the Lord our God,' is He not the one Whose high places and altars Hezekiah has removed? He has said to Judah and to Jerusalem, 'Before this altar in Jerusalem shall you prostrate yourselves.' 23. And now, wager now with my Lord the king of Assyria, and I will give you two thousand horses if you are able to supply riders upon them of your men. 24. And how can you

repulse

Assyria." It was but words of the lips. As long as he did not leave his place to march upon you, you did not require counsel and might. Now, however, that he has left his place *and come upon you, you require counsel and might for this war. Now tell upon whom you have depended?* [*Rashi*].

Alternatively, you have said but with your lips to your soldiers that you have counsel and might for war [*Ibn Ezra,* Isaiah 36, quoted here by *Redak*].

21. **and it will go into his palm**—*When a person supports himself on a support of a splintered reed, which has broken in his hand, the ends of the scaly envelope will come and puncture his palm* [*Rashi*].

so is Pharaoh—His support, instead of being a help, will prove to your detriment [*Mezudath David, Rashi* Isaiah 36:6].

22. **Is He not the one Whose high places and altars Hezekiah has removed . . .**—*It can be deduced from here that Rabshakeh was an apostate Jew, for he admits that the Holy One, Blessed be He, is God, but His will is that we worship idols* [*Rashi*]. Possibly, *Rashi* means that even though Rabshakeh believed in the existence of God, his will was, nevertheless, to worship idols.

He has said to Judah and to Jerusalem—i.e. to the people of Judah and Jerusalem [*Redak* after *Jonathan*].

'Before this altar—When he abolished the high places and all the other altars throughout the land, he meant only for his own honor and glory, that everyone would come to his altar in Jerusalem to prostrate themselves. How, then, can he expect God's aid when he destroyed His altars? [*Redak*].*

23. **wager now**—*boast over him. Enter a wager on the condition that if you are able to supply riders for two thousand horses. wager-gajjer in O.F.* [*Rashi*].

This is analogous to one who says to his opponent, "If only I had a sword, I would kill you." His opponent replies, "Here is a sword. Let me see whether you can defeat me." Similarly, the Judeans were threat-

פחת אחד עבדי אדני הקטנים ותבטח
לך על־מצרים לרכב ולפרשים:
כה עתה המבלעדי יהוה עליתי על־
המקום הזה להשחתו יהוה אמר אלי
עלה על־הארץ הזאת והשחיתה:
כו ויאמר אליקים בן־חלקיהו ושבנה
ויואח אל־רבשקה דבר־נא אל־
עבדיך ארמית כי שמעים אנחנו ואל־
תדבר עמנו יהודית באזני העם אשר
על־החמה: כז ויאמר אליהם רבשקה
העל אדניך ואליך שלחני אדני לדבר

לאתבא ית אפי חד
משלטוני עבדי רבוני
זעיריא ואתרחיצת לך
על מצראי לרתיכין
ולפרשין: כה כען הבר
ממימרא דיי סליקית
על אתרא הדין
לחבלותה יי אמר לי סק
לאתרא הדין וחבלינה:
כו ואמר אליקים בר
חלקיה ושבנה ויואח
לרבשקה מלל כען עם
עבדך ארמית ארי
שמעין אנחנא ולא
תמליל עמנא יהודית
קדם עמא דעל שורא:
כז ואמר להון רבשקה
העל רבונך ועלך
שלחני רבוני למללא
ית

ת"א המבלעדי. סנהדרין לד:

רש"י

וחמשה אלף שנפלו עם סנחריב הקטן שבהם שר על אלפים היה שמו: (כה) המבלעדי ה'. וכי שלא ברשות באתי כבר נתנבא ישעיה (ז' י"ז) בימי אחז אביך יביא ה' עליך ועל עמך וגו' את מלך אשור: והשחיתה. את זו הוסיף משלו: (כו) כי שומעים אנחנו. אנו בני פלטין ומכירין

רד"ק

שיהיו פרשים: (כה) המבלעדי ה'. להפחיד' אמר כן או פירושו אחר שכל הארצות נתן ה' בידי וגם כל ארץ ישראל הוא אמר אלי עלה אל הארץ והשחית' ואם רבשקה היה ישראל מומר אמר זה לפי שישעיה ניבא ואמר הנני מעלה את מי הנהר העצומים והרבים את מלך אשור וגו': (כו) כי שומעים אנחנו. מבינים' ומכירים בלשון ארמית: (כז) העל אדניך. כמו האל וכן הוא בישעיה וכן על האנשים כמו אל ולאליקים אמר שהוא

חגדול וכן הוא אומר ויאמר אליקים וגו': חריהם. כן כתיב וקרי צואתם וענין אחד הוא והקרי הוא לשון נקיה: שיניהם.

רלב"ג

מהגדול שאין ראוי לחזקיה להשי' פני פחת' אחד שהוא מעבדיו הקטנים גם כי אחד מעבדיו הקטנים גדול מאד עד שאין ראוי להשיב פניו ולבטוח על מצרים לרכב ולפרשים שיעזרהו במלחמ' כנגד מלך אשור: (כה) עתה המבלעדי ה'. אמר זה כאילו יאמר איך תבטח על ה' שיצילך והוא אמר אלי שאעלה על הארץ הזאת להשחיתה:

מנחת שי

(כה) אמר אלי עלה על הארץ הזאת. כן ראיתי בספרי הדפוס חדשים גם ישנים וגם בס"א כ"י מדוייק כתוב על אבל בספרים אחרים כ"י כתוב אל הארץ וכן בתרגום סק לאתרא ואולם בישעיה ל"ו הביא בעל המסורת כמה חילופים שבין פסוק דמלכים לפסוק דישעיה בזה הענין וכתב שזה על הארץ ודישעיה אל הארץ עיין שם: (כו) ויאמר אליקים בן חלקיהו ושבנה. ב' כתוב ה"א הדין ואידך

(כו) באזני העם אשר על החומ'. אמרו זה כי לא היו רוצים שישמע אלו הדברים העם אשר על החומה כדי שלא ירפא ידיהם משמירת החומה: (כז) העל אדניך ואליך. ר"ל האם בעבור אדניך ובעבורך שלחני מלך אשור: לאכול את צואתם ולשתות את מימי רגליהם עמכם. כאילו אמר שאם ישמרו את החומה שלא יכנסו חיל מלך אשור הנה יכנה עליה מלך אשור מצור עד שמריב הרעב יאכלו צואתם ויבתו

מצודת דוד

ותבטח. א"כ בוודאי כל בטחונך ברכב ובפרשים על מצרים אשר הוא כקנה רצוץ: (כה) המבלעדי ה'. וכי מבלי גזירת המקום: ה' אמר. כבר ניבא ישעיה ישא וגו' ואת שלל שומרון (ישעיה ח') וטעה לומר שכן יעשה לירושלים: (כו) ארמית. בלשון ארמית:

כי שומעים. כי מבינים אנחנו ארמית: יהודית. בלשון יהודית: באזני העם. בפניהם כשהם שומעים כי הכל מכירים בו וכאומר שנה אין מהדרך לפרסם דברי מלחמה בפני המון העם: (כז) העל אדוניך. וכי רק אל אדוניך ואליך שלחני אדוני לדבר דברי: לאכול.

מצודת ציון

מה וכ"א מחייב עלמו בממון באם לא יהיה כדבריו הדרך הוא שכ"א נותן ערבון להיות בטוח ומקיים: (כד) פחת. ענין שררה: (כה) המבלעדי. ענינו כמו זולת: (כז) העל. כמו האל: הוריהם.

family and he would take pity upon them [Some versions of *Rashi*, Is. 36:11].

It is not customary to reveal matters of the war to the populace [*Mezudath David*].

They did not want the people to lose courage and give up protecting the wall [*Ralbag*].

27. **to your master**—lit. concerning your master. *Redak* explains as we have translated in the text. *Ralbag* explains it literally, Has my master sent me because of your

one captain of the smallest of my master's servants, and you rely on Egypt for chariots and horsemen? 25. Now is it with other than the Lord that I have come up against this place to destroy it? The Lord said to me, 'Go up against this land and destroy it.'" 26. And Eliakim the son of Hilkiah and Shebnah and Joah said to Rabshakeh, "Please speak to your servants in Aramaic for we understand it; do not speak with us in Judean within the hearing of the people who are on the wall." 27. And Rabshakeh said to them, "Did my master send me to speak these words to your master and to you?

that the smallest of them was captain over two thousand men that were with him [*Rashi*].

repulse—lit. turn away from the face of.

and you rely—Obviously, you rely on Egypt for chariots and horsemen [*Mezudath David*].

25. **is it with other than the Lord**—*Did I come without permission? Isaiah already prophesied in the days of Ahaz your father,* "(Is. 7:17) *The Lord shall bring upon you and upon your people . . . the king of Assyria*" [*Rashi*].

Another prophecy was, "(ibid. 8:7) And therefore, the Lord brings up upon them the mighty and massive waters of the river—the king of Assyria— . . ." [*Redak*].

According to the Rabbis, who say that Rabshakeh was an apostate Jew, it is very likely that he was familiar with the prophecies of Isaiah. Otherwise, we may theorize that he made this statement to threaten the Jews by telling them that just as God had delivered other lands into the hands of the king of Assyria, so had He delivered the land of Judah into his hands [*Redak*].

and destroy it—*This he added of his own* [*Rashi*].

I.e. this was not part of the prophecy. This he added of his own, to frighten the people.

26. **for we understand**—lit. we hear [*Redak*].

We are residents of the palace, and understand the Aramaic language and other languages. Do not speak to us Judean, which all the people understand, and we do not want them to hear [*Rashi*].

within the hearing of the people—*For all the people understand Judean, and they are frightened by your words. Since he said to them, "Say now to Hezekiah," they thought that he did not come to frighten the people. Since Rabshakeh was an apostate Jew, they thought that even though his master's orders were incumbent upon Rabshakeh* to observe, *but his heart was attracted to his*

את־הדברים האלה הלא על־האנשים
הישבים על־החמה לאכל את־
חריהם ולשתות את־שיניהם עמכם:
כח ויעמד רבשקה ויקרא בקול־גדול
יהודית וידבר ויאמר שמעו דבר־
המלך הגדול מלך אשור: כט כה אמר
המלך אל־ישיא לכם חזקיהו כי־לא
יוכל להציל אתכם מידו: ל ואל־יבטח
אתכם חזקיהו אל־יהוה לאמר הצל
יצילנו יהוה ולא תנתן את־העיר הזאת
ביד מלך אשור: לא אל־תשמעו אל־
חזקיהו כי כה אמר מלך אשור עשו

יָת כָּל פִּתְגָמַיָא הָאִלֵין הֲלָא עַל גֻבְרַיָא דְיָתְבִין עַל שׁוּרָא לְמֵיכַל יָת מַפְּקַתְהוֹן וּלְמִשְׁתֵּי יָת מֵימֵי רַגְלֵיהוֹן בְּצַיְרָא עִמְּכוֹן: כח וְקָם רַבְשָׁקֵה וּקְרָא בְּקָל רַב יְהוּדִית וּמַלֵּיל וַאֲמַר שְׁמַעוּ פִּתְגָמָא דְמַלְכָּא רַבְּרְבָתָנָא מַלְכָּא דְאַתּוּר: כט כִּדְנַן אֲמַר מַלְכָּא לָא יַטְעֵי יַתְכוֹן חִזְקִיָה אֲרֵי לָא יִכּוּל לְשֵׁיזָבָא יַתְכוֹן מִן יְדֵיהּ: ל וְלָא יַרְחִיץ יַתְכוֹן חִזְקִיָה עַל מֵימְרָא דַיְיָ לְמֵימַר שֵׁיזָבָא יְשֵׁיזְבִינָנָא יְיָ וְלָא תִתְמְסַר קַרְתָּא הָדָא בְּיַד מַלְכָּא דְאַתּוּר: לא לָא תְקַבְּלוּן מִן חִזְקִיָה אֲרֵי כִדְנַן אֲמַר מַלְכָּא דְאַתּוּר עֲבִידוּ עִמִּי

רד"ק
צואתם קרי מימי רגליהם

כן כתיב וקרי מימי רגליהם הכתוב הוא רמז להתחתוניות וכן בדברי רז"ל המקנח בדבר שהאור שולט בשיניו נושרות וענין לאכול את צואת' שחושבי' להיות במצור עד שיאכלו צואת'

רש"י
בלשון ארמי ובשאר לשונות ואל תדבר אלינו יהודית שכל העם מכירין בו ואין אנו רוצים שישמעו: (כז) לאכול את צואתם. ברעב המצור: חוריהם. רעי היוצא דרך חור פי הטבעת. ורבותינו פירשו לכנותם לשון נאה צואתם: שיניהם. צואה לשון שיני דכרכשא דקיימא אתלת שני או לשון גלל שבא על ידי לעיסת השינים: (לא) עשו אתי ברכה. שאילת שלום כמו ויברך יעקב את פרעה (בראשית

מנחת שי
ויקראו אל המלך דלעיל: (כז) היושבים על החמה. בספרים מדויקים חסר וא"ו: חריהם. צואתם קרי ועיין מה שכתוב בישעיה ל"ו: שיניהם. מימי רגליהם קרי ומתקני הנקוד שמו זה הנקודות על שתי המלות ... בקמ' תחת הקמץ אף על פי שאינה אלא מלה אחת ועיין מה שכתוב בזה בישעיה ל"ו בשייעתא דשמיא: (כט) אל ישיא לכם חזקיהו. בספרי הדפוס האחרונים מלא יו"ד אבל בספרים כתובי יד ודפוסים ישנים חסר וכן מצאתי במסורת כ"י ה' ב' מנהון חסר וסימנהון אל ישיא לכם חזקיהו דמלכים ודישעיהו חסר. ודד"ה. והויה בו. תלים פ"ט מלא. וחד יבימות עלומו תלים ל"ה כתיב חד מלא וקריא ב' יולין: להציל אתכם מידו. הספרים שכתוב בהם מידי הם כבני בבל אבל לבני ארץ ישראל אני כותבים עליהם בחילופי המקרא כתוב מידו: כי לא יוכל להציל אתכם מידי. (הנ"ל) מי יוכל לתקן את אשר עותו הסופרים והמדפיסים מימים קדמונים וכ"ש שהקיים בנו בעוונותינו לכן הנני יוסיף להפליא את העם הזה הפלא ופלא ואבדה חכמת חכמיו ובינת נבוניו תסתתר והנה אנחנו מגששים כעורים באפלת המחלוקה ואין אנו גואליהם את דרכינו למלא חפצנו. בבלות ספרים ישנים מהדפוס כתוב מידי וכן מצאתי בס"א מדוייק כ"י מספרד ובספר אחד כ"י נכתב בפסיק מידו ונרשם מבחוץ נ"א מידי ובספר אחד כתוב מידו בוא"ו ונקוד חירק ואין בידי להכריע כי בספרים אחדים כתוב מידו וכן מתורגם מן ידיה. ה' יגיה הכבנו מאפל ומחשך עיני עורים תראינה: (ל) ולא תנתן את־העיר הזאת. בספרים כ"י ודפוסים ישנים כתוב את העיר:

רלב"ג
מי רגליהם והיא השתן: (לא) עשו אתי ברכה ולאו. ר"ל אם תהיו אתי להשלים עמי ולצאת אני עשו ברכה כי אז תוכלו לעבוד האדמה

מצודת ציון
מגזרון חור ונקב ור"ל צואה היוצאת מנקב פי הטבעת: שיניהם. הוא מ"ר והוא קרוב מל' שתן: (כט) ישיא. ענין הסתה ופתוי כמו הנחש השיאני (בראשית ג'): (לא) ברכה. ענינו מנחה ותשורת שלום כמו

מצודת דוד
להזהירם כי יבאו במצור ומעקת רעבון ולמאון יוכרחו לאכול צואה ולשתות מי רגלים: עמכם. ר"ל גם הם גם אתם: (כח) וידבר ויאמר. כפל דבריו לחזקם: (לא) עשו אתי ברכה. ר"ל עשו עמי

gift, which he referred to as *birchathi*. See *Rashi* Gen. 33:10.

each man will eat of his vine and each man of his fig tree—If you make peace with me, you will be able to leave the city to gather the fruit of your vines and trees and to drink the water of your cisterns which are outside the city [*Redak, Mezudath David*].

Is it not to the men who sit on the wall to eat their dung and drink their urine with you?" 28. And Rabshakeh stood and called out in a loud voice in Judean, and he spoke and said, "Listen to the word of the great king, the king of Assyria! 29. So has the king said, 'Let not Hezekiah deceive you, for he will not be able to deliver you from his hand. 30. And let not Hezekiah make you rely on the Lord, saying, 'The Lord will save us, and this city will not be given into the hand of the king of Assyria.' 31. Do not listen to Hezekiah, for so has the king of Assyria said, "Make

master and you? Is it not because of the men . . .?

to eat their dung—*in the hunger* brought about *by the siege* [*Rashi*].

If they continue to guard the wall to prevent the king of Assyria from entering, he will lay siege to the city, and the people will starve during the siege [*Ralbag, Mezudath David*].

their dung—The *k'thib* reads חֲרֵיהֶם—*dung that is excreted through the orifice of the anus. Our Rabbis explained to euphemize and read,* צוֹאָתָם, *i.e. their dung* [*Rashi*].

Our Rabbis explained that we are to read צוֹאָתָם as the *k'ri* because it is a more agreeable term than חֲרֵיהֶם, lit. *their holes.*

R. Joseph Kara states, "Our Rabbis instituted to euphemize צוֹאָתָם. It appears that this reading is a rabbinical enactment. See *Megillah* 25b. See also *Rashi,* Is. 36:12.

their urine—This is according to the *k'ri,* מֵימֵי רַגְלֵיהֶם. According to *k'thib,* שֵׁינֵיהֶם, however, we explain it as *loose excrement, the glands of the rectum, which is held by three glands.* They are called שְׁנַיִם because they are shaped like teeth. *Alternatively, an expression of excrement which comes about through the chewing of the teeth* [*Rashi*].

28. **the great king**—in contrast to the insignificant king, Hezekiah [*Malbim,* Is.].

It was common for the Assyrian monarchs to sign their names in this manner [*Antiquities* by Aaron Marcus, p. 168].

31. **"Make peace with me**—*Jonathan, Redak.* Lit. Make a blessing with me,—an expression of *a greeting, like* "(Gen. 47:7) *and Jacob greeted Pharaoh."* [*Rashi*].

Rashi, Is. 36:16, elaborates that the *b'rachah* is the customary gift offered to a monarch upon greeting him. *Mezudoth,* too, follows this interpretation. We find that Jacob presented Esau with such a greeting

אִתִּי בְרָכָה וּצְאוּ אֵלַי וְאִכְלוּ אִישׁ־גַּפְנוֹ
וְאִישׁ תְּאֵנָתוֹ וּשְׁתוּ אִישׁ מֵי־בֹרוֹ׃
לב עַד־בֹּאִי וְלָקַחְתִּי אֶתְכֶם אֶל־אֶרֶץ
כְּאַרְצְכֶם אֶרֶץ דָּגָן וְתִירוֹשׁ אֶרֶץ לֶחֶם
וּכְרָמִים אֶרֶץ זֵית יִצְהָר וּדְבַשׁ וִחְיוּ
וְלֹא תָמֻתוּ וְאַל־תִּשְׁמְעוּ אֶל־חִזְקִיָּהוּ
כִּי־יַסִּית אֶתְכֶם לֵאמֹר יְהוָה יַצִּילֵנוּ׃
לג הַהַצֵּל הִצִּילוּ אֱלֹהֵי הַגּוֹיִם אִישׁ אֶת־
אַרְצוֹ מִיַּד מֶלֶךְ אַשּׁוּר׃ לד אַיֵּה אֱלֹהֵי

עִמִּי שְׁלָמָא וּפוּקוּ
לְוָתִי וְאִכְלוּ גְּבַר פֵּרֵי
גוּפְנֵיהּ וּגְבַר פֵּרֵי תְינוֹהִי
וּשְׁתוֹ גְּבַר מֵי גוּבֵּיהּ׃
לב עַד מֵיתִי וְאַדְבַּר
יָתְכוֹן לְאַרְעָא טָבָא
כְּאַרְעֲכוֹן אַרְעָא עֲבוּר
נְחַמַר אַרְעָא חַקְלִין
וְכַרְמִין אַרְעָא דְזֵיתָהָא
עָבְדִין מִשְׁחָא וְהִיא
עָבְדָא דְבַשׁ וְחִיוּן וְלָא
תְמוּתוּן וְלָא תְקַבְּלוּן
מִן חִזְקִיָּה. אֲרֵי יַטְעֵי
יָתְכוֹן לְמֵימַר יְיָ
יְשֵׁיזְבִינָנָא׃ לג הֲשֵׁיזָבָא
שֵׁיזִיבָא דַחֲלַת עַמְמַיָּא
גְּבַר יַת אַרְעֵיהּ מִיַּד
מַלְכָּא דְאַתּוּר׃ לד אָן

רש"י

מ"ז ו'): (לב) אל ארץ כארצכם. כן דרכי להעביר את האומות ממדינה למדינה היה לו לומר אל ארץ טובה משלכם שהרי לפתותם בא אלא שידע שיכירו שדבריו שקר: ארץ

רד"ק

וכן הוסיף יהונתן בציירא עמכון: (לא) ברכה. ר"ל פשרה ושלום וכת"י שלמא: איש מי בורו. הבורות שהם חוצה לעיר בגנות: (לב) עד בואי ולקחתי אתכם. כי כן עשה בכל הגוים אשר כבש היה מגלה אותם מארצ' ומשכן אחרים תחתיה' כדי שיהיו כלם נכבשים תחתיו וכן עשה יוסף באנשי מצרים ואת העם

העביר אותו לערים: ארץ לחם וכרמים. אמר זה אחר שאמר ארץ דגן ותירוש כי אפשר שהדגן והתירוש יבואו לה מעיירות אחרות לרוב כמו שאמר בצור לפיכך אמר ארץ לחם וכרמים כי הארץ ההיא עושה לחם ויש בה כרמים וכת"י ארע' חקלין וכרמין ארע' דזיתה' עבדין משחא והיא עבדא דבש: כי יסית אתכ'. הדגש תמור' הנח כויסת דוד וכן בדגש הסיתוך ויכלו

רלב"ג

ולאכל פריה: (לב) ולקחתי אתכם אל ארץ כארצכם. ר"ל וכהגתי אתכם אל ארץ טובה כמו ארצכם ואמר זה להם לבאר שלא יזוקו אם אלה אותם לארץ אחרת כמו שעשה מעשרת שבטים והנה היה מניע ומבלבל האומות בזה הדרך כדי שלא יוכלו למרוד בו ולזה היה מרחיק

מנחת שי

(לב) וחיו ולא תמותו. במקצת ספרים תמותו מלא וא"ו אך כפי המסורת דגנו

מצודת דוד

שלום לאת תבורת שלום: ואכלו וגו'. ר"ל לא תהיו עוד כלואים בתוך העיר מבלי לצאת וללקוט פירות האילנות ולשאוב מי הבורות: (לב) ולקחתי. אקח אתכם משם להוליך אל ארץ טובה כארצכם כי כן היה דרכו להעביר את האומות שכבש מארצם לארץ אחרת: וחיו. משא"כ אם תעמדו במרד: כי יסית. אבל יסית: (לג) איש וגו'.

מצודת ציון

קח לא את ברכתי (שם ל"ג): (לב) ותירוש. ענבי היין: זית יצהר. זיתים המוכנין שמן: יסית. מלשון הסתה ופיתוי:

and you may live—If you rebel, however, you shall die [*Mezudath David*].

34. **Hamath . . . Sepharvaim**—mentioned above, 17:30, 31, among the nations repatriated in Samaria.

He exiled them and twisted them—Heb. הֵנַע וְעִוָּה. *The King of Assyria* exiled them and twisted *them*; i.e. *he destroyed them and exiled them* [*Rashi* after *Jonathan*]. *Redak* suggests that these were names of provinces or deities, Hena and Ivvah. *Ralbag* too considers them names of provinces.

Now, did they save Samaria—*and the inhabitants of Samaria worshipped the gods of the Arameans, who were their neighbors* [*Rashi*].

Rashi, Is. 36:19, adds: *And Hamath was from Aram.*

Redak suggests that the antecedent is "the Lord," mentioned in v. 32. Did the Lord save Samaria from my hand? What makes you think He will save Jerusalem?

Alternatively, did the calves in Dan and Bethel save Samaria from my hand? What makes you think that your God will save Jerusalem? [*Redak*].

The prophet Isaiah depicts the

peace with me, and come out to me, and each man will eat of his vine and each man of his fig tree, and each man will drink the water of his cistern.
32. Until I come and take you to a land like your land, a land of grain and wine, a land of bread and vineyards, a land of oil yielding olives and honey, and you may live and not die, and do not heed Hezekiah for he will mislead you, saying, 'The Lord will save us.'
33. Have the gods of the nations saved each one his land, from the hand of the king of Assyria?

32. **to a land like your land**—*So is my wont to repatriate the nations from province to province. He should have said, "to a land better than yours," since he came to entice them, but he knew that they would recognize that his statement was false* [*Rashi* from *San.* 94a]. Cf. *Rashi* Is. 36:17.

Rashi follows those who say that Sennacherib was a clever king. He knew that it would be more effective were he to praise his land over and above theirs. He knew, however, that they would not believe him were he to do so. Others claim that Sennacherib behaved foolishly by saying, "a land like your land," rather than "a land better than your land."

The Talmud states further that for refraining from denigrating the Holy Land, Sennacherib was rewarded with the title, "the great and noble Asenappar (Ezra 4:10)." Even though he refrained from doing so in order to gain his own ends, he was, nevertheless, rewarded. This follows the view that Sennacherib was a clever king [*K'li Y'kar*].

As we see, Sennacherib (and his father, Sargon), exiled all the nations they conquered in order to facilitate their subordination. Joseph, too, repatriated the Egyptians from city to city to demonstrate that they no longer had any claim to their land [*Redak, Mezudath David*].

He would exile them from their country, where they had allies among their neighbors, and brought them near to Assyria, where he would have full control over them. Lest they fear disaster, he promised them a land as good as their own as he had done to the ten tribes [*Ralbag*].

a land of grain and wine—*This is Africa* [*Rashi* from *Yerushalmi Sh'viith* 6:1].

a land of bread and vineyards—Lest we think that the land is replete with grain and wine through extensive import trade, like Tyre, Rabshakeh proceeded to clarify the matter, that this land is a land of bread and vineyards, a land which produces bread from its own grain and which has its own vineyards [*Redak* from *Jonathan*].

חֲמָת וְאַרְפָּד אַיֵּה אֱלֹהֵי סְפַרְוַיִם הֵנַע וְעִוָּה כִּי־הִצִּילוּ אֶת־שֹׁמְרוֹן מִיָּדִי׃ לה מִי בְּכָל־אֱלֹהֵי הָאֲרָצוֹת אֲשֶׁר־הִצִּילוּ אֶת־אַרְצָם מִיָּדִי כִּי־יַצִּיל יְהוָה אֶת־יְרוּשָׁלִַם מִיָּדִי׃ לו וְהֶחֱרִישׁוּ הָעָם וְלֹא־עָנוּ אֹתוֹ דָּבָר כִּי־מִצְוַת הַמֶּלֶךְ הִיא לֵאמֹר לֹא תַעֲנֻהוּ׃ לז וַיָּבֹא אֶלְיָקִים בֶּן־חִלְקִיָּה אֲשֶׁר־עַל־הַבַּיִת וְשֶׁבְנָא הַסֹּפֵר וְיוֹאָח בֶּן־אָסָף הַמַּזְכִּיר אֶל־חִזְקִיָּהוּ קְרוּעֵי בְגָדִים וַיַּגִּדוּ לוֹ אֵת דִּבְרֵי רַבְשָׁקֵה׃
יט א וַיְהִי כִּשְׁמֹעַ הַמֶּלֶךְ חִזְקִיָּהוּ וַיִּקְרַע

תרגום

דַחֲלַת חֲמָת וְאַרְפָּד וְאָן דַחֲלַת סְפַרְוַיִם הֲלָא טַלְטִילוּנוּן וְאַגְלִיאוּנוּן אֲרֵי שֵׁיזִיבוּ יַת שֹׁמְרוֹן מִן יְדִי׃ לה מַן בְּכָל דַחֲלַת מְדִינָתָא דְשֵׁיזִיבוּ יַת אַרְעֲהוֹן מִן יְדִי אֲרֵי יְשֵׁיזִיב יְיָ יַת יְרוּשְׁלֶם מִן יְדִי׃ לו וּשְׁתִיקוּ עַמָּא וְלָא אֲתִיבוּ יָתֵיהּ פִּתְגָמָא אֲרֵי תַפְקֵידַת מַלְכָּא הִיא לְמֵימַר לָא תְתִיבוּנֵיהּ׃ לז וַאֲתָא אֶלְיָקִים בַּר חִלְקִיָּה דִּמְמַנָּא עַל בֵּיתָא וְשֶׁבְנָא סָפְרָא וְיוֹאָח בַּר אָסָף דִּמְמַנָּא עַל דָכְרָנַיָּא לְוָת חִזְקִיָּהוּ מְבַזְּעִין לְבוּשֵׁיהוֹן וְחַוִּיאוּ לֵיהּ יַת פִּתְגָמֵי רַבְשָׁקֵה׃ א וַהֲוָה כַּד שְׁמַע מַלְכָּא חִזְקִיָּה וּבְזַע יַת לְבוּשׁוֹהִי

ת״א ויהי כשמוע. (מ״ק כג):

רד״ק

לד: (לד) הנה ועוה. שמות מדינו׳ או שמות אלהים אחרי׳ ולדעת יונתן פירושו הניע ועוה אותם מארצם שתרג׳ הלא טלטילונון ואגליאונון: כי הצילו את שומרון מידי. בתמיה וכי ה׳ אלהיכם שאתם בוטחי׳ בו הצילו את שומרון מידי שתחשבו שיציל את ירושל׳ מידי וכן הוא אומר בישעיה וכי הצילו בוי״ו שידמה ענין תמיהה וי״מ וכי הצילו העגלים את שמרון מידי: (לז) קרועי בגדים. רז״ל פי׳ כי בעבור ששמער ברכ׳ השם קרעו בגדיהם וסמכו מזה הפ׳ כי כל השומע ברכת ה׳ חייב לקרוע ואותו קרע אינו מתאחה לעולם ואינו חייב לקרוע אלא א״כ שומע הגדוף מישר׳ והם שקרעו ששמעו מרבשקה לפי שקבלה היתה בידם כי רבשקח ישראל מומר היה ומה חירוף אמר רבשקה שקרעו בגדיהם כששמעו שאמר מי בכל אלהי הארצו׳ אשר הצילו את ארצם מידי כי יציל ה׳ את ירושל׳ מידי אין לך גידוף גדול מזה שהשוה בורא הכל לאלהי עץ ואבן והסיר היכולת מהבורא וכן האל ית׳ השב לו דבריו לחירוף וגידוף ואמר עליו את מי חרפת וגדפת ואמר ביד מלאכיך חרפת ה׳: (א) ויקרע את בגדיו. על מה שהגידו

רש״י

דגן והירוש. זו אפריקי: (לד) הנע ועוה. אותם מלך אשור החריבם והגלם: כי הצילו את שומרון. והשומרונים היו עובדים את אלהי ארם שהיו שכיניהם: (לז) קרועי

מנחת שי

להיות חסר בלא נחתב זה עם ז׳ מלאים בסדר מקץ: (לז) ויבא אליקים וגו׳ ויגידו לו דברי רבשקה. אי מסכתא נסחי דכתוב בהו לו את דברי. הם אליבא דמדינחאי אבל למערבאי כתיב ויגידו לו דברי וכן מלאתי בספרי׳ המדוייקים ובאחד מהם נכתב בלדו יפה חסר את:

רלב״ג

אותה מעוזריהם והיה מקרב אותם אליו ואל עמו: (לד) חמת וארפד ספרוים הנע ועוה. הם שמות מדינות ויעיד ע״ז מ״ש אחר זה ומלך לעיר ספרוים הנע ועוה: כי הצילו את שומרון מידי. הנה קלר בזה המחמר בהתחלתו קלר הכונה ובסופו קלר הכונה והרלון בו איה אלהי חמת וארפד האם הצילו חמת וארפד מידי איה אלהי ספרוים הנע ועוה האם הצילו אלו המדינות מידי איה אלהי שומרון כי הצילו את שומרון מידי והנה הקים ודמה הש״י לאלו האלילים אשר הם הבל ואין בם מועיל ועל זה קרעו בגדיהם השומעי׳ דבריו מפני זה בקרף

מצודת ציון

(לד)הנע. מלשון נע: ועוה. מל׳ עוות ועקום:(לו) והחרישו. שתקו:

מצודת דוד

ר״ל כל אלוה את ארלו: (לד) הנע ועוה. הניעם ממקומ׳ והעקימם: כי הצילו. וכי אלהי שומרון הצילו את שומרון מידי: (לז) קרועי בגדים. על ששמעו דברי רבשקה המחרף ומגדף כלפי מעל להדמותו לאלהי עמי הארלות:

1. **that he rent his garments**—since his emissaries reported to him that Rabshakeh had blasphemed the Name of God [*Redak* from *San.* ibid.].

and covered himself with sack-

34. Where are the gods of Hamath and Arpad, where are the gods of Sepharvaim? He exiled them and twisted them. Now, did they save Samaria from my hand? 35. Who are they among all the gods of the lands who saved their land from my hand, that the Lord should save Jerusalem from my hand?'" 36. And the people remained silent and did not answer him even one word, for it was the king's order, saying, "Do not answer him." 37. And Eliakim the son of Hilkiah who was appointed over the palace and Shebna the scribe and Joah the son of Asaph the recorder, came to Hezekiah, with torn garments, and they related to him the words of Rabshakeh.

19

1. And it was when king Hezekiah heard that he rent

king of Assyria assuming that the inhabitants of both Samaria and Jerusalem were idolators. They supplied all the idolatrous nations with their images. He quotes the king of Assyria saying, "(Is. 10:10, 11) As I was able to seize the idolatrous kingdoms, whose graven images were from Jerusalem and from Samaria, is it not so, that as I have done to Samaria and her idols, so will I do to Jerusalem and her idols?" Perhaps he made that statement at this point, but Jeremiah, the author of Kings, did not wish to dwell on these blasphemies [*Daath Soferim*].

R. Joseph Kara, too, explains that Rabshakeh meant that the idols with which Samaria and Jerusalem had been supplying the nations, saved neither the nations who worshipped them nor Samaria. Why should they save Jerusalem?

37. **with torn garments**—*because they heard blasphemies of the Name of God* [*Rashi* from *Sanhedrin* 60a].

The Talmud learns from here that if one hears God's Name blasphemed, he is required to rend his clothing, and never completely repair the rend. This applies only if one hears blasphemy from a Jew, not from a non-Jew. Rabshakeh was, as mentioned before, an apostate Jew. Therefore, his blasphemy required rending the garments.

His blasphemy constituted his comparing God to the pagan deities, by saying that He would not be able to save Jerusalem anymore than they were able to save their worshippers [*Redak*].

את־בְּגָדָיו וַיִּתְכַּס בַּשָּׂק וַיָּבֹא בֵּית
יְהוָה׃ ב וַיִּשְׁלַח אֶת־אֶלְיָקִים אֲשֶׁר־
עַל־הַבַּיִת וְשֶׁבְנָא הַסֹּפֵר וְאֵת זִקְנֵי
הַכֹּהֲנִים מִתְכַּסִּים בַּשַּׂקִּים אֶל־יְשַׁעְיָהוּ
הַנָּבִיא בֶּן־אָמוֹץ׃ ג וַיֹּאמְרוּ אֵלָיו כֹּה
אָמַר חִזְקִיָּהוּ יוֹם־צָרָה וְתוֹכֵחָה וּנְאָצָה
הַיּוֹם הַזֶּה כִּי־בָאוּ בָנִים עַד־מַשְׁבֵּר
וְכֹחַ אַיִן לְלֵדָה׃ ד אוּלַי יִשְׁמַע יְהוָה
אֱלֹהֶיךָ אֵת ׀ כָּל־דִּבְרֵי רַבְשָׁקֵה אֲשֶׁר
שְׁלָחוֹ מֶלֶךְ־אַשּׁוּר ׀ אֲדֹנָיו לְחָרֵף
אֱלֹהִים חַי וְהוֹכִיחַ בַּדְּבָרִים אֲשֶׁר

לְבוּשׁוֹהִי וְאִתְכַּסִּי בְסַקָּא וַעֲל לְבֵית מַקְדְּשָׁא דַיְיָ׃ ב וּשְׁלַח יָת אֶלְיָקִים דִּי מְמַנָּא עַל בֵּיתָא וְשֶׁבְנָא סָפְרָא וְסָבֵי כָהֲנַיָּא כַּד מְכַסַּן סַקַּיָּא לְוָת יְשַׁעְיָהוּ נְבִיָּא בַּר אָמוֹץ׃ ג וַאֲמָרוּ לֵיהּ כִּדְנַן אֲמַר חִזְקִיָּהוּ יוֹם עָקָא וְחִיסוּדִין וְנִיאוּצָא יוֹמָא הָדֵין אֲרֵי אֲקִיפְתָּנָא עָקָא כְּאִתְּתָא דְיָתְבָא עַל מַתְבְּרָא וְחֵיל לֵית לַהּ לְמֵילַד׃ ד מָאִים שְׁמִיעַ קֳדָם יְיָ אֱלָהָךְ יָת כָּל פִּתְגָמֵי רַבְשָׁקֵה דִשְׁלְחֵיהּ מַלְכָּא דְאַתּוּר רִבּוֹנֵיהּ לְחַסָּדָא עַמָּא דַיְיָ קַיָּמָא וְיַעֲבֵּיד פּוּרְעָנוּתָא עַל כָּל פִּתְגָמַיָּא דִשְׁמָעִין קדמוהי

רש"י

בגדים. על ששמעו גידופי השם: (ג) **והוכחה.** שהרשעים מתווכחין ומראין פנים לדבריהם לאמר לנו הכח והגבורה: **בנים.** ישראל: **עד משבר.** עד צרה הדומה לאשה יושבת על משבר ואין בה כח לילד: **משבר.** שם מושב אשה הכורעת לילד: (ד) **והוכיח.** אישפרובי"ר בלע"ז הראה

רד"ק

לו שחירף וגידף רבשקה הש"י שמו: ויתכס בשק. לענו' **עצמו** שירחם האל עליו ועל העם: (ג) יום צרה ותוכחה **ונאצה.** תוכחה שרבשקה הוכיחנו בדברי הפחד וחרופין או פי' שהאל מוכיח אותנו על עונותינו. ונאצ'. שנאץ רבשקה האל וי"ת יום עקא וחיסודין וניאוצא: באו בני' עד משבר. המשיל הצרה לאשה אשר יאחזוה חבליה ובא הבן עד המשבר והו' הרח' מקום יציאת הולד **כי** אז **חבליה** יותר קשים כשהולד קרוב לצאת ואם אין כח ליולד' לחזק עצמ' להוליד הולד חנה היא בחוזק חבליה בלי תקוה למנוחה כן הצרה גדול' עלינו **ואין לנו** כח לצאת ממנה אם לא יעזרנו האל: ללידה. שם תואר ות"י הפסו' כן **ארי אקיפנ'** עקא כאתתא דיתב' על מתבר' וחיל לית לה למילד: (ד) לחרף אלהים חי. כמו שאו' **כי יציל** את ירושל' מידי וי"ת לחסד' עמא דה' קיים': והוכיח בדברים.

רלב"ג

וגדף רבשקה הש"י והמלך קרע בגדיו ונתכס' בבגדי שק לצער עצמו כדי שירחם הש"י עליו ובא בית ה' להתפלל שם: (ג) יום צרה ותוכחה ונאצה היום הזה. ר"ל שהוא יום צרה חזקה מפני מה שגזר מלך אשור להשחית את ירושל' עד שמרוב הצרות הנה המעוכרות הכורעו' ללדת אין להן כח ללדת ואע"פ שבאו בנים עד משבר והוא המקום מהרחם שיהיה בו הולד בעת יציאתו ועיקו מרחם והוא ג"כ

מנחת שי

יט (ב) ושבנא הספר. בהרבה מדוייקים חסר וא"ו ומילתא פסיקתא **נמסר** בשמואל ב' סימן ט' סופר הסופר כל הנביאים חסר בר **מן ב' מלאים**

מצודת דוד

יט (ג) ותוכחה. האויב התווכח להשתבח בהצלחתו ואומר ידי רמה: ונאצה. מנאץ את ה' בדברי חרוף: כי באו בנים. דימה בני הדור לאשה הכורעת ללדת בנים ויושבת על המשבר ואין בה כח להוליד הבנים: (ד) אולי ישמע ה'. הלואי יתן לב לשמוע: והוכיח. התווכח בדברים כאשר שמע ה': ונשאת. כאומר לזה שאלתי מעמך שתשא תפלה לה': השארית הנמצאה, שאריח

מצודת ציון

יט ג () ותוכחה. מלשון ויכוח וברור דברים: **ונאצה.** ענין בזיון כמו כי נאצו האנשים (ש"א ב'): משבר. הוא מקום מושב הילדות וכן במשבר בנים (הושע י"ג): (ד) אולי. הלואי כמו אולי

Alternatively, **and may He castigate for the words that the Lord your God has heard** [*Redak, Jonathan*].

his garments, and covered himself with sackcloth, and came to the house of the Lord.
2. And he sent Eliakim who was appointed over the palace, and Shebna the scribe and the elders of the priests, covered with sackcloth, to Isaiah the prophet, the son of Amoz.
3. And they said to him, "So has Hezekiah said, 'This day is a day of distress, debate, and blasphemy, for the children have come as far as the birthstool and there is no strength to give birth.
4. Perhaps the Lord your God will take note of all the words of Rabshakeh whom the king of Assyria, his master, sent to blaspheme the living God, and he brought proof with the words that

cloth—to mortify himself, so that God would pity him and his people [*Redak*].

3. **and debate**—*that the wicked are debating and showing evidence to their words, saying, "We have power and strength"* [*Rashi*].

Alternatively, this may be rendered as *reproof,* i.e. a day when the Almighty is reproving us, or that Rabshakeh is reproving us with his threats [*Redak*].

Jonathan renders: disgrace.

children—*Israel.*

as far as the birthstool—*as far as a distress analogous to a woman sitting on the birthstool, and she has no strength to give birth.* The Hebrew is מַשְׁבֵּר—*the name of the seat* used *by a woman who kneels to give birth* [*Rashi*].

for the birth—[*Redak*]. *Jonathan* renders: to give birth.

Just as in the case of a woman in labor, when the fetus comes to the birth canal, her pains become the strongest, and if she has no strength to give birth, she will have no relief from them, so are we experiencing a great distress, and we have no way of extricating ourselves therefrom unless God helps us [*Redak*].

4. **Perhaps**—[*Jonathan*]. Others render: *If only* [*Mezudath Zion*]. See *Rashi,* Gen. 50:15.

to blaspheme the living God—by saying, "will the Lord save Jerusalem from my hand?" *Jon.* paraphrases: to disgrace the people of the living God [*Redak*].

and he brought proof with the words—*éprover in French, to prove. He showed evidence to his statement, that he prospered wherever he went* [*Rashi, Mezudoth*].

I.e. he proved with his blasphemous words that God would not save Jerusalem [*Ralbag, Redak*].

שְׁמַע יְהוָה אֱלֹהֶיךָ וְנָשָׂאתָ תְפִלָּה
בְּעַד הַשְּׁאֵרִית הַנִּמְצָאָה: ה וַיָּבֹאוּ
עַבְדֵי הַמֶּלֶךְ חִזְקִיָּהוּ אֶל־יְשַׁעְיָהוּ:
ו וַיֹּאמֶר לָהֶם יְשַׁעְיָהוּ כֹּה תֹאמְרוּן אֶל־
אֲדֹנֵיכֶם כֹּה ׀ אָמַר יְהוָה אַל־תִּירָא
מִפְּנֵי הַדְּבָרִים אֲשֶׁר שָׁמַעְתָּ אֲשֶׁר
גִּדְּפוּ נַעֲרֵי מֶלֶךְ־אַשּׁוּר אֹתִי: ז הִנְנִי נֹתֵן
בּוֹ רוּחַ וְשָׁמַע שְׁמוּעָה וְשָׁב לְאַרְצוֹ
וְהִפַּלְתִּיו בַּחֶרֶב בְּאַרְצוֹ: ח וַיָּשָׁב
רַבְשָׁקֵה וַיִּמְצָא אֶת־מֶלֶךְ אַשּׁוּר נִלְחָם
עַל־לִבְנָה כִּי שָׁמַע כִּי נָסַע מִלָּכִישׁ:

תרגום

קֳדָם יְיָ אֱלָהָךְ וְתִתְחַנַּן בִּצְלוֹ עַל שְׁאָרָא הָדֵין דְאִשְׁתְּאַר: ה וַאֲתוֹ עַבְדֵי מַלְכָּא חִזְקִיָּהוּ לְוָת יְשַׁעְיָהוּ: ו וַאֲמַר לְהוֹן יְשַׁעְיָהוּ כִּדְנַן תֵּימְרוּן לְרִבּוֹנְכוֹן כִּדְנַן אֲמַר יְיָ לָא תִדְחַל מִן קֳדָם פִּתְגָמַיָּא דִשְׁמַעְתָּ דְחַסִידוּ עוּלֵימֵי מַלְכָּא דְאַתּוּר קֳדָמַי: ז הָא אֲנָא יָהֵיב בֵּיהּ רוּחָא וְיִשְׁמַע בְּסוּרָא וִיתוּב לְאַרְעֵיהּ וְאַפְּלֵינֵיהּ בְּחַרְבָּא בְּאַרְעֵיהּ: ח וְתָב רַבְשָׁקֵה וְאַשְׁכַּח יָת מַלְכָּא דְאַתּוּר מַגִיחַ קְרָבָא עַל לִבְנָה אֲרֵי שְׁמַע אֲרֵי נטל

רד"ק

רבשקה הוכיח בדברי גדופין או פירושו האל יוכיח בדברים אשר שמע וכן ת"י ויעביד פורענותא על כל פתגמי' דשמעין קדמוהי: (ו) נערי. עבדי כי המשרת יקר' נער והם רבשקה והביריו: (ז) רוח. רצון: ושמע שמועה. זהו ששמע שמלך כוש יצא להלח' אתו: ושב לארצו. כי מלך כיש יצא לארץ מלך אשור להלח' בארצו בעוד שהיה מלך אשור בארץ ישראל ואני אתן בו רוח שישוב לארצו להלהם עם מלך כוש ויניח מלחמ' העיר הזאת ואח"כ אפילנו בחרב בארצו וזה היה אחר שישב ממלחמ' כיש לירושל' ונגף מחנהו על ידי המלאך ושב לארצו ושם נפל בחרב כלו שכתוב אבל נבואת המגפה לא אמר להם ישעיה בפי' ואין לשאול טעם למעשה האל ית' כי ח' נורא עלילו' למה לא נגפו אז אלא עד שהלך להלח' עם

רש"י

פנים לדבריו שהלאיח בכל אשר הלך: (ז) ושמע שמועה. ויעלה מעליכם ושב לארצו ולא מהמת השמועה אלא לאחר זמן ישוב לארצו בבושת פנים והפלתיו שם בחרב. ומה היא השמועה וישמע אל תרהקה שמע שילא תרהקה להלחם עמו ועלה מעל ירושלם והלך לכוש ונלחם עם תרהקה ופוט ומצרים שעמו ונלחם ונטל חמדת אוצרותיהם ובא לירושלים ונפל שם הוא שאמר ישעיה (מ"ה י"ד) יגיע מצרים וסחר

מנחת שי

ולים דין נגווייסו: (ז) הנני נתן בו רוח. דמלכים חסר דישעיה מלא:

רלב"ג

יום תוכח' ונאלה כי הוכיח רבשקה בדברי נאלה וחרוף וגדוף שהש"י לא יציל את ירושל' מיד מלך אשור וזה אמרו אחר זה והוכיח בדברי' אשר שמע ה' אלהיך: (ו) נערי מלך אשור. עבדי מלך אשור: (ז) הנני נותן בו רוח. ר"ל רצון: ושמע שמועה ושב לארצו. הנה השמועה היתה בשמע על תרהקה מלך כוש שילא אליו להלחם אתו ואולי הגיעו הש"י משם כדי שילאו נוהמלודה בזמן שהוא ויבימו לעיר מה שילטרך להם מהמזון מחוץ ואחר זה ישוב לארצו אחר היות המגפה במחנו ושם בארצו יפול בחרב כי בניו יהרגוהו והנה

מצודת ציון

ירלה ר' בעניי (ש"ב ט"ז): והוכיח. נתוכה: (ו) גדפו. חרפו: (ז) רוח. רלון כמו אל אשר יהיה שמה הרוח ללכת (יחזקאל א'):

מצודת דוד

ישראל הנמלאה בירושלים כי כבר כבש כל ערי הבלורות שביהודה: (ז) נותן בו רוח. אעיר רלונו ללכת מפה כאשר ישמע שמועה היא

thought of lending credulity to the rumor. Second, he returned to his land, taking his entire army with him. He did not leave any portion of his vast army to lay siege to Jerusalem [*Malbim,* Isaiah 37:7].

return to his land—of his own volition, lest the Jews believe that it was their military power that caused him to withdraw [*Daath Soferim*].

Alternatively, he alone will return to his land without his massive army. Here the prophet alludes to Sennacherib's miraculous defeat, when the angel will smite his entire camp and leave them all corpses [*Abarbanel*].

8. **against Libnah**—another Judean city. Some say that he encountered Tirhakah in Libnah, and

the Lord your God heard, and you shall offer up a prayer for the remnant that is found.'" 5. And King Hezekiah's servants came to Isaiah. 6. And Isaiah said to them, "So shall you say to your master, 'So has the Lord said, "Have no fear of the words that you have head, that the servants of the king of Assyria blasphemed Me. 7. Behold I will imbue him with a desire, and he will hear a rumor and return to his land, and I will cause him to fall by the sword in his land.'" 8. And Rabshakeh returned and found the king of Assyria waging war against Libnah, for he heard that he had left Lachish.

that is found—in Jerusalem, for all the other fortified cities had already been conquered [*Mezudath David*].

6. **the servants**—Heb. נְעָרֵי, usually youths [*Redak, Ralbag*].

The emissaries were actually high officials, not properly referred to as servants or youths. God commanded Hezekiah not to respect their exalted position, but to look at them as mere servants or youths [*Daath Soferim*].

7. **I will imbue him with a desire**—lit. I will place a spirit in him. The word רוּחַ, *spirit,* is sometimes used in the sense of desire. See Ezekiel 1:12 [*Mezudath Zion, Redak*].

and he will hear a rumor—*and he will withdraw from you and return to his land.* He will *not* return *because of the rumor, but after a while he will return shamefacedly, and I will cause him to fall there by the sword. Now what was the rumor?* "(v. 9) *And he heard* [*a rumor*] about Tirhakah." He heard that Tirhakah had gone out to wage war against him. Consequently, he withdrew from Jerusalem and went to Cush, and waged war with Tirhakah and Put and Egypt, who were with him. He defeated him and took their most coveted treasures, and came to Jerusalem, where he fell. In reference to this, Isaiah stated, "(45:14) The toil of Egypt and the merchandise of Cush . . . will pass by you . . ." [*Rashi* (See above 18:14)].

Redak explains that the words, "and he will return to his land," refer to Sennacherib's return to Assyria to defend it against Tirhakah, king of Cush. His ultimate downfall, i.e. his assassination however, would take place after his miraculous defeat outside Jerusalem, and his shameful return to his land. His defeat is not mentioned here by Isaiah [*Redak*].

Malbim explains that Sennacherib's withdrawal from Jerusalem was in itself a series of miracles. First, Sennacherib heard but a rumor, not an official report, that Tirhakah had marched on Assyria. Yet, he believed it. That was the "spirit" God imbued him with, the

ט וישמע אל־תרהקה מלך־כוש לאמר
הנה יצא להלחם אתך וישב וישלח
מלאכים אל־חזקיהו לאמר: י כה
תאמרון אל־חזקיהו מלך־יהודה
לאמר אל־ישאך אלהיך אשר אתה
בטח בו לאמר לא תנתן ירושלם ביד
מלך אשור: יא הנה | אתה שמעת את
אשר עשו מלכי אשור לכל־הארצות
להחרימם ואתה תנצל: יב ההצילו
אתם אלהי הגוים אשר שחתו אבותי
את־גוזן ואת־חרן ורצף ובני־עדן
אשר בתלאשר: יג איו מלך־חמת
ומלך ארפד ומלך לעיר ספרוים הנע

תרגום

נטל מלכיש: ט ושמע
על תרהקה מלכא דכוש
למימר הא נפק לאגחא
קרבא עמך ותב ושלח
אזגדין לות חזקיה
למימר: י כדנן תימרון
לחזקיה מלך שבטא
דבית יהודה למימר לא
יטעינך אלהך דאת
רחיץ ביה למימר לא
תתמסר ירושלם ביד
מלכא דאתור: יא הא
את שמעתא ית דעבדו
מלכי דאתור לכל
מדינתא לגמרותהון
ואת מדמי לאשתיזבא:
יב השיזבא יתהון דחלת
עממיא דחבילו אבהתי
ית גוזן וית חרן ורצף
ובני עדן דבתלסר:
יג אן מלכא דחמת
ומלכא דארפד ומלכא
דלקרתא ספרוים הא
טלטילונון

רש"י

כוש וגו' עליך יעבורו וגו': (ט) וישב וישלח מלאכים. להודיע שאינו שב לארצו אלא להלחם עם כוש ולהזור כאן: (יב) עדן. שם מדינה: (יג) הנע ועוה. אותן מלך אשור לירושלם עמו להפחיד יושבי ירושלם עוד: (יג) איו מלך חמת. על האלהים אמ' אשר לא יוכלו להציל ארצות עובדיהם וגם

רד"ק

מלך כוש ואח"כ שב לירושלם והטעם הנראה לנו בזה כדי שיהיה להם לישראל בזת כוש ומצרים ועוד שיראו כוש ומצרים הנפלאות שעשה לאוהביו ולדורשי שמו כי מלך אשור נצח אותם וכל הארצות כבש ובירושל' נגף בלא חרב ובלא חנית והאל נתן בלב מלך אשור להביא חיל מלך כוש ומצרים

רלב"ג

כשקה שב אל אדוניו אחרי עשותו שליחותו ומצא מלך אשור נלחם אלא לנה שהיתה מישראל כי שם בא אליו מלך כוש להלחם עמו ומשם שב מלך אשור אל המלור שלר בו על ירושל' ושלח מלאכים אל חזקיה לאמר כמו הדברים הראשונים ודמה ממה שנאמר אחר זה שהם היו מלאכים

מצודת דוד

שמועת תרהקה מלך כוש: וישב לארצו. סוף הדבר יהיה שישוב לארצו: בפחי נפש ובארצו אפיל אותו בחרב: (ט) וישמע אל תרהקה. ר"ל קבל דבריו ויצא גם הוא לקראתו למלחמה: וישב. שלח שוב מלאכים להודיע שאינו מבטל נגמרי כ"א על מנת לשוב: (יא) ואתה. וכי אתה תנצל בתמיה: (יב) ההצילו. וכי אלהי העמים הצילו את העמים: (יג) לעיר ספרוים. לפי שהיתה גדולה

מצודת ציון

(י) ישיאך. יסית ויפתה אותך:

to his view, they were to be vanquished and humbled, not appealed to. It appears that Rabshakeh's appeal had been his own fabrication, not Sennacherib's orders. (See above 18:32). Additionally, Rabshakeh had added his appeal to Hezekiah to abandon his reliance upon Egypt and upon his own military prowess. Sennacherib attempted only to destroy Hezekiah's reliance on Divine Providence [*Abarbanel*].

12. **Eden**—*the name of a province* [*Rashi*].

13. **Where are the king of Hamath**—In addition to destroying the nations who worshipped these

9. And he heard [a rumor] about Tirhakah the king of Cush, saying, "He has gone out to wage war against you." And he again sent emissaries to Hezekiah, saying, 10. "So shall you say to Hezekiah the king of Judah, saying, 'Let your God in Whom you trust, not delude you, saying, 'Jerusalem shall not be given into the hand[s] of the king of Assyria. 11. Behold you have heard what the kings of Assyria have done to all the lands to destroy them. Now will you be saved? 12. Did the gods of the nations whom my forefathers destroyed—Gozan and Haran, and Rezeph and the children of Eden which is in Telassar save them? 13. Where are the king of Hamath and the king of Arpad, and the king of the city of Sepharvaim? He exiled [them] and twisted [them]!

vanquished him there [*Ralbag, Abarbanel*].

According to them, verses 8 and 9 are not in chronological order, since Sennacherib went to Libnah after he heard the rumor of Tirhakah. We may, however, render: And he *had* heard a rumor concerning Tirhakah . . . Additionally, according to this interpretation, he did not return to his land to wage war with Tirhakah. *Redak*'s interpretation of v. 7 cannot conform with that view.

Now, why did God lure Sennacherib away from Jerusalem and not cause his immediate downfall then and there? *Ralbag* replies that God wished to give the besieged Jerusalemites an opportunity to leave the city in order to obtain food and other necessities.

Redak explains that Sennacherib was lured to battle Cush and Egypt so that the Jews would benefit from the plunder of these nations. Moreover, God wished to demonstrate to the Cushites and the Egyptians the wonders He would perform for His beloved people. He wished to show them that the mighty armies that had vanquished them and many other nations, would be destroyed instantly with the aid of neither sword nor spear, but by means of a divinely visited plague. Moreover, the Lord inspired Sennacherib to bring all his captives to Jerusalem, in order to frighten the Jews more intensely. (Perhaps then they would turn more readily to God and repent of their transgressions.)

9. **and he again sent messengers**—*to notify him that he was returning to his land only to wage war with Cush, and then to return here* [*Rashi*].

to Hezekiah—not to the people. Sennacherib, in his arrogance, did not appeal to the people. According

וָעִוָּה׃ יד וַיִּקַּח חִזְקִיָּהוּ אֶת־הַסְּפָרִים
מִיַּד הַמַּלְאָכִים וַיִּקְרָאֵם וַיַּעַל בֵּית
יְהוָה וַיִּפְרְשֵׂהוּ חִזְקִיָּהוּ לִפְנֵי יְהוָה׃
טו וַיִּתְפַּלֵּל חִזְקִיָּהוּ לִפְנֵי יְהוָה וַיֹּאמַר
יְהוָה אֱלֹהֵי יִשְׂרָאֵל יֹשֵׁב הַכְּרֻבִים
אַתָּה־הוּא הָאֱלֹהִים לְבַדְּךָ לְכֹל
מַמְלְכוֹת הָאָרֶץ אַתָּה עָשִׂיתָ אֶת־
הַשָּׁמַיִם וְאֶת־הָאָרֶץ׃ טז הַטֵּה יְהוָה ׀
אָזְנְךָ וּשְׁמָע פְּקַח יְהוָה עֵינֶיךָ וּרְאֵה
וּשְׁמַע אֵת דִּבְרֵי סַנְחֵרִיב אֲשֶׁר שְׁלָחוֹ
לְחָרֵף אֱלֹהִים חָי׃ יז אָמְנָם יְהוָה
הֶחֱרִיבוּ מַלְכֵי אַשּׁוּר אֶת־הַגּוֹיִם וְאֶת־
אַרְצָם׃ יח וְנָתְנוּ אֶת־אֱלֹהֵיהֶם בָּאֵשׁ כִּי

תרגום

טלטילונון ואגליאונון׃
יד ונסיב חזקיהו ית
אגרתא מיד אזגדיא
וקרינן וסליק לבית
מקדשא דיי ופרסינן
חזקיהו קדם יי׃ טו וצלי
חזקיהו קדם יי ואמר
יי אלהא דישראל
דשכנתיה שריא עיל מן
כרוביא את הוא יי ולית
בר מנך לכל מלכות
ארעא את עבדתא ית
שמיא וית ארעא׃ טז גלי
קדמך יי ודון ושמיע
קדמך יי ואתפרע ביד
פורענותא על כל
פתגמי דסנחריב
דשלחיה לחסדא עמא
דיי קימא׃ יז בקושטא
יי אחריבו מלכי אתור
ית עממיא וית ארעהון׃
יח ומוקדין ית טעותהון
בנורא

רד"ק קמץ בז"ק

המלכים איה הם שלא עמדו לפני כלם ואמר עם ספרוים לעיר שהיתה גדולה מכלם: (יד) ויפרשהו. אחד מהספרי׳ או כל א׳ מהם ואדוני אבי ז"ל פי׳ ויפרשהו על הספר שבו הי׳ גדוף האלהים: (טז) אשר שלחו. שלח המדבר החירוף:

רש"י

(יז) אמנם. אמת הוא שהחריבו מלכי אשור את העמים ונתנו את אלהיהם באש:

מנחת שי

(טז) הטה ה׳ אזנך ושמע. הוא״ו במאריך וקצת ספרים הסי״ן בגוא לבדו ובמקצתם בגוא ופתח ועיין מה שכתוב בפרשת בלק על פסוק קום בלק ושמע ושופטים ה׳ על ושבה שביך: ושמע את דברי סנחריב. בדפוס ישן כתוב את כל דברי וכן בספר ה׳ כ״י היה כתוב בתחלה את דברי ואחר כך הוסיף הסופר מלת כל וכן מתורגם על כל פתגמי ועולם בכל שאר ספרים אין כאן מלת כל רק הוא בספר ישעיה כמו שנזכר במסורת שם וכן בתרגום מדפוס ישן כתוב על פתגמי: אשר שלחו. בס״א כ״י טעה הסופר בין שלח לשלחו ואין ספק בזה שכתוב שלחו וזהו גם כן אחד מהחילופים שיש בין שני הספרים:

רלב"ג

הלשונות ושהבקשה אמר הדברים האלו: (יד) ויפרשהו. ר״ל הספר שהיה בו אלו החרופין והגדופין כי הם נשאו ספרים על זה ממלך אשור ועוד דברו בפיהם אלו החירופין ולזה אמר אחר זה את דברי סנחריב אשר שלחו לחרף אלהים חיים: (טו) ויתפלל חזקיהו. רוצה לומר ה׳ אלהי ישראל אשר השגחתו דבקה בהם ושכינתו תגלה

מצודת ציון

(טז) פקח. פתח כמו אפקח את עיני (זכריה י״ב):

מצודת דוד

ותשובה אמר בה לעיל: (יד) הספרים. כי במכתב שלח הדברים האלה: ויפרשהו. פרש כל אחד ואחד: (טו) הכרובים. שעל הכפורת אשר על הארון. וכאומר ואיך א״כ תמסור בידו את ירושלים ויבאו הכרובים ביד לר: (טז) אשר שלחו. את המלאך המכים הספרים: (יז) אמנם ה׳. אתה ה׳ הנה אמת הוא שהחריבו את העמים: (יח) כי לא אלהים המה. אבל כ״ז היה בעבור שאין בהם

doms of the earth—and Sennacherib is not the "great king" he calls himself [*Abarbanel*].

You made the heavens and the earth—from absolutely nothing. Destroying Sennacherib with his hosts presents no difficulty for You [*Abarbanel*].

who sent him—i.e. the messenger who spoke these blasphemous words [*Redak*].

Apparently, Sennacherib sent his message both written and oral. For this reason, Hezekiah prayed to God to both listen and to see.

17. **Indeed**—*It is true that the*

14. And Hezekiah took the letters from the hand of the messengers and read them; he went up to the house of the Lord, and Hezekiah spread it out before the Lord. 15. And Hezekiah prayed before the Lord and said, "O Lord God of Israel, Who dwells between the cherubim, You alone are the God of all the kingdoms of the earth. You made the heavens and the earth. 16. O Lord, incline Your ear and listen, O Lord, open Your eyes and see. And listen to the words of Sennacherib, who sent him to blaspheme the living God. 17. Indeed, O Lord, the kings of Assyria have destroyed the nations and their land.

18. And they have committed their gods to the fire, for

deities, the kings were not able to resist the power of Assyria. And as evidence, where are the king of Hamath and the king of Arpad . . .? [*Redak*].

the city of Sepharvaim—i.e. the metropolis of Sepharvaim, the largest city of the nation [*Redak*].

he exiled and twisted—I.e. *the king of Assyria exiled and twisted them* [*Rashi* (See above 18:34.)].

14. **the letters . . . read them . . . spread it out**—We may explain that Hezekiah spread out each of the letters before the Lord, hence the singular, or he spread out one of the letters, i.e. the one containing blasphemous statements [*Redak*].

Since this letter blasphemed the Name of God, he spread it out in the house of God [*Abarbanel*].

Obviously, Hezekiah was concerned only with the letter that blasphemed God, not with the other letters, those that belittled his military prowess. According to this, it is possible that the other letters contained the entire argument presented by Rabshakeh. The author is concerned, however, only with the one blasphemous letter, which Hezekiah spread out before the Almighty to pray for His honor. In the Book of Isaiah, we find, "(37:14) and he read *it*," which *Jonathan* renders: and he read one of them. This indicates that Hezekiah merely skimmed through the other letters, or that the author of Isaiah is not interested in what he did with the other letters. The important point here is that Hezekiah read the one letter in which Sennacherib blasphemed the Name of God.

15. **"O Lord God of Israel**—Since You are God of Israel, it is proper that You take pity on Your people Israel [*Abarbanel*].

Who dwells between the cherubim—Since your Shechinah dwells between the cherubim in the Holy of Holies, how can You permit Sennacherib to destroy it? [*Abarbanel*].

You alone are God of all the king-

לֹא אֱלֹהִים הֵמָּה כִּי אִם־מַעֲשֵׂה יְדֵי־
אָדָם עֵץ וָאֶבֶן וַיְאַבְּדוּם: יט וְעַתָּה יְהוָה
אֱלֹהֵינוּ הוֹשִׁיעֵנוּ נָא מִיָּדוֹ וְיֵדְעוּ כָּל־
מַמְלְכוֹת הָאָרֶץ כִּי אַתָּה יְהוָה אֱלֹהִים
לְבַדֶּךָ: כ וַיִּשְׁלַח יְשַׁעְיָהוּ בֶן־אָמוֹץ אֶל־
חִזְקִיָּהוּ לֵאמֹר כֹּה־אָמַר יְהוָה אֱלֹהֵי
יִשְׂרָאֵל אֲשֶׁר הִתְפַּלַּלְתָּ אֵלַי אֶל־
סַנְחֵרִב מֶלֶךְ־אַשּׁוּר שָׁמָעְתִּי: כא זֶה
הַדָּבָר אֲשֶׁר־דִּבֶּר יְהוָה עָלָיו בָּזָה לְךָ
לָעֲגָה לְךָ בְּתוּלַת בַּת־צִיּוֹן אַחֲרֶיךָ
רֹאשׁ הֵנִיעָה בַּת יְרוּשָׁלִָם: כב אֶת־מִי
חֵרַפְתָּ וְגִדַּפְתָּ וְעַל־מִי הֲרִימוֹתָ קּוֹל
וַתִּשָּׂא מָרוֹם עֵינֶיךָ עַל־קְדוֹשׁ יִשְׂרָאֵל:
כג בְּיַד מַלְאָכֶיךָ חֵרַפְתָּ ׀ אֲדֹנָי וַתֹּאמֶר

בנורא ארי לא טעון
דאית בהון צרוך אינון
אלהין עובד ידי אנשא
אעא ואבנא ואבדונון:
יט וכען יי אלהנא
פרוקנא כען מן ידיה
וידעון כל מלכות ארעא
ארי את יי אלהים לית
בר מנך: כ ושלח
ישעיהו בר אמוץ לות
חזקיהו למימר כדנן
אמר יי אלהא דישראל
דבעיתא מן קדמי על
סנחריב מלכא דאתור
שמיע קדמי: כא דין
פתגמא די מליל יי עלוהי
מבסרא לך מעיקא עלך
מלכות כנשתא דציון
בתרך רישיהון מנידין
עמא דירושלם: כב ית
מן חסידתא וגלית מן
אתרברבתא וקדם מן
ארימתא קלא וזקיפתא
לרומא עינך אמרת
מלין דלא כשרין קדם
קדישא דישראל:
כג ביד אזגדך חסידתא
עמא דיי ואמרת

רד"ק

(כ)אל סנחרב. בעבור סנחריב:(כא)בזה לך. פועל עבר בנחיה"ע ן והו' מלרע שלא כמנהג ברוב: בתולה בת ציון. מלכות כנישתא ד'ציון: בת ירושלם. עמא דירושלם ופי' בתולה כבתולה שלא נכבשה וכן בכ"מ שזוכ' בתול' על עם ועל עדה וזהו עניינו:(כב)על

רלב"ג

ותראה על דבק המופת במקום הכרובים בקדש הקדשים כמו שנהפרסם זה מספורי התורה ונתבאר ג"כ במה שסופר בעניני שלמה וזה לאות כי הש"י השגחתו דבק' בישראל אתה הוא המנהיג לבדך לכל ממלכות הארץ כי אתה שליט להשפיל מלכים ולהקימם והם אין להם מסודר ממערכת הכוכבים לפי שאתה מושל על הכוכבים ועל השפע השופע מהם כי אתה עשית את השמים ואת הארץ: (יט) וידעו כל ממלכו' הארץ כי אתה ה' אלהים לבדך. ר"ל שראוי לנצטוות זה כדי שלא יתהלל שמך והם אין ישראל ראויים שתעשה להם נס: (כא) בזה לך לעגה לך. ר"ל שהיא מבזה ומלעגת על דבריך ואינה יראה מהם כי מהש"י יהיה עזרה בסוף כמו שבאר ולזה גם הניע' ראש אחריך וזה אמר להודיע שאינה צריכה שתירא מאלו הדברים הע"פ שבכבר היו ישראל מתפחדים מאד מהם כמו שקדם: (כב) ותשא מרו' עיניך על קדוש ישראל. ר"ל הנה הגדל' לעבו' מאד עד שהשיאך גודל לבבך לחרף ולגד' מי שהוא בתכלית הרוממו' והוא קדוש ישראל: (כג) הנה ביד מלאכיך חרפת ה' ואמרת כי בגבורתך ורב רכביך עלית לכבוש מרום הרים והם המקומות החזקים הבנויים בהרים:

מצודת דוד

אלהות ולזה האבידם: (כ) אל סנחריב. בעבור דברי סנחריב: (כא) עליו. על סנחריב: בזה לך. בת ציון תבזה אותך ותלעג עליך. וקראה בתולה על כי לא נכבשה עדיין מעולם למשול בה עם אחר כבתולה זו שלא באה ברשות הבעל וכן בתולת בת צידון (ישעיה כ"ג): אחריך. אחרי מפלתך תניע בראשה בדרך לעג: (כב) את מי. למה לא שמת על לבך להבין את מי חרפת: מרום. לגובה רקיע:

blasphemed—It is not necessary to answer you on behalf of the people of Jerusalem, for they mock you. However, it is necessary to answer you concerning your blasphemies. Not only have you insulted and blasphemed Me . . . [*Abarbanel*].

And upon Whom have your raised your voice?— . . . but you have also raised your voice and shouted against Me [*Abarbanel*].

And you have lifted your eyes on

they are not gods, but the handiwork of man, wood and stone, and they destroyed them. 19. And now, O Lord our God, please deliver us from his hand, so that all the kingdoms of the earth may know that You are the Lord God alone." 20. And Isaiah the son of Amoz sent to Hezekiah, saying, "So has the Lord God of Israel said, 'I have heard what you prayed to me concerning Sennacherib, king of Assyria. 21. This is the word that the Lord has spoken about him: 'The virgin daughter of Zion has despised you and has mocked you. The daughter of Jerusalem has shaken her head at you. 22. Whom have you insulted and blasphemed, and upon whom have you raised [your] voice? And you have lifted your eyes on high against the Holy One of Israel. 23. Through your messengers you have insulted the Lord, and you said,

kings of Assyria destroyed the peoples and committed their deities to the fire [*Rashi*].

18. **for they are not gods**—i.e. they have no power [*Jonathan*].

They were committed to the fire because they are not gods . . . therefore, they destroyed them [*Mezudath David*].

In contrast to the "living God" of Israel, Whom Sennacherib blasphemed (v. 16) [*Abarbanel*].

19. **so that all the kingdoms of the earth may know**—I, therefore, beseech You to save us, so that all the nations of the earth will know that You are the Only God, and all others are worthless things [*Abarbanel*].

It is proper for You to save Israel so that Your Name will not be profaned, even if Israel does not deserve to be saved [*Ralbag*].

21. **'The virgin duaghter of Zion**—the kingdom of the community of Zion [*Jonathan*].

Zion is like a virgin, never having been conquered by a foreign power [*Redak, Mezudath David*].

has despised you and has mocked you—You, Sennacherib, should know that although you have threatened Jerusalem, its inhabitants are mocking you, as one who boasts of future achievements when his listener knows that he will die that day. He will mock him and shake his head at him [*Abarbanel*].

This was a message to the people to forget their fears and to expect God's salvation from the threat of Assyrian conquest [*Mezudath David*].

The daughter of Jerusalem—the people of Jerusalem [*Jonathan*].

22. **Whom have you insulted and**

ברכב רכבי אני עליתי מרום הרים
ירכתי לבנון ואכרת קומת ארזיו
מבחור ברשיו ואבואה מלון קצה
יער כרמלו: כד אני קרתי ושתיתי מים
זרים ואחרב בכף פעמי כל יארי מצור

בסגיאות רתיכי אנא סליקית לתקוף כרכיהון אף איחוד בית מקדשהון ואקטול שפר גבריהון מבחר שלטוניהון ואכביש קרית תוקפיהון ואשיצי סגי משריתהון: כד אנא הויתי חפיר גובין ושתי מין נוכראין ומפחית בפרסת רגלי עמא דעמי

ה"א ביד מלאכיך. סנהדרין לד: מלון קצו. שם: אני קרתי. שם: ברב קרי קצו קרי

רד"ק

קדוש ישראל. כמו אל קדוש וכן כתוב בישעיה: (כג) מרום הרי'. ארץ ישר' שהיא גבוה' מכל הארצות והמשיל' ללבנון לפי שהלבנון הוא יער עצים בארץ ישראל נקרא כן ולפי שהמשיל גדולי ישראל שריו וגבוריו לברושים וארזים המשיל הארץ ללבנון ר"ל עליתי על הארץ וכבשתי אותה ועתה אבא לירושלם ולפי שהיא טובה ונכבדת מכל הארץ קרא' מלון קיצו יער כרמלו כי הכרמל הוא טוב מן היער וכי הכרמל הוא מקום זרע ואילני פירות ויער לבנון הוא אילני סרק ומה שקראה מלון בעבור בית המקדש שבה שהוא משכן האל ומלונו ובישעיה מרום קיצו והענין אחד כי בית המקדש במקום גבוה בהר המוריה ומה שאמר קצו כאילו היתה ירושלם קץ כל ארץ ישראל לפי שכבש כל ארץ ישראל זולתי ירושלם כלומר מלון קצו שאין לו עוד על דרך ובא עד קצו ואין עוזר לו ות"ת סליקי' לתקוף כרכיהון וגו' ובדברי רז"ל כתיב מלון קצו וכתיב מרום קצו אמר אותו רשע בתחילה אחריב דירת של מטה ואח"כ אחריב דירה של מעלה: מבחור. בחול' בישעי' מבחר בפתח והענין אחד: (כד) אני קרתי. באתי עד המקור כלו' חפשתי אחר מקור המי' כי לא היו מספיקין לי מרוב חיילותי המים הנמצאים על הארץ וזהו שאמר ואחריב בכף פעמי כל יאורי מצור וקראם זרים לפי שלא היו ידועים ונראים לבני אדם ועל הדרך הזה ת"י הפסוק אנא הויתי חפיר גובין וגו' כבעמוד ויש מפרשים יאורי מציר כמו מצרים לפי שהוא נהר

רש"י

(כג) מרום הרים. הר הבית: ירכתי לבנון. בית המקדש שמלבין עונות: ואכרית קומת ארזיו. לא אשוב עד שאחריבנו: קצו. סופו: יער כרמלו. מליאת ארצו ויופי הדרו: (כד) אני קרתי ושתיתי מים זרים. כלומר התחלתי בכל מעשי וגמרתי כזה הכורה בור ומוצא מים זרים ושותה. מים נובעים קורא זרים לפי שעד הנה לא הכירו בהם: ואחריב בכף פעמי. אם צרתי על עיר הבוטח' בנהרותי' הבאתי עליה גייסות רבות שהוביש יאוריה בשתייתם ושתיית בהמתם ומרמס רגליהם: ואחריב. לשון

מנחת שי

(כג) ביד מלאכיך חרפת | אדני. יש פסוק בין חרפת לאדני להרחיק החירוף כן הוא בפסיקתא דנביאים ובספרים מדוייקים וכן הוא חברו דישעיה: ברכב רכבי. ברב ק': מבחור ברשיו. החי"ת בחולם ובישעיה מ ב ח ר בפתח וסימנהון ראשי כפריהון (פי' תמצא לקמן כ' ג') וכן במסורת מבחור ב' ומצא הדין דמכבים וחברו וכל עיר מ ב ח ו ר דהאי סיפרא סימן ג': מלון קצה. קצו ק' ועין מה שכתוב בישעיה סימן ל"ז ג (כד) כל יארי מצור. פליגי ספרי כ"י אם

רלב"ג

ירכתי לבנון. הם קצות יער הלבנון וכל זה משל לארץ ישראל שהיא גבוה מכל הארצות והיה מתפאר על שכבש רוב ארץ ישראל ולזה אמר ירכתי כי ירושלם היתה באמצע ולא כבש אותה והנה התפאר שיכרות קומת ארזים אשר באמצע היער ובמקום הגבוה יותר ממנו והנה קרא ארזים וברושים המלכות והשרים או העיירות יותר חזקות: ואבואה מלון קצו. ובישעיה כתוב מרום קצו והנה קרא מלון קצו בית המקדש כי הוא קץ וסוף המעלות והרוממות אשר בארץ ישראל ורצה לומר שכבר יחריב בית המקדש ואחר כך יחריב יער המישור אשר לפניו אשר מגדל פירות ולמחיה לרוב הם בני ירושלים: (כד) אני קרתי ושתיתי מים זרים. ר"ל לא היה פלא אם שתיתי מים המוכנים לשתותם אבל אני חפרתי והוצאתי מים זרים אשר לא עלה על לב איש שיוכל לשתות משם מים וזה משל למקומו שכבש בפית כלם חזקים שלא עלה בלב איש שיוכל לכבשם ובכף פעמי לבד בלי השתדלות אחר החרבתי והובשתי כל היאורים אשר בערי המצור והם הערים החזקים שלא יתכן לכבשם כי אם בבניית המצור עליהם ואפשר שיאמר אומר שכבר אמר אני קרתי ושתיתי בעבור חזקיה שסתם המעינות כמו שנזכר בספר ד"ה והבאור הראשון יותר נכון לפי מה שאחשוב:

מצודת ציון

(כג) כרמלו. מקו' שדות וכרמי' משובחים קרוי כרמל: (כד) קרתי. חפרתי אחר מקור והוא מלשון יקרוה עורבי נחל (משלי ל') שהוא ענין נקב ובקוע: זרים. שוטפים כמו זרם מים עבר (חבקוק ג'): ואחריב. מלשון חורב ויובש: פעמי. רגלי: יאורי. ענין נהר

מצודת דוד

(כג) מרום הרים. זה הר הבית: ירכתי לבנון. בסוף יער הלבנון מקום הארזים הגבוהים: קומת ארזיו. ר"ל הגבורים והגבורים: מלון קצו. הוא בה"מ שהוא מלון ומשכן השכינה והיא הקץ מכל הדברים הנחמדים אשר בעולם: יער כרמלו. ר"ל מיטב שבתו וכובד חזקו: (כד) אני קרתי ושתיתי מים. ר"ל מעולם הצלחתי במעשי כמו הכורה באר ומצליח למצוא המקור ושותה מימיו הזרים: ואחריב בכף פעמי. כאשר באתי להלחם בעיר הבטוחה בהוזה

Temple below is "the lodge," in the words of King Solomon, "(Song of Songs 1:13) Between my breasts He will lodge," referring to the Shechinah, which lodges between the two staves of the Holy Ark, which pressed against the *parocheth,* the dividing curtain, like the two breasts of a woman. See I Kings 8:8.

to its farmland forest—In contrast with the forest of Lebanon, whose cedars and cypresses produce no fruit, the farmland forest affords place for sowing seeds and is replete with fruit frees. Likewise, Jerusalem was highly esteemed above the entire land of Judah [*Redak*].

24. **I dug**—I.e. I dug until I came to the sources, קַרְתִּי from מָקוֹר, *a source* [*Redak*].

"With my many chariots I have ascended to the heights of mountains, to the end of the Lebanon, and I will cut down its tallest cedars, its choice cypresses, and I will come to its remotest lodge, to its farmland forest. 24. I dug and drank strange water, and I dry up with the soles of my feet all rivers of the siege."

high—Your expressions and gesticulations have compounded your crime [*Abarbanel*].

Why have you not given thought Who it was Whom you insulted? [*Mezudath David*].

23. **Through your messengers you have insulted the Lord**—Not only have *you* blasphemed, but you have sent others to commit the same sin [*Abarbanel*].

to the heights of mountains—*the Temple mount* [*Rashi*].

to the end of the Lebanon—*the Temple which whitens the sins* (Heb. מַלְבִּין). *Rashi* (see *Gittin* 56b, *Rashi*).

The sacrifices offered up in the Temple would atone for the sins of the people, and figuratively, whiten them, as in the words of the prophet Isaiah, "(1:18) If your sins will be like scarlet, they will become white as snow."

and I will cut down its tallest cedars—*I will not return until I have destroyed it* [*Rashi*].

its remotest lodge—lit. the lodge of *its end* [*Rashi*].

its farmland forest—*the fullness of its land and the beauty of its splendor* [*Rashi*].

Hence, *Rashi* explains the entire verse as referring to the Temple. Alternatively,

to the heights of mountains—*Eretz Israel,* which is higher than all other lands [*Redak, R. Joseph Kara*].

to the end of the Lebanon—Since the Lebanon is a forest in Eretz Israel, and Scripture is referring to the greats of Israel, their princes and mighty warriors as cedar and cypress tress, it refers to the land as the forest of Lebanon. Sennacherib boasts that he has already conquered all the land of Judah except Jerusalem [*Redak*].

and I will come to its remotest lodge—Now I will come to the end of the forest, to its remotest lodge, i.e. now I will complete my conquest when I conquer Jerusalem, the site of the Temple, the lodging place of the Shechinah. In Isaiah 19:24, the wording is: "and I will come to its remotest height," since the Temple was situated on Mt. Moriah. According to the *derash* (San. 94b), Sennacherib said, "First I will destroy His dwelling below, and then I will destroy His dwelling above [*Redak*].

Apparently, Sennacherib believed that by destroying the Temple, he would destroy God's power completely. *Rashi* ad loc. explains that the Temple below is known as "the height" in Jer. 17:12, and the Temple above is known as the lodge, since that is God's permanent dwelling. *Maharsha* suggests that the

כָּל מֵי נַהֲרִין עֲמִיקִין: כה הֲלָא שְׁמַעְתָּא מִלְּקַדְמִין מָה בַעֲבָדִית לְפַרְעֹה מַלְכָּא דְמִצְרַיִם הֲלָא עַל דְּשַׁלִּיט בְּהוֹן וְאַף עֲלָךְ אִתְנַבִּיאוּ נְבִיֵּי יִשְׂרָאֵל וְלָא תַבְתָּא וְדָא חֲזָא קֳדָמַי מִיּוֹמֵי קֶדֶם לְמֶעְבַּד לָךְ אַף אַתְקֵינְתַּהּ כְּעַן אַיְתִיתַהּ וְדָא הֲוָת לָךְ לְהַקְלָא עַל דַּהֲוָאָה קֳדָמָךְ כְּאִתְרְגוּשַׁת גַּלִּין דְּיִשְׁחוּ קִירְוִין כְּרִיכָן: כו וְיָתְבֵיהוֹן אִתְקְצַר חֵילֵיהוֹן אִתְּבָרוּ וּבְהִיתוּ הֲווֹ כְּעֶשֶׂב חַקְלָא וְכִירוֹק דִּתְאָה כְּעֶשֶׂב אִגְּרַיָּא דְיִשְׁלוֹק עַד דְּלָא

מָצוֹר: כה הֲלֹא־שָׁמַעְתָּ לְמֵרָחוֹק אֹתָהּ עָשִׂיתִי לְמִימֵי קֶדֶם וִיצַרְתִּיהָ עַתָּה הֲבֵיאתִיהָ וּתְהִי לַהְשׁוֹת גַּלִּים נִצִּים עָרִים בְּצֻרוֹת: כו וְיֹשְׁבֵיהֶן קִצְרֵי־יָד חַתּוּ וַיֵּבֹשׁוּ הָיוּ עֵשֶׂב שָׂדֶה וִירַק דֶּשֶׁא

להשאות קרי — חציר

רש"י

הוה כן דרכי תמיד: (כה) הלא שמעת למרחוק. למה תתפאר ותתגדל בזאת לא שלך היא כי שמעת למרחוק על ידי הנביאים שגזרתי על העובדי כוכבים להביאך עליהם כענין שנאמר הוי אשור שבט אפי (ישעיה י' ה'): למימי קדם. משנבראה העולם עלתה במחשבה שנאמר (ישעיה ל' ל"ג) כי ערוך מאתמול תפתה גם הוא למלך הוכן זה סנחריב שנשרף בלא ניכר שנ' (שם ל"א ט') נאם ה' אשר אור לו בציון: עתה הבאתיה. וזה הכח שבידך: ותהי. ביאתה של גזרתי להשאות ערים בצורות להיות לגלים נצים לגלי אדמה שצומחין בהן ירקות שאתה מחריבן בגזרתי: להשאות. לשון שאיה גלמודה: (כו) ויושביהן קצרי יד. הם שאני התשתי את כחן לפניך ואין הגבורה שלך אין אתה גבור אבל הניעה הלמ"ד וההא מפני חסרון האלף: גלים נצים ערים בצורות.

רד"ק

גדול אמר כן על דרך ההפלגה: (כה) הלא שמעת למרחוק אמר לו הקב"ה הלא שמעת מזמן רחוק הגזרה שגזרתי על האומות להחריבם אותה הגזרה עתה הביאותיה משמלכו מלכי אשור הבאתי הגזר' על ידם ועל ידך על האומה ועל ישראל אני הוא שגזרתי שיהיו ערים בצורות לגלים נצים ויהיו יושבי הערים קצרי יד ויהיו כעשב השדה וירק דשא וכיותר חלוש מהם והוא חציר גגות שלא היה כח ביושבי הערים להלחם כנגדך והכל היה מאתי ואני גזרתי ואמרתי ע"י נביאי טרם שהיתה הגזרה ואיך תתפאר על מה שעשיתי אני וכן אמר עליו הנביא ז"ל היתפאר הגרזן על החוצב בו וי"ת כן הלא שמעת מלקדמין וגו' כבעמוד וא"א ז"ל פי' כן אותה עשיתי ירושלם וכן אמר ויוצרה מרחוק לא ראיתם אמר כי מימים קדמונים אני עשיתיה ועתה הביאותיה בתמיה אמר הביאותית עתה שתהי להשות גלים נצים ערים ושיהיו יושביהם קצרי יד וחתו ובשו ושיהיו כעשב השדה: להשות. שרשו שאת ומשפטו בתשלומו להשאות כמו שכתוב בישעיה ונשתנו הניעה הלמ"ד וההא מפני חסרון האלף. להשות ערים בצורות להיות גלים נצים ופי' נצים

רלב"ג

(כה) הלא שמעת למרחוק אותה עשיתי. ר"ל על מה תתפאר על אלהיך במלחמות הלא שמעת כי למרחוק הודעתי אלו הדברים מהלחמותיך על כל הגוים ע"י עבדי הנביאים וזה לאות כי אותה עשיתי כמו שאמר ישעיה מי פעל ועשה קורא הדורות מראש ר"ל שמי שיקרא הדורות מראש ויודע מה שעתיד להיות הוא מחוייב שיהיה הוא הפועל כי לולי זה איך יתכן שידע הוא מה שיעשה זולתי האלהים אלא אם היה הזולת ההוא מצרף אותו כזה ויהיה הפועל מסודר מהמודיע זה טרם היותו לא מהמצרף כי איננו הראשון בזה וכבר הארכנו המאמר בזה בראשון מספר מלחמות ה' ובספר ישעיה: למימי קדם וילדתיה. ר"ל כי מימי קדם השכתיה ודמיתיה והוא מענין וילדי כלל כלם והנה עתה הבאתיה בימי מלכי אשור ותהי זאת המחשבה בהבנתי ועשיתי אותה להשאו' ולהחריב עד שיהיו ערים בצורות לגלים הרבים ועשיתי יושבי הערים קצרי יד כאילו אין להם כח חתו ובושו כי נהיו לשמה כרגע מה שלא השבו זה מלפנים הנה לא היה להם כח להלחם כאילו הם עשב שדה וירק דשא שאיננו זז ממקומו כי יכרתו אותו וכמו חציר הגגות שהוא יותר נקל להכרת

מנחת שי

חסר הוא או מלא ועיין מה שכתוב בזכריה י': (כה) עתה הביאתיה. עיין מ"ש בזה בישעיה ל"ז ובמיעוט ספרים דין דמלכים הבי"ת בחירק והאל"ף בחולם וליכא למיסמך עליהון: ותהי להשות גלים נלים. במקצת ספרים כן כתוב בפנים להשות ובחוץ להשאות קרי וזה טעות גמור הוא כי אותו של ישעיה כתוב להשאות כמו שנזכר בחילופים שהובאו שם וכ"כ ן' פרחון בישעיה אבל זה דמלכים כתיב וקרי להשות וכן נמנה במסו' לעיל סימן ס"ז עם מלין דלא מפקין אל"ף בקריאה ולית להון זוג והוא גם כן חד מן ד' זוגים מתחלפים מן ב' קדמאה חסר אל"ף בתראה מלא אל"ף וסימנא ברים פרשת תולדות יצחק ודברי הימים א' ז' וכן ראיתי בספרים כתובי יד מדוייקים ודפוסים ישנים הלמ"ד פתוחה והה"א בשוא נח וכן כתב רד"ק במכלול דף קס"ו ובשרשים שרש שאה ושרש נשה על פי ספרים מדויקים וכן כתב הגויה חן בפ"ד פ"ה ובס"ה כ"י כתוב עליו במחזורה רבה להשות וכן הביאו רד"ק בתחלת ולקדילה האחת יהיה בפתח הכ"א והשין דגושה ושרשו נשא:

מצודת דוד

נכבותיה אשר סביב לה אז הבאתי עליה חיילות רבות והחריבו הבצורות במדרך כף רגליהם: (כה) למרחוק. מזמן רחוק: אותה. את הגזירה הזאת עשיתי מימים קדמונים: ויצרתיה. ואני ילדתי את הדבר הזה וכפל הדבר במ"ש: עתה הבאתיה. אני הבאתי עתה את הדבר על ידך: ותהי. אתה תהיה למקל מרדות להחריב ערים בצורות לעשות' שממה וגלי' מלאים' גלים ופרחים: (כו) ויושביהן. יושבי הערים ההם עשיתים להיות קצרה ידם מלהלחם למולך: עשב שדה. כעשב בדה: חציר גגות. כחציר הגדל על הגגות שהוא

מצודת ציון

ונהל: מצור. ענין חוזק והוא מלשון צור: (כה) להשות. מלשון שאיה ובמשמון כמו אמש שואה ומשואה (איוב ל'): גלים. הוא כענין תל: נצים. פרחים כמו הנצו הרמונים (ש"ה ז'): (כו) חתו.

and it shall be—*the coming of My decree* shall be *to make desolate fortified cities into blossoming hills, into piles of earth upon which vegetables grow, for you destroy them because of My decree* [*Rashi*].*

to make desolate—לַהְשׁוֹת in Heb., *an expression of desolation, loneliness* [*Rashi*].

For the correct version here and in Isaiah, see *Redak, Minhath Shai.*

26. **And their inhabitants became short of strength**—*Those whom I weakened before you, and the might*

25. Have you not heard from afar what I did in days of yore, and what I formed? Now I have brought it, and it shall be to make desolate, blossoming hills, [of] fortified cities. 26. And their inhabitants became short of strength, broken and ashamed; they were [like] the grass of the field and green herbage,

I dug and drank strange water—*I.e. to say, I started all my deeds and completed* them, *as one who digs a hole and finds strange water and drinks it. Flowing water he calls "strange" since until now no one knew of them* [*Rashi* after *Jonathan, Redak*].

Others identify זָרִים with זֶרֶם, a stream, rendering: *flowing water* [*Mezudath Zion*].

and I will dry up with the soles of my feet—*If I would besiege a city reliant upon its rivers, I would bring many troops upon it who would dry up its rivers with their drinking and the drinking of their cattle and by the treading of their feet* [*Rashi*].

and I will dry up—*This is the present tense. So is my wont always* [*Rashi*].

I.e. even though the structure of the word is that of the future, the sense is the present. It is very common for a continual or repeated action to be written in the future tense. See *Rashi* Ex. 15:1.

rivers of the siege—*all the rivers of the city that is besieged by me* [*Rashi* Is. 37:25]. *Jonathan* renders: all deep rivers.

Redak suggests that מָצוֹר is short for מִצְרַיִם, *Egypt,* i.e. all great rivers, which can be compared to the rivers of Egypt.

Now God replies to Sennacherib:

25. **Have you not heard from afar**—*Why do you boast and aggrandize yourself with this? This is not yours, for you have heard from afar through the prophets, that I decreed upon the nations to bring you upon them, as the matter that is written,* "(Is. 7:4) *Ho, Assyria, the staff of My wrath*" [*Rashi*].

The expression "from afar" denotes time, not distance. Have you not heard long ago? In Is. 37:26, *Rashi* adds: *More than seventy years since Amos prophesied two years before the earthquake. "(Amos 7:17) and Israel shall be exiled from upon its land." Since then, you should have heard that I wrought and prepared this retribution* [*Rashi*].

See *Rashi* Amos 1:1, that the earthquake took place when Uzziah entered the Temple to offer up the incense.

in the days of yore—*Since the world was created, it entered* My *thought, as it is said,* "(Is. 30:33) *For Gehinnom is arranged from days of yore; that too was prepared for the king." This refers to Sennacherib, who was burned in the fire of Gehinnom, as it is said,* "(Is. 31:9) The *word of the Lord, Who has fire in Zion*" [*Rashi*].*

Now I have brought it—*and this is the power that is in your hand* [*Rashi*].

חֲצִיר גַּגּוֹת וּשְׁדֵפָה לִפְנֵי קָמָה:
כז וְשִׁבְתְּךָ וְצֵאתְךָ וּבֹאֲךָ יָדָעְתִּי וְאֵת
הִתְרַגֶּזְךָ אֵלָי: כח יַעַן הִתְרַגֶּזְךָ אֵלַי
וְשַׁאֲנַנְךָ עָלָה בְאָזְנָי וְשַׂמְתִּי חַחִי
בְּאַפֶּךָ וּמִתְגִּי בִּשְׂפָתֶיךָ וַהֲשִׁבֹתִיךָ
בַּדֶּרֶךְ אֲשֶׁר־בָּאתָ בָּהּ: כט וְזֶה־לְּךָ
הָאוֹת אָכוֹל הַשָּׁנָה סָפִיחַ וּבַשָּׁנָה

מְטָא לְמֶהֱוֵי שׁוּבְלִין:
כז וּמִיתְּבָךְ בְּעֵיצָה
וּמִיפְּקָךְ לְאַגָּחָא קְרָבָא
וּמֵיתָךְ לְאַרְעָא דְיִשְׂרָאֵל
גְּלֵי קֳדָמַי וְיַת
דְּאַרְגֵּיזְתָּא קֳדָמַי גְּלֵי:
כח חֲלַף דְּאַרְגֵּיזְתָּא עַל
מֵימְרִי וְאִתְרַבְּרְבוּתָךְ
סְלֵיקַת לְקֳדָמַי וַאֲשַׁוֵּי
שֵׁירִין בְּלִיסְתָךְ וְזִמָּם
בְּסִפְוָתָךְ וַאֲתֵיבִינָךְ
בְּאוֹרְחָא דַּאֲתֵיתָא בַּהּ:
כט וְדֵין לָךְ אָתָא אֱכוֹל
בְּשַׁתָּא הָדָא כְּתִין

רד"ק

הרבים מן עריך תצינה: (כו) ושדפה לפני קמה. העשב שהכה השדפון טרם היותו קמה כלומר שלא הספיק להיותה קמה ולהיות נגמר בשולו והוכח בשדפון ובישעיה ושדמה במ"ם והוא כמו בפ"א כי המ"ם והפ"א ממוצא אחד: (כז) ושבתך וצאתך ובאך. שבתך בארצך וצאתך מארצך ובואך הנה הכל גלוי וידוע לפני: ואת התרגזך אלי. ג"כ ידעתי שהקצפת אלי ודברת בי כדבר באלהי עץ ואבן ות"י שבתך ומיתבך בעיצה: (כח) ושאננך. כמו ושאנך וכפל הנו"ן להפלגת השאנן כן כתבו רבי יונה וכן הו' דעתי ודעת יונתן שתרגם ואתרברבותך סליקת לקדמי ויש לפרשו כמשמעו בעבור כי התרגזו היה בעבור שהיה שלו שקט ושאנן: ושמתי חחי באפך. הוא הברזל כמין מחט וראשו כפוף נוקב אף הדג ולחיו ומעלין אותו מן המים וכן ובחוח תקוב לחיו ונתתי חחי' בלחיך: ומתגי בשפתיך. המתג הוא הברזל שמשימין בפה הבהמה להנהיגה וכת"י וזמם בספותך והרגם ורסן מתע' וזמ' דמעי ר"ל אני ארא' לך שאתה ברשותי ואנהיג אותך למקום שארצ' כמו שמנהיג האד' הבהמ' ומושכ' למקו' שירצ' וכמו שהדייג מושך הדג אליו מן המים בחכתו': בדרך אשר באת בה. כמו אשר תבא בה כי עתה ע"י מלאכים שלח הדברים והוא הלך להלחם עם מלך כוש אלא אחר המלחמה שב לירושל' ועל אותו הדרך אמר שעתיד לשוב ולבוא לירושלים כי באותו הדרך שיבא ישוב לארצו אחר שינגף מחנהו: (כט) וזה לך האות. אמר לחזקיהו זה שאמרתי לך בנבוא' הראשונ' ושמע

רש"י

הם הלשים: חציר גגות. הממהר ליבש: ושדפה לפני קמה. כשבלים השדופות בטרם יתקשו לבא לידי קמה: (כז) ושבתך וצאתך ובאך. תירגם יונתן ומיתבך בעצה ומיפקך לאגחא קרבא ומיתך לארעא דישראל גלי קדמי אתי נהיתה: ואת התרגזך אלי. ואת אשר סופך להתגאות ולהתעורר אלי ברוגז ורעש (אשטרימי"ה בלע"ז): (כח) ושאננך. כמו ושאונך: חחי. כמין שיר הוא שמושכין בו בהמה שעסקיה רעים כמו שענינו כל בעלי השיר יובלון בשיר: ומתגי. תרגום יונתן זמם והוא של ברזל ותוחבין אותו בנחירי הגאקה ונמשכת בו לפי שעסקיה רעים והוא שענינו וגאקה בחוטם: (כט) וזה לך האות.

מנחת שי

מבית שאנן: (כח) ושאננך. במקצת ספרים כ"י ודפוסים קדמונים נו"ן ראשונה בקמץ וכן הביאו דישעיה והם בנים במסורת וכיון הקבולים הם יבאו כניהם

רלב"ג

וכמו העשב השרוף טרם הגיעו להיות קמה: (כז) ושבתך וצאתך ובאך ידעתי. ר"ל שבתך בארצך וצאתך למלחמה ובאך לעיירות שלכדת הכל ידעתי טרם היותו וגם ידעתי התרגזך אלי. ר"ל היותך מרגיז עצמך אלי גורא מאד עד שחשבת שלא אוכל לך ושאני צריך לירא ממך ולפי שכבר עלה באזני התרגזך אלי והיה סבת זה היותך שלו ושאנן ולזה יחסת לעצמך אלו ההצלחות לא כי הנה אראה לך שאני האדון והמנהיג ואתה העבד ולזה אשים חח באפך והוא הברזל שילכדו בו הדגים ואשים בשפתיך המתג שמשימין בשפתי הבהמות להנהיגם באשר ירצו: (כח) והשיבותיך בדרך אשר באת בה. ידמה שאחר שנלחמו עם מלך כוש שב אל ירושלם ושם נגף ה' את כל חילו: (כט) וזה לך האות אכול השנה ספיח. אמר זה לפי שלא היה בלי פחד עדיין אעפ"י שימותו חיל מלך אשור כי אולי ישוב עליהם עם

מצודת ציון

נשברו: ושדפה. מלשון שדפון ירקון (מ"א ח') והוא לקות הזרע: (כז) התרגזך. ענין תנועת הדדת המהירות וכן סרגיז ממלכות (ישעיה כ"ג): (כח) ושאננך. הוא מלשון שאון והמייה: חחי. הוא הטבעת ההוסם כפי הבהמה שעסקיה רעים למושכה ע"י וכן ונתתי חחים בלחייך (יחזקאל ל"ח): ומתגי. הוא כענין רסן כמו מתג לחמור (משלי כ"ו): (כט) ספיח. הוא הצומח מהגרעין הנופל

מצודת דוד

חלש למאד: ושדפה. כשבלים הנשדפים טרם נגמר בשולם לבוא לכלל קמה כי אז המה חלושים עד למאד ור"ל הנה אני הוא הממית ומחליש לפניך את העובדי כוכבי' ולא בכחך בעולם ידך: (כז) ושבתך. ת"י ומיתבך בעצה: ואת התרגזך. ואף את התרגזך ידעתי: (כח) אלי. באה אלי: והשיבותיך. בע"כ אשיב אותך: (כט) וזה לך האות. אל מול חזקיה ידבר הנה התבועה הזאת תהיה לך לאות

animal that is difficult to control. He explains מֶתֶג just as he does here. *Shem Ephraim* questions these definitions in view of the wording of the verse, which places חָח in the nose and מֶתֶג in the lips.*

by which you have come—or, will come, since he had not yet arrived in Jerusalem [*Redak*].

29. **And this will be the sign for you**—*The prophet said this to Hezekiah. And this* prophecy *which I said to you* that *Sennacherib will fall here, will be a sign for you also for the approaching days, for you are afraid of dying from hunger, since Sennacherib destroyed the land and chopped down the trees* [Rashi].

like grass of the roofs, and blast before becoming standing grain. 27. And your sitting and your going out and your coming I know, and your raging against Me. 28. Because you have raged against Me, and your tumult has ascended into My ears, I will place my ring in your nose and My bit in your lips, and I will return you by the road by which you have come. 29. And this shall be the sign for you, this year you shall eat what grows by itself, and the next year,

is not yours. You are not mighty, but they are weak [*Rashi*].

I weakened the inhabitants of the cities that you attacked, so that they could not defend themselves against you [*Mezudath David*].

they were like the grass of the field—unable to move, to defend themselves [*Ralbag*].

like grass of the roofs—*which hastens to dry* [*Rashi*].

and blast before becoming standing grain—*like ears of grain, blasted before they hardened to become standing grain* [*Rashi*].

I.e. before they ripened, when the grain is very frail.

All these nations were weakened so that Assyria could conquer them [*Mezudath David*].

27. **And your sitting and your going out and your coming**—*Jonathan paraphrased: And your sitting in counsel, and your going out to wage war, and your coming to the land of Israel, is revealed to Me. It emanated from Me* [*Rashi*].

Alternatively, your staying in your land . . . [*Redak*].

and your raging against Me—And the fact *that you will become arrogant and aroused against Me with anger and tumult.* (Or, *that you will provoke Me . . .*) [*R. Joseph Kara*]. (*Estomir in O.F.*)

28. **Because you have raged against me**—[*Jonathan*].

Or, because your raging has come before Me [*Mezudath David*].

and your tumult—*like* וּשְׁאוֹנְךָ [*Rashi, Redak, Jonathan, Mezudath Zion*].

The word שַׁאֲנָן usually means tranquility, which apparently is inappropriate here. It is, therefore, explained as "tumult." According to Mesorah, this and the identical word in Isaiah are to be rendered as "tumult." See *Parshandatha*, Isaiah 37:29.*

My ring—חַחִי in Heb., *a kind of ring by which they pull an animal whose behavior is bad, as we learned,* "(*Shabbath* 5:1) *And all animals that are usually pulled with a ring may go out with a ring*" [*Rashi*].

and my bit—Heb. מְתְגִּי, *Jonathan rendered* זְמָם, *which is* made *of iron, and which they insert into the nostrils of a female camel, and she is pulled with it, since her behavior is bad. This is what we learned,* "(*Shabbath* ibid) *and the female camel with a nose ring*" (*Rashi*].

Rashi Is. 37:29, explains חָח as a ring inserted through the lip of an

הַשֵּׁנִית סָחִישׁ וּבַשָּׁנָה הַשְּׁלִישִׁית זִרְעוּ וְקִצְרוּ וְנִטְעוּ כְרָמִים וְאִכְלוּ פִרְיָם:
ל וְיָסְפָה פְּלֵיטַת בֵּית־יְהוּדָה הַנִּשְׁאָרָה שֹׁרֶשׁ לְמָטָּה וְעָשָׂה פְרִי לְמָעְלָה:
לא כִּי מִירוּשָׁלִַם תֵּצֵא שְׁאֵרִית וּפְלֵיטָה מֵהַר צִיּוֹן קִנְאַת יְהוָה * תַּעֲשֶׂה־זֹּאת:
לב לָכֵן כֹּה־אָמַר יְהוָה אֶל־מֶלֶךְ אַשּׁוּר

לא

וּבְשַׁתָּא תִּנְיָנֵיתָא כַּתְכְּתִין וּבְשַׁתָּא תְלִיתָאָה זְרוּעוּ וַחֲצוּדוּ וְצוּבוּ כַּרְמִין וְאֱכוּלוּ אִבֵּיהוֹן: וְיוֹסְפוּן מְשֵׁיזְבָא דְבֵית יְהוּדָה דְאִשְׁתְּאָרוּן כְּאִילָן דִּי מְשַׁלַּח שׁוּרְשׁוֹהִי לְרַע וּמָרִים נוֹפֵיהּ לְעֵילָא: לא אֲרֵי מִירוּשְׁלֶם יִפְּקוּן שְׁאָר צַדִּיקַיָּא וְשֵׁיזְבַת מְקַיְּמֵי אוֹרַיְתָא מִטּוּרָא דְצִיּוֹן בְּמֵימְרָא דַיְיָ צְבָאוֹת תִּתְעֲבֵיד דָּא: לב בְּכֵן כִּדְנַן אֲמַר יְיָ

רש״י
צבאות קרי ולא כתיב

לחזקיהו אמר הנביא וזה שאמרתי לך סנחריב יפול כאן יהי לך לאות אף לימים הבאים שאתם יראים למות ברעב לפי שסנחריב החריב את הארץ וגדע את האילנות: אכול השנה ספיח. בשנה הזאת ימלאו לכם למחי' ותתפרנסו מהם: סחיש. גדועי אילנות שילמהו וכתרגמו דברי קיים במפלת האוכלוסין יהיה לך לאות שאף הבטחה זו תתקיים: (לא) קנאת ה' צבאות. שיקנא לכבודו ולשמו ולא שיש

רד״ק

שמוע' ושב לארצו וכן עשה שהרי ראית ששלח מלאכיו ישב לארצ' להלחם עם מלך כוש ובזה האות שנתאמת אצלך דברי תדע כי גם נבואה זאת תהיה אמת בזה לך לענה לך בתולת בת ציון לא יבא מלך אשור אל העיר הזאת שיכבוש אותה ועוד אני אומר שתאכלו השנה ספיח כי אותה השנה לא זרעו מפני חיל מלך אשור ואכלו הספיחים אם כן מה אמר להם הנביא כי יודעים היו שיאכלו הספיחים אחר שלא זרעו לא היה להם קציר אחר אלא אמר להם הנביא שיתברך להם התבואה שבשדות ויספיקו להם אותם הספיחי' כל השנה ההיא ובשנה השנית ג"כ לא תצטרכו לזרוע כי האכלו הסחיש והוא היוצא מהנופל מהספיח ובשנה הג' תזרעו כמותר הסחיש על אכלכם ותקצרו בשלום כי לא יהיה לכם פחד מאויב ותטעו כרמים ותאכלו פרים בהשקט ובבטחה. ובסדר עולם באחד עשר ביובל עלה סנחריב בשנה הרביעי' בשבוע וכן הוא אומר אכול השנה ספיח שעלה בפרס הפסח ולא יכלו לזרוע ואכלו הספיחים ובשנה השנית סחיש שנדעו לגיינות את האילנות ובשנה השלישית זרעו מלמד שלא נשתייר בשבוע אלא שנה אחת: (ל) שרש למטה. ת"י כאילן די משלח שרשוהי לרע ומרים נופיה לעילא: (לא) כי מירושלים תצא שארית. יפקון שאר צדיקיא ושיזבת מקיימי אורייתא מטורא דציון: קנאת ה' צבאות. קרי

רלב״ג

היו אחר ולזה אמר הנביא לחזקיה וזה הדבר אשר תראה מסנחריב שישיב בדרך אשר בא בה ולא יבא על ירושלים יהיה לך אות על ייעוד אחר שמיעד אותך הש"י והוא השנה הזאת תאכלו הספיחים אשר בשדות בהון ולא יהיה אויב בחוץ שימנע אתכם מזה ויתברכו הספיחים באופן שיספיקו כל השנה: ובשנה השנית תאכלו סחיש. והם ספיחים הצומחים מהנופל מהספיחים הראשונים וידמה שאותה השנה היתה שנת השמטה שאם לא היה כן מה זה שלא יזרעו ולא יקצרו: (ל) ויספה פליטת בית יהודה הנשארה. ממלך אשור ומלכי ישראל וזולתם מלך ארם לעשות שרש למטה ותשתרש באופן שתעשה פרי למעלה: (לא) כי מירושלים תצא שארית ופליטה מהר ציון.

מנחת שי

בקריאה אחת וספרים אחרים שניהם בפתח כמו שכתוב בישעיה: (לא) קנאת ה' ***** תעשה זאת. צבאות קרי ולא כתיב והוא חד מן י' מלין דקריין

מצודת דוד

על הבטחה אחרת כי הנה הלגיונות החריבו וקלקלו הזרעים וגדעו האילנות והקב"ה מבטיחך לכלכל אתכ' בשנה ההיא בספיחי הארעי': ובשנה השנית סחיש. אולי היתה שנת השמיטה והיו אסורים בחרישה וזריעה ולזה נתברכו ספיחי הספיחים: ובשנה השלישית זרעו. ולא תפחדו עוד מאת הבדה מפחד האויב: (ל) שורש למטה. ר"ל יהיו ממולאים בכל טוב כהאילן הנטוע במקום לטוב שמוסיף שורש למטה ומרבה לעשות פרי למעלה: (לא) כי מירושלים וגו'. ר"ל ירושלים תהיה השארית להנצל מיד סנחריב וכן ופליטה

מצודת ציון

מאליו כמו ספיח קצירך (ויקרא כ"ה): סחיש. ענינו ספיחי

depleted. This does not appear in all editions. See *Parshandatha* ad loc.

Jonathan renders simply:—By the word of the Lord of Hosts this will be accomplished.*

32. **concerning the king of Assyria**—Lit. to the king of Assyria.

He shall not enter this city—Lit. He shall not come to this city. I.e. he shall not come to this city to conquer it. Indeed, he came to the city and encamped outside of it, where his entire army was smitten. Our translation is also plausible [*Redak*].

nor shall he advance upon it with a shield—*He shall not set a shield before it* [*Rashi*]. In Isaiah 37:33, *Rashi* adds, *Since the Aramaic translation of "before" is* קֳדָם.

Alternatively, the first soldiers to advance upon a city were the shield-bearers [*Redak*].

what grows from the tree stumps, and in the third year, sow and
reap, and plant vineyards and eat their fruit. 30. And the
remaining survivors of the house of Judah shall continue to
take root below and they will produce fruit above. 31. For
from Jerusalem shall come out a remnant, and survivors from
Mt. Zion; the zeal of the Lord of Hosts shall do this. 32. Therefore, so has the Lord said concerning the king of Assyria:

this year you shall eat what grows by itself—*This year plants will grow for you, and you will be sustained by them* [*Rashi*].

In Isaiah 37:30, *Rashi* is more explicit. He adds, *And the Holy One, Blessed be He, promises you that you will have sufficient from the shoots of the plants that will grow by themselves.**

what grows from the tree stumps—*the chopped off trees that will grow* (according to ms. and Lublin ed. of R. Jos. Kara—*the products of the trees that will grow, and when you see My word fulfilled concerning the fall of the armies, it will be a sign for you that this promise, too, will be fulfilled* [*Rashi*].*

and in the third year—you shall sow the remnants of the second year and reap its crops, for then you will have no more fear of the enemies, and will be able to go about your affairs as in normal times.

According to *Seder Olam*, ch. 23, Sennacherib invaded in the eleventh year following the jubilee, two weeks before Passover. At that time, they were unable to sow anymore. Therefore, God blessed the crops that grew by themselves, and they sufficed for the remainder of the year. The following year they ate the fruits that grew from the trees the Assyrians had chopped down. In the third year, which immediately preceded the Sabbatical Year, they sowed their seeds and reaped their crops [*Redak*].

30. **shall continue to take root below**—They shall be replete with all good, like a tree planted in a moist location, whose roots spread out below, and which produces much fruit above [*Mezudath David*].

Jonathan, apparently understands this to mean that it will raise its branches on high, not fruit in the usual sense. See *Methurgeman, Lexicon Chaldaicum Authore Elia Levita.*

31. **For from Jerusalem shall come out a remnant**—the remnant of the righteous [*Redak* from *Jonathan*].

and survivors from Mt. Zion—the survivors of those who keep the Torah [*Redak* from *Jonathan*].

Since the rest of the country has been conquered by Assyria, the survivors will be solely from Jerusalem [*R. Jos. Kara*].

the zeal of the Lord of Hosts—*that He will be zealous for His honor and for His name, not that you have any merit, for Ahaz your father committed many wicked deeds* [*Rashi*].

In Is. 37:32, he adds, *We learn that the merit of the Patriarchs has been*

לֹ֣א יָבֹא֙ אֶל־הָעִ֣יר הַזֹּ֔את וְלֹֽא־יוֹרֶ֥ה
שָׁ֖ם חֵ֑ץ וְלֹֽא־יְקַדְּמֶ֣נָּה מָגֵ֔ן וְלֹֽא־יִשְׁפֹּ֥ךְ
עָלֶ֖יהָ סֹלְלָֽה׃ לג בַּדֶּ֥רֶךְ אֲשֶׁר־יָבֹ֖א בָּ֑הּ
יָשׁ֕וּב וְאֶל־הָעִ֥יר הַזֹּ֛את לֹ֥א יָבֹ֖א נְאֻם־
יְהוָֽה׃ לד וְגַנּוֹתִ֛י אֶל־הָעִ֥יר הַזֹּ֖את
לְהֽוֹשִׁיעָ֑הּ לְמַֽעֲנִ֔י וּלְמַ֖עַן דָּוִ֥ד עַבְדִּֽי׃
לה וַֽיְהִי֙ בַּלַּ֣יְלָה הַה֔וּא וַיֵּצֵ֖א ׀ מַלְאַ֣ךְ

לְמַלְכָּא דְאָתוּר לָא יֵיעוֹל לְקַרְתָּא הָדָא וְלָא יַקְשֵׁית תַּמָּן גִּיר וְלָא יְקַדְּמִינַהּ בִּתְרִיסִין וְלָא יִצְבַּר עֲלַהּ מְלִיתָא׃ לג בְּאוֹרְחָא דַאֲתָא בַהּ יְתוּב וּלְקַרְתָּא הָדָא לָא יֵיעוֹל אֲמַר יְיָ׃ לד וְאָגֵין עַל קַרְתָּא הָדָא לְמִפְרְקַהּ בְּדִיל מֵימְרִי וּבְדִיל דָּוִד עַבְדִּי׃ לה וַהֲוָה בְּלֵילְיָא הַהוּא וּנְפַק מַלְאֲכָא דַיְיָ

רד"ק

ולא כתיב שקנא האל לשמו לפי שחירף וגדף מלך אשור ביד מלאכיו וי"ת במימרא דה' צבאו' תתעביד דא: (לג) לא יבא אל העיר הזאת. שיכבשנה כי אל העיר בא עם מחנהו מחוץ לירושלם ושם נגף מחנהו או פי' לא יבא לא יכנס תוך העיר וכן תרגום יונתן לא יעול לקרתא הדא: ולא יקדמנה מגן. חסר בי"ת השמוש במגן כי בעלי המגינים באים ראשוני' אל העיר כשנלחמים עליה וכת"י לא יקדמנה בתריסין: ולא ישפוך עליה סוללה. כתרגומו ולא יצבר עלה מליתא. ומליתא הוא תל עפר מדברי רבותינו ז"ל מוליא בנצא והוא שציברין עפר לעשות תל ולהגביה כנגד חומת העיר ללכוד העיר וכן אמר ויצבור עפר וילכדה: (לה) ויהי בלילה ההוא. היות שחזר מלך אשור על ירושלם עם מהנהו ועם כל השבי באותה הלילה יצא מלאך ה' והכה במחנה אשור ורבותינו ז"ל אמרו כי ליל פסח היה ועוד אמרו כי לפני מפלתו של סנחריב חלה חזקיהו ויו' שלישי להליו היתה מפלתו של סנחריב ואותה הלילה אמרו ישר' שירה שנ' השיר יהיה לכם כליל התקדש חג ואמרו מאה ושמנים אלף שהכה במחנה אשור כולם היו קשורים כתרים בראשיהם וכדבריה' נראה בדברי הימים שנאמר ויכחד כל גבורי חיל ונגיד ושר במחנה מלך אשור וכן מה שנא' בישעיה במשמניו רזון ואמרו כי מכתם היתה שריפ' נשמה וגוף קיים שנ' ותחת

רש"י

זכות בידכם כי הרבה הרשע אחז אביך: (לב) ולא יקדמנה. לא יערך לפניה מגן: סוללה. לבור אדמה להגביה תל לעמוד עליו להלחם על העיר ועל שם שהוא כובשו וחובטו ברגלים ומקבות כדי שיהא נדוש וכבוש בחוזק קורהו סוללה ל' סולו סולו המסלה: (לה) ויהי בלילה ההוא. כששב סנחריב מעל כוש ובא עד נוב שהיתה סמוכה

מנחת שי

ולא כתב; שנמסר ברים סדר אלה הדברים וברות ומה שכתוב שם במסורת לבאות כי מירושלם תלא דישעיה טעות הוא וצריך להגיה דמלכים שכן הוא בכל הספרים דישעיה לבאות כתיב וקרי ובסדר קרי ולא כתיב ופירושו מלאתי כתוב כלשון הזה חסר לבאות מבפנים ואלה אותו מבחוץ להודיע כי שתי נקמות נקם האלהים בו אחת ע"י עצמו ואחרי כן ע"י לבאות מלאכיו וכן הוא אומר ויצא מלאך ה' ויך במחנה אשור וגו': (לד) וגנותי אל העיר. בס"א כתיבא יד על העיר אבן בשאר ספרים כתוב אל וכן במסורת ירמיה ל"ב כל וגנותי על העיר בר מן

רלב"ג

יעשה זה הש"י לקנאתו על החירופין שחרף אותו מלך אשור ואע"פ שאין ישראל ראוין לזה הנס: (לב) ולא יקדמנה מגן. לפי שההורסים החומות מקדמים לפניהם מגן והם בהים תחתיו והורסי' החומה בכשיל וכלפות אמר לא יקדמנה מגן ולא ישפוך עליה סוללה להפיל החומה והוא כלי שמשליכין בו אבנים גדולות מאד להפיל החומה בחוזק או ירצה באמרו ולא יקדמנה מגן ולא יקדמנה איש מגן ויהיה חסר הנושא כאמרו ומאכלו בריאה שהרצון בו ומאכלו שם בריאה:

(לד) וגנותי. הוא מענין מגן: למעני ולמען דוד עבדי. ר"ל למען כבוד שמי ובעבור בריתי עם דוד עבדי שאם יכמדו בניו את מלותי לא תסור המלכות מהם: (לה) ויהי בלילה ההוא. ר"ל בליל היום ההוא שאמר בו ישעיה אלו הדברים והנה א"כ אמרה אחר שבא סנחריב על ירושלים במצור כמו שפירשנו: וישכימו בבקר והנה כולם פגרים מתים. ר"ל רובם וכזה רבי' בדברי הנביאים והנה הנגלבים היו מעטים כמו שזכר ישעיה בספרו והנה פגרים מתים הם גופים מתים כי הגוף המי יקרא ג"כ פגר והנה בניו המיתוהו אח"ז כמו

מצודת ציון

ספיחים או ספיחי האילנות ואין לו דומה: (לב) יורה. ישליך: ולא יקדמנה. לא יערך לפניה כי התרגום של לפני הוא קדם וכן במה אקדם ה' (מיכה ו'): סללה. הוא לבור העפר שמשפכין מול העיר ועולים בה להלחם וכן שפכו על ירושלים סוללה (ירמיה ו): (לד) וגנותי. מלשון הגנה:

מצודת דוד

מהר ציון וכפל הדבר במ"ש: קנאת ה'. כי יקנא כמו אבר הרף רבשקה וסנחריב: (לד) למעני. למען כבוד שמי: (לה) ויצא מלאך

turn to Nineveh after his defeat. He remained in Nineveh, never again to go out in battle, and died an ignoble death at the hands of his own sons, rather than a hero's death on the battlefield [*Abarbanel*].

and dwelt in Nineveh—*That is the capital of the land of Assyria* [*Rashi*]. In Isaiah 37:37, *Rashi* adds, *as it is said,* "(Gen. 10:11) *From that land Ashur came out, and he built Nineveh . . .*"

According to inscriptions, Sennacherib rebuilt Nineveh as the capital of Assyria [*The Mizvah Candle, Maharal,* p. 23].

37. **the temple of Nisroch his god**—*a board from Noah's ark* [*Rashi* from *San.* 96a].

Sennacherib prostrated himself

'He shall not enter this city, neither shall he shoot there an arrow, nor shall he advance upon it with a shield, nor shall he pile up a siege mound against it. 33. By the way he comes he shall return, and this city he shall not enter,' says the Lord. 34. 'And I will protect this city to save it, for My sake and for the sake of My servant David.'" 35. And it came to pass on that night that an angel of the Lord went out

Hence, we render a shield-bearer shall not advance upon it [*Ralbag*].

Thus, we explain קדם as the first or earliest.

a siege mound—Heb. סֹלְלָה, *a heap of earth to raise a mount upon which to stand to embattle the city. Since one presses it down and beats it with sticks and sledge hammers, so that it be trodden and pressed down with strength, it is called* סֹלְלָה, *an expression* similar to "(Is. 62:10) *Beat down, beat down the highway.*" Heb. סֹלּוּ סֹלּוּ הַמְסִלָּה [*Rashi*].*

35. **And it came to pass on that night**—*when Sennacherib returned from* warring *with Cush, and he came as far as Nob, which was near Jerusalem* [*Rashi*].*

one hundred eighty-five thousand—*All of them were heads of companies* [*Rashi* from *Sanhedrin* 95b]. The Talmud elaborates on the enormity of Sennacherib's camp. There were 45,000 princes sitting in coaches, accompanied by queens and prostitutes, 80,000 mighty warriors, clothed in mail, sixty thousand swordsmen running before him, and the rest were horsemen. See above 18:24, *Rashi,* where we find that the lowest of the officers governed two thousand men. Thus, we have an idea of the millions of soldiers who accompanied Sennacherib and the reason for his delaying the attack until the following day. Since he thought that his success was due to his own strength, there was no reason to rush the attack. With his enormous army, he could just as easily conquer Jerusalem on the following day.

And they arose in the morning—Sennacherib, his two sons, Nebuzaradan and Nebuchadnezzar [*Sanhedrin* 95b]. When Nebuchadnezzar threw Hananiah, Mishael, and Azariah into the furnace, he saw instead four people. "(Dan. 3:25) The appearance of the fourth one was like an angel," Nebuchadnezzar cried. He knew the appearance of an angel because he was in Sennacherib's camp when Gabriel slew the entire camp.

dead corpses—They were slain just as Nadab and Abihu had been on the day of the inauguration of the Tabernacle; their souls were burnt out while their bodies remained intact [*Abarbanel* from *San.* 94a].

36. **and he returned**—The Chronicler elaborates, "(II Chron. 32:21) and he returned shamefacedly."

Sennacherib was spared death at the hand of the angel, in order to suffer disgrace in the wake of his re-

יְהֹוָה וַיַּךְ בְּמַחֲנֵה אַשּׁוּר מֵאָה שְׁמוֹנִים
וַחֲמִשָּׁה אָלֶף וַיַּשְׁכִּימוּ בַבֹּקֶר וְהִנֵּה
כֻלָּם פְּגָרִים מֵתִים: לו וַיִּסַּע וַיֵּלֶךְ וַיָּשָׁב
סַנְחֵרִיב מֶלֶךְ־אַשּׁוּר וַיֵּשֶׁב בְּנִינְוֵה:
לז וַיְהִי הוּא מִשְׁתַּחֲוֶה בֵּית | נִסְרֹךְ
אֱלֹהָיו וְאַדְרַמֶּלֶךְ וְשַׂרְאֶצֶר * הִכֻּהוּ
בַחֶרֶב וְהֵמָּה נִמְלְטוּ אֶרֶץ אֲרָרָט וַיִּמְלֹךְ
אֵסַר־חַדֹּן בְּנוֹ תַּחְתָּיו: כ א בַּיָּמִים
הָהֵם חָלָה חִזְקִיָּהוּ לָמוּת וַיָּבֹא אֵלָיו
יְשַׁעְיָהוּ בֶן־אָמוֹץ הַנָּבִיא וַיֹּאמֶר אֵלָיו

* בניו קרי ולא כתיב

תרגום

דַיְיָ וּקְטַל בְּמַשְׁרִיַת אֲתוּרָאָה מְאָה וְתַמְנַן וַחֲמֵשָׁא אַלְפִין וְאַקְדִימוּ בְצַפְרָא וְהָא כוּלְהוֹן פִּגְרִין מֵתִין: לו וּנְטַל וַאֲזַל וְתָב סַנְחֵרִיב מַלְכָּא דְאַתּוּר וִיתֵיב בְּנִינְוֵה: לז וַהֲוָה הוּא סָגִיד בֵּית נִסְרוֹךְ טַעֲוָתֵיהּ וְאַדְרַמֶּלֶךְ וְשַׂרְאֶצֶר בְּנוֹהִי קַטְלוּהִי בְחַרְבָּא וְאִינוּן אִשְׁתֵּיזָבוּ לַאֲרַעְא קַרְדוּ וּמְלַךְ אֲסַרְחַדּוֹן בְּרֵיהּ תְּחוֹתוֹהִי: א בְּיוֹמַיָּא הָאִינוּן מְרַע חִזְקִיָּהוּ לִמְמָת וַאֲתָא לְוָתֵיהּ יְשַׁעְיָה בַר אָמוֹץ נְבִיָא וַאֲמַר לֵיהּ כִּדְנַן אמר

ת"א בימים ההם. ברכות י ב"ב קמז:

רש"י

לירושלים: מאה שמונים וחמשה אלף. כולם ראשי גייסות: (לו) וישב בנינוה. היא ראש לארץ אשור: (לז) בית נסרוך אלהיו. נסר מתיבתו של נח: הכהו בחרב. שמעו אותו שאמר לשוחטן לפניו אם ינצלוהו שלא יהרגוהו שרי המלכות שמתו בניהם על ידו:
כ (א) בימים ההם. שלשה ימים לפני מפלתו של סנחריב: חלה חזקיהו. ויום שלישי כשעלה בית ה' יום

רד"ק

כבודו יקד יקוד כלומר תחת הלבוש שהוא כבודו של אדם כשרפת בני אהרן שנא' וישאום בכתנותם: (לו) וישב בנינוה. שלא יצא במלחמה עוד: (לז) בניו. קרי ולא כתיב: הכוהו בחרב. באגדה סנחריב שאל את הכמיו כאשר הכה המלאך מחנהו מה זכות של אומה זו שאלהיהם נלחם להם אמרו לו אברהם אביה' העל' את בנו עולה אמר אף אני אעלה את שני בני לאלהי כששמעו בניו הכוהו בהרב בעוד שהיה משתחוה: (א) כי מת אתה ולא תחיה. לא תרפא מחולי זה כי מתוך זה החולי תמות וכת"י ולא תיחי ממרעך ורז"ל אמרו כי מת אתה בעולם הזה

רלב"ג

שייעד לו הנביא: (א) בימים ההם חלה חזקיה למות. אחשוב כי אחר הספור הקודם היה זה ונלא הפלא ממה שאמר ומכף מלך אשור

מנחת שי

הד אל העיר וכימן וגנותי אל העיר הזאת להושיעה קדמאה דמלכים והתרגום בתרגם על יש לומר דפרושי קא מפרש: (לז) וְאַדְרַמֶּלֶךְ. הוא בגעיא בספרים מדוייקים כתובי יד ובספרי' אה"יס כתוב זו"ן: עליו נ"א
וְאַדְרַמֶּלֶךְ וּבראשר *** הכהו. בניו קרי ולא כתיב ע"פ המסורת ואלו נכתב ואדרמלך ושראצר הכהו לא נודע כי בניו הכוהו בחרב לכן תלה בניו מבחוץ להודיע נקמת ה' בו לכל העולם כענין שכתוב הנני מקים עליך רעה מביתך כן מצאתי: אסרחדן. במקצת ספרים מלה חדא ומקצתן תרין מלין כמ"ש בישעיה:

מצודת דוד

ה'. לאחר שנלחם בכוש חזר ובא לירושלים ואז יצא מלאך ה' וגו': וישכימו בבוקר. סנחריב והמעט אשר נשארו חיים: (לו) בנינוה. היא ראש למלכות אשור: (לז) בית נסרוך. נסר מתיבתו של נח היה לו לאלוה ובעת אשר השתחוה לה הכוהו בניו: והמה. בני סנחריב אשר הכוהו:
כ (א) בימים ההם. אחז"ל שהיה שלשה ימים לפני מפלת סנחריב:

1. **In those days**—*Three days before Sennacherib's downfall, Hezekiah became ill, and the third day, when he went up to the house of the Lord, was the day of Sennacherib's downfall, and it was the* first *festive day of Passover* [*Rashi* from *Seder Olam* ch. 23].

and slew one hundred eighty-five thousand of the camp of Assyria. And they arose in the morning, and behold they were all dead corpses. 36. And Sennacherib, the king of Assyria, left and went away, and he returned and dwelt in Nineveh. 37. And he was prostrating himself in the temple of Nisroch his god, and Adramelech and Sharezer, his sons, slew him with a sword, and they fled to the land of Ararat, and his son Esarhaddon reigned in his stead.

20

1. In those days Hezekiah became critically ill, when Isaiah the son of Amoz the prophet came to him, and said to him,

before a portion of Noah's ark, believing it to be the "great god who saved Noah from the Deluge" [*San.* ibid.].

Adramelech—probably named after the pagan deity mentioned above 17:31.

Sharezer—According to ancient inscriptions, his name was Nergal Sharezer. Since Nergal was the name of a pagan deity, Scripture deleted it [*Antiquities* by Aaron Marcus, p. 169].

his sons—This is written in Isaiah, but omitted from the written text of Kings. According to the *Midrash K'ri velo K'thib,* this word is read orally to identify the two assassins as Sennacherib's sons. It does not clarify, however, why it is not written in the text.

slew him—*They heard him that he said he would slaughter them before him if they (sic) (he-Kara*) would save him so that the princes of the kingdom, whose sons perished because of him, would not kill him [*Rashi* from *San.* ibid].

Sennacherib asked his wise men what merit the Jewish people had that God saved them from his hand and destroyed his camp. They replied, "Their patriarch, Abraham, brought his son for a burnt-offering."

"If so," he replied, "I will offer my two sons to my god." When his sons heard this, they slew him while he was prostrating himself [*Redak* from unknown Midrashic source].

and his son Esarhaddon reigned in his stead—Ancient inscriptions reveal that Esarhaddon did not assume the throne until he avenged his father's death at the hands of his two brothers. He defeated them in heavy warfare in the land of Ararat. [*Marcus* p. 169].

כֹּה־אָמַר יְהוָה צַו לְבֵיתֶךָ כִּי מֵת אַתָּה
וְלֹא תִחְיֶה׃ ב וַיַּסֵּב אֶת־פָּנָיו אֶל־הַקִּיר
וַיִּתְפַּלֵּל אֶל־יְהוָה לֵאמֹר׃ ג אָנָּה יְהוָה
זְכָר־נָא אֵת אֲשֶׁר הִתְהַלַּכְתִּי לְפָנֶיךָ
בֶּאֱמֶת וּבְלֵבָב שָׁלֵם וְהַטּוֹב בְּעֵינֶיךָ
עָשִׂיתִי וַיֵּבְךְּ חִזְקִיָּהוּ בְּכִי גָדוֹל׃ ד וַיְהִי
יְשַׁעְיָהוּ לֹא יָצָא הָעִיר הַתִּיכֹנָה וּדְבַר־
יְהוָה הָיָה אֵלָיו לֵאמֹר׃ ה שׁוּב וְאָמַרְתָּ
אֶל־חִזְקִיָּהוּ נְגִיד עַמִּי כֹּה־אָמַר יְהוָה
אֱלֹהֵי דָּוִד אָבִיךָ שָׁמַעְתִּי אֶת־תְּפִלָּתֶךָ
רָאִיתִי אֶת־דִּמְעָתֶךָ הִנְנִי רֹפֵא לָךְ
בַּיּוֹם הַשְּׁלִישִׁי תַּעֲלֶה בֵּית יְהוָה׃

אֲמַר יְיָ פַּקֵיד עַל אֱנָשׁ בֵּיתָךְ אֲרֵי מָאִית אַתְּ וְלָא תֵיחֵי מִמַּרְעָךְ׃ ב וְאַסְחַר יָת אַפּוֹהִי לְכוֹתֶל בֵּית מַקְדְּשָׁא וְצַלֵּי קֳדָם יְיָ לְמֵימַר׃ ג קַבֵּל בְּעוּתִי יְיָ אַדְכַּר כְּעַן יָת דִּפְלָחִית קֳדָמָךְ בְּקוּשְׁטְ וּבְלִבַּב שְׁלִים וּדְתַקִּין קֳדָמָךְ עַבְדִית וּבְכָא חִזְקִיָּה בִּכְיָא סַגִּיאָה׃ ד וַהֲוָה יְשַׁעְיָה לָא נְפַק לְדַרְתָּא מְצִיעָאָה וּפִתְגָם נְבוּאָה מִן קֳדָם יְיָ הֲוָה עִמֵּיהּ לְמֵימַר׃ ה תּוּב וְתֵימַר לְחִזְקִיָּה מַלְכָּא דְעַמִּי כִּדְנַן אֲמַר יְיָ אֱלָהֵיהּ דְּדָוִד אֲבוּךְ שְׁמִיעַ קֳדָמַי צְלוֹתָךְ גְּלֵיא קֳדָמַי דִּמְעָתָךְ הָא אֲנָא מַסֵּי לָךְ בְּיוֹמָא תְלִיתָאָה תֵּיסַק לְבֵית מַקְדְּשָׁא

דיו

ה״א ויסב. ברכות י׳: זכר נא. שם: והטוב בעיניך. סנהדרין קד: ויהי ישעיהו. ערובין כו: חצר קרי

רד״ק

ולא תחיה לעולם הבא מאי טעמא דלא עסקת בפריה ורביה ואמת הוא כי בניו נולדו אחר חליו שנ׳ בן שתי׳ עשרה שנה מנשה במלכו: (ב) אל הקיר. כדי לכוין לבו בתפל׳ כי היה תמי׳ בלבו למה היה האל מקצר ימיו שהרי לא היה אלא בן ל״ט שנים כשחלה חלי זה וי״ת אל הקיר לכותל בית מקדשא: (ג) התהלכתי לפניך. זה עבודת הלב ואחר כך זכר המעשה: והטוב בעיניך עשיתי. כמו שהעיד עליו הכתוב ויעש הישר בעיני ה׳ ככל אשר עשה דוד אביו ואומר יישמור מצותיו אשר צוה ה׳ את משה. ובדרש והטוב בעיניך עשיתי שגנז ספר רפואות שעשה שלמה והיו העם בוטחים בו ולא היו דורשים את ה׳ בלבם: (ד) לא יצא העיר התיכונה. העיר כתיב וחצר קרי ובדברי רז״ל כתיב העי׳ וקרינן חצר מכאן שהסרטיא של מלכים כעיירות בינוניות ובמקום אחר אמר בירושלמי כתיב העיר לומר מהר הקב״ה להודיע רפואתו בטרם יצא קול הברת

רש״י

תפלתו של סנחריב וי״ט של פסח היה: כי מת אתה. בעולם הזה: ולא תחיה. לעולם הבא משום דלא עסקת אבה כדאיתא בברכות: (ד) לא יצא חצר וגו׳. מיהר הקב״ה להודיע רפואתו בטרם יצא קול הברה בעיר שנקנסה

מנחת שי

כ (ג) אנה ה׳. תר מן ו׳ כתיבין ה״א לבסוף בשופה ובס״ה כ״י בבני טעמים כזה **אנה** ובאחר ספרים בטעם ה׳ לבד כמו״ן ועיין מ״ש בתלים סימן קי״ח: דגש ובלבב שלם. וביעשיה סימן ל״ח ובלב שלם וסימן ראשי ספריהון פי׳ מלכים המתחיל והמלך שיש לו ה׳ אותיות כתוב ובלבב בתוה כל ה״א אותיות ישעיה המתחיל חזון שיש לו ד׳ אותיות כ׳ ובלב של ד׳ אותיות: (ד) העיר. חצר ק׳ ונדרש בבבלי דעירובין פרק עושין פסין ובירושלמי פ׳ חלק בענין מנשה עיין ילקוט מלכים רמז רמ״ב ובפי׳ רש״י ורד״ק וכלי יקר: (ה) רפא לך. בב׳ ספרים כ״י הפ״א בסגול וזהו גם דעת רד״ק במכלול דף קנ״ב

רלב״ג

הגיד כי כבר הסכים שהסרחדון היה מגזם אל ירושלם:

many remedies that were involved with astrology, and many people were misled by them.

4. **had not gone out to the inner court . . .**—*The Holy One, Blessed be He, hastened to inform him of his cure before the report would spread in the city that the death sentence had been decreed as a punishment upon Hezekiah, as is stated in Yerushalmi* (*Sanhedrin* 10:2) [*Rashi*].

This accounts for the *K'thib* הָעִיר, *the city*. The *Bavli* (*Eruvin* 26a) explains that the inner court חָצֵר behind the king's palace was the size of an average city הָעִיר [*Redak*].

"So has the Lord said, 'Give orders to your household, for you
are going to die and you shall not live.'" 2. And he turned his
face toward the wall and prayed to the Lord, saying,
3. "Please, O Lord, remember now, how I walked before You
truly and wholeheartedly, and I did what is good in Your eyes."
And Hezekiah wept profusely. 4. And it was when Isaiah had
not gone out to the inner court, and the word of the Lord came
to him, saying, 5. "Return and say to Hezekiah the ruler of My
people, 'So has the Lord God of your father David said, "I
have heard your prayer; I have seen your tears. Behold I shall
heal you. On the third day you shall go up to the house of the
Lord.

for you are going to die—*in this world* [*Rashi*].

and you shall not live—*in the world to come, for you have not married, as it is stated in Berachoth* 10b [*Rashi*].

Hezekiah had been informed through divine inspiration that he would beget wicked children. He, therefore, refrained from marrying. Isaiah explained to him that he should not interfere with God's secrets, and he should do as he was commanded by the Torah.

2. **toward the wall**—in order to concentrate on his prayer. He wondered why God should shorten his years, since he was only thirty-nine years old. *Jonathan* renders: toward the wall of the Temple [***Redak***].

3. **"Please**—Heb. אָנָּה. Jonathan renders: Accept my plea. Although this spelling usually means "where," the *Masorah* points out that in six instances in the Scriptures, אָנָּה in this sense is spelled with a *he* instead of an *aleph*. In Isaiah 38:8, *Rashi* explains thus: Where, O Lord—*Where is your mercy?*

how I walked before You truly and wholeheartedly—This refers to his serving God in his heart, i.e. with fervent prayer [*Redak*].

and I did what is good in Your eyes."—Here he refers to his serving God through his deeds, as the Scripture testifies above 18:3, "And he did what was right in the eyes of the Lord, like all that his father David had done." Our Rabbis explained that he suppressed the book of medicines, composed by King Solomon, since the people commenced to depend solely on the medicines and did not seek God in their hour of distress [*Redak, Rashi Berachoth* 10b].

Rambam (*Commentary on Mishnayoth, Pesachim* 4:9) explains that the book of medicines contained

ו וְהֹסַפְתִּי עַל־יָמֶיךָ חֲמֵשׁ עֶשְׂרֵה שָׁנָה
וּמִכַּף מֶלֶךְ־אַשּׁוּר אַצִּילְךָ וְאֵת הָעִיר
הַזֹּאת וְגַנּוֹתִי עַל־הָעִיר הַזֹּאת לְמַעֲנִי
וּלְמַעַן דָּוִד עַבְדִּי׃ ז וַיֹּאמֶר יְשַׁעְיָהוּ קְחוּ
דְּבֶלֶת תְּאֵנִים וַיִּקְחוּ וַיָּשִׂימוּ עַל־הַשְּׁחִין
וַיֶּחִי׃ ח וַיֹּאמֶר חִזְקִיָּהוּ אֶל־יְשַׁעְיָהוּ מָה
אוֹת כִּי־יִרְפָּא יְהוָה לִי וְעָלִיתִי בַּיּוֹם
הַשְּׁלִישִׁי בֵּית יְהוָה׃ ט וַיֹּאמֶר יְשַׁעְיָהוּ
זֶה־לְּךָ הָאוֹת מֵאֵת יְהוָה כִּי יַעֲשֶׂה

דַיְיָ׃ ו וְאוֹסִיף עַל יוֹמָךְ
חֲמֵשׁ עַסְרֵי שְׁנִין וּמִיַּד
מַלְכָּא דְאַתּוּר אֲשֵׁיזְבִינָךְ
וְיַת קַרְתָּא הָדָא וְאַגֵּין
עַל קַרְתָּא הָדָא בְּדִיל
מֵימְרִי וּבְדִיל דָּוִד
עַבְדִּי׃ ז וַאֲמַר יְשַׁעְיָהוּ
יִסְבוּן דְּבֶלֶת תְּאֵינִין
וּנְסִיבוּ וְשַׁוִּיאוּ עַל
שִׁיחֲנָא וְאִתַּסִי׃ ח וַאֲמַר
חִזְקִיָּהוּ לִישַׁעְיָהוּ מָא
אָת אֲרֵי יַסֵּי יְיָ לִי וְאֶסַּק
בְּיוֹמָא תְלִיתָאָה לְבֵית
מַקְדְּשָׁא דַיְיָ׃ ט וַאֲמַר
יְשַׁעְיָה דֵּין לָךְ אָתָא
מִן קֳדָם יְיָ אֲרֵי יַעְבֵּד

ת"א והוספתי על ימיך. יבמות מט ע׳: וגנותי. ברכות י׳: כי יעשה. עקידה שער יג:

רש"י

עליו מיתה כדאיתא ביהו׳: (ו) ומכף מלך אשור אצילך. למדנו שלפני תפלתו כל סנחריב הלה: (ז) דבלת תאנים. כשהם לחים קרוין תאנים וכשנדרסים בעיגול קרוין דבלה: וישימו על השחין ויחי. וגם בתוך נס שהרי אף בבשר חי כשמתה נותן עליו דבלה נסרח והקב"ה נותן דבר המחבל

רד"ק

בעיר שנקנסה עליו מיתה: (ו) והוספתי על ימיך. שהיו קצובים לך ובזה מחלוקת בדברי רז"ל י"א משלו הוסיפו לו כי ימיו הקצובים היו יותר ולעונש עון היו מחסרין לו ויש אומרים תוספת עשו לו על הקצובים לו ובספר שמואל בפס׳ כי אם יי׳ יגפנו פירשנו זה הענין: ומכף מלך אשור אצילך. זה ראיה כי קוד׳ מפלתו של סנחרב חלה חזקיה: (ז) דבלת תאנים. בדברי רז"ל והלא אם אתה נותן שרף של תאנים על הבשר מיד הבשר מתחבל אלא נס בתוך נס כיוצא בדבר ויורהו ה׳ עץ עץ מר היה כך הוא דרכו של הקב"ה במר הוא ממתיק את המר: (ח) מה אות. שאל אות לפי שאמר לו הגזר׳ כפילה כי מת אתה ולא תחיה חשב כי מה שאמר לו ישעיה הנני רופא לך לא אמר אלא לנחמו לפי שרא׳ אותו שבכה בבכי גדול ואף על פי שראה שנתרפא השחין לא חשב שנתרפא עד שיתחזק ויוכל לעלות בית יי׳ כי אפש׳ שישוב השחין עדיין או שלא סר החולי ממנו:

רלב"ג

(ז) קחו דבלת תאנים. ידוע כי הב"י כשיעשה מופתים יקבל להם קלת סבות כשאפשר זה ביהיה בהם יותר מעט מהזרות אל הטבע ולזה נוה לקחת דבלת תאנים כי אע"פ שאין בו כח לעבות זה הנה בו קלת מבול לרפואת המורסות והבועות: (ח) ויאמר חזקיהו אל ישעיהו מה אות כי ירפא ה׳ לי. ראוי שתדע שלא היה זה מיעוט אמונה לחזקיהו אם בקש אות כזה וזה שבכבר הודיעו ישעיה כי גזרת הב"י היתה בימות ועתה כשהשכים להוסיף על ימיו חמש עשרה שנה אילו היה תנאי ר"ל אם יהיה חזקיהו באופן מהשלימות שיתכן שתדבק בו

מנחת שי

תאנים בספרי הדפוס ובס"ס כ"י בלידי והאנה מלעיל בכל הספרים: (ו) והוספתי. זלו ה׳ מן ב׳ מלרע על פי המסורת ותכדו והוספתי על כל חטאתך (תהלים ע"ה) ובניס דקהלת (ה׳ ט"ז י"ב ט׳) מלעיל (כי הם וה"ו החבור) ומסורת חביב להו ואת בנתוב נתן במסורת בנמקרא גדולה ב׳ בההיי מלעיל טעות מפורש הוה ור"ל ב׳ בההיי מלרע וכן מלאתי במסורת כ"י ובספר תהלים נמסר יפה והדין חסר וה"ו בתר ה"ה ותלת התריני מלרע. ועיין עוד מה שכתוב בתהלים ע"ה:

מצודת דוד

מגוה על עניני ביתך: (ח) מה אות. ר"ל מה מאד יהיה לאות גדול ונפלא כאשר ירפאני ה׳ מכל מכאוב החלי ואעלה ביום השלישי אל בית ה׳: (ט) זה לך האות מאת ה׳. המקום מעלתו אמר לתת לך אות על הדבר הזה אשר תעלה ביום הג׳ לבית ה׳: הלך הצל עשר מעלות. מעלות היו עשויים מול החמה לבחון בהם שעות היום כי כל שעה יורד הצל מעלה אחת ובאל לו שיהיה אות יבחר יותר אם ילך הצל במהלכו לפנים עשר מעלות פתאום וברגע אחד (ויהיה הלך כמו ילך עשר במקום עתיד וכמוהו רבים במקרא) או אם תשוב

מצודת ציון

עתה: (ד) התיכונה. האמצעית: (ז) דבלת תאנים. הם התאנים הנדרסים יחד: השחין. מין נגע בנחלה על ידה וכן לבהין פורח אבעבועות (שמות ט׳): ויחי. ענין רפואה כמו עד היותם (יהושע ה׳): (ח) מה אות. מלת מה יורה על גודל הדבר והבינתו כמו מה אדיר שמך (תהלים ח): אות. מופת:

return, or perhaps, his malaise had not yet been healed, and he considered himself unable to enter the Temple on the third day [*Redak*].

Abarbanel adds that Hezekiah believed that the remedy of the figs was Isaiah's own remedy, not divinely inspired. He, therefore, requested "a sign that God will heal me."

Ralbag suggests that perhaps the fulfillment of the prophecy was contingent on Hezekiah's worthiness. Hezekiah, being modest and unassuming, doubted that he was worthy. He, therefore, requested a sign that it would be fulfilled in any case.

Mezudath David renders: How great is this sign that the Lord will heal me, and I will go up to the

6. And I will add fifteen years to your life, and I will save you from the hand of the king of Assyria, I will save you and this city, and I will protect this city for My sake and for the sake of My servant David.'" 7. And Isaiah said, "Take a cake of pressed figs." And they took [one] and placed it on the boil, and it was healed. 8. And Hezekiah said to Isaiah, "What is the sign that the Lord will heal me, and that I will go up to the house of the Lord on the third day?" 9. And Isaiah said, "This is your sign from the Lord, that the Lord will

6. **And I will add fifteen years to your life**—lit. to your days, to the days that had been allotted to you. Some say that he had originally been allotted these fifteen years, but because of his sin, they would have been taken away. Others maintain that these years were augmented to the days that had originally been allotted to him [*Redak* from *Yebamoth* 50a].

and I will save you from the hand of the king of Assyria—*We learn that before Sennacherib's downfall he became ill* [*Rashi, Redak*].

Ralbag (v. 1) explains this entire episode in chronological order, i.e. following Sennacherib's downfall delineated in ch. 19. Still, he is undaunted by our verse. He suggests that Esarhaddon threatened to march on Jerusalem.

and for the sake of My servant David—Since he prayed to be healed in his own merit, God replied that he would be healed for the sake of King David [*Berachoth* 10b].

7. **a cake of pressed figs**—Heb. דְּבֶלֶת תְּאֵנִים, lit. a pressed cake of figs. *When they are fresh, they are called* תְּאֵנִים, *figs, and when they are pressed into a round cake, they are called* דְּבֵלָה [*Rashi*].

and placed it on the boil, and it was healed—This was *a miracle within a miracle, for even healthy flesh—when you place a cake of pressed figs upon it, decays, yet the Holy One, Blessed be He, puts an injurious substance upon vulnerable tissue and it becomes healed* [*Rashi* from *Mechilta,* Ex. 15:25].

The *Mechilta* lists two other instances in which God performed "a miracle within a miracle," i.e. used detrimental substances to produce a beneficial effect. The first one was when Moses cast a bitter tree into the waters of Marah and thereby sweetened them, and the second one was when Elisha cast salt into the waters of Jericho and rendered them fit to drink (above 2:19–22).

8. **"What is the sign**—Since the decree was twofold, ". . . for you are going to die, and you shall not live," he thought that when Isaiah said to him, "Behold I will heal you," he said this only to console him because he had wept profusely. Even though he saw that the boil had been healed, he suspected that it would

יְהוָה֙ אֶת־הַדָּבָ֖ר אֲשֶׁ֣ר דִּבֵּ֑ר הָלַ֤ךְ הַצֵּל֙ עֶ֣שֶׂר מַעֲל֔וֹת אִם־יָשׁ֖וּב עֶ֥שֶׂר מַעֲלֽוֹת׃
י וַיֹּ֙אמֶר֙ יְחִזְקִיָּ֔הוּ נָקֵ֣ל לַצֵּ֔ל לִנְט֖וֹת עֶ֣שֶׂר מַעֲל֑וֹת לֹ֣א כִ֔י יָשׁ֥וּב הַצֵּ֛ל אֲחֹרַנִּ֖ית עֶ֥שֶׂר מַעֲלֽוֹת׃
יא וַיִּקְרָ֛א יְשַׁעְיָ֥הוּ הַנָּבִ֖יא אֶל־יְהוָ֑ה וַיָּ֣שֶׁב אֶת־הַצֵּ֗ל בַּֽמַּעֲל֞וֹת אֲשֶׁ֣ר יָרְדָ֗ה בְּמַעֲל֥וֹת אָחָ֛ז אֲחֹרַנִּ֖ית

יְיָ יָת פִּתְגָמָא דְמַלִיל הָיְהֵךְ טוּלָא עֲסַר שָׁעִין אִם יְתוּב עֲסַר שָׁעִין׃ י וַאֲמַר חִזְקִיָה קַלִילָא דָא דִיהַךְ טוּלָא עֲסַר שָׁעִין בְּרַם נִסָא יְתוּב טוּלָא לַאֲחוֹרוֹהִי עֲסַר שָׁעִין׃ יא וְצַלִי יְשַׁעְיָה נְבִיָא קֳדָם יְיָ וַאֲתֵיב יָת טוּלָא בְּצוּרַת אֶבֶן שָׁעַיָא דְנַחֲתַת בְּמַסְקָנָא דְאָחָז

ת"א הצל אחורנית. שם: פס תום. (סנהדרין לו):

רד"ק

(ט) הלך הצל. כמו ילך שאל לו באיזה אות יבחר אם ילך הצל לפנים עשר מעלות ברגע אחד או ישוב אחורנית עשר מעלות ואמר חזקיהו נקל לצל לנטות עשר מעלות כי הגלגל במרוצתו יהיה נקל האות שימהר כרוצתו יותר ממנהגו אבל האות יהיה יותר חזק אם ישוב אחורנית ממהלכו: (יא) במעלות אשר ירדה. אשר ירד׳ השמש והלך הצל עשרה מעלות ושב השמש אחורנית והיה הצל במעלה הראשונה: במעלות אחז. כי זוא בנה אותם המעלות. ובדרש אשר ירדה במעלות אחז כי במות אחז נתקצר היום ונטה הצל עשר מעלות וירדה השמש עשר מעלות טרם זמנו כדי שלא יספדוהו לפי שהיה רשע ואותם עשר מעלות שירדה לאחז חזר׳ אחורנית לחזקיה לאות וי"ת וצלי ישעיה נביאה קדם יי ואתיב ית טולא בצורת

רש"י

לתוך דבר שנתקלקל ומתרפה: (ט) הלך הצל עשר מעלות אם ישוב עשר מעלות. הרי זה מקרי קצר כבר ירד הצל למעלות העשוי׳ לשעות היום כמו (אורלויי"ן בלע"ז) שעושין האנשים לבחון שעות היום הפך אתה שימתין במקום שהוא שם כדי מהלך עשר שעות או ישוב למעלה עשר מעלות ויהא נראה כאילו הוא שחרית: (י) ויאמר יחזקיהו נקל לצל לנטות עשר מעלות. דבר קל הוא לנטות במקומו ונוטה ועומד עבר מעלות אינו דבר הניכר כ"כ לא כן אלא ישוב הצל ויהיה הדבר תימה שראו שפנה היום לערוב וחוזר להיות בוקר: (יא) אשר ירדה במעלות אחז. יום שמת אחז נתקצר היום ומיהר הצל לירד עשר מעלות כדי שלא יהא נספד ואותן עשר שעות חזרו עכשיו לחזקיהו:

רלב"ג

כמו ההשגחה ולזה לא היה סומך בזה חזקיהו אם לא שיתן לו אות שבזולת תנאי נתן לו השם יתברך זאת המחיה: (ט) הלך הצל עשר מעלות אם ישוב עשר מעלות. ר"ל אם ישוב ללכת עשר מעלות אחרות בדרך שיהיו עשרים מעלות: (י) ויאמר חזקיהו נקל לצל לנטות עשר מעלות. הנה זה הפסוק קשה מאד בפירושו וזה כי ידוע כי נטית הצל הוא׳ מצד תנועת השמש ולפי תנועת השמש מעט מעט יטה הצל מעט מעט וזה מבוא׳ בעצמו ובהיות הענין כן מה זה שאמר חזקיהו נקל לצל לנטות עשר מעלות איך השב חזקיהו נקל מה שהוא מהמופת נפלא מאד לא רהיו כמוהו בביאור הפילו נמצא אשר לא קם כמוהו לכל האותות והמופתים אשר עשה כי במופתים ההם היו לשנות סדר אלו הדברים השפלים והוא יותר נפלא לאין שיעור מה שישתנה בו סדר הגרמים העליונים ובהיות הענין כן הנה יהיה זה המאמר מחזקיה בתכלית הסכלות ואיך ראוי שנחשוב זה עליו עם שלמותו הנראה מדבריו ואם אמרנו שלא היה זה המופת בתנועת השמש בעצמ׳ יקשה מה שאמר בספר דברי הימים על מליצי שרי בבל שבאו לדרוש המופת אשר היה בארץ כי ידמה מזה המקום שזה המופת היה על דבר אליו לפי שבזה המקום אמר כי שמע כי חלה חזקיהו והנראה בעיני מפני כל זה שזה המופת היה בצל לא בשמש בעצמו וכבר ידעת כי הענינים המתנועעים תחת השמש יביאו לפעמים שילון השמש בזולת מקומו הראוי לו וזה כבר נמצא בחוש הרבה ולפי שראה חזקיה מתנועת הרוח אז וקלות אידים שהיו תחת השמש שיקל להם בתנועתם המהירה להשיב הצל עשר מעלות כי באותו לד היתה תנועתם בקש מישעיה שיהיה הענין בהפך זה כדי שיוכר לו מופת הש"י והנה התפלל הנביא אל הש"י ושב הצל אחורנית עשר מעלות כמו ששאל חזקיה וזה המופת יתכן שנהיה כשחדש הש"י על דרך המופת אידים מתנועעים לצד הרוח ונראה בהם גילון השמש והביאוהו בתנועתם במהירות נפלא אל המקום ההוא עד שכבר היה זה תכף: (יא) במעלות אחז אחורנית. יתכן שבנה אחז אלו המעלות בבית המלכות. והנה שמע מלך בבל כי חלה חזקיה ולזה שלח מלאכיו שם ולזה אותם ג"כ שידרשו המופת אשר היה בארץ אז מחיל סנחריב שמתו כלם בזולת יד אדם אך הכם מלאך ה׳ ולזה אמר ג"כ אשר היה בארץ ואם היה זה שב אל המופת מהשמש הנה לא היה בארץ לבד אך בכל העולם:

מצודת דוד

שישוב הצל אחורנית עשר מעלות: (י) נקל לצל לנטות. האות הזה שיטה הצל במהירות הוא נקל מול אות החזרת הצל כי בנטיות הצל במהירות הלא חלף גלגל החמה במהלכו ואך ימהר ללכת במרוצה ואין האות ניכר כ"כ ולזה ישוב הצל אחורנית כי האות הזה יותר חזק וקשה: (יא) ויקרא וגו׳. לעשות האות אשר בחר חזקיה: במעלות אחז. ר"ל זה האות נעשה בהמעלות אשר עשה אחז ובהם שב הצל אחורנית עשר מעלות. ורז"ל אמרו שבא לאחור כחשבון שמיהרה לרדת בהמעלות ביום שמת אחז לקצר את היום להמעיט

hours returned now to Hezekiah [*Rashi* from *San.* 96a].

Alternatively, Ahaz made the sundial. Therefore, it was called the steps of Ahaz [*Redak*; *R. Joseph Kara,* Jerusalem ed.].

According to *Pirke d' R. Eliezer,* the sun had set early in Ahaz' time to prevent him from worshipping it [Ch. 52].

fulfill the word that He spoke. Shall the shade advance ten steps or shall it come back ten steps?" 10. And Hezekiah said, "It is easy for the shade to advance ten steps. Not so; let it return ten steps." 11. And the prophet Isaiah called to the Lord, and He brought back the shade on the steps that it had gone down on the steps of Ahaz, backwards ten steps.

house of the Lord on the third day! (The fact that this was merely a side remark rather than a question, makes it easier to understand its absence in the account of the Book of Isaiah. According to all other interpretations, the sign was given only after Hezekiah had requested it. Yet, that request is absent in Isaiah. Ed. note.)

9. **Shall the shade advance ten steps or shall it come back ten steps?**—I.e. which sign do you prefer, that the shade advance ten steps on the sundial, or that it come back ten steps? [*Redak, Mezudath David*].

10. **"It is easy for the shade to advance**—I.e. between the two wonders, it is easier for the shade to advance ten steps than to return ten steps [*Redak, Mezudath David*].

Rashi explains v. 9 in the past tense according to its literal translation, thus:

9. **The shade has advanced ten steps. Shall it come back ten steps?**—*This is an abbreviated verse. The shade has already advanced to the steps (from the steps—Rashi ms., on the steps—R. J. Kara) that are made for the hours of the day like the clocks (horloge in French) that people* (sic) (*craftsmen*—R. J. Kara; *Rashi,* Isaiah 38:8; *the sectarians—Parshandatha* ibid.; *R. J. Kara* in Lublin ed.) *make to determine the hours of the day. Do you wish it to wait in the place where it is, as long as it takes to go in ten hours, or should it go back up ten steps so that it will appear as though it is morning?* [*Rashi*].

Rashi refers to the sun clocks made by the Catholic priests in the Middle Ages. See *Parshandatha.* In Isaiah he elaborates more by explaining, *A sort of steps made opposite the sun to determine the hours of the day . . .*

Rashi explains *ma'aloth* with the French word, *orlein,* as it appears in its Hebrew transliteration. There is no known French word of that spelling. In Isaiah 38:8, *Rashi* brings the word, *horloge,* a clock. In II Kings 9:13, for *gerem hama'aloth, Rashi* uses the word, *ourle,* a border, a recessed line, a cut out sundial. Either one may be correct here.

10. **It is easy for the shade to recline for ten steps**—*It is an easy thing to recline in its place, reclining and standing still for ten steps. It is not so conspicuous. Not so, but let the shade go back, and the thing will be a marvel, for they saw that the day was turning toward evening, and it returns to be morning* [*Rashi*].

11. **that it had gone down on the steps of Ahaz**—*The day that Ahaz died, the day was shortened, and the shade hastened to advance ten steps, lest he be eulogized, and those ten*

עֶשֶׂר מַעֲלוֹת: יב בָּעֵת הַהִיא שָׁלַח בְּרֹאדַךְ בַּלְאֲדָן בֶּן־בַּלְאֲדָן מֶלֶךְ־בָּבֶל סְפָרִים וּמִנְחָה אֶל־חִזְקִיָּהוּ כִּי שָׁמַע כִּי חָלָה חִזְקִיָּהוּ: יג וַיִּשְׁמַע עֲלֵיהֶם חִזְקִיָּהוּ וַיַּרְאֵם אֶת־כָּל־בֵּית נְכֹתֹה אֶת־הַכֶּסֶף וְאֶת־הַזָּהָב וְאֶת־הַבְּשָׂמִים וְאֵת ׀ שֶׁמֶן הַטּוֹב וְאֵת כָּל־בֵּית כֵּלָיו וְאֵת כָּל־

דְאָחָז שִׁמְשָׁא לַאֲחוֹרוֹהִי עֲסַר שָׁעִין: יב בְּעִדָּנָא הַהִיא שְׁלַח בְּרֹאדַךְ בַּלְאֲדָן בַּר בַּלְאֲדָן מַלְכָּא דְבָבֶל אִגְרַן וְקֻרְבָּנִין לְוָת חִזְקִיָּה אֲרֵי שְׁמַע אֲרֵי אִתְמְרַע חִזְקִיָּה: יג וְקַבֵּל מִנְהוֹן חִזְקִיָּה וְאַחְזִינוּן יָת כָּל בֵּית גִּנְזוֹהִי יָת כַּסְפָּא וְיָת דַּהֲבָא וְיָת בּוּסְמַנַיָּא וְיָת מִשְׁחָא טָבָא וְיָת בֵּית מָנוֹהִי וְיָת כָּל

ת״א בלאדן. סנהדרין לו:

נכתו קרי

רש״י

(יב) כי שמע כי חלה. ועד אותו היום לא היה אדם חולה והיה ואיך שמע למוד היה לאכול בשלש שעות ביום וישן עד תשע כיון שחזר גלגל חמה לחזקיהו ניעור בתשע שעות ומלא שהוא שחרית בקש להרוג את עבדיו אמר אתם הנחתם אותי לישן יום ולילה אמרו גלגל חמה חזר אמר להם מי החזירו אמרו לו אלהיו של חזקיה כדאיתא בפסיקתא: (יג) בית נכתו. בית גנזי בשמיו כמו נכאות וצרי ולוט (בראשית ל״ז כ״ד): ואת שמן הטוב. יש פותרין שמן המשחה ויש פותרים שמן אפרסמון (בלסמון) שהוא מצוי בא״י שנאמר (ביחזקאל כ״ז י״ז) יהודה וישראל המה זין או כלי זין הרא׳ להם וכהם אמרו בית גנזיו הראה להם: שמן הטוב. זה שמן אפרסמון שלא היה בכל העולם אלא בירחו

רד״ק

אבן שעיא דנחתת במסקנא דאחז שמשא לאחורוהי עשר שעין ר״ל במעלות היתה אבן מסומנת לדעת שעות היום: (יב) בראדך. ובישעיה מראדך כתיב במ״ם ואחד הוא כי הם ממוצא אחד ובלאדן הוא שם כנוי נסמך לאביו שהיה שמו בלאדן וזה מלך אסרחדון כי סנחריב מלך בבל היה וכן בימי מנשה נאמר בדברי הימים ויבא עליה׳ את שרי הצבא אשר למלך אשור וגו׳ ויוליכם בבלה: כי שמע כי חלה. לא היה עיקר שליחותו על חליו אלא על המופת שנעשה לו על חליו וכן הוא בדברי הימים לדרוש המופת אשר היה בארץ: (יג) וישמע עליהם. כמו אליהם ועל כמו אל ורבים כמוהו כמו וילך אלקנה הרמתה על ביתו כמו אל ביתו ומה שאמר וישמע נראה שהם בקשו ממנו להראותם נכתה ושמע אליהם ועשה כן וכת״י וקביל מנהון ובישעיה וישמח עליהם: את כל בית נכתה. כל בית חמדתו כלומר כל חדברי׳ שהיו לו ואחר כך פרט מה הם הדברים הנחמדים וכן נכאת וצרי ולוט דבר נחמד ובדברי רז״ל מאי בית נכותה מהם אמרו אשתו היתה משקה להם ומהם אמרו

רלב״ג

(יב) בעת ההיא שלח בראדך בלאדן. ראוי שתדע כי אע״פ שהיה סנחריב מושל בבבל כמו שיראה ממה שאמר במה שקדם ויבא מלך אשור מבבל הנה היה שם מלך והיה תחת סנחריב והיה נותן לו מס בנה בנה כי כן היה מנהגו עם כל המלכים שהיה כובש אותם והנה לפי דעתי נמשכה המלוכה למלכי אשור עד שבא נבוכדנצר מלך בבל והחזיק במלכות הוא וכאשר המלכות לו ולבנו ולבן בנו עד שבעים שנה: ספרים ומנחה אל חזקיהו. כבר ספר בספר ד״ה כי רבים היו מביאים מנחה לה׳ בירושלים ומגדנות לחזקיה והיה זה כן מפני מה ששמעו מהמופת שעשה ה׳ בחיל מלך אשור אז ידעו כל ממלכות הארץ כי ה׳ הוא האלהים ולזה ספר זה שם אחר ספור זה המופת אשר עשה ה׳ בחיל מלך אשור: (יג) וישמע עליהם חזקיהו. ר״ל שקבל במעט בעבורם מה שבקשו ממנו והגיד להם כל אשר שאלו והראם את כל בית נכתה הנה הוא קבוץ על חמודותיו ואחר זה פרט מה שהיה שם והיא כסף וזהב ובשמים ושמן הטוב הוא שמן אפרסמון שלא היה נמצא כי אם בארצו ובמקום אחד ממנו לבד והוא נקרא בלשון חכמי בלע״ז: ואת כל בית כליו ואת כל אשר נמצא באוצרותיו. יתכן שהראה אותם ג״כ הדברים החמודים שהיו לו בממשלתו ושנם שיש

מנחת ש״י

(יג) וישמע עליהם חזקיהו. במקרא דפוס ישן מוויניציאה נכתב בגליון וישמח וכן בתרגום שלה והדי עליהון חזקיה וזהו טעות גדול שכל הספרים והמסורתיים מסכימים שזה דמלכים וישמע ודישעיה וישמח וי״א. פסוק סימן שמעה ושמחה ציון וזהו ג״כ א׳ מן הנמנים במסורת דסמיך על לשון שמיעה ותרגומו וקביל מנהון חזקיה: וישמע עליהם חזקיה. (הנ״ל) בס״א ישן מטוליטולא כתוב אליהם וכ״כ החכם לומאטו שכן מצא בספרים כ״י ואיני שומע אליהם לבטל ספרים אחרים שהמסורה אומרת כל לשון שמיעה אל בר מן י״ב על וזה א׳ מהם וכ״כ רד״ק וישמע עליהם כמו אליהם וכן מצאתי מסרה כ״י שאומרת בפ׳ סימן מלכים וישמע עליהם חזקיהו. ישעיה וישמח עליהם חזקיהו: נכתה. נכתו קרי: ואת בית כליו. בס״א כ״י ואת כל בית וכן הוא בנביאים עם פי׳ פרי״א

מצודת דוד

בהספדו: (יב) כי חלה. על בהתפלא שלח לדרוש בשלומו דרך אהבה וכד״ה נאמר בבלה לדרוש המופת הנעשה בחליו: (יג) וישמע

מצודת ציון

(יג) נכתו. ענין אוצר נחמד וכן נכאת וצרי (בראשית ל״ז) שר״ל דברי נחמדים:

greater than our god?" They replied, "Yes, Hezekiah's God is greater than your god." *Tanhuma* words it thus,—"Is there a greater god than mine?" "Yes," they replied, "Hezekiah's God is greater than all the gods in the world." Since Merodach-baladan was a sun worshipper, he was astounded to learn that Hezekiah's God had overruled his god, the sun [*Etz Yosef* on *Tanhuma*].

"Is there such a man, and I should not want to send him a greeting?" [*Sanhedrin* 96a].

Immediately, he sent letters and a gift to Hezekiah [*Pesikta* ibid.].

13. **listened to them**—They apparently requested of him that he show them his treasure-house, and he

12. At that time, Berodach-baladan the son of Baladan, the king of Babylonia, sent letters and a gift to Hezekiah for he heard that Hezekiah had been ill. 13. And Hezekiah listened to them, and he showed them his entire treasure-house, the silver, the gold, the spices, and the good oil, and the entire house in which he kept his vessels, and everything

12. **Berodach-baladan the son of Baladan, the king of Babylonia**—Although Sennacherib ruled over Babylonia, as above 17:24, there was, nevertheless, a king in Babylonia. He was subordinate to the king of Assyria and paid tribute annually, as was the custom of all the nations conquered by Assyria. This continued until Nebuchadnezzar became king, when he became the independent ruler of Babylonia. He occupied the throne, followed by his son and his grandson, for a total of seventy years [*Ralbag*].

Others identify him with Esarhaddon, king of Assyria, who ruled also over Babylonia. In Isaiah, he is called Merodach-baladan. Since his father was named Baladan, he was called Merodach of Baladan [*Redak*].

The Talmud (*San.* 96a) relates that King Baladan's face became like that of a dog. His son, Merodach, assumed the throne and reigned as a substitute for his father. In honor of his father, he adopted the name Merodach-Baladan to indicate that he was merely representing his father Baladan on the throne. The name Merodach the son of Baladan did not suffice to convey that idea, because everyone used such appelations.

Abarbanel places him after Esarhaddon. This view cannot be reconciled with the tradition that Hezekiah was cured of his illness on the day of Sennacherib's defeat, because some time elapsed from then until he fled to Nineveh, was assassinated, succeeded by Esarhaddon, and then for Esarhaddon to be succeeded by Merodach. Even *Redak*'s view is difficult to reconcile with this tradition, since Esarhaddon did not become king immediately after Sennacherib's defeat. See above 19:37.

for he heard that Hezekiah had been ill—*and until that time no person had ever been ill and had become well. Now, how did he hear? He was accustomed to eating after three hours had elapsed in the day, and he would sleep until after the ninth hour. Since the sphere of the sun had gone backwards, he awoke after nine hours and found that it was morning. He sought to kill his servants. He said, "You let me sleep a day and a night!" They replied, "The sphere of the sun went back." He said to them, "Who brought it back?" They said to him, "The God of Hezekiah." As is stated in Pesikta* (*d'Rav Kahana* p. 14a) [*Rashi*].

Rashi, Isaiah adds that the account is also found in *Tanhuma.* We find it in *Ki Thissa* 5.

The Midrashim conclude,—He said to them, "Is Hezekiah's God

אֲשֶׁר נִמְצָא בְּאוֹצְרֹתָיו לֹא־הָיָה דָבָר אֲשֶׁר לֹא־הֶרְאָם חִזְקִיָּהוּ בְּבֵיתוֹ וּבְכָל־מֶמְשַׁלְתּוֹ׃ יד וַיָּבֹא יְשַׁעְיָהוּ הַנָּבִיא אֶל־הַמֶּלֶךְ חִזְקִיָּהוּ וַיֹּאמֶר אֵלָיו מָה־אָמְרוּ הָאֲנָשִׁים הָאֵלֶּה וּמֵאַיִן יָבֹאוּ אֵלֶיךָ וַיֹּאמֶר חִזְקִיָּהוּ מֵאֶרֶץ רְחוֹקָה בָּאוּ מִבָּבֶל׃ טו וַיֹּאמֶר מָה רָאוּ בְּבֵיתֶךָ וַיֹּאמֶר חִזְקִיָּהוּ אֵת כָּל־אֲשֶׁר בְּבֵיתִי רָאוּ לֹא־הָיָה דָבָר אֲשֶׁר לֹא־הִרְאִיתִם בְּאֹצְרֹתָי׃ טז וַיֹּאמֶר יְשַׁעְיָהוּ אֶל־חִזְקִיָּהוּ שְׁמַע דְּבַר־יְהוָה׃ יז הִנֵּה יָמִים בָּאִים

דְאִשְׁתְּכַח בְּגִנְזוֹהִי לָא הֲוָה מִדַעַם דְלָא אַחֲזִינוּן חִזְקִיָה בְּבֵיתֵיהּ וּבְכָל שׁוּלְטָנֵיהּ׃ יד וַאֲתָא יְשַׁעְיָה נְבִיָא לְוַת מַלְכָּא חִזְקִיָה וַאֲמַר לֵיהּ מָה אֲמַרוּ לָךְ גֻבְרַיָא הָאִלֵין וּמְנָן אֲתוֹ לְוָתָךְ וַאֲמַר חִזְקִיָה מֵאַרְעָא רְחִיקָא אֲתוֹ לְוָתִי מִבָּבֶל׃ טו וַאֲמַר מָה חֲזוֹ בְּבֵיתָךְ וַאֲמַר חִזְקִיָה יָת כָּל דִי בְּבֵיתִי חֲזוֹ לָא הֲוָה מִדַעַם דִי לָא אַחֲזֵיתִינוּן בְּגִנְזַי׃ טז וַאֲמַר יְשַׁעְיָהוּ לְחִזְקִיָה קַבֵּל פִּתְגָמָא דַיָי׃ יז הָא יוֹמַיָא אָתָן וִיתְנְטִיל

רד"ק

ואמרו כי לפיכך נקרא יריחו. והיה רע בעיני ה' כי הרא' להם בית נכתה כי נתגא' בבא אליו השלוחים מארץ רחוקה וכי היה מצליח בכל דרכיו וכן אומר בדברי הימים כי גבה לבו ואמר בשלוחים האלה שבאו לכבודו והיה לו לומ' שבאו לכבוד האל כי לדרוש המופת באו וכן אומר בדברי הימים וכן במליצי שרי בבל המשולחים עליו לדרוש המופת אשר היה בארץ עזבו

רש"י

רוכליך בחטי מנית ופנג וראיתי בס' יוסיפון פנג הוא אפרסמון וגדל ביריחו ועל שם הריח נקרא יריחו: לא היה דבר. את הארון והלוחות וספר התורה: (יד) מארץ רחוקה באו. זה אחד משלשה שבדקן הקב"ה ומצאן עביט של מים עכורים. קין. יחזקיהו. ובלעם. קין לא ידעתי השומר אחי אנכי (בראשית ד' ה') היה לו לומר רבונו של עולם הלא כל הנסתרות גלויות לך כדאיתא בתנחומא. בלעם

מנחת שי

ובדפוס ישן יש הערה מחילוף אבן בכל אחד כפרים אין בהם אלא כל רק הוא בס' ישעיהו: (יד) ויבא ישעיהו הנביא אל המלך חזקיהו. בכ"א נכתב בלדו

רלב"ג

רע בעיני ה' אבל עשה כי גבה לבו על הש"י כי הם באו לדרוש את המופ' לכבוד הש"י ולא הי' ראוי לחזקיה להגדיל עצמו בזה אבל היה ראוי שיתן הגדולה והכבוד לש"י ויראה להם גדולת הש"י כי על זה באו ולזה גנה אותו בספר ד"ה על זה כי הוא לא השיב לש"י מהכבוד על זה המופת בשבה לו שהוסיף על ימיו מה שהוא ראוי אבל גבה לבו ולזה היה עליו קצף על יהודה וירושלם והנה הקצף היה מה

מצודת ציון

(יד) ומאין. מאיזה מקום:

מצודת דוד

עליהם. יתכן בקשו להראות להם את כל בית נכתו ושמע אליהם

turbid water: Cain, Balaam, and Hezekiah. Cain said, "(Gen. 4:9) *I know not. Am I my brother's keeper?" He should have said, "Lord of the Universe! Are all hidden things not revealed to You? As it is stated in Tanhuma.* (In our versions of *Tanhuma* this is not found. It is found, however, *Num. Rabbah* 20:6. See *Parshandatha* Is. 39:3.) *Balaam, when the Omnipresent said to him,* "(Num. 22:9) *Who are these men with you?" he should have said, "O Lord God, You know!" as it is said concerning Ezekiel* (37:3). *Yet he retorted arrogantly,* "(Num. 22:10 *Balak, son of Zippor, king of Moab, sent them to me." Many people seek me. Hezekiah should have replied to Isaiah, "You are the prophet of the Omnipresent. Yet you ask me?"* Instead, *Hezekiah commenced to become haughty, and said,* "(Is. 39:3) *They have come to me from a distant land." Therefore, he was punished, and because he rejoiced over them and*

that was found in his treasuries; there was nothing that Hezekiah did not show them in his palace and in his kingdom.
14. And Isaiah the prophet came to King Hezekiah and said to him, "What did these men say, and whence did they come to you?" And Hezekiah said, "They have come from a distant country—from Babylonia."
15. And he said, "What did they see in your palace?" And Hezekiah said, "They saw everything that is in my palace. There was nothing that I did not show them in my treasuries."
16. And Isaiah said to Hezekiah, "Hearken to the word of the Lord.
17. Behold a time will come

complied with their wishes. Isaiah states, "and he rejoiced over them (39:2).

his treasure-house—Heb. בֵּית נְכֹתוֹ, *the storehouse of his spices, like* "(Gen. 37:25) *spices* (נְכֹאת), balm and lotus" [*Rashi*].

Alternatively, the term נְכֹאת includes all his choice possessions. Subsequently, they are enumerated. In the Talmud, *San.* 104a there is a variance of opinion concerning בֵּית נְכֹתוֹ. Some say that his wife was waiting on them. Some say he showed them iron that could destroy other iron, or his most powerful weapons. Some say that he showed them his treasure-house [*Redak*].

and the good oil—*Some interpret this as the anointment oil* (Ex. 30:22–33), *and others interpret it as balsam oil, which is found in Eretz Israel, as it is said,* "(Ezek. 27:17) *Judah and the land of Israel, they were your merchants, with wheat of Minnith and Pannag. I saw in the book of Josephon* (book 4, ch. 22), *Pannag is balsam, and it grows in Jericho. Because of the aroma* (רֵיחַ), *it is called Jericho* (יְרִיחוֹ) [*Rashi, Redak*].

there was nothing—*even the Ark, the Tablets, and the Scroll of the Law* [*Rashi* from *Pirkei d' R. Eliezer,* ch. 52]. He told them, "With this we wage war and are victorious [Ibid.].

It displeased God when Hezekiah showed the emissaries from Babylon all his treasures, for it demonstrated arrogance, assuming that they had come from a distant land, to do him honor since he prospered in all his undertakings, as the Chronicler states (II 32:25), ". . . for his heart became haughty." He should have realized that the visitors came in honor of the Almighty. He concludes (v. 31) "And so with the messengers of the princes of Babylonia, whom they sent to him to inquire of the wonder that was in the land, God allowed him; to test him, to know all that was in his heart" [*Redak*].

14. **"They have come from a distant country**—*This is one of the three whom the Holy One, Blessed be He, tested and found them to be a vessel of*

ויתנטיל כל די בביתך
ודגנזו אבהתך עד יומא
הדין ויתוב לבבל לא
ישתאר מדעם אמר יי:
יח ומבנך די יפקון מנך
דתוליד ידבר ויהון
רברבין בהיכלא
דמלכא דבבל: יט ואמר
חזקיה לישעיהו תקין
פתגמא דיי דמלילתא
ואמר הלא אם שלם
וקשוט יהי ביומי:
כ ושאר פתגמי חזקיה
וכל גבורתיה ודעבד
ית בריכתא וית
מזיקתא ואיתי ית מיא
לקרתא הלא · אינון
כתיבין

וְנִשָּׂא ׀ כָּל־אֲשֶׁר בְּבֵיתֶךָ וַאֲשֶׁר אָצְרוּ
אֲבֹתֶיךָ עַד־הַיּוֹם הַזֶּה בָּבֶלָה לֹא־יִוָּתֵר
דָּבָר אָמַר יְהוָה: יח וּמִבָּנֶיךָ אֲשֶׁר־יֵצְאוּ
מִמְּךָ אֲשֶׁר תּוֹלִיד יִקָּח וְהָיוּ סָרִיסִים
בְּהֵיכַל מֶלֶךְ בָּבֶל: יט וַיֹּאמֶר חִזְקִיָּהוּ
אֶל־יְשַׁעְיָהוּ טוֹב דְּבַר־יְהוָה אֲשֶׁר
דִּבַּרְתָּ וַיֹּאמֶר הֲלוֹא אִם־שָׁלוֹם וֶאֱמֶת
יִהְיֶה בְיָמָי: כ וְיֶתֶר דִּבְרֵי חִזְקִיָּהוּ וְכָל־
גְּבוּרָתוֹ וַאֲשֶׁר עָשָׂה אֶת־הַבְּרֵכָה וְאֶת־
הַתְּעָלָה וַיָּבֵא אֶת־הַמַּיִם הָעִירָה הֲלוֹא־

תולדות אהרן

לא יותר דבר. יומא לג: ומבניך סנהדרין צג קד:

*יקחו קרי פתח באתנח

רש"י

שאמר לו המקום (במדבר כ"ב ט') מי האנשים האלה עמך היה לו לומר ה' אלהים אתה ידעת כמו שנאמר (יחזקאל ל"ז ג') והוא השיב בגאוה בלק בן צפור מלך מואב שלח אלי הרבה מבקשים יש לי חזקיהו היה לו להשיב לישעיה אתה נביאו של מקום ואתה שואל אלי התחיל חזקיה מתגאה ואמר מארץ רחוקה באו אלי לכך נענש ועל ששמח עליהם והאכילם על שלחנו: (יז) לא יותר דבר. מדה כנגד מדה לא היה דבר: (יח) ומבניך. חנני' מישאל ועזריה: (יט) טוב דבר ה'. מאחר שבימי יהיה שלום: (כ) ואשר עשה את הברכה וגו'. בדברי הימים:

רד"ק

האלהים לנסותו לדעת כל אשר בלבבו: (יח) אשר תוליד יקחו. יקח כתיב וקרי יקחו ואמרו זה דניאל חנניה מישאל ועזריה: והיו סריסים. מחלוקת בדברי רז"ל מהם אמרו סריסי' ממש ומהם אמרו שנסתרס' ע"ג בימיהם כלומר שהכירו הכל שאין בה ממש וי"ת רברבין כמו שרים ועל דניאל חנניה מישאל ועזריה אמר שהם היו בהיכלי מלך בבל ונאמר עליה' מבני

רלב"ג

שאמר לו ישעיה הנביא על זה: (יח) אשר יצאו ממך אשר תוליד. זה לאות שלא היו בנים לחזקיה בעת זאת הנבואה אך אחר שלש שנים הוליד מנשה שמלך אחריו והנה אמר ובניך על זרעו ואם הוא רחוק כי כל זרע אדם יקראו בניו אפי' לאלף דור כמו שנקרא אנחנו היום ב"י:

מנחת שי

יש ספרים שכתוב ישעיה: (יח) יקח*. יקחו קרי:

מצודת דוד

והראם: (יז) ונשא. יהיה נשא ונלקח: ואשר אצרו. אשר טמנו באוצר: לא יותר דבר. מכל אשר בביתך: (יח) ומבניך. הם דניאל חנניה מישאל ועזריה: אשר יצאו ממך אשר תוליד. כפל הדבר פעמים ובלשון שונה כדרך המקרא: (יט) טוב דבר ה'. טוב הדבר בעיני ופירש דבריו ואמר הלוא אם יהיה שלום בימי וה' יאמת לו הבטחתו זו איני חושש במה שיהיה אחרי מותי: (כ) את המים. מוצא מי גיחון שהיתה מחוץ לעיר הביא העירה:

מצודת ציון

(יח) סריסים. שרים וממונים: (כ) הברכה. בנין אבנים על אסיפת המים: התעלה. חפירה למים:

He felt, too, that perhaps this gloomy prophecy would be revoked if they would improve their ways [*Malbim*].

peace and truth—The prophecy of peace in my days will surely come true, since favorable prophecies are never revoked [*Malbim*].

20. **and how he made the conduit and the pool**—*in Chronicles* [*Rashi*].

In II Chron. 32:3, 4, the Chronicler relates that when Sennacherib seized the fortified cities of Judah and marched toward Jerusalem, Hezekiah "took counsel with his officers and his mighty warriors to close off the waters of the springs that were outside the city, and they assisted him. And a large multitude gathered, and they closed off all the springs, and the stream that flowed in the midst of the land, saying,

when everything in your palace and what your forefathers have
stored up, will be carried off to Babylonia; nothing shall
remain," said the Lord. 18. And they will take [some] of your
sons, who will issue from you, whom you will beget, and they
will be officers in the palace of the king of Babylonia." 19. And
Hezekiah said to Isaiah, "The word of the Lord that you have
spoken is good." For he thought, "Is it not so, if there will be
peace and truth in my days?" 20. And the rest of the events of
Hezekiah and all his mighty deeds, and how he made the conduit and the pool, and he brought the water into the city, they

are

served them at his table [*Rashi*].

17. **nothing shall remain**—*You shall be paid in kind,* corresponding to "*There was nothing* (v. 15)" [*Rashi*].

I.e. Hezekiah would be punished for showing off all his treasures, by having all those treasures carried off to Babylonia.

18. **And ... [some] of your sons**—*Hananiah, Mishael, and Azariah* [*Rashi*].

officers—Heb. *sarisim,* usually interpreted as eunuchs. There is a dispute in the Babylonian Talmud (*Sanhedrin* 93b). Some say that Hananiah, Mishael, and Azariah were actually eunuchs, as was the custom of the kings to castrate those who were to serve in their palace, so that they would not marry, and would be completely dedicated to his service. Others maintain that the expression is figurative. It represents the fact that paganism was emasculated in their time. I.e. its impotency and folly were generally recognized. Although no harm was done to them, it was, nevertheless, an evil decree that they would be exiled to Babylonia. *Jonathan* renders: officers. This prophecy alludes to Daniel as well as Hananiah, Mishael, and Azariah, all of whom were chosen to stand in Nebuchadnezzar's court. They were all of royal descent, as is mentioned in the beginning of the Book of Daniel, 1:3. According to some, only Daniel was of royal blood, whereas Hananiah, Mishael, and Azariah were of other tribes and were not included in this prophecy —*Redak,* also *San.* 93b, *Rashi* ad loc.*

19. **"The word of the Lord ... is good**—*since there will be peace in my days* [*Rashi*].

Alternatively, the word of the Lord is good, i.e. it is justified, both because of my political error, and because of my haughtiness, which is a sin against God [*Malbim*].

For he thought—lit. And he said. This may be interpreted as a second statement. First he justified God's retribution upon his descendants.

הֵ֣ם כְּתוּבִ֔ים עַל־סֵ֛פֶר דִּבְרֵ֥י הַיָּמִ֖ים
לְמַלְכֵ֥י יְהוּדָֽה׃ כא וַיִּשְׁכַּ֥ב חִזְקִיָּ֖הוּ עִם־
אֲבֹתָ֑יו וַיִּמְלֹ֛ךְ מְנַשֶּׁ֥ה בְנ֖וֹ תַּחְתָּֽיו׃
כא א בֶּן־שְׁתֵּ֤ים עֶשְׂרֵה֙ שָׁנָ֔ה מְנַשֶּׁ֖ה
בְמָלְכ֑וֹ וַחֲמִשִּׁ֣ים וְחָמֵ֗שׁ שָׁנָ֔ה מָלַ֖ךְ
בִּירוּשָׁלִָ֑ם וְשֵׁ֥ם אִמּ֖וֹ חֶפְצִי־בָֽהּ׃ ב וַיַּ֥עַשׂ
הָרַ֖ע בְּעֵינֵ֣י יְהוָ֑ה כְּתוֹעֲבֹת֙ הַגּוֹיִ֔ם אֲשֶׁר֙
הוֹרִ֣ישׁ יְהוָ֔ה מִפְּנֵ֖י בְּנֵ֥י יִשְׂרָאֵֽל׃ ג וַיָּ֗שָׁב
וַיִּ֙בֶן֙ אֶת־הַבָּמ֔וֹת אֲשֶׁ֥ר אִבַּ֖ד חִזְקִיָּ֣הוּ
אָבִ֑יו וַיָּ֨קֶם מִזְבְּחֹ֜ת לַבַּ֗עַל וַיַּ֤עַשׂ אֲשֵׁרָה֙
כַּאֲשֶׁ֣ר עָשָׂ֗ה אַחְאָב֙ מֶ֣לֶךְ יִשְׂרָאֵ֔ל
וַיִּשְׁתַּ֙חוּ֙ לְכָל־צְבָ֣א הַשָּׁמַ֔יִם וַיַּעֲבֹ֖ד
אֹתָֽם׃ ד וּבָנָ֥ה מִזְבְּחֹ֖ת בְּבֵ֣ית יְהוָ֑ה
אֲשֶׁר֙ אָמַ֣ר יְהוָ֔ה בִּירוּשָׁלִַ֖ם אָשִׂ֥ים אֶת־

תרגום

כְּתִיבִין עַל סְפַר פִּתְגָמֵי
יוֹמַיָא לְמַלְכֵי דְבֵית
יְהוּדָה׃ כא וּשְׁכִיב
חִזְקִיָהוּ עִם אֲבָהָתוֹהִי
וּמְלַךְ מְנַשֶּׁה בְּרֵיהּ
תְּחוֹתוֹהִי׃ א בַּר תַּרְתָּא
עַסְרֵי שְׁנִין מְנַשֶּׁה כַּד
מְלַךְ וְחַמְשִׁין וְחַמֵשׁ
שְׁנִין מְלַךְ בִּירוּשְׁלֵם
וְשׁוּם אִמֵיהּ חֶפְצִי בַהּ׃
ב וַעֲבַד דְבִישׁ קֳדָם יְיָ
כְּתוֹעֲבַת עַמְמַיָא דְתָרִיךְ
יְיָ מִן קֳדָם בְּנֵי יִשְׂרָאֵל׃
ג וְתָב וּבְנָא יַת בָּמָתָא
דְאַבֵּיד חִזְקִיָהוּ אֲבוּהִי
וַאֲקֵים אֱגוֹרִין לְבַעְלָא
וַעֲבַד אֲשֵׁירְתָא כְּמָא
דַעֲבַד אַחְאָב מַלְכָּא
דְיִשְׂרָאֵל וּסְגִיד לְכָל
חֵילֵי שְׁמַיָא וּפְלַח
יַתְהוֹן׃ ד וּבְנָא אֱגוֹרִין
בְּבֵית מַקְדְשָׁא דַיְיָ
דַאֲמַר יְיָ בִּירוּשְׁלֵם
אשרי

ת"א מנשה. שם קב ג

רד"ק

יהודה והם היו מזרע המלוכה כי כן אמר נבוכדנצר לבקש מזרע המלוכה ומן הפרתמים: (ג) כאשר עשה אחאב. כי הוא החל לעשו' אשרה במלכי ישראל כי עד שמלך אחאב לא ראינו לאחד מן המלכים שעשו אשרה אלא שהיו הולכי' בחטאת

מנחת שי

כא (ג) ויקם מזבחות לבעל. במלה זו וחברותיה שבסמוך רבו החלופים בספרים אם הם חסרים וא"ו או מלאים והעיקר כמו שמלאתי בס"ס כ"י שזה ויבן ובנה מזבחת שבסמוך חסרים ועל אלו נמסר ב' חסרים ובענין וכל אורייתא כוותיה חסר. והכי איתמר בהדיא במסרא רבתא אבל

מצודת ציון

כא (ב) הוריש. גירש: (ג) צבא השמים. כוכבים ומזלות:

מצודת דוד

כא (ד) אשר אמר וגו'. כאלו המקרא קורא עליו לומר כאו מס

written in the book of the chronicles of the kings of Judah. 21. And Hezekiah slept with his forefathers, and Manasseh his son reigned in his stead.

21.

1. Manasseh was twelve years old when he became king, and he reigned in Jerusalem fifty-five years, and his mother's name was Hephzibah. 2. And he did what was evil in the eyes of the Lord; like the abominations of the nations that the Lord had driven out from before the children of Israel. 3. And he rebuilt the high places that Hezekiah his father had destroyed, and he erected altars to the Baal, and he made an *asherah* as Ahab the king of Israel had made, and he prostrated himself to the entire host of the heaven, and he worshipped them. 4. And he built altars in the house of the Lord, concerning which the Lord had said, "In Jerusalem I will establish My Name."

'Why should the kings of Assyria come and find many waters?'"

In v. 30, he explains in detail, "And he, Hezekiah closed off the source of the waters of the upper Gihon and diverted them downstream westward to the city of David." By this maneuver, he diverted the stream into the city of Jerusalem [*Mezudath David*].

3. **as Ahab the king of Israel had made**—Until Ahab, none of the kings had worshipped the *asherah*. They merely followed the sins of Jeroboam, son of Nebat. Ahab introduced the worship of the *asherah* [*Redak*].

4. **which the Lord had said . . .**—Scripture decries Manasseh's evil deeds that in the very place the Lord chose to cause His Name to dwell, Manasseh built altars to pagan deities [*Mezudath David*].

שמי: ה ויבן מזבחות לכל־צבא
השמים בשתי חצרות בית־יהוה:
ו והעביר את־בנו באש ועונן ונחש
ועשה אוב וידענים הרבה לעשות
הרע בעיני יהוה להכעיס: ז וישם את־
פסל האשרה אשר עשה בבית אשר
אמר יהוה אל־דוד ואל־שלמה בנו
בבית הזה ובירושלם אשר בחרתי
מכל שבטי ישראל אשים את־שמי
לעולם: ח ולא אסיף להניד רגל
ישראל מן־האדמה אשר נתתי
לאבותם רק | אם־ישמרו לעשות ככל
אשר צויתים ולכל־התורה אשר־צוה
אתם עבדי משה: ט ולא שמעו ויתעם

אשרי ית שכינתי:
ה ובנא אגורין לכל
חילי שמיא בתרתין
דרתא דבית מקדשא
דיי: ו ועבר ית בריה
בנורא ועגין ונחיש
ועבד בידין וזכורו אסגי
למעבד דביש קדם יי
לארגזא קדמוהי:
ז ושוי ית צלם אשירתא
דעבד בביתא דאמר
יי לדוד ולשלמה בריה
בביתא הדין ובירושלם
דאיתרעיתי מכל
שבטיא דישראל אשרי
ית שכינתי לעלם:
ח ולא אוסיף לטלטלא
ית ישראל מן ארעא
דיהבית לאבהתהון
לחוד אם יטרון למעבד
ככל תפקידתא
דפקידתינון ולכל
אוריתא דפקיד יתהון
עבדי משה: ט ולא
קבילו וצטעינון מנשה
למעבד

רד"ק

ירבעם: (ו) לעשו' הרע בעיני ה' להכעיס. אמרו שסילק האש העליונה שהיתה במזבח מעת שירד' שם בימי שלמה עמד הוא וסלקה וזה המעש' הי' להכעיס: (ח) ולא אסיף להניד. אמר אוסיף כי כשהיו חוטאי' היה משליט בהם אויבית' והיו מנידי'

מנחת שי

ויבן מזבחות שבפסוק לאחריו ראוי להיות מלא: (ו) ועונן. יש ספרים חסר וא"ו אחר עי"ן: לעשות הרע בעיני ה' להכעיס. ובדפוס ישן מויניציאה כתוב ל ה כ ע י ס ו וכן הוא בקונקורדאנציאה אך בשאר ספרים כתוב להכעיס בלא וא"ו ומה שמתורגם לארגזא קדמוהי כן דרך התרגום בכל מלת ל ה כ ע י ס מפני כבוד המקום ברוך הוא: (ח) להניד רגל ישראל. ראיתי מי שנסתפק אם כתוב את רגל וכן נראה מהתרגום ואין ספק מוציא מידי ודאי כל הספרים

מצודת דוד

פה אשר ה' אמר כי שמה ישכון והוא שם שמה מזבחות לאשרה: בירושלים. בבית העומד בירושלים: אשים את שמי. ר"ל אשרה שכינתי: (ה) בשתי חצרות. עזרת כהנים ועזרת ישראל: (ו) והעביר וגו'. היא עבודת המולך: ועונן וגו'. המה מעשה כשפים: (ז) בבית וגו'. פסל האשרה שעשה שם אותם בבית ה': (ח) ולא אוסיף. גם זה מדברי ה' שאמר לדוד ולשלמה: אשר צויתים. הם אנכי ולא יהיה לך וגו' ששמעו מפי הגבורה: אשר צוה אותם עבדי משה. הם שאר המצות כולם ששמעו ממשה הנאמר לו מפי ה': (ט) ולא שמעו. אבל המה לא

מצודת ציון

(ח) להניד. ענ' נדידה: (ט) ויתעם. ענ' תועה:

7. **the image of the *asherah* . . . in the house**—Ahaz had placed it in the attic over the *heichal*. Manasseh brought it into the *heichal* itself. Amon outdid his father by placing it in the Holy of Holies [*San.* 103b].

8. **And I will not cause Israel's feet to wander**—This is part of the quotation. God had promised David and Solomon that He would not continue to exile Israel as long as they kept His commandments. Although they had not been completely exiled before Solomon's time, they, nevertheless, had suffered partial exile at the hands of their adversaries when the people were not scrupulous in their observance of the commandments [*Redak*].

all that I have commanded them—

5. And he built altars for the entire host of Heaven in the two courts of the house of the Lord. 6. And he passed his son through fire; he practiced soothsaying and divination, and he consulted necromancers and those divine by the Jidoa bone; he did much that was evil in the eyes of the Lord, to provoke [Him]. 7. He placed the graven image of the *asherah* that he made, in the house concerning which the Lord had said to David and to his son Solomon, "In this house and in Jerusalem, which I have chosen from all the tribes of Israel, will I establish My Name forever. 8. And I will not continue to cause Israel's feet to wander from the land that I have given their forefathers; if they will but observe to act in accordance with all that I have commanded them, and according to all the Law that Moses My servant commanded them." 9. But they did not obey, and Manasseh led them astray

5. **in the two courts of the house of the Lord**—the court of the priests and the court of the Israelites [*Mezudath David*].

6. **And he passed his son through fire**—*This was the Molech worship* [*Mezudath David*].

he practiced soothsaying—as those who believe that certain times are auspicious for commencing undertakings and others are not [*Rashi*, Lev. 19:26].

and divination—like those who divine with weasels and birds. If his bread fell out of his mouth or a deer ran across his path, he considers it an evil omen [*Rashi* ibid.].

and he consulted necromancers—who would conjure up the dead. See I Sam. 28:3–25, especially v. 19, where the validity of necromancy is discussed in the Commentary Digest. See also *Rashi*, Lev. 19:31, *San.* 65a, that the necromancer would bring up the dead and seat him under his armpit, where he would talk.

the Jidoa bone—the bone of an animal whose navel is always attached to the ground. The sorcerer would take a bone of this animal, insert it in his mouth, and cause it to speak [*San.* 65b; *Sifthei hachamim*, Lev. 19:31].

he did much that was evil in the eyes of the Lord, to provoke Him—Our Rabbis say that he removed the heavenly fire, which had descended upon the altar in Solomon's time. He did this purely to provoke God [*Redak* from unknown Midrashic source].

מנשה לעשות את־הרע מן־הגוים
אשר השמיד יהוה מפני בני ישראל:
י וידבר יהוה ביד־עבדיו הנביאים
לאמר: יא יען אשר עשה מנשה מלך־
יהודה התעבות האלה הרע מכל
אשר־עשו האמרי אשר לפניו ויחטא
גם־את־יהודה בגלוליו: יב לכן כה־אמר
יהוה אלהי ישראל הנני מביא רעה
על־ירושלם ויהודה אשר כל־שמעיו
תצלנה שתי אזניו: יג ונטיתי על־
ירושלם את קו שמרון ואת־משקלת
בית אחאב ומחיתי את־ירושלם

תרגום

למעבד ית דביש מן
עממיא דשיצי יי מן
קדם בני ישראל:
י ומליל יי ביד עבדוהי
נביאיא למימר: יא חלף
דעבד מנשה מלך
שבטא דבית יהודה ית
תועבתא האלין אבאיש
מכל דעבדו אמוראי
דקדמוהי וחייב אף ית
דבית יהודה בפולחן
טעותיה: יב בכן כדנן
אמר יי אלהא דישראל
הא אנא מיתי בישתא
על ירושלם ויהודה
דכל דישמעיניה יצלן
תרתין אודנוהי:
יג ואגוד על ירושלם ית
חוט חורבן שמרון וית
מתקולת צרות בית
אחאב ואמחי ית
ירושלם

קמץ בז"ק שמעה קרי

רש"י

כא (י) ביד עבדיו הנביאים. נחום וחבקוק ולפי שהיה מנשה רשע לא נקראו על שמו לפרש שבימיו היו: (יב) תצלנה. ל' מללתים (טינטני"ר בלע"ז): (יג) משקולת.

רד"ק

ומגלי' אותם מארצם אע"פ שלא גלו גלות שלימ' לפני דוד: (י) וידב' ה' ביד עבדיו הנביאי'. בסדר עולם יואל נחום וחבקוק נתנבאו בימי מנשה ולפי שלא היה מנשה כשר לא נקראו על שמו: (יב) כל שמעיו. כתי' וקרי שמעה והקרי בעבור כי רעה לשון נקבה והכתי' על הענין: תצלנה שתי אזניו. שרשו צלל מבנין נפעל מפעלי הכפל מענין לקול צללו שפתי והוא ענין תנודת הרעשה (סנדימנ"ט בלע"ז): (יג) את קו שומרון. קו החרבן על דרך ונטיתי עליה קו תהו ואבני בהו וכן ת"י ואגוד על ירושלם ית חוט חורבן שמרון וית מתקולת צרות

מנחת שי

(יא) התעבות האלה. הד מן ט' כתיבין כן חסר וא"ו קדמאה ומלא וא"ו בתרא כמו שנמסר בהאי ספרא ריש סימן ט"ז ובסוף סדר אחרי מות: (יב) שמעיו. שמעה קרי ונראה שכן צריך להיות בחילופי המקרא כתובים בלא מלת את:

רלב"ג

(יב) אשר כל שומעיו תצלנה שתי אזניו. ר"ל שמרוב התרועה וההפעלות שיקרה לו מזאת השמועה הרבה ידמה לו שיהי' קול הברה באזניו: (יג) ונטיתי על ירושלם וגו'. ר"ל שתנתן ביד מלך אשור: ואת משקול' בית אחאב. הוא אבן העופרת שבונין בו ואמר זה על צד המשל לענין חורבן בית טו"ב כמו שנתנה שומרון ביד מלך אשור:

מצודת ציון

(יב) תצלנה. ענין תנועות הרעדה כמו צללו שפתי (חבקוק ג): (יג) קו. חבל: ומחית. מל' מחיה ומחיקה ור"ל אקנה: הצלחת.

מצודת דוד

(י) וידבר ה'. ולכן דבר ה' וכו': (יב) תצלנה. כ"א מאזניו תרעד ותתנועע מגודל החרדה: (יג) קו שומרון. ר"ל כדרך הבנאי אשר ינטה קו לייסר ולהשוות הבנין כ"כ הרעה אשר תבוא לירושלים תדמה לרעת שמרון: ואת משקולת. היא העופרת הקשורה בהקו לשקול ולהכביד למטה: ומחיתי. אקנה אותה מכל אשר בה כמו שמקנחין את הצלחת ומהפכין אותה על פיה אחר הקנוח שלא תתעף כן שמעו כי מנשה התעה אותם לעשות הרע עוד יותר מן העמים וכו':

11. Manasseh outdid his predecessors in wickedness, both through the evil of his deeds and through his influence on the nation at large. Therefore, Scripture states—

he has done more wickedly than all that the Amorites who were before him did—He surpassed Ahaz, who had sealed the Torah and abolished the Temple service, by cutting out God's Name from the Torah and dismantling the altar (San. 103b). Ahaz sinned in order to break off the yoke of Heaven and to emancipate himself from his obligations to observe commandments. Manasseh, however, sinned in order to provoke the Almighty. This is evidenced by

to do what was evil, more than the nations that the Lord had destroyed from before the children of Israel. 10. And the Lord spoke through His servants the prophets, saying, 11. "Since Manasseh has committed these abominations, he has done more wickedly than all the Amorites who were before him did, and he caused Judah to sin with his idols. 12. Therefore, has the Lord God of Israel said, 'Behold I bring calamity on Jerusalem and Judah, concerning which the two ears of all those who hear it will tingle. 13. And I will stretch over Jerusalem the measuring line of Samaria and the plumb line of the house of Ahab, and I will wipe Jerusalem

the first two commandments of the Decalogue, "I am the Lord your God," and "You shall have no other gods in My presence," which they heard directly from God [*Abarbanel, Mezudath David*].

all the Law that Moses My servant commanded them—the remainder of the commandments, which Moses heard from God and relayed to Israel [*Abarbanel, Mezudath David*].

9. **and Manasseh led them astray**—i.e. because Manasseh led them astray [*Abarbanel, Mezudath David*].

Alternatively, they went astray without Manasseh's influence. In addition to their straying, however, Manasseh encouraged them to worship idols, convincing them that their only success would be through idolatry [*Daath Soferim*].

Alternatively, since they did not follow the teachings of the Torah, Manasseh was able to mislead them. Had they been faithful to the Torah, they would have revolted and not allowed him to place an image in the Temple, a place belonging to the nation at large, over which the king had no jurisdiction. Through his sins, he caused the people to sin, and to commit greater abominations than the Canaanites, who were destroyed from before them [*Malbim*].

10. **through His servants the prophets**—*Nahum and Habakkuk, but since Manasseh was wicked, they were not referred to with his name to explain that they were in his time* [*Rashi* from *Seder Olam,* ch. 20].

Redak, quoting *Seder Olam,* includes Joel, whose name indeed appears in our editions of *Seder Olam. Rashi,* intentionally, omitted Joel, since in Joel 1:1, he cites variant opinions concerning the period in which Joel flourished. There he quotes *Halachoth Gedoloth* as placing Joel, Nahum, and Habakkuk in Manasseh's time. *Rashi, Megillah* 14a, however, quotes *Halachoth Gedoloth* as placing all three prophets in Amon's time. Only Isaiah prophesied during Manasseh's reign, and was eventually executed by him. See *Rashi,* Isaiah 1:1.

כַּאֲשֶׁר־יִמְחֶה אֶת־הַצַּלַּחַת מָחָה וְהָפַךְ
עַל־פָּנֶיהָ׃ יד וְנָטַשְׁתִּי אֵת שְׁאֵרִית
נַחֲלָתִי וּנְתַתִּים בְּיַד אֹיְבֵיהֶם וְהָיוּ לְבַז
וְלִמְשִׁסָּה לְכָל־אֹיְבֵיהֶם׃ טו יַעַן אֲשֶׁר
עָשׂוּ אֶת־הָרַע בְּעֵינַי וַיִּהְיוּ מַכְעִסִים
אֹתִי מִן־הַיּוֹם אֲשֶׁר יָצְאוּ אֲבוֹתָם
מִמִּצְרַיִם וְעַד הַיּוֹם הַזֶּה׃ טז וְגַם דָּם נָקִי
שָׁפַךְ מְנַשֶּׁה הַרְבֵּה מְאֹד עַד אֲשֶׁר־
מִלֵּא אֶת־יְרוּשָׁלַםִ פֶּה לָפֶה לְבַד
מֵחַטָּאתוֹ אֲשֶׁר הֶחֱטִיא אֶת־יְהוּדָה

ירושלם כמא דמתמחיא צלוחיתא מתמחיא ומתהפכא על אפהא׃ יד וארטוש ית שארא דאחסנתי ואמסרינון ביד בעלי דבביהון ויהון לבז ולהבר לכל סנאיהון׃ טו חלף דעבדו ית דביש קדמי והוו מרגזין קדמי מן יומא דנפקו אבהתהון ממצרים ועד יומא הדין׃ טז ואף דם זכאי דאשד מנשה סגי לחדא עד די מלא ית ירושלם סיפא בסיפא בר מחובוהי דחייב ית דבית יהודה

ת"א וגם דם נקי. יומא ט כג סנהדרין קג קט(פס כח):

רש"י

הוא היא שהבונים הומה קושרין בה עופרת לכוין בו את ההומה: **ימחה את הצלחת**. יקנה את הקערה:

רד"ק

בית אחאב: ומחיתו. ענין קנוח: הצלחת. הקערה: **כאשר** ימחה. חסר איש וכן כאשר ישבור כלי היוצר כאשר **ישבור** איש: מחה. פי' כאשר ימחה האדם את הצלחת שמחה אותה **ואח"כ** הפכה על פני' כי כן דרך המקנח הקערה שהופך אותה אח"כ על פניה כדי שלא תתטנף כן ימחה ירושלם וינקת אותה מאנשיה ואח"כ יחריבנה: (טז) הרבה מאד. יש מרז"ל שדרשו בו שהרג ישעיהו:

רלב"ג

לאחאב והכלותו וכן אמר שיכלו מירושלים יושביו: ומחיתי. והכיתי: **כאשר** ימחה את הצלחת. ר"ל כמו שיכה איש את הקערה מגאה **בעבור** שבהכותו אותה תתהפך על פניה ולא ישאר בקערה דבר מהתבשיל שיהיה בה: (יד) ונטשתי את שארית נחלתי. הנה קרא **מלכות** יהודה שארית נחלתו כי הוא לבדו נשאר מנחלת הש"י שהוא עם ישראל כי השאר הגלה מלך אשור: (טז) וגם דם נקי שפך מנשה **הרבה** מאד. ידמה שהוא היה הורג כל מי שלא השכים לעבוד ע"ג והנביאים המוכיחי' אותו' כמו שעשתה איזבל שהרג' את נביאי ה':

מנחת שי

אליבא דמערבאי: (טו) ויהיו מכעיסים. במקצת ספרים כ"י מלא יו"ד **גם**

מצודת דוד

יהיה סוף הקנוח של ירושלים כי לאחר שתתרוקן מכל תהיה נהפכת **ונחרבה**: (יד) שארית נחלתי. כי שאר שבטי ישראל כבר הגלו: **(טו)** ועד היום הזה. ולכן עתה נתמלא הסאה: (טז) עד אשר **מלא**. כי בראות העם שהקל מנשה בשפיכת דם למדו ממנו ושפכו גם המה ויחשב העון אף למנשה כאלו הוא היה הממלא: **פה לפה**.

מצודת ציון

הוא ענין קדירה כמו ובדודים ובצלחת (דה"ב לה): (יד) ונטשתי. ועזבתי: ולמשסה. ענין דריסה ורמיסה כמו מי נתן למשסה יעקב

poor of the land, whom Nebuchadnezzar had left in the land as vinedressers and farmers, and who later fled to Egypt, where they were massacred by Nebuchadnezzar's armies [*Malbim*].

15. **until this day**—when the measure has become full, and it is time for retribution [*Mezudath David*].

16. **shed very much innocent blood**—It appears that he executed anyone who did not comply with his wishes to practice idolatry [*Ralbag*].

until he filled Jerusalem—When the people saw that human blood meant very little to Manasseh, they followed suit and murdered all their enemies. These murders are accounted as though Manasseh himself had committed them [*Mezudath David*].

The Rabbis interpret this verse as alluding to Manasseh's murder of the prophet Isaiah. Since Isaiah was a righteous man, his life was considered equivalent to the lives of many people. It is, therefore, considered as though he had shed very

as one wipes a dish, he wipes and turns it upside down. 14. And I will forsake the remnant of My heritage, and I will deliver them into the hands of their enemies, and they will become plunder and prey for all their enemies. 15. Since they did what was evil in My eyes, and they constantly provoked Me since the day that their forefathers left Egypt until this day.'" 16. Moreover, Manasseh shed very much innocent blood, until he filled Jerusalem from one end to the other, besides his sin that he caused Judah to commit,

the fact that Ahaz was ashamed to show his face before Isaiah, whereas Manasseh had the audacity to execute him (ibid. 104a). Moreover, Ahaz did not influence the populace to follow his evil deeds, whereas Manasseh—

caused Judah to sin with his idols—Therefore, Manasseh dared to place his image in the Temple without fear of rebellion, while Ahaz placed his in the attic [*Malbim*].

12. **will tingle**—The root is צלל, *an expression* similar to מְצִלְתַּיִם, *cymbals (tentir in French), to ring, resound* [*Rashi*].

13. **the measuring line of Samaria**—It is customary for a builder to stretch out a string over the building stones to make certain that they are straight. Just as I stretched out the line over Samaria, I will stretch out the line over Jerusalem. Just as Samaria was destroyed by enemies, so will Jerusalem be destroyed [*Mezudath David*].

and the plumb line—*That is the line upon which the builders of a wall tie a lead weight to make the wall exact* [*Rashi*].

The measuring line is used to even out the length and width of the wall, whereas the plummet is hung above and is let down to even out the height of the wall. The analogy is that Jerusalem would be destroyed below just as Samaria had been destroyed, and Manasseh would be destroyed from above, i.e. he would lose his share in the World to Come, just as Ahab and his dynasty had lost their share in the World to Come [*Malbim*].

as one wipes a dish—[*Rashi, Redak*].

and turns it upside down—to prevent it from becoming soiled. So will Jerusalem be emptied of its inhabitants and then destroyed [*Redak, Mezudath David*].

Alternatively, just as one turns over a recently washed dish to prevent others from refilling it, so will Jerusalem be destroyed to prevent the Jews from returning there to resettle [*Malbim*].

14. **And I will forsake the remnant of My heritage**—Since the ten tribes had already been exiled, Judah is referred to as the remnant [*Mezudath David, Ralbag*].

Alternatively, this refers to the

לעשות הרע בעיני יהוה: יז ויתר דברי
מנשה וכל־אשר עשה וחטאתו אשר
חטא הלא־הם כתובים על־ספר דברי
הימים למלכי יהודה: יח וישכב מנשה
עם־אבתיו ויקבר בגן־ביתו בגן־עזא
וימלך אמון בנו תחתיו: יט בן־עשרים
ושתים שנה אמון במלכו ושתים
שנים מלך בירושלם ושם אמו
משלמת בת־חרוץ מן־יטבה: כ ויעש
הרע בעיני יהוה כאשר עשה מנשה
אביו: כא וילך בכל־הדרך אשר־הלך
אביו ויעבד את־הגללים אשר־עבד
אביו וישתחו להם: כב ויעזב את־יהוה
אלהי אבתיו ולא הלך בדרך יהוה:
כג ויקשרו עבדי־אמון עליו וימיתו את־

יהודה למעבד דביש
קדם יי: יז ושאר
פתגמי מנשה וכל דעבד
וחובוהי דחב הלא
אינון כתיבין על ספר
פתגמי יומיא למלכי
דבית יהודה: יח ושכיב
מנשה עם אבהתוהי
ואתקבר בגנן ביתיה
בגנן עזא ומלך אמון
בריה תחותוהי: יט בר
עסרין ותרתין שנין אמון
כד מלך ותרתין שנין
מלך בירושלם ושום
אמיה משלמת בת חרוץ
מן יטבה: כ ועבד
דביש קדם יי כמא
דעבד מנשה אבוהי:
כא ואזל בכל אורחא
דהליך אבוהי ופלח
ית טעותא דפלח
אבוהי וסגיד להון:
כב ושבק ית פולחנא דיי
אלהא דאבהתוהי ולא
הליך באורחא דתקנא
קדם יי: כג ומרדו עבדי
אמון עלוהי וקטלו ית
מלכא

מנחת שי

אחר העי"ן וכן נכון לפי המסורת דריש שמואל: (יז) הלא הם כתובים. בספרים חדשים מהדפוס מלא וא"ו והוא טעות כי אין זה מן י"ז מלאים שנמנו במסורת בסוף ספר ראשון ממלכים וכן בספרים כ"י ודפוסים ישנים חסר: (יט) יטבה. היו"ד בקמץ חטוף במדוייקים כ"י ודפוסים ראשונים ובדפוסים חדשים היו"ד במאריך ומוטעים הם: (כא) הגלולים. י"ס כתוב הגללים:

רלב"ג

(כב) ויעזוב את ה' אלהי אבתיו ולא הלך בדרך ה'. ר"ל שבכבר נפרד

מצודת ציון

(ישעיה מב): (יח) בגן עזא. כך שם הגן: (כג) ויקשרו. ענין מרד:

מצודת דוד

ר"ל משער לשער: בעיני ה'. שבין האדם למקום: (יח) בגן ביתו.

himself before God as Manasseh his father had done. See II Chron. 33:23 [*Abarbanel*].

21. **in all the way that his father had gone**—He surpassed his father in wickedness. In the Talmud (*San.* 103b) Amon is described as endeavoring to outdo his forebears in sin. Whereas Ahaz sealed the Torah, and Manasseh cut out the holy Names, Amon burnt it completely. Whereas Ahaz permitted incest, and Manasseh was intimate with his sister, Amon was intimate with his mother, merely for the sake of provoking God. The Chronicler sums this up with the words, "(II 33:23) for he was Amon; he increased guilt."

23. **And Amon's servants conspired against him**—Just as he had

to do what was evil in the eyes of the Lord. 17. And the rest of the events of Manasseh and all that he did and his sin which he sinned, are written in the book of the chronicles of the kings of Judah. 18. And Manasseh slept with his forefathers and was buried in the garden of his house in the garden of Uzza, and his son Amon reigned in his stead. 19. Amon was twenty-two years old when he became king, and he reigned two years in Jerusalem, and his mother's name was Meshullemeth the daughter to Haruz of Jotbah. 20. And he did what was evil in the eyes of the Lord, as Manasseh his father had done. 21. And he went in all the ways that his father had gone, and he worshipped pagan deities that his father had worshipped, and he prostrated himself to them. 22. And he forsook the Lord God of his forefathers and did not follow the Lord's way. 23. And Amon's servants conspired against him and assassinated the king in his palace.

much innocent blood and filled Jerusalem with it (*San.* 103b). He alleged to have found discrepancies between Isaiah's prophecies and those of Moses in the Torah. Isaiah knew that Manasseh would not accept his explanations. He, therefore, did not attempt to defend himself. Instead, he pronounced the Name of God and became concealed in a cedar tree. Manasseh commenced to saw into the tree. When the saw reached Isaiah's mouth, he died (*Yebamoth* 49b) [*Redak*].*

18. **and was buried**—Note the expression, "and was buried," instead of the usual, "and they buried him." This denotes that he, himself, requested that he be buried in his own garden, rather than in the grave of the kings. He was ashamed to enter into their compartment despite his partial repentance [*K'li Y'kar*].

19. **he reigned two years**—like the sons of the wicked kings, who did not merit long reigns for their posterity, such as the sons of Jeroboam, Baasha, Ahab, and others. This is in accordance with the Torah's admonition, "(Deut. 17:20) and not to turn away from the commandment right or left, in order to have long days on his throne, he and his sons, in the midst of Israel" [*Abarbanel*].

20. **evil . . .as Manasseh his father had done**—but he did not humble

הַמֶּלֶךְ בְּבֵיתוֹ׃ כד וַיַּךְ עַם־הָאָרֶץ אֵת כָּל־הַקֹּשְׁרִים עַל־הַמֶּלֶךְ אָמוֹן וַיַּמְלִיכוּ עַם־הָאָרֶץ אֶת־יֹאשִׁיָּהוּ בְנוֹ תַּחְתָּיו׃
כה וְיֶתֶר דִּבְרֵי אָמוֹן אֲשֶׁר עָשָׂה הֲלֹא־הֵם כְּתוּבִים עַל־סֵפֶר דִּבְרֵי הַיָּמִים לְמַלְכֵי יְהוּדָה׃
כו וַיִּקְבֹּר אֹתוֹ בִּקְבֻרָתוֹ בְּגַן־עֻזָּא וַיִּמְלֹךְ יֹאשִׁיָּהוּ בְנוֹ תַּחְתָּיו׃
כב א בֶּן־שְׁמֹנֶה שָׁנָה יֹאשִׁיָּהוּ בְמָלְכוֹ וּשְׁלֹשִׁים וְאַחַת שָׁנָה מָלַךְ בִּירוּשָׁלִָם וְשֵׁם אִמּוֹ יְדִידָה בַת־עֲדָיָה מִבָּצְקַת׃
ב וַיַּעַשׂ הַיָּשָׁר בְּעֵינֵי יְהוָה וַיֵּלֶךְ בְּכָל־דֶּרֶךְ דָּוִד אָבִיו וְלֹא־סָר יָמִין וּשְׂמֹאול׃
ג וַיְהִי בִּשְׁמֹנֶה עֶשְׂרֵה שָׁנָה לַמֶּלֶךְ יֹאשִׁיָּהוּ שָׁלַח הַמֶּלֶךְ אֶת־שָׁפָן בֶּן־אֲצַלְיָהוּ בֶן־מְשֻׁלָּם הַסֹּפֵר בֵּית יְהוָה

מַלְכָּא בְּבֵיתֵיהּ׃ כד וּקְטַל עַמָּא דְאַרְעָא יָת כָּל דִּמְרָדוּ עַל מַלְכָּא אָמוֹן וְאַמְלִיכוּ עַמָּא דְאַרְעָא יָת יֹאשִׁיָּהוּ בְרֵיהּ תְּחוֹתוֹהִי׃ כה וּשְׁאָר פִּתְגָמֵי אָמוֹן וְכָל דַּעֲבַד הֲלָא אִינוּן כְּתִיבִין עַל סְפַר פִּתְגָמֵי יוֹמַיָּא לְמַלְכֵי יְהוּדָה׃ כו וּקְבַר יָתֵיהּ בִּקְבוּרְתֵּיהּ בְּגִנַּת עֻזָּא וּמְלַךְ יֹאשִׁיָּהוּ בְרֵיהּ תְּחוֹתוֹהִי׃ א בַּר תְּמָנֵי שְׁנִין יֹאשִׁיָּהוּ כַּד מְלַךְ וּתְלָתִין וַחֲדָא שְׁנִין מְלַךְ בִּירוּשְׁלֵם וְשׁוּם אִמֵּיהּ יְדִידָה בַּת עֲדָיָה מִבָּצְקַת׃ ב וַעֲבַד דְּכָשַׁר קֳדָם יְיָ וַאֲזַל בְּכָל אוֹרַח דָּוִד אֲבוּהִי וְלָא סְטָא לְיַמִּינָא וְלִסְמָלָא׃ ג וַהֲוָה בִּתְמָנֵי עַסְרֵי שְׁנִין לְמַלְכָּא יֹאשִׁיָּהוּ שְׁלַח מַלְכָּא יָת שָׁפָן בַּר אֲצַלְיָה בַר מְשֻׁלָּם סַפְרָא לְבֵית מַקְדְּשָׁא דַיְיָ לְמֵימַר

רלב"ג

מכל וכל מדרך ה׳: (ב) וילך בכל דרך דוד אביו ולא סר ימין ושמאל. ר"ל אע"פ בשלחה לו חולדה הנביאה יען רך לבבך ותכנע מפני ה׳ אין הרצון בזה שחטא יאשיה קודם זה אך הרצון בו שבעת שמעו את הרעה הזאת אשר נגזרה מאת ה׳ על ירושלים השתדל עכ"פ לתקן את אשר עותוהו הראשונים כי קודם זה לא היה יודע הרע שנגזר עליהם אך היה עושה הישר בעיני ה׳ ולזה לא היה מספיק לו להשיב חרון אף ה׳ ממנו אבל היה ראוי שיוסף לו דבקות בש"י בדרך שיהי׳ מושגח השגחה ומלטו בה מזה הרע הנגזר מאת הש"י ולזה תמצא שהשתדל יאשיה להשיב ישראל לעם לה׳ כדי שיסור מהם זה הרע ונבער בשלמות את כל הנעשה לע"ג:

מלא ואי

מנחת שי

(כה) ויתר דברי אמון וגו׳ הלא הם כתובים. במדוייקים חסר וא"ו וכן נכון מהטעם שכתבתי למעלה: **כב** (א) מבצקת. הבי"ת בקמ"ץ חטוף והקו"ף בפתח

מצודת דוד

בהגן שהיה לו בביתו: (כו) בקבורתו. אשר כרה לעצמו בחייו:

rectified the evils that his forebears had instituted in the land. She, therefore, mentioned that he had humbled himself before the Lord because of his failure as yet to rectify those evils [*Ralbag*]. (See below 23:25.)

3. **in the eighteenth year**—of his

24. And the people of the land slew all the conspirators against
King Amon, and the people of the land appointed his son
Josiah in his stead. 25. And the rest of the deeds of Amon that
he did, are written in the book of the chronicles of the kings of
Judah. 26. And he buried him in his grave in the garden of
Uzza, and his son Josiah reigned in his stead.

22

1. Josiah was eight years old when he became king, and he
reigned in Jerusalem thirty-one years. His mother's name was
Jedidah the daughter of Adaiah of Bozkath. 2. And he did
what was right in the eyes of the Lord, and he walked in all the
ways of David his father, and he turned away neither right nor
left. 3. And it was in the eighteenth year of King Josiah, that
the king sent Shaphan the son of Azaliah the son of Meshullam
the scribe to the house of the Lord, saying,

estranged himself from his Master, so did his servants estrange themselves from him [*Abarbanel*].

24. **And the people of the land slew . . .**—This shows the wickedness of the populace, who sympathized with Amon and avenged his death. Since he was an idolator, they loved him, and, therefore, punished his assassins [*Abarbanel*].

26. **And he buried him in his grave**—Josiah buried him in the grave he had dug during his lifetime near that of his father Manasseh, for he had chosen Manasseh's earlier ways. Alternatively, Josiah buried him in his grave, i.e. in the grave that was fitting for him, not in the grave of the kings of the Davidic dynasty [*K'li Y'kar*].

2. **And he did what was right**—Although the people who had avenged Amon's death probably expected his son Josiah to follow in his footsteps, he, nevertheless, deceived them and followed the way of King David [*K'li Y'kar*].

Although the prophetess Huldah later sent a message to Josiah in which she mentions that he humbled himself before the Lord, this is no indication that previously he had sinned. He had not yet completely

לֵאמֹר: ד עֲלֵה אֶל־חִלְקִיָּהוּ הַכֹּהֵן
הַגָּדוֹל וְיַתֵּם אֶת־הַכֶּסֶף הַמּוּבָא בֵּית
יְהוָה אֲשֶׁר אָסְפוּ שֹׁמְרֵי הַסַּף מֵאֵת
הָעָם: ה וְיִתְּנֻה עַל־יַד עֹשֵׂי הַמְּלָאכָה
הַמֻּפְקָדִים בְּבֵית יְהוָה וְיִתְּנוּ אֹתוֹ
לְעֹשֵׂי הַמְּלָאכָה אֲשֶׁר בְּבֵית יְהוָה
לְחַזֵּק אֶת־בֶּדֶק הַבָּיִת: ו לֶחָרָשִׁים
וְלַבֹּנִים וְלַגֹּדְרִים וְלִקְנוֹת עֵצִים וְאַבְנֵי
מַחְצֵב לְחַזֵּק אֶת־הַבָּיִת: ז אַךְ לֹא־
יֵחָשֵׁב אִתָּם הַכֶּסֶף הַנִּתָּן עַל־יָדָם כִּי
בֶאֱמוּנָה הֵם עֹשִׂים: ח וַיֹּאמֶר חִלְקִיָּהוּ

תרגום

למימר: ד סק לות חלקיה כהנא רבא ויתקים ית כספא דאתעל בבית מקדשא דיי די כנשו אמרכליא מן עמא: ה ויתגוניה על ידי עבדי עבידתא דממנן בבית מקדשא דיי ויתנון יתיה לעבדי עבידתא דבבית מקדשא דיי לתקפא ית בדקא דביתא: ו לנגריא ולארדיכליא ולארגובליא ולמזבן אעין ואבנין פסילן לתקפא ית ביתא: ז ברם לא מתחשב עמהון כספא דמתיהב על ידיהון ארי בהמנותא אינון עבדין: ח ואמר חלקיה כהנא רבא

ויתנהו קרי בית קרי

רד"ק

(ד) ויתם את הכסף. וישלי' כלומר לגבותו ויתנוהו לעושי המלאכה. כי היה צריך הבית חזוק ובנין לפי שנהרס מימי יהואש שחזק בדק הבית עד היום ההוא שהיו רכ"ד שנה ובס"ע מאתים ושמנה עשרה: שומרי הסף. שומרי כלי בית המקדש וי"ת אמרכלי' והם הגזברי' וכבר פירשנו כל הענין הזה בבדק יהואש: (ה) ויתנה.

מנחת שי

ובהרבה ספרים בקמ"ץ:(ה) ויתנה. ויתנהו קרי: בבית. בית קרי: לחזק בדק הבית. ברוב ספרי הדפוס כתוב לחזק את בדק וכן ת"י לתקפא ית בידקא וברוב הספרים כ"י שלפני ליכא מלת את וגם בדפוס יבן ומאיר נתיב שרש חזק ושרש בדק איננה:

רלב"ג

(ד) ויתם את הכסף המובא בית ה'. ידמה שהיה הכסף נתון בארון כמו שהיה הענין בימי יהואש המלך ושם זכר דומה למה שזכר בזה המקום והנה אמרו ויתם את הכסף ר"ל ויכלה וזה יהיה בשערו את הארון אשר אספו בו את הכסף שומרי כלי בית המקדש והמונים הכסף הוא יתנוהו מנוי על ידי עושי המלאכה הממונים בבית ה' להזקו והם הכהן הגדול וסופר המלך ומהכסף ההוא יפרעו שכירות' לאומנין העושי' המלאכה בבית ה' לחזק את בדק הבית ר"ל מה שראוי שיבדק לתקן מפני הראותו בלתי חזק והאומנים הם חרשי העץ והבונים הקירות והתקרה והגודרים הם הגודלים גדר סביב אלו הכהנים וזולתו ומהכסף

מצודת ציון

כב (ד) ויתם. מל' תם והשלמה: שומרי הסף. הם השוערים: (ה) על יד. ביד: בדק הבית. רעוע הבית ע"ש שנבדקים ומחפשים אחר מקום השבור והרעוע: (ו) ואבני מחצב. אבנים הנכרתים ממקום גדלם:

מצודת דוד

כב (ד) ויתם את הכסף. ר"ל יאסף כל הכסף בשלימות: (ה) עושי המלאכה. הם האומנים הגדולים הנקראים בדרז"ל אדרכלין והיו ממונים בבית ה' ומתחת ידם היו בונים האומנים הפועלים כפי מה שיורו אותם: ויתנו. והם יתנו את הכסף לאומנים הפועלים בבנין: (ו) לחרשים. הם כורתי העצים בתמונה הנרצה: ולבונים. הם הבונים העצים בקירות הבית: ולגודרים. הם הבונים קירות האבנים: (ז) אך לא יחשב. לא עשו חשבון על הכסף וגו'

4. "Go up to Hilkiah the high priest and let him gather up all the silver that was brought to the house of the Lord, that the keepers of the utensils collected from the people. 5. And let them give it into the hands of the foremen of the work, who are appointed in the house of the Lord, and let them give it to the workers who are in the house of the Lord, to repair the damage of the Temple. 6. To the carpenters and to the builders and to the masons, and to purchase wood and quarried stones, to strengthen the Temple. 7. However, no reckoning shall be made with them of the silver that is given into their hands, for they deal honestly."

reign [II Chron. 34:8].

4. **and let him gather up all the silver**—lit. let him complete the silver. Let him complete the gathering (*Mezudath David*) or the collection of the silver. Since Jehoash had repaired the Temple, 224 years had elapsed. According to *Seder Olam,* ch. 24, 218 years had elapsed. Therefore, by now, it was necessary to repair it again [*Redak*].

Alternatively, Let him perfect the silver, i.e. by melting it and removing the dross. Impure silver used in the construction of holy vessels is like blemished animals offered on the altar [*K'li Y'kar*].

the keepers of the utensils—i.e. the keepers of the utensils used in the Temple. *Jonathan* renders: the treasurers. See above 12:10 [*Redak*].

Alternatively, this verse refers to two types of silver, that which was brought voluntarily to the Temple, and that which the keepers of the utensils, the Levites, had collected from the people [*Malbim*].

5. **And let them give it**—i.e. let the keepers of the utensils give the silver to the foremen, who would in turn give it to the workers for their wages and for the building materials. According to the *K'thib,* we render: and let him give it, i.e. let Hilkiah give the collection to the foremen [*Redak*].

6. **To the carpenters**—See above 12:11–13.

7. **no reckoning**—See above 12:16.

הכהן הגדול על־שפן הספר ספר התורה מצאתי בבית יהוה ויתן חלקיה את־הספר אל־שפן ויקראהו: ט ויבא שפן הספר אל־המלך וישב את־המלך דבר ויאמר התיכו עבדיך את־הכסף הנמצא בבית ויתנהו על־יד עשי המלאכה המפקדים בית יהוה: י ויגד שפן הספר למלך לאמר

רבא לשפן ספרא ספרא דאוריתא אשכחית בבית מקדשא דיי ויהב חלקיה ית ספרא לשפן וקרהי: ט ואתא שפן ספרא למלכא ואתיב ית מלכא פתגמא ואמר טקיסו עבדך ית כספא דאשתכח בביתא ויהבוהי על ידי עבדי עבידתא דממנן בבית מקדשא דיי: י וחוי שפן ספרא למלכא למימר

ת"א ספר התורה. עקרים מג פ׳ כח: ויקראהו. סוכה לח:

רש"י

כב (ח) ספר התורה מצאתי. טמון תחת הנדבך שהטמינו שם כשסרף אחז את התורה:

רד"ק

כתיב וקרי ויתנוהו הכת׳ אומר על הלקיהו וה״א הכנוי על המגב׳ והקרי ויתנוהו על שומרי הסף שיתנוהו הכסף וה״א וי״ו הכנוי על הכסף: המופקדים בית ה׳. כמו בבית: (ח) על שפן הסופר. כמו אל שפן וכן וילך אלקנה הרמתה על ביתו כמו אל ביתו: ספר התו׳ מצאתי בבית ה׳. דרשו כי אחז שרף את התור׳ והטמינו מפני׳ ספר תורה אחת והטמינוהו תחת הנדבך ועכשיו מצא חלק׳ ספר התורה הזה ורחוק הוא זה שחזקיהו שבא אחריו שרבץ תור׳ בישראל איך לא הוציאו וכמה ספרי תור׳ הניח חזקיהו במותו אלא מנשה מלך זמן רב שהרי מלך נ״ה שנה ועשה הרע בעיני ה׳ כתועבות הגוים ובנה מזבחות לע״ג בבית ה׳ והוא השביח התו׳ מישראל ואין פונה אליה כי כלם היו פונים אל האלהים אחרים ואל תקית הגוים ובנ״ה שנה נשתכחה התור׳ ועכשיו כאשר צוה יאשיהו לחפש בית ה׳ לכל אשר ימצא שם בדק ולהוציא הכסף המובא בית ה׳ והיה חלקיהו מחפש בבית ה׳ ובבית קה״ק ובדביר מצא ס״ת שהיה מונח במקומו מצד הארון וכן הוא אומר בד״ה ובהוציאם את הכסף המובא בית ה׳ מצא חלקיהו הכהן את ספר תורת ה׳ ופתח וקראו ונתנו אל סופר המלך שיביאהו אל המלך שיקרא בו ויראה איך שכחו התורה המונעת כל המעשים הרעים שהיו עושים בישראל ואם תאמר והרי מנשה עשה תשובה כמ״ש בדברי הימים כשהגלו אותו שרי מלך אשור והוליכוהו בבל אמר ובהצר לו חל׳ את פני ה׳ ויכנע מאד ויתפלל אליו ויעתר לו וישיבהו ירושל׳ וידע מנשה כי ה׳ הוא האלהים ואמר שהסיר את אלהי הנכר ואת הסמל מבית ה׳ ויאמר ליהודה לעבוד את ה׳ א״כ היאך לא החזיר את התו׳ ליושנ׳ ולא קרא בה ואיך היה אצל חלקיה ואצל אחרים חדוש דברי התורה אפשר כי הגלו׳ שגלה מנשה היה בזקנותו ואחר שעשה תשובה לא האריך ימים כ״כ אלא שידע ושמע כי ע״ג רע בעיני ה׳ כמו שהעידו בו הנביאים בעידו ברשעו והע״ג בער כשעשה תשובה

רלב"ג

הה:א היו ג״כ קונין עלים והאבני מחצב ולא יחשב את עושי המלאכה הממונים בבית ה׳ הכסף כי באמונה הם עושים וכבר באלנו הספה בזה בענין יואש ושם באלנו התועלת המגיעות מזה הספור אשר נכתב שם ולזה לא נשוב למנותם בזה המקום: (ח) ויאמר הלקיהו הכהן הגדול על שפן הסופר. הנה זכר כי הכהן הגדול היה לאש על שפן הסופר בזה הממוי שהיו עושים אותו בניהם ולזה יחס יאשיה הפעל כלו בהוצאת הכסף לכהן הגדול ולזה אמר ויתם את הכסף אע״פ שבניהם היו שם: (ט) ויתנוהו על יד עושי המלאכה. והנה לא זכר למי אמר זה כי נבטן במה שזכר שפן הסופר ועוד שכבר אמר אח״ז ויתן הלקיה את הספר אל שפן: התיכו עבדיך את הכסף. אי

מנחת שי

(ח) ויאמר הלקיהו הכהן הגדול. הראשון שבפ׳ חלקיהו בוא״ו והשני חלקיה בלא וא״ו וכן ראוי על פי המסורת ד״ה ב׳ ל״ג שבמ״ג וכן נמצאו ברובן של

מצודת דוד

כי ידוע היו שעושים באמונה ולזה נבהרו אלו: (ח) ספר התורה מצאתי. יתכן שבעל כי אחז שרף את התורה כמ״ש רז״ל לזה פחדו הכהנים פן ישלח ידו וגם בספר התורה המונח מצד הארון אשר כתב משה מפי ה׳ ולקחו הס״ת ההיא והטמינו מפניו ולאחר מותו חפשו אחריה ולא מצאוה וכאשר היה הכ״ג מחפש אחר הכסף המובא ואחרי בדקו הבית מצאה והרז״ל שמצאה כשהיתה מגוללת בפרשה תוכחות והיה התחלת הדף יולך ה׳ אותך ואת מלכך ועל כי מאז חפשו אחריה ולא מצאוה אמר כמבשר ספר התורה הסיא מצאתיה בבית ה׳: ויתן וגו׳. ר״ל הראה לו הנמצא כתוב בתחלת הדף כי השב את הדבר לאות ורמז להחריד את העם: ויקראהו. כמתמיה ומשתומם: (ט) התיכו. לעשות מטבעות להוליאם בהולאה:

מצודת ציון

(ח) על שפן. אל שפן: (ט) התיכו. ענין הלקה שע״י האור כמו כהתוך כסף (יחזקאל כ״ב):

seh cut out the holy Names from the Torah. Since they were in possession of the Scroll written by Moses himself, by divine command, they made sure to hide it from Manasseh. Consequently, it was put between two rows of stones in the Temple. During Josiah's reign, they searched for it, but were unable to find it. When Josiah ordered that the Temple be repaired, Hilkiah the priest searched through the entire Temple to determine the necessary repairs. In doing so, he discovered it in its hiding place, between two rows of stones. They were overwhelmed, not by the discovery of a *sefer Torah,* but by the discovery of the first, original *sefer*

8. And Hilkiah the high priest said to Shaphan the scribe, "I have found the Scroll of the Law in the house of the Lord," and Hilkiah gave the scroll to Shaphan, and he read it. 9. And Shaphan the scribe came to the king and brought back word to the king, and said, "Your servants have melted the silver that was found in the Temple, and they have given it into the hands of the foremen of the work who were appointed over the house of the Lord. 10. And Shaphan the scribe told the king, saying,

8. **And Hilkiah the high priest said to Shaphan the scribe**—The word for "to" in this case is עַל, usually rendered "on," instead of the usual אֶל [*Redak*].

This may be an allusion to the fact that Hilkiah was appointed *over* Shaphan, although Shaphan had been ordered directly by the king to go to Hilkiah. Hence we would render, "And Hilkiah, the high priest who was over Shaphan the scribe,. said, . . .

I have found the Scroll of the Law—*It was hidden under a layer of stones where they had concealed it when Ahaz burned the Torah* [*Rashi* from unknown Rabbinic source].

This is quoted by *Redak, Abarbanel, Mezudath David.* We have, however, no knowledge of any Talmudic or Midrashic source stating that Ahaz burnt the Torah. We mentioned above that Ahaz sealed the Torah, Manasseh cut out the holy Names, and Amon burnt the Torah [*Shem Ephraim*].

Moreover, it is difficult to understand the surprise in finding the *sefer Torah.* Is it possible that Hezekiah who spread the knowledge of the Torah throughout Israel did not take it out? Did not Hezekiah leave over many scrolls after his death? Did not the prophets have copies of the *sefer Torah? Redak,* therefore, rejects this view. Instead, he conjectures that during Manasseh's reign the Torah was all but forgotten. Since idolatry was rampant, no one thought of the Torah. This continued through Amon's reign. During Josiah's reign, however, when Hilkiah the priest searched through the entire Temple to determine what repairs were required, he fell upon the Torah in its proper place, in the Holy of Holies, on the side of the Ark. Since they had not seen a Torah for the fifty-five years of Manasseh's reign, the two years of Amon's reign, and the first eighteen years of Josiah's reign, they were overwhelmed by this discovery. The reason for their alarm will be discussed in the following verses.

Abarbanel questions this explanation on the grounds that Manasseh repented thirty-three years before his death. How is it possible that during that long period, he did not make an effort to take out the Torah and read it? He, therefore, concludes that, as mentioned before, Manas-

ספר נתן לי חלקיה הכהן ויקראהו שפן לפני המלך: יא ויהי כשמע המלך את־דברי ספר התורה ויקרע את־בגדיו: יב ויצו המלך את־חלקיה הכהן ואת־אחיקם בן־שפן ואת־עכבור בן־מיכיה ואת ׀ שפן הספר ואת עשיה עבד־המלך לאמר: יג לכו דרשו את־יהוה בעדי ובעד־העם ובעד כל־יהודה על־דברי הספר הנמצא הזה כי־גדולה חמת יהוה

תרגום

למימר ספרא יהיב לי חלקיה כהנא וקרהי שפן קדם מלכא: יא והוה כד שמע מלכא ית פתגמי ספרא דאוריתא ובזע ית לבושוהי: יב ופקיד מלכא ית חלקיה כהנא וית אחיקם בר שפן וית עכבור בר מיכיה וית שפן ספרא וית עשיה עבדא דמלכא למימר: יג אזילו תבעו מן קדם יי עלי ועל עמא ועל כל דבית יהודה על פתגמי ספרא דאשתכח הדין ארי סגיאה חימתא

רד"ק

ולא נתן אל לבו לחפש ספ' התור' ויאשיהו היה קטן בימי מנש' בן שש שני' ולא למד תור' עדיין ואמון אביו היה רשע ואחז בדרכי אביו הרעים שגדל בהם ובשוב מנשה מרשעו לא הכין הוא את לבבו כמו שכתוב ולא נכנע מלפני ה' כהכנע מנשה אביו ומפני זה היה חדוש אצלם ספר התור' אבל למה שמצינו בסדר עולם ובדברי רז"ל כי בשנת כ"ב למנשה גלה ואח"כ עשה תשובה וסמכו זה למה שכתוב ויעש אשרה כאשר עשה אחאב וכמה מלך אחאב כ"ב ר"ל כי מנשה הרע כאחאב ואחאב עשה הרע כ"ב שנה כל ימי מלכותו ומנשה עשה הרע ג"כ כ"ב שנה הנה ל"ג שנים היה מנשה בתשובה והוא רחוק ואיך היה זה שעמד ל"ג שנים בתשובה רוב ימי מלכותו ולא דרש ספר התורה זה רחוק מאד: (יא) ויהי כשמוע המלך. אמרו כי מצאו הספר נגלל בפרשת תוכחות יולך ה' אותך ואת מלכך וגו' כי שם נרמז ענין גלות שומרון וגלות יהודה עם מלך יהודה כמו שבארנו שם ואולם חלקיה קרא זה אל שפן לסבב שיקראהו שפן אל מלך ויקח עצה להסיר ממנו זה הרע לפי מה שאפשר: (יב) ואת עכבור. ובדברי הימים ואת עבדון ושני שמות היו לו וכמוהו רבים: (יג) נצתה בנו. נדלקה בנו כמו

רש"י

(יג) דרשו את ה' בעדי. ראה כתוב יולך ה' אותך ואת

מנחת שי

מדוייקים: (יב) ויצו המלך את חלקיה הכהן ואת אחיקם בן שפן. בכל הספרים כתוב חלקיה בה"א וא"ו. ובמסורה בפ' הסמוכה כתוב ויצו המלך את חלקיהו בוא"ו. וסמ"ג חלקיהו הכהן ה' וסימן עלה אל חלקיהו. ויאמר חלקיהו

רלב"ג

הרלון בו שהשיכוהו באש אך הרלון בו מענין כלוי כטע' ותחך חמתי: (יא) ויהי כשמוע המלך את דברי ספר התורה ויקרע את בגדיו. יתכן שראה התוכחות והנמשך להם שבמשנה תורה כי שם נרמז ענין גלות שומרון וגלו' יהודה עם מלך יהודה כמו שבארנו שם ואולי חלקיה קרא זה אל שפן לסבב שיקראהו שפן אל המלך ויקח עצה

מצודת ציון

(יג) נצתה. מל' הלתה והבערה:

מצודת דוד

(י) ספר נתן לי. ר"ל נתן לי ספר האבד כשהיא מגוללת בדף הזה: ויקראהו. בהדף ההוא: (יא) ויקרע וגו'. בעבור החרדה כי גם הוא הבנה לאות וסימן: (יג) דרשו את ה'. שאלו לנביאים עלי ועל העם הנמצא פה ועל כל יהודה בעבור דברי הספר הנמצא כתוב בה בתחלת

along with the people, because "you will appoint over yourselves," i.e. because you will appoint him, he will be led away with you. Additionally, the Torah goes on to say that the people would be punished "for the iniquities of their forefathers (Lev. 26:39)." This troubled Josiah intensely. He feared that he would be doomed because of the sins of the people and because of the sins of his forebears [*K'li Y'kar*].

concerning the words of this scroll which has been found—The order of the Hebrew words indicates that primary importance was attached to the fact that it was found, i.e. that God had predestined the finding of the scroll rolled to that ominous passage [*K'li Y'kar*].

for great is the Lord's wrath—as is indicated by the passage at the head of the column to which the scroll is open [*Mezudath David*].

"Hilkiah the priest gave me a scroll," And Shaphan read it
before the king. 11. And it was when the king heard the words
of the scroll of the Law, that he rent his garments. 12. And the
king commanded Hilkiah the priest and Ahikam the son of
Shaphan and Achbor the son of Micaiah and Shaphan the
scribe and Asaiah the king's servant, saying, 13. "Go, inquire
of the Lord on my behalf and on the behalf of the people and
on behalf of all of Judah concerning the words of this scroll
which has been found, for great is the Lord's wrath

Torah, the most holy Torah existing. Therefore, Hilkiah announced, "I have found *the* Scroll of the Law."

This may also be a reflection on the deeds of the priests and the other dignitaries. While we work to repair the physical condition of the outer Temple, we have sadly neglected the Torah, which is the inner Temple of God, wherein His Shechinah rests [*Malbim*].

and he read it—overwhelmed and astounded [*Mezudath David*].

10. **"Hilkiah the priest gave me a scroll."**—Hilkiah the priest gave me this lost scroll rolled to this place [*Mezudath David*].

He hinted to the king that just as we are concerned with the physical condition of the Temple, we must be concerned with the deteriorated condition of Torah observance [*Malbim*].

11. **heard the words of the Scroll of the Law**—Instead of being rolled to the beginning, as the *sefer Torah* of the Temple always was, they found it rolled to the section dealing with the curses that God would visit upon the Jews for non-observance of His commandments. What struck them was the verse reading, "The Lord will lead you and your king, whom you will appoint over yourselves, to a nation that neither you nor your ancestors have known . . . (Deut. 28:36)." This was the prediction of the exile of both Samaria and Judah with its king. Hilkiah intentionally gave the scroll to Shaphan to read to the king, perhaps something could be done to alleviate the situation [*Redak, Abarbanel*].

that he rent his garments—He understood this as a precursor of imminent exile [*Mezudath David*].

12. **Achbor the son of Micaiah**—In II Chron. 34:20, he is known as Abdon the son of Micah. It is common for one person to be called by two similar names [*Redak*].

13. **inquire of the Lord on my behalf**—*He saw written, "The Lord will lead you and your king . . ."* [*Rashi*].

Ask the prophets on my behalf and on behalf of the people found here and on behalf of the entire nation of Judah [*Mezudath David*].

Josiah understood the implication of the verse to mean that even if the king is righteous, he would be exiled

אֲשֶׁר־הִיא נִצְּתָה בָּנוּ עַל אֲשֶׁר לֹא־שָׁמְעוּ אֲבֹתֵינוּ עַל־דִּבְרֵי הַסֵּפֶר הַזֶּה לַעֲשׂוֹת כְּכָל־הַכָּתוּב עָלֵינוּ: יד וַיֵּלֶךְ חִלְקִיָּהוּ הַכֹּהֵן וַאֲחִיקָם וְעַכְבּוֹר וְשָׁפָן וַעֲשָׂיָה אֶל־חֻלְדָּה הַנְּבִיאָה אֵשֶׁת | שַׁלֻּם בֶּן־תִּקְוָה בֶּן־חַרְחַס שֹׁמֵר הַבְּגָדִים וְהִיא יֹשֶׁבֶת בִּירוּשָׁלַםִ בַּמִּשְׁנֶה וַיְדַבְּרוּ אֵלֶיהָ: טו וַתֹּאמֶר אֲלֵיהֶם כֹּה־אָמַר יְהוָה אֱלֹהֵי יִשְׂרָאֵל אִמְרוּ לָאִישׁ אֲשֶׁר־שָׁלַח אֶתְכֶם אֵלָי:

חֵימְתָא דַיְיָ דְהִיא דְלִיקַת בָּנָא עַל דְלָא קַבִּילוּ אֲבָהָתָנָא לְפִתְגָמֵי סִפְרָא הָדֵין לְמֶעְבַּד כְּכָל דִכְתִיב עֲלָנָא: יד וַאֲזַל חִלְקִיָה כָהֲנָא וַאֲחִיקָם וְעַכְבּוֹר וְשָׁפָן וַעֲשָׂיָה לְוַת חֻלְדָה נְבִיָיתָא אִתַּת שַׁלֻּם בַּר תִּקְוָה בַּר חַרְחַס נָטַר לְבוּשַׁיָא וְהִיא יָתְבָא בִּירוּשְׁלֵם בְּבֵית אוּלְפָנָא וּמַלִילוּ עִמַהּ: טו וַאֲמַרַת לְהוֹן כִּדְנַן אֲמַר יְיָ אֱלָהָא דְיִשְׂרָאֵל אֲמָרוּ לְגַבְרָא דִשְׁלַח יתכון

ת"א כן תקוה. סוכה לח:

רש"י

מלכך: (יד) אל חולדה. אמרו רבותינו לפי שהאשה מרחמת יותר מן האיש לכך לא שלח אל ירמיהו. ויש אומרים ירמיהו לא היה שם שהלך להחזיר עשרת השבטים: במשנה. בבית אולפנא שער יש בעזרה ששמו שער הולדה במסכת מדות. ויש ספותרים במשנה חוץ לחומה בין ב' החומות שהיא משנה לעיר: (במשנה. היתה מלמדה התורה שבע"פ לזקנים שלדור והיא היא המשנה הג"ה דר"ע): (במשנה. מאלה הדברים עד לעיני כל ישראל וכן כל הדברים הכפלים בתורה דרשה ברבים וגלתה העונשים והגליות הכפלים לעוברים על סודו ורמזי התורה) (סוד מישרי'):

רד"ק

הנני מצית בך אש מדליק: על דברי הספר. כמו אל: (יד) אל חולדה הנביאה. אמרו במדרש כי מבני בניה של רחב היתה ולמה הלכו אל חולדה ולא הלכו אל ירמי' יש מרבות' ז"ל שאמרו מפני שהנשי' רחמניו' ומהם אמרו כי ירמיה לא היה שם כי הלך להחזיר עשרת השבטים ואמרו כי ירמיה היה אז נביא שהרי תחלת נבואת' היתה בי"ג שנה ליאשיה וזה הענין היה בשנת י"ח אלא שלא היה שם בירושלם אז כשנמצאו התורה אולי היה בענתות או במקום אחר והולדה היתה יושבת בירושלים לפיכך שלח אליה ואמרו רבות' ז"ל כי שלשה

רלב"ג

להסיר ממנו זה הרע לפי מה שאפשר: (יג) נצתה בנו על אשר לא שמעו אבותינו. ר"ל נבערה בנו: (יד) והיא יושבת בירושלם במשנה. תרגם יונתן במשנה בבית המדרש:

מנחת שי

הכהן. ויצו המלך את. וילך חלקיהו הכהן. ויצו המלך הגיגה דכיפדה ע"כ. והאי קרא דמסיר מסורתא דלעיל באמלעיתא ויצו המלך את. על הכוה דכתיב בד"ה ב' ל"ד איתמר וקראי אחריני כולהון כתיבין בעניגא דהכא הכל ויצו המלך את קדמאה דהאי סיפרא כתיב חלקיה בלא וא"ו כדכתבינן לעיל: (יד) חרחס. בקצת ספרים במ"ס אבל ברוב מדוייקים בסמ"ך וכן כתב רד"ק במשנה. בדפוסים חדשים הנו"ן בציירי וביבנים בסגול וכן בכ"י בסגול:

מצודת דוד

סדף אשר מהגראה שהוא לאות אשר גדולה חמת ה' וכו': לעשות. אשר רולה לעשות ככל הכתוב בתחילת הדף ההוא: (יד) אל חולדה. אכז"ל מפני שהנשים רחמניות הן הלכו אליה שהיא תתפלל בעדם. או יתכן אשר שאר הנביאים לא היו אז בירושלים: שומר הבגדים. של המלך: במשנה. בין שתי החומות שהיא משנה להעיר וכן ויללה מן המשנה (צפניה א): וידברו אליה. את דברי המלך:

same root, which sometimes means "to repeat," or double. It is used in the sense of לֶחֶם מִשְׁנֶה, double bread, מִשְׁנֶה לַמֶּלֶךְ, second to the king, etc. (בַּמִּשְׁנֶה,—*She was teaching the Oral Law to the elders of the generation. That is the Mishnah.*—Annotation of R.A.) His identity is unknown. (בַּמִּשְׁנֶה,—From "(Deut. 1:1) *These are the words,*" *until* "(ibid. 34:12) *before the eyes of all Israel,*" *and likewise all the things that are repeated in the Torah, she expounded on in public, and revealed the punishments and the exiles which were doubled for those who transgress the secrets and the allusions of the Torah, the secret of equity.*) This authority interprets "*mishneh*" again as double. She taught the Book known as *Mishneh Torah*, Deuteronomy. She also expounded on any part of

which is kindled against us, since our forefathers did not obey the words of this scroll, to do according to all that is written concerning us." 14. And Hilkiah the priest and Ahikam and Achbor and Shaphan and Asaiah went to Huldah the prophetess, the wife of Shallum the son of Tikvah the son of Harhas, the keeper of the raiment, and she was sitting in Jerusalem in the study-hall, and they spoke to her. 15. And she said to them, "So has the Lord God of Israel spoken, 'Say to the man who sent you to me,

since our fathers did not obey—As mentioned above, Josiah feared that he would be punished for the sins of his forebears [*K'li Y'kar*].

As is recorded in II Chron. 34, Josiah had already been conducting a campaign to "purify" the land. Apparently, his efforts were not yet great enough [*Daath Soferim*].

14. **to Huldah**—*Our Rabbis said that because a woman is more merciful than a man, he, therefore, did not send to Jeremiah. Others say that Jeremiah was not there since he went to bring back the ten tribes* [*Rashi* from *Megillah* 14b].

Since women are more merciful than men, Huldah would undoubtedly pray for Josiah and his people that any evil decree be averted [*Maharsha, Meg. ibid.*].

Jeremiah commenced his prophecies during the thirteenth year of Josiah's reign (Jer. 1:1). This was already the eighteenth year. Either he had gone back to bring back the ten tribes, or he was in Anathoth or elsewhere at the time of the discovery of the scroll. As is mentioned in *Meg.* ad loc, both Jeremiah and Huldah were descended from Rahab the innkeeper whom Joshua married. Together with Zephaniah, they were the sole prophets of that generation. Jeremiah prophesied in the streets, Zephaniah in the synagogues, and Huldah to the women [*Redak* from *Pesikta Rabbathi* 28:2].

Shallum the son of Tikvah—See above 13:21, Comm. Dig. for information concerning the merits of Shallum the son of Tikvah. Because of his meritorious deeds, his wife attained prophecy.

the keeper of the raiment—i.e. the royal robes [*Mezudath David*].

It is also possible that he was the keeper of the priestly garb [*Pseudo-Rashi,* II Chron. 34:22].

in the study-hall—Heb. בַּמִּשְׁנֶה. (*Jonathan* renders:) *in the study-hall.* The root would be שנה, to study. *There is a gate in the Temple court, named "the Gate of Huldah."* This is found in *Tractate Middoth,* 1:3. (Ed. note. The Mishnah states that the two gates of Huldah led to the Temple mt., not to the Temple court.) *Others interpret* בַּמִּשְׁנֶה *as "outside the wall," between the two walls, which are double* around *the city.* They trace the word מִשְׁנֶה from the

טז כֹּה אָמַר יְהוָה הִנְנִי מֵבִיא רָעָה אֶל־
הַמָּקוֹם הַזֶּה וְעַל־יֹשְׁבָיו אֵת כָּל־דִּבְרֵי
הַסֵּפֶר אֲשֶׁר קָרָא מֶלֶךְ יְהוּדָה׃ יז תַּחַת
אֲשֶׁר עֲזָבוּנִי וַיְקַטְּרוּ לֵאלֹהִים אֲחֵרִים
לְמַעַן הַכְעִיסֵנִי בְּכֹל מַעֲשֵׂה יְדֵיהֶם
וְנִצְּתָה חֲמָתִי בַּמָּקוֹם הַזֶּה וְלֹא תִכְבֶּה׃
יח וְאֶל־מֶלֶךְ יְהוּדָה הַשֹּׁלֵחַ אֶתְכֶם
לִדְרֹשׁ אֶת־יְהוָה כֹּה תֹאמְרוּ אֵלָיו
כֹּה־אָמַר יְהוָה אֱלֹהֵי יִשְׂרָאֵל הַדְּבָרִים
אֲשֶׁר שָׁמָעְתָּ׃ יט יַעַן רַךְ־לְבָבְךָ וַתִּכָּנַע
מִפְּנֵי יְהוָה בְּשָׁמְעֲךָ אֲשֶׁר דִּבַּרְתִּי עַל־
הַמָּקוֹם הַזֶּה וְעַל־יֹשְׁבָיו לִהְיוֹת לְשַׁמָּה
וְלִקְלָלָה וַתִּקְרַע אֶת־בְּגָדֶיךָ וַתֵּבְךְּ
לְפָנָי וְגַם אָנֹכִי שָׁמַעְתִּי נְאֻם־יְהוָה׃

תרגום: יתכון לותי: טז כדנן אמר יי הא אנא מיתי בישתא על אתרא הדין ועל יתבוהי ית כל פתגמי ספרא דקרא מלך שבטא דבית יהודה: יז חלף דשבקו פולחני ואסיקו בוסמין לטעות עממיא בדיל לארגזא קדמי בכל עובדי ידיהון וידלק רוגזי באתרא הדין ולא יטפי: יח ולמלך שבטא דבית יהודה דשלח יתכון למתבע אולפן מן קדם יי כדנן תמרון ליה כדנן אמר יי אלהא דישראל פתגמא די שמעתא: יט חלף דנע לבך ואתכנעתא מן קדם יי במשמעך דגזרית על אתרא הדין ועל יתבוהי למהוי לצדו וללוטא ובזעתא ית לבושך ובכיתא קדמי ואף קדמי שמיע אמר

ת"א את כל דברי. סוטה לה:

רד"ק

נביאים נתנבאו בימי יאשיהו והם ירמיהו וצפניה וחולדה כי ירמיה היה מתנבא בשוקי' וצפניה בבתי כנסיות וחולדה אל הנשים: בן חרחס. בסמ"ך: במשנ'. כתרגו' בבית אולפנא: (טז) אשר קרא מלך יהודה. צוה לקראם כאילו קראם וכן ויבן שלמה את הבית והדומים להם וכן הוא בד"ה אשר קרא לפני מלך יהודה ובדברי רז"ל אשר קרא מלך יהודה וכי מלך יהודה

מצודת ציון

(יז) תכבה. מל' כבוי: (יט) רך לבבך. הוא ההפוך מקשה הלב: ותכנע. מל' הכנעה: לשמה. מלשון שממה:

מצודת דוד

(טז) הנני מביא. ר"ל הזאת הזה לא במקרה בא כ"א מה' וכאלו אמר הנני מביא רעה וגו': אשר קרא. אשר לזה לקרות לפניו: (יח) ואל מלך יהודה. ר"ל דבר הנוגע אל המלך עצמו: הדברים אשר שמעת. ר"ל אף שהגזירה גזורה כאשר שמעת לא תהיה כלול עמהם: (יט) בשמעך אשר דברתי. ר"ל בעת השכלת בדברי המקום הזה אשר הוא מה': ולקללה. מי שיקלל את זולתו יתלה הקללה בהם לומר שיקולל כהם:

18. **And concerning the king of Judah**—i.e. as regards the king of Judah [*Abarbanel*], who was not involved in these sins [*Mezudath David*].

"The words are what you heard—I.e. the facts are as you understood them, that a great calamity will befall the nation for its abandoning God's worship in favor of the worship of pagan idols. But—

19. **Since your heart has become soft**—and since you had no part in the idolatry of the nation [*Abarbanel, Mezudath David*].

when you heard what I spoke—i.e when you comprehended from the reading [*Mezudath David*].

16. "So has the Lord said, 'Behold I bring calamity to this place and upon its inhabitants—all the words of the scroll that the king of Judah read. 17. Because they have forsaken Me and have burned incense to pagan deities, in order to provoke Me with all the deeds of their hands, My wrath is kindled against this place, and it shall not be quenched.' 18. And concerning the king of Judah who has sent you to inquire of the Lord, so shall you say to him, 'So has the Lord God of Israel said, "The words are what you heard. 19. Since your heart has become soft, and you have humbled yourself before the Lord, when you heard what I spoke about this place and about its inhabitants, to become a desolation and a curse, and you rent your garments and wept before Me, I, too, have heard [it],' says the Lord.

the Torah that was repeated, illustrating that the laws that are derived from the seemingly redundant words are just as binding and stringent as those explicitly written in the Torah. The authors of these addenda are unknown. Additionally, the last two words are unintelligible.

According to *pseudo-Rashi, Huldah had a chamber adjacent to the "Chamber of Hewn Stone,"* (where the Great Sanhedrin convened). *Huldah's chamber was open to the outside and closed toward the Sanhedrin, which was in the "Chamber of Hewn Stone." So it is written in Tractate Middoth* (?). *This was because of propriety.*

15. **the man who sent you**—The Rabbis (*Meg.* 14b) criticize Huldah for her arrogance in referrng to Josiah as "the man," rather than "the king."

16. **'Behold I bring calamity**—This sign was no coincidence, but a sign from God, as though He said, "Behold I bring calamity . . ." [*Abarbanel*].

that the king of Judah read—Since he ordered these words read, it is considered as though he himself read them. The Rabbis (*Sukkah* 38b) derive from this passage that hearing is tantamount to reciting. (As regards blessings, Hallel, Megillah reading, and most other precepts fulfilled by recitation, hearing the recitation is acceptable as well as actually reciting it.) [*Redak*].

17. **Because they have forsaken Me and have burned incense to pagan gods**—I.e. they deserve this retribution because they have forsaken My worship completely, and have worshipped only pagan deities [*Abarbanel*].

כ לָכֵ֗ן הִנְנִי֮ אֹסִפְךָ֣ עַל־אֲבֹתֶ֒יךָ֒ וְנֶאֱסַפְתָּ֣ אֶל־קִבְרֹתֶ֘יךָ֮ בְּשָׁלוֹם֒ וְלֹא־תִרְאֶ֣ינָה עֵינֶ֔יךָ בְּכֹל֙ הָֽרָעָ֔ה אֲשֶׁר־אֲנִ֥י מֵבִ֖יא עַל־הַמָּק֣וֹם הַזֶּ֑ה וַיָּשִׁ֥בוּ אֶת־הַמֶּ֖לֶךְ דָּבָֽר׃ כג א וַיִּשְׁלַ֖ח הַמֶּ֑לֶךְ וַיַּאַסְפ֣וּ אֵלָ֔יו כָּל־זִקְנֵ֥י יְהוּדָ֖ה וִירוּשָׁלִָֽם׃ ב וַיַּ֣עַל הַמֶּ֣לֶךְ בֵּית־יְהוָ֡ה וְכָל־אִ֣ישׁ יְהוּדָ֩ה וְכָל־יֹשְׁבֵ֨י יְרוּשָׁלִַ֜ם אִתּ֗וֹ וְהַכֹּֽהֲנִים֙ וְהַנְּבִיאִ֔ים וְכָל־הָעָ֖ם לְמִקָּטֹ֣ן וְעַד־גָּד֑וֹל וַיִּקְרָ֣א בְאָזְנֵיהֶ֗ם אֶת־כָּל־דִּבְרֵי֙ סֵ֣פֶר הַבְּרִ֔ית הַנִּמְצָ֖א בְּבֵ֥ית יְהוָֽה׃ ג וַיַּעֲמֹ֣ד הַמֶּ֣לֶךְ עַֽל־הָ֠עַמּוּד וַיִּכְרֹ֨ת אֶֽת־הַבְּרִ֜ית לִפְנֵ֣י יְהוָ֗ה לָלֶ֜כֶת אַחַ֤ר יְהוָה֙ וְלִשְׁמֹ֨ר

אֲמַר יְיָ׃ כ בְּכֵן הָא אֲנָא כְּנִישׁ לָךְ לְוָת אֲבָהָתָךְ וְתִתְכְּנִישׁ לְקִבְרָךְ בִּשְׁלָם וְלָא יֶחֱזְיָן עֵינָךְ בְּכָל בִּישְׁתָא דִי אֲנָא מֵיתֵי עַל אַתְרָא הָדֵין וַאֲתִיבוּ יָת מַלְכָּא פִּתְגָמָא׃ א וּשְׁלַח מַלְכָּא וּכְנַשׁוּ לְוָתֵיהּ כָּל סָבֵי יְהוּדָה וִירוּשְׁלֵם׃ ב וּסְלֵיק מַלְכָּא לְבֵית מַקְדְּשָׁא דַיְיָ וְכָל אֱנָשׁ יְהוּדָה וְיָתְבֵי יְרוּשְׁלֵם עִמֵּיהּ וְכַהֲנַיָא וְסָפְרַיָא וְכָל עַמָּא לְמִזְעֵירָא וְעַד רַבָּא וּקְרָא קֳדָמֵיהוֹן יָת כָּל פִּתְגָמֵי סִפְרָא דִקְיָמָא דְאִשְׁתְּכַח בְּבֵית מַקְדְּשָׁא דַיְיָ׃ ג וְקָם מַלְכָּא עַל אִסְטְוָנָא וּגְזַר יָת קְיָמָא קֳדָם יְיָ לִמְהַךְ בָּתַר פּוּלְחָנָא דַיְיָ ולמטר

תולדות אהרן

הנני אוסף. מ"ק כח:

רש"י

(כ) ונאספת אל קברותיך בשלום. ומהו השלום ולא תראינה עיניך בחורבן הבית:
כג (ג) על העמוד. מקום מעמד המלך בבה"מ:

רד"ק

(כ) אספך. קראם והלא שפן קראם אלא מכאן לשומע כעונה: בחיר"ק בשקל אויבך ויבא ג"כ בסגול על משקל אצרך בבטן: על אבותיך. כמו אל: ונאספת אל קברותיך בשלום. והלא כתי' וירו המורים למלך יאשיהו מהו בשלום שלא חרב ב"ה בימיו וכן הוא מפרש והולך ולא תראינה עיניך בכל הרעה אשר אני מביא אל המקו' הזה: קברותיך. ר"ל קברות אבותיך: (ב) והכהני' והנביאי'. ת"י וכהניא וספריא תרגם הנביאי' ספרי' כלומר תלמידים לפי שלא היו שם נביאים אחרים שהרי המלך שלח אל חולדה מלמד שלא היו שם נביאי' אחרי' וכן תרגם שופט ונביא דיין וסופר ונוכל לפרש נביאים כמשמעו כי ירמיה וצפניה בן כושי היו נביאים בזמן ההוא ואוריהו בן שמעיהו אפשר שהיה נביא ג"כ בזמן ההוא ולא היו בירושל' בעת שמצא חלקי' הכהן את ספר התורה ועתה כאשר שלח המלך לאסוף איש יהוד' באו ג"כ לירושל': (ג) על העמוד. כתרגומו על אסטונא וכבר פי' למעלה בדבר יהואש

רלב"ג

(כ) לכן הנני אוסיפך אל אבותיך. ר"ל בהמותו יהיה נקבר אצל אבותיו ולא תהיה הרעה בימיו ידמה שהיו בישראל אז נביאים זולת חולדה אך שלח אליה מפני היותה קרובה לו כי היתה אז בירושלם: (ג) ויעמוד המלך על העמוד. ידמה שהנו שם עמוד והיה בו המלך בעת קראו

מנחת שי

(כ) הנני אספך. עיין מ"ש בשמואל א' ט"ו ובהרבה ספרים אין כאן בוס מאריך:

מצודת דוד

(כ) אל קברותיך. ולא תקבר בארץ העובדי גלולים: בשלום. עם כי מת במלחמה מ"מ תחשב לו לשלום על כי לא ראה ברעה הבאה על ישראל: וישיבו. חלקיה וחבריו:
כג (ב) ספר הברית. ספור התוכחות הנאמרים בברית: הנמצא בבית ה'. והוא על כי בספר ההוא מלאו התוכחות גוללה בפתיחתו ואף היא כתובה בידי משה המקודשת ומפי ה' והמה סיבות עצומות להחריד את העם לשוב לה': (ג) על העמוד. על המקום

מצודת ציון

(כ) אוספך. ענין מיתה כמו יאסף אהרן (במדבר כ): ונאספת. ענין הכנסה כמו ואין איש מאסף אותי (שופטים יט):

were summoned to assemble in Jerusalem [*Redak*].

the scroll of the covenant—Since it was open to the section of the curses, which ends with the passage, "(Deut. 29:69) These are the words of the covenant," it was called the scroll of the covenant. Immediately following this section is the section entitled "nizabim," in which Moses enters Israel into a covenant with God. Following this precedent,

20. Therefore, behold I gather you in to your forefathers, and you shall be gathered into your graves in peace, and your eyes shall not see any of the calamity that I am bringing upon this place." And they brought back word to the king.

23

1. And the king summoned, and they assembled before him all the elders of Judah and Jerusalem. 2. And the king went up to the house of the Lord, and all the people of Judah and all the inhabitants of Jerusalem were with him, and the priests and the prophets, and all the people from small to great, and he read within their hearing all the words of the scroll of the covenant that was found in the house of the Lord. 3. And the king stood on his place, and enacted the covenant before the Lord, to follow the Lord and to observe

20. **I gather you in to your forefathers**—I.e. you will be interred near your forefathers [*Ralbag*].

and you shall be gathered into your graves in peace—*And what is the peace?* As Scripture continues—

and your eyes shall not see— *the destruction of the Temple* [*Rashi, Redak*].*

and you shall be gathered into your graves—Although you will fall in battle, your body will be buried in the graves of the house of David.

in peace—No one will hinder those transporting your body for burial. The burial will take place with the proper respect due a monarch. He intentionally omits the word בְּשָׁלוֹם, *in peace,* in conjunction with the demise, since that will take place on the battlefield, where Josiah was riddled with arrows. The third promise is:—

and your eyes shall not see any of the calamity . . —The destruction of the Temple and the exile will not take place during your lifetime [*Abarbanel, Malbim*].

2. **and the prophets**—*Jonathan* renders: and the scribes, i.e. the students. Since Josiah sent to Huldah, apparently there were no other prophets at that time. It is, however, possible that Jeremiah and Zephaniah, who were known to have flourished at that time, were present at this assembly. It is also possible that Uriah the son of Shemaiah (Jer. 26:20–23) prophesied at that time. When the scroll was found, they were not available, but now, they

מִצְוֺתָיו וְאֶת־עֵדְוֺתָיו וְאֶת־חֻקֹּתָיו בְּכָל־לֵב וּבְכָל־נֶפֶשׁ לְהָקִים אֶת־דִּבְרֵי הַבְּרִית הַזֹּאת הַכְּתֻבִים עַל־הַסֵּפֶר הַזֶּה וַיַּעֲמֹד כָּל־הָעָם בַּבְּרִית׃
ד וַיְצַו הַמֶּלֶךְ אֶת־חִלְקִיָּהוּ הַכֹּהֵן הַגָּדוֹל וְאֶת־כֹּהֲנֵי הַמִּשְׁנֶה וְאֶת־שֹׁמְרֵי הַסַּף לְהוֹצִיא מֵהֵיכַל יְהוָה אֵת כָּל־הַכֵּלִים הָעֲשׂוּיִם לַבַּעַל וְלָאֲשֵׁרָה וּלְכֹל צְבָא הַשָּׁמָיִם וַיִּשְׂרְפֵם מִחוּץ לִירוּשָׁלַ͏ִם בְּשַׁדְמוֹת קִדְרוֹן וְנָשָׂא אֶת־עֲפָרָם בֵּית־אֵל׃
ה וְהִשְׁבִּית אֶת־הַכְּמָרִים

וּלְמִטַּר פִּקּוּדוֹהִי וְיָת סָהִידְוָתוֹהִי וְיָת קְיָמוֹהִי בְּכָל לִבָּא וּבְכָל נְפַשׁ לְקַיָּמָא יָת פִּתְגָמֵי קְיָמָא הָדֵין דִּכְתִיבִין עַל סִפְרָא הָדֵין וְקַבִּילוּ כָּל עַמָּא עֲלֵיהוֹן קְיָמָא׃ ד וּפַקִּיד מַלְכָּא יָת חִלְקִיָּהוּ כָּהֲנָא רַבָּא וְיָת סְגַן כָּהֲנַיָּא וְיָת אֲמַרְכְּלַיָּא לְאַפָּקָא מֵהֵיכְלָא דַּייָ יָת כָּל מָנַיָּא דַּעֲבִידִין לְבַעֲלָא וְלַאֲשֵׁירְתָא וּלְכָל חֵילֵי שְׁמַיָּא וְאוֹקְדִינוּן מִבָּרָא לִירוּשְׁלֵם בְּמִישַׁר קִדְרוֹן וְאוֹבִיל יָת עַפְרְהוֹן לְבֵית אֵל׃ ה וּבַטֵּיל יָת כּוּמְרַיָּא דִּי

רד"ק

ובדברי הימים ויעמוד המלך על עמדו כלומר במקום שהיה רגיל לעמוד שם: עדותיו. בהנעת הוי"ו: ויעמוד כל העם בברית. עמדו והתחזקו בפיהם ובלבם בברית וכן היעמוד לבך אם תחזקנה ידיך ות"י וקבילו כל עמא עליהון קימא: (ד) ואת כהני המשנה. שהיו שניים לכהן גדול וכת"י וית סגן כהניא: שומרי הסף. פירשנוהו: להוציא מהיכל ה'. והלא מנשה הוציא הכל כשעשה תשובה כמו שאומר בד"ה ויסר את אלהי הנכר ואת הסמל מבית ה' וגו', אלא שאמון החזירם שם ובשנת שתים עשרה למלכו החל לטהר ולהעביר את השקוצים כמו שאומר בד"ה אבל לא כלה עד שנת שמנה עשרה אחר שמצא הספר כמו שאמר הנה: בשדמו' קדרון. כתרגומו במישר קדרון: ונשא את עפרם בית אל. כי שם היה עיקר הע"ג שהיה שם העגל וטמא אותו המקום שהיה בו העגל והמזבח ונשא עפר שריפת הבעל והאשר' וכליהם ששרף בירושלם השדמו' קדרון נשא את עפרם שם: (ה) והשבית את הכמרי'. האנשי' העובדים לפני הבעל נקראין כמרי' וכן תרגם הכהנים

רש"י

(ד) ואת כהני המשנה. סגני כהונה שהם שניים לכהנים גדולים: שומרי הסף. אמרכלים הממונים על כל צרכי הבית ומפתחות העזרה בידם: בשדמות קדרון. במישר קדרון: ונשא את עפרם בית אל. אל

מנחת שי

כג (ג) ואת עדותיו. בהנעת הוא"ו רד"ק ובמסורת עדותיו ה' מפקין וא"ו בליש' וסימנהון ושמרת את משמרת. ויעמדו את חקיו. ויעמד המלך על העמוד דמלכים. ותכרו דד"ה מפני אשר קשרתם כן מלאתי במסרות כ"י ובמסורת שבדפוס במלכים א' ב' גם זו לעמת זו עדתיו ה' בליש' וסימן בסדר ואתחנן ותהלים סימן ל"ט וכה חמש כנגד חמש:

רלב"ג

את התורה כמו שנזכר בפרשת הקהל: (ד) ואת כהני המשנה. הם הכהני' השניים לו כמו סגן הכהנים והנמשכים לו לפי מדרגותיהם על הסדר: בשדמות קדרון. הוא כמו נחל קדרון והוא מישור שהיה בו: (ה) והשבית את הכמרי'. ר"ל שבטל והשבית את הכמרים בקטל

מצודת ציון

כג (ד) שומרי הסף. השוערים: בשדמות קדרון. במישור הסמוך לנחל קדרון: (ה) והשבית. ענין בטול: הכמרים.

מצודת דוד

המיוחד למלך לעמוד בו: להקים. לקיים את דברי התורה הכתובה בברית: ויעמוד וגו'. ר"ל קבלו הברית: (ד) כהני המשנה. הכהנים שהמה שניים לו כסגן ומשוח מלחמה: בית אל. כי שם היה מקום טומאה כי העמיד בה ירבעם עגל הזהב: (ה) והשבית וגו'. ביטל הכמרים אשר העמידו מלכי יהודה להיות ויקטר וגו'.

the necessities of the Temple, and the keys of the Temple court were in their charge [Rashi].

See above 12:10, Commentary Digest.

to take out of the Temple of the Lord—Did not Manasseh remove all the images from the Temple when he repented of his sins, as is delineated in II Chron. 33:15? How then does Josiah find the Temple full of idols accompanied by their paraphernalia? The answer is that Amon replaced the idols in the Temple, even in the Holy of Holies, as is mentioned above. In the twelfth year of his reign, Josiah commenced to purify the land. He did not com-

His commandments and His testimonies and His statutes with all their heart and soul, to fulfill the words of this covenant, which are written in this scroll. And all the people were steadfast in their acceptance of the covenant. 4. And the king commanded Hilkiah the high priest and the priests of the second rank and the guards of the threshold, to take out of the Temple of the Lord all the utensils that were made for the Baal and for the *asherah,* and for the entire host of the heaven, and he burnt them outside Jerusalem in the plains of Kidron, and he carried their ashes to Bethel. 5. And he abolished the pagan priests

Josiah did likewise. See v. 3 [*Malbim*].

3. **on his place**—*the place where the king would stand in the Temple* [*Rashi*].

Jonathan renders: on the collonade. The Chronicler words this as, "on his stand," that is the place where he would usually stand. See above 11:14.

to fulfill the words of the covenant—i.e. the words of the Torah which was given through a covenant [*Mezudath David*].

and all the people were steadfast—I.e. they accepted the covenant wholeheartedly [*Jonathan, Mezudath David*].

This was done in commemoration of the covenant entered into by the Israelites before the demise of Moses [*Malbim*].

Scripture emphasizes the fact that *all* the people accepted the covenant, without any dissenters [*Abarbanel*].

According to tradition (*Yoma* 52b), that Josiah, aware of the impending exile, and fearing for the preservation of the sanctity of the Holy Ark, commanded the Levites to conceal it under the Temple. This is based on the verse in II Chron. 35:3, which reads, "And he said to the Levites who taught all Israel understanding, those who were holy to the Lord, 'Place the Holy Ark in the Temple which Solomon, son of David, king of Israel, built . . .'" I.e. hide it there, lest it be discovered by the invaders, who will undoubtedly defile its sanctity [*Abarbanel*].

4. **and the priests of the second rank**—*the assistants of the priesthood, who were in second rank to the high priests* [*Rashi*].

These were the assistants to the high priest, who would substitute for him in case of his incapacity to perform the Temple service. This includes also those of lower ranks, who assisted them [*Ralbag, Abarbanel*].

The priest anointed for war was also included [*Mezudath David*].

and the guards of the threshold—*the superintendents appointed over all*

אשר נתנו מלכי יהודה ויקטר בבמות
בערי יהודה ומסבי ירושלם ואת־
המקטרים לבעל לשמש ולירח
ולמזלות ולכל צבא השמים: ו ויצא
את־האשרה מבית יהוה מחוץ
לירושלם אל־נחל קדרון וישרף אתה
בנחל קדרון וידק לעפר וישלך את־
עפרה על־קבר בני העם: ז ויתץ את־
בתי הקדשים אשר בבית יהוה אשר
הנשים ארגות שם בתים לאשרה:

די יהבו מלכיא דבית
יהודה ואסיקו בוסמין
על במתא בקרויא
דבית יהודה ובסחרני
ירושלם וית דאסיקו
בוסמין לבעלא
לשמשא ולסיהרא
ולמזלתא ולכל חילי
שמיא: ו ואפיק ית
אשירתא מבית מקדשא
די מברא לירושלם
למישר קדרון ואוקיד
יתה בנחלא דקדרון
ואדקה לעפרא ורמא ית
עפרה לקברי בני גליא:
ז ותרע ית בתי הקדש
טעותא די בבית
מקדשא די נשיא
מחן תמן מכולין

ת"א על קבר. שבת פג סנהדרין מז:

רש"י

מקום טמא אשר טמא שם את המזבח שעשה ירבעם ושרף עליו את כהני הבמות: (ה) ויקטר בבמות. ואותן שקטרו בבמות בערי יהודה: (ז) את בתי הקדשים. בתי הזמה:

רד"ק

ויקטר בבמות. ויקטר כל אחד מהמלכים וכת"י ואסיקו בוסמין על במת': ומסבי. כמו ובמסיבי: ואת המקטרים. פירוש והשבית ג"כ את המקטרים לבעל לשמש ולירח: (ו) על קבר בני העם. העם שהיו עובדים להם בחייה' השליך עפר השריפה על קבריה' לבזיונם כלו' ראו מה שהייתם עובדים בחייכם כדי שיוסרו החיים וכן אומר בדברי הימים ויזרק על פני הקברים הזובחים להם והוא חכר הנסמך קברי הזובחים להם כמו העם המלחמה וי"ת לקברי גליא וגליא שם ע"ג וכן בדברי רבותינו ז"ל בית גליא קורין לה בית כריא: (ז) ויתץ את בתי הקדשים. ת"י ית בתי הקדש טעותא והענין מורה עליו אשר הנשים אורגות שם בתים לאשרה אבל וגם קדש היה בארץ ויעבר את הקדשים מן הארץ תרגם כמשמעו נפקת ברא כי אם היה הקדשים זה ענין זמה מה ענין בבית ה' אבל האשרה שעשה מנשה בבית ה' עשה שם בתים לנשים שיארגו יריעות לכבוד האשרה: בתים לאשרה. יריעות היו בתים לאשרה כמו בתים לבדים אפשר שהיו אותן יריעות תלויות סביב האשרה והיה לאשרה בית ומקום וי"ת די נשיא מחין תמן מכולין לאשירתא ופי' בעל הערוך כמו שהם עובדים ע"ג כומריא ומה שאמר שם הכמרי' עם הכהני' ושניהם עובדי ע"ג אלא שמשתנין בלבושיהם כי הכמרים הם לובשים שחורים לפיכך נקראו כמרי' מענין עורנו כתנור נכמרו ואומר כי הכמרים האלה נתני אותם מלכי יהודה לזו העבודת ויאשיה בטל הע"ג ובטל העובדים מעבודתם והחזירם למוטב:

רלב"ג

כל אחד מהם בבמות בערי יהודה ובמסבי ירושלם והשבית ג"כ המקטרים לבעל ולשמש ולירח ולמזלות ולכל צבא השמים וידמה שככר החזירם למוטב ובטל העבודה ההוא שהיו עושים לע"ג: (ו) וישלך את עפרה על קבר בני העם. ר"ל על קבר העם שהיו עובדים ע"ג ומזה המקום למדנו שככר אסור בהנאה שאם היה מותר בהנאה היה לו להשמר מזה שלא יהנו בקברי העם ונמלאו נהנין מע"ג: (ז) ויתץ את בתי הקדשים אשר בבית ה'. אפשר כי עם החזקם בפעולות המגונות ההם החזיקו בזמה ובתועבות שהיו עושים אחר הגוים וידמה כי מעבודות קצת האשרות היה שיהיו שם מוכנים למשגל מגונה והנשים היו אורגות שם בתים בעבור האשרה והיו עושים יריעות יהיו מחילה ובית נבאים לעבוד האשרה הפעולה המגונה וככר זכר הרב המורה קצת מאותם המשגלים המגונים שהיו מנהג

מצודת דוד

מקטירים בבמות בערי יהודה וסביבות ירושלים: ואת המקטרים וגו'. גם אותם השבית: (ו) בנחל קדרון. סמוך להנחל: וידק לעפר. שרפה עד שהיתה דק כעפר: בני העם. אותם שהיו עובדים להם בחייהם ועשה כזאת לבזותם: (ז) בתי הקדשים. העשויים לשבת בהן המיוחדים לעבודת האשרה: בתים. ר"ל יריעות לתלות סביבה

מצודת ציון

הם כהני עו"ג הלובשים שחורים וכן וכמריו עליו יגילו (הושע י): (ז) ויתץ. מל' נתיצה: הקדשים. דבר המובדל מן האדם ואף

east of Jerusalem, between the Temple Mt. and the Mt. of Olives. Mezudath David insists that he burned the *asherah* next to *Nahal* Kidron. He, apparently, renders *nahal* as stream, rather than valley. Since there was water running through it, he could, obviously, not burn the asherah there. In *Zohar* vol. 2, p. 214, there is indication that there was water in *Nahal* Kidron.

7. **the houses devoted to pagan worship**—Heb. בָּתֵּי הַקְּדֵשִׁים, *the houses of immorality* [*Rashi*].

The context indicates that these houses were related to pagan wor-

whom the kings of Judah had appointed and who had burnt
incense on the high places in the cities of Judah and the environs of Jerusalem, and those who burnt incense to the Baal,
to the sun, to the moon, and to the constellations, and to all the
host of heaven. 6. And he took the *asherah* out of the house of
the Lord to the outside of Jerusalem, to the Kidron Valley, and
he burnt it in the Kidron Valley and he pulverized it into dust;
and he threw its dust on the graves of the members of the
people. 7. And he demolished the houses devoted to pagan
worship that were in the house of the Lord, where the women
weave enclosures for the *asherah*.

plete this project until the eighteenth year, after the discovery of the scroll. See II Chron. 34:3 [*Redak*].

in the plains of Kidron—[*Rashi, Redak,* from *Jonathan*].

I.e. in the plains adjacent to the Kidron Valley [*Mezudath Zion*].

and he carried their ashes to Bethel—*to an unclean place, where he defiled the altar that Jeroboam had made, and he burnt the priests of the high places upon it* [*Rashi*].

There was the home of idol worship in Israel. There Jeroboam erected one of his golden calves and built an altar. Therefore, the ashes of Baal and the *asherah* and their trappings were appropriately deposited there [*Redak*].

5. **And he abolished the pagan priests**—These were the black garbed priests, in opposition to the *kohanim,* who were the white garbed priests [*Redak, Abarbanel*].

He abolished the priests by reforming them and leading them to repent [*Redak, Ralbag, Abarbanel*].

Malbim conjectures that by destroying their paraphernalia, the cult automatically discontinued to function.

and who had burnt incense—*and those who had burnt incense on the high places in the cities of Judah* [*Rashi*].

Alternatively, and each of the kings had burnt incense in the cities of Judah [*Redak*].

and those who burnt incense—These, too, Josiah abolished [*Abarbanel, Mezudath David*].

to the sun—The Baal represented the sun [*Abarbanel*].

See I Kings 18:16, Commentary Digest.

on the graves of the members of the people—who had worshipped it during their lifetime. This was done to degrade them, as if to say, "See the futility of the gods you worshipped during your lifetime." The Chronicler (II 34:4) makes this point clear by stating that "he threw it on the graves of those who sacrificed to them" [*Redak*].

6. **the Kidron Valley**—a valley

ח ויבא את־כל־הכהנים מערי יהודה
ויטמא את־הבמות אשר קטרו־שמה
הכהנים מגבע עד־באר שבע ונתץ
את־במות השערים אשר־פתח שער
יהושע שר־העיר אשר־על־שמאול
איש בשער העיר: ט אך לא יעלו כהני
הבמות אל־מזבח יהוה בירושלם כי
אם־אכלו מצות בתוך אחיהם: י וטמא

לאשירתא: ח ואיתי ית כל כומריא מקרויא דבית יהודה וסאיב ית במתא דאסיקו בוסמין תמן כומריא מגבע עד באר שבע ותרע ית במת תרעיא די קדם תרע יהושע רב קרתא די על שמאלא גברא במיעליה תרע קרתא: ט ברם לא סלקין כהניא כומרי במתא לדבחא על מדבחא דיי בירושלם אלהין אכלו פטיר בגו אחיהון: י וסאיב ית תופת די

בחילת

ת"א אך לא יעלו. מנחות קט: מלא ואו

רד"ק

מכילתא שהם מדות: (ח) ויבא את כל הכהנים. אלה הכהנים היו מזרע אהרן ותרגם אותם יונתן כומריא לפי שנעשו כומרים לע"ג והביא אותם לירושלים והחזירם בתשובה: ויטמא. שם אותם מקום טומאה להשליך שם נבלות וכל טומאה להרחיק הע"ג מלב העם: אשר פתח שער. כמו ואשר פתח השער וכמוהו שמש ירח ופי' נתץ את במות השערים והבמה אשר היתה פתח שער יהושע שר העיר גם כן נתץ אולי היתה גדולה משאר הבמות לפיכך זכר אותה לבדה: אשר על שמאל איש בשער העיר. כלומר הבא איש בשער העיר היתה זאת הבמה לשמאלו וכן ת"י במיעליה תרע קרתא: (ט) כי אם אכלו מצות. פירשו רבותינו ז"ל הרי הם כבעלי מומין חולקין ואוכלין אבל לא מקריבין ומה שאומר מצות פי' מנחות שהיו נאפות מצות והוא הדין לכל חקדשים: (י) וטמא את התופת. שם מקום שהיו מעבירין שם בניהם למולך היה שם המקום תופת ואמרו כי נקרא כן כי היו מרקדים ומכים בתופים בשעת העבודה כדי שלא ישמע האב צעקת בנו כשהיו מעבירין אותו באש וינהם לבו עליו ויקחהו מידם והמקום הזה היה גיא שהיה לאדם הנקרא הנם ונקרא גי הנם וגי בן הנם והכתיב בזת בני הנם והקרי בן הנם כי לבני הנם היה זה הגיא או לאחד מהם וטמא

רש"י

אורגות שם בהים. יריעות: (ט) לא יעלו. הכהנים שקטרו בבמות לעכומ"ז לא יעלו עוד לשרת על מזבח ה': כי אם אכלו מצות. כלומר כי אם בדבר זה לא יצאו מכהונתם שמותרין לאכול בקדשים הרי הם כבעלי מומין וחולקין ואוכלים אבל לא מקריבין: אכלו מצות. מנחות

רלב"ג

הקדומים מעובדי ע"ג להתנהג בהם: (ח) ויבא את כל הכהנים מערי יהודה. כבר באר בספר יחזקאל כי הכהנים בני צדוק הם אשר לא עבדו ע"ג אך שאר הכהנים חטאו בחטא בני יהודה והנה טמא את הבמות בששם בהם דבר טומאה: (ט) אך לא יעלו כהני הבמות. ר"ל שהכהנים שעבדו ע"ג לא יעלו אל מזבח ה' בירושלם. להקריב אשה לה' אך יאכלו במלות המנחות חלקם ובמה שידמה להם עם אחיהם כאילו הם בעלי מומין: (י) וטמא את התופת. הנה עשו שם בנין כדי להעביר בנו ובתו באש למולך והיה את מכאן ואת מכאן

מצודת ציון

בעבור הטומאה והאיסור נקרא בלשון קודש וכן הן תקדש המלאה

מצודת דוד

ודוגמתו בתים לבדים (שמות כ"ה): (ח) ויבא וגו'. הכהנים מזרע אהרן אשר נעשו כומרים לעכו"ם הביאם לירושלים להחזירם בתשובה: ויטמא. השליך שם נבלות וכדומה: מגבע. הבמות אשר עמדו מגבע וגו': במות השערים. אשר עמדו מול השערים: אשר פתח. כמו ואשר בפתח וגו' ולפי שהיתה גדולה מכולם זכרה לעצמה: שמאל איש. בבואו אל העיר: (ט) אך לא יעלו. עם שהחזירם למוטב מ"מ לא הניחם לעבוד במזבח ה': אכלו מצות. משירי מנחה הנאפה מצות וה"ה לשאר קדשים: בתוך אחיהם.

boundary of the Holy Land. See Jos. 19:2.

the high places near the gates—These high places stood opposite **the one that was at the entrance of the gate**—also the high place that was at **the entrance of the gate of Joshua.** In addition to all the high places near the gates of the cities, Josiah demolished the one at the entrance of the gate of Joshua. Perhaps this one was outstanding for its size, and was therefore mentioned separately [*Redak*].

on a person's left in the gate—As one enters the gate of the city, the high place is on his left [*Redak*].

Josiah did not destroy all the high places because most of them had been used for sacrifices to God. He, therefore, sufficed with defiling them [*Malbim*].

9. **However, . . . would not go up**—*The priests who burnt incense on*

8. And he brought all the priests from the cities of Judah, and
he defiled the high places where the priests had burnt incense,
from Geba as far as Beersheba, and he demolished the high
places near the gates, the one that was at the entrance of the
gate of Joshua the mayor of the city, which is on a person's left
in the gate of the city. 9. However, the priests of the high places
would not go up to the Lord's altar in Jerusalem, but they
would eat unleavened cakes among their brethren.

ship, since the women would weave there the enclosures for the *asherah*. Manasseh had constructed houses in the Temple, designated for the women who would stay there and weave enclosures for the *asherah* [*Redak*].

Alternatively, the houses of the dedicated ones—houses for men and women who dedicated their lives to live in seclusion and worship the *asherah*. These women would weave curtains to enclose the *asherah* [*Abarbanel, Mezudath David*].

where the women weave enclosures—*curtains* [*Rashi*]. They would weave curtains to hang around the *asherah,* to enclose it. These were called *battim*, houses or enclosures [*Redak, Mezudath David*].

Ralbag maintains that these were houses of immorality. The *asherah* cult would engage in immoral acts in their worship. The women would weave enclosures to conceal those who engaged in those acts while worshipping the *asherah*.

8. **the priests**—As is apparent from the following verse, these were actually *kohanim* of the seed of Aaron. Since they had become idolatrous priests, *Jonathan* refers to them as כּוּמְרַיָּא. See above v. 5. Josiah brought them to Jerusalem and influenced them to repent of their idolatrous practices [*Redak*].

he defiled the high places—I.e. he made it a place of ritual contamination, to cast carcasses and other forms of uncleanness there, in order to induce the people to forget their liason with the idol cult [*Redak*].

It is noteworthy that people who were capable of worshipping idols, could be deterred from doing so because the site of their idol worship was contaminated. This illustrates that although the people were attracted to paganism, they, nevertheless, observed the commandments and would not enter a contaminated place. The Talmud tells us that during the period we are discussing, the temptation to worship idols was very strong. Manasseh appeared to Rav Ashi in a dream and told him that had he lived at that time, he would have picked up the skirt of his coat and run to worship idols (*San.* 102b). See "Behold a People," p. 351, paragraph 589.

from Geba—a city belonging to Benjamin, given to the Levites, as in Jos. 21:17.

as far as Beersheba—a city belonging to Simeon, on the southern

אֶת־הַתֹּפֶת אֲשֶׁר בְּגֵי בְנֵי־הִנֹּם לְבִלְתִּי
לְהַעֲבִיר אִישׁ אֶת־בְּנוֹ וְאֶת־בִּתּוֹ בָּאֵשׁ
לַמֹּלֶךְ׃ יא וַיַּשְׁבֵּת אֶת־הַסּוּסִים אֲשֶׁר
נָתְנוּ מַלְכֵי יְהוּדָה לַשֶּׁמֶשׁ מִבֹּא בֵית־
יְהוָה אֶל־לִשְׁכַּת נְתַן־מֶלֶךְ הַסָּרִיס
אֲשֶׁר בַּפַּרְוָרִים וְאֶת־מַרְכְּבוֹת הַשֶּׁמֶשׁ
שָׂרַף בָּאֵשׁ׃ יב וְאֶת־הַמִּזְבְּחוֹת אֲשֶׁר

בְחֵילַת בַּר הִנּוֹם בְּדִיל
דְּלָא לְאַעֲבָרָא גְבַר יָת
בְּרֵיהּ וְיָת בְּרַתֵּיהּ בְּנוּרָא
לְמוֹלֶךְ׃ יא וּבַטֵּיל יָת
סוּסְוָתָא דִיהָבוּ מַלְכַיָּא
דְבֵית יְהוּדָה לְשִׁמְשָׁא
מִמֵּעֲלָנָא דְבֵית מַקְדְּשָׁא
דַיְיָ לְלִשְׁכַּת נְתַן מֶלֶךְ
גַּוָּזָאָה דִּבְפַרְוָרַיָּא וְיָת
רְתִיכֵי שִׁמְשָׁא אוֹקֵיד
בְּנוּרָא׃ יב וְיָת אֱגוֹרַיָּא
די

רש"י

וה"ה לכל הקדשים: (י) התופת. הוא המולך ועל שם שהיו הכהנים מקישין בתופים שלא ישמע האב את נהמת הבן כשהוא נכוה בידי הגורה של עכו"ם מולך קראוהו תופת: (יא) את הסוסים. אותם המשתחוים לחמה היו להם סוסי' מוכנים לצאת לקראת החמה בבקר: נתן מלך.

בן קרי

רד"ק

יאשיהו אותו המקום כלומר שם אותו מקום טומאה להשליך שם נבלות וכל טומאה שלא יעלה עוד על לב איש להעביר עוד את בנו ואת בתו באש למולך ומעשה המולך פירשו בדרש אמרו רז"ל אע"פ שהיו כל בתי ע"ג בירושלים המולך היה חוץ לירושלים והיה עשוי צלם חלול נתון לפנים משבעה קנקנים וכל מי שמקריב סלת פותחין לו אחד מהם תורין ובני יונה פותחין לו שנים כבש פותחין לו ג' איל פותחין לו ד' עגל פותחין לו חמשה שור פותחין לו ששה וכן מי שהיה מקריב בנו פותחין לו שבעה והיו פניו של עגל וידיו פשוטות כאדם שפותח ידיו לקבל מחבירו והיו מסיקין אותו באש והכומרים נוטלין את התינוק ונותנין תוך ידיו של מולך והתינוק מוציא נפשו ולמה נקרא תפת והנם תפת שהיו מנהמין בתופים שלא ישמע אביו קול הנער וירחם עליו ויחזור בו הנם שהיה התינוק מנהם וקול נהמותיו עולה. דבר אחר הנם שהיו הכומרים אומרים הנה לך יערב לך יתבסם לך: (יא) וישבת את הסוסים. ובטל ג"כ זה המעשה שהיו עושים מלכי יהודה שהיו עובדים לשמש ונתנו שם סוסים שהיו מוכנים לזאת העבודה שהיו רוכבים עליהם והולכים לקראת השמש בבקר בזרחה והיו הולכים לקראתו ממקום שהיה מבוא בית ה' עד לשכת נתן מלך וזהו שאמר מבוא בית ה' אל לשכת נתן מלך ובוא הוא שם כמו מבוא וכן תרגם ממעלנא דבית מקדשא דה': לשכת נתן מלך והסרים. כמשמעו וכת"י גוזאה וככר פירשנו זה הענין בפסוק ויתן לה המלך סריס אחד: אשר בפרורים. פירוש

רלב"ג

הכומרים מעבירים אותו בין שני האשים: (יא) וישבת את הסוסים. הנה מלכי יהודה נתנו לשמש סוסים מיוחדים שהיו רוכבים בהם ממבוא בית ה' אל לשכת מי שיהוא המלך להיות שר על המגרשים וידמה שהלשכה ההיא היו עושים דבר מה לשמש והנה הם היו הולכים מבית ה' לפאת המזרח אל הלשכה ההיא להשתחוות לשמש הפך מה שכוונה התורה ולזה סדרה שיהיה קדש הקדשים לפאת

מנחת שי

(י) בגי כתי. בן קרי ג (יא) בפרורים. בר"ס וכן הוא בתרגום ירושלמי

מצודת דוד

ר"ל לקחו חלק בין הכהנים והיו א"כ כבעלי מומין שאינם עובדים ואוכלין: (י) את התופת. היא המקום שהיו מעבירים שם בניהם למולך ונקרא כן ע"ש שהיו מכים בתופים לבל ישמע האב נהמת הבן כשהוא נשרף בין המדורות ולבל יכמרו רחמיו: לבלתי להעביר. ר"ל טמא המקום ההוא לבל יעלה עוד על לב אדם להעביר שם למולך: (יא) לשמש. כי מלכי יהודה היו מיחדים סוסים לעבודת השמש לרכוב בהם לקראתו בבוקר ממקום שבאים בה לבית ה' אל

מצודת ציון

(דברים כב): (יא) וישבת. ענין בטול: נתן מלך. כך שמו: בפרורים יבעתו מגרשות (יחזקאל כז) תרגום ירושלמי פרוריא

his daughter in the fire—Josiah defiled it so that no one would think anymore of going to that site to pass his son or daughter through the fire to Molech [*Mezudath David*].

11. **the horses**—*Those who prostrated themselves to the sun, had horses ready to go out toward the sun in the morning* [*Rashi*].

from the entrance of the house of the Lord . . .—I.e. the idolatrous Judean kings would ride these horses from the entrance of the Temple until the chamber of Nethan-melech [*Redak, Mezudath David*].

Nethan-melech—*That was his name* [*Rashi*].

in the outskirts—Heb. בַּפַּרְוָרִים *I do not know what they are* [*Rashi*].

Redak points out that this word is used in the Talmud for the cleared space outside the city, the outskirts. Nethan-melech was in charge of the outskirts.

This chamber was on the east of the city, where the sun-worshippers would go every morning to welcome

10. And he defiled the Topheth that was in the Valley of Ben Hinnom, so that no man would pass his son or his daughter in the fire to the Molech. 11. And he abolished the horses that the kings of Judah had dedicated to the sun, from the entrance of the house of the Lord until the chamber of Nethan-melech the eunuch who was in the outskirts, and he burnt the sun chariots with fire. 12. And the altars that were

the high places to idols, may not ascend anymore to serve on the altar of the Lord [*Rashi*].

But they would eat unleavened cakes—That is to say, but in this thing they would not be disqualified from their priesthood, that they are permitted to eat hallowed things. They are like priests who are blemished, in that they share and eat the sacrifices, but they may not sacrifice [*Rashi, Redak* from *Menahoth* 13:10].

they would eat unleavened cakes—*meal-offerings, and likewise, all hallowed things* [*Rashi*].

10. **the Tofeth**—*This was the Molech. Since priests would bang on drums so that the father would not hear the groans of the child when he would be burned by the hands of the pagan image, Molech, they called it Topheth* [*Rashi* from *Yelam'denu,* a lost Midrash, quoted by *Redak, Abarbanel, Mezudath David, Yalkut Shimoni* Jer. 7, *Aruch.* Also found in addenda to *Tanhuma Buber, Va'ethhannan,* 2].

The Midrash, in its entirety, reads as follows: Although all the pagan shrines were in Jerusalem, the Molech was outside Jerusalem. It was made as a hollow idol within seven rooms. If one would sacrifice fine flour, they would open one room for him. If he would sacrifice turtledoves or young pigeons, they would open two rooms for him. If he would sacrifice a lamb, they would open three rooms for him. If he would sacrifice a ram, they would open four rooms for him. If he would sacrifice a calf, they would open five rooms for him. If he would sacrifice an ox, they would open six rooms for him. If he sacrificed his son, they would open all seven rooms for him. Its face was like that of a calf. Its hands were extended as one does to receive something from his friend. They would heat it with fire. Then the priests would take the child and place him in the hands of the Molech, where he would let out his soul. Why was it called Topheth and Hinnom? Topheth, because . . . and have pity on him and renege. Hinnom, because the child would moan (*nohem*), and his moans would ascend.

Ralbag and *Abarbanel* describe this as two fires between which the priests would pass the child.

According to the simple explanation, this valley belonged to a man named Hinnom, who left it to his sons or to one of them [*Redak*].

so that no one would pass his son or

על־הגג עלית אחז אשר־עשו ׀ מלכי
יהודה ואת־המזבחות אשר עשה
מנשה בשתי חצרות בית־יהוה נתץ
המלך וירץ משם והשליך את־עפרם
אל־נחל קדרון: יג ואת־הבמות אשר ׀
על־פני ירושלם אשר מימין להר־
המשחית אשר בנה שלמה מלך־
ישראל לעשתרת ׀ שקץ צידנים
ולכמוש שקץ מואב ולמלכם תועבת
בני־עמון טמא המלך: יד ושבר את־
המצבות ויכרת את־האשרים וימלא

תרגום

די על אגר עלית אחז
דעבדו מלכיא דבית
יהודה וית אגוריא
דעבד מנשה בתרתין
דרת בית מקדשא דיי
תרע מלכא וארחיק
מתמן ורמא ית עפריהון
לנחלא דקדרון: יג וית
במתא די על אפי
ירושלם דמדרום לטור
זיתיא די בנא שלמה
מלכא דישראל
לעשתורת שקץ
צידונאי ולכמוש שקץ
מואבאי ולמלכום
ריחוק בני עמון סאיב
מלכא: יד ותבר ית
קמתא וקץ ית אשירתא
ומלא

תולדות אהרן

עלית אחז. סנהדרין קג: ואת הבמות. שבת נו:

רד"ק

מגרשי הערים ותרגום ירעשו מגרשות יזועון פרורים ובדברי רז"ל בבל וכל פרורהא. ונתן מלך זה היה פקיד על מגרשי העיר: מרכבות השמש. מרכבות הסוסים שהיו הולכים בהם לקראת השמש: (יב) הגג עלית אחז. חסר הנסמך הגג גג עלית אחז וכן הארון הברית הארון ארון הברית וסמך גג העליה לאחז אולי הוא בנה אותו לזאת העבודה · וירץ משם. מן הקל והוא פעל יוצא כלומר הריצם משם ויש לפרשו ענין שבר ונתיצה כמו כי בך ארוץ גדוד לדעת רבים ואפשר שיהיה שרשו רצץ ויהיו לו חברים רבים בענינו ות"י ופלינון מתמן ר"ל ביערם משם נ"א וארחיק מתמן: (יג) להר המשחית. הר הזיתים ונקרא הר המשחה ולגנאי מפני הע"ג שהיה שם קראו הר המשחית ובן תרגם יונתן לטור זיתיא: אשר בנה שלמה. והיאך לא ביערו אותם אסא ויהושפט שביערו כל ע"ג אשר היתה בארץ ישראל לפניהם ע"ג בערו אבל הבמות לא בערו כי היו אז מקריבים עליהם לאל כי בכלם נאמר והבמות לא סרו עוד העם מזבחים ומקטרים בבמות ויאשיהו נתץ ג"כ הבמות כיון שנעשו מתחלה לע"ג או כדי שלא יקריבו עליהם אפילו לשם שמים שכיון שהיה בית המקדש קיים אסורות היו הבמות לפיכך כתוב עליו לא היה לפניו מלך אשר שב אל ה' בכל

רש"י

כך שמו: אשר בפרורים. לא ידעתי מה הם: (יב) וירץ משם. ונערס משם: (יג) להר המשחית. הר הזיתים הוא הר המשחה וכיון שהזכיר את שמו ע"י עכו"ם שינה שמו

מנחת שי

ובגמרא דילן ומד"ר כמו שפירוש הערוך ערך פרוור: (יב) ואת המזבחות אשר על הגג. הוא"ו בגעיא בס"ס: (יג) ואת הבמות אשר על פני. הוא"ו בגעיא בס"ס: להר המשחית. בסוף פרק במה בהמה כתוב בספרי הגמרא להר המשחה וטעות הוא מהמדפיסים וכן בפירש"י כ"י כתוב להר המשחית ופי' המפרשים שהוא הר המשחה הנקרא ג"כ הר הזיתים וכנהו הכתוב בלשון המשחית לגנאי מפני בנין ע"ג שבנו בו: שקץ צידנים. בספרים מדוייקים מלא ב' יודי"ן וכן נכון על פי המסורת דשופטים י"ח כמו שכתוב שם:

רלב"ג

מטרך כמו שבארנו בבאורנו לדברי התורה: ואת מרכבות השמש שרף באש. ר"ל שמרכבות אשר לסוסים הנזכרים: (יב) אל נחל קדרון. מישור קדרון:(יג) אשר בנה שלמה מלך ישראל. כבר בארנו במה שקדם שלא בנה אותה שלמה אך העלים עיניו מנשותיו שבנו הבמות האלו ולזה יחס הכתוב בנייתם אל שלמה: (יד) וימלא את מקומם עצמות אדם. לטמא אותם וידמה שמעצמות עובדי ע"ז עשם

מצודת ציון

ובדרז"ל בבל וכל פרורהא (כתובות כד): (יב) נתץ. שבר וכתת: ישראל: וירץ משם. הוליאם משם במרוצה ובמהירות: (יג) להר המשחית. הוא הר המשחה ובעבור שעכו"ם כנהו לגנאי: אשר

מצודת דוד

לשכת וגו': מרכבות השמש. אשר משכו בם הסוסים ההם: (יב) עלית אחז. שעל עלית אחז: בשתי חצרות. של הכהנים ושל

pieces and removed them from there. In the *Targum*, we find two versions: וּפַלִּינוּן, *and he eliminated them,* and וְאַרְחֵק, *and he took them far away* [*Redak*].

13. **the Mount of the Destroyer**— *The Mount of Olives, which is known as the Mount of Oil* (הַר הַמִּשְׁחָה). *Since he mentioned its name in reference to idolatry, he changed its name to a pejorative* [*Rashi*].

I.e. he changed its name from הַר הַמִּשְׁחָה to הַר הַמַּשְׁחִית, *the Mount of the* Destroyer, as a derogatory name because of the idols mentioned in its connection.

on the roof, [the roof of] Ahaz's upper chamber, which the kings of Judah had made, and the altars that Manasseh had made in the two courts of the house of the Lord, the king demolished, and he hurriedly removed [them] from there and threw their dust into the Kidron Valley. 13. And the high places that were before Jerusalem, that were on the right of the *Mount of the Destroyer,* which Solomon king of Israel had built for Ashtoreth the abomination of the Sidonians and for Chemosh the abomination of Moab and for Milcom the abomination of the children of Amon, did the king defile. 14. And he broke down the monuments, and cut down the *asherim,* and filled

the sunrise [*Ralbag, Malbim*].

the sun chariots—the chariots to which the horses were hitched for the daily sun-worshipping [*Rashi, Redak, Mezudath David*].

12. **the roof, [the roof of] Ahaz's upper chamber**—Perhaps Ahaz built this upper chamber for this service [*Redak*].

This alludes to the tradition that Ahaz placed an idol in the attic of the Temple [*San.* 103b].

and the altars that Manasseh had made—and which he abandoned when he repented. Ahaz's altars had likewise been abandoned when Hezekiah came to power. Josiah, nevertheless, wished to abolish every trace of idolatry.

in the two courts of the house of the Lord—i.e. the court of the Israelites and the court of the priests [*Mezudath David*].

It is also possible that Scripture is referring to the court of the women and the court of the Israelites. It is unlikely that Manasseh would leave an altar in the court of the priests, where the sacrificial service took place. We can assume that Hezekiah removed tha altar that Ahaz had erected after the model of the one he saw in Damascus. Otherwise, Josiah would have done so, and it is not mentioned here. Likewise, when Manasseh repented, he, undoubtedly, would have cleared that area. Therefore, it seems more likely that the two courts referred to are the court of the women and the court of the Israelites.

and he hurriedly removed them—*and he eliminated them from there* [*Rashi*].

The root of the Hebrew word וַיָּרָץ, may be רוץ, *to run.* In that case, we render, *and he hurriedly removed them from there.* It is also possible that the root is רצץ, *to smash.* In that case, we render, *and he smashed them from there.* I.e. after he had dismantled the altars, he smashed the

את־מקומם עצמות אדם: טו וגם את־
המזבח אשר בבית־אל הבמה אשר
עשה ירבעם בן־נבט אשר החטיא
את־ישראל גם את־המזבח ההוא
ואת־הבמה נתץ וישרף את־הבמה
הדק לעפר ושרף אשרה: טז ויפן
יאשיהו וירא את־הקברים אשר־שם
בהר וישלח ויקח את־העצמות מן־
הקברים וישרף על־המזבח ויטמאהו
כדבר יהוה אשר קרא איש האלהים
אשר קרא את־הדברים האלה:
יז ויאמר מה הציון הלז אשר אני ראה

וּמַלֵא יַת אַתְרֵהוֹן גַרְמֵי אֱנָשָׁא: טו וְאַף יַת אֱגוֹרָא דִי בְבֵית אֵל בָּמָתָא דַעֲבַד יָרָבְעָם בַּר נְבָט דְחַיֵב יַת יִשְׂרָאֵל אַף יַת אֱגוֹרָא הַהִיא וְיַת בָּמָתָא פְּרַע וְאוֹקִיד יַת בָּמָתָא אַדְקָהּ לְעַפְרָא וְאוֹקִיד אֲשֵׁירָתָא: טז וְאִתְפְּנֵי יֹאשִׁיָהוּ וַחֲזָא יַת קִבְרַיָא דְתַמָן בְּטוּרָא וּשְׁלַח וּנְסִיב יַת גַרְמַיָא מִן קִבְרַיָא וְאוֹקִיד עַל אֱגוֹרַיָא וְסַאֲבֵיהּ כְּפִתְגָמָא דַיְיָ דְמַלֵיל נְבִיָא דַיְיָ דְאִתְנַבֵּי יַת פִּתְגָמַיָא הָאִלֵין: יז וַאֲמַר מָה צִיוּנָא הָדֵין דִי אֲנָא חָזֵי

ת"א מה הציון הלז. מגלה יד ערכין לג:

רש"י

לגנהי: (יז) מה הציון הלז. ראה קבר מלדו א' עלי קמשוני' וחרולי' ולדו א' הדסים ובשמים ותמה עליו ואמר

רד"ק

לבבו ובכל נפשו ובכל מאודו כי המלכים אשר היו לפניו לא הסירו הבמות אע"פ שהיו מלכים טובים: (יד) עצמות אדם. עצמות עובדי ע"ג שהיה מוציא אותם מקבריהם ונותנם במקום האשרות והמצבות לבזיון ישרפם שם: (יז) מה הציון הלז. נראה כי הנביא הזקן צוה לבניו שיעשו על הקבר ציון גדול שיהא ניכר בין הציונים האחרים כי ידע כי תתקיים נבואת הנביא כמו שאמר כי היה יהיה הדבר והנביא אמר מה שיעשה יאשיהו שיוציא העצמות מקבריהם וישרפו אותם לפיכך צוה להם שיהיה ציון אותו הקבר ניכר בין האחרים כי עצמות נביא האמת ידע שלא יוציאו מקברו לפיכך שאל יאשיהו מה הציון הלז. ובדרש ראה שצדו אחד עלו בו חרולים וקמשונים וצדו אחד עלו בו הדסים ועשבי בשמים לפיכך תמה ושאל מה הציון הלז והיה זה כי צדיק ורשע היו נקברים בו נביא אמת ונביא השקר: ויאמרו אליו אנשי העיר. קבלה היתה בידם כי מעת שנקבר שם הנביא עד הזמן ההוא יותר משלש מאות וחמשים שנה אלא קבלה היתה בידם בן מפי אב: הקבר איש האלהים. חסר הנסמך חקבר קבר איש האלהים וכן הארון הברית: על המזבח בית אל. בא בה"א הידיעה עם הסמוך שלא כמנהג וכמוהו הלשכות הקדש היתד הארג והדומים להם שכתבנו

רלב"ג

אם: (טז) ויקח את העצמות מן הקברים. זה לאות שלא היה משים אם רק עצמות החטאים ולזה לא הסכים לשרוף עליהם עצמות איש האלהים ומלטו עצמותיו עצמות הנביא אשר בא משומרון ולולי זה כבר היו עצמותו נשרפים כי היה מנביאי ע"ג: (יז) מה הציון הלז.

מצודת דוד

בנה שלמה. ר"ל הניח לנשיו לבנות: (יד) עצמות אדם. כי הוליא מהקברים עצמות הטכומ"ז: (טו) וגם את המזבח אשר בבית אל. עם שבית אל לא היתה מארץ יהודה מדינת מלכותו: הבמה. כמו והבמה והוא הבנין אשר עשה להעמיד בה הטכומ"ז והמזבחות: הדק לעפר. להיות דק דק דומה לעפר: (טז) בהר. של בית אל: וישרוף. כי היו עובדי כוכבים: אשר קרא. מאז בימי ירבעם קרא ולתוספות ביאור אמר שוב אשר קרא הדברים האלה: (יז) מה הציון. ראה ציון על קבר משונה בגדלו ושאל עליו

מצודת ציון

(יז) הציון. הוא סימן נעלבת מת וכן ובנה אצלו ציון (יחזקאל לט):

pers of Jeroboam's calves. Therefore, he sent and took out the bones and burnt them, as is stated further on in this verse [*Malbim*].

that the man of God had called—during the days of Jeroboam, as in I Kings 13:16 [*Mezudath David*].

who called out—*Jonathan* renders: who prophesied. This is an additional explanation [*Mezudath David*].

17. **"What is this marker?"**—*He saw a grave, one side of which was overgrown with thorns and thistles, and whose other side was* graced with *myrtles and spices. He wondered*

their place with human bones. 15. And also the altar that was
in Bethel, the high place that Jeroboam the son of Nebat—who
caused Israel to sin—had made, also that altar and the high
place he demolished, and he burnt the high place; he pulverized
it and burnt the *asherah*. 16. And Josiah turned and saw the
graves that were there on the mount, and he sent and took the
bones out of the graves and burned them on the altar and
defiled it, according to the word of the Lord that the man of
God had called, who had called out these words. 17. And he
said, "What is this marker that I see?"

which Solomon, king of Israel, had built—Since he did not protest their building, it is considered as though he, himself, had built them [*Ralbag*].

Alternatively, Solomon had thought that they would be used for idolatry. In reality, however, they were used in God's service. Since there had been a thought of using them for idolatry, Josiah destroyed them [*Malbim*].

Alternatively, since Josiah destroyed all the high places, even those used for God's service, since they were now forbidden to be used from the time of the building of the Temple, these altars, too, fell into that category. Asa and Jehoshaphat, however, who did not abolish the high places, left these altars, since they were not being used for idolatrous purposes [*Redak*].

As mentioned above, *Malbim*'s view is that the high places that were used only in service of God, were defiled but not destroyed. He, therefore, rejects *Redak*'s explanation.

Ashtoreth—a god in the form of a sheep.

Milcom—identified with Molech. See I Kings 11:5–7.

14. **the monuments**—See above 10:26, where the term, monument, is discussed at length.

Since the monuments and the *asherim* were used for idolatrous purposes, Josiah destroyed them, not being satisfied with merely defiling them [*Malbim*].

human bones—He would remove the bones of the idolators from their grave, and fill the places of the monuments and the *asherim* with them to disgrace them. Then he would burn them [*Redak*].

15. **And also the altar that was in Bethel**—Although it was not in his kingdom, he destroyed it, in order to cleanse the entire country of idolatry [*Malbim*].

16. **And Josiah turned**—It was customary for the idolators to make graveyards neighboring the shrines of their deities, since they clung to defilement, inherent in the graves. The proximity of these graves was sufficient evidence to Josiah, that their occupants had been worship-

וַיֹּאמְרוּ אֵלָיו אַנְשֵׁי הָעִיר הַקֶּבֶר אִישׁ־
הָאֱלֹהִים אֲשֶׁר־בָּא מִיהוּדָה וַיִּקְרָא דן
אֶת־הַדְּבָרִים הָאֵלֶּה אֲשֶׁר עָשִׂיתָ עַל
הַמִּזְבַּח בֵּית־אֵל׃ יח וַיֹּאמֶר הַנִּיחוּ לוֹ
אִישׁ אַל־יָנַע עַצְמֹתָיו וַיְמַלְּטוּ עַצְמֹתָיו
אֵת עַצְמוֹת הַנָּבִיא אֲשֶׁר־בָּא
מִשֹּׁמְרוֹן׃ יט וְגַם אֶת־כָּל־בָּתֵּי הַבָּמוֹת
אֲשֶׁר ׀ בְּעָרֵי שֹׁמְרוֹן אֲשֶׁר עָשׂוּ מַלְכֵי
יִשְׂרָאֵל לְהַכְעִיס הֵסִיר יֹאשִׁיָּהוּ וַיַּעַשׂ
לָהֶם כְּכָל־הַמַּעֲשִׂים אֲשֶׁר עָשָׂה
בְּבֵית־אֵל׃ כ וַיִּזְבַּח אֶת־כָּל־כֹּהֲנֵי
הַבָּמוֹת אֲשֶׁר־שָׁם עַל־הַמִּזְבְּחוֹת
וַיִּשְׂרֹף אֶת־עַצְמוֹת אָדָם עֲלֵיהֶם וַיָּשָׁב
יְרוּשָׁלִָם׃ כא וַיְצַו הַמֶּלֶךְ אֶת־כָּל־הָעָם

תרגום

חֲזֵי וַאֲמַרוּ לֵיהּ אֱנָשֵׁי קַרְתָּא קְבוּרָא דִנְבִיָא דַיְיָ דַאֲתָא מִשִּׁבְטָא דִיהוּדָה וְאִתְנַבֵּי יָת פִּתְגָמַיָא הָאִלֵּין דַעֲבַדְתָּא עַל אֱגוֹרָיָא בְּבֵית אֵל׃ יח וַאֲמַר שְׁבוּקוּ מִנֵּיהּ אֱנָשׁ לָא יָנִיד גַרְמוֹהִי וְשַׁזִּיבוּ גַרְמוֹהִי (עִם) יָת גַרְמֵי נְבִיָא שִׁקְרָא דַאֲתָא מִשֹּׁמְרוֹן׃ יט וְאַף יָת כָּל בָּתֵּי בָּמָתָא דִי בְּקִרְוֵי שֹׁמְרוֹן דִי עֲבַדוּ מַלְכֵי יִשְׂרָאֵל לְאַרְגָזָא פַּלֵּי יֹאשִׁיָהוּ וַעֲבַד לְהוֹן כְּכָל עֲבִידְרָא דַעֲבַד בְּבֵית אֵל׃ כ וּנְכַס יָת כָּל כּוּמְרֵי בָמָתָא דִי תַמָן עַל אֱגוֹרַיָא וְאוֹקִיד יָת גַרְמֵי אֱנָשָׁא עֲלֵיהוֹן וְתָב לִירוּשְׁלֵם׃ כא וּפַקִּיד מַלְכָּא יָת כָּל עַמָּא לְמֵימַר

רש"י

מה זה והשיבו: הקבר איש האלהים. ונביא השקר שלוה לבניו שיקברוהו אצלו: (יט) אשר בערי שמרון. שהי' יאשיהו מלך על כל ישר' מה שחזרו מעשרת השבטים על ידי ירמיהו:

רד"ק

בספר מכלול: (יח) וימלטו. כי בקבר אחד היו עצמותיו אצל עצמות הנביא אשר בא משומרון הוא הנביא הזקן נביא השקר ובבית אל היה יושב אז אבל משומרון בא שם כמו שפירשנו למעלה במקומו: (יט) אשר בערי שומרון. והלא הכותים היו יושבים בשמרון וישראל גלו מהם אלא הבמות היו עדיין קיימים וגם שארית נשארה בארץ אחר גלות ישראל מפוזרים בארץ זעיר שם זעיר שם והיו עובדים ע"ג עדיין כמו שאמר

רלב"ג

הנה כנו כנין על קבר איש האלהים להכירו והכנין ההוא נקרא ציון ובאלו יאשיה מה הציון הלז: (כ) ויזבח את כל כהני הבמות אשר שם על המזבחות. ידמה שעדין נשארו שם קצת ישראל כמו שנזכר אחר זה ועדין היו מחזיקים ברשעתם והיו שם כהני במות ויאשיה זבח

מצודת ציון

הלז. הזה: (יח) ינע. מלשון תנועה:

מצודת דוד

של מי הוא: הקבר. זה הקבר הוא של איש האלהים וגו': (יח) וימלטו עצמותיו. בעבור שלא יניעו עצמות איש האלהים הציל מקמת עצמות הנביא שקבור סמוך לו כי חשש פן יניעו בזה עצמות איש האלהים: אשר בא משומרון. להשיב עמו את איש האלהים כאשר נאמר שם: (כ) אשר שם. אף שכבר גלו משומרון עכ"ז המעט אשר נשארו עבדו עכומ"ז כמאז:

scattered throughout the land. These Israelites still worshipped idols, as is mentioned in v. 20. The Chronicler, too, mentions the tribes of Ephraim and Manasseh, still in Samaria during Josiah's reign (II Chron. 34:9) [*Redak*].

20. **who were there**—As mentioned above, the remnant continued to worship pagan deities as was their wont [*Mezudath David*].

he burnt human bones—an allusion to the bones of Jeroboam the son of Nebat, as in I Kings 13:2.

21. **"Perform a Passover sacrifice**—After abolishing the high

And the people of the city said to him, "The grave of the man of God who came from Judah and called out these things that you did on the altar of Bethel." 18. And he said, "Let him be. Let no one move his bones." And they spared his bones with the bones of the prophet who came from Samaria. 19. And also all the temples of the high places that were in the cities of Samaria that the kings of Israel had made [in order] to anger, Josiah removed, and he did to them like all the deeds he had done in Bethel. 20. And he slaughtered all the priests of the high places who were there, on the altars, and he burnt human bones upon them, and he returned to Jerusalem. 21. And the king commanded all the people,

about it and said, "What is this?" And they replied, . . . —Rashi, Redak, from unknown Rabbinic source.

Alternatively, he noticed a large marker on one grave, unlike the markers on all the other graves. The old prophet from Samaria had ordered that an outstanding marker be placed on the grave of the prophet from Judah, since he was confident that his prophecy would be fulfilled. He was confident also that Josiah would spare the bones of the prophet from Judah and hoped that his bones too would be spared because of their proximity [*Redak, Abarbanel*].

And the people of the city said to him—This was a tradition handed down from father to son for over three hundred years that Josiah would burn the bones of the idolators on the altar in Bethel, and that the prophet who had prophesied this was buried on that site [*Redak*].

"The grave of the man of God—*and the false prophet, who commanded his sons that they bury him next to him* [*Rashi*].

18. **And they spared his bones with the bones of the prophet who came from Samaria**—Since they were buried in the same grave, they feared that if they removed his bones, they would move the bones of the prophet from Judah [*Redak*].

This may also be rendered: And his bones saved the bones of the prophet who came from Samaria. See I Kings 13:31, 32.

19. **that were in the cities of Samaria**—*for Josiah was king over all Israel, those who returned from the ten tribes through Jeremiah* [*Rashi*].

See above 22:14.

Additionally, although the Cuthites inhabited Samaria, there remained high places which the kings of Israel had built. Moreover, there was a small remnant of Israelites

לֵאמֹר עֲשׂוּ פֶּסַח לַיהוָה אֱלֹהֵיכֶם
כַּכָּתוּב עַל סֵפֶר הַבְּרִית הַזֶּה׃ כב כִּי לֹא
נַעֲשָׂה כַּפֶּסַח הַזֶּה מִימֵי הַשֹּׁפְטִים
אֲשֶׁר שָׁפְטוּ אֶת־יִשְׂרָאֵל וְכֹל יְמֵי מַלְכֵי
יִשְׂרָאֵל וּמַלְכֵי יְהוּדָה׃ כג כִּי אִם־
בִּשְׁמֹנֶה עֶשְׂרֵה שָׁנָה לַמֶּלֶךְ יֹאשִׁיָּהוּ
נַעֲשָׂה הַפֶּסַח הַזֶּה לַיהוָה בִּירוּשָׁלִָם׃
כד וְגַם אֶת־הָאֹבוֹת וְאֶת־הַיִּדְּעֹנִים
וְאֶת־הַתְּרָפִים וְאֶת־הַגִּלֻּלִים וְאֵת כָּל־

לְמֵימַר עֲבִידוּ פִסְחָא
קֳדָם יְיָ אֱלָהֲכוֹן כְּמָא
דִכְתִיב עַל סִפְרָא
דִקְיָמָא הָדֵין׃ כב אֲרֵי
לָא אִתְעֲבִיד כְּפִסְחָא
הָדֵין מִיוֹמֵי נְגִידַיָא
דְדָנוּ יַת יִשְׂרָאֵל וְכָל
יוֹמֵי מַלְכֵי יִשְׂרָאֵל
וּמַלְכַיָא דְבֵית יְהוּדָה׃
כג אֱלָהֵין בִּתְמָנֵי עַסְרֵי
שְׁנִין לְמַלְכָּא יֹאשִׁיָהוּ
אִתְעֲבַד פִּסְחָא הָדֵין
קֳדָם יְיָ בִּירוּשְׁלֵם׃
כד וְאַף יַת בִּידִין וְיַת
זְכוּרוּ וְיַת צַלְמָנַיָא וְיַת
טעותא

רש"י

(כב) לא נעשה כפסח הזה. לא נתקבלו רוב עם בכל פסח כמו שנתקבלו בזה: מימי השופטים. מימי שמואל כתוב (בד"ה ב' ל"ה י"ח) לפי שאף שמואל החזיר ישראל למוטב וקבלם המלפתה. ד"ר לא נעש' כפסח הזה לה' בירושלים אבל משמלכו מלכי ישראל ומלכי יהודה לא עשו פסח כל ישראל בירושלים לפי שנחלקה המלכות לשנים מירבעם והיו הולכים לעגל שבבית אל וכן עד עכשיו שגלו עשרת השבטים והחזירם ירמיהו ומלך עליהם יאשיהו ובאו כולם לירושלים:(כד)התרפים. צורות שמדברי' ע"י כשפים והעושה אותן צריך לכוין שעה א' בשנה ושנה א' ראויה לכך:

רד"ק

ויזבח את כל כהני הבמות אשר שם וכן אמר בדברי הימים כי מאפרים וממנשה היה שם שארית בימי יאשיהו וכן בימי חזקיהו היה שארת בארץ מזבולון ומאשר ומשמעון ואפרים ומנשה ורבותינו ז"ל אמרו כי ירמיהו החזיר מעשרת השבטים ומלך עליהם יאשיהו: (כב) כי לא נעשת כפסח הזה. תכלית הספור הוא זה כי מלת כי נותן טעם למה שקדם וכן כי נתן ה' בידינו את כל הארץ ר"ל כי עשו הפסח כמו שצוה אותם יאשיהו ונתקבצו כולם לירושלם וארך הספור ההוא כמו שכתוב בדברי הימים וסוף הספור כי לא נעשה כפסח הזה: מימי השופטים. ובד"ה כתיב מימי שמואל הנביא וזמן אחד היא כי שמואל בימי השופטים היה ובימיו החלה המלוכה בישראל ומה שאמר כי לא נעשה כפסח הזה שהיו כל ישראל בלב אחד לעבוד את ה' וכן אמר בשמואל וינהו כל בית ישראל אחרי ה' ואמר ויסירו בני ישראל את הבעלים ואת העשתרות ויעבדו את השם לבדו וגם פסח שעשה חזקיהו רבים מישראל שלא היו שם ולא עוד אלא שהיו מלעיבים ברצים שהיה שולח חזקיהו ואף אותם שהיו בירושלים רבים היו טמאים ואכלו את הפסח בטומאה: (כד) ואת התרפים. כתרגומו צלמניא והם

רלב"ג

אותם אלא המזבחות ושרף על המזבחות עצמות אדם: (כב) כי לא נעשה כפסח הזה מימי השופטים. ר"ל מימי סוף השופטים שהוא שמואל כי בחייו שבו ג"כ כל ישראל אל ה' ובימי שאול ודוד היו בישראל במות בהסך כונת התורה אע"פ שהיו מותרות ובימי שלמה נשארו ג"כ הבמות ונעשו במות לע"ג ובימי חזקיהו לא שבו ג"כ כל ישראל אל ה' אך קצת ישראל היו מלעיגים לדברי חזקיהו אך בימי יאשיהו בזאת השנה שבו כל ישראל אל ה' והנה זכר הפסח הנעשה אז לפי שמתנאי הפסח שלא יאכל ממנו ישראל מומר וידמה כי בזאת השנה לבד היה לב כל ישראל לש"י אך אחר זה חטאו בסתר גם בימי יאשיהו ולזה אמר כי בשמנה עשרה שנה למלך יאשיהו נעשה הפסח הזה לה' והנה לזאת הסבה לא שב הש"י מחרון אפו הגדול כמו שספר כי בלי ספק אם היו ישראל שבים לה' בכל נפשם היתה ההשגחה האלהית דבקה בהם וישוב חרון ה' מהם ולזה אמר אך לא שב ה' מחרון אפו הגדול ולזאת הסבה ג"כ מת יאשיהו בעון העם כי הוא חשב שיהיו כל ישראל הולכים אחר מצות הש"י ויהיו ראוים מפני זה שידבקו בהם כל הברכות הכתובות בתורה אשר כתוב בהם וחרב לא תעבור בארצכם אפילו חרב של שלום ובחטא העם מת ונענשו בעבור מהם מי שחיו בללו בגוים ועליו קונן ירמיהו כמו שכתוב בספר הקינות לפי מה שזכר בד"ה ממנו ואמרו רבותינו ז"ל שמה שכתוב שם מזה הוא אמרו רוח אפינו משיח ה' נלכד בשחיתום וגו' וזה

מצודת דוד

(כב) כי לא נעשה. ר"ל עם שגם לפניו עשו פסח מ"מ הוכרח לצאת נעשות ככתוב בטהרה גדולה כי לא נעשה כפסח הזה העשוי בטהרה מימי השופטים ובד"ה נאמר מימי שמואל כי שמואל היה סוף השופטים: וכל ימי מלכי ישראל. מוסב על לא נעשה לומר בלא נעשה

מצודת ציון

(כד) התרפים. הם העשויים בצורת אדם ומגידים עתידות ע"י

23. **Except in the eighteenth year**—Apparently, the following year they reverted to their previous ways. Many sinned clandestinely even during Josiah's reign. Because of this shortcoming, God's wrath did not subside, as below, v. 26. This led, too, to Josiah's death. Had the people really returned to the Lord wholeheartedly, they would have merited the fulfillment of the blessings of the Torah, wherein it is stated, "(Lev. 26:6) . . . and a sword will not pass through your land,"

saying, "Perform a Passover sacrifice to the Lord your God, as it is written in this scroll of the covenant." 22. For such a Passover sacrifice had not been performed since the time of the judges who judged Israel, and all the days of the kings of Israel and the kings of Judah. 23. Except in the eighteenth year of King Josiah, this Passover sacrifice was performed to the Lord, in Jerusalem. 24. And also the necromaneers and those who divine by the Jidoa bone and the *teraphim* and the idols and all

places and the idols, Josiah commanded that the people perform the annual Passover sacrifice, since the purpose of the original Passover sacrifice was to abolish the worship of Aries the Ram, the first sign of the zodiac, which the Egyptians worshipped [*Malbim*].

22. **such a Passover sacrifice had not been performed**—*So many people had not assembled at any Passover sacrifice as assembled at this one.* [*Rashi*].

since the days of the judges—*In* II *Chron.* 35:18, *it is written, "Since the days of Samuel," because Samuel, too, led Israel to improve* their ways, *and he assembled them to Mizpah* (I Sam. 7:5, 6). *Alternatively, such a Passover had not been performed to the Lord in Jerusalem. Since the kings of Israel and the kings of Judah reigned, all Israel did not perform a Passover sacrifice in Jerusalem, because the kingdom had been divided in two since Jeroboam, and they would go to the calf in Bethel and in Dan until now that the ten tribes were exiled, and Jeremiah brought them back, and Josiah reigned over them, and they all came to Jerusalem* [*Rashi*].

With slight variation, *Redak* explains that since the days of the judges, there was never a Passover sacrifice performed by all Israel of one accord. In Samuel's time, which was the end of the period of the judges, Scripture tells us, "(I Sam. 7:2) . . . and all the house of Israel were drawn after the Lord." "(v. 4) And the children of Israel removed the Baalim and the Ashtaroth, and served the Lord alone." Even during Hezekiah's reign, many Jews did not attend the performance of the Passover sacrifice. Moreover, many "(II Chron. 30:10) mocked them and jeered at them." I.e. at Hezekiah's couriers. Even of those who were in Jerusalem, many were unclean and ate the sacrifice in their unclean state.

Even in the time of Saul, David, and Solomon, many sacrificed on high places which remained during Solomon's reign even after the building of the Temple. Hence no Passover sacrifice had been performed in unity, in purity, in the absence of any idolatry in the land, according to all its requirements, between the time of Samuel and the time of Josiah [*Ralbag, Abarbanel*].

הַשִּׁקֻּצִים אֲשֶׁר נִרְאוּ בְּאֶרֶץ יְהוּדָה
וּבִירוּשָׁלַםִ בִּעֵר יֹאשִׁיָּהוּ לְמַעַן הָקִים
אֶת־דִּבְרֵי הַתּוֹרָה הַכְּתֻבִים עַל־
הַסֵּפֶר אֲשֶׁר מָצָא חִלְקִיָּהוּ הַכֹּהֵן בֵּית
יְהוָה: כה וְכָמֹהוּ לֹא־הָיָה לְפָנָיו מֶלֶךְ
אֲשֶׁר־שָׁב אֶל־יְהוָה בְּכָל־לְבָבוֹ וּבְכָל־
נַפְשׁוֹ וּבְכָל־מְאֹדוֹ כְּכֹל תּוֹרַת מֹשֶׁה
וְאַחֲרָיו לֹא־קָם כָּמֹהוּ: כו אַךְ לֹא־שָׁב
יְהוָה מֵחֲרוֹן אַפּוֹ הַגָּדוֹל אֲשֶׁר־חָרָה
אַפּוֹ בִּיהוּדָה עַל כָּל־הַכְּעָסִים אֲשֶׁר
הִכְעִסוֹ מְנַשֶּׁה: כז וַיֹּאמֶר יְהוָה גַּם אֶת־
יְהוּדָה אָסִיר מֵעַל פָּנַי כַּאֲשֶׁר הֲסִרֹתִי

טָעֲוָתָא וְיָת כָּל שִׁקוּצַיָא
דְאִתְחֲזִיאוּ בְּאַרְעָא
דְבֵית יְהוּדָה וּבִירוּשְׁלֵם
פַּלֵי יֹאשִׁיָהוּ בְּדִיל
לְקַיָמָא יָת פִּתְגָמֵי
אוֹרַיְתָא דִכְתִיבִין עַל
סִפְרָא דְאַשְׁכַּח חִלְקִיָה
כָּהֲנָא בְּבֵית מַקְדְשָׁא
דַיָי: כה וּכְוָתֵיהּ לָא הֲוָה
קֳדָמוֹהִי מַלְכָּא דְתָב
לְפוּלְחָנָא דַיָי בְּכָל לִבֵּיהּ
וּבְכָל נַפְשֵׁיהּ וּבְכָל
נִכְסוֹהִי כְּכֹל אוֹרַיְתָא
דְמֹשֶׁה וּבָתְרוֹהִי לָא קָם
כְּוָתֵיהּ: כו בְּרַם לָא תָב
יְיָ מִתְּקוֹף רוּגְזֵיהּ רַבָּא
דִתְקִיף רוּגְזֵיהּ בִּדְבֵית
יְהוּדָה עַל כָּל אַרְגָזוּתָא
דִי אַרְגֵיז קֳדָמוֹהִי
מְנַשֶּׁה: כז וַאֲמַר יְיָ אַף
יָת דְבֵית יְהוּדָה אַגְלֵי
מֵאַרְעָא בֵּית שְׁכִנְתִּי
כמא

ת״א וכמהו לא היה. שבת נו:

רד״ק

צלמים עשויים לדעת העתידות וכבר פירשנוהו עוד בספר שמואל: (כה) אשר שב אל ה׳. שחרד לדברי תורה ועשה ככל הכתוב בה והסיר הבמות לא השאיר אחד ולא הקריבו בימיו כי אם בבה״מ לבדו והמלכים אשר לפניו אף על פי שהיו בהם טובים לא הסירו הבמות כמו שאמר עוד העם מזבחים ומקטרים בבמות ונמצא באסא דברי׳ אשר לא כן שנשען על מלך ארם והוציא כסף וזהב מאוצרות בית ה׳ ושלח לו ונאמר וגם בחליו לא דרש את ה׳ ויהושפט ג״כ היה עוזר למלכי ישראל הרשעים ונתחתן עמהם וחזקיה ג״כ נאמר עליו ולא כגמול עליו השיב חזקיהו כי גבה לבו ויהי עליו קצף ועל יהודה ועל ירושלים אבל יאשיהו נאמר עליו ככל תורת משה ויש מחלוקת בזה בדברי רז״ל מהם אמרו כי יאשיהו חטא אלא שעשה תשובה גדולה אשר שב אל ה׳ וגו׳ ומהם אמרו שלא חטא אלא מה אני מקיים אשר שב אל ה׳ שכל דין שדן מבן שמנה ועד י״ח החזירו להם שמא תאמר נטל מזה ונתן לזה תלמוד לומר ובכל מאודו שהחזיר להם משלו:

מנחת שי

(כד) חלקיהו הכהן בית ה׳. בכל הספרים כתוב בית לא בבית:

רלב״ג

מספים למה שאמרנו: (כה) וכמוהו לא היה לפניו מלך אשר שב אל ה׳ וגו׳. עד שבכר היה מגזה כל הדברים זולת השם יתברך ובכל הקניינים היה בז לרוב חשקו לעבוד הש״י ואיך הרלון שלא יהיה יאשיהו בתחלת ענינו טוב עם הש״י כי כבר נזכר בדברי הימים כי מקטנותו החל לעבוד הש״י אך לא בער בשלמות האלילים ממלכותו והיו חוטאים עדיין ישראל בהם ומפני ראותו הכתוב בספר התורה שיבא מהרע למי שלא יקיים את התורה ויעבור על ברית הש״י התעורר בכל עוז להשיב ישראל לעבודתו ובער האלילים שעשו ישראל

מצודת ציון

כישוף: בער. ענין הסרה: הקים. מל׳ קיום: בית ה׳. בבית ה׳: (כה) מאודו. עשרו כמו ובכל מאדך (דברים ו):

מצודת דוד

כפסח הזה כל ימי מלכי ישראל והם דוד ושלמה שמלכו על כל ישראל: (כד) על הספר. ר״ל בעבור הספר אשר מצא חלקיה כי הספר הזה היתה סיבה לכל זה: (כה) וכמהו לא היה לפניו. ומה שנאמר בחזקיה ואחריו לא קם כמוהו הוא בדבר הבטחון בה׳ וכמ״ש שם אבל בדבר התשובה לא היה כיאשיהו ויש מרז״ל באמרו במעולם לא חטא ותשובתו היתה להחזירו מכלו כל דין שדן מבן ח׳ עד י״ח וז״ש ובכל מאודו: (כו) אך לא שב וגו׳. אף ביאשיה עשה תשובה בכל לבבו והורה להעם דרכי ה׳: על כל הכעסים. בעבור כי בהלגע אחזו ישראל בהכעסים אשר הכעים מנשה לעבוד כוכבים כמוהו:

author of Kings, omitted the account of Manasseh's repentance [*Abarbanel*].

The Rabbis of the Talmud (*Shabbath* 56b) disagree as to whether Josiah sinned and repented, or whether he was righteous from the start. One explains this verse according to its simple sense. The other explains that Josiah rescinded all the legal decisions he had issued between the ages of eight and eighteen, for fear that he had erred in his youth [*Redak*].

the abominations that were seen in the land of Judah and in
Jerusalem, Josiah abolished, in order to fulfill the words of the
Torah which were written in the scroll that Hilkiah the priest
had found in the house of the Lord. 25. Now, before him there
was no king like him, who returned to the Lord with all his
heart and with all his soul and with all his possessions, according to the entire Torah of Moses, and after him no one arose.
26. Nevertheless, the Lord did not turn back from His great
wrath, for His wrath was kindled against Judah, because of all
the provocations that Manasseh had provoked Him. 27. And
the Lord said, "I will remove Judah too from before Me as I
have removed Israel,

meaning even a sword of peace, armies passing through to attack other countries (*Rashi* ad loc.). Pharaoh-Neco would not have passed through Judah, and Josiah would not have fallen. This coincides with the Rabbinical explanation of "(Lam. 4:20) The breath of our nostrils, the anointed of the Lord, was caught in their traps," which identifies this verse with Josiah, who was killed by Egyptian archers because of the sins of the people [*Ralbag*].

24. **the necromancers . . .**—See above 21:6.

the teraphim—*images that speak through sorcery, and the one who makes them must determine one hour in the year and one year that is fit for this* [*Rashi*].

These were made in the form of a man and were used to foretell the future [*Redak, Mezudath Zion*].

See I Sam. 19:13, Comm. Dig.

25. **who returned to the Lord**—who kept the words of the Torah scrupulously and conscientiously. Although there were other righteous kings before him, none of them abolished the high places completely. In his time, however, everyone sacrificed in the Temple only. Moreover, some fault could be found with each of Josiah's forebears, even with the righteous ones. Asa relied on the king of Aram and took silver and gold from the treasuries of the Temple, which he sent to him. Additionally, he did not seek God in his illness. Jehoshaphat aided the kings of Israel and intermarried with them. Hezekiah, too, became haughty when the king of Babylon sent emissaries to him. Josiah, however, was completely beyond reproach [*Redak*].

with all his heart . . .—as opposed to Manasseh who repented only in order to be extricated from his troubles, as the Chronicler explains. For this reason, Jeremiah, the

אֶת־יִשְׂרָאֵל וּמָאַסְתִּי אֶת־הָעִיר הַזֹּאת אֲשֶׁר־בָּחַרְתִּי אֶת־יְרוּשָׁלַםִ וְאֶת־הַבַּיִת אֲשֶׁר אָמַרְתִּי יִהְיֶה שְׁמִי שָׁם: כח וְיֶתֶר דִּבְרֵי יֹאשִׁיָּהוּ וְכָל־אֲשֶׁר עָשָׂה הֲלֹא־הֵם כְּתוּבִים עַל־סֵפֶר דִּבְרֵי הַיָּמִים לְמַלְכֵי יְהוּדָה: כט בְּיָמָיו עָלָה פַרְעֹה נְכֹה מֶלֶךְ־מִצְרַיִם עַל־מֶלֶךְ אַשּׁוּר עַל־נְהַר־פְּרָת וַיֵּלֶךְ הַמֶּלֶךְ יֹאשִׁיָּהוּ לִקְרָאתוֹ וַיְמִיתֵהוּ בִּמְגִדּוֹ כִּרְאֹתוֹ אֹתוֹ: ל וַיַּרְכִּבֻהוּ עֲבָדָיו מֵת מִמְּגִדּוֹ וַיְבִאֻהוּ יְרוּשָׁלַםִ וַיִּקְבְּרֻהוּ בִּקְבֻרָתוֹ וַיִּקַּח עַם־הָאָרֶץ

כְּמָא דְאַגְלֵיתִי יַת יִשְׂרָאֵל וְאַרְחֵיק יַת קַרְתָּא הָדָא דְאִתְרְעֵיתִי בִירוּשְׁלֵם וּבְבֵיתָא דַאֲמָרִית יְהֵי שְׁמִי תַּמָּן: כח וּשְׁאָר פִּתְגָמֵי יֹאשִׁיָּהוּ וְכָל דִּי עֲבַד הֲלָא אִינוּן כְּתִיבִין עַל סְפַר פִּתְגָמֵי יוֹמַיָּא לְמַלְכַיָּא דְבֵית יְהוּדָה: כט בְּיוֹמוֹהִי סְלֵיק פַּרְעֹה חֲגִירָא מַלְכָּא דְמִצְרַיִם עַל מַלְכָּא דְאַתּוּר עַל נְהַר פְּרָת נָאזַל מַלְכָּא יֹאשִׁיָּהוּ לְקַדְמוּתֵיהּ וְקַטְלֵיהּ בִּמְגִדּוֹ כַּד חֲזָא יָתֵיהּ: ל וְאַחֲתוּהִי עַבְדוֹהִי כַּד מִית מִמְּגִדּוֹ וְאַיְתִיאוּהִי לִירוּשְׁלֵם וְקַבְרוּהִי בִּקְבוּרְתֵּיהּ וּדְבַר עַמָּא דְאַרְעָא יַת יְהוֹאָחָז

רד"ק

(כט) פרעה נכה. כתרגומו פרעה חגירא שהיה נכה רגלים: וילך המלך יאשיהו לקראתו. להלחם אתו לפי שהיה עובר בגבולו בכרכמיש על פרת והוא היה הולך להלחם על מלך אשור שכבש כרכמיש ממלך ארם ושלח לו מה לי ולך מלך ישראל לא עליך אתה היום כי אל בית מלחמתי כמו שכתוב בדברי הימים ולא שמע אל דברי פרעה נכה ואמרו רבותינו ז"ל מאי דרש יאשיהו וחרב לא תעבור בארצכם אפילו חרב של שלום כיון שהיו עושין רצונו של מקום והוא לא היה ידע שכל דורו עובדי ע"ג היו אלא שהיו עושין בסתר שהרי בימי יאשיהו היה ירמיהו מוכיח כי מספר עריך היו אלהיך יהודה: וימיתהו במגידו כראותו אותו. בכ"ף בבקעת מגידו היתה המלחמה כמו שאומר בדברי הימים ופי' כראותו אותו כשראה אותו שדעתו להלחם עמו שהתרה בו וראה אותו לבוש כלי מלחמה כמו שאומר בדברי הימים כי להלחם בו התחפש ונענש יאשיהו לפי שלא שמע יאשיהו אליו כי מפי אלהים היה אומר לו כמו שאומר בדברי הימים ולא שמע אל דבר נכה כי ירמיהו התנבא בזה וכן אמרו רז"ל כי אלהים האמור ביאשיהו קדש ומהם אמרו כי חדל לך מאלהים אשר עמי ע"ג ובעוד פרעה שם נלחם בכרכמיש על פרת לקח הש"י נקמת יאשיהו ממנו שצר שם ימים רבים עד השנה הרביעית ליהויקים בן יאשיהו ובא עליו נבוכדנצר והוא שהתנבא ירמיהו למצרים על חיל פרעה נכה מלך מצרים אשר היה על נהר פרת בכרכמיש אשר הכה נבוכדנצר מלך בבל וגו' ואומר והיה היום ההוא לה' צבאות יום נקמה להנקם מצריו הוא נקמת המלך יאשיהו: (ל) בקבורתו. בקברות המלכים כמו שאומר בדברי הימים בקברות אבותיו ומה שאמר בקבורתו אפשר שהוא כרה לו

רלב"ג

מכל הכן ישראל כדי שיסור זכר ע"ג מישראל ולא יוסיפו לחטוא עוד: (ל) ויקח עם הארץ את יהואחז בן יאשיהו וימשחו אותו. ידמה שמשחו אותו מפני המחלוקת שהיתה בין האחים וידמה מפני זה כי הוא לא היה יהואחז הבכור וכבר יתבאר זה ממה שזכר כי בן עשרים ושלש שנה יהואחז במלכו ולא מלך כי אם שלשה חדשים ומלך אחריו יהויקים והיה בן עשרים וחמש שנה יהויקים במלכו וזה לאות שכבר היה גדול ממנו כמו שתי שנים וכבר נמנו בספר ד"ה בני יאשיהו וזכר שם כי הבכור יוחנן השני יהויקים השלישי לדקיהו הרביעי שלום וכבר באר ר' אברהם בן עזרא ע"ה כי שלום הוא יהואחז כי כתוב בירמיהו כי כה אמר ה' אל שלום בן יאשיהו מלך יהודה המולך תחת יאשיהו אביו אשר יצא מן המקום הזה לא ישוב עוד והנה אחריו מלך יהויקים ובנו ואחריהם מלך לדקיה ולא מלך יוחנן ואם הוא הבכור מלך בבל המליך הישר בעיניו ואמנם הנה זכר בספר ד"ה כי הבכור יוחנן לפי מה שהחשוב להודיע שכבר עשו ישראל שלא כהוגן בהמליכם הקטן מהבנים אך המליכוהו בהיותו

מנחת שי

(כט) כראתו. בכ"ף וכן במסורת כראתו לית חסר וא' מלא. כי אין הנעד (בראשית מ"ד ל"א): (ל) ויבאהו ירושלם. בס"ס חסר יו"ד אחר הבי"ת וכן הוא במקצת דפוסים ישנים ועיין מה שאני עתיד לכתוב בירמיה סימן כ"ו בס"ד:

מצודת דוד

(כט) לקראתו. למנעו ללכת דרך הלוו: כראותו אותו. ר"ל כשהלחמו עמו וכמו ויתראו פנים (לעיל י"ד) שר"ל נלחמו פנים בפנים והוא לשון המלחמה: (ל) בקברתו. אשר כרה לעצמו בחייו:

מצודת ציון

(כט) נכה. ת"י חגורא והוא מענין צולע וכן בן נכה רגלים (ש"ב

was unaware that many of his subjects worshipped idols clandestinely. The prophet Jeremiah announced, "(Jer. 2:29) . . . for the number of your cities were your gods, O Judah!" [*Redak* from *Taanith* 22b].

Pseudo-Rashi, II Chron. ibid. quotes R. Eleazar the Kalir in the *Kinoth* for *Tisha b'Av,* that the scornful of the generation concealed idols behind their doors.

and he killed him in Megiddo—

and I will reject this city, which I have chosen—Jerusalem—and the Temple concerning which I said, 'My Name shall be there.'" 28. And the rest of the events of Josiah and all that he did, are written in the book of the chronicles of the kings of Judah. 29. In his days, Pharaoh-Neco went up against the king of Assyria by the Euphrates River, and King Josiah went toward him, and he killed him in Megiddo when he saw him. 30. And his servants transported him dead from Megiddo, and they brought him to Jerusalem and buried him in his grave.

And the people of the land took

and with all his possessions—When he rescinded his legal decisions, he paid the litigant against whom he had decided originally, from his own pocket [*Shabbath* ibid.].

26. **because of all the provocations that Manasseh had provoked Him**—As mentioned above, Manasseh's repentance was not wholehearted. Consequently, he did not influence the people to mend their ways. When he died, Amon reverted openly to Manasseh's early sins, and the people followed him. Even during Josiah's reign, there were among the ignorant masses, people who worshipped idols clandestinely. After the momentous revival experienced during the Passover celebration of the eighteenth year, many of them reverted to their old ways, as mentioned above [*Abarbanel*].

29. **Pharaoh-Neco**—He was given this appelation because he was lame. See II Sam. 4:4 [*Redak*].*

by the Euphrates River—Assyria had seized Carchemish from Aram and was encamped there on the Euphrates River. In order to attack them, Pharaoh-Neco had to pass through Eretz Israel [*Redak* from II Chron. 35:20].

King Josiah went toward him—to prevent him from traversing his land to attack Assyria. Instead of inquiring of Jeremiah whether he should march against Pharaoh-Neco, he expounded on the passage of Lev. 26:6, ". . . and a sword will not pass through your land," to mean that even friendly armies passing through the land to attack other countries, would not pass through Eretz Israel. He, therefore, had the courage to attempt to repulse the Egyptian forces. When he heard Pharaoh-Neco admonish him to "desist from the god who is with me, and he will not destroy you (II Chron. 35:21)," he thought that since Pharaoh-Neco depended on the pagan deities for aid, he would surely vanquish him, and he continued his campaign. The truth of the matter was, however, that his generation was not worthy to be spared the intrusion of friendly armies. He

אֶת־יְהוֹאָחָז בֶּן־יֹאשִׁיָּהוּ וַיִּמְשְׁחוּ אֹתוֹ
וַיַּמְלִיכוּ אֹתוֹ תַּחַת אָבִיו: לא בֶּן־עֶשְׂרִים
וְשָׁלֹשׁ שָׁנָה יְהוֹאָחָז בְּמָלְכוֹ וּשְׁלֹשָׁה
חֳדָשִׁים מָלַךְ בִּירוּשָׁלָםִ וְשֵׁם אִמּוֹ
חֲמוּטַל בַּת־יִרְמְיָהוּ מִלִּבְנָה: לב וַיַּעַשׂ
הָרַע בְּעֵינֵי יְהוָה כְּכֹל אֲשֶׁר־עָשׂוּ
אֲבֹתָיו: לג וַיַּאַסְרֵהוּ פַרְעֹה נְכֹה בְרִבְלָה
בְּאֶרֶץ חֲמָת בִּמְלֹךְ בִּירוּשָׁלָםִ וַיִּתֶּן־
עֹנֶשׁ עַל־הָאָרֶץ מֵאָה כִכַּר־כֶּסֶף וְכִכַּר

ממלך קרי

תרגום

יְהוֹאָחָז בַּר יֹאשִׁיָהוּ וּמְשַׁחוּ יָתֵיהּ וְאַמְלִיכוּ יָתֵיהּ תְּחוֹת אֲבוּהִי: לא בַּר עַסְרִין וּתְלָת שְׁנִין יְהוֹאָחָז כַּד מְלַךְ וּתְלָתָא יַרְחִין מְלַךְ בִּירוּשְׁלֶם וְשׁוּם אִמֵּיהּ חֲמוּטַל בַּת יִרְמְיָה מִן לִבְנָה: לב וַעֲבַד דְבִישׁ קֳדָם יְיָ כְּכֹל דַעֲבָדוּ אֲבָהָתוֹהִי: לג וְאַסְרֵיהּ פַּרְעֹה חֲגִירָא בְרִבְלָה בְּאַרְעָא דַחֲמָת מִלְמִמְלַךְ בִּירוּשְׁלֶם וּרְמָא מַגְבִּיתָא עַל עַמָּא דְאַרְעָא מְאָה כִּכְּרֵי כַסְפָּא וְכִכְּרָא דְדַהֲבָא: ואמליך

רש"י

(ל) וימשחו. לא היה צריך משיחה אלא מפני שהיה יהויקים אחיו גדול ממנו שתי שנים כמו שכתוב בענין:

רד"ק

קבורה בחייו: וימשחו אותו. מפני מה משחו אותו והלא אין מושחין מלך בן מלך ולא משחו שלמה אלא מפני מחלוקתו של אדוניהו ואת יהואש מפני מחלוקתו של עתליה ויהואחז ג"כ משחו מפני מחלוקתו של יהויקים שהיה גדול ממנו שתי שנים ומשחו יהואחז אע"פ שהיה קטן ממנו מפני שהיה ממלא מקום אבותיו ויהויקים לא היה ממלא מקום אבותיו כך פירשו רז"ל ויהויקים שהיה גדול מיהואחז שתי שנים ראו מהפסוקים שנאמר בן עשרים ושלש שנה יהואחז במלכו וכתיב בן עשרים וחמש יהויקים במלכו ולא מלך יהואחז אלא שלשה חדשים והנה מצאנו בדברי הימים ובני יאשיהו הבכור יוחנן השני יהויקים השלישי צדקיהו הרביעי שלום והנה לא נזכר שם יהואחז והם אמרו כי יוחנן הוא יהואחז וקראו בכור שהי' בכור למלכו' ושלום הוא צדקיהו ואמר השלישי צדקיהו שהיה שלישי לבני יאשיהו ואמר עליו הרביעי שלום שהיה רביעי למלכות יאשיהו וקראו שלום ששלמה מלכות בית דוד בימיו ואני פרשתי בד"ה כי שלום הוא יהויכין ובזכרו בן הבן בסדר הבנים רבי' כמוהו בספ' והחכם רבי אברהם בן עזרא כתב כי יוחנן היה בכור ולא מלך ושלום הוא יהואחז והנה יהואחז היה במות אביו בן כ"ג וצדקיה שהיה גדול ממנו בן כ"ד ויהויקים בן כ"ה והנה במלוך צדקיהו לפי זה החשבון היה בן ל"ה והכתוב אומר בן כ"א צדקיהו במלכו אלא שהמליכו יאשיהו אביו בחייו שלש שנים לפני מותו וכשמת יאשיהו לא רצו העם במלכותו והמליכו את יהואחז שהוא שלום וזהו שאמר ויקח עם הארץ את יהואחז בן יאשיהו וימשחו אותו וימליכו אותו תחת אביו נראה כי בחזקה המליכוהו והביא ראיה ממה שכתוב בירמיה בראשית ממלכת יהויקים וגו' ואומר עשה לך מוסרות ומוטות וגו' ביד המלאכים הבאים ירושלם אל צדקיהו מלך יהודה והיאך היה צדקיהו מלך בראשית ממלכת יהויקים אלא שהיה נודע בגוים כי יאשיה המליך צדקיהו בחייו אלא שלא רצו בו עם הארץ אחרי מות אביו ואנחנו נפרש זה הענין בספר ירמיה בע"ה: (לג) ויאסרהו פרעה נכה. נראה כי יהואחז במלכו חשב לנקום נקמת אביו מפרעה נכה והלך ופשט בארץ מצרים והכה בהם מכה גדולה ובשובו פגע בו פרעה בארץ חמת ולכדו ואסרו וזהו שאמר יחזקאל וילמד לטרוף טרף אדם אכל כי מה ענין ויאסרהו מבלי שיקדם לו ענין שנלחם עמו או עלה על ארצו והלא פרעה התנצל ליאשיהו ואמר לו לא עליך אתה היום שכן נראה הענין כמו שפירשנו ומשל יחזקאל מורה עליו: במלך בירושלם. כן כתיב רוצה לומר בעוד מלכו בירושלם מעט הזמן הזה לקחו וקרי ממלוך שהסירו מהמלוכה לפי שהחל להלח' עמו והוא לא פשע במיתת אביו לפי דעתו כי הוא לא היה בא להלחם עמו ואעפ"כ לקח האל ית' נקמתו ממנו כמו שכתוב והמליך פרעה נכה את אחיו כדי שיהי' לו עבד וידע כי מידו הוא מולך: וככר זהב. כמשמעו ככר א' זהב וי"ת וככרי דהבא ר"ל ככרים ולא זכר כמה:

מנחת שי

(לג) במלך. ממלך קרי:

רלב"ג

כמשך לפעולות המגונות אשר היו עושים מועדות אליהם ולזה נמשך אליהם מהרע מה שנמשך כי אולי היה יוחנן אחיו מעטה יאשיהו אביו: (לב) ככל אשר עשו אבותיו. ר"ל אבותיו אשר עשו הרע בעיני ה' כמו אחז ומנשה והדומים להם: (לג) ויתן עונש על הארץ. ר"ל שיתנו זה הממס מדי שנה בשנה והוא המליך להם את אליקים:

מצודת ציון

ד): על נהר. כמוך לנהר: (לג) ויאסרהו. קשרו:

מצודת דוד

(לב) אבותיו. מנשה ואמון: (לג) ממלוך. להסירו ממלוך בירושלים: ויתן

is depicted as one who learned to prey and devoured a man, consequently being taken to Egypt in chains [*Redak*].

from reigning—Heb. מִמְּלֹךְ. The *Kethib* is בִּמְלֹךְ, *while reigning*. I.e. while he was yet reigning his brief reign, Pharaoh-Neco captured him and removed him from his throne. Pharaoh-Neco considered himself justified in slaying Josiah, since he did not march on Judah, but was merely passing through the land on his way to attack Assyria. He, there-

Jehoahaz the son of Josiah and anointed him and made him king instead of his father. 31. Jehoahaz was twenty-three years old when he became king, and he reigned three months in Jerusalem. And his mother's name was Hamutal the daughter of Jeremiah of Libnah. 32. And he did what was evil in the eyes of the Lord, like all that his forefathers had done. 33. And Pharaoh-Neco imprisoned him in Riblah in the land of Hamath, to prevent him from reigning in Jerusalem, and he imposed a fine on the land consisting of one hundred talents of silver and a talent of gold.

The battle transpired in the Valley of Megiddo, as is related in II Chron. [*Redak*].

when we saw him—dressed for battle, as the Chronicler explains. Josiah was punished for not consulting Jeremiah to hear God's word concerning attacking the Egyptian armies, and for not heeding the words of Neco which he repeated from the prophecy of Isaiah, that he was destined to battle Assyria. Because of this shortcoming, Josiah was riddled by the arrows of the Egyptian archers. Since he was a righteous man all his life, his death was avenged when Nebuchadnezzar attacked the Egyptians in Carchemish and destroyed them. This revenge was prophesied by Jeremiah (46:10), "And that day will be for the Lord God of Hosts, a day of revenge to be avenged of His adversaries . . . in the north land on the River Euphrates." This refers to the revenge for the death of King Josiah [*Redak*].

30. **in his grave**—in the graves of the kings, as in II Chron. 35:24. Perhaps he had dug this grave for himself [*Redak*].

and anointed him—*He required anointment only because Jehoiakim his brother was two years older than he, as is explained in this episode* [*Rashi* from *Horioth* 11b].*

32. **his forefathers**—Manasseh and Amon. [*Mezudath David*].

As mentioned above, Jehoahaz was originally righteous, but reverted to the ways of his forebears after he became king.

33. **imprisoned him**—It appears that Jehoahaz attempted to avenge his father's death at the hands of Pharaoh-Neco. He, therefore, marched on Egypt during his absence, dealing it a severe blow. On his return home, he confronted Pharaoh-Neco in the land of Hamath. Pharaoh-Neco captured him and imprisoned him, and levied a penalty on the land for their attacking his country. Ezekiel's elegy on the princes of Israel (19), in which he depicts Josiah's sons as lion whelps supports this theory. The first one, alluding to Jehoahaz,

זָהָב׃ לד וַיַּמְלֵךְ פַּרְעֹה נְכֹה אֶת־אֶלְיָקִים
בֶּן־יֹאשִׁיָּהוּ תַּחַת יֹאשִׁיָּהוּ אָבִיו וַיַּסֵּב
אֶת־שְׁמוֹ יְהוֹיָקִים וְאֶת־יְהוֹאָחָז לָקַח
וַיָּבֹא מִצְרַיִם וַיָּמָת שָׁם׃ לה וְהַכֶּסֶף
וְהַזָּהָב נָתַן יְהוֹיָקִים לְפַרְעֹה אַךְ
הֶעֱרִיךְ אֶת־הָאָרֶץ לָתֵת אֶת־הַכֶּסֶף
עַל־פִּי פַרְעֹה אִישׁ כְּעֶרְכּוֹ נָגַשׂ אֶת־
הַכֶּסֶף וְאֶת־הַזָּהָב אֶת־עַם הָאָרֶץ לָתֵת
לְפַרְעֹה נְכֹה׃ לו בֶּן־עֶשְׂרִים וְחָמֵשׁ שָׁנָה
יְהוֹיָקִים בְּמָלְכוֹ וְאַחַת עֶשְׂרֵה שָׁנָה
מָלַךְ בִּירוּשָׁלָם וְשֵׁם אִמּוֹ זְבִידָה בַת־
פְּדָיָה מִן־רוּמָה׃ לז וַיַּעַשׂ הָרַע בְּעֵינֵי
יְהוָה כְּכֹל אֲשֶׁר־עָשׂוּ אֲבֹתָיו׃
כד א בְּיָמָיו עָלָה נְבֻכַדְנֶאצַּר מֶלֶךְ בָּבֶל

זבודה קרי

לד וְאַמְלֵיךְ פַּרְעֹה חֲגִירָא יַת אֶלְיָקִים בַּר יֹאשִׁיָּהוּ תְּחוֹת יֹאשִׁיָּהוּ אֲבוּהִי וְשַׁוִּי יַת שְׁמֵיהּ יְהוֹיָקִים וְיַת יְהוֹאָחָז דְּבַר וַאֲתָא לְמִצְרַיִם וּמִית תַּמָּן׃ לה וְכַסְפָּא וְדַהֲבָא יְהַב יְהוֹיָקִים לְפַרְעֹה בְּרַם רְמָא מַגְבִּיתָא עַל עַמָּא דְאַרְעָא לְמִתַּן יַת כַּסְפָּא עַל מֵימְרָא דְפַרְעֹה גְּבַר כַּד חֲזֵי טַקִּים יַת כַּסְפָּא וְיַת דַּהֲבָא מִן עַמָּא דְאַרְעָא לְמִתַּן לְפַרְעֹה חֲגִירָא׃ לו בַּר עַסְרִין וְחָמֵשׁ שְׁנִין יְהוֹיָקִים כַּד מְלַךְ וַחֲדָא עַסְרֵי שְׁנִין מְלַךְ בִּירוּשְׁלֵם וְשׁוּם אִמֵּיהּ זְבוּדָה בַּת פְּדָיָה מִן רוּמָה׃ לז וַעֲבַד דְּבִישׁ קֳדָם יְיָ כְּכֹל דַּעֲבָדוּ אֲבָהָתוֹהִי׃ א בְּיוֹמוֹהִי סְלֵיק נְבוּכַדְנֶאצַּר מַלְכָּא דְבָבֶל

מנחת שי

(לו) זבידה. זבודה קרי בוא״ו עם דגש בדל״ת רד״ק:

רש״י

(לה) איש כערכו. כפי עשרו:

רד״ק

(לד) ויסב את שמו יהויקים. הטע׳ כדי שידמה שברשותו הוא והמלוכה לו מאתו כי השם לא מאסו: (לה) אך העריך. כתרגו׳ ברם רמא מגביתא על עמא דארעא: איש כערכו. גבר כד חזי כל אחד כמו שהיה ראוי לתת לו לפי ממונו: נגש את הכסף ואת הזהב את עם הארץ. נגש את עם הארץ לתת את הכסף ואת הזהב: (לו) זבידה. כתוב ביו״ד וקרי זבודה בוי״ו עם הדגש: (לז) אבותיו. אמון ומנשה:

מצודת דוד

עונש. על שהמליכוהו לפני יהויקים אחיו הגדול ממנו אשר לו משפט המלוכה: (לה) אך העריך. לא לקח הכסף כפי אשר ישר בעיניו אך לקח מכ״א לפי ערך עשרו: על פי פרעה. מה שאמר פרעה בעבור העונש: איש כערכו נגש. בחוזק יד ובכפיה נגש מכ״א לפי ערכו: (לו) בן עשרים וחמש. כי היה גדול ב׳ שנים מיהואחז אחיו:

מצודת ציון

(לד) ויסב. ויסבב: (לה) נגש. דחק וכפה:

mine which year Nebuchadnezzar conquered Jehoiakim and how long he rebelled against him, we must turn to *Seder Olam,* ch. 25, where we find the following computation. "(Dan. 1:1) In the third year of the reign of Jehoiakim, king of Judah, Nebuchadnezzar, king of Babylon, came upon Jerusalem and besieged it." Is this possible to say? Did he not commence to reign in the fourth year of Jehoiakim? I.e. in Jer. 25:2, we read, "The word that was to Jeremiah concerning the entire people of Judah in the fourth year of Jehoiakim, son of Josiah, king of Judah; this is the first year of Nebuchadnezzar, king of Babylon." Hence it is impossible that Nebuchadnezzar should have besieged Jerusalem in the third year of Jehoiakim. We must, therefore, say

34. And Pharaoh—Neco crowned Eliakim the son of Josiah instead of his father Josiah, and he changed his name to Jehoiakim, and he took Jehoahaz, and he came to Egypt and died there. 35. And Jehoiakim gave the silver and gold to Pharaoh but he assessed the land to give the silver according to Pharaoh's orders; each one according to his assessment, he exacted the silver and gold from the people of the land to give to Pharaoh-Neco. 36. Jehoiakim was twenty-five years old when he became king, and he reigned eleven years in Jerusalem. And his mother's name was Zebudah the daughter of Pedaiah of Rumah. 37. And he did what was evil in the eyes of the Lord, like all that his forefathers had done.

24

1. In his days, Nebuchadnezzar went up,

fore, considered Josiah's attack as unprovoked. As a penalty to Jehoahaz, he removed him from the throne and placed his brother Jehoiakim there in his stead. Thus, the Judean king would be his vassal, and would recognize that he had him to thank for his throne [*Redak*].

a talent of gold—According to *Jonathan,* talents of gold. The number is not specified [*Redak*].

This is not true in our edition of *Targum Jonathan,* which has the word in the singular.

Abarbanel maintains that Pharaoh-Neco punished the people for making Jehoahaz king instead of his older brother, Jehoiakim.

34. **instead of his father Josiah**—Not instead of Jehoahaz, but instead of Josiah. This was to indicate that Jehoahaz' reign was null and void, since he was not appointed by Pharaoh-Neco [*K'li Y'kar*].

he changed his name to Jehoiakim—to impress upon him that he was Pharaoh-Neco's vassal, since even his name was given him by Pharaoh-Neco. The meanings of the two names are identical, "the Lord shall uphold," since God did not forsake him [*Redak*].

35. **he assessed the land**—He levied a tax on the inhabitants of the land [*Redak* from *Jonathan*].

each one according to his assessment—*according to his wealth* [*Rashi*].

he exacted—by force and coercion [*Mezudath David*].

37. his forefathers —**Manasseh and Amon [*Redak*].**

1. **In his days**—In order to deter-

ויהי־לו יהויקים עבד שלש שנים
וישב וימרד־בו: ב וישלח יהוה ׀ בו
את־גדודי כשדים ואת־גדודי ארם
ואת ׀ גדודי מואב ואת גדודי בני־עמון
וישלחם ביהודה להאבידו כדבר
יהוה אשר דבר ביד עבדיו הנביאים:
ג אך ׀ על־פי יהוה היתה ביהודה
להסיר מעל פניו בחטאת מנשה ככל
אשר עשה: ד וגם דם־הנקי אשר
שפך וימלא את־ירושלם דם נקי

דבבל והוה ליה יהויקים עבדא תלת שנין ותב ומריד ביה: ב וגרי יי ביה ית משרית כסדאי וית משרית ארם וית משרית מואב וית משרית בני עמון וגרינון בדבית יהודה לאובדיהון כפתגמא דיי די מליל ביד עבדוהי נביא: ג ברם על דארגיזו קדם יי הות דא בדבית יהודה לאגליותהון מארעא בית שכנתיה בחובי מנשה ככל דעבד: ד ואף דם זכאי דאשד ומלא ית ירושלם חובת דם זכאי הות רעוא

רד"ק קמץ בז"ק

רש"י

כד (ג) אך על פי ה' היתה. כל הרעה הבאה ביהודה

רד"ק

(א) ויהי לו יהויקים עבד שלש שנים. הנה מצאנו כי נבוכדנצר מלך בשנה הרביעית ליהויקים כי כן כתיב בירמיהו הדבר אשר היה אל ירמיהו שעל כל עם יהודה בשנה הרביעית ליהויקי' בן יאשיהו מלך יהודה היא השנה הראשונה לנבוכדנצר מלך בבל ובדניאל אומר בשנת שלש למלכות יהויקים בא נבוכדנצר וגו' ויתן ה' בידו את יהויקים מלך יהודה ומקצ' כלי בית האלהים ויביאם ארץ שנער יהנה אמר כי יהויקים הגלה בבל. וכן אומר בדברי הימים להוליכו בבלה וירמיה נתנבא עליו סחוב והשלך מהלאה לשערי ירושלם נראה כי בדרך מת ואמר כי בשנת שלש למלכו' יהויקים שהמליכו פרעה נכה ובסוף ג' שנים ליהויקים בתחלת שנה רביעית לו התנבא ירמיהו שיבא נבוכדנצר על ירושלים ובא בשנה ההיא ויצר עליה ולכדה ולקח את יהויקים והוליכו בבל כמו שאומר בספר דניאל והשיבו לירושלם ועמד בירושלם שלש שנים באמונתו עם מלך בבל ומרד בו זהו שאמר ויהי לו יהויקים עבד שלש שנים וישב וימרד בו וזהו שאמר וישב כי כבר לקחו יהוליכו בבל ואחר כך שב ומרד בו והנה היו לו ממלכותו ז' שנים או יותר כי לא ידענו כמה היה בבבל טרם שובו לירושלם כי אם נאמר כי בשנה ההיא שהוליכו בבל השיבו לירושלם יעמד שלש שנים באמונתו ומרד הנה עברו שבע שנים ממלכותו ונשארו ד' שנים ממלכותו א"כ לא באו גדידי כשדים לירושלם עד סוף ארבע שנים אלו ועמד במרדו ד' שנים ישבע שעברו הרי י"א שנה שמלך יהויקים ואם נאמר שהיה שם בבבל יותר נוכל לומר כי עד ד' שנים היה שם ובשובו לירושל' עברו ח' שנים ממלכותו ונשארו שלש שנים ממלכותו ואותן שלש עמד באמונתו עם מלך בבל והיה לו עבד ובסוף שלש שנים שהיא שנת י"א לו מרד ובאו גדודי כשדים ולכדוהו וסחבו אותו ובדרך מת ולא נקבר והיתה נבלתו מושלכת לחורב ביום ולקרח בליל' ובסדר עולם אומר וכן בדברי רבותינו ז"ל כי בשנה הראשונה שמלך נבוכדנצר כבש נינוה שניה כבש יהויקים והיא השנה החמישית ליהויקים והיה לו עבד ועמד שלש שנים שהרי שמנה שנים שמלך ארבע קודם מלכות נבוכדנצר ושנה שנכבש בידו ושלש שנים שהיה לו עבד הרי שמנה שנים שמרד בו ולבסוף ג' שנים למרדו בא נבוכדנצר וכבשו פעם שניה וזהו שאומר בדניאל בשנת שלש הרי י"א ליהויקים ושמנה למלכות נבוכדנצר ואותה שנה שמינית המליך יהויכין ומלך ג' חדשים והגלהו עם החרש והמסגר וזהו שאמר גלו בשנת שבע גלו בשמנה ושבע לכבוש יהויקים שהיה שמנה למלכות נבוכדנצר שהרי שנה א' מלך קודם כביש יהויקים: (ב) ואת גדודי ארם ואת גדודי מואב ואת גדודי בני עמון. כלם באו בשליחות נבוכדנצר הרשע שנתן ה' בלבם לבא להאבידו לפי שעשה הרע בעיני ה' וזהו שאמר וישלח ה' בו ולא אבה האל ית' להאריך לו עוד לפיכך אמ' וישלח ה' בו: (ג) אך על פי ה' היתה ביהודה. כלומר קודם מלכית יהויקים היתה הגזירה על פי ה' שדבר ביד עבדיו הנביאי' בחטאת מנשה כי לולי חטאותיו שרבו היה סולח לחטאי' הבאי' אחריו אך בחטאתיו נגזרה הגזירה להחריב

מצודת ציון

כד (ב) גדודי. חילי לבא:

מצודת דוד

כד (א) וישב. אחרי שלשה שנים: (ב) וישלח ה'. העיר את לב גדודי כשדים וגו' לבוא עליו למלחמה: וישלחם. לפי שהלכו הדברים לכן הזר ואמר וישלחם וכן דרך המקרא: (ג) אך על פי ה'. רלה לומר לא נגזרו העכו"ם בעולם ידם אך דבר ה' היתה: בחטאת מנשה. בעבור שאחזו בחטאת מנשה לעשות ככל אשר עשה הוא: (ד) וגם דם הנקי. גם דם הנקי גרם הדבר: אשר שפך. ר"ל על שהקיל מנשה בשפיכת דם למדו העם גם הם לשפוך דם א"כ מילא הוא את הדם לעשות את כולם רולחים: ולא אבה.

had been already decreed [*Redak*].

4. **And also because of the innocent blood**—That too was instrumental in bringing about the doom of Jerusalem [*Mezudath David*].

that he had shed—Since bloodshed was taken lightly by Manasseh, the people, too, became accustomed to shed blood [*Mezudath David*]. See above 21:16.

and Jehoiakim was his vassal for three years, then he turned and rebelled against him. 2. And the Lord incited against him bands of Chaldeans and bands of Arameans and bands of Moabites and bands of the children of Ammon, and he incited them against Judah to destroy it, according to the word of the Lord which He had spoken through His servants, the prophets. 3. Indeed, it was by the order of the Lord against Judah to remove them from before Him, because of the sins of Manasseh, according to all that he had done. 4. And also [because of] the innocent blood that he had shed, and he filled Jerusalem with innocent blood

that it means in *the third year of his revolt.*

Below we read, "(v. 12) . . . and the king of Babylon took him in the eighth year of his reign." I.e. Nebuchadnezzar exiled Jehoiachin in the eighth year of his reign. In Jeremiah 52:28, we read, "This is the people whom Nebuchadnezzar had exiled in the seventh year . . ." How do we reconcile this discrepancy? It was in the seventh year after the conquest and the eighth year of Nebuchadnezzar's reign. We find that Nebuchadnezzar vanquished Jehoiakim in the fifth year of the latter's reign, which was the second of the former's. Jehoiakim was faithful to Nebuchadnezzar for three years, making eight years from the beginning of his reign. He, then, rebelled against Nebuchadnezzar for three years, making eleven years that he reigned. After the third year of his revolt, Nebuchadnezzar vanquished him again and carried him off to Babylon.*

2. **and bands of Arameans . . .**—All of these were sent by Nebuchadnezzar. Because of Jehoiakim's evil deeds, God put into their hearts the desire to attack Israel. Therefore, Scripture states, "And the Lord incited . . ." I.e. he did not extend anymore grace to Israel, but incited bands of the neighboring nations against him to bring about the ultimate destruction of the Temple and the exile of the people of Judah [*Redak*].

and He incited them—Because of the length of the verse, this is repeated [*Mezudath. David*].

3. **Indeed, it was by the order of the Lord**—*all the calamity that befell Judah through these bands* [*Rashi*].

Before Jehoiakim's reign, the doom had been preordained from the time of Manasseh's reign because of the abominable sins he had committed. Were it not for his numerous sins, God would have forgiven his successors. Now, however, the destruction of Jerusalem

וְלֹא־אָבָה יְהוָה לִסְלֹחַ׃ ה וְיֶתֶר דִּבְרֵי
יְהוֹיָקִים וְכָל־אֲשֶׁר עָשָׂה הֲלֹא־הֵם
כְּתוּבִים עַל־סֵפֶר דִּבְרֵי הַיָּמִים לְמַלְכֵי
יְהוּדָה׃ ו וַיִּשְׁכַּב יְהוֹיָקִים עִם־אֲבֹתָיו
וַיִּמְלֹךְ יְהוֹיָכִין בְּנוֹ תַּחְתָּיו׃ ז וְלֹא־
הֹסִיף עוֹד מֶלֶךְ מִצְרַיִם לָצֵאת מֵאַרְצוֹ
כִּי־לָקַח מֶלֶךְ בָּבֶל מִנַּחַל מִצְרַיִם עַד־
נְהַר־פְּרָת כֹּל אֲשֶׁר הָיְתָה לְמֶלֶךְ
מִצְרָיִם׃ ח בֶּן־שְׁמֹנֶה עֶשְׂרֵה שָׁנָה

קדם יי דלא למשבק׃ ה ושאר פתגמי יהויקים וכל די עבד הלא אינון כתיבין על ספר פתגמי יומיא למלכי דבית יהודה׃ ו ושכיב יהויקים עם אבהתוהי ומלך יהויכין בריה תחותוהי׃ ז ולא אוסיף עוד מלכא דמצרים למפק מארעיה ארי נסיב מלכא דבבל מנחל מצרים עד נהר פרת כל דהוה למלכא דמצרים׃ ח בר תמני עסרי

רש"י

על ידי הגדודים האלה׃ (ו) וישכב יהויקים. לא על מטתו כי אסרו נבוכדנאצר בנחושתים להוליכו בבלה והיו מגררין אותו ומת בידם כמו שנאמר (ירמיה כ"ב י"ט) קבורת חמור יקבר סחוב והשלך (ובדברי הימים ב' ל"ו ו') כתיב שאסרו נבוכדנאצר להוליכו בבלה׃ (ז) לצאת מארצו. לעזור ליהויקים׃ כי לקח מלך בבל וגו'. שגלהו במלחמ'

רד"ק

ירושלם׃ (ה) למלכי יהוד'. ושם כתיב בסתם ותעבתיו אשר עשה והנמצא עליו הנם כתובים על ספר מלכי ישראל ויהודה ואם אמר על זה הס' אין כאן כתוב דבר ממעשיו אלא בסתם ויעש הרע ונראה כי על ספר ירמיהו אמר כי שם מספר תועבותיו בפרשת הוי בונה ביתו׃ (ו) וישכב יהויקים עם אבותיו. רוצה לומר שמת אבל לא נקבר עם אבותיו שהרי לא נקבר כלל כמו שכתוב אלא בא על דרך ויאסף על עמיו׃ (ז) ולא הוסיף עוד מלך מצרים. פי' באותו הזמן עד שמלך צדקיהו ואז יצא כמו שכתוב בירמיהו וימלך מלך צדקיהו וגו' וחיל פרעה יצא ממצרים וישמעו הכשדי' הצרים על ירושל' את שמעם ויעלו מעל ירושלם וכמוהו ולא יספו עוד גדודי ארם לבא בארץ ישראל ר"ל בזמן ההוא אבל אח"כ באו כמו שכתוב׃ (ח) בן

רלב"ג

(ד) ולא אבה ה' לסלוח. ר"ל כי אף ע"פ שעשה מנשה תשובה לא אבה הש"י לסלוח שפיכתו הדם הנקי וידמה שבכלל עבדי ה' אשר הרג ישעיהו בן אמוץ על אשר היה מוכיח אותו וכן אמרו רז"ל כי מנשה הרג ישעיהו׃ (ז) ולא הוסיף עוד מלך מצרים לצאת מארצו.

מצודת דוד

לזה לא רצה ה' לסלוח כי היו אוחזים ברשעת מנשה ואף בשפיכת הדם׃ (ו) עם אבותיו. ר"ל שמת עם אבותיו אבל לא נקבר עמהם כי אסר אותו להוליכו בבלה ומת בדרך ולא נקבר כלל כמ"ש בד"ה ובירמיה׃ (ז) לצאת מארצו. להמליך מלך ביהודה כמו שהמליך

him to Babylon [*Rashi*].

This is similar to the *Seder Olam* 25, which states that Jehoiakim died as soon as he was bound. Then they took him out and dragged him, to fulfill Jeremiah's prophecy.

Lev. Rabbah relates that when Nebuchadnezzar came to destroy Jerusalem, he encamped in Riblah. The Great Sanhedrin came down to him. They asked him, "Has the time arrived for the Temple to be destroyed?" He replied, "No, but Jehoiakim has rebelled against me. Deliver him to me, and I will go. They went to him and told him, "Nebuchadnezzar wants you." After refuting his protests, they lowered him over the wall into the Chaldean camp. Some say that they lowered him alive, and some say that they lowered him dead. Some say that he died in their hands because of his frailty. Some say that Nebuchadnezzar judged him and executed him and inserted his body into the carcass of a donkey, to fulfill the prophecy that he would be buried "a donkey's burial." He was then dragged around all the cities of Judea. Still others say that Nebuchadnezzar dragged him around while he was alive, then killed him and fed his flesh to the dogs, as

and the Lord did not want to forgive. 5. And the rest of the events of Jehoiakim and all that he did are written in the book of the chronicles of the kings of Judah. 6. And Jehoiakim slept with his forefathers, and Jehoiachin his son reigned in his stead. 7. And the king of Egypt no longer went out of his land, for the king of Babylonia had taken from the river of Egypt until the Euphrates River, all that belonged to the king of Egypt.

8. Jehoiachin was eighteen years old

5. **and all that he did**—The Chronicler (II 36:8) elaborates, ". . . and his abominations which he committed and that which was found on him . . ." The Rabbis (*San.* 103b) explain that Jehoiakim believed that once God had created this world, its inhabitants were given complete jurisdiction over it. Divine Providence was not needed except for the sunlight, which comes from the heavens. Jehoiakim denied the necessity of sunlight. He believed that the gold of Parvaim, a reddish gold, would shed enough light to substitute for the light of the sun. His denial of God's bounty was termed as "his abominations." See *Maharsha, Etz Yosef* on *Ein Yaakov.*

Pseudo-Rashi ad loc. explains that he was intimate with his mother. This follows Leviticus *Rabbah* 19:6, which lists this among Jehoiakim's sins, among which is also listed the wearing of *shaatnes,* wool and linen, a sin one commits only to provoke the Almighty, since there is no temptation involved in it.

"And that which was found on him," is explained by *Pseudo-Rashi* as tattoo. The Talmud elaborates by telling us that he tattooed the Name of God on his genitals. This was meant as a provocation against God. Others say that he tatooed the name of pagan deities on his genitals. He was ashamed to do this on the exposed parts of the body since there were many pious Jews in his generation. This tattoo was found after his death [*Maharsha* ad loc.].

The Chronicler states that these abominations are written in the book of Chronicles of the kings of Israel and Judah. This could not refer to our Book of Kings, since no details of his evil deeds are mentioned here. It appears, therefore, that the reference is to the Book of Jeremiah, 22:13–30 [*Redak*]. (Ed. note. Perhaps Jeremiah was at one time considered part of the Book of Kings, which precedes it immediately according to the order of the prophets in *Baba Bathra* 14b.)

6. **And Jehoiakim slept with his forefathers**—*not in his bed, for Nebuchadnezzar bound him with copper chains to take him to Babylon, and they were dragging him, and he died in their hands, as it is said,* "(Jer. 22:19) *The burial of a donkey you shall be buried, dragged and thrown* past the gates of Jerusalem." *And in* II *Chron.* 36:6, *it is written that Nebuchadnezzar bound him to take*

יְהוֹיָכִין בְּמָלְכוֹ וּשְׁלֹשָׁה חֳדָשִׁים מָלַךְ בִּירוּשָׁלִָם וְשֵׁם אִמּוֹ נְחֻשְׁתָּא בַת־אֶלְנָתָן מִירוּשָׁלִָם: ט וַיַּעַשׂ הָרַע בְּעֵינֵי יְהוָה כְּכֹל אֲשֶׁר־עָשָׂה אָבִיו: י בָּעֵת הַהִיא עָלָה עַבְדֵי נְבֻכַדְנֶאצַּר מֶלֶךְ־בָּבֶל יְרוּשָׁלִָם וַתָּבֹא הָעִיר בַּמָּצוֹר: יא וַיָּבֹא נְבֻכַדְנֶאצַּר מֶלֶךְ־בָּבֶל עַל־הָעִיר וַעֲבָדָיו צָרִים עָלֶיהָ: יב וַיֵּצֵא יְהוֹיָכִין מֶלֶךְ־יְהוּדָה עַל־מֶלֶךְ בָּבֶל הוּא וְאִמּוֹ וַעֲבָדָיו וְשָׂרָיו וְסָרִיסָיו וַיִּקַּח אֹתוֹ מֶלֶךְ בָּבֶל בִּשְׁנַת שְׁמֹנֶה לְמָלְכוֹ: יג וַיּוֹצֵא מִשָּׁם אֶת־כָּל־אוֹצְרוֹת בֵּית

עֲסַרֵי שְׁנִין יְהוֹיָכִין כַּד מְלַךְ וּתְלָתָא יַרְחִין מְלַךְ בִּירוּשְׁלֶם וְשׁוּם אִמֵּיהּ נְחֻשְׁתָּא בַּת אֶלְנָתָן מִירוּשְׁלֶם: ט וַעֲבַד דְּבִישׁ קֳדָם יְיָ כְּכֹל דַּעֲבַד אֲבוּהִי: י בְּעִדָּנָא הַהִיא סְלִיקוּ עַבְדֵי נְבוּכַדְנֶאצַּר מַלְכָּא דְבָבֶל לִירוּשְׁלֶם וְעָלַת קַרְתָּא בִּצְיָרָא: יא וַאֲתָא נְבוּכַדְנֶאצַּר מַלְכָּא דְבָבֶל עַל קַרְתָּא וְעַבְדוֹהִי צָיְרִין עֲלַהּ: יב וּנְפַק יְהוֹיָכִין מֶלֶךְ שִׁבְטָא דְבֵית יְהוּדָה עַל מַלְכָּא דְבָבֶל הוּא וְאִמֵּיהּ וְעַבְדוֹהִי וְרַבְרְבָנוֹהִי וְגִבָּרוֹהִי וּדְבַר יָתֵיהּ מַלְכָּא דְבָבֶל בִּשְׁנַת תְּמָנֵי לְמַלְכֵיהּ: יג וְאַפֵּיק מִתַּמָּן יָת כָּל אוֹצְרֵי בֵית

רד"ק עלו קרי

שמונה עשרה שנה יהויכין במלכו. ובדברי הימים בן שמנה שנים יהויכין במלכו ושלשה חדשים ועשרת ימים מלך בירושלים אפשר כי יהויקים אביו המליכו בשנה ראשונ' שמלך הוא שימלוך תחתיו אחר מותו אולי היו לו בנים אחרים ועוד כי ראה שמלכותו תלוי' ביד אחרים לא ידע אם יסירוהו מהמלוכה כמו שעשו לאחיו והמליך בנו יהויכין שימלוך תחתיו אחריו והיה אז יהויכין בן שמנה שנים ועתה כשמת אביו ומלך הוא היה בן י"ח שנה ומלך ג' חדשי' ולא חשש כאן לכתוב עשרה ימים היתרים ובסדר עולם י"ח של מלך נבוכדנצר שבנה משנחתם גזר דין לגלות: (י) בעת ההוא. כמו שאומר בדברי הימים ולתשובת השנה שלח המלך: עלו עבדי נבוכדנצר. כתיב עלה וקרי עלו כי הוא עלה אחר כן ומצא' צרי' על העיר וקרי עלו כי עבדיו עלו בתחילה: (יב) ויצא יהויכין. יצא אל מלך בבל שיעשה בו רצונו והוא לקחו ולמה העבירו מהמלוכה אמרו חשב מלך בבל שיהיה מורד יהויכין כמו שהיה אביו מורד אמר מכלבא בישא גורא טבא לא נפיק לפיכך העבירו והמליך דודו תחתיו: ושריו וסריסיו. ת"י ורברבנוהי וגברוהי: בשנת שמנה למלכו. בתחלת ח' שהרי יהויקים מלך י"א שנה ונבוכדנצר מלך בשנת

רש"י

בשנת הרביעי' ליהויקים בכרכמיש על נהר פרת ככתוב בספר (ירמי' מ"ו ב'): (יב) ויצא יהויכין מלך יהודה

מנחת שי

כד (י) בעת ההיא עלה. עלו קרי: (יב) ויצא יהויכין מלך יהודה על מלך בבל. בדפוס ישן כתוב אל מלך וטעות הוא כי בכל אלה ספרי הדפוס וגם בכ"י כתוב על מלך אמנם בספר כ"י כתוב עליו בגליון למלך ע"פ המסורת ומנה כ"ט למלך בקריאה וזה מכלום אך כמ"ג שלנו בדפוס לא נמנה זה עמהם והמסרה כ"י השמיטה להיות למלך על ישראל דד"ה סימן כ"ח ונסחא דדפוסא טפי עדיפא ועלה סמכינן דבמסרה אחריתי איתמסר ט' על מלך ודין חד

רלב"ג

אמר זה להעיר כי לקח השם יתברך נקמת יאשיהו ממנו שהרגו בעלותו להלחם על נהר פרת: (יב) ויצא יהויכין מלך יהודה על מלך בבל. ר"ל שיצא במלוך מלך בבל כשמעו שהיה בא שם להשלים עמו ולשום לוארו תחת עולו והנה לא רצה להשלים עמו אך הגלה אותו אל בבל הוא ואמו ועבדיו ושריו וסריסיו בשנת שמנה למלכות

מצודת דוד

את יהויקים: (י) ותבוא העיר במצור. בנו סביבה כרקום לכבשה וכן וכנית מליך (דברים כ') ונקראה כן ע"ש כי העם היושב בה המה במצור ובמצוק: (יא) צרים עליה. מסבבים עליה להצר להעם: (יב) ויצא יהויכין. מסר א"ע בידו לעשות בו חפצו בחשבו כי יחמול עליו בעבור הכנעהו: בשנת שמנה. והושב בנים מקוטעות: למלכו. למלכות נ"נ וכירמיה (נ"ב) נא' בשנת שבע ור"ל בשבע לכיבוש

fore, stayed in Riblah and sent his servants to besiege the city [*Maharzav, Lev. Rabbah* 19:6, *Pesikta Rabbathi*, p. 227].

12. **And Jehoiachin, the king of Judah, came out to the king of Babylonia**—*that he should do to him as he wishes, not for war* [*Rashi, Redak*].

and the king of Babylonia took him—He deposed him because he suspected that he would rebel as his father had done. He said, "From a bad dog no good pup is born"

when he became king, and he reigned three months in Jerusalem, and his mother's name was Nehushta the daughter of Elnathan of Jerusalem. 9. And he did what was evil in the eyes of the Lord like all that his father had done. 10. At that time, the servants of Nebuchadnezzar went up against Jerusalem and the city was brought under siege. 11. And Nebuchadnezzar the king of Babylonia came to the city, and his servants were besieging it. 12. And Jehoiachin, the king of Judah, came out to the king of Babylonia, he and his mother and his servants and his officers and his mighty warriors, and the king of Babylonia took him in the eighth year of his reign. 13. And he removed from there all the treasures of the house of

donkey flesh is usually "buried."

7. **went out of his land**—*to aid Jehoiakim* [*Rashi*].

for the king of Babylonia had taken . . .—*for he defeated him in battle in the fourth year of Jehoiakim in Carchemish on the Euphrates River, as is written in the Book of Jeremiah* (46:2) [*Rashi*].

After his defeat, the king of Egypt did not leave his land to aid Israel until the reign of Zedekiah, when his presence became a threat to the Chaldees who had laid siege to Jerusalem, and caused them to return to their land, as is reported in Jeremiah 37:5 [*Redak*].

8. **Jehoiachin was eighteen years old**—In Chron. 36:9, we read, "Jehoiachin was eight years old. Possibly, Jehoiakim had placed him on the throne at the beginning of his reign, since he knew that his throne was dependent upon other rulers, and was not stable. Therefore, even though Jehoiachin did not exercise any authority during his father's lifetime, it is considered as though he reigned [*Redak*].

The Rabbis say that he became king in the eighth year of Nebuchadnezzar's reign, when it was decreed that the exile take place. He was, however, eighteen years old, as appears in our text [*Seder Olam* ch. 25 according to *Elijah Gaon*].

As mentioned above, Nebuchadnezzar became king in the fourth year of Jehoiakim, who reigned eleven years. Hence Nebuchadnezzar was in the eighth year of his reign when Jehoiachin became king.

10. **At that time**—as is mentioned in II Chron. 36:10, "And at the end of the year, King Nebuchadnezzar sent and brought him to Babylon . . ." [*Redak*].

11. **and his servants were besieging it**—Nebuchadnezzar, himself, did not accompany him. He feared he would meet Sennacherib's fate if he would attack Jerusalem. He, there-

יְהוָה וְאוֹצְרוֹת בֵּית הַמֶּלֶךְ וַיְקַצֵּץ אֶת־
כָּל־כְּלֵי הַזָּהָב אֲשֶׁר עָשָׂה שְׁלֹמֹה מֶלֶךְ־
יִשְׂרָאֵל בְּהֵיכַל יְהוָה כַּאֲשֶׁר דִּבֶּר
יְהוָה׃ יד וְהִגְלָה אֶת־כָּל־יְרוּשָׁלִַם וְאֶת־
כָּל־הַשָּׂרִים וְאֵת ׀ כָּל־גִּבּוֹרֵי הַחַיִל
עֲשָׂרָה* אֲלָפִים גּוֹלֶה וְכָל־הֶחָרָשׁ
וְהַמַּסְגֵּר לֹא נִשְׁאַר זוּלַת דַּלַּת עַם־
הָאָרֶץ׃ טו וַיֶּגֶל אֶת־יְהוֹיָכִין בָּבֶלָה וְאֶת־
אֵם הַמֶּלֶךְ וְאֶת־נְשֵׁי הַמֶּלֶךְ וְאֶת־
סָרִיסָיו וְאֵת אֱוִלֵי* הָאָרֶץ הוֹלִיךְ גּוֹלָה
מִירוּשָׁלִַם בָּבֶלָה׃ טז וְאֵת כָּל־אַנְשֵׁי

עשרת קרי אילי קרי

בֵּית מַקְדְּשָׁא דַיְיָ וְיַת אוֹצְרֵי בֵית מַלְכָּא וְקַצֵּיץ יַת כָּל מָנֵי דַהֲבָא דַעֲבַד שְׁלֹמֹה מַלְכָּא דְיִשְׂרָאֵל בְּהֵיכְלָא דַיְיָ כְּמָא דִי מַלֵּיל יְיָ׃ יד וְאַגְלֵי יַת כָּל יְרוּשְׁלֵם וְיַת כָּל רַבְרְבַיָא וְיַת כָּל גִּבָּרֵי חֵילָא עַסְרָא אַלְפִין בְּגָלוּתָא וְכָל אוּמָנַיָא וְתַרְעַיָא לָא אִשְׁתְּאַר אֱלָהֵין חֲשִׁיכֵי עַמָא דְאַרְעָא׃ טו וְאַגְלֵי יַת יְהוֹיָכִין לְבָבֶל וְיַת אִמָא דְמַלְכָּא וְיַת נְשֵׁי דְמַלְכָּא וְיַת רַבְרְבָנוֹהִי וְיַת רַבְרְבֵי אַרְעָא אוֹבֵיל בְּגָלוּתָא מִירוּשְׁלֵם לְבָבֶל׃ טז וְיַת כָּל גִּבָּרֵי חילא

ת״א והחרש והמסגר. גיטין פח סנה׃ רין לח (בס יט נדרים מ)׃

רש״י

על מלך בבל. לעשות לו כרצונו ולא למלחמ׳: (יד) החרש והמסגר. תרגום יונתן אומניא ותרעיא ורבותינו אמרו הכמים גדולים בתורה שכשאחד פותח הכל שותקין כמו שכתוב (ישעיה מ״א א׳) החרישו אלי איים. מסגר הכל יושבין לפניו ולמדין הימנו כמו שנאמר (ישעיה כ״ב) ופתח ואין סוגר וסגר ואין פותח: (טו) ואת אילי הארץ. אלו חורי יהודה ובנימין ולדיקים היו עליהם הכתוב אומר (ירמיה כ״ד ה׳) כתאני׳ הטובות האלה כן אכיר את

רד״ק

הרביעית ליהויקים ואם היה בסוף ח׳ היה י״ב אלא כך פירו׳ בתחלת שמנה וכן בירמיה אומ׳ וזה העם אשר הגלה נבוכדנצר בשנת ז׳ סוף ז׳ ותחלת ח׳ והרבה פיר׳ כזה בזה הספר ולדברי בעל סדר עולם שנת ז׳ לכיבוש יהויקים הוא שנת שמנת לנבוכדנצר: (יד) גבורי החיל עשרת אלפי׳ גול׳. כתיב עשרה ועשרת קרי ואחד הוא ואמר עוד ואת כל אנשי החיל ז׳ אלפים ובירמיה אומר בשנת שבע יהודים שלשת אלפים ועשרים ושלשה היאך הוא זה החשבון הראשון שהוא עשרת אלפים הוא כלל לכל ופרט אחר כן ז׳ אלפים והם מבני בנימין ושאר שבטים ופרט עוד בירמיה ג׳ אלפים והם אנשים מקובצים שהיו מבני יהודה כמו שאומר יהודים והכל י׳ אלפים וכ״ג הוא מספר מועט ולא חשש לספרו עם י׳ אלפים זה הוא גלות שגלה עם יהויכין ובספר ירמיה אומר מה שגלו בגלות צדקי׳ שהוא שנר י״ח לנבוכדנצר והיו בשמנה מאות ול״ב ואחר החורבן שנת כ״ג לנבוכדנצר היו הגולי׳ תשמ״ה אותם שהיו בעמון ומואב ואמר גולה כמו גולים והוא דרך כלל בלשון יחיד ולדעת יונתן הוא שם שתרגם בגלותא: וכל החרש והמסג׳. ת״יאומי א ותרעיא: (טו) ואת אילי הארץ. אלה חורי יהודה ובנימין עליהם הכתוב אומר כתאנים הטובות האלה וגו׳:

רלב״ג

כנוכדנלר מלך בבל שעברו לו ז׳ שנים שלמות: (יד) וכל החרש והמסגר. הם האומנים והשוערים ושומרי החומה וסוגרים פתחיה: (טו) ואת אילי הארץ. ר״ל שרי הארץ: (טז) ואת כל אנשי החיל שבעת אלפים. והנה אמר למעלה י׳ אלפים ובספר ירמיה אמר

מנחת שי

מינייהו עיין לקמן בשילהי סיפרא: (יד) ואת כל השרים הוא״ו בגעיא בס״ס: עשרה. עשרת קרי: (טו) אולי. אילי קרי:

מצודת דוד

יהויקים כי בשני למלכותו והיא ה׳ ליהויקים כבש את יהויקים והוליכו לבבל וקבל על עלמו להיות לו לעבד והחזירו ועבדו ג׳ שנים וחזר ומרד בו וכבשו שנית בשנת ג׳ למרדו הוא האמור בד״ה כ׳ (לו) ובזה השנה מלך יהויכין וגלהו אחר ג׳ חדשים: (יג) ויקצץ. כרת וקלף את הזהב מהכלים: (יד) עשרת אלפים. ובירמיה נאמר יהודים שלשת אלפים וכ״ג ור״ל מבני יהודה היה החשבון האמור והמותר היו מבני בנימין ושאר השבטים אשר התגוררו בירושלים וזהו שאמר למטה שבעת אלפים וכולם יחד המה עשרת אלפים ולא הבט לחשוב עוד אותן הכ״ג האמור בירמיה: וכל החרש והמסגר. הם האומנים ושומרי השערים אשר סגרו אותם בעתם וכן ת״י:

מצודת ציון

(יד) זולת. רק: (טו) אילי. הם השרים הגדולים והחזקים כי הוא ברחבונה

three thousand were of the tribe of Judah and seven thousand of Benjamin and other tribes. Also in Seder Olam ch. 25 *I learned this* [*Rashi, Redak* v. 14].

one thousand—These were not included in the ten thousand exiles mentioned in v. 14. According to *Seder Olam*, however, this thousand is included in the ten thousand [*Redak*]. (I have not found this in *Seder Olam*.—Ed. note)

the Lord and the treasures of the king's palace, and he stripped off all the golden decorations that Solomon king of Israel had made in the Temple of the Lord, as the Lord had spoken.
14. And he exiled all Jerusalem and all the officers and all the mighty warriors, ten thousand exiles, and all the craftsmen and the sentries of the gates. No one remained except the poorest of the people of the land. 15. And he exiled Jehoiachin to Babylon, and the king's mother and the king's wives, and his officers and the dignitaries of the land, he led in exile from Jerusalem to Babylon. 16. And all the military men

[*Redak* from *Seder Olam* ch. 25, *Lev. Rabbah* 19:6].

and his mighty warriors—[*Redak* following *Jonathan*].

in the eighth year of his reign—I.e. in the beginning of the eighth year of Nebuchadnezzar's reign, since he ascended the throne in the fourth year of Jehoiakim, who reigned eleven years. If it were at the end of the eighth year, it would be the twelfth year of Jehoiakim. According to *Seder Olam*, the conquest of Jehoiachin took place in the seventh year from the conquest of Jehoiakim, which was the eighth year of Nebuchadnezzar [*Redak*].

14. **the craftsmen and the sentries of the gates**—Heb. הֶחָרָשׁ וְהַמַּסְגֵּר *Jonathan rendered: the craftsmen and the sentries of the gates,* translating *harash* as craftsmen, as in Ex. 28:11, and *masger* as closing, i.e. those who close the gates. *Our Rabbis,* however, *said that these were great Torah scholars, that when one would open his mouth to speak, all would remain silent, as it is written,* "(Is. 41:1) *Keep silence* (הַחֲרִישׁוּ) *before Me, O islands.*" "*Masger,*" *all would sit before him and learn from him, as it is said,* "(Is. 22:22) *And he will open, and no one will close, and he will close, and no one will open*" [*Rashi* from *Gittin* 88a, *San.* 38a, *Seder Olam* ch. 25].

In *Gittin, Rashi* explains more clearly, that these were such great scholars, that when they would leave a question unanswered, no one could volunteer any information to reopen the question.

15. **and the dignitaries of the land**—*These are the dignitaries of Judah and Benjamin, who were righteous men. Concerning them the Scripture states,* "(Jer. 24:5) *Like these good figs, so will I recognize the exiles of Judah* [*Rashi, Redak* from *Seder Olam*, ch. 25].

16. **seven thousand**—*Yet above* (v. 14) *he states, "ten thousand." The third verse comes to reconcile the difference between them. In Jeremiah* 52:28, we read, "*This is the people whom Nebuchadnezzar exiled in the seventh year, three thousand Judeans.*" *We deduce from here that*

הַחַיִל שִׁבְעַת אֲלָפִים וְהֶחָרָשׁ וְהַמַּסְגֵּר אֶלֶף הַכֹּל גִּבּוֹרִים עֹשֵׂי מִלְחָמָה וַיְבִיאֵם מֶלֶךְ־בָּבֶל גּוֹלָה בָּבֶלָה׃
יז וַיַּמְלֵךְ מֶלֶךְ־בָּבֶל אֶת־מַתַּנְיָה דֹדוֹ תַּחְתָּיו וַיַּסֵּב אֶת־שְׁמוֹ צִדְקִיָּהוּ׃ יח בֶּן־עֶשְׂרִים וְאַחַת שָׁנָה צִדְקִיָּהוּ בְמָלְכוֹ וְאַחַת עֶשְׂרֵה שָׁנָה מָלַךְ בִּירוּשָׁלָ͏ִם וְשֵׁם אִמּוֹ חֲמִיטַל בַּת־יִרְמְיָהוּ מִלִּבְנָה׃
יט וַיַּעַשׂ הָרַע בְּעֵינֵי יְהוָה כְּכֹל אֲשֶׁר־עָשָׂה יְהוֹיָקִים׃ כ כִּי ׀ עַל־אַף יְהוָה

חמוטל קרי

תרגום

חֵילָא שִׁבְעָא אַלְפִין אוּמָנַיָא וְתַרְעַיָא אַלְפִין כּוּלְהוֹן גֻּבְרִין גִּבָּרֵי עָבְדֵי קְרָבָא וְאַיְתִינוּן מַלְכָּא דְבָבֶל בְּגָלוּתָא לְבָבֶל׃ יז וְאַמְלִיךְ מַלְכָּא דְבָבֶל יָת מַתַּנְיָה אַח אֲבוּהִי תְּחוֹתוֹהִי וְשַׁוִּי יָת שְׁמֵיהּ צִדְקִיָּהוּ׃ יח בַּר עַסְרִין וְחָדָא שְׁנִין צִדְקִיָּה כַּד מְלַךְ וְחָדָא עַסְרֵי שְׁנִין מְלַךְ בִּירוּשְׁלֵם וְשׁוּם אִמֵּיהּ חֲמוּטַל בַּת יִרְמְיָה מִן לִבְנָה׃ יט וַעֲבַד דְּבִישׁ קֳדָם יְיָ כְּכֹל דַּעֲבַד יְהוֹיָקִים׃ כ אֲרֵי עַל

דארגיזו

ת״א ויסב את שמו . הוריות יא כריתות ה (שקלים יט סוטה כב הוריות ז) : ויעש הרע . סנהד׳ קג :

רש״י

גלות יהודה : (טז) שבעת אלפים. ולמעלה הוא אומר עשרת אלפים בא הכתוב השלישי והכריע בספר ירמיה (כ״ב כ״ח) זה העם אשר הגלה נבוכדנצר בשנת שבע יהודי׳ שלשת אלפים אמור מעתה ג׳ אלפים היו משבט יהודה ושבעת אלפים מבנימין ושאר שבטי׳ ואף בסדר עולם למדט כן : (יז) ויסב את שמו צדקיהו. יה ילדיק עליך את הדין אם תמרוד בי : (כ) כי על אף ה׳ היתה וגו׳. לפיכך וימרוד צדקיהו במלך בבל נתן הקב״ה בלבו למרוד בו כדי שיגלה :

רד״ק

תוליך גולה. בגולה והוא שם בשקל שואה וכן כלי גולה : (טז) והחרש והמסג׳ אלף. אלה אינם בכלל הי״ד אלפי׳ שזכר במספר שלמעלה ובסדר עולם הוא אומר ומתוכן החרש והמסג׳ אלף היו כלומר שמכלל העשרת אלפים היו ואין דרך המקרא לכלול מספר ואחר כן לפרט אם לא לחדש על ענין הראשון וא״כ לבד אלה הראשונים היו : הכל גבורים עושי מלחמה. בסדר עולם וכי מה גבורה הם עושים בני אדם תהולכי׳ בגולה ומה מלחמה עושין בני אדם האסורי׳ בזיקי׳ הנתוני׳ בשלשלאות של ברזל אלא גבורי׳ בגבורה של תורה וכן הוא אומר גבורי כח עושי דברו עושי מלחמה עושין מלחמ׳ של תור׳ וכן הוא אומר על כן יאמר בספר מלחמות ה׳. חרש אחד מדבר והכל שותקין . מסגר שהכל יושבין לפניו ולמדין ממנו לקיים מה שנאמ׳ ופתח ואין סוגר וסגר ואין פותח : (יז) ויסב את שמו צדקיהו. הטעם פי׳ למעלה ומה ששנה כ״כ שמו וקראו צדקיהו אומר בדרש אמר לו יה יצדיק עליך את הדין אם תמרוד בי : (יח) בן עשרים ואחת שנה צדקיהו. היאך הוא זה והלא בן ל״ה שנה היה לפי חשבון של אחיו שהרי הבן השלישי ליאשיהו היה ויהויקים שהי׳ גדול ממנו נאמר בו בן כ״ה שנה יהויקים במלכו וי״א שנה מלך הרי ל״ח לצדקיהו וכבר כתבנו למעלה לדעת החכם ראב״ע כי הוא אומר שמלך ג׳ שנים בחיי אביו ואז היה בן כ״א וכל זה היה צריך לדעתו שאמר כי שלום הוא יהואחז הוא היה הקטן שבבני יאשיהו וכתיב בן כ״ג במלכו אבל דברי רז״ל שאמרו כי שלום הוא צדקיהו אין כאן קושיא כלל כי צדקיהו היה הקטן שבבני יאשיהו והיה במות אביו בן עשר שנים ועתה כשמלך בן אחד ועשרים אלא שרחוק והוא שזכר שני בנים בסדר והאחד איננו לפירושנו כי שלום הוא יהויכין הנה צדקיהו היה הקטן שבבני יאשיהו ואין צריך כאן תיקון : (כ) כי על אף ה׳. והוא טעם

מנחת שי

(יח) חמיטל. חמוטל קרי :

רלב״ג

שבשנת שבע למלכות נבוכדנצר הגלה יהודים שלשת אלפים ועשרים ושלשה וידמה שמה שאמר בספר ירמיה בשנת שבע ר״ל שעברו לנבוכדנצר שבע שנים ולזה אמר בזה המקום בשנת שמנה ואולם מספר הגבורים ידמ׳ כמו שפי׳ רבינו דוד קמחי כי בתחלה ספר כל גבורי החיל הגולים מיהודה ובנימין ואחר כן פרט בזה המקום הגבורי׳ שהיו משבט בנימין ובספר ירמי׳ פרט הגבורי׳ שהיו משבט יהודה ולזה קראם יהודים : (כ) כי על אף ה׳ היתה בירושלם וביהודה עד השליכו אותם מעל פניו. ר״ל כי מחמת מוקצי העם וכעס הש״י עליהם נסיה שימליכו עליהם אלו הרעים ולזה ג״כ היתה הסבה שמרד צדקי׳ במלך בבל כי לולי מרדו לא נתבסס

מצודת ציון

פנין חוזק רב כמו יש לאל ידי (בראשית לא) : (יז) תחתיו. במקומו :

מצודת דוד

(טז) הכל גבורים. על אנשי החיל יאמר לא על החרש והמסגר : (כ) כי על אף. כי בעבור שהיתה אף ה׳ בירושלים וביהודה כ״כ גדולה עד להשליך אותם מעל פניו לזה העיר לב צדקיה למרוד במלך בבל להיות סיבה אל הגלות לשלחם מעל פניו :

strengthened the temptation of his heart from returning to the Lord God of Israel.''*

20. **Because the wrath of the Lord was . . .**—*Therefore, Zedekiah rebelled against the king of Babylonia. The Holy One, Blessed be He, gave* the desire *into his heart to rebel against him in order that he would be exiled* [*Rashi*].*

seven thousand, and the craftsmen and the gate sentries one
thousand, all mighty warriors; and the king of Babylonia
brought them into exile to Babylon. 17. And the king of Babylonia crowned Mattaniah his uncle in his stead, and changed
his name to Zedekiah. 18. Zedekiah was twenty-one years old
when he became king, and he reigned twenty-one years in Jerusalem. His mother's name was Hamutal the daughter of
Jeremiah from Libnah. 19. And he did what was evil in the
eyes of the Lord, like all that Jehoiakim had done. 20. Because
the wrath of the Lord

all mighty warriors—Now, what might do people going in exile show? And what war do people bound in chains wage? Rather, they were mighty men of Torah, who wage the war of Torah, as mentioned above [*Redak* from *Seder Olam* ch. 25].*

17. **his uncle**—son of Josiah. See above 23:30.

and he changed his name to Zedekiah—*May the Lord justify* (יָהּ יַצְדִּיק) *the judgment upon you if you rebel against me* [*Rashi* from *Horioth* 11b].

Nebuchadnezzar said to Zedekiah, "May the Lord agree that any judgment I pass upon you for rebelling against me is just." As mentioned above, it was customary for the king to change the names of his vassals to impress upon them that they are completely dependent upon him, even for their names [*Redak*].

18. **Zedekiah was twenty-one years old**—According to *Ibn Ezra* mentioned above, 23:30, that Shallum is identified with Jehoahaz, who was twenty-three when he was anointed, and Jehoiakim was twenty-five, this makes Zedekiah, who came between them, twenty-four. After eleven years of Jehoiakim's reign, he was thirty-five. Yet, Scripture states that he was twenty-one when he became king. For the solution, see above. According to the Talmud, however, that identifies Shallum with Zedekiah, there is no problem. Since Zedekiah was the youngest son, he could very well have been ten yers old when his father died, and was, therefore, twenty-one after Jehoiakim's eleven-year reign. Also, according to *Redak* above, that Shallum was Jehoiachin, Zedekiah was the youngest of Josiah's sons, again giving us no problem [*Redak*].

19. **And he did what was evil**—The Chronicler (II 36:12) elaborates on the evil deeds that Zedekiah was guilty of. "He did not humble himself before Jeremiah the prophet from the mouth of the Lord." He proceeds to state, "(v. 13) Also he rebelled against King Nebuchadnezzar, who had adjured him by God, and he stiffened his nape and

הָיְתָה בִירוּשָׁלַםִ וּבִיהוּדָה עַד־הִשְׁלִכוֹ אֹתָם מֵעַל פָּנָיו וַיִּמְרֹד צִדְקִיָּהוּ בְּמֶלֶךְ בָּבֶל׃ כה א וַיְהִי בִשְׁנַת הַתְּשִׁיעִית לְמָלְכוֹ בַּחֹדֶשׁ הָעֲשִׂירִי בֶּעָשׂוֹר לַחֹדֶשׁ בָּא נְבֻכַדְנֶאצַּר מֶלֶךְ־בָּבֶל הוּא וְכָל־חֵילוֹ עַל־יְרוּשָׁלַםִ וַיִּחַן עָלֶיהָ וַיִּבְנוּ עָלֶיהָ דָּיֵק סָבִיב׃ ב וַתָּבֹא הָעִיר בַּמָּצוֹר עַד עַשְׁתֵּי עֶשְׂרֵה שָׁנָה לַמֶּלֶךְ צִדְקִיָּהוּ׃ ג בְּתִשְׁעָה לַחֹדֶשׁ וַיֶּחֱזַק הָרָעָב בָּעִיר וְלֹא־הָיָה לֶחֶם לְעַם הָאָרֶץ׃ ד וַתִּבָּקַע הָעִיר וְכָל־אַנְשֵׁי

דְאַרְגִיזוּ קֳדָם יְיָ הֲוַת בִּירוּשְׁלֵם וּבִיהוּדָה עַד דְּאַגְלֵי יָתְהוֹן מֵאַרְעָא בֵּית שְׁכִינְתֵּיהּ וּמְרִיד צִדְקִיָּהוּ בְּמַלְכָּא דְבָבֶל׃ א וַהֲוָה בִּשְׁתָּא תְּשִׁיעֵיתָא לְמַלְכֵיהּ בְּיַרְחָא עֲשִׂירָאָה בְּעַשְׂרָא לְיַרְחָא אֲתָא נְבוּכַדְנֶאצַּר מַלְכָּא דְבָבֶל הוּא וְכָל מַשִׁרְיָתֵיהּ עַל יְרוּשְׁלֵם וּשְׁרָא עֲלַהּ וּבְנוֹ עֲלַהּ כַּרְקוֹם סְחוֹר סְחוֹר׃ ב נְעַלַת קַרְתָּא בִּצְיָרָא עַד חֲדָא עַשְׂרֵי שְׁנִין לְמַלְכָּא צִדְקִיָּהוּ׃ ג בְּתִשְׁעָא לְיַרְחָא וּתְקִיף כַּפְנָא בְּקַרְתָּא וְלָא הֲוָה מֵיכַל לְעַמָּא דְאַרְעָא׃ ד וְאִתְרְעַת קַרְתָּא וְכָל גַּבְרֵי עָבְדֵי

רש"י

כה (א) בשנת התשיעי' למלכו. של צדקיהו:

רד"ק

למה שאמר אחר כן וימרוד. האל ית' שם בלבו שימרוד במלך בבל כדי שימצא מלך בבל טענה להחריב הכל: היתה בירושלם. חפלטה הנשארה היתה בירושלם על אפו ועל חמתו בעבור המעשי' רעי' שהיו עושים: (א) בשנת התשיעית למלכו. למלכות צדקיהו והיא שנת י"ז לנבוכדנצר: ויבנו עליה דיק. הוא מגדל עץ שבונין נגד העיר לכבש': (ג) בתשעה לחדש. ולא זכר באיזה חדש ובספר ירמיה אמר בחדש הרביעי בתשעה לחדש: (ד) ותבקע העיר. בקעו הכשדים חומת העיר וכיון שראו אנשי המלחמה אשר בעיר כי בקעו העיר ברחו בלילה ההוא וזהו שאמר וכל אנשי המלחמה הלילה רוצה לו' ברחו

רלב"ג

ירושלים ולא גלו מעל אדמתם כמו שהיה אומר לו ירמיהו: (א) ויבנו עליה דיק סביב. הוא מגדל שבונין סביב העיר לכבש': (ג) בתשע' לחדש ויחזק הרעב בעיר. הנה לא באר באי זה חדש ואולם בספר ירמיה באר שזה היה בחדש הרביעי בתשעה לחדש: (ד) ותבקע העיר. ר"ל ע"י חיל כשדים: וכל אנשי המלחמה הלילה. ר"ל ברחו

מנחת שי

(כ) עד השלכו. בספרים מעטים הה"א בפתח ואין לחוש עליהם שכן במסורה ב' א' חסר ואחד מלא וזהו החסר וחברו דסוף ירמיה מלא ושניהם בחירק:

כה (א) ויהי בשנת התשיעית. במ"ג כתוב בשנת ומסור עליה בשנת כתיב למדנחאי וכן בנסחאי כ"י נכתב כן בלדם ובחילופי דידן ליתיה ומ"מ כבר איבטילא ההיא נסחא דכמערבאי נקטינן ובנסחא עתיקא כ"י בשנת כתיב בשנת קרי ולפום מאי דחזי לי לאו דסמלא היא דהאי ככי הוה ליה גבעל המסורת למיתתביה בהדי ז' מלין דכתיבין חי"ו ולא קרינן כמ"ש לעיל בהאי סיפרא תניינא דמלכים סימן י"א ואיכא נוסחא אחרינא דכתיב בשנה וקרי בשנת וליכא למיסמך נמי עלה דא"כ ה"ל למימניה עם י"א מלין דקריין חי"ו ולא כתבן ואינון כתיבין ברים שופטים ובריש קהלת וכיון דאיתבטילו כולהו נסחי דאמרן אית לן למימר על כרחין דנסחא דילן עדיפא טפי הילכך לא נעדי מינה: (ג) ולא היה לחם. בס"א כ"י היה מלרע ובספרים אחרים שלפני מלעיל ובמכלול מקבל מלרע שלא כמנהג וכתב אח"כ ודמלכים פליגין עליה וכן כתב המכלול יופי יש אומרים פָּעַל מנה ולא היה לחם לעם הארץ דירמיה עם דומים אחרים שבאו שהוא מלעיל כמנהג ויש אומרים שהוא מלרע שלא כמנהג ועיין

מצודת דוד

כה (א) למלכו. למלכות צדקיה: דיק. הוא מגדל הבננה מול העיר ללכדה: (ב) ותבוא העיר במצור. עמדה העיר והמצור סביבה עד וגו': (ג) בתשעה לחודש. בירמיהו נאמר בחודש הרביעי: (ד) ותבקע העיר. חיל בבל בקעו החומה וכאלו

מצודת ציון

כה (א) ויחן. מל' חניה:

was breached on the seventeenth before the first destruction as well as before the second. Since the people were very upset and distraught about the siege and the famine resulting therefrom, they miscalculated. Lest the people believe that the prophet erred, he recorded the date according to their calculation.

The siege lasted two years to give the people an opportunity to repent and be saved. They, however, neglected to avail themselves of this opportunity. Moreover, this taught the Babylonians that they did not take the city by their strength, since they were unable to take it for the duration of the siege. It was only

was against Jerusalem and against Judah until He cast them away from before His presence, Zedekiah rebelled against the king of Babylonia.

25

1. And it was in the ninth year of his reign, in the tenth month, on the tenth of the month, that Nebuchadnezzar the king of Babylonia came, he and his entire army, against Jerusalem and encamped against it, and they built works of siege around it. 2. And the city came under siege until the eleventh year of King Zedekiah. 3. On the ninth of the month, the famine became severe in the city, and the people of the land had no food.

4. The city was broken into, and all the men of war

1. **in the ninth year of his reign**—i.e. the reign *of Zedekiah* [*Rashi*].

This was the seventeenth year of Nebuchadnezzar [*Redak*].

in the tenth month—This is the month of *Tebeth.*

works of siege—*Jonathan renders: Karkom.* This is the Aramaic term for works of siege [*Rashi*].

This is a tower built around a city placed under siege, in order to attack from its top [*Redak, Ralbag, Mezudath David*].

2. **came under siege**—remained under siege [*Mezudath David*].

3. **On the ninth of the month**—This is explained in Jer. 52:6, as the fourth month. I.e. the month of *Tammuz.*

4. **The city was broken into**—The Chaldeans broke into the city [*Redak*].

The passive is used here instead of the active, since the breaking into the city met with virtually no resistance, because of the weakness of its inhabitants. It was, therefore, considered as though it was broken into by itself [*Mezudath David*].

According to the *Mishnah Taanith* 4:6, the wall was breached on the seventeenth of Tammuz, for which a fast was declared. Yet, here we learn that the wall was breached on the ninth of *Tammuz.* The commonly accepted answer to this question is that before the destruction of the Second Temple, the wall was breached on the seventeenth. Before the destruction of the first Temple, it was broken on the ninth. Since the second destruction had more severe consequences to the Jewish people, since it led to the Diaspora in which we find ourselves today, the later date was chosen for the fast rather than the earlier one. It is too difficult to fast on both days [*Taanith* 28b].

According to *Yerushalmi,* the wall

הַמִּלְחָמָה ׀ הַלַּיְלָה דֶּרֶךְ שַׁעַר ׀ בֵּין הַחֹמֹתַיִם אֲשֶׁר עַל־גַּן הַמֶּלֶךְ וְכַשְׂדִּים עַל־הָעִיר סָבִיב וַיֵּלֶךְ דֶּרֶךְ הָעֲרָבָה:
ה וַיִּרְדְּפוּ חֵיל־כַּשְׂדִּים אַחַר הַמֶּלֶךְ וַיַּשִּׂגוּ אֹתוֹ בְּעַרְבוֹת יְרֵחוֹ וְכָל־חֵילוֹ נָפֹצוּ מֵעָלָיו:
ו וַיִּתְפְּשׂוּ אֶת־הַמֶּלֶךְ וַיַּעֲלוּ אֹתוֹ אֶל־מֶלֶךְ בָּבֶל רִבְלָתָה וַיְדַבְּרוּ אִתּוֹ מִשְׁפָּט:
ז וְאֶת־בְּנֵי צִדְקִיָּהוּ

קְרָבָא בְּלֵילְיָא בְּאוֹרַח תַּרְעָא בֵּין שׁוּרַיָּא דִי עַל גִּינְתָא דְמַלְכָּא וְכַסְדָּאֵי שָׁרָן עַל קַרְתָּא סְחוֹר סְחוֹר וַאֲזַל בְּאוֹרַח מֵישְׁרָא: ה וּרְדָפוּ מַשִּׁרְיַת כַּסְדָּאֵי בָּתַר מַלְכָּא וְאַדְבִּיקוּ יָתֵיהּ בְּמֵישְׁרֵי יְרִיחוֹ וְכָל מַשִּׁרְיָתֵיהּ אִתְבַּדְרַת מִנֵּיהּ: ו וַאֲחָדוּ יַת מַלְכָּא וְאַסִּיקוּ יָתֵיהּ לְוָת מַלְכָּא דְבָבֶל לְרִבְלַת וּמַלִּילוּ עִמֵּיהּ פִּתְגָּמֵי דִינִין: ז וְיַת

ת"א ויעלו אתו. סנהדרין לו:

רד"ק

בלילה ההיא וכן אמר בספר ירמיה וכל אנשי המלחמה ברחו ויצאו מן העיר לילה: דרך שער בין החומותי׳ אשר על גן המלך. יצאו דרך השער שהיה בין שתי החומות בסתר שלא ירגישו בהם הכשדי׳: וילך דרך הערבה. וילך צדקיהו ואשר יצאו עמו. ובדרש בין החומותי׳ מערה היתה מבית צדקיהו עד ערבות יריחו וברח לו דרך המערה והקב"ה זימן צבי שהלך על גג המערה ורדפו כשדים אחר הצבי וכשהגיעו לפתח המערה בערבות יריחו היה צדקי׳ יוצא וראהו ולכדוהו הוא שאמר יחזקאל ופרשתי רשתי עליו ונתפש במצודתי: (ו) אל מלך בבל רבלתה. והרי נבוכדנצר בא לירושלם כמו שכתוב בא נבוכדנצר מלך בבל וכל חילו על ירושלם אלא שארכו ימי המצור כמו שאומר והלך לו נבוכדנצר בארץ חמת רבלתה והניח חילו במצור וכשכבשו ירושלם היה הוא ברבלתה והעלו את צדקיהו אליו. ובדרש לא עלה נבוכדנצר לירוש׳ אלא מה שאומר בא נבוכדנצר נבוזראדן הוא שעלה ודמות דיוקנו של נבוכדנצר היתה חקוקה לו במרכבתו והית׳ אימתו מוטלת עליו כאילו הוא עומד לפניו כמו שאומר בספר ירמיה עמד בפני מלך בבל בירושלם: וידברו אתו משפט. הוכיחו על

רש"י

דיק. יתרגוס יונתן כרקוס: (ד) דרך שער בין החומתים. מערה הולכת מביתו עד ערבות יריחו וברח לו דרך המערה והקב"ה זימן לבי הולך על גג המערה חוץ לעיר ורדפו כשדים אחרי הלבי וכשהגיעו לפתח המערה בערבות יריחו ראוהו ולכדוהו הוא שאמר (ביחזקאל י"ב י"ג) ופרשתי רשתי עליו ונתפש במצודתי: (ו) וידברו אתו

מנחת שי

במברה גדולה אות הה"א ומ"ש במלכים א׳ י"ז: (ה) וירדפו חיל כשדים אחר המלך. כן כתיב לא אחרי; בערבות ירחו. הרי"ש בליפי וחסר יו"ד ובמקצת ספרים הוסיפו יו"ד, ולפי מה שכתוב כאן במסורת חסר דכלנא כייל וכל אורייתא דכוותיה. וכן כתב הרמ"ה ז"ל גבי פ׳ מעבר לירדן ירחו פ׳ חקת חסר יו"ד ריש לחי"ת וכל אורייתא דכוותיה: (ו) וידברו אתו משפט. ובירמיה (נ"ב

רלב"ג

הלילה לפי שראו שחיל כשדים נכנסו לעיר: דרך שער בין החומותי׳. ר"ל שילאו דרך שהיה בין שתי חומות כדי שלא ירגישו בהם: אשר על גן המלך. ר"ל אצל גן המלך: וילך דרך הערבה. ר"ל כי המלך הלך דרך המדבר שלא ירגישו בו כשדים: (ו) וידברו אתו משפט. אמר לו משפט המורד והעובר על שבועתו ולזה הרג בניו ועור עיני צדקיהו ויאסרהו בנחשתים ונתנוהו בבית האסורים עד יום מותו כמו שנזכר בספר ירמיה:

מצודת ציון

(ה) נפצו. נתפזרו: (ו) ויתפשו. אחזו בחזקה:

מצודת דוד

נעשית מעלמה כי אנשי ירושלים היו חלושים ברעב ולא עמדו למולם לערך עלידם: הלילה. ר"ל ברחו בלילה ובירמיה נאמר ויברחו ויצאו מן העיר לילה: דרך שער וגו׳. בדרך השער העומד בין שתי החומות אשר אצל גן המלך: וילך. המלך וכל אשר עמו: דרך הערבה. בדרך ההולך אל ערבות יריחו: (ה) וירדפו. אחז"ל שברח דרך מערה ההולכת עד ערבות יריחו ונזדמן לבי הולך ממעל על המערה ורדפו הכשדים אחר הלבי ובבואם לפתח המערה מלאו את המלך יולא ותפשוהו: (ו) רבלתה. כי בהאריך ימי המצור הלך ל"נ לרבלה: משפט. התווכחו עמו על

against him [*Redak*].

According to the Talmud (*Nedarim* 65a) Zedekiah found Nebuchadnezzar eating a raw (or live) rabbit. He made him swear that he would not reveal what he had seen. He did, however, have his oath nullified, and he revealed Nebuchadnezzar's uncivilized habit. For this he was sternly reprimanded.

[fled] at night by way of the gate between the two walls that was near the king's garden, and the Chaldees were surrounding the city, and he went by way of the Arabah. 5. And the army of the Chaldees pursued the king, and they overtook him on the plains of Jericho, and all his army had scattered and deserted him. 6. And they seized the king and brought him up to the king of Babylonia, to Riblah, and called him to account.

that God gave it into their hands [*K'li Y'kar*].

fled at night—The word "fled" does not appear in our text. It does, however, appear in Jer. 52:7.

by way of the gate between the two walls—*A cave went from his house until the plains of Jericho, and he fled through the cave. The Holy One, Blessed be He, ordained a deer walking on the roof of the cave. The Chaldeans pursued the deer, and when they reached the entrance of the cave in the plains of Jericho, they saw him and captured him. This is what Ezekiel said,* "(12:13) *And I will spread My net over him, and he shall be caught in My net . . ." [Rashi* from unknown Midrashic source].

According to tradition, this cave is found outside the old city of Jerusalem, near the Shechem gate. It is open to the public for a short distance.

Zedekiah and those with him left through the gate between the walls. This was a secret gate, unknown to the Chaldees [*Redak*].

6. **to the king of Babylonia, to Riblah**—According to the Talmud (*San.* 96b) and the *Midrash* (*Lev. Rabbah* 19:6), Riblah is Antioch, a city outside of *Eretz Israel.* Nebuchadnezzar never came to Jerusalem. As we explained above, he feared that he would meet Sennacherib's fate. He, therefore, established his headquarters in Antioch, from where he directed his campaign. V. 1, which states that Nebuchadnezzar and his entire army encamped against Jerusalem, means that Nebuzaradan came with Nebuchadnezzar's image engraved in his chariot. It was as though he was standing before his master. He stood in awe as though Nebuchadnezzar was there personally. In Jeremiah 52:12, Scripture states, "He stood before the king of Babylon in Jerusalem" [*Redak* from *San.* 96b].

and called him to account—*He debated with him concerning the oath* [*Rashi*].

He rebuked him for rebelling against him and for violating the oath that he had sworn to him, as the Chronicler puts it, "(II 36:13) And also against King Nebuchadnezzar he rebelled, who had adjured him by God . . ." I.e. he had adjured him by God that he would not rebel

שַׁחֲטוּ לְעֵינָיו וְאֶת־עֵינֵי צִדְקִיָּהוּ עִוֵּר וַיַּאַסְרֵהוּ בַנְחֻשְׁתַּיִם וַיְבִאֵהוּ בָּבֶל׃
ח וּבַחֹדֶשׁ הַחֲמִישִׁי בְּשִׁבְעָה לַחֹדֶשׁ הִיא שְׁנַת תְּשַׁע־עֶשְׂרֵה שָׁנָה לַמֶּלֶךְ נְבֻכַדְנֶאצַּר מֶלֶךְ־בָּבֶל בָּא נְבוּזַרְאֲדָן רַב־טַבָּחִים עֶבֶד מֶלֶךְ־בָּבֶל יְרוּשָׁלִָם׃
ט וַיִּשְׂרֹף אֶת־בֵּית־יְהוָה וְאֶת־בֵּית הַמֶּלֶךְ וְאֵת כָּל־בָּתֵּי יְרוּשָׁלִַם וְאֶת־כָּל־בֵּית גָּדוֹל שָׂרַף בָּאֵשׁ׃
י וְאֶת־חוֹמֹת

בְנוֹהִי דְצִדְקִיָהוּ נְכִיסוּ לְעֵינוֹהִי וְיָת עֵינֵי צִדְקִיָהוּ עֲוַר וְאַסְרֵיהּ בְּשַׁלְשְׁלָן דִנְחָשׁ וְאוֹבִילֵיהּ לְבָבֶל׃
ח וּבְיַרְחָא חֲמִישָׁאָה בְּשַׁבְעָא לְיַרְחָא הִיא שְׁנַת תְּשַׁע עַסְרֵי שְׁנִין לְמַלְכָּא נְבוּכַדְנֶאצַּר מַלְכָּא דְבָבֶל אֲתָא נְבוּזַרְאֲדָן רַב קַטוֹלַיָא עַבְדָא דְמַלְכָּא דְבָבֶל לִירוּשְׁלֵם׃
ט וְאוֹקִיד יָת מַקְדְשָׁא דַיְיָ וְיָת בֵּית מַלְכָּא וְיָת כָּל בָּתֵּי יְרוּשְׁלֵם וְיָת כָּל בָּתֵּי רַבְרְבַיָא אוֹקִיד בְּנוּרָא׃
י וְיָת שׁוּרֵי יְרוּשְׁלֵם סְחוֹר

ת״א וּבחדש החמישי. תענית כט סנהדרין לו: וישרף. מגלה יב סנהדרין לו (מגילה כג):

רש״י
משפט. נתווכח עמו על השבועה: (ט) ואת כל בית גדול. בתי כנסיות שמגדלין בהן תורה ותפלה ובתי השרי׳:

רד״ק
שמרד בו ועבר על שבועתו כמו שכתוב וגם במלך נבוכדנצר מרד אשר השביעו באלהים: (ח) בשבעה לחדש. ובירמיה כתוב בעשור לחודש פי׳ רז״ל בשבעה בו נכנסו גוים להיכל ואכלו ושתו וקלקלו בו שמיני ותשיעי ובתשיעי סמוך לחשכה הציתו בו את האור והי׳ דולק והולך עד סוף עשירי: הוא שנת י״ט למלך נבוכדנצר. וכן כתוב בירמיה ובזה הפסוק ה״א שנת י״ט אבל בסוף אמר בשנת י״ח לנבוכדנצר הגלה מירושל׳ נפש ח׳ מאות כמו שפי׳ בז׳ ובח׳ סוף ז׳ ותחלת ח׳ וכן הוא שנת י״ח בסוף י״ח והתחלת י״ט ורבותינו ז״ל אמרו גלו בי״ט גל בי״ח וחשבינן א׳ הוא אלא י״ט למלכו׳ נבוכדנצר וי״ח לכבוש יהויקי׳ שהיה בשנה שניה לנבוכדנצר: (ט) ואת כל בית גדול. כל בית אדם גדול ר״ל בתי הגדולים וכן ת״י בתי רברביא:

רלב״ג
(ח) ובחדש החמישי בשבעה לחדש. וכבר אמר בספ׳ ירמיה בעשור לחדש וידמה שהתחלת החרבן היה בז׳ לחדש כי אז נכנסו בירושלים וסוף החורבן היה בעשור לחדש כי אז נשרף בית המקדש: (ט) ואת

מנחת שי
ט״ו) וידבר אתו משפטים: (ז) ויאסרהו בס״ה ישן ויאסרהו הרי״ם בגלא נקודות ומשקלו בלדו ויבאהו בבל ופני טעיות הן שכל א׳ גורם לחברו טעות ראשון מבואר מזה שנמסר במסורת ויאסרהו ג׳ בקריאה וסימן ויאסרהו בשנים עבתים חדשים (שופטים ט״ו) וינקרו את עיניו (בס סימן ט״ו) ויקדו את מנשה בחוחים דד״ה (ב׳ ל״ג) למדנו מכאן שזה כתוב ויאסרהו בלידי וכיון שכ״ל ג״כ ויבאהו בלידי כמ״ש בסוף ירמיה וכמ״ש כאן בספרים כ״י מדוייקים ודפוסים ישנים לא בגלא נקודות כמו שהוא בדפוסים חדשים ומי שלא יתפייס בזה יעיין במסורת ירמיה סוף סימן כ״ד שנמסר ז׳ ויבאהו ואין זה ממניים וכן תרגם יונתן ואסריה ואוביליה וכן הם במאיר נתיב ופי׳ רלב״ג: (ז) בנחשתים. הנו״ן בלא דגש והבי״ת במאריך כמ״ש בשופטים ט״ז וכן הוא במדוייקים. ויביאהו בבל. בחתי דפוסי כתוב בבלה ואינהו הטעו המעתיקים במאי דאשכחו במ״ר סימנא מן עשרים ותשע בבלה וחד מינייהו ואת עיני צדקיהו עור ויאסרהו בסבי דהדין הוא ולא בית דהתם בסוף ירמיה קיימא והוא: (ח) ובחדש החמישי וגו׳ למלך נבוכדנאצר. תלא מלא כתיב כחבריו שבענין:

מצודת דוד
מה שמרד בו ועבר על שבועתו כמ״ש בד״ה: (ח) תשע עשרה. כי בעת שכבש את יהויכין היה ח׳ למלכו ולצדקיהו מלך י״א שנה הרי י״ט ובסוף ירמיה נאמר י״ח ור״ל לכבוש יהויקים בראשונה שהיתה בשניה למלכות נ״נ: רב טבחים. שר על ההורגים במלאכת המלך: (ט) בית גדול. הוא פי׳ על מה שאמר כל בתי ירושלים לומר בהם כל בית אדם גדול אשר בירושלים ואותם לבד שרף ולא זולתם:

מצודת ציון
(ז) בנחשתים. בשלשלאות נחושת:

tenth of the month." Our Rabbis answer that on the seventh of the month of *Av, the Chaldees entered the Temple, ate, drank, and reveled on the seventh and eighth days of the month. On the ninth, toward evening, they ignited the Temple, which continued to burn through the tenth day [Redak* from *Taanith* 29a].

the nineteenth year of Nebuchadnezzar king of Babylonia—The identical verse appears in Jer. 52:12. In v. 29, however, we read that the exile took place in the eighteenth year. It may have been the end of the eighteenth year and the beginning of the nineteenth. The Rabbis (*Meg.* 11b), however, explain that Zedekiah's exile took place in the nineteenth year of Nebuchadnezzar's reign, which was the eighteenth year counting from the conquest of

7. And they slaughtered Zedekiah's sons before his eyes, and they blinded Zedekiah's eyes, and he bound him with copper chains and brought him to Babylon. 8. And in the fifth month, on the seventh of the month (that was the nineteenth year of Nebuchadnezzar king of Babylonia) Nebuzaradan, chief executioner, servant of the king of Babylonia, came to Jerusalem. 9. And he burnt the house of the Lord and the king's palace, and all the houses of Jerusalem and all the houses of the dignitaries he burnt with fire.

7. **and they blinded Zedekiah's eyes**—This had already been prophesied by Ezekiel (12:13), "And I will bring him to Babylon, the land of the Chaldees, but he will not see it."

This heartrending incident of the slaughter of Zedekiah's children and the blinding of Zedekiah is narrated in various Midrashim, partially quoted by *Yalkut Shimoni* ad loc. One account states as follows:

When Zedekiah saw this, he went out to escape through the cave that extended to Jericho, the place through which the water conduit ran. He exerted himself to run through this tunnel with his ten sons preceding him. Nebuzaradan saw them, seized him and his ten sons, and sent them to Nebuchadnezzar. He said to him, "Tell me, Zedekiah, what did you see that encouraged you to rebel against me? With which system of laws shall I judge you? If with the law of your God, you are deserving of death, since you swore falsely by His Name. If with the law of the kingdom, you are deserving of death, since anyone who transgresses the king's oath, is liable to death." Then Zedekiah spoke up and said, "Slay me first, lest I see the blood of my sons." His sons said, "Slay us first, lest we see our father's blood spilt on the ground." So he did to them. He slaughtered them before him and then gouged out his eyes and put them into an oven. Then he led him to Babylon. Zedekiah was crying out, "Come, all peoples, and see what Jeremiah prophesied concerning me. He said to me, 'You shall go to Babylon; you shall die in Babylon, but your eyes will not see Babylon.' Yet, I did not heed his words. Now I am in Babylon, yet my eyes do not see it" [*Pesikta Rabbathi,* p. 229].

A second version of this tragic event is as follows:

Zedekiah's eyes resembled those of Adam. (I.e. he was able to see his way through the cave when he fled from Jerusalem [*Maharsha Sotah* 10a]. They thrust spears into his eyes, yet they were not blinded. When they slaughtered his sons before his eyes, (and he wept—*Yalkut*) however, he became blind [*Tanhuma Va'ethhanan* 1].

8. **on the seventh of the month**—In Jeremiah 52:12, we read, ". . . on the

ירושלם סביב נתצו כל־חיל כשדים
אשר רב־טבחים: יא ואת יתר העם
הנשארים בעיר ואת־הנפלים אשר
נפלו על־המלך בבל ואת יתר ההמון
הגלה נבוזראדן רב־טבחים: יב ומדלת
הארץ השאיר רב־טבחים לכרמים
ול*גבים: יג ואת־עמודי הנחשת אשר
בית־יהוה ואת־המכנות ואת־ים
הנחשת אשר־בבית יהוה שברו
כשדים וישאו את־נחשתם בבלה:
יד ואת־הסירות ואת־היעים ואת־
המזמרות ואת־הכפות ואת כל־כלי

*וליוגבים קרי

סחור סחור תרעו כל
משרית כסדאי דעם רב
קטוליא: יא וית שאר
עמא דאשתארו בקרתא
וית שמיעיא דאשתמעו
על מלכא דבבל וית
שאר המונא אגלי
נבוזראדן רב קטוליא:
יב ומחשיבי עמא
דארעא אשאר רב
קטוליא למהוי מפלחין
בחקלין ובכרמין:
יג וית עמודי נחשא
דבבית מקדשא דיי וית
בסיסיא וית ימא
דנחשא די בבית
מקדשא דיי תברו
כסדאי ואובילו ית
נחשיהון לבבל: יד וית
דודיא וית מגרופיתא
וית מזמריא וית בזיכיא
וית כל מני נחשא דהוו
משמשין

רד"ק

(י) אשר רב טבחים. אשר עם רב הטבחים וכן כתוב בירמיה אשר את רב טבחים: (יא) ואת הנופלים אשר נפלו. שיצאו אליו קודם כבוש העי' ומסרו עצמם אליו כמו אל הכשדים אתה נופל ות"י וית שמיעיא דאשתמעו כלומר שסרו אל משמעתו: על המלך בבל. סמוך ה"א הידיעה כמו הארון הברי': (יב) לכורמי' וליוגבים. כורמים עובדי הכרמי' יוגבים עובדי השדות וכן ת"י למהוי מפלחין בכרמין ובחקלין וכתוב ולגבי' בלא י' פ' הפעל ובדברי רבותינו ז"ל תני רב יוסף לכורמים אלו מלקטי אפרסמון מעין גדי עד רמתא וליוגבים אלו צדי חלזון

רש"י

(יא) ואת הנופלים. ששמעו לקול נבוכדנצר ויצאו אליו מן העיר כמו בלכתו אל נקלג נפלו עליו ממנשה וגו' (ד"ה א' י"ב כ"א): (יב) וליוגבים. חופרי הארץ לשון יקבים

מנחת שי

(י) אשר רב טבחים. בספר אחד כ"י כתוב אשר את רב וגם בדפוס ישן מויניליאה יש הערה מזה החילוף ואין כן בשאר הספרים: (יא) ואת יתר העם הנשארים וגו' ואת יתר ההמון. ובסוף ירמיה הוא אומר יתר האמון וסימן הא לכם זרע ובמלכי' יו"ד ומדלת הארץ. ובירמיה ומדלות הארץ וסימן מניושא בתר עניותא אולא פירש ירמיה שמדבר מעניות החרבן נכתב ומדלות לשון רבים. ובמלכים שהם עשירים נכתב ומדלת לשון יחיד: (יב) ולגבים. וליגבים קרי ובמקצת ספרים כתיב וליגבים ואין הפרש בין קרי לכתיב ובאחד מהם נכתב בחוץ ולגבים כתוב למדנחאי וליגבים קרי. ובחילופים שלנו שבין מערבאי למדינחאי לא נזכר מזה כלל ומה שכתבתי בתחלה היא דעת רד"ק שכתב זה לשונו: וכתוב ולגבים בלא יו"ד פ"א הפעל: (יג) ואת המכנות. הוא"ו בגעיא בס"ס: (יד) המזמרות. הה"א סמוכה במאריך והמ"ם רפה ובמקצת ספרים

רלב"ג

כל בית גדול. ר"ל ואת כל בית איש גדול: (י) אשר רב טבחים. ר"ל אשר את רב טבחים: (יב) לכורמים וליוגבים. ר"ל לעבוד השדות והכרמים: (יג) ואת עמודי הנחשת אשר בית ה'. וכבר התבאר בענין לורת אלו הכלים בזכרון בניית שלמה בית המקדש ומשם ילקח

מצודת דוד

(י) אשר רב טבחים. אשר עם רב טבחים: (יא) הנשארים אשר לא נהרגו: ואת יתר ההמון. הנשארים בכל ערי יהודה:

מצודת ציון

(י) נתצו. שברו וכתתו: (יא) הנופלים. הם היוצאים מעצמן למסור עצמן ולשכון בינותם וכן אל הכשדים אתה נופל (ירמיה לז): ההמון. העם הרב: (יב) לכורמים. לעבוד הכרמים: וליוגבים. ענין בורות כמו עשה הנחל הזה גבים גבים (לעיל ג') ור"ל לעבוד השדות בחפירות ובורות או הוא כמו ליוקבים מל' יקב היין כי ניכ"ק מתחלף ור"ל לדרוך ולהמשיך היין אל היקב: (יג) בית ה'. בבית ה': המכונות. הם כני ובסיסי הכיורות: ים. כענין גיגית גדולה עשויה לרחוץ בה · (יד) הסירות הקדרות: היעים. המכבדות והמגרפות עשוים לגרוף בהם הדשן: המזמרות. כלי

as grapes are pressed to extract their juice. Hence the similarity to יֶקֶב, *the wine-vat*. These fish were caught in the Mediterranean between the

10. The entire army of the Chaldeans that was [with] the chief executioner demolished the walls of Jerusalem around.
11. And Nebuzaradan the chief executioner exiled the remnant of the people who remained in the city, and the defectors who defected to the king of Babylonia, and the rest of the populace.
12. Now the chief executioner left over some of the poorest of the land as vine-dressers and farmers. 13. And the Chaldeans broke the copper pillars that were in the house of the Lord and the bases and the copper sea that was in the house of the Lord, and they carried off their copper to Babylon. 14. And they
took the pots and the shovels and the musical instruments and the spoons and all the copper vessels with which they served.

Jehoiakim, which took place during Nebuchadnezzar's second year [*Redak*].

Thus we figure that Jehoiachin's exile took place during the eighth year of Nebuchadnezzar's reign, and Zedekiah reigned for eleven years thereafter, totalling nineteen years [*Mezudath David*].

9. **and all the houses of the dignitaries**—lit. the house of every great one. *Synagogues wherein Torah and prayer are aggrandized, and the houses of the princes* [*Rashi* from *Meg*. 27a and *Targum Jonathan*].

10. **with the chief executioner**—The word "with" is absent in our text, but appears in Jeremiah 52:14 [*Redak*].

11. **who remained in the city**—i.e. those who were not killed [*Mezudath David*].

and the defectors—*who obeyed Nebuchadnezzar and went out to him from the city, like* "(I Chron. 12:20) *When he went to Ziklag, of Manasseh . . . defected to him* [*Rashi*]".

In both instances the root נפל, usually meaning *to fall,* is used.

They had already defected before the conquest of the city [*Redak*].

the rest of the populace—from the other cities of Judah [*Mezudath David*].

and farmers—Heb. יֹגְבִים, *diggers of the earth, an expression of wine-vats* (יְקָבִים) [*Rashi*].

The *gimel* and the *kuf* are interchangeable. We, therefore, interpret יֹגְבִים, as those who dig holes in the ground. Others explain it as farmers [*Redak* from *Jonathan*].

The Rabbis (*Shabbath* 26a) interpret this as gatherers of balsam and fishermen who catch the *hilazon,* a fish from which the blue dye for *techeleth* is obtained. The fish were pressed to extract their blood, much

הַנְּחֹ֤שֶׁת אֲשֶֽׁר־יְשָׁרְתוּ־בָם֙ לָקָֽחוּ׃
טו וְאֶת־הַמַּחְתּוֹת֙ וְאֶת־הַמִּזְרָק֔וֹת
אֲשֶׁ֤ר זָהָב֙ זָהָ֔ב וַאֲשֶׁר־כֶּ֖סֶף כָּ֑סֶף לָקַ֖ח
רַב־טַבָּחִֽים׃ טז הָעַמּוּדִ֣ים ׀ שְׁנַ֗יִם הַיָּ֤ם
הָאֶחָד֙ וְהַמְּכֹנ֔וֹת אֲשֶׁר־עָשָׂ֥ה שְׁלֹמֹ֖ה
לְבֵ֣ית יְהוָ֑ה לֹא־הָיָ֣ה מִשְׁקָ֔ל לִנְחֻ֖שְׁתָּ֥ם
כָּל־הַכֵּלִ֥ים הָאֵֽלֶּה׃ יז שְׁמֹנֶה֩ עֶשְׂרֵ֨ה
אַמָּ֜ה קוֹמַ֣ת ׀ הָעַמּ֣וּד הָאֶחָד֮ וְכֹתֶ֣רֶת
עָלָ֣יו ׀ נְחֹשֶׁת֒ וְקוֹמַ֨ת הַכֹּתֶ֜רֶת שָׁלֹ֣שׁ
אַמָּ֗ה וּשְׂבָכָ֨ה וְרִמֹּנִ֜ים עַל־הַכֹּתֶ֛רֶת
סָבִ֖יב הַכֹּ֣ל נְחֹ֑שֶׁת וְכָאֵ֛לֶּה לַֽעַמּ֥וּד
הַשֵּׁנִ֖י עַל־הַשְּׂבָכָֽה׃ יח וַיִּקַּ֣ח רַב־טַבָּחִ֗ים
אֶת־שְׂרָיָה֙ כֹּהֵ֣ן הָרֹ֔אשׁ וְאֶת־צְפַנְיָ֖הוּ
כֹּהֵ֣ן מִשְׁנֶ֑ה וְאֶת־שְׁלֹ֖שֶׁת שֹׁמְרֵ֥י הַסַּֽף׃

תרגום

מְשַׁמְשִׁין בְּהוֹן נְסִיבוּ: טו וְיַת מַחְתְּיָתָא וְיַת מִזְרְקַיָא דִי דַהֲבָא דַהֲבָא וְדִי כַסְפָּא כַסְפָּא נְסִיב רַב קָטוֹלַיָא: טז עַמּוּדַיָא תְרֵין וְיַמָּא חַד וּבְסִיסַיָא דַעֲבַד שְׁלֹמֹה לְבֵית מַקְדְשָׁא דַיְיָ לָא הֲוָה מַתְקַל לִנְחָשְׁתְּהוֹן דְכָל מָנַיָא הָאִלֵין: יז תַּמְנֵי עַסְרֵי אַמִין רוּמֵיהּ דְעַמּוּדָא חַד וְקַרְוֹנְתְּהוֹן עֲלוֹהִי דִנְחָשָׁא וְרוּמָא דְקַרְוֹנְתְּהוֹן תְּלַת אַמִין וּסְרִגְתָא וְרִמּוֹנַיָא עַל קַרְוֹנְתְהוֹן סְחוֹר סְחוֹר כּוּלָא נְחָשָׁא וּכְאִלֵין לְעַמּוּדָא תִנְיָנָא עַל סְרִגְתָא: יח וּדְבַר רַב קָטוֹלַיָא יַת שְׂרָיָה כַּהֲנָא רַבָּא וְיַת צְפַנְיָה סְגַן כַּהֲנַיָא וְיַת תְּלָתָא אמרכליא

ת״א שלשת שמרי הסף . מגלה כג :

רש״י

שהם הפירות בקרקע: (יז) וקומת הכותרת שלש אמות. ובתחלת הספר (ז׳ ט״ז) הוא אומר חמש אמות ושם ישבתי את המקראות: ושבכה. (כופייא בלע״ז) כמין

אמות קרי

רד״ק

מסולמא דצור עד חיפא: (יח) כהן הראש. כהן גדול שהוא ראש לשאר הכהנים: כהן משנה. שני לכהן גדול והוא הסגן וכן תרג׳ יונתן סגן כהניא: שומרי הסף. שומרי כלי בית

רלב״ג

ביאור כל מה שזכר בזה המקום מאלו הכלים: (יח) שריה כהן הראש. הוא כהן גדול: ואת לפניה כהן משנה. הוא סגן הכהנים: ואת שלשת שומרי הסף. הם שומרי בית המקדש:

מנחת שי

הה״א בלא מאריך והמ״ם דגושה: (יז) וכתרת עליו וגו׳. בספרים מדוייקים חסר וא״ו אחר כ״ף וכן שנים אחרים שבפ׳: שלש אמה. אמות קרי ובמלכים א׳ ז׳ כתוב חמש אמות. עיין שם במפרשים וכלי יקר: (יח) שמרי הסף.

מצודת דוד

(יד) אשר ישרתו בם. העשוים לעבוד ולשרת בהם בבה״מ: (טו) אשר זהב זהב וגו׳. רלה לומר בין של זהב בין של כסף הכל לקח: (יז) שמנה עשרה אמה וגו׳. כבר נתבאר ענינ׳ במ״א בספור מלאכתו ואין צורך א״כ בהשנות הנה: וכאלה. מספר

מצודת ציון

זמר: חכפות, הבזיכים: (טו) המחתות. כלים להתות בהן האש: המזרקות. הספלים: (יז) ושבכה. עשויה היא כרשת: ורמונים. עשוי׳ מנחושת: (יח) כהן הראש. זה כהן גדול: משנה. שני לו זה הסגן: שומרי הסף. הם השוערים כי מזוזות השער יקרא סף

the priest of second rank—the assistant to the high priest.

keepers of the utensils—See above 23:4.

15. And the chief executioner took the censers and the basins, both of gold and of silver. 16. The two pillars, the one sea, and the bases that Solomon had made for the house of the Lord; there was no weight for the copper of all these vessels. 17. The height of one pillar was eighteen cubits and there was a capital of copper upon it, and the height of the capital was three cubits, and a net and pomegranates on the capital around, all was copper. And such did the second pillar have on the net. 18. And the chief executioner took Seraiah the head priest and Zephaniah the priest of second rank, and the three keepers of the utensils.

Ladder of Tyre and Haifa. Nebuzaradan allowed these people to remain in Eretz Israel to supply him with dye for the royal robes [*Rashi* ad loc.].

Alternatively, they were winepressers [*Mezudath Zion*].

13. **and the bases**—of the washbasins [*Mezudath Zion*]. See I Kings 7:27.

the copper sea—a huge vat, used for ritual immersion [*Mezudath Zion]. See I Kings 7:23.*

the shovels—used to pick up the ashes from the altar [*Mezudath Zion*].

with which they served—i.e. which were used for the sacrificial service [*Mezudath David*].

and they carried off their copper—To the uncouth Chaldean soldiers, the fixtures of the Temple had no value but for their copper. They did not even consider them as objects of art. Consequently, they smashed them and carried off their copper to Babylon. The holy vessels, which they carried off intact, were probably packed when they came upon them, and they never saw them [*Daath Soferim*].

15. **both of gold and of silver**—lit. that which was gold, gold, and that which was silver, silver [*Mezudath David*].

17. **and the height of the capital was three cubits**—*and in the beginning of the book* (I Kings 7:16) *he says, "five cubits." There I reconciled the verses* [*Rashi*].

and a net—(*coiffe in French*) *like a sort of hat* [*Rashi*].

and such—Lit. like these; i.e. like these pomegranates [*Rashi*].

The entire structure of the Temple was discussed in I Kings 7.

18. **the head priest**—i.e. the high priest [*Redak, Mezudath Zion*].

יט וּמִן־הָעִיר לָקַח סָרִיס אֶחָד אֲשֶׁר־הוּא פָקִיד ׀ עַל־אַנְשֵׁי הַמִּלְחָמָה וַחֲמִשָּׁה אֲנָשִׁים מֵרֹאֵי פְנֵי־הַמֶּלֶךְ אֲשֶׁר נִמְצְאוּ בָעִיר וְאֵת הַסֹּפֵר שַׂר הַצָּבָא הַמַּצְבִּא אֶת־עַם הָאָרֶץ וְשִׁשִּׁים אִישׁ מֵעַם הָאָרֶץ הַנִּמְצְאִים בָּעִיר:
כ וַיִּקַּח אֹתָם נְבוּזַרְאֲדָן רַב־טַבָּחִים וַיֹּלֶךְ אֹתָם עַל־מֶלֶךְ בָּבֶל רִבְלָתָה:
כא וַיַּךְ אֹתָם מֶלֶךְ בָּבֶל וַיְמִיתֵם בְּרִבְלָה בְּאֶרֶץ חֲמָת וַיִּגֶל יְהוּדָה מֵעַל אַדְמָתוֹ:
כב וְהָעָם הַנִּשְׁאָר בְּאֶרֶץ יְהוּדָה אֲשֶׁר הִשְׁאִיר נְבוּכַדְנֶאצַּר מֶלֶךְ בָּבֶל וַיַּפְקֵד עֲלֵיהֶם אֶת־גְּדַלְיָהוּ בֶּן־אֲחִיקָם בֶּן־שָׁפָן:

תרגום

אֲמַרְכְּלַיָא: יט וּמִן קַרְתָּא דְבַר גַּוָּזָא חַד דְּהוּא מְמַנָּא עַל גַּבְרֵי עָבְדֵי קְרָבָא וְחַמְשָׁא גֻּבְרִין דְּחָזַן אַפֵּי מַלְכָּא דְּאִשְׁתְּכָחוּ בְקַרְתָּא וְיָת סָפְרָא רַב חֵילָא דִּכְנֵשׁ יָת עַמָּא דְאַרְעָא וְשִׁתִּין גֻּבְרָא מֵעַמָּא דְאַרְעָא דְּאִשְׁתְּכָחוּ בְקַרְתָּא: כ וּדְבַר יָתְהוֹן נְבוּזַרְאֲדָן רַב קָטוֹלַיָא וְאוֹבֵיל יָתְהוֹן לְוָת מַלְכָּא דְבָבֶל לְרִבְלָת: כא וּמְחָא יָתְהוֹן מַלְכָּא דְבָבֶל וְקַטְלִינוּן בְּרִבְלָא בְּאַרְעָא דַּחֲמָת וּגְלוֹ דְּבֵית יְהוּדָה מֵעַל אַרְעֲהוֹן: כב וְעַמָּא דְּאִשְׁתְּאַר בְּאַרְעָא דְבֵית יְהוּדָה דְּאַשְׁאַר נְבוּכַדְנֶאצַּר מַלְכָּא דְבָבֶל וּמַנִּי עֲלֵיהֶן יָת גְּדַלְיָה בַּר אֲחִיקָם בַּר שָׁפָן

ת"א וחמשה אנשים. סנהדרין י (סנהדרין יח):

רש"י

כובע: **וכאלה**. רמונים: **(יט) הסופר שר הצבא**. שהיה יודע מנין כל עיר ועיר כמה אנשים מוציא' לצבא:

רד"ק

המקדש: (יט) ומן העיר לקח. לפי שאלו שזכר היו מבית המקדש אמר ומן העיר לקח: סריס אחד. סרים ממש כתרגומו גוזא: וחמישה אנשים מרואי פני המלך. ובירמיהו אומר שבעה אנשים מראי פני המלך השנים לא היו גדולים כמו החמשה לפיכך לא מנאן כאן ובדברי רבותינו ז"ל כתוב אחד

מנחת שי

הסמ"ך בפתח במדוייקים ועיין מה שכתבתי בשופטים סימן י"ט*: (יט) אשר היא פקיד. ג' פסוקים מטעים וסימן אשר הוא פקיד דסוף מלכים. ירמיה אשר היה פקיד. וא' פסוק סימן הוא היה גבר ליד. מלכים ואת הספר שר הצבא. ירמיה ואת ספר שר הצבא. ואחד פסוק סימן וזה פרשגן הנשתון עד כאן לשון המסורת. פי' בגלותו פסוק כתיב לעזרא הכהן הספר ספר דברי וגו' (עזרא ז'): וחמשה אנשים. חלוף. מלכים וחמשה אנשים. ירמיה ושבעה אנשים. וכן צריך לגרוס בבמדבר רבה פרשה י"א והכי איתא בירושלמי פרקא קמא דסנהדרין סימן ד' עיין כלי יקר: מלכים מביא כלא. ירמיה מבית הכנוה. מלכים מעל כסא המלכים. ירמיה ממעל לכסא המלכים: (כ) על מלך בבל רבלתה. זהו א' מן ט"ו על הסמוך למלת מלך וסימנם במקרא גדולה יחזקאל כ"ח ודניאל י"א ובנביאים עם פירוש הרי"א כתוב אל מלך ואחלף ליה נביא בנביא: (כא) ויגל יהודה. היו"ד בחירק על פי

*עיין מסר' ריש (ויקרא) ובפירוש הרב מנ"ש שם שלפי גודל בקיאותו לא עיין כאן (ובשופטים שם):

רלב"ג

(יט) ואת הסופר שר הצבא. ר"ל ואת הסופר שהיה סופר שר הצבא והנה שר הצבא הוא המצביא את כל עם הארץ על פי הסופר: (כ) ויולך אותם על מלך בבל. ר"ל אל מלך בבל:

מצודת ציון

כמו וסף הספר (יחזקאל ח): (יט) סרים. שר: פקיד. ממונה: המצבא. מלשון צבא: (כ) על מלך. אל מלך: (כב) ויפקד. מענין מנוי

מצודת דוד

הרמונים שהיו באחד היו בהשני: (יט) מרואי פני המלך. ר"ל היושבים תמיד עם המלך ובירמיה נאמר שבעה אנשים וזהו לפי שהשנים מהם לא היו חשובים כמו החמשה ולא כללם כאן עמהם: אשר נמצאו בעיר. ולא ברחו ממנה כיתר השרים: הספר שר הצבא. סופר של שר הצבא: המצבא. על פיו הוציאה כל עיר

to. Perhaps the intention is that he brought them by the command of the king of Babylonia, who demanded more victims upon whom to wreak his vengeance. Nebuzaradan, himself, had already relented of his cruelty and showed sympathy to the Jewish people, as is recorded in Jeremiah 40 [*Daath Soferim*].

and Judah went in exile—By this time, the people had completely despaired of remaining in the Holy Land. Whereas until now, they were willing to risk their lives rather than

19. And from the city he took one eunuch who was appointed over the men of war, and five men of those who saw the king's face, who were found in the city, and the scribe of the general of the army, who would muster out the people of the land, and sixty men of the people of the land who were found in the city.
20. And Nebuzaradan the chief executioner took them and brought them to the king of Babylonia, to Riblah. 21. And the king of Babylonia struck them down and killed them in Riblah in the land of Hamath, and Judah went in to exile off its land.
22. And [as for] the people who remained in the land of Judah whom Nebuchadnezzar king of Babylonia had left over, he appointed over them Gedaliah the son of Ahikam the son of Shaphan.

19. **And from the city**—Heretofore he delineated what was taken from the Temple. Now, Scripture delineates what Nebuzaradan took from the city at large [*Redak*].

one eunuch—This one was actually a eunuch, as *Jonathan* renders [*Redak*]. He was perhaps castrated by the wicked kings who preceded Zedekiah, or he may have been captured in war and returned in that condition. The righteous kings never practiced castration, which is forbidden by the Torah. See above 8:6. Alternatively, we render, *one officer* [*Mezudath Zion*].

According to the Rabbis, this refers to the seventy-first member of the Great Sanhedrin, whose word would decide the verdict [*Korban Ha-edah, Yerushalmi Sanhedrin* 1:2].

and five men of those who saw the king's face—I.e. of the king's intimates, who sat with him constantly [*Mezudath David*].

Regarding the identical incident, we read in Jer. 52:25, "seven men of those who saw the king's face." The exegetes explain that two of them did not occupy as high a position as the other five. Therefore, they are not mentioned here [*Redak, Mezudath David, Rashi* on Jer.].

According to the Rabbis, the extra two men were the scribes of the judges, who would record the opinions of the judges and their verdicts [*Redak* from *Yerushalmi Sanhedrin* 1:2].

19. **the scribe of the general of the army**—*who knew the number of every city, how many men it sends forth to the army* [*Rashi*].

who would muster out the people of the land—By his orders, each city would muster out the required number of soldiers [*Mezudath David, Redak*].

20. **to the king of Babylonia**—Heb. עַל *on,* instead of the usual אֶל,

כג וישמעו כל־שרי החילים המה
והאנשים כי־הפקיד מלך־בבל את־
גדליהו ויבאו אל־גדליהו המצפה
וישמעאל בן־נתניה ויוחנן בן־קרח
ושריה בן־תנחמת הנטפתי ויאזניהו
בן־המעכתי המה ואנשיהם: כד וישבע
להם גדליהו ולאנשיהם ויאמר להם
אל־תיראו מעבדי הכשדים שבו
בארץ ועבדו את־מלך בבל וייטב לכם:
כה ויהי בחדש השביעי בא ישמעאל
בן־נתניה בן־אלישמע מזרע המלוכה
ועשרה אנשים אתו ויכו את־גדליהו
וימת ואת־היהודים ואת־הכשדים

שפן: כג ושמעו כל רבני חילותא אינון וגבריהון ארי מני עליהון מלכא דבבל ית גדליה ואתו לות גדליה למצפיא וישמעאל בר נתניה ויוחנן בר קרח ושריה בר תנחמת דמנטופה ויאזניה בר מעכת אינון וגבריהון: כד וקיים להון גדליה ולגבריהון ואמר להון לא תדחלון מעבדי כסדאי תבו בארעא ופלחו ית מלכא דבבל ויטב לכון: כה והוה בירחא שביעאה אתא ישמעאל בר נתניה בר אלישמע מזרעא דמלכותא ועסרא גברין עמיה ומחו ית גדליה ומית וית יהודאי וית

ת"א כה ישמעאל. (הוריות ח):

רש"י

(כג) כל שרי החילים. שיצאו מן העיר להחבא במחילות ובטינריס ובצורים וביערים:

רד"ק

אומר חמשה וכתוב אחד אומר שבע' להביא שני סופרי הדיינין: המצביא את עם הארץ. שעל פיו היו יוצאים העם לצבא:

מנחת שי

המסורת וכמ"ש במלכים ב' י"ז וכן כתב רש"י שם הע"פ שלא כתב כן ברים פרשת שמות על פסוק וייטב אלהים ובהיכה על פסוק וירב בבת יהודה: (כג) אל גדליהו המצפה. בספר א' כ"י המצפתה ובמה נתחלף לו בין זה דמלכים ובין אותו של ירמיה בסימן מ' ובמקרא גדולה כתיב על זה בספר מוגה. ובלשון הזה מצאתי בספר כ"י ור"ל שכן ראוי להיות המצפה ולא המצפתה עוד יש ראיה ממסרה הגדולה שבמערכת מ"ס נמסר ו' המצפתה ולא נמנה זה בתוכם. והוי יודע שמסרה זו צריכה תיקון מחסרון יוכל להמנות שבדי בירמיה סימן הנ"ל יש עוד ב' המצפתה ויבאו ארץ יהודה אל גדליהו המצפתה והסימן

מצודת דוד

אנשיה לצאת במלחמה: מעם הארץ. מהמכובדים שבהם אשר נמצאו בעיר ולא ברחו: (כג) והאנשים. אשר היו עמהם: המצפה. מקום מושב גדליהו: וישמעאל וגו'. גם ישמעאל וגו' באו אליו עם אנשיהם: (כד) וישבע להם. גדליהו נשבע להשרים ההם שאין להם לפחוד מן הכשדים כי לא יקחם בשבי: ועבדו. במס: (כה) מזרע המלוכה. כאומר בעבור זה הרג לגדליהו בחשבו שאליו ראוי הממשלה כי הוא מזרע המלוכה ולא לגדליה: ואת היהודים. גם היהודים והכשדים שהיו עם גדליה הרג ישמעאל ואנשיו:

מצודת ציון

ונזכרות: (כג) החילים. לצאות עם:

by the Chaldees, since he was authorized by the king to be the guardian of the people, and could prevent any attempted attack on them. He instructed them to till the soil in the towns they had occupied.

Undoubtedly, had Gedaliah remained alive, Jews from the neighboring countries, those who had been exiled, would surely have returned to Judea, and a new community would have flourished. Since Gedaliah was assassinated, however, this community never reached fruition [*Abarbanel*].

25. **in the seventh month**—*Redak* Jer. 41:1, explains this as "on the seventh New Moon." Hence Gedaliah was assassinated on the first day of Tishri, on *Rosh Hashanah*. In

23. And all the officers of the armies, they and the men, heard that the king of Babylonia had appointed Gedaliah, and they came to Gedaliah to Mizpah, and Ishmael the son of Nethaniah and Johanan the son of Kareach and Seraiah the son of Tanhumeth the Netophathite, and Jaazaniah the son of the Maachathite, they and their men. 24. And Gedaliah swore to them and to their men, and said to them, "Fear not the servants of the Chaldeans; dwell in the land and serve the king of Babylonia, and it will go well with you." 25. And it was in the seventh month that Ishmael the son of Nethaniah the son of Elishama of the royal descent, came with ten men with him, and they struck down Gedaliah and he died, and the Judeans and the Chaldeans

leave the land, now they went into exile of their own free will. Hence the simple conjugation of the verb גלה, *to go in exile* [*Daath Soferim*].

22. **who remained in the land . . ., whom Nebuchadnezzar . . . had left over**—I.e. those who preferred to remain in the land, and whom Nebuchadnezzar allowed to remain—those who would pose no threat to his authority [*Daath Soferim*].

23. **all the officers of the armies**—*who had vacated the city to hide in the strongholds and in the boulders and in the rocks* (sic) *and in the forests* [*Rashi*].

Rashi's wording appears redundant. *Kara* words it, *in the strongholds and in the towns.*

24. **And Gedaliah swore to them . . .**—They feared that Gedaliah, being an appointee of Nebuchadnezzar, would disclose their whereabouts to him. Since they had fled from the Chaldees, they feared for their lives. Consequently, Gedaliah swore to them that they had nothing to fear from the Chaldees as long as they would serve them and not revolt [*K'li Y'kar*].

"Fear not the servants of the Chaldeans—Since they lived in constant fear of the Chaldeans, that they would attack them and kill them, Gedaliah swore to them that they would be protected from the Chaldeans, and that they need not fear them or their servants [*Abarbanel*].

In Jeremiah 40:9, the version is, "Do not be afraid of serving the Chaldeans." I.e. do not fear that they will place undue burdens upon you [*Mezudath David* ad loc.].

In Jer. 40, the prophet elaborates on the event of the assassination of Gedaliah. Gedaliah promised to remain in Mizpah, where he would protect the people from any attack

אשר־היו אתו במצפה: כו ויקמו כל־
העם מקטן ועד־גדול ושרי החילים
ויבאו מצרים כי יראו מפני כשדים:
כז ויהי בשלשים ושבע שנה לגלות
יהויכין מלך־יהודה בשנים עשר חדש
בעשרים ושבעה לחדש נשא אויל
מרדך מלך בבל בשנת מלכו את־
ראש יהויכין מלך־יהודה מבית כלא:
כח וידבר אתו טבות ויתן את־כסאו
מעל כסא המלכים אשר אתו בבבל:
כט ושנא את בגדי כלאו ואכל לחם

וית כסדאי דהוו עמיה במצפיא: כו וקמו כל עמא מזעירא ועד רבא ורבני חילותא ואתו למצרים ארי דחילו מן קדם כסדאי: כז והוה בתלתין ושבע שנין לגלות יהויכין מלך שבטא דבית יהודה בתרי עשר ירחין בעשרין ושבעא לירחא רבי אויל מרודך מלכא דבבל בשנת ממלכיה ית ריש יהויכין מלך שבטא דבית יהודה מבית אסירי: כח ומליל עמיה פתגמין תקנין ויהב ית כורסיה עיל מן כורסי מלכיא די עמיה בבבל: כט ושני ית לבושי אסוריה ואכיל לחמא תדירא

רש"י

(כז) **נשא אויל מרודך.** שמת נבוכדנצר ומלך אויל מרודך תחתיו: **בעשרים ושבעה לחודש.** (ובירמיה נ"ב ל"א) הוא אומר בעשרים וחמשה אלא בעשרים וחמשה מת נבוכדנצר ונקבר בעשרים וששה בעשרים ושבעה הוציאו אויל מרודך מקברו וגררוהו בשביל לבטל גזירותיו כמו שנא' בישעיה (סי' י"ד י"ט) ואתה השלכת מקברך כנצר נתעב וגו': (כח) **וידבר אתו טובות.** דברי נחומים:

רד"ק

(כז) בעשרים ושבעה לחדש נשא אויל מרודך. שמת נבוכדנצר ומלך אויל מרודך בני ובירמיה אומר בעשרים וחמשה פירשו רז"ל בכ"ה מת נבוכדנצר בכ"ו נקבר בכ"ז הוציאו אויל מרודך בני מקברו כי פחד שמא ישוב עדיין כמו שעשה אחר שנטרד ודר עם החיו' והמית בן אהד שהמליכו תחתיו ובקצ' הנסחאות בדרש כתוב אויל מרודך הוא שהמליכו תחתיו וכששב נבוכדנצר ומצאו על כסאו נתנו בבית האסורי' ועכשיו פחד אויל מרודך אולי ישוב ויהרגהו והוציאו מקברו לראות אם מת בלא ספק לקיים עליו מ"ש ואתה השלכת מקברך כנצר נתעב: (כט) ושנא.

מנחת שי

נ"ל ח' המלפחה וכו על כל אחד מהם נמסר ח': (כט) ושנא. באל"ף (ודירמיה) בה"א מסורת תילים יו"ד ומכלול דף ק"י קמ"ד ובברשים שרש שנה: ואכל לחם.

רלב"ג

(כו) כי יראו מפני כשדים. על שהומתו הכשדים שהיו עם גדליה והומת גדליה אשר מנה אותו מלך בבל על שארית הגולה: (כז) ויהי בשלשים ושבע שנה לגלות יהויכין. לפי שזה היתה השנה הראשונה מלכות אויל מרודך וכבר היה גלות יהויכין בשנה השמיני לנבוכדנצר למדנו שנבוכדנצר מלך מ"ד שנה. והנה אמר פה בכ"ז לחדש ובספר ירמיה בעשרים וחמשה וידמה כי בכ"ה לחדש היה זה המעשה ולא נשלם עד עשרים ושבעה לחדש והנה אמרו רבותינו ז"ל כי אויל מרודך רצה לנסות אם מת אביו קודם שימלוך כי היה ירא ממנו מאד ולזה השליכו מקברו לדעת אם הוא מת כמו שכתוב ואתה השלכת מקברך כנצר נתעב ואמנם היה ירא אויל מרודך ממנו כי כשנטרד נבוכדנצר והוסר ממנו שכלו המליכו אויל מרודך כי כן היה ראוי בלי ספק וכאשר שב לדעתו ומלאו מולך שמהו בית האסורין ואולי קבלה היתה בידם: (כט) ואכל

מצודת ציון

(כז) נשא. הגביה והרים: מבית כלא. מבית המאסר כמו ובבתי כלאים החבאו (ישעיה מב): (כח) מעל. ממעל: (כט) ושנא. כמו ושנה בה"א והוא מענין חלוף ותמורה: כלאו. מאסרו:

מצודת דוד

(כו) כי יראו. פן יאמרו הכשדים אשר בעלתם נהרג גדליה פקיד המלך והכשדים אשר עמו: (כז) בעשרים ושבעה. ובירמיה (נ"ב) נאמר בעשרים וחמשה כי בכ"ה מת נ"נ שטני ובכ"ו נקבר והוציאהו אויל מרודך בנו מקברו וגררו בחוצות להודיע לכל שמת ובכ"ז מלך ונשא את ראש יהויכין: מבית כלא. ר"ל מיד כשהוציאו מבית הכלא נשאו וגדלו: (כח) טובות. דברים טובים ונחומים: מעל. עליון לכסאי שאר המלכים אשר היו עמו: (כט) ושנא. היה משנה את בגדיו אשר ישב בהן בבית הכלא להחליפם באחרות: לחם. כל הסעודה קרויה ע"ש

persuaded Ishmael to assassinate Gedaliah. Ishmael consented to do so because of his own jealousy toward Gedaliah. Johanan the son of Kareah warned Gedaliah of the imminent peril and offered to slay Ishmael. Gedaliah, however, would not suspect anyone of doing wrong, and refused to allow Johanan to assassinate Ishmael [*Abarbanel*].

and they struck down Gedaliah— not in battle, but at a festive meal on Rosh Hashanah [*Abarbanel*].

and the Judeans and the Chal-

who were with him at Mizpah. 26. And all the people, young and old, and the officers of the armies, got up and came to Egypt, because they were afraid of the Chaldeans. 27. And it was in the thirty-seventh year of the exile of Jehoiachin king of Judah, in the twelfth month, on the twenty-seventh day of the month, that Evil-merodach, king of Babylonia, in the year of his coronation, lifted up the head of Jehoiachin, king of Judah and released him from prison. 28. And he spoke with him kindly and placed his throne above the throne of the kings who were with him in Babylon. 29. And he changed his prison garb, and he ate meals

order to avoid fasting on *Rosh Hashanah,* the fast commemmorating his death was proclaimed for the day following the festival.

Ishmael the son of Nethaniah—Since we know nothing of his father, we assume that just as he was wicked, so was his father [*Megillah* 15a].

of the royal descent—of the house of David. He was jealous of Gedaliah's position, which he believed, should rightfully have belonged to him since he was of royal descent. The Rabbis, however, identify Gedaliah's grandfather, Elishama with the Elishama mentioned in I Chron. 2:41. In v. 26, it is mentioned that Jerachmeal, the first-born of Hezron, married a woman named Atarah, a gentile woman whom he took to "crown himself with." Hence the name Atarah, a *crown.* She was of a royal family, into which Jerachmeal married to gain prestige. She was a forebear of Ishmael. Thus, he was descended from proselytes [*Redak,* Jer. 41:16 from *Yerushalmi San.* 2:3].

The source of this statement that she was of royal descent is not found there. *Pseudo-Rashi,* I Chron. 2:26, cites *Yerushalmi Yebamoth.* This source, too, is unknown to us.

In addition to Ishmael's descent from proselytes, we find among his forebears an emancipated Egyptian slave, named Jarha (I Chron. 2:35), which is considered a stigma and valid grounds to doubt his veracity for fifteen or sixteen generations [*Pseudo-Rashi* ibid. from *Yerushalmi* end of *Horioth*].

He goes on to quote a Midrash, which states that Ishmael was called "*mizera hameluchah*" because he gave of his children to *Molech,* not because he was descended from the royal family. This Midrash is unknown to us.

Jeremiah relates that Ishmael was sent by Baalis, king of Ammon, who was opposed to a governor being appointed by Nebuchadnezzar. He

תמיד לפניו כל ימי חייו: ל וארחתו ארחת תמיד נתנה לו מאת המלך דבר יום ביומו כל ימי חיו:

קדמוהי כל יומי חיוהי: ל ושירותיה שירות תדירא מתיהבא ליה מן קדם מלכא פתגם יום ביומיה כל יומי חיוהי:

ת"א וארוחתו. סנהדרין מח (קדושין ה):

סכום פסוקי של ספר מלכים אלף וחמש מאות ושלשים וארבעה וסימנו **אשרי הגוי** אשר ה' אלהיו. וסדריו שלשי' וחמשה וסימנו חן חן **לה** (ואצלנו מ"ז) וקאפיטולין שבספר ראשון כ"ב סימן **בך** יברך ישראל וספר שני כ"ה. סימן **כה** תברכו את בני ישראל. בין הכל מ"ז. והסימן **יזל** מים מדליו:

רד"ק

באל"ף במקו' ה"א ושל ירמיהו כתיב בה"א: לפניו. לא לפניו ועל שולחנו שהרי אומר ארוחת תמיד נתנה לו מאת המלך דבר יום ביומו: (ל) כל ימי חייו. ימי חייו של יהויכין ובדברי רז"ל רב ולוי חד אמר ימי חייו של אויל מרודך וחד אמר ימי חייו של יהויכין ומסתברא כמאן דאמר ימי חייו של יהויכין שכשהקב"ה נותן שלו' לצדיקים אינו נוטל' מהם אלא הולכת עמה' לגן עדן:

מנחת שי

ואכל מלרע שלא כמנהג. מכלול שקל **פָּעַל** וכן חברו דירמיה: (ל) כל ימי חיו. ביו"ד אחת בלבד והוא חד מן ד' הסרים על פי המסורת אבל כל ימי חייו שבפסוק הקודם בשני יודי"ן כי לא בא במנין החסרים. וכן מלאתי במקצת ספרים ובמקצת שניהם מלאים והמסורת חולקת עליהם: ה' יקיים בנו מקרא שכתוב יחיינו מימים ביום השלישי יקמנו ונחיה לפניו ונדעה ונרדפה לדעת את ה' כשחר נכון מוצאו וגו':

רלב"ג

להם תמיד לפניו. אחשוב כי הוא היה מאוכלי שולחנו ועכ"ז היה שולח לו ארוחה ומשאת לפרנס ב"ב ואפשר שהוא לא היה מאוכלי שולחנו ואמר שהוא אוכל לחם תמיד לפניו כי אללו היה בבית או סמוך לו: (ל) כל ימי חייו. אפשר ששב אל יהויכין ואפשר ששב אל אויל מרודך ואין לנו הכרע בזה ואין אללנו ספורים מדברי אויל מרודך ומקרהו בחייו שנוכל לעמוד בבירור על זה מהם. הנה זה הוא מה שראינו שיצטרך אל ביאור בזאת הפרשה שהגבלנו באורה בזה המקום: ואולם התועלת המגיעות מאלו הספורים הנה הם אלו: הראשון לבאר מדרך העדות שהש"י משגיח על אישי המין האנושי לענוש הרשעים על רשעם ולגמול טוב לצדיקים על צדקם ולזה ספר כי מפני שעשה יהואחז בן יהוא הרע בעיני ה' חרה אף ה' בישראל ונתנם ביד חזאל מלך ארם וביד בנו עד שלא השאיר חזאל ליהואחז כי אם חמשים פרשים ועשרה רכב ועשרת אלפים רגלי' ולזה גם כן ספר כי ההצלחה שהיתה ליואש בן יהואחז על מלך ארם לא היתה כי אם מפני ברית הש"י עם האבות כי בזולת זה תוספר בריתו עם האבות כמו שזכרנו בביאורנו בזה המקום עם מה שעזר בזה אלישע על דרך המופת במה שלוה ליואש לקחת קשת וחצים כי מההשגחה הדבקה לנביא נמשכה אז ההשגחה לישראל בתפלתו ולזה גם כן ספר כי תכף שמת אלישע פשטו גדודי מואב על ארץ ישראל כי בזכותו היו נצולים מזה בחייו ולזה גם כן ספר כי אמציה בעשות הישר בעיני ה' הצליח במלחמה והכה את אדום בגיא מלח י' אלפים ומן אז עבד לאלהי אדום והשתחוה להם וקטר להם נפל ביד אויביו הוא ויהודה עמו וקשרו עליו קשר בירושלים והמיתוהו ולזה גם כן ספר שההצלחה שהיתה לירבעם בן יואש מלך ישראל היתה בעבור ברית השם עם האבות שלא ימחה שם ישראל מתחת השמים ולזה ג"כ ספר כי עוזיה נצטרע מפני החטא שעשה בגשתו אל המזבח להקטיר כמו שנזכר בד"ה ובראשונה כאשר עשה הישר בעיני ה' הצליח במלחמות מאד ובכל ענינו כמו שנזכר בד"ה ולזה גם כן ספר שזכריהו בן ירבעם לא מלך כי אם ששה חדשים ונהרג מפני עשותו הרע בעיני ה' ומפני חטא אבותיו ולא המית אבותיו בזה האופן כי דבר ה' היה שיהיו ליהוא בנים רבעים על כסא ישראל לזה גם כן ספר כי מנחם בן גדי מפני עשותו הרע בעיני ה' קשר עליו פקח בן רמליהו והרגו ולזה גם כן ספר כי פקח מפני עשותו הרע בעיני ה' בא עליו מלך אשור ולקח הרבה מעריו והגלה יושביהם לאשור ומפני זה גם כן קשר עליו הושע בן אלה והרגו ולזה גם כן ספר כי מפני שעשה יותם הישר בעיני ה' שכב עם אבותיו קודם שישלח ה' ביהודה רצין מלך ארם ופקח בן רמליהו וזה היה בעבור חטא העם כי עם יהודה היו משחיתים כמו שנזכר בספר ד"ה ולזה גם כן ספר פה ובד"ה כי מפני שעשה אחז הרע בעיני ה' והפליג בזה הנה בא עליו רע נפלא על יד רצין ופקח וזולתם כמו שנזכר בספר ד"ה ולזה ג"כ ספר כי מפני שעשה הושע בן אלה את הרע בעיני ה' ומפני החטאים שעשו עליהם מלכי ישראל בכללם הנה בא קץ הכרתת ישראל מעל אדמתם ולזה עלה עליו מלך אשור ובאחרית הדבר לכד שמרון ויגל את ישראל אשורה וזכר אחר זה כי זה היה מפני החטאים הנפלאים שהתמידו בהם כל המלכים והעם וזה שהם מאסו את ברית הש"י וכל עדותיו אשר העיד בהם ועזבו כל מצותיו ולא אבו שמוע לדברי הנביאים המוכיחים אותם ולזה היה רבליתם לזה הרע הנפלא כמו שיעדה התורה ולזה גם כן ספר שהש"י שלח האריות להמית העם אשר הביא מלך אשור בעם שומרון עד התקרבו לעבודת ה' קצת התקרבו' ולזה ג"כ ספר כי מפני שהפליג חזקיה לעשות הישר בעיני ה' וביער מן הארץ כל מה שיש בו רושם להסיר ישראל מאחרי ה' הצליח הצלחות רבות ועשה לו הש"י מופתים נפלאים והטיב לו בזה שהוא יצא מעבודת מלך אשור והכה את הפלשתים מכה רבה ונמלט מסנחריב מלך אשור שהיה מולך בכל הממלכות בזה האופן הנפלא שנזכר בזה הספור והוסיף הש"י על ימיו ט"ו שנה ורפאו מחליו הכבד בקלות רב עד שביום הג' עלה בבית ה' ולזאת הסבה ספר כי מפני שנתן חזקיהו כבוד לעצמו במה שהראה למלאכי מלך בבל נכבוד עשרו ולא נתן הכבוד לש"י לפרסם להם גדולות הש"י מצד המופת שהיה בארץ אשר באו לדרוש עליו כמו שנזכר בספר ד"ה הנה היה קצף ה' עליו אלא שלא היה הרע בימיו מפני התהלכו את הש"י תמיד רק בזה הדבר לבד חטא ולזה ג"כ ספר כי מפני שחטא מנשה זה החטא הנפלא בע"ג ושפיכות דמים נגזר על מלכות יהודה לגלות מעל האדמה אשר נתן להם ה' כמו שגלו עשרת השבטים והנה ספר בד"ה שכבר עשה מנשה תשובה אחרי נתנו ה' ביד מלך אשור ואסר אותו ושמהו בבית כלא ולזה לא נהיה הרע בימיו והאריך ימיו על ממלכתו אך אמון בנו שהלך בדרכיו הרעים הנך בלא חמדה ולא מלך כ"א שתי שנים וקשרו עליו והכוהו והמיתוהו כאילו היה זה להשגחת הש"י על יהודה ובנימין שלא יכשלו בחטאיו ולזה ג"כ ספר כי יאשיה מפני שעשה הישר בעיני ה' השגיח בו הש"י שלא היה

מצודת דוד

לחם: לפניו. ר"ל עמו יחד: כל ימי חייו. של יהויכין: (ל) וארחתו ארחת תמיד. פרס הנתונה לו היתה פרס הנתונה תמיד מבלי הפסק והיה לנאכל לאנשי ביתו כי הוא בעצמו אכל לחם לפני המלך תמיד: דבר יום ביומו. דבר הצריך לו בכל יום נתנו לו ביומו ולא העבירו המועד:

מצודת ציון

(ל) וארחתו. הוא ענין פרס קבוע וכן ארחה ומשאת (ירמיה מ):

experienced a flow of blood as red as a rose. Immediately, he took heed and did not touch her until she left, counted the required number of days, and immersed herself. This was the indication that Jehoiachin repented of the sins he had committed in Jerusalem. Consequently, God forgave all his sins, and he was then considered a righteous man [*K'li Y'kar*].

before him regularly all the days of his life. 30. And his meals, regular meals were given him from the king, each day's need in its day, all the days of his life.

deans—Not only did he slay Gedaliah, but also the Judeans and the Chaldeans who accompanied him [*Abarbanel*].

26. **And came to Egypt**—After taking counsel of Jeremiah and hearing his prophecy that they should remain in Eretz Israel, they, nevertheless, lacked courage, and fled to Egypt where they deemed themselves safe from the vengeance of Nebuchadnezzar. Alas, they were sadly mistaken, for Nebuchadnezzar conquered Egypt, and destroyed the remnant of Israel that was found there. This is recorded in detail in the Book of Jeremiah 41–46.

27. **Evil-Merodach . . . lifted**—*for Nebuchadnezzar died, and Evil-Merodach reigned in his stead* [*Rashi*].

on the twenty-seventh day of the month—*In Jeremiah* (52:31), *Scripture states, "On the twenty-fifth." Rather, on the twenty-fifth Nebuchadnezzar died. He was buried on the twenty-sixth. On the twenty-seventh, Evil-Merodach removed him from his grave and dragged him about, in order to nullify his decrees, as it is said, "and you have been cast out of your grave like a despised sapling* . . . (Is. 14:19) [*Rashi* from *Seder Olam*].

This is elaborated upon in *Lev. Rabbah,* 18:2. When Nebuchadnezzar lived with the beasts for seven years, Evil-Merodach his son occupied his throne. When he was restored to his human state, he returned to find his son sitting on his throne, and he imprisoned him. This time, when Nebuchadnezzar died, the people came to Evil-Merodach and again offered him the throne. He replied, "This time I will not listen to you. The first time, I listened to you, and my father took me and imprisoned me. Now, he will kill me." He did not believe them until they removed him from his grave and dragged him and cast him before him, as it is said . . . [*Redak*].*

28. **And he spoke with him kindly**—words of consolation [*Rashi, Mezudath David*].

30. **all the days of his life**—In the Midrash (*Sam.* 18) there is a dispute between Rav and Levi. One takes this to mean all the days of Evil-Merodach, and one maintains that it means all the days of Jehoiachin. The Midrash concludes that it means all the days of Jehoiachin, because when the Holy One, Blessed be He, grants tranquility to the righteous, He does not take it away from them, but it accompanies them to Paradise [*Redak* from *Mid. Sam. 18*].

Although Jehoiachin was considered wicked above 24:9, "And he did what was evil in the eyes of the Lord, like all that his father had done," he is now deemed a *zaddik* because he repented of his sins while in prison. The Midrash (*Lev. Rabbah* 19) relates that Nebuchadnezzar's queen arranged a conjugal visit for Jehoiachin. His wife was lowered through the roof of the prison. When she alighted in his prison cell, she told him that she had

הרע שנגזר על יהודה וירושלים בימיו אך נהי' בימי בניו וכבר מת על ידי פרעה נכה בעבור אשמת ישראל ולזה גם כן ספר מה שקרה מהרע לבני יאשיהו כלם מפני עשייתם הרע בעיני ה' עד שכבר השליך הש"י בחטאיהם יהודה ובנימין מעל פניו והחריב ירושלים ובית המקדש יהי רצון שיבנה במהרה בימינו : השני הוא להודיע שאף על פי שישראל חוטאים לש"י הנה תדבק ההשגחה בהם מצד האבות הקדושים באופן שלא ישמידם ולזה ספר כי מפני ראות הש"י את לחץ ישראל על יד חזאל שהיה כשעור שיכלם לולי ה' שהיה להם כי לא השאיר ליהואחז עם כי אם מתי מספר הנה חנן הש"י אותם ורחמם ופנה אליהם למען בריתו את אברהם את יצחק ואת יעקב והציל אותם מכף חזאל ובזה נתבאר כי כמו שההשגחה הכוללת תמשך מהאב לזרעו זמן ארוך כן הענין בהשגחה הפרטית אבל היא יותר אמתית בזה ולזה נתבאר מן התורה שלא יכלה שבט מן השבטים. השלישי לפרסם דבר המופתים המתחדשים על יד הנביא כי באמונתם קיום פנת התורה ולזה זכר ענין הנבואה וההצלחה שנתחדשה ליואש עם הלחמו על ארם מפני מה ששם הנביא ידיו על ידי המלך שהיו על הקשת ומספר החצים שירה אז כן היה מספר המלחמות שהצליח בם והכה את ארם ובאמר לו הנבי' שאם היה מכה מהחצים באלן פעמים יותר היה מכה ארם פעמים יותר כאילו התבאר מזה שההצלחה בשעה. לו על דרך מופת מהנביא מפני שומו ידיו על ידיו בהכאות ההם שהיה משל להכאות ארם ולזה גם כן ספר שהאיש שקברו בנגעו בעצמות אלישע חיה וקם על רגליו בעבור כבוד אלישע והנה זה המופת היה נפלא מאד ולזה ג"כ ספר מה שנגע הש"י המלך עוזיהו בצרעת בעלותו על המזבח להקטיר ולזה גם כן ספר מה ששלח הש"י האריות להמית השמרונים עד שהסכימו לעבוד את ה' באופן מה והתקרבו קירוב מה לעבודתו ולזה ג"כ ספר המופת הנפלא שעשה הש"י בנגפו חיל מלך אשור שהיה מתפאר על הש"י עד שבלילה ההוא מת חיל מלך אשור על יד מלאך ה' והוא שב לארצו ושם סבב הש"י שהכוהו בניו בחרב והרגוהו כמו שייעד ע"י נביאו ולזה ג"כ ספר מה שרפא הש"י על דרך המופת את חזקיה מחליו אשר היה ראוי שימות בו וענין המופת שעשה בהשבתו הצל אחורנית י' מעלות : הרביעי הוא לפרסם קיום ייעודי השם יתברך על יד נביאו ולזה ספר הרע שעשה חזאל לישראל כמו שייעד הש"י לאליהו וזכר אלישע זה הייעוד לחזאל בעת שלא היה מלך ונתבאר מזה הספור שכן היה הענין בסוף כמו שייעד אלישע ולזה זכר ג"כ שכבר ייעד אלישע שלש פעמים יכה יהואש את ארם ושכן היה הענין בסוף ולזה זכר גם כן מירבעם בן יואש שהוא השיב את גבול ישראל מלבא חמת עד ים הערבה כמו שייעד הנביא יונה ולזה ג"כ ספר שהיו ליהוא בנים רבעים על כסא ישראל כמו שייעד לו הש"י על יד נביאו וספר ג"כ רוב הרעות שבאו לישראל שכבר ייעד אותם אחיה לאשת ירבעם באמרו והכה ה' את ישראל כאשר ינוד הקנה במים ונתש את ישראל מעל האדמה הטובה ונתבאר ג"כ מזה הספור ששבט ראובן והנספחים אליו גלו ראשונה ואל זה רמז בתורה באומר יחי ראובן ואל ימות ויהי מתיו מספר כמו שביארנו שם ולזה ג"כ זכר שכבר הסיר הש"י את ישראל מעל פניו כאשר דבר ביד כל עבדיו הנביאים ולזה ג"כ זכר שכבר ייעד הש"י בסנחריב שכבר ישמע שמועה ושב לארצו ויפול בחרב בארצו ושלא יבא אל ירושלים ולא יורה שם חץ ולא יקדמנה מגן ולא ישפוך עליה סוללה וכן היה הענין בסוף ולזה ג"כ זכר שכבר ייעד הנביא שירפא ה' לחזקיה ויוסיף על ימיו ט"ו שנה וכן היה ולזה ג"כ זכר שכבר ייעד ישעיה לחזקיה הנה ימים באים ונשא את כל אשר בביתו ואשר אצרו אבותיו בבלה ומבניו אשר יוליד יהיו סריסים בהיכל מלך בבל וכן היה הענין בסוף ולזה ג"כ זכר מה שדבר הש"י ביד עבדיו הנביאים על חטא מנשה שיבין מן הרעה על יהודה וירושלם מה שנתאמת בזה הספור שכבר באה להם הרעה ההיא ולזה ג"כ ספר שכבר עשה יאשיהו מה שייעד הנביא אשר בא מיהודה שכבר ישרף יאשיהו על המזבח ההוא עצמות אדם: החמישי הוא להודיע שאין ראוי שיתחבר הרשע עם הצדיק אפילו אחר המות ולזה ספר שכאשר קבר איש בקבר אלישע הנה תכף שנגע בעצמותיו חיה וקם על רגליו כי לא רצה הש"י שיהיה רשע נקבר אצל צדיק : הששי הוא להודיע שאין ראוי לענוש הבנים על חטא האבות ולא האבות על הבנים ולזה ספר שבני המכים לא המית ככתוב בספר תורת משה לא יומתו אבות על בנים ובנים לא יומתו על האבות : השביעי הוא להודיע שאין ראוי שיתגאה האדם בדבר המלחמה ויעורר מדנים מפני ראותו שכבר הצליח במלחמה מה כי כבר אפשר שינוצח במלחמה הזאת אע"פ שכבר הצליח במלחמה האחרת ולזה ספר כי אמציה שעורר מדנים ליהואש מפני מה שראה מהצלחתו על האדומיים במלחמה נפל בידו הוא ויהודה עמו ולזאת הסבה ג"כ ספר ענין הגאוה שאמר יהואש לאמציה שכבר אמר לו שיפול הוא ויהודה עמו ונמשך לו מזה שכבר חיה אמציה אחר יהואש ט"ו שנה : השמיני הוא להודיע שאין ראוי להתחרות במצליח דרכו ולזה ספר מה שקרה מהרע לישראל בעבור שמרדו מלכיהם במלכים המצליחים אשר היו נותנים מס להם כי זה היה סבת החורבן והגלות ולזה ספר שכבר מצא מלך אשור בהושע קשר ולזה צר על שומרון והגלה ישר' מעל אדמתם ולזאת הסבה ג"כ זכר כי חזקיה בראותו כי מלך אשור תפש כל הערים. הבצורות אשר ליהודה נכנע אליו ועבדו וזהו אמרו חטאתי שוב מעלי את אשר תתן עלי אשא ולזה ג"כ ספר כי כבר היו ישראל בסכנה גדולה בימי חזקיה מלך יהודה מפני מרדו במלך אשור לולא ה' שהיה לו ולזאת הסבה ג"כ זכר מרד יהויקים בנבוכדנצר שהיה סבה אל שהגלה שם כל ביתו ובנו יהויכין ועמו גלו היותר נכבדים שבירושל' ולזאת הסבה ג"כ זכר מרד צדקיה במלך בבל שהיה סבה לחרבן ירושל' ולגלות יהודה מעל אדמתו ולזאת הסבה ג"כ זכר כי יהויכין מפני ששם צוארו תחת עול מלך בבל היתה לו נפשו לשלל וממנו לבד נשארו בנים לבית יאשיהו והנה היה זרובבל בן שאלתיאל מזרעו כמו שנזכר בספר ד"ה ואחר מות נבוכדנצר נשא אויל מרודך את ראש יהויכין והוציאהו מבית כלא ונתן כסאו מעל כסא המלכים אשר אתו בבבל : התשיעי הוא להודיע כי זה הרע הנפלא שהביא הש"י על עשרת השבטים לא הביאו עליהם כי אם אחרי הפליגם בעשיית הרע מאד. עד שכבר מאסו כל מצות הש"י ועדותיו ועזבום ועבדו אלהים אחרים בכל מקומותיה' ועשו פעולות היותר מגונות והיותר רעות שיוכלו לעשות ולא קבלו מוסר מדברי הש"י על יד נביאיו שהעיד בהם כל הרע שהיה בא עליהם קודם בואו מפני עזבם ברית הש"י והיה זה סבה שמאס הש"י בכל זרע ישראל ויענה אותם במיני ענוים כמו הרעב ומה שידמה לו ואחר זה נתנם ביד שוסים ובוזזים אותם ולבסוף השליכם מעל פניו כמו שנזכר בקללות הכתובות בתורה : העשירי הוא להודיע כי מה שימשך ממנו רע אע"פ שכוון לתכלית טוב ראוי להרחיקו ואע"פ שגודל ענינו על יד השלם שבאנשים וכל שכן כשהיה מביא לעבוד עבודת אלילים הלא תראה כי נחש הנחשת שנעשה במצות הש"י ע"י משה רבינו להציל הנשוכים כשיראו אותו כתת אותו חזקיה בראותו שהיו ישראל תועים אחריו : האחד עשר הוא להודיע שהוא ראוי שיקרע האדם בגדיו בשמעו חלול השם הנכבד ולזה ספר שקרעו בגדיהם שומעי אלו החרופים והגדופין מפי רבשקה וגם חזקיה קרע בגדיו כששמע זה מפי שלוחיו ששלח שם אל רבשקה : השנים עשר הוא להודיע כי אחת מן התחבולות הטובות למלחמה הוא להפחיד אנשי המלחמה ולזה אמר רבשקה כי אדניו שלחו בעבור האנשים אשר על החומה ליראם ולבהלם : השלשה עשר הוא להודיע שהמלך ימשול בעם בהטבתו להם כי בזה ימשך רצונם אליו וזהו אמרו עשו אתי ברכה וצאו אלי ואכלו איש גפנו ואיש תאנתו : הארבעה עשר הוא להודיע שאין ראוי לאדם שיענה על הדברים שיאמרו לו בעתו' הרעה והצרה אך ישבע בחרפה אולי יתעשת האלהים לו וירחמהו ויצילהו מהצרה ההיא ולזה ספר שלא ענו העם דבר לרבשקה כי מצות המלך היא לאמר לא תענהו : החמשה עשר הוא להודיע כי לעתות בצרה ראוי שיכנע האדם לפני הש"י ויתפלל אליו כדי שירחמהו ויראה בעניו ולזה ספר שכבר התפלל המלך בשק והתפלל לפני הש"י ובקש מישעיה שישא תפלה בעד השארית הנמצאה ולזאת הסבה ג"כ ספר שכבר נכנע יאשיה לפני הש"י וקרע את בגדיו ובכה לפניו על דבר הרע המוכן לבא עליו ועל עמו מאת ה' על חטאת אבותיו : הששה עשר הוא להודיע כי היות הש"י מגיד מראשית אחרית הוא המופת על שהוא פועל הדברים כי לולי זה לא יתכן שיודיע אותם טרם היותם כי איך ידע הוא מה שיפעלהו זולתו : השבעה עשר הוא להודיע כי מהשגחת הש"י בצדיקים ימשך לדחות מעליהם הרע שכבר התחיל לבא כאמרו הן יקטלני לו איחל ולזה ספר שאע"פ שכבר נגזר על חזקיה שימות מחליו החולי הנה שמע הש"י תפלתו ורפא אותו והאריך ימיו חמש עשרה שנה ולזאת הסבה ג"כ ספר שאף על פי שכבר היה נגזר שיבא הרע בימי יאשיהו הנה נעתר לו הש"י והיה שלום ואמת בימיו : השמנה עשר הוא להודיע כי כשנגזר שימשך רע מה מהחטאים מה הנה ראוי לנקות מהחטאים ההם כדי שיסור הרע ההוא ולזה תמצא כי כשידע יאשיהו שהאריך הש"י את הרע עד אחר מותו מפני הכנעו לפניו רצה לנקות ישראל מהחטא ההיא והעמיד כל העם בברית עם הש"י ובער כל האלילים והמזבחות והבמות ומשמשיהם והשבית את הכומרים וזבח כל כהני הבמות אצל המזבחות לא השאיר לע"א שום זכר בישראל ובארצם והנה היה כלי כל זה להסיר הרע לגמרי מישראל כי הייעודים הרעים יסורו בסור החטאים אשר בעבורם היו אף ישראל חטאו אז כמו שזכר הנביא שהיה מוכיח אותם בימי יאשיהו ולזה לא נמשך מזה התכלית שכיון אליו יאשיהו : התשעה עשר הוא להודיע שכהן שעבד עבודת אלילים הוא פסול לעבודה אך הוא אוכל בקדשים עם אחיו הכהנים וזהו אמרו אך לא יעלו כהני הבמות אל מזבח ה' בירושלים כי אם אכלו מצות בתוך אחיהם :

א"ה, מראשית כזאת הודענו (בסוף ספר שופטים ובפתיחתנו לשמואל) כי הפי' מהר"י קרא על ספרי יהושע שופטים ומלכים. לא ישוה עם פירושו על כל הנביאים כולם. כי פירושו באלו הספרים בדרך אחד יהלך עם פירש"י בפירוש המקרא ובסגנון הלשון. ואין ביניהם בעצם הפי' כמלא נימא. ורק במקומות מועטים ישנם בם שנוים קלים אשר שם יתפרדו מעט זה מזה. ויען כי בראשית קרבנו אל מלאכתנו הנכבדה הזאת הי' כל כונתנו אך לעשות צדקה וחסד עם כל דורשי ה'. להכן להם מטעמים למען יתענגו על מי מנוחות פירושי המקראות היותר פשוטים קלים ונאוהים. על כן לא יכולנו לעבור במעוף עין מעל הפי' הזה. מבלי הת מהודו גם על הספרים האלה. ולקטנו פנינים יקרים מתוך הפי'. את הדברים אשר יראו כי שונים הם מפירש"י. בפירושו או בסגנון לשונו. והצגנום יחד בסוף הספר. למען יהיו לאבני נזר להתנוסס לעיני כל מבין בתורת ה'. כי הלומדים אשר ידעו מאוד להוקיר כל הגה קל היוצא מפי אחד הראשונים ישמחו בעל כל הון על הגרגרים האלה. כי שרשם מספר קדמון אשר מחברו הוא עמוד התוך אשר כל בית ישראל נשען עליו. אכן מספר זה והלאה עד תשלים כל הנביאים. תבא הפי' מהר"י קרא במקום יתר המפורשים בפנים הספר. (כאשר בספר שמואל ונוסף עליו ספר ישעי' אשר שם ישתרע הפי' הזה מאוד. יש אשר יכיל על פסוק אחד דף אחד שלם ויש גם שנים) ויתענגו הלומדים כי ימצאו להם כר נרחב להגות בו—ואנחנו נקיה כי נפיק רצון טוב מאת כל הוגה בם. כי ישימו על ראשנו כל יקר יהוד. על פעולתנו הרצויה והטובה מאוד. כן יחננו ה'. ויערב נא דברי תורתו בפינו ובפי צאצאינו. ולא תמיש התורה מפינו ומפי זרעינו וזרע זרעינו עד עולם. אמן:

מהר"י — מלכים א — קרא

א (ע) עין רגל. ת"י קצרא הוא כובס שמתקן בגדי צמר ברגליו על ידי בעיטה. אבן גבוה שהיו עולין עליה לראות למרחוק כשהיו זוחלין מן החיילות. וכן משמעות התרגום: (מ) בחלילים. קלימלי"ש:

ג (ג) רק העם. גנותו העיר הכתוב שדחה לבנות עד ארבע למלכותו וגרם העם להקטיר בבמות:

ה (כ) כצדונים. שכנים לצור היו וממשלתו (על) [של] חירם: (ל) שלשת אלפים ושלש מאות. היו ממונים על מאה וחמשים שכל אחד ואחד ממונה על ארבעים וחמשה והשלש מאות שנוספים וכו' אבל יש לנו לפרש שני מקראות האחרונים בממונים על כולם ולשלמה וכו' וספר מלכים מנה את נציבי הגרים וכו':

ו (א) בחודש זיו. יש אומרים הוא אייר וכו': (ח) ובלולים יעלו על התיכונה. תרג' מסעתא התאים הללו לא היו פתוחים אל החוץ אלא שלשה פתחים לכל אחד ואחד כך וכו' ולולים תרג' יונ' מסיבתא וכו' והעולה בהם דומה לו כמקיף ועולה סביבות וכו': (ט) גבים ושדרות בארזים. שתי וכו' ואני אומר שהם לבנים חלולים כמין חצי קנה חלול שעושין וכו': גבים. לשון גובתא דקניא. והם היו למעלה והשדרות למטה וכו': (טו) מביתה בצלעות ארזים. קירות וכו' שאי אפשר לטוח זהב על האבנים כי אם על העצים ובמסמרות: קירות הספון. תיקרת העלייה: בצלעות ברושים. הקפים לרקבון מליחלוח הקרקעות: (טז) את עשרים אמה מירכתי הבית עשרים שהם מסוף ההיכל והלאה זאף הרצפה של דביר בכלל: (כא) [ברתוקות זהב]. לתלות בהן פרוכת דבבא. שהדלתות שעשה לפתח הדביר אי אפשר לנעול שכן משהכניסו הארון ויאריכו הבדים על ידי נס וכולטין בפתח וקבע שרשרות ממזוזה למזוזה וקבע בהן פרוכת לצניעות ונראין הבדים כשני דדי האשה. כך אמר ר': (כג) עשר אמות קומתו. ורגליהם בקרקע עומדים וכו' סוככים על הארון כולו ארך כנפים. ועל בדיו מקצתו ברחב הכנפים וכו' ובדיו נתונים ארכו בראשו כדי וכו': (כז) ותגע כנף. הכרוב האחד בקיר המערב: וכנף הכרוב השני נוגעת בקיר. מזרחי: (לא) האיל. אילי הפתח וכו' כמין אילים אלה ואלון וכן כל בנין יחזקאל ספות הפתחים קרוין אילים: (לח) בירח בול. הוא מרחשון שהעשב כלה בשדה ובוללין וכו':

ז (ב) וכרותות ארזים. קורות וכו' והטור השני למול טור הראשון ברוחב הבית וכן ארבעת הטורים לסכך הבית ברצפת הבית מטור הראשון אל טור שעל הכרותות לדריסת הרגל הילוך בני אדם ברגל הקרקע: (ג) על הצלעות. מחיצות וכו' קירוי הסיפון ארבעה וחמשה. נסרים היה הסיפון של טורים נסרים על ארבעה טורי עמודים חמשה עשר נסרים הטור ממעל לרצפה עשה מחיצות כותל הבית כנגד כל טור וטור ארבעה כתלים הן הן צלעות ולא הוצרך הכתוב לפרש הרצפה והצלעות שכל כך נתן הכריתות על העמודים להושיב עליהם רצפה וצלעות: (ז) ואולם הכסא. עשה מלכותא דארעא מעין מלכותא דרקיעא. וזהו שיסד הקליר שופט אם ירצה משבת באולם הכסא: (ח) ובית יעשה לבת פרעה. לפנים מאולם הכסא. אמר ר' ולא מאולם הלבנון: (יב) ולחצר בית ה' הפנימית. כבר פירש ויבן את החצר הפנימית שלשה טורי גזית וגו' אלא משבא לומר חצרו ואולם שבנה כענין זה כלל עמהם העזרה שהיתה כמותו:

י (טו) וכל מלכי הערב. תרגם יונתן ומלכי סומכוותא לשון ערובה. המלכים שהיו בערבותו וסומכים עליו.

(כח) ומקוה. אסיפת סוחרי סוסים וכו'. ועוד ראיתי ביסודו של ר' מאיר שליח החסיד זצ"ל ומקוה לשון מיני מעשה אורג. לשון כלי קיואוי. וכן וקורי עכביש מתורגם וקווי לפי שהיו כלי פשתן באים ממצרים כענין שנ' עובדי פשתים שריקות ואורגים חורי ואומר שש ורקמה היה ממצרים ואומר חטובות אטון מצרים:

יא (כז) וירם יד במלך. הוכיחו בדברים:

יג (ד) ותיבש ידו. אם הקב"ה וכו' ובשביל הצדיק יבשה ידו:

יד (י) משתין בקיר. ידע מדע תירגם יונתן. שיודע להשית מחשבה מקירות לבו:

טו (יג) בשנת שלש לאסא. מלך בעשא. שנת שלישית נמנית לאסא ולבעשא:

טז (ז) וגם ביד יהוא בן חנני. דבר ה' אל בעשא. אחרי שמלך אלה בן בעשא גם זאת היה דבר ה' ביד יהוא וכו':

יז (ט) צרפתה. שם העיר. מעשים של צרפית. משל מעשה באחד שגנב נרתיקו של רופא כשהוא יוצא נפלט בנו וחזר אצלו ואמר לו אדוני הרופא רפא את בני אמר לו לך והחזר הנרתק של מיני רפואות נתונים בו וארפא את בנך כך אמר הקב"ה לאליהו התר נדרו של טל שאין המתים חיים אלא בטללים ואני מחיה בנה של צרפית. בברכות ירושלמי: (יב) מעוג. כדי עוגה:

יח (כא) שתי הסעיפים. שתי מחשבות שאינכם מבחינים להכריע וכו': ולא ענו העם אותו דבר. שלא היו יודעין היאך להבחין: (לז) וידעו [וגו'] כי אתה ה'. ואני עבדך ונשתלחתי לבשרם לעתיד לבוא שלא יאמינו כי אם היום לא תענני: (מד) אסור ורד. אסור מרכבתיך ורד מן הכרמל לשוב פן יחזק אותך הגשמים בדרך:

יט (כא) ובכלי הבקר. פר"ש העול והמחרשה והעגלה:

כ (כד) ושים פחות תחתיהם. מתוך שלא יהיו נושאי הרמה יתנו וכו': (כז) התפקדו. הם כלי זיין וכל צרכי המלחמה: וכלכלו. וכו': ויחלטוה. לשון למיתות וכו' וה"א של ויחלטוה נוטה וכו':

כב (לח) והזונות רחצו. והכלי זיין רחצו שהתיז מן הדם כך ת"י וכו': (מח) ומלך אין באדום. מימי דוד השיב הוא המלך וכאן וכו' וימליכו עליהם מלך ופו' כפופים לו ולא היה באדום מלך אלא נציב היה להם במקום מלך: (נב) בשנת שבע עשרה ליהושפט. וכאן הוא אומר וכו' ומצאתי ברוב מלכי ישראל שאינן מדקדקים במנין שנותיהן וכו' וגם שנה של יהושפט לא נמנית בשבע עשרה הללו:

מלכים ב

ב (ח) ויגלום. לא כריכה ממש אלא לוקט שקורין קולקולי"ד: (י) אם תראה אותי לוקח מאתך. וכו' לתת לך יותר וכו': (יא) ויהי (בעלות) וגו' בשנת ב' לאחזיה בן אחאב נגנז אליהו. ואינו נראה עד שיבא משיח. וכשיבא ונגנז שוב אינו נראה עד שיבא גוג. ועכשיו הוא כותב מעשה הדורות כולם כסדר:

ג (ד) נקד. רועה: (יג) אל כי קרא ה' וגו'. בבעו לא תמלל הוכין בשעתא דא בעי רחמין עלנא אחרי זמין ה' וגו':

ד (ב) אסוך שמן. כדי וכו' ואלף שבתוכה יסוד נופל וכו' וכן אשורים ולטושים: (יג) מה לעשות לך. מה וכו' שבשבילו עסקתה כל זה: (לט) וילקט ממנו. מלא בגדו. פר"ש פקועות כמהין. פקועות שדה והן בלויין סם המות ומשום ר' מנחם שמעתי וילקט ממנו מלא בגדו פקועות שדה:

ה (א) ונעמן שר צבא וגו'. נסים שעשה עשר שנעשו על ידי אלישע מסדר והולך: (כו) פר"ש. העת לך. ראוי היה לך מן אמיתת הדין לקנות נכסים בעת הזאת לולי דבר זה שעשית שנשבעת לשקר ועכשיו מיכן ואילך זה יהיה שכרך וצרעת נעמן יהיה בו וכו':

ט (יג) אל גרם המעלות. על וכו' כשהצל יורד מעלה אחת היא השעה:

י (ב) ואתכם הרכב והסוסים. ויש בכם כחול לרוב:

יא (ה) השלישית מכם באי שבת. המשמרות וכו' ומשמר הנכנס היה צריך להתחלק וכו': (יב) את הנזר ואת העדות. ספר תורה. ורבותינו אמרו הנזר הוא הכתר של מלכם תועבת בני עמון שכל הראוי למלכות הולמתו ואינו ראוי למלכות אינו הולמתו:

יב (ג) כל ימיו אשר הורהו יהוידע הכהן. מכל משמרת יהוידע. ואחרי מות יהוידע וכו': (יב) ולבונים. הם אדריכלים חרשי וכו': (יג) ולגודרים. בוני החומה תלמידי האדריכלים: (יד) ספות כסף מזמרות. אף הן כלי שיר:

יד (ט) ותעבור חית השדה ותרמוס וגו'. לפי שנתגאה אף וכו':

יז (לד) אינם יראים את ה'. יראה וכו' יראה שלימה כמו שמפרש והולך שאינם עושים כתורה וכמצוה אשר וכו':

יח (כב) הלא הוא אשר הסיר חזקיהו וגו'. הלא חזקיה הסיר את במותיו ואת מזבחותיו שלא היה מקום בארץ ישראל שלא היה שם מזבח לשם ה' והיו מקטרין עליו בזמן הזה. ובא חזקיה והסיר את כולם. ולא השאיר לה' אלא מזבח אחד בלבד בעירו ירושלים. ואדם שהכעים כל כך לאלהים היים איך יעמוד לו בשעת דוחקו. וחזקיה לשם מצוה הסיר אותם שהרי משנבנה הבית נאסרו הבמות. יש ללמוד מכאן וכו' אלא שדימהו בעכו"ם: (כג) התערב נא. התפאר. לשון ערבון על מנת וכו': (כז) חוריהם. ריע וכו' ורבותינו תיקנו לשון נאה וכו':

יט (כג) יער כרמילו. מלואת ארצו ויופי הכרמל: (כד) אני קרתי ושתיתי מים. התחלתי וכו' ומוציא מים קרים ושותה. מים נובעים קורא מים קרים, לפי וכו': ואחריב בכף פעמי. אם צרתי על העיר הובשתי נהרותיה הבאתי וכו': (כט) אכול השנה ספיח. בשנה זו יצאו לכם ספוחים ותתפרנסו מהם: סחיש. גדולי אילנות וכו':

כ (ח) (וימרחו) [וישימו]. יחלקוה לדקה על השחין וגם וכו': (ט) הלך הצל עשר מעלות. הרי מקרא קצר וכו' לשעות היום כמין אורולוגין שעושין המינים לבהון וכו': (יג) ואת שמן הטוב. יש וכו' ויש פותרין שמן כל שמן שהיה בארץ ישראל מצוי שנאמר ביחזקאל וכו': לא היה דבר. את הארון והלוחות וכתר תורה:

כג (כד) התרפים. צלמים שמדברים וכו' והעושה אותם צריך לכוין שעה אחת בשנה הראויה לכך:

כד (יד) החרש והמסגר. ת"י וכו' גדולים בתורה. חרש כשאחד מהן פותח וכו' איים. מסגר. הכל וכו':

נשלם ספר מלכים שבח למלך המלכים

APPENDIX

4:42

Since this was a famine year, grain was very scarce. Nowhere was there any ripe grain except in Baal-Shalishah, where grain ripens the earliest. Even there, only the barley was ripe. Otherwise, the disciples of the prophets would surely have many supporters, and much more food would have been available. At that time, however, the shortage was so acute that only one man came with a small donation of twenty loaves of barley bread and sheaves of fresh grain.

The Talmud relates that the year should ideally have been made a leap year according to the regulations governing that procedure. Because of the acute famine, however, the Sanhedrin decided to refrain from declaring it so, in order to make the little grain they had, available after the *Omer* a month earlier [*K'li Y'kar* from *TB San.* 12a]. (The *Omer* is brought on the second day of Passover. On that day, the new grain becomes permissible for consumption.)

5:26

Alternatively, even if he offered you olive trees, vineyards, sheep, and cattle, you would not be allowed to accept them [*Mezudath David*].

The Rabbis explain that Elisha had performed the miracle with the sole intention of sanctifying the Name of God. He, therefore, refused to accept any reward for it. He went so far as to swear by God's Name that he would accept nothing. Gehazi, by accepting the gifts, and by swearing falsely that Elisha had sent him, destroyed the effect of Elisha's *kiddush hashem,* thus making a *chillul hashem,* a profanation of the Name of God [*Num. Rabbah* 7:5].

Alternatively, Naaman had come to Elisha expecting a miraculous cure for his *zaraath.* When Elisha ordered him to immerse himself in the Jordan, he was disappointed, since this seemed like a natural cure, similar to the cure of certain ailments effected by bathing in the hot springs of Tiberias and similar waters. His servants convinced him that this was not a natural cure, but a miraculous one since these waters do not possess therapeutic properties. In order to stress this point, Elisha refused to accept any reward, since he was not a physician. He was merely an agent of the Divine in the performance of a miracle.

Gehazi, however, felt that Elisha should accept reward as a physician. By accepting this reward Gehazi destroyed the effect of Elisha's *kiddush hashem,* and made it appear as though he had cured Naaman by natural means. Therefore, Elisha decreed upon him that he and his sons would be afflicted with *zaraath* for the rest of their lives, to demonstrate that there was no natural cure for that ailment [*Maharsha San.* 107b].

17:28

In what way, then, did the Jews differ from the pagans? Some say that among the pagan nations, when they would worship their gods, the intellectuals among them were aware that the images themselves were of no avail to them. They worshipped them merely as intermediaries, because they believed that God desired such worship. The unlearned multitudes, however, directed their thoughts only to the images they worshipped, believing that they themselves had power to benefit or harm.

Among the Jews, however, this was not so. Everyone had inherited the knowledge of God from his forebears, that God is the God of the gods. They were, however, misled to follow the practice of the pagan nations. Since they were separate from the other nations, when they perceived that their neighbors were prosperous, they attributed their prosperity to the aid of these intermediaries, and they would say, "(Deut. 12:30) How do these nations worship their gods? I will do likewise." We find Ahaz saying, "(II Chron. 28:23) For the gods of the kings of Aram are helping them; to them I will sacrifice, and they will help me."

Even the wickedest among them would inquire of the Lord, for Jeroboam said, "(I Kings 13:6) Please beseech the Lord your God." It is obvious that he meant to beseech God to heal his paralyzed hand because He is the one Who does benefits or harms. He did not say that his paralysis was a mere coincidence. Likewise, when his son became ill, he sent his wife to inquire of God from Ahijah the Shilonite.

Ahab concurred with Elijah concerning the matter of the prophets of Baal. He became frightened when the prophet told him, "(I Kings 20:42) Your life shall be forfeit instead of his life." He likewise became frightened by Elijah's prophecy, rent his clothing, fasted, and lay in sackcloth (I Kings 21:27).

Jehoram, too, demonstrated his belief in God by saying, "(above 3:10) for the Lord has called these three kings to deliver them into the hands of Moab!"

This much fear of God they had in their hearts, to believe that both good and evil emanated from God.

Indeed there were a number of disbelievers, who said, "(Zeph. 1:12) God does neither good nor harm," and there were those who said, "(Is. 29:15) Who sees us and who knows us?" These were, however, a small minority. Moreover, they entertained a different idea. They would state their beliefs clandestinely, as it is said, "(above 17:9) And the children of Israel attributed concealment." Those people believed that good and evil were not directed by any power, neither by God nor by any of the worshipped deities.

The idol cult, however, were numerous. They believed in God, but worshipped him through intermediaries. They did not possess this fear of God to heed what the Almighty had enjoined them, "(Ex. 20:20) You shall not make with Me, gods of silver or gods of gold . . ." I.e. you shall not make images as intermediaries between Me and you. In this they went astray. Additionally, they followed the practices of the heathens in many things that the Lord had prohibited. Therefore, the land ejected them, as it is said,

"(Lev. 20:23) And you shall not follow the statutes of the nations," and "(ibid. 18:28) And the land will not eject you."

Now why were these nations punished when they came to Samaria and not when they were living in their native countries? For Eretz Israel is hallowed over all other lands, and it can, therefore, not bear those abominations, as it is said, "(Deut. 31:15) the strange gods of the land." Therefore, Scripture states, "And he would direct them how they should fear the Lord." And it is stated, "(Lev. 18:28) as it has ejected the nation that was before you."

Now, if this priest who came to instruct these people in Samaria, had admonished them to abandon idolatry, completely, they would not believe him, since all nations had been reared from time immemorial, with this belief until it had become axiomatic to them. He, therefore, permitted them to continue worshipping their idols, provided that they direct their thoughts toward God, for these deities can do no good or harm except with God's will. Thus he permitted them to worship their gods as intermediaries between themselves and the Creator. He instructed them also to abstain from committing abominations, e.g. sodomy, and incest, as the Torah states, "(Lev. 18:27) For the people of the land who were before you, committed all these abominations, and the land became defiled." This is "the law of the God of the land." This is the fear that they should fear Him. They should ascribe power to Him, viz. that He is the God over all the gods, and abstain from these defilements because of fear of Him and because of His admonition that they abstain from these acts in that land more than in other lands [*Redak*].

18:4

Asa and Jehoshaphat did not destroy it, since at their time, it was not worshipped. According to the Babylonian Talmud, (*Hullin* 7a), it was through Divine Providence that Asa and Jehoshaphat neglected to destroy the copper serpent, in order to give Hezekiah the opportunity to attain greatness by destroying it [*Redak*].

They mistakenly believed that we may not destroy any article made in fulfillment of a Divine command [*Tos.* ad loc.].

18:4

Alternatively, he called it Nehushtan to denote that it was but copper. The *nun* was added for the diminutive, as though to say, "Of what avail is this? It is nothing but an insignificant piece of copper." *Jonathan* renders: And *they* called it Nehushtan, i.e. the Jews who worshipped it called it Nehushtan [*Redak*].

18:14

The account of Hezekiah's relations with Sennacherib and his agents may be pieced together from the account given here, in II Chron., and in Isaiah. In order to make the matter easier to understand, we will outline it according to the combined material of all three sources. When Hezekiah humbled himself before Sennacherib and offered to pay him tribute, Sennacherib left Judah and returned to Assyria. Hezekiah paid tribute for a few years and then stopped paying. Upon Hezekiah's failure to pay tribute, Sennacherib returned to Lachish, whence he sent Rabshakeh with troops to Jerusalem to confront Hezekiah and the people. Hezekiah did not surrender to Assyria. His agent Shebna, however, did surrender. Rabshakeh withdrew from Jerusalem to find Sennacherib besieging Libnah. There he heard a rumor that Tirhakah the king of Cush had attacked Assyria. He returned to Assyria to combat Tirhakah, warning Hezekiah that he would soon return after his war with Cush. After defeating Cush and Egypt, Sennacherib returned to Jerusalem with all his captives and encamped outside the city. That night, an angel of God smote the entire camp, leaving only a handful of survivors. The Jews went out and plundered the camp, taking all the plunder of Cush and Seba. The survivors converted to Judaism and went to Egypt.

The prophet Isaiah alludes to Shebna's dissent by saying, "(8:12) You shall not say conspiracy to all that this people says conspiracy." I.e. you shall not take into consideration the conspiracy of Shebna and his company against Hezekiah and his company, since a union of the wicked is not counted even if they are the majority. See *Rashi* ad loc.

He alludes to the defeat of Cush and Seba as a ransom for Israel, "(Is. 43:3) I gave Egypt as your ransom, Cush and Seba in your stead." Also, "(45:14) The toil of Egypt and the merchandise of Cush and the Sebaites, men of stature will pass by you, and they will be yours. They will follow you; in fetters will they pass. And to you they shall prostrate themselves; they will beseech you, saying, 'Only among you is there a true God, and there is no other God.'"

Concerning these survivors the prophet states, "On that day, there will be five cities in the land of Egypt speaking the language of Canaan and swearing by the Lord of Hosts . . . (Is. 19:18)" [*Redak*].

18:17

Redak ventures to say that Rabshakeh was the spokesman for the group, but all three came together. Our Rabbis (San. 60a) state that Rabshakeh was an apostate Jew. The fact that he spoke Hebrew is no proof of his Jewishness, just as Hezekiah's officers speaking Aramic is no proof of their affiliation with Aram. There was probably an oral tradition to that effect [*Redak*].

From the context of that statement, it appears that the evidence was the fact that Hezekiah and his emissaries rent their garments upon hearing Rabshakeh's blasphemy. Were Rabshakeh a non-Jew, there would have been no necessity to rend the garments, as is explained in the Talmud ad loc. See below v. 22, 25.

18:17

Archeological excavations have yielded information concerning these names. *Rabshakeh* is a combination of two words: *rab sak,* the great head. *Tartan* means the general. *Rabsaris* is the chief of the eunuchs, the guard over the king's harem. Rabshakeh was the second in rank after Tartan. Rabsaris, too, was familiar with the language of Canaan, and was, therefore, sent as an emissary [*Antiquities* by Aaron Marcus, p. 167].

Perhaps Rabshakeh, being a Jew, was considered the most effective, and was, therefore, sent first.

18:22

Alternatively, how can he expect God's aid when he diminished His worship? [*Mezudath David, Ralbag*].

Rashi, Isaiah 36:7, expresses himself thus: **Whose high places Hezekiah removed**—*He abolished all the temples of idolatry and the altars and high places, and forced all of Judah to prostrate themselves before one altar.* It is noteworthy that *Rashi* includes the temples of idolatry. Apparently, Rabshakeh sincerely believed that it was God's will that we worship idols as intermediaries. Since Hezekiah abolished them, he diminished God's worship and cannot expect God's aid.

R. Joseph Kara explains that Rabshakeh contrasted Hezekiah with his father Ahaz. Whereas Ahaz spread the worship of God by erecting altars throughout the entire land of Judah, Hezekiah destroyed them all, and confined God's worship to one solitary altar. Did he not anger God by abolishing His shrines?

19:25

The prophet recalls the prophecies predicting Assyria's victory over all the nations including Israel, who had already been exiled. Hence, it is obvious that these victories came about because of a divine decree, not because of any strength possessed by Assyria. Isaiah rebuked Assyria in a similar vein when he stated, "(Is. 10:15) Will the axe boast over the one who wields it?" [*Redak*].

19:25

Alternatively, and *you* shall be to make desolate . . . [*Mezudath David*].

Others interpret: Have you not heard from afar that I made it in days of yore? I.e. that I have made Jerusalem. And that I formed it? Is it possible that now I have brought it that it should be made desolate . . .? [*Redak* from his father, *R. Joseph Kimchi*].

19:28

Redak, however, suggests that it may be rendered "your tranquility." Sennacherib raged against God because of his tranquility; i.e. because he felt tranquil and sure of himself, he dared to rage against God.

19:28

Redak defines חָח as a fishhook, which pierces the jaws of the fish, (or the nose), and מֶתֶג as a bit, inserted in the mouth of an animal to lead it. Thus, God announces to Sennacherib that he is under His control, and He will lead him where He so desires. *Ralbag,* too, follows the same definitions.

19:29

Alternatively, you have already witnessed the fulfillment of the first part of my prophecy, that Sennacherib will hear a rumor and return to his land (v. 7). When he returned to Assyria to defend it from Tirhakah, king of Cush, this was fulfilled. This fulfillment will be a sign to you that the remainder of the prophecy, viz. that he will fall by the sword in his land, will likewise be fulfilled, and you will never again be threatened by Sennacherib. Another prophecy, which I am revealing to you is that this year you shall eat . . . [*Redak*].

19:29

It was obvious that they would have to eat the plants that grew by themselves, since the invasion had prevented them from sowing that year. The promise was that the plants which grew by themselves would suffice the population for the remainder of the year [*Redak*].

19:29

Alternatively, during the second year you will not find it necessary to sow seeds because the seeds that fall from the plants of the first year will take root and suffice for the entire second year [*Redak, Ralbag, Mezudath, R. Jos. Kara* in name of *R. Menahem, Jonathan*].

19:31

The word צְבָאוֹת, *Hosts,* does not appear in the written text. It is in the category of קְרִי וְלֹא כְּתִיב, *words read but not written.* The purpose of its omission is to denote that God performed two acts of vengeance upon Sennacherib, one which He himself wrought upon him, and one which was wrought by His heavenly hosts, as in v. 35, ". . .an angel of the Lord went out . . ." [*Midrash K'ri velo K'thib*]. See *Minhath Shai*; *Otzar Midrashim,* p. 194.

What the two acts of vengeance were, is not made clear by the Midrash. Moreover, according to the *Babylonian Talmud, San.* 94, since Sennacherib blasphemed through his messengers, he was punished through a messenger, i.e. the angel who destroyed his camp. This was greater humiliation than to be punished by the Almighty Himself (*Rashi* ad loc.). According to the Midrash, however, he was punished by God Himself.

19:32

In Isaiah, *Rashi* quotes exegetes who interpret this in reference to a pile of rocks which is thrown near the wall of the city in order to embattle the city from upon it. *Rashi* rejects this interpretation on the grounds that the element of pressing down is absent in the case of the pile of rocks. Additionally, the word יִשְׁפֹּךְ, *he will pile up,* lit. he will spill, applies only to earth, not to rocks.

19:35

In Isaiah 10, the prophet lists the ten cities Sennacherib traversed on that day. He concludes with "(10:32) Yet today we will stay in Nob; he raises his hand toward the mount of the daughter of Zion, the hill of Jerusalem." *Rashi* comments:—*All this way he hurried, in order to stand in Nob when it was yet day, for his astrologers had said to him, "If you wage war with it today, you will conquer it. And when he stood in Nob and saw the small Jerusalem, he did not heed the words of his astrologers, and began to raise his hand arrogantly. "For such a small city have I agitated all these armies? Lodge here tonight, and tomorrow each man will cast his stone upon it."* I.e. each one will break a stone off the wall and destroy the entire wall [*Rashi San.* 95a].

The Rabbis tell us that the Jews were still to be punished for Saul's murder of the priests of Nob. At the end of the day, they were no longer to be punished for it. Had Sennacherib attacked Jerusalem on that day, he would have been victorious.

Because of his arrogance, he met his downfall [*San.* 95a].

20:18

It is not clear why *Rashi* does not include Daniel, who was definitely meant in this prophecy according to all opinions in the aforementioned Talmudic passage.

Malbim, Is. 39, explains that God had performed the miracle of turning back the sun, a miracle such as had not taken place since the time of Joshua, for a much greater purpose than merely to grant Hezekiah a sign that he would be cured of his illness. As stated above, most of Israel was now living in Assyrian exile. God desired to help them, lest the "lost sheep" be devoured by the many "wolves." He, therefore, afforded them this sign that they would be returned to their land. Indeed, Hezekiah did bring some of them back to their land without any opposition from the nations, as prophesied by Isaiah 18, 24:13, 17. Had Hezekiah not sinned, the entire nation would have been restored to their land. When this miracle took place, the Babylonians were greatly impressed, and forthwith sent emissaries to Hezekiah. This was not a friendly gesture. On the contrary, they were pained greatly by the miserable defeat of their sister nation, Assyria. They sent these emissaries as spies, to discover the secret of Hezekiah's success. At that time, Merodach-baladan heard that Hezekiah had been ill and was miraculously cured.

Hezekiah, upon receiving the emissaries, made two mistakes: (1) he believed that the miracle had come about for his sake only, and therefore, became haughty, as the Chronicler states; and (2) he expressed that sentiment to the Babylonian emissaries. This caused them to believe that after his death, they need not fear the strength of his people.

Isaiah rebuked him on two counts: (1) for his political error of revealing his secrets to a potential enemy; and (2) for his sin against God, Who proscribed acquisition of wealth by a monarch lest he become haughty (Deut. 17:17). Here Hezekiah had amassed treasures and was boasting of them before the pagans.

Abarbanel maintains that Hezekiah was not punished for his haughtiness. As the Chronicler relates, "(II 32:26) And Hezekiah humbled himself from his haughtiness, he and the inhabitants of Jerusalem, and God's ire did not come upon them in Hezekiah's days." Hence, Hezekiah was but a sign of the impending exile, not its cause. Manasseh's misdeeds were the cause of the destruction of the Temple and the exile. When Hezekiah heard of the exile from Isaiah, he became very sad, to the point that he regretted having prayed for his life. He would have preferred to die rather than experience the exile. Thereupon, the prophet informed him that the exile would not take place during his days. He, then, was relieved, and announced, "The word of the Lord . . . is good." I.e. the word of the Lord, that He added fifteen years to my life, is good, since I will not experience the exile.

21:16

The Chronicler elaborates on the remaining years of Manasseh, how he was captured by the Assyrian generals and led to Babylon in chains. There he repented of his sins. He prayed to God to save him; his prayers were accepted, and he was returned to his kingdom. The Chronicler concludes the episode with the words, "(II Chron. 33:13) and He returned him to Jerusalem, to his kingdom, and Manasseh knew that the Lord is God."

We find in *Pirkei d' R. Eliezer* (ch. 43) and in *Targum Rav Yosef* that the Chaldeans placed him in a huge pan under which they built a fire. Manasseh prayed to all his gods, but to no avail. He finally turned to the God of his fathers, praying fervently and repenting of his sins. God accepted his repentance and his prayers and returned him to Jerusalem.

The Talmud (*San.* 103a) states that Manasseh lived in penitence for thirty-three years. Some say that he has a share in the World to Come.

This entire episode is not mentioned in Kings. *Malbim* opines that Manasseh repented only of his sins of idolatry, not of his other sins, including murder. Since these sins remained on his record, it is not mentioned here that he repented.

22:20

Although Josiah was killed in war with Pharaoh Neco, it is considered that he died in peace and contentment, since he did not live to see the Temple being destroyed.

Abarbanel interprets thus: *I gather you in above your forefathers* — God promises Josiah that He will gather in his soul under the Throne of Glory in a more exalted place than his righteous ancestors: Asa, Jehoshaphat, Hezekiah, and others have merited.

23:29

According to *Midrash Abba Gurion,* Esther 1:2, he became lame after capturing Solomon's throne from Josiah and attempting to mount it. Since he was unfamiliar with its mechanism, the "lion" struck him on his thigh and lamed him. Accordingly, he received this appelation after his attack on Judah. Nevertheless, Scripture calls him by the name he was called later, as in many other instances in the Bible. See *Kethuboth* 10b.

23:30

Redak elaborates on this topic. According to the Talmud, a king whose father, too, was a king, requires no anointment, since the kingship is hereditary. Solomon was anointed only because of Adonijah's contesting his right to the throne. Similarly, Jehoash was anointed only because of Athaliah's usurpation of the throne. Likewise, Jehoahaz was anointed because of Jehoiakim's contesting this right to the throne, since he was two years older. He was chosen instead of his elder brother because he could replace his forefathers, whereas Jehoiakim could not. I.e. before he became king, he was righteous. He turned "sour" after occupying the throne. Jehoiakim, however, was unworthy from the start. The Rabbis based the conclusion that Jehoiakim was two years Jehoahaz' senior, on v. 31, which states that Jehoahaz was twenty-three when he became king, and on v. 36 which states that Jehoiakim was twenty-five. Since

Jehoahaz reigned but three months, we deduce that Jehoiakim was twenty-five during the same year that Jehoahaz was twenty-three, making a difference of two years between their ages. In view of this reasoning, the Talmud must explain the verse in Chron. (I 3:14), which reads as follows: "And the sons of Josiah, the first-born was Johanan, the second Jehoiakim, the third Zedekiah, the fourth Shallum." Johanan is identified with Jehoahaz, and Zedekiah with Shallum. This would place Jehoahaz as the first-born rather than Jehoiakim. Concerning this, the Talmud explains that Johanan was considered the first-born as regards the throne. Zedekiah is counted both as third and fourth, being the third son, but the fourth to ascend the throne. since Jecaniah preceded him. *Redak* identifies Shallum with Jehoiachin, counting a grandson together with the sons, found sometimes in the Scriptures. *Ibn Ezra* identifies Jehoahaz with Shallum. Johanan, the first-born, never occupied the throne. Jehoahaz was twenty-three when he ascended the throne, his brother Zedekiah twenty-four, and Jehoiakim twenty-five. Since Jehoiakim reigned eleven years, Zedekiah would be thirty-five years of age when he occupied the throne. Yet, Scripture (below 24:18) makes him twenty-one when he became king. We must, therefore, surmise that Josiah placed him on the throne three years prior to his demise. When Josiah died, the populace anointed Jehoahaz instead, as is denoted by the expression, "The people of the land *took* Jehoahaz," implying that they took him forcefully. *Ibn Ezra* brings further proof from Jer. 27:1, which states, "In the beginning of the kingdom of Jehoiakim . . ." In v. 3, the prophet refers to "messengers coming to Jerusalem to Zedekiah, king of Judah. This implies that the nations knew Zedekiah as king of Judah since his father had placed him on the throne during his lifetime. Actually, Jehoiakim was king at that time [*Redak* quoting *Ibn Ezra*]. See commentaries ad loc for other views.

24:1

Redak and *Abarbanel* venture another reckoning, viz. that at the end of the third year, the beginning of the fourth year of Jehoiakim's reign, which was the beginning of Nebuchadnezzar's, he attacked Jehoiakim and carried him off to Babylonia. How long he detained him we do not know. He, then, returned to Jerusalem, where he was faithful to Nebuchadnezzar for three years, after which he rebelled. Again, we do not know how many years he remained in a state of rebellion.

24:16

These men showed their might in their prodigious erudition in Torah and in their ability to debate over all halachic matters until arriving at an accurate conclusion. As mentioned, when they were unable to reach a conclusion, there was no one existing who was able. It was this group of one thousand Torah scholars that preserved Torah in Babylonia, transferring the entire Torah community to that location. In Eretz Israel remained only the poor of the land, who would have forgotten

Torah completely, were it not for the exile of Zedekiah ten years later, which was an act of kindness bestowed on Israel by the Almighty, lest the *harash* and the *masger* die out before the final exiles would arrive in Babylon. See *Gittin* 88a, *Rashi* ad loc.

24:19

He refers to 38, wherein the prophet commanded Zedekiah to surrender to the Chaldeans, and he would be spared, whereas if he would continue to battle against them, the city would be destroyed. Zedekiah was afraid to do so, and disobeyed the command of Jeremiah.

The Chronicler continues, "(v. 14) Also, all the dignitaries of the priests and the people committed many betrayals, like all the abominations of the nations, and they defiled the house of the Lord . . ."

Contrary to the apparent meaning of our verse, Zedekiah himself was innocent of the abominations of Jehoiakim. He is blamed for them because the people committed these sins, and he did not protest. His generation was no longer under the influence of the *harash* and the *masger*—the great Torah scholars—who had already been exiled during the reign of Jeconiah. Consequently, they reverted to all the abominations of the nations surrounding them. Zedekiah, however, was considered a *zaddik,* a righteous man. He was called Shallum because he was perfect in his deeds (*shalem,* perfect) (*Horioth* 11a). The Talmud (*San.* 103b) relates that God wished to destroy the world because of the sins of Jehoiakim. He looked at his generation, however, and spared it. Later, he wished to destroy the world because of the generation of Zedekiah, but when He looked at Zedekiah, He spared it. See *Pseudo-Rashi* II Chron. ad loc.

24:20

Since he rebelled, Nebuchadnezzar had an excuse for destroying Jerusalem [*Redak*].

Redak explains: Since the remnant was in Jerusalem and in Judah contrary to the Lord's will, i.e. because of their evil deeds and abominable acts, the Lord inspired Zedekiah to rebel against Nebuchadnezzar and bring about the destruction.

25:27

He cites another version that when Nebuchadnezzar lived with the beasts, another son occupied the throne. When he returned, he executed him. Consequently, Evil-Merodach feared that he would meet his brother's fate.

In our edition of *Seder Olam,* we read that Nebuchadnezzar died on the twenty-fifth, was exhumed on the twenty-sixth, and Jehoiachin was released on the twenty-seventh.

Malbim conjectures that Evil-Merodach released Jehoiachin on the twenty-fifth and honored him on the twenty-seventh.

BIBLIOGRAPHY

I. Background Material

1. Bible with commentaries ("Mikraoth Gedoloth"(, commonly known as "Nach Lublin," including Rashi, Ralbag (Rabbi Levi ben Gershon, also known as Gersonides), and Redak (R. David Kimchi).

2. Talmud Bavli or Babylonian Talmud. Corpus of Jewish law and ethics compiled by Ravina and Rav Ashi 500 C.E. All Talmudic quotations, unless otherwise specified, are from the Babylonian Talmud.

3. Talmud Yerushalmi or Palestinian Talmud. Earlier and smaller compilation of Jewish law and ethics, compiled by R. Johanan, first generation *Amora* in second century C.E.

4. Midrash Rabbah. Homiletic explanation of Pentateuch and Five Scrolls. Compiled by Rabbi Oshia Rabbah (the great), late Tannaite, or by Rabbah bar Nahmani, third generation *Amora.* Exodus Rabbah, Numbers Rabbah, and Esther Rabbah are believed to have been composed at a later date.

5. Midrash Tanhuma. A Midrash on Pentateuch, based on the teachings of R. Tanhuma bar Abba, Palestinian *Amora* of the fifth century C.E. An earlier Midrash Tanhuma was discovered by Solomon Buber. It is evident that this is the Tanhuma usually quoted by medieval scholars, e.g. Rashi, Yalkut Shimoni, and Abarbanel.

6. Pirke d'Rabbi Eliezer. Eighth century aggadic compilation, attributed to Rabbi Eliezer ben Hyrcanus, early Tannaite of first generation after destruction of second Temple. Also called Baraitha d'Rabbi Eliezer, or Haggadah d'Rabbi Eliezer. Commentary—Radal (R. David Luria) 1798–1855. Om Publishing Co., New York 1946

7. Yalkut Shimoni. Talmudic and Midrashic anthology on Bible, composed by R. Simon Ashkenazi, thirteenth century preacher of Frankfort on the Main. Earliest known edition is dated 1308, in Bodlian Library. Sources traced by Arthur B. Hyman, M.D. in "The Sources of the Yalkut Shimeoni," Mossad Harav Kook, Jerusalem 1965.

8. Pesikta d'Rav Kahana. Homiletic dissertations of special Torah readings and haftaroth. Composed by Rav Kahana, early *Amora,* at time of compilation of Talmud Yerushalmi. Solomon Buber, latest edition Jerusalem 5723.

9. Pesikta Rabbathi. Later compilation similar to that of Rav Kahana. Composed 4605. Warsaw, 5673, Jerusalem—Bnei Brak 5729.

10. Elijah Rabba—Midrash revealed by Elijah the prophet to Rav Anan. See Kethuboth 106a. Together with Elijah Zuta, this is known as Tanna d'vei Elijah. New Square 5720, with commentary Tuvei chaim. Jerusalem 5723, with commentary Meorei haeish.

11. Elijah Zuta—Smaller part of Tanna d'vei Elijah. See Elijah Rabba.

12. Midrash Tehillim, Or Shoher Tov. Homiletic explanation on Book of Psalms. Authorship not definitely established. New York 1947

13. Midrash Samuel, or Agadath Sh'muel. Also known as Midrash "Eth La'asoth." Compendium of early Midrashim on the Book of Samuel. Composed in Eretz Israel by unknown author. Date of compilation unknown. Jerusalem 1965.

14. Mechilta. Tannaitic work on Book of Exodus. Some ascribe its authorship to Rabbi Ishmael, some to Rabbi Akiva, and others to Rav, first generation *Amora.* Printed with Malbim below text of Exodus.

15. Sifrei. Tannaitic work on Numbers and Deuteronomy. Some attribute its authorship to Rav, first generation *Amora.* Printed with Malbim below text of Numbers and Deuteronomy.

16. Seder Olam. Early Tannaitic work, recording chronology of entire Biblical era. Composed by Rabbi Jose son of Halafta. Jerusalem 5715

17. Zohar. Kabbalistic exposition on the Pentateuch. Composed by Tannaite R. Shimon ben Yochai and his disciples. Third generation after the destruction of the Second Temple. New York 1954

II. Medieval Commentaries and Source Material

1. Don Isaac Abarbanel or Abravanel. Commentary on Kings, by renowned scholar, onetime finance minister of Spain. 1437–1509

2. Commentary of Rabbenu Joseph Kara on the Prophets, contemporary of Rashi. Published by Rabbi S. Epenstein under Mossad Harav Kook 1972. Other version appears in Nach Lublin. 1060-1130

III. Modern Commentaries

1. R. Chaim Joseph David Azulai. Author of Homath Anach and other commentaries on the Bible by a famous 18th century authority on all fields of Torah study.

2. R. Meir Leibush Malbim. Commentary on Biblical literature, which combines ancient tradition with keen insight into nuances of meanings in the Hebrew language, by a leading nineteenth century scholar. 1809–1879

3. Shem Ephraim on Tanach by the renowned authority, R. Ephraim

Zalman Margolis of Brodi, emendations on Rashi text, Munkacz 5673, Eretz Israel 5732

4. K'li Y'kar by Rabbi Sh'muel Laniado, commentary on N'viim Rishonim, containing comments on early commentaries and original exegesis. Venice (5363) 1603

5. Daath Soferim, by Rabbi Chaim Rabinowitz. Biblical exegesis by contemporary historian, exegete, and educator, Jerusalem

6. Mezudath David and Mezudath Zion, by Rabbi Yechiel Hillel Altschuller. Simple and concise 18th century Bible commentary

IV. Other Sources

1. Kadmonioth—Antiquities. Aaron Marcus, nineteenth scholar and archeologist. Records of ancient inscriptions relevant to the period of Kings.

2. Behold a People by Rabbi Avigdor Miller, contemporary Torah scholar, author of Rejoice, O Youth, A Torah Nation, and other works. History of first commonwealth. New York (5728) 1968

3. Sefer Hashorashim, Redak. Lexicon of Biblical roots. Berlin 5607, New York, 5708

4. Sefer Hashorashim, R. Jona ibn Ganah, earlier lexicon of Biblical roots, Berlin (5656) 1896, Jerusalem 5726

5. Aruch, R. Nathan of Rome. Talmudic dictionary by early medieval scholar. Died 4866

6. Otzar Midrashim. Encyclopedia of all Midrashim. J.D. Eisenstein. New York, 1915, 1956

7. Methurgeman. Lexicon Chaldaicum. Aramaic lexicon, comprising all roots found in *Targumim* and in Bible. Composed by Eliia Levita, grammarian and lexicographer. 1541. No date on reprint.

8. Parshandatha. Critical edition of Rashi on Isaiah. I. Maarsen. Jerusalem, 5732

ARAM
HERMON
DAN
ZIDON
CANAANITE
IJON
LAJISH
TYRE
ABEL BETH MAACHA
KANAH
BETH REHOB
ASHER
KEDESH
ACHSIB
YIRON
NAPHTALI
ARGOB
BET HAEMEK
BETH DAGON
HORMAH
Hazor
MEROM
ACCO
KABUL
BASHAN
HANATON
RIMON
ZEBULUN
KINERET
ACHSAPH
KITRON
Sea of Kineres
Shomron
Mt. Carmel
GATH CHEFER
ASHTAROTH KARNAJIM
KISHON R.
RAKAT
DOR
YAFIA
HAMATH
YAKNEAM
SARID
Mt. TABOR
TIBERIA
YABNEL
Aphek
MEGIDDO
SHUNAM
EN DOR
KENATH
ISSACHAR
YISREEL
ANHARATH
YARMUK R.
MEDITERRANEAN SEA
TANOCH
EDREI
KINGDOM OF ISRAEL
MANASSEH
LO DEBAR
RAMOTH GILEAD
BETH SHEAN
BETH HAGAN
CHEFER
Yabesh Gilead
MAHANAIM
MITZPAH
SALCHAH
SOCHO
TEBETS
SAMARIA
TIRTSAH
ZAPHON
SHOMRON
PNUEL
Mt. EBAL
SUCCOTH
Yabok R.
SHECHEM
GILEAD
Mt. GERIZIM
YANUAH
HAGALGAL
arkon R.